AutoCAD®
and its applications
BASICS

by

Terence M. Shumaker
Faculty Emeritus
Former Chairperson
Drafting Technology
Autodesk Premier Training Center
Clackamas Community College, Oregon City, Oregon

David A. Madsen
Faculty Emeritus
Former Chairperson
Drafting Technology
Autodesk Premier Training Center
Clackamas Community College, Oregon City, Oregon

Former Board of Director
American Design Drafting Association

Publisher
The Goodheart-Willcox Company, Inc.
Tinley Park, Illinois
www.g-w.com

Manufactured in the United States of America.

Library of Congress Catalog Card Number 2004047558
International Standard Book Number 1-59070-370-7

1 2 3 4 5 6 7 8 9 – 05 – 09 08 07 06 05 04

Goodheart-Willcox Publisher Brand Disclaimer: Brand names, company names, and illustrations for products and services included in this text are provided for educational purposes only and do not represent or imply endorsement or recommendation by the author or the publisher.

The Goodheart-Willcox Company, Inc. Safety Notice: The reader is expressly advised to carefully read, understand, and apply all safety precautions and warnings described in this book or that might also be indicated in undertaking the activities and exercises described herein to minimize risk of personal injury or injury to others. Common sense and good judgment should also be exercised and applied to help avoid all potential hazards. The reader should always refer to the appropriate manufacturer's technical information, directions, and recommendations; then proceed with care to follow specific equipment operating instructions. The reader should understand these notices and cautions are not exhaustive.

The publisher makes no warranty or representation whatsoever, either expressed or implied, including but not limited to equipment, procedures, and applications described or referred to herein, their quality, performance, merchantability, or fitness for a particular purpose. The publisher assumes no responsibility for any changes, errors, or omissions in this book. The publisher specifically disclaims any liability whatsoever, including any direct, indirect, incidental, consequential, special, or exemplary damages resulting, in whole or in part, from the reader's use or reliance upon the information, instructions, procedures, warnings, cautions, applications or other matter contained in this book. The publisher assumes no responsibility for the activities of the reader.

Library of Congress Cataloging-in-Publication Data

Shumaker, Terence M.
AutoCAD and its applications: basics 2005 / by Terence M. Shumaker, David A. Madsen.
p. cm.
ISBN 1-59070-370-7
1. Computer graphics. 2. AutoCAD. I. Madsen, David A. II. Title.
T385.S46146 2005
620.0042'0285536—dc22 2004047558

Introduction

AutoCAD and its Applications—Basics is a text providing complete instruction in mastering fundamental AutoCAD® 2005 commands and drawing techniques. Typical applications of AutoCAD are presented with basic drafting and design concepts. The topics are covered in an easy-to-understand sequence and progress in a way that allows you to become comfortable with the commands as your knowledge builds from one chapter to the next. In addition, ***AutoCAD and its Applications—Basics*** offers the following features:

- Step-by-step use of AutoCAD commands.
- In-depth explanations of how and why commands function as they do.
- Extensive use of font changes to specify certain meanings.
- Examples and discussions of industry practices and standards.
- Actual screen captures of AutoCAD and Windows features and functions.
- Professional tips explaining how to use AutoCAD effectively and efficiently.
- Over two hundred exercises to reinforce the chapter topics. These exercises also build on previously learned material.
- Chapter tests for review of commands and key AutoCAD concepts.
- A large selection of drafting problems supplementing each chapter. Problems are presented as 3D illustrations, industrial drawings, and engineering sketches.

With ***AutoCAD and its Applications—Basics,*** you learn AutoCAD commands and become acquainted with information in other areas:

- Office practices for firms using AutoCAD systems.
- Preliminary planning and sketches.
- Linetypes and their uses.
- Drawing geometric shapes and constructions.
- Special editing operations that increase productivity.
- Making multiview drawings (orthographic projection).
- Dimensioning techniques and practices, based on accepted standards.
- Drawing section views and designing graphic patterns.
- Creating shapes and symbols for different uses.
- Creating and managing symbol libraries.
- Sketching with AutoCAD.
- Basic 3D drawing and display.
- Plotting and printing drawings.
- Using Windows Explorer for organizing and managing files and directories.

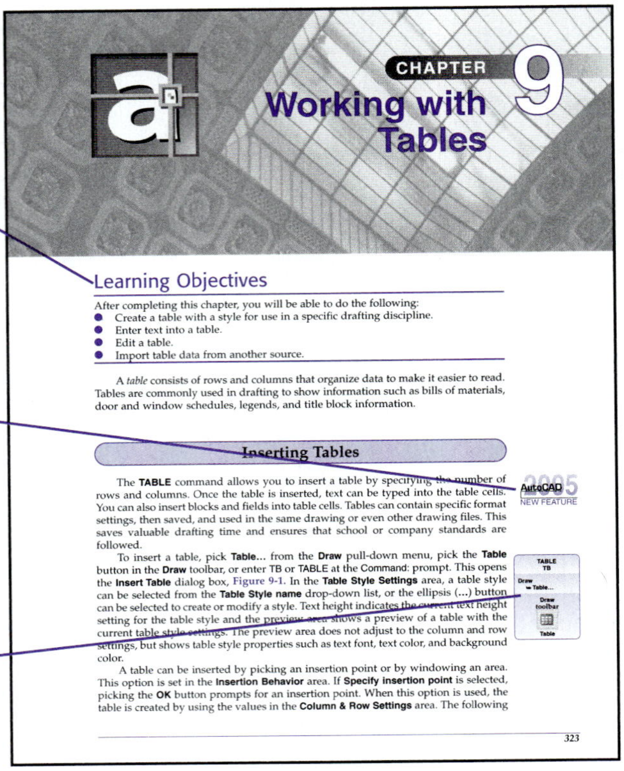

CHAPTER 9

Working with Tables

Learning Objectives

After completing this chapter, you will be able to do the following:

- Create a table with a style for use in a specific drafting discipline.
- Enter text into a table.
- Edit a table.
- Import table data from another source.

A *table* consists of rows and columns that organize data to make it easier to read. Tables are commonly used in drafting to show information such as bills of materials, door and window schedules, legends, and title block information.

Inserting Tables

The **TABLE** command allows you to insert a table by specifying the number of rows and columns. Once the table is inserted, text can be typed into the table cells. You can also insert blocks and fields into table cells. Tables can contain specific format settings, then saved, and used in the same drawing or even other drawing files. This saves valuable drafting time and ensures that school or company standards are followed.

AutoCAD 2005 NEW FEATURE

To insert a table, pick **Table...** from the **Draw** pull-down menu, pick the **Table** button in the **Draw** toolbar, or enter TB or TABLE at the Command: prompt. This opens the **Insert Table** dialog box, Figure 9-1. In the **Table Style Settings** area, a table style can be selected from the **Table Style name** drop-down list, or the ellipsis (...) button can be selected to create or modify a style. Text height indicates the current text height setting for the table style and the preview area shows a preview of a table with the current table style settings. The preview area does not adjust to the column and row settings, but shows table style properties such as text font, text color, and background color.

TABLE TB

Draw ➡ Table...

Draw toolbar

Table

A table can be inserted by picking an insertion point or by windowing an area. This option is set in the **Insertion Behavior** area. If **Specify insertion point** is selected, picking the **OK** button prompts for an insertion point. When this option is used, the table is created by using the values in the **Column & Row Settings** area. The following

323

Learning Objectives identify the key items you will learn in the chapter.

New Feature Graphics identify new and updated features for AutoCAD 2005.

Command Entry Graphics show command prompt, toolbar, and pull-down menu entry.

Drawing Problems require application of chapter concepts and problem-solving techniques. Icons identify problems from various drafting disciplines.

Mechanical

Civil

Architectural Structural

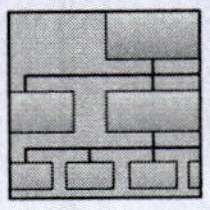

Graphic Design

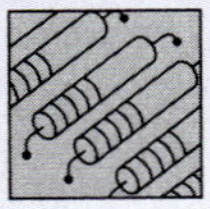

Electronics

Piping

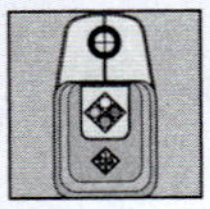

General

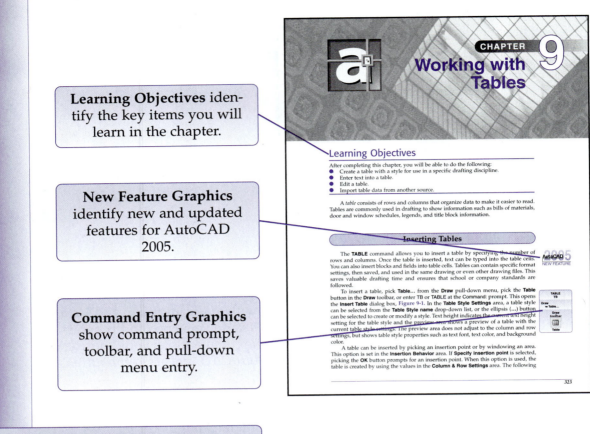

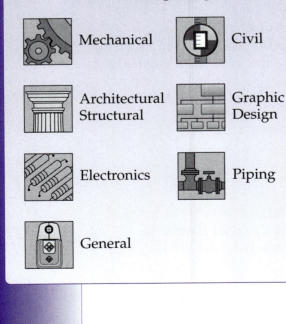

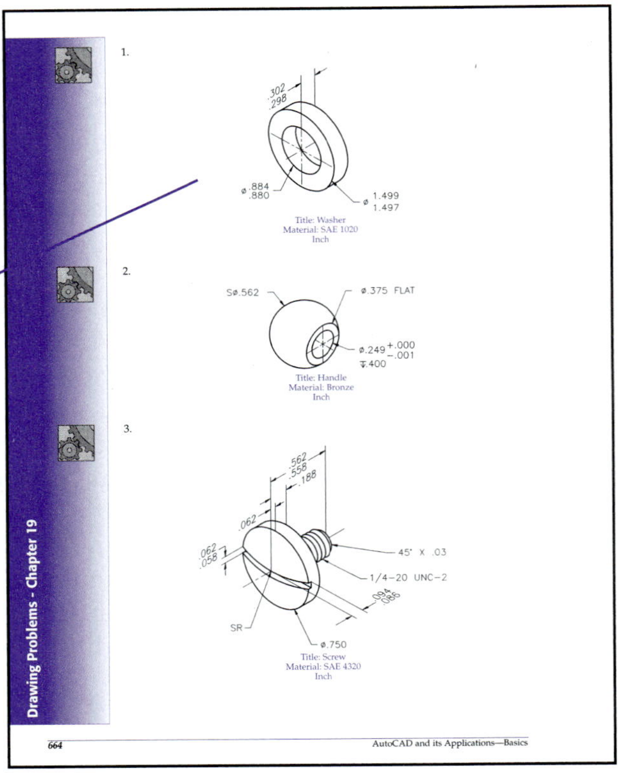

Features of the Textbook

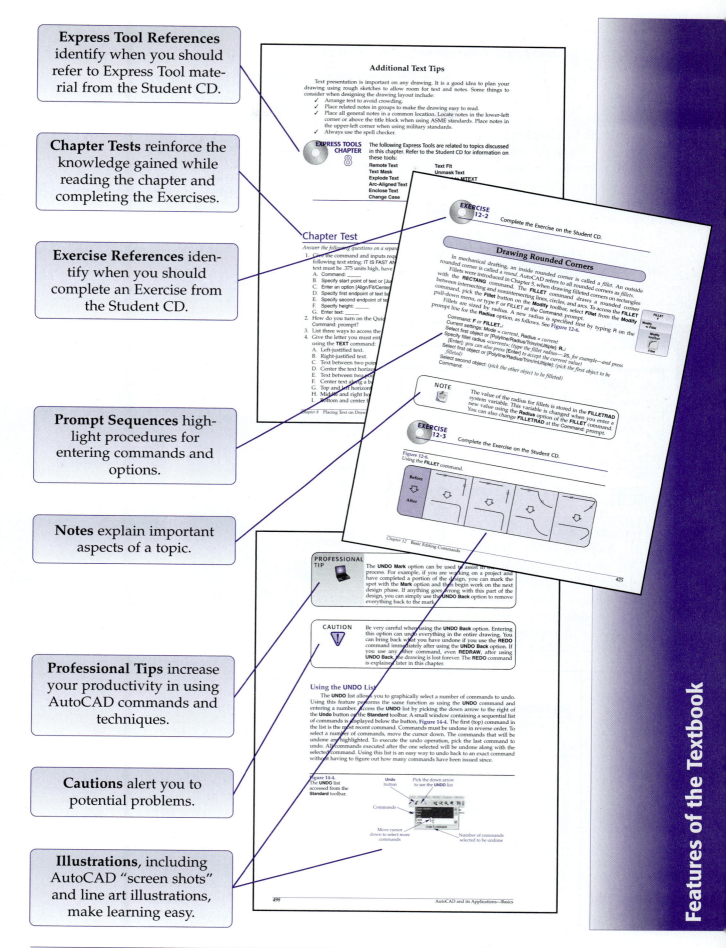

Features of the Textbook

Express Tool References identify when you should refer to Express Tool material from the Student CD.

Chapter Tests reinforce the knowledge gained while reading the chapter and completing the Exercises.

Exercise References identify when you should complete an Exercise from the Student CD.

Prompt Sequences highlight procedures for entering commands and options.

Notes explain important aspects of a topic.

Professional Tips increase your productivity in using AutoCAD commands and techniques.

Cautions alert you to potential problems.

Illustrations, including AutoCAD "screen shots" and line art illustrations, make learning easy.

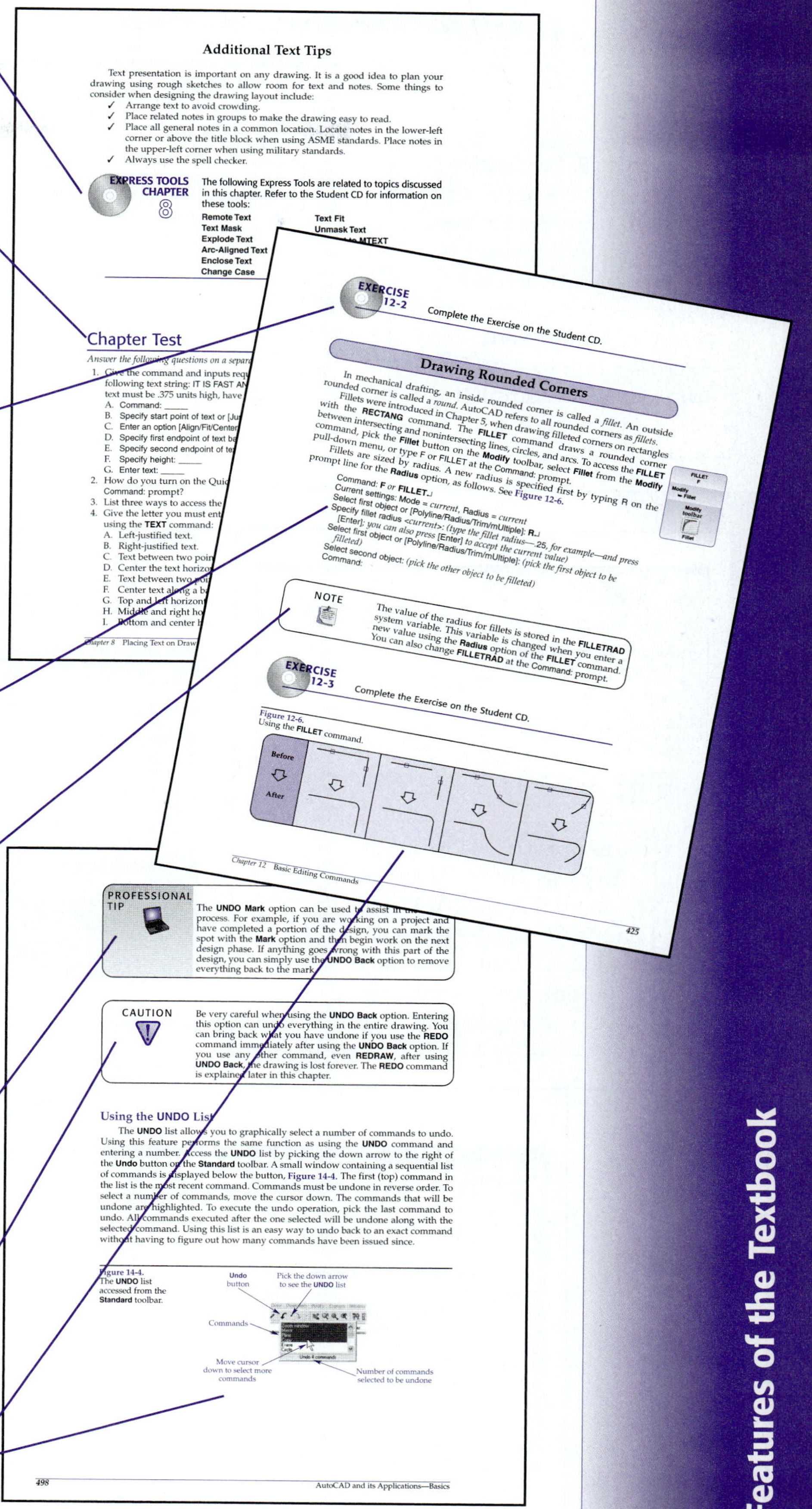

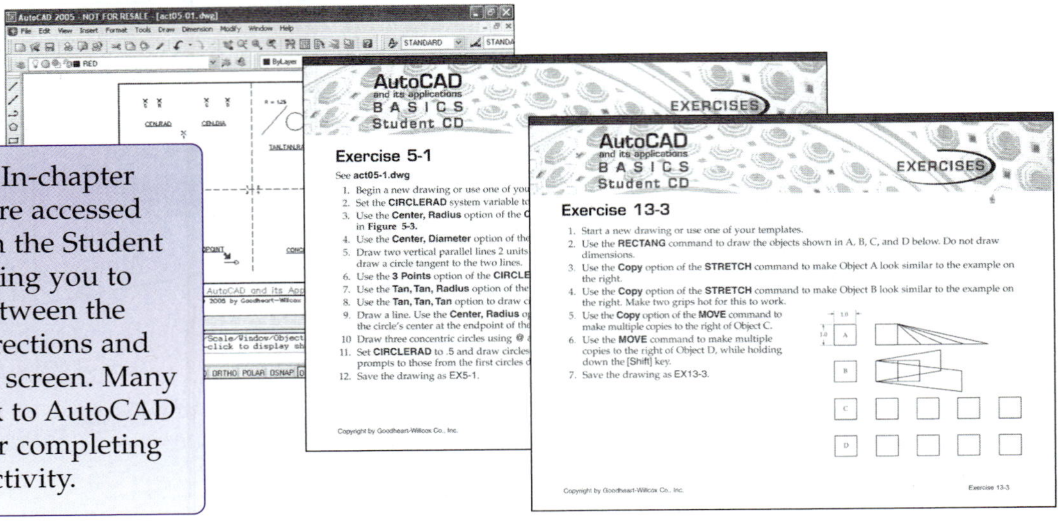

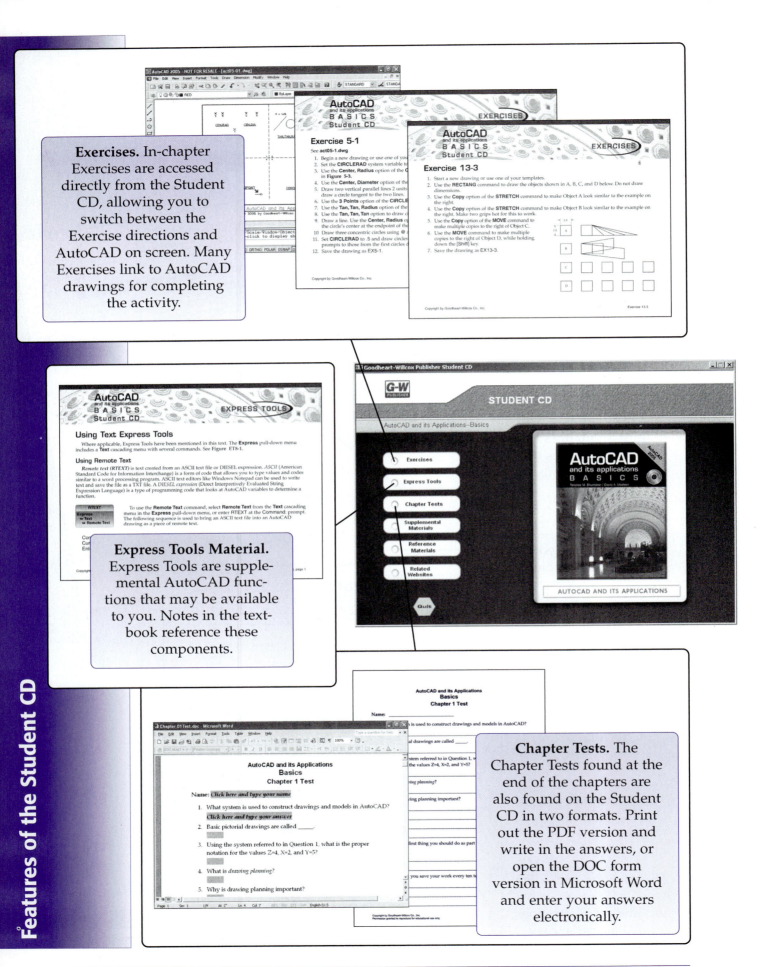

Exercises. In-chapter Exercises are accessed directly from the Student CD, allowing you to switch between the Exercise directions and AutoCAD on screen. Many Exercises link to AutoCAD drawings for completing the activity.

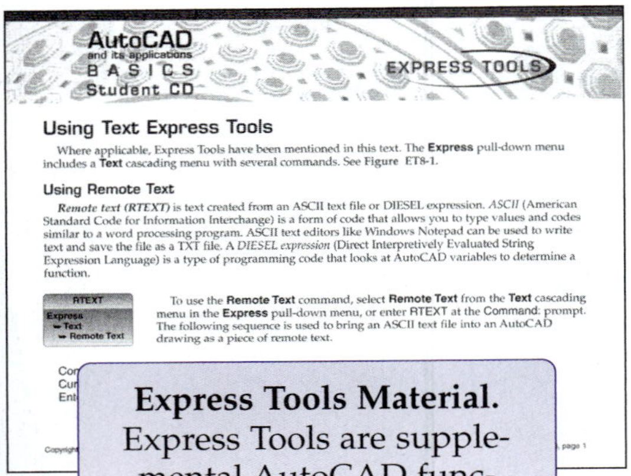

Express Tools Material. Express Tools are supplemental AutoCAD functions that may be available to you. Notes in the textbook reference these components.

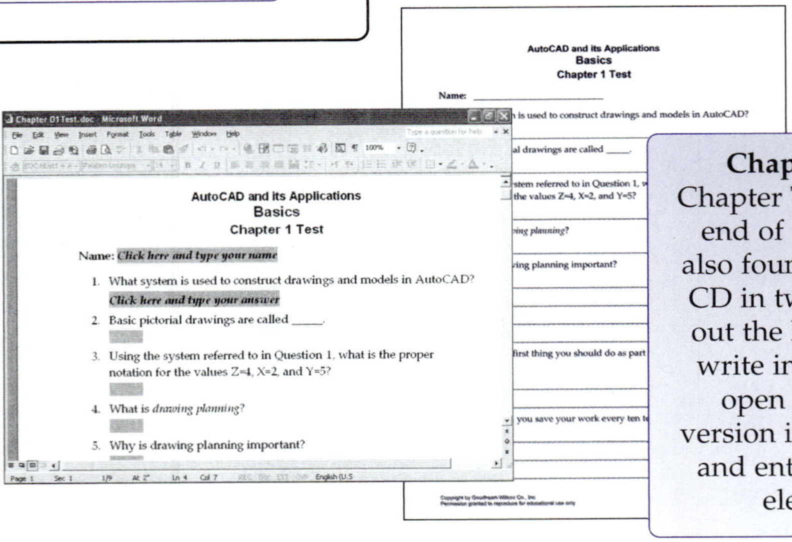

Chapter Tests. The Chapter Tests found at the end of the chapters are also found on the Student CD in two formats. Print out the PDF version and write in the answers, or open the DOC form version in Microsoft Word and enter your answers electronically.

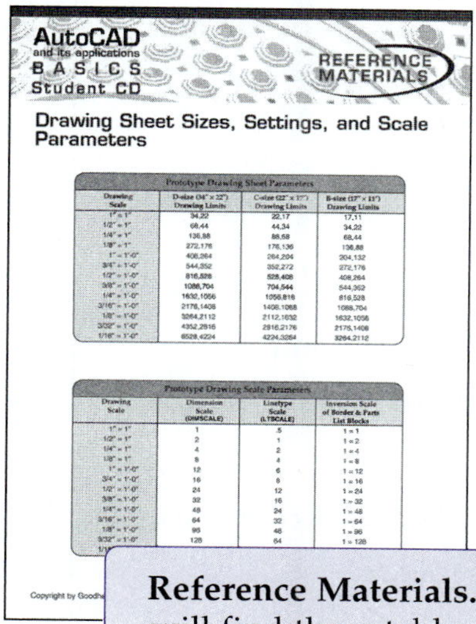

Reference Materials. You will find these tables and charts useful both in the classroom and in the workplace. Access the material from your desktop, or print them and store in a binder.

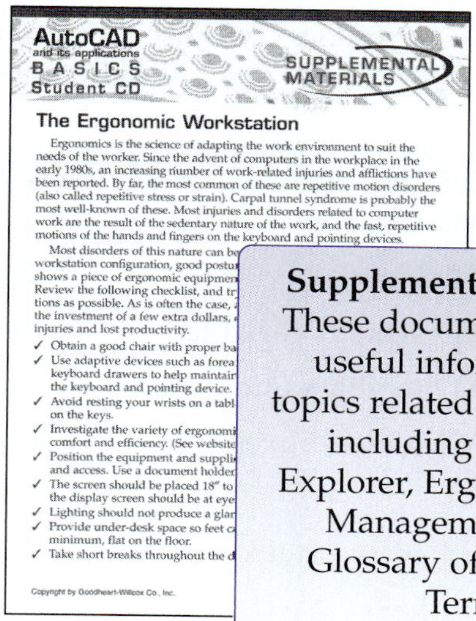

Supplemental Materials. These documents provide useful information on topics related to AutoCAD, including Windows Explorer, Ergonomics, File Management, and a Glossary of Computer Terms.

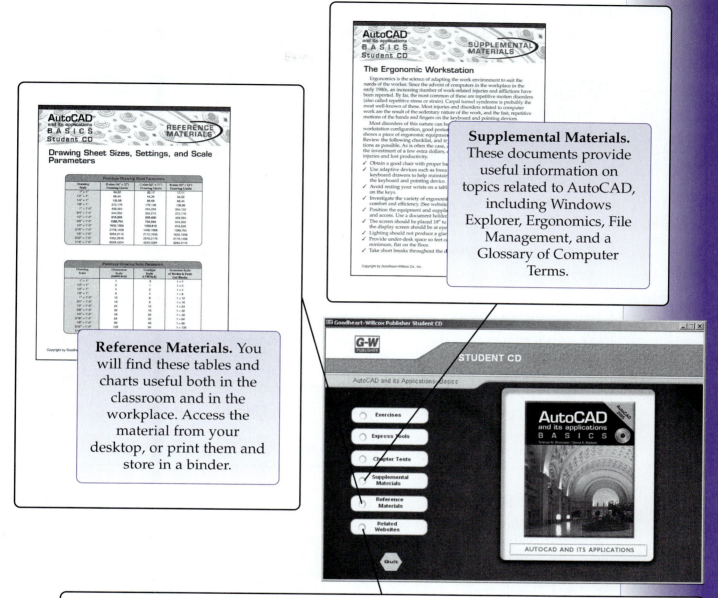

Internet Resources. Use this to access a wide variety of CAD/drafting web sites.

Fonts Used in This Text

Different typefaces are used throughout this text to define terms and identify AutoCAD commands. The following typeface conventions are used in this textbook:

Text Element	Example
AutoCAD commands	**LINE** command
AutoCAD menu	**Draw** pull-down menu
AutoCAD system variables	**FILEDIA** system variable
AutoCAD toolbars and buttons	**Edit** toolbar, **Offset** button
AutoCAD dialog boxes	**Insert Table** dialog box
Keyboard entry (in text)	Type **LINE** at the Command: prompt
Keyboard keys	[Ctrl]+[1] key combination
File names, folders, and paths	C:\Program Files\AutoCAD 2005\my drawing.dwg
Microsoft Windows features	Start menu, Programs folder
Prompt sequence	Command:
Keyboard input at prompt sequence	Command: **L** *or* **LINE**↵
Comment at prompt sequence	Specify first point: *(pick a point or press* [Enter]*)*

Other Text References

For additional information, standards from organizations, such as ANSI (American National Standards Institute) and ASME (American Society of Mechanical Engineers) are referenced throughout the text. These standards are used to help you create drawings that follow industry, national, and international practices. The Student CD includes a list of many of these standards.

Also for your convenience, other Goodheart-Willcox textbooks are referenced. Referenced textbooks include ***AutoCAD and its Applications—Advanced***, ***Geometric Dimensioning and Tolerancing***, and ***Process Pipe Drafting***. All these textbooks can be ordered directly from Goodheart-Willcox.

AutoCAD and its Applications—Basics covers basic AutoCAD applications. For a text covering the advanced AutoCAD applications, please refer to ***AutoCAD and its Applications—Advanced***.

Contents in Brief

1	Introduction to AutoCAD Features	19
2	Working with Drawings and Templates	51
3	Introduction to Drawing and Editing	85
4	Using Layers, Modifying Object Properties, and Making Prints	117
5	Drawing Basic Shapes	157
6	Object Snap, Geometric Constructions, and Multiview Drawings	191
7	Using the Geometry Calculator and Filters	241
8	Placing Text on Drawings	275
9	Working with Tables	323
10	Drawing Display Options	337
11	Layouts, Plotting, and Printing	371
12	Basic Editing Commands	419
13	Automatic Editing	467
14	Introduction to Polylines and Multilines	491
15	Drawing and Editing Polylines and Splines	521
16	Obtaining Information about the Drawing	551
17	Basic Dimensioning Practices	567
18	Editing Dimensions	639
19	Dimensioning with Tolerances	653
20	Geometric Dimensioning and Tolerancing	667
21	Drawing Section Views and Graphic Patterns	697
22	Creating Symbols for Multiple Use	729
23	Assigning Attributes and Generating a Bill of Materials	773
24	External References	799
25	Sheet Sets	833
26	Isometric Drawing	869
27	Introduction to Three-Dimensional Drawing	885
28	External Commands, Script Files, and Slide Shows	907
	Index	921

About the Authors

Terence M. Shumaker is Faculty Emeritus, the former Chairperson of the Drafting Technology Department, and former Director of the Autodesk Premier Training Center at Clackamas Community College. Terence taught at the community college level for over 25 years. He has professional experience in surveying, civil drafting, industrial piping, and technical illustration. He is the author of Goodheart-Willcox's ***Process Pipe Drafting*** and coauthor of the ***AutoCAD and its Applications*** series.

David A. Madsen is Faculty Emeritus, the former Chairperson of Drafting Technology and the Autodesk Premier Training Center at Clackamas Community College and former member of the American Design and Drafting Association Board of Directors. David was an instructor and a department chair at Clackamas Community College for nearly thirty years. In addition to community college experience, David was a Drafting Technology instructor at Centennial High School in Gresham, Oregon. David also has extensive experience in mechanical drafting, architectural design and drafting, and construction practices. He is the author of several Goodheart-Willcox drafting and design textbooks, including ***Geometric Dimensioning and Tolerancing,*** and coauthor of the ***AutoCAD and its Applications*** series and ***Architectural Drafting Using AutoCAD.***

Acknowledgments

Special thanks from David Madsen to Ethan Collins, Eugene O'Day, and Ron Palma for their professional expertise in providing in-depth research and testing, technical assistance, reviews, and development of new materials for use throughout the text.

Special thanks from Terence Shumaker to Craig Black for his expert reviews, technical assistance, and contribution of new material for several chapters in this book. Craig is manager of the Autodesk Premier Training Center at Fox Valley Technical College in Appleton, Wisconsin.

Technical Assistance and Contribution of Materials

Margo Bilson of Willamette Industries, Inc.
Fitzgerald, Hagan, & Hackathorn
Bruce L. Wilcox, Johnson and Wales University School of Technology

Contribution of Photographs or Other Technical Information

Arthur Baker
Autodesk, Inc.
CADalyst magazine
CADENCE magazine
Chris Lindner
EPCM Services Ltd.
Harris Group, Inc.
International Source for Ergonomics
Jim Webster
Kunz Associates
Myonetics, Inc.
Norwest Engineering
Schuchart & Associates, Inc.
Willamette Industries, Inc.

Trademarks

Autodesk, the Autodesk logo, 3ds max, Autodesk VIZ, AutoCAD, DesignCenter, AutoCAD Learning Assistance, AutoSnap, and AutoTrack are either registered trademarks or trademarks of Autodesk, Inc. in the U.S.A. and/or other countries.

Microsoft, Windows, and Windows NT are registered trademarks of Microsoft Corporation in the United States and/or other countries.

Contents

Introduction to AutoCAD

CHAPTER 1 **Introduction to AutoCAD Features**

The Tools of CAD ... 19
The AutoCAD Toolbox ... 20
The Applications of AutoCAD ... 20
Establishing an AutoCAD Drawing Method ... 22
Starting AutoCAD ... 26
The AutoCAD Window ... 28
Selecting AutoCAD Commands ... 39
Getting Help ... 42
Keys and Buttons ... 44

CHAPTER 2 **Working with Drawings and Templates**

Starting a New Drawing ... 51
Saving Drawings ... 57
Opening Existing Drawings ... 61
Closing a Drawing ... 69
Exiting AutoCAD ... 70
Creating and Using Drawing Templates ... 70
Establishing a Grid on the Screen ... 72
Setting Increments for Cursor Movement ... 74
Drawing Settings ... 77

CHAPTER 3 **Introduction to Drawing and Editing**

Line Conventions ... 85
Drawing Lines with AutoCAD ... 90
Canceling a Command ... 102
Introduction to Editing ... 102

Drawing and Printing with AutoCAD

CHAPTER 4

Using Layers, Modifying Object Properties, and Making Prints

Introduction to Layers 117
Changing Object Properties 140
Overriding Layer Settings 141
Reusing Drawing Content 143
Introduction to Printing and Plotting 147

CHAPTER 5

Drawing Basic Shapes

Watching Objects Drag into Place 157
Drawing Circles 158
Drawing Arcs 162
Drawing Ellipses 170
Drawing Regular Polygons 174
Drawing Rectangles 175
Drawing Donuts and Solid Circles 179
Using the Revision Cloud 180

CHAPTER 6

Object Snap, Geometric Constructions, and Multiview Drawings

Snapping to Specific Features 191
Object Snap Modes 192
Setting Running Object Snaps 203
AutoSnap Settings 205
Using Temporary Tracking to Locate Points 207
Using AutoTracking to Locate Points 209
Coordinate Filters 214
Drawing Parallel Lines and Curves 217
Dividing an Object 218
Dividing Objects at Specified Distances 219
Drawing Points 220
Orthographic Multiview Drawings 221
Drawing Auxiliary Views 224
Drawing Construction Lines 227

CHAPTER 7

Using the Geometry Calculator and Filters

Using the Geometry Calculator 241
Creating Selection Sets 258

CHAPTER 8

Placing Text on Drawings

Text Standards 275
Scale Factors for Text Height 276
Text Composition 277
Using AutoCAD to Draw Text 277
AutoCAD Text Fonts 295
AutoCAD Text Styles 296
Redrawing Text Quickly 302
Revising Text with **DDEDIT** 303
Changing Text with the **Properties** Window 304
Working with Fields 308
Checking Your Spelling 311
Finding and Replacing Text 313
Additional Text Tips 315

CHAPTER 9

Working with Tables

Inserting Tables 323
Editing Tables 326
Table Styles 331

CHAPTER 10

Drawing Display Options

Redrawing and Regenerating the Screen 337
Getting Close to Your Work 339
Moving around the Display Screen 343
Setting View Resolution for Quick Displays 345
Creating Your Own Working Views 347
Using Transparent Display Commands 351
Using the Aerial View 352
Model Space and Paper Space 354
Tiled Viewports 355
Floating Viewports 359
Introduction to 3D Display Commands 362
Redrawing and Regenerating Viewports 365
Controlling the Order of Display 366
Clearing the Screen 367

CHAPTER 11

Layouts, Plotting, and Printing

Plotting Procedure 371
Layout and Plotting Terms 372
Layout Settings 373
Plot Device Selection and Management 384
Plot Styles 386
Plotting Settings 399
Alternative Plotting 410
Plotting Hints 412

Editing the Drawing

CHAPTER 12

Basic Editing Commands

Drawing Chamfers 420
Drawing Rounded Corners 425
Removing a Section from an Object 427
Trimming Sections of Lines, Circles, and Arcs 429
Extending Lines 431
Changing Lines and Circles 433
Moving an Object 434
Copying Objects 435
Drawing a Mirror Image of an Object 437
Rotating Existing Objects 438
Moving and Rotating an Object at the Same Time 440
Creating Multiple Objects with **ARRAY** 441
Changing the Size of an Object 446
Stretching an Object 447
Changing the Length of an Object 449
Selecting Objects for Future Editing 452
Creating Object Groups 453

CHAPTER 13

Automatic Editing

Automatic Editing with Grips 467
Basic Editing versus Automatic Editing 476
Using the **Properties** Window 477
Changing the Properties of an Object at the Command: Prompt . 481
Editing between Multiple Drawings 481
Matching Properties 483

AutoCAD Applications

CHAPTER 14

Introduction to Polylines and Multilines

Introduction to Drawing Polylines 491
Using the **UNDO** Command 495
Redoing the Undone 499
Filling Polylines and Traces 499
Drawing Multilines 499
Editing Multilines 508
Sketching with AutoCAD 512

CHAPTER 15

Drawing and Editing Polylines and Splines

Drawing Polyline Arcs 521
Revising Polylines Using the **PEDIT** Command 525
Revising a Polyline As One Unit 526
Converting a Polyline into Individual Line and Arc Segments . 535
Additional Methods for Smoothing Polylines 536
Drawing Curves Using the **SPLINE** Command 537
Editing Splines 539
Creating a Polyline Boundary 544

CHAPTER 16 Obtaining Information about the Drawing

Finding the Area of Shapes and Objects 552
Displaying Information with Fields 554
Listing Drawing Data 556
Listing Drawing Data for All Objects 558
Finding the Distance between Two Points 558
Identifying Point Locations 559
Checking the Time 559
Determining the Drawing Status 560

Dimensioning and Tolerancing

CHAPTER 17 Basic Dimensioning Practices

Dimension Arrangement 569
Drawing Dimensions with AutoCAD 570
Drawing Linear Dimensions 570
Dimensioning Angled Surfaces and Auxiliary Views 574
Dimensioning Angles 574
Dimensioning Practices 577
Location Dimensions 580
Datum and Chain Dimensioning 581
Using **QDIM** to Dimension 585
Including Symbols with Dimension Text 586
Drawing Center Dashes or Centerlines in a Circle or Arc 587
Dimensioning Circles 588
Dimensioning Arcs 591
Drawing Leader Lines 593
Alternate Dimensioning Practices 599
Thread Drawings and Notes 603
Dimension Styles 605
Creating Dimension Styles 605
Making Your Own Dimension Styles 619
Overriding Existing Dimensioning Variables 620

CHAPTER 18 Editing Dimensions

Erasing Dimensions 639
Editing Dimension Text Values 640
Editing Dimensions with the **QDIM** Command 641
Editing Dimension Text Placement 642
Using the **DIMEDIT** Command 644
Shortcut Menu Options 644
Changing the Dimension Style 645
Copying Dimension Styles between Drawings 646
Using the **Properties** Window to Edit Dimensions 646
Using the **MATCHPROP** Command 647
Editing Associative Dimensions 648
Exploding an Associative Dimension 649
Dimension Definition Points 650

CHAPTER 19

Dimensioning with Tolerances

Tolerancing Fundamentals .654
Assigning Decimal Places to Dimensions and Tolerances .655
Setting Primary Units .656
Setting Tolerance Methods .658

CHAPTER 20

Geometric Dimensioning and Tolerancing

Dimensioning Symbols .668
Geometric Characteristic Symbols .668
Material Condition Symbols .669
Feature Control Frame .671
Basic Dimensions .673
Additional Symbols .674
Datum Feature Symbols .675
Geometric Dimensioning and Tolerancing with AutoCAD .678
Introduction to Projected Tolerance Zones .682
Drawing a Double Feature Control Frame .685
Drawing Datum Feature Symbols .686
Controlling the Height of the Feature Control Frame .688
Drawing Basic Dimensions .688
Editing Feature Control Frames .689
Sample GD&T Applications .689

Advanced Drawing Construction

CHAPTER 21

Drawing Section Views and Graphic Patterns

Types of Sections .699
Section Line Symbols .700
Drawing Section Lines and Hatch Patterns .702
Editing Hatch Patterns .718
Drawing Objects with Solid Fills .719

CHAPTER 22

Creating Symbols for Multiple Use

Creating Symbols As Blocks .729
Using Blocks in a Drawing .734
Editing Blocks .744
Creating a Block from a Drawing File .749
Creating Blocks As Drawing Files .750
Symbol Libraries .752
Renaming Blocks .755
Deleting Named Objects .755
Using and Customizing Tool Palettes .756

CHAPTER 23
Assigning Attributes and Generating a Bill of Materials
Assigning Attributes to Blocks .773
Editing Attribute Definitions .776
Inserting Blocks with Attributes .778
Changing Attribute Values .780
Changing Attribute Definitions .783
Using Attributes to Automate Drafting Documentation .786
Collecting Attribute Information .791

CHAPTER 24
External References
Using Reference Drawings .799
Binding Dependent Objects to a Drawing .811
Editing Reference Drawings .813
Using Xrefs in Multiview Layouts .818

CHAPTER 25
Sheet Sets
Sheet Sets Overview .834
Introduction to the **Sheet Set Manager** .834
Creating Sheet Sets .835
Working with Sheet Sets .842
Working with Subsets .844
Working with Sheets .845
Publishing a Sheet Set .847
Sheet Views .849
Sheet Set Fields .858
Creating a Sheet List Table .861
Archiving a Sheet Set .863

Basic 3D Drawing and Advanced Applications

CHAPTER 26
Isometric Drawing
Pictorial Drawing Overview .869
Isometric Drawing .871
Isometric Dimensioning .878

CHAPTER 27
Introduction to Three-Dimensional Drawing
3D Coordinates .885
The Right-Hand Rule .887
Displaying 3D Views .888
3D Construction Techniques .891
Hiding and Shading .899

CHAPTER 28

External Commands, Script Files, and Slide Shows

Using Text Editors 907
The ACAD.PGP File 908
Creating Script Files to Automate AutoCAD 912
Slides and Slide Shows 914
Creating and Using Slide Libraries 916

Student CD Content

Textbook Exercises

Express Tools

Chapter Tests

Supplemental Materials

Working with AutoCAD Files
The Ergonomic Workstation
Managing the AutoCAD File System
Glossary of Computer Terms

Reference Materials

Drawing Sheet Sizes, Settings, and Scale Parameters
Command Aliases
AutoCAD 2005 Menu Tree
Drafting Standards and Related Documents
Drafting Symbols
Standard Tables
AutoCAD System Variables
Planning Sheet

Internet Resources

CHAPTER 1

Introduction to AutoCAD Features

Learning Objectives

After completing this chapter, you will be able to do the following:

- Describe the methods and procedures used in computer-aided drafting.
- Explain the value of planning your work and system management.
- Load AutoCAD from the Windows desktop.
- Describe the AutoCAD screen layout and user interface.
- Describe the function of dialog boxes.
- Identify the function of **DesignCenter** and the **Properties** window.
- Use the features found in the **AutoCAD Help** window.
- Review the online product support.
- Define the use of function, control, and shortcut keys.

The Tools of CAD

The computer and software are the principal components of the present-day design and drafting workstation. These tools make up a *system* referred to as *CAD*—computer-aided design or computer-aided drafting. Drafters, designers, and engineers use CAD to develop designs and drawings and to plot them on paper or film. Additionally, drawings and designs can be displayed as 3D models and animations or used in analysis and testing.

CAD has surpassed the use of manual drafting techniques because of its speed, power, accuracy, and flexibility. However, it is not totally without its attendant problems and trade-offs. Although the uses of CAD designs are limited only by the imagination, it should be remembered that the computer hardware is sensitive to the slightest electrical impulses and the human body is sensitive to the repetitive motions required when using the tools.

The AutoCAD Toolbox

Drawings and models are constructed in AutoCAD using XYZ coordinates. The *Cartesian (rectangular)* coordinate system is used most often and is discussed in Chapter 3. Angular layouts are created by measuring angles in a counterclockwise direction. Drawings can be annotated with text and described with a variety of dimensioning techniques. In addition, objects can be given colors, patterns, and textures. AutoCAD also provides you with the tools to create basic pictorial drawings, called *isometrics,* and powerful 3D solids and surface models.

The Applications of AutoCAD

Using AutoCAD software and this text, you will learn how to construct, lay out, dimension, and annotate two-dimensional drawings. Should you wish to continue your study into 3D modeling, 3D rendering, and customization, ***AutoCAD and its Applications—Advanced*** can provide you with detailed instruction. Your studies will enable you to create a wide variety of drawings, designs, and 3D models in any of the drafting, design, and engineering disciplines.

AutoCAD drawings can have hundreds of colors and *layers,* which contain different kinds of information. Objects can also be shown as exploded assemblies or displayed in 3D. See **Figure 1-1.** In addition, objects in the drawing can be given "intelligence" in the form of ***attributes***. These attributes are various kinds of data that turn a drawing into a graphical database. You can then ask questions of your drawing and receive a variety of information.

Using AutoCAD, you have the ability to construct 3D models that appear as wireframes or have surface colors and textures. The creation of solid models that have mass properties and can be analyzed is also possible with AutoCAD. The display in **Figure 1-2** is an example of a solid model created in AutoCAD. 3D drawings and models can be viewed in several ways. These models can also be colored and shaded, or ***rendered***, to appear in a realistic format.

Figure 1-1.
A 3D model shown as an exploded assembly. (Thomas Short, Anthony Dudek)

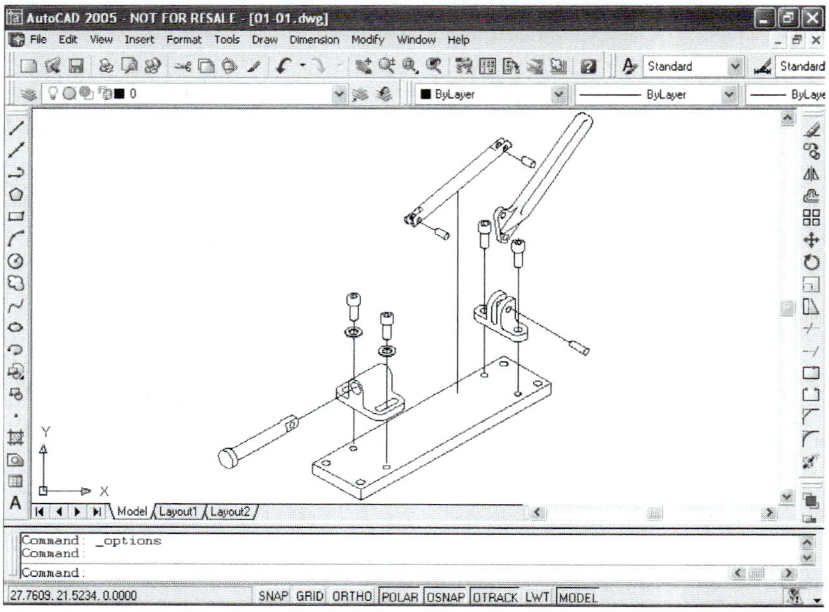

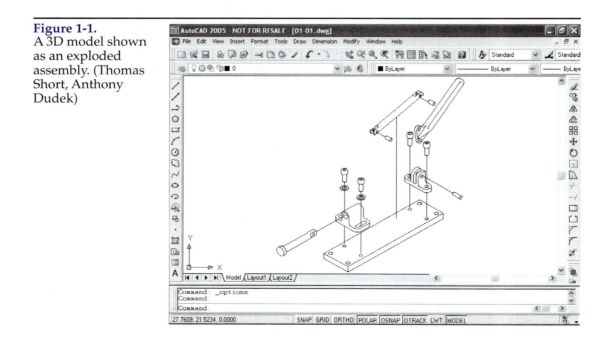

Figure 1-2.
A 3D model of a connecting rod. A—Model shown as a wireframe with edges marked by lines. B—Color and shading are added when the model is rendered. (Autodesk, Inc.)

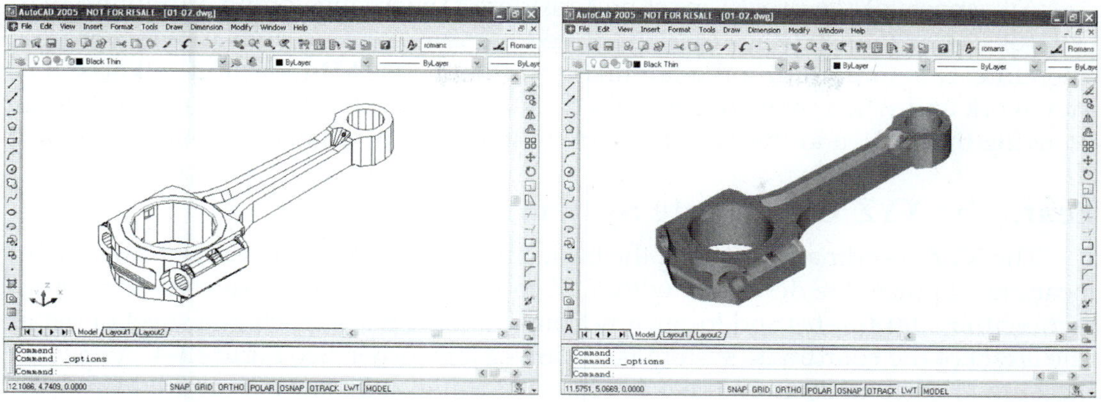

A B

A powerful application of CAD software and 3D models is animation. The simplest form of animation is to dynamically rotate the model in order to view it from any direction. See **Figure 1-3.** Drawings and models can also be animated so the model appears to move, rotate, and even explode into its individual components. An extremely useful form of animation is called a ***walkthrough***. Using specialized software, you can plot a path through or around a model and replay it just like a movie. The logical next step in viewing the model is to actually be inside it and have the ability to manipulate and change the objects in it. This is called ***virtual reality***, and it is achieved through the use of 3D models and highly specialized software and hardware.

Figure 1-3.
This 3D piping model can be rotated and viewed from any location in 3D space. (Autodesk, Inc.)

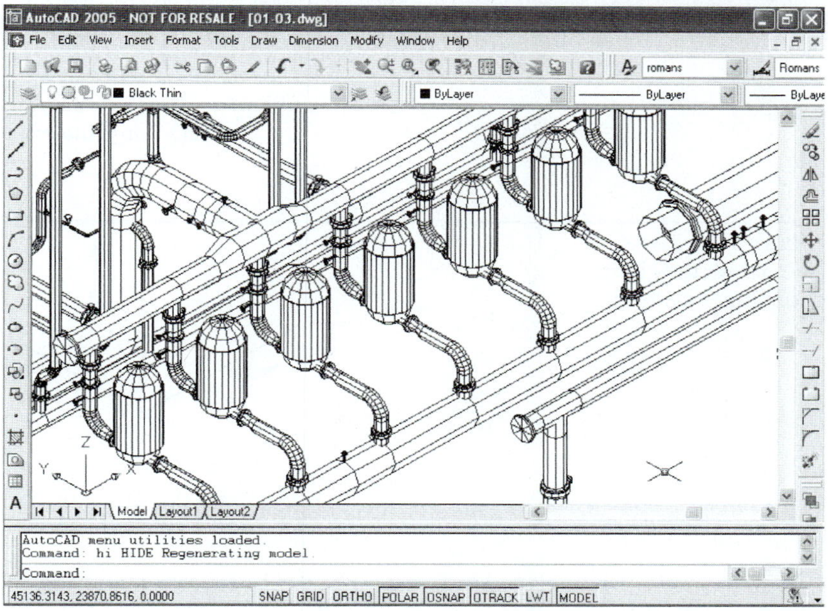

Establishing an AutoCAD Drawing Method

All aspects of the project must be considered when developing a drawing plan. Careful use of the CAD system is required for the planning and drawing process. Therefore, it is important to be familiar with the AutoCAD tools and to know how they work and when they are best suited for a specific job. There is no substitute for knowing the tools, and the most basic of these is the Cartesian coordinate system.

Learn the XYZ Coordinate System

The XYZ coordinate system is the basic building block of any CAD drawing. The locations of points are described with XYZ coordinate values. These values are called ***rectangular coordinates*** and locate any point on a flat plane, such as a sheet of paper. The *origin* of the coordinate system is the lower-left corner. See **Figure 1-4.** A distance measured horizontally from the origin is an X value. A distance measured vertically from the origin is a Y value.

Rectangular coordinates can also be measured in three-dimensional space. The third dimension rises up from the surface of the paper and is given a Z value. See **Figure 1-5.** When describing coordinate locations the X value is first, the Y value second, and the Z value third. Each value is separated by a comma. For example, the coordinate location of 3,1,6 represents three units from the X origin, one unit from the Y origin, and six units from the Z origin. A detailed explanation of rectangular coordinates is provided in Chapter 3.

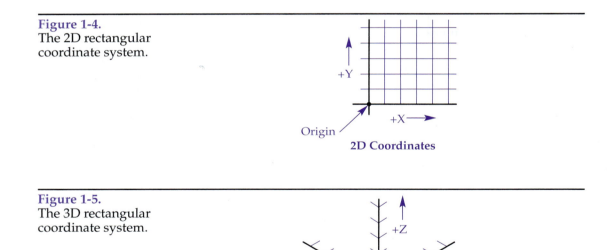

Figure 1-4.
The 2D rectangular coordinate system.

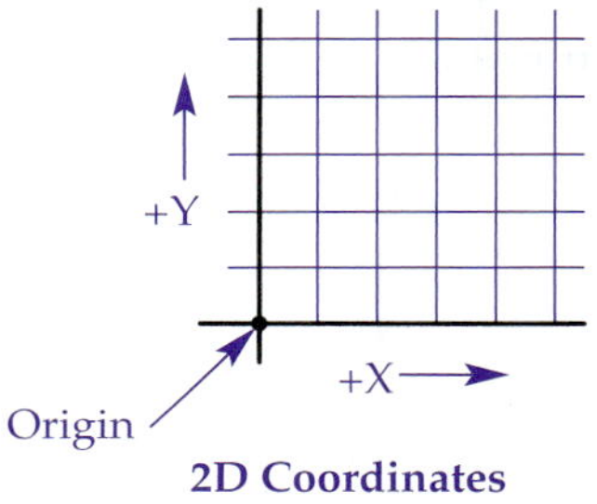

Figure 1-5.
The 3D rectangular coordinate system.

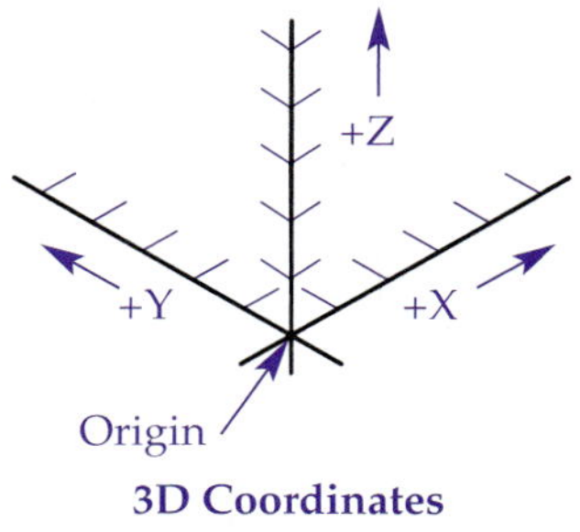

Planning Your Drawing

Drawing planning involves looking at the entire process or project in which you are involved. A plan determines how a project is going to be approached. It includes the drawings to be created, the title and numbering conventions, the information to be presented, and the types of symbols needed to show the information.

More specifically, drawing planning applies to how you create and manage a drawing or set of drawings. This includes which view or feature you draw first and the coordinates and AutoCAD commands you use to draw it. Drafters who begin constructing a drawing from the seat of their pants—creating symbols and naming objects, shapes, and views as they go—do not possess a good drawing plan. Those who plan, use consistent techniques, and adhere to school or company standards are developing good drawing habits.

Throughout this text you will find aids to help you develop good drawing habits. One of the first steps in developing your skills is to learn how to plan your work. The importance of planning cannot be emphasized enough. There is no substitute.

Using Drawing Standards

Standards are guidelines for operating procedures, drawing techniques, and record keeping. Most schools and companies have established standards. It is important that standards exist and are used by all CAD personnel. Drawing standards may include the following items:

- Methods of file storage (location and name).
- File naming conventions.
- File backup methods and times.
- Drawing templates and title blocks.
- Drawing symbols.
- Dimensioning styles and techniques.
- Text styles.
- Table styles.
- Layer settings.
- Plot styles.

Your standards may vary in content, but the most important aspect of standards is that they are used. When standards are used, your drawings are consistent, you become more productive, and the classroom or office functions more efficiently.

Planning Your Work

Study the planning pyramids in **Figure 1-6.** The horizontal axes of the pyramids represent the amount of time spent on the project. The vertical axes represent the life of the project. The top level is the planning stage and the bottom level is the final execution of the project.

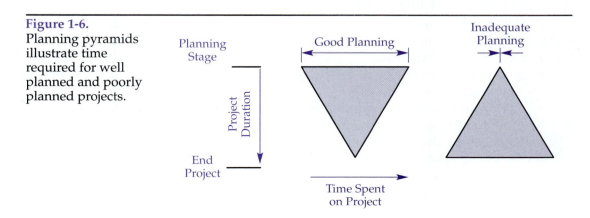

Figure 1-6.
Planning pyramids illustrate time required for well planned and poorly planned projects.

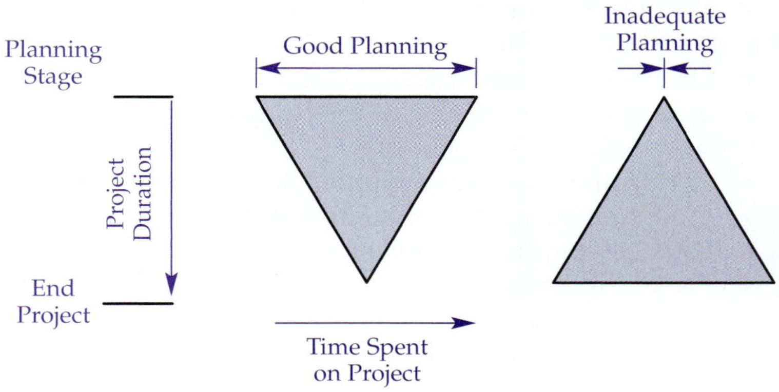

The right pyramid is pointed at the top and indicates a small amount of initial planning. As the project progresses, more and more time is devoted to planning, and less time is available for other tasks. This is *not* an ideal situation. The left pyramid is inverted and shows a lot of time devoted to initial planning. As the project advances, less planning time is needed, thus freeing more time for tasks related to the completion of the project.

As you begin your CAD training, plan your drawing sessions thoroughly to organize your thoughts. Sketch the problem or design, noting the sizes and locations of features. List the drawing commands needed in the order they are to be used. Schedule a regular time to use the computer and adhere to that time. Follow the standards your school or firm has set. These might include specific drawing names, project planning sheets, project logs, drawing layout procedures, special title blocks, and a location for drawing storage. Everyone using the computers in your school or company must follow the standards and procedures. Confusion may result if your drawings do not have the proper name, are stored in the wrong place, or have the wrong title block.

Develop the habit of saving your work regularly—at least every ten to fifteen minutes. The automatic save tool can be set to automatically save your drawings at predetermined intervals. Automatic save is covered in detail in Chapter 2. Drawings may be lost due to a software error, hardware malfunction, power failure, or your own mistakes. This is not common, but you should still be prepared for such an event.

You should develop methods of managing your work. This is critical to computer drafting and is discussed throughout the text. Keep the following points in mind as you begin your AutoCAD training:

- ✓ Plan your work and organize your thoughts.
- ✓ Learn and use your classroom or office standards.
- ✓ Save your work often.

If you remember to follow these three points, your grasp of the tools and methods of CAD will be easier. In addition, your experiences with the computer will be more enjoyable.

Remember the planning pyramids as you begin your study of AutoCAD. When you feel the need to dive blindly into a drawing or project, restrain yourself. Take the time needed for development of the project goals. Then proceed with the confidence of knowing where you are heading.

During your early stages of AutoCAD training, write down all the instructions needed to construct your drawing. Do this especially for your first few assignments. This means documenting every command and every coordinate point (dimension) needed. Develop a planning sheet for your drawings. Your time spent at the computer with AutoCAD will be more productive and enjoyable.

Using Drawing Plan Sheets

A good work plan can save drawing time. Planning should include sketches. A rough preliminary sketch and a drawing plan can help by:

- Determining the drawing layout.
- Setting the overall size of the drawing by laying out the views and required free space.
- Confirming the drawing units, based on the dimensions provided.
- Predetermining the point entry system and locating the points.
- Establishing the grid and snap settings.
- Presetting some of the drawing variables, such as layers, linetypes, and line widths. (These items are explained in Chapters 3 and 4.)
- Establishing how and when various activities are to be performed.

- Determining the best use of AutoCAD.
- Resulting in an even workload.
- Providing maximum use of equipment.

Planning Checklist

In the early stages of your AutoCAD training, it is best to plan your drawing projects carefully. There is a tendency to want things to happen immediately—for things to be "automatic"—but if you hurry and do little or no planning, you will become more frustrated. Therefore, as you begin each new project, step through the following planning checklist so the execution of your project goes smoothly:

- ✓ Analyze the problem.
- ✓ Study all engineering sketches.
- ✓ Locate all available resources and list for future use.
- ✓ Determine the applicable standards for the project.
- ✓ Sketch the problem.
- ✓ Decide on the number and kinds of views required.
- ✓ Determine the final plotted scale of the drawing and of all views.
- ✓ Determine the drawing sequence, such as lines, features, dimensions, and notes.
- ✓ List the AutoCAD commands to be used.
- ✓ Follow the standards and refer to resources as you work.

PROFESSIONAL TIP

AutoCAD is designed so you can construct drawings and models using the actual dimensions of the object. *Always draw in full scale.* The proper text and dimension size is set using scale factors. This is covered in detail in later chapters. The final scale of the drawing should be planned early, and it is shown on the plot.

Working Procedures Checklist

As you begin learning AutoCAD, you will realize that several skills are required to become a proficient CAD user. The following checklist provides you with some hints to help you become comfortable with AutoCAD. These hints will also allow you to work quickly and efficiently. The following actions are discussed in detail in later chapters:

- ✓ Plan all work with pencil and paper before using the computer.
- ✓ Check the **Layers** and **Properties** toolbars at the top of the display screen and the status bar at the bottom to see which object property settings and drawing aids are in effect.
- ✓ Read the command line at the bottom of the display screen. Constantly check for the correct commands, instructions, or keyboard entry of data.
- ✓ Read the command line after keyboard entry of data before pressing the [Enter] key. Backspacing to erase incorrect typing is quicker than redoing the command.
- ✓ If using a multibutton puck, develop a good hand position that allows easy movement. Your button-pressing finger should move without readjusting your grip of the puck.
- ✓ Learn the meanings of all the buttons on your puck or mouse and use them regularly.

- ✓ Watch the disk drive lights to see when the disks are being accessed. Some disk access may take a few seconds. Knowing what is happening will lessen frustration and impatience.
- ✓ Think ahead. Know your next move.
- ✓ Learn new commands every day. Do not rely on just a few that seem to work. Find commands that can speed your work and do it more efficiently.
- ✓ Save your work every ten to fifteen minutes, in case a power failure or system crash deletes the drawing held in computer memory.
- ✓ If you are stumped, ask the computer for help. Use the online help to display valuable information about each command on the screen. Using AutoCAD's online help is discussed in detail later in this chapter.

EXERCISE 1-1 Complete the Exercise on the Student CD.

Starting AutoCAD

AutoCAD 2005 is designed to operate with Windows 2003 Server Edition, Windows XP Professional, Windows 2000 Server Edition, Windows 2000, Windows XP Home, and Windows XP Tablet PC. If you see illustrations in this text that appear slightly different than your screen, do not be concerned, as the AutoCAD feature is the same.

When AutoCAD is first installed, Windows creates a ***program icon***, which is displayed on the desktop. An ***icon*** is a small picture representing an application, accessory, file, or command. In addition to the icon, the program name is listed as an item in the Start menu, under the Autodesk item, which is found in the Programs menu.

NOTE AutoCAD must first be installed properly on the computer before it can be used. Refer to the AutoCAD help system for detailed instructions on AutoCAD installation and configuration of peripheral devices, such as plotters, printers, and digitizers.

AutoCAD can be started using several different techniques. The quickest way to start AutoCAD is to double-click on the AutoCAD 2005 icon on the Windows desktop. See **Figure 1-7.**

PROFESSIONAL TIP When AutoCAD is installed using unaltered settings, the label for the AutoCAD icon is AutoCAD 2005. The name can be quickly changed by picking the label, typing a new name, and pressing [Enter].

Figure 1-7.
Double-click the AutoCAD 2005 icon on the Windows desktop to start AutoCAD.

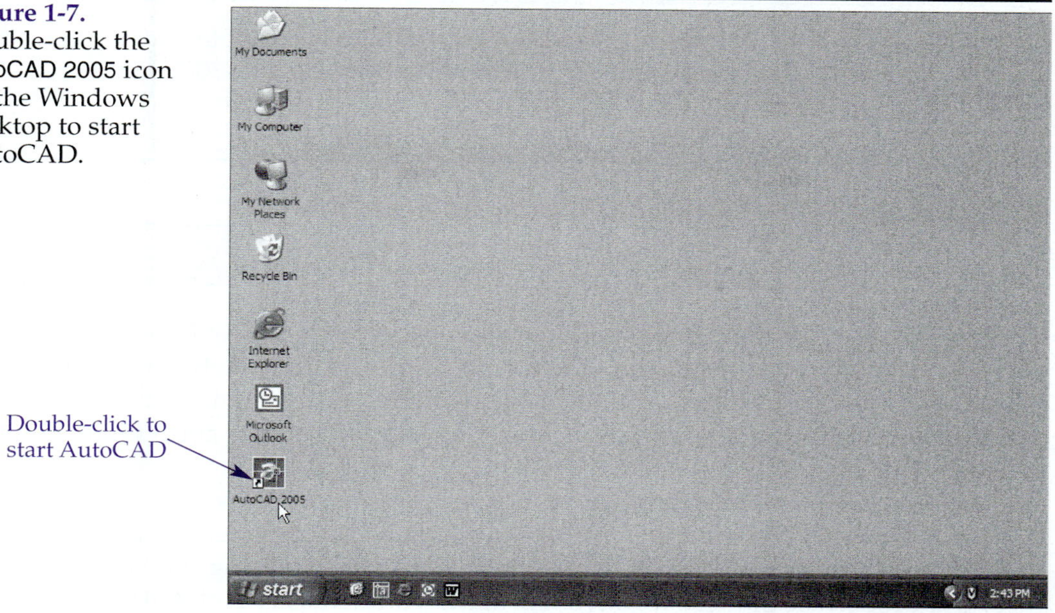

The second method for starting AutoCAD is to pick the Start button at the lower-left corner of the Windows desktop. This displays the Start menu. Next, move the pointer to Programs and either hold it there or pick to display the Programs menu. Move the pointer to Autodesk and click to show the Autodesk menu. Now move the pointer to the AutoCAD 2005 item and click. This displays all the items in the AutoCAD 2005 program group. Pick AutoCAD 2005 to start the software. See **Figure 1-8.**

Figure 1-8.
Pick AutoCAD 2005 in the AutoCAD 2005 menu to load AutoCAD.

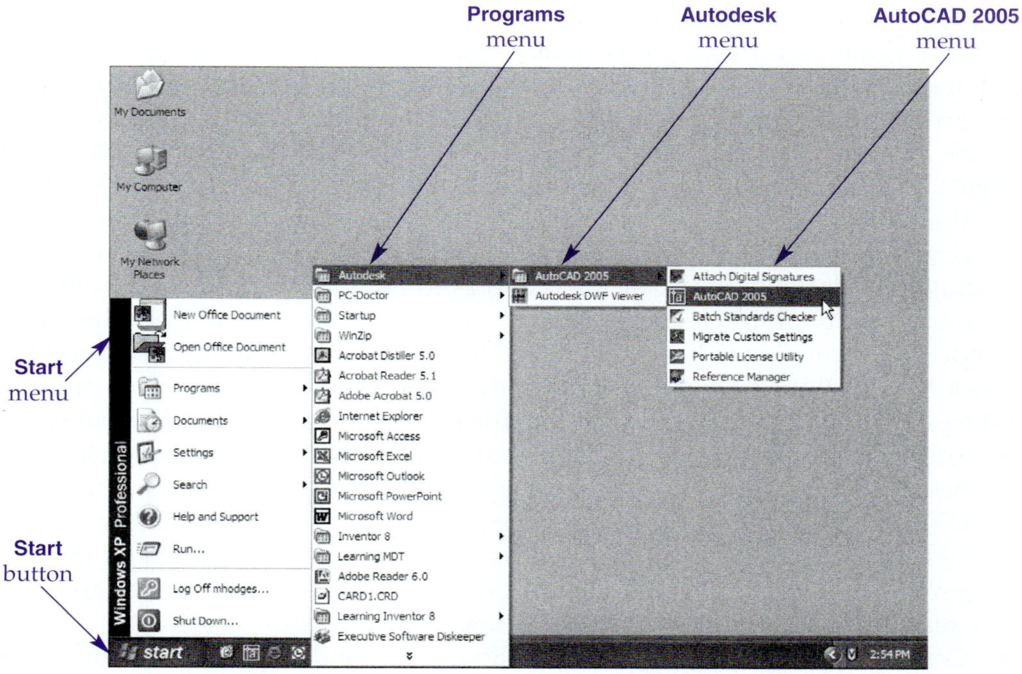

NOTE You can also start AutoCAD by double-clicking on the acad.exe file in the Program Files/AutoCAD 2005 folder.

The AutoCAD Window

The AutoCAD window is similar to any other window within the Windows operating system. Picking the small control icon in the upper-left corner displays a standard window control menu, and the icons in the upper-right corner are used for minimizing, maximizing, and closing the program window or individual drawing windows. See **Figure 1-9.**

Window sizing operations are done as with any other window. AutoCAD uses the familiar Windows style interface, with buttons, pull-down menus, and dialog boxes. Each of these items is discussed in detail in this chapter. Learning the layout, appearance, and proper use of these features will allow you to master AutoCAD quickly.

Standard Screen Layout

The standard screen layout provides a large graphics, or drawing, area. The drawing area is bordered by ***toolbars*** at the left, right, and top and by the ***command window*** at the bottom. Look at your screen now and study the illustration in **Figure 1-9.** Note that the proportional size of the AutoCAD window features may vary depending on the display resolution of your computer system.

Many of the elements of the AutoCAD window are referred to as ***floating***. This means the item can be freely resized or moved about the screen into new positions. Floating features are contained within a standard Windows border and display a title bar at the top. When you run AutoCAD for the first time, the AutoCAD window is displayed in a floating position on the desktop. A smaller window inside the AutoCAD window displays the drawing area for the currently open drawing file. Floating windows are moved and adjusted for size in the same manner as any other window; however, the drawing windows can only be adjusted and positioned within the AutoCAD window.

Some floating features, such as toolbars and the **Tool Palettes** and **Sheet Set Manager** windows, can also be ***docked*** around the edges of the AutoCAD window. The toolbars displayed initially after installing AutoCAD are docked by default and do not display a title bar. To place a docked toolbar in a floating position, you can either double-click the grab bar or press and hold the pick button while pointing at the grab bar, and then move your mouse to drag the toolbar away from the edge of the window. The term ***grab bar*** refers to the two thin bars at the top or left edge of a docked toolbar. To dock a floating toolbar, double-click on the title bar or press and hold the pick button while pointing at the title bar and drag the toolbar to an edge of the AutoCAD window (top, bottom, left, or right). Then release the pick button. When the item is docked, it loses its border and title bar and becomes a part of the AutoCAD window. Floating features may be moved or docked at any time as needed.

Become familiar with these unique areas of the AutoCAD window and the information provided by each. The following list describes the function of each area. Each of these features will be discussed in detail later in this text:

- **Command window.** In its default position, this window is docked at the bottom of the AutoCAD window. It displays the Command: prompt and reflects any command entries you make. It also displays prompts that supply information to you or request input. This is where your primary communications with AutoCAD are displayed, so watch for any information shown on this line.

Figure 1-9.
The standard AutoCAD window.

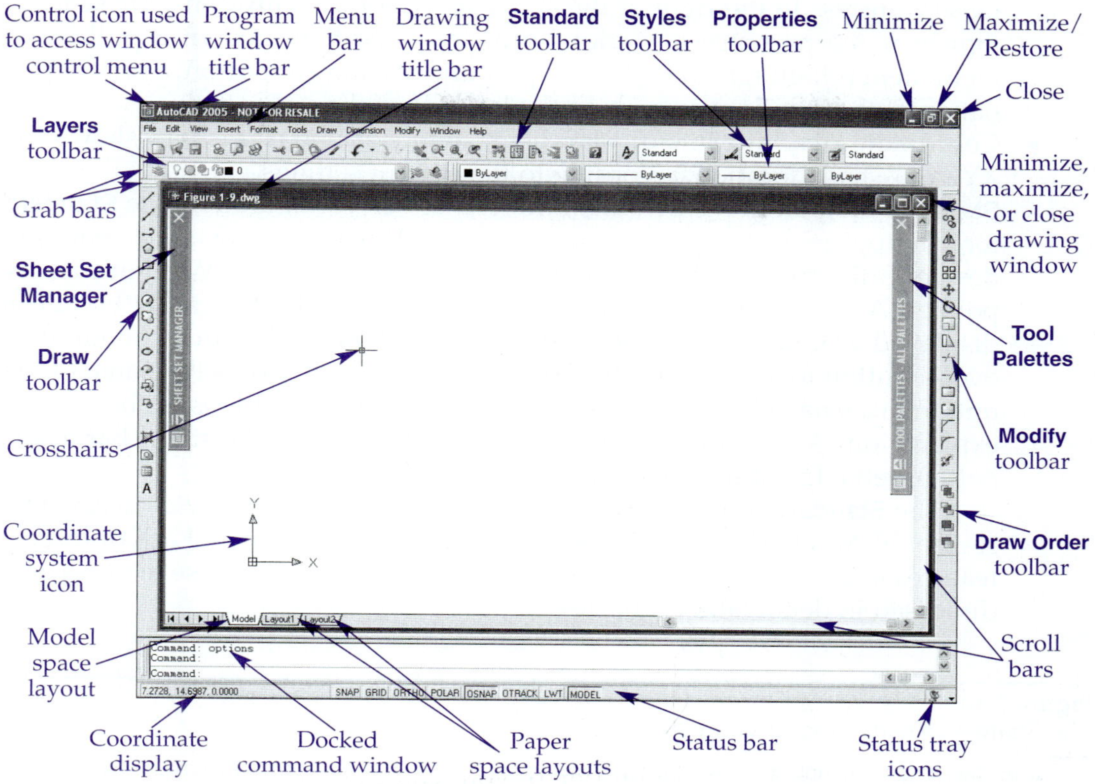

- **Menu bar.** The menu bar appears just below the title bar and displays a number of menu names. As with standard Windows menus, use the cursor to point at a menu name and press the pick button. This causes a ***pull-down menu*** to be displayed. Any time you pick an item followed by an ***ellipsis*** (…), a dialog box is displayed. A ***dialog box*** is a rectangular area that appears on the screen after you type or select certain commands. It contains a variety of options related to a specific command or function and provides a convenient means of supplying information to AutoCAD.
- **Scroll bars.** The scroll bars allow you to adjust your view of the drawing area by "sliding" the drawing from side to side or up and down.
- **Crosshairs.** This is your primary means of pointing to objects or locations within a drawing.
- **Coordinate system icon.** This indicates the current coordinate system and view orientation.
- **Toolbars.** Toolbars contain various buttons that activate AutoCAD commands. These toolbars can be moved, resized, modified, hidden, or docked as needed. Some toolbar buttons show a small black triangle in the lower-right corner. These buttons are called ***flyouts***. Press and hold the pick button while pointing at a flyout to display a set of related buttons.
- **Tool Palettes window.** The **Tool Palettes** window is similar to floating toolbars and contains frequently used block symbols and fill patterns that can be used in your drawings. Tool palettes are typically user customized with block symbols and hatch patterns to meet your specific needs. AutoCAD includes three sample palettes. Customizing tool palettes is covered later in this text.
- **Sheet Set Manager window.** The **Sheet Set Manager** window helps you organize, display, and manage sheet sets. A *sheet set* is a named collection of drawing sheets. Sheet sets are covered later in this text.

- **Status bar.** This bar contains several buttons that display the current state of specific drawing control features and allow access for changing the settings of these features. To the right of the status bar is a tray with icons. These icons represent the presence of various drawing conditions. When a pull-down menu item is highlighted or you are pointing at a toolbar button, a brief explanation of the item is shown along the left side of the status bar.
- **Coordinate display.** This display field, found on the status bar, shows the XYZ crosshairs location, according to the current settings.
- **Standard toolbar.** In the default AutoCAD screen configuration, the **Standard** toolbar appears just above the **Layers** toolbar. When you move your pointing device to the toolbar, the crosshairs change to the familiar Windows arrow pointer. As you move your cursor across a toolbar button, a 3D border is displayed around the previously flat button. Holding the cursor motionless over a button for a moment displays a ***tooltip***, which shows the name of the button in a small box at the cursor location. While the tooltip is visible, a brief explanation of what the button does is displayed along the status bar at the bottom-left edge of the window.

  The **Standard** toolbar contains a series of buttons that provide access to several of AutoCAD's drawing setup and control commands. Each of these features is identified and briefly described in **Figure 1-10.** These features are discussed in detail later in this text.

Figure 1-10.
The **Standard** toolbar and its components.

A—**Grab Bar.** A "grab" handle for relocating toolbars.
B—**New.** Begins a new drawing.
C—**Open.** Opens an existing drawing for editing and revision.
D—**Save.** Writes the drawing information currently in memory to a file.
E—**Plot.** Sends the drawing information to a hardcopy device, such as a printer or plotter.
F—**Plot Preview.** Displays a preview of the drawing layout prior to plotting.
G—**Publish.** Prints drawing sheets to an electronic file.
H—**Cut to Clipboard.** "Cuts" (removes) a specified portion of your drawing geometry, storing it in the Windows Clipboard.
I—**Copy to Clipboard.** Copies a specified portion of the drawing geometry, storing it in the Windows Clipboard.
J—**Paste from Clipboard.** "Pastes" (inserts) the contents of the Windows Clipboard to a specified location in your drawing.
K—**Match Properties.** Copies the properties from one object to one or more objects.
L—**Undo**. Cancels the effects of the last command or operation.
M—**Undo Drop-Down.** Provides a list of previous operations that can be undone.
N—**Redo.** Can be used to "redo" or restore operations previously canceled by the **Undo** command.
O—**Redo Drop-Down.** Provides a list of previously undone operations to restore in the current drawing.
P—**Pan Realtime.** Displays the hand cursor and moves the display in the graphics screen dynamically in "real-time."
Q—**Zoom Realtime.** Displays the Zoom cursor and increases or decreases the displayed size of objects in the drawing area.
R—**Zoom Flyout.** Displays a series of buttons that activate the **ZOOM** command options.
S—**Zoom Previous.** Restores the previous display to the drawing area.
T—**Properties.** Displays the **Properties** window, where you can set properties for new objects or modify the properties of existing objects.
U—**DesignCenter.** Activates **DesignCenter**, allowing drawing information to be shared between multiple drawings.
V—**Tool Palettes.** Turns the **Tool Palettes** window on or off.
W—**Sheet Set Manager.** Toggles on and off the **Sheet Set Manager** window, which allows you to manage the drawings associated with a project.
X—**Markup Set Manager.** Displays the **DWF Markup** window, which is used when working with markup files.
Y—**Help.** Activates AutoCAD's online help facility.

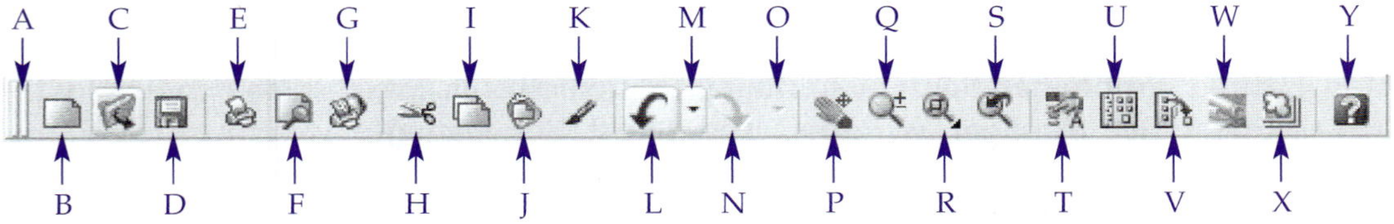

- **Styles toolbar.** In the default AutoCAD screen configuration, the **Styles** toolbar appears to the right of the **Standard** toolbar. This toolbar contains buttons and display fields relative to text, dimension, and table styles. These features are identified and briefly explained in Figure 1-11.
- **Layers and Properties toolbars.** In the default AutoCAD screen configuration, the **Layers** and **Properties** toolbars appear just above the drawing area, below the **Standard** and **Styles** toolbars. These toolbars contain buttons and display fields for setting and adjusting the properties of objects in a drawing. Each of these features is identified and briefly explained in Figure 1-12.

Figure 1-11.
The **Styles** toolbar and its components.

A—**Text Style Manager**. Displays the **Text Style** dialog box where text styles can be created and managed.

B—**Text Style Control**. Displays the current text style and provides a list of available text styles in the drawing.

C—**Dimension Style Manager**. Displays the **Dimension Style Manager** dialog box where dimension styles can be created and managed.

D—**Dim Style Control**. Displays the current dimension style and provides a list of available dimension styles in the current drawing.

E—**Table Style Manager**. Displays the **Table Style** dialog box where table styles can be created and managed.

F—**Table Style Control**. Displays the current table style and provides a list of the available table styles in the current drawing.

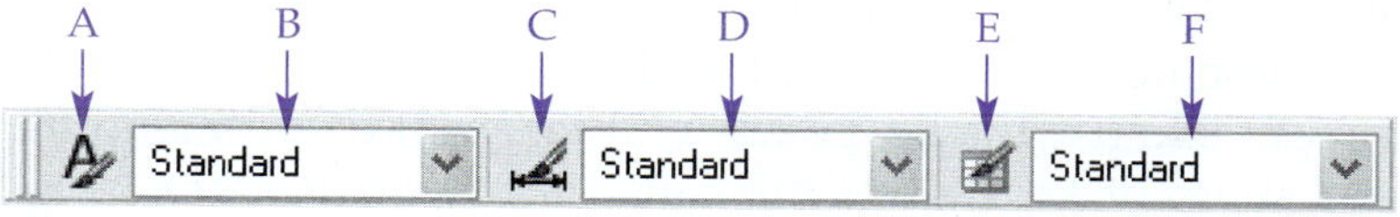

Figure 1-12.
The **Layers** and **Properties** toolbars and their components.

Layers Toolbar:

A—**Layer Properties Manager**. Displays the **Layer Properties Manager**, where drawing layers can be created and managed.

B—**Layer Control Drop-Down**. Displays the current drawing layer, provides a list of available drawing layers, and allows the control of different display properties of each.

C—**Make Object's Layer Current**. Allows the selection of a drawing object to change the current drawing layer to that of the selected object.

D—**Layer Previous**. Activates the previous layer control display.

Properties Toolbar:

E—**Color Control**. Displays the current object creation color, provides a list of colors, and allows the accessing of the **Select Color** dialog box.

F—**Linetype Control**. Displays the current object creation linetype, provides a list of loaded linetypes in the current drawing, and allows access to the **Linetype Manager** dialog box.

G—**Lineweight Control**. Displays the current object creation lineweight and provides a list of available lineweights.

H—**Plot Style Control**. Displays the current object creation plot style and provides a list of additional plot styles and the accessing of the **Current Plot Style** dialog box.

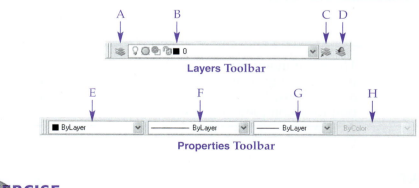

Layers Toolbar

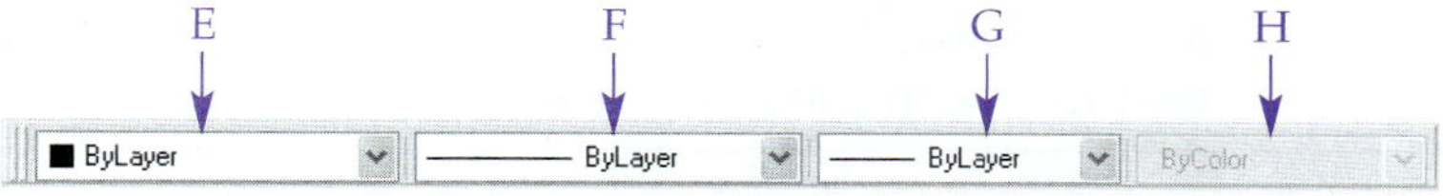

Properties Toolbar

EXERCISE 1-2 Complete the Exercise on the Student CD.

Pull-Down Menus

The AutoCAD pull-down menus are located on the menu bar at the top of the screen. As with a toolbar, when you move your pointing device to the menu bar, the crosshairs change to the arrow pointer. The default menu bar has eleven pull-down menu items: **File**, **Edit**, **View**, **Insert**, **Format**, **Tools**, **Draw**, **Dimension**, **Modify**, **Window**, and **Help**.

> **NOTE**
>
> During the AutoCAD installation process, an additional Express Tools menu is available. Installing this menu provides you with an **Express** pull-down menu, which includes additional tools for improved functionality and productivity during your drawing processes. Express Tools are discussed on the Student CD and referenced where appropriate throughout this textbook.

Menu items and commands are easily selected by picking a menu item with your pointing device. Some commands in the pull-down menu may have a small arrow to the right. When one of these items is selected, a ***cascading menu*** appears that has additional options. Some of the menu selections are followed by an ellipsis (...). If you pick one of these items, a dialog box is displayed.

It is also possible to use the keyboard to access pull-down menu items by typing shortcuts. These shortcut keystrokes are called ***menu accelerator keys.*** The [Alt] key turns on the menu accelerator keys. To access any pull-down menu selection, use an [Alt]+[*key*] combination on the keyboard. For instance, the **View** menu can be accessed by first pressing the [Alt] key and then pressing the [V] key.

One character of each pull-down menu title or command is underlined on screen. Once a pull-down menu is displayed, a menu item can be selected using that single character key. For example, to zoom in closer to your work, press [Alt]+[V] to access the **View** menu. Then, press [Z] to select the **Zoom** command, and [I] to select the **In** option.

> **PROFESSIONAL TIP**
>
> Once a pull-down menu is displayed, you can use the up, down, right, and left arrow keys to move to different items in the menu and to display cascading menus. When an item followed by an arrow is highlighted, press the right arrow key to display the cascading menu. Remove the menu by pressing the left arrow. Press [Enter] to select a highlighted item.

> **NOTE**
>
> There are many individual character key and key combination shortcuts available for Windows and Windows-based applications. Refer to your Microsoft Windows documentation for a complete list of keyboard shortcuts.

EXERCISE 1-3 Complete the Exercise on the Student CD.

Dialog Boxes

One of the most important aspects of AutoCAD is the graphical user interface (GUI) offered by the Microsoft Windows operating environment. A *graphical user interface* is how the software displays information, options, and choices for you. The most common component of the GUI is the dialog box. A *dialog box* is a box that may contain a variety of information. You can set variables and select items in a dialog box using your cursor. This eliminates typing, saving time and increasing productivity.

A pull-down selection followed by an ellipsis (...) displays a dialog box when picked. An example of a simple dialog box is shown in **Figure 1-13.** This dialog box is displayed when you pick **Block...** from the **Insert** pull-down menu.

Buttons in a dialog box that are followed by an ellipsis (...) display another dialog box when they are picked. You must make a selection from the second dialog box before returning to the original dialog box. A button in a dialog box with an arrow symbol (**<**) requires you to make a selection in the drawing area.

There are standard parts to all dialog boxes. Knowing these parts will make it much easier to work with the dialog boxes. Detailed discussions are provided in later chapters.

- **Command buttons.** When you pick a command button, something happens immediately. The most common buttons are **OK**, **Cancel**, and **Help**. See **Figure 1-13.** If a button has a dark border, it is the default. Pressing the [Enter] key accepts the default. If a button is "grayed-out," it cannot be selected.
- **Text box.** You can enter a name or single line of information using the text box. Refer to the text box in **Figure 1-13.**
- **Check box.** A check box, or toggle, displays a "✓" when it is on (active). If the box is empty, the option is off. See **Figure 1-14.**
- **Radio buttons.** Only one item in a group of radio buttons can be highlighted or active at one time. See **Figure 1-14.**
- **Tab.** A dialog box tab is much like an index tab used to separate sections of a notebook or the label tabs on the top of a manila file folder. Many dialog boxes in AutoCAD contain two or more "pages" or "panels," each with a tab at the top. See **Figure 1-14.**
- **List box.** A list box contains a list of items or options that you can scan through using the scroll bar (if present) or the keyboard arrow keys. Either highlight the desired item with the arrow keys and press [Enter] or simply select it using your pointing device. See **Figure 1-15.**

Figure 1-13.
A dialog box is displayed when you pick an item that is followed by an ellipsis. The dialog box shown here appears after you select **Block...** from the **Insert** pull-down menu. You can enter a name, number, or single line of information in a text box.

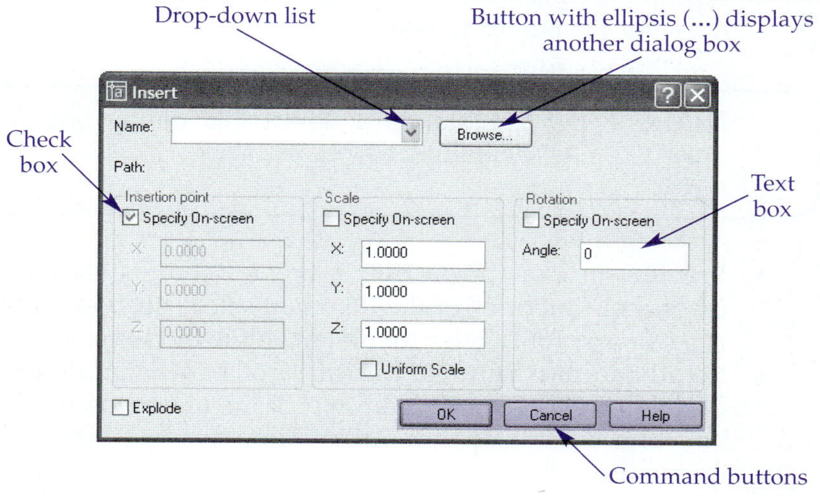

Figure 1-14.
Only one radio button in a group can be highlighted at a time. A "✓" in a check box indicates the item is active (on). Any number of check boxes can be active in a given group. A dialog box tab is much like an index tab used to separate sections of a notebook. Each tab displays a new set of related options.

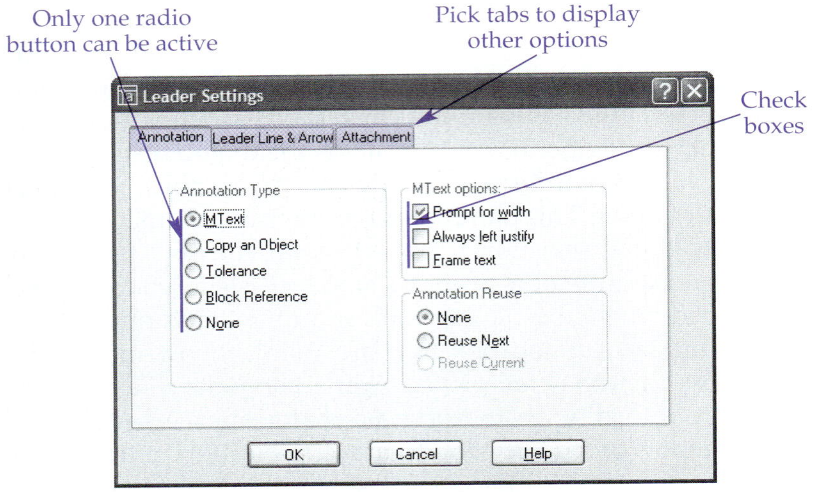

Figure 1-15.
A list box contains a list of items related to the dialog box. A drop-down list is displayed when you pick the drop-down arrow.

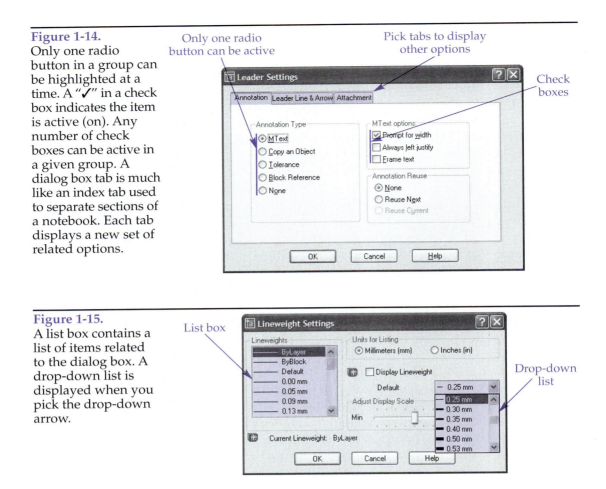

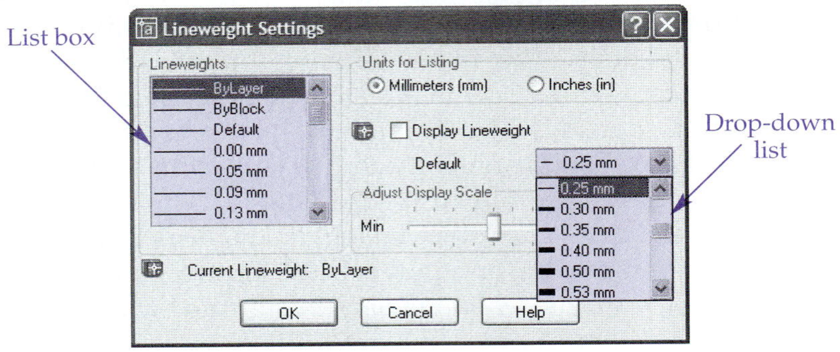

- **Drop-down list box.** The drop-down list box is similar to the standard list box, except only one item is initially shown. The remaining items are hidden until you pick the drop-down arrow. When you pick the drop-down arrow, the drop-down list is displayed below the initial item. You can then pick from the expanded list or use the scroll bar to find the item you need. See Figure 1-15.
- **File dialog box.** The file dialog box provides a simple means of locating and specifying file names using the familiar Windows style dialog box. The example in Figure 1-16 shows a file dialog box for selecting one or more drawing file names to open for editing.

NOTE

The standard **Select File** dialog box is discussed in more detail in Chapter 2.

- **Preview box or image tile.** A preview box is an area of a dialog box that displays a "picture" of the item you select, such as a file, hatching style, linetype, or text font. Refer to the image tile in Figure 1-16.
- **Scroll bars and buttons.** Vertical scroll bars and buttons allow you to scroll up or down a list of items. Simply pick the up or down arrows. Horizontal scroll bars and buttons operate in the same manner. Figure 1-17 shows the operation of a scroll bar.
- **Alerts.** Alerts may appear in the lower-left corner of the original dialog box, or as a separate alert dialog box. See Figure 1-18.

Figure 1-16.
The file dialog box provides a simple means of locating files. An image tile displays the selected setting or file.

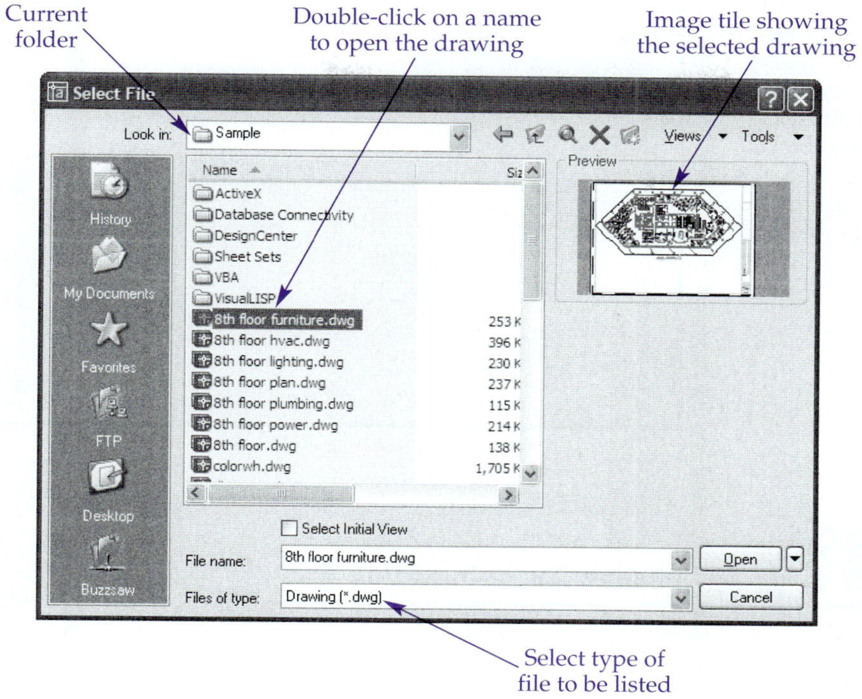

Figure 1-17.
Use scroll bars and buttons to scroll through a listing or to view sections of a drawing.

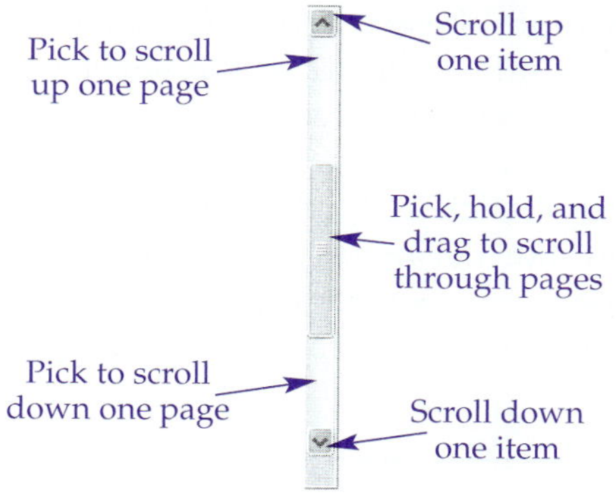

- **Help.** If you are unsure of any features of a dialog box, pick the question mark button in the upper-right corner of the dialog box. When the question mark appears next to your cursor, you can pick any feature in the dialog box to see a description of what it does.
- **... (Ellipsis button).** Some dialog box features have an ellipsis button. The ellipsis button provides access to a related dialog box. See **Figure 1-19.**

Figure 1-18.
An alert may appear as a separate dialog box.

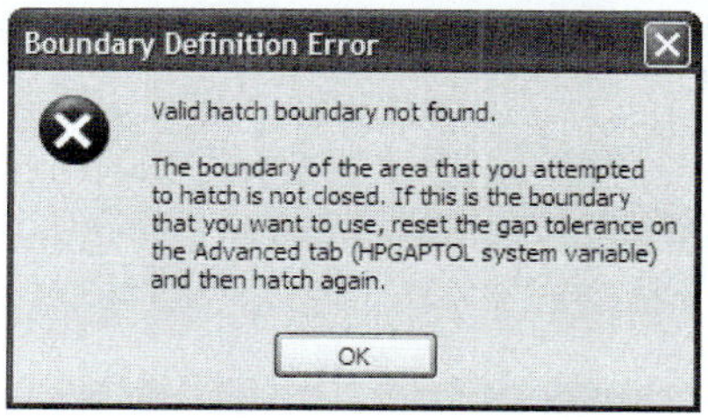

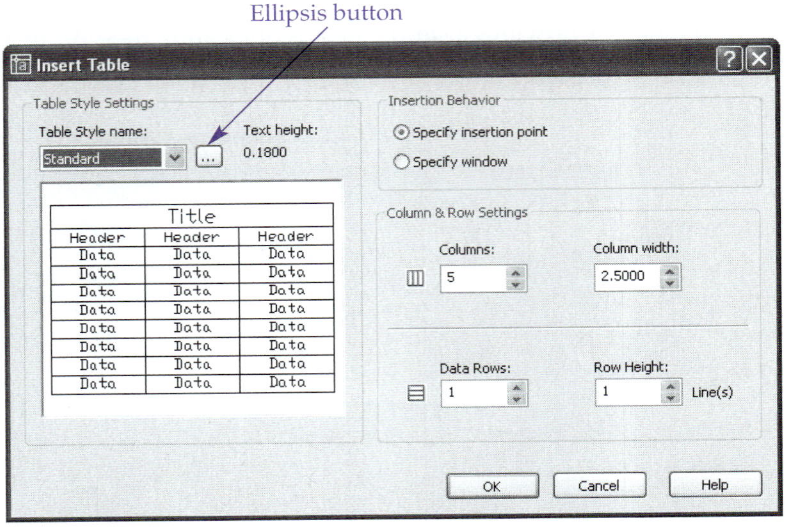

Figure 1-19. The ... (ellipsis) button displays a dialog box providing additional options related to the dialog feature it is next to. The ellipsis button shown here is picked to display a dialog box for defining and modifying table styles.

EXERCISE 1-4

Complete the Exercise on the Student CD.

Shortcut Menus

AutoCAD makes extensive use of shortcut menus to simplify and accelerate command entries. Sometimes referred to as ***cursor menus*** because they are displayed at the cursor location, these context sensitive menus are accessed by right-clicking. Because they are context sensitive, the shortcut menu content varies based on the location of the pointer when you right-click and the current conditions, such as whether a command is active or whether an object is selected.

When you right-click in the drawing area with no command active, the first item displayed on the shortcut menu is typically an option to repeat the previously used command or operation. See **Figure 1-20A.** If you right-click while a command is active, the shortcut menu contains options specific to the command. See **Figure 1-20B.**

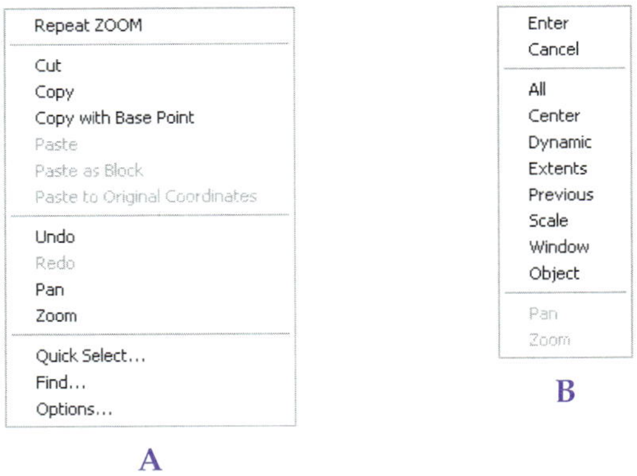

Figure 1-20. The context sensitive shortcut menus in AutoCAD provide instant access to commands and options related to what you are doing at the time. A—If a command is not currently active, the top menu pick repeats the previous command. B—This menu displays options for the **ZOOM** command. This is accessed by right-clicking after the **ZOOM** command is activated.

EXERCISE 1-5 Complete the Exercise on the Student CD.

Image Tile Menus

An image tile appears similar to a preview box and displays an image of the available object, pattern, or option. AutoCAD uses several menus composed of images. See Figure 1-21. To choose the object you want to use, simply pick the image tile or text label in the list box. Image tile menus allow for easy selection, since you can see the shape or item represented by the image. To select an image, move your pointing device to it and pick.

Figure 1-21.
Image tile menus graphically display options or selections.

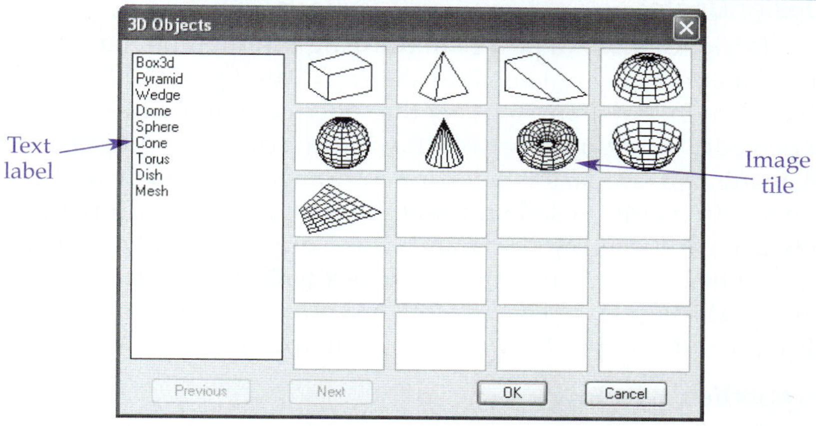

EXERCISE 1-6 Complete the Exercise on the Student CD.

Modeless Dialog Boxes

Some AutoCAD features are presented in a special type of window that is sometimes referred to as a ***modeless dialog box*** or window. Features displayed in this manner include the **DesignCenter**, the **Properties** window, the **Sheet Set Manager** window, and the **Tool Palettes** window. Unlike standard dialog boxes, these windows can be docked or resized and do not need to be closed in order to enter commands and work within the drawing. See Figure 1-22. If one of these windows has been docked, double-click on the grab bar to change to the floating state. Double-click on the title bar to return to the docked position. When docked, the window's resizing bar allows you to adjust the size to suit your needs.

The **Auto-hide** button allows the window to minimize out of your way when the cursor is away from the window. Each modeless dialog box also contains a **Properties** button, which allows you to control how the window operates and displays within AutoCAD.

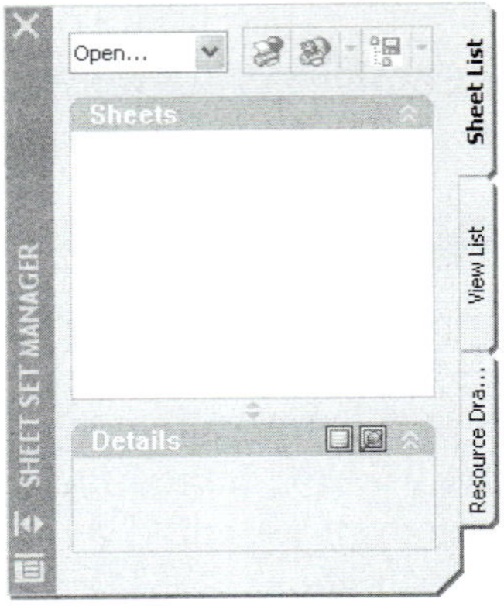

Figure 1-22. Modeless dialog boxes include buttons in the title bar to control their behavior.

DesignCenter

DesignCenter is a powerful drawing information manager that provides a simple tool for effectively reusing and sharing drawing content. One of the primary productivity benefits of using CAD is that once something has been created, you can use it repeatedly in any number of drawings or drawing projects. Many types of drawing elements are similar or the same in numerous drawings, such as common drawing details, frequently used subassemblies or parts, and drawing layouts. **DesignCenter** lets you conveniently "drag and drop" drawing content to copy it from one drawing to another. When you first start **DesignCenter**, it is opened in the center of the AutoCAD window. The use of this powerful information management system is discussed throughout the text where it applies.

Properties window

The **Properties** window lets you manage the properties of new and existing objects in a drawing. The actual use of the **Properties** window is explained where it applies throughout this text.

Sheet Set Manager window

The **Sheet Set Manager** lets you create, organize, and manage sheets in a sheet set. A *sheet set* is a named collection of drawing sheets. The use of the **Sheet Set Manager** is explained in detail in Chapter 25.

Tool Palettes window

The default **Tool Palettes** window includes four sample palettes. See **Figure 1-23.** These different tabs provide access to frequently used commands, block symbols, and hatch fill patterns. These palettes can be customized with your own symbols or hatch patterns, and new palettes can also be created. This process is explained later in this text. The **Properties** button on this modeless dialog box includes a **Transparency...** option, which allows the palette to display transparently so drawing geometry behind the palette can be viewed, as shown in **Figure 1-24.**

PROFESSIONAL TIP

You can move the modeless dialog boxes to the side of the AutoCAD window without docking them by holding the [Ctrl] key while positioning the windows where desired.

Figure 1-23.
Four sample palettes are included with AutoCAD 2005.

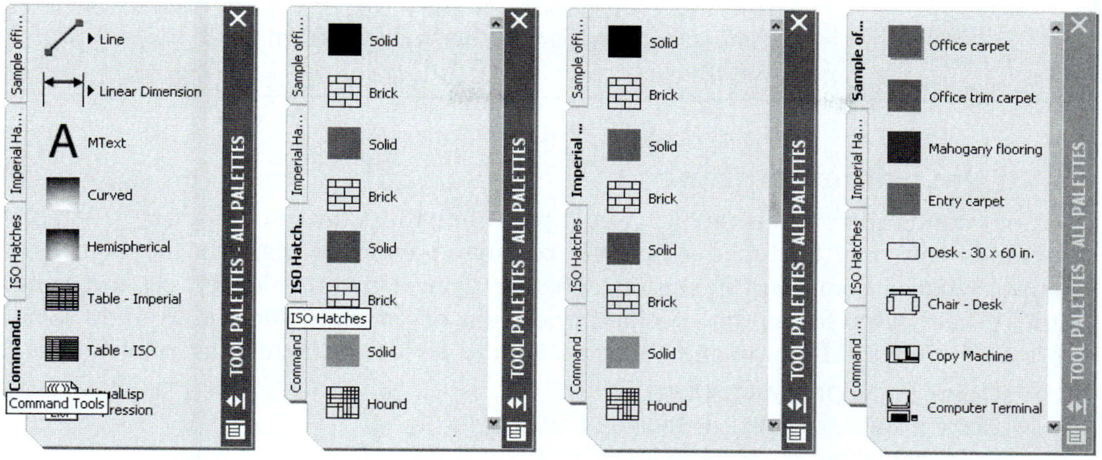

Figure 1-24.
Tool palettes can be set to be transparent by picking the **Properties** button in the title bar.

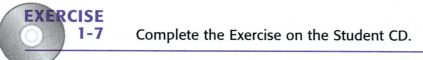

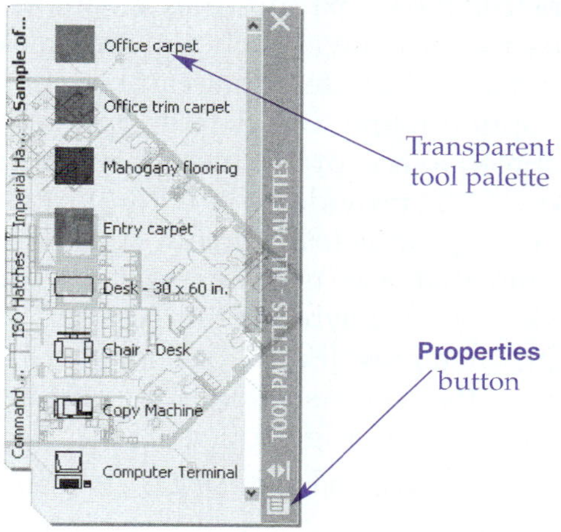

EXERCISE 1-7 Complete the Exercise on the Student CD.

Selecting AutoCAD Commands

AutoCAD commands may be selected in these four different ways:

- By picking a toolbar button or icon.
- By selecting from one of the pull-down or shortcut menus (or screen menus, if so configured).
- By selecting from a digitizer tablet menu overlay.
- By typing at the keyboard.

The advantage of using toolbar buttons and on-screen shortcut menus is you do not need to remove your eyes from the screen. Typing commands may not require you to turn your eyes from the screen. You can also learn commands quickly by typing them. When using a digitizer tablet, however, you must look down to pick tablet menu commands. On the other hand, a tablet menu overlay can show almost every command. Also, when configured as both a Windows pointer and a digitizer, a tablet is a powerful and efficient input device.

NOTE

The examples shown in this text illustrate each of the AutoCAD commands as they appear when typed at the Command: prompt and when picked from toolbars and pull-down menus.

Using the Command Line

Commands and options can be typed directly into the command window. AutoCAD commands can only be typed when the command window displays the Command: prompt. When a command is started, whether from a menu selection or by typing, AutoCAD either performs the specified operation or prompts you for any additional information. AutoCAD commands have a standard format, structured as follows:

Command: **COMMANDNAME**↵
Current settings: Setting1 Setting2 Setting3
Instructional text [Option1/oPtion2/opTion3/...] <default option or value>:

If the command has associated settings or options, these are displayed as shown. The instructional text indicates what you should do at this point, and all available options are shown within the square brackets. Each option has a unique combination of uppercase characters that can be entered at the prompt rather than entering the entire option name. If a default option is displayed in the angle brackets, you can press [Enter] to accept it rather than entering the value again.

AutoCAD provides you with the ability to select previously used commands by using the up and down arrow keys. For example, if you want to use the **CIRCLE** command that was used a few steps prior to your present position, press the up arrow key on the keyboard until the command you need is displayed at the Command: prompt. Then press [Enter] to activate it. This capability can be used to execute a typed command that is misspelled. For example, suppose you type LINE3 and press [Enter]. The following message appears:

Unknown command "LINE3". Press F1 for help.

Just press the up arrow key, then press [Backspace] to delete the number three (3) and press [Enter] to execute the **LINE** command. This is a timesaving feature if you like to type commands at the Command: prompt.

Right-clicking in the command window displays a shortcut menu with a cascading menu showing a list of commands you have used recently. See Figure 1-25. This list shows up to six recently used command names. Pick a command name from the list to use that command again.

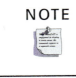

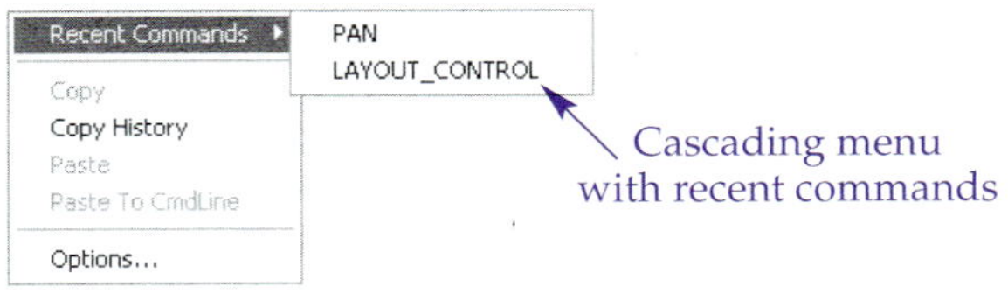

Figure 1-25.
The shortcut menu displayed when you right-click in the command window offers a cascading menu listing commands you have used recently.

EXERCISE 1-8 Complete the Exercise on the Student CD.

AutoCAD Tablet Menu

A digitizer tablet can accept an overlay or menu containing a large selection of AutoCAD commands. Other specialized programs that operate with AutoCAD can have similar menus. This text presents commands as if they are typed at the keyboard or selected from menus, dialog boxes, or toolbars. If you want to use a digitizer tablet to pick commands, the tablet must first be configured (arranged) before the menu can be used.

When you use a digitizer with AutoCAD, the cursor can be moved within only the active drawing area on screen. Therefore, menu selections can be made only from the tablet menu overlay. Since all the AutoCAD commands do not fit on the tablet, you still need to select toolbar buttons or make selections from the pull-down menus. In addition, using the tablet requires you to take your eyes off the screen and look down at the overlay. After picking a tablet command, look at the command line to be sure you picked what you desired.

The AutoCAD tablet menu is shown in **Figure 1-26.** If you plan on using a digitizer with a tablet menu, take some time and study its arrangement. Become familiar

Figure 1-26.
The AutoCAD tablet menu. (Autodesk, Inc.)

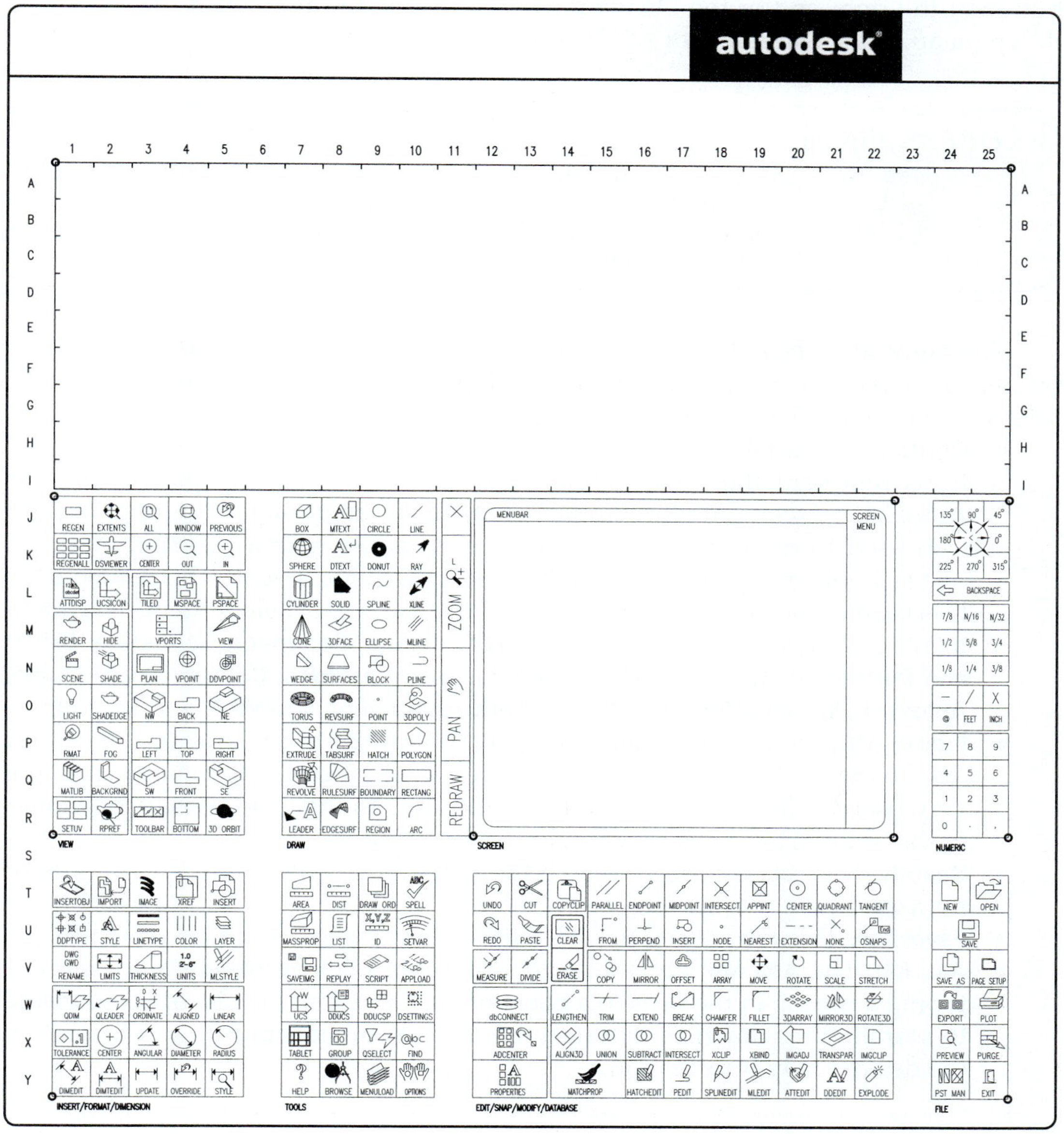

with the command groups and try to remember where each command is located. The quicker you learn the layout of the menu, the more efficient your drawing sessions will be.

EXERCISE 1-9 Complete the Exercise on the Student CD.

Getting Help

HELP
?
[F1]

Help
➥ Help

Standard toolbar
Help

If you need help with a specific command, option, or program feature, AutoCAD provides a powerful and convenient online help system. There are several ways to access this feature. The fastest method is to press the [F1] function key. This displays the **AutoCAD 2005 Help** window. The first time you use the help system, the **Contents** tab lists the names of the available online reference guides for the AutoCAD help system. You can also display the **AutoCAD 2005 Help** window by selecting the **?** button at the right end of the **Standard** toolbar, by picking **Help** from the **Help** pull-down menu, or by entering ? or HELP at the Command: prompt.

PROFESSIONAL TIP

If you are unfamiliar with how to use a Windows help system, it is suggested you spend time now exploring all the topics under **AutoCAD Help** in the **Contents** tab of the **AutoCAD 2005 Help** window.

The **AutoCAD 2005 Help** window consists of two frames. See Figure 1-27. The left frame, which has five tabs, is used to locate help topics. The right frame displays the selected help topics. The five tabs in the left frame are as follows:

- **Contents.** This tab displays a list of book icons and topic names. The book icons represent the organizational structure of books of topics within the AutoCAD documentation. Topics contain the actual help information; the icon used to represent a topic is a sheet of paper with a question mark. To open a book or a help topic, double-click on its name or icon. The **Contents** tab lists each of the help documents within the AutoCAD help system. The documents available are **AutoCAD Help**; **User's Guide**; **Command Reference**; **Driver and Peripheral Guide**; **Installation and Licensing Guides**; **Customization Guide**; **AutoLISP**, **Visual LISP**, **and DXF**; **ActiveX Automation and VBA**; and **My Help**.
- **Index.** Although the **Contents** tab of the **AutoCAD Help** window is useful for displaying all the topics in an expanded table of contents manner, it is not very useful when searching for a specific item. In this case, most people refer to the index. This is the function of the **Index** tab.
- **Search.** This tab is used to search the help documents for specific words or phrases.
- **Favorites.** This tab is used to save a list of help topics for future reference.
- **Ask Me.** The **Ask Me** tab is used to sort help topics by posing a question or typing a phrase in the **Type in a question** text box. Use the **List of components to search:** drop-down list to select the help documents most likely to contain the desired help information.

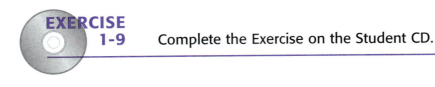

Figure 1-27.
The **AutoCAD 2005 Help** window.

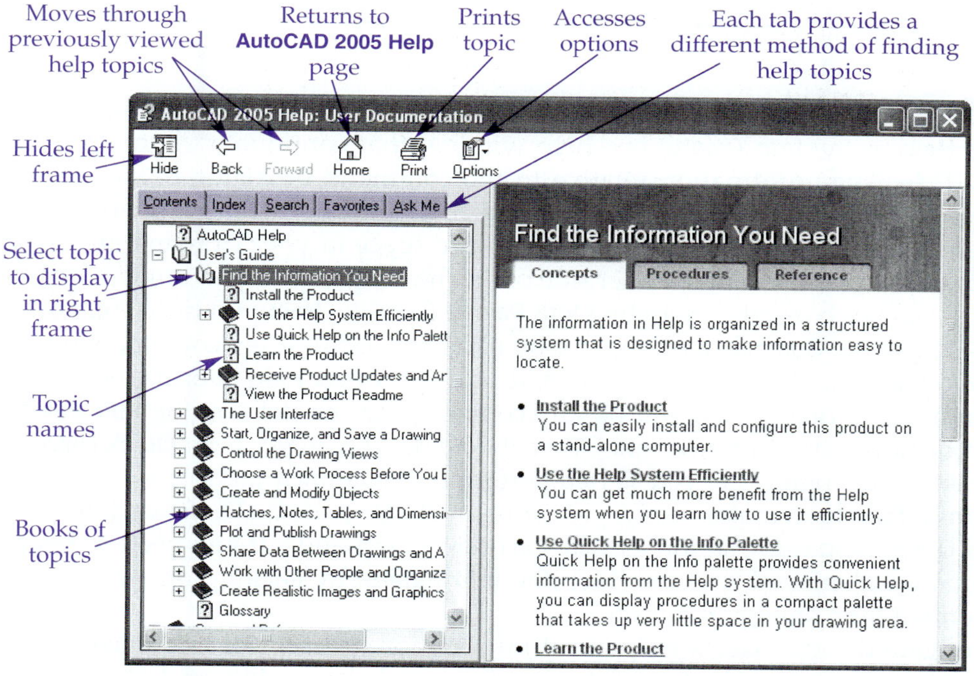

PROFESSIONAL TIP

While a help window is displayed, pressing the right mouse button displays a shortcut menu containing many of the items found in the pull-down menus.

In addition to the two frames and five tabs, there are six buttons located at the top of the **AutoCAD 2005 Help** window. The **Hide/Show** button controls the visibility of the left frame. The **Back** button is used to view the previously displayed help topic. The **Forward** button is used to go forward to help pages you viewed before pressing the **Back** button. The **Home** button takes you to the AutoCAD 2005 Help page. The **Print** button is used to print a help topic. The **Options** button contains a cascading menu with a variety of items used to control other aspects of the **AutoCAD 2005 Help** window.

PROFESSIONAL TIP

AutoCAD's help function can also be used while you are in the process of using a command. For example, suppose you are using the **ARC** command and forget what type of information AutoCAD requires for the specific prompts on screen. Get help by pressing the [F1] function key, and the help information for the currently active command is displayed. This ***context oriented help*** saves valuable time, since you do not need to scan through the help contents or perform any searches to find the information.

EXERCISE 1-10 Complete the Exercise on the Student CD.

AutoCAD 2005
NEW FEATURE

ASSIST
[Ctrl]+[5]
Help
➥ **Info Palette**

The Info Palette

Quick Help in the **Info Palette** is a help window that continually monitors your actions and displays information relative to the command or dialog box currently being accessed. With **Quick Help** on the **Info Palette**, you can display a list of procedures in a compact palette that takes up very little space in your drawing area. The **Info Palette** can also be docked on either side of the drawing area so you can work more efficiently. It can be accessed by selecting **Info Palette** from the **Help** pull-down menu, by typing ASSIST at the Command: prompt, or by using the [Ctrl]+[5] key combination.

The **Info Palette** is shown in Figure 1-28. It provides **Quick Help** information for the active command or dialog box. During any command, **Quick Help** on the **Info Palette** displays context-sensitive information. Often, the guidance you get from **Quick Help** on the **Info Palette** is enough to get you started performing unfamiliar tasks.

The **Info Palette** remains active as you work in AutoCAD. It updates the displayed **Quick Help** information as you start new commands. If you need to freeze the information displayed, you can lock the **Info Palette** by clicking on the **Lock to prevent content from changing** button.

To navigate through **Quick Help**, print information, or lock the **Info Palette**, you can use the buttons across the top of the window, as shown in Figure 1-28. You can also right-click in the **Info Palette** to display the **Info Palette** shortcut menu. This menu includes the following options:

- **Home.** This option displays the Tips on Quick Help topic in the window. This information describes how to use **Quick Help**, the **Info Palette**, and the various options.
- **Back.** This option displays the previous **Quick Help** topics you have viewed.
- **Forward.** This option returns to the **Quick Help** topic displayed prior to using the **Back** option. It is only enabled after the **Back** option is used.
- **Print.** This option prints the displayed **Quick Help** topic.
- **Lock/Unlock.** This option locks the **Quick Help** information displayed in the **Info Palette** into place until you unlock it. You can lock the information displayed at any time. This may be helpful when you want to follow the steps in a procedure.

Figure 1-28.
The **Info Palette** provides **Quick Help** information for the current command.

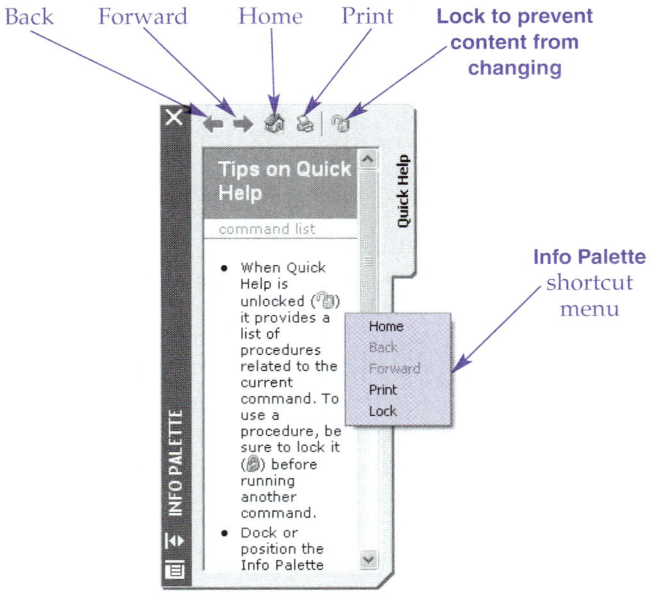

The **Info Palette** has properties that can be changed when it is in the undocked state. To change these settings, click the **Properties** button at the lower end of the **Info Palette** title bar, as shown in Figure 1-29. The following options are available:

- **Move.** This option allows you to move the **Info Palette**.
- **Size.** This option allows you to change the size of the **Info Palette**.
- **Close.** This option closes the **Info Palette**.
- **Allow Docking.** This option controls whether or not the **Info Palette** docks when you drag it over a docking area at the side of the drawing area.
- **Auto-hide.** This option sets the **Info Palette** to display information only when the cursor is over the title bar. Make sure this option does not have a check mark if you want to display the **Info Palette** content at all times.
- **Transparency.** This option accesses the **Transparency** dialog box. This dialog box sets the display for the **Info Palette** to be opaque or transparent.

When you are finished using the **Info Palette**, you can click on the X to exit. You can also type ASSISTCLOSE at the Command: prompt to close **Quick Help** and the **Info Palette**. The system variable **ASSISTSTATE** can be accessed at any time to determine whether the **Info Palette** that displays **Quick Help** is active (1) or not active (0).

Figure 1-29.
The **Info Palette** properties can be changed by choosing an option from the **Properties** menu.

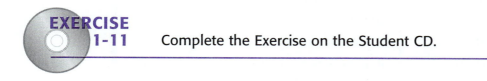

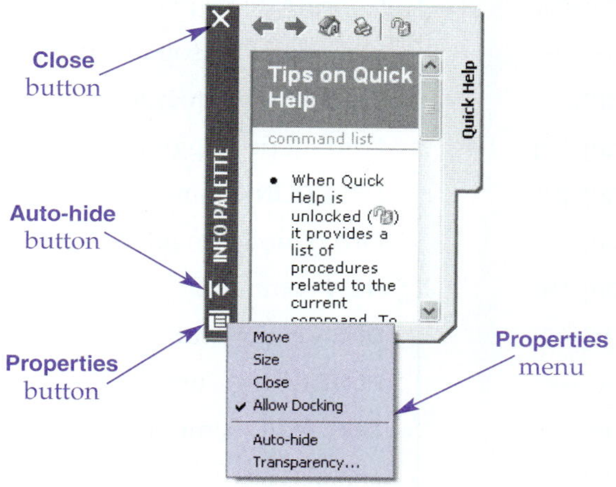

Using the Online Product Support

Help
➡ Online Resources
➡ Product Support

Product support is a comprehensive support tool. It is accessed by picking the **Online Resources** cascading menu in the **Help** pull-down menu, and then selecting **Product Support**. This powerful support tool features a knowledge base of information designed to help you find fast answers to questions, solutions for problems, and guidance for finding additional support and technical assistance.

EXERCISE 1-11 Complete the Exercise on the Student CD.

Keys and Buttons

AutoCAD provides several ways of performing a given task. Many keys on the keyboard allow you to quickly perform many functions. In addition, multibutton pointing devices also use buttons for AutoCAD commands. Become familiar with the meaning of these keys and buttons to help improve your performance with AutoCAD.

The [Esc] Key

Any time it is necessary to cancel a command and return to the Command: prompt, press the ***escape key*** [Esc] on your keyboard. This key is found on the upper-left corner of most keyboards and is typically labeled Esc. Some command sequences may require the [Esc] key to be pressed twice to completely cancel the operation.

Control Keys

Most computer programs use ***control key*** functions to perform common tasks. Control key functions are used by pressing and holding the [Ctrl] key while pressing a second key. These keys are also called ***accelerator keys***. Keep the following list close at hand and try them occasionally. If a command or key is noted as a "toggle," it is either on or off—nothing else.

Key Combination	Result
[Ctrl]+[A]	Select all
[Ctrl]+[B]	Snap mode (toggle)
[Ctrl]+[C]	**COPYCLIP** command
[Ctrl]+[D]	Coordinate display on status line (toggle)
[Ctrl]+[E]	Crosshairs in isoplane positions left/top/right (toggle)
[Ctrl]+[F]	Osnap mode (toggle)
[Ctrl]+[G]	Grid mode (toggle)
[Ctrl]+[K]	**HYPERLINK** command
[Ctrl]+[L]	Ortho mode (toggle)
[Ctrl]+[N]	**NEW** command
[Ctrl]+[O]	**OPEN** command
[Ctrl]+[P]	**PLOT** (print) command
[Ctrl]+[Q]	**QUIT** (exit) command
[Ctrl]+[R]	Toggle viewport
[Ctrl]+[S]	**SAVE** command
[Ctrl]+[T]	Tablet mode (toggle)
[Ctrl]+[U]	Polar mode (toggle)
[Ctrl]+[V]	**PASTECLIP** command
[Ctrl]+[W]	Object Snap Tracking (toggle)
[Ctrl]+[X]	**CUTCLIP** command
[Ctrl]+[Y]	**REDO** command
[Ctrl]+[Z]	**UNDO** command
[Ctrl]+[0]	Clean Screen mode (toggle)
[Ctrl]+[1]	**Properties** window (toggle)
[Ctrl]+[2]	**DesignCenter** (toggle)
[Ctrl]+[3]	**Tool Palettes** window (toggle)
[Ctrl]+[4]	**Sheet Set Manager** (toggle)
[Ctrl]+[5]	**Info Palette** window (toggle)
[Ctrl]+[6]	**dbConnect Manager** (toggle)
[Ctrl]+[7]	**Markup Set Manager** (toggle)

Function Keys

Function keys provide instant access to commands. They can also be programmed to perform a series of commands. The function keys are located along the top of the keyboard. Depending on the brand of keyboard, there will be either ten or twelve function keys. These are numbered from [F1] to [F12]. AutoCAD uses eleven function keys. These are listed below. As you become proficient with AutoCAD, you might program the function keys to do specific tasks using other computer programs.

Function Key	Result
[F1]	**HELP** command
[F2]	Flip screen between graphics and text windows (toggle)
[F3]	Object Snap mode (toggle)
[F4]	Tablet mode (toggle)
[F5]	Isoplane mode (toggle)
[F6]	Coordinate display (toggle)
[F7]	Grid mode (toggle)
[F8]	Ortho mode (toggle)
[F9]	Snap mode (toggle)
[F10]	Polar mode (toggle)
[F11]	Object Snap Tracking (toggle)

Button Functions

If you are using a multibutton pointing device, you can select control key functions by pressing a single button. The default settings of the pointing device buttons are as follows:

Button	Result
0	Pick
1	Return
2	**Object Snap** shortcut menu
3	Cancel
4	Snap mode (toggle)
5	Ortho mode (toggle)
6	Grid mode (toggle)
7	Coordinate display (toggle)
8	Crosshairs isoplane positions top/left/right (toggle)
9	Tablet mode (toggle)

EXERCISE 1-12 Complete the Exercise on the Student CD.

Understanding Terminology

The following terms are used throughout the text and will help you select AutoCAD functions. You should become familiar with them.

- **Default.** A value maintained by the computer until you change it.
- **Pick** or **click.** Use the pointing device to select an item on the screen or tablet.
- **Button.** One of the screen toolbar or pointing device (puck) buttons.
- **Key.** A key on the keyboard.
- **Function key.** One of the keys labeled [F1]–[F12] along the top or side of the keyboard.
- **[Enter] (↵).** The [Enter] or [Return] key on the keyboard.
- **Command.** An instruction issued to the computer.
- **Option.** An aspect of a command that can be selected.

Chapter Test

Answer the following questions on a separate sheet of paper.

1. What system is used to construct drawings and models in AutoCAD?
2. Basic pictorial drawings are called _____.
3. Using the system referred to in Question 1, what is the proper notation for the values Z=4, X=2, and Y=5?
4. What is *drawing planning*?
5. Why is drawing planning important?
6. What is the first thing you should do as part of your planning checklist?
7. Why should you save your work every ten to fifteen minutes?
8. What are *standards*?
9. What scale should you use to draw in AutoCAD?
10. Why should you read the command line at the bottom of the screen?
11. How is AutoCAD represented on the Windows desktop?
12. What is the quickest method for starting AutoCAD?
13. Which toolbars are displayed by default when AutoCAD is launched?
14. What is a *grab bar*?
15. Which area displays the communication between you and AutoCAD?
16. What is the difference between a docked toolbar and a floating toolbar?
17. What are *menu accelerator keys*? How are they used? Give an example.
18. What is an *option*?
19. List the AutoCAD pull-down menus.
20. What is a *flyout menu*?
21. What is the function of tabs in a dialog box?
22. What must you do to a tablet before it can be used?
23. What are the functions of the following control keys?
    A. [Ctrl]+[B]
    B. [Ctrl]+[C]
    C. [Ctrl]+[D]
    D. [Ctrl]+[G]
    E. [Ctrl]+[O]
    F. [Ctrl]+[S]

24. Name the function keys that execute the same tasks as the following control keys:
    A. [Ctrl]+[B]
    B. [Ctrl]+[D]
    C. [Ctrl]+[G]
    D. [Ctrl]+[L]
    E. [Ctrl]+[T]
25. What is the difference between a *button* and a *key*?
26. What do you call a value that is maintained by the computer until you change it?
27. What type of pull-down menu item has an arrow to the right?
28. What type of menu contains a group of symbols or patterns?
29. What is an *image tile*?
30. What is *context oriented help,* and how is it accessed?
31. How do you open a folder in a file dialog box in order to see its contents?
32. What is the area in a dialog box that displays a "picture" of the item you select?
33. What is the function of the **...** (ellipsis) button?
34. How do you access a shortcut menu?
35. What is the purpose of a shortcut menu?
36. Why are shortcut menus considered context sensitive?
37. Name a powerful drawing information manager that provides a simple tool for efficiently reusing and sharing drawing content.
38. Name the window that lets you manage the properties of new and existing objects in a drawing.
39. How do you access previously used commands?
40. Identify the quickest way to access the **AutoCAD 2005 Help** window.
41. What happens to the cursor when you pick the question mark in the upper-right corner of a dialog box? What is the purpose of the cursor?
42. Describe the purpose of the book icons in the **Contents** tab of the **AutoCAD 2005 Help** window.
43. Identify the tab in the **AutoCAD 2005 Help** window that allows you to do a detailed search based on one or more words.
44. How do you access help regarding a currently active command?
45. What is Online Product Support?

Problems

1. Interview your drafting instructor or supervisor and try to determine what type of drawing standards exist at your school or company. Write them down and keep them with you as you learn AutoCAD. Make notes as you progress through this text on how you use these standards. Also note how the standards could be changed to better match the capabilities of AutoCAD.

2. Research your drafting department standards. If you do not have a copy of the standards, acquire one. If AutoCAD standards have been created, make notes as to how you can use these in your projects. If no standards exist in your department or company, make notes as to how you can help develop standards. Write a report on why your school or company should create CAD standards and how they would be used. Discuss who should be responsible for specific tasks. Recommend procedures, techniques, and forms, if necessary. Develop this report as you progress through your AutoCAD instruction and as you read through this book.

3. Develop a drawing planning sheet for use in your school or company. List items you think are important for planning a CAD drawing. Make changes to this sheet as you learn more about AutoCAD.

4. Load AutoCAD from the Windows desktop using one of the three methods discussed in this chapter. Perform the following tasks:
   A. Open the **AutoCAD 2005 Help** window.
   B. In the **Contents** tab, expand the User's Guide category.
   C. Pick the Find the Information You Need topic, then pick the Use the Help System Efficiently hyperlink in the right pane.
   D. If you have access to a printer, print the topic.
   E. Close the **AutoCAD 2005 Help** window, and then close AutoCAD.

5. Load AutoCAD by selecting the proper items, using the Start button on the Windows task bar.
   A. Move the pointer over the buttons in the **Standard** toolbar and read the notes on the status bar at the bottom of the screen.
   B. Move the pointer to the second button in the **Standard** toolbar and read the note on the status bar.
   C. Slowly move the pointer over each of the buttons on the **Styles** and **Layers** toolbars and read the tooltips. Do the same on the **Draw** and **Modify** toolbars at the sides of the screen.
   D. Pick the **File** pull-down menu to display it. Using the right arrow key, move through all the pull-down menus. Use the left arrow key to return to the **Draw** pull-down menu. Use the down arrow key to move to the **Circle** command, then use the right arrow key to display the **Circle** options in the cascading menu.
   E. Press the [Esc] key to dismiss the menu.
   F. Close AutoCAD by picking **Exit** in the **File** pull-down menu.

6. Draw a freehand sketch of the screen display. Label each of the screen areas. To the side of the sketch, write a short description of each screen area's function.

CHAPTER 2

Working with Drawings and Templates

Learning Objectives

After completing this chapter, you will be able to do the following:

- Start a new drawing.
- Save a drawing under a different name.
- Specify how often your work is automatically saved.
- Save AutoCAD drawings for older releases.
- Open a saved drawing.
- Search for AutoCAD files.
- Manage drawings in the Multiple Design Environment (MDE).
- Use the **CLOSE** and **EXIT** commands.
- Adjust grid and snap settings.
- Select linear and angular units and precision.
- Set the model space drawing limits.
- Create a template drawing.

When using AutoCAD, you work with drawing files. In this chapter, you will learn how to create new drawing files, save drawing files, and open existing drawing files.

New drawings are typically created using templates. Templates allow you to start a new drawing with preset drawing aids and objects. Some of the basic drawing aids are discussed in this chapter. Many templates are provided with AutoCAD, and you can also create custom templates.

Starting a New Drawing

In AutoCAD, new drawings are typically started from templates. ***Templates*** store standard drawing settings and objects. All settings and contents of the template file are included in the new drawing.

Templates can be incredible productivity boosters. The provided template files may meet some personal needs, but creating new custom templates is where the greatest benefit is found. Custom templates allow you to use an existing drawing as a starting point for any new drawing. This option is extremely valuable for ensuring that everyone in a department, class, school, or company uses the same standards within their drawings.

When using a template, values defining the drawing settings are automatically set. Templates usually have values for the following drawing elements:

- ✓ Standard layouts with a border and title block.
- ✓ Grid and snap settings.
- ✓ Units and angle values.
- ✓ Text standards and general notes.
- ✓ Dimensioning styles.
- ✓ Layer definitions.
- ✓ Plot styles.

These items are discussed later in this textbook.

NEW
[Ctrl]+[N]
File
➥ **New**

To start a drawing , select **New...** from the **File** pull-down menu, enter NEW at the Command: prompt, or use the [Ctrl]+[N] key combination. This displays the **Select template** dialog box, as seen in **Figure 2-1.**

The **Select template** dialog box lists the templates found in the default template folder. A variety of templates conforming to accepted industry standards are included with AutoCAD. You will notice all the files have a .dwt extension, which stands for ***drawing template***. If you just want to open a blank file, use the acad.dwt template for English settings or the acadiso.dwt template for metric settings. To open a template file, double-click on the file or select the file and then pick the **Open** button.

Figure 2-1.
The **Select template** dialog box allows you to begin a new drawing by selecting a template.

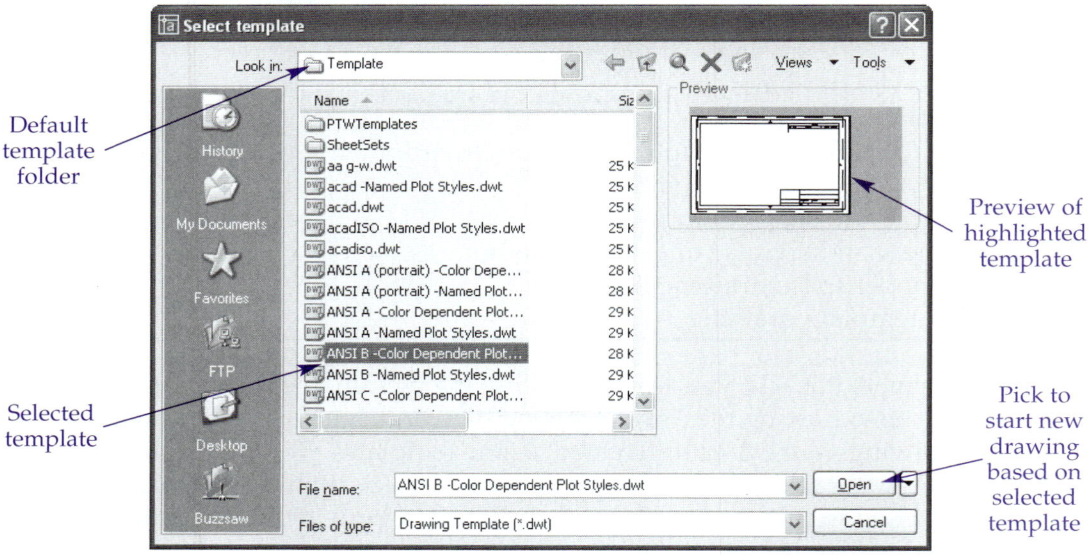

Standard Templates

The template files provided with AutoCAD use a naming system indicating the drafting standard referenced, the size of the title block in the preset layout, and the plot style settings used. Plot styles are introduced in Chapter 11.

Drafters often think of the drawing size as sheet size. The ***sheet size*** is the size of the paper you will use to lay out and plot the final drawing. It takes into account the size of the drawing and additional space for dimensions, notes, and clear area between the drawing and border lines. The sheet size also includes the title block, the revision block, zoning, and an area for general notes. In AutoCAD, the sheet size is specified in the **Page Setup** dialog box when defining your drawing layout. The **Page Setup** dialog box is discussed in Chapter 11.

ASME/ANSI standard sheet sizes and formats are specified in the documents ASME Y14.1, *Decimal Inch Drawing Sheet Size and Format*, and ASME Y14.1M, *Metric Drawing Sheet Size and Format*. ASME Y14.1 lists sheet size specifications in inches, as follows:

Size Designation	Size (in inches)
A	8 1/2 × 11 (horizontal format)
	11 × 8 1/2 (vertical format)
B	11 × 17
C	17 × 22
D	22 × 34
E	34 × 44
F	28 × 40
Sizes G, H, J, and K are roll sizes.	

ASME Y14.1M provides sheet size specifications in metric units. Standard metric drawing sheet sizes are designated as follows:

Designation	Size (in millimeters)
A0	841 × 1189
A1	594 × 841
A2	420 × 594
A3	297 × 420
A4	210 × 297

Longer lengths are referred to as elongated and extra-elongated drawing sizes. These are available in multiples of the short side of the sheet size. **Figure 2-2** shows standard ANSI/ASME sheet sizes.

All generic and ANSI templates provided with AutoCAD are based on decimal inches as the unit of measure. The architectural templates are set up for feet and inches measurements, which are typical in architectural applications. DIN, ISO, and JIS template files are based on metric measurement settings.

NOTE

DIN refers to the German standard *Deutsches Institut Für Normung*, which was established by the German Institute for Standardization. ***ISO*** is the International Organization for Standardization, and ***JIS*** is the Japanese Industry Standard.

The ANSI, DIN, ISO, and JIS templates provide layouts with the title block located in the lower-right corner. The architectural templates provide a title block on the right side of the sheet, which is common in the architectural industry. The Template folder also contains the acad.dwt template, for starting a drawing using feet and inches, and the acadiso.dwt template, for using metric units. These options do not have layouts or title blocks.

Figure 2-2.
A—Standard drawing sheet sizes (ANSI Y14.1). B—Standard metric drawing sheet sizes (ASME Y14.1M).

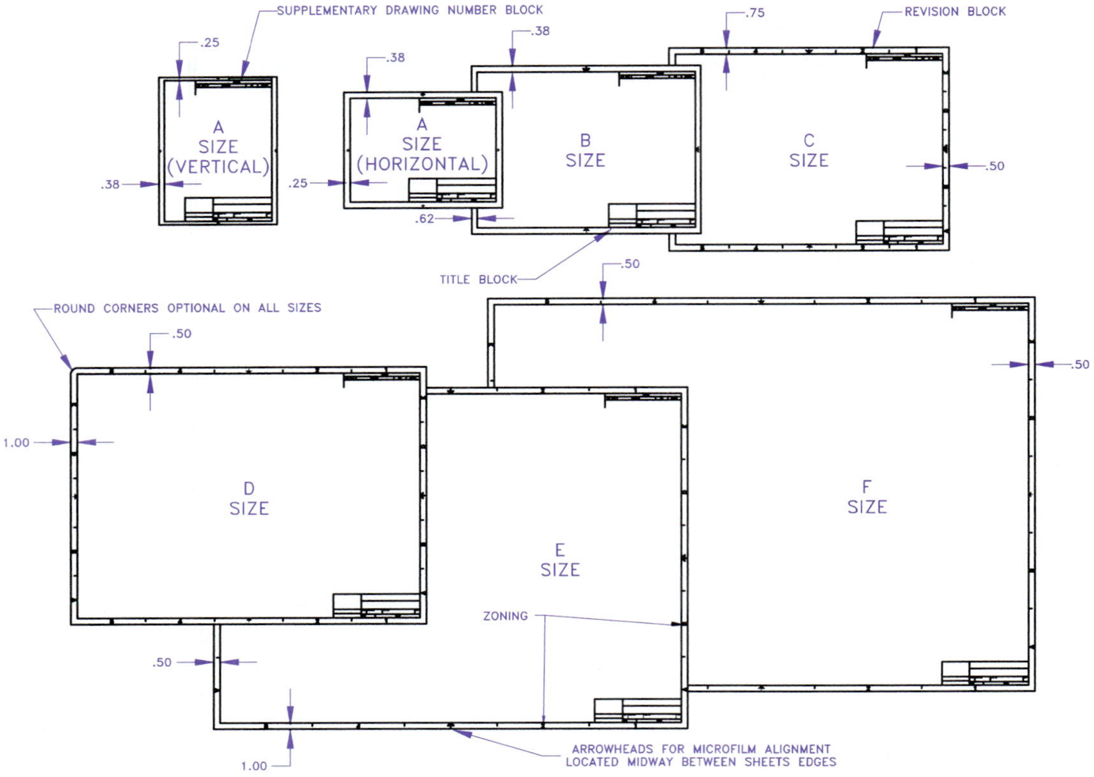

A

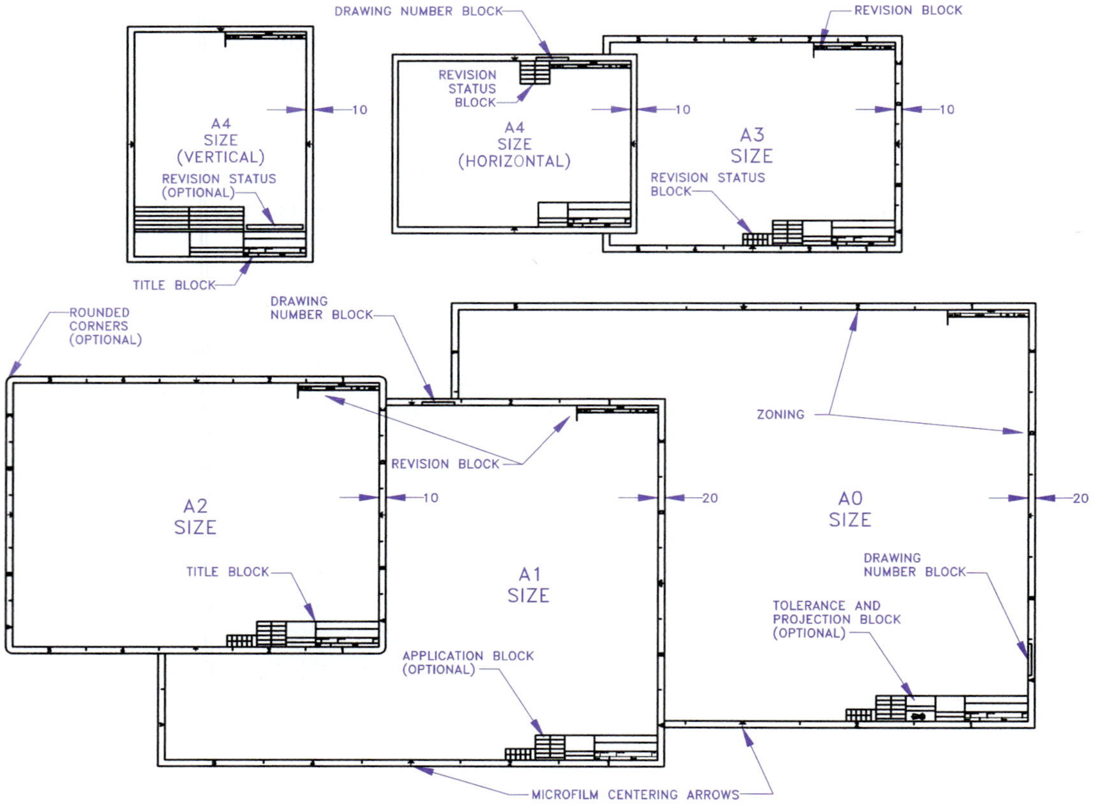

B

PROFESSIONAL TIP

If you wish to change the default template folder, you can do so in the **Options** dialog box. To access this dialog box, pick **Options...** from the **Tools** pull-down menu. In the **Files** tab of the **Options** dialog box, expand Template Settings, and then expand Drawing Template File Location.

EXERCISE 2-1 Complete the Exercise on the Student CD.

Starting a Drawing Quickly

AutoCAD also provides methods of starting a new drawing from a preset template. This allows you to begin a drawing more quickly.

QNEW
Standard toolbar
QNew

Before using the "quick start" feature, you must specify the template to be used for quick starts. This is done in the **Options** dialog box. To access the dialog box, pick **Options...** from the **Tools** pull-down menu. In the **Files** tab of the **Options** dialog box, expand Template Settings, and then expand Default Template File Name for QNEW item. Either a template file name or None is displayed. See **Figure 2-3.** Pick the **Browse...** button to select a template.

To start a new drawing using this template, pick the **QNew** button from the **Standard** toolbar or type QNEW at the Command: prompt. A new drawing is started.

If the Default Template File Name for QNEW setting is None, both the **QNEW** command and **QNew** button open the **Select template** dialog box.

Figure 2-3.
Specifying a template file for the **QNEW** command.

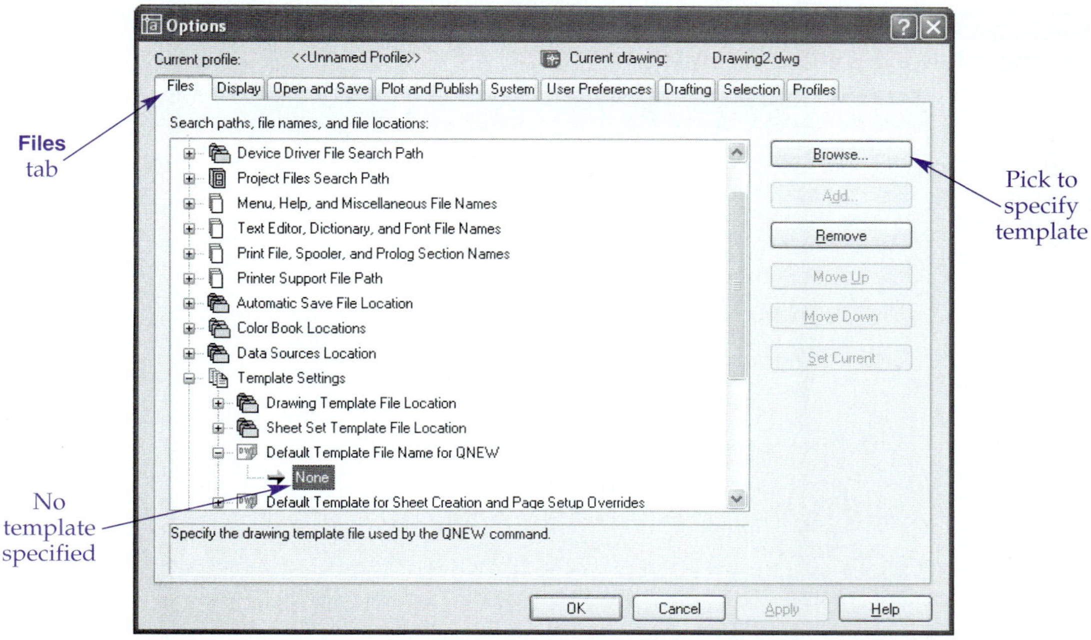

PROFESSIONAL TIP

When you begin a session of AutoCAD, a new drawing is started. If a template is specified for the **QNEW** command, it is used for the initial drawing. If there is no template specified for the **QNEW** command, the initial drawing is based on the acad.dwt template.

Other Options for Starting Drawings

You can also start a drawing without using a template. This is also called starting a drawing "from scratch." Doing so provides a "blank" drawing without a title block, layouts, or customized drawing settings. Use this option to "play it by ear" when just sketching or when the start or end of a drawing project is unknown.

To create a new drawing from scratch, pick the arrow next to the **Open** button in the **Select template** dialog box. See Figure 2-4. Select one of the **Open with no Template** options. Pick the option corresponding to the type of units to be used in the drawing.

PROFESSIONAL TIP

AutoCAD provides an alternative method for drawing startup using a **Startup** dialog box. This method is inactive by default, but can be selected from the **System** tab of the **Options** dialog box. When this method is active, a **Startup** or **Start New Drawing** dialog box appears when AutoCAD is started and when the **NEW** command is issued. These dialog boxes allow you to select a template, start a drawing from scratch, or use a startup wizard to set some drawing settings. It is recommended that you use the default settings and do not use this alternative method.

Figure 2-4.
Starting a drawing without a template.

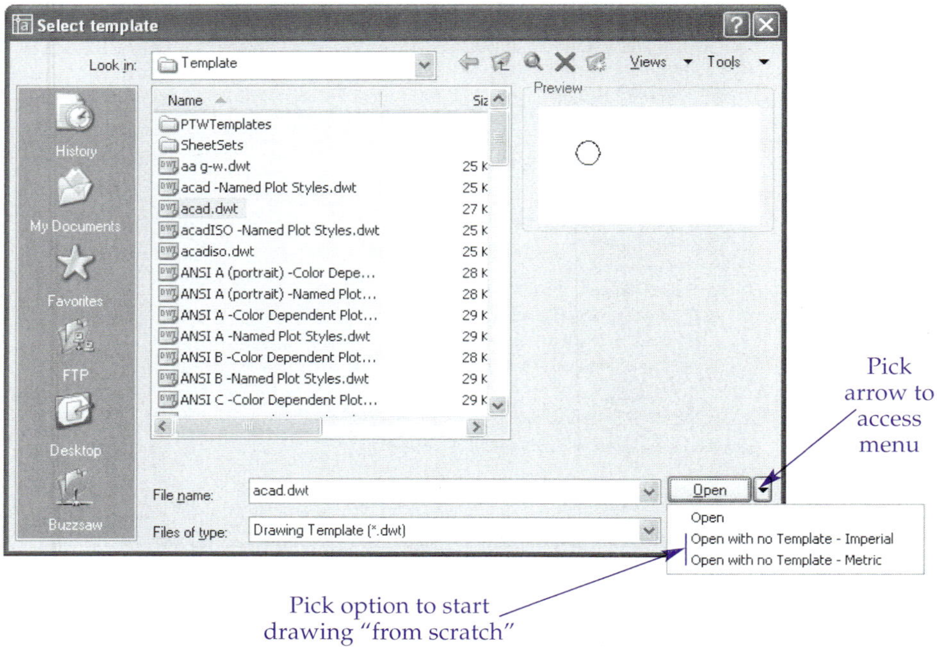

Saving Drawings

After starting a drawing, you need to assign a name to the new drawing and save it. The following discussion provides you with detailed information about saving and quitting a drawing. When saving drawing files using either the **QSAVE** or **SAVEAS** command, you can use a dialog box or type everything at the Command: prompt.

PROFESSIONAL TIP

Dialog boxes are controlled by the **FILEDIA** system variable. A ***system variable*** is a setting that lets you change the way AutoCAD works. These variables are remembered by AutoCAD and remain in effect until you change them again. If **FILEDIA** system variable is set to 1, the default, dialog boxes are displayed at the appropriate times. If **FILEDIA** is set to 0, dialog boxes do not appear. You must then type the desired information at the prompt line.

Naming Drawings

Drawing names may be chosen to identify a product by name and number—for example, VICE-101, FLOORPLAN, or 6DT1005. Your school or company probably has a drawing numbering system you can use. These drawing names should be recorded in a part numbering or drawing name log. Such a log serves as a valuable reference long after you forget what the drawings contain.

It is important to set up a system that allows you to determine the content of a drawing by the drawing name. Although it is possible to give a drawing file an extended name, such as Details for Top Half of Compressor Housing for ACME, Inc., Part Number 4011A, Revision Level C, this is normally not a practical way of sorting drawing information. Drawing titles should be standardized and may be most effective when making a clear and concise reference to the project, part number, process, sheet number, and revision level.

When a standardized naming system exists, a shorter name like ACME.4011A.C provides all the necessary information. If additional information is desirable for easier recognition, it can be added to the base name, for example: ACME 4011 A.C Compressor Housing.Top.Casting Details. Always record drawing names and provide information related to the drawings. The following rules and restrictions apply to naming all files, including AutoCAD drawings:

- A maximum of 256 characters can be used.
- Alphabetical and numeric characters and spaces, along with most punctuation symbols, can be used.
- The following characters cannot be used: quotation mark ("), asterisk (*), question mark (?), forward slash (/), and backward slash (\).

Saving Your Work

You must save your drawing periodically to protect your work by writing the existing status of your drawing to disk. While working in AutoCAD, you should save your drawing every ten to fifteen minutes. This is very important! If there is a power failure, a severe editing error, or another problem, all the work saved prior to the problem will be usable. If you save only once an hour, a power failure could result in an hour of lost work. Saving your drawing every ten to fifteen minutes results in less lost work if a problem occurs.

The **QSAVE**, **SAVEAS**, and **SAVE** commands allow you to save your work. Also, any command or option ending the AutoCAD session provides a warning asking if you want to save changes to the drawing. This gives you a final option to either save or not save changes to the drawing.

QSAVE
[Ctrl]+[S]

File
➥ **Save**

Standard toolbar
Save

Using the QSAVE Command

Of the three available saving commands, the most frequently used is the **QSAVE** command. **QSAVE** stands for *quick save*. The **QSAVE** command is accessed by picking the **Save** button from the **Standard** toolbar, picking the **Save** option from the **File** pull-down menu, entering QSAVE at the Command: prompt, or by pressing [Ctrl]+[S].

The **QSAVE** command response depends on whether or not the drawing already has a name. If the current drawing has a name, the **QSAVE** command updates the file based on the current state of the drawing. In this situation, **QSAVE** issues no prompts and displays no messages.

If the current drawing has not yet been named, the **QSAVE** command displays the **Save Drawing As** dialog box. See **Figure 2-5.** You must complete three steps in order to save your file:

1. Select the folder in which the file is to be saved.
2. Select the type of file to save, such as drawing (.dwg) or template (.dwt).
3. Enter a name for the file.

When selecting the folder in which the file will be stored, first select the disk drive from the **Save in:** drop-down list. Using this option, you can save to any available hard disk, floppy disk, or network drive. To move upward from the current folder, pick the **Up one level** button. To create a new folder in the current location, pick the **Create New Folder** button and type the name for the folder.

Figure 2-5.
The **Save Drawing As** dialog box.

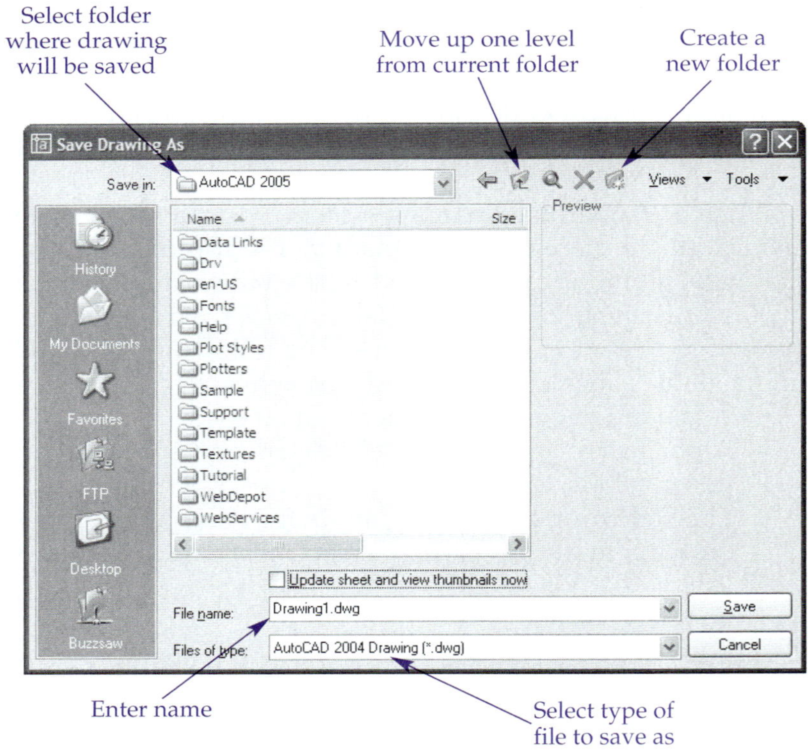

The **Files of type:** drop-down list offers options to save the drawing file in alternate formats. For most applications, this should be set to AutoCAD 2004 Drawing (*.dwg) when saving drawings. When saving a template file, this is set as AutoCAD Drawing Template (*.dwt).

> **NOTE**
> Drawings created in AutoCAD 2005 are saved as AutoCAD 2004 drawings. You will not see an option for saving as AutoCAD 2005 drawing file in the **Files of type:** drop-down list.

If the drawing has not yet been named, the name Drawing1 appears in the **File name:** text box. Change this to the desired drawing name. You do not need to include the .dwg extension.

Once you have specified the correct location and file name, pick the **Save** button to save the drawing file. Keep in mind that you can either pick the **Save** button or just press the [Enter] key to activate the **Save** button and save the drawing.

> **NOTE**
> The **Save Drawing As** dialog box is a standard file selection dialog box. The features of this dialog box are discussed more thoroughly later in this chapter.

Using the SAVEAS Command

The **SAVEAS** command is used in the following situations:

- When the current drawing already has a name and you need to save it under a different name.
- When you need to save the current drawing in an alternate format, such as a drawing file for a previous AutoCAD release format.
- When you open one of your drawing template files and create a drawing. This leaves the drawing template unchanged and ready to use for other drawings.

SAVEAS
File
➥ **Save As...**

The **SAVEAS** command is accessed by picking **Save As...** from the **File** pull-down menu or by entering SAVEAS at the Command: prompt. This command always displays the **Save Drawing As** dialog box. If the current drawing has already been saved, the current name and location are displayed. Confirm that the **Save in:** box displays the current drive and directory folder you want and that the **Files of type:** box displays the desired file type. Type the new drawing name in the **File name:** box and pick the **Save** button.

Using the SAVE Command

The third command provided for saving a drawing is the **SAVE** command. The **SAVE** command is not commonly used and is only available at the command line by entering SAVE. The **SAVE** command displays the **Save Drawing As** dialog box, regardless of whether or not the drawing has been previously saved. Because of this, the **QSAVE** command is better for saving a drawing in progress, and the **SAVEAS** command is better for saving a drawing with a new name or location.

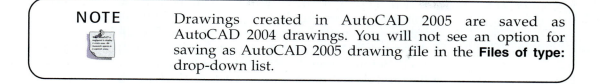

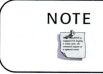

If you try to save the current drawing using the same name and location as another drawing file, AutoCAD issues a warning message in an alert box and allows you to cancel the operation or replace the current drawing with the one you are working on. If you actually need to replace the existing file, pick the **Yes** button to overwrite the file with the information in the current drawing. If you do not wish to overwrite the file, pick the **No** button to return to the **Save Drawing As** dialog box. To cancel the operation, pick the **Cancel** button. Be very careful—if you pick the **Yes** button, the current drawing replaces the other drawing.

> **NOTE**
>
> When saving a drawing to a different name, the **SAVE** command saves the drawing file with a different name, but leaves you in the current drawing. The **SAVEAS** command discards all changes to the original drawing file up to the last save. Before using the **SAVEAS** command, close the drawing file, and then reopen it to make sure all changes remain.

Saving Your Work Automatically

AutoCAD can create an automatic backup copy of the active drawing. The backup file has a .bak extension and is created in the same folder where the drawing is located. When you save the drawing, the .dwg file is updated, and the .bak file is overwritten by the old .dwg file. Therefore, the backup file is always "one save behind" the drawing file.

This feature can be activated using the **Create backup copy with each save** check box in the **Open and Save** tab of the **Options** dialog box. See Figure 2-6. This dialog box can be accessed by selecting **Options...** from the **Tools** pull-down menu.

Before you can access a backup file, you must rename it. Use Windows Explorer to rename the file and change the file extension from .bak to .dwg. Once the file has been renamed, it can be opened in AutoCAD.

AutoCAD provides you with an automatic work-saving tool called *automatic save (autosave).* Enter the amount of time (in minutes) between saves in the **Open and Save** tab of the **Options** dialog box. The value is entered in the **Minutes between saves** text box in the **File Safety Precautions** area. See Figure 2-6, which shows a setting of ten minutes.

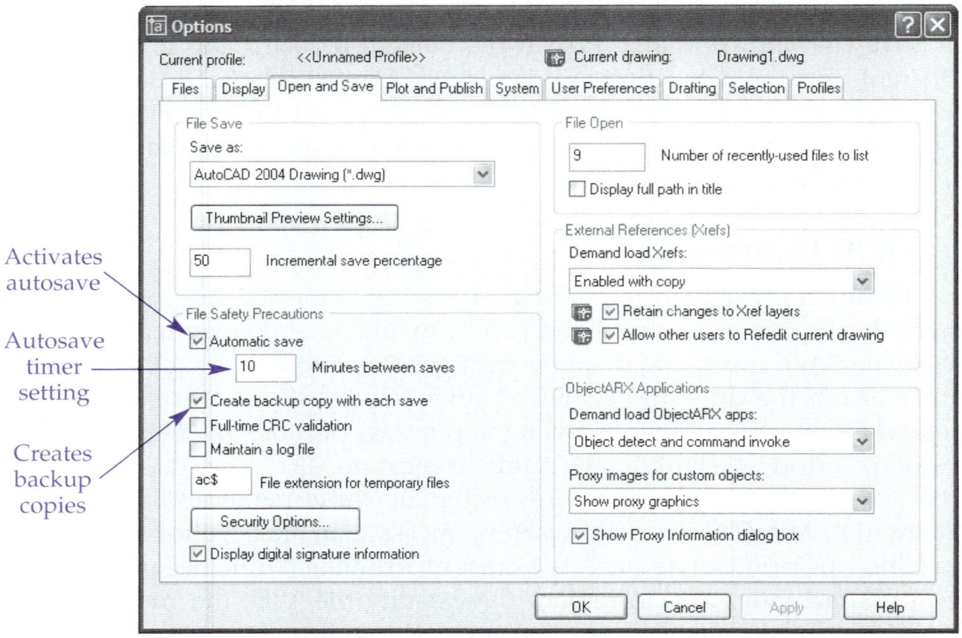

Figure 2-6.
Use the **Open and Save** tab in the **Options** dialog box to set the autosave timer value.

The autosave timer starts as soon as a change is made to the drawing. The timer is reset when the **QSAVE**, **SAVEAS**, or **SAVE** command is used. The drawing is saved when the first command is given after the autosave timer has been reached. For example, if you set the timer to fifteen minutes, work for fourteen minutes, and then let the computer remain idle for five minutes, an automatic save is not executed until the nineteen-minute interval, when you perform a command. Therefore, be sure to manually save your drawing if you plan to be away from your computer for an extended period of time.

The autosave feature is intended to be used in case AutoCAD shuts down unexpectedly. Therefore, when you close a drawing file, the autosave file associated with that drawing is automatically deleted from Windows. If AutoCAD does shut down unexpectedly, the autosave file remains and can be used. The autosave drawing is always saved with the name of *DrawingName_n_n_nnnn*.sv$. If you need to use the autosaved file, it can be renamed with a .dwg file extension using Windows Explorer. Refer to the Student CD for more information on Windows Explorer.

> **NOTE**
>
> The **Automatic Save File Location** in the **Files** tab of the **Options** dialog box determines the folder where the autosaved files are saved. Pick **Options...** from the **Tools** pull-down menu to access this dialog box.

Saving AutoCAD Drawings As Older Releases

The drawing file type saved by AutoCAD 2005 is a different file format than the file types saved by previous releases of AutoCAD. AutoCAD 2005 drawings can be saved in an AutoCAD 2000 format. This allows you to send AutoCAD 2005 drawings to businesses where older releases of AutoCAD are being used.

To save as an older release, use the **SAVEAS** command. The **Save Drawing As** dialog box appears. Using the **Files of type:** drop-down list, select the AutoCAD 2000/LT2000 Drawing (*.dwg) to save the drawing as an AutoCAD 2000 format. AutoCAD 2002, AutoCAD 2000i, and AutoCAD 2000 all use AutoCAD 2000 format files.

After selecting the file format, specify the file name and location as previously discussed. When you save a version of a drawing in an earlier format, be sure to give it a different name than the AutoCAD 2005 version. This prevents you from accidentally overwriting your working drawing with the older format.

> **NOTE**
>
> Additional information on saving AutoCAD drawings in alternative formats can be found in the Windows Explorer material on the Student CD.

Opening Existing Drawings

OPEN
[Ctrl]+[O]

File
➥ Open

Standard toolbar
Open

An existing drawing is one that has been previously saved. You can easily access any existing drawing with the **OPEN** command. To use the **OPEN** command, pick the **Open** button on the **Standard** toolbar, pick **Open...** from the **File** pull-down menu, press the [Ctrl]+[O] key combination, or enter OPEN at the Command: prompt. The **Select File** dialog box appears. See **Figure 2-7.** This dialog box contains a list of folders and files. Double-click on a file folder to open it, and then double-click on the desired

Figure 2-7.
The **Select File** dialog box is used to select a drawing to open. Notice the 8th floor drawing has been selected from the file list box and appears in the **File name:** text box.

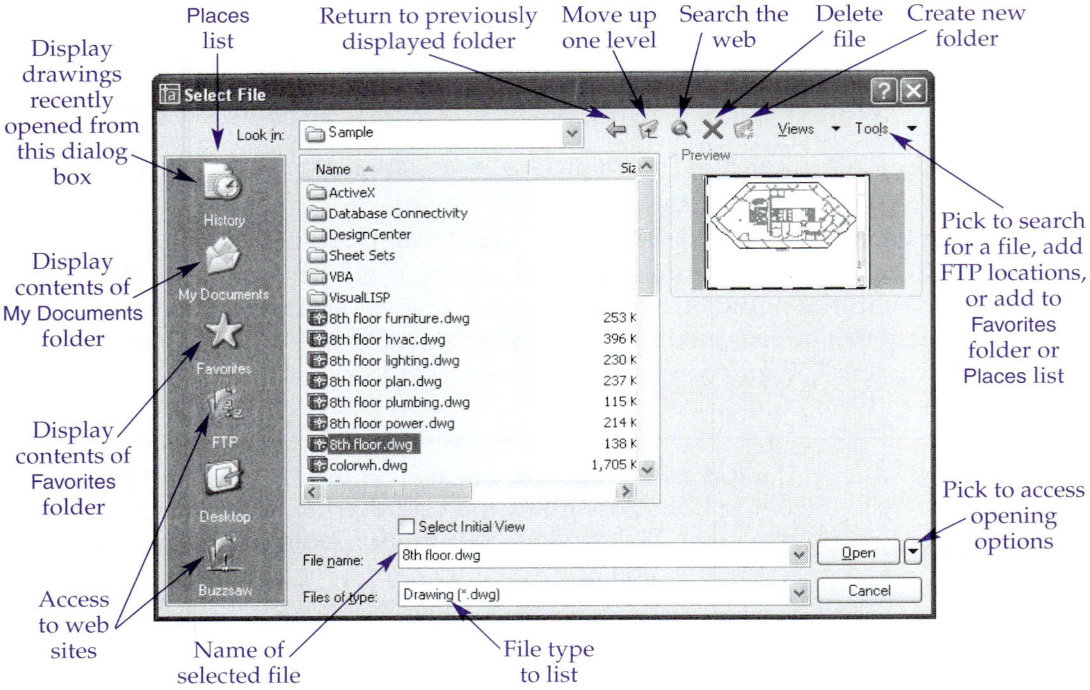

file to open it. The AutoCAD 2005\Sample folder is open, with the sample drawings displayed.

When you pick an existing drawing, a picture of the drawing is displayed in the **Preview** area. This is an easy way for you to get a quick look at the drawing without loading the drawing into AutoCAD. You can view each drawing until you find the one you want.

After picking a drawing file name to highlight it, you can quickly highlight another drawing in the list by using the keyboard arrow keys. Use the up and down arrow keys to move vertically between files and use the left and right arrow keys to move horizontally. This enables you to scan through the drawing previews very quickly. An easy way to become familiar with the **Preview** image tile feature is to look at the sample drawings that come with AutoCAD. To do the following exercise, the sample drawings must have been loaded during the AutoCAD installation process.

EXERCISE 2-2 Complete the Exercise on the Student CD.

Accessing Files

The **Select File** dialog box includes the Places list along its left side. The Places list provides instant access to certain folders. The following buttons are available:

- **History.** Lists drawing files opened recently from the **Select File** dialog box.
- **My Documents/Personal.** Displays the files and folders contained in the My Documents or Personal folder for the current user. Whether you see My Documents or Personal depends on your operating system version.

- **Favorites.** Displays files and folders located in the Windows\Favorites folder.
- **FTP.** Displays available FTP (file transfer protocol) sites. To add or modify the listed FTP sites, select **Add/Modify FTP Locations** from the **Tools** menu in the **Select File** dialog box.
- **Desktop.** Lists the files, folders, and drives located on your desktop.
- **Buzzsaw.** Displays projects on the Buzzsaw web site. Buzzsaw.com is designed for the building industry. After setting up a project hosting account, users can access project drawings from the Web site. This allows the various companies involved in the construction process to have instant access to the drawing files.

The **Select File** dialog box includes other features for selecting folders and files:

- **Back button.** Shows the previously displayed folder contents.
- **Up one level button.** Displays the contents of the folder containing the currently displayed file or folder.
- **Search the Web button.** Accesses the **Browse the Web** dialog box, from which you can open files from the Internet.
- **Delete button.** Deletes the selected file or folder.
- **Create New Folder button.** Creates a new folder within the folder being displayed.

Finding Files

You can search for files from the **Select File** dialog box by picking **Find...** in the **Tools** menu. This accesses the **Find** dialog box, which is shown in **Figure 2-8.** If you know the file name for the drawing, enter it in the **Named:** text box. If you do not know the name, you can use wildcard characters (such as *) to narrow the search.

Choose the type of file from the **Type:** drop-down list. You can search for .dwg, .dws, .dxf, or .dwt files from the **Find** dialog box. If you are searching for another type of file, use the Windows Explorer search tool.

A search can be completed more quickly if you do not search the entire hard drive. If you know the folder in which the file is located, specify the folder in the **Look in:** text box. Pick the **Browse** button to select a folder from the **Browse for Folder** dialog box. Select the **Include subfolders** check box if you want the subfolders within the selected folder to be searched.

You can also search for files based on when they were last modified. The **Date Modified** tab provides options to search for files modified within a certain time

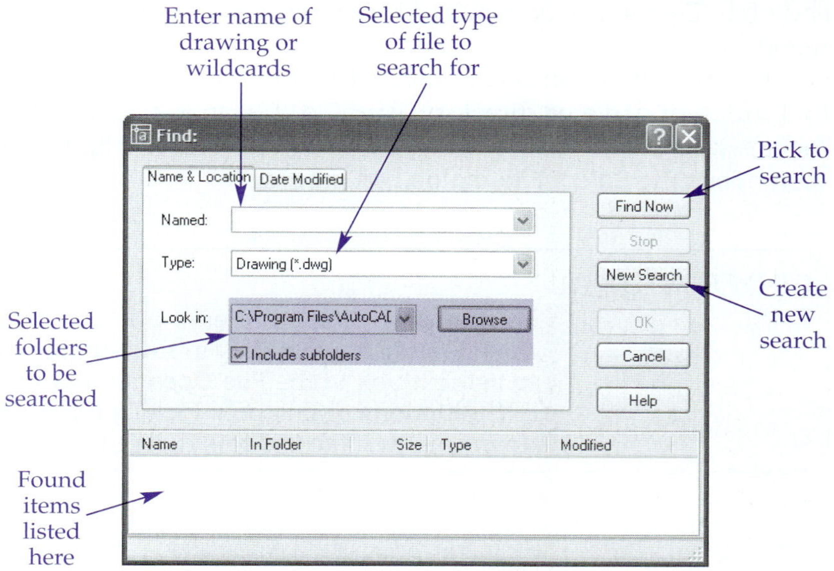

Figure 2-8.
Use the **Find** dialog box to locate drawing files.

period. This option is very useful if you wish to list all drawings modified within a specific week or month.

PROFESSIONAL TIP

While working in file dialog boxes, certain file management capabilities are available, similar to when you are using the Windows Explorer. To rename an existing file or folder, pick it once and pause for a moment, then pick the name again. This places the name in a text box for editing. Type the new name and press [Enter].

For a full listing of all the available options, point to a desired file folder, and then right-click. This displays a shortcut menu of available options for working with the file folder. Use one of the options or pick somewhere off the menu to close it.

CAUTION

Use extreme caution when deleting or renaming files and folders. Never delete or rename anything if you are not absolutely certain you should. If you are unsure, ask your instructor or system administrator for assistance.

Opening Drawings from Previous Releases of AutoCAD

In AutoCAD 2005, you can open drawing files created in Release 12 or later. When you open a drawing from a previous release and work on it, AutoCAD automatically updates the drawing to the AutoCAD 2004 file format when you save. Remember, AutoCAD 2005 files are saved in the AutoCAD 2004 file format. After the previous release drawing is saved in AutoCAD 2005, it can be viewed in the **Preview** image tile during future applications.

Opening a Drawing from the File Pull-Down Menu List

By default, AutoCAD stores the names and locations of the last nine drawing files opened. These file names are listed at the bottom of the **File** pull-down menu, as shown in Figure 2-9. Any one of these files can be quickly opened by picking the file name.

If you try to open one of these drawing files after it has been deleted or moved to a different drive or directory, AutoCAD is unable to locate it. AutoCAD displays the message Cannot find the specified drawing file. Please verify that the file exists. AutoCAD then opens the **Select File** dialog box.

PROFESSIONAL TIP

You can select the number of previous drawings displayed in the **File** pull-down menu in the **Number of recently-used files to list** text box in the **File Open** area of the **Open and Save** tab of the **Options** dialog box. Pick **Options...** from the **Tools** pull-down menu to access this dialog box.

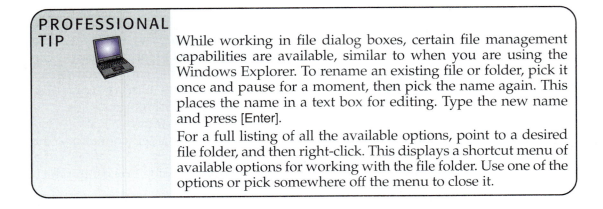

Figure 2-9.
The **File** pull-down menu contains a list of the last nine edited drawings.

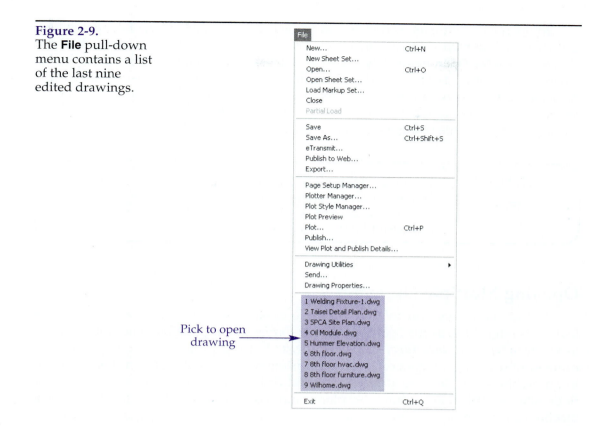

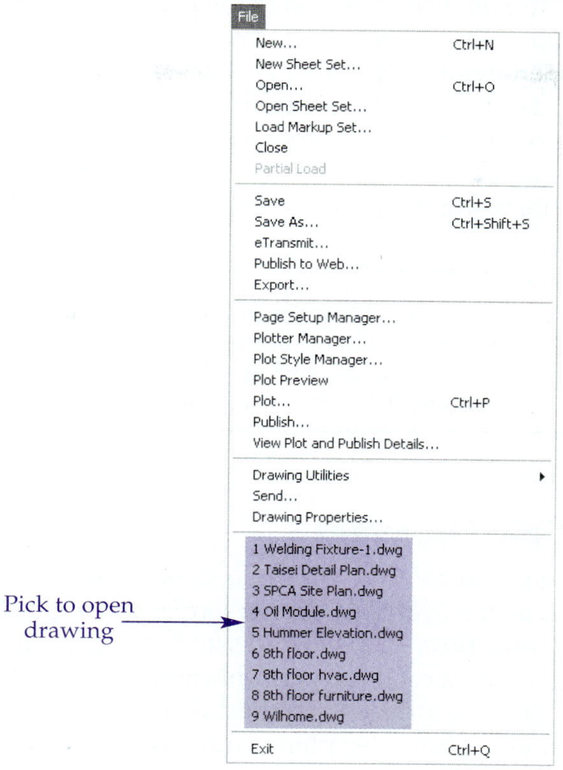

Using Windows Explorer to Open Drawings

You can open drawing files through the Windows Explorer program. This can be done in two ways. You can double-click on the file, and it will open in AutoCAD. If AutoCAD is not already running, it will start and the file will be opened. You can also drag-and-drop a file to the AutoCAD command line, and AutoCAD will open it. If AutoCAD is not running, you can drag-and-drop the file to the AutoCAD icon on your desktop. AutoCAD will then start and open the drawing file. Refer to the Student CD for more information about the Windows Explorer.

Opening DXF Files

You can open DXF files from Release 12 or later. When you open a DXF file and work on it, AutoCAD automatically updates the DXF file to the AutoCAD 2004 DXF file format when you save. As with drawing files, AutoCAD 2005 DXF files are saved in the AutoCAD 2004 file format. After the previous release DXF is saved in AutoCAD 2004 format, it can be viewed in the **Preview** image tile during future applications. To open a DXF file, use the **OPEN** command and select DXF (*.dxf) in the **Files of type:** drop-down list. See the Windows Explorer material on the Student CD for more information on DXF files.

EXERCISE 2-3 Complete the Exercise on the Student CD.

Opening a Drawing As Read-Only

Drawings can be opened as read-only. When a drawing is opened as read-only, the drawing changes cannot be saved to the original file. This ensures that the original drawing file will remain unchanged.

To open a drawing as read-only, select the drawing in the **Select File** dialog box, and then pick the **Open Read-Only** option from the **Open** drop-down menu. You can also select **Partial Open Read-Only** to use the **Partial Open** option with a read-only file. Opening part of a file is covered later in this textbook. You can make changes to a drawing opened as read-only, but AutoCAD will not allow you to save the changes to the original file name. However, you can use the **SAVEAS** command to save the modified drawing file using a different name.

NOTE

When working with large drawings, you can use the **Partial Open** option to open only part of a drawing by selecting specific views and layers to be opened. Views and layers are discussed later in this textbook.

Opening Multiple Drawings

AutoCAD allows you to have multiple drawings open at the same time. This feature is referred to as the ***Multiple Design Environment (MDE)*** (sometimes called a ***multiple document interface***, or ***MDI***). Most drafting projects are composed of a number of drawings, where each presents different aspects of a project. For example, in an architectural drafting project, required drawings might include a site plan, a floor plan, electrical and plumbing plans, and assorted detail drawings. Consider a mechanical assembly composed of several unique parts. The required drawings might include an overall assembly view, plus individual detail drawings of each component part. The drawings in such projects are closely related to one another. By opening two or more of these drawings at the same time, you can easily reference information contained in existing drawings, while working in a new drawing. AutoCAD even allows you to directly copy all or part of the contents from one drawing directly into another, using a simple drag-and-drop operation.

There are many ways to increase your drafting productivity through effective use of the MDE. These more advanced topics are covered throughout the text where they apply to the discussion material. The following information introduces the basic features and behaviors of the MDE.

Controlling Drawing Windows

Each drawing you open or start in AutoCAD is placed in its own drawing window. Based on AutoCAD's initial default behavior, drawing windows are displayed in a floating state. This means the drawing area is displayed within a smaller window inside the main AutoCAD window. When multiple drawings are open at the same time, they are placed in a cascading arrangement by default. The name of each drawing is displayed on the left side of its title bar.

AutoCAD's drawing windows have the same control options as program windows on your desktop. They can be resized, moved, minimized, maximized, restored, and closed, using the same methods used for program windows on your desktop. **Figure 2-10** shows a summary of the standard window control functions available for drawing windows.

The drawing windows and the AutoCAD window have the same relationship as program windows have with the Windows desktop. When a drawing window is maximized, it fills the available area in the AutoCAD window. Minimizing a drawing window displays it as a reduced size title bar along the bottom of AutoCAD's drawing area. Drawing windows cannot be moved outside the AutoCAD window. **Figure 2-11** illustrates drawing windows in a floating state and minimized.

Figure 2-10.
Drawing window control options.

Window Control Buttons		
Button	**Function**	**Description**
	Minimize	Displays window as a button along bottom of drawing window space in AutoCAD window.
	Restore	Returns window to floating state, at previous size and position, displays title bar.
	Maximize	Displays window at largest possible size, hides title bar.
	Close	Closes drawing, provides option to save drawing if any changes remain unsaved.
	Display window control menu	Displays pull-down menu with window control options.

Resizing Controls		
Cursor	**Function**	**Usage**
	Size window vertically	Press and hold pick button while pointing at top or bottom border of window, then move mouse.
	Size window horizontally	Press and hold pick button while pointing at left or right border of window, then move mouse.
	Size window diagonally	Press and hold pick button while pointing at any corner on border of window, then move mouse.
	Move window	Press and hold pick button while pointing at title bar of window, then move mouse.

Figure 2-11.
Drawing windows can be displayed in several ways. A—By default, drawings are displayed in floating windows. When multiple drawings are open, the windows are placed in a cascading arrangement. B—Minimized drawing windows are displayed as a reduced size title bar. Pick the title bar to display a window control menu.

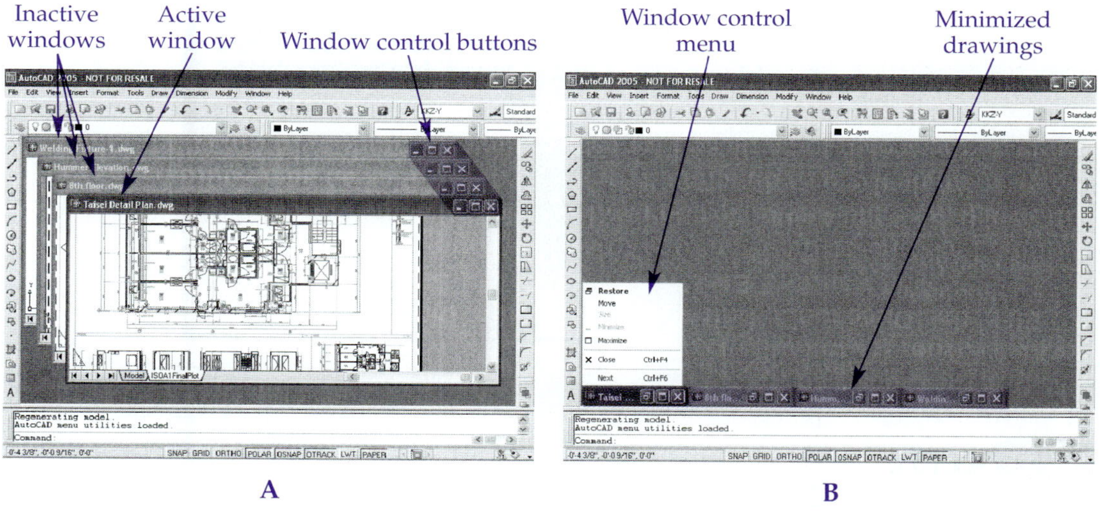

To work on any currently open drawing, just pick its title bar if it is visible. Pressing either the [Ctrl]+[F6] or [Ctrl]+[Tab] key combination allows you to cycle through all open drawings. To go directly to a specific drawing when the title bars are not visible, access the **Window** pull-down menu in AutoCAD. The name of each open drawing file is displayed, and the active drawing shows a check mark next to it. See **Figure 2-12A.** Pick the name of the desired drawing to make it current. Up to nine drawing names are displayed on this menu. If more than nine drawings are open, a **More Windows...** selection is displayed. Picking this displays the **Select Window** dialog box, shown in **Figure 2-12B.**

The additional control options available in the **Window** pull-down menu include:

- **Close.** Closes the active window.
- **Close All.** Closes all open drawings.
- **Cascade.** Arranges the drawing windows that are not currently minimized in a cascade of floating windows, with the active drawing placed at the front.
- **Tile Horizontally.** Tiles the drawing windows that are not currently minimized in a horizontal arrangement, with the active drawing window placed in the top position.
- **Tile Vertically.** Tiles the drawing windows that are not currently minimized in a vertical arrangement, with the active drawing window placed in the left position.
- **Arrange Icons.** Arranges minimized drawings neatly along the bottom of the AutoCAD drawing window area.

The effects of tiling the drawing windows vary, based on the number of windows being tiled and whether they are tiled horizontally or vertically. See **Figure 2-13.**

NOTE

Typically, you can change the active drawing as desired. There are some situations, however, when you cannot switch between drawings. For example, you cannot switch drawings during a dialog session. You must either complete or cancel the dialog box before switching is possible.

Figure 2-12.
Selecting the active drawing window. A—Pick the name of a drawing displayed on the **Window** pull-down menu to make it current. This menu also offers additional drawing window control options. B—When more than nine drawings are open, pick **More Windows...** from the **Window** pull-down menu to display the **Select Window** dialog box.

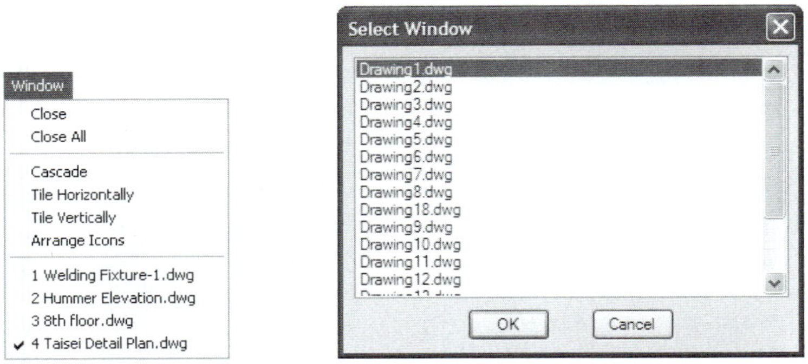

A B

EXERCISE 2-4 Complete the Exercise on the Student CD.

Figure 2-13.
Tiled drawing windows. A—Three drawing windows, tiled horizontally. B—Three drawing windows, tiled vertically. C—Four drawing windows, tiled either horizontally or vertically.

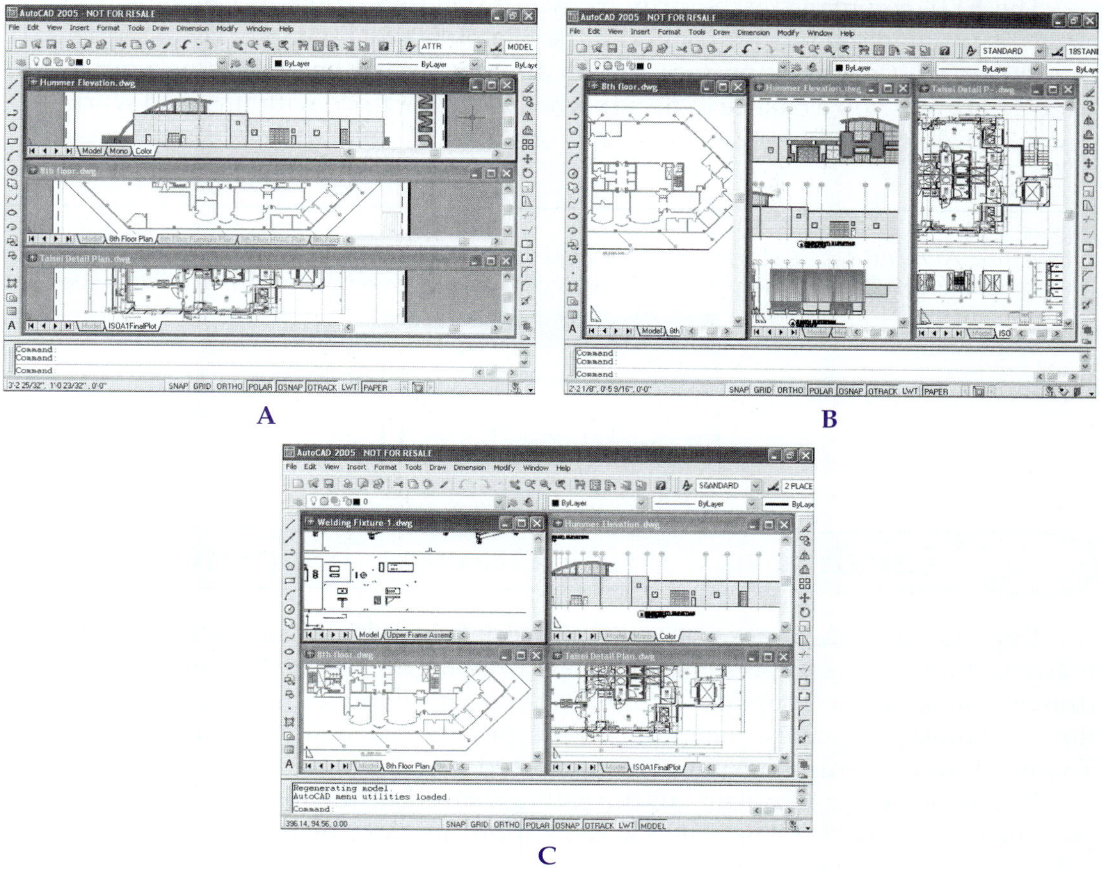

Closing a Drawing

The **CLOSE** command is the primary way to exit out of a drawing file without ending the AutoCAD session. You can close the current drawing file by picking **Close** from the **File** pull-down menu or by entering CLOSE at the Command: prompt. If you enter the **CLOSE** command before saving your work, AutoCAD gives you a chance to decide what you want to do with unsaved work. The AutoCAD alert box shown in **Figure 2-14** appears. Press [Enter] to activate the highlighted **Yes** button. This saves the drawing. If the drawing is unnamed, the **Save Drawing As** dialog box appears. You can also pick the **No** button if you plan to discard any changes made to the drawing since the previous save. Pick the **Cancel** button if you decide not to close the drawing and want to return to the graphics window.

CLOSE
File
➥ **Close...**

If you have multiple drawing windows open, you can close all of them simultaneously by selecting **Close All** from the **Window** pull-down menu. This command closes all open drawing files. Picking **Close** in the **Window** pull-down menu closes only the active drawing. This option is identical to the **CLOSE** command.

Exiting AutoCAD

EXIT
QUIT

File
➥ Exit...

The **EXIT** command is the primary way to end an AutoCAD session. You can close the program by picking **Exit** from the **File** pull-down menu or by entering EXIT or QUIT at the Command: prompt. If you attempt to exit before saving your work, AutoCAD gives you a chance to decide what you want to do with unsaved work. The AutoCAD alert box shown in Figure 2-14 appears.

Figure 2-14.
This AutoCAD alert box is shown if you try to exit AutoCAD or close a drawing file without saving your work. This is an opportunity to decide what will be done with unsaved work.

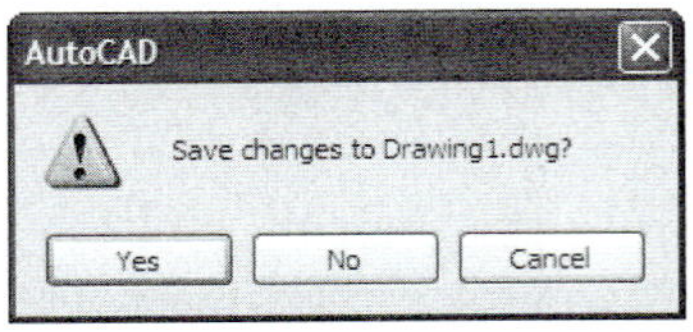

Creating and Using Drawing Templates

Depending on the types of drawing projects with which you work, there may be many settings that are the same from one drawing to the next. These can include drawing aids, such as snap and grid settings, and drawing settings, such as units and limits. In most companies, standard borders and title blocks are used in all drawings. To save drawing setup time, templates are used.

When you use a template, all the settings saved in the template are applied to your new drawing. The template file can supply any information normally saved in a drawing file, including settings and drawing objects. Many of the templates already have standard borders and title blocks, which are then created in your new drawing. The template drawing contains the setup options you choose, plus any snap and grid settings you use. As you continue through this text, you can add items to your templates, such as layer settings, company information, logos, text styles, plot styles, dimension styles, and table styles. All these settings are designed to your company or school specifications and based on your drawing applications.

Creating Your Own Templates

If none of the predefined templates meet your needs, you can create and save your own custom templates. AutoCAD allows you to save *any* drawing as a template. A drawing template should be developed whenever several drawing applications require the same setup procedure. The template then allows the setup to be applied to any number of future drawings. Creating templates increases drafting productivity by decreasing setup requirements.

Some existing AutoCAD templates may be close to what you need and simply need fine-tuning. Some basic parameters that can be specified in a drawing template include units, limits, snap settings, and grid settings. These are discussed later in this chapter. You can also draw your own border and title block.

As you learn more about working with AutoCAD, you will find many other settings that can be included in your drawing templates. When you have everything needed in the template, the template is ready to save. Use the **SAVEAS** command to save a drawing template. Picking **Save As...** from the **File** pull-down menu or typing SAVEAS at the Command: prompt accesses the **SAVEAS** command. This command displays the **Save Drawing As** dialog box, as shown in Figure 2-15. To specify that the

Figure 2-15.
Saving a template.

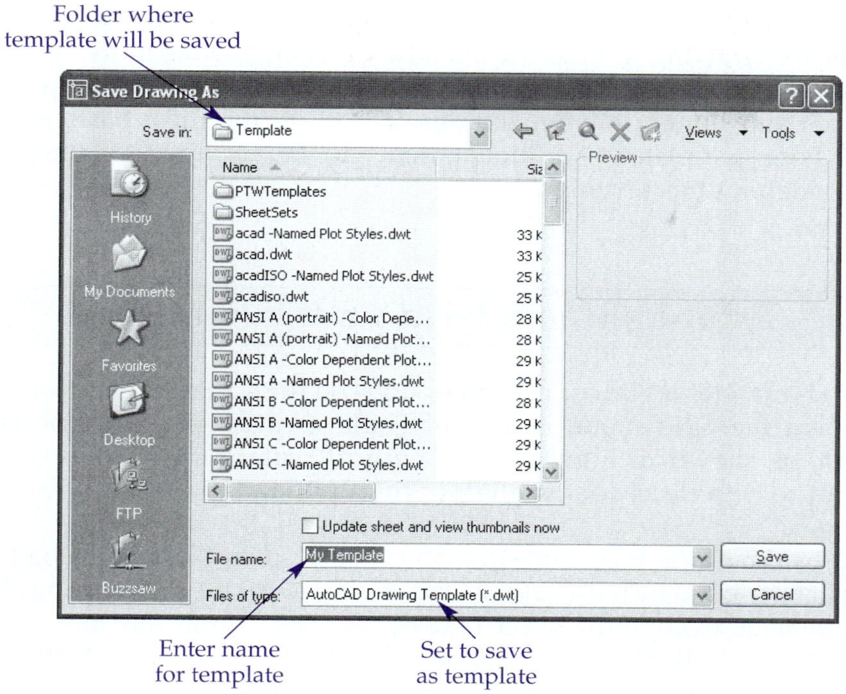

drawing is to be saved as a drawing template, pick AutoCAD Drawing Template (*.dwt) from the **Files of type:** drop-down list. The file list window then shows all the drawing templates currently found in the Template folder. You can store custom templates in another location, but it is recommended that they be stored in the Template folder. After specifying the name and location for the new template file, pick the **Save** button in the **Save Drawing As** dialog box. The **Template Description** dialog box is now displayed, as shown in Figure 2-16. Use the **Description** area to enter a brief description of the template file you are saving. You can enter up to two hundred characters, but a brief description usually works best. Under the **Measurement** drop-down list, specify whether the units used in the template are English or Metric, and then pick the **OK** button.

The template name should relate to the template, such as Mechanical A size, for a mechanical drawing on an A-size sheet. The template might be named for the drawing application, such as Architectural floor plans. The template name might be as simple as Template 1. The name should be written in a reference manual, along with documentation about what is included in the template. This provides future reference for you and other users. The template drawing you create is saved for you to open and use whenever it is needed. Now, you can exit AutoCAD, and when you start up again, the template you created is ready for you to use for preparing a new drawing.

Figure 2-16.
Enter a description of the new template in the **Template Description** dialog box.

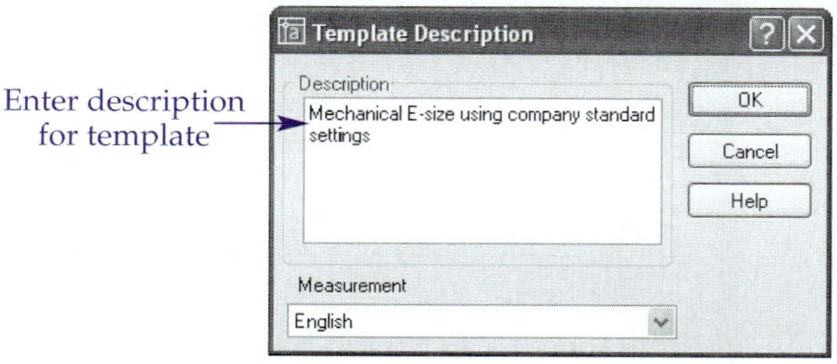

Planning Your AutoCAD Templates

Effective planning can greatly reduce the amount of time it takes to set up and complete a drawing. By creating a variety of templates with various setups, the basic drawing aids and drawing settings are already set when you begin the drawing.

The next sections discuss the basic drawing aids Grid mode and Snap mode and the basic units and limits drawing settings. These are the most basic items to be included in your templates. Additional items to be included in templates are discussed throughout this textbook.

Establishing a Grid on the Screen

AutoCAD provides a grid, or pattern of dots, on the screen to help you lay out a drawing. When the Grid mode is activated, this pattern of dots appears in the drawing area, as shown in Figure 2-17. The grid pattern shows only within the drawing limits to help clearly define the working area, and the spacing between dots can be adjusted.

Figure 2-18 shows the **Snap and Grid** tab of the **Drafting Settings** dialog box. This dialog box can be used to turn the grid on and off and to set the grid spacing. To access the **Drafting Settings** dialog box, select **Drafting Settings...** from the **Tools** pull-down menu; right-click on the **GRID** or **SNAP** button in the status bar and select **Settings...** from the shortcut menu; or type DSETTINGS, DS, or SE at the Command: prompt. The grid can be turned on (displayed) or off (not displayed) by selecting the **Grid On** check box. Other methods for turning the grid on and off include using the **ON** and **OFF** options of the **GRID** command, picking the **GRID** button on the status bar, using the [Ctrl]+[G] key combination, pressing the [F7] function key, and using puck button 6.

The grid spacing can be set in the **Grid** area of the **Drafting Settings** dialog box. You can also set the grid spacing using the **GRID** command. Entering GRID at the Command: prompt provides the following prompt:

Command: **GRID**↵
Specify grid spacing(X) or [ON/OFF/Snap/Aspect] <*current*>: **.25**↵

Figure 2-17.
Dots represent the grid spacing.

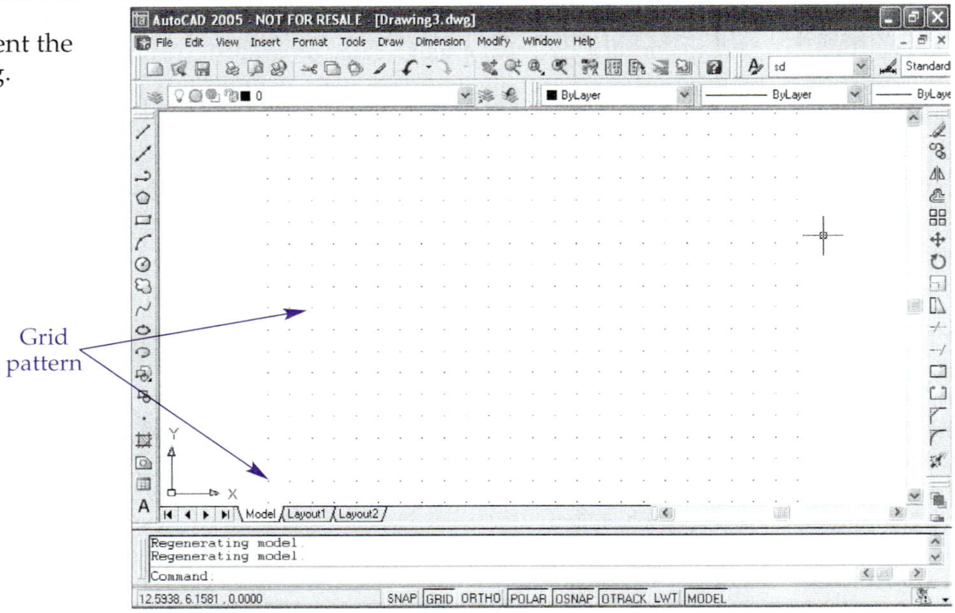

Figure 2-18.
Grid setting can be made in the **Snap and Grid** tab of the **Drafting Settings** dialog box.

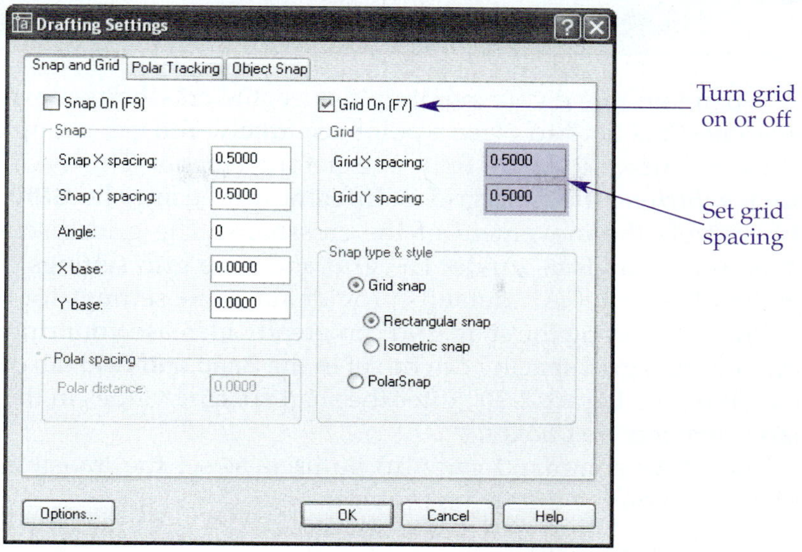

You can press [Enter] to accept the default spacing value shown in brackets or enter a new value, as shown. If the grid spacing you enter is too close to display on the screen, you get the Grid too dense to display message. In this case, a larger grid spacing is required.

Different Horizontal and Vertical Grid Units

To set different values for horizontal and vertical grid spacing, enter the appropriate values in the **Grid X spacing:** and **Grid Y spacing:** text boxes in the **Drafting Settings** dialog box. For example, Figure 2-19 shows a horizontal spacing of 1 and a vertical spacing of .5. This can also be done using the **GRID** command. Type A (for the **Aspect** option) to set different values for the horizontal and vertical grid spacing.

Figure 2-19.
The X and Y grid spacing units can be set to different values. Notice that, here, the horizontal spacing is greater than the vertical spacing.

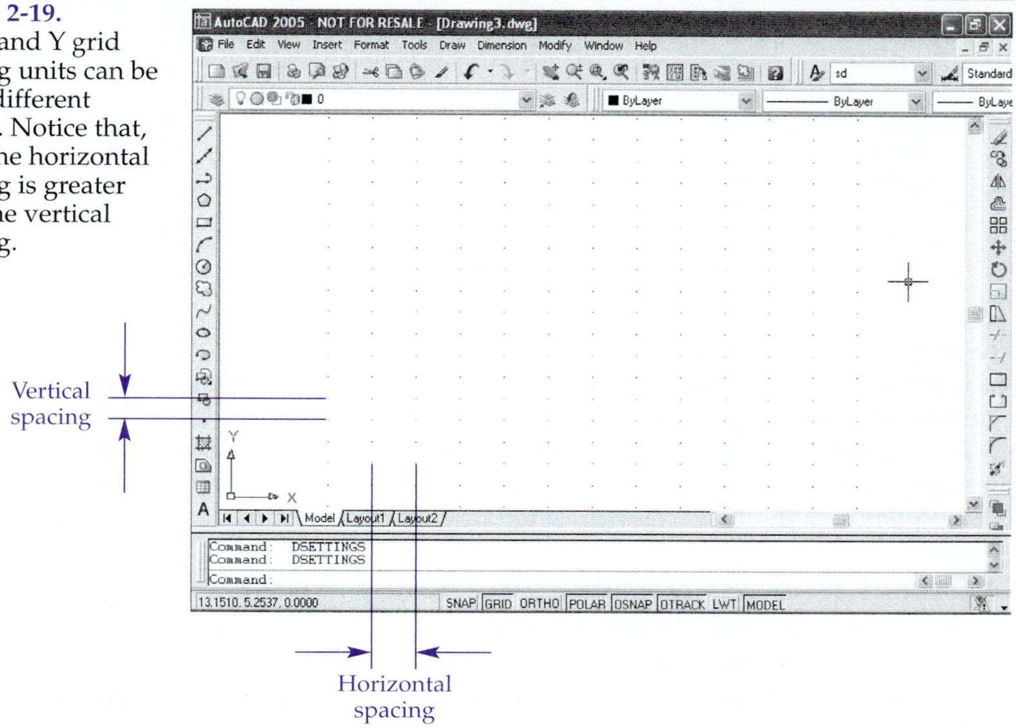

Setting Increments for Cursor Movement

When you move your pointing device, the crosshairs move freely on the screen. Sometimes it is hard to place a point accurately. You can set up an invisible grid that allows the cursor to move only in exact increments. This is called the ***snap grid***, or ***snap resolution***. The snap grid is different from using the **GRID** command. The snap grid controls the movement of the crosshairs. The grid discussed in the previous section is only a visual guide. The grid and snap grid settings can, however, be used together. The AutoCAD defaults provide the same settings for both.

Properly setting the snap grid can greatly increase your drawing speed and accuracy. The snap grid spacing can be set in the **Snap and Grid** tab of the **Drafting Settings** dialog box. See **Figure 2-20.** Enter the snap spacing values in the **Snap X spacing:** and **Snap Y spacing:** text boxes.

The **SNAP** command can also be used to set the invisible snap grid. Entering SNAP gives you the following prompt:

Command: **SNAP**↵
Specify snap spacing or [ON/OFF/Aspect/Rotate/Style/Type] <*current*>:

Figure 2-20.
Snap grid settings can be made in the **Snap and Grid** tab of the **Drafting Settings** dialog box.

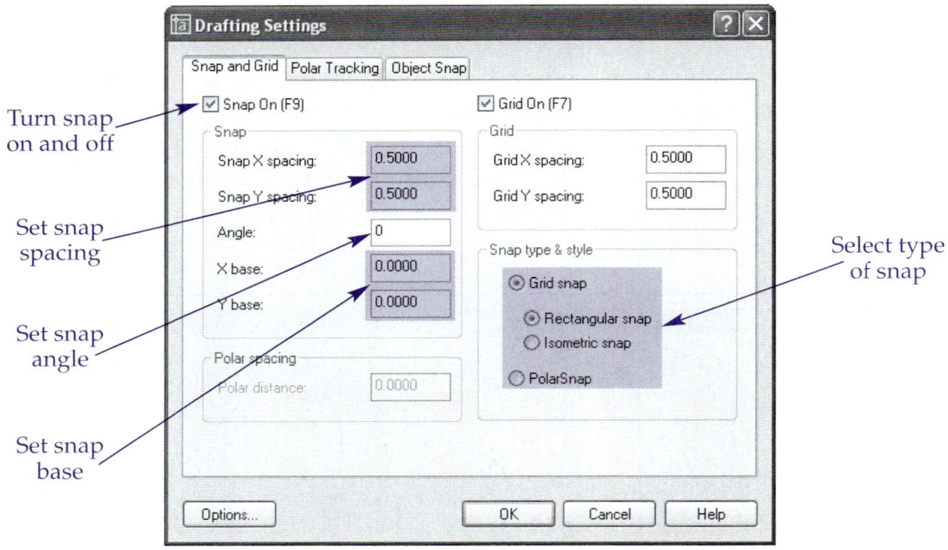

Pressing [Enter] accepts the value shown in brackets. The value you set remains the same until changed. The **OFF** option turns snap off, but the same snap spacing is again in effect when you turn snap on again. The snap spacing can be turned on or off at any time by clicking the **SNAP** button on the status bar, pressing [Ctrl]+[B], pressing the [F9] function key, selecting or deselecting the **Snap On** check box in the **Drafting Settings** dialog box, or pressing puck button 4.

Different Horizontal and Vertical Snap Grid Units

The snap grid is usually set up with equal horizontal and vertical snap grid units. It is possible, however, to set different horizontal and vertical snap grid units. To do this, enter different values in the **Snap X spacing:** and **Snap Y spacing:** text boxes in the **Drafting Settings** dialog box. This can also be done using the **Aspect** option of the **SNAP** command.

PROFESSIONAL TIP

The most effective use of the Snap mode quite often comes from setting an equal X and Y spacing to the lowest, or near lowest, increment of the majority of the feature dimensions. For example, this might be .0625 units in a mechanical drawing or 6″ in an architectural application. If many horizontal features conform to one increment and most vertical features correspond to another, then a snap grid can be set up using different X and Y values.

Rotating the Snap Grid

The normal snap grid pattern consists of horizontal rows and vertical columns. Another option, however, is to rotate the snap grid. This technique is helpful when drawing an auxiliary view at an angle to other views of the drawing. When the snap grid is rotated, you are given the option of setting a new base point. The base point is the pivot around which the snap grid is rotated. The base point of a normal snap grid is the lower-left corner. It may be more convenient to set the base point at the location where you will begin the view.

Using the **Drafting Settings** dialog box, enter the snap angle in the **Angle:** text box and the new base point in the **X base:** and **Y base:** text boxes. These values can also be set using the **Rotate** option of the **SNAP** command. The grid automatically rotates counterclockwise about the base point when a positive rotation angle is given and clockwise when a negative rotation angle is given. Figure 2-21 shows the relationship between the regular and rotated snap grids. Remember, the snap grid is invisible.

Figure 2-21.
The snap grid is usually horizontal rows and vertical columns. It can be rotated, however, to help you draw. Notice the angle of the crosshairs. (The snap grid is invisible, but it is represented here by dots.)

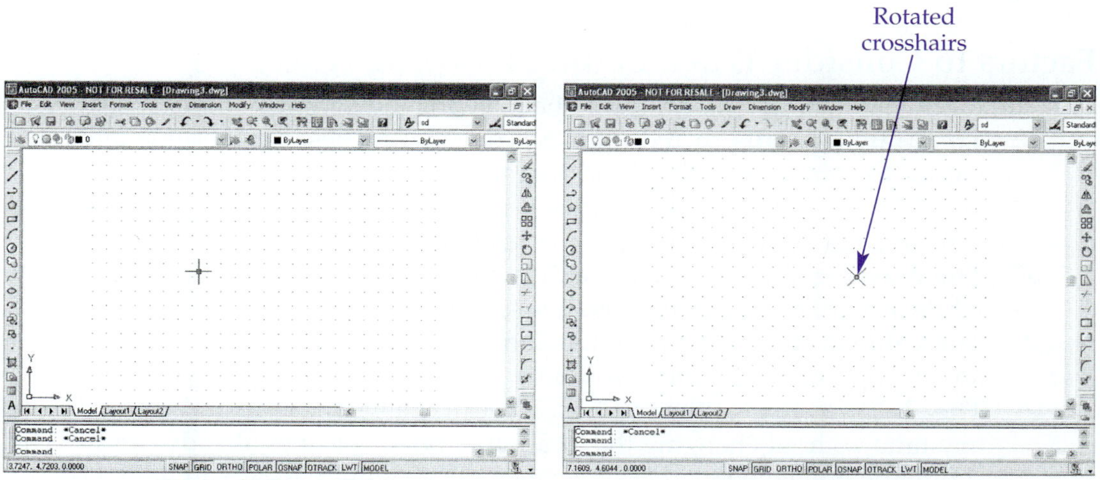

Default Snap Grid　　Rotated Snap Grid

Setting the Snap Type and Style

The **Snap type & style** area of the **Drafting Settings** dialog box allows you to select one of two types of snap grids: **Grid snap** or **PolarSnap**. **PolarSnap** allows you to snap to precise distances along alignment paths when using polar tracking. Polar tracking is discussed in Chapter 6. **Grid snap** has two styles: **Rectangular snap** and **Isometric snap**. **Rectangular snap** is the standard style. **Isometric snap** is useful when creating isometric drawings (discussed in Chapter 26). Select the radio button(s) for the snap type and style you desire and pick the **OK** button. You can also use the **Type** and **Style** options of the **SNAP** command to change these settings. Use the **Type** option to select **Polar** or **Grid** and use the **Style** option to select **Standard** (Rectangular) or **Isometric**.

Setting the Grid Spacing Relative to the Snap Spacing

The visible grid can be set to coincide with the invisible snap grid by choosing the **Snap** option after entering the **GRID** command. You can also set the dot spacing as a multiple of the snap units by entering the number of snap units between grid points. For example, 2X places grid points at every other snap unit. If the snap spacing is .25, and you specify 2X at the Specify grid spacing(X) or [ON/OFF/Snap/Aspect] <*current*>: prompt, the grid spacing will be .5 units.

Command: **GRID**↵
Specify grid spacing(X) or [ON/OFF/Snap/Aspect] <0.5000>: **2X**↵

> **PROFESSIONAL TIP**
>
> The Snap and Grid modes may be set at different values to complement each other. For example, the grid may be set at .5, and the snap may be set at .25. With this type of format, each mode plays a separate role in assisting drawing layout. This may also keep the grid from being too dense. You can quickly change these values at any time to have them best assist you.

Factors to Consider When Setting Drawing Aids

The following factors will influence the drawing aid settings you choose to use:

- ✓ **The drawing units.** If the units are decimal inches, set the grid and snap values to standard decimal increments, such as .0625, .125, .25, .5, and 1 or .05, .1, .2, .5, and 1. For architectural units, use standard increments, such as 1, 6, and 12 (for inches) or 1, 2, 4, 5, and 10 (for feet).
- ✓ **The drawing size.** A very large drawing might have a grid spacing of 1.00, while a small drawing may use a spacing of .5 or less.
- ✓ **The value of the smallest dimension.** If the smallest dimension is .125, then an appropriate snap value would be .125, with a grid spacing of .25.
- ✓ **The ability to change the settings.** You can change the snap and grid values at any time without changing the location of points or lines already drawn. This should be done when larger or smaller values would assist you with a certain part of the drawing. For example, suppose a few of the dimensions are in .0625 multiples, but the rest of the dimensions are .250 multiples. Change the snap spacing from .250 to .0625 when laying out the smaller dimensions.
- ✓ **Sketches prepared before starting the drawing.** Use the visible grid to help you place views and lay out the entire drawing.
- ✓ **Efficiency.** Use whatever method works best and quickest for you when setting or changing the drawing aids.

Drawing Settings

Drawing settings determine the general characteristics of a drawing. This includes the type of units used for linear and angular measurements, and the precision to which these measurements are displayed. The limit of the drawing area is another drawing setting discussed in this section. The drawing units and drawing limits can be changed within a drawing, but it is best if the settings found in the template on which the drawing is based are not modified.

Drawing Units

UNITS
UN

Format
➥ **Units...**

The **UNITS** command is the quickest way to set the units and angles. The **UNITS** command opens the **Drawing Units** dialog box for easy control of the settings. Picking **Units...** in the **Format** pull-down menu or typing UN or UNITS at the Command: prompt accesses this dialog box, shown in Figure 2-22.

Linear units are specified in the **Length** area of the **Drawing Units** dialog box. Select the desired linear units format from the **Type:** drop-down list and use the **Precision:** drop-down list to specify the linear unit's precision. The following options are illustrated in Figure 2-23:

- **Decimal.** These units are used to create drawings in decimal inches or millimeters. Decimal units are normally used on mechanical drawings for manufacturing. This option conforms to the ASME Y14.5M dimensioning and tolerancing standard. The initial default precision is four decimal places.
- **Engineering.** These units are often used in civil drafting projects, such as maps, plot plans, dam and bridge construction, and topography. The initial default precision is four decimal places.
- **Architectural.** Architectural, structural, and other drawings use these units when measurements are in feet, inches, and fractional inches. The initial default precision is 1/16″.
- **Fractional.** This option is used for drawings having fractional parts of any common unit of measure. The initial default precision is 1/16.
- **Scientific.** These units are used when very large or small values are applied to a drawing. These applications take place in industries such as chemical engineering and astronomy. The initial default precision is four decimal places. The E+01 means the base number is multiplied by 10 to the first power.

Figure 2-22.
The **UNITS** command accesses the **Drawing Units** dialog box.

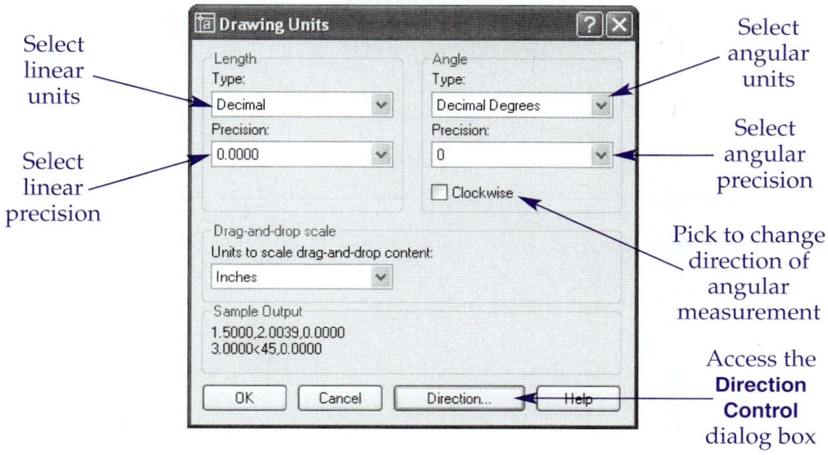

Figure 2-23.
Select the linear unit format from the **Drawing Units** dialog box.

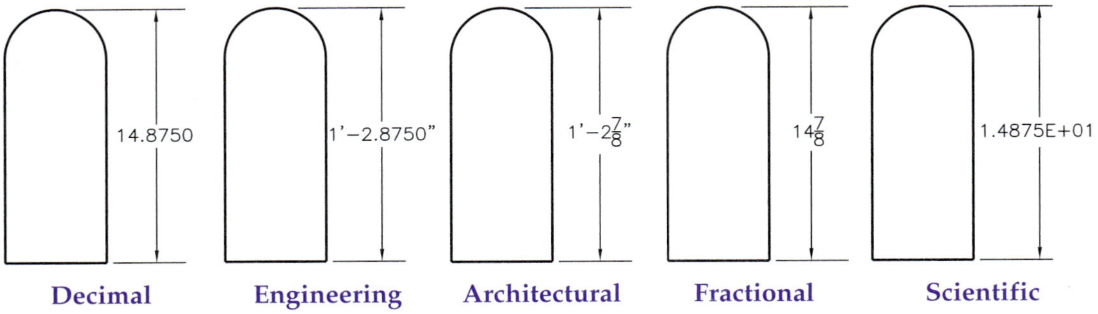

Access the **Type:** and **Precision:** drop-down lists located in the **Angle** area of the **Drawing Units** dialog box to set the desired angular unit's format and precision. Selecting the **Clockwise** check box changes the direction for angular measurements to clockwise from the default of counterclockwise.

Pick the **Direction...** button to access the **Direction Control** dialog box. See **Figure 2-24.** The standard **East**, **North**, **West**, and **South** options are offered as radio buttons. Pick one of these buttons to set the compass orientation. The **Other** radio button activates the **Angle:** text box and the **Pick an angle** button. The **Angle:** text box allows an angle for zero direction to be entered. The **Pick an angle** button allows two points on the screen to be picked for establishing the angle zero direction.

The angular units available are illustrated in **Figure 2-25** and described as follows:

- **Decimal Degrees.** This is the initial default setting. It is normally used in mechanical drafting, where degrees and decimal parts of a degree are commonly used.
- **Deg/Min/Sec.** This style is sometimes used in mechanical, architectural, structural, and civil drafting. There are sixty minutes in one degree and sixty seconds in one minute.

Figure 2-24.
Picking the **Direction...** button in the **Drawing Units** dialog box displays the **Direction Control** dialog box.

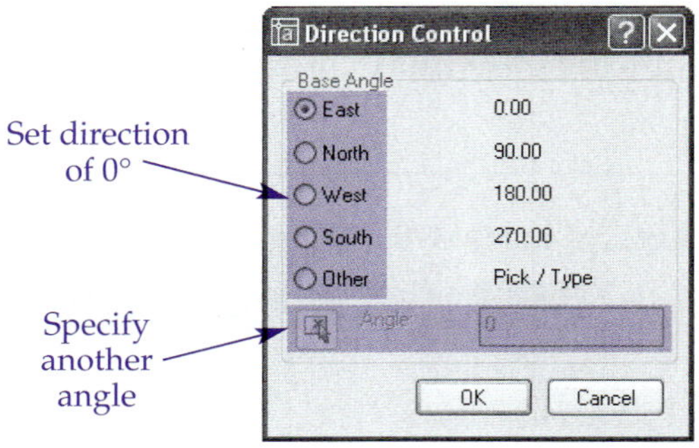

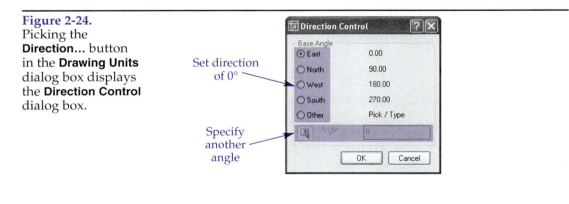

Figure 2-25.
Select the angular unit format from the **Drawing Units** dialog box.

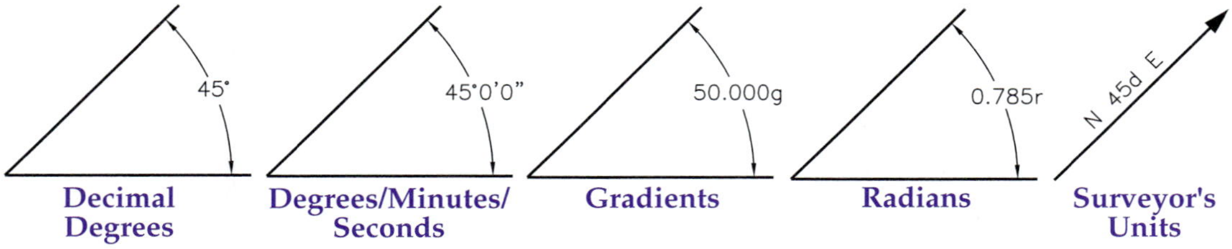

- **Grads.** *Grad* is the abbreviation for ***gradient.*** The angular value is followed by a g. Gradients are units of angular measurement based on one-quarter of a circle having one hundred grads. A full circle has four hundred grads.
- **Radians.** A ***radian*** is an angular unit of measurement in which 2π radians = 360° and π radians = 180°. For example, a 90° angle has $\pi/2$ radians and an arc length of $\pi/2$. Changing the precision displays the radian value rounded to the specified decimal place.
- **Surveyor.** Surveyor angles are measured using bearings. A ***bearing*** is the direction of a line with respect to one of the quadrants of a compass. Bearings are measured clockwise or counterclockwise (depending on the quadrant), beginning from either north or south. Bearings are measured in degrees, minutes, and seconds. An angle measuring 55°45′22″ from north toward west is expressed as N55°45′22″W. An angle measured 25°30′10″ from south toward east is expressed as S25°30′10″E. Use the **Precision:** drop-down list to set measurement to degrees, degrees/minutes, or degree/minutes/seconds, or use it to set decimal display accuracy of the seconds part of the measurement.

After selecting the linear and angular units and precision, pick the **OK** button to exit the **Drawing Units** dialog box.

Drawing Limits

AutoCAD refers to the drawings you create as ***models.*** Models are drawn full-size in ***model space.*** Model space is active when the **Model** tab is selected. When you finish drawing the model, you then switch to ***layout space***, where the drawing layout is organized as necessary to be printed on paper. Model space and layout space are fully explained in Chapter 11 of this text. All text material prior to Chapter 11 is presented based on model space being active.

An AutoCAD drawing is created in actual size, using the desired units of measure. If you are drawing an object measured in feet and inches, you draw using feet and inches in AutoCAD. If you are creating a mechanical drawing for manufacturing, the drawing is full-size, using decimal inches or millimeters. You draw the objects full-size, regardless of the type of drawing, the units used, or the size of the final layout on paper. AutoCAD allows you to specify the size of the actual area required for your drawing and refers to this as the ***model space drawing limits***. The model space drawing limits are typically set in the template, but can be changed at any time during the drawing process.

LIMITS

Format
➥ Drawing Limits

The model space drawing limits can be set using the **LIMITS** command. Entering LIMITS at the Command: prompt or picking **Drawing Limits** from the **Format** pull-down menu accesses the **LIMITS** command. The **LIMITS** command asks you to specify the coordinates for the lower-left corner and the upper-right corner of the drawing area. The lower-left corner is usually 0,0, but you can specify a different value. Press [Enter] to accept the 0,0 value for the lower-left corner default or type a new value. The upper-right corner setting usually identifies the upper-right corner of the drawing area. If you want a 17″ × 11″ drawing area, then the upper-right corner setting should be 17,11. The first value is the horizontal measurement, and the second value is the vertical measurement of the limits. A comma separates the values. The command works like this:

Command: **LIMITS**↵
Reset Model space limits:
Specify lower left corner or [ON/OFF] <0.0000,0.0000>: ↵
Specify upper right corner <12.0000,9.0000>: **17,11**↵
Command:

The **LIMITS** command can also be used to turn the limits on or off by typing ON or OFF at the prompt. When the limits are turned on, AutoCAD restricts you from drawing outside of the rectangular area defined by the limits settings. Limits are typically turned off for most drafting applications.

The drawing limits should be large enough for the model being created. For example, if you are designing a 50′ × 30′ building, your drawing limits will need to be larger than 50′ × 30′ to allow room for dimensions, notes, and other features.

Keep in mind that the size of your drawing area does not need to conform to standard sheet sizes because the sheet size is specified when you define the drawing layout. Additionally, you can change the drawing limits at any time if more or less space is required to complete the drawing. This is accomplished with the **LIMITS** command. The following list provides some professional guidelines you can use to set the drawing area width and length based on different units:

- **Inch and metric drawings.** Calculate the total widths and lengths of the objects included in all views, adding extra space between views and room for dimensions and notes. Use these values for your drawing area settings.
- **Architectural drawings.** The actual size of architectural drawings is based on foot and inch measurements. If you are drawing a 48′ × 24′ floor plan, allow 10′ on each side for dimensions and notes to make a total drawing area 68′ × 44′. When you select architectural units, AutoCAD automatically sets up the drawing for you to draw in feet and inches.
- **Civil drawings.** The actual size of civil drawings used for mapping is often measured in units of feet. This allows you to set up the drawing limits similar to the architectural application just discussed. Civil drawings often represent very large areas, such as a plot plan requiring 200′ × 100′ to accommodate all the property lines, dimensions, and notes.

EXERCISE 2-5 Complete the Exercise on the Student CD.

PROFESSIONAL TIP

Generalized templates that set the units, limits, snap settings, and grid settings to specifications are useful, but keep in mind you can create any number of drawing templates. Templates containing more detailed settings can dramatically increase drafting productivity. As you refine your setup procedure, you can revise the template files. When using the **SAVE** command, you can save a new template over an existing one. You can also use the **SAVEAS** command to save a new template from an existing one.

EXERCISE 2-6 Complete the Exercise on the Student CD.

Chapter Test

Answer the following questions on a separate sheet of paper.

1. By default, what is the name of the dialog box that opens when using the **NEW** command?
2. What is a template drawing?
3. What is *sheet size*?
4. What are the dimensions of an ANSI/ASME B-size sheet?
5. Is the size of an ANSI/ASME A2 sheet specified in inches or millimeters?
6. What does the .dwt file extension stand for?
7. How often should work be saved?
8. Name the command allowing you to quickly save your work without displaying the dialog box.
9. Name the system variable allowing you to control the dialog box display.
10. Name the pull-down menu where the **SAVE**, **SAVEAS**, and **OPEN** commands are located.
11. How do you set AutoCAD to automatically save your work at designated intervals?
12. What command do you use to save a drawing to a floppy disk?
13. If a drawing has been previously saved, what is the difference between using the **QSAVE** and **SAVE** commands?
14. How do you search for a drawing file from the **Select File** dialog box?
15. What is displayed when you select the **Favorites** button in the **Select File** dialog box?
16. From which pull-down menu can you select the name of a recently opened drawing file and open it?
17. How can you set the number of files listed in the pull-down menu described in Question 16?
18. How do you quickly cycle through all the currently open drawings in sequence?
19. Identify the command you would use if you wanted to exit a drawing file, but remain in the AutoCAD session.
20. What happens if you use the **CLOSE** command before saving your work?
21. How can you simultaneously close all open drawing windows?
22. How do you set grid spacing of .25?
23. How do you set snap spacing of .125?
24. Name the command used to place a pattern of dots on the screen.
25. How do you activate the snap grid so the screen cursor will automatically move in precise increments?
26. How do you set different horizontal and vertical snap units?
27. Name three ways to access the **Drafting Settings** dialog box.
28. What command opens the **Drawing Units** dialog box?
29. Name three settings that can be specified in the **Drawing Units** dialog box.
30. What is the result of pressing the [Ctrl]+[B] key combination or the [F9] function key?

Drawing Problems

1. Create a new drawing, based on one of the templates supplied by AutoCAD. Save the new drawing as an AutoCAD 2000 drawing file named P2-1.dwg.

The following problems can be done if the AutoCAD 2005\Sample file folder is loaded. All drawings listed are found in that folder.

2. Locate and preview or open the 8th Floor drawing. Describe the drawing in your own words.

3. Locate and preview or open the Stadium Plan drawing. Describe the drawing in your own words.

4 Locate and preview or open the Wilhome drawing. Describe the drawing in your own words.

5. Locate and preview or open the Tablet drawing. Describe the drawing in your own words

6. Locate and preview or open the SPCA Site Plan drawing. Describe the drawing in your own words.

7. Locate and preview or open the Hotel Model drawing. Describe the drawing in your own words.

The following problems can be saved as templates for future use.

8. Create a template with an 11″ × 8.5″ area and decimal units. Name it QK A SIZE (H) INCHES.dwt and include QUICK A SIZE (H) INCHES SETUP for its description. You now have a template for doing inch drawings on 11″ × 8.5″ (horizontal) sheets.
9. Create a template with an 8.5″ × 11″ area and decimal units. Name it QK A SIZE (V) INCHES.dwt and include QUICK A SIZE (V) INCHES SETUP for its description. You now have a template for doing inch drawings on 11″ × 8.5″ (vertical) sheets.
10. Create a template with a 594 mm × 420 mm area and decimal units. Name it QK A2 SIZE METRIC.dwt and include QUICK A2 SIZE METRIC SETUP for its description. You now have a template for doing metric (millimeters) drawings on 594 mm × 420 mm sheets.
11. Create a template with a 17″ × 11″ area, decimal units with 0.000 precision, decimal degrees with 0.0 precision, and default angle measure and orientation. Name it ADV B SIZE INCHES.dwt and include ADVANCED B SIZE INCHES SETUP for its description. You now have a template for doing inch drawings on 17″ × 11″ sheets.
12. Create a template with a 420 mm × 297 mm area, decimal units with 0.0 precision, decimal degrees with 0.0 precision, and default angle measure and orientation. Name it ADV ISO A3 SIZE MM.dwt and include ADVANCED ISO A3 SIZE MILLIMETERS SETUP for its description. You now have a template for doing metric (millimeters) drawings on 420 mm × 297 mm sheets.

13. Begin a new drawing and select the Ansi c -color dependent plot styles.dwt template. Use the **UNITS** command to set decimal units with 0.000 precision and decimal angles with 0.0 precision. The direction control should be set to the default values. Set the limits to 0,0 and 17,11. Name the drawing TEMP ANSI B.dwt and include ANSI B TEMPLATE SETUP for its description. You now have a template for doing inch drawings on 17″ × 11″ sheets with a border and a title block.

14. Begin a new drawing and select the Iso a3 -color dependent plot styles.dwt template. Use the **UNITS** command to set decimal units with 0.000 precision and decimal angles with 0.0 precision. The direction control should be set to the default values. Set the limits to 0,0 and 420,297. Name the drawing TEMP ISO A3.dwt and include ISO A3 TEMPLATE SETUP for its description. You now have a template for doing metric (millimeters) drawings on 420 mm × 297 mm sheets with a border and a title block.

15. Begin a new drawing and select the Architectural, english units -color dependent plot styles.dwt template. Use the **UNITS** command to set architectural units with 1/16″ precision and degrees/minutes/seconds angles with 0d00′00″ precision. The direction control should be set to the default values. Set the limits to 0,0 and 22,17. Name the drawing TEMP ARCH.dwt and include ARCHITECTURAL TEMPLATE SETUP for its description. You now have a template for doing architectural drawings on 22″ × 17″ sheets with a border and a title block.

16. Begin a new drawing from scratch. Select 0.00 as decimal units, 0.00 as decimal degrees, and 90° (North) for direction of the 0° angle. Make angles measure counterclockwise. Set the limits to 0,0 and 17,11. Save as a drawing template named SFS B SIZE INCHES and include START FROM SCRATCH B SIZE INCHES SETUP for its description. You now have a template for doing inch drawings on 17″ × 11″ sheets.

17. Begin a new drawing from scratch. Select 0.00 as decimal units, 0.00 as decimal degrees, and 0° (East) for direction of the 0° angle. Make angles measure counterclockwise. Set the limits to 0,0 and 420,297. Save as a drawing template named SFS A3 SIZE METRIC and include START FROM SCRATCH A3 METRIC SETUP for its description. You now have a template for doing metric (millimeters) drawings on 420 mm × 297 mm sheets.

AutoCAD includes many standard templates. These templates include settings and title blocks for many standard sheet sizes. Three such templates are shown here.

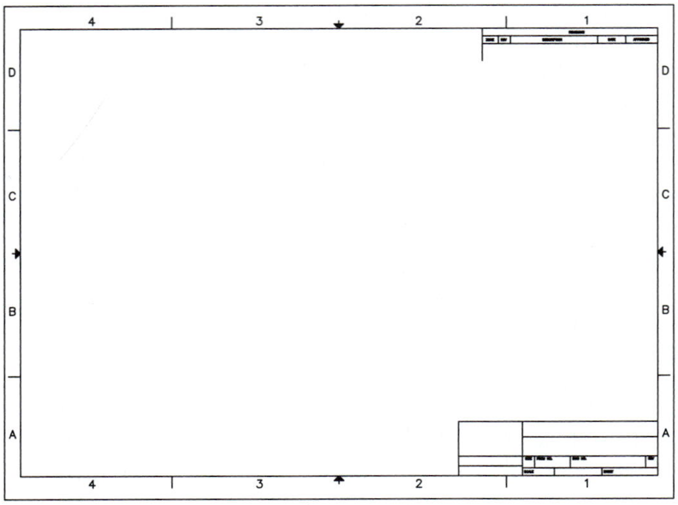

ANSI C Title Block

Architectural Title Block

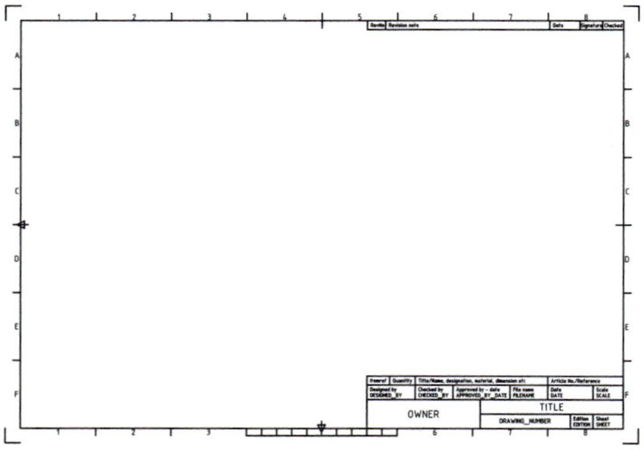

ISO A3 Title Block

CHAPTER 3

Introduction to Drawing and Editing

Learning Objectives

After completing this chapter, you will be able to do the following:

- Use a variety of linetypes to construct an object.
- Select the **LINE** command to draw given objects.
- Use absolute, relative, and polar coordinate point entry systems.
- Use the screen cursor for point entry.
- Use the **MULTIPLE** command modifier.
- Use the Ortho mode and polar tracking.
- Use direct distance entry.
- Make revisions to objects using the **ERASE** command and its options.
- Make selection sets using the **Window**, **Crossing**, **WPolygon**, **CPolygon**, and **Fence** options.
- Remove and add objects to a selection set.
- Clean up the screen with the **REDRAW** command.
- Use the **OOPS** command to bring back an erased object.
- Use the **U** command to undo a command.
- Select stacked objects.

This chapter introduces drawing and editing using the **LINE** command and **ERASE** command. There are many other drawing and editing commands discussed in later chapters of this textbook.

All drawing commands require that you select points in the drawing area. AutoCAD provides many point entry methods, including coordinate entry, cursor selection, and direct distance entry. These point entry methods are discussed in this chapter.

Similarly, nearly all editing commands require that you select one or more objects. There are many object selection methods. Several object selection methods are introduced in this chapter.

Line Conventions

Drafting is a graphic language using lines, symbols, and words to describe products to be manufactured or constructed. Line conventions are standards based on line thickness and type. These standards are designed to enhance the readability of drawings. This section introduces line standards.

The American National Standards Institute (ANSI) recommends two line widths to establish contrasting lines in a drawing. Lines are described as thick or thin. For manual drafting, thick lines are twice as thick as thin lines, with recommended widths of 0.6 mm and 0.3 mm, respectively. A single line width for all types of lines is acceptable, however, on drawings prepared with a CAD system. **Figure 3-1** shows recommended line width and type as defined in ASME Y14.2M, *Line Conventions and Lettering*.

Figure 3-1.
Line conventions. (Adapted from ASME Y14.2M)

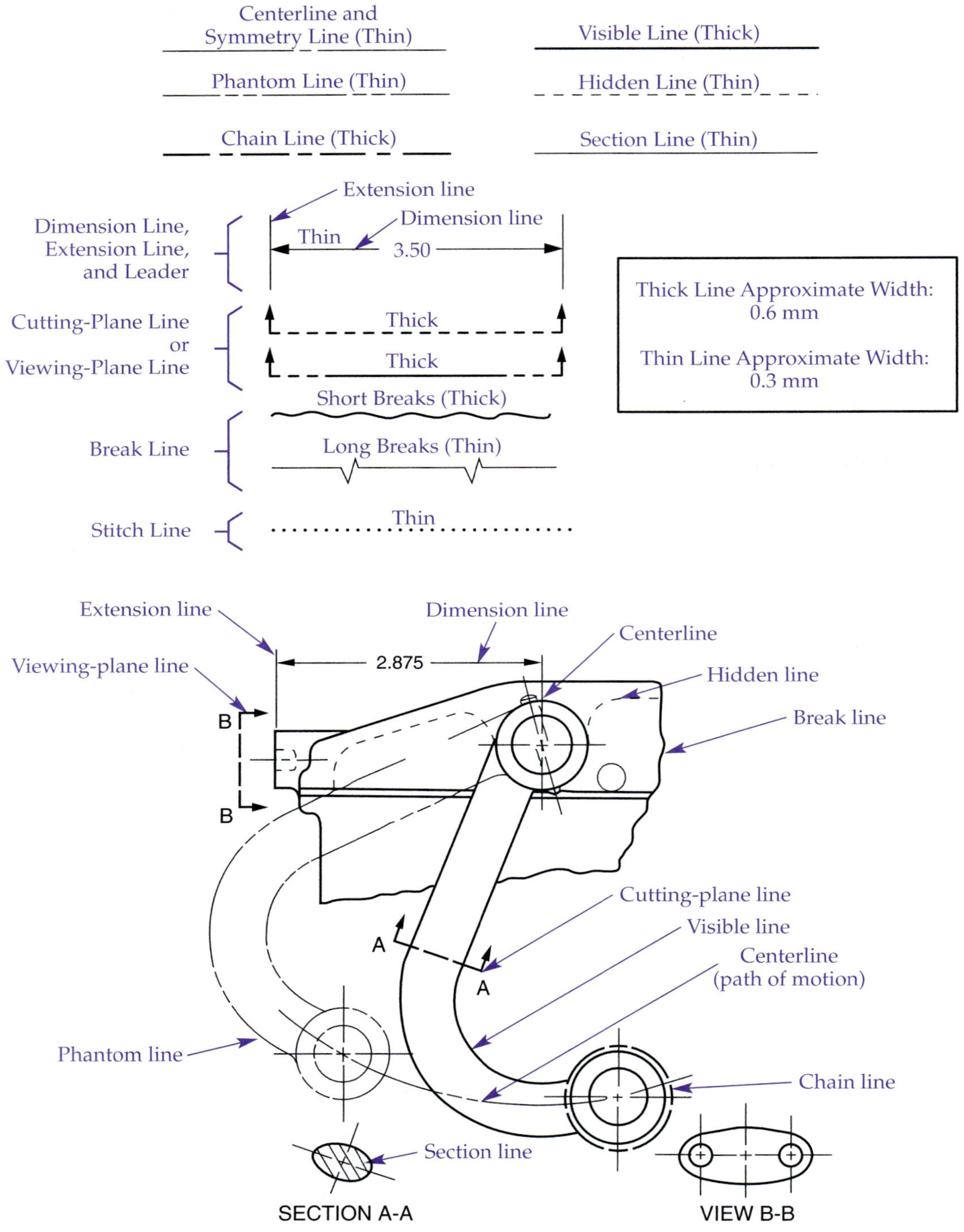

Object Lines

Object lines, also called ***visible lines***, are thick lines used to show the outline or contour of an object. See **Figure 3-2.** Object lines are the most common type of lines used in drawings. These lines should be twice as thick as thin lines.

Figure 3-2.
Object lines and hidden lines.

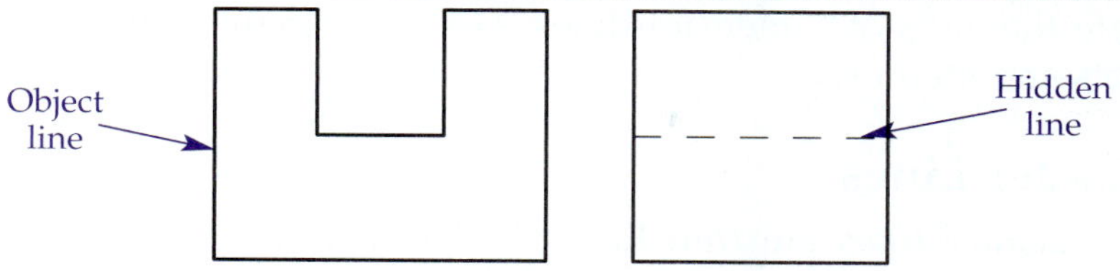

Hidden Lines

Hidden lines, often called ***dashed lines***, are used to represent invisible features of an object, as shown in **Figure 3-2.** They are drawn thin so they clearly contrast with object lines. When properly drawn at full size, the dashes are .125″ (3 mm) long and spaced .06″ (1.5 mm) apart. Be careful if the drawing is to be greatly reduced or scaled down during the plotting process. Reduced dashes may appear too small.

Centerlines

Centerlines locate the centers of circles and arcs and show the axis of a cylindrical or symmetrical shape, as shown in **Figure 3-3.** They are thin lines consisting of alternating long and short dashes. The recommended dash lengths are .125″ (3 mm) for the short dashes and .75″ to 1.5″ (19 mm to 38 mm) for the long dashes. These lengths can be altered, depending on the size of the drawing. Spaces approximately .06″ (1.5 mm) long should separate the dashes. The small centerline dashes should cross only at the center of a circle.

Extension Lines

Extension lines are thin lines used to show the "extent" of a dimension, as shown in **Figure 3-3.** They begin a small distance from an object and extend .125″ (3 mm) beyond the last dimension line. Extension lines may cross object lines, hidden lines, and centerlines, but they may not cross dimension lines. Centerlines become extension lines when they are used to show the extent of a dimension. When this is done, there is no space where the centerline joins the extension line.

Figure 3-3.
This simple drawing shows centerlines, extension lines, dimension lines, and leader lines.

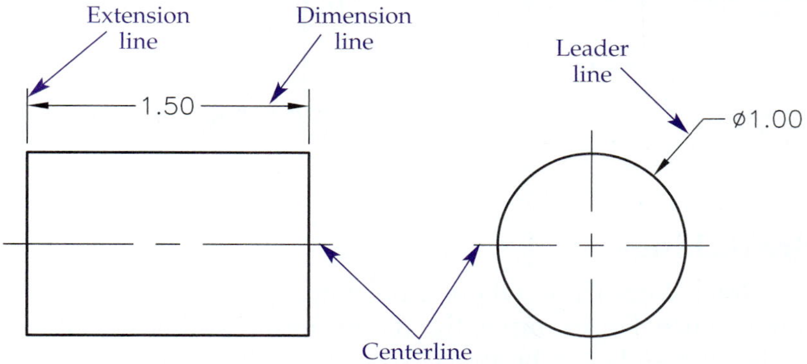

Dimension Lines

Dimension lines are thin lines placed between extension lines to indicate a measurement. In mechanical drafting, the dimension line is normally broken near the center for placement of the dimension numeral, as shown in **Figure 3-3.** The dimension line normally remains unbroken in architectural and structural drawings. The dimension numeral is placed on top of an unbroken dimension line. Arrows terminate the ends of dimension lines, except in architectural drafting, where slashes or dots are often used.

Leader Lines

Leader lines are thin lines used to connect a specific note to a feature on a drawing. A leader line terminates with an arrowhead at the feature and has a small shoulder at the note. See **Figure 3-3.** Dimension and leader line usage is discussed in detail in Chapters 17 and 18.

Cutting-Plane and Viewing-Plane Lines

Cutting-plane lines are thick lines identifying the location of a section. ***Viewing-plane lines*** are drawn in the same style as cutting-plane lines, but identify the location of a view. Cutting-plane and viewing-plane lines may be drawn one of two ways, as shown in **Figure 3-1.** The use of viewing-plane and cutting-plane lines is discussed in detail in Chapters 6 and 21.

Section Lines

Section lines are thin lines drawn in a section view to show where material has been cut away, as shown in **Figure 3-4.** Types of section lines and applications are discussed in Chapter 21.

Figure 3-4.
Section lines and cutting-plane lines.

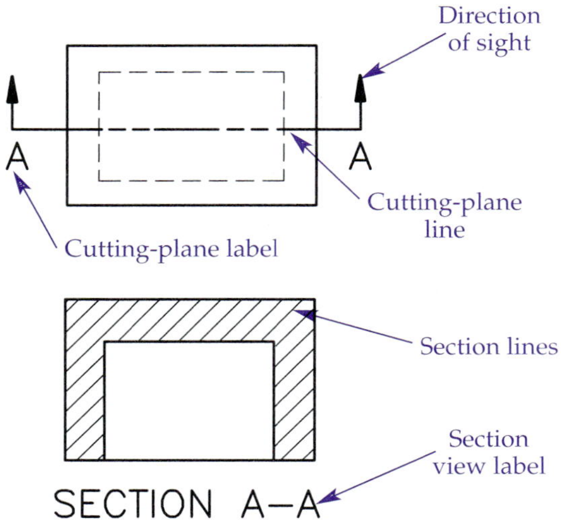

Break Lines

Break lines show where a portion of an object has been removed for clarity or convenience. For example, the center portion of a very long part may be broken out so the two ends can be moved closer together for more convenient representation. There are several types of break lines shown in **Figure 3-5.**

Figure 3-5.
Standard break lines.

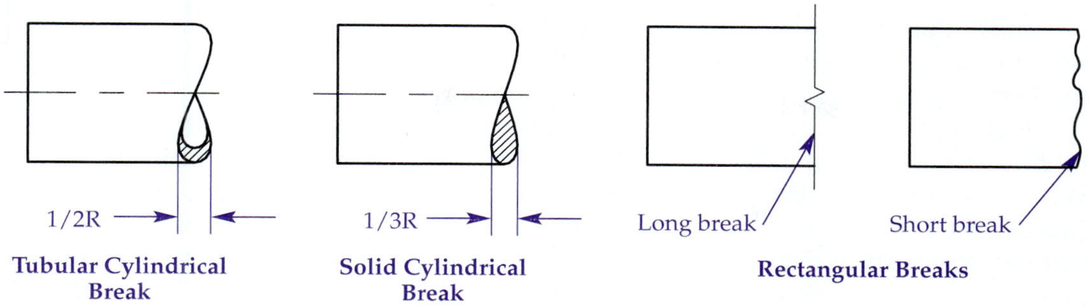

Phantom Lines

Phantom lines are thin lines with two short dashes alternating with long dashes. The short dashes are .125″ (3 mm) long, and the long dashes range from .75″ to 1.5″ (19 mm to 38 mm) in length, depending on the size of the drawing. Spaces between dashes are .06″ (1.5 mm). Phantom lines identify repetitive details, show alternate positions of moving parts, and locate adjacent positions of related parts. See **Figure 3-6.**

Figure 3-6.
Phantom lines.

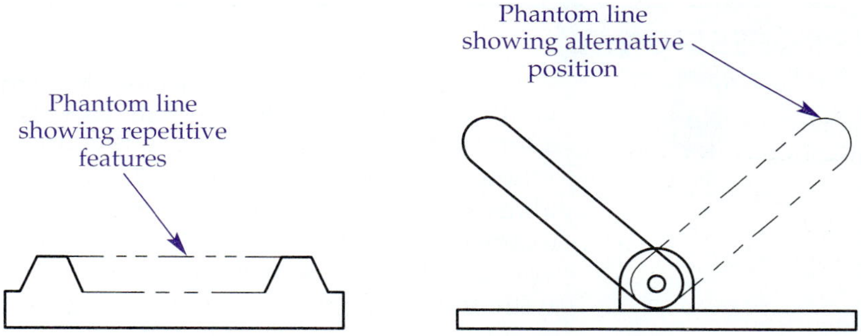

Chain Lines

Chain lines are thick lines of alternating long and short dashes. They show that the portion of the surface next to the chain line has special features or receives unique treatment. See **Figure 3-7.**

Figure 3-7.
Chain lines.

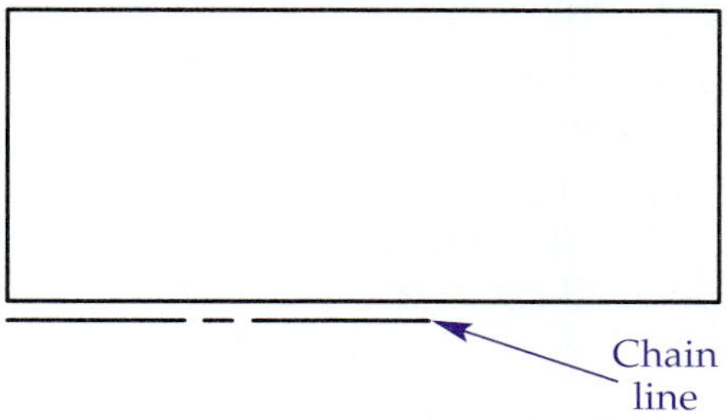

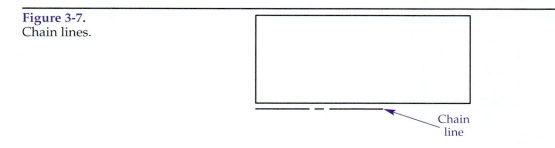

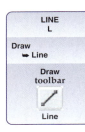

Drawing Lines with AutoCAD

LINE
L

Draw
➡ Line

Draw
toolbar

Line

Individual line segments are drawn between two points on the screen. This is referred to as ***point entry***. Point entry is the simplest form of drafting. After selecting the **LINE** command, simply enter the endpoints of the line.

Picking the **Line** button in the **Draw** toolbar, picking **Line** in the **Draw** pull-down menu, or typing L or LINE at the Command: prompt accesses the **LINE** command. When you use the **LINE** command, a prompt asks you to select a starting point (Specify first point:). When the first point is selected, you are asked for the second point (Specify next point or [Undo]:). When the next Specify next point or [Undo]: prompt is given, continue selecting additional points if you want to connect a series of lines. When you are finished, press the [Enter] key or the space bar to get back to the Command: prompt. The following command sequence is used for the **LINE** command:

Command: **L** *or* **LINE**↵
Specify first point: *(select the first point)*
Specify next point or [Undo]: *(select the second point)*
Specify next point or [Undo]: *(select the third point or press* [Enter] *or the space bar to finish)*
Command: *(this appears if you pressed* [Enter] *or the space bar at the previous prompt)*

PROFESSIONAL TIP

AutoCAD provides a set of abbreviated commands called ***command aliases***. Command aliases are also called ***keyboard shortcuts*** because they reduce the amount of typing needed when entering a command at the keyboard. Using command aliases allows you to enter commands more quickly. For example, instead of typing LINE at the Command: prompt, you can type L, which takes less time. Becoming familiar with the available command aliases can help you become more productive with AutoCAD.

Responding to AutoCAD Prompts with Numbers

Many of the AutoCAD commands require specific types of numeric data. Some of AutoCAD's prompts require you to enter a whole number. For example, later in this book, you will learn how to draw a polygon using the **POLYGON** command. This command requires you to specify the number of sides, as follows:

Command: **POLYGON**↵
Enter number of sides <*current*>: **6**↵
Specify center of polygon or [Edge]: *(pick the center of the polygon)*
Enter an option [Inscribed in circle/Circumscribed about circle] <I>: ↵
Specify radius of circle: **2**↵
Command:

The Enter number of sides <*current*>: prompt illustrates the simplest form of numeric entry in which any whole number may be used. Other entries require whole numbers that may be positive or negative. A number is understood to be positive without placing the plus (+) sign before the number. The minus (-) sign must, however, precede a negative number.

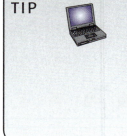

Much of your data entry may not be whole numbers. In these cases, any real number can be used and expressed as a decimal, as a fraction, or in scientific notation. These numbers may be positive or negative. Here are some examples of acceptable real numbers:

4.250
-6.375
1/2
1-3/4
2.5E+4 *(25,000)*
2.5E-4 *(0.00025)*

When entering fractions, the numerator and denominator must be whole numbers greater than zero. For example, 1/2, 3/4, and 2/3 are all acceptable fraction entries. Fractional numbers greater than one must have a dash between the whole number and the fraction. For example, 2-3/4 is entered for two and three quarters. The dash (-) separator is needed because a space acts just like pressing [Enter] and automatically ends the input. The numerator may be larger than the denominator, as in 3/2, *only* if a whole number is not used with the fraction. For example, 1-3/2 is not a valid input for a fraction. When you enter coordinates or measurements, the values used depend on the units of measurement.

- Values on inch drawings are understood to be in inches without placing the inch marks (″) after the numeral. For example, 2.500 is automatically understood to be 2.500″.
- When your drawing is set up for metric values, any entry is automatically expressed as millimeters.
- If you are working in an engineering or architectural environment, any value greater than 1′ is expressed in inches, feet, or feet and inches. The values can be whole numbers, decimals, or fractions.
  - For measurements in feet, the foot symbol (′) must follow the number, as in 24′.
  - If the value is in feet and inches, there is no space between the feet and inch value. For example, 24′6 is the proper input for the value 24′-6″.
  - If the inch part of the value contains a fraction, the inch and fractional part of an inch are separated by a dash, such as 24′6-1/2.

  Never mix feet with inch values greater than one foot. For example, 24′18″ is an invalid entry. In this case, you should enter 25′6.

PROFESSIONAL TIP

Placing the inch mark (″) after an inch value at the prompt line is acceptable, but not necessary. It takes more time and reduces productivity.

NOTE

AutoCAD accepts the inch (″) and foot (′) symbols in the command line only when the **UNITS** are set to either **Architectural** or **Engineering**. If the **UNITS** are not set to one of these, a message on the command line will read Requires numeric distance or second point.

Point Entry Methods

There are several point entry techniques for drawing lines. Being familiar and skillful with these methods is very important. A combination of point entry techniques should be used to help reduce drawing time.

Each of the point entry methods uses the Cartesian, or rectangular, coordinate system. The ***Cartesian coordinate system*** is based on selecting distances from three intersecting axes. The point's distance from the intersection point, called the ***origin***, in respect to each of these axes defines a ***location***. In standard two-dimensional (2D) drafting applications, objects are drawn in the XY plane, and the Z axis is not referenced. Using the Z axis is discussed in Chapter 28 with three-dimensional (3D) drafting.

In 2D drafting, the origin divides the coordinate system into four quadrants within the XY plane. Points are located in relation to the origin, or (0,0), where X = 0, and Y = 0. **Figure 3-8** shows the X,Y values of points located in the Cartesian coordinate system.

When using AutoCAD, the origin (0,0) is usually at the lower-left corner of the drawing. This point also coincides with the lower-left corner of the drawing limits. This setup places all points in the upper-right quadrant, where both X and Y coordinate values are positive. See **Figure 3-9.** Methods of establishing points in the Cartesian coordinate system include using absolute coordinates, relative coordinates, and polar coordinates.

Figure 3-8.
The Cartesian coordinate system.

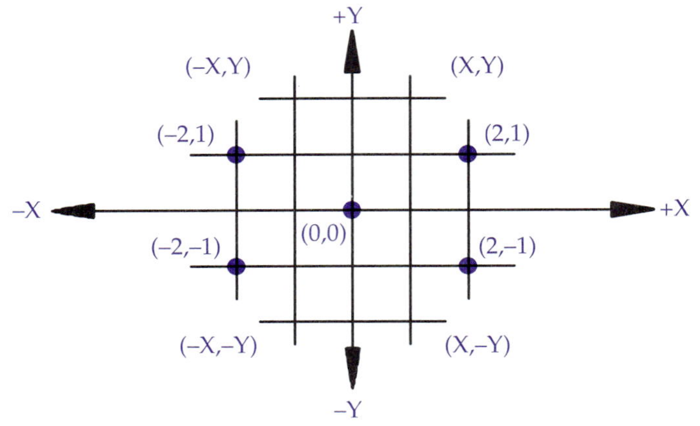

Figure 3-9.
The XY coordinate axes on the screen.

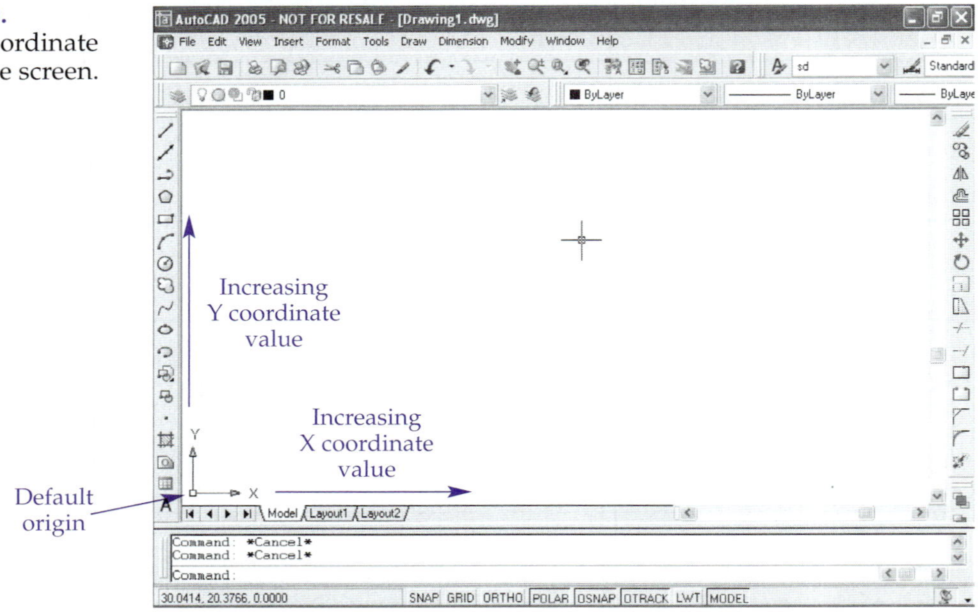

Using absolute coordinates

Points located using the absolute coordinate system are measured from the origin (0,0). For example, when X = 4, and Y = 2, (4,2), a point is located four units horizontally and two units vertically from the origin, as shown in **Figure 3-10.** The coordinate display on the status bar registers the location of the selected point in XYZ coordinates.

The discussion and examples in this chapter reference only the XY coordinates for 2D drafting. Also note that the coordinate display reflects the current system of working units. Remember, when the absolute coordinate system is used, each point is located from 0,0. Follow these commands and point placements at your computer, as you refer to **Figure 3-11:**

Command: **L** *or* **LINE**↵
Specify first point: **4,2**↵
Specify next point or [Undo]: **7,2**↵
Specify next point or [Undo]: **7,6**↵
Specify next point or [Close/Undo]: **4,6**↵
Specify next point or [Close/Undo]: **4,2**↵
Specify next point or [Close/Undo]: ↵
Command:

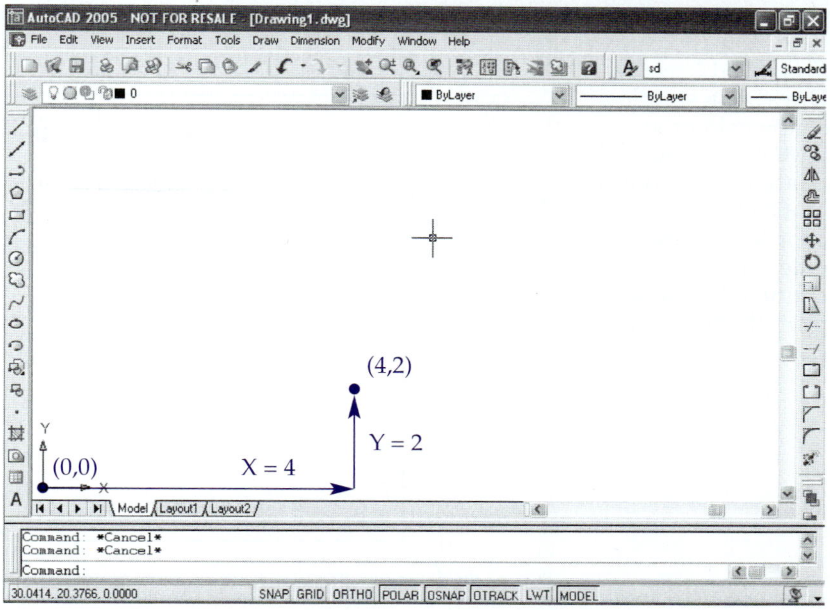

Figure 3-10. Locating points with absolute coordinates.

Figure 3-11. Drawing simple shapes using the **LINE** command and absolute coordinates.

EXERCISE 3-1 Complete the Exercise on the Student CD.

Using relative coordinates

Relative coordinates are located from the previous position, rather than from the origin. The relationship of points in the Cartesian coordinate system, shown in **Figure 3-8,** must be clearly understood before using this method. For relative coordinates, the @ symbol must precede your entry. Holding the [Shift] key and pressing the [2] key at the top of the keyboard selects this symbol. Follow these commands and relative coordinate point placements, as you refer to **Figure 3-12:**

Command: **L** *or* **LINE**↵
Specify first point: **2,2**↵
Specify next point or [Undo]: **@6,0**↵
Specify next point or [Undo]: **@2,2**↵
Specify next point or [Close/Undo]: **@0,3**↵
Specify next point or [Close/Undo]: **@-2,2**↵
Specify next point or [Close/Undo]: **@-6,0**↵
Specify next point or [Close/Undo]: **@0,-7**↵
Specify next point or [Close/Undo]: ↵
Command:

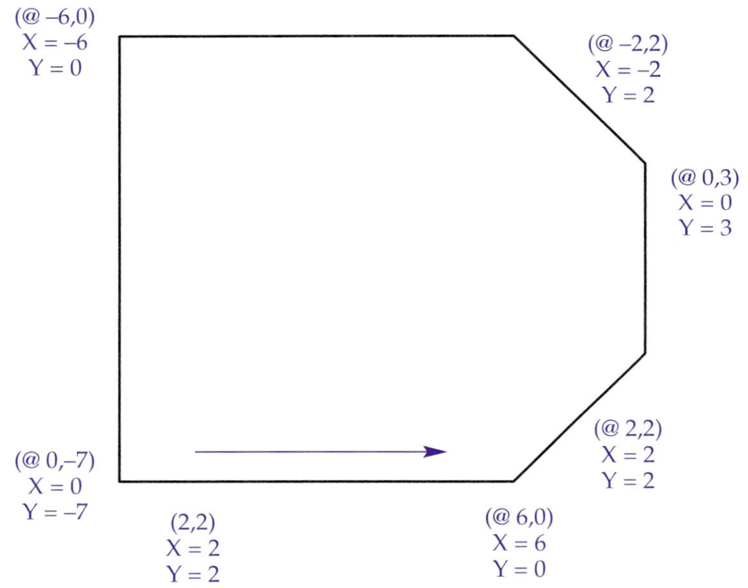

Figure 3-12. Drawing a simple shape using the **LINE** command and relative coordinates. Notice that the coordinates are entered counterclockwise from the first point (2,2).

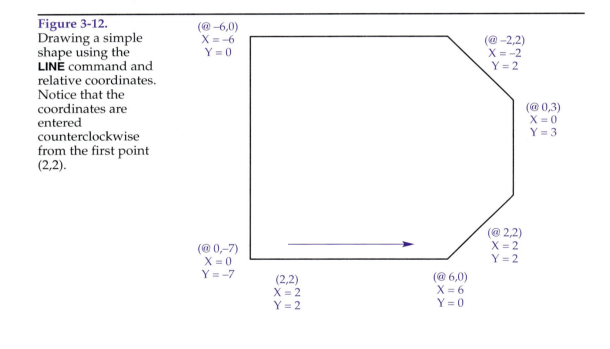

EXERCISE 3-2 Complete the Exercise on the Student CD.

Using polar coordinates

A point located using ***polar coordinates*** is based on the distance from a fixed point at a given angle. First the distance is entered, then the angle. A < symbol separates the two values.

The angular values used for the polar coordinate format are shown in **Figure 3-13.** Consistent with standard AutoCAD convention, 0° is to the right, or east. Angles are then measured counterclockwise.

When preceded by the @ symbol, a polar coordinate point is measured from the previous point. If the @ symbol is not included, the coordinate is located relative to the origin. If you want to draw a line four units long from point 1,1, at a 45° angle, the following information must be typed:

Command: **L** *or* **LINE**↵
Specify first point: **1,1**↵
Specify next point or [Undo]: **@4<45**↵
Specify next point or [Undo]: ↵

Figure 3-14 shows the result of this command. The entry @4<45 means the following:

- **@.** Tells AutoCAD to measure from the previous point. This symbol must precede all relative coordinate inputs.
- **4.** Gives the distance, such as 4 units, from the previous point.
- **<.** Establishes that a polar or angular increment is to follow.
- **45.** Determines the angle, such as 45°, from 0°.

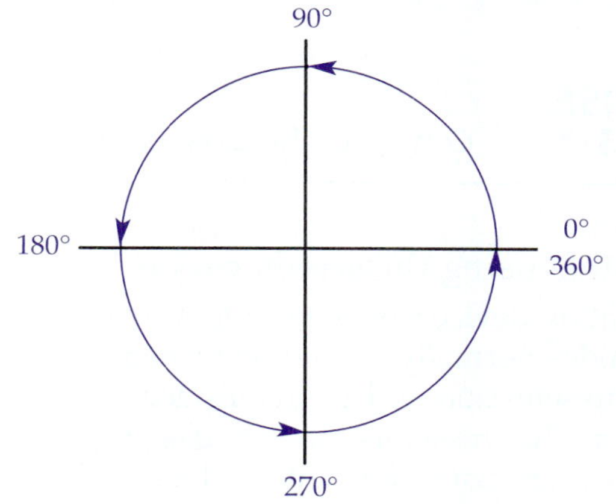

Figure 3-13. Angles used in the polar coordinate system.

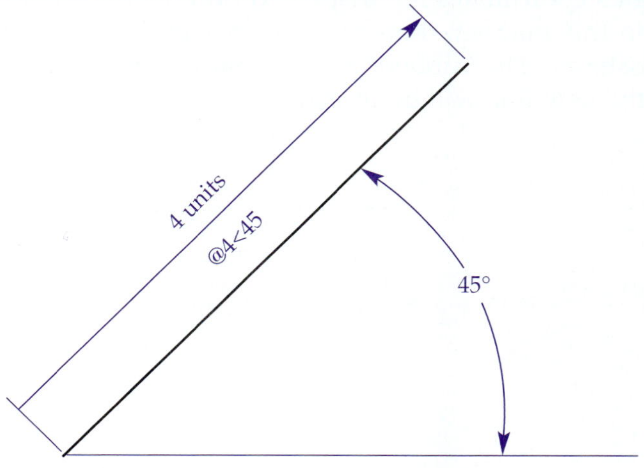

Figure 3-14. Using polar coordinates for the **LINE** command.

Now, follow these commands and polar coordinate points on your computer, as you refer to **Figure 3-15:**

Command: **L** *or* **LINE**↵
Specify first point: **2,6**↵
Specify next point or [Undo]: **@2.5<0**↵
Specify next point or [Undo]: **@3<135**↵
Specify next point or [Close/Undo]: **2,6**↵
Specify next point or [Close/Undo]: ↵
Command: ↵
LINE Specify first point: **6,6**↵
Specify next point or [Undo]: **@4<0**↵
Specify next point or [Undo]: **@2<90**↵
Specify next point or [Close/Undo]: **@4<180**↵
Specify next point or [Close/Undo]: **@2<270**↵
Specify next point or [Close/Undo]: ↵
Command:

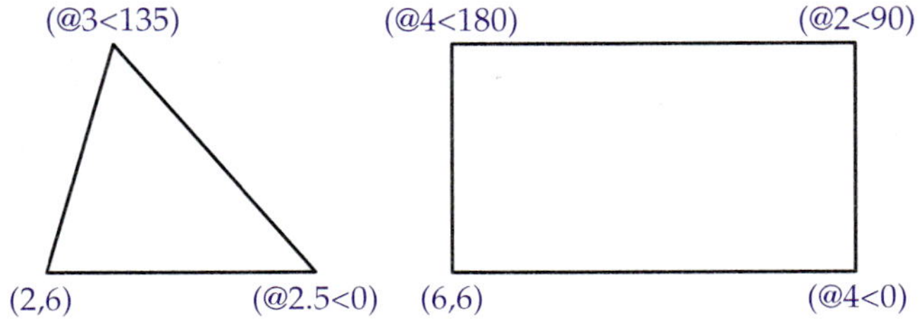

Figure 3-15.
Using polar coordinates to draw.

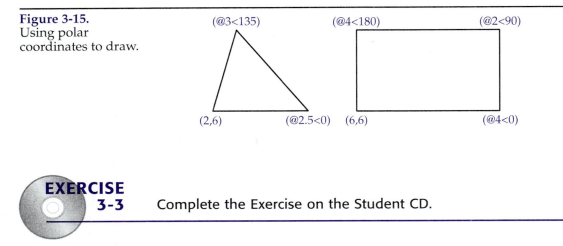

EXERCISE 3-3 Complete the Exercise on the Student CD.

Picking points using the screen cursor

The pointing device can be used to move the crosshairs and pick points. The Grid and Snap modes normally should be turned on for precise point location. This assists in drafting presentation and maintains accuracy when using a pointing device. With Snap mode on, the crosshairs move in designated increments without any guesswork.

When you are using a pointing device, the command sequence is the same as when you are using coordinates. Points are picked when the crosshairs are at the desired location. After the first point is picked, the distance to the second point and the point's coordinates are displayed on the status line for reference. When picking points in this manner, there is a "rubberband" line connecting the "first point" and the crosshairs. The rubberband line moves as the crosshairs are moved, showing where the new line will be placed.

Drawing Multiple Lines

The **MULTIPLE** command is used to automatically repeat commands issued at the keyboard. This technique can be used to draw repetitive lines, polylines, circles, arcs, ellipses, or polygons. For example, if you plan to draw several sets of line segments, type **MULTIPLE** at the Command: prompt, press the space bar or [Enter], and then type L or LINE. AutoCAD automatically repeats the **LINE** command until you have finished drawing all the desired lines. You must cancel to get back to the Command: prompt. The **MULTIPLE** command is used as follows:

Command: **MULTIPLE**↵
Enter command name to repeat: **L** *or* **LINE**↵
Specify first point: *(pick the first point)*
Specify next point or [Undo]: *(pick the second point)*
Specify next point or [Undo]: *(pick the third point or press* [Enter]*)*
Specify next point or [Close/Undo]: ↵
LINE Specify first point: *(pick the first point)*
Specify next point or [Undo]: *(pick the second point)*
Specify next point or [Undo]: *(pick the third point or press* [Enter]*)*
Specify next point or [Close/Undo]: ↵
LINE Specify first point: *(press* [Esc] *to cancel)* *Cancel*

As you can see, AutoCAD automatically reissues the **LINE** command so you can draw another line (or lines). Press [Esc] to cancel the repeating command.

The Coordinate Display

The area to the left side of the status bar shows the coordinate display window. The units setting determines the number of places displayed to the right of the decimal point. The coordinate display changes to represent the location of the cursor in relation to the origin. Each time a new point is picked or the pointing device is moved, the coordinates are updated.

Picking the coordinate display in the status bar or pressing the [Ctrl]+[D] key combination, the [F6] function key, or puck button 7 turns the coordinate display on and off. With coordinates on, the coordinates constantly change as the crosshairs move. With coordinates off, no coordinates are displayed.

There are three coordinate modes, and they are controlled by the **COORDS** system variable. Set this variable to 0 for a static display. This displays coordinates only when points are selected. Set the **COORDS** variable to 1 for a dynamic absolute display. Set the variable to 2 for a dynamic length/angle (polar) display. A typical absolute coordinate display gives X, Y, and Z coordinates, such as 6.2000,5.9000,0.0000. A polar coordinate display shows the distance and angle from the last point and the Z axis distance, such as 3.4000<180, 0.0000.

EXERCISE 3-4 Complete the Exercise on the Student CD.

Drawing in Ortho Mode

The term ***ortho*** comes from *orthogonal*, which means "at right angles." The Ortho mode constrains points selected while drawing and editing to be only horizontal or vertical. The directions are in alignment with the current Snap grid.

The Ortho mode has a special advantage when drawing rectangular shapes because all corners are guaranteed to be square. See **Figure 3-16.** Picking the **ORTHO** button on the status bar; using the [F8] function key, puck button 5, or the [Ctrl]+[L] key combination; or typing ORTHO at the Command: prompt can activate and deactivate Ortho mode.

Figure 3-16.
Using Ortho mode.
A—Angled lines cannot be drawn with a pointing device while Ortho mode is turned on.
B—With Ortho mode turned off, angled lines can be drawn.

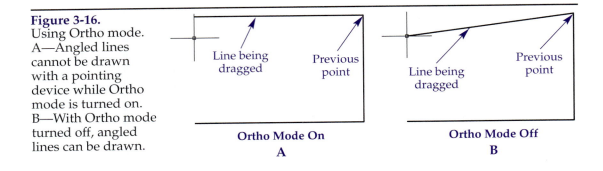

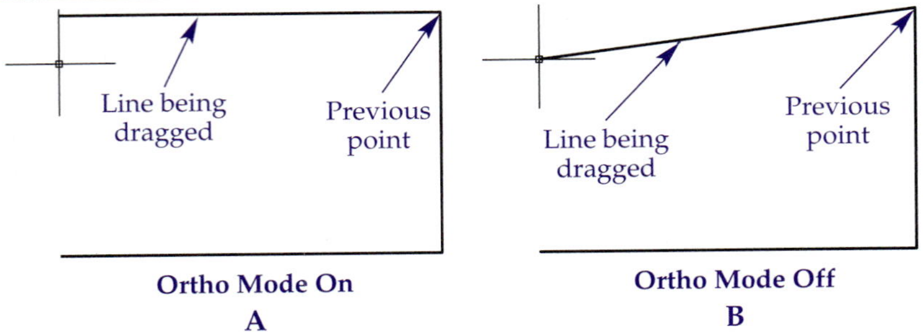

Using Direct Distance Entry

Direct distance entry is a method of entering points allowing you to use the cursor to specify the direction and use a keyboard entry to specify a distance. To draw a line using this point entry method, drag the cursor in any desired direction from the first point of the line. Then type a numerical value indicating the distance from that point.

The direct distance entry method works best in combination with the Ortho mode or polar tracking. **Figure 3-17** shows how to draw a rectangle using direct distance entry. Note that the Ortho mode is on for this example:

Command: **L** *or* **LINE**↵
Specify first point: **2,2**↵
Specify next point or [Undo]: *(drag the cursor to the right)* **3**↵
Specify next point or [Undo]: *(drag the cursor up)* **2**↵
Specify next point or [Close/Undo]: *(drag the cursor to the left)* **3**↵
Specify next point or [Close/Undo]: *(drag the cursor down)* **2**↵
Specify next point or [Close/Undo]: ↵
Command:

PROFESSIONAL TIP

Direct distance entry is a convenient way to find points quickly and easily with a minimum amount of effort. Use direct distance entry with Ortho or Snap mode to draw objects with perpendicular lines. Direct distance entry can be used whenever AutoCAD expects a point coordinate value, including in both drawing and editing commands.

Figure 3-17.
Using direct distance entry to draw lines a designated distance from a current point. With Ortho mode on, move the cursor in the desired direction and type the distance.

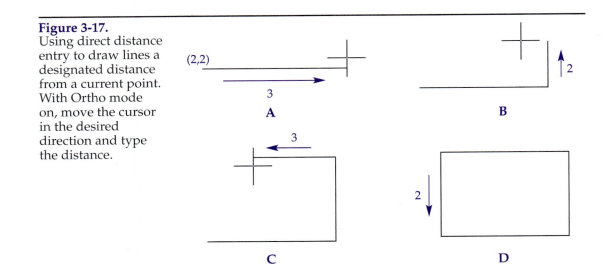

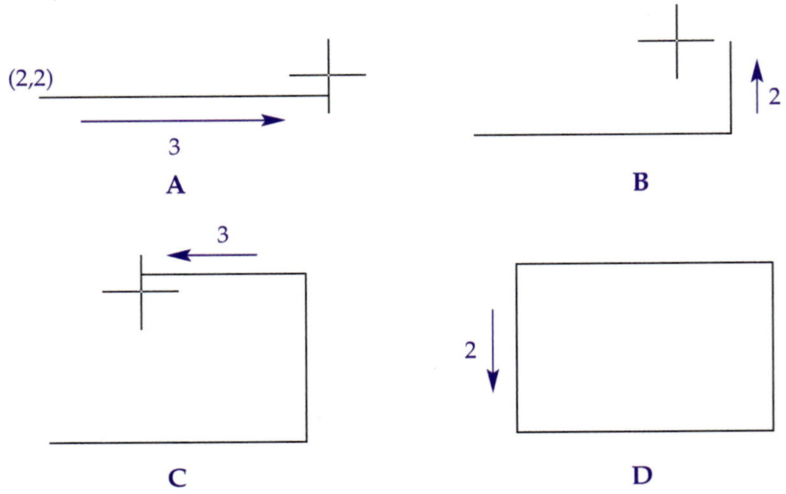

Using Polar Tracking

Polar tracking is similar to Ortho mode, except you are not limited to 90° angles. With polar tracking toggled on, you can cause the drawing crosshairs to "snap" to any predefined angle increment. To turn on polar tracking, pick the **POLAR** button on the status bar or use the [F10] function key. Polar tracking provides visual aids. As you move the cursor in the desired direction, AutoCAD displays an alignment path and tooltip when the cursor crosses the default polar angle increments of 0°, 90°, 180°, or 270°. Setting different polar alignment angles is explained in Chapter 6.

After you have specified a starting point in the **LINE** command and moved the cursor in alignment with a polar tracking angle, all you have to do is type the desired distance value and press [Enter] to have the line drawn. Polar tracking is used, as follows, to draw the lines shown in **Figure 3-18:**

Command: **L** *or* **LINE**↵
Specify first point: **2,2**↵
Specify next point or [Undo]: **2** *(drag the crosshairs while watching the tooltip; at 0°, press* [Enter]*)*
Specify next point or [Undo]: **3** *(drag the crosshairs while watching the tooltip; at 90°, press* [Enter]*)*
Specify next point or [Close/Undo]: ↵
Command:

Polar tracking is discussed in detail in Chapter 6.

Figure 3-18.
Using polar tracking to draw lines at predefined angle increments.

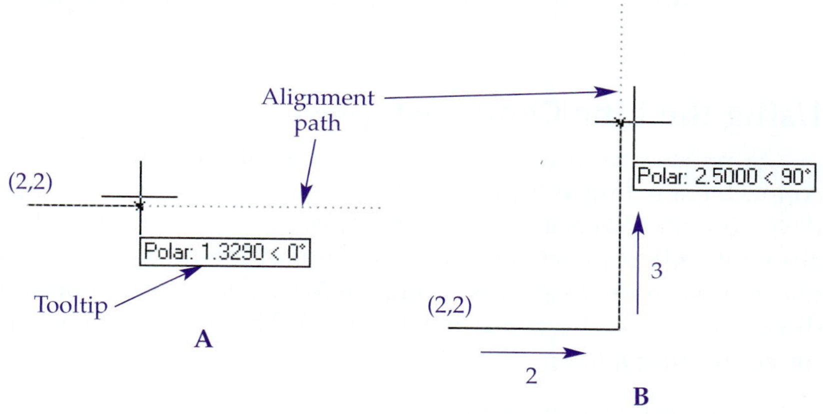

PROFESSIONAL TIP

Practice using the different point entry techniques and decide which method works best for certain situations. Keep in mind that you may mix methods to help enhance your drawing speed. For example, absolute coordinates may work best to locate an initial point or to draw a simple shape. These calculations are easy. Polar coordinates may work better to locate features in a circular pattern or at an angular relationship. Practice with Ortho mode, polar tracking, and snap settings to see the advantages and disadvantages of each. Change the snap settings to assist in drawing layout accuracy.

EXERCISE 3-5 Complete the Exercise on the Student CD.

Using the Close Line Option

A ***polygon*** is a closed plane figure with at least three sides. Triangles and rectangles are examples of polygons. Once you have drawn two or more line segments of a polygon, the endpoint of the last line segment can be connected automatically to the first line segment, using the **Close** option. To use this option, type C or CLOSE at the prompt line. In **Figure 3-19,** the last line is drawn using the **Close** option, as follows:

Command: **L** *or* **LINE**↵
Specify first point: *(pick Point 1)*
Specify next point or [Undo]: *(pick Point 2)*
Specify next point or [Undo]: *(pick Point 3)*
Specify next point or [Close/Undo]: *(pick Point 4)*
Specify next point or [Close/Undo]: **C**↵
Command:

Figure 3-19.
Using the **Close** option to complete a box.

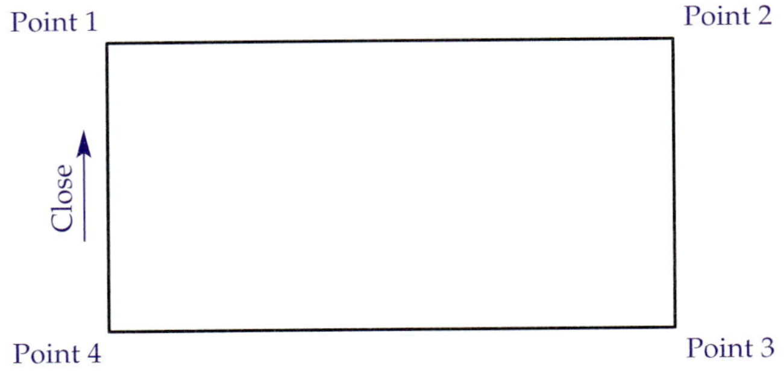

Using the Line Continue Option

Suppose you draw a line, then exit the **LINE** command, but decide to go back and connect a new line to the end of the previous one. Type L to begin the **LINE** command. At the Specify first point: prompt, simply press the [Enter] key or the space bar. This action automatically connects the first endpoint of the new line segment to the endpoint of the previous one, as shown in **Figure 3-20.** The **Continue** option can also be used for drawing arcs, as discussed in Chapter 5. The following command sequence is used for continuing a line:

Command: **L** *or* **LINE**↵
Specify first point: *(press* [Enter] *or the space bar, and AutoCAD automatically picks the last endpoint of the previous line)*
Specify next point or [Undo]: *(pick the next point)*
Specify next point or [Undo]: *(press* [Enter] *to exit the command)*
Command:

PROFESSIONAL TIP

Pressing the space bar or [Enter] repeats the previous command. If no other commands have been used since the line to be continued was drawn, pressing the space bar or [Enter] repeats the **LINE** command.

Figure 3-20.
Using the **Continue** option.

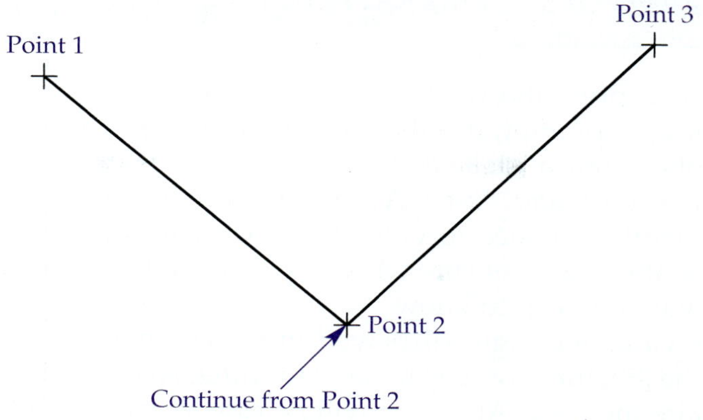

Undoing the Previously Drawn Line

When drawing a series of lines, you may find you made an error. To delete the mistake while still in the **LINE** command, type U at the Specify next point or [Undo]: prompt and press [Enter]. Doing this removes the previously drawn line and allows you to continue from the previous endpoint. You can use the **Undo** option repeatedly to continue deleting line segments until the entire line is gone. The results of the following prompt sequence are shown in **Figure 3-21:**

Command: **L** *or* **LINE**↵
Specify first point: *(pick Point 1)*
Specify next point or [Undo]: *(pick Point 2)*
Specify next point or [Undo]: *(pick Point 3)*
Specify next point or [Close/Undo]: *(pick Point 4)*
Specify next point or [Close/Undo]: **U**↵
Specify next point or [Close/Undo]: **U**↵
Specify next point or [Undo]: *(pick Point 5)*
Specify next point or [Close/Undo]: *(press* [Enter] *to exit the command)*
Command:

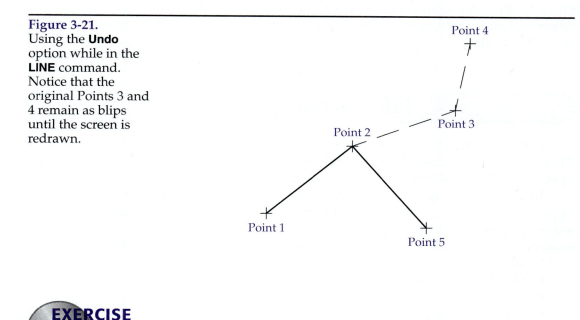

Figure 3-21.
Using the **Undo** option while in the **LINE** command. Notice that the original Points 3 and 4 remain as blips until the screen is redrawn.

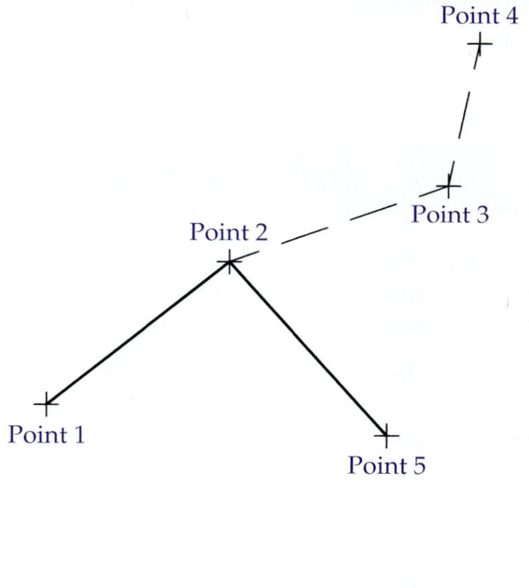

EXERCISE 3-6 Complete the Exercise on the Student CD.

Canceling a Command

If you press the wrong key or misspell a word when entering a command or answering a prompt, use the [Backspace] key to correct the error. This works only if you notice your mistake *before* the [Enter] key is pressed. If you do enter an incorrect option or command, AutoCAD usually responds with an error message. You are then given another chance to enter the correct information or return to the Command: prompt. If you are not sure what has happened, reading the error message should tell you what you need to know.

Previous messages displayed in the command window are not always visible. Press the [F2] function key to display AutoCAD's text screen. This allows you to read the entire message. Also, you will be able to review the commands and options you entered. This may help you better understand what happened. You can press the [F2] key again to return to the graphics screen or use your cursor to pick any visible portion of the graphics screen to make it current again.

It is often necessary to stop the currently active command and return to AutoCAD's Command: prompt to either reenter a command or use another command. This can occur if an incorrect entry is made and you need to restart the command using the correct method or even if you simply decide to do something different. Pressing the [Enter] key or the space bar discontinues some commands, such as the **LINE** command. This exits the command and returns to the Command: prompt, where AutoCAD awaits a new command entry. There are many situations, however, where this does not work. One example of this is using the **Window** option of the **ZOOM** command. Pressing [Enter] does not discontinue the command. In this case, you must cancel the command. (The **ZOOM** command is discussed in detail in Chapter 10.)

You can cancel any active command or abort any data entry and return to the Command: prompt by pressing the [Esc] key. This key is usually located in the upper-left corner of your keyboard. It may be necessary to press the [Esc] key twice to completely cancel certain commands. Many multibutton digitizer pucks use button number 3 to cancel a command. Additionally, most of the toolbar buttons and pull-down menu options automatically cancel any currently active command before entering the new command. In a case in which you wish to abort the current command and start a new one, simply pick the appropriate pull-down menu option or toolbar button.

Introduction to Editing

Editing is the procedure used to correct mistakes or revise an existing drawing. There are many editing functions that help increase productivity. The basic editing operations **ERASE**, **OOPS**, and **U** are introduced in the next sections.

To edit a drawing, you must select items to modify. The Select objects: prompt appears whenever you need to select items in the command sequence. Whether you select only one object or hundreds of objects, you create a ***selection set***. You can create a selection set using a variety of selection options, including the following:

- Window selection.
- Crossing selection.
- Window polygon selection.
- Crossing polygon selection.
- Selection fence.

When you become familiar with the selection set options, you will find that they increase your flexibility and productivity.

In the following discussion and examples, several of the selection set methods are introduced using the **ERASE** command. Keep in mind, however, that these techniques can be used with most of the editing commands in AutoCAD whenever the Select objects: prompt appears. Any of the selection set methods can be enabled from the prompt line.

Using the ERASE Command

ERASE
E

Modify
➡ Erase

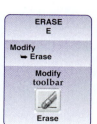

Modify
toolbar

Erase

The **ERASE** command is similar to using an eraser in manual drafting to remove unwanted information. With the **ERASE** command, however, you have a second chance. If you erase the wrong item, it can be brought back with the **OOPS** or **UNDO** command. Picking the **Erase** button in the **Modify** toolbar, picking **Erase** in the **Modify** pull-down menu, or typing E or ERASE at the Command: prompt accesses the **ERASE** command.

When you enter the **ERASE** command, you are prompted to select an object to be erased, as follows:

Command: **E** *or* **ERASE**↵
Select objects: *(select the object(s) to be erased)*
Select objects: ↵
Command:

When the Select objects: prompt appears, a small box replaces the screen crosshairs. This box is referred to as the ***pick box***. Move the pick box over the item to be erased and pick that item. The object is highlighted. Press the [Enter] key or the right mouse button, and the object is erased.

NOTE

The terms *entity* and *object* are interchangeable in AutoCAD. An entity or object is a predefined element you place in a drawing by means of a single command. For example, a line, a circle, an arc, or a single line of text is an entity or object.

After you pick the first object, the Select objects: prompt is redisplayed. You can then select another object to erase, as shown in **Figure 3-22.** If you are finished selecting objects, press the [Enter] key at the Select objects: prompt to "close" the selection set. The **ERASE** operation is completed, and you are returned to the Command: prompt.

Figure 3-22.
Using the **ERASE** command to erase a single object.

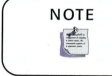

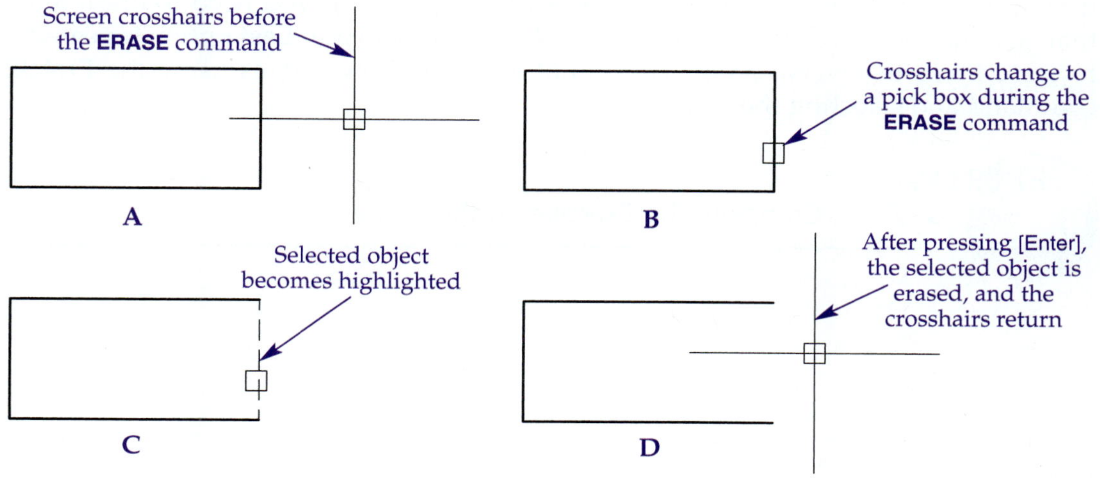

Making a single selection automatically

Normally, AutoCAD lets you pick as many items as you want for a selection set, and selected items are highlighted to let you know what has been picked. You also have the option of selecting a single item and having it automatically edited without first being highlighted. To do this, enter SI (for single) at the Select objects: prompt. To select several items with this method, use the **Window** or **Crossing** selection options (discussed later in this chapter). The command sequence is as follows:

Command: **E** *or* **ERASE**↵
Select objects: **SI**↵
Select objects: *(pick an individual item or use the* **Window** *or* **Crossing** *option to pick several items)*
Command:

Note that the Select objects: prompt did not return after the items were picked. The entire group is automatically edited (erased in this example) when you press [Enter] or pick the second corner of a window or crossing box.

PROFESSIONAL TIP

The **SI** (single) selection option is not commonly used as a command line option. This is because the option of picking an object and pressing [Enter] requires less keystrokes than the option of typing SI and pressing [Enter] does. The **SI** option is most commonly used when developing menu macros requiring single object selection.

Using the Last selection option

The **ERASE** command's **Last** option saves time if you need to erase the last entity drawn. For example, suppose you draw a line and then want to erase it. The **Last** option will automatically select the line. Typing L at the Select objects: prompt selects the **Last** option:

Command: **E** *or* **ERASE**↵
Select objects: **L**↵
1 found
Select objects: ↵
Command:

Keep in mind that using the **Last** option only highlights the last visible item drawn. You must press [Enter] for the object to be erased. If you need to erase more than just the last object, you can use the **ERASE** command and **Last** option repeatedly to erase items in reverse order. This is not as quick, however, as using the **ERASE** command and selecting the objects.

EXERCISE 3-7 Complete the Exercise on the Student CD.

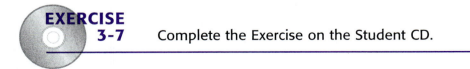

Using the Window selection option

The **W** or **Window** option can be used at any Select objects: prompt. This option allows you to draw a box, or "window," around an object or group of objects to select for editing. Everything entirely within the window can be selected at the same time. If portions of entities project outside the window, those entities are not selected. The command sequence looks like this:

> Command: **E** *or* **ERASE**↵
> Select objects: *(select a point below and to the left of the object(s) to be erased)*

When the Select objects: prompt is shown, select a point clearly below and to the left of the object to be erased. After you select the first point, the screen crosshairs change to a box-shaped cursor. It expands in size as you move the pointing device to the right. The box is a solid line. The next prompt is as follows:

> Specify opposite corner: *(pick the other corner above and to the right of the object(s) to be erased)*
> Select objects: ↵
> Command:

When the Specify opposite corner: prompt is shown, move the pointing device up and to the right so the box totally encloses the object(s) to be erased. Pick to locate the second corner, as shown in **Figure 3-23.** All objects within the window become highlighted. When finished, press [Enter] or pick the right mouse button to complete the **ERASE** command.

You can also manually specify the **Window** selection option from the command line. You need to do this if the **PICKAUTO** variable (discussed later in this chapter) is set to 0. The command sequence is as follows:

> Command: **E** *or* **ERASE**↵
> Select objects: **W**↵
> Specify first corner: *(select a point outside of the object)*
> Specify opposite corner: *(pick the opposite corner of the window)*
> Select objects: ↵
> Command:

When you manually enter the **Window** option, you do not need to pick the first point to the left of the object(s) being erased. The "box" remains the **Window** box whether you move the cursor to the left or right.

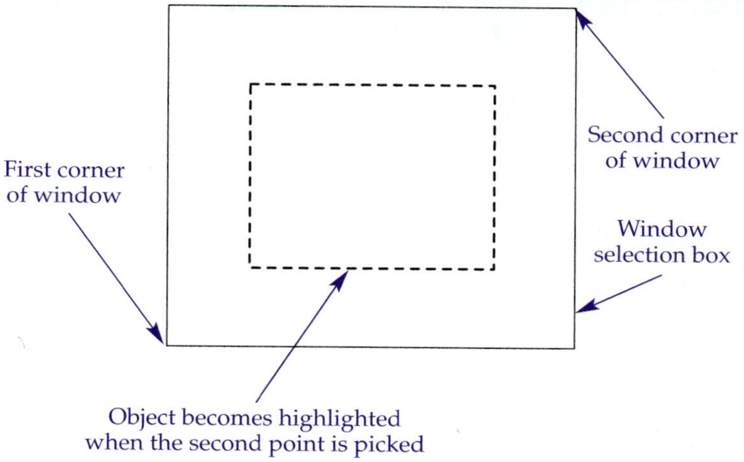

Figure 3-23. Using the **Window** selection option with the **ERASE** command.

Using the **Crossing** selection option

The **Crossing** selection option is similar to the **Window** option. Entities within the box and those *crossing* the box, however, are selected. The **Crossing** box outline is dotted to distinguish it from the solid outline of the **Window** box. The command sequence for the **Crossing** option is as follows:

Command: **E** *or* **ERASE**↵
Select objects: *(pick a point to the right of the object(s) to be erased)*

When the Select objects: prompt is shown, select a point to the right of the object to be erased. After you select the first point, the screen crosshairs change to a box-shaped cursor. The cursor expands in size as you move the pointing device to the left. The next prompt is as follows:

Specify opposite corner: *(move the cursor to the left so the box encloses or crosses the object(s) to be erased and pick)*
Select objects: ↵
Command:

Remember, the crossing box does not need to enclose the entire object to erase it as the window box does. The crossing box needs only to "cross" part of the object. **Figure 3-24** shows how to erase three of the four lines of a rectangle using the **Crossing** option.

You can also manually specify the **Crossing** option from the command line. You need to do this if the **PICKAUTO** variable (discussed later in this chapter) is set to 0. The command sequence is as follows:

Command: **E** *or* **ERASE**↵
Select objects: **C**↵
Specify first corner: *(pick a point outside of the object)*
Specify opposite corner: *(pick the opposite corner of the box)*
Select objects: ↵
Command:

When you manually enter the **Crossing** option, you do not need to pick the first point to the right of the object(s) being erased. The "box" remains the **Crossing** box whether you move the cursor to the left or right.

Figure 3-24.
Using the **Crossing** box to erase objects.

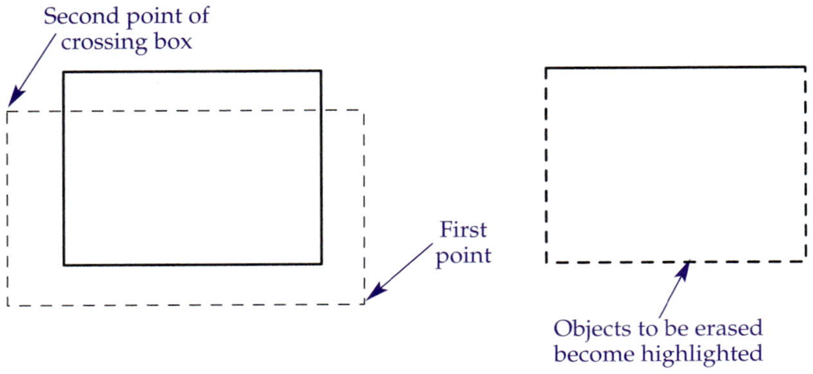

Using the PICKAUTO system variable

The **PICKAUTO** system variable controls automatic windowing when the Select objects: prompt appears. The **PICKAUTO** settings are ON = 1 (default) and OFF = 0. Change the **PICKAUTO** value by typing PICKAUTO at the Command: prompt and then entering the new value. By default, **PICKAUTO** is set to 1. At this setting, you can automatically use the **Window** or **Crossing** selection process.

With **PICKAUTO** set to 1, pick any left point outside the object, and then move the cursor to the right for a **Window** selection. The **Window** box outline is a solid line. Pick any right point outside the object and move the cursor to the left for a **Crossing** selection. The **Crossing** box is a dashed line.

You can use the automatic **Window** or **Crossing** option even if **PICKAUTO** is 0 (off). To do this, enter W (for window) or C (for crossing) at the Select objects: prompt, and then proceed as previously discussed.

Using the Box selection option

Another way to begin the **Window** or **Crossing** selection option is to type BOX at the Select objects: prompt. You are then prompted to pick the first corner, which is the bottom left corner of a **Window** box or the right corner of a **Crossing** box. The command sequence is as follows:

Command: **E** *or* **ERASE**↵
Select objects: **BOX**↵
Specify first corner: *(pick the bottom left corner of a* **Window** *box or the right corner of a* **Crossing** *box)*
Specify opposite corner: *(pick the opposite corner of the box)*
Select objects: ↵
Command:

EXERCISE 3-8 Complete the Exercise on the Student CD.

Using the WPolygon selection option

The **Window** selection option requires you to place a rectangle completely around the entities to be erased. Sometimes it is awkward to place a rectangle around the items to erase. When this situation occurs, you can place a polygon (closed figure with three or more sides) of your own design around the objects with the **WPolygon** selection option.

To use the **WPolygon** option, type WP at the Select objects: prompt. Draw a polygon enclosing the objects. As you pick corners, the polygon drags into place. The command sequence for erasing the five middle squares in **Figure 3-25** is as follows:

Command: **E** *or* **ERASE**↵
Select objects: **WP**↵
First polygon point: *(pick Point 1)*
Specify endpoint of line or [Undo]: *(pick Point 2)*
Specify endpoint of line or [Undo]: *(pick Point 3)*
Specify endpoint of line or [Undo]: *(pick Point 4)*
Specify endpoint of line or [Undo]: ↵
Select objects: ↵
Command:

If you do not like the last polygon point you picked, use the **Undo** option by entering U at the Specify endpoint of line or [Undo]: prompt.

Figure 3-25.
Using the **WPolygon** selection option to erase objects.

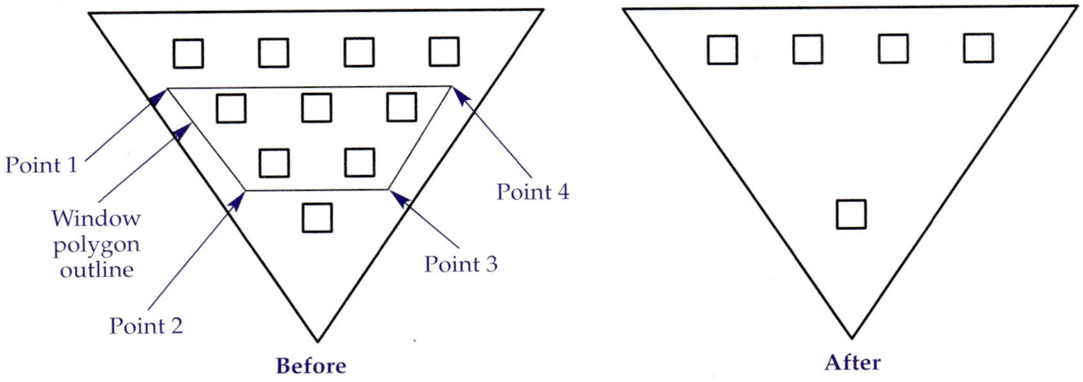

Using the CPolygon selection option

The **Crossing** selection option lets you place a rectangle around or through the objects to be erased. Sometimes it is difficult to place a rectangle around or through the items to be erased without coming into contact with other entities. When you want to use the features of the **Crossing** selection option, but prefer to use a polygon instead of a rectangle, enter CP at the Select objects: prompt. Proceed to draw a polygon enclosing or crossing the objects to erase. As you pick the points, the polygon drags into place. The **CPolygon** line is a dashed rubberband cursor. Suppose you want to erase everything inside the large triangle in Figure 3-26, except for the top and bottom horizontal lines. The command sequence to erase these lines is as follows:

Command: **E** *or* **ERASE**↵
Select objects: **CP**↵
First polygon point: *(pick Point 1)*
Specify endpoint of line or [Undo]: *(pick Point 2)*
Specify endpoint of line or [Undo]: *(pick Point 3)*
Specify endpoint of line or [Undo]: *(pick Point 4)*
Specify endpoint of line or [Undo]: ↵
Select objects: ↵
Command:

Figure 3-26.
Using the **CPolygon** selection option. Everything enclosed within and crossing the polygon is selected.

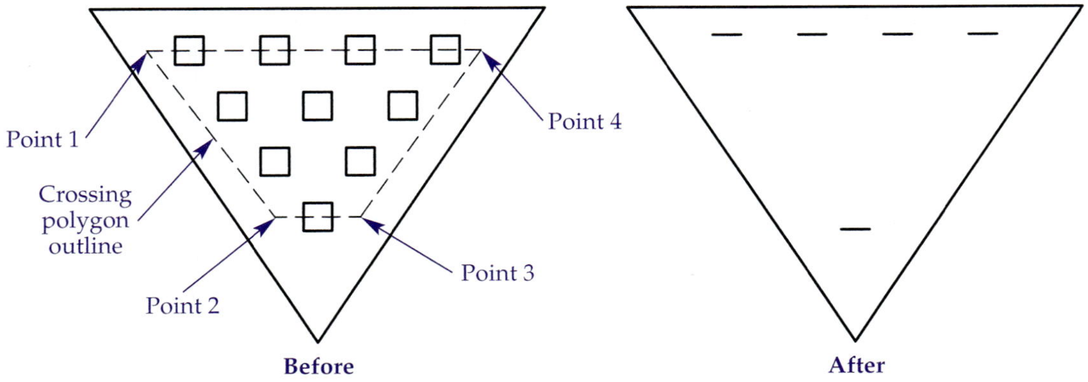

PROFESSIONAL TIP

When using **WPolygon** or **CPolygon**, AutoCAD does not allow you to select a point that causes the lines of the selection polygon to intersect each other. Pick locations that do not result in an intersection. Use the **Undo** option if you need to go back and relocate a preceding pick point.

Using the Fence selection option

Fence is another selection option used to select several objects at the same time. When using the **Fence** option, you simply need to place a fence through the objects you want to select. Anything the fence passes through is included in the selection set. The fence can be straight or staggered, as shown in **Figure 3-27.** Type F at the Select objects: prompt and continue as follows:

Command: **E** *or* **ERASE**↵
Select objects: **F**↵
First fence point: *(pick Point 1)*
Specify endpoint of line or [Undo]: *(pick Point 2)*
Specify endpoint of line or [Undo]: *(pick Point 3)*
Specify endpoint of line or [Undo]: *(pick Point 4)*
Specify endpoint of line or [Undo]: *(pick Point 5)*
Specify endpoint of line or [Undo]: *(pick Point 6)*
Specify endpoint of line or [Undo]: ↵
Select objects: ↵
Command:

Figure 3-27.
Using the **Fence** selection option to erase entities. The fence can be either straight or staggered.

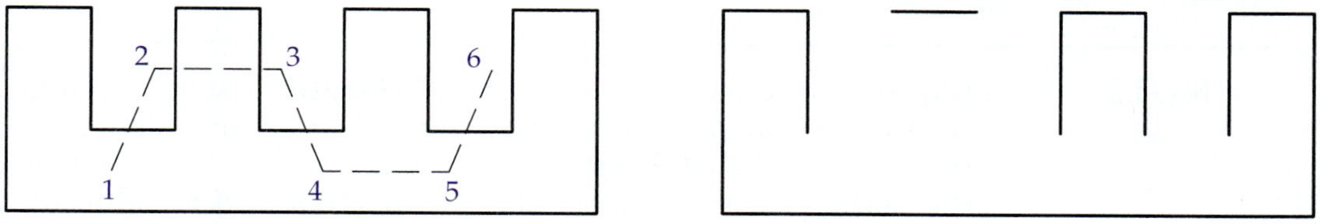

Before After

EXERCISE 3-9 Complete the Exercise on the Student CD.

Removing from and adding to the selection set

When editing a drawing, a common mistake is to accidentally select an object you do not want to select. The simplest way to remove one or more objects from the current selection set is by holding down the [Shift] key and reselecting the objects. This is possible only for individual picks and implied windows. For an implied window, the [Shift] key must be held down while picking the first corner and then can be released for picking the second corner. If you accidentally remove the wrong object from the selection set, release the [Shift] key and pick it again.

To use other methods for removing objects from a selection set or for specialized selection needs, you can switch to the Remove objects mode by typing R at the Select objects: prompt. This changes the Select objects: prompt to Remove objects:. The command sequence is as follows:

Command: **E** *or* **ERASE**↵
Select objects: *(pick several objects, using any technique)*
Select objects: **R**↵
Remove objects: *(pick the objects you want removed from the selection set)*
Remove objects: ↵
Command:

Switch back to the selection mode by typing A (for Add) at the Remove objects: prompt. This restores the Select objects: prompt and allows you to select additional objects. This is how the **Add** feature works:

Remove objects: **A**↵
Select objects: *(continue selecting objects as needed)*
Select objects: ↵
Command:

Cleaning up the Screen

After you draw and edit a number of objects, the screen is cluttered with small crosses or markers called ***blips***. In addition, many of the grid dots may be missing. This can be distracting.

REDRAW
R
View
➡ Redraw

The **REDRAW** command cleans the screen in the current viewport. To access the **REDRAW** command, pick **Redraw** from the **View** pull-down menu or type R or REDRAW at the Command: prompt. The screen goes blank for an instant, and the cleaned drawing and screen return. The **REDRAW** and **REDRAWALL** commands are discussed in Chapter 10.

NOTE

Blips are used as visual aids. The **BLIPMODE** system variable controls whether or not blips are used. Blips are displayed when the **BLIPMODE** setting is 1 and are not displayed when the setting is 0 (default). Change the **BLIPMODE** value by typing BLIPMODE at the Command: prompt and then entering the new value.

Using the OOPS Command

The **OOPS** command brings back the last object you erased. It is issued by typing OOPS at the Command: prompt. If you erased several objects in the same command sequence, all are brought back to the screen. Only the objects erased in the most recent erase procedure can be returned using **OOPS**.

Using the U Command

While the **OOPS** command brings back the last object you erased, the **U** command undoes the last command. The **U** command is issued by typing U at the Command: prompt or by using the [Ctrl]+[Z] key combination. **OOPS** can be used only one time in sequence, while **U** can be issued until every command used since the editing session began has been undone. Even **OOPS** can be undone with the **U** command.

Using the Previous Selection

The object selection options given up to this point in the chapter have used the example of the **ERASE** command. These selection options are also used when moving objects, rotating objects, and performing other editing functions. These basic editing commands are explained in Chapter 12.

Often, more than one sequential editing operation needs to be carried out on a specific group of objects. In this case, the **Previous** selection option allows you to select the same object(s) you just edited for further editing. You can select the **Previous** selection set by typing P at the Select objects: prompt. In the following example, a group of objects is erased, and the **OOPS** command is used to recover them. The **ERASE** command is then issued again, this time using the **Previous** selection option to access the previously selected objects:

Command: **E** *or* **ERASE**↵
Select objects: *(pick several items, using any selection technique)*
Select objects: ↵
Command: **OOPS**↵
Command: **E** *or* **ERASE**↵
Select objects: **P**↵
Select objects: ↵
Command:

Selecting All Objects in a Drawing

Sometimes, you may want to select every object in the drawing. To do this, type ALL at the Select objects: prompt, as follows:

Command: **E** *or* **ERASE**↵
Select objects: **ALL**↵
Select objects: ↵
Command:

This procedure erases everything in the drawing. You can use the **Remove** option at the second Select objects: prompt to remove certain objects from the set. You can also enter ALL after typing R to remove all objects from the set.

NOTE

When you are selecting objects to be erased, AutoCAD accepts only qualifying objects. *Qualifying object* refers to an object that is not on a locked layer and that passes through the pick box area at the point selected. Layers are discussed later in this book.

EXERCISE 3-10

Complete the Exercise on the Student CD.

Cycling through Stacked Objects

One way to deal with stacked objects is to let AutoCAD cycle through the overlapping objects. ***Cycling*** is repeatedly selecting one item from a series of stacked objects until the desired object is highlighted. This works best when several objects cross at the same place or are very close together. To begin cycling through objects, hold down the [Ctrl] key while you make your first pick.

For the objects in **Figure 3-28,** pick the point where the four circles intersect. If there are two or more objects found crossing through the pick box area, the top object is highlighted. Now, you can release the [Ctrl] key. When you pick again, the top object returns, and the next one is highlighted. Every time you pick, another object becomes highlighted. In this way, you cycle through all the objects. When you have the desired object highlighted, press [Enter] to end the cycling process and return to the Command: prompt. The following command sequence is used to erase one of the circles in **Figure 3-28,** but you can use this for any editing function:

Command: **E** *or* **ERASE**↵
Select objects: *(hold down the* [Ctrl] *key and pick)* <Cycle on> *(pick until you highlight the desired object and press* [Enter]*)*
<Cycle off>1 found
Select objects: *(select additional objects or press* [Enter]*)*
Command:

Figure 3-28.
Cycling through a series of stacked circles until the desired object is highlighted.

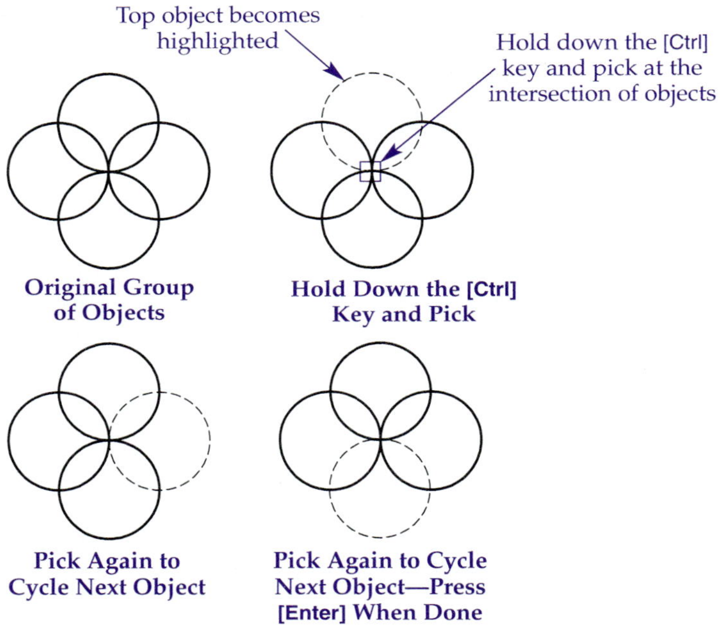
Top object becomes highlighted
Hold down the [Ctrl] key and pick at the intersection of objects
Original Group of Objects
Hold Down the [Ctrl] Key and Pick
Pick Again to Cycle Next Object
Pick Again to Cycle Next Object—Press [Enter] When Done

Chapter Test

Answer the following questions on a separate sheet of paper.

1. Give the commands and entries to draw a line from Point A to Point B to Point C and back to Point A. Return to the Command: prompt:
   A. Command: _____
   B. Specify first point: _____
   C. Specify next point or [Undo]: _____
   D. Specify next point or [Undo]: _____
   E. Specify next point or [Close/Undo]: _____
2. Give the command sequence used to erase a group of objects using the **Windows** selection option and then bring them all back:
   A. Command: _____
   B. Select objects: _____
   C. Specify first corner: _____
   D. Specify opposite corner: _____
   E. Select objects: _____
   F. Command: _____
3. Give the command necessary to refresh the screen.
4. Identify the following linetypes:

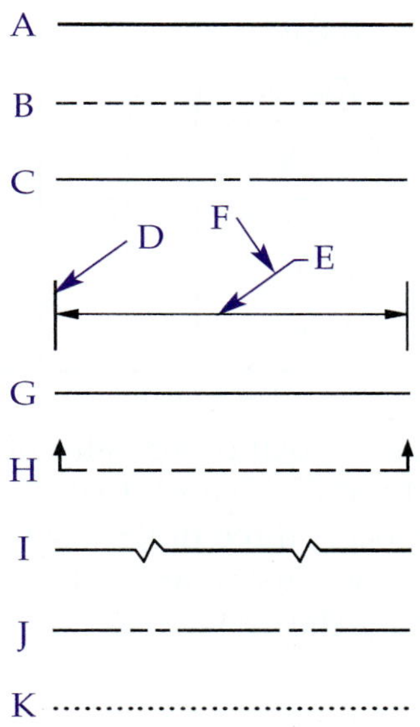

5. List two ways to discontinue drawing a line.
6. Name five point entry methods.
7. Identify three ways to turn on the coordinate display.
8. What does the coordinate display 2.750<90 mean?
9. What does the coordinate display 5.250,7.875 mean?
10. List four ways to turn on the Ortho mode.
11. Identify how you can continue drawing another line segment from a previously drawn line.
12. Define *stacked objects*.
13. How do the appearances of a window and a crossing box differ?
14. Name the command used to bring back the last object(s) erased before issuing another command.
15. List at least five ways to select an object to erase.
16. Explain, in general terms, how direct distance entry works.

Drawing Problems

1. Open one of your templates from Chapter 2. Draw the specified objects as accurately as possible with grid and snap turned off. Use the **LINE** command and draw the following objects on only the left side of the screen:
   - Right triangle.
   - Isosceles triangle.
   - Rectangle.
   - Square.

   Save the drawing as P3-1.
2. Draw the same objects specified in Problem 1 on the right side of the screen. This time, make sure the snap grid is turned on. Observe the difference between having snap on in this problem and off in the previous problem. Save the drawing as P3-2.
3. Draw an object by connecting the following point coordinates. Save your drawing as P3-3. Make a print of your drawing if a printer is available.

Point	Coordinates	Point	Coordinates
1	2,2	8	@-1.5,0
2	@1.5,0	9	@0,1.25
3	@.75<90	10	@-1.25,1.25
4	@1.5<0	11	@2<180
5	@0,-.75	12	@-1.25,-1.25
6	@3,0	13	@2.25<270
7	@1<90		

4. With the absolute, relative, and polar coordinate entry methods, draw the following shapes. Set the limits to 0,0 and 22,17; units to decimal; grid spacing to .5; and snap spacing to .0625. Draw Object A three times, using a different point entry system each time. Draw Object B once, using at least two methods of coordinate entry. Do not draw dimensions. Save the drawing as P3-4. Make a print of your drawing if a printer is available.

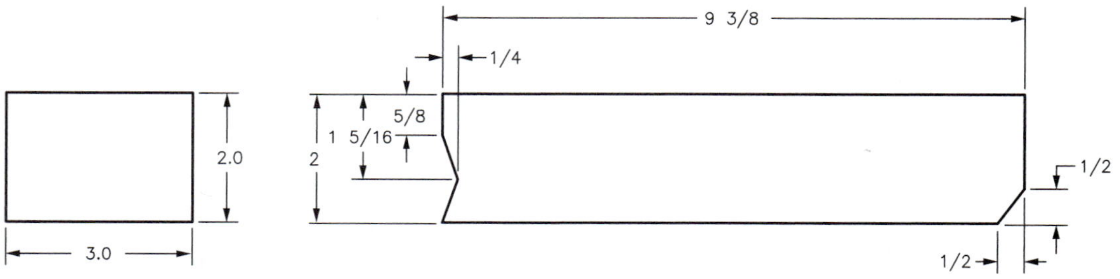

A B

5. Draw the front elevation of this house. Create the features proportional to the given drawings. Save the drawing as P3-5.

6. Use Ortho mode and direct distance entry to draw the outline shown. Each grid square is one unit. Do not draw the grid lines. Save the drawing as P3-6.

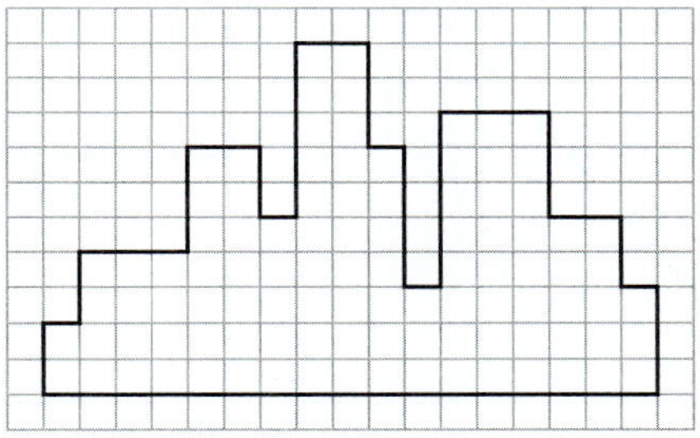

7. Use polar coordinate entry to draw the hexagon shown. Each side of the hexagon is 2 units. Begin at the start point, and draw the lines in the direction indicated by the arrows. Do not draw dimensions. Save the drawing as P3-7.

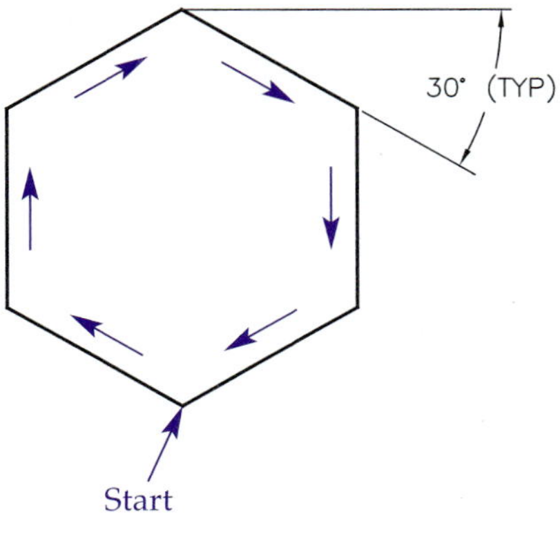

8. Draw the objects shown at A and B below. Begin at the start point and then discontinue the **LINE** command at the point shown. Complete each object using the **Continuation** option. Do not draw dimensions. Save the drawing as P3-8.

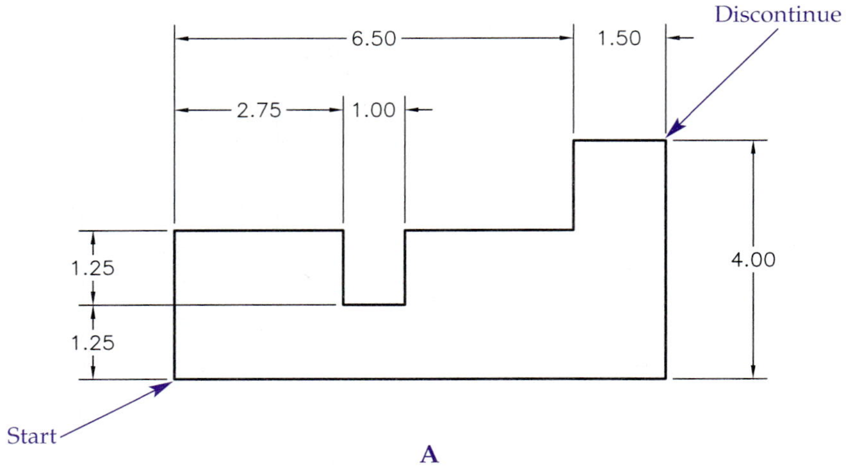

A

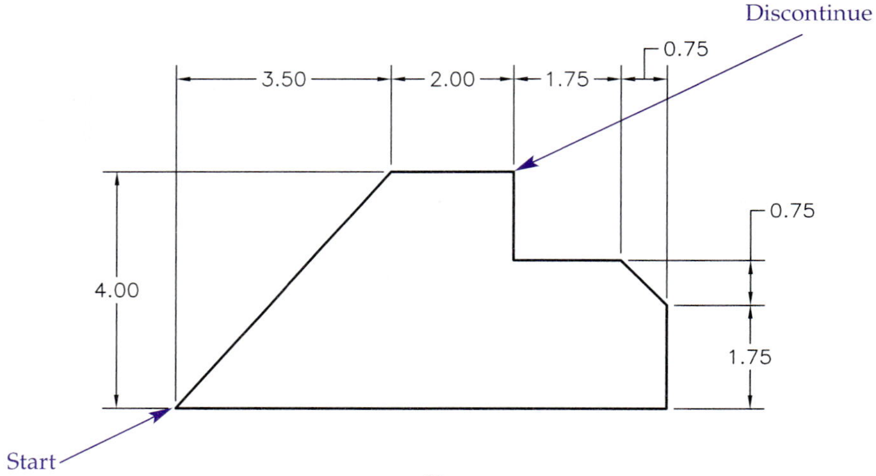

B

CHAPTER 4

Using Layers, Modifying Object Properties, and Making Prints

Learning Objectives

After completing this chapter, you will be able to do the following:

- Draw objects on separate layers.
- Create and manage drawing layers.
- Draw objects with different colors, linetypes, and lineweights.
- Filter a list of layers.
- Use the **Properties** window to change layers, colors, linetypes, and lineweights.
- Use **DesignCenter** to copy layers and linetypes between drawings.
- Make prints of your drawings.

Chapter 3 introduced you to drawing and editing in AutoCAD. In addition to lines, many other types of objects are created in the course of producing most drawings. Many of these objects will be introduced in Chapter 5.

Regardless of the type of object drawn, all AutoCAD objects have properties. Some object properties—such as color and linetype—are common to many types of objects. Other properties—such as text height—are specific to a single object type. AutoCAD uses a layer system to simplify the process of assigning and modifying object properties. In addition, when using layer display options, you can create several different drawing sheets, views, and displays from a single drawing.

This chapter introduces the AutoCAD layer system and basic object properties. It also provides a brief introduction to printing and plotting. Printing and plotting will be covered in greater detail in Chapter 11.

Introduction to Layers

In drafting, different elements or components of drawings might be separated by placing them on different sheets. When each sheet is perfectly aligned with the others, you have what is called an *overlay system*. In AutoCAD, the components of this overlay system are referred to as ***layers***. All the layers can be reproduced together to reflect the entire design drawing. Individual layers might also be reproduced to show specific details or components of the design. Using layers increases productivity in several ways:

- ✓ Specific information can be grouped on separate layers. For example, the floor plan can be drawn on one layer, the electrical plan on another, and the plumbing plan on a third.
- ✓ Several plot sheets can be referenced from the same drawing file by modifying layer visibility.
- ✓ Drawings can be reproduced in individual layers, or the layers can be combined in any desired format. For example, the floor plan and electrical plan can be reproduced together and sent to an electrical contractor for a bid. The floor plan and plumbing plan can be reproduced together and sent to a plumbing contractor.
- ✓ Each layer can be assigned a different color, linetype, and lineweight to help improve clarity.
- ✓ Each layer can be plotted in a different color or pen width, or it can be not plotted at all.
- ✓ Selected layers can be turned off or frozen to decrease the amount of information displayed on the screen or to speed screen regeneration.
- ✓ Changes can be made to a layer promptly, often while the client watches.

Layers Used in Different Drafting Fields

In mechanical drafting, views, hidden features, dimensions, sections, notes, and symbols might each be placed on separate layers. In architectural or civil drafting, there may be over one hundred layers. Layers can be created for floor plans, foundation plans, partition layouts, plumbing systems, electrical systems, structural systems, roof drainage systems, reflected ceiling systems, and HVAC systems. Interior designers may use floor plan, interior partition, and furniture layers. In electronics drafting, each level of a multilevel circuit board can be drawn on its own layer.

Current Layer

As you have worked through the exercises in this book, you may have noticed that "0" appears in the **Layer Control** drop-down list on the **Layers** toolbar. See Figure 4-1. Layer 0 is the AutoCAD default current layer. Until another layer is defined and set current, all objects drawn are placed on and belong to Layer 0.

PROFESSIONAL TIP

Although Layer 0 is often the current layer when a new drawing is started, it is advisable to draw on layers you create other than Layer 0. Layer 0 is typically reserved for the creation of block symbols, which is discussed later in this text.

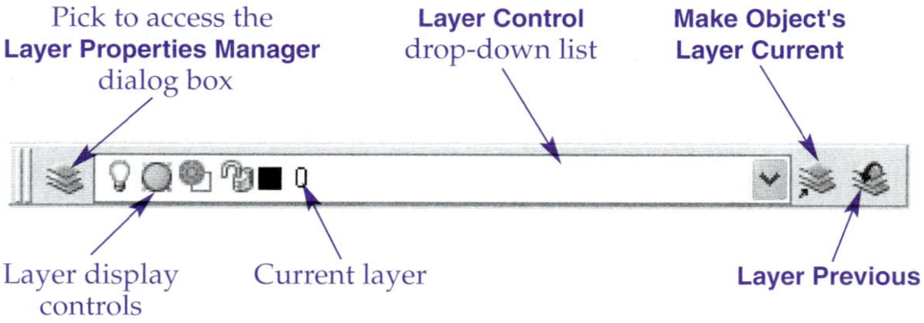

Figure 4-1.
0 appears in the **Layer Control** drop-down list on the **Layers** toolbar. Layer 0 is the AutoCAD default layer.

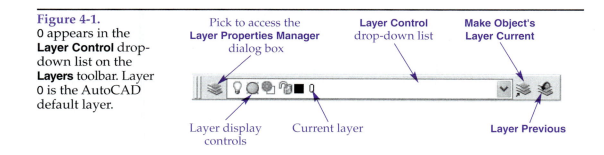

Naming Layers

Layers should be given names to reflect what is drawn on them. Layer names can have up to 255 characters and can include letters, numbers, and certain special characters, including spaces. Typical mechanical, architectural, and civil drafting layer names are as follows:

Mechanical	Architectural	Civil
Object	Walls	Property Line
Hidden	Windows	Structures
Center	Doors	Roads
Dimension	Electrical	Water
Construction	Plumbing	Contours
Hatch	Furniture	Gas
Border	Lighting	Elevations

For very simple drawings, layers can be named by linetype and color. For example, the layer name Continuous-White may have a continuous linetype drawn in white. The layer usage and color number, such as Object-7, can also be used to indicate an object line with color 7. Another option is to assign the linetype a numerical value. For example, object lines can be 1, hidden lines can be 2, and centerlines can be 3. If you use this method, keep a written record of your numbering system for reference.

Layers can also be given more complex names. The name might include the drawing number, color code, and layer content. The layer name Dwg100-2-Dimen, for example, could refer to drawing DWG100, color 2, and the fact that this layer is used for dimensions. The American Institute of Architects (AIA) has established a layer naming system for architectural and related drawings. This standard is found in the document *CAD Layer Guidelines*, published by AIA.

The Layer Properties Manager

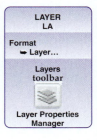

LAYER
LA

Format
➥ Layer...

Layers toolbar

Layer Properties Manager

The **LAYER** command opens the **Layer Properties Manager** dialog box. To display this dialog box, pick the **Layer Properties Manager** button from the **Layers** toolbar, select **Layer...** from the **Format** pull-down menu, or type LA or LAYER at the Command: prompt. Figure 4-2 shows the **Layer Properties Manager** dialog box. Only one layer is required in an AutoCAD drawing. This layer is named 0 and cannot be renamed or purged from the drawing. As discussed earlier, however, it is often useful to have more than one layer in a drawing. The most important layer is the *current* layer because whatever you draw is placed on this layer. It is useful to think of the current layer as the *top* layer.

Figure 4-2.
The **Layer Properties Manager** dialog box.

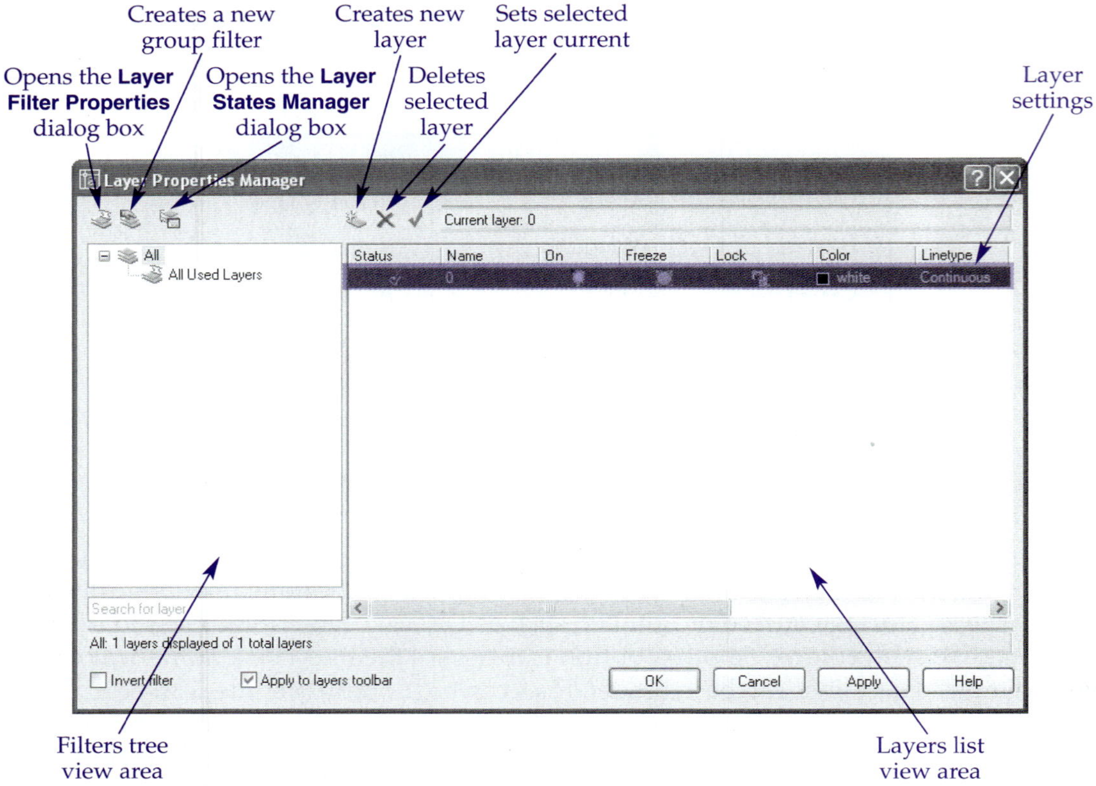

Creating Layers

Layers should be added to a drawing to meet the needs of the current drawing project. To add a new layer, pick the **New Layer** button from the **Layer Properties Manager** dialog box. A new layer listing appears, using a default name of Layer1. See **Figure 4-3.** The layer name is highlighted when the listing appears, allowing you to type a new name.

You can also enter several new layer names at the same time. Typing a layer name and then pressing the comma key enters the first layer name and moves on to the next one. This drops the Layer1 listing below the previously entered name. Entering several layer names in this manner saves time because it keeps you from having to pick the **New Layer** button each time. Pick the **OK** button when you are finished typing the new layer names. When you reopen the **Layer Properties Manager** dialog box, the new layer names are alphabetized, as shown in **Figure 4-4.**

Figure 4-3.
A new layer is named Layer1 by default.

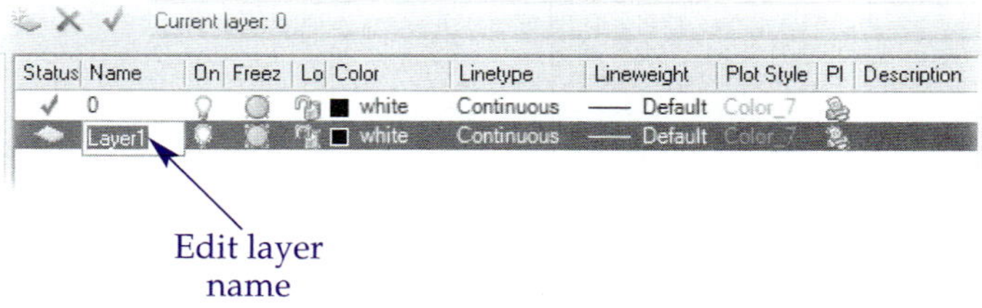

Figure 4-4.
Layer names are automatically placed in numerical and alphabetical order.

Status	Name	On	Freez	Lo	Color	Linetype	Lineweight	Plot Style	PI	Description
✓	0	◉	◉	◪	■ white	Continuous	—— Default	Color_7	●	
⌣	1	◯	◯	◪	■ white	Continuous	—— Default	Color_7	●	
⌣	2	◯	◯	◪	■ white	Continuous	—— Default	Color_7	●	
⌣	3	◯	◯	◪	■ white	Continuous	—— Default	Color_7	●	
⌣	Electrical	◯	◯	◪	■ white	Continuous	—— Default	Color_7	●	
⌣	Judy	◯	◯	◪	■ white	Continuous	—— Default	Color_7	●	
⌣	Plumbing	◯	◯	◪	■ white	Continuous	—— Default	Color_7	●	
⌣	Walls	◯	◯	◪	■ white	Continuous	—— Default	Color_7	●	

Current layer: 0

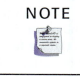

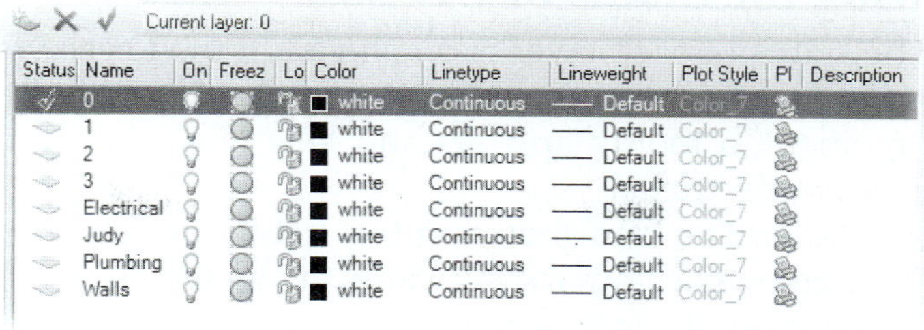

NOTE

Selecting the headings in the layer names window controls sorting. Each time the **Layer Properties Manager** dialog box is reopened, however, the layers are sorted alphanumerically by default.

The **MAXSORT** system variable controls the sorting of layers. The default **MAXSORT** value is 1000. As long as the number of layers is less than the **MAXSORT** value, the layers are sorted numerically and alphabetically. If there are more layers than the **MAXSORT** value, the layers are sorted in the order in which they were created. The **MAXSORT** system variable also controls the sorting of symbol names and block names.

PROFESSIONAL TIP

If you need to exit the **Layer Properties Manager** dialog box after creating layers, pick the **OK** button to accept the creation of the new layers. Picking the **Close** button (**X**) causes the dialog box to be closed without saving the list of layers you created.

Deleting Layers

Deleting a layer no longer in use is a simple process. First, select the layer, and then pick the **Delete Layer** button. Pick the **Apply** button, and then the layer is erased from the list box. If the selected layer is not deleted, an object in the drawing has been drawn on this layer.

Setting the Current Layer

You can set a new current layer by double-clicking the layer name or highlighting the layer name in the layer list and then picking the **Set Current** button. To highlight the layer name, simply pick on top of the name. The current layer is specified in the status line above the layer list in the **Layer Properties Manager** dialog box and in the **Layer Control** drop-down list in the **Layers** toolbar.

EXERCISE 4-1 Complete the Exercise on the Student CD.

Viewing the Status of Layers

The status of each layer is displayed in the **Layer Properties Manager** with icons to the right of the layer name. See **Figure 4-5.** If you position the pointer over an icon for a moment, a tooltip appears and tells what the icon refers to. Picking the icons changes layer settings.

- **Status.** The icon shown in this field indicates the status property of the layer. A green check mark indicates this is the current layer. If there are objects on the layer, the icon is a blue sheet of paper. A white sheet of paper indicates that there are no objects on the layer. If the filters are shown in the layer list, the same icons associated with the filters in the filter tree view list are used.
- **Changing the layer name.** The layer name list box contains all the layers in the drawing. To change an existing name, pick the name once to highlight it, pause for a moment, and then pick it again. When you pick the second time, the layer name is highlighted with a text box around it and a cursor for text entry, allowing you to type a new layer name. Layer 0 cannot be renamed.

On Off

- **Turning layers on and off.** The lightbulb shows whether a layer is on or off. The yellow lightbulb means the layer is on; objects on that layer are displayed on-screen and can be plotted. If you pick on a yellow lightbulb, it turns gray, turning the layer off. If a layer is off, the objects on it are not displayed on-screen and are not plotted. Objects on a layer that has been turned off can still be edited when using advanced selection techniques and are regenerated when a drawing regeneration occurs.

Thawed Frozen

- **Thawing and freezing layers.** Layers are further classified as thawed or frozen. Similar to turned off layers, frozen layers are not displayed and do not plot. Objects on a frozen layer, however, cannot be edited and are not regenerated when the drawing regenerates. Freezing layers containing objects that do not need to be referenced for current drawing tasks can greatly speed up your system performance. The snowflake icon is displayed when a layer is frozen. Layers are normally thawed, which means objects on the layer are displayed on-screen. The sun icon is displayed for thawed layers. Picking the sun/snowflake icon toggles it to the other icon.

NOTE

It is important to note that objects on frozen layers cannot be modified, but objects residing on turned off layers can be modified. For example, if you turn off half your layers and use the **All** selection option with the **ERASE** command, even the objects on the turned off layers will be erased! The **ERASE** command does not, however, affect frozen layers.

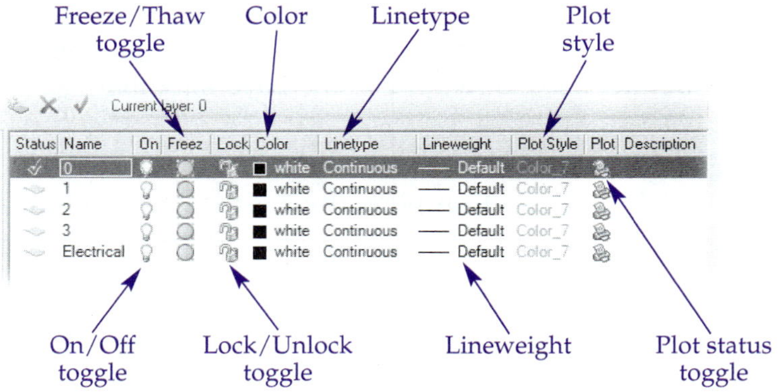

Figure 4-5. Layer settings can be changed by picking the icons in the **Layer Properties Manager** dialog box.

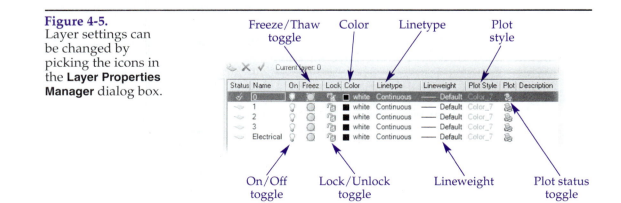

- **Unlocked and locked layers.** The unlocked and locked padlock symbols are for locking and unlocking layers. Layers are unlocked by default, but you can pick on an unlocked padlock to lock it. A locked layer remains visible, but objects on it cannot be edited. New objects can be added to a locked layer.

Locked Unlocked

- **Layer color.** The color swatch shows the current default color for objects created on each layer. When you need to change the color for an existing layer, pick the swatch to display the **Select Color** dialog box. Working with colors is discussed later in this chapter.
- **Layer linetype.** The current linetype setting for each layer is shown in the **Linetype** list. Picking the linetype name opens the **Select Linetype** dialog box, where you can specify a new linetype. Working with linetypes is discussed later in this chapter.
- **Layer lineweight.** The current lineweight setting for each layer is shown in the **Lineweight** list. Picking the lineweight name opens the **Lineweight** dialog box, where you can specify a new lineweight. Working with lineweights is discussed later in this chapter.
- **Layer plot styles.** This setting changes the plot style associated with the selected layers. The plot style setting is disabled when you are working with color-dependent plot styles (the **PSTYLEPOLICY** system variable is set to 1). Otherwise, picking the plot style displays the **Select Plot Style** dialog box. Plot styles are discussed in Chapter 11.
- **Layer plot/no plot.** Select this toggle to turn off plotting for a particular layer. The "no plot" symbol is displayed over the printer image when the layer is not available to be plotted. The layer is still displayed, but not plotted.

Plot No Plot

- **Description.** Provides an area to type a short description for the layer.

The following layer options appear only in paper space layout mode, which is discussed in Chapter 11:

- **Thawing and freezing layers in active and new viewports.** These settings, for floating model space views on layouts, are detailed later in this textbook. The options are visible only when a layout tab is active.

EXERCISE 4-2 Complete the Exercise on the Student CD.

Working with Layers

Any setting you change affects all currently highlighted layer names. Highlighting layer names employs the same techniques used in file dialog boxes. You can highlight a single name by picking it. Picking another name deselects the previous name and highlights the new selection. You can use the [Shift] key to select two layers and all layer names between them on the listing. Holding the [Ctrl] key while picking layer names highlights or deselects each selected name without affecting any other selections.

A shortcut menu is also available while your cursor is in the layer list area of the **Layer Properties Manager** dialog box. Press the right mouse button to display the shortcut menu shown in **Figure 4-6.** The options available on this menu are as follows:

- **Show Filter Tree.** Opens or closes the filter tree view area.
- **Show Filters in Layer List.** Displays all the layer filters, along with the layers, in the layer list area.
- **Set current.** Sets the selected layer current.
- **New Layer.** Creates a new layer.
- **Delete Layer.** Sets the selected layer to be deleted.
- **Change Description.** Allows you to modify the description for the selected layer.

Figure 4-6.
Right-clicking in the list box of the **Layer Properties Manager** dialog box produces this shortcut menu.

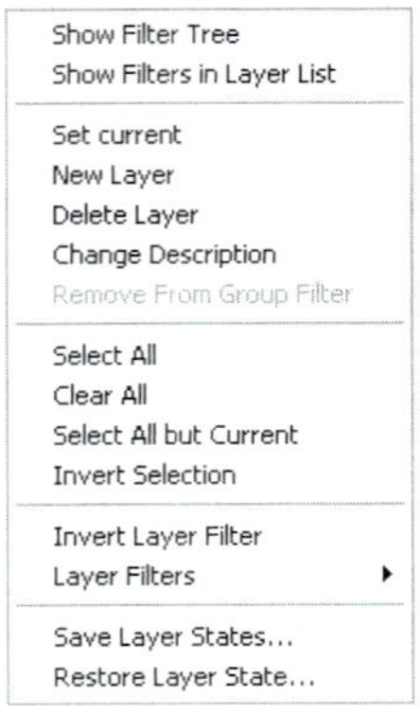

- **Remove From Group Filter.** This is only available if the selected layer is part of a group filter. When this option is available and chosen, the selected layer is removed from the group filter.
- **Select All.** Selects all layers.
- **Clear All.** Deselects all layers.
- **Select All but Current.** Selects all layers, except the current layer.
- **Invert Selection.** Deselects all selected layers and selects all deselected layers.
- **Invert Layer Filter.** Inverts the current filter setting. Filters are discussed later in this chapter.
- **Layer Filters.** Displays a submenu with predefined filters. The choices are the following:
  - **All.**
  - **All Used Layers.**
- **Save Layer States.** Opens the **New Layer State to Save** dialog box, which is discussed later in this chapter.
- **Restore Layer State.** Opens the **Layer States Manager** dialog box, which allows you to restore a previously saved layer state.

EXERCISE 4-3 Complete the Exercise on the Student CD.

Setting the Layer Color

The number of layer colors available depends on your graphics card and monitor. Color systems usually support at least 256 colors, while many graphics cards support up to 16.7 million colors. Color settings can affect the appearance of plotted drawings. Lineweights can also be associated with drawing colors. This is discussed in Chapter 11. Colors should highlight the important features on the drawing and not cause eyestrain. AutoCAD allows you to assign colors to layers by selecting a color from the **Select Color** dialog box.

In order to assign a color to a layer, first highlight a layer name in the **Layer Properties Manager**, and then pick the color swatch associated with the layer name. AutoCAD displays the **Select Color** dialog box. See Figure 4-7. This dialog box includes three different color tabs from which a color can be selected for use in your highlighted layer. These tabs are the **Index Color** tab, the **True Color** tab, and the **Color Books** tab. Each of these tabs includes different methods of obtaining colors for assignment to a layer. The tabs are described in the following sections.

Figure 4-7.
The **Select Color** dialog box.

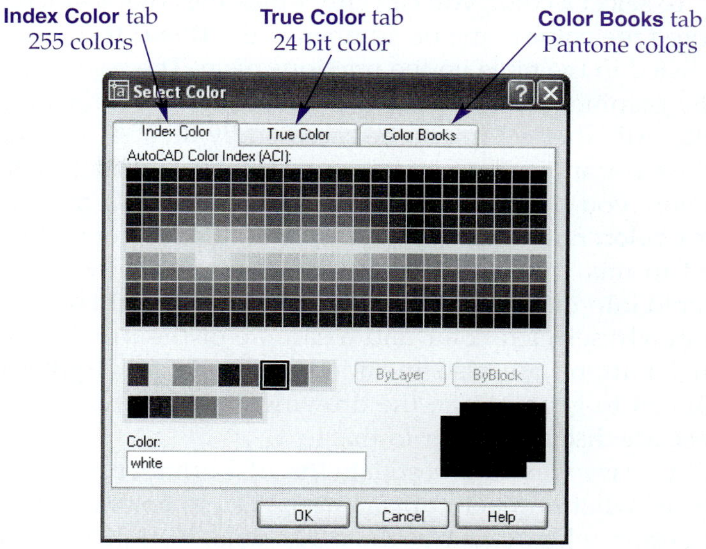

Index Color tab

This tab includes 255 color swatches from which you can choose a color. See Figure 4-8. This tab is commonly referred to as the AutoCAD Color Index (ACI), as layer colors are coded by name and number. The first seven colors in the ACI include both a numerical index number and a name:

Number	Color
1	red
2	yellow
3	green
4	cyan
5	blue
6	magenta
7	white

Figure 4-8.
The **Index Color** tab uses 255 indexed colors.

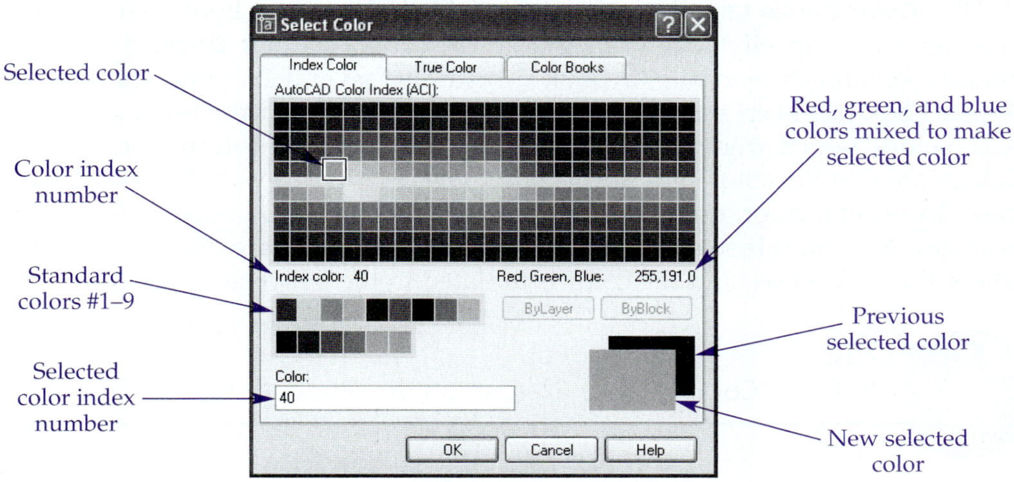

To select a color, you can either pick the color swatch displaying the desired color or type the color name or number in the **Color:** text box. The first seven basic colors are listed in the table on the previous page. The color white (number 7) refers to white if the graphics screen background is black, and it refers to black if the background is white. All other colors can be accessed by their ACI numbers.

As you move the cursor around the color swatches, the **Index color:** note updates to show you the number of the color over which the cursor is hovering. Beside the **Index color:** note is the **Red, Green, Blue:** (RGB) note. This indicates the RGB numbers used to mix the highlighted color. Once you pick a color, the **Index color:** note is entered into the **Color:** text box. On the lower right of the dialog box are a preview of the newly selected color and a sample of the previously assigned color. Two additional buttons are also included: **ByLayer** and **ByBlock**. These are special colors assigned to geometry in the drawing, but they cannot be assigned to a layer name. These are discussed later in this text.

An easy way to investigate the ACI numbering system is to pick a color swatch and see what number appears in the **Color:** text box. After selecting a color, pick the **OK** button when you are ready. The color you picked is now displayed as the color swatch for the highlighted layer name in the **Layer Properties Manager** dialog box.

True Color tab

The **True Color** tab allows you to specify a true color (24 bit color) using either Hue, Saturation, and Luminance (HSL) or Red, Green, and Blue (RGB) color models. Figure 4-9A shows the **True Color** tab with the **HSL** color model selected. The **True Color** tab is shown in Figure 4-9B with the **RGB** color model selected.

The **HSL** color model includes three text boxes allowing you to control the properties of the color. The **Hue:** value represents a specific wavelength of light within the visible spectrum. Valid hue values range from 0–360 degrees. The **Saturation:** value refers to the purity of the color. Valid saturation values range from 0–100 percent. Finally, the **Luminance:** value specifies the brightness of the color. Valid luminance values range from 0–100 percent, where 0 percent represents black, 100 percent represents white, and 50 percent represents the optimal brightness of the color. Instead of adjusting the HSL colors through the text boxes, you can move the cursors in the spectrum preview screen and luminance slider bar and pick the approximate color you want. The true color specified is then translated to RGB values, which are displayed in the **Color:** text box.

The **RGB** color model includes four text boxes and three slider bars. Adjusting the values in the **Red:**, **Green:**, and **Blue:** text boxes causes the slider bars to be adjusted, with the mixed color displayed in the new color preview. The cursors can also be used to slide the markers along each bar to mix the colors.

Color Books tab

The **Color Books** tab allows you to use third party color books, such as Pantone color books, to specify a color. See Figure 4-10. The **Color Book:** drop-down list includes several different color books, including several Pantone and RAL books. Once a book has been selected, the available colors within the book are displayed. (RAL colors, which were developed in Germany, are used internationally.) You can pick an area on the color slider or use the up and down keys to browse through the book. To select a color, use your pick button to pick on top of one of the color book swatches. As a color is selected, the equivalent RGB values are displayed on the right side of the dialog box, and the color is updated in the new color preview.

EXERCISE 4-4 Complete the Exercise on the Student CD.

Figure 4-9.
The **True Color** tab uses 24 bit color. A—HSL color model. B—RGB color model.

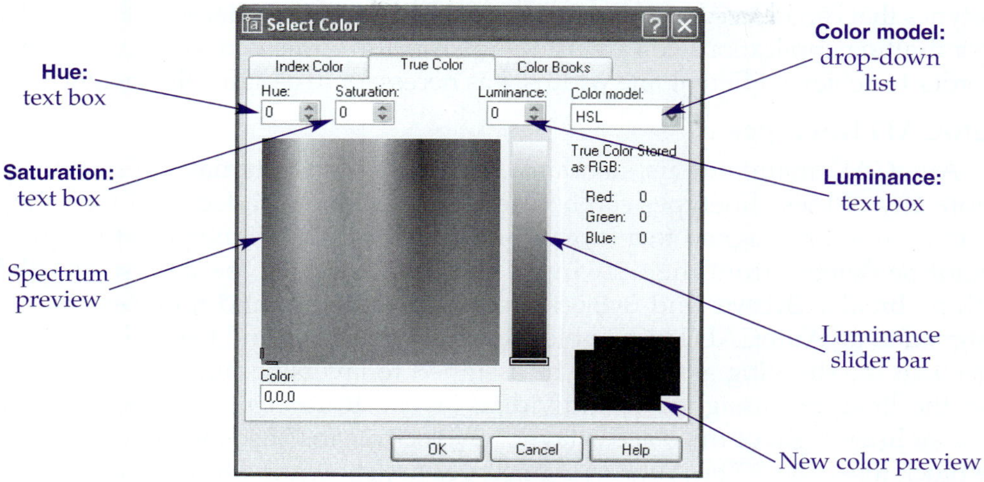

HSL Color Model
A

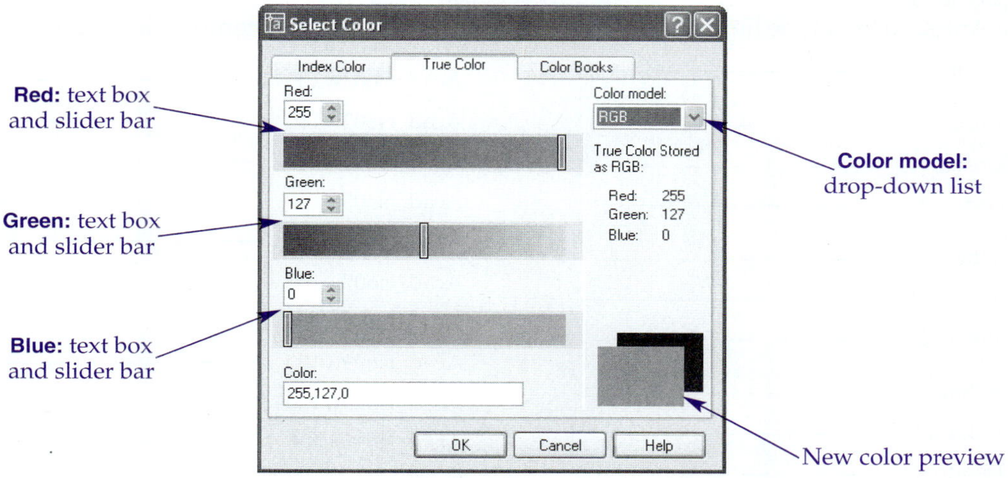

RGB Color Model
B

Figure 4-10.
The **Color Books** tab uses Pantone and RAL colors.

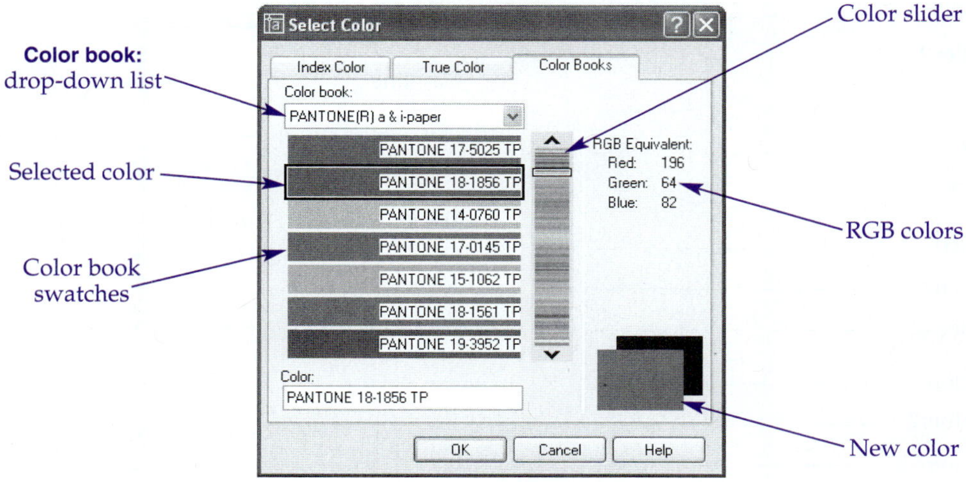

Setting the Layer Linetype

You were introduced to line standards in Chapter 3. AutoCAD provides standard linetypes that can be used at any time to match the ASME standards or the standards for other drafting applications you are using. You can also create your own custom linetypes. In order to achieve different line widths, it is necessary to assign a lineweight.

AutoCAD linetypes

AutoCAD maintains its standard linetypes in an external file named acad.lin. Before any of these linetypes can be used, they must be loaded, and then they must be set current or assigned to a layer. Three of AutoCAD's linetypes are required and cannot be deleted from the drawing. The Continuous linetype represents solid lines with no breaks. ByLayer and ByBlock are logical linetypes and represent the linetype assigned to an AutoCAD layer or block insertion. ByLayer and ByBlock are assigned to objects in the drawing and cannot be assigned to layers because they already represent the linetypes assigned to individual layers. ByLayer means "use the linetype, color, or lineweight of the object's layer." ByBlock means "use the linetype assigned to the block insertion." The AutoCAD linetypes are shown in **Figure 4-11.**

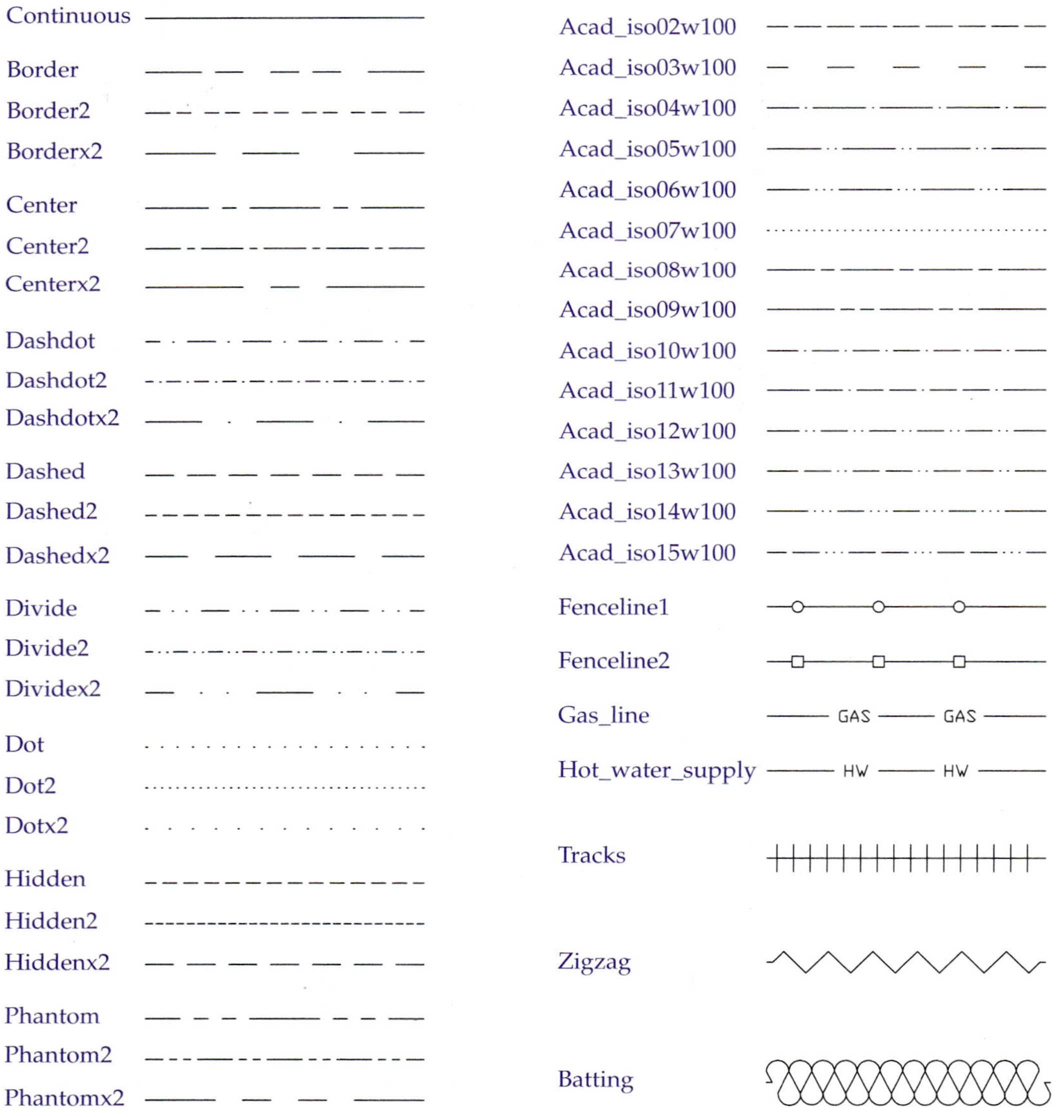

Figure 4-11.
The AutoCAD linetype library contains ACAD ISO, standard, and complex linetypes.

PROFESSIONAL TIP

Two linetype definition files are available, acad.lin and acadiso.lin. The ACAD ISO linetypes found in both files are identical, but the non-ISO linetype definitions are scaled up 25.4 times in the acadiso.lin file. The scale factor of 25.4 is used to convert from inches to millimeters. The ACAD ISO linetypes are for metric drawings.

Changing linetype assignments

To change linetype assignments, select the layer name you want to change and pick its linetype name. This displays the **Select Linetype** dialog box, shown in **Figure 4-12.** The first time you use this dialog box, you may find only the Continuous linetype listed in the **Loaded linetypes** list box. You need to load any other linetypes to be used in the drawing.

If you need to add linetypes not included in the list, pick the **Load...** button to display the **Load or Reload Linetypes** dialog box, shown in **Figure 4-13.** The ACAD ISO, standard, and complex linetypes are named and displayed in the **Available Linetypes** list. Standard linetypes use only dashes, dots, and gaps. Complex linetypes can also contain special shapes and text.

Figure 4-12.
The **Select Linetype** dialog box.

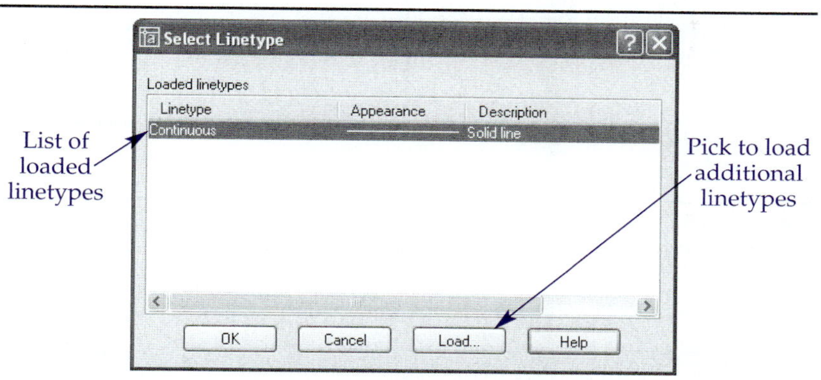

Figure 4-13.
The **Load or Reload Linetypes** dialog box.

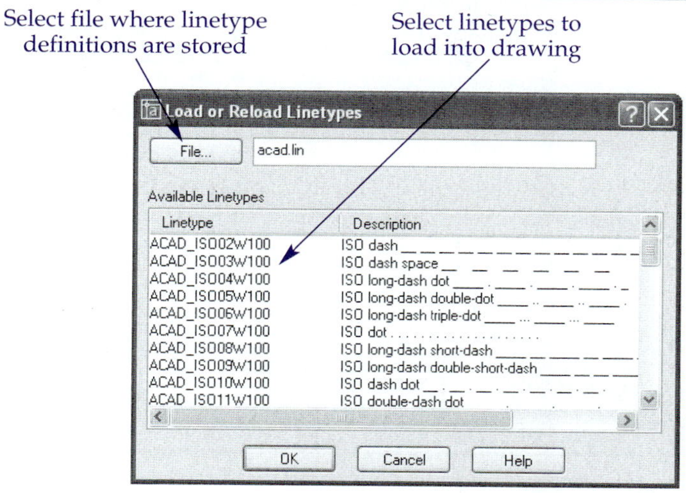

Use the down arrow to look at all the linetypes. Select the linetypes you want to load. Use the [Shift] key and pick to select linetypes between your two picked linetypes. You can also use the [Ctrl] key and pick to select nonconsecutive linetypes. Pick the **OK** button to return to the **Select Linetype** dialog box, where the linetypes you selected are listed, as shown in **Figure 4-14.** In the **Select Linetype** dialog box, pick the desired linetype, and then pick **OK**. The HIDDEN linetype selected in **Figure 4-14** is now the linetype assigned to Layer 2, as shown in **Figure 4-15.**

> **NOTE**
>
> The acad.lin file is used by default. You can switch to the ISO library by picking the **File...** button in the **Load or Reload Linetypes** dialog box. This displays the **Select Linetype File** dialog box, where you can select the acadiso.lin file.

Figure 4-14.
Linetypes loaded from the **Load or Reload Linetypes** dialog box are added to the **Loaded linetypes** list box.

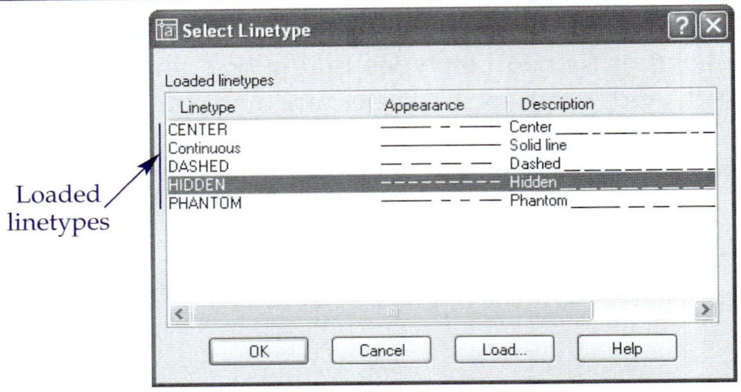

Figure 4-15.
Objects drawn on Layer 2 now have a HIDDEN linetype.

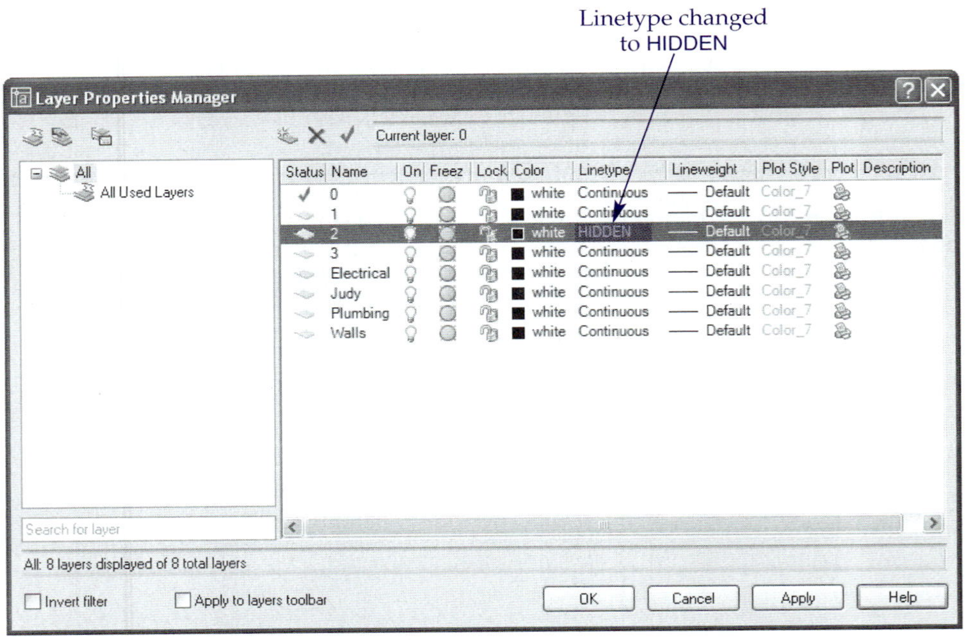

Managing linetypes

The **Linetype Manager** dialog box is a convenient place to load and access linetypes. This dialog box can be accessed by selecting **Linetype...** from the **Format** pull-down menu, selecting **Other...** in the **Linetype Control** drop-down list in the **Properties** toolbar, or typing LT or LINETYPE at the Command: prompt. See **Figure 4-16.**

LINETYPE
LT

Format
➥ Linetype...

This dialog box is similar to the **Layer Properties Manager** dialog box. Picking the **Load...** button opens the **Load or Reload Linetypes** dialog box. Picking the **Delete** button deletes any selected nonused linetypes.

Changing lineweight assignments

Like linetypes, lineweights can also be assigned to objects. ***Lineweight*** adds width to objects for display and plotting. Lineweights can be set for objects or assigned to layers. Assigning lineweights to layers allows you to have the objects on specific layers set to their own lineweights. This allows you to control the display of line thickness to match ASME or other standards related to your drafting application.

The layer lineweight settings are displayed on the screen when the lineweight is turned on. To toggle screen lineweights, click the **LWT** button on the status bar. You can also right-click on the **LWT** button and pick the **On** or **Off** option from the shortcut menu.

To change lineweight assignments in the **Layer Properties Manager**, select the layer name you want to change and pick its lineweight setting. This displays the **Lineweight** dialog box, shown in **Figure 4-17.** Scroll through the **Lineweights:** list to select the desired lineweight. The **Lineweight** dialog box displays fixed lineweights available in AutoCAD for you to apply to the selected layer. The Default lineweight is the lineweight initially assigned to a layer when it is created.

The area near the bottom of the **Lineweight** dialog box displays **Original:**, which is the lineweight previously assigned to the layer, and **New:**, which is the new lineweight assigned to the layer. In **Figure 4-17,** the **Original:** and **New:** specifications are the same, because the initial layer lineweight has not been changed from the default.

Figure 4-16.
The **Linetype Manager** dialog box.

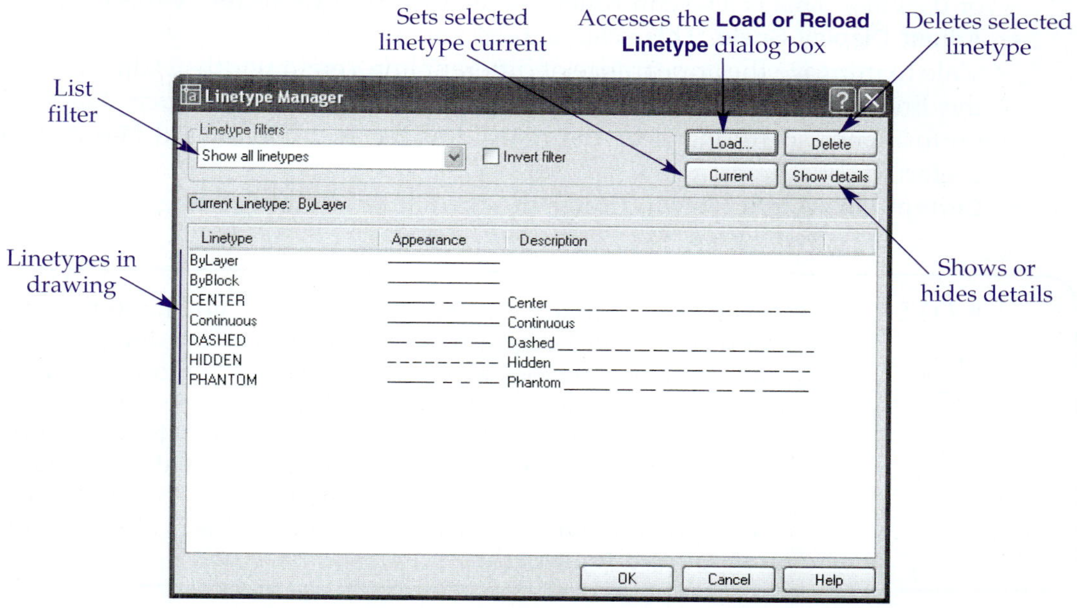

Figure 4-17.
The **Lineweight** dialog box.

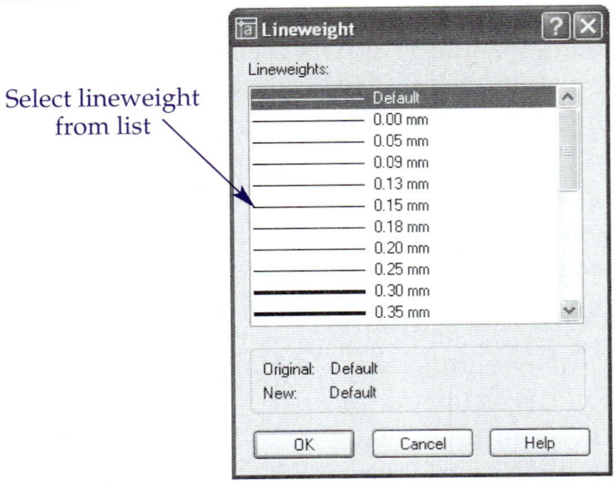

Setting the current lineweight

LINEWEIGHT
LWEIGHT
LW

Format
➡ Lineweight...

Current lineweights are set in the **Lineweight Settings** dialog box, shown in Figure 4-18. The **Lineweight Settings** dialog box can be accessed by picking **Lineweight...** from the **Format** pull-down menu; typing LW, LWEIGHT, or LINEWEIGHT at the Command: prompt; or right-clicking on the **LWT** button on the status bar and then selecting **Settings...** from the shortcut menu. The following describes the features of the **Lineweight Settings** dialog box:

- **Lineweights.** Set the current lineweight by selecting the desired setting from the list. If lineweight is set to ByLayer, the object lineweight corresponds to the lineweight of its layer. The Default option lineweight width is controlled by the Default list options. Settings other than ByLayer, ByBlock, or Default are used as overrides for lineweights of objects drawn with the selected option.
- **Units for Listing.** This area allows you to set the lineweight thickness to **Millimeters (mm)** or **Inches (in)**.
- **Display Lineweight.** This is another way to turn lineweight thickness on or off. Check this box to turn lineweight on.
- **Default.** Select a lineweight default value from the drop-down list. This becomes the default lineweight for layers. The initial default setting is 0.010" or 0.25 mm. This is also controlled by the **LWDEFAULT** system variable.
- **Adjust Display Scale.** This scale allows you to adjust the lineweight display scale to improve the appearance of different lineweight widths. Adjustment of the lineweight display scale toward the **Max** value can reduce AutoCAD performance. A setting near the middle of the scale or toward **Min** may be preferred.
- **Current Lineweight.** This indicates the current lineweight setting.

NOTE

An object's individual properties, such as color, linetype, and lineweight, can be assigned "by layer" or "by object." It is important to note that assigning properties "by object" overrides any assignments made "by layer." For example, if a line's color property is ByLayer, the line obtains its color from the color of the layer on which it is drawn. If that same line's color is changed "by object" to a green color, however, the line is green regardless of the layer color. This is also true for linetype and lineweight.

Figure 4-18.
The **Lineweight Settings** dialog box.

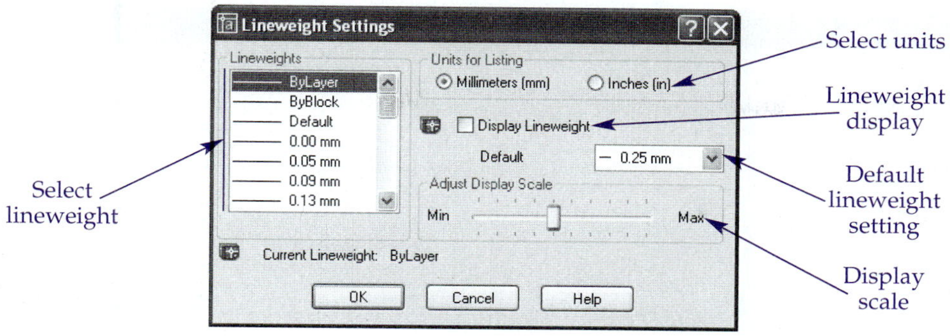

EXERCISE 4-5 Complete the Exercise on the Student CD.

Layer States

Layer settings, such as on/off, frozen/thawed, plot/no plot, and locked/unlocked, determine whether or not a layer is displayed, plotted, and editable. The status of layer settings for all layers in the drawing can be saved as a named *layer state*. Once a layer state is saved, layer settings can be readjusted to meet your needs, giving you the ability to restore the previously saved layer state at anytime.

For example, a basic architectural drawing uses the layers shown in **Figure 4-19.** From this drawing file, three different drawings are plotted: a floor plan, a plumbing plan, and an electrical plan. The following chart shows the layer settings for each of the three drawings:

	Floor Plan	Plumbing Plan	Electrical Plan
0	Off	Off	Off
Dimension-Electrical	Frozen	Frozen	On/Thawed
Dimension-Floor Plan	On/Thawed	Frozen	Frozen
Dimension-Plumbing	Frozen	On/Thawed	Frozen
Electrical	Frozen	Frozen	On/Thawed
Floor Plan Notes	On/Thawed	Frozen	Frozen
Plumbing	Frozen	On/Thawed	Frozen
Title Block	On/Thawed	Locked	Locked
Walls	On/Thawed	Locked	Locked
Windows and Doors	On/Thawed	Frozen	Frozen

Each of the three groups of settings can be saved as an individual layer state. Once the layer state is created, the settings can be restored by simply restoring the layer state. This is easier than changing the settings for each layer individually.

To save a layer state, pick the **Layer States Manager** button from the **Layer Properties Manager** dialog box. The **Layer States Manager** dialog box appears as shown in **Figure 4-20.** In the **Layer settings to restore** area, place a check mark next to

Figure 4-19.
Layers for a basic architectural drawing.

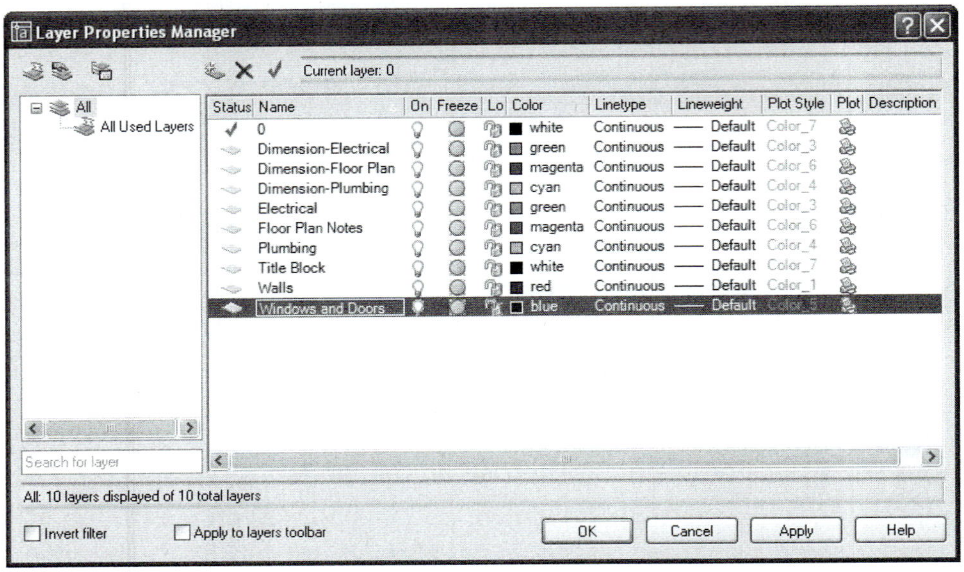

the layer properties you want to have saved with your layer state. To create a new layer state, pick the **New...** button. Type a name for the layer state in the **New layer state name:** field and enter a description (optional). Pick the **OK** button to save the new layer state. To restore a layer state, select the layer state in the **Layer States Manager** dialog box and pick the **Restore** button. The following buttons are available in the **Layer States Manager** dialog box:

- **New.** Opens the **New Layer State to Save** dialog box, in which a layer state can be saved.
- **Delete.** Deletes the selected layer state.
- **Import.** Accesses the **Import layer state** dialog box, where you can select an LAS file containing an existing layer state. Imported layer states are listed in the **Layer states** list in the **Layer State Manager**. Select the imported layer state and pick the **Restore** button to have the settings restored.

Figure 4-20.
The **Layer States Manager** allows you to save layer settings so they can be used later.

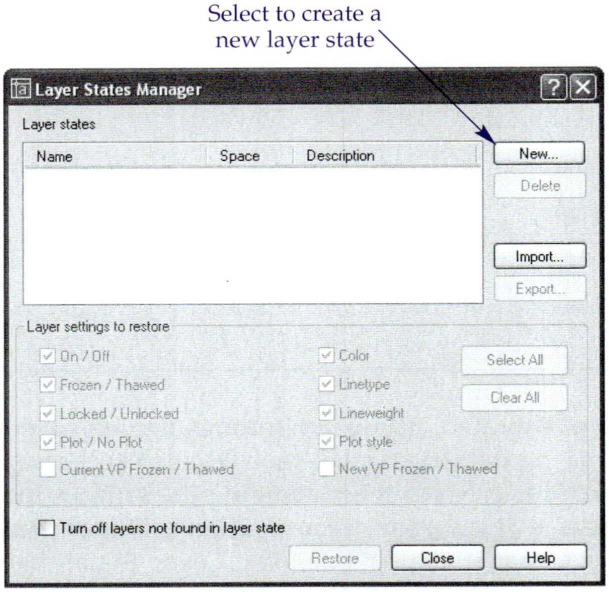

- **Export.** Saves the layer state as a LAS file and imports it into other drawings. This allows you to share layer states between drawings containing identical layers. Pick this button to access the **Export layer state** dialog box, where you can specify a name and location for the LAS file.
- **Restore.** Restores the layer settings saved in the selected layer state.

PROFESSIONAL TIP

If you have a drawing that does not contain layer names, importing a layer state file (.las) causes the layers from the layer state to be added to your drawing.

NOTE

The **Express** pull-down menu includes a **Layer Manager...** tool found in the **Layers** cascading menu. The **Layer Manager...** tool also creates layer states in a drawing, but it allows you to save these as LAY files. This utility is very similar to the **Layer States Manager** dialog box discussed previously. The **Layer Manager...** tool is primarily for pre–AutoCAD 2000 users, who would have used this older routine to create layer states.

Layer Filters

In some applications, large numbers of layer names may be used to assist in drawing information management. Having all layer names showing at the same time in the layer list can make it more difficult to work with your drawing layers. *Layer filters* are used to screen, or filter, out any layers you do not want displayed in the **Layer Properties Manager** dialog box. The filters tree view area in the **Layer Properties Manager** dialog box was created to make working with filters easier. The options are explained below:

- **Invert filter.** You can invert, or reverse, the layer filter setting. For example, there is a choice to show all used layers, but what if you want to show all unused layers? In this case, you would check the **Invert filter** toggle to invert, or reverse, your choice.
- **Apply to layers toolbar.** Check this toggle if you want only the layers matching the current filter displayed in the **Layers** toolbar. The **Layer Control** drop-down list tooltip shows when a filter is active.

The filters tree view area of the **Layer Properties Manager** dialog box is shown in **Figure 4-21.** The **All Used Layers** filter is a default filter created by AutoCAD. Selecting this filter hides all the layers that have no objects on them. To create a new filter, pick the **New Property Filter** button. This displays the **Layer Filter Properties** dialog box, **Figure 4-22.** Enter a name for the new filter in the **Filter name:** text box. The **Filter definition** area is where the parameters are defined to hide the unwanted layers from the **Layer Properties Manager** dialog box and the **Layer Control** drop-down list on the **Layers** toolbar. To create a definition, pick in any of the layer settings fields. Depending on the layer setting, the appropriate options become available. For most, there is a drop-down list from which to choose. Here are the filter definition options for each setting:

- **Status.** Use this filter to display the names of all layers, only used layers, or only nonused layers.
- **Name.** This is a text field in which you can type a layer name or a partial layer name using the * wildcard character. If you want to see all the layers that start with an *A*, type **a***.

Figure 4-21.
Layer filters can be created and restored from the filters tree view area of the **Layer Properties Manager** dialog box.

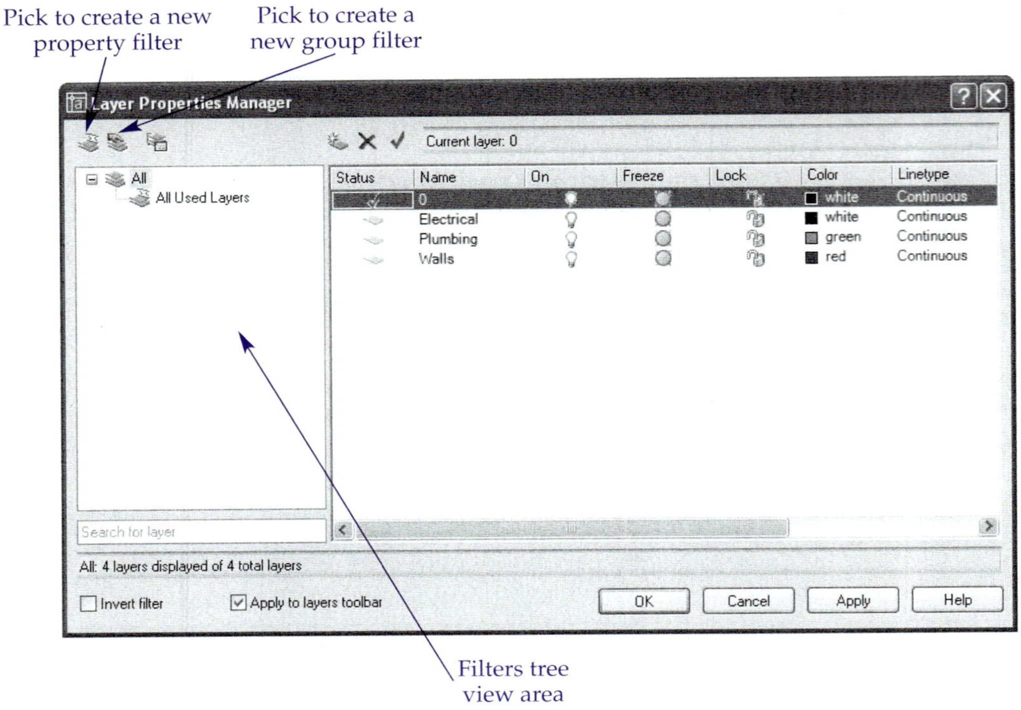

Figure 4-22.
New layer filters are created in the **Layer Filter Properties** dialog box.

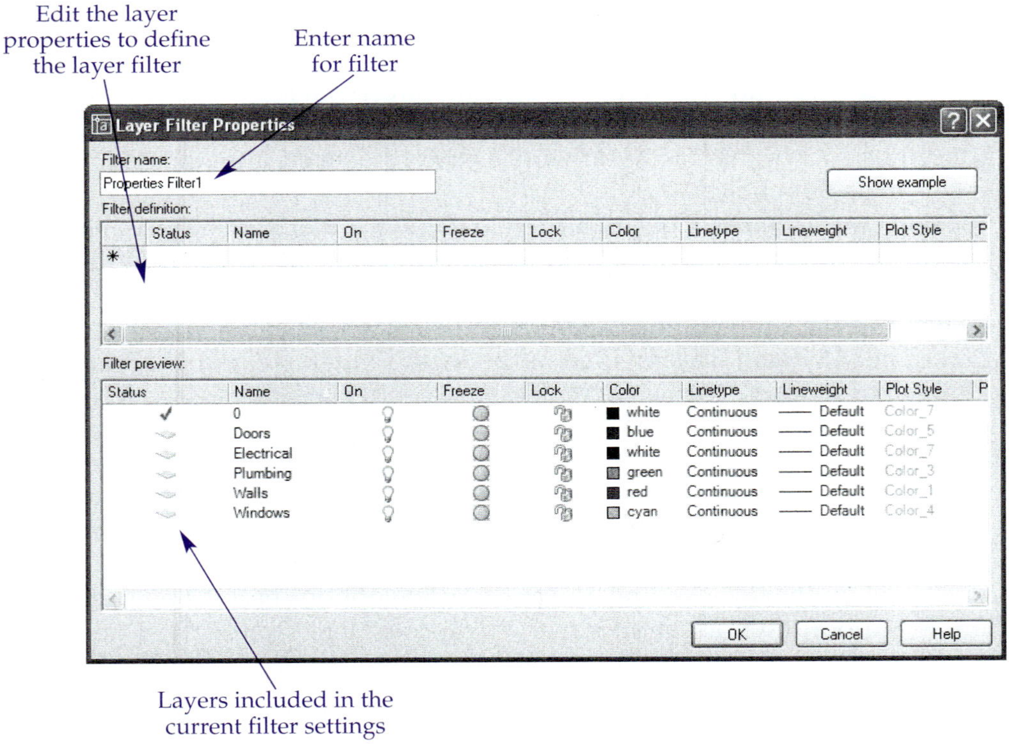

- **On.** Use this filter to display only the names of layers that are on or only those that are off.
- **Freeze.** Use this filter to display only frozen or only thawed layer names.
- **Lock.** Use this filter to display only locked or only unlocked layer names.
- **Color.** A color number or name can be typed, or the **...** button can be used to select a color from the **Select Color** dialog box.
- **Linetype.** A linetype name can be typed, or the **...** button can be used to select a linetype from the **Select Linetype** dialog box.
- **Lineweight.** A lineweight can be typed, or the **...** button can be used to select a lineweight from the **Lineweight** dialog box.
- **Plot Style.** Type a plot style name or select a plot style from the **Select Plot Style** dialog box by picking the **...** button. This option is only available if the current drawing is using named plot style tables.
- **Plot.** Use this filter to display the names of layers that plot or the names of layers that do not plot.
- **Current VP Freeze.** Use this filter to display only frozen or only thawed layer names. This option is only available in paper space.
- **New VP Freeze.** Use this filter to display only frozen or only thawed layer names. This option is only available in paper space.

Once a definition has been edited, another row is added to the **Filter definition:** area. This allows you to create simple to advanced filters. Figure 4-23 shows a filter named Walls and Electrical, where two rows are used to filter out all the layers except for Walls and Electrical. To save the filter, pick the **OK** button. The new filter now displays in the filter tree view area. To set it current, just select it once. The layers the filter defined are now displayed in the layer list area. To view all the layers again, pick the **All** filter at the top of the filter tree view area.

Another type of filter that can be created is a group filter. Layers can be added to a group filter, but the individual settings of the layers cannot be defined, as in a property filter. To add a group filter, select the **New Group Filter** button above the filter tree view area. A new group filter is created in the filter tree view area, and a name can be typed. To add a layer to a group filter, select a layer in the layer list, and then drag and drop it onto the group filter name. You can also add layers to a group filter by

Figure 4-23.
Multiple rows in the **Filter definition:** area can be used to create a filter.

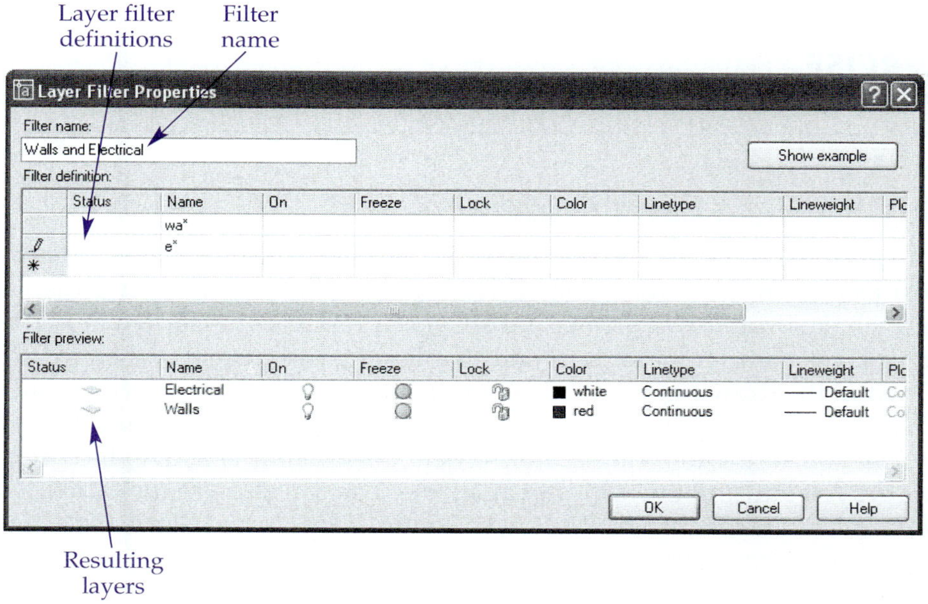

selecting the group filter and then right-clicking. From the shortcut menu, choose **Select Layers**. Select **Add** from the **Select Layers** cascading menu. The **Layer Properties Manager** temporarily hides, allowing you to select objects on the layers you wish to add to the group filter. After the objects are selected, right-click or press the [Enter] key to add the layers to the group filter.

Other options associated with filters are only accessible from the shortcut menu. To display the shortcut menu, right-click in the filters tree view area. The shortcut menu is displayed in **Figure 4-24.** Most of the options in the shortcut menu are the same for the filter types, but there are some options that are only available for a certain filter. Here is an explanation for the shortcut menu options:

- **Visibility.** Allows you to change the **On/Off** and **Thawed/Frozen** states of all the layers associated with the filter.
- **Lock.** Locks or unlocks all the layers.
- **Viewport.** Allows you to freeze or thaw all the layers in the current paper space viewport.
- **Isolate Group.** Turns off all the layers in the drawing that are filtered out by the filter. It can be applied to all the viewports or just the current one.
- **New Properties Filter.** Opens the **Layer Filter Properties** dialog box so a new layer filter can be created.
- **New Group Filter.** Creates a new group filter.
- **Convert to Group Filter.** Converts a property filter to a group filter.
- **Rename.** Allows you to rename the selected filter.
- **Delete.** Deletes the selected filter.
- **Properties.** Allows you to edit a property filter.
- **Select Layers.** Gives the options to **Add** or **Replace** layers to an existing group filter.

Figure 4-24.
The filter tree view shortcut menu displays options for the selected filter type.

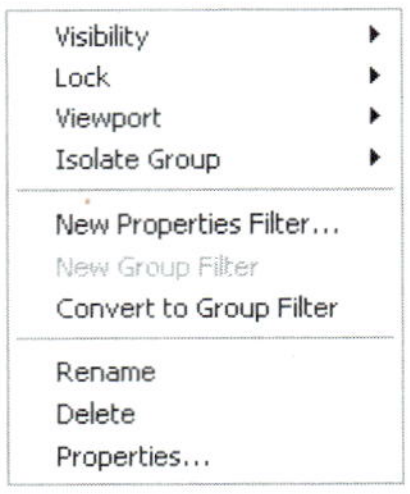

EXERCISE 4-6 Complete the Exercise on the Student CD.

Quickly Setting a Layer Current

You can quickly make another layer current by using the **Layer Control** drop-down list located in the **Layers** toolbar. The name of the current layer is displayed in the box. Pick the drop-down arrow, and a layer list appears, as shown in **Figure 4-25.**

Pick a layer name from the list, and that layer is set current. When many layers are defined in the drawing, the vertical scroll bar can be used to move up and down through the list. Selecting a layer name to set as current automatically closes the list and returns you to the drawing editor. When a command is active, the drop-down button is grayed out, and the list is not available. You can also use the **CLAYER** system variable to make a layer current. The **Layer Control** drop-down list has the same status icons as the **Layer Properties Manager** dialog box. By picking an icon, you can change the state of the layer.

Figure 4-25.
The **Layer Control** drop-down list is located on the left side of the **Layers** toolbar. All layers are listed with icons representing their state and color. Pick on a layer name to make it current.

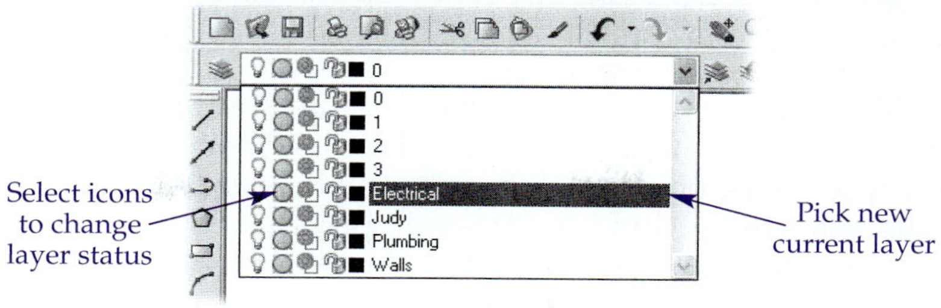

> **PROFESSIONAL TIP**
>
> Layers are meant to simplify the drafting process. They separate different details of the drawing and can reduce the complexity of what is displayed. If you set color and linetype by layer, do not reset and mix entity linetypes and color on the same layer. Doing so can mislead you and your colleagues when trying to find certain details. Always maintain accurate records of your template drawings.

Making the Layer of an Existing Object Current

Layers toolbar
Make Object's Layer Current

Another quick way to set the current layer is to use the **Make Object's Layer Current** button in the **Layers** toolbar. When you pick this button, AutoCAD asks you to select an object on the layer you want to make current:

Command: _ai_molc
Select object whose layer will become current: *(pick an object to make its layer current)*
X is now the current layer.
Command:

Restoring the Previous Layer Settings

LAYERP
Layers toolbar
Layer Previous

After changing layer properties, you can restore the previous layer settings by picking the **Layer Previous** button in the **Layers** toolbar or typing LAYERP at the Command: prompt. Once the command has been executed, the Command: prompt displays a message stating if the command was successful or if it failed:

Command: **LAYERP**↵
Restored previous layer status.
Command:

The **Layer Previous** command only affects layer operations. Therefore, after using commands to draw, modify, and zoom, you can use the **Layer Previous** command to restore the last layer state without affecting any other functions. The following layer properties are restored by the **Layer Previous** command:

- On/Off.
- Freeze/Thaw.
- Lock/Unlock.
- Color.
- Linetype.
- Lineweight.
- Plot style (if using named plot styles).
- Freeze/Thaw in current viewport.

Layer Previous does not affect layer name changes, recreate layers that have been purged, or delete layers that have been added.

Changing Object Properties

You should always draw objects on an appropriate layer, but layer settings are not permanent. You can change an object's layer if needed. You can also change other properties of the object, such as color and linetype. Using the **Properties** toolbar or the **Properties** window modifies these properties.

PROPERTIES
PROPS
CH
MO

Modify
➥ Properties

Standard toolbar

Properties

To modify properties using the **Properties** toolbar, select the object, and then use the drop-down lists in the appropriate control boxes to change the properties. After you have changed the properties, press [Esc] to deselect the object. To modify an object's properties using the **Properties** window, pick the **Properties** button in the **Standard** toolbar; select **Properties** from the **Modify** pull-down menu; or type PROPS, CH, MO, or PROPERTIES at the Command: prompt. If an object has been selected, you can right-click on it and pick **Properties** from the shortcut menu. When you use one of these options, AutoCAD displays the **Properties** window, shown in **Figure 4-26.** You can also double-click on many objects to automatically select the object and open the **Properties** window.

The properties of the selected object are listed in the **Properties** window. The specific properties listed vary, depending on the type of object selected. Properties such as layer, linetype, and color are listed in the **General** category.

To modify a particular object property, first find the property in the **Properties** window, and then select its value. Depending on the type of value, a specific editing method is activated. Use this tool to change the value. For example, if you want to change an object's layer, pick **Layer** to highlight it, as in **Figure 4-26.** A drop-down arrow is displayed to the right of the layer name. Pick the arrow to access the **Layer** drop-down list. Pick the layer name you want to use for the selected object's layer. You can use this same process to change the color, linetype, or lineweight of a selected object.

You can work in AutoCAD with the **Properties** window open and available for use. By picking and holding on the title bar while you move the mouse, you can move the **Properties** window. If you want to close the **Properties** window, select the **X** in the upper-left corner.

> **NOTE**
>
> Modifying object properties using the **Properties** window is covered in greater depth in Chapter 13.

Figure 4-26.
The **Properties** window is used to modify the properties of the selected object.

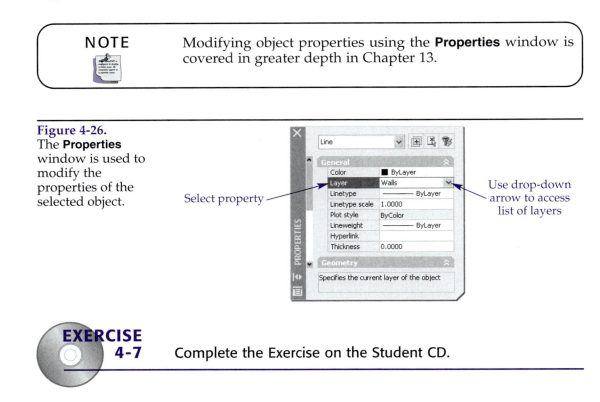

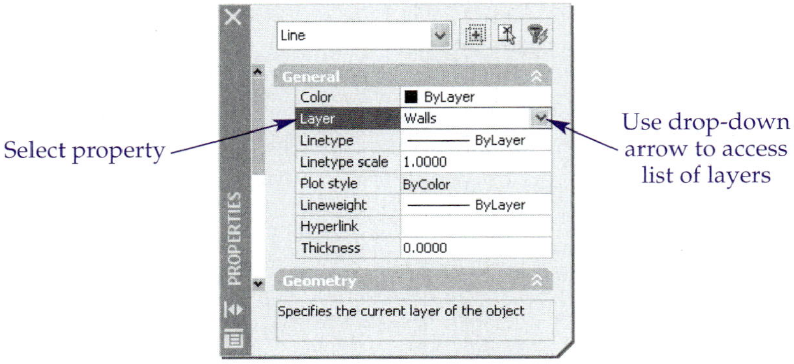

EXERCISE 4-7 Complete the Exercise on the Student CD.

Overriding Layer Settings

Color, linetype, and lineweight settings reference layer settings by default. This means when you create a layer, you also establish a color, linetype, and lineweight to go with the layer. This is what it means when the color, linetype, and lineweight are specified as ByLayer. This is the most common method for managing these settings. Sometimes, however, you may need objects to reference a specific layer, but have specific color, linetype, or lineweight properties different than the layer settings. In such a situation, the color, linetype, and lineweight can be set to an *absolute* value, and current layer settings are ignored. The term ***absolute***, as used here and in future content, refers to an object being assigned specific properties that are not reliant on a layer or block for their definitions.

EXERCISE 4-8 Complete the Exercise on the Student CD.

Setting Color

The current object color can be easily set by selecting the **Color Control** drop-down list from the **Properties** toolbar. See **Figure 4-27.** The default setting is ByLayer. This is the recommended setting for most applications. To change this setting, pick another color from the list. If the color you want is not on the list, you can pick the item at the bottom of the list, labeled **Select Color...**, to display the **Select Color** dialog box, or you can type COL or COLOR at the Command: prompt. Once an absolute color is specified, all new objects are drawn in the specified color, regardless of the current layer settings. Another way to set the current object color is by using the **CECOLOR** system variable. **CECOLOR** stands for *current entity color*. This variable is set as follows:

Command: **CECOLOR**↵
Enter new value for CECOLOR <"BYLAYER">: *(enter new color value)*
Command:

Setting Lineweight

Similar to the current object color, you can set the current object lineweight to differ from the layer settings. To set the current object lineweight, pick the **Lineweight Control** drop-down list from the **Properties** toolbar and select the desired linetype. See **Figure 4-28.** You can also directly adjust the system variable controlling the current object linetype. This variable is called **CELWEIGHT**. Set the **CELWEIGHT** system variable in a similar manner as you set the **CECOLOR** system variable. If ByLayer is desired, you must enter –1.

Figure 4-27. The current object color is easily set by opening the **Color Control** drop-down list in the **Properties** toolbar. This control box is also used to change the color of selected objects.

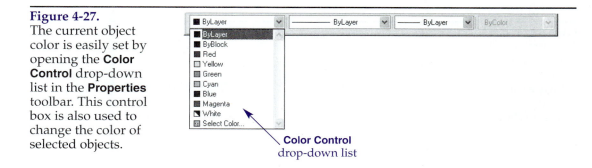

Figure 4-28.
The current object lineweight is easily set by opening the **Lineweight Control** drop-down list in the **Properties** toolbar.

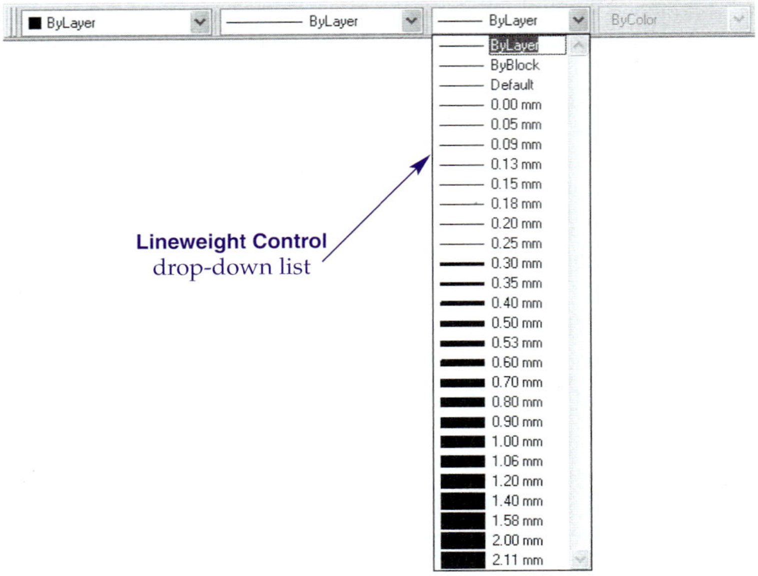

Setting Linetype

Similar to the current object lineweight, you can set the current object linetype to be separate from any layer settings. To set the current object linetype, pick the **Linetype Control** drop-down list from the **Properties** toolbar and select the desired linetype. See **Figure 4-29.** If the linetype you want has not been loaded into the current drawing yet, it will not appear in the listing. You can select **Other...** from the list to load the **Linetype Manager** so new linetypes can be loaded.

You can also directly adjust the system variable controlling the current object linetype. This variable is called **CELTYPE**, for *current entity linetype*. Set the **CELTYPE** system variable in the same manner as you set the **CECOLOR** and **CELWEIGHT** system variables.

NOTE

Colors, linetypes, and lineweights are often set as ByLayer. ByLayer is known as a logical color, while red, for instance, is known as an explicit color. If an object uses ByLayer as its color, its color is displayed as the color assigned to the layer on which the object resides. Explicit properties, however, override logical properties. Therefore, if an object's color is set explicitly to red, it will appear red regardless of the layer on which it resides. Change its color to ByLayer, and it will use the layer color. It is a common AutoCAD mistake for users to set **CECOLOR**, **CELTYPE**, or **CELWEIGHT** to some value other than ByLayer and then wonder why new objects do not use the color of the current layer!

Figure 4-29.
The current object linetype is easily set by opening the **Linetype Control** drop-down list in the **Properties** toolbar.

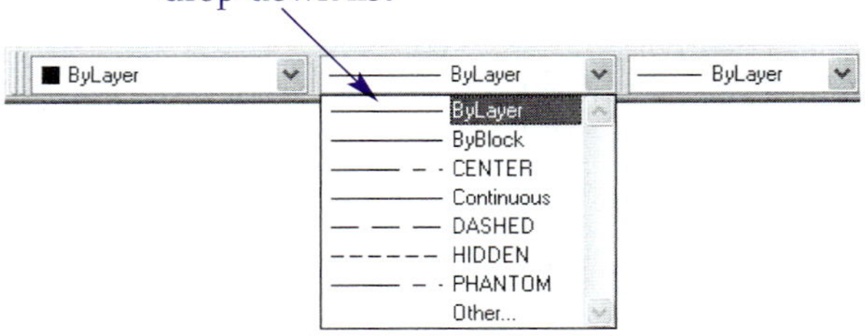

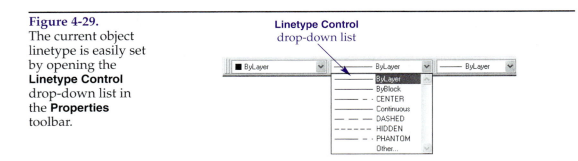

Setting the linetype scale

The linetype scale sets the lengths of dashes and spaces in linetypes. When you start AutoCAD with a wizard or template, the global linetype scale is automatically set to match the units you select. The global linetype scale can, however, be overridden at the object level. A ***global change*** is a change affecting all linetypes in the current drawing.

The default object linetype scale factor is 1.0000. As with layers, the linetype scale can be changed at the object level. One reason for changing the default linetype scale is to make your drawing more closely match standard drafting practices.

Earlier, you were introduced to the **Properties** window. When a line object is selected to modify, a **Linetype scale** property is listed. You can change the linetype scale of the object by entering a new value in this field. A value less than 1.0 makes the dashes and spaces smaller than those in the global setting, while a value greater than 1.0 makes the dashes and spaces larger than those in the global setting. Using this information, you can experiment with different linetype scales until you achieve your desired results. Be careful when changing linetype scales to avoid making your drawing look odd, with a variety of line formats. **Figure 4-30** shows a diagram comparing different linetype scale factors.

Figure 4-30.
Drawing the same linetype at different linetype scales.

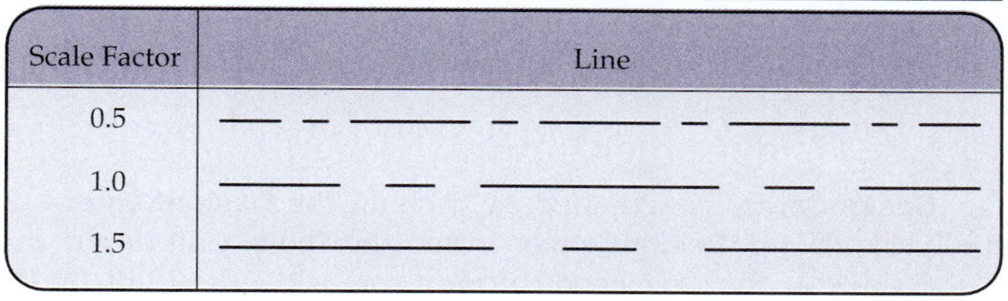

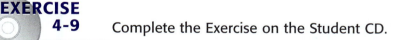

Changing the global linetype scale

The **LTSCALE** variable can be used to make a global change to the linetype scale. The default global linetype scale factor is 1.0000. Any line with dashes initially assumes this factor.

To change the linetype scale for the entire drawing, type **LTSCALE** at the Command: prompt. The current value is listed. Enter the new value and press [Enter]. A Regenerating model. message appears, as the global linetype scale is changed for all lines on the drawing.

EXERCISE 4-9 Complete the Exercise on the Student CD.

Reusing Drawing Content

In nearly every drafting discipline, individual drawings created as part of a given project are likely to share a number of common elements. All the drawings within a specific drafting project generally have the same set of standards. Drawing features, such as the text size and font used for annotation, standardized dimensioning methods and appearances, layer names and properties, drafting symbols, drawing layouts, and even typical drawing details, are often duplicated in many different drawings. These and other components of CAD drawings are referred to as ***drawing content***. One of the most fundamental advantages of CAD systems is the ease with which content can be shared between drawings. Once a commonly used drawing feature has been defined, it can be used again as needed, in any number of drawing applications.

The creation and use of drawing template files was covered in Chapters 2 and 3. Drawing templates represents one way to reuse drawing content that has already been defined. Creating your own customized drawing template files provides an effective way to start each new drawing using standard settings.

Drawing templates, however, provides only a starting point. During the course of a drawing project, you may need to add content to the current drawing that has been defined previously in another drawing. Some drawing projects may require you to revise an existing drawing rather than start a completely new drawing. For other projects, you may need to duplicate the standards used in a drawing a client has supplied.

AutoCAD provides a powerful drawing content manager called **DesignCenter**. **DesignCenter** allows you to reuse drawing content that has already been defined in previous drawings by using a drag-and-drop operation. **DesignCenter** was introduced in Chapter 1.

DesignCenter is used to manage several categories of drawing content, including blocks, dimension styles, layers, layouts, linetypes, text styles, and externally referenced drawings. Layers and linetypes are discussed in this chapter, but the other content types are introduced in the chapters where they apply. The following discussion details the features of **DesignCenter** and shows how layer and linetype content found in existing drawings can be reused in other drawing projects.

ADCENTER
ADC
[Ctrl]+[2]

Tools
➥ **DesignCenter**

Standard toolbar
DesignCenter

Using DesignCenter to Copy Layers and Linetypes

DesignCenter is activated by picking the **DesignCenter** button on the **Standard** toolbar, picking **DesignCenter** from the **Tools** pull-down menu, typing ADC or ADCENTER at the Command: prompt, or using the [Ctrl]+[2] key combination. This displays **DesignCenter**. See **Figure 4-31.**

Figure 4-31.
DesignCenter is used to copy content from one drawing to another.

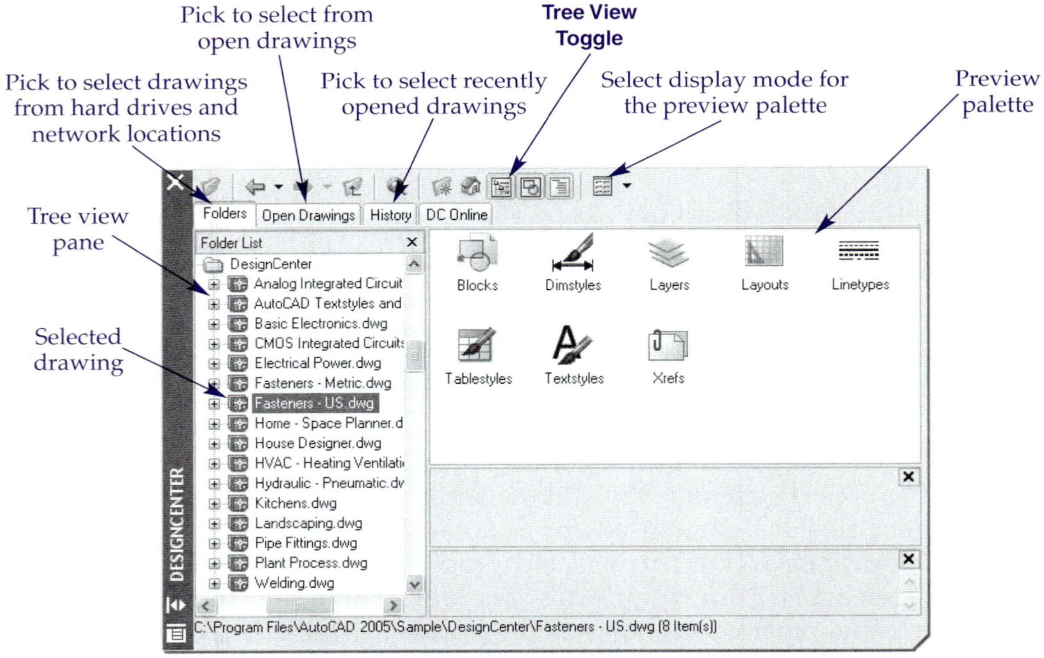

It is not necessary to open a drawing in AutoCAD in order to view or access its content. **DesignCenter** allows you to directly load content from any accessible drawing. You can also use **DesignCenter** to browse through existing drawing files and view their contents, or you can use its advanced search tools to look for specific drawing content.

DesignCenter allows you to easily share content between drawings currently open in AutoCAD. To copy content, first select the drawing from which the content is to be copied. The drawing is selected from the tree view pane. If the tree view is not already visible, toggle it on by picking the **Tree View Toggle** button in the **DesignCenter** toolbar. The first three tabs on the **DesignCenter** toolbar control the tree view display:

- **Folders.** Pick this tab to display the folders and files found on the hard drive and network.
- **Open Drawings.** Pick this tab to list only the currently opened drawings.
- **History.** Pick this tab to list recently opened drawings.

Pick the plus sign (+) next to a drawing icon to view the content categories for the drawing. Each category of drawing content is listed with a representative icon. Pick the Layers icon to load the palette with the layer content found in the selected drawing. The preview palette now displays all the available layer content. See **Figure 4-32.**

To select layers from the palette, use standard Windows selection methods. The [Shift] and [Ctrl] keys are used for selecting multiple items. In this example, the drawing is selected first, and the **Layers** content is picked. The preview palette displays the available content. Select the desired layers and use one of the following options to import them into the current drawing:

- **Drag and drop.** Move the cursor over the top of the desired icon in the preview palette. Press and hold down the pick button on your pointing device. Drag the cursor to the opened drawing. See **Figure 4-33.** Release the pick button, and the selected content is added to your current drawing file.
- **Add from shortcut menu.** Select the desired icon(s) in the preview palette and right-click to open the shortcut menu. Pick the **Add Layer(s)** option, and the selected content is added to your current drawing.
- **Copy from shortcut menu.** This option is identical to the **Add Layer(s)** option, except you select **Copy** from the shortcut menu instead of **Add Layer(s)**. Now, move the cursor to the drawing where you want the content added and right-click to open the shortcut menu. Select **Paste**, and the selected contents are added to the current drawing.

Figure 4-32.
Displaying the layers found in a drawing using **DesignCenter**.

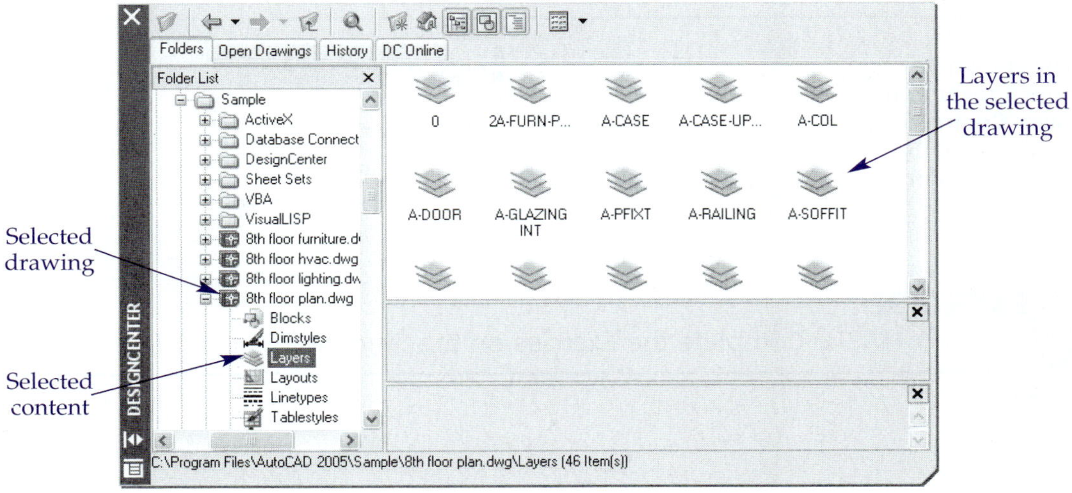

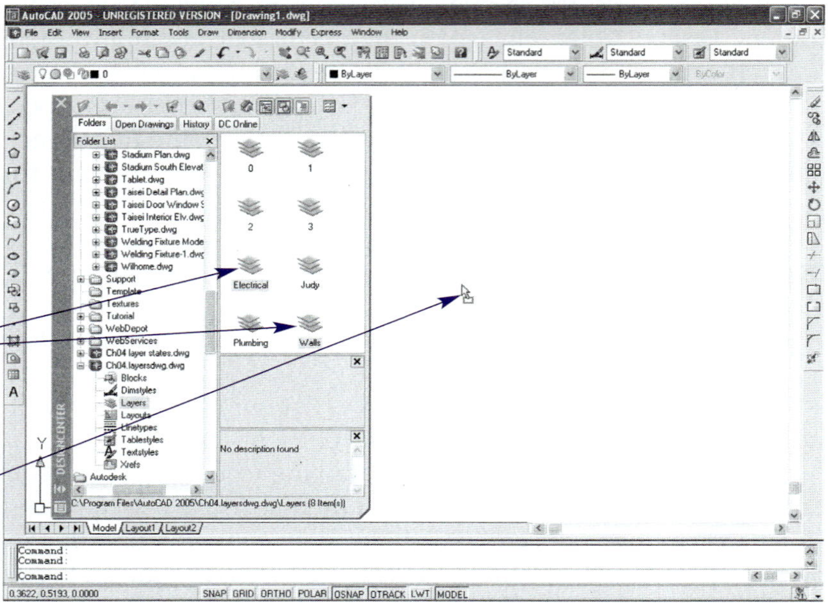

Figure 4-33.
To copy layers shown in **DesignCenter** into the current drawing, first select the layers to be copied, and then drag and drop them into the drawing area of the current drawing.

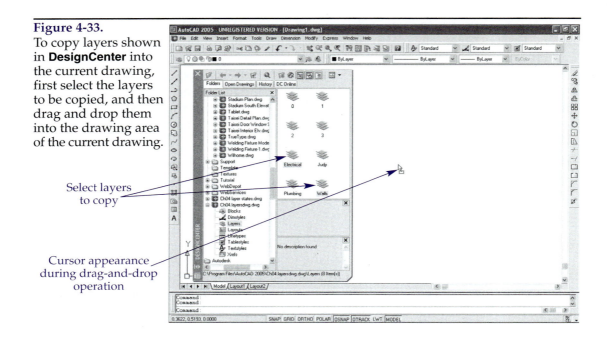

To select more than one icon at one time, hold down the [Shift] key and pick the first and last icons in a group. You can also hold down the [Ctrl] key to select multiple icons individually. The copied layers are now available in the active drawing. See **Figure 4-34.** If the name of a layer being loaded already exists in the destination drawing, that layer name and its settings are ignored. The existing settings for the layer are preserved, and a message is displayed at the command line indicating the duplicate settings were ignored.

Linetypes can be copied using the same procedure. In the tree view, select the drawing containing the linetypes to be copied. Select **Linetypes** to display the linetypes in the preview palette. See **Figure 4-35.** Select the linetypes to be copied, and then use drag and drop or the shortcut menu to add the linetypes to the current drawing.

NOTE

DesignCenter is a very powerful tool. Specific applications of **DesignCenter** are provided throughout this text.

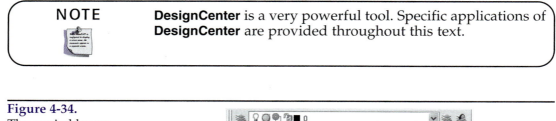

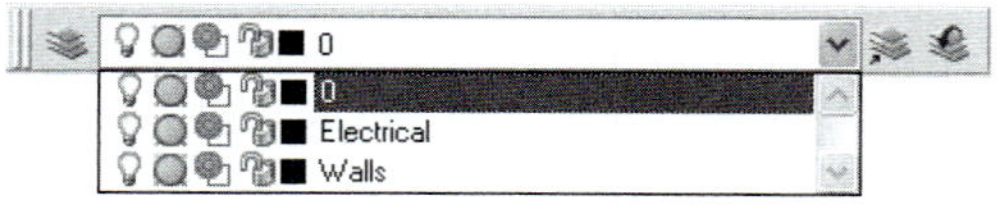

Figure 4-34.
The copied layers now appear in the **Layer Control** drop-down list of the current drawing.

EXERCISE 4-10

Complete the Exercise on the Student CD.

Figure 4-35.
Linetypes can also be displayed in the preview palette.

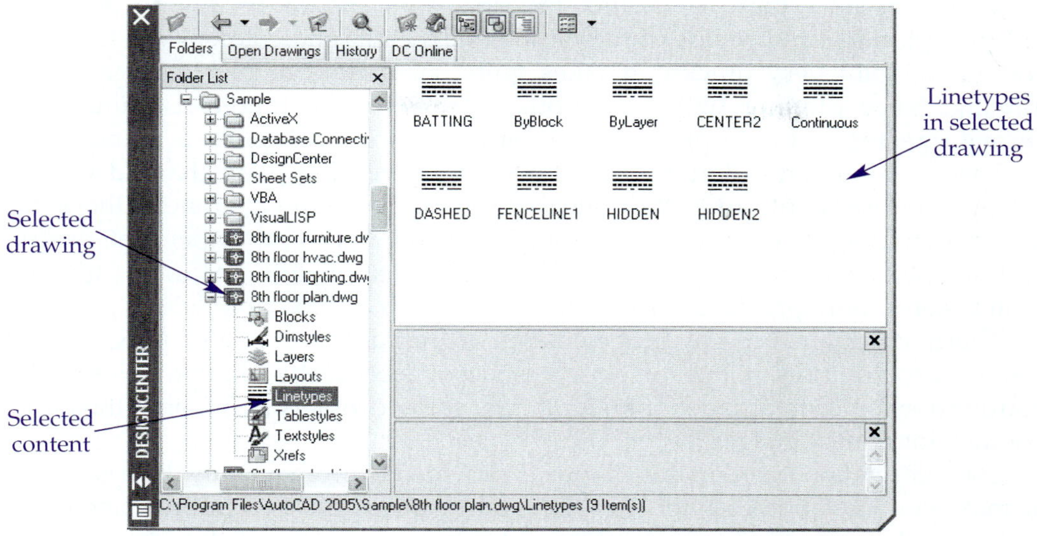

EXPRESS TOOLS CHAPTER 4

The following Express Tools are related to topics discussed in this chapter. Refer to the Student CD for information on these tools:

Change to Current Layer	**Copy Objects to New Layer**	**Isolate Layer in Current Viewport**
Layer Delete	**Layer Freeze**	**Layer Isolate**
Layer Manager	**Layer Match**	**Layer Merge**
Layer Off	**Layer Lock**	**Layer Unlock**
Layer Walk	**Thaw All Layers**	**Turn All Layers On**

Introduction to Printing and Plotting

A drawing created with CAD can exist in two distinct forms: hard copy and soft copy. The term ***hard copy*** refers to a physical drawing a printer or plotter produces on paper. The term ***soft copy*** refers to the computer software version of the drawing, or the actual data file. The soft copy can only be displayed on the computer monitor, making it inconvenient to use for many manufacturing and construction purposes. If the power to the computer is turned off, the soft copy drawing is not available.

A hard copy drawing is extremely versatile. It can be rolled up or folded and taken down to the shop floor or out to a construction site. A hard copy drawing can be checked and redlined without a computer or CAD software. Although CAD is the standard throughout the world for generating drawings, the hard copy drawing is still a vital tool in industry.

AutoCAD supports two types of hard copy devices—printers and plotters. Printers and plotters take the soft copy images you draw in AutoCAD and transfer them onto paper. There are several types of ***printers***, including dot matrix, ink-jet, laser, and thermal transfer. Dot matrix printers are normally used to make low-quality check prints, while the better quality ink-jet, laser, and thermal printers may be used for quick check prints of formal drawings. Print size for most of these printers is 8.5″ × 11″ or 8.5″ × 14″.

Large format hard copy devices are commonly referred to as ***plotters***. These include ink-jet, thermal, electrostatic, pen, and pencil plotters. Plotters are capable of producing a hard copy with varying line widths and color output. Pen plotters have been the industry standard for preparing large format hard copies. They are called *pen plotters* because they use liquid ink, fiber tip pens, or pens with pencil lead. Multipen plotters can provide different line thicknesses and colors. Even though pen plotters can plot very quickly, it takes quite some time to plot a large, complex drawing. Since plotting with pen plotters can often be time-consuming, ink-jet, thermal transfer, and laser plotters are rapidly replacing pen plotters in industry.

Laser printers and plotters draw lines on a revolving plate charged with high voltage. The laser light causes the plate to discharge, while an ink toner adheres to the laser-drawn image. Pressure or heat then bonds the ink to the paper. The quality of the laser printer or plotter depends on the number of dots per inch (dpi). Laser printers commonly produce hard copies that are 600 or 1200 dpi.

Thermal printers use tiny heat elements to burn dots into treated paper. The electrostatic process uses a line of closely spaced, electrically charged, wire nibs to produce dots on coated paper. Ink-jet plotters spray droplets of ink onto the paper to produce dot matrix images.

PLOT
[Ctrl]+[P]

File
➥ **Plot...**

Standard toolbar

Plot

The information found in this chapter is provided to give you only the basics, so you can make your first plot. Chapter 11 explores the detailed aspects of printing and plotting. Prints and plots are made using the **Plot** dialog box. Access this dialog box by selecting **Plot...** from the **File** pull-down menu, picking the **Plot** button in the **Standard** toolbar, pressing the [Ctrl]+[P] key combination, or typing PLOT at the Command: prompt. You can also right-click on a **Model** or **Layout** tab and select **Plot...** from the shortcut menu.

The first step in making an AutoCAD drawing is to create a model. The ***model*** is composed of various objects, such as lines, circles, and text. The model is created by drawing in the **Model** tab at the bottom of the drawing area. See **Figure 4-36.** The model is created in an environment called ***model space***.

Once the model is completed, a layout can be created. A ***layout*** can contain various views of the model, a title block, and other annotations. In addition, the layout includes page setup information (such as paper size and margins) and plotter configuration data (information related to the specific model of printer or plotter being used). Layouts are created using the **Layout** tabs at the bottom of the drawing area. They are created in an environment called ***paper space***, and a single drawing can have multiple layouts.

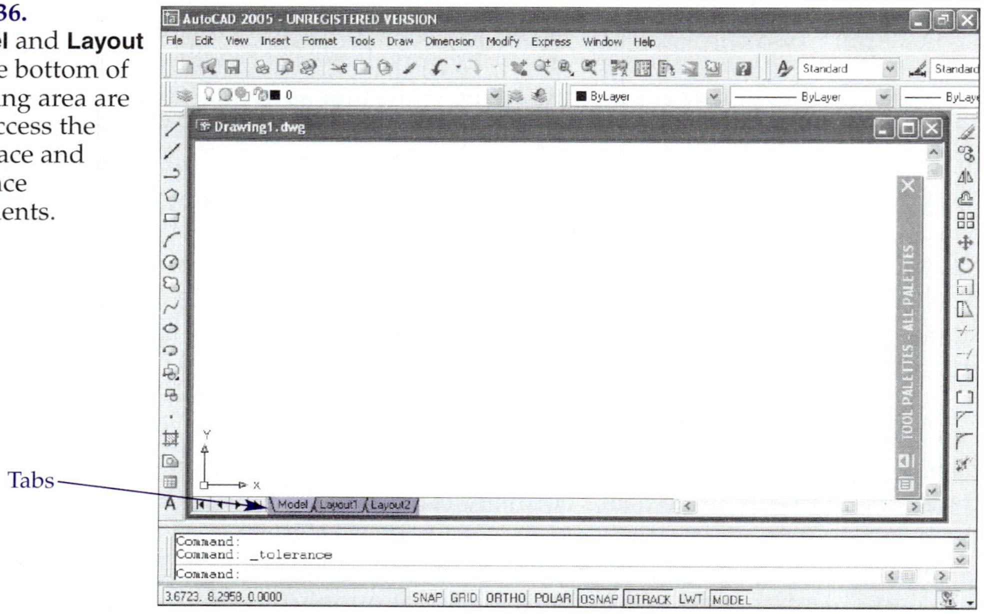

Figure 4-36.
The **Model** and **Layout** tabs at the bottom of the drawing area are used to access the model space and paper space environments.

Drawings can be plotted from the **Model** tab of the drawing area or from one of the **Layout** tabs. The following discussion will address plotting from the **Model** tab only. Creating and plotting layouts is addressed in Chapter 11.

In the **Plot** dialog box, there is a **More Options** button that extends the dialog box to show other available settings. The **Plot** dialog box is shown in Figure 4-37A in its default state. Figure 4-37B shows it with the **More Options** button activated.

Figure 4-37.
A—The **Plot** dialog box. B—The **Plot** dialog box with **More Options** selected.

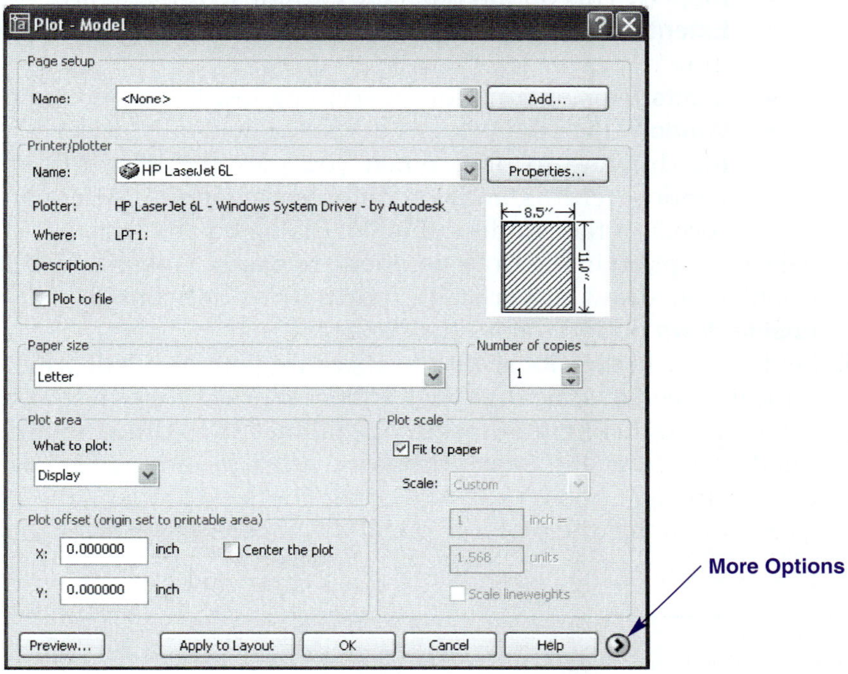

A

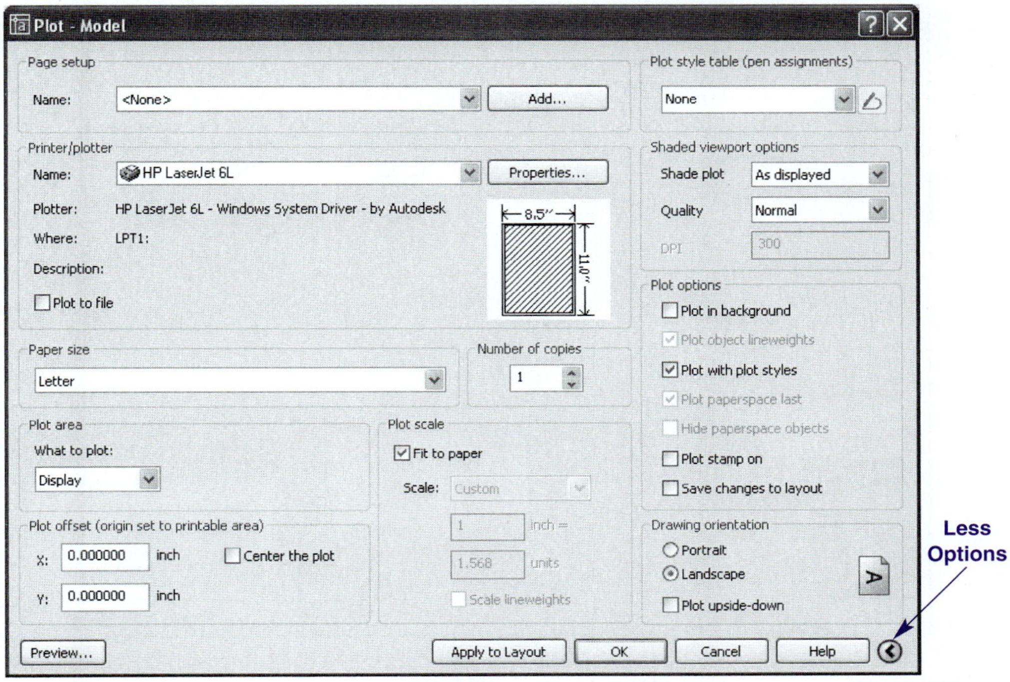

B

Making a Plot

There are many plotting options available. In this section, one method of creating a plot from the **Model** tab is discussed. Refer to **Figure 4-38** as you read through the following plotting procedure:

1. Access the **Plot** dialog box.
2. Check the plot device and paper size specifications in the **Printer/plotter** and **Paper size** areas.
3. Select what is to be plotted in the **Plot area** section. The following options are available:
   - **Display.** This option plots the current screen display.
   - **Extents.** This option plots only the area of the drawing where objects are drawn.
   - **Limits.** This option plots everything inside the defined drawing limits.
   - **Window.** Pick the **Window** option to manually select a rectangular area of the drawing to plot. When you pick the **Window** button, the drawing window returns, and you can select a window. After you select the second corner of the window, the **Plot** dialog box returns.
4. Select an option in the **Drawing orientation** area. Choose **Portrait** or **Landscape** to orient your drawing vertically (portrait) or horizontally (landscape). The **Plot upside-down** option rotates the paper 180°.
5. Set the scale in the **Plot scale** area. Because you draw full-scale in AutoCAD, you typically need to scale drawings either up or down to fit the paper. Scale is measured as a ratio of either inches or millimeters to drawing units. Select a predefined scale from the **Scale:** drop-down list or enter your own values into the custom fields. Choose the **Fit to paper** check box to let AutoCAD automatically shrink or stretch the plot area to fill the paper.

Figure 4-38.
The **Plot** dialog box.

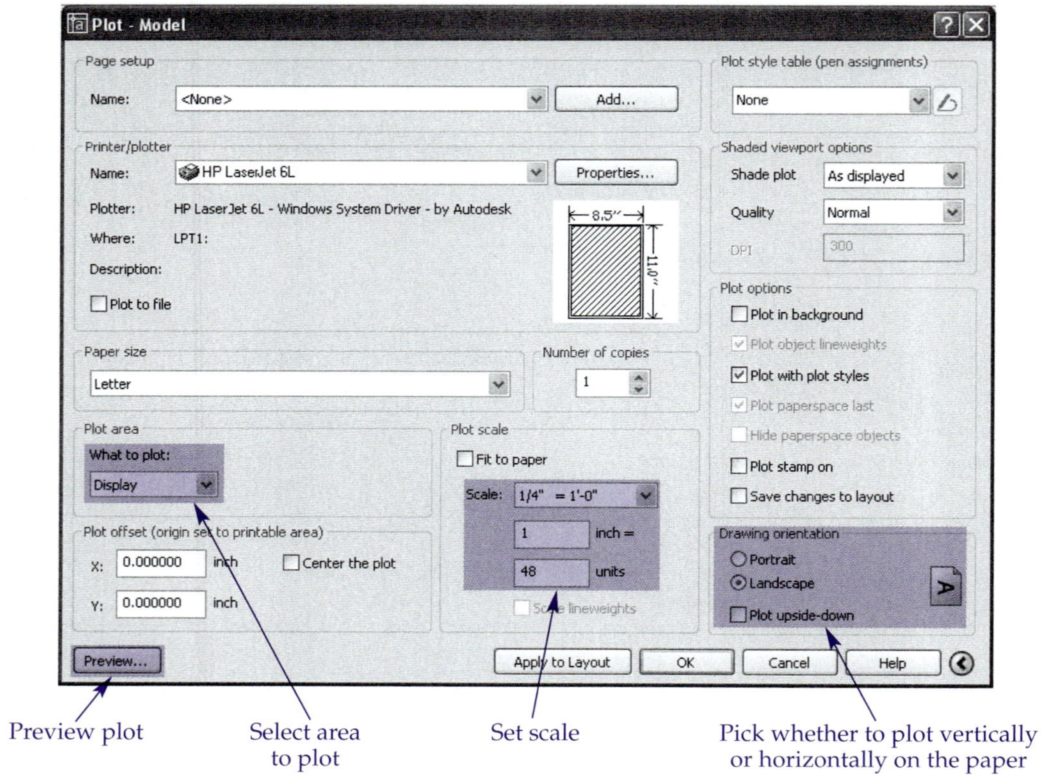

6. If desired, use the **Plot offset (origin set to printable area)** area to set additional left and bottom margins around the plot or to center the plot.
7. Preview the plot. Pick the **Preview...** button to display the sheet as it will look when it is plotted. See **Figure 4-39.** The cursor appears as a magnifying glass with + and – symbols. The plot preview image zooms if you hold the left mouse button and move the cursor. Press [Esc] to exit the preview.
8. Pick the **OK** button in the **Plot** dialog box to send the data to the plotting device.

Before you pick the **OK** button to send your drawing to the plotter, there are several items you should check:

- ✓ The printer or plotter is plugged in.
- ✓ The cable from your computer to printer or plotter is secure.
- ✓ The printer has paper.
- ✓ Paper is properly loaded in the plotter, and grips or clamps are in place.
- ✓ Ink cartridges or plotter pens are inserted correctly.
- ✓ The plotter area is clear for paper movement.

PROFESSIONAL TIP

You can stop a plot in progress at any time by using the [Esc] key. Keep in mind that it may take a while for some plotters or printers to terminate the plot, depending on the amount of the drawing file that has already been sent. Turning the plotter off purges all plot data from the plotter's internal buffer.

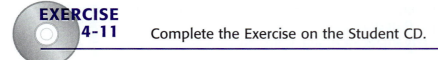

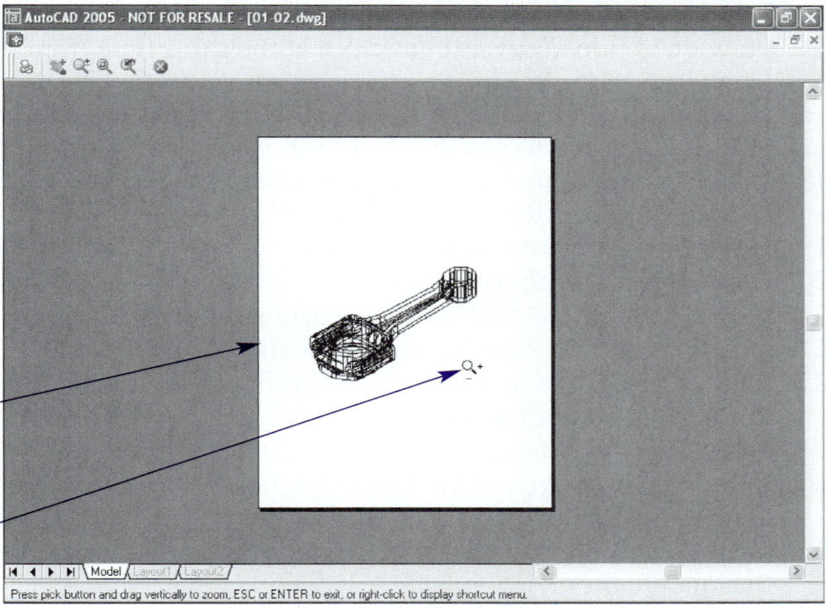

Figure 4-39.
A preview of the plot shows exactly how the drawing will appear on the paper.

EXERCISE 4-11

Complete the Exercise on the Student CD.

Chapter Test

Answer the following questions on a separate sheet of paper.

1. Which pull-down menu contains the **Layer...** option?
2. Identify three ways to access the **Layer Properties Manager** dialog box.
3. How are new layer names entered when creating several layers at the same time without using the **New Layer** button in the **Layer Properties Manager** dialog box?
4. How do you make another layer current in the **Layer Properties Manager** dialog box?
5. How do you know if a layer is off, thawed, or unlocked in the **Layer Properties Manager** dialog box?
6. What is the state of a layer *not* displayed on the screen and *not* calculated by the computer when the drawing is regenerated?
7. Identify the following layer status icons:

   A. 
   B. 
   C. 
   D. 
   E. 
   F. 

8. Are locked layers visible?
9. Describe the purpose of locking a layer.
10. How is the **Select Color** dialog box displayed from the **Layer Properties Manager** dialog box?
11. List the seven standard color names and numbers.
12. What is the default linetype in AutoCAD?
13. Name at least ten of AutoCAD's standard linetypes.
14. What condition must exist before a linetype can be used in a layer?
15. How do you load several linetypes at the same time from the **Load or Reload Linetypes** dialog box?
16. How do you change a layer's linetype in the **Layer Properties Manager** dialog box?
17. Why is ByLayer referred to as a logical color, linetype, and lineweight?
18. Which button in the **Layer Properties Manager** allows you to save layer settings so they can be restored at a later time?
19. Describe the purpose of layer filters.
20. Name the two types of filters.
21. How do you make another layer current by using the **Layers** toolbar?
22. How do you make the layer of an existing object current?
23. Identify two ways to directly access property options for changing the layer, linetype, or color of an existing object.
24. Define a *global change*.
25. In the tree view area of **DesignCenter**, how do you view the content categories of one of the listed open drawings?
26. How do you display all the available layer contents from a drawing in the **DesignCenter** preview palette?
27. Briefly explain how drag and drop works.
28. Define *hard copy* and *soft copy*.
29. Identify four ways to access the **Plot** dialog box.
30. Describe the difference between the **Display** and **Window** options in the **Plot area** section of the **Plot** dialog box.
31. What is a major advantage of doing a plot preview?

Drawing Problems

Before beginning these problems, set up template drawings with layer names, colors, linetypes, and lineweights for the type of drawing you are creating. Do not draw dimensions. Be sure to do preliminary planning for each drawing as discussed in this chapter.

1. Draw the plot plan shown below. Use the linetypes shown, which include Continuous, HIDDEN, PHANTOM, CENTER, FENCELINE2, and GAS_LINE. Make your drawing proportional to the example. Save the drawing as P4-1.

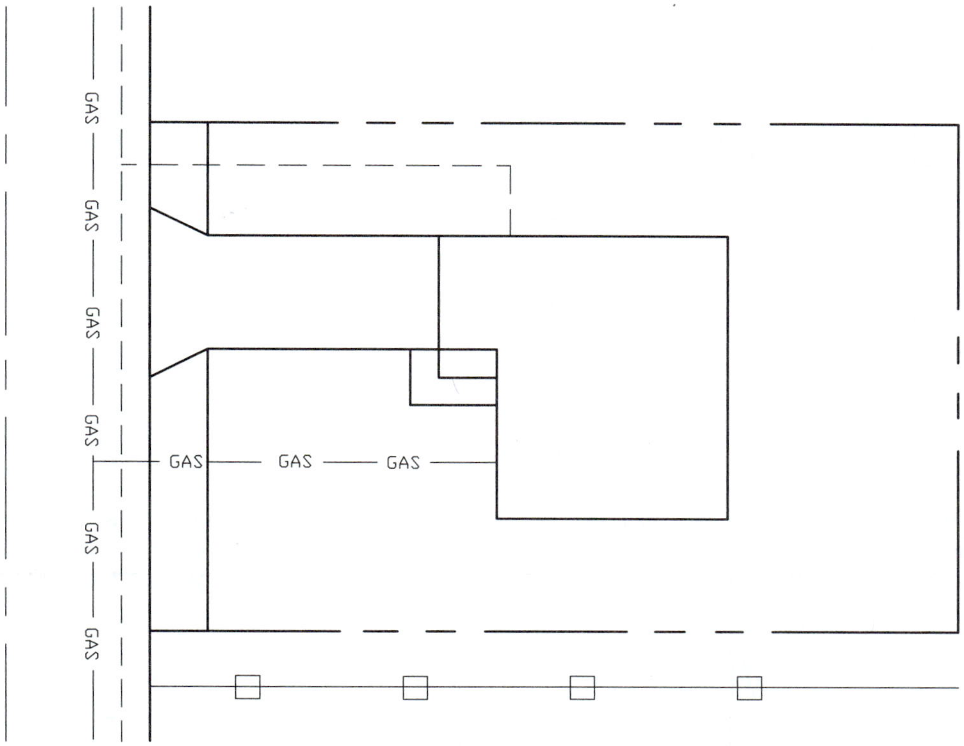

2. Draw the chart for the door schedule. Make the measurements for the rows and columns approximately the same as in the given problem. Do not draw the text. It will be added in Chapter 8. Save the drawing as P4-2.

DOOR SCHEDULE			
SYM.	SIZE	TYPE	QTY.
①	36 x 80	S.C. RP. METAL INSULATED	1
②	36 x 80	S.C. FLUSH METAL INSULATED	2
③	32 x 80	S.C. SELF CLOSING	2
④	32 x 80	HOLLOW CORE	5
⑤	30 x 80	HOLLOW CORE	5
⑥	30 x 80	POCKET SLDG.	2

3. Draw the line chart shown below. Use the linetypes shown, which include Continuous, HIDDEN, PHANTOM, CENTER, FENCELINE1, and FENCELINE2. Make your drawing proportional to the given example. Save the drawing as P4-3.

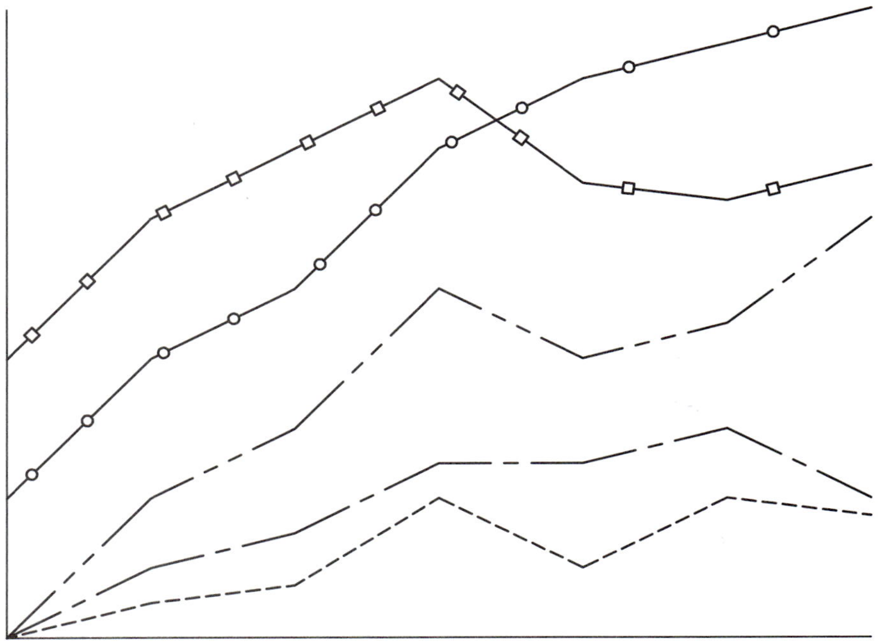

4. Draw the chart for the window schedule. Make the measurements for the rows and columns approximately the same as shown. Do not draw the hexagons or text. They will be added in Chapter 8. Save the drawing as P4-4.

WINDOW SCHEDULE				
SYM.	SIZE	MODEL	ROUGH OPEN	QTY.
A	12 x 60	JOB BUILT	VERIFY	2
B	96 x 60	W4N5 CSM.	8'-0 3/4" x 5'-0 7/8"	1
C	48 x 60	W2N5 CSM.	4'-0 3/4" x 5'-0 7/8"	2
D	48 x 36	W2N3 CSM.	4'-0 3/4" x 3'-6 1/2"	2
E	42 x 42	2N3 CSM.	3'- 6 1/2" x 3'-6 1/2"	2
F	72 x 48	G64 SLDG.	6'-0 1/2" x 4'-0 1/2"	1
G	60 x 42	G536 SLDG.	5'-0 1/2" x 3'-6 1/2"	4
H	48 x 42	G436 SLDG.	4'-0 1/2" x 3'-6 1/2"	1
J	48 x 24	A41 AWN.	4'-0 1/2" x 2'-0 7/8"	3

5. Draw the chart for the interior finish schedule. Make the measurements for the rows and columns approximately the same as in the given problem. Do not draw the solid circles or the text. They will be added in Chapter 8. Save the drawing as P4-5.

INTERIOR FINISH SCHEDULE

ROOM	FLOOR					WALLS				CEILING		
	VINYL	CARPET	TILE	HARDWOOD	CONCRETE	PAINT	PAPER	TEXTURE	SPRAY	SMOOTH	BROCADE	PAINT
ENTRY					●							
FOYER			●			●			●			●
KITCHEN			●				●			●		●
DINING				●		●			●		●	●
FAMILY		●				●			●		●	●
LIVING		●				●		●			●	●
MSTR. BATH			●			●				●		●
BATH #2			●			●			●	●		●
MSTR. BED		●				●		●			●	●
BED #2		●				●			●		●	●
BED #3		●				●			●		●	●
UTILITY	●					●			●	●		●

6. Draw the integrated circuit block diagram. Make your drawing proportional to the given problem. Do not draw the circle, line connections, or text. Save the drawing as P4-6.

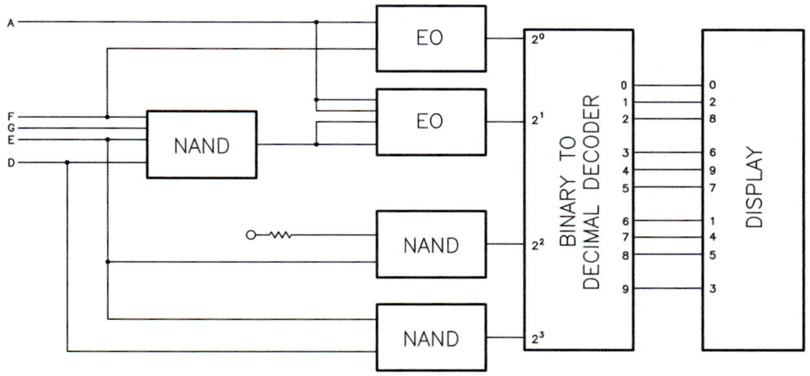

7. Draw the robotics system block diagram. Make your drawing proportional to the given problem. Do not draw the arrowheads or text. Save the drawing as P4-7.

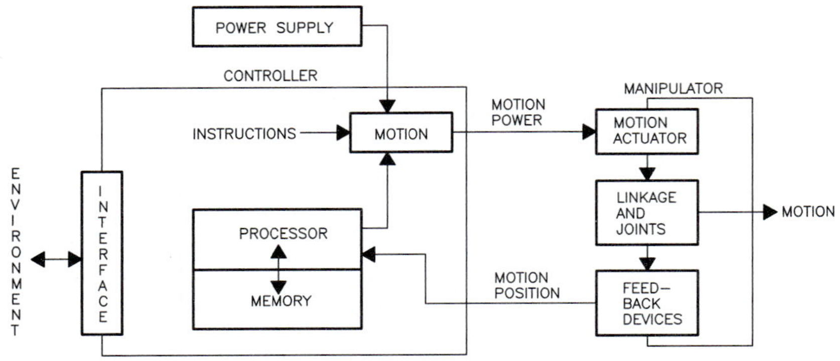

Drawing Problems - Chapter 4

CHAPTER 5

Drawing Basic Shapes

Learning Objectives

After completing this chapter, you will be able to do the following:

- Use **DRAGMODE** to observe an object being dragged into place.
- Draw circles using the **CIRCLE** command options.
- Identify and use the @ symbol function.
- Draw arcs using the **ARC** command options.
- Use the **ELLIPSE** command to draw ellipses and elliptical arcs.
- Draw polygons.
- Use the **RECTANG** command to draw rectangles and explore other rectangle options.
- Draw donuts.
- Use the **Revision Cloud** tool to mark up drawings.

The decisions you make when drawing circles and arcs with AutoCAD are similar to those made when drawing the items manually. AutoCAD provides many ways to create circles and arcs using the **CIRCLE** and **ARC** commands. These methods require inputting the center location and radius or diameter or entering where the outline of the circle or arc should be located. AutoCAD also includes additional drawing tools, such as the **ELLIPSE**, **POLYGON**, **RECTANG**, and **DONUT** commands, to draw a wide variety of shapes. Other provided tools include the **Revision Cloud** tool, which is used to mark up drawings.

Watching Objects Drag into Place

Chapter 3 showed how the **LINE** command displays an image that is "dragged" across the screen before the second endpoint is picked. This image is called a ***rubberband***. The **CIRCLE**, **ARC**, **ELLIPSE**, **POLYGON**, and **RECTANG** commands also display a rubberband image to help you decide where to place the object.

For example, when you draw a circle using the **Center, Radius** option, a circle image appears on the screen after you pick the center point. This image gets larger or smaller as you move the pointer. When the desired circle size is picked, a solid-line circle replaces the dragged image. See **Figure 5-1.**

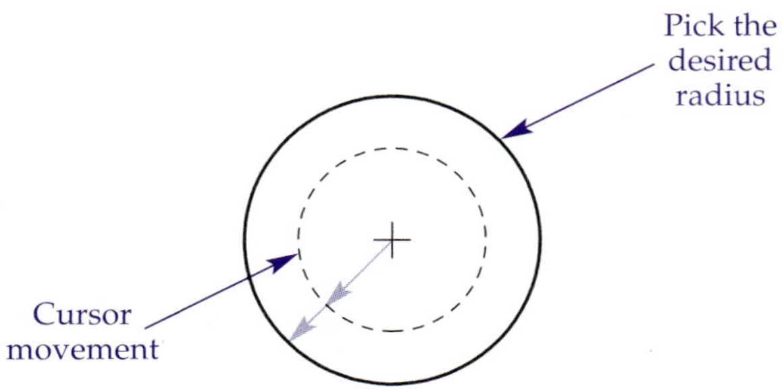

Figure 5-1.
Dragging a circle to its desired size.

The **DRAGMODE** system variable affects the visibility of the rubberband. The **DRAGMODE** can be set to **ON**, **OFF**, or **Auto** by typing DRAGMODE at the Command: prompt and pressing [Enter] as follows:

Command: **DRAGMODE**↵
Enter new value [ON/OFF/Auto] <Auto>: *(type* ON, OFF, *or* A, *and press* [Enter]*)*

The current (default) mode is shown in brackets. Pressing the [Enter] key keeps the existing status. When **DRAGMODE** is on, you must enter DRAG during a command sequence to see the objects drag into place.

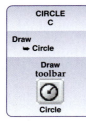

CIRCLE
C

Draw
➥ **Circle**

Draw toolbar
Circle

Drawing Circles

The **CIRCLE** command is activated by picking the **Circle** button in the **Draw** toolbar. You can also select **Circle** from the **Draw** pull-down menu or enter C or CIRCLE at the Command: prompt. The options available in the **Circle** cascading menu are shown in **Figure 5-2.**

Drawing a Circle by Radius

Draw
➥ **Circle**
➥ **Center, Radius**

A circle can be drawn by specifying the center point and the radius. The ***radius*** is the distance from the center to the circumference of a circle or arc. The ***circumference*** is the perimeter or distance around the circle.

After accessing the **Center, Radius** option, you are asked to pick the center point, followed by the radius. If the radius is picked on the screen, watch the coordinate display to help you locate the exact radius. The following command sequence is used to draw the circle in **Figure 5-3:**

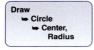

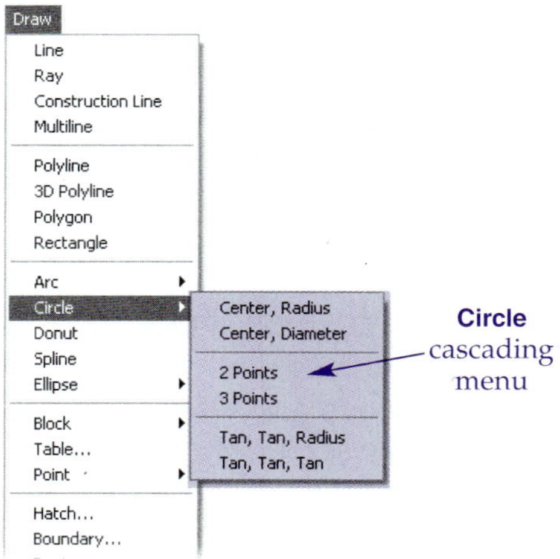

Figure 5-2.
The **Circle** cascading menu in the **Draw** pull-down menu.

Figure 5-3.
Drawing a circle by specifying the center point and radius.

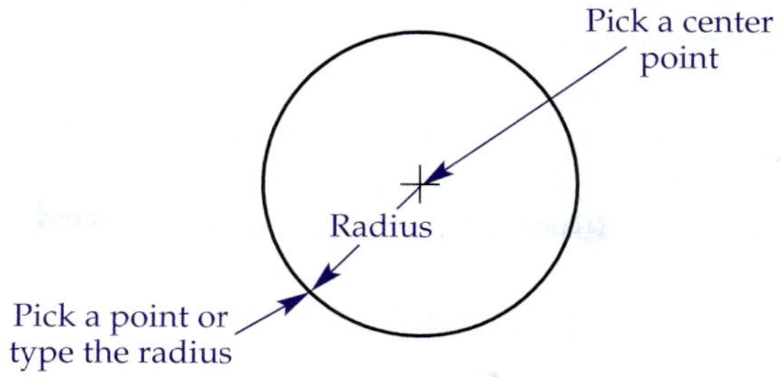

Command: **C** *or* **CIRCLE**↵
Specify center point for circle or [3P/2P/Ttr (tan tan radius)]: *(select a center point)*
Specify radius of circle or [Diameter] <*current*>: *(drag the circle to the desired radius and pick, or type the radius size and press* [Enter]*)*

NOTE The radius value you enter is stored as the **CIRCLERAD** system variable. This system variable is the default radius setting the next time you use the **CIRCLE** command. If **CIRCLERAD** is set to 0, no default radius is provided the next time you use the **CIRCLE** command.

Drawing a Circle by Diameter

Draw
➥ **Circle**
➥ **Center, Diameter**

A circle can also be drawn by specifying the center point and the diameter. The command sequence for the **Center, Diameter** option is as follows:

Command: **C** *or* **CIRCLE**↵
Specify center point for circle or [3P/2P/Ttr (tan tan radius)]: *(select a center point)*
Specify radius of circle or [Diameter] <*current*>: **D**↵
Specify diameter of circle <*current*>: *(drag the circle to the desired diameter and pick, or type the diameter size and press* [Enter]*)*

Watch the screen carefully when using the **Center, Diameter** option. The pointer measures the diameter, but the circle passes midway between the center and the cursor. See **Figure 5-4.** The **Center, Diameter** option is convenient because most circle dimensions are given as diameters.

Figure 5-4.
Drawing a circle using the **Center, Diameter** option. Notice that AutoCAD calculates the circle's position as you move the cursor.

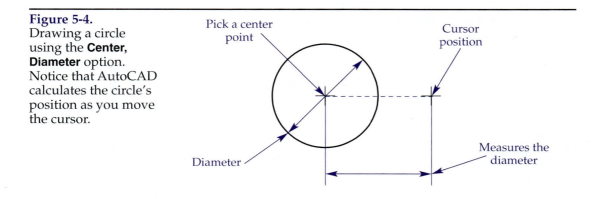

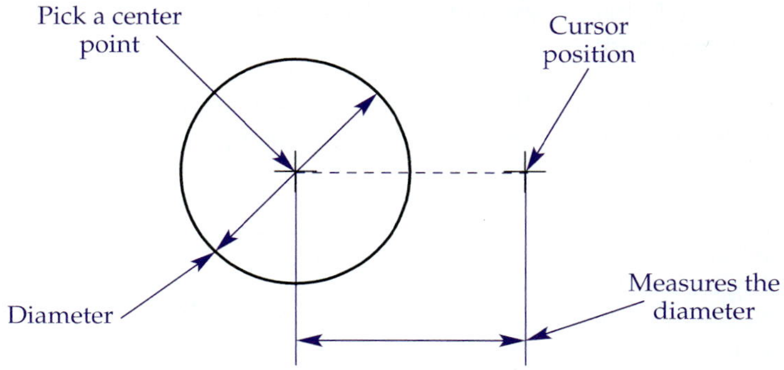

After you draw a circle, its radius becomes the default for the next circle. If you use the **Diameter** option, the previous default setting is converted to a diameter. If you use the **Radius** option to draw a circle after using the **Diameter** option, AutoCAD changes the default to a radius measurement based on the previous diameter. If you set **CIRCLERAD** to a value such as .50, the default for a circle drawn with the **Diameter** option is automatically 1.00 (twice the default radius).

Drawing a Two-Point Circle

Draw
➥ Circle
➥ 2 Points

A two-point circle is drawn by picking two points on opposite sides of the circle. See **Figure 5-5.** The **2 Points** option is useful if the diameter of the circle is known, but the center is difficult to find. One example of this is locating a circle between two lines. The command sequence is as follows:

Command: **C** *or* **CIRCLE**↵
Specify center point for circle or [3P/2P/Ttr (tan tan radius)]: **2P**↵
Specify first end point of circle's diameter: *(select a point)*
Specify second end point of circle's diameter: *(select a point)*

AutoCAD automatically calculates the radius of the circle. This is the default radius the next time the **CIRCLE** command is used.

Figure 5-5.
Drawing a circle by selecting two points.

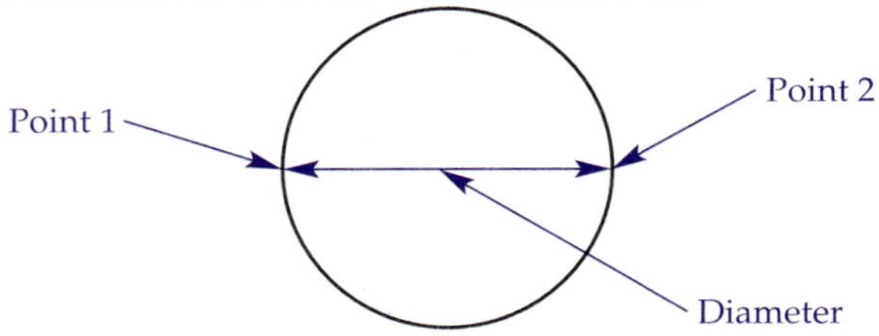

Drawing a Three-Point Circle

Draw
➥ Circle
➥ 3 Points

If three points on the circumference of a circle are known, the **3 Points** option is the best method to use. The three points can be selected in any order. See **Figure 5-6.** The command sequence is as follows:

Command: **C** *or* **CIRCLE**↵
Specify center point for circle or [3P/2P/Ttr (tan tan radius)]: **3P**↵
Specify first point on circle: *(select a point)*
Specify second point on circle: *(select a point)*
Specify third point on circle: *(select a point)*
Command:

AutoCAD automatically calculates the radius of the circle. This becomes the default radius the next time the **CIRCLE** command is used.

Figure 5-6.
Drawing a circle by picking three points on the circle.

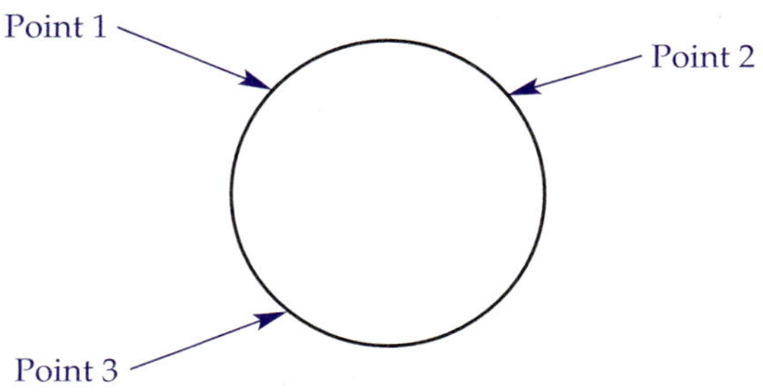

Drawing a Circle Tangent to Two Objects

The term ***tangent*** refers to a line, circle, or arc that comes into contact with an arc or circle at only one point. That point is called the ***point of tangency***. A line drawn from the circle's center to the point of tangency is perpendicular to the tangent line. One drawn between the centers of two tangent circles passes through the point of tangency. You can draw a circle tangent to given lines, circles, or arcs.

Draw
➥ Circle
➥ Tan, Tan, Radius

The **Tan, Tan, Radius** option creates a circle having a specific radius and tangent to two objects. Once the **Tan, Tan, Radius** option is selected, select the lines, arcs, or circles to which the new circle will be tangent. The radius of the circle is also required. To assist you in picking the objects, AutoCAD uses the **Deferred Tangent** object snap by default. (Object snap modes are covered in Chapter 6.) When you see the **Deferred Tangent** symbol, move it to the objects you want to pick. The command sequence is as follows:

Command: **C** *or* **CIRCLE**↵
Specify center point for circle or [3P/2P/Ttr (tan tan radius)]: **T**↵
Specify point on object for first tangent of circle: *(pick the first line, circle, or arc)*
Specify point on object for second tangent of circle: *(pick the second line, circle, or arc)*
Specify radius of circle *<current>*: *(type a radius value and press* [Enter]*)*

If the radius entered is too small, AutoCAD gives you the message Circle does not exist. AutoCAD automatically calculates the radius of the circle. This is the default radius the next time the **CIRCLE** command is used. Two examples of this option are shown in **Figure 5-7.**

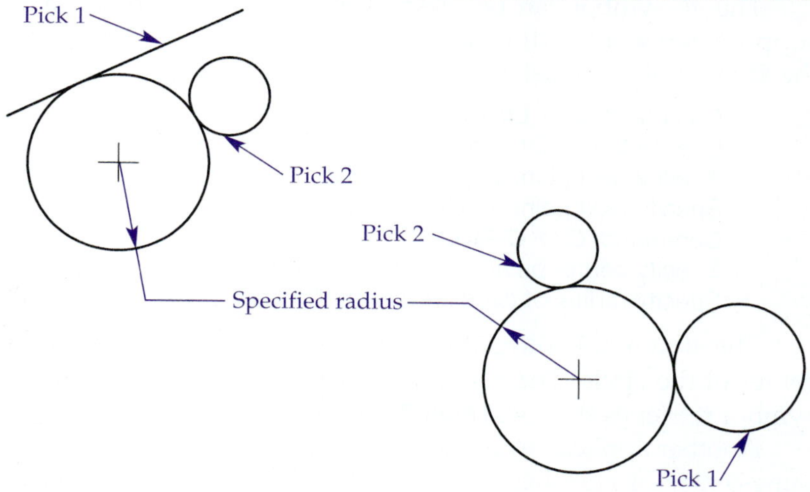

Figure 5-7.
Two examples of drawing circles tangent to two given objects using the **Tan, Tan, Radius** option.

Drawing a Circle Tangent to Three Objects

Draw
➥ Circle
➥ Tan, Tan, Tan

The **Tan, Tan, Tan** option allows you to draw a circle tangent to three existing objects. This option creates a three-point circle using the three points of tangency. See **Figure 5-8.** Selecting the pull-down option is the same as using the **3 Points** option at the Command: prompt with the **TAN** object snap:

Command: **C** *or* **CIRCLE**↵
Specify center point for circle or [3P/2P/Ttr (tan tan radius)]: **3P**↵
Specify first point on circle: **TAN**↵
to *(pick an object)*
Specify second point on circle: **TAN**↵
to *(pick an object)*
Specify third point on circle: **TAN**↵
to *(pick an object)*
Command:

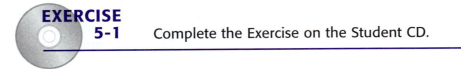

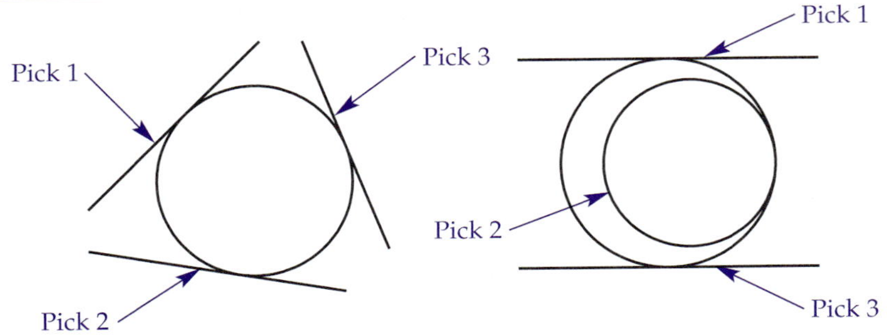

Figure 5-8.
Two examples of drawing circles tangent to three given objects.

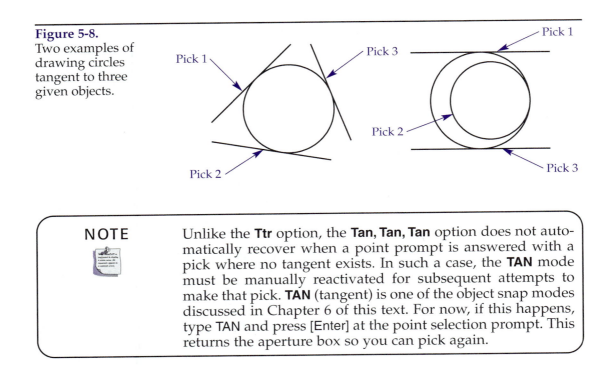

> **NOTE**
>
> Unlike the **Ttr** option, the **Tan, Tan, Tan** option does not automatically recover when a point prompt is answered with a pick where no tangent exists. In such a case, the **TAN** mode must be manually reactivated for subsequent attempts to make that pick. **TAN** (tangent) is one of the object snap modes discussed in Chapter 6 of this text. For now, if this happens, type TAN and press [Enter] at the point selection prompt. This returns the aperture box so you can pick again.

Using the @ Symbol to Specify the Last Coordinates

The @ symbol can be used to input the coordinates last entered. For example, suppose you want to draw a circle with a center at the end of the line just drawn. Enter the @ symbol when asked for a center point. The command sequence is as follows:

Command: **L** *or* **LINE**↵
Specify first point: **4,4**↵
Specify next point or [Undo]: **8,4**↵
Specify next point or [Undo]: ↵
Command: **C** *or* **CIRCLE**↵
Specify center point for circle or [3P/2P/Ttr (tan tan radius)]: **@**↵
Specify radius of circle or [Diameter] <*current*>:

The @ symbol automatically issues the coordinate 8,4 (end of the last line) as the center of the circle. The 8,4 value is saved in the **LASTPOINT** system variable. The @ symbol retrieves the **LASTPOINT** value.

Another application of the @ symbol is drawing concentric circles (circles with the same center). To do this, draw a circle using the **Center, Radius** or the **Center, Diameter** option. Enter the **CIRCLE** command again and type @ when asked for the center point. This automatically places the center of the new circle at the center of the previous circle.

EXERCISE 5-1 Complete the Exercise on the Student CD.

Drawing Arcs

> **ARC**
> **A**
>
> **Draw**
> **➡ Arc**
>
> **Draw** toolbar
> **Arc**

An *arc* is defined as any portion of a circle or curve. Arcs are commonly dimensioned with a radius, but they can be drawn by a number of different methods. The **ARC** command can be accessed by selecting **Arc** from the **Draw** pull-down menu. There are eleven arc construction options accessible in the **Arc** cascading menu. See **Figure 5-9.** This is the easiest way to access the **ARC** command and an arc option. The

Figure 5-9.
The **Arc** cascading menu in the **Draw** pull-down menu.

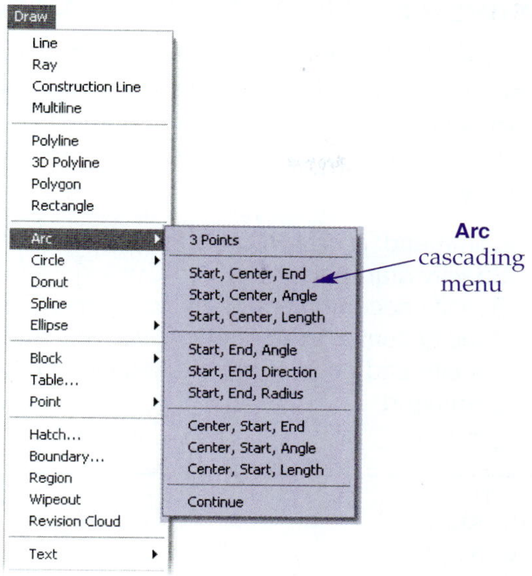

ARC command and its options, however, also can be accessed by picking the **Arc** button in the **Draw** toolbar or by typing A or ARC at the Command: prompt. The **3 Points** option is the default when using the toolbar button or the Command: prompt.

PROFESSIONAL TIP

It is easiest to select the desired **ARC** option using the **Arc** cascading menu in the **Draw** pull-down menu. When an **ARC** option is selected, AutoCAD automatically prompts you for the next required input.

Drawing a Three-Point Arc

Draw
➥ Arc
➥ 3 Points

The **3 Points** option asks for the start point, the second point along the arc, and then the endpoint. See **Figure 5-10.** The arc can be drawn clockwise or counterclockwise and is dragged into position as the endpoint is located. The command sequence is as follows:

Command: **A** *or* **ARC**↵
Specify start point of arc or [Center]: *(select the first point on the arc)*
Specify second point of arc or [Center/End]: *(select the second point on the arc)*
Select end point of arc: *(select the arc's endpoint)*
Command:

Figure 5-10.
Drawing an arc by picking three points.

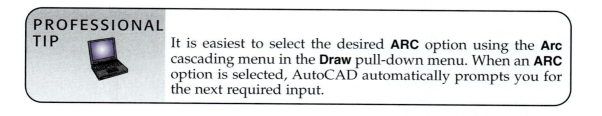

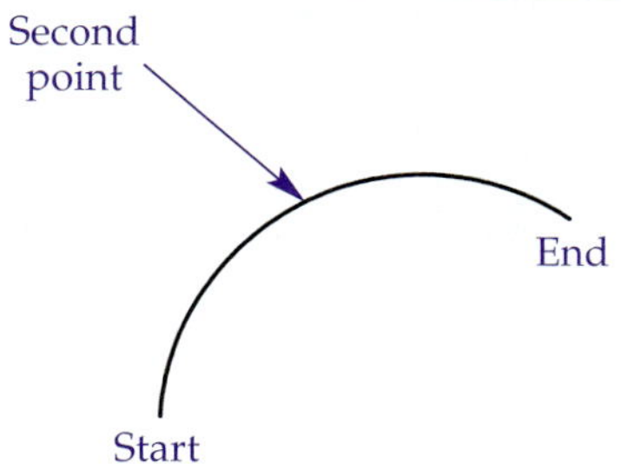

Drawing Arcs Using the **Start, Center, End** Option

Draw
➥ Arc
➥ Start, Center, End

Use the **Start, Center, End** option when you know the start, center, and endpoint locations for the arc. Picking the start and center points establishes the arc's radius. The point selected for the endpoint determines the arc length. The selected endpoint does not have to be on the radius of the arc. See **Figure 5-11.** The command sequence is as follows:

Command: **A** *or* **ARC**↵
Specify start point of arc or [Center]: *(select the first point on the arc)*
Specify second point of arc or [Center/End]: **C**↵
Specify center point of arc: *(select the arc's center point)*
Specify end point of arc or [Angle/chord Length]: *(select the arc's endpoint)*
Command:

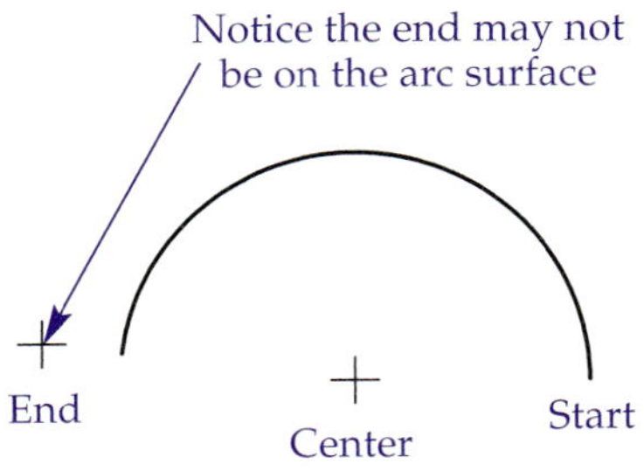

Figure 5-11.
Using the **Start, Center, End** option. Notice the endpoint does not have to be on the arc.

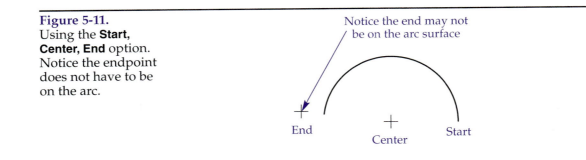

Drawing Arcs Using the **Start, Center, Angle** Option

Draw
➥ Arc
➥ Start, Center, Angle

When the arc's included angle is known, the **Start, Center, Angle** option may be the best choice. The ***included angle*** is an angle formed between the center, start point, and endpoint of the arc. The arc is drawn counterclockwise, unless a negative angle is specified. See **Figure 5-12.** The following shows the command sequence with a 45° included angle:

Command: **A** *or* **ARC**↵
Specify start point of arc or [Center]: *(select the first point on the arc)*
Specify second point of arc or [Center/End]: **C**↵
Select center point of arc: *(select the arc's center point)*
Specify end point of arc or [Angle/chord Length]: **A**↵
Specify included angle: **45**↵
Command:

Figure 5-12.
How positive and negative angles work with the **Start, Center, Angle** option.

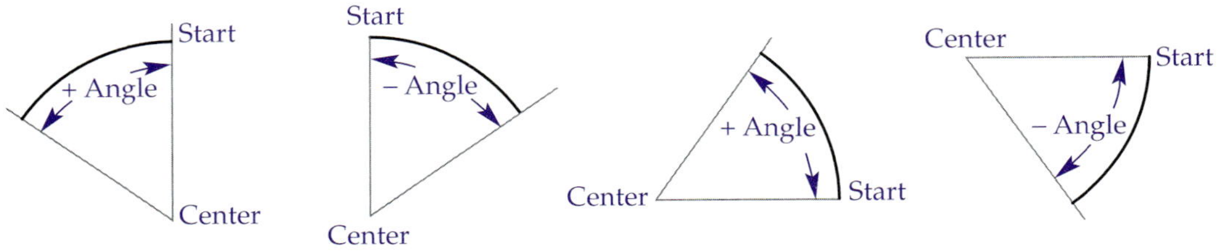

Drawing Arcs Using the **Start, Center, Length** Option

Draw
➥ **Arc**
➥ **Start, Center, Length**

The chord length can be determined using a chord length table (provided on Student CD). A one-unit radius arc with an included angle of 45° has a chord length of .765 units. Arcs are drawn counterclockwise. Therefore, a positive chord length gives the smallest possible arc with that length. A negative chord length results in the largest possible arc. See **Figure 5-13.** The following shows the command sequence with a chord length of .765:

Command: **A** *or* **ARC**↵
Specify start point of arc or [Center]: *(select the first point on the arc)*
Specify second point of arc or [Center/End]: **C**↵
Specify center point of arc: *(select the arc's center point)*
Specify end point of arc or [Angle/chord Length]: **L**↵
Specify length of chord: *(type* .765 *for the smaller arc or* –.765 *for the larger arc, and press* [Enter]*)*
Command:

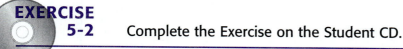

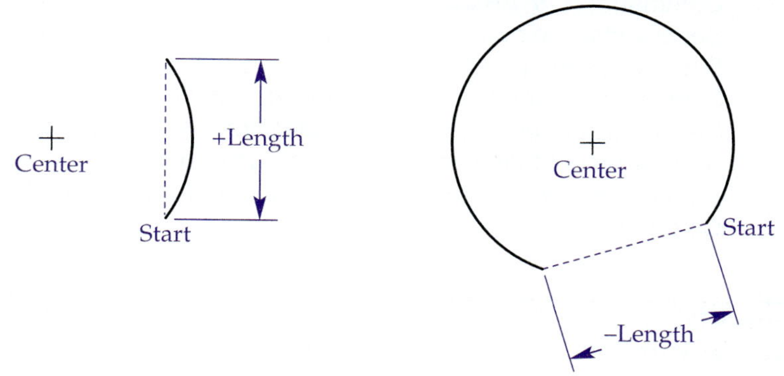

Figure 5-13.
How positive and negative chord lengths work with the **Start, Center, Length** option.

EXERCISE 5-2 Complete the Exercise on the Student CD.

Drawing Arcs Using the **Start, End, Angle** Option

Draw
➥ **Arc**
➥ **Start, End, Angle**

An arc can also be drawn by picking the start point and endpoint and entering the included angle. A positive included angle draws the arc counterclockwise, while a negative angle produces a clockwise arc. See **Figure 5-14.** The command sequence is as follows:

Command: **A** *or* **ARC**↵
Specify start point of arc or [Center]: *(select the first point on the arc)*
Specify second point of arc or [Center/End]: **E**↵
Specify end point of arc: *(select the arc's endpoint)*
Specify center point of arc or [Angle/Direction/Radius]: **A**↵
Specify included angle: *(type a positive or negative angle and press* [Enter]*)*
Command:

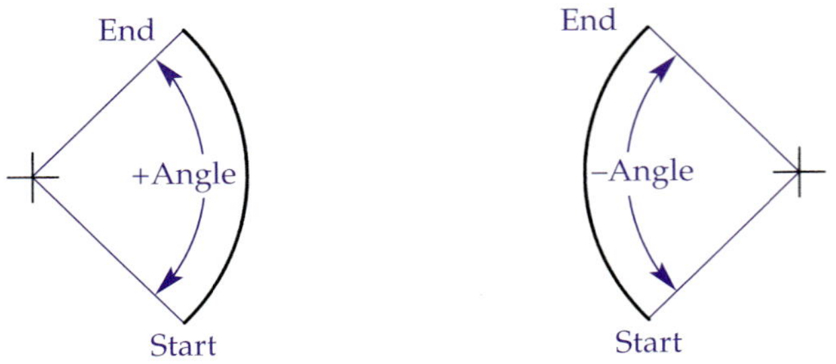

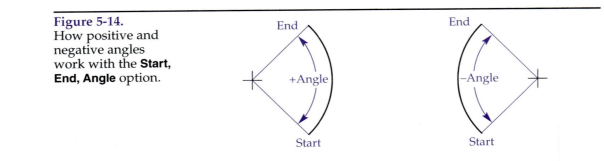

Figure 5-14.
How positive and negative angles work with the **Start, End, Angle** option.

Drawing Arcs Using the **Start, End, Direction** Option

Draw
➥ Arc
➥ Start, End, Direction

An arc can be drawn by picking the start point and endpoint and entering the direction of rotation in degrees. The distance between the points and the number of degrees determine the arc's location and size. The arc is started tangent to the direction specified, with the direction being measured from the 0° mark, as shown in **Figure 5-15.** The command sequence is as follows:

Command: **A** *or* **ARC**↵
Specify start point of arc or [Center]: *(select the first point on the arc)*
Specify second point of arc or [Center/End]: **E**↵
Specify end point of arc: *(select the arc's endpoint)*
Specify center point of arc or [Angle/Direction/Radius]: **D**↵
Specify tangent direction for the start point of arc: *(pick the direction from the start point, or type the direction in degrees and press* [Enter]*)*
Command:

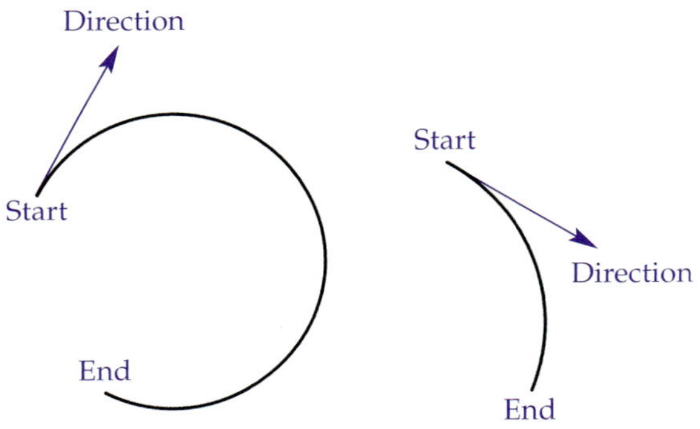

Figure 5-15.
Using the **Start, End, Direction** option.

Drawing Arcs Using the Start, End, Radius Option

Draw
➥ Arc
➥ Start, End, Radius

A positive radius value for the **Start, End, Radius** option results in the smallest possible arc between the start point and endpoint. A negative radius gives the largest arc possible. See **Figure 5-16.** Arcs can only be drawn counterclockwise with this option. The command sequence is as follows:

Command: **A** *or* **ARC**↵
Specify start point of arc or [Center]: *(select the first point on the arc)*
Specify second point of arc or [Center/End]: **E**↵
Specify end point of arc: *(select the arc's endpoint)*
Specify center point of arc or [Angle/Direction/Radius]: **R**↵
Specify radius of arc: *(pick or type a positive or negative radius and press* [Enter]*)*
Command:

Figure 5-16.
Using the **Start, End, Radius** option with a positive and negative radius.

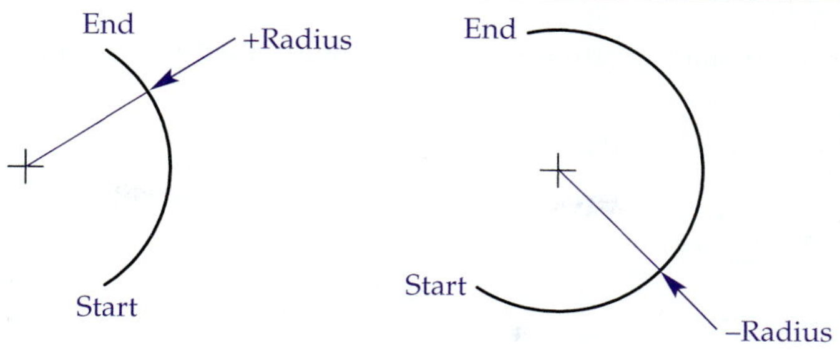

EXERCISE 5-3 Complete the Exercise on the Student CD.

Drawing Arcs Using the Center, Start, End Option

Draw
➥ Arc
➥ Center, Start, End

The **Center, Start, End** option is a variation of the **Start, Center, End** option. See **Figure 5-17.** Use the **Center, Start, End** option when it is easier to begin by locating the center. The command sequence is as follows:

Command: **A** *or* **ARC**↵
Specify start point of arc or [Center]: **C**↵
Specify center point of arc: *(pick the center point)*
Specify start point of arc: *(pick the start point)*
Specify end point of arc or [Angle/chord Length]: *(pick the arc's endpoint)*
Command:

Figure 5-17.
Using the **Center, Start, End** option. Note that the endpoint does not have to be on the arc.

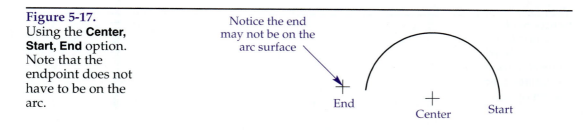

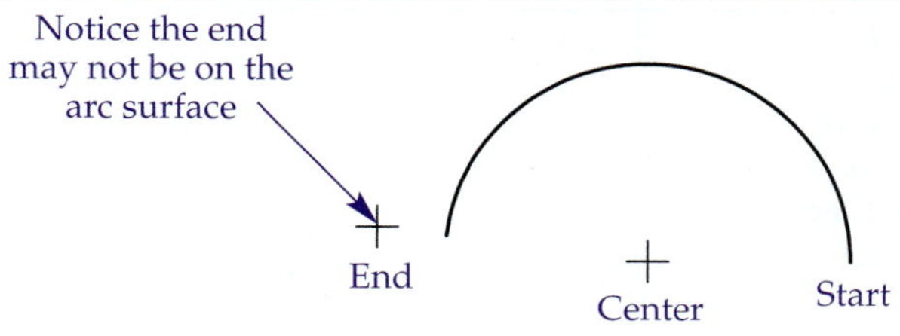

Drawing Arcs Using the Center, Start, Angle Option

Draw
➥ Arc
➥ Center, Start, Angle

The **Center, Start, Angle** option is a variation of the **Start, Center, Angle** option. Use the **Center, Start, Angle** option when it is easier to begin by locating the center. **Figure 5-18** shows how positive and negative angles work with this option. The command sequence is as follows:

Command: **A** *or* **ARC**↵
Specify start point of arc or [Center]: **C**↵
Specify center point of arc: *(pick the center point)*
Specify start point of arc: *(pick the start point)*
Specify end point of arc or [Angle/chord Length]: **A**↵
Specify included angle: *(pick the included angle, or type a positive angle or negative angle and press* [Enter]*)*
Command:

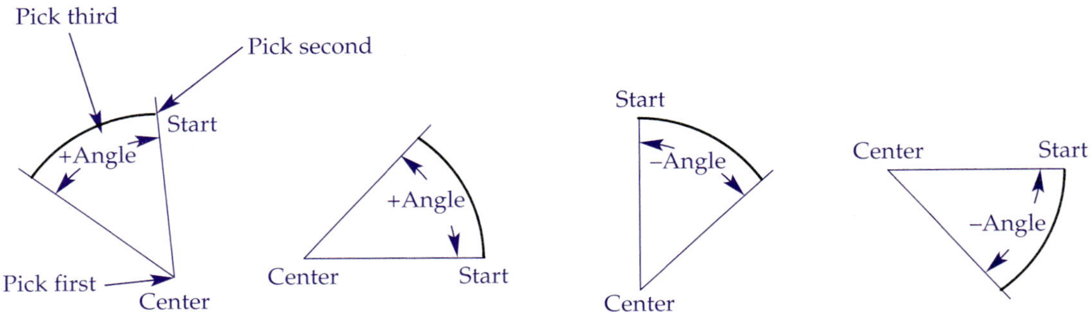

Figure 5-18.
How positive and negative angles work with the **Center, Start, Angle** option.

Drawing Arcs Using the Center, Start, Length Option

Draw
➥ **Arc**
➥ **Center, Start, Length**

The **Center, Start, Length** option is a variation of the **Start, Center, Length** option. Use the **Center, Start, Length** option when it is easier to begin by locating the center. **Figure 5-19** shows how positive and negative chord lengths work with this option. The command sequence is as follows:

Command: **A** *or* **ARC**↵
Specify start point of arc or [Center]: **C**↵
Specify center point of arc: *(pick the center point)*
Specify start point of arc: *(pick the start point)*
Specify end point of arc or [Angle/chord Length]: **L**↵
Specify length of chord: *(pick or type the chord length, and press* [Enter]*)*
Command:

Figure 5-19.
How positive and negative chord lengths work with the **Center, Start, Length** option.

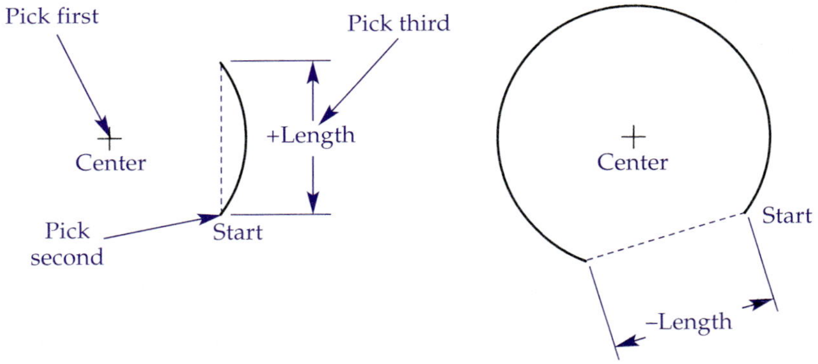

Continuing Arcs from a Previously Drawn Arc or Line

Draw
➥ **Arc**
➥ **Continue**

An arc can be continued from the previous arc or line. To do so, pick **Continue** from the **Arc** cascading menu in the **Draw** pull-down menu. The **Continue** option can also be accessed by beginning the **ARC** command and then pressing the [Enter] key, pressing the space bar, or selecting **Enter** from the shortcut menu when prompted to specify the start point of the arc:

Specify start point of arc or [Center]: *(press the space bar or* [Enter] *to place the start point of the arc at the end of the previous line or arc)*

When a series of arcs are drawn in this manner, each consecutive arc is tangent to the object before it. The start point and direction are taken from the endpoint and direction of the previous arc. See **Figure 5-20.**

Figure 5-20.
Using the **Continue** option to draw three arcs.

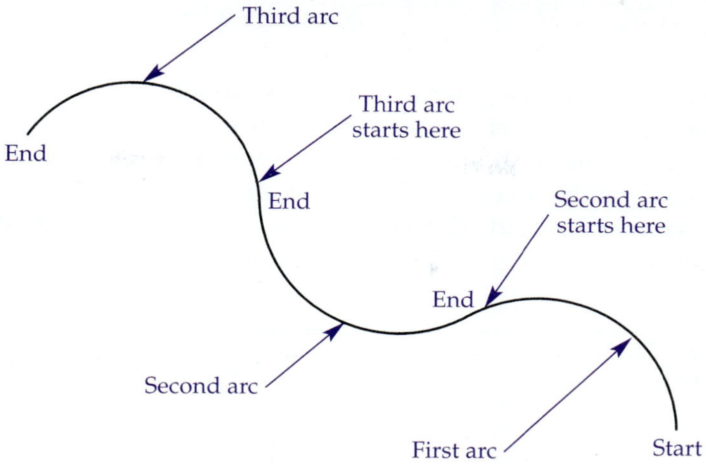

The **Continue** option can also be used to quickly draw an arc tangent to the endpoint of a previously drawn line. See **Figure 5-21.** The command sequence is as follows:

Command: **L** *or* **LINE**↵
Specify first point: *(select a point)*
Specify next point or [Undo]: *(select a second point)*
Specify next point or [Undo]: ↵
Command: **A** *or* **ARC**↵
Specify start point of arc or [Center]: *(press the space bar or* [Enter] *to place the start point of the arc at the end of the previous line)*
Specify end point of arc: *(select the endpoint of the arc)*
Command:

Figure 5-21.
An arc continuing from the previous line. Point 2 is the start of the arc, and Point 3 is the end of the arc.

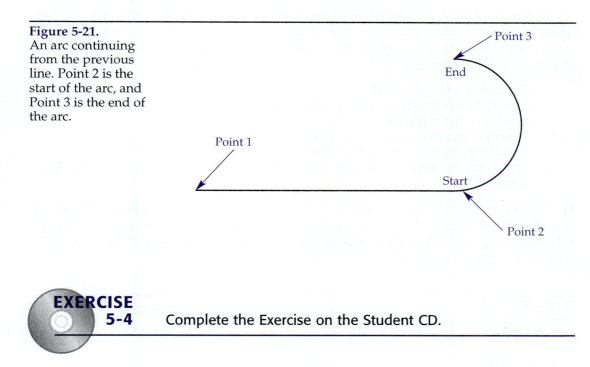

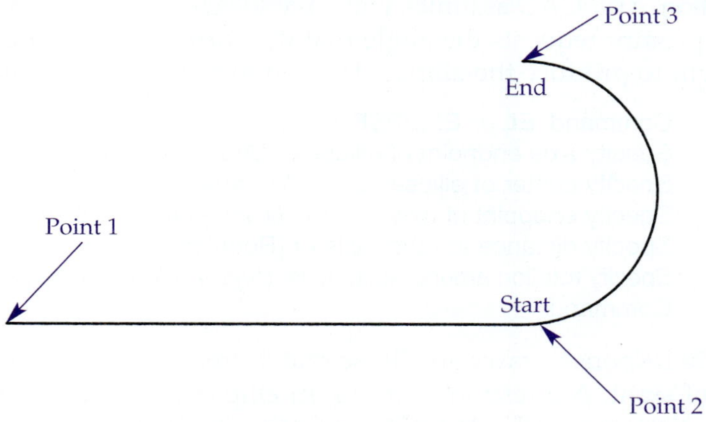

EXERCISE 5-4 Complete the Exercise on the Student CD.

Drawing Ellipses

ELLIPSE
EL

Draw
➡ Ellipse

Draw
toolbar

Ellipse

When a circle is viewed at an angle, an elliptical shape is seen. For example, a 30° ellipse is created if a circle is rotated 60° from the line of sight. The parts of an ellipse are shown in **Figure 5-22.** The longer of the two axes is always the major axis. The **ELLIPSE** command can be accessed by selecting **Ellipse** from the **Draw** pull-down menu, picking the **Ellipse** button in the **Draw** toolbar, or entering EL or ELLIPSE at the Command: prompt. An ellipse can be drawn using different options of the **ELLIPSE** command.

Figure 5-22.
Parts of an ellipse.

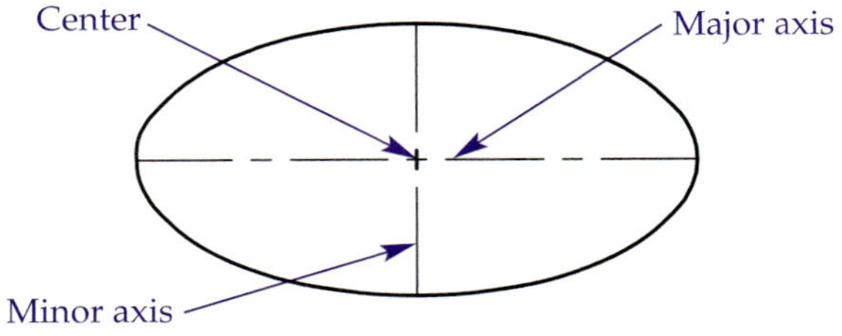

Drawing an Ellipse Using the Center Option

Draw
➡ Ellipse
➡ Center

An ellipse can be constructed by specifying the center point and one endpoint for each of the two axes. See **Figure 5-23.** The command sequence for this option is as follows:

Command: **EL** *or* **ELLIPSE**↵
Specify axis endpoint of ellipse or [Arc/Center]: **C**↵
Specify center of ellipse: *(select the ellipse's center point)*
Specify endpoint of axis: *(select the endpoint of one axis)*
Specify distance to other axis or [Rotation]: *(select the endpoint of the other axis)*

If you respond to the Specify distance to other axis or [Rotation]: prompt with R for **Rotation**, AutoCAD assumes you have selected the major axis with the first point. The next prompt requests the angle that the corresponding circle is rotated from the line of sight to produce the ellipse. The command sequence is as follows:

Command: **EL** *or* **ELLIPSE**↵
Specify axis endpoint of ellipse or [Arc/Center]: **C**↵
Specify center of ellipse: *(select the ellipse's center point)*
Specify endpoint of axis: *(select the endpoint of one axis)*
Specify distance to other axis or [Rotation]: **R**↵
Specify rotation around major axis: *(type a rotation angle, such as* 30*, and press* [Enter]*)*
Command:

The 30 response draws an ellipse that is created when a circle is rotated 30° from the line of sight. A 0 response draws an ellipse with the minor axis equal to the major axis—that is, a circle. AutoCAD rejects any rotation angle between 89.42° and 90.57° or between 269.42° and 270.57°.

Figure 5-23.
Drawing an ellipse by picking the center and endpoints of two axes.

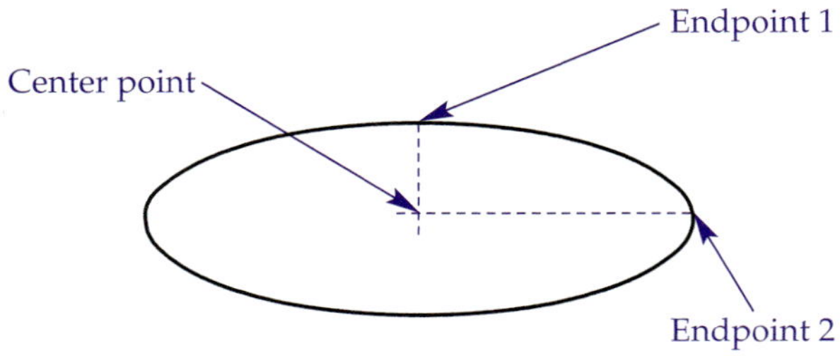

Drawing an Ellipse Using the **Axis, End** Option

Draw
➥ Ellipse
➥ Axis, End

The **Axis, End** option establishes the first axis and one endpoint of the second axis. The first axis may be either the major or minor axis, depending on what is entered for the second axis. After you pick the first axis, the ellipse is dragged by the cursor until the point is picked. The command sequence for the ellipses in Figure 5-24 is as follows:

Command: **EL** *or* **ELLIPSE**↵
Specify axis endpoint of ellipse or [Arc/Center]: *(select an axis endpoint)*
Specify other endpoint of axis: *(select the other endpoint of the axis)*
Specify distance to other axis or [Rotation]: *(select a distance from the midpoint of the first axis to the end of the second axis and press* [Enter]*)*
Command:

The **Rotation** option can be used instead of selecting a distance to the end of the second axis. Figure 5-25 shows the relationship between several ellipses having the same major axis length, but different rotation angles.

Figure 5-24.
Constructing the same ellipse by choosing different axis endpoints.

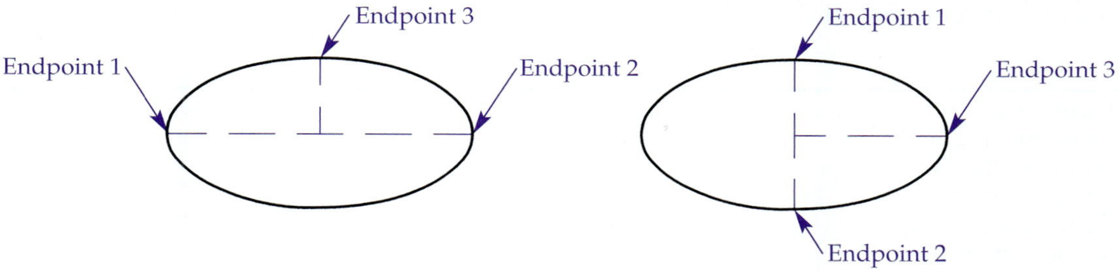

Figure 5-25.
Ellipse rotation angles.

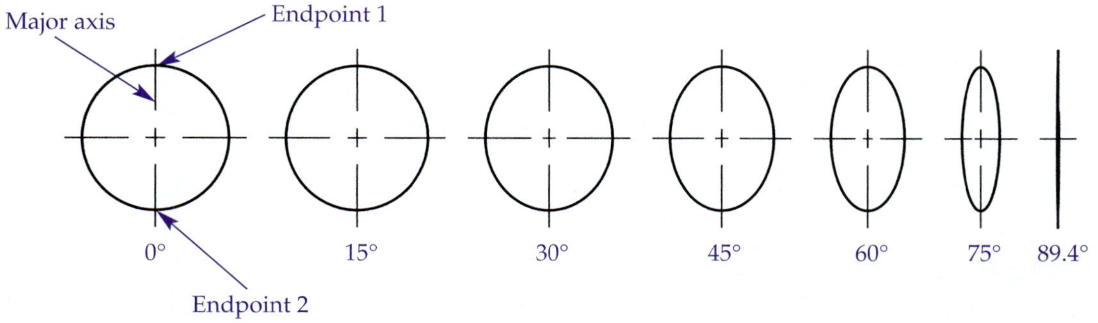

EXERCISE 5-5 Complete the Exercise on the Student CD.

Drawing Elliptical Arcs

Draw
➥ Ellipse
➥ Arc

The **Arc** option of the **ELLIPSE** command is used to draw elliptical arcs. The command sequence for the **Arc** option is as follows:

Command: **EL** *or* **ELLIPSE**↵
Specify axis endpoint of ellipse or [Arc/Center]: **A**↵
Specify axis endpoint of elliptical arc or [Center]: *(pick the first axis endpoint)*
Specify other endpoint of axis: *(pick the second axis endpoint)*
Specify distance to other axis or [Rotation]: *(pick the distance for the second axis)*
Specify start angle or [Parameter]: **0**↵
Specify end angle or [Parameter/Included angle]: **90**↵
Command:

Once the second endpoint of the first axis is picked, you can drag the shape of a full ellipse. This can help you visualize the other axis. The distance for the second axis is from the ellipse's center to the point picked. Enter a start angle. The start and end angles are the angular relationships between the ellipse's center and the arc's endpoints. The angle of the elliptical arc is established from the angle of the first axis. A 0° start angle is the same as the first endpoint of the first axis. A 45° start angle is 45° counterclockwise from the first endpoint of the first axis. End angles are also established counterclockwise from the start point. **Figure 5-26** shows the elliptical arc drawn with the previous command sequence and displays sample arcs with different start and end angles.

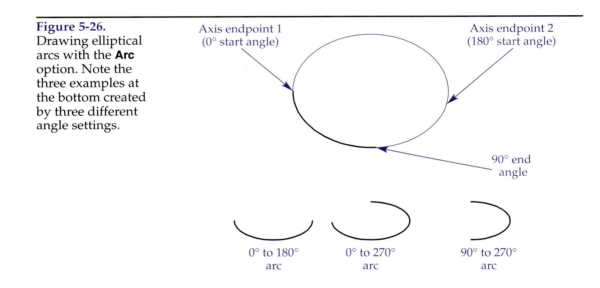

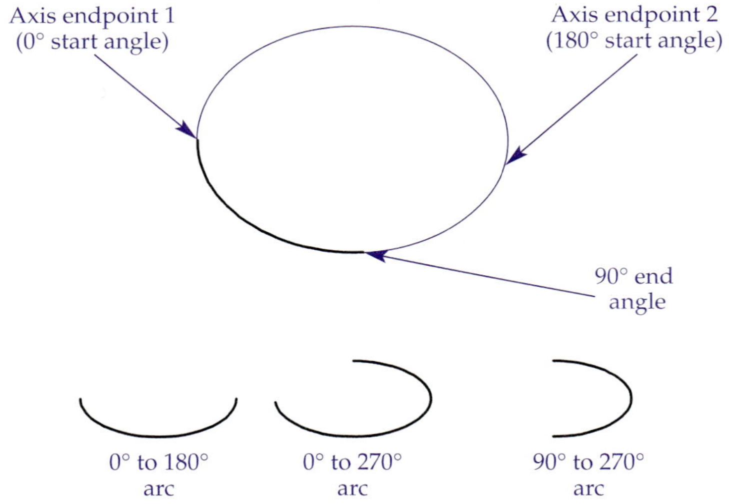

Figure 5-26. Drawing elliptical arcs with the **Arc** option. Note the three examples at the bottom created by three different angle settings.

Using the **Parameter** option

The **Parameter** option requires the same input as the other elliptical arcs, until the Specify start angle or [Parameter]: prompt. The difference is that AutoCAD uses a different means of vector calculation to create the elliptical arc. The results are similar, but the command sequence is as follows:

Specify start angle or [Parameter]: **P**↵
Specify start parameter or [Angle]: *(pick the start point)*
Specify end parameter or [Angle/Included angle]: *(pick the endpoint)*
Command:

Using the **Included** option

The **Included** option establishes an included angle beginning at the start angle. An included angle is an angle that is formed by two sides, or in this case, the angle formed by the endpoints and center of the arc. This option requires the same input as the other elliptical arcs until the Specify end angle or [Parameter/Included angle]: prompt. The command sequence is as follows:

Specify end angle or [Parameter/Included angle]: **I**↵
Specify included angle for arc <*current*>: *(enter the included angle)*
Command:

Rotating an elliptical arc around its axis

The **Rotation** option for drawing an elliptical arc is similar to the **Rotation** option when drawing a full ellipse, which was discussed earlier. This option allows you to rotate the elliptical arc about the first axis by specifying a rotation angle. Refer back to **Figure 5-25** for examples of various rotation angles. This option requires the same input as the other elliptical arcs, until the Specify distance to other axis or [Rotation]: prompt. The command sequence is as follows:

Specify distance to other axis or [Rotation]: **R**↵
Specify rotation around major axis: *(enter rotation value)*
Specify start angle or [Parameter]: *(enter start angle)*
Specify end angle or [Parameter/Included angle]: *(enter end angle)*
Command:

Drawing an elliptical arc using the Center option

The **Center** option for drawing an elliptical arc lets you establish the center of the ellipse. See **Figure 5-27.** This option requires the same input as the other elliptical arcs, until the Specify axis endpoint of elliptical arc or [Center]: prompt. The command sequence is as follows:

Specify axis endpoint of elliptical arc or [Center]: **C**↵
Specify center of elliptical arc: *(select the ellipse's center point)*
Specify endpoint of axis: *(select the endpoint of the axis)*
Specify distance to other axis or [Rotation]: *(select the endpoint of the other axis)*
Specify start angle or [Parameter]: *(enter start angle)*
Specify end angle or [Parameter/Included angle]: *(enter end angle)*
Command:

NOTE

The setting of the **PELLIPSE** system variable affects the way an ellipse can be edited. An ellipse drawn when **PELLIPSE** is set at 0 is a true elliptical object, while an ellipse drawn when **PELLIPSE** is set at 1 is a polyline ellipse. A true elliptical object maintains its elliptical shape during grip editing. (Grip editing is discussed in Chapter 13 of this text.) The vertices of a polyline ellipse can be moved out of the elliptical shape. The **Arc** option of the **ELLIPSE** command is not available when **PELLIPSE** is set to 1.

Figure 5-27.
Drawing elliptical arcs with the **Center** option.

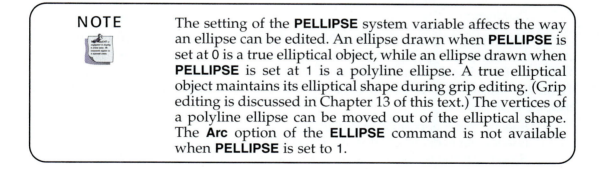

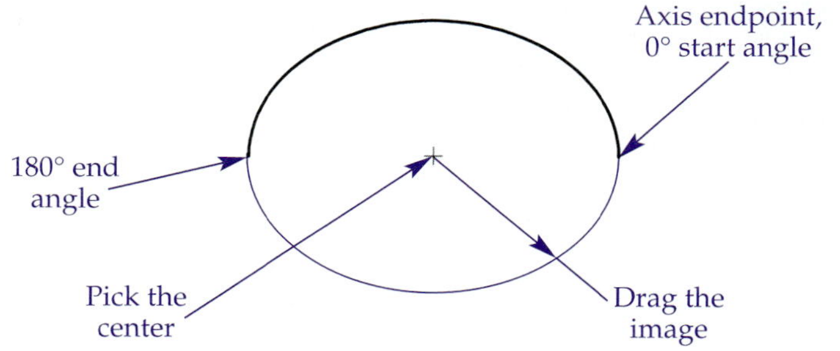

EXERCISE 5-6 Complete the Exercise on the Student CD.

Drawing Regular Polygons

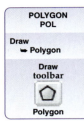

> **POLYGON**
> **POL**
>
> **Draw**
> ➥ **Polygon**
>
> **Draw toolbar**
> **Polygon**

A ***regular polygon*** is any closed-plane geometric figure with three or more equal sides and equal angles. For example, a hexagon is a six-sided regular polygon. The **POLYGON** command is used to draw any regular polygon with up to 1024 sides.

The **POLYGON** command can be accessed by selecting **Polygon** from the **Draw** pull-down menu, picking the **Polygon** button in the **Draw** toolbar, or entering POL or POLYGON at the Command: prompt. Regardless of the method used to select the command, you are first prompted for the number of sides. If you want an octagon (a polygon with eight sides), enter 8 as follows:

> Command: **POL** *or* **POLYGON**↵
> Enter number of sides <*current*>: **8**↵
> Specify center of polygon or [Edge]:

The number of sides you enter becomes the default for the next time you use the **POLYGON** command. Next, AutoCAD prompts for the center or edge of the polygon. If you reply by picking a point on the screen, this point becomes the center of the polygon. You are then asked if you want to have the polygon inscribed within or circumscribed outside of an imaginary circle. See **Figure 5-28.**

A polygon is ***inscribed*** when it is drawn inside a circle and its corners touch the circle. ***Circumscribed*** polygons are drawn outside of a circle, where the sides of the polygon are tangent to the circle. With either option, you must then specify the radius of the circle. The command continues as follows:

> Specify center of polygon or [Edge]: *(pick the center of the polygon)*
> Enter an option [Inscribed in circle/Circumscribed about circle] <*current*>: *(respond with* I *or* C*, and press* [Enter]*)*
> Specify radius of circle: *(type the radius, such as* 2*, and press* [Enter]*, or pick a point on the screen at the desired distance from the center)*
> Command:

The **I** or **C** option you select becomes the default for the next polygon. The Specify center of polygon or [Edge]: prompt allows you to pick the center or specify the edge. Notice that picking the center is the default. If you want to draw the polygon by specifying the length of one of the edges, enter E for the **Edge** option and pick edge endpoints as follows:

> Specify center of polygon or [Edge]: **E**↵
> Specify first endpoint of edge: *(pick a point)*
> Specify second endpoint of edge: *(pick a second point)*
> Command:

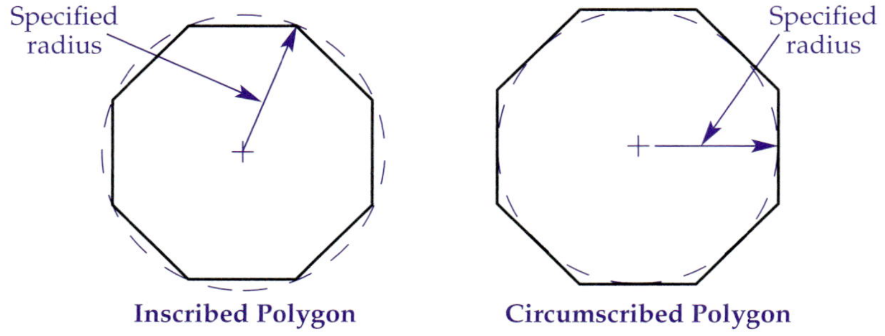

Figure 5-28. Drawing an inscribed and a circumscribed polygon.

After you pick the endpoints of one side, the rest of the polygon sides are drawn counterclockwise, using the length specified by the two picked endpoints.

Polygons are polylines and can be easily edited using the **PEDIT** (polyline edit) command. The **PEDIT** command is discussed in Chapter 15 of this text. For example, a polygon can be given width using the **Width** option of the **PEDIT** command.

Hexagons (six-sided polygons) are commonly drawn as bolt heads and nuts on mechanical drawings. Keep in mind that these features are normally dimensioned across the flats. To draw a polygon to be dimensioned across the flats, circumscribe it. The radius you enter is equal to one-half the distance across the flats. The distance across the corners (inscribed polygon) is specified when the polygon must be confined within a circular area. One example is the boundary of a swimming pool deck in architectural drafting. Notice the distance across the flats and the distance across the corners in **Figure 5-29.**

Figure 5-29.
Specifying the distance across the flats and between the corners of a polygon.

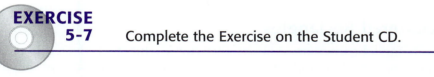

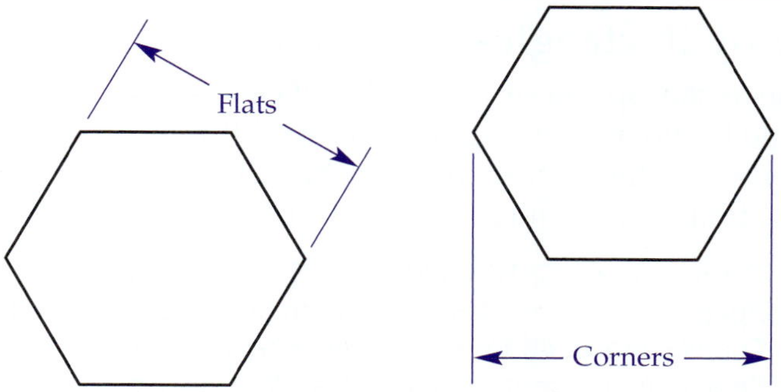

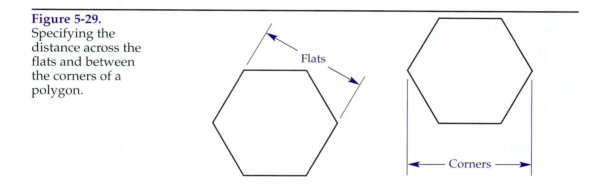

Setting the Number of Polygon Sides

AutoCAD allows you to set the default number of polygon sides with the **POLYSIDES** system variable. This value can be set in your template for future use, but is automatically reset to 4 in a new drawing. Type POLYSIDES at the Command: prompt and enter the number of default sides for the **POLYGON** command. The value you specify for the default is used until you change the value again using the **POLYSIDES** system variable or the **POLYGON** command.

EXERCISE 5-7 Complete the Exercise on the Student CD.

Drawing Rectangles

RECTANGLE
RECTANG
REC

Draw
➡ Rectangle

Draw toolbar

Rectangle

AutoCAD's **RECTANG** command allows you to easily draw rectangles. When using this command, pick one corner and then the opposite diagonal corner to establish the rectangle. See **Figure 5-30.** The **RECTANG** command can be accessed by picking **Rectangle** in the **Draw** pull-down menu; by picking the **Rectangle** button in the **Draw** toolbar; or by entering REC, RECTANG, or RECTANGLE at the Command: prompt:

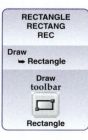

Command: **REC**, **RECTANG**, *or* **RECTANGLE**↵
Specify first corner point or [Chamfer/Elevation/Fillet/Thickness/Width]: *(select the first corner of the rectangle)*
Specify other corner point or [Dimensions]: *(select the second corner)*
Command:

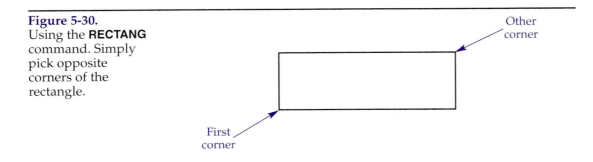

Figure 5-30.
Using the **RECTANG** command. Simply pick opposite corners of the rectangle.

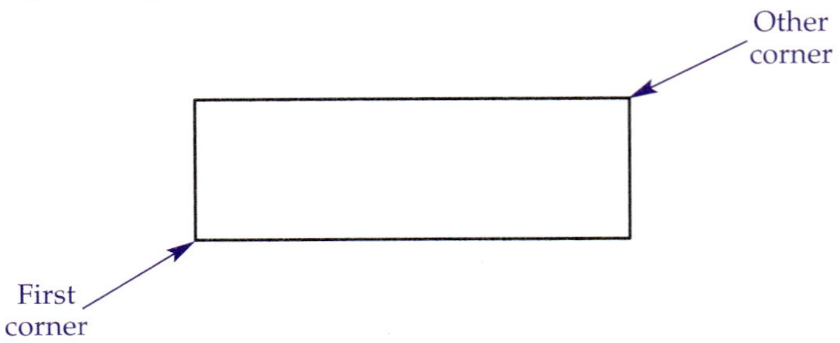

Rectangles are polylines and can be edited using the **PEDIT** command. Since a rectangle is a polyline, it is treated as one entity until it is exploded. After it is exploded, the individual sides can be edited separately. The **EXPLODE** command is discussed in Chapter 15 of this text.

Drawing Rectangles with Line Width

The **Width** option of the **RECTANG** command is used to adjust the width of the rectangle in the XY plane. Setting line width for rectangles is similar to setting width for polylines. This is discussed in Chapters 14 and 15.

The following sequence is used to create a rectangle with .03 wide lines:

Command: **REC**, **RECTANG**, *or* **RECTANGLE**↵
Specify first corner point or [Chamfer/Elevation/Fillet/Thickness/Width]: **W**↵
Specify line width for rectangles <*current*>: **.03**↵
Specify first corner point or [Chamfer/Elevation/Fillet/Thickness/Width]:

You can press [Enter] at the Specify line width for rectangles: prompt to have the rectangle polylines drawn with the default polyline width. If you enter a value at this prompt, the polylines are drawn using the specified width.

After setting the rectangle width, you can either select another option or draw the rectangle. Continue selecting options until you have set the characteristics correctly, and then draw the rectangle. If a width is set, any new rectangles drawn use the width you entered. To reset the width to the initial default, enter the **Width** option, and then specify a width of 0. Now, new rectangles are drawn using a standard "0 width" line.

Drawing Chamfered Rectangles

A ***chamfer*** is an angled corner on an object. Drawing chamfers is covered in detail in Chapter 12 of this text. This is a brief introduction to drawing chamfers on rectangles. To draw chamfers on rectangles, use the **Chamfer** option of the **RECTANG** command. The rectangle created will have chamfers drawn automatically.

After you select the **Chamfer** option, you must provide the chamfer distances. See **Figure 5-31.** The command sequence is as follows:

Command: **REC**, **RECTANG**, *or* **RECTANGLE**↵
Specify first corner point or [Chamfer/Elevation/Fillet/Thickness/Width]: **C**↵
Specify first chamfer distance for rectangles <*current*>: *(enter the first chamfer distance)*
Specify second chamfer distance for rectangles <*current*>: *(enter the second chamfer distance)*
Specify first corner point or [Chamfer/Elevation/Fillet/Thickness/Width]:

After setting the chamfer distances, you can either draw the rectangle or select another option. If you select the **Fillet** option, the chamfers will not be drawn.

Figure 5-31.
A chamfer is an angled corner. Two distances are used to calculate the chamfer.

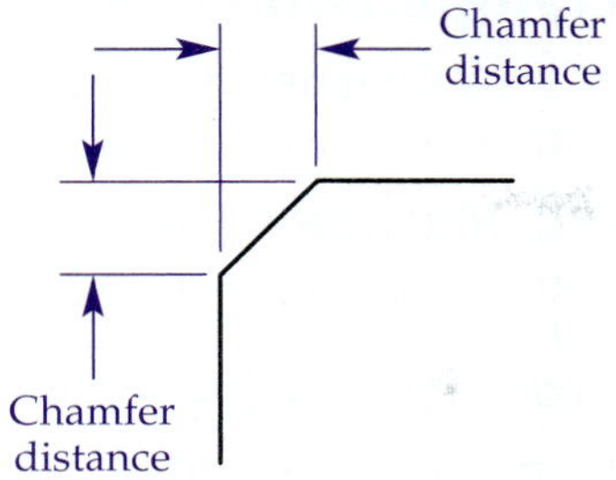

The default chamfer distances are the chamfer distances or fillet radius used to draw the previous rectangle. If the default for the first chamfer distance is zero, and you enter a different value, the new distance becomes the default for the second chamfer distance. If the default chamfer distances are nonzero values, however, a new value entered for the first distance does *not* become the default for the second distance. As with the **Width** option, if you set the **Chamfer** option's distances to a value greater than 0, any new rectangles created are automatically chamfered. New rectangles will continue to be created with chamfers until you reset the chamfer distances to 0 or use the **Fillet** option to create rounded corners.

Drawing Filleted Rectangles

A ***fillet*** is a rounded corner on an object. See **Figure 5-32.** Drawing fillets is covered in detail in Chapter 12 of this text. This is a brief introduction to drawing fillets on rectangles.

Fillets are automatically drawn on rectangles using the **Fillet** option of the **RECTANG** command. After selecting the option, you must enter the fillet radius:

Command: **REC**, **RECTANG**, *or* **RECTANGLE**↵
Specify first corner point or [Chamfer/Elevation/Fillet/Thickness/Width]: **F**↵
Specify fillet radius for rectangles <*current*>: *(enter a fillet radius or press* [Enter] *to accept the default)*
Specify first corner point or [Chamfer/Elevation/Fillet/Thickness/Width]:

The default fillet radius is the radius of the previously drawn rectangle. Once a fillet radius is specified, the **RECTANG** command will automatically draw fillets on rectangles. In order to draw rectangles without fillets, the fillet radius must be set to 0. **Figure 5-33** shows examples of rectangles drawn with chamfers and fillets.

Figure 5-32.
A fillet is a rounded corner.

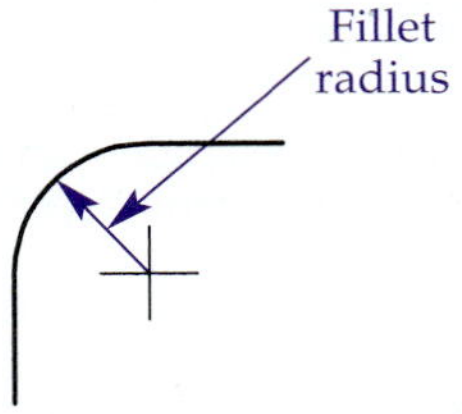

Figure 5-33.
Chamfered and filleted rectangles. A—A rectangle drawn with chamfers. B—A rectangle drawn with fillets.

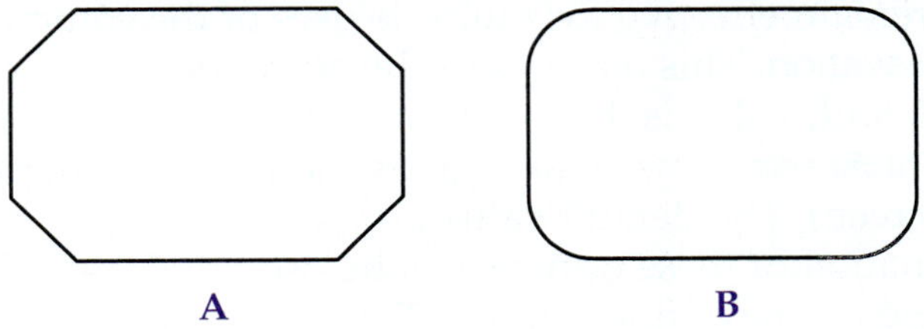

Specifying Rectangle Dimensions

AutoCAD provides a **Dimensions** option for the **RECTANG** command. The option is available after the first corner of the rectangle is picked:

> Command: **REC**, **RECTANG**, *or* **RECTANGLE**↵
> Specify first corner point or [Chamfer/Elevation/Fillet/Thickness/Width]: *(pick first corner point)*
> Specify other corner point or [Dimensions]:

Enter D to access the **Dimensions** option. You are then prompted to enter the length and width of the rectangle. In the following example, a 5 × 3 rectangle is specified:

> Specify other corner point or [Dimensions]: **D**↵
> Specify length for rectangles <*current*>: **5**↵
> Specify width for rectangles <*current*>: **3**↵
> Specify other corner point or [Dimensions]: *(move the crosshairs to the desired quadrant and pick a point)*
> Command:

After specifying the length and width, the Specify other corner point or [Dimensions]: prompt is displayed. If you wish to change the dimensions, select the **Dimensions** option again. If the dimensions are correct, you can specify the other corner point to complete the rectangle. When using the **Dimensions** option, the second corner point determines which of four possible rectangles is drawn. See **Figure 5-34.**

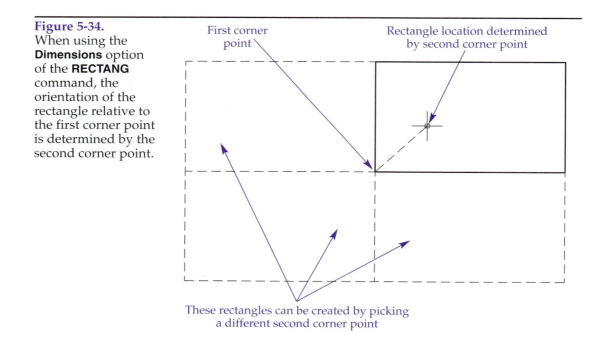

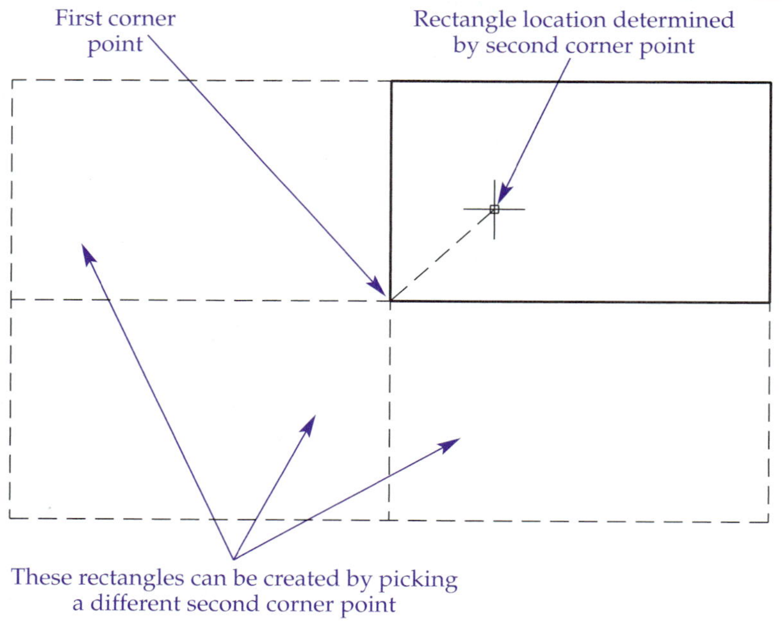
First corner point
Rectangle location determined by second corner point
These rectangles can be created by picking a different second corner point

Figure 5-34. When using the **Dimensions** option of the **RECTANG** command, the orientation of the rectangle relative to the first corner point is determined by the second corner point.

Additional RECTANG Options

There are two other options available when using the **RECTANG** command. These options remain effective for multiple uses of the command:

- **Elevation.** This option sets the elevation of the rectangle along the Z axis. The default value is 0.
- **Thickness.** This option gives the rectangle depth along the Z axis (into the screen). The default value is 0.

A combination of these options can be used to draw a single rectangle. For example, a rectangle can have fillets and a .03 line width.

EXERCISE 5-8 Complete the Exercise on the Student CD.

Drawing Donuts and Solid Circles

DONUT
DOUGHNUT
DO

Draw
➥ Donut

Donuts drawn in AutoCAD are actually polyline arcs with width. Drawing polylines is introduced in Chapter 14 and is covered in detail in Chapter 15. The **DONUT** command allows you to draw a thick circle. It can have any inside and outside diameters or be completely filled. See **Figure 5-35.**

The **DONUT** command can be accessed by selecting **Donut** from the **Draw** pull-down menu or by entering DO, DONUT, or DOUGHNUT at the Command: prompt, as follows:

Command: **DO**, **DONUT**, *or* **DOUGHNUT**↵
Specify inside diameter of donut <*current*>: *(enter inside diameter)*
Specify outside diameter of donut <*current*>: *(enter outside diameter)*
Specify center of donut or <exit>: *(select the donut's center point)*
Specify center of donut or <exit>: *(select the center point for another donut, or press* [Enter] *to discontinue the command)*

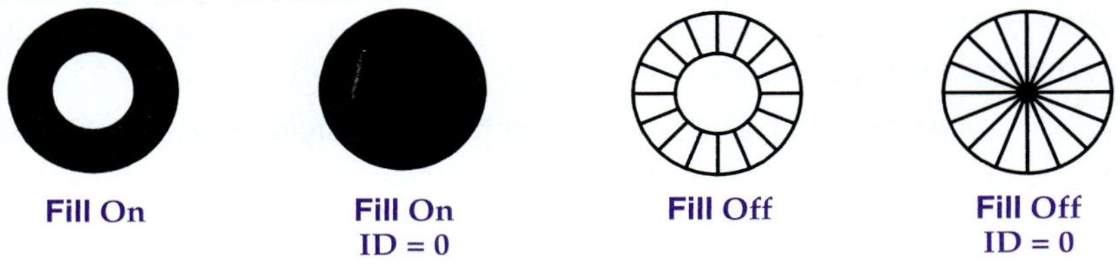

Figure 5-35.
Examples of donuts.

The current diameter settings are shown in brackets. New diameters can be entered, or the current value can be accepted by pressing the [Enter] key. An inside diameter of 0 produces a solid circle.

After selecting the center point, the donut appears on the screen. You may pick another center point to draw the same size donut in a new location. The **DONUT** command remains active until you press [Enter] or cancel by pressing [Esc].

When the **FILL** mode is turned off, donuts appear as segmented circles or concentric circles. **FILL** can be used transparently by entering 'FILL while inside the **DONUT** command. Enter ON or OFF as needed. The fill display for previously drawn donuts is updated when the drawing is regenerated.

NOTE

The setting for the inside diameter of a donut is stored in the **DONUTID** system variable. The setting for the outside diameter is stored in the **DONUTOD** system variable. If the value of **DONUTID** is greater than the value of **DONUTOD**, the values are switched when the next donut is drawn.

EXERCISE 5-9 Complete the Exercise on the Student CD.

Using the Revision Cloud

A ***revision cloud*** is a polyline of sequential arcs that forms a cloud-shaped object. See **Figure 5-36.** Revision clouds are typically used by people who review drawings and mark notes and changes. The revision cloud points the drafter to a specific portion of the drawing that may need to be edited.

REVCLOUD
Draw
➥ Revision Cloud
Draw toolbar
Revcloud

To create a revision cloud, pick a starting location, move the cursor to shape the cloud, and then move the cursor toward the beginning of the cloud. AutoCAD automatically closes the cloud and ends the command. This command can be entered by selecting **Revision Cloud** from the **Draw** pull-down menu, picking the **Revcloud** button from the **Draw** toolbar, or by entering REVCLOUD at the Command: prompt. The following prompt is displayed after entering this command:

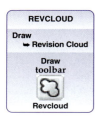

Command: **REVCLOUD**↵
Minimum arc length: *current* Maximum arc length: *current* Style: *current*
Specify start point or [Arc length/Object/Style] <*current option*>:

To begin drawing the revision cloud, pick a starting point in the drawing. After picking the starting point, the prompt tells you to Guide crosshairs along cloud path.... Move the cursor around the objects to be enclosed, until you come close to the starting point. AutoCAD then closes the cloud and prompts you with the message Revision cloud finished.

The size of the arcs is determined by entering the **Arc length** option. This value measures the length of an arc from its starting point to its ending point. You can change this value to any desired value. Upon entering the **Arc length** option, you are prompted for the following:

Specify start point or [Arc length/Object/Style] <*current option*>: **A**↵
Specify minimum length of arc <*current size*>: *(enter a minimum arc length)*
Specify maximum length of arc <*current size*>: *(enter a maximum arc length)*
Specify start point or [Arc length/Object/Style] <*current option*>: *(pick a starting point for the cloud)*

Figure 5-36.
The revision cloud can be used to identify areas of a drawing that have been modified.

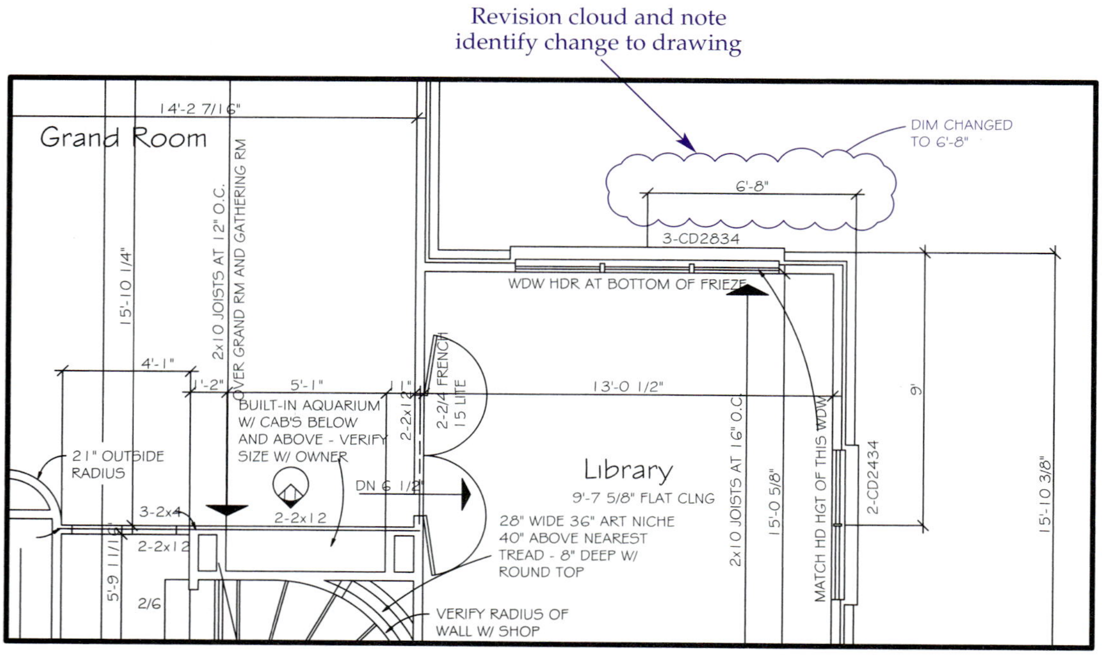

Varying the minimum and maximum values causes the revision cloud to have an uneven, hand-drawn look. The actual size of the arc is the length value multiplied by the dimension scale (**DIMSCALE** variable), so revision clouds appear the same size in drawings with different scales.

Circles, closed polylines, ellipses, polygons, and rectangles can be converted to revision clouds by selecting the **Object** option. The command sequence follows:

Command: **REVCLOUD**↵
Minimum arc length: *current*   Maximum arc length: *current*   Style: *current*
Specify start point or [Arc length/Object/Style] <*current option*>: **O**↵
Select object: *(pick the object to convert to a revision cloud)*
Reverse direction [Yes/No] <*default*>: *(enter* N*, or enter* Y *to reverse the cloud arcs)*
Revision cloud finished.
Command:

The polyline and dimension scale topics related to this discussion are covered in detail later in this text.

AutoCAD 2005 NEW FEATURE

The **Style** option of the **REVCLOUD** command offers two different style choices: **Normal** and **Calligraphy**. The default style is **Normal**, in which the arcs are a consistent width. With the **Calligraphy** style, the individual arcs' start and end widths are different, creating a more stylish revision cloud. See Figure 5-37. To change the revision cloud style, the command sequence is as follows:

Command: **REVCLOUD**↵
Minimum arc length: *current*   Maximum arc length: *current*   Style: *current*
Specify start point or [Arc length/Object/Style] <*current option*>: **S**↵
Select arc style [Normal/Calligraphy] <*current*>: **C**↵
Arc style = Calligraphy
Specify start point or [Arc length/Object/Style] <*current option*>: *(pick a starting point for the cloud)*
Guide crosshairs along cloud path… *(move the cursor around the objects to be enclosed, until you come close to the starting point)*
Revision cloud finished.
Command:

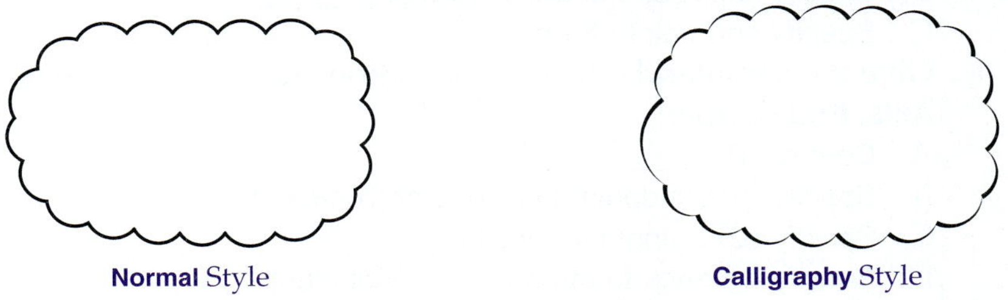

Figure 5-37.
Revision clouds can be created in two different styles, the **Normal** style and the **Calligraphy** style.

EXERCISE 5-10 Complete the Exercise on the Student CD.

Chapter Test

Answer the following questions on a separate sheet of paper.

1. Give the command, entries, and actions required to draw a circle with a 2.5 unit diameter:
   A. Command: _____
   B. Specify center point for circle or [3P/2P/Ttr (tan tan radius)]: _____
   C. Specify radius of circle or [Diameter] <*current*>: _____
   D. Specify diameter of circle <*current*>: _____
2. Give the command, entries, and actions required to draw a circle that has a 1.75 unit radius and is tangent to an existing line and circle:
   A. Command: _____
   B. Specify center point for circle or [3P/2P/Ttr (tan tan radius)]: _____
   C. Specify point on object for first tangent of circle: _____
   D. Specify point on object for second tangent of circle: _____
   E. Specify radius of circle <*current*>: _____
3. Give the command, entries, and actions needed to draw a three-point arc:
   A. Command: _____
   B. Specify start point of arc or [Center]: _____
   C. Specify second point of arc or [Center/End]: _____
   D. Specify end point of arc: _____
4. Give the command, entries, and actions needed to draw an arc, beginning with the center point and having a 60° included angle:
   A. Command: _____
   B. Specify start point of arc or [Center]: _____
   C. Specify center point of arc: _____
   D. Specify start point of arc: _____
   E. Specify end point of arc or [Angle/chord Length]: _____
   F. Specify included angle: _____
5. Give the command, entries, and actions required to draw an arc tangent to the endpoint of a previously drawn line:
   A. Command: _____
   B. Specify start point of arc or [Center]: _____
   C. Specify end point of arc: _____
6. Give the command, entries, and actions needed to draw an ellipse with the **Axis, End** option:
   A. Command: _____
   B. Specify axis endpoint of ellipse or [Arc/Center]: _____
   C. Specify other endpoint of axis: _____
   D. Specify distance to other axis or [Rotation]: _____
7. Give the command, entries, and actions necessary to draw a hexagon measuring 4″ (102 mm) across the flats:
   A. Command: _____
   B. Enter number of sides <*current*>: _____
   C. Specify center of polygon or [Edge]: _____
   D. Enter an option [Inscribed in circle/Circumscribed about circle] <*current*>: _____
   E. Specify radius of circle: _____

8. Give the responses required to draw two donuts with a .25 inside diameter and a .75 outside diameter:
   A. Command: _____
   B. Specify inside diameter of donut <*current*>: _____
   C. Specify outside diameter of donut <*current*>: _____
   D. Specify center of donut or <exit>: _____
   E. Specify center of donut or <exit>: _____
   F. Specify center of donut or <exit>: _____
9. Describe why the @ symbol can be used by itself for point selection.
10. Define the term *included angle*.
11. List the three input options that can be used to draw an arc tangent to the endpoint of a previously drawn arc.
12. Given the distance across the flats of a hexagon, would you use the **Inscribed** or **Circumscribed** option to draw the hexagon?
13. Describe how a solid circle can be drawn.
14. Identify how to access the option that allows you to draw a circle tangent to three objects.
15. Identify two ways to access the **Arc** option for drawing elliptical arcs.
16. Name the AutoCAD system variable that lets you draw a true ellipse or a polyline ellipse with the **ELLIPSE** command.
17. Name the pull-down menu where the **RECTANGLE** command is found.
18. What is the default option if the **ARC** command is typed at the Command: prompt?
19. Give the easiest keyboard shortcut for the following commands:
    A. **CIRCLE**
    B. **ARC**
    C. **ELLIPSE**
    D. **POLYGON**
    E. **RECTANG**
    F. **DONUT**
20. Name the command option designed specifically for drawing rectangles with line width.
21. Name the command option used to draw rectangles with rounded corners.
22. Describe how you would draw a rectangle with different chamfer distances at each corner.
23. What is the **ELLIPSE** rotation angle that causes you to draw a circle?
24. Explain how to turn the **FILL** mode off while inside the **DONUT** command.
25. Name the system variable used to set the default radius when drawing circles.
26. How do you close a revision cloud?

Drawing Problems

Start AutoCAD and use one of the setup options or use a template. Do not draw dimensions or text. Use your own judgment and approximate dimensions if needed.

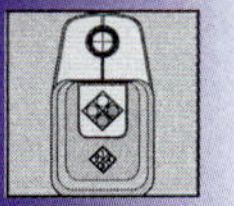

1. You have just been given the sketch of a new sports car design (shown below). You are asked to create a drawing from the sketch. Use the **LINE** command and selected shape commands to draw the car. Do not be concerned with size and scale. Consider the commands and techniques used to draw the car, and try to minimize the number of entities. Save your drawing as P5-1.

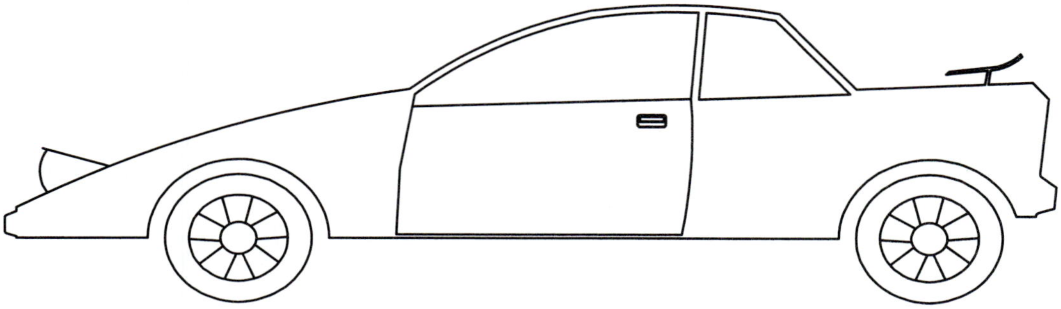

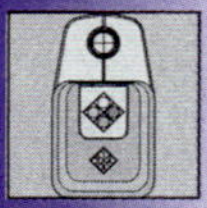

2. You have just been given the sketch of an innovative new truck design (shown below). You are asked to create a drawing from the sketch. Use the **LINE** command and selected shape commands to draw a truck resembling the sketch. Do not be concerned with size and scale. Save your drawing as P5-2.

3. Use the **LINE** and **CIRCLE** command options to draw the objects below. Do not include dimensions. Save the drawing as P5-3.

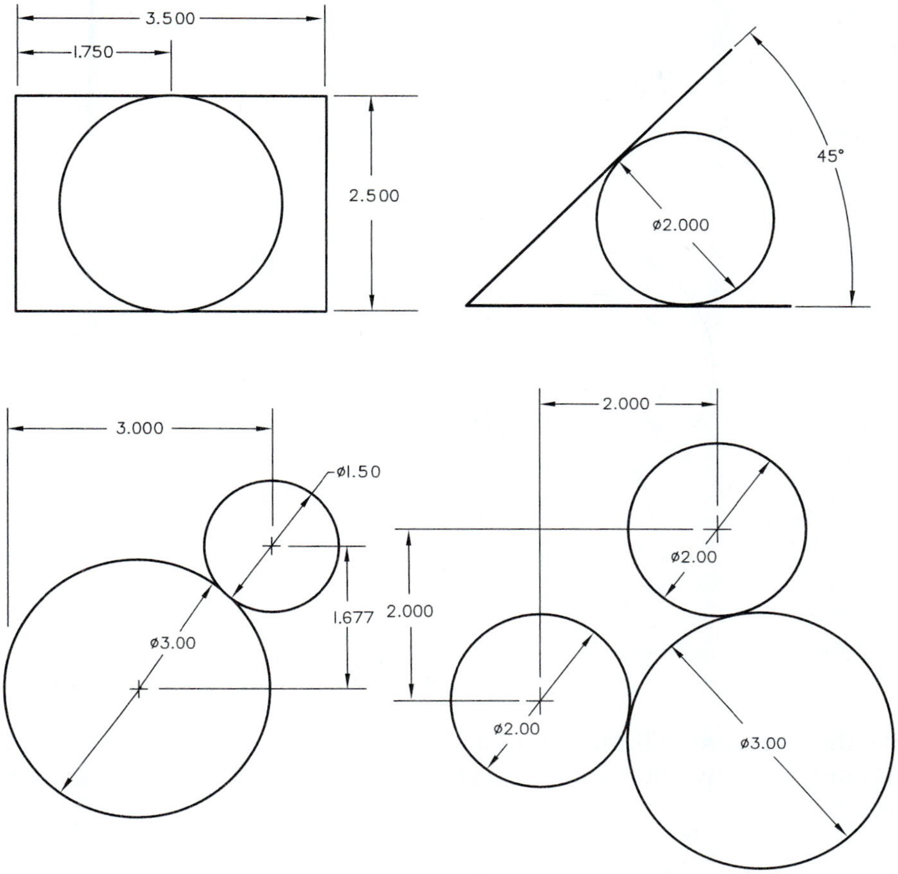

4. Use the **CIRCLE** and **ARC** command options to draw the object below. Do not include dimensions. Save the drawing as P5-4.

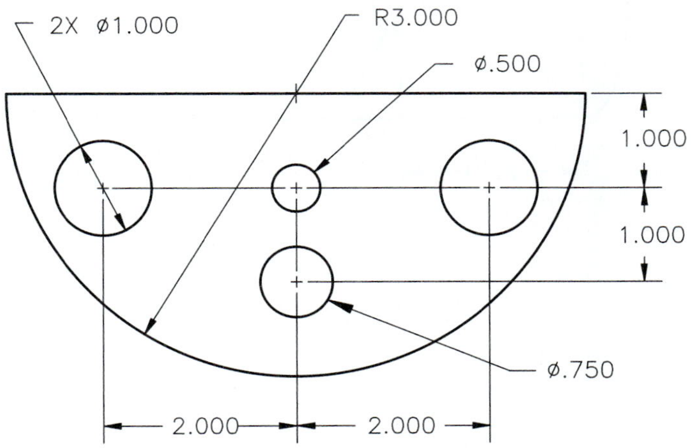

5. Draw the following object. Do not include dimensions.

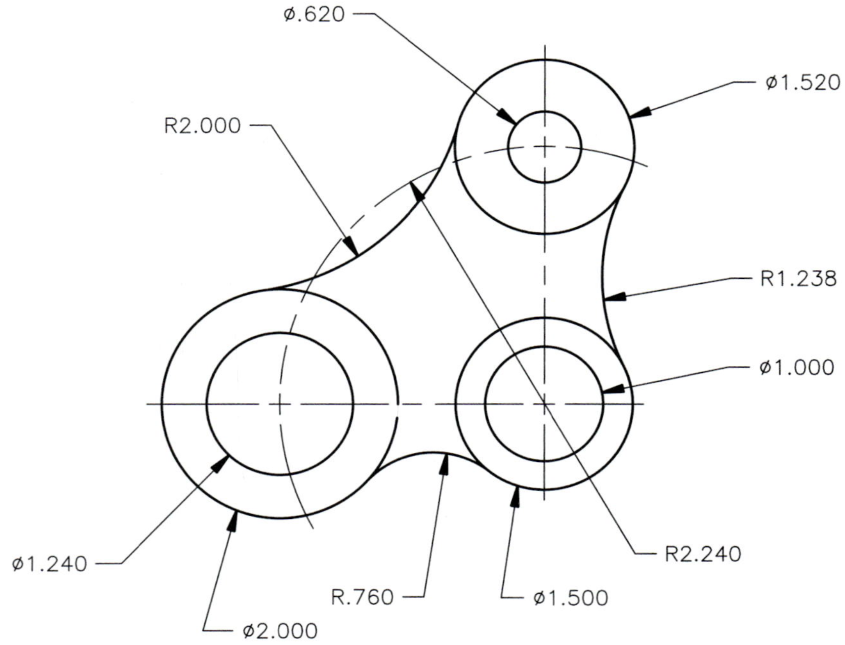

(Art courtesy of Bruce L. Wilcox)

6. Draw the pressure cylinder shown below. Use the **Arc** option of the **ELLIPSE** command to draw the cylinder ends. Do not draw the dimensions. Save the drawing as P5-6.

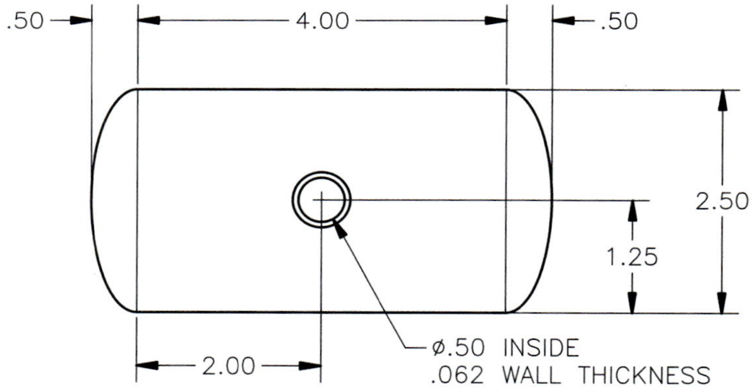

7. Draw the hex head bolt pattern shown below. Do not draw dimensions. Save the drawing as P5-7.

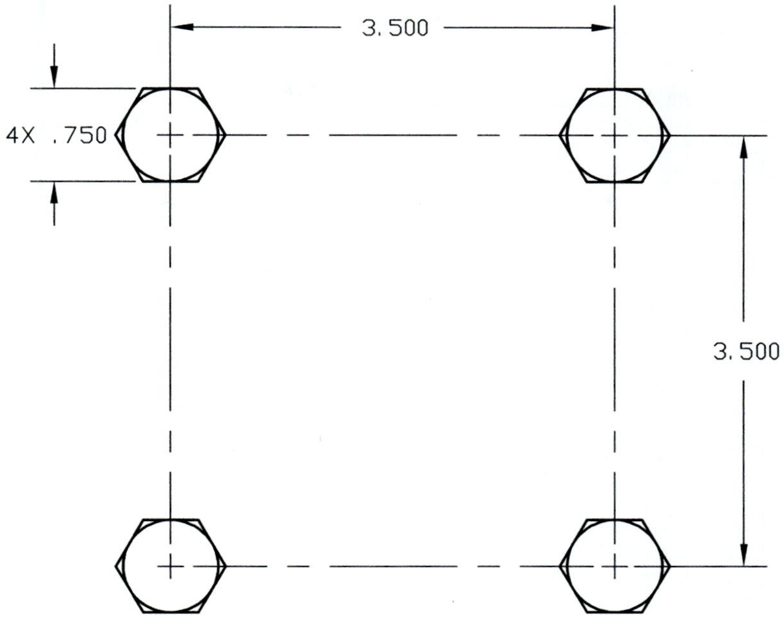

8. Draw the spacer below. Do not draw the dimensions.

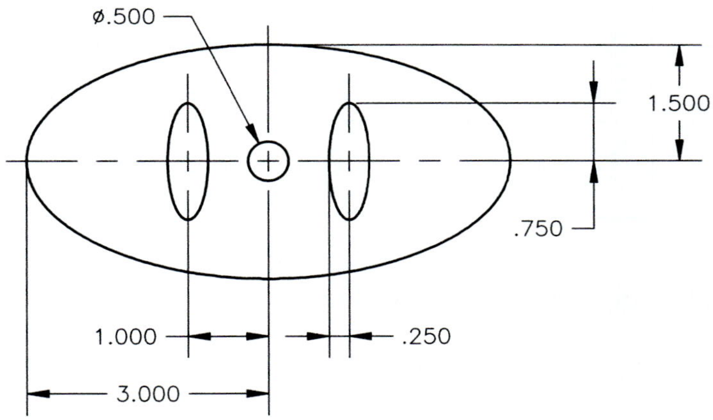

Drawing Problems - Chapter 5

9. Draw the following object. Do not include dimensions.

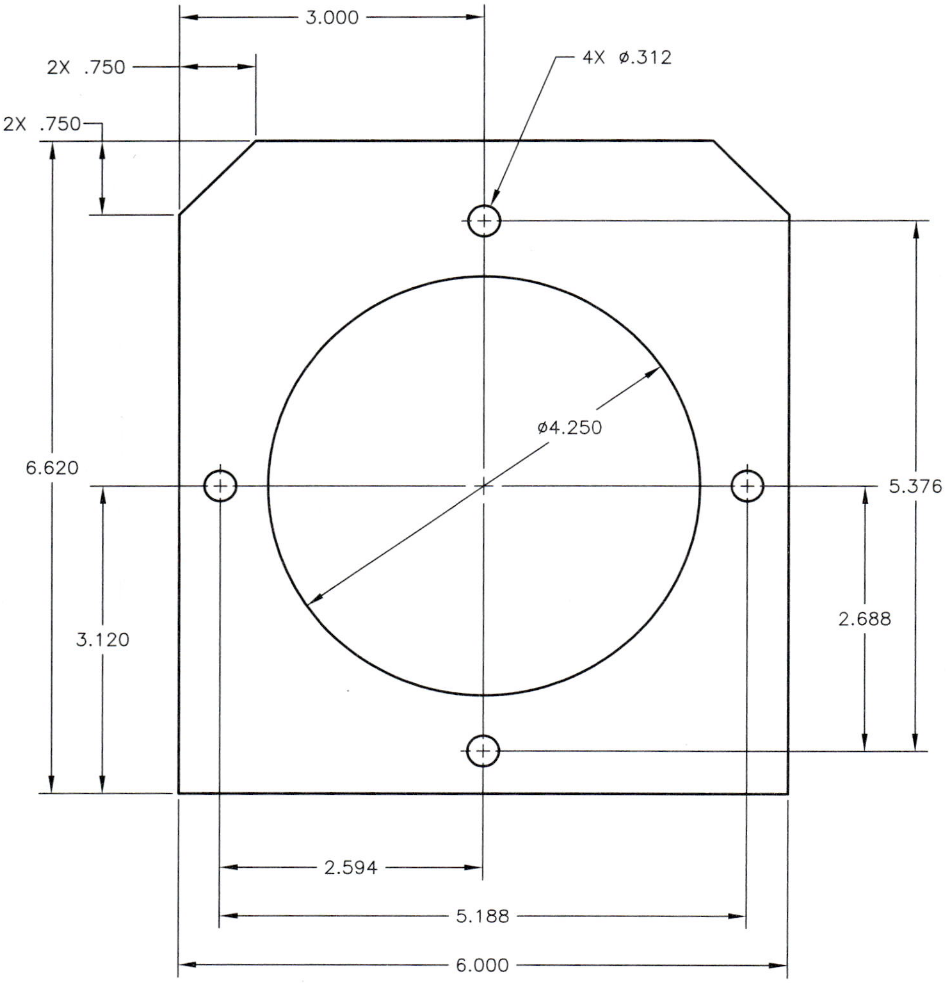

10. Draw the following object. Do not include dimensions.

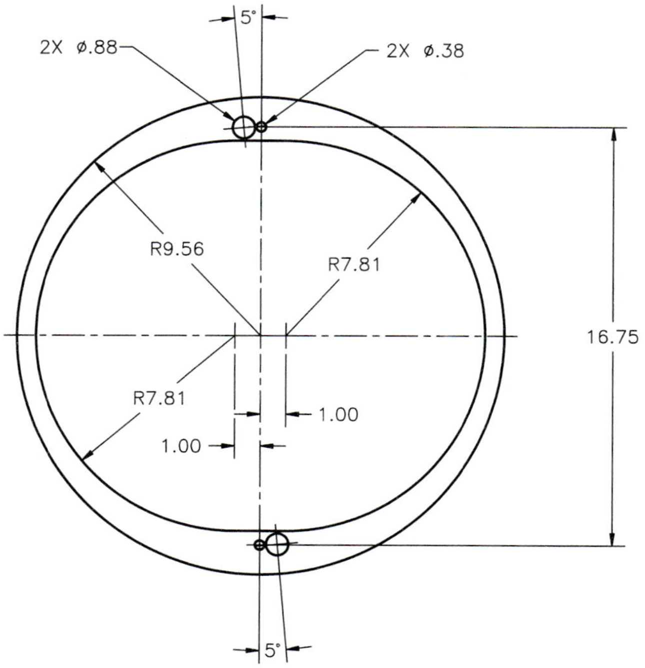

11. Create this controller integrated circuit diagram. Use a ruler or scale to keep the proportion as close as possible. Do not include the text.

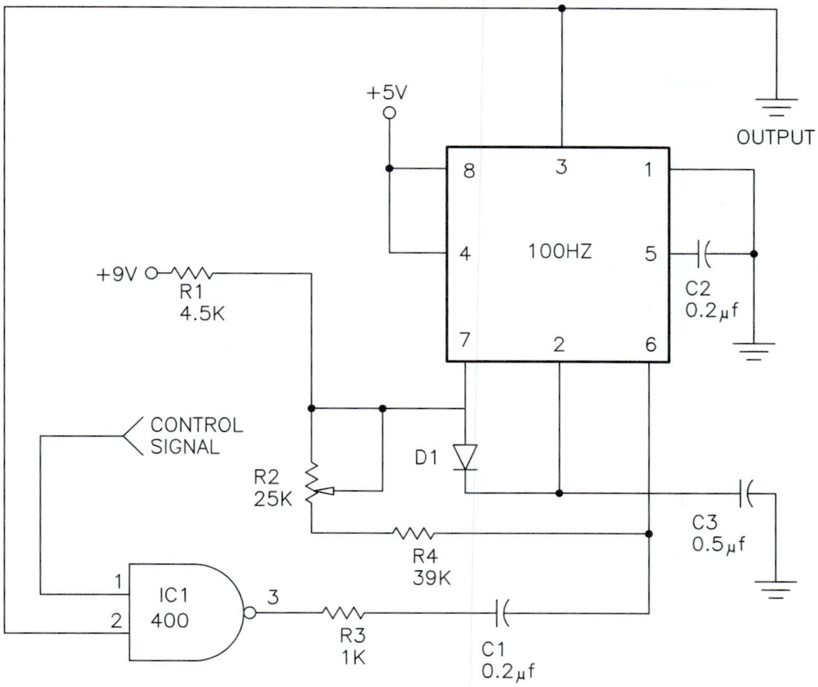

12. Draw this elevation using the **ARC**, **CIRCLE**, and **RECTANG** commands. Do not be concerned with size and scale.

Drawing Problems - Chapter 5

13. Create a 1/2″ hex nut with 3/4″ across the flats and a .422″ root diameter as shown. Save the drawing as P5-13.

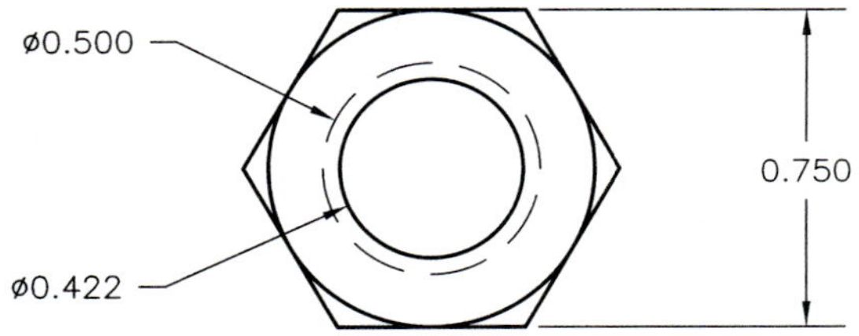

14. Open P4-5 and add the donuts to the cells in the schedule. Save the drawing as P5-14.

CHAPTER 6

Object Snap, Geometric Constructions, and Multiview Drawings

Learning Objectives

After completing this chapter, you will be able to do the following:

- Use object snap modes to create precision drawings.
- Use object snap overrides for single point selections.
- Set running object snap modes for continuous use.
- Use the AutoSnap features to speed up point specifications.
- Adjust marker size based on point selection needs.
- Use temporary tracking and AutoTrack modes to locate points relative to other points in a drawing.
- Use polar tracking and polar snap.
- Make point selections using coordinate filters.
- Use the **OFFSET** command to draw parallel lines and curves.
- Divide existing objects into equal lengths using the **DIVIDE** command.
- Use the **MEASURE** command to set designated increments on an existing object.
- Create orthographic multiview drawings.
- Adjust snap grid and UCS settings to construct auxiliary views.
- Use construction lines to assist in drawing orthographic views and auxiliary views.

This chapter explains how the powerful **OSNAP** command features are used when creating and editing your drawing. **OSNAP** means *object snap*. Object snap allows you to instantly locate exact points relative to existing objects. A feature called ***AutoSnap***™ can be used to visually preview and confirm snap point options prior to point selection. Other point selection methods, such as object snap tracking, polar tracking, and X and Y coordinate filters, allow you to locate points relative to existing points. This chapter continues with an explanation of how to create parallel offset copies, divide objects, and place point objects. Creating multiview drawings using orthographic projection and construction lines is also covered.

Snapping to Specific Features

Object snap is one of the most useful tools found in AutoCAD. It increases your drafting ability, performance, and productivity. The term ***object snap*** refers to the cursor's ability to "snap" exactly to a specific point or place on an object. The advantage of object snap is that you do not have to pick an exact point.

The AutoSnap feature is enabled by default. With AutoSnap active, visual cues are displayed while using object snap. This helps you in visualizing and confirming candidate points for object snap.

These visual cues appear as ***markers*** displayed at the current selection point. **Figure 6-1** shows two examples of visual cues provided by AutoSnap. The endpoint of a line object is being picked in **Figure 6-1A.** The visual cue for an **Endpoint** object snap is shown as a square when the cursor is placed close to the line object. After a brief pause, a tooltip is displayed, indicating the object snap mode. In **Figure 6-1B,** a point that is tangent to an existing circle is being selected. The AutoSnap symbol for a tangency point is shown as a circle with a tangent horizontal line.

Another visual clue that is displayed with some object snaps, and also with AutoTrack options, is an alignment path. An ***alignment path*** is a dashed line that shows the path upon which an object would be drawn if aligned as desired with another object. For example, you will see a parallel alignment path created when drawing parallel objects using the **Parallel** object snap. An ***extension path*** is a type of alignment path that is displayed when using the **Extension** object snap to find the imaginary extension of an existing object. The default settings for AutoSnap are used for this discussion of the object snap features. Changing AutoSnap settings and features is discussed later in this chapter.

Figure 6-1.
AutoSnap displays markers and related tooltips for object snap modes.

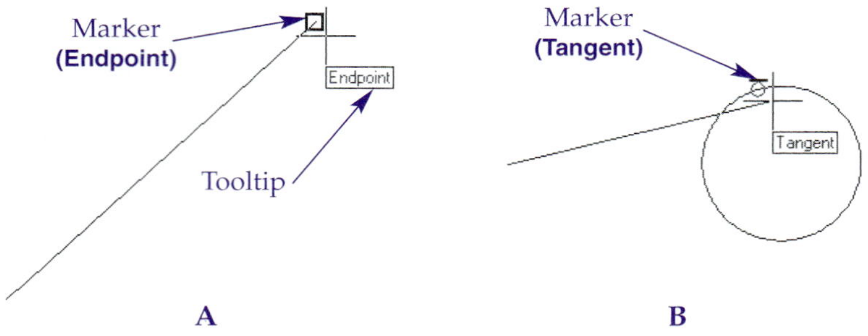

Object Snap Modes

Object snap modes determine the point to which the cursor snaps. These modes can be activated using one of several different methods. After entering a command, an object snap override can be typed at the prompt line or selected from the **Object Snap** shortcut menu shown in **Figure 6-2.** To activate this menu, hold down the [Shift] key and right-click your mouse or pick the [Enter] button on your puck. Object snap overrides are also available as buttons in the **Object Snap** toolbar. See **Figure 6-3.**

To activate the **Object Snap** toolbar, select **Toolbars...** from the **View** pull-down menu. Select **Object Snap** in the **Toolbars** tab of the **Customize** dialog box. Pick the **Close** button to close the **Customize** dialog box. You can keep the **Object Snap** toolbar floating, or you can dock it at the edge of the graphics window in a location that is convenient to access.

Object snap override refers to the entry of an object snap mode at a point specification prompt. A ***point specification prompt*** is any prompt that asks you to enter or pick a point coordinate. Object snap overrides are active for one point specification only, and they override any previously set object snap modes for that one entry. A ***running object snap mode*** stays active for all point selections until it is changed. Running object snap modes are discussed later in this chapter.

Figure 6-2.
The **Object Snap** shortcut menu provides quick access to object snap overrides.

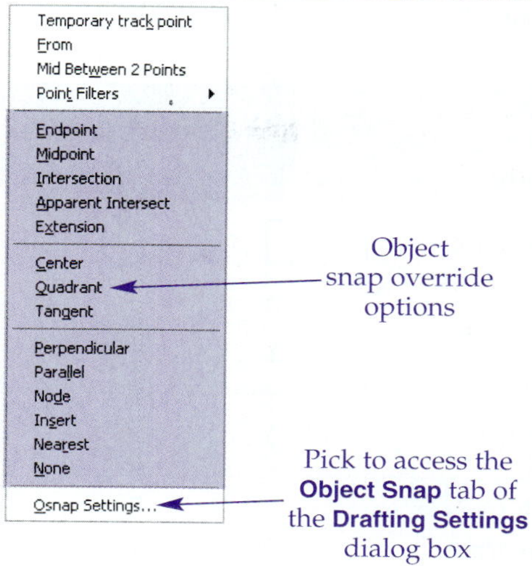

Figure 6-3.
The **Object Snap** toolbar.

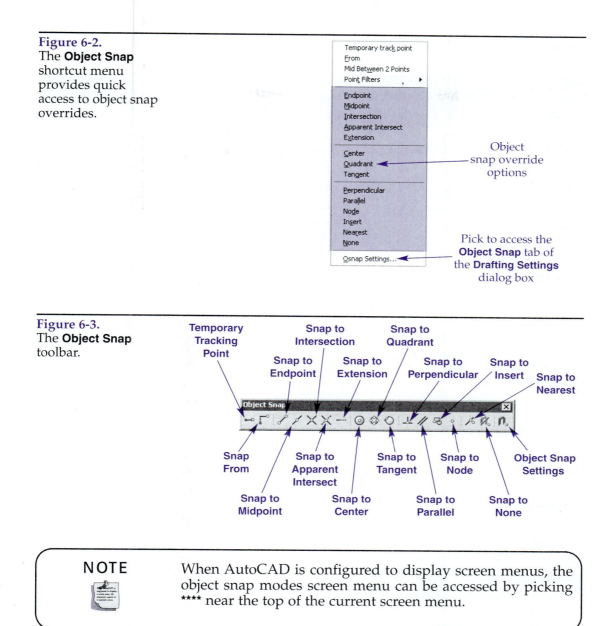

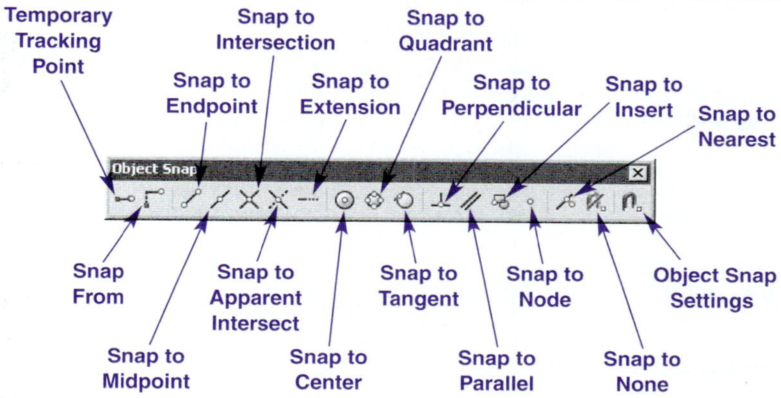

NOTE

When AutoCAD is configured to display screen menus, the object snap modes screen menu can be accessed by picking **** near the top of the current screen menu.

The table in **Figure 6-4** summarizes the object snap modes. Included with each mode is the marker that appears on-screen and its button from the **Object Snap** toolbar. Each object snap mode selects a different portion of an object. When you activate an object snap override from the prompt line, you only need to enter the first three letters of the desired object snap mode.

PROFESSIONAL TIP

Remember that object snap overrides are not commands. They are, however, used in conjunction with commands. If you type MID at the Command: prompt, for example, AutoCAD displays an Unknown command "MID". Press F1 for help. error message.

Figure 6-4.
The object snap modes.

Object Snap Modes			
Mode	**Marker**	**Button**	**Description**
Endpoint	□		Finds the nearest endpoint of a line, arc, polyline, elliptical arc, spline, ellipse, ray, solid, or multiline.
Midpoint	△		Finds the middle point of any object having two endpoints, such as a line, polyline, arc, elliptical arc, polyline arc, spline, ray, solid, xline, or multiline.
Center	○		Locates the center point of a radial object, including circles, arcs, ellipses, elliptical arcs, and radial solids.
Quadrant	◇		Picks the closest of the four quadrant points that can be found on circles, arcs, elliptical arcs, ellipses, and radial solids. (Not all of these objects may have all four quadrants.)
Intersection	✕		Picks the closest intersection of two objects.
Apparent Intersection	⊠		Selects a visual intersection between two objects that appear to intersect on screen in the current view, but may not actually intersect each other in 3D space.
Extension	+		Finds a point along the imaginary extension of an existing line, polyline, arc, polyline arc, elliptical arc, spline, ray, xline, solid, or multiline.
Insertion	⊐		Finds the insertion point of text objects and blocks.
Perpendicular	⌐		Finds a point that is perpendicular to an object from the previously picked point.
Parallel	⫽		Used to find any point along an imaginary line parallel to an existing line or polyline.
Tangent	○̄		Finds points of tangency between radial and linear objects.
Nearest	⋈		Locates the point on an object closest to the crosshairs.
Node	⊗		Picks a point object drawn with the **POINT**, **DIVIDE**, or **MEASURE** command.
None			Turns running object snap off.

Practice with the different object snap modes to find the ones that work best in various situations. Object snap can be used during many commands, such as **LINE**, **CIRCLE**, **ARC**, **MOVE**, **COPY**, and **INSERT**. The most common uses for object snap are discussed in the following sections.

Endpoint Object Snap

In many cases, you need to connect a line, an arc, or a center point of a circle to the endpoint of an existing line or arc. Select the **Endpoint** object snap mode and move the cursor past the midpoint of the line or arc, toward the end to be picked. A small square marks the endpoint that will be picked.

In **Figure 6-5,** the following command sequence is used to connect a line to the endpoint of an existing line:

Figure 6-5.
Using **Endpoint** object snap.

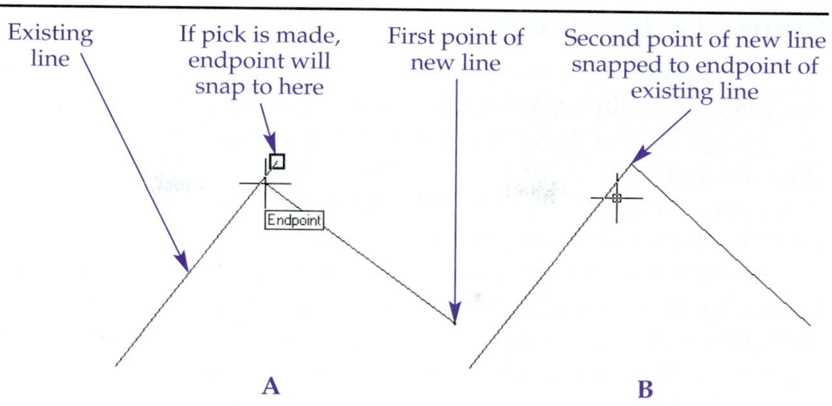

Command: **L** *or* **LINE**↵
Specify first point: *(pick a point)*
Specify next point or [Undo]: *(pick the* **Snap to Endpoint** *button on the* **Object Snap** *toolbar, type* END, *or pick* **Endpoint** *from the* **Object Snap** *shortcut menu)*
of *(move the cursor near the end of the line and pick)*
Specify next point or [Undo]: ↵
Command:

The **Endpoint** object snap can be used to quickly select the endpoints of all types of lines and arcs. It is often selected as a running object snap.

Midpoint Object Snap

The **Midpoint** object snap mode finds and picks the midpoint of a line, a polyline, or an arc. During a command, type MID at the prompt, pick the **Snap to Midpoint** button on the **Object Snap** toolbar, or select **Midpoint** from the **Object Snap** shortcut menu to activate this object snap mode. Next, position the cursor near the midpoint of the object. A small triangle will mark the midpoint. See Figure 6-6.

Figure 6-6.
Using **Midpoint** object snap.

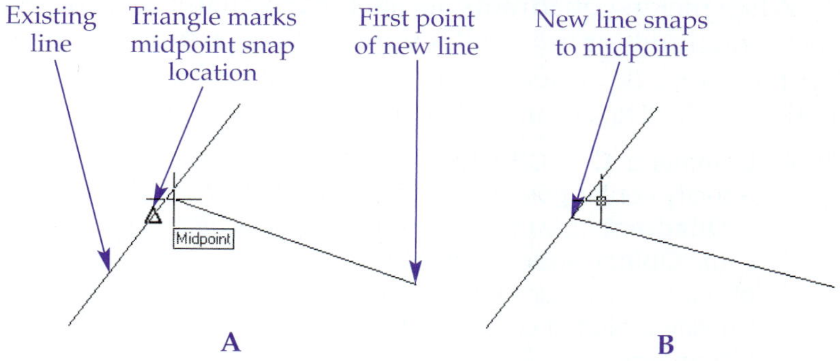

EXERCISE 6-1

Complete the Exercise on the Student CD.

Center Object Snap

The **Center** object snap mode allows you to snap to the center point of a circle, a doughnut, an ellipse, an elliptical arc, a polyline arc, or an arc. The mode is activated by typing CEN at the selection prompt, picking the **Snap to Center** button on the **Object Snap** toolbar, or picking **Center** from the **Object Snap** shortcut menu. When you move the cursor onto the object whose center point is to be located, a small circle and plus sign will mark the center point.

Be sure to move the cursor near the perimeter, not the center point, of the object. For example, when locating the center of a large circle, the **Center** object snap mode will *not* locate the center if the cursor is not near the perimeter of the circle. In Figure 6-7, the **Center** object snap is used to draw a line to the center of a circle.

Figure 6-7.
Using **Center** object snap.

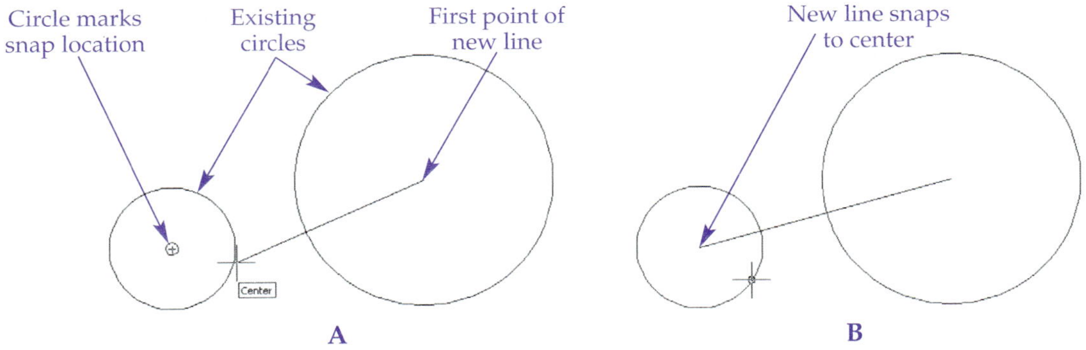

Quadrant Object Snap

A ***quadrant*** is a quarter section of a circle, a doughnut, an ellipse, an elliptical arc, a polyline arc, or an arc. The **Quadrant** object snap mode finds the 0°, 90°, 180°, and 270° positions on a circle, a doughnut, or an arc. See Figure 6-8.

When picking quadrants, locate the crosshairs near the intended quadrant on the circle, doughnut, or arc. For example, Figure 6-9 illustrates the use of the **Quadrant** object snap mode to locate the center point of a new circle at the quadrant of an existing circle. The command sequence is as follows:

Command: **C** *or* **CIRCLE**↵
Specify center point for circle or [3P/2P/Ttr (tan tan radius)]: *(pick the* **Snap to Quadrant** *button in the* **Object Snap** *toolbar, type* QUA, *or pick* **Quadrant** *from the* **Object Snap** *shortcut menu)*
of *(move the cursor near the desired quadrant and pick)*
Specify radius of circle or [Diameter] <*current*>: *(pick a radius)*
Command:

Figure 6-8.
The quadrants of a circle.

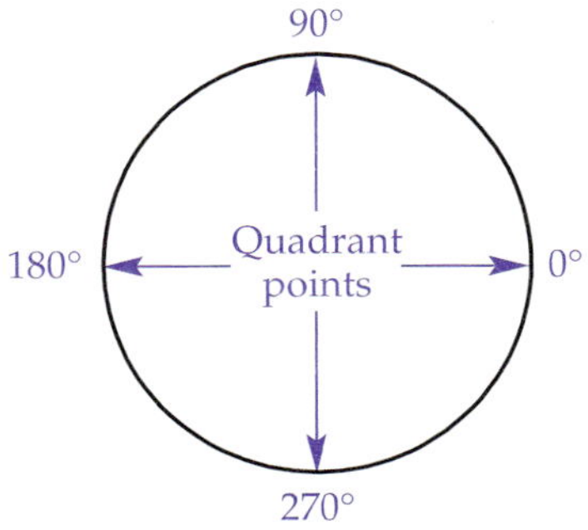

Figure 6-9.
Using **Quadrant** object snap.

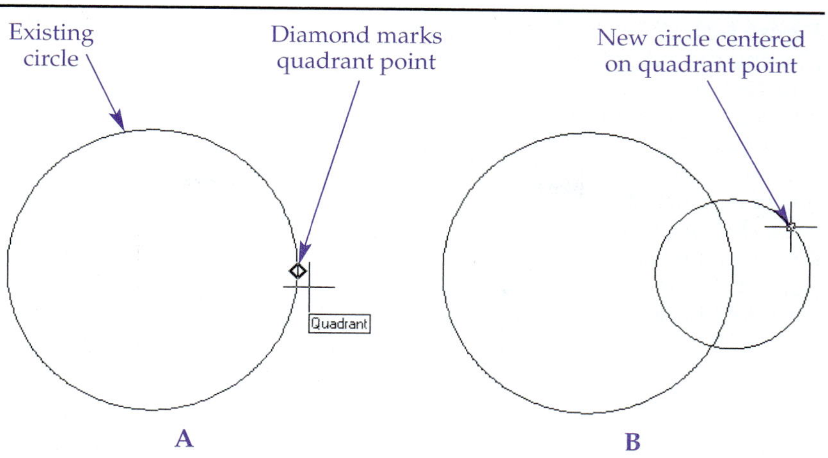

> **NOTE**
>
> Quadrant positions are unaffected by the current angle zero direction, but they always coincide with the current WCS (world coordinate system). The WCS is discussed later in this chapter. The quadrant points of a circle, a doughnut, or an arc are at the top, bottom, left, and right, regardless of the rotation of the object. The quadrant points of ellipses and elliptical arcs, however, rotate with the objects.

EXERCISE 6-2 Complete the Exercise on the Student CD.

Intersection Object Snap

The **Intersection** object snap mode is used to snap to the intersection of two or more objects. This mode is activated by typing INT at the selection prompt, picking the **Snap to Intersection** button on the **Object Snap** toolbar, or picking **Intersection** from the **Object Snap** shortcut menu. Move the cursor near the intersection. A small "X" marks the intersection. See Figure 6-10.

When picking a point for an **Intersection** object snap, the "X" appears only when the cursor is close to the intersection point of two objects. If the cursor is near an object, but not close to an actual intersection, the tooltip reads Extended Intersection, and the AutoSnap marker is followed by an ellipsis (...). When using **Extended Intersection**, you select the objects one at a time, and the intersection point is automatically located. This is especially useful when two objects do not actually intersect, and you need to access the point where these objects would intersect if they were extended. Figure 6-11 shows the use of **Extended Intersection** to find an intersection point between a line and an arc.

Figure 6-10.
Using **Intersection** object snap.

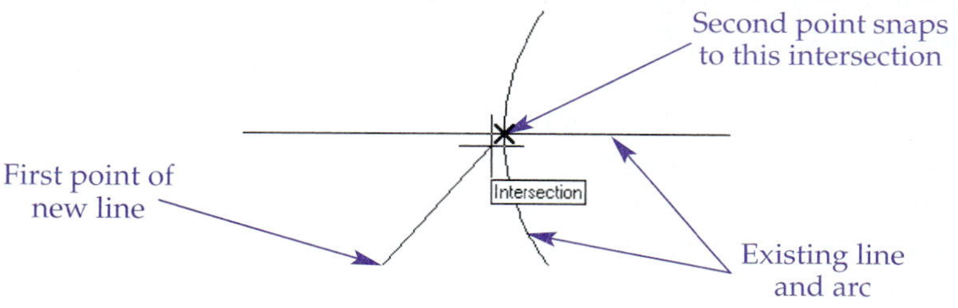

Figure 6-11.
Finding the extended intersection of two objects. A—Select the first object. B—When the second object is selected, the extended intersection becomes the snap point. C—The completed line.

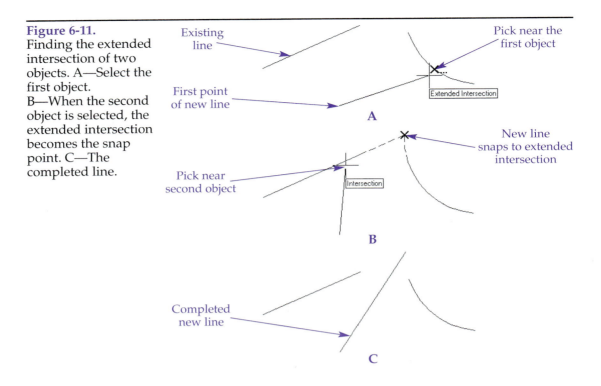

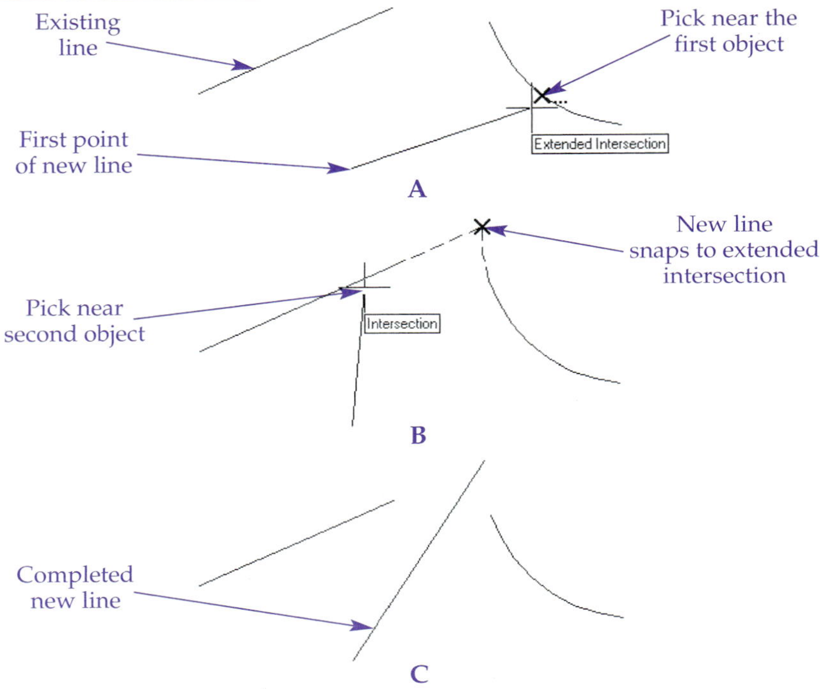

If the intersection point is not in the currently visible screen area, the AutoSnap marker is not displayed when selecting the second object. You can still confirm the point, however, before picking. Keeping the cursor motionless over the second object will display the tooltip, which confirms the objects intersect somewhere beyond the currently visible area. When selecting two objects that could not intersect, no AutoSnap marker or tooltip is displayed, and no intersection point is found if the pick is made.

Apparent Intersection Object Snap

The ***apparent intersection*** is the point where two objects created in 3D space appear to intersect based on the current view. Three-dimensional objects that are far apart may appear to intersect when viewed from certain angles. Whether they intersect or not, this option returns the coordinate point where the objects appear to intersect. This is a valuable option when working with 3D drawings. Creating and editing 3D objects is discussed in Chapter 27 of this text and in ***AutoCAD and its Applications—Advanced***.

Extension Object Snap

The **Extension** object snap mode is used to find any point along the imaginary extension of an existing line, polyline, or polyline arc. This mode is activated by typing EXT at the selection prompt, picking the **Snap to Extension** button on the **Object Snap** toolbar, or picking **Extension** from the **Object Snap** shortcut menu. The extension object snap differs from most other snaps because it requires more than one selection point. The initial point, called the ***acquired point***, is not selected in the typical manner, but is found by simply moving the cursor over the line, polyline, or polyline arc from which the new object is to be extended. When the object is found, a (+) symbol marks the location. If the new object is to be created at the intersection of extensions from two objects, the cursor must be placed over the second object to locate its extension path. The last point, which is the actual snap point, can be placed anywhere along the extension path, including the intersection of two extension paths. The ***extension path***, represented by a dashed line or arc, extends from the acquired point to the current location of the mouse.

Line A in Figure 6-12 is an example of the way the **Extension** object snap can create a new line at the intersection of extension paths from two existing objects. The first acquired point is found by moving the cursor directly over the corner of the rectangle. The tooltip for the extension is displayed, and the (+) marker becomes visible at the corner. The second acquired point is found in the same manner at the endpoint of the existing line. Dragging the cursor upward, toward the intersection point of the extension paths, causes the extension paths to be displayed as dashed lines. The snap point is located at the intersection of the dashed lines, as shown in Figure 6-12.

The **Extension** object snap can also be used in a manner similar to temporary tracking and the **From** object snap, which are discussed later in this chapter. In Figure 6-12, the **Extension** snap and direct distance entry are used to start Line B 1.5 units away from the corner of the rectangle.

Figure 6-12.
The **Extension** object snap being used on a line and rectangle.

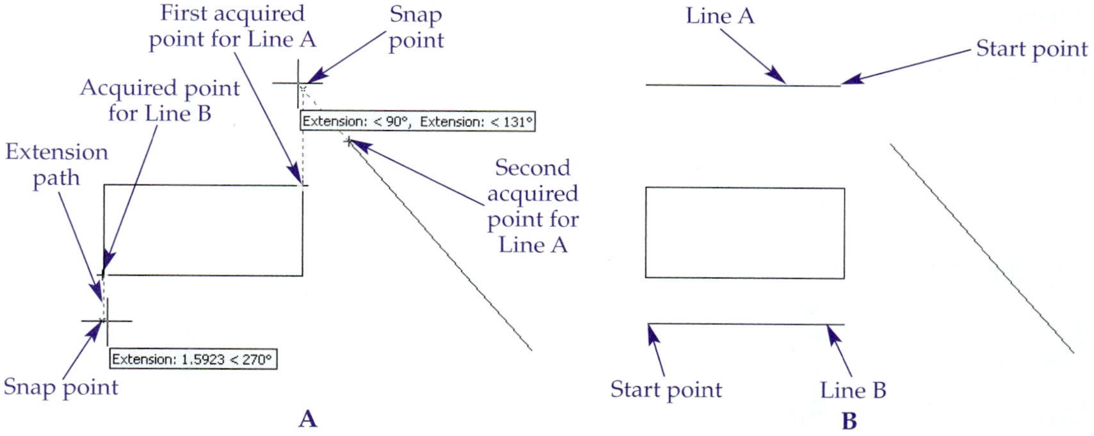

EXERCISE 6-3 Complete the Exercise on the Student CD.

Perpendicular Object Snap

In geometric construction, it is common to draw one object perpendicular to another. This is done using the **Perpendicular** object snap mode. To activate this mode, type PER at the selection prompt, pick the **Snap to Perpendicular** button in the **Object Snap** toolbar, or pick **Perpendicular** from the **Object Snap** shortcut menu. A small right-angle symbol appears at the snap point. This mode can be used with arcs, elliptical arcs, ellipses, splines, xlines, multilines, polylines, solids, traces, or circles.

Figure 6-13 shows an example of the **Perpendicular** object snap being used to locate the endpoint of a line. The endpoint is positioned so the new line is perpendicular to the existing line. In Figure 6-14, the first point of the line is selected with the **Perpendicular** object snap. The tooltip reads Deferred Perpendicular, and the AutoSnap marker is followed by an ellipsis (...). The term ***deferred perpendicular*** means the calculation of the perpendicular point is delayed until another point is picked. The second endpoint determines the location of the first endpoint.

It is important to understand that perpendicularity is calculated from points picked and not as a relationship between objects. Also, perpendicularity is measured at the point of intersection. Therefore, it is possible to draw a line perpendicular to a circle or an arc.

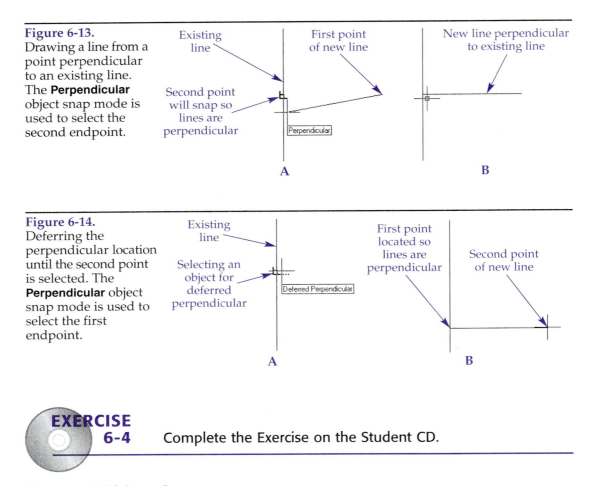

Figure 6-13.
Drawing a line from a point perpendicular to an existing line. The **Perpendicular** object snap mode is used to select the second endpoint.

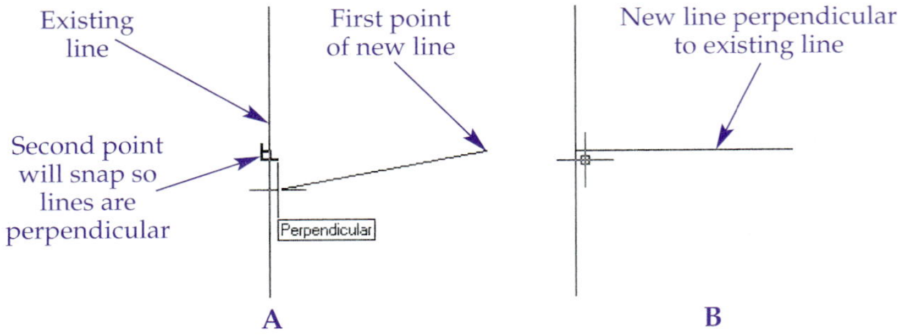

Figure 6-14.
Deferring the perpendicular location until the second point is selected. The **Perpendicular** object snap mode is used to select the first endpoint.

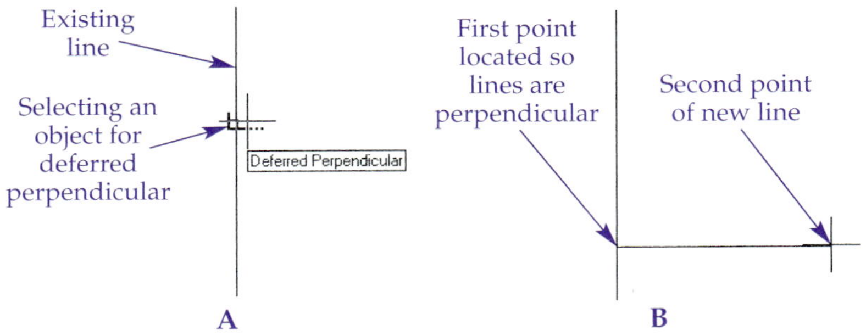

EXERCISE 6-4 Complete the Exercise on the Student CD.

Tangent Object Snap

The **Tangent** object snap is similar to the **Perpendicular** object snap. Instead of aligning the objects perpendicularly, however, it aligns objects tangentially. To activate this mode, type TAN at the selection prompt, pick the **Snap to Tangent** button on the **Object Snap** toolbar, or pick **Tangent** from the **Object Snap** shortcut menu. A small circle with a horizontal line appears at the snap point.

In Figure 6-15, the endpoint of a line is located using the **Tangent** object snap mode. The first point is selected normally. The **Tangent** object snap mode is then activated, and the cursor is placed near the tangent point on the circle. AutoCAD determines the tangent point and places the snap point (and the endpoint) there.

When creating an object tangent to another object, multiple points may be needed to fix the tangency point. For example, the point where a line is tangent to a circle cannot be found without knowing the locations of both ends of the line. Until both points have been specified, the object snap specification is for ***deferred tangency***. Once both endpoints are known, the tangency is calculated, and the object is drawn in the correct location. In Figure 6-16, a line is drawn tangent to two circles. The command sequence is as follows:

Command: **L** *or* **LINE**↵
Specify first point: *(pick the* **Snap to Tangent** *button on the* **Object Snap** *toolbar, type* TAN, *or pick* **Tangent** *from the* **Object Snap** *shortcut menu)*
tan to *(pick the first circle)*
Specify next point or [Undo]: *(pick the* **Snap to Tangent** *button on the* **Object Snap** *toolbar, type* TAN, *or pick* **Tangent** *from the* **Object Snap** *shortcut menu)*
tan to *(pick the second circle)*
Specify next point or [Undo]: ↵
Command:

Figure 6-15.
Using **Tangent** object snap.

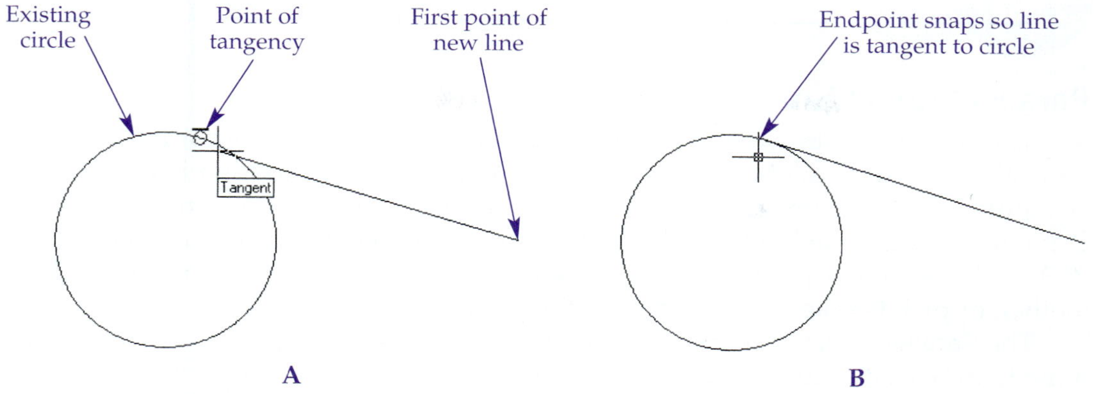
Existing circle
Point of tangency
First point of new line
Tangent
A
Endpoint snaps so line is tangent to circle
B

Figure 6-16.
Drawing a line tangent to two circles.

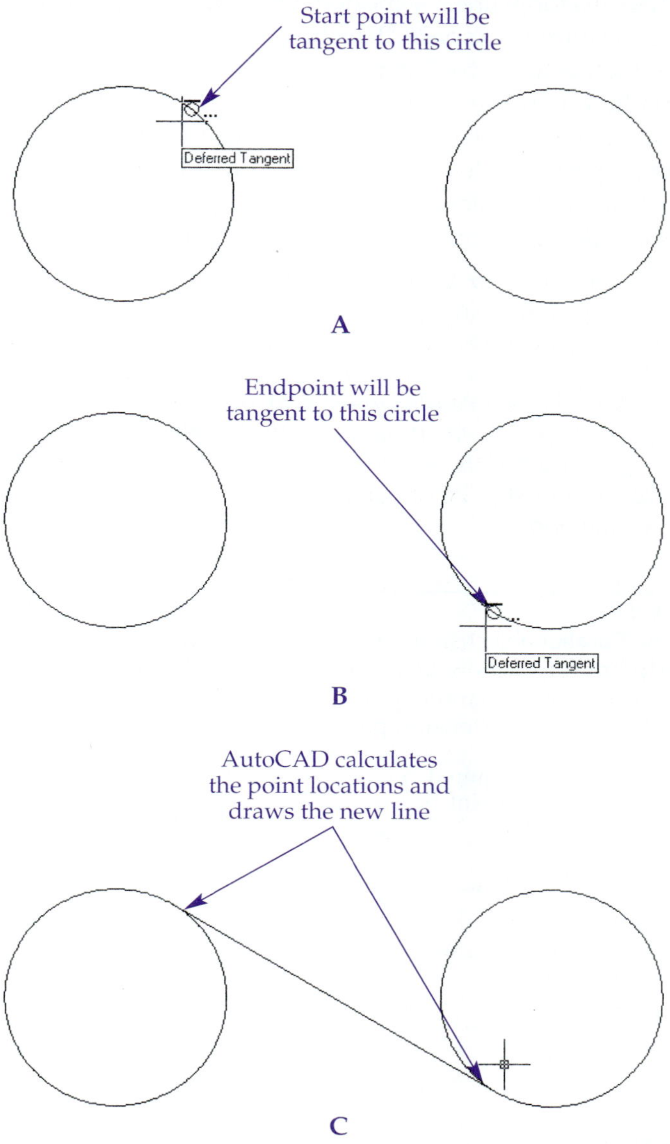
Start point will be tangent to this circle
Deferred Tangent
A
Endpoint will be tangent to this circle
Deferred Tangent
B
AutoCAD calculates the point locations and draws the new line
C

EXERCISE 6-5 Complete the Exercise on the Student CD.

Parallel Object Snap

The process of drawing, moving, or copying objects that are not horizontal or vertical is improved with the **Parallel** object snap mode. This option is used to find any point along an imaginary line that is parallel to an existing line or polyline. Polylines are discussed in Chapter 14. To activate the **Parallel** object snap mode, type PAR at the selection prompt, pick the **Snap to Parallel** button on the **Object Snap** toolbar, or pick **Parallel** from the **Object Snap** shortcut menu.

The **Parallel** object snap is similar to the **Extension** object snap because it requires more than one selection point. The first point, called the ***acquired point***, is found by pausing the cursor over the line to which the new object is to be parallel. When the object is found, and you move the cursor in a direction parallel to the existing line, a (//) symbol marks the existing line. A dashed line, parallel to the existing line, extends from the cursor's location into space. This line is known as the ***parallel alignment path***. The last point, which is the actual snap point, can be placed anywhere along the parallel alignment path. When the alignment path is displayed, the **Parallel** snap marker appears on the line from which the parallel is used. Picking any location along the parallel alignment path creates the second point of the parallel line. Figure 6-17 shows an example of the **Parallel** object snap being used to draw a line parallel to an existing line. The following command sequence is used:

Command: **L** *or* **LINE**↵
Specify first point: *(pick the first point of the new line)*
Specify next point or [Undo]: **PAR**↵
to *(Move the cursor over the existing line until you see the acquired point symbol, and then move the cursor near the first endpoint of the new line. At this time, the parallel alignment path and the* **Parallel** *snap marker are displayed. Pick the endpoint of the new line.)*
Specify next point or [Undo]: ↵
Command:

Figure 6-17.
Using the **Parallel** object snap option to draw a line parallel to an existing line. A—Select the first endpoint for the new line, and then move the crosshairs near the existing line to acquire a point. B—After the parallel point is acquired, move the crosshairs near the location of the parallel line, and an extension path appears.

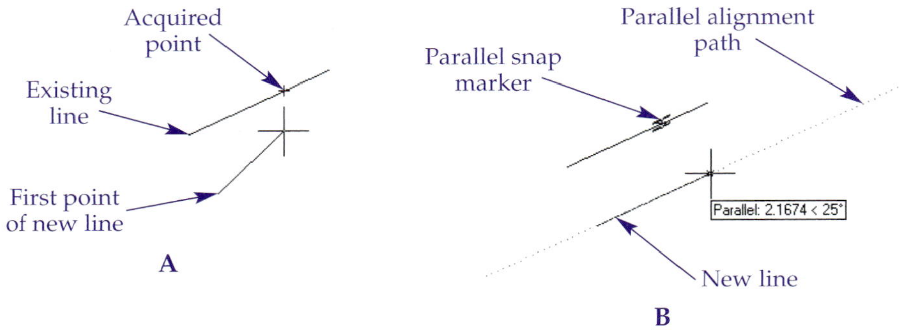

EXERCISE 6-6 Complete the Exercise on the Student CD.

Node Object Snap

Point objects can be snapped to using the **Node** object snap mode. In order for object snap to find the point object, the point must be in a visible display mode. Controlling the point display mode is covered later in this chapter.

Nearest Object Snap

When you need to specify a point that is on an object, but cannot be located with any of the other object snap modes, the **Nearest** mode can be used. This object snap locates the point on the object closest to the crosshair location. It should be used when you want an object to touch an existing object, but the location of the intersection is not critical.

Consider drawing a line object that is to end on another line. Trying to pick the point with the crosshairs is inaccurate because you are relying only on your screen and mouse resolution. The line you draw may fall short or extend past the line. Using **Nearest** ensures that the point is precisely on the object.

PROFESSIONAL TIP

When AutoCAD uses object snap modes, it searches the entire drawing database for the specified type of point nearest to the crosshairs. When working on a complex drawing, you may want to use the **Quick** mode, which selects the first point satisfying the snap mode. The **Quick** mode must be activated at the Command: prompt and is only effective for a single selection. It is activated by preceding the object snap mode with QUI and a comma. For example, the following command sequence would be used to activate the **Tangent** object snap mode in **Quick** mode:

Command: **L** *or* **LINE**↵
Specify first point: **QUI,TAN**↵
to

Setting Running Object Snaps

The previous discussion explained how to use object snaps by activating the individual mode at the selection prompt. If you plan to use object snaps continuously, however, you can set ***running object snaps***. You preset the running object snap modes, and AutoCAD automatically activates them at all point selection prompts.

You can set a running object snap mode using the **Object Snap** tab in the **Drafting Settings** dialog box. Pick **Drafting Settings...** from the **Tools** pull-down menu; pick the **Object Snap Settings** button from the **Object Snap** toolbar; right-click on the **OSNAP** or **OTRACK** button on the status bar and select **Settings...** from the shortcut menu; or type OS, OSNAP, or DDOSNAP at the Command: prompt. You can also type DSETTINGS at the Command: prompt to access the **Drafting Settings** dialog box.

DDOSNAP
OSNAP
OS

Tools
➥ Drafting Settings...

Object Snap toolbar
Object Snap Settings

The **Object Snap** tab of the **Drafting Settings** dialog box is shown in Figure 6-18. Notice that the **Endpoint**, **Intersection**, **Extension**, and **Parallel** modes are active. You can use this dialog box at any time to discontinue a running object snap or to set additional modes.

Figure 6-18.
Running object snap modes can be set in the **Drafting Settings** dialog box.

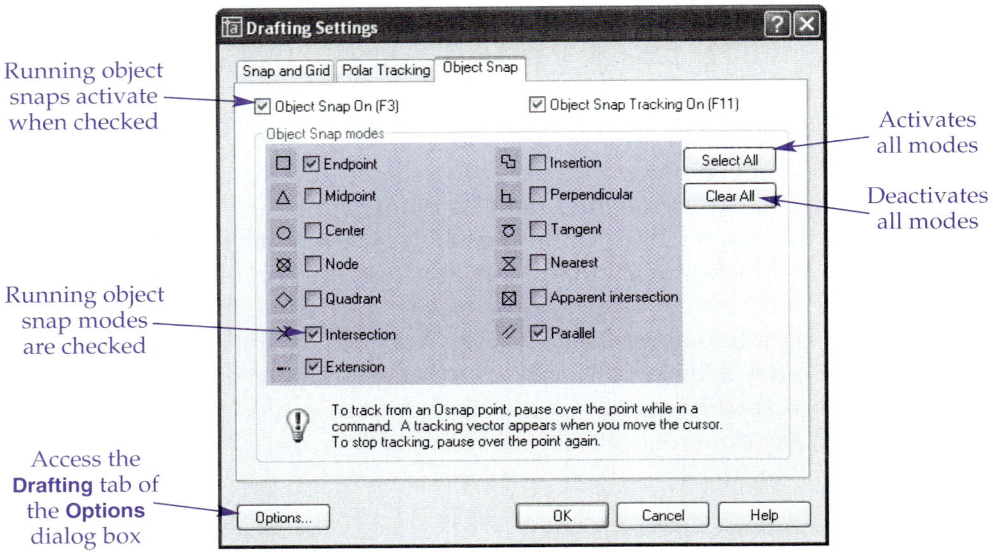

Toggling, Disabling, and Overriding Running Object Snap

Running object snap is active at all point selection prompts, but it is temporarily suspended when an object snap override is entered. The override is temporary and active for a single point selection only. Any currently running object snap mode is reactivated for the next pick. To make a single point selection without the effects of any running object snap modes, enter the **None** object snap mode. To activate the **None** object snap mode, type NON at the selection prompt, select the **Snap to None** button on the **Object Snap** toolbar, or select **None** from the **Object Snap** shortcut menu.

When you need to make several point specifications without the aid of object snap, you can toggle it off by clicking the **OSNAP** button on the status bar at the bottom of the AutoCAD window. The advantage of this method is that you can make several picks and then restore the same running object snap modes by clicking **OSNAP** again. You can also right-click on the **OSNAP** button and pick **Off** from the shortcut menu (pick **On** to restore the running object snaps), pick the **Object Snap On (F3)** check box in the **Drafting Settings** dialog box, or press the [F3] key on your keyboard. Any of these options can be used to reactivate running object snaps.

You can remove the active checks in the **Drafting Settings** dialog box as needed to disable running object snaps. You can also pick the **Clear All** button to disable all running modes. Select desired running object snaps by picking the associated boxes or pick the **Select All** button to activate all object snaps.

Using Multiple Object Snap Modes

As shown with the examples of running object snap, more than one object snap mode can be made active at once. When multiple modes are running at the same time, each of the modes is checked for possible points, and the closest point is selected.

For example, assume the **Endpoint** and **Midpoint** object snap modes are active. The AutoSnap marker locates either an endpoint or the midpoint of a line, depending on which is closest to the location of the crosshairs. This can cause conflicts between some object snap modes. For example, no matter where you pick a circle, the closest quadrant point is always closer than the center of the circle. This means that when **Quadrant** and **Center** are both active, a quadrant point is always selected when moving the crosshairs over a circle. To make the **Center** snap marker appear, move the crosshairs over the circle and then over the circle's center.

The **Nearest** object snap mode causes conflicts with almost every other mode. The **Nearest** mode does not move the selection point to a nearby feature of an object, but it picks the point on the object closest to the current cursor location. This means the **Nearest** mode always locates the closest point.

The [Tab] key on your keyboard can be used to cycle through available snap points. This works well when multiple object snap modes are active. For example, use this feature if you are trying to select the intersection between two objects where several other objects intersect nearby. To use this feature, when the AutoSnap marker appears, press the [Tab] key until the desired point is marked.

PROFESSIONAL TIP

By default, a keyboard entry overrides any currently running object snap modes. This behavior is controlled by the **OSNAPCOORD** system variable. The value of **OSNAPCOORD** can be set as follows:

- 0. Running object snap settings override absolute coordinate entry.
- 1. Keyboard entry overrides object snap settings.
- 2. Keyboard entry overrides object snap settings except in scripts.

This can also be changed by selecting **Options...** from the **Tools** pull-down menu, selecting the **User Preferences** tab in the **Options** dialog box, and selecting the appropriate radio button in the **Priority for Coordinate Data Entry** section.

PROFESSIONAL TIP

Use the object snap modes not only when drawing, but also when editing. With practice, using object snaps will become second nature and greatly increase your productivity and accuracy.

EXERCISE 6-7 Complete the Exercise on the Student CD.

AutoSnap Settings

The AutoSnap feature makes object snap much easier to use. If you do not wish to have the additional visual cues while using object snap, however, you can turn the AutoSnap feature off. To customize the appearance and functionality of the AutoSnap feature, access the **Object Snap** tab of the **Drafting Settings** dialog box and pick the **Options...** button in the lower left-hand corner. This opens the **Drafting** tab of the **Options** dialog box, shown in Figure 6-19. To activate an AutoSnap option, check the corresponding check box:

- **Marker.** Toggles the AutoSnap marker display.
- **Magnet.** Toggles the AutoSnap magnet. When active, the magnet snaps the cursor to the object snap point.

Figure 6-19.
Setting AutoSnap features.

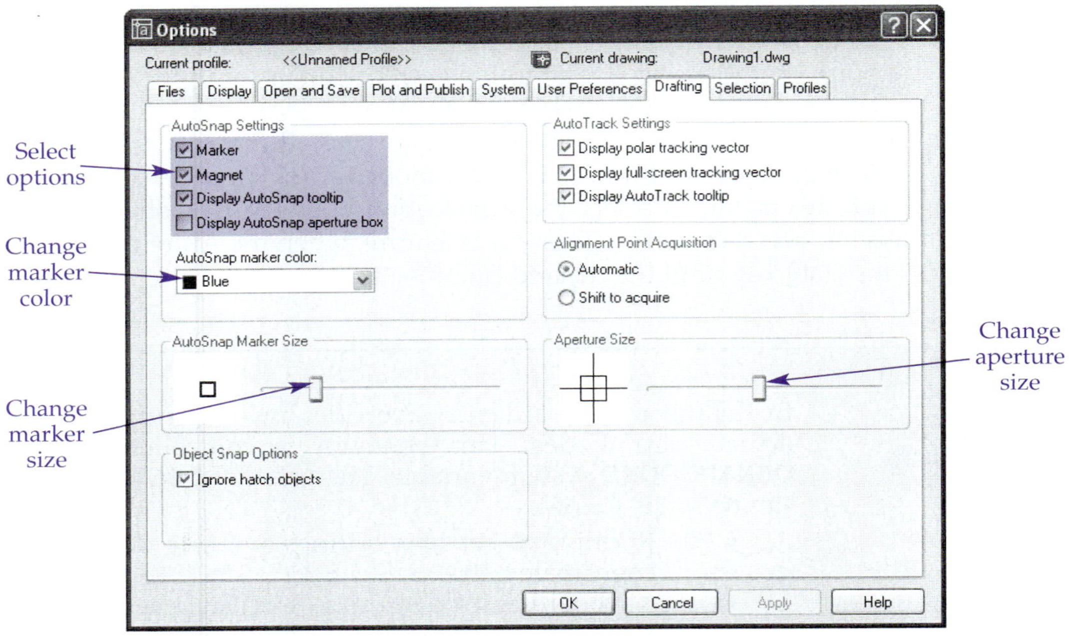

- **Display AutoSnap tooltip.** Toggles the tooltip display.
- **Display AutoSnap aperture box.** Toggles the display of the aperture.

The marker size and color can also be adjusted to suit your needs. For example, the default marker color is yellow, but this is difficult to see if you have the graphics screen background set to white. Pick the down arrow to access the **AutoSnap marker color:** drop-down list, and select the desired color. At higher screen resolutions, a larger marker size improves visibility. Move the slider at the **AutoSnap Marker Size** area to change the size. **Ignore hatch objects** determines whether or not you can snap to hatch patterns. Hatching is discussed in Chapter 21. The **AUTOSNAP** system variable controls the display of AutoSnap markers and tooltips and turns the AutoSnap magnet on or off. The **OSMODE** system variable uses bit codes to set object snap modes.

EXERCISE 6-8 Complete the Exercise on the Student CD.

Changing the Aperture Size

When selecting a point using object snaps, the cursor must be within a specific range of a candidate point before the point is located. The object snap detection system finds everything within a square area centered at the cursor location. This square area is called the ***aperture*** and is invisible by default.

To display the aperture, open the **Drafting Settings** dialog box and pick the **Options...** button from the **Object Snap** tab. The **Drafting** tab of the **Options** dialog box appears. Activate the **Display AutoSnap aperture box** check box. Having the aperture visible may be helpful when you are first learning to work with object snap. The **APBOX** system variable turns the AutoSnap aperture box on or off.

To change the size of the aperture, move the slider in the **Aperture Size** area. Various aperture sizes are shown in Figure 6-20. The aperture size can also be set by typing APERTURE at the Command: prompt. The size of the aperture is measured in ***pixels***. Pixels are the dots that make up a display screen.

Figure 6-20.
Aperture box size is measured in pixels. The three examples here are not shown in actual size, but they are provided to show the size relationships among different settings.

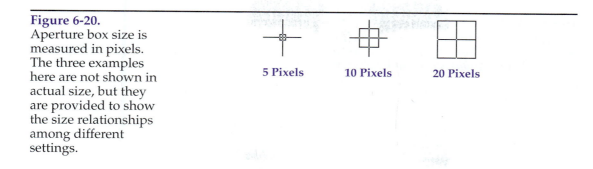

Keep in mind that the *aperture* and the *pick box* are different. The aperture is displayed on the screen when object snap modes are active. The pick box appears on the screen for any command that activates the Select objects: prompt.

EXERCISE 6-9 Complete the Exercise on the Student CD.

Using Temporary Tracking to Locate Points

Tracking is a system that allows you to visually locate points in a drawing, relative to other points. This system creates a new point using the X coordinate of one tracking point and the Y coordinate of another. The tracking feature can be used at any point specification prompt, just like object snap. Tracking can also be used in combination with object snap.

To activate temporary tracking, pick the **Temporary Tracking Point** button from the **Object Snap** toolbar, type TT at the selection prompt, or pick **Temporary track point** from the **Object Snap** shortcut menu. For example, tracking can be used to place a circle at the center of a rectangle. See Figure 6-21. The X coordinate of the rectangle's center corresponds to the midpoint of the horizontal lines. The Y coordinate of the rectangle's center corresponds to the midpoint of the vertical lines. Temporary tracking can be used to combine these two points to find the center of the rectangle using this sequence:

Command: **C** *or* **CIRCLE**↵
Specify center point for circle or [3P/2P/Ttr (tan tan radius)]: **TT**↵
Specify temporary OTRACK point: **MID**↵
of *(pick one of the vertical lines and move the cursor horizontally)*
Specify center point for circle or [3P/2P/Ttr (tan tan radius)]: **TT**↵
Specify temporary OTRACK point: **MID**↵
of *(pick one of the horizontal lines and move the cursor vertically)*
Specify center point for circle or [3P/2P/Ttr (tan tan radius)]: *(select the point where the two alignment paths intersect)*
Specify radius of circle or [Diameter] <*current*>: ↵
Command:

The direction of the orthogonal line determines whether the X or Y component is used. In the previous example, after picking the first tracking point, the cursor is moved horizontally. This means the Y axis value of the previous point is being used, and tracking is now ready for an X coordinate specification.

After moving the cursor horizontally, you may notice movement is locked in a horizontal mode. If you need to move the cursor vertically, move the cursor back to the previously picked point, and then drag vertically. Use this method anytime you need to switch between horizontal and vertical movements.

Figure 6-21.
Using temporary tracking to locate the center of a rectangle. A—The midpoint of the left line is acquired. B—The midpoint of the bottom line is acquired. C—The center point of the circle is located at the intersection of the alignment paths.

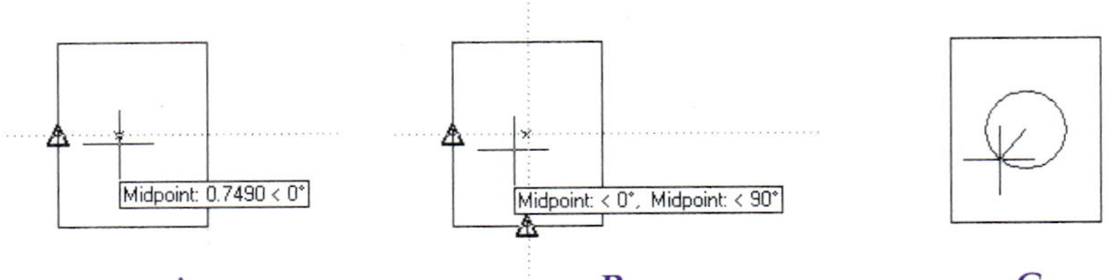

Using the From Point Selection Option

The **From** point selection mode is another tracking tool that can be used to locate points based on existing geometry. It allows you to establish a relative coordinate, polar coordinate, or direct distance entry from a specified reference base point. Access the **From** option by selecting the **Snap From** button in the **Object Snap** toolbar, selecting **From** in the **Object Snap** shortcut menu, or typing FRO at a point selection prompt. The example in Figure 6-22 shows the center point for a circle being established as a polar distance from the midpoint of an existing line. The command sequence is shown here:

Command: **C** *or* **CIRCLE**↵
Specify center point for circle or [3P/2P/Ttr (tan tan radius)]: **FRO**↵
Base point: **MID**↵
of *(pick line)*
<Offset>: **@2<45**↵
Specify radius of circle or [Diameter] <*current*>: *(pick a radius)*
Command:

Figure 6-22.
Using the **From** point selection mode, following the command sequence given in the text.

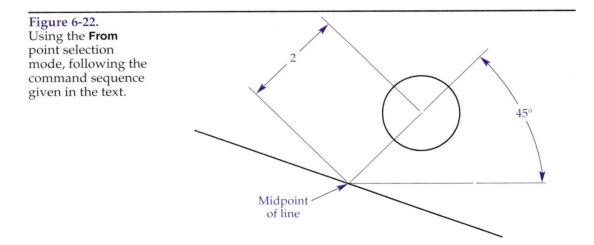

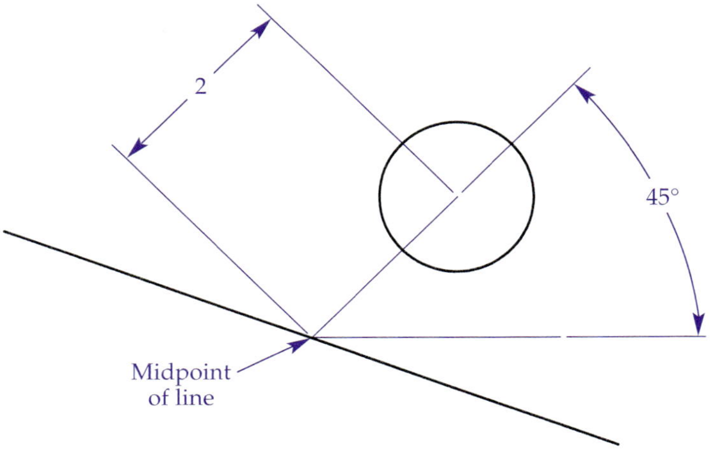

Using the Mid Between 2 Points Option

AutoCAD 2005 NEW FEATURE

A point can be located at the midpoint of two picks by using the **Mid Between 2 Points** feature. This is different from the **Midpoint** object snap, which finds the midpoint of a selected object. **Mid Between 2 Points** can be any two picked points in the drawing area and can be used in conjunction with **OSNAPS**.

Mid Between 2 Points can only be accessed by the **Object Snap** shortcut menu. To use this feature, start a command, such as **CIRCLE**, and then pick the [Shift] key and right-click to open the **Object Snap** shortcut menu. Pick **Mid Between 2 Points**, and then pick two points on the screen. The center of the circle will then be started from the midpoint of the two selected points, as in Figure 6-23.

Command: **C** *or* **CIRCLE**↵
Specify center point for circle or [3P/2P/Ttr (tan tan radius)]: *(pick the* [Shift] *key and right-click to select* **Mid Between 2 Points***)*
_m2p First point of mid: *(select first point)*
Second point of mid: *(select second point)*
Specify radius of circle or [Diameter] <*current*>: *(pick a radius)*
Command:

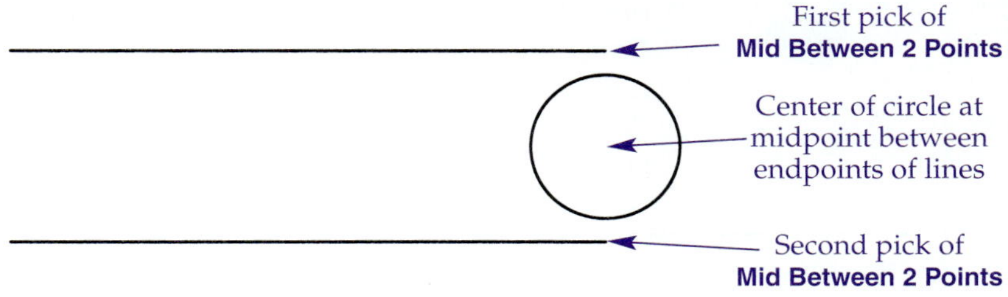

Figure 6-23.
Creating a circle, in which the center is an exact equal distance between two points, using the **Mid Between 2 Points** option.

EXERCISE 6-10 Complete the Exercise on the Student CD.

Using AutoTracking to Locate Points

The temporary tracking mode, discussed earlier, allows the relative placement of a point for a single task. The AutoTrack™ mode enables this feature to be activated at all times, similar to running object snaps. The purpose of AutoTracking is to reduce the need for construction lines and keyboard entry.

There are two AutoTrack modes: object snap tracking and polar tracking. Both modes provide alignment paths to aid in precise point location, relative to existing points. Any commands requiring a point selection, such as the **COPY**, **MOVE**, and **LINE** commands, can make use of these modes.

Object Snap Tracking

Object snap tracking is always used in conjunction with object snaps. When this mode is active, placing the crosshairs near an AutoSnap marker will acquire the point. Once a point is acquired, horizontal and vertical alignment paths are available for locating points.

The [F11] function key and the **OTRACK** button on the status bar toggle object snap tracking on and off. This mode is only available for points selected by the currently active object snap modes. When running object snaps are active, all selected object snap modes are available for object snap tracking. These modes are not available for object snap tracking, however, if running object snaps are deactivated.

In Figure 6-24, object snap tracking is used in conjunction with the **Perpendicular** and **Midpoint** running object snaps to draw a line that is 2 units long and perpendicular to the existing, slanted line. The running object snap modes are set before the following command sequence is initiated. The **OSNAP** and **OTRACK** buttons on the status are active.

Command: **L** *or* **LINE**↵
Specify first point: *(pick the midpoint of the existing line)*
Specify next point or [Undo]: *(pause the crosshairs near the first point to acquire it, and then position the crosshairs as shown in Figure 6-24A to activate perpendicular alignment path)* **2**↵
Specify next point or [Undo]: ↵
Command:

PROFESSIONAL TIP

AutoTracking is similar in performance to the **Extended** object snap. Experiment with a combination of just the **Endpoint** object snap mode and AutoTracking. Try a combination of **Endpoint** and **Extended** object snap modes without AutoTracking to see the difference. Notice that without object snap tracking, you cannot drag in a direction perpendicular to an endpoint.

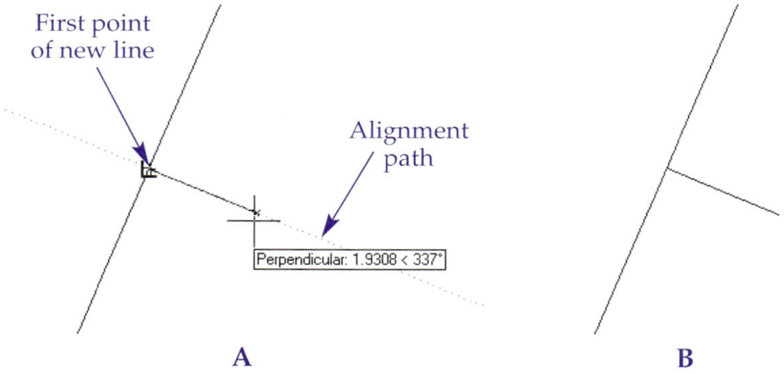

Figure 6-24.
Using object snap tracking to draw a line. A—First endpoint located at midpoint of existing line. The alignment path is displayed when the crosshairs are near. B—The completed line, with the second endpoint identified using direct distance entry along the alignment path.

EXERCISE 6-11 Complete the Exercise on the Student CD.

Polar Tracking

The Ortho mode, discussed in Chapter 3, forces the cursor movement to orthogonal (horizontal and vertical) orientations. When Ortho mode is turned on, and the **LINE** command is in use, all new line segments are drawn at 0°, 90°, 180°, or 270°. Polar tracking works in much the same way, but it allows for a greater range of angles.

Polar tracking can be turned on and off by selecting the **POLAR** button from the status bar or by using the [F10] function key. AutoCAD automatically turns Ortho off when polar tracking is on, and it turns polar tracking off when Ortho is on. You cannot use polar tracking and Ortho at the same time.

When the polar tracking mode is turned on, the cursor snaps to preset incremental angles if a point is being located relative to another point. For example, when using the **LINE** command, polar tracking is not active for the first endpoint selection, but it is available for the second and subsequent point selections. Polar alignment paths are displayed as dashed lines whenever the cursor comes into alignment with any of these preset angles.

To set incremental angles, use the **Polar Tracking** tab in the **Drafting Settings** dialog box. To access this dialog box, right-click on the **POLAR** button from the status bar, and then select **Settings...**; pick **Drafting Settings...** from the **Tools** pull-down menu; or type DSETTINGS or DS at the Command: prompt. Figure 6-25 shows the **Polar Tracking** tab of the **Drafting Settings** dialog box.

The following features are found in the **Polar Tracking** tab:

- **Polar Tracking On (F10).** Check this box, press the [F10] key, or pick the **POLAR** button on the status bar to turn polar tracking on.
- **Polar Angle Settings area.** This area of the dialog box allows you to set the desired polar angle increments. It contains the following items:
    - **Increment angle.** This drop-down list is set at 90.0 by default. This setting provides angle increments every 90°. Open the drop-down list to select from a variety of preset angles. The setting in Figure 6-25 (30) provides polar tracking in 30° increments. The increment angle can also be adjusted by changing the value of the **POLARANG** system variable.

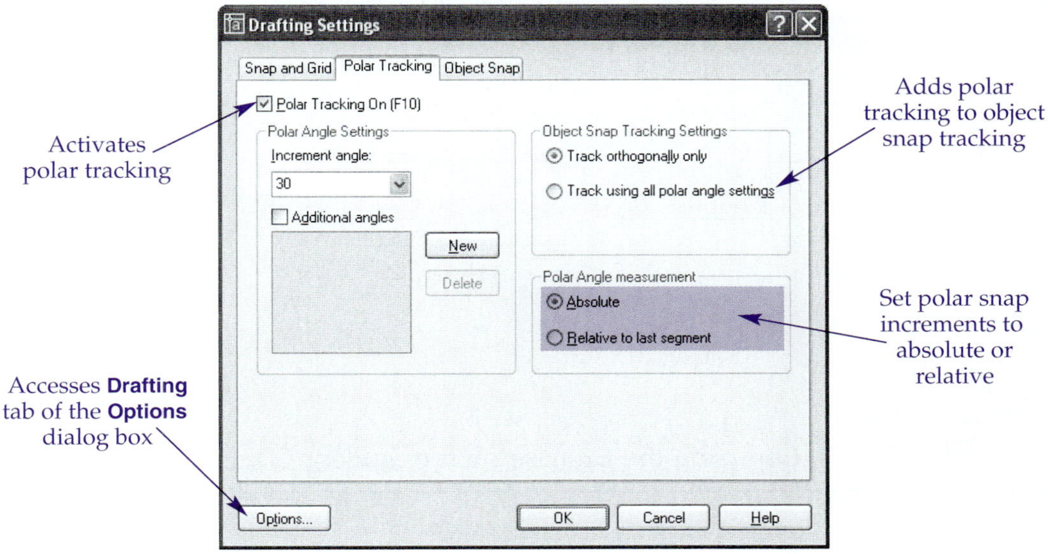

Figure 6-25.
The **Polar Tracking** tab of the **Drafting Settings** dialog box.

- **Additional angles.** This check box activates your own angle increments. To do this, pick the **New** button to open a text box in the window. Type the desired angle. Pick the **New** button each time you want to add another angle. The additional angles are used together with the incremental angle setting when you use polar tracking. Use the **Delete** button to remove angles from the list. You can make the additional angle(s) inactive by turning off the **Additional angles** check box. An additional angle can also be added or changed using the **POLARADDANG** system variable.

- **Object Snap Tracking Settings area.** This area is used to set the angles available with object snap tracking. If **Track orthogonally only** is selected, only horizontal and vertical alignment paths are active. If **Track using all polar angle settings** is selected, alignment paths for all polar snap angles are active.
- **Polar Angle measurement area.** This setting determines if the polar snap increments are constant or relative to the previous segment. If **Absolute** is selected, the polar snap angles are measured from the base angle of 0° set for the drawing. If **Relative to last segment** is selected, each increment angle is measured from a base angle established by the previously drawn segment.

Figure 6-26 shows a parallelogram being drawn with polar tracking active and set for 30° angle increments and absolute polar angle measurements. The following command sequence creates the parallelogram:

Command: **L** *or* **LINE**↵
Specify first point: *(select the first point)*
Specify next point or [Undo]: *(drag the cursor to the right while the polar alignment path indicates <0°)* **3**↵
Specify next point or [Undo]: *(drag the cursor to the 60° polar alignment path)* **1.5**↵
Specify next point or [Close/Undo]: *(drag the cursor to the 180° polar alignment path)* **3**↵
Specify next point or [Close/Undo]: **C**↵
Command:

Figure 6-26.
Using polar tracking with 30° angle increments to draw a parallelogram. A—After the first side is drawn, the alignment path and direct distance entry are used to create the second side. B—Horizontal alignment path is used for the third side. C—Parallelogram completed with the **Close** option.

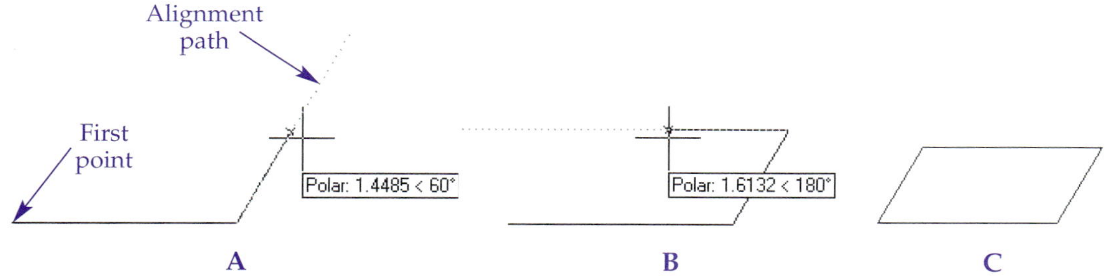

EXERCISE 6-12 Complete the Exercise on the Student CD.

Polar tracking with polar snaps

Polar tracking can also be used in conjunction with polar snaps. If polar snaps are used when drawing the parallelogram in Figure 6-26, there is no need to type the length of the line, because you set both the angle increment and a length increment. The desired angle and length increments are established in the **Snap and Grid** tab of the **Drafting Settings** dialog box. You can open this dialog box as previously described, or you can right-click on the status bar **SNAP** button and pick **Settings...** from the shortcut menu. This opens the **Drafting Settings** dialog box, as shown in Figure 6-27.

To activate polar snap, pick the **PolarSnap** button in the **Snap type & style** area of the dialog box. Picking this button activates the **Polar spacing** area and deactivates the **Snap** area. The length of the polar snap increment is set in the **Polar distance:** box. If the **Polar distance:** setting is 0, the polar snap distance will be the orthogonal snap distance. Figure 6-28 shows a parallelogram being drawn with 30° angle increments and length increments of .75. The lengths of the parallelogram sides are 1.5 and .75.

Figure 6-27.
The **Snap and Grid** tab of the **Drafting Settings** dialog box is used to set the polar snap spacing.

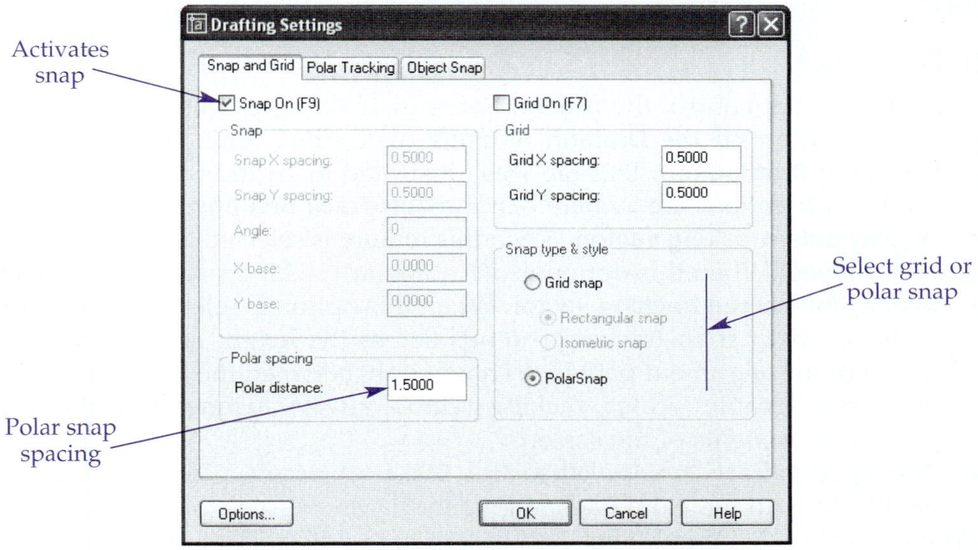

Figure 6-28.
Drawing a parallelogram with polar snap.

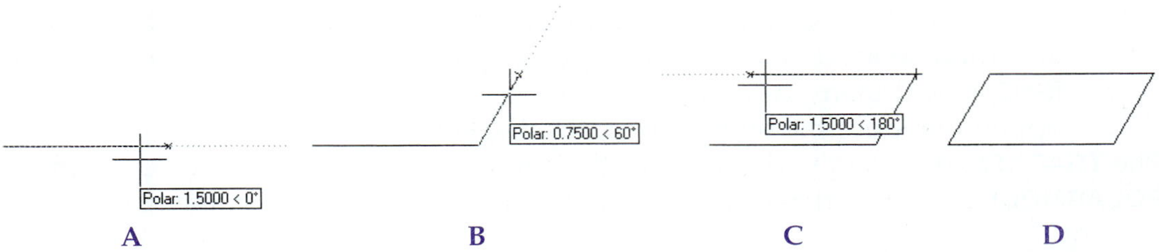

Using polar tracking overrides

It takes some time to set up the polar tracking and the polar snap options, but it is worth the effort if you have several objects to draw that can take advantage of this feature. If you want to perform polar tracking for only one point, you can use the polar tracking override to do this easily. This works for the specified angle if polar tracking is on or off. To activate a polar tracking override, enter a left angle bracket (<) followed by the desired angle when AutoCAD asks you to specify a point. The following command sequence uses a 30° override to draw a line 1.5 units long:

Command: **L** *or* **LINE**↵
Specify first point: *(pick a start point for the line)*
Specify next point or [Undo]: **<30**↵
Angle override: 30
Specify next point or [Undo]: *(move the cursor in the desired 30° direction)* **1.5**↵
Specify next point or [Undo]: ↵
Command:

EXERCISE 6-13 Complete the Exercise on the Student CD.

AutoTrack Settings

The settings that control the function of AutoTracking can be accessed through the **Options...** button on the **Drafting Settings** dialog box. This opens the **Options** dialog box to the **Drafting** tab. This tab was illustrated in Figure 6-19.

The following options are available in the **AutoTrack Settings** area:

- **Display polar tracking vector.** When this feature is selected, the alignment path is displayed. When this option is off, no polar tracking path is displayed.
- **Display full-screen tracking vector.** When this option is selected, the alignment path for object snap tracking extends across the length of the screen. If not checked, the alignment paths are shown only between the acquired point and the cursor location. Polar tracking vectors always extend from the original point to the extents of the screen.
- **Display AutoTrack tooltip.** When this box is checked, a temporary tooltip is displayed with the AutoTrack alignment paths.

The options in the **Alignment Point Acquisition** area determine how the object snap tracking alignment paths are selected:

- **Automatic.** When this option is selected, points are acquired whenever the cursor is paused over an object snap point.
- **Shift to acquire.** When this option is selected, the [Shift] key must be pressed to acquire an object snap point and use object snap tracking. AutoSnap markers are still displayed, and normal object snap can be used without pressing the [Shift] key. If many running object snaps are set, it may be useful to use this option to reduce the number of paths displayed across the screen.

The **TRACKPATH** system variable stores the alignment path display settings, and the **POLARMODE** system variable stores the alignment point acquisition method.

Coordinate Filters

Filters allow you to select some aspects of an object on the screen while "filtering out" other objects, items, or features. Several types of filters are available, including layer filters and selection set filters. These filters are discussed at appropriate locations in this textbook. The following sections discuss coordinate filters.

Drawing with X and Y Filters

There are three coordinate filters: an X filter, a Y filter, and a Z filter. Coordinates filters are used to select an X, Y, or Z coordinate value of an existing point. The Z filter is used in 3D applications. This discussion will focus on the X filter and Y filter.

Suppose you want to construct an isosceles triangle with a height of 2″ from a previously drawn baseline. Refer to **Figure 6-29.** First, use this command sequence to establish the base of the triangle:

Command: **L** *or* **LINE**↵
Specify first point: **2,2**↵
Specify next point or [Undo]: **@3<90**↵

Now, place the vertex 2″ from the midpoint of the baseline:

Specify next point or [Undo]: **.Y**↵
of **MID**↵
of *(pick the baseline)*
of (need XZ): **@2,0**↵

When not specified, as in @2,0, the Z value is assumed to be 0. Finally, complete the triangle with the **Close** option:

Specify next point or [Undo]: **C**↵
Command:

In Chapter 5, you learned to construct a circle at the center of a rectangle using the geometry calculator expression **(END+END)/2** (or **MEE** shortcut function). The same operation can be performed using X and Y filters. As an example, suppose you want to place the center of a circle at the center of a rectangle, as shown in **Figure 6-30.** The command sequence is:

Command: **C** *or* **CIRCLE**↵
Specify center point for circle or [3P/2P/Ttr (tan tan radius)]: **.X**↵
of **MID**↵
of *(pick a horizontal line)*
of (need YZ): **MID**↵
of *(pick a vertical line)*
Specify radius of circle or [Diameter] <*current*>: *(specify the radius)*
Command:

In this example, the X value is filtered before the YZ value. However, the same operation can be performed by filtering the Y value first, and then the XZ value.

Figure 6-29.
Constructing an isosceles triangle using a Y filter.

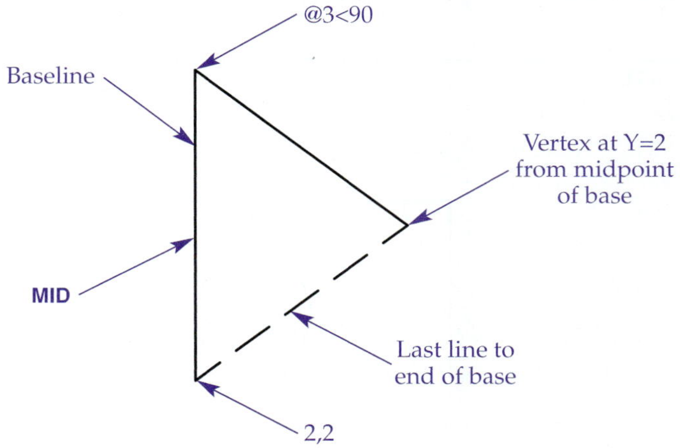

Figure 6-30.
Centering a circle inside a rectangle using X and Y filters.

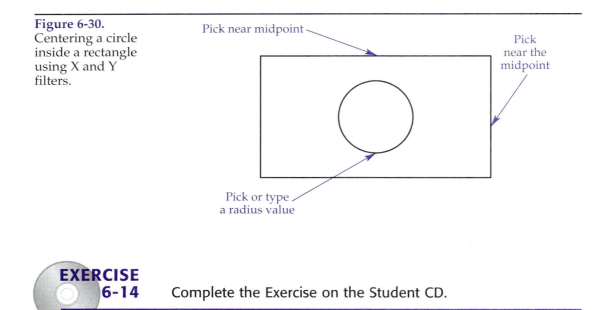

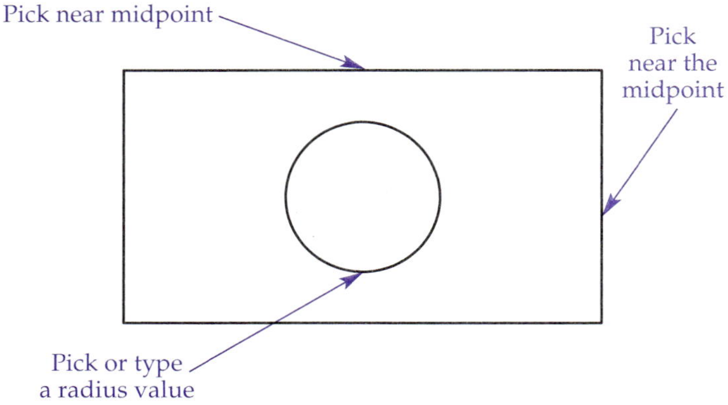

EXERCISE 6-14 Complete the Exercise on the Student CD.

Using Coordinate Filters to Project Views

If you draw the object shown in **Figure 6-31** on a drafting board, you would probably draw the front view first. Then, using drafting instruments, you might project construction lines and points from the front view to complete the right-side view. Filters can be used to perform similar projection operations.

The front view of a rectangular object can be drawn very efficiently using the **RECTANG** command. The circle can then be constructed using X and Y filters, as previously described. Then, the command sequence to draw the side view is:

Command: **REC** *or* **RECTANG**↵
Specify first corner point or [Chamfer/Elevation/Fillet/Thickness/Width]: **.Y**↵
of **END**↵
of *(pick near the endpoint of the bottom horizontal line)*
of (need XZ): *(pick a point to set distance between the views)*
Specify other corner point or [Dimensions]: **@2.5,5**↵
Command:

The rectangle that represents the side view is now complete. Since the lower-left corner of the side view is located by filtering the Y value of the lower-right corner of the front view, it is aligned orthographically with that view. The @2.5,5 entry locates the upper-right corner of the side view rectangle relative to the filtered point.

Figure 6-31.
A simple orthographic drawing.

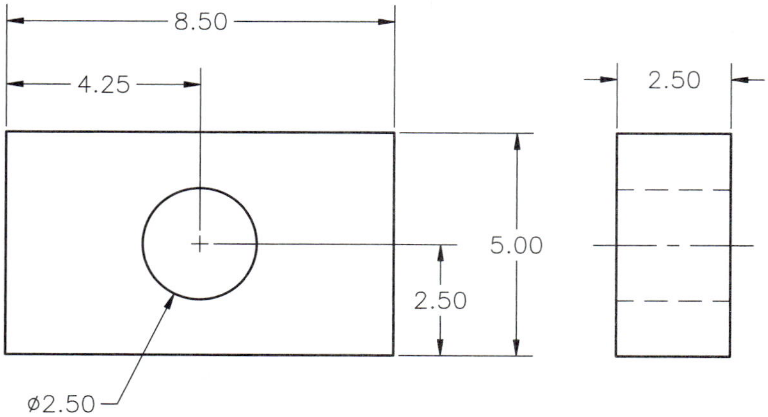

PROFESSIONAL TIP

You can greatly increase your productivity when you use object snaps in conjunction with coordinate filters by setting running object snaps and using the AutoSnap feature. This is similar to using object snap tracking to locate points.

EXERCISE 6-15 Complete the Exercise on the Student CD.

Drawing Parallel Lines and Curves

OFFSET
O
Modify ➡ Offset
Modify toolbar
Offset

The **OFFSET** command is used to draw concentric circles, concentric arcs, concentric curves, parallel polylines, and parallel lines. This command is accessed by picking **Offset** in the **Modify** pull-down menu, picking the **Offset** button in the **Modify** toolbar, or typing O or OFFSET at the Command: prompt. When selected, the command produces the following prompt:

Command: **O** *or* **OFFSET**↵
Specify offset distance or [Through] <*current*>:

Type a distance or pick a point through which the parallel object is to be drawn. The last offset distance used is shown in brackets. If you want to draw two parallel circles a distance of .1 unit apart, use the following command sequence. Refer to **Figure 6-32.**

Command: **O** *or* **OFFSET**↵
Specify offset distance or [Through] <*current*>: **.1**↵
Select object to offset or <exit>: *(pick the object)*
Specify point on side to offset: *(pick the side of the object for the offset to be drawn)*
Select object to offset or <exit>: *(select another object or press* [Enter]*)*

When the Select object to offset or <exit>: prompt first appears, the screen cursor turns into a pick box. After the object is picked, the screen cursor turns back into crosshairs. No other selection option (such as window or crossing) works with the **OFFSET** command. The other option is to pick a point through which the offset is drawn. Type T, as follows, to produce the results shown in **Figure 6-33:**

Command: **O** *or* **OFFSET**↵
Specify offset distance or [Through] <*current*>: **T**↵
Select object to offset or <exit>: *(pick the object)*
Specify through point: *(pick the point through which the offset will be drawn)*
Select object to offset or <exit>: ↵

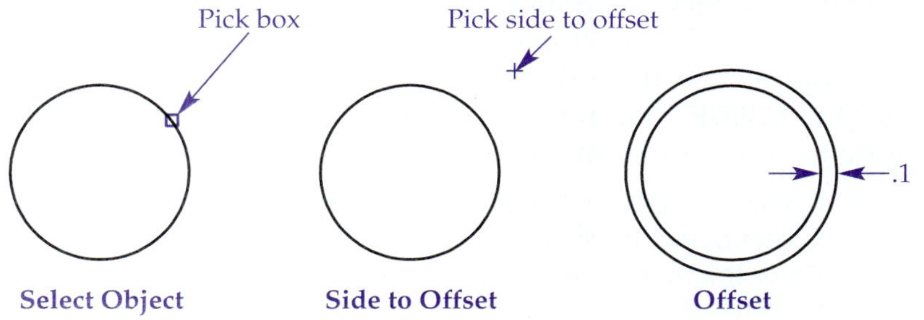

Figure 6-32.
Drawing an offset using a designated distance.

Figure 6-33.
Drawing an offset through a given point.

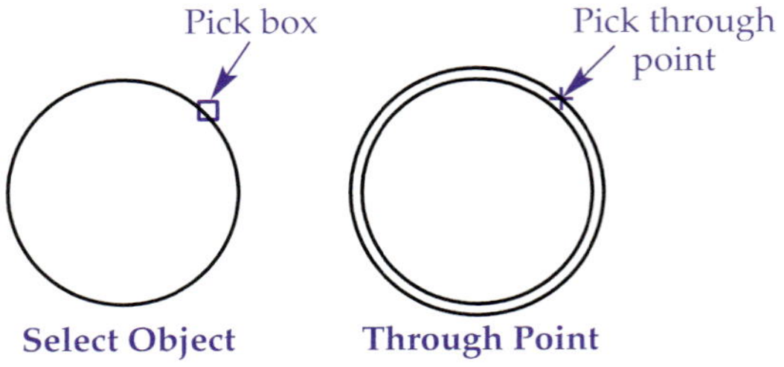

Object snap modes can be used to assist in drawing an offset. For example, suppose you have a circle and a line and want to draw a concentric circle tangent to the line. Refer to **Figure 6-34** and the following command sequence:

Command: **O** *or* **OFFSET**↵
Specify offset distance or [Through] <*current*>: **QUA**↵
of *(pick the existing circle)*
Specify second point: **PER**↵
to *(pick the existing line)*
Select object to offset or <exit>: *(pick the existing circle)*
Specify point on side to offset: *(pick between the circle and line)*
Select object to offset or <exit>: ↵
Command:

Figure 6-34.
Using **OFFSET** to draw a concentric circle tangent to a line.

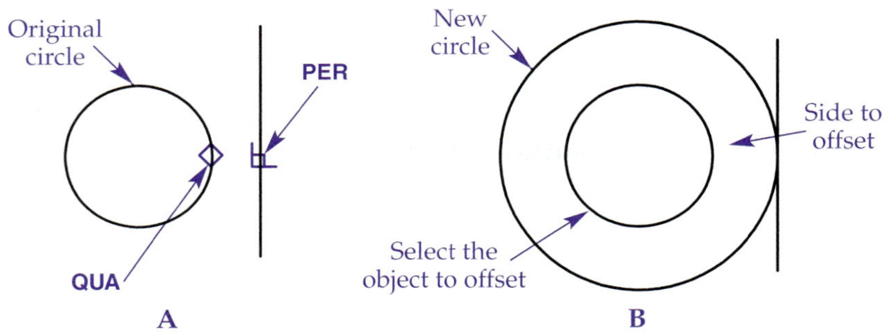

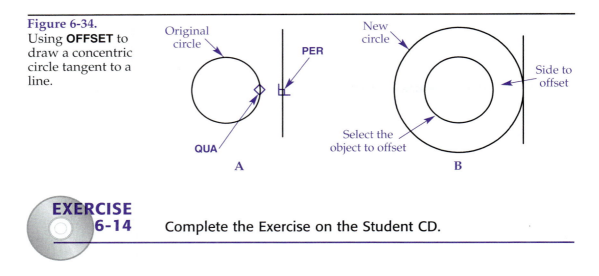

EXERCISE 6-14

Complete the Exercise on the Student CD.

Dividing an Object

DIVIDE
DIV

Draw
➥ **Point**
➥ **Divide**

A line, a circle, an arc, or a polyline can be divided into an equal number of segments using the **DIVIDE** command. To start the **DIVIDE** command, select **Divide** from the **Point** cascading menu of the **Draw** pull-down menu, or type DIV or DIVIDE. The **DIVIDE** command does not physically break an object into multiple parts. It places point objects or blocks at the locations where the breaks would occur if the object were actually divided into multiple segments.

Suppose you have drawn a line and want to divide it into seven equal parts. Enter the **DIVIDE** command, select the object to divide, and then enter the number of segments. Refer to **Figure 6-35.** The procedure is as follows:

Command: **DIV** *or* **DIVIDE**↵
Select object to divide: *(pick the object)*
Enter the number of segments or [Block]: **7**↵
Command:

Figure 6-35.
Using the **DIVIDE** command. Note that the default marks (points) have been changed to Xs.

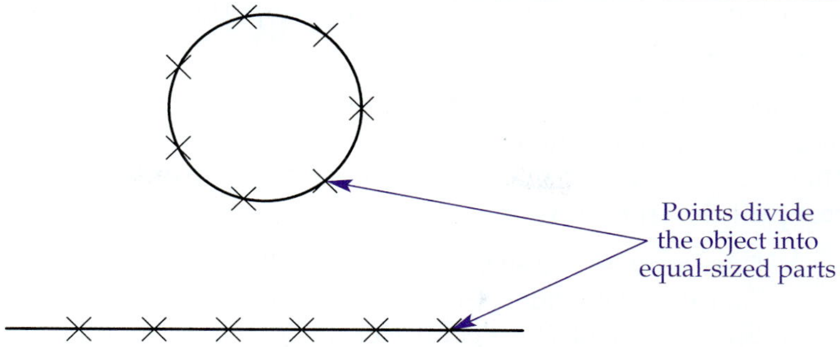

The **Block** option of the **DIVIDE** command allows you to place a block at each division point. To initiate the **Block** option, type B at the Enter the number of segments or [Block]: prompt. You are then asked if the block is to be aligned with the object. A ***block*** is a previously drawn symbol or shape. Blocks are discussed in detail in Chapter 22 of this text.

After the number of segments is given, the object is divided with points. By default, however, points are displayed as dots, which may not show very well. Notice that the appearance of the marks has been changed in Figure 6-35 by changing the point style. To change the point style, select **Point Style...** from the **Format** pull-down menu and select a new point style from the **Point Style** dialog box. Drawing points and setting point style are discussed later in this chapter.

Dividing Objects at Specified Distances

MEASURE
ME

Draw
➥ **Point**
➥ **Measure**

Unlike the **DIVIDE** command, in which an object is divided into a specified number of parts, the **MEASURE** command places marks a specified distance apart. To activate the **MEASURE** command, pick **Measure** from the **Point** cascading menu of the **Draw** pull-down menu, or type ME or MEASURE at the Command: prompt. The line shown in Figure 6-36 is measured with .75 unit segments, as follows:

Command: **ME** *or* **MEASURE**↵
Select object to measure: *(pick an object)*
Specify length of segment or [Block]: **.75**↵

Measuring begins at the end closest to where the object is picked. All increments are equal to the entered segment length, except the last segment, which may be shorter. The point style determines the type of marks placed on the object, just as it does with the **DIVIDE** command. Blocks can be inserted at the given distances using the **Block** option of the **MEASURE** command.

Figure 6-36.
Using the **MEASURE** command. Notice that the last segment may be shorter than the others, depending on the total length of the object.

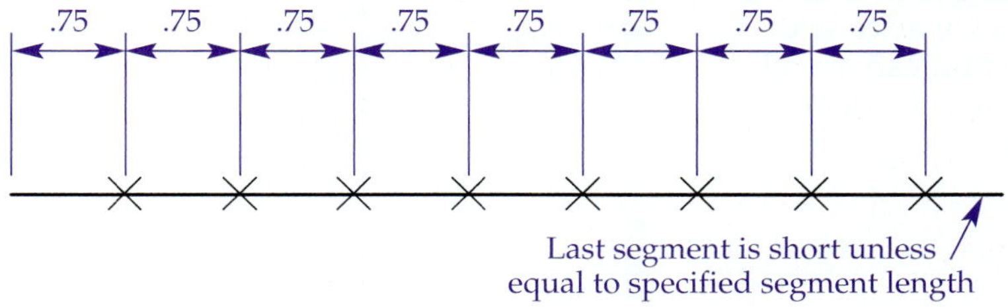

EXERCISE 6-15 Complete the Exercise on the Student CD.

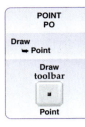

Drawing Points

POINT
PO

Draw
➥ Point

Draw
toolbar

Point

You can draw points anywhere on the screen using the **POINT** command. To access this command, pick the **Point** button from the **Draw** toolbar, type PO or POINT at the Command: prompt, or select one of the options from the **Point** cascading menu in the **Draw** pull-down menu. The command sequence is as follows:

Command: **PO** *or* **POINT**↵
Current point modes: PDMODE=<*current*> PDSIZE=<*current*>
Specify a point: *(type point coordinates or pick with the pointing device)*
Command:

If you need to place only a single point object, use the keyboard command or select the **Single Point** option from the **Point** cascading menu. After drawing a single point, you are returned to the Command: prompt. If you need to draw multiple points, use the **Point** button on the **Draw** toolbar or the **Multiple Point** option from the **Point** cascading menu. Press [Esc] to exit the command.

When the **POINT** command is used, the current point modes are listed at the command line. The **PDMODE** system variable specifies the type of point marker, and the **PDSIZE** system variable specifies the size of the point marker. The appearance of the point is controlled by the point style, which is set in the **Point Style** dialog box.

NOTE If the point style is set as dots, and blips are active, the blip covers the dot when the point is selected. Enter REDRAW at the Command: prompt. Press [Enter] to erase the blip.

Setting Point Style

DDPTYPE

Format
➥ Point Style...

The style and size of points are set using the **Point Style** dialog box. See Figure 6-37. This dialog box is accessed by selecting **Point Style...** from the **Format** pull-down menu or by entering DDPTYPE at the Command: prompt.

The **Point Style** dialog box contains twenty different point styles. The current point style is highlighted. To change the style, simply pick the graphic image of the desired style.

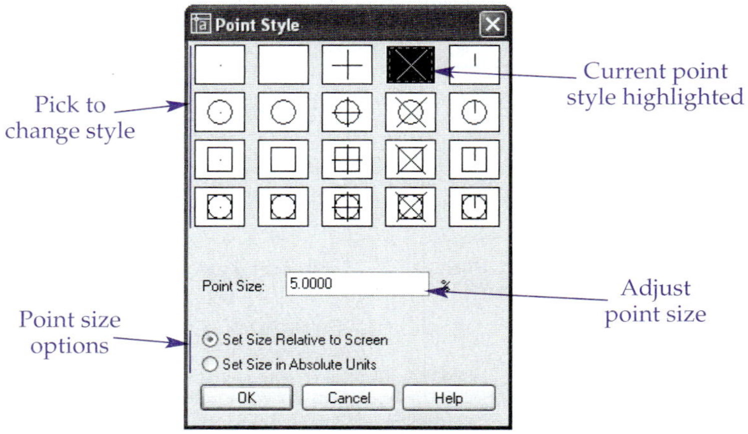

Figure 6-37.
The **Point Style** dialog box. This is a quick way to select the point style and change the point size.

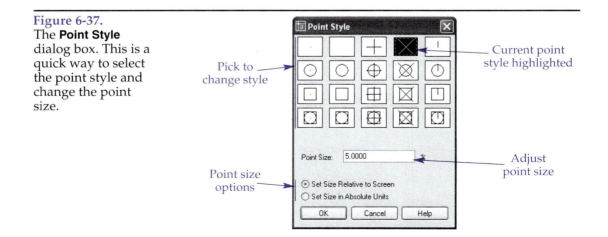

> **NOTE**
>
> The point style is stored in the **PDMODE** system variable. This variable can be changed at the Command: prompt. The **PDMODE** values of the point styles shown in the top row of the **Point Style** dialog box are 0 through 4, from left to right. These are the basic point styles. Add a circle (second row in dialog box) by adding 32 to the basic **PDMODE** value. Add 64 to draw a square (third row), and add 96 to draw a circle and square (bottom row). For example, a point display of an X inside a circle has a **PDMODE** value of 35. This is the sum of the X value of 3 and the circle value of 32.

Set the point size by entering a value in the **Point Size:** text box of the **Point Style** dialog box. Pick the **Set Size Relative to Screen** option button if you want the point size to change in relation to different display options. Picking the **Set Size in Absolute Units** option button makes the points appear the same size no matter what display option is used. The effects of these options are shown in **Figure 6-38.**

> **NOTE**
>
> The point size and relative/absolute settings can also be modified by changing the **PDSIZE** (point display size) system variable. Positive **PDSIZE** values change size in relation to different display options (relative to screen). Negative **PDSIZE** values make the points appear the same size no matter how much you **ZOOM** the drawing (absolute units).

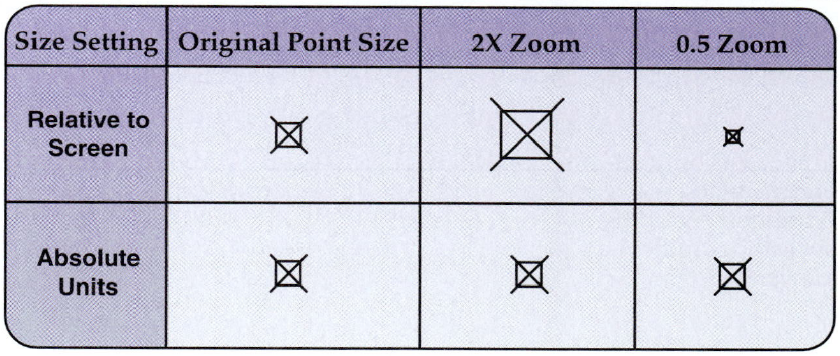

Figure 6-38. Points sized with the **Set Size Relative to Screen** setting change size as the drawing is zoomed. Points sized with the **Set Size in Absolute Units** setting remain a constant size.

EXERCISE 6-16 Complete the Exercise on the Student CD.

Orthographic Multiview Drawings

Each field of drafting has its own method to present views of a product. Architectural drafting uses plan views, exterior elevations, and sections. In electronics drafting, symbols are placed in a schematic diagram to show a circuit layout. In civil drafting, contour lines are used to show the topography of land. Mechanical drafting uses ***multiview drawings***.

This section discusses multiview drawings. Multiview drawings are based on the standard ASME Y14.3M, *Multiview and Sectional View Drawings*. The use of construction lines for view alignment and geometric construction is also explained.

The views of a multiview drawing are created through orthographic projection. ***Orthographic projection*** involves projecting object features onto an imaginary plane. This imaginary plane is called a ***projection plane***. The imaginary projection plane is placed parallel to the object. Thus, the line of sight is perpendicular to the object. This results in views that appear two-dimensional. See **Figure 6-39.**

Six two-dimensional views show all sides of an object. The six views are the front, right side, left side, top, bottom, and rear. The views are placed in a standard arrangement so others can read the drawing. The front view is the central, or most important, view. Other views are placed around the front view. See **Figure 6-40.**

There are very few products that require all six views. The number of views needed depends on the complexity of the object. Use only enough views to completely describe the object. Drawing too many views is time-consuming and can clutter the drawing. In some cases, a single view may be enough to describe the object. The object shown in **Figure 6-41,** needs only two views. These two views completely describe the width, height, depth, and features of the object.

Figure 6-39.
Obtaining a front view with orthographic projection.

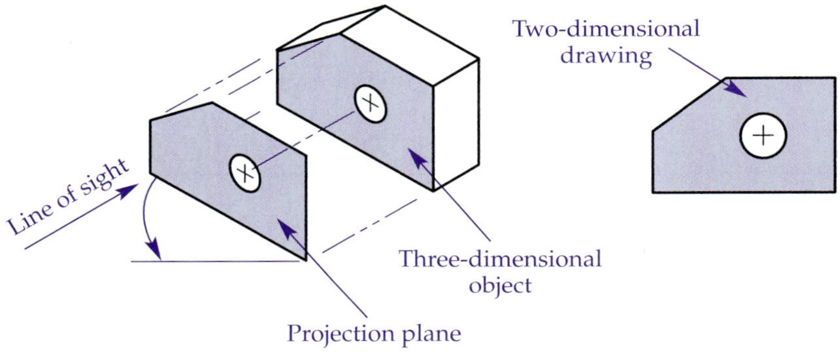

Figure 6-40.
Arrangement of the six orthographic views.

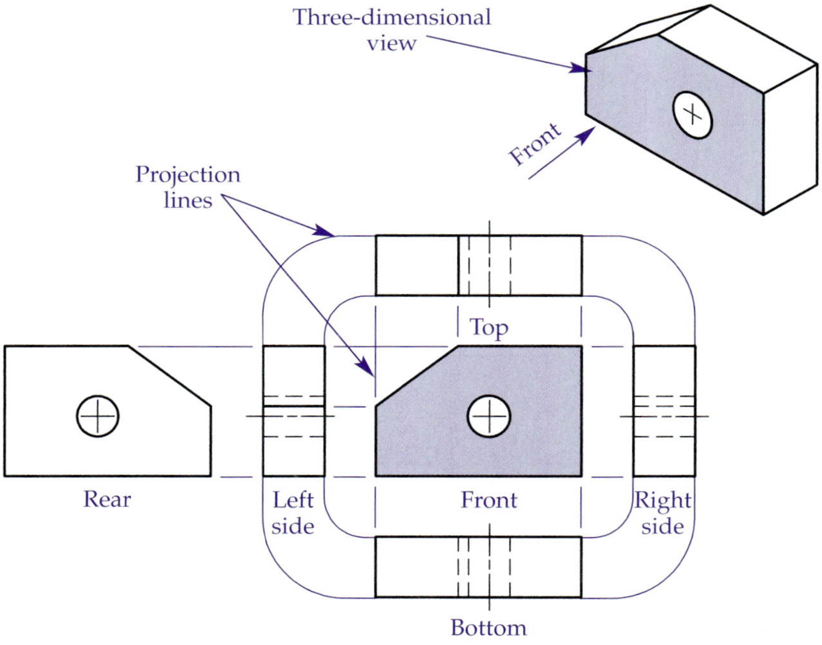

Figure 6-41.
The views you choose to describe the object should show all height, width, and depth dimensions.

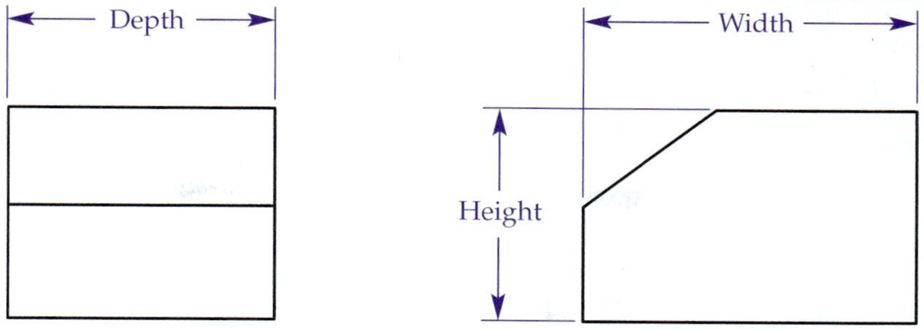

Selecting the Front View

The front view is usually the most important view. The following guidelines should be considered when selecting the front view:

- ✓ Look for the best shape or most contours.
- ✓ Show the most natural position of use.
- ✓ Display the most stable position.
- ✓ Provide the longest dimension.
- ✓ Contain the least hidden features.

Additional views are selected relative to the front view. Remember to choose only the number of views needed to completely describe the object's features.

Showing Hidden Features

Hidden features are parts of the object not visible in the view at which you are looking. A visible edge appears as a solid line. A hidden edge is shown with a hidden line. Hidden lines were discussed in Chapter 3. Notice in **Figure 6-42** how hidden features are shown as hidden lines. Hidden lines are thin to provide contrast to object lines.

Figure 6-42.
Hidden features are shown with hidden lines.

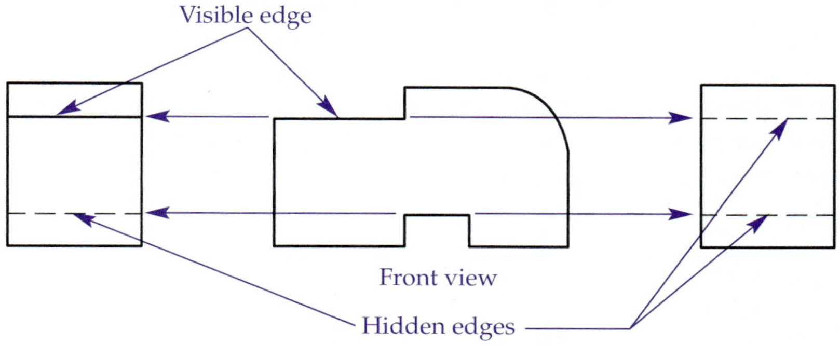

One-View Drawings

In some instances, an object can be fully described using one view. A thin part, such as a gasket, can be drawn with one view. See **Figure 6-43.** The thickness is given as a note in the drawing or in the title block. A cylindrical object can also be drawn with one view. The diameter dimension is given to identify the object as round.

Showing Symmetry and Circle Centers

The centerlines of symmetrical objects and the centers of circles are shown with centerlines. For example, in one view of a cylinder, the axis is drawn as a centerline. In the other view, centerlines cross to show the center in the circular view. See **Figure 6-44.** The only place that the small centerline dashes should cross is at the center of a circle.

Figure 6-43.
A one-view drawing of a gasket. The thickness is given in a note.

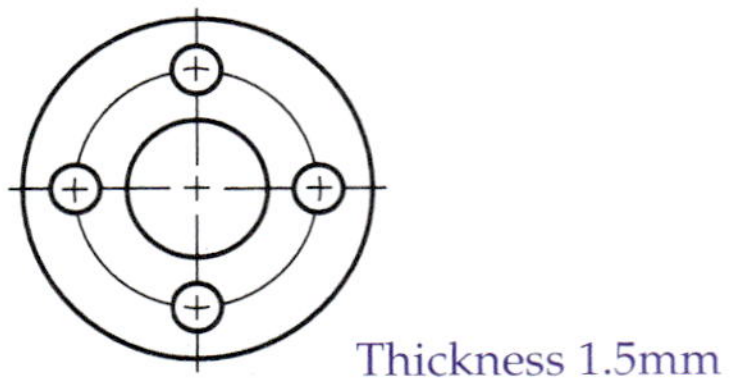

Figure 6-44.
Drawing centerlines.
A—For a cylinder.
B—For a round hole.

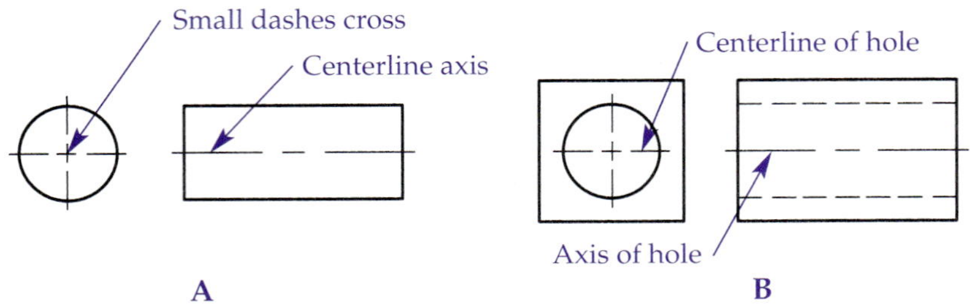

Drawing Auxiliary Views

In most cases, an object is completely described using a combination of one or more of the six standard views. Sometimes, however, the multiview layout is not enough to properly identify some object surfaces. It may then be necessary to draw auxiliary views.

Auxiliary views are typically needed when a surface on the object is at an angle to the line of sight. These slanted surfaces are ***foreshortened,*** meaning they are shorter than the true size and shape of the surface. To show this surface in true size, an auxiliary view is needed. Foreshortened dimensions are not recommended.

Auxiliary views are drawn by projecting lines perpendicular (90°) to a slanted surface. Usually, one projection line remains on the drawing. It connects the auxiliary view to the view where the slanted surface appears as a line. The resulting auxiliary view shows the surface in true size and shape. For most applications, the auxiliary view needs only to show the slanted surface, not the entire object. This is called a ***partial auxiliary view*** and is shown in **Figure 6-45.**

Figure 6-45.
Auxiliary views show the true size and shape of an inclined surface.

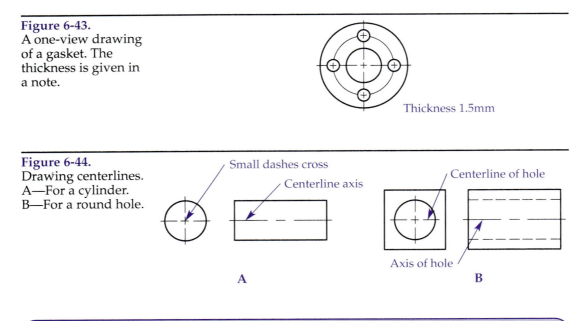

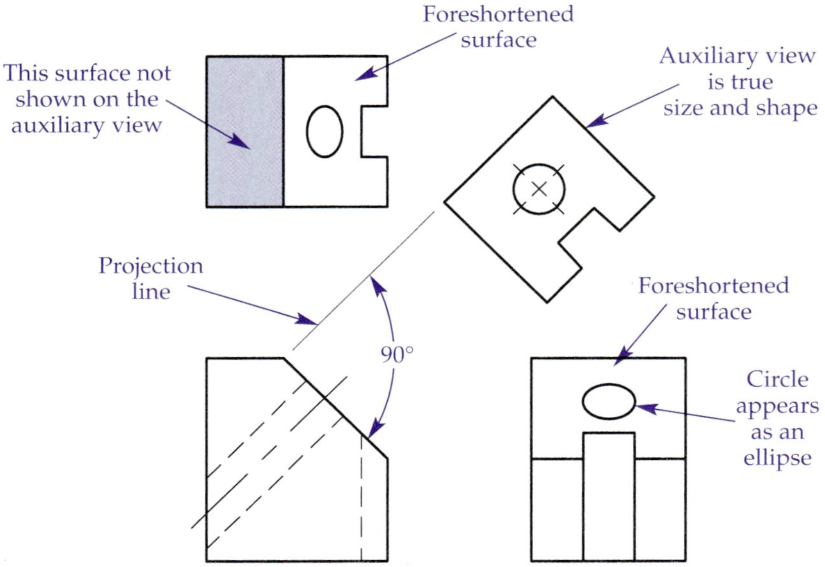

In many situations, there may not be enough room on the drawing to project directly from the slanted surface. The auxiliary view is then placed elsewhere. See **Figure 6-46.** A viewing-plane line is drawn next to the view where the slanted surface appears as a line. The ***viewing-plane line*** is drawn with a thick dashed or phantom line in accordance with ASME Y14.2M. It is terminated with bold arrowheads that point toward the slanted surface.

Each end of the viewing-plane line is labeled with a letter. The letters relate the viewing-plane line with the proper auxiliary view. A title such as VIEW A-A is placed under the auxiliary view. When more than one auxiliary view is drawn, labels continue with B-B through Z-Z (if necessary). The letters *I*, *O*, and *Q* are not used because they may be confused with numbers. An auxiliary view drawn away from the standard view retains the same angle as if it is projected directly.

PROFESSIONAL TIP

Changing the rotation angle of the snap grid is especially useful for drawing auxiliary views. After the views have been drawn, access the **SNAP** command. Pick the base point for rotation on the line that represents the slanted surface. Enter the snap rotation angle equal to the angle of the slanted surface. If you do not know the angle, use object snap modes and pick points on the slanted surface to define the angle. Rotating the snap grid is discussed completely in Chapter 3.

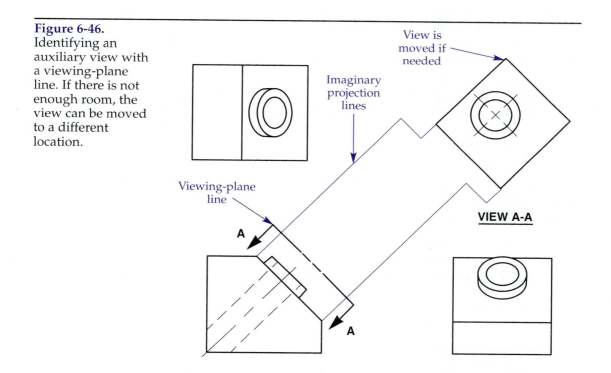

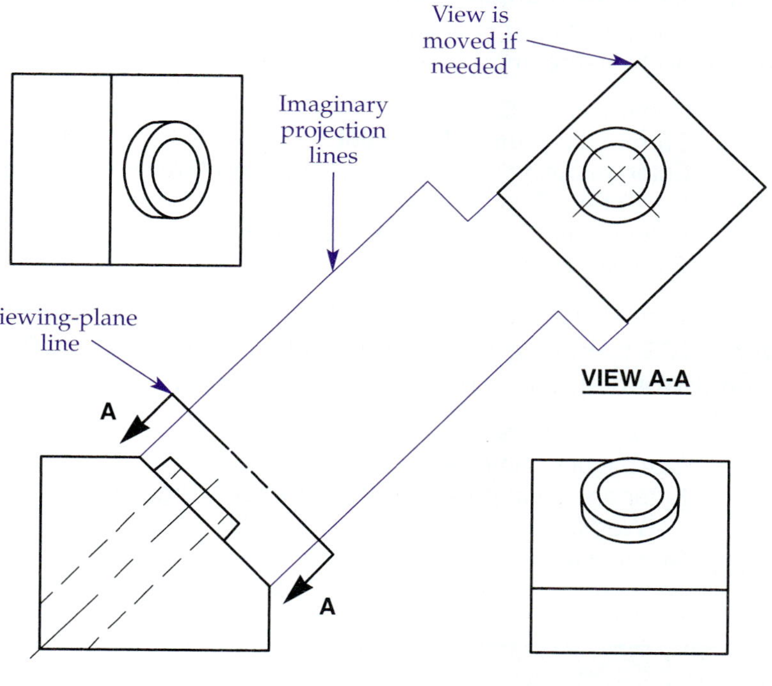

Figure 6-46. Identifying an auxiliary view with a viewing-plane line. If there is not enough room, the view can be moved to a different location.

Using the User Coordinate System for Auxiliary Views

All the features on your drawing originate from the ***world coordinate system (WCS)***. This system includes the X, Y, and Z coordinate values measured from the origin (0,0,0). The WCS is fixed. The ***user coordinate system (UCS)***, on the other hand, can be moved to any orientation. The UCS is discussed in detail in ***AutoCAD and its Applications—Advanced***.

In general, the UCS allows you to set your own coordinate origin. The UCS 0,0,0 origin has been in the lower-left corner of the screen for the drawings you have done so far. In many cases, this is fine, but when drawing an auxiliary view, it is best to have the measurements originate from a corner of the view. This, in turn, makes all auxiliary view features and the coordinate display true, as measured from the corner of the view. This method makes it easier to locate and later dimension the auxiliary view features.

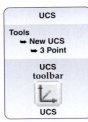

Figure 6-47 shows an example of aligning the UCS to the auxiliary view. Draw the principal views, such as the front, top, and right side. Move the UCS origin to a location that coincides with a corner of the auxiliary view.

UCS
Tools
➥ New UCS
➥ 3 Point
UCS
toolbar
UCS

To move the UCS origin, type UCS at the Command: prompt, select the **UCS** button on the **UCS** toolbar, or select the **3 Point** option in the **New UCS** cascading menu of the **Tools** pull-down menu. The command sequence is as follows:

Command: **UCS**↵
Current ucs name: *WORLD*
Enter an option [New/Move/orthoGraphic/Prev/Restore/Save/Del/Apply/?/World]
<World>: **N**↵
Specify origin of new UCS or [ZAxis/3point/OBject/Face/View/X/Y/Z] <0,0,0>: **3**↵
Specify new origin point <0,0,0>: *(select Point A, as shown in* ***Figure 6-47****)*
Specify point on positive portion of X-axis <*current*>: *(select Point B)*
Specify point on positive-Y portion of the UCS XY plane <*current*>: *(select Point C)*
Command:

The icon is rotated and moved, as shown in **Figure 6-47B.** If you want the UCS displayed in the lower-left corner of the drawing area, select **Named UCS...** from the **Tools** pull-down menu. This displays the **UCS** dialog box. In the **Settings** tab, uncheck the **Display at UCS origin point** check box.

Before you begin drawing the auxiliary view, use the **Save** option of the **UCS** command to name and save the new UCS:

Command: **UCS**↵
Current ucs name: *NO NAME*
Enter an option [New/Move/orthoGraphic/Prev/Restore/Save/Del/Apply/?/World]
<World>: **S**↵
Enter name to save current UCS or [?]: **AUX**↵
Command:

Now, proceed by drawing the auxiliary view. When you have finished, select the **World UCS** button from the **UCS** toolbar or enter the UCS command and use the default **World** option to reset the UCS back to the WCS origin:

Command: **UCS**↵
Current ucs name: AUX
Enter an option [New/Move/orthoGraphic/Prev/Restore/Save/Del/Apply/?/World]
<World>: ↵
Command:

PROFESSIONAL TIP

Polar tracking is another method that can be used to draw auxiliary views. It can be used in place of or in addition to the UCS method described in the previous section. Polar tracking was covered earlier in this chapter.

Figure 6-47.
Relocating the origin and rotating the Z axis of the UCS system. A—Rotating the UCS to align with the auxiliary view angle. B—The UCS icon displayed at the current UCS origin at the corner of the auxiliary view.

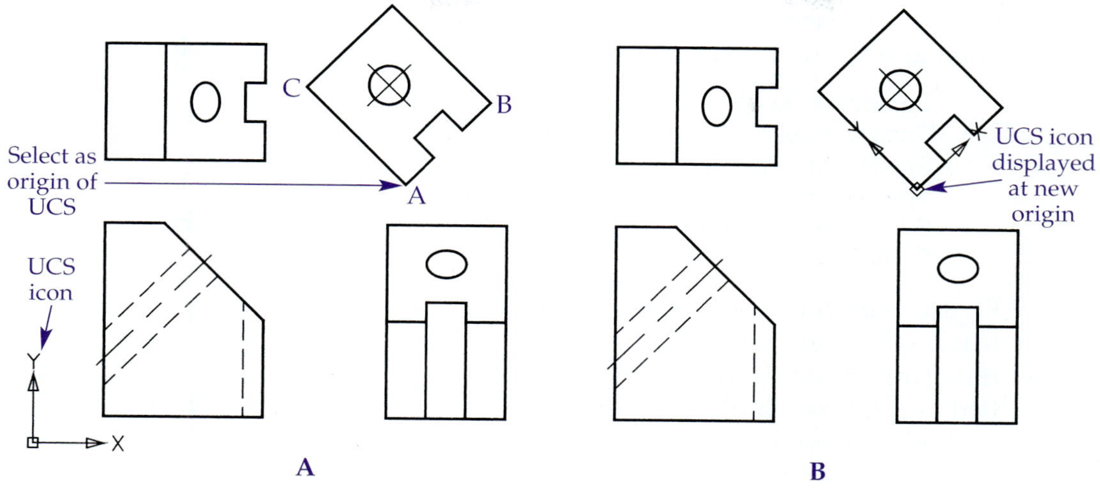

Drawing Construction Lines

In drafting terminology, ***construction lines*** are lines used for layout purposes. They are not part of the drawing. In manual drafting, they are either drawn very lightly or removed so they do not reproduce.

AutoCAD has construction lines and rays that can be used for such purposes. For example, you can use construction lines and rays to project features between views for accurate placement, for geometric constructions, or to coordinate geometric locations for object snap selections. The AutoCAD command that lets you draw construction lines is **XLINE**, while rays are drawn with the **RAY** command. Both commands can be used for similar purposes. The **XLINE** command, however, has more options and flexibility than the **RAY** command has.

Using the XLINE Command

The **XLINE** command creates xline objects. An ***xline object*** is an infinite length line designed for use as a construction line. Although these lines are infinite, they do not change the drawing extents. This means that they have no effect on zooming operations.

The xlines can be modified by moving, copying, trimming, and other editing operations. Editing commands such as **TRIM** or **FILLET** change the object type. For example, if one end of an xline is trimmed off, it becomes a ray object. A ***ray*** is considered semi-infinite because it is infinite in one direction only. If the infinite end of a ray is trimmed off, it becomes a line object.

Construction lines and rays are drawn on the current layer and plot the same as other objects. This may cause conflict with the other lines on that layer. A good way to handle this problem is to set up a special layer just for construction lines.

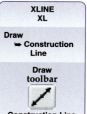

XLINE
XL

Draw
➥ Construction Line

Draw toolbar
Construction Line

The **XLINE** command can be accessed by picking the **Construction Line** button in the **Draw** toolbar, picking **Construction Line** in the **Draw** pull-down menu, or typing XL or XLINE at the Command: prompt. The **XLINE** command sequence appears as follows:

Command: **XL** *or* **XLINE**↵
Specify a point or [Hor/Ver/Ang/Bisect/Offset]:

The following **XLINE** options are available:

- **Specify a point.** This **XLINE** default allows you to specify two points through which the construction line passes. The first point of an xline is called the ***root point***. After you pick the first point, the Specify through point: prompt allows you to select as many points as you would like. Xlines are created between every point and the root point. Use the object snap modes to accurately pick points:

  Command: **XL** *or* **XLINE**↵
  Specify a point or [Hor/Ver/Ang/Bisect/Offset]: *(pick a point)*
  Specify through point: *(pick a second point)*
  Specify through point: *(pick another second point)*
  Specify through point: *(draw more construction lines or press* [Enter]*)*
  Command:

  Figure 6-48 shows how construction lines can be used to help project features between views.
- **Hor.** This option draws a horizontal construction line through a single specified point. It serves the same purpose as the default option. The line is automatically drawn horizontally, however, and you only have to pick one point.
- **Ver.** This option draws a vertical construction line through the specified point.

EXERCISE 6-17 Complete the Exercise on the Student CD.

- **Ang.** This option draws a construction line at a specified angle through a specified point. The default lets you specify an angle and then pick a point through which the construction line is to be drawn. This works well if you know the angle. You can also pick two points in the drawing to describe the angle:

Figure 6-48.
Using the **XLINE** command default option. You can also use the **XLINE** command **Hor** option.

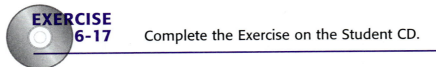

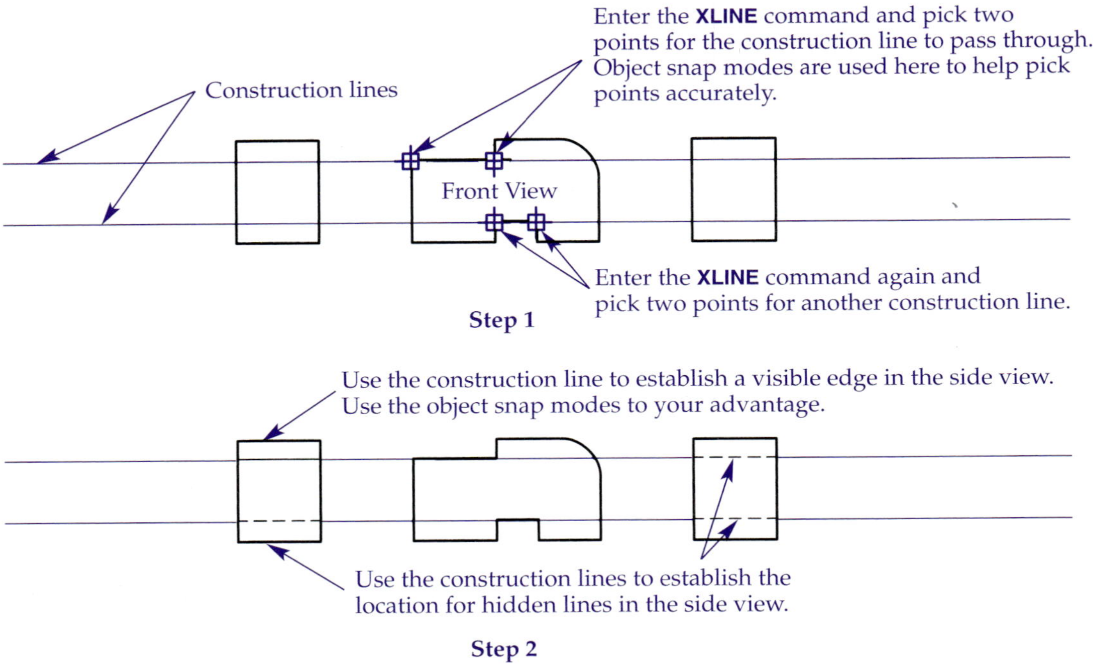

Command: **XL** *or* **XLINE**↵
Specify a point or [Hor/Ver/Ang/Bisect/Offset]: **A**↵
Enter angle of xline (0) or [Reference]: *(enter an angle, such as* 45*)*
Specify through point: *(pick a point)*
Specify through point: *(draw more construction lines or press* [Enter]*)*
Command:

The **Reference** option allows you to use the angle of an existing line object as a reference angle for construction lines. This option is useful when you do not know the angle of the construction line, but you know the angle between an existing object and the construction line:

Command: **XL** *or* **XLINE**↵
Specify a point or [Hor/Ver/Ang/Bisect/Offset]: **A**↵
Enter angle of xline (0) or [Reference]: **R**↵
Select a line object: *(pick a line)*
Enter angle of xline <*current*>: **90**↵
Specify through point: *(pick a point)*
Specify through point: *(draw more construction lines or press* [Enter]*)*
Command:

Figure 6-49 shows the **Ang** option used to draw construction lines establishing the location of an auxiliary view.

EXERCISE 6-18 Complete the Exercise on the Student CD.

- **Bisect.** This option draws a construction line that bisects a specified angle. This is a convenient tool for use in some geometric constructions, as shown in Figure 6-50:

Command: **XL** *or* **XLINE**↵
Specify a point or [Hor/Ver/Ang/Bisect/Offset]: **B**↵
Specify angle vertex point: *(pick the vertex)*
Specify angle start point: *(pick a point on a side of the angle)*
Specify angle end point: *(pick a point on the other side of the angle)*
Specify angle end point: *(draw more construction lines or press* [Enter]*)*
Command:

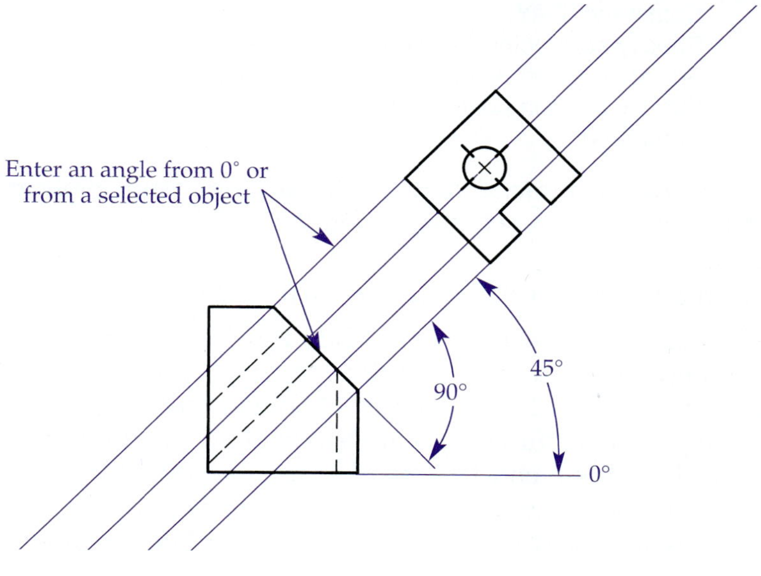

Figure 6-49.
Using the **XLINE** command **Ang** option.

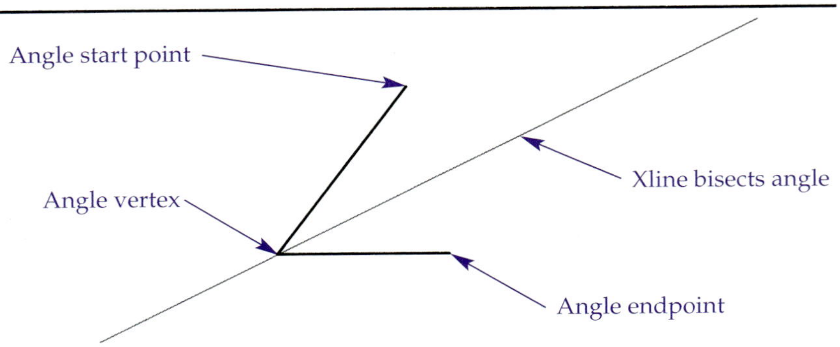

Figure 6-50.
Using the **XLINE** command **Bisect** option.

- **Offset.** This **XLINE** option draws a construction line a specified distance (offset) from a selected line object. It works just like the **OFFSET** command. You have the option of specifying an offset distance or using the **Through** option to pick a point through which to draw the construction line:

  Command: **XL** *or* **XLINE**↵
  Specify a point or [Hor/Ver/Ang/Bisect/Offset]: **O**↵
  Specify offset distance or [Through] <*current*>: **0.75**↵
  Select a line object: *(pick a line)*
  Specify side to offset: *(pick any point on the side for the xline to be drawn)*
  Select a line object: *(draw more construction lines or press* [Enter]*)*
  Command:

EXERCISE 6-19 Complete the Exercise on the Student CD.

Using the RAY Command

The **RAY** command is limited, compared to the **XLINE** command. The **RAY** command allows you to specify the point of origin and a point through which the ray passes. In this manner, the **RAY** command works much like the default option of the **XLINE** command. The ray, however, extends beyond only the second pick point. The **XLINE** command results in a construction line that extends both ways from the pick points.

Ray
Draw
➥ Ray

The **RAY** command can be accessed by picking **Ray** in the **Draw** pull-down menu or by typing RAY at the Command: prompt. The **RAY** command sequence is as follows:

Command: **RAY**↵
Specify start point: *(pick a point)*
Specify through point: *(pick a second point)*
Specify through point: *(draw more construction lines or press* [Enter]*)*
Command:

Both the **RAY** command and the **XLINE** command allow the creation of multiple objects. You must press [Enter] to end the command.

Editing Construction Lines and Rays

The construction lines you create using the **XLINE** and **RAY** commands can be edited and modified using standard editing commands. These commands are introduced in Chapter 12 and Chapter 13. The construction lines will change into a new object type when infinite ends are trimmed off. A trimmed xline becomes a ray. A ray that has its infinite end trimmed becomes a normal line object. Therefore, in many cases, your construction lines can be modified to become part of the actual drawing. This approach can save a significant amount of time in many drawings.

Chapter Test

Answer the following questions on a separate sheet of paper.

1. Give the command and entries needed to draw a line to the midpoint of an existing line:
   A. Command: ______
   B. Specify first point: ______
   C. Specify next point or [Undo]: ______
   D. of ______
2. Give the command and entries needed to draw a line tangent to an existing circle and perpendicular to an existing line:
   A. Command: ______
   B. Specify first point: ______
   C. to ______
   D. Specify next point or [Undo]: ______
   E. to ______
3. Give the command sequence required to draw a concentric circle inside an existing circle at a distance of .25:
   A. Command: ______
   B. Specify offset distance or [Through] <*current*>: ______
   C. Select object to offset or <exit>: ______
   D. Specify point on side to offset: ______
   E. Select object to offset or <exit>: ______
4. Give the command and entries needed to divide a line into 24 equal parts:
   A. Command: ______
   B. Select object to divide: ______
   C. Enter the number of segments or [Block]: ______
5. Define *AutoSnap*.
6. Define *object snap*.
7. What is an AutoSnap tooltip?
8. How do you activate the **Object Snap** shortcut menu?
9. Describe the object snap override.
10. Define *running object snap mode*.
11. Name the following AutoSnap markers:

A.  B.  C. 

D.  E.  F. 

G.  H.  I. 

J.  K.  L. 

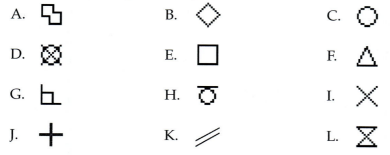

12. Define *quadrant*.
13. What is the situation when the tooltip reads Extended Intersection?
14. What does it mean when the tooltip reads Deferred Perpendicular?
15. What is a deferred tangency?
16. What conditions must exist for the tooltip to read Tangent?
17. Which object snaps depend on "acquired points" to function?
18. How do you set running object snaps?
19. How do you access the **Drafting Settings** dialog box to change object snap settings?
20. If you are using running object snaps, and you want to make a single point selection without the effects of the running object snaps, what do you do?

21. If you are using running object snaps and want to make several point specifications without the aid of object snap, but want to continue the same running object snaps after making the desired point selections, what is the easiest way to temporarily turn off the running object snaps?
22. How is the running object snap discontinued?
23. What do you do if there are multiple AutoSnap selection possibilities within range of the cursor, and you want to select a specific one of the possibilities?
24. How do you turn off AutoSnap?
25. How do you change the color of the AutoSnap marker?
26. How do you change the aperture size?
27. What value would you specify to make the aperture half the default value?
28. Define *AutoTracking*.
29. Which feature should be used in conjunction with AutoTracking?
30. What is the purpose of X, Y, and Z filters?
31. List two ways to establish an offset distance using the **OFFSET** command.
32. If you use the **DIVIDE** command and nothing appears to happen, what should you do?
33. How do you access the **Point Style** dialog box?
34. What is the difference between the **DIVIDE** and **MEASURE** commands?
35. How do you draw a single point, and how do you draw multiple points?
36. How do you change the point size in the **Point Style** dialog box?
37. Provide at least four guidelines for selecting the front view of an orthographic multiview drawing.
38. When can a part be shown with only one view?
39. When is an auxiliary view needed, and what does an auxiliary view show?
40. What is the angle of projection from the slanted surface into the auxiliary view?
41. Name the AutoCAD command that allows you to draw construction lines.
42. Why is it a good idea to put construction lines on their own layer?
43. Name the option that can be used to bisect an angle with a construction line.
44. What is the difference between the construction lines drawn with the command identified in Question 41 and rays drawn with the **RAY** command?

Drawing Problems

Load AutoCAD for each of the following problems, and use one of your templates or start a new drawing using your own variables.

1. Draw the object below using the object snap modes. Do not draw the dimensions. Save the drawing as P6-1.

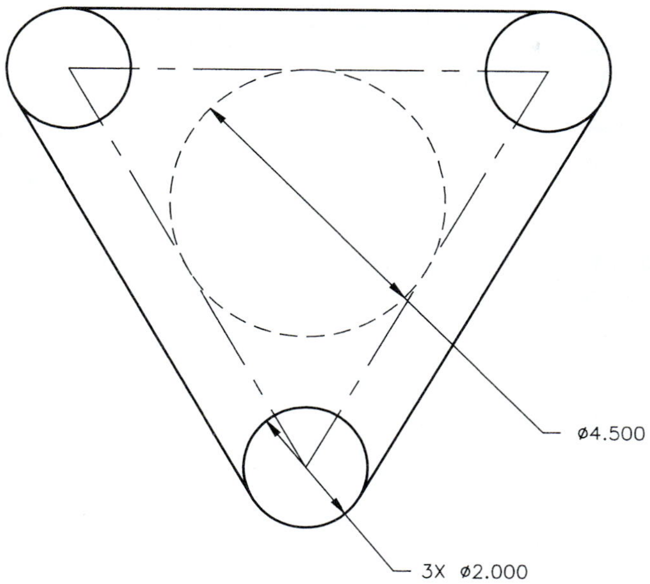

2. Draw the highlighted objects below, and then use the object snap modes indicated to draw the remaining objects. Save the drawing as P6-2.

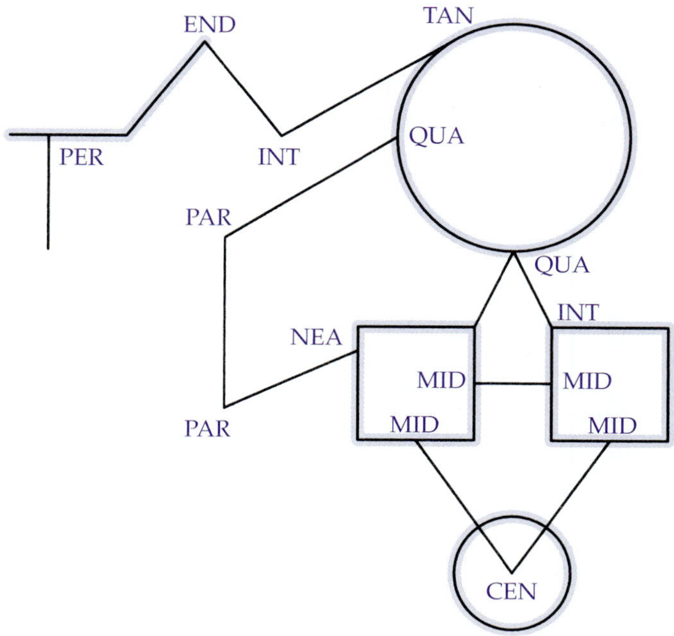

Drawing Problems - Chapter 6

3. Draw the object below using the **Endpoint**, **Tangent**, **Perpendicular**, and **Quadrant** object snap modes. Save the drawing as P6-3.

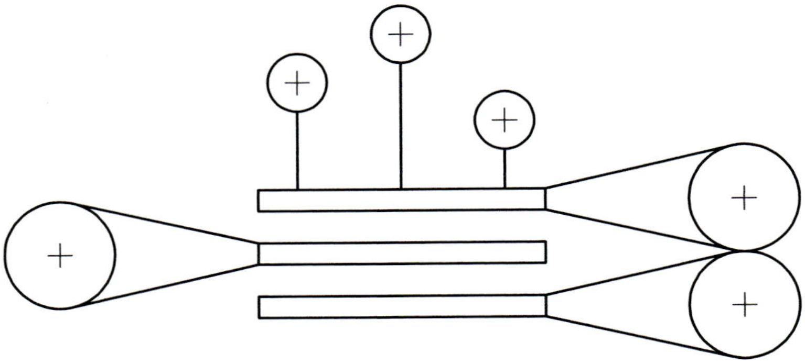

4. Use the **Midpoint**, **Endpoint**, **Tangent**, **Perpendicular,** and **Quadrant** object snap modes to draw these electrical switch schematics. Do not draw the text. Save the drawing as P6-4.

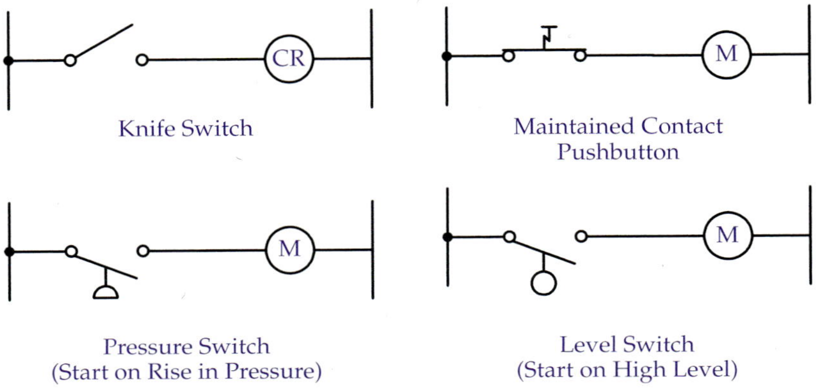

5. Draw the front and side views of this offset support. Use construction lines. Do not draw the dimensions. Save your drawing as P6-5.

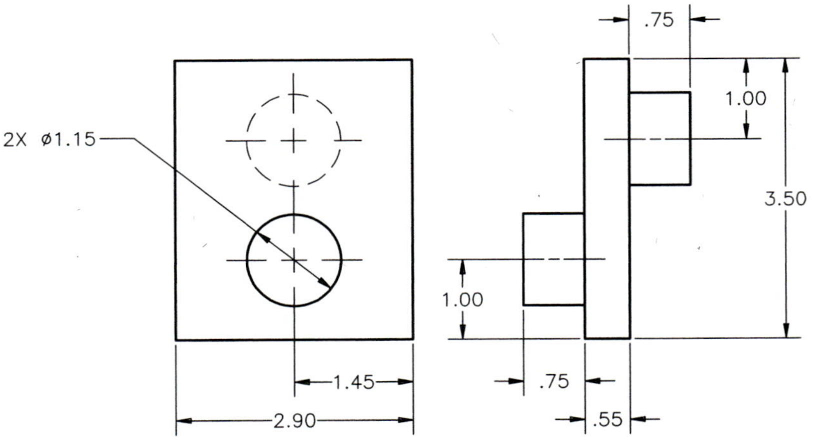

6. Draw the top and front views of this hitch bracket. Use construction lines. Do not draw the dimensions. Save your drawing as **P6-6**.

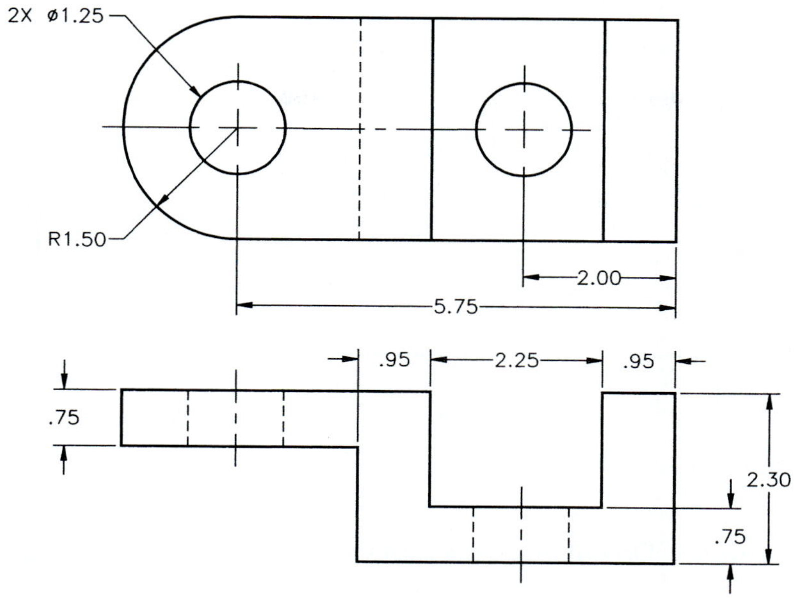

7. Draw this aluminum spacer. Use object snap modes and construction lines. Do not draw the dimensions. Save the drawing as **P6-7**.

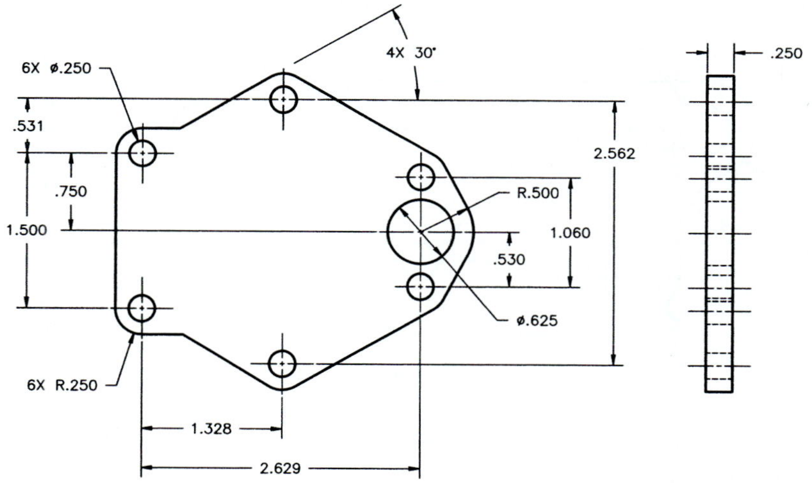

8. Draw this spring using the **OFFSET** command for material thickness. Do not draw the dimensions. Save the drawing as P6-8.

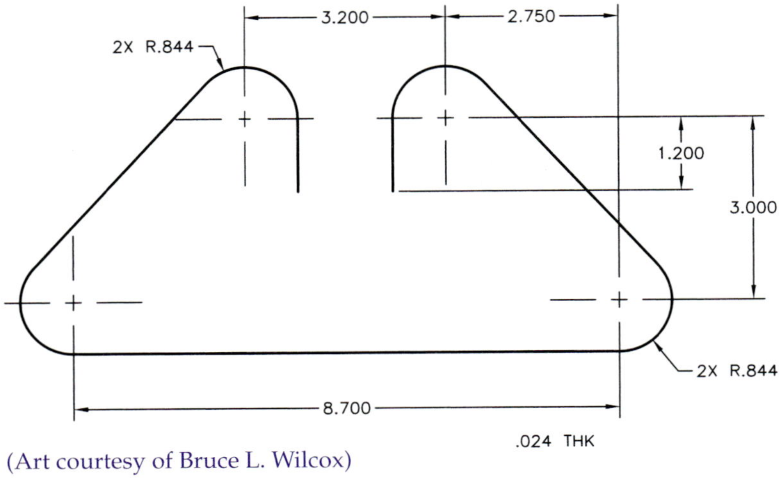

(Art courtesy of Bruce L. Wilcox)

9. Draw this gasket. Do not draw the dimensions. Save the drawing as P6-9.

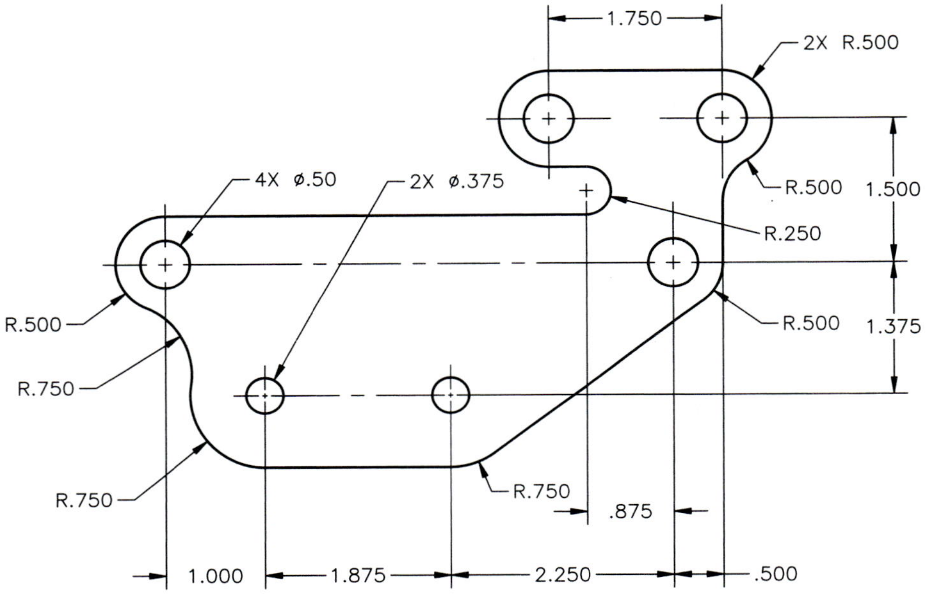

(Art courtesy of Bruce L. Wilcox)

10. Draw this sheet metal chassis. Do not draw the dimensions. Use object snap tracking and polar tracking to your advantage. Save the drawing as **P6-10**.

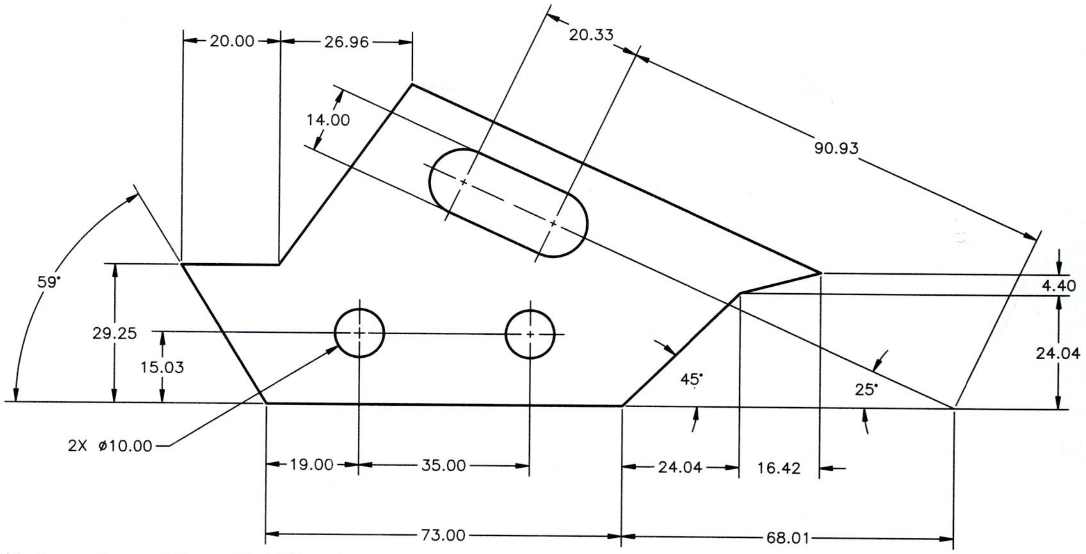

(Art courtesy of Bruce L. Wilcox)

11. Use the X and Y filters to draw an isosceles triangle with a vertical baseline measuring 4.5″ long and 5.75″ high. Save the drawing as **P6-11**.

In Problems 12 through 16, draw the views needed to completely describe the objects. Use object snap modes, AutoTrack modes, coordinate filters, and construction lines as needed. Do not dimension. Save the drawings as **P6-(problem number)**, *such as* **P6-12**, **P6-13**, *and so forth.*

12.

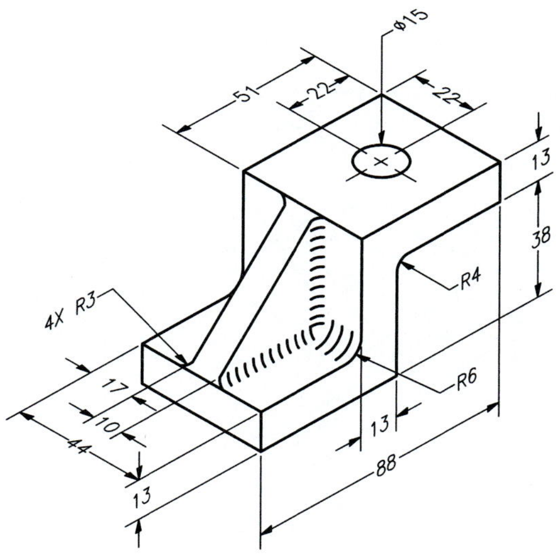

Brace

13.

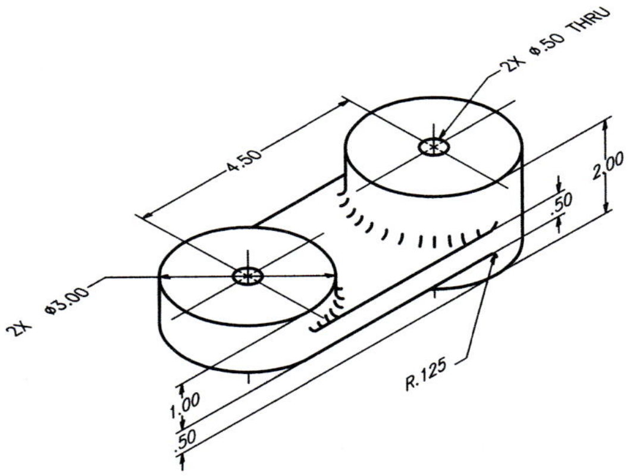

Connector

14.

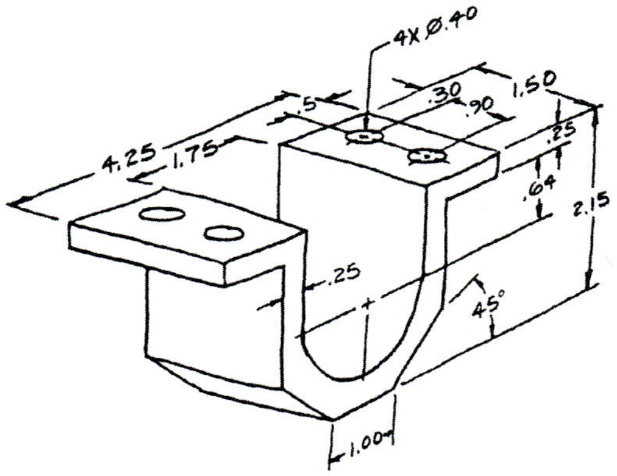

Journal Bracket

15.

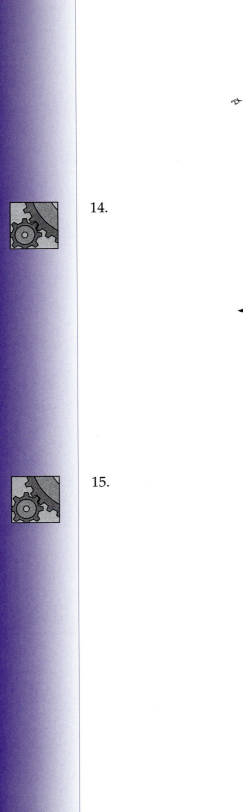

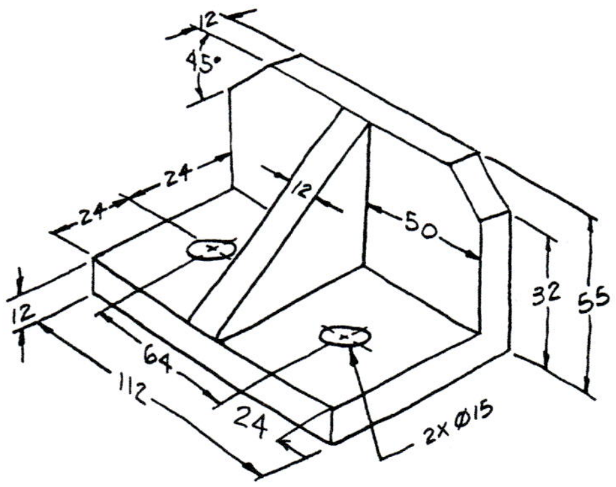

Angle Bracket
(Metric)

16.

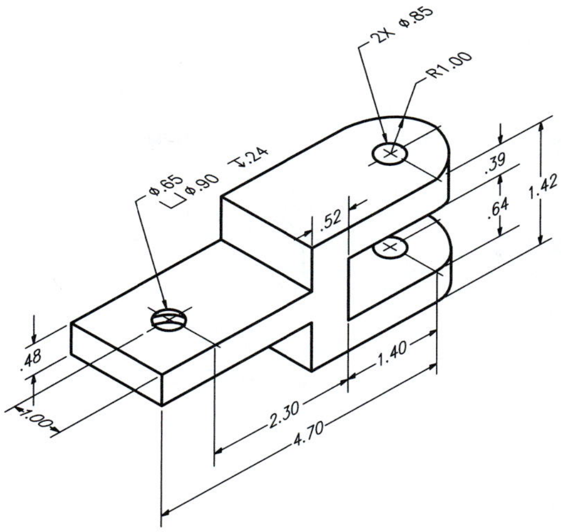

Hitch Bracket

17. Draw the views of this pillow block, including the auxiliary view. Use construction lines. Do not draw the dimensions. Save your drawing as P6-17.

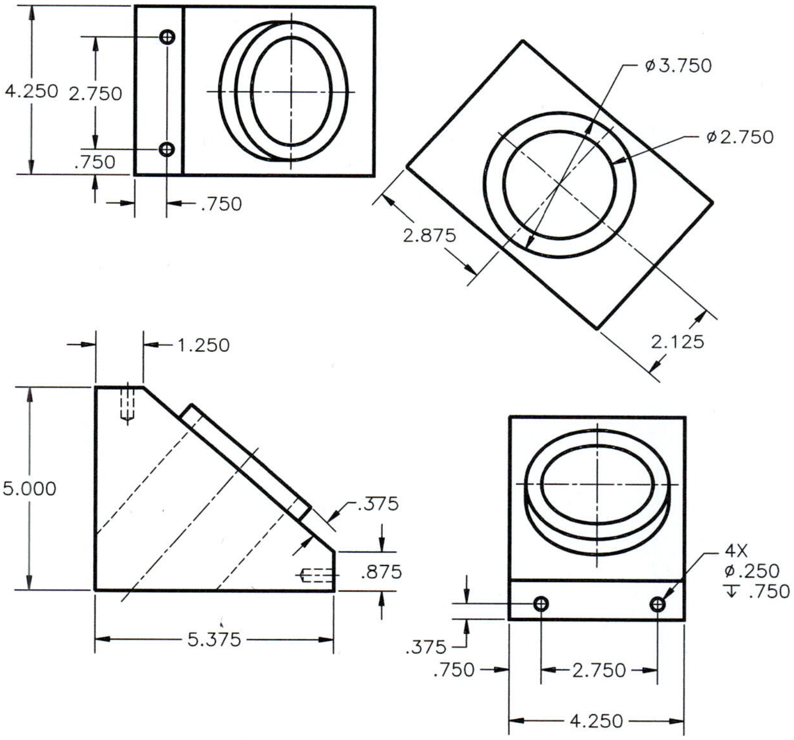

18. Use object snap modes to draw this elementary diagram. Do not draw the text. Save the drawing as P6-18.

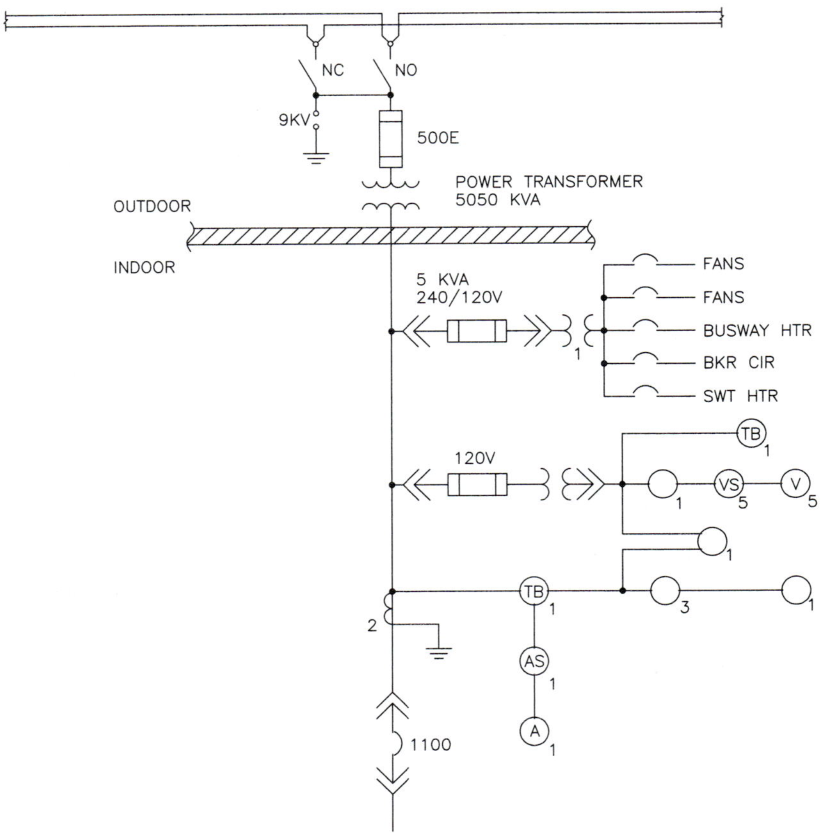

CHAPTER 7

Using the Geometry Calculator and Filters

Learning Objectives

After completing this chapter, you will be able to do the following:

- Use the geometry calculator to make mathematical calculations.
- Make calculations and use information based on existing drawing geometry.
- Add objects to drawings using the geometry calculator and object snaps.
- Use selection set filters to create custom selection sets according to object types and object properties.

AutoCAD commands require precise input. Often, the input is variable and based on objects or locations within a drawing. AutoCAD provides a feature known as the ***geometry calculator*** to help find and use this type of information.

The geometry calculator and its use are explained in this chapter. Fundamental math calculations and drafting applications are presented. Complex mathematical calculations are also possible. Also covered in this chapter is the **FILTER** command, which allows you to customize a selection set by filtering objects based on object type and object properties.

Using the Geometry Calculator

AutoCAD's geometry calculator allows you to extract and use existing information in your drawing. The geometry calculator also allows you to perform basic mathematical calculations at the command line or supply an expression as input to a prompt.

The geometry calculator is accessed by typing CAL at the Command: prompt. You are then prompted for an expression. After you type the mathematical expression and press [Enter], AutoCAD automatically simplifies, or "solves," the expression and returns the result. For example:

Command: **CAL**↵
>> Expression: **2+2**↵
4
Command:

Basics of the Geometry Calculator

The geometry calculator is more powerful than most hand-held calculators because it can directly access drawing information and can supply input to an AutoCAD prompt. The types of expressions that can be entered include numeric expressions and vector expressions. A ***numeric expression*** refers to a mathematical process using numbers, such as the expressions solved using normal calculators. A ***vector expression*** is an expression involving a point coordinate location.

To use the geometry calculator, you must understand the sequence and format of an expression. The geometry calculator evaluates expressions according to the standard mathematical rules of precedence. This means that expressions within parentheses are simplified first, starting with the innermost set and proceeding outward. Mathematical operators are evaluated in the standard order: exponents first, multiplication and division next, addition and subtraction last. Operators of equal precedence are evaluated from left to right.

Making Numeric Entries

The same methods of entering numbers at AutoCAD prompts are also acceptable for calculator expressions. When entering feet and inches, either of the accepted formats can be used. This means that 5′-6″ can also be entered as 5′6″. The 5′-6″ value can also be entered as 66 inches. When a number expressed in feet and inches is entered, AutoCAD automatically converts that number to inches:

Command: **CAL**↵
>> Expression: **24'6"**↵
294.0

> **NOTE** An entry at the Expression: prompt must be completed by pressing [Enter]. Pressing the space bar adds a space to your entry; it does not act as a return at this prompt.

Using Basic Math Functions

The basic mathematical functions used in numeric expressions include addition, subtraction, multiplication, division, and exponential notation. Parentheses are used to group symbols and values into sets. The symbols used for the basic mathematical operators are shown in the following table:

Symbol	Function	Example
+	Addition	3+26
–	Subtraction	270–15.3
*	Multiplication	4*156
/	Division	256/16
^	Exponent	22.6^3
( )	Grouped expressions	2*(16+2^3)

The following examples use the **CAL** command to solve each type of mathematical functions:

Command: **CAL↵**
>> Expression: **17.375+5.0625↵**
22.4375

Command: **CAL↵**
>> Expression: **17.375–5.0625↵**
12.3125

Command: **CAL↵**
>> Expression: **12*18.25↵**
219.0

Command: **CAL↵**
>> Expression: **27'8"/4↵**
83.0

Command: **CAL↵**
>> Expression: **9^2↵**
81.0

Command: **CAL↵**
>> Expression: **(17.375+5.0625)+(4.25*3.75)–(18.5/2)↵**
29.125

An *integer* is a whole number; it has no decimal or fractional part. The geometry calculator has limits when working with integer values. Integers greater than 32,767 or less than –32,768 must be presented as real numbers. When working with values outside this range, type a decimal point and a zero (.0) after the value.

EXERCISE 7-1 Complete the Exercise on the Student CD.

Making Unit Conversions

The calculator has a function called **CVUNIT** that lets you convert one type of unit into another. For example, inches can be converted to millimeters or liters can be converted to gallons. The order of elements in the **CVUNIT** function is:

CVUNIT(*value*,*from units*,*to units***)**

For example, to convert 4.7 kilometers to the equivalent number of feet:

Command: **CAL↵**
>> Expression: **CVUNIT(4.7,kilometers,feet)↵**
15419.9

If the units of measure you specify are either incompatible or are not defined in the acad.unt file, the message

>> Error: CVUNIT failed to convert units

is displayed and the prompt is reissued.

The **CVUNIT** function can work with units of distance, angles, volume, mass, time, and frequency. The units available for conversion are specified in the file acad.unt found in the AutoCAD \Support folder. This file can be edited to include additional units of measure if needed.

EXERCISE 7-2 Complete the Exercise on the Student CD.

Point Entry

While the numeric functions of the calculator provide many useful capabilities, the most powerful use of the geometry calculator is its ability to find and use geometric information. Information such as point coordinates can be entered as input to the geometry calculator.

A point coordinate is entered as one, two, or three numbers separated by commas and enclosed in square brackets. The numbers represent the XYZ coordinates. For example [4,7,2], [2.1,3.79], or [2,7.4,0]. Any value that is zero can be omitted, as well as commas immediately in front of the right bracket. For example:

[2,2] is the same as [2,2,0]
[,,6] is the same as [0,0,6]
[5] is the same as [5,0,0]
[] is the same as [0,0,0]

Direction can be entered using any accepted AutoCAD format, including polar and relative coordinates, as shown in the following table.

Coordinate entry	Entry format
Polar	[*dist*<*angle*]
Relative	[@*x*, *y*, *z*]

These options provide the ability to determine locations, distances, and directions within a drawing. For example, to determine a point coordinate value for a location that is 6 units at an angle within the XY plane of 45° from the point 2,2,0, use the sequence:

Command: **CAL**↵
>> Expression: **[2,2,0]+[6<45]**↵
(6.24264 6.24264 0.0)

In an application of this type, the point answer is returned in parentheses with spaces to separate the numbers instead of commas. Calculations can also be performed within the point coordinate specification. For example:

>> Expression: **[2+3,2+3,0]+[1,2,0]**↵
(6.0 7.0 0.0)

A point location can be specified using the @ symbol. Entering this symbol supplies the current value of the **LASTPOINT** system variable:

Command: **CAL**↵
>> Expression: **@**↵
(point coordinates)

The reference to (*point coordinates*) in this command sequence represents the point coordinate values returned by AutoCAD. The actual coordinate values will vary based on user input.

Besides entering coordinates at the prompt, you can also specify point coordinates by picking with the cursor. The **CUR** function is used to specify a point picked with the cursor:

Command: **CAL**↵
>> Expression: **CUR**↵
>> Enter a point: *(pick a point)*
(point coordinates)

This method can also be used as part of a calculation:

>> Expression: **CUR+[1,2]**↵
>> Enter a point: *(pick a point)*
(point coordinates)

EXERCISE 7-3 Complete the Exercise on the Student CD.

Using the CAL Command Transparently

The **CAL** command can also be used transparently (within another command). To use the geometry calculator transparently, enter the command as **'CAL** (an apostrophe followed by CAL). When the **CAL** command is used transparently, the result is supplied as input to the current prompt.

The following example uses direct distance entry combined with the geometry calculator to provide the correct length of a line. The line being drawn is 8.0″ times 1.006.

Command: **L** *or* **LINE**↵
Specify first point: *(pick first point)*
Specify next point or [Undo]: **'CAL**↵ *(drag cursor in appropriate direction to set the angle of the line)*
>> Expression: **8*1.006**↵
8.048
Specify next point or [Undo]: ↵

The calculator evaluates the expression and automatically supplies the result of 8.048 at the Specify next point or [Undo]: prompt. When AutoCAD receives a single numeric value at a point prompt, it is automatically understood as a direct distance entry value. An application of this type of calculation may include a shrinkage allowance for a casting or forging pattern.

EXERCISE 7-4 Complete the Exercise on the Student CD.

Using the Object Snap Modes

Object snap points can also be specified as point coordinates to the geometry calculator. The object snaps provide the accuracy that is often needed when finding points on an object. The following example shows the **Endpoint** object snap used to identify a specific point on an object. Note that you *must* use the letter abbreviation. Typing the full snap name will result in an error.

Command: **CAL**↵
>> Expression: **END**↵
>> Select entity for END snap: *(pick an object)*
(point coordinates)

The next example uses the **Endpoint** object snap to find the end of a line and add the point coordinate of 2 at 45°.

Command: **CAL**↵
>> Expression: **END+[2<45]**↵
>> Select entity for END snap: *(pick an object)*
(point coordinates)

You can use the geometry calculator to provide information based on selected points. For example, the following sequence can be used to find the point midway between two points selected with the cursor.

Command: **CAL**↵
>> Expression: **(CUR+CUR)/2**↵
>> Enter a point: *(pick a point)*
>> Enter a point: *(pick a point)*
(point coordinates)

This same technique can be used with any desired object snap mode. For example, to divide the distance between the center of a circle and the endpoint of a line by two:

Command: **CAL**↵
>> Expression: **(CEN+END)/2**↵
>> Select entity for CEN snap: *(pick the circle)*
>> Select entity for END snap: *(pick the line)*
(point coordinates)

The previous sequence can be used within the **LINE** command to draw a line that starts halfway between the center of an existing circle and the endpoint of an existing line, as shown in Figure 7-1.

Command: **L** *or* **LINE**↵
Specify first point: **'CAL**↵
>> Expression: **(CEN+END)/2**↵
>> Select entity for CEN snap: *(pick the circle)*
>> Select entity for END snap: *(pick the line)*
(point coordinates)
Specify next point or [Undo]:

The following sequence is used to create a circle with its center located two units along the X axis from the midpoint of an existing line, as shown in Figure 7-2.

Command: **C** *or* **CIRCLE**↵
Specify center point for circle or [3P/2P/Ttr (tan tan radius)]: **'CAL**↵
>> Expression: **MID+[2,0]**↵
>> Select entity for MID snap: *(pick the line object)*
(point coordinates)
Specify radius of circle or [Diameter] <*current*>:

Figure 7-1.
Finding a point halfway between the center of a circle and the endpoint of a line.

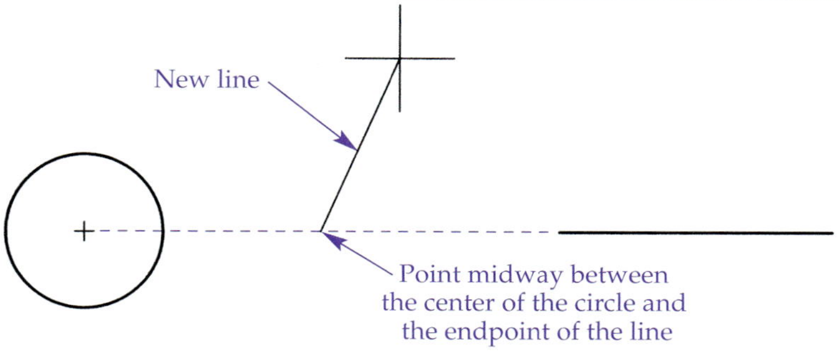

Figure 7-2.
Locating the center of a circle two units to the right of the midpoint of a line.

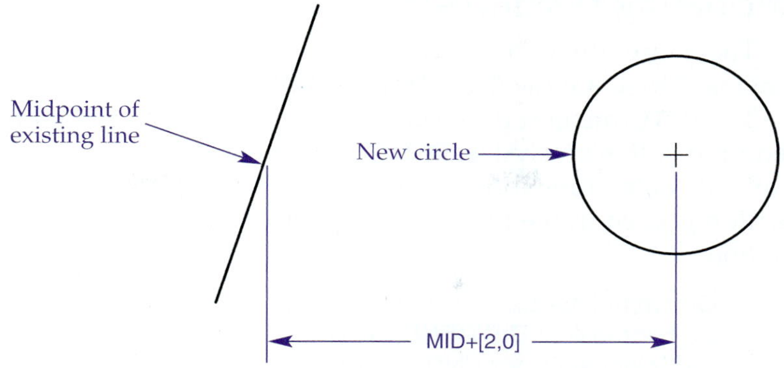

The next sequence determines the centroid (center of mass) of a triangle defined by picking three endpoints, as shown in **Figure 7-3.**

Command: **CAL↵**
>> Expression: **(END+END+END)/3↵**
>> Select entity for END snap: *(pick first corner of the triangle)*
>> Select entity for END snap: *(pick second corner of the triangle)*
>> Select entity for END snap: *(pick third corner of the triangle)*
(*point coordinates*)

PROFESSIONAL TIP

The snaps entered within a **CAL** command expression are not the same as those used with **OSNAP**. If **OSNAP** is on when using object snaps within the **CAL** command, you may get incorrect results. Turn **OSNAP** off before using an object snap in an expression within the **CAL** command. You can, however, use **OSNAP** to precisely locate points with the **CUR** function of the **CAL** command.

Figure 7-3.
Locating the center of mass of a triangle.

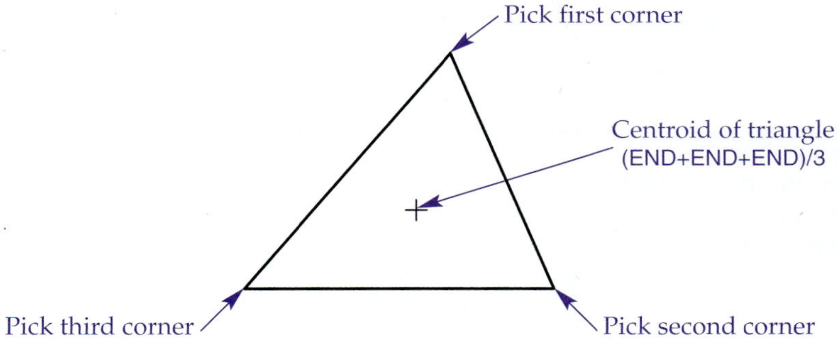

EXERCISE 7-5 Complete the Exercise on the Student CD.

Calculating Distances

There are three basic calculator functions used to calculate distances in a drawing. These are the **DIST**, **DPL**, and **DPP** functions.

The **DIST** function performs a simple distance calculation between the two specified points. It is entered as **DIST(***P1*,*P2***)** where *P1* = Point 1 and *P2* = Point 2. Similar to all calculator functions, the points can be entered manually or picked. The **DIST** function is used in the following sequence to find a distance between two endpoints of a line:

Command: **CAL↵**
>> Expression: **DIST(END,END)↵**
>> Select entity for END snap: *(pick an object)*
>> Select entity for END snap: *(pick an object)*
(*distance*)

The **DPL** function calculates the perpendicular distance between a point (*P*) and a line passing through two other points (*P1* and *P2*). It is written as **DPL(***P*,*P1*,*P2***)**. See Figure 7-4. The following is an example using **DPL** with the endpoint object snap. The order of selection is *P*, *P1*, and then *P2*:

Command: **CAL↵**
>> Expression: **DPL(END,END,END)↵**
>> Select entity for END snap: *(pick an object)*
>> Select entity for END snap: *(pick an object)*
>> Select entity for END snap: *(pick an object)*
(*distance*)

DPP function is much like the **DPL** function except it finds the shortest distance between a point (*P*) and a plane defined by three other points (*P1*, *P2*, and *P3*). See Figure 7-5. The **DPP** function is written as **DPP(***P*,*P1*,*P2*,*P3***)**. The points for **DPP** can be entered manually or picked. The following example calculates the distance between the point 2,2,6 and three random points on the XY plane:

Command: **CAL↵**
>> Expression: **DPP([2,2,6],CUR,CUR,CUR)↵**
>> Enter a point: *(pick a point)*
>> Enter a point: *(pick a point)*
>> Enter a point: *(pick a point)*
6.0

Figure 7-4.
Finding the shortest distance between a point and a line.

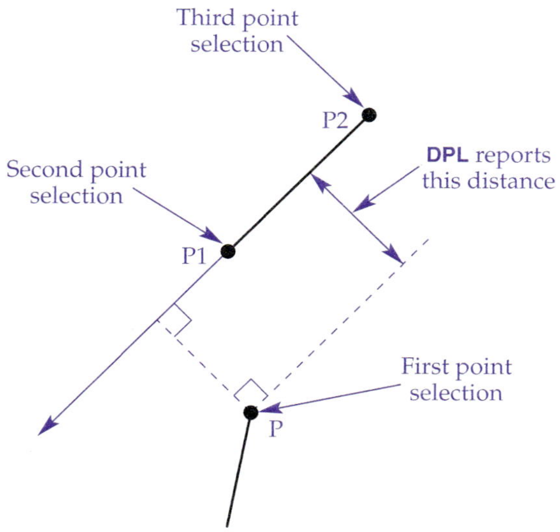

Figure 7-5.
Finding the shortest distance between a point and a plane.

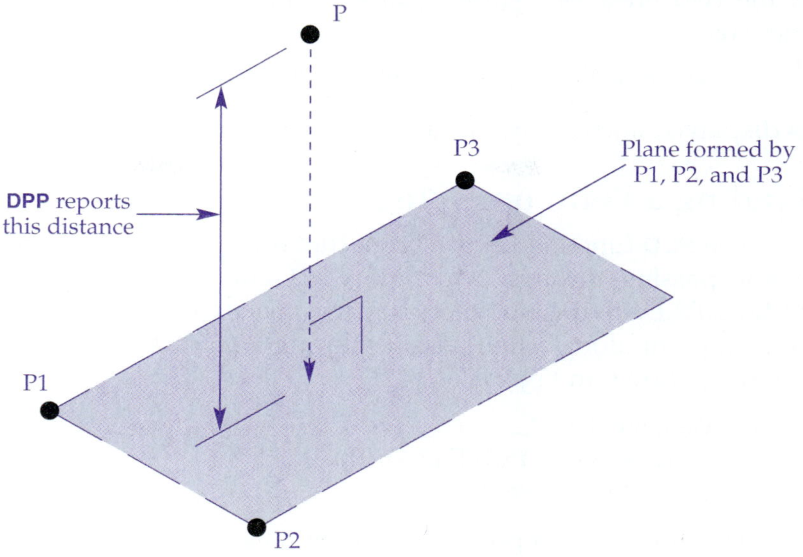

If point *P* is on the same plane as the three points picked to define the plane, the returned value is 0. Notice in the command sequence that point *P* is defined with the coordinates 2,2,6, which means it is located six units above the XY plane.

EXERCISE 7-6 Complete the Exercise on the Student CD.

Finding Intersection Points

The **ILL** function locates an intersection point between two nonparallel lines. This function is written as **ILL(***P1*,*P2*,*P3*,*P4***)**. The point location where the line containing *P1* and *P2* intersects the line containing *P3* and *P4* is identified. An actual line between *P1* and *P2* (or *P3* and *P4*) is not necessary. This function finds a hypothetical intersection as though the lines are infinite in length. The following sequence shows the use of the **ILL** function to find the intersection of the lines shown in **Figure 7-6:**

Command: **CAL**↵
>> Expression: **ILL([2,5,0],[4,6,0],[4,5,0],[2,6,0])**↵
(3.0 5.5 0.0)

Figure 7-6.
Finding the point of intersection of two nonparallel lines.

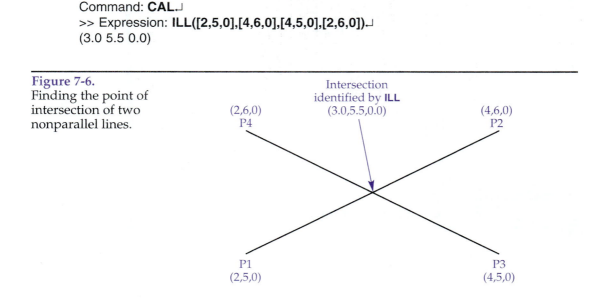

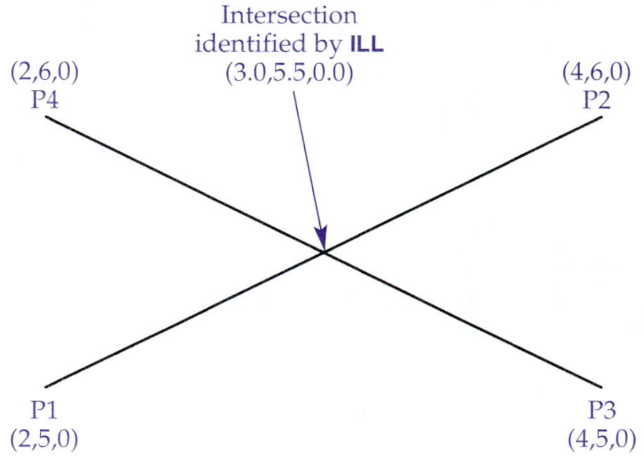

If the two lines, or hypothetical extensions of the two lines, do not intersect, the message:

>> Error: The two lines in function ILL do not intersect or are collinear.

is displayed and the >>Expression: prompt is returned.

Finding a Point on a Line

The **PLD** function finds a point that is a specified distance from the start point of a line passing through two points (*P1* and *P2*) and on the line. It is written as **PLD(***P1*,*P2*,*Dist***)**. It is not necessary for an actual line to exist. The following sequence finds a point along a line passing through 0,0 and 3,1 that is 10 units from the start point, as shown in **Figure 7-7.**

Command: **CAL**↵
>> Expression: **PLD([],[3,1],10)**↵
(9.48683 3.16228 0.0)

The **PLT** function provides another means of finding a point along a line. It finds a point that is along a line passing through two points (*P1* and *P2*) and located from the start point based on a specified scale (*T* parameter). The *T* parameter is simply a scale factor relative to the distance between *P1* and *P2*. The function is written as **PLT(***P1*,*P2*,*T***)**. The following sequence locates a point that is three-quarters of the way along the length of the specified line:

Command: **CAL**↵
>> Expression: **PLT([],[2,2],.75)**↵
(1.5 1.5 0.0)

If *T*=0, then the point location is the same as *P1*. If *T*=1, then the point location is the same as *P2*. A *T* value of .5 identifies the midpoint between *P1* and *P2*. A *T* value of 2 locates a point along the line that is a distance from the start point equal to twice the length of the line. **Figure 7-8** shows several examples.

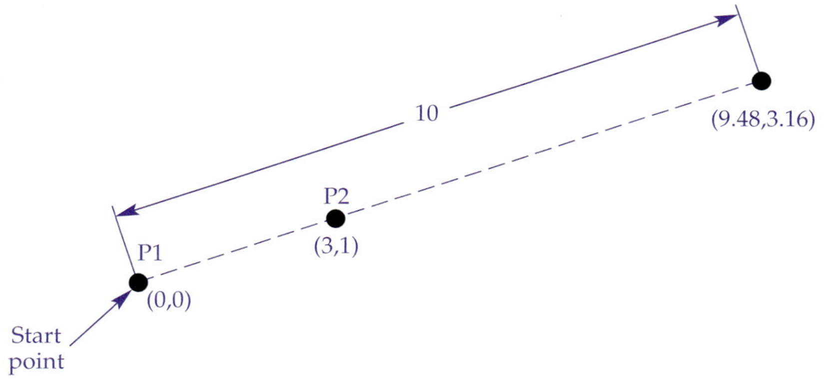

Figure 7-7.
Finding a point along a line that is a specified distance from the start point.

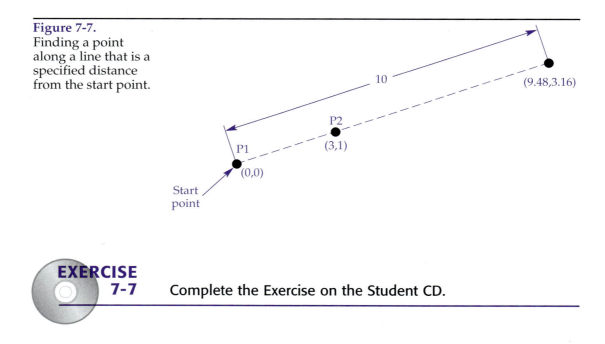

EXERCISE 7-7 Complete the Exercise on the Student CD.

Figure 7-8.
Finding a point along a line based on the scale of the line length.

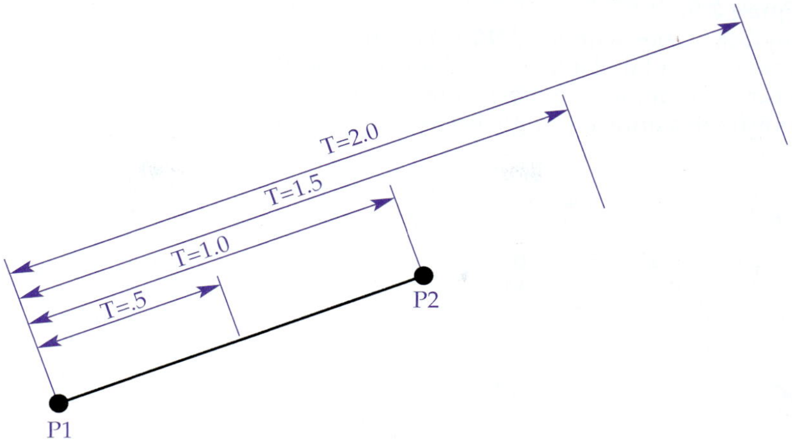

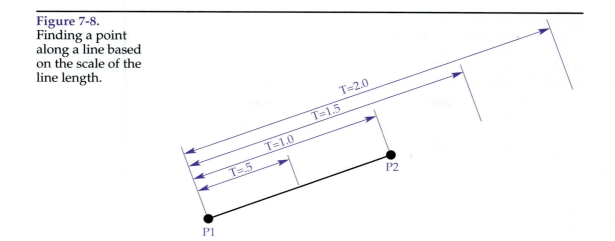

Finding an Angle

The **ANG** function finds the angle between two lines. As with other calculator functions, the lines need not physically exist in the drawing. This function can be entered several different ways, depending on the nature of the angle you are trying to calculate.

To find the angle of a vector from the X axis in the XY plane, enter **ANG(***coordinates***)**. The coordinate values are entered within parentheses. The coordinates can be manually entered or a point can be selected using object snap options. The following sequence shows this method being used to enter the coordinates of a point along the line shown in Figure 7-9A.

Command: **CAL**↵
>> Expression: **ANG([1,1,0])**↵
45.0

If the vector is not known, two points along a line can be used to determine the angle of the line in the XY plane from the X axis. The function is **ANG(***P1, P2***)**, as shown in Figure 7-9B and in the following sequence:

Command: **CAL**↵
>> Expression: **ANG([2,2],[4,4])**↵
45.0

You can also calculate an included angle by specifying a vertex and a point on each side, or leg, of the angle. A ***vertex*** is the intersection of two lines. An ***included angle*** is the angle formed between the vertex and the sides of the angle. The formula is entered as **ANG(***vertex,P1,P2***)**, Figure 7-9C. The following example determines the angle between two lines. The **Endpoint** object snap is used to precisely pick points.

Command: **CAL**↵
>> Expression: **ANG(END,END,END)**↵
>> Select entity for END snap: *(pick vertex)*
>> Select entity for END snap: *(pick end of first line)*
>> Select entity for END snap: *(pick end of second line)*
(angle)

EXERCISE 7-8 Complete the Exercise on the Student CD.

Figure 7-9.
Finding angles with the **ANG** function. A—Entering a single coordinate returns the angle from horizontal of a line containing 0,0 and the specified point. B—Entering two coordinates returns the angle from horizontal of a line containing the points. C—Entering three coordinates finds the angle between the two lines formed by the three points.

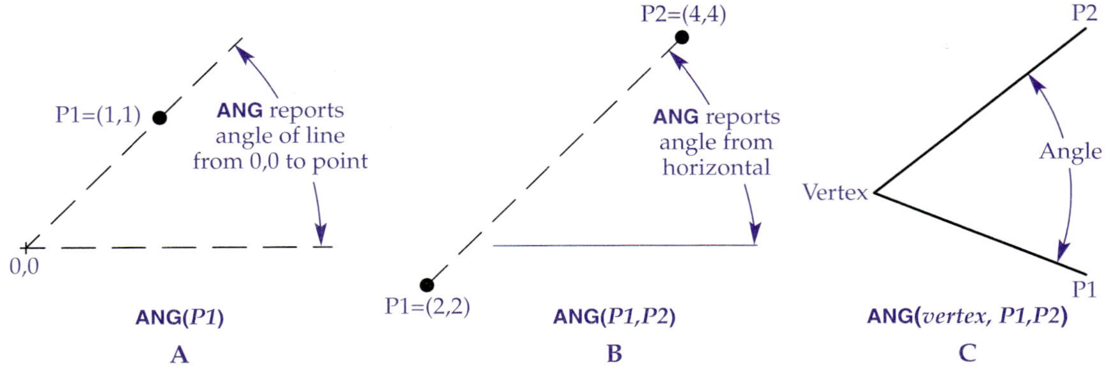

Finding a Radius

You can use the **RAD** function to find the radius of an arc, circle, or 2D polyline arc. The command sequence is:

Command: **CAL↵**
>> Expression: **RAD↵**
>> Select circle, arc or polyline segment for RAD function: *(select a circle)*
(*radius*)

You can easily draw objects to match the radius of an existing object using the **RAD** function. The following example uses **RAD** to supply the radius value for a circle to match that of the existing circle, as shown in Figure 7-10.

Command: **C** *or* **CIRCLE↵**
Specify center point for circle or [3P/2P/Ttr (tan tan radius)]: *(pick the center point of the new circle)*
Specify radius of circle or [Diameter] <*current*>: **'CAL↵**
>> Expression: **RAD↵**
>> Select circle, arc or polyline segment for RAD function: *(select the existing circle)*
(*radius of existing circle*)
Command:

Figure 7-10.
Using the **RAD** function to create a circle equal in diameter to an existing circle.

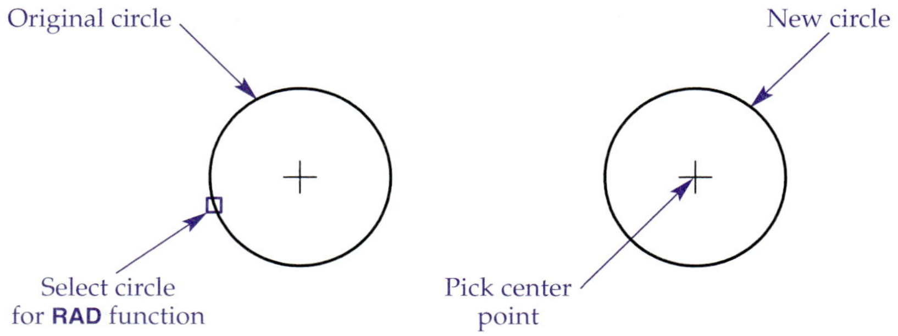

Combining Calculator Functions

Calculator functions can be combined. For example, suppose you want to draw a new circle that is 25% the size of the original circle and placed in a new position that also needs to be calculated. Look at **Figure 7-11** as you use the following command sequence:

Command: **C** *or* **CIRCLE**↵
Specify center point for circle or [3P/2P/Ttr (tan tan radius)]: **'CAL**↵
>> Expression: **(MID+MID)/2**↵
>> Select entity for MID snap: *(pick Line 1)*
>> Select entity for MID snap: *(pick Line 2)*
(*point coordinates*)

This locates the center point of the new circle halfway between the midpoints of Line 1 and Line 2. Now, instruct AutoCAD to calculate a new radius that is 25% of the size of the original circle:

Specify radius of circle or [Diameter] <*current*>: **'CAL**↵
>> Expression: **.25*RAD**↵
>> Select circle, arc, or polyline segment for RAD function: *(pick one of the original circles)*
Command:

A new circle that is 25% of the size of the original circle is drawn at the calculated location.

Another application of the **CAL** command is shown in **Figure 7-12** where a new circle is placed 3″ along a centerline from an existing circle. The new circle is 1.5 times larger than the original circle. The command sequence is:

Command: **C** *or* **CIRCLE**↵
Specify center point for circle or [3P/2P/Ttr (tan tan radius)]: **'CAL**↵
>> Expression: **PLD(CEN,END,3)**↵
>> Select entity for CEN snap: *(pick the original circle)*
>> Select entity for END snap: *(pick near the right end of the centerline)*
(*point coordinates*)
Specify radius of circle or [Diameter] <*current*>: **'CAL**↵
>> Expression: **1.5*RAD**↵
>> Select circle, arc, or polyline segment for RAD function: *(pick the original circle)*

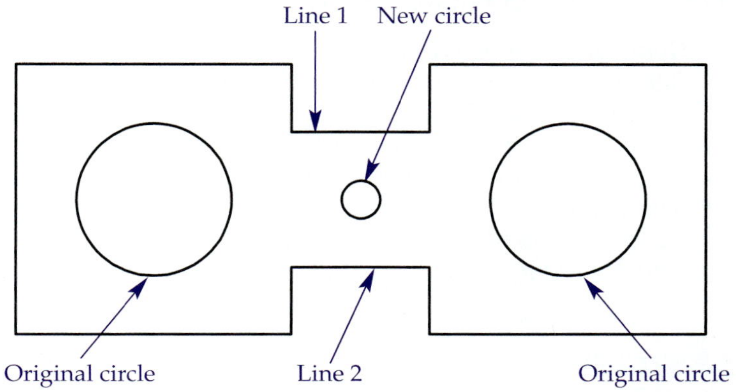

Figure 7-11. Combining calculator functions to revise a circle and place it in a new position.

EXERCISE 7-9 Complete the Exercise on the Student CD.

Figure 7-12.
Copying a circle along a centerline and resizing it.

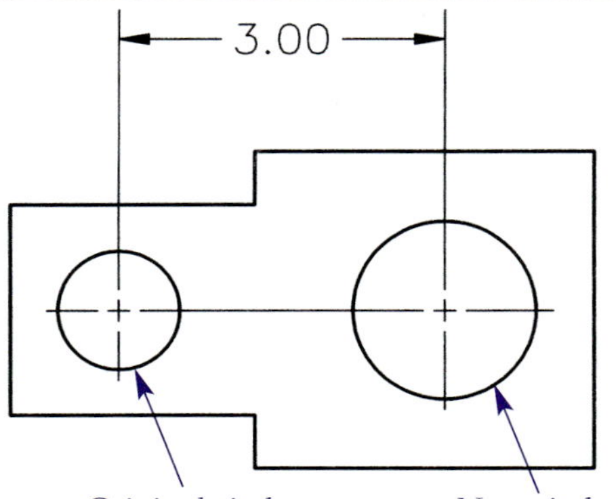

Geometry Calculator Shortcut Functions

To make using the geometry calculator as efficient as possible, some of the most commonly used calculator tasks have shortcuts. The basic abbreviations are shown in the following table.

Function	Replaces	Description
DEE	**DIST(END,END)**	Distance between two selected endpoints
ILLE	**ILL(END,END,END,END)**	Intersection of two lines defined by four selected endpoints
MEE	**(END+END)/2**	Point midway between two selected endpoints

These functions work exactly the same way as the longer format that you have already learned. Look at each of the shortcut options as you review earlier discussions covering the actual functions used by the shortcuts. For example, you can use the **DEE** shortcut to determine the length of a line:

Command: **CAL↵**
>> Expression: **DEE↵**
>> Select one endpoint for DEE: *(pick one end of the line)*
>> Select another endpoint for DEE: *(pick the other end)*
(distance)

The command sequence to draw a circle at the center of a rectangle using the **MEE** function, as shown in Figure 7-13, is:

Command: **C** *or* **CIRCLE↵**
Specify center point for circle or [3P/2P/Ttr (tan tan radius)]: **'CAL↵**
>> Expression: **MEE↵**
>> Select one endpoint for MEE: *(pick one corner of the rectangle)*
>> Select another endpoint for MEE: *(pick the opposite corner of the rectangle)*
(coordinates)
Specify radius of circle or [Diameter] <*current*>: *(type a radius and press* [Enter] *or pick a radius)*

EXERCISE 7-10 Complete the Exercise on the Student CD.

Figure 7-13.
Centering a circle within a rectangle using the **CAL** command.

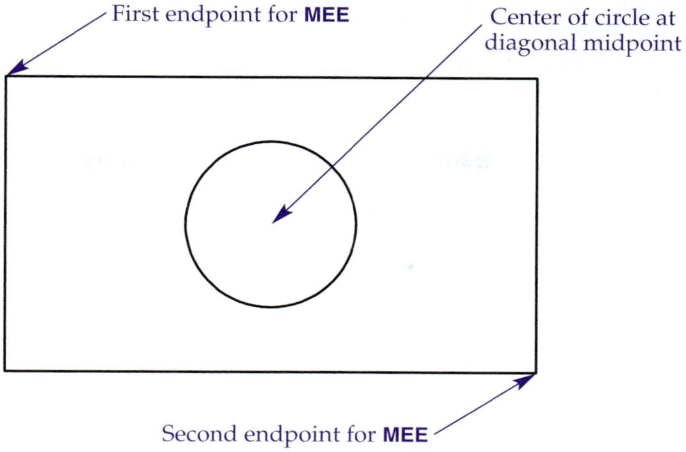

Using Advanced Math Functions

A number of advanced mathematical functions are also supported by the geometry calculator. These include logarithmic and exponential functions, as well as some data modification and conversion functions. For example, you can calculate the square root of 25:

Command: **CAL**↵
>> Expression: **SQRT(25)**↵
5.0

The following table shows each of the advanced math operators supported by the geometry calculator:

Function	Description
LN(*x***)**	Returns the natural log of a number.
LOG(*x***)**	Returns the base-10 log of a number.
EXP(*x***)**	Returns the natural exponent (or antilog) of a number.
EXP10(*x***)**	Returns the base-10 exponent of a number.
SQR(*x***)**	Returns a number squared.
SQRT(*x***)**	Returns the square root of a number.
ABS(*x***)**	Returns the absolute value (magnitude) of a number.
ROUND(*x***)**	Rounds a number to the nearest integer value.
TRUNC(*x***)**	Removes the decimal value of a number, returning the integer value.

Using Trigonometric Functions

When creating drawings, you often need to work with distances and angles. The geometry calculator supports several trigonometric functions for the calculations of distances and angles in a drawing. **Figure 7-14** shows the basic trigonometric operators and formulas.

The geometry calculator assumes the input for angular values is in degrees unless otherwise specified. This is regardless of the current angular units setting in AutoCAD. To enter angular data as degrees (d), minutes (′) and seconds (″), use the format 30d45′15″. If the minute or second value is zero, it can be omitted from the entry. For example, 42d0′30″ can be written as 42d30″. However, the degree value must be given, even if it is zero.

Figure 7-14.
The elements of a right triangle and related trigonometric functions.

$$sine = \frac{length\ of\ opposite\ side}{length\ of\ hypotenuse}$$

$$cosine = \frac{length\ of\ adjacent\ side}{length\ of\ hypotenuse}$$

$$tangent = \frac{length\ of\ opposite\ side}{length\ of\ adjacent\ side}$$

$$\sin A = \frac{a}{c}$$

$$\cos A = \frac{b}{c}$$

$$\tan A = \frac{a}{b}$$

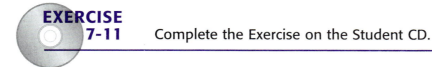

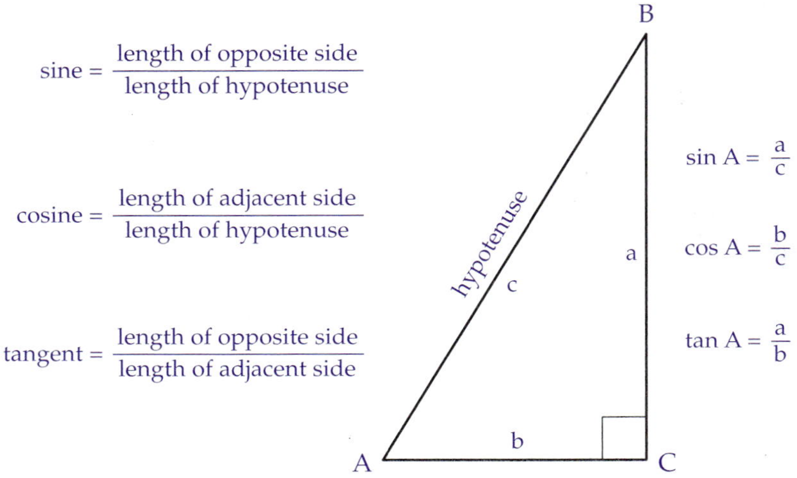

To enter a value in radians, use an *r* as a suffix for the number, such as 1.2r. A suffix of *g* indicates that the value is in grads, such as 50.00g. The geometry calculator output is always decimal degrees, regardless of the angular units style used for the input, except for the **D2R**(*angle*) function. The available trigonometric operators are shown in the following table.

Function	Description
SIN(*angle*)	Returns the sine of the angle.
COS(*angle*)	Returns the cosine of the angle.
TANG(*angle*)	Returns the tangent of the angle.
ASIN(*angle*)	Returns the arcsine of the angle.
ACOS(*angle*)	Returns the arccosine of the angle.
ATAN(*angle*)	Returns the arctangent of the angle.
D2R(*angle*)	Converts from degrees to radians.
R2D(*angle*)	Converts from radians to degrees. (Note: Do not use *r* suffix for this function.)
PI	The constant pi (π, 3.14159…)

To provide an example of using trigonometric functions in the geometry calculator, the following sequence solves for angle *A* in **Figure 7-14**. The length of side *a* is 4.182 and side *c* is 5.136. Since the length of side *a* divided by the length of side *c* is equal to the sine of angle *A*, the arcsine of *a* ÷ *c* is equal to angle *A*:

```
Command: CAL↵
>> Expression: ASIN(4.182/5.136)↵
54.5135
```

The returned value of 54.5135 indicates that angle *A* is 54.5135°. Using the information in **Figure 7-14** and the geometry calculator, you can quickly solve for missing information needed to complete a drawing.

The constant *pi* (π) is presented in the trigonometry functions table. This constant is also used in circular formulas, such as πR^2 (area) or $2\pi R$ (circumference).

EXERCISE 7-11 Complete the Exercise on the Student CD.

Setting and Using Variables with the Geometry Calculator

The geometry calculator has the ability to save values by assigning them to a user-defined variable. A ***variable*** is a text item that represents a value stored for later use. Calculator variables can store only numeric, point, or vector data. The following example sets a variable named *X* to a value of 1.2.

Command: **CAL↵**
>> Expression: **X=1.25↵**
1.25

The variable can be entered at a prompt by using the transparent **CAL** command:

Command: **C** *or* **CIRCLE↵**
Specify center point for circle or [3P/2P/Ttr (tan tan radius)]: *(pick a center point)*
Specify radius of circle or [Diameter] <*current*>: **'CAL↵**
>> Expression: **X**
1.25

This extracts the value of the variable *X* (1.25) and uses this as the radius of the circle. The following example sets a variable named *P1* to the coordinates of a user-selected endpoint, then uses *P1* in the **LINE** command:

Command: **CAL↵**
>> Expression: **P1=END↵**
>> Select entity for END snap: *(pick an object)*
(*point coordinates*)
Command: **L** *or* **LINE↵**
Specify first point: **'CAL↵**
>> Expression: **P1↵**
(*coordinates of P1*)
Specify next point or [Undo]: ↵

PROFESSIONAL TIP

The variables used by the geometry calculator are actually AutoLISP variables. ***AutoLISP*** is an easy-to-learn programming language for AutoCAD. An introduction to AutoLISP is given in ***AutoCAD and its Applications— Advanced.***

Using AutoCAD System Variables in the Geometry Calculator

In AutoCAD, many values are given a special name and stored for access whenever needed. These are called ***system variables,*** and their values depend on the current drawing or environment. The geometry calculator has a specialized function named **GETVAR** that allows you to use values stored in AutoCAD system variables. To retrieve a system variable, type **GETVAR(***variable name***)** at the Expression: prompt. The following example shows the drawing area being increased by multiplying the upper-right limits by 4:

Command: **LIMITS↵**
Reset Model space limits:
Specify lower left corner or [ON/OFF] <0.0000,0.0000>: ↵
Specify upper right corner <12.0000,9.0000>: **'CAL↵** *(notice the current maximum limits are 12,9)*
>> Expression: **4*GETVAR(LIMMAX)↵**
(48.0 36.0 0.0)
Command:

If you use the **LIMITS** command again, you will see the upper-right value has increased to 48,36.

A complete listing of system variables is available by typing **SETVAR** at the Command: prompt, followed by typing **?**. This gives you the Enter variable(s) to list <*>: prompt. The default * lists all of the variables:

Command: **SETVAR**↵
Enter variable name or [?]: **?**↵
Enter variable(s) to list <*>: ↵

This opens the **AutoCAD Text Window**, where all the system variables and their settings are listed. Continue pressing [Enter] to see the complete list. Press the [F2] key to return to the graphics window.

Creating Selection Sets

When creating complex drawings, you often need to perform the same editing operation to many objects. For example, assume you have designed a complex metal part with over 40 holes for 1/8″ bolts. A design change occurs, and you are notified that 3/16″ bolts will be used instead of 1/8″ bolts. Therefore, the hole size will also change. You could select and modify each circle individually, but it would be more efficient to create a selection set of all the circles and then modify them simultaneously.

AutoCAD provides two methods of creating selection sets: the **QSELECT** (quick select) command and the **FILTER** command. The **QSELECT** command is used to create simple selection sets by specifying object types and property values for selection. The **FILTER** command provides additional selection criteria and allows you to save selection sets.

Using Quick Select to Create Selection Sets

QSELECT

Tools
➡ Quick Select...

Properties window

Quick Select

One way to filter for different objects in a drawing is by using the **QSELECT** command. With **QSELECT**, you can quickly create a selection set based on the filtering criteria you specify. To access the command, pick **Quick Select...** in the **Tools** pull-down menu, type QSELECT at the Command: prompt, or right-click in the drawing area and choose **Quick Select...** from the shortcut menu. This displays the **Quick Select** dialog box. See Figure 7-15. You can also open the **Quick Select** dialog box by picking the **Quick Select** button in the **Properties** window.

A selection set can be defined in several ways using the **Quick Select** dialog box:

- Pick the **Select objects** button and select the objects on screen.
- Specify an object type (such as text, line, or circle) to be selected throughout the drawing.
- Specify a property (such as a color or layer) that objects must possess in order to be selected.

Once the selection criteria are defined, you can use the radio buttons in the **How to apply:** area to include or exclude the defined objects.

Look at Figure 7-16 as you follow this example that uses the **Quick Select** command:

1. Select **Quick Select...** from the **Tools** pull-down menu to open the **Quick Select** dialog box.
2. In the **Apply to:** drop-down list, select **Entire drawing**. If you access the **Quick Select** dialog box after a selection set is defined, there is also a **Current selection** option that allows you to create a subset of the existing set.
3. In the **Object type:** drop-down list, select **Multiple**. This will allow you to select any object type. The drop-down list contains all the object types in the drawing.
4. In the **Properties:** list, select **Color**. The items in the **Properties:** list vary depending on what is specified in the **Object type:** drop-down list.
5. In the **Operator:** drop-down list, select **= Equals**.

Figure 7-15.
Selection sets can be defined in the **Quick Select** dialog box.

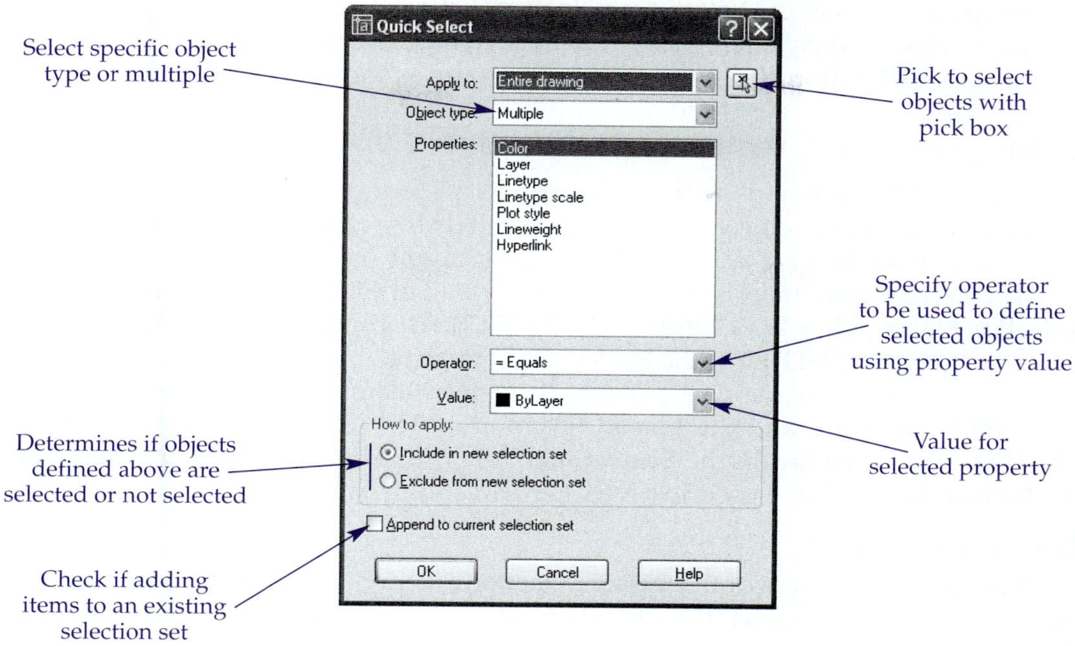

6. The **Value:** drop-down list contains values corresponding to the entry in the **Properties:** drop-down list. In this case, color values are listed. Select the color of the right-hand objects in Figure 7-16A.
7. Under the **How to apply:** area, pick the **Include in new selection set** radio button.
8. Pick the **OK** button.

AutoCAD selects all objects with the color specified in the **Value:** drop-down list, as shown in Figure 7-16B.

Once a set of objects has been selected, the **Quick Select** dialog box can be used to refine the selection set. Use the **Exclude from new selection set** option to exclude objects or use the **Append to current selection set** option to add objects. The following procedure refines the selection set created above to include any circles in the drawing that have a black color.

1. While the initial set of objects is selected, right-click in the drawing area and select **Quick Select...** from the shortcut menu to open the **Quick Select** dialog box.
2. Check the **Append to current selection set** check box at the bottom of the dialog box. AutoCAD automatically selects the **Entire drawing** option in the **Apply to:** drop-down list.

Figure 7-16.
Creating selection sets with the **Quick Select** dialog box. A—Objects in drawing. B—Selection set containing objects with the display color specified. C—Circle object added to initial selection set.

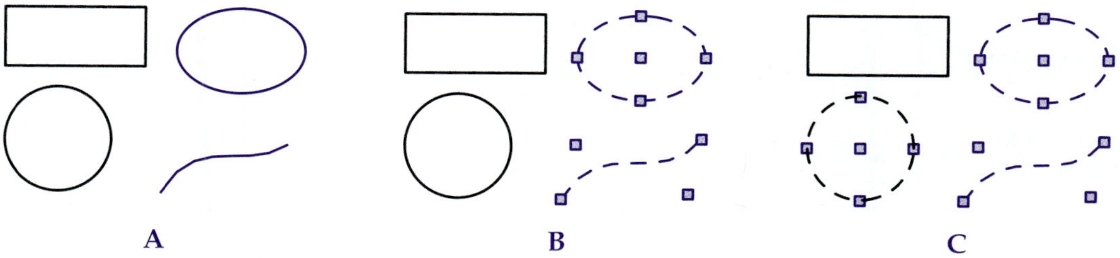

3. Select **Circle** in the **Object type:** drop-down list, **Color** in the **Properties:** drop-down list, **= Equals** in the **Operator:** drop-down list, and **Black** (or **ByLayer**, as appropriate) in the **Value:** drop-down list.
4. In the **How to apply:** area, pick the **Include in new selection set** radio button.
5. Pick the **OK** button. The selection now appears as shown in **Figure 7-16C.**

Using Filters to Create a Selection Set

FILTER
FI

The **FILTER** command is used to create a list of property criteria that must be met in order for a specific object to be selected. Filter lists can be created for use at any time. These filter lists are accessed at any Select object: prompt.

The **FILTER** command is accessed by typing FI or FILTER. This opens the **Object Selection Filters** dialog box, **Figure 7-17.** The **FILTER** command can also be used transparently by typing 'FILTER at the Select object: prompt.

The three major areas of the **Object Selection Filters** dialog box are the list box, the **Select Filter** area, and the **Named Filters** area. The list box is where the current filter list data is displayed, the **Select Filter** area is used to specify filter criteria, and the **Named Filters** area is used to save filters for future use.

Entering filter data

The **Select Filter** area of the **Object Selection Filters** dialog box is where filter data are entered. The drop-down list and edit boxes can be used to enter the values for the filters. Objects in a drawing can even be selected to develop a filter.

The three edit boxes correspond to X, Y, and Z point coordinates. They are enabled as needed for entering different types of filter information. When the filter drop-down list reads **Arc**, it refers to an object type. Since no further information is required about the object type, the edit boxes are all disabled. Setting the filter to **Arc Center** enables all three edit boxes, which are used to define the center point. When **Arc Radius** is selected, only the top edit box is enabled because only a single value is required. An example of each of these situations is shown in **Figure 7-18.**

For many filter specifications, such as layer, linetype, and color, the **Select...** button is enabled. When picked, this button displays the appropriate dialog box for showing the available options. For example, if **Color** is the specified filter, the **Select...** button displays the standard **Select Color** dialog box.

Once the desired filter and value(s) are specified, you must add these data to the list. Pick the **Add to List** button to add the new item to the existing filter list. The list at the top of the dialog box is updated.

Figure 7-17.
The **Object Selection Filters** dialog box.

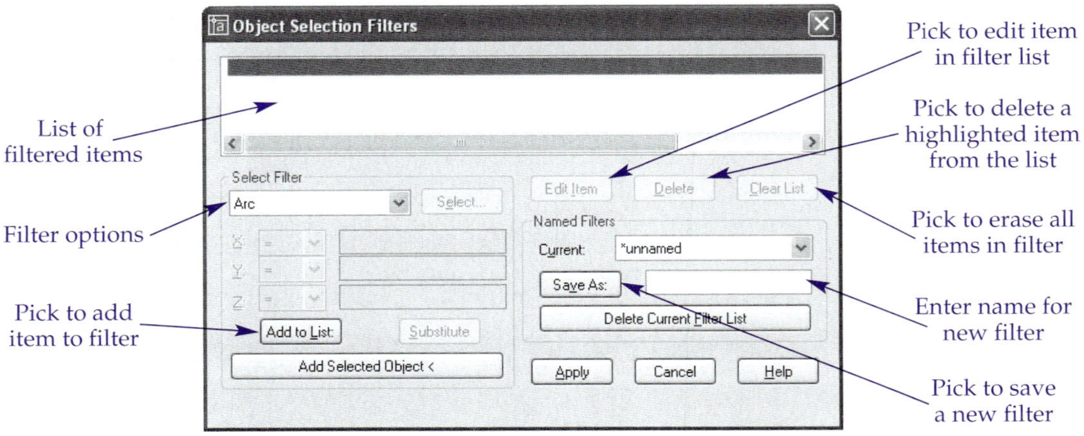

Figure 7-18.
This shows examples of filter items with the **X:**, **Y:**, and **Z:** edit boxes enabled as needed.

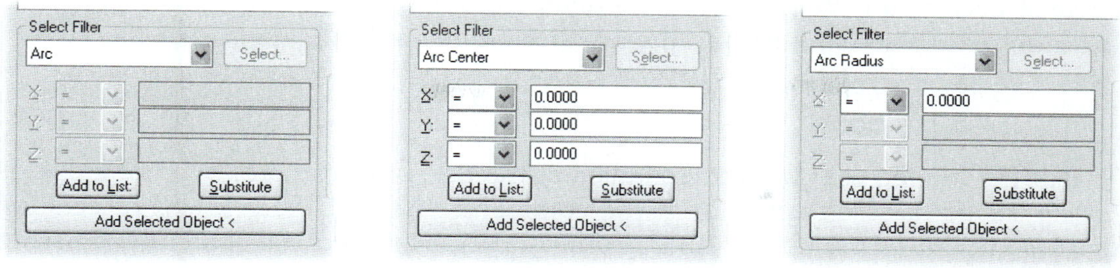

Object Filter
Edit boxes deactivated

Point Filter
All three edit boxes active

Distance/Length Filter
One edit box active

To use an existing object as a basis for a filter list, pick the **Add Selected Object** button. This temporarily closes the **Object Selection Filters** dialog box and gives you a Select object: prompt. Once an object is selected, you are returned to the dialog box. The information from the selected object is placed in the filter list. Since you may not need all of the filter list specifications that result from picking an object, the filter list can now be edited as needed.

To remove an item from the filter list, highlight it and pick the **Delete** button. To clear the entire list and start over, pick the **Clear List** button. To edit an item in the list, highlight the item and pick the **Edit Item** button. Editing the filter list is discussed in more detail later in this chapter.

To introduce applications of selection filters, the following example creates a simple filter list that selects only circle objects:

Command: **FI** *or* **FILTER**↵

This displays the **Object Selection Filters** dialog box. In the **Select Filter** area, pick the drop-down list to see the selection filter options. From this list, select **Circle**. To add this specification to the filter list, pick the **Add to List** button. The list box now displays this selection criteria as **Object = Circle**. This shows that only circle objects will be selected. See **Figure 7-19.** To use the selection filter, pick the **Apply** button. The dialog box is closed, and the following prompt is issued:

Applying filter to selection.
Select objects: *(use window, crossing, fence, or* ALL *to select objects)*

Figure 7-19.
Setting the filter so that only circles are selected.

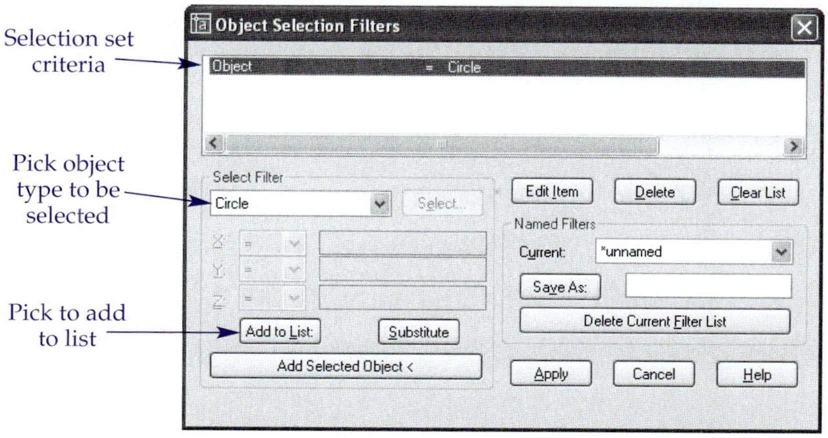

The prompt tells you that the filter is active. In Figure 7-20, a selection window is created around a group of lines, arcs, and circles. Because the filter is set to allow only circle objects, all other object types are filtered out of the selection. AutoCAD reports the number of objects found and the number filtered out (not selected):

```
13 found 8 were filtered out.
Select objects:
```

To exit the filtered selection, press [Enter] at the Select objects: prompt. The message Exiting filtered selection appears on the command line and the selected objects are displayed with grips. If the **FILTER** command was entered transparently, pressing [Enter] displays the message Resuming *(command)* command. That command's normal Select objects: prompt is displayed.

Filter lists can be expanded to select only objects with specific properties. The next example creates a filter list that selects only line objects that have a CENTER linetype. The steps are:

1. Enter the **FILTER** command and clear the list box by picking the **Clear List** button. This starts a new filter list.
2. From the drop-down list in the **Select Filter** area, select **Line**, then pick the **Add to List** button. This adds the filter **Object = Line** to the list box.
3. Select **Linetype** in the drop-down list and then pick the **Select...** button to display the **Select Linetype(s)** dialog box. Select the CENTER linetype and pick the **OK** button.
4. Pick the **Add to List** button. The **Object Selection Filters** dialog box should appear as shown in Figure 7-21.

By adding additional filters to the filter list, a filter can be extremely specific when needed. Filters for a specific location or a specific text string can be useful when selecting items in very large, complex drawings.

Figure 7-20.
All objects are filtered out except for the circles.

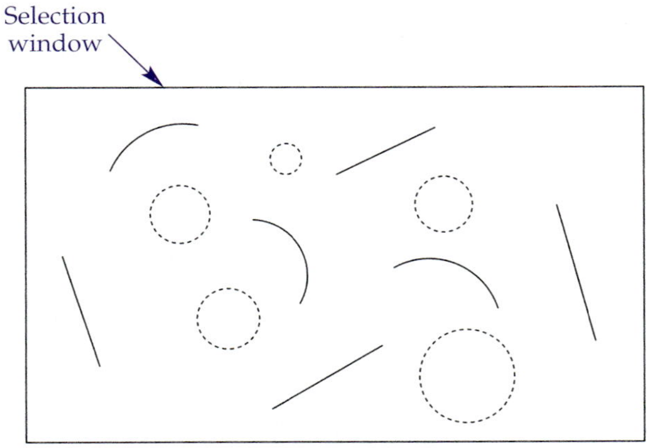

EXERCISE 7-12 Complete the Exercise on the Student CD.

Figure 7-21.
Line objects with CENTER linetype will be selected by this filter.

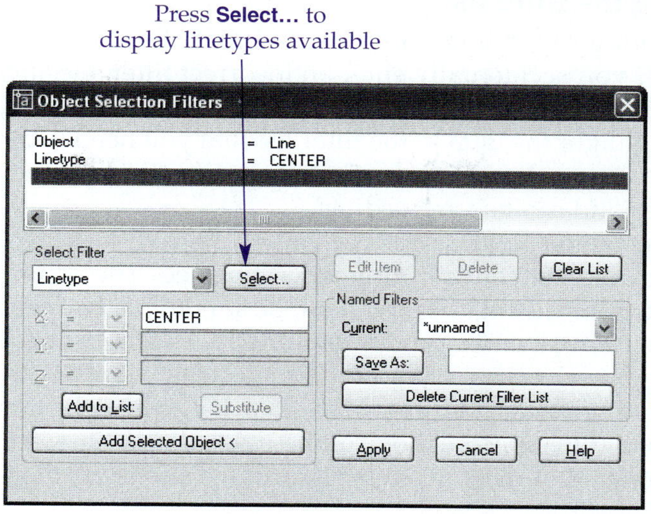

Working with relative operators

The term ***relative operator*** refers to functions that determine the relationship between data items. These relationships include equality, inequality, greater than, less than, and combinations such as greater than or equal to and less than or equal to. Each of the three edit boxes in the **Select Filter** area are preceded by a relative operator drop-down list. By default, the operator is "equal to" when the list is enabled. An appropriate relative operator can be selected for each data field.

For example, a relative operator can be used to select all arcs that have a radius of 2.5 or greater. To do this, the filter specification is **Arc Radius** with 2.5 entered in the enabled edit box. Then, select the greater than or equal to symbol (**>=**) in the relative operator drop-down list. See Figure 7-22. The following chart shows the relative operator functions:

Symbol	Meaning
=	Equal to
!=	Not equal to
<	Less than
<=	Less than or equal to
>	Greater than
>=	Greater than or equal to
×	Equal to any value

Figure 7-22.
The greater-than-or-equal-to filtering option.

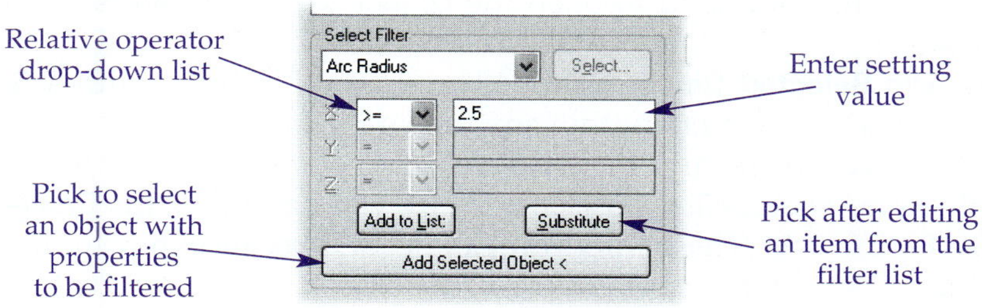

Editing the filter list

Editing capabilities are provided that allow you to modify and delete filter list items. If you accidentally enter an incorrect filter specification, you can easily correct it using these steps.

1. Highlight the item in the filter list that you need to edit and pick the **Edit Item** button. The values for the selected specification are then entered in the **Select Filter** area and can be freely edited.
2. Change the values as necessary.
3. Pick the **Substitute** button when finished. The edited filter specification is substituted for the highlighted item. Be sure to pick **Substitute** and not **Add to List**; otherwise, you end up with two different values for the same filter specification in the filter list.

To remove an item from the filter list, highlight it and select the **Delete** button. Only one filter specification can be deleted at a time using this method. If you need to remove all of the current specifications and start over, pick the **Clear List** button.

Creating named filters

The most powerful feature of CAD is being able to benefit from work you have already done. By reusing previous work instead of repeating the work to produce duplicate results, you increase your efficiency and overall productivity levels.

Complex filter lists can be time-consuming to develop. However, AutoCAD allows you to name and save filter lists. Then, you can recall the lists for future use. The **Named Filters** area of the **Object Selection Filters** dialog box is used to create and manage these lists.

When you have created a filter list that you plan to use again, it should be named and saved. When the filter list is completed and tested, follow these steps to name and save the list.

1. Pick in the edit box to the right of the **Save As:** button.
2. Type a short, descriptive name in the edit box. The name for a filter list can be up to 18 characters in length. These named filter lists are stored in a file named filter.nfl and are available until deleted.
3. Pick the **Save As:** button to save the named filter.

To delete a saved filter list, make it current by picking the filter name in the **Current:** drop-down list. Then, pick the **Delete Current Filter List** button.

EXERCISE 7-13 Complete the Exercise on the Student CD.

Using filters on a drawing

Filters can increase productivity, but you must learn to recognize situations when they can be used. Imagine that you have just created the flowchart in **Figure 7-23.** You are then asked to change all of the text inside the flowchart to a new layer and color for plotting considerations. You could use the **Properties** window and individually select each word on the chart, but you decide to use the **FILTER** command to make the job easier. Access the command to open the **Object Selection Filters** dialog box, and follow these steps.

1. Pick the **Add Selected Object** button. The drawing returns with a Select object: prompt. Pick a text element within any one of the boxes.
2. The dialog box returns and displays the characteristics of the text you picked. Highlight items such as Text Position and Text Value and pick the **Delete** button for each. See **Figure 7-24.** These filters are not needed because they limit the filter list to specific aspects of the text.

Figure 7-23.
Original flowchart requiring modification.

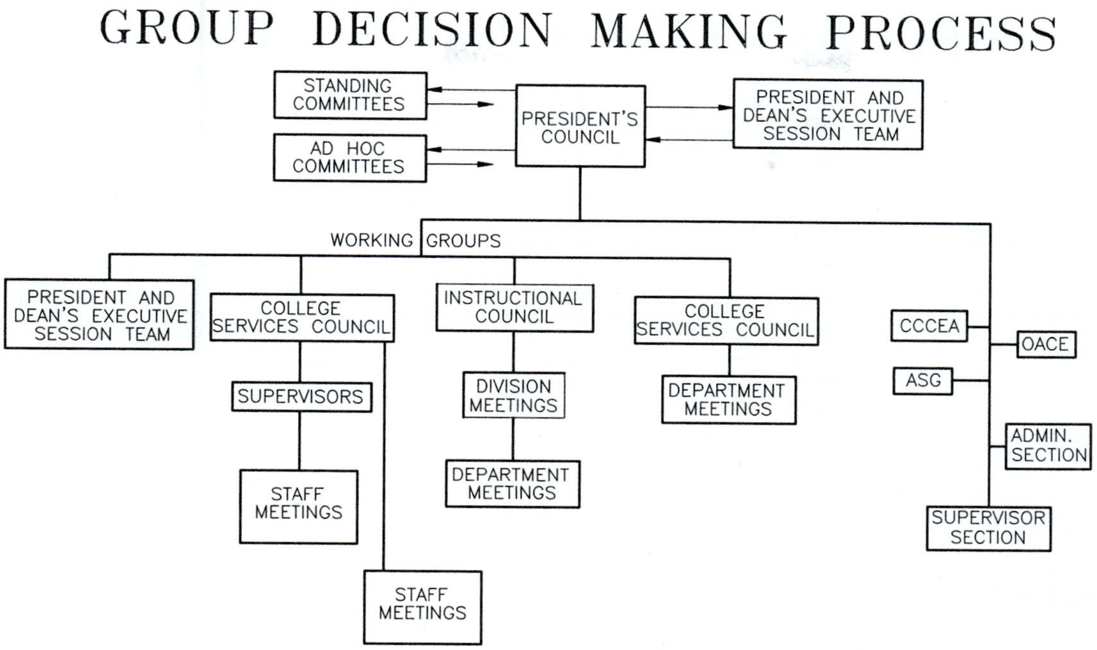

Figure 7-24.
Deleting selection filters that are too specific.

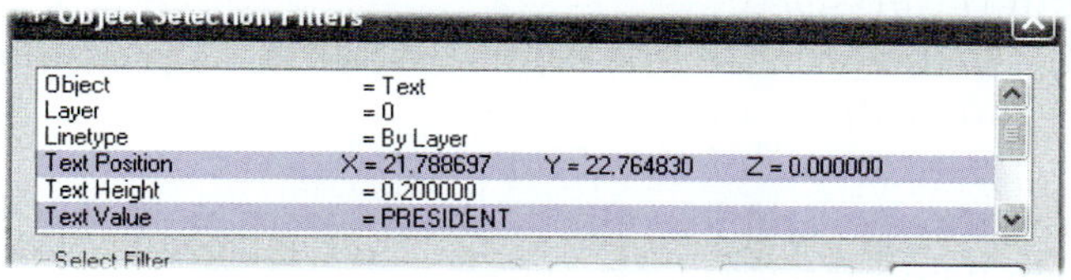

3. Enter a filter name, such as TEXT, in the **Save As:** text box and then pick the **Save As:** button. TEXT becomes the current filter name.
4. Pick the **Apply** button. The drawing returns and you are prompted:

Select object:
Applying filter to selection.
Select objects: **ALL**↵
Select objects: Specify opposite corner: 144 found
106 were filtered out.
(the text within the flowchart is now highlighted)
Select objects: ↵
Exiting filter selection.
Command:

5. All text is selected and displayed with grips.
6. Use the **Properties** window or other editing method to modify the selected text. The revised flowchart is shown in Figure 7-25.

EXPRESS TOOLS CHAPTER 7

The following Express Tool is related to topics discussed in this chapter. Refer to the Student CD for information on this tool:
Get Selection Set

Figure 7-25.
Revised flowchart. All text in the flowchart is now displayed in color.

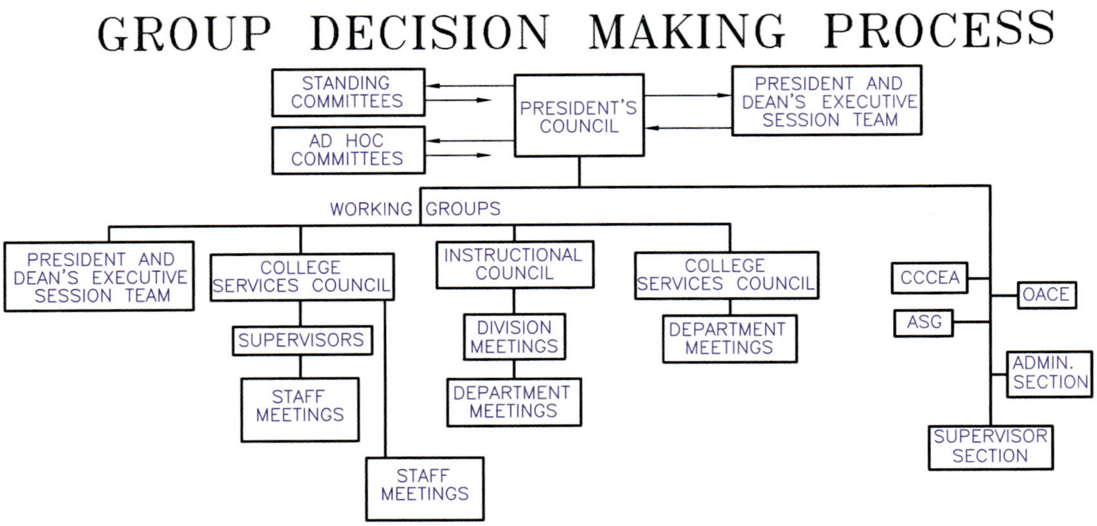

Chapter Test

Answer the following questions on a separate sheet of paper.

1. Identify the command that starts the geometry calculator.
2. Define *expression.*
3. What is the order of operations within an expression?
4. Give an example of an integer.
5. Give an example of a real number.
6. Show three examples of how the measurement *five feet six inches* can be entered when using the **CAL** command.
7. Give the proper symbol to use for the following math functions:
   A. Addition.
   B. Subtraction.
   C. Multiplication.
   D. Division.
   E. Exponent.
   F. Grouped expressions.
8. Give the expression used to calculate the conversion of 8″ to millimeters.
9. Given the following geometry calculator point coordinate entries, provide the shorter format:
   A. [2,2,0]
   B. [0,0,6]
   C. [5,0,0]
   D. [0,0,0]
10. Show the entry format for the following coordinate systems:
    A. Polar.
    B. Relative.
11. Which expression do you enter if you want to use the cursor to specify a point?
12. Give the expression that you would use to find a point that is added to the cursor location at X=1 and Y=2.
13. How do you enter the geometry calculator transparently?
14. Why are object snaps often used when finding points for the geometry calculator?
15. How do you enter an object snap within the geometry calculator?
16. Give the expression used to find the distance halfway between the endpoints of two lines.

17. Give the expression used to calculate the distance between the center of two circles.
18. Give the expression used to find the shortest distance from the end of a line to another line with two available endpoints.
19. Give the expression needed to find the distance between the last point used in AutoCAD and the point located at coordinates 4,4,0.
20. Identify the function that is used to find the intersection point between two nonparallel lines.
21. Name the function that is used to find an angle.
22. Give the expression used to identify the included angle when the vertex and sides are available.
23. Provide the function that is used to find the radius of a circle, arc, or 2D polyline.
24. Give the shortcut functions for the following applications:
    A. Distance between two selected endpoints.
    B. Intersection of two lines defined by four selected endpoints.
    C. Point midway between two selected endpoints.
25. Give the function for the following math operations:
    A. Returns a number squared.
    B. Returns the square root of a number.
26. Give an example of the full format for entering degrees, minutes, and seconds in the geometry calculator.
27. Give the trigonometric functions for the following operations:
    A. Returns the sine of angle.
    B. Returns the cosine of angle.
    C. Returns the tangent of angle.
28. Give the function for calculating the constant pi.
29. A _____ is a text item that represents another value that can be accessed later as needed.
30. Name the command that allows you to quickly create a selection set based on the filtering criteria that you specify.
31. Identify four ways to open the **Quick Select** dialog box.
32. Define *filters.*
33. How do you enter the **FILTER** command transparently?
34. What happens when you enter the **FILTER** command?
35. What is the purpose of the list box in the **Object Selection Filters** dialog box?
36. What is the purpose of the **Select Filter** area in the **Object Selection Filters** dialog box?
37. What is the purpose of the **Named Filters** area in the **Object Selection Filters** dialog box?
38. How do you remove an item from the filter list?
39. How do you clear the entire filter list and start over again?
40. Which relative operator is used to select all arcs that have a radius of 4.3 or less?
41. If you want to use filters to make changes to the text on your drawing and you pick one of the text objects, the dialog box displays the characteristics of the text you picked. Why is it best to delete items such as Text Position and Text Value?
42. If you add circles to the filter list, what happens when a selection window is placed around a group of lines, arcs, and circles?
43. Identify two ways to specify a linetype in a filter list.
44. Provide the following relative operator symbols:
    A. Not equal to.
    B. Less than.
    C. Less than or equal to.
    D. Greater than.
    E. Greater than or equal to.
    F. Equal to any value.

Drawing Problems

Use the **CAL** *command to calculate the result of the following equations.*

1. 27.375 + 15.875
2. 16.0625 – 7.1250
3. 5 × 17′-8″
4. 48′-0″ ÷ 16
5. (12.625 + 3.063) + (18.250 – 4.375) – (2.625 – 1.188)
6. 7.25^2
7. Show the calculation and answer that would be used with the **LINE** command to make an 8″ line 1.006 in./in. longer in a pattern to allow for shrinkage in the final casting. Show only the expression and answer.
8. Solve for the deflection of a structural member. The formula is written as $PL^3/48EI$, where P = pounds of force, L = length of beam, E = Modulus of Elasticity, and I = moment of inertia. The values to be used are P = 4000 lbs, L = 240″, and E = 1,000,000 lbs/in^2. The value for I is the result of the beam (Width × Height^3)/12, where Width = 6.75″ and Height = 13.5″.
9. Convert 4.625″ to millimeters.
10. Convert 26 mm to inches.
11. Convert 65 miles to kilometers.
12. Convert 5 gallons to liters.
13. Calculate the coordinate located at 4,4,0 + 3<30.
14. Calculate the coordinate located at (3 + 5,1 + 1.25,0) + (2.375,1.625,0).
15. Find the square root of 360.
16. Calculate 3.25 squared.

Given the following right triangle, make the required trigonometry calculations.

17. Length of side c (hypotenuse).
18. Sine of angle *A*.
19. Sine of angle *B*.
20. Cosine of angle *A*.
21. Tangent of angle *A*.
22. Tangent of angle *B*.

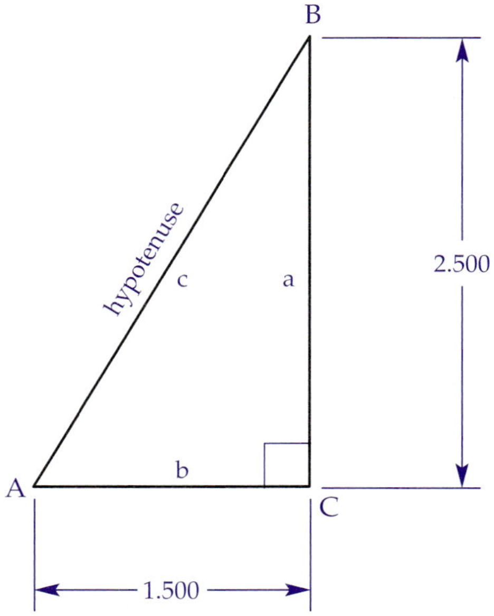

23. Create the following drawing. Use the **CAL** command and object snaps as needed to help you. Do not draw dimensions. Save the drawing as P7-23.

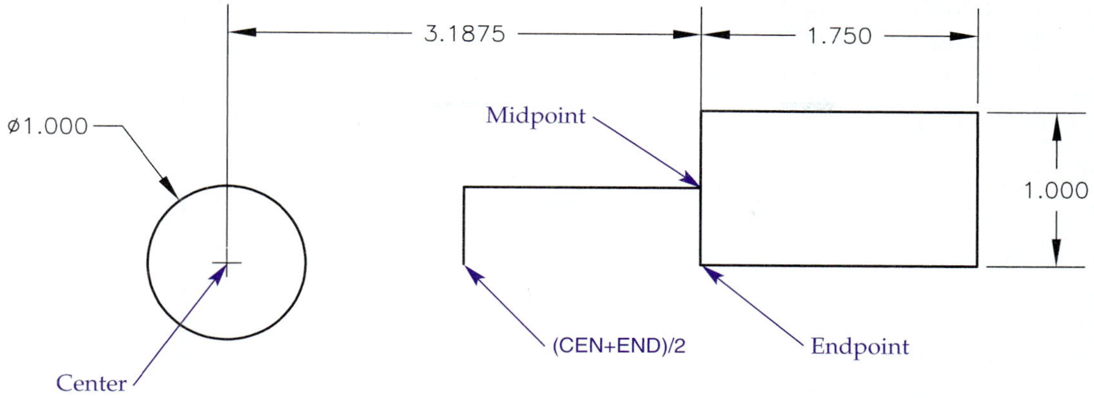

24. Open P7-23 and add the circle as shown below. Save the drawing as P7-24.

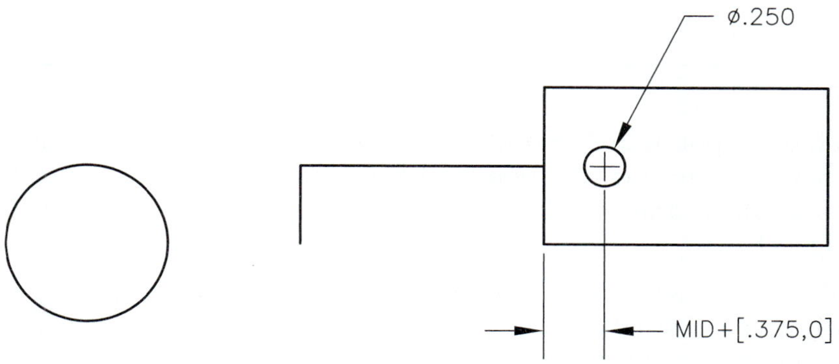

25. Create the following drawing. Use the **CAL** command and object snaps as needed to help you. Place the circle with its center at the centroid (center of mass) of the triangle. Do not draw dimensions. Save the drawing as P7-25.

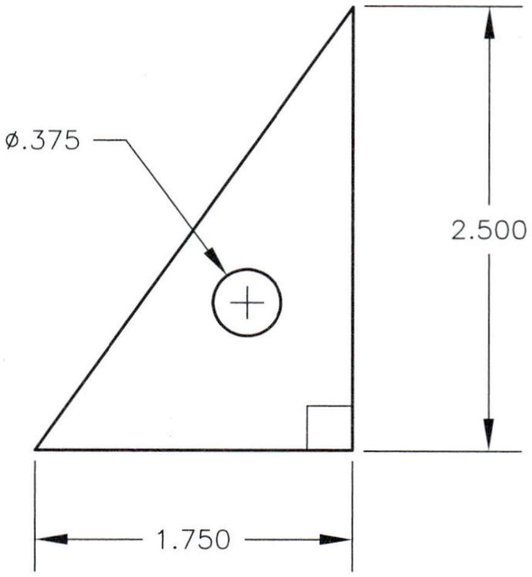

Drawing Problems - Chapter 7

26. Draw the lines shown below using the dimensions given. Do not draw dimensions or labels. Save the drawing as P7-26. Then, calculate:
   A. Length of Line A.
   B. Length of Line B.
   C. Shortest distance between Point P and Line B.

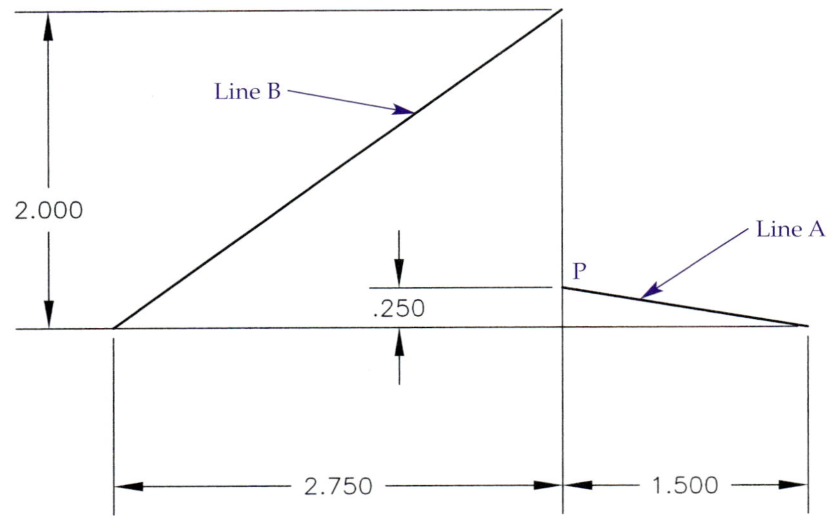

27. Line A has endpoints at 2.88,8.88 and 6.50,6.75. Line B has endpoints at 1.75,7.25 and 6.5,8.5. Determine the point where these lines intersect using the **CAL** command. Then, draw the lines and check your solution graphically. Save the drawing as P7-27.

28. Draw the line shown below using the coordinates and dimensions given. Do not draw dimensions or labels. Calculate the coordinate at the other end of the line and the coordinate of a point along the line that is two and one-quarter times the length of the given line. Write your answer and save the drawing as P7-28.

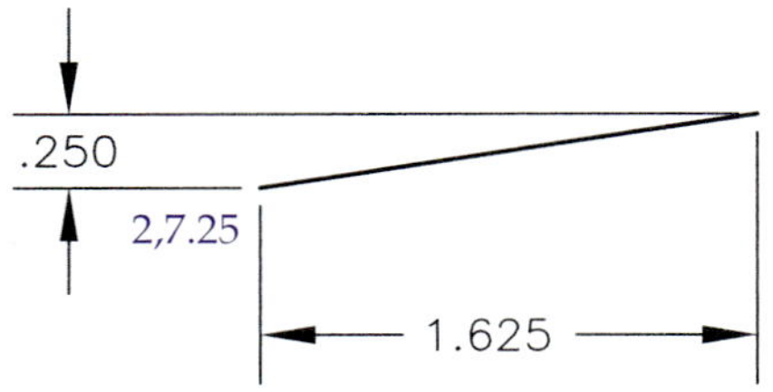

29. Draw the lines shown below. Use the **CAL** command to determine the angle between the lines. Save the drawing as P7-29.

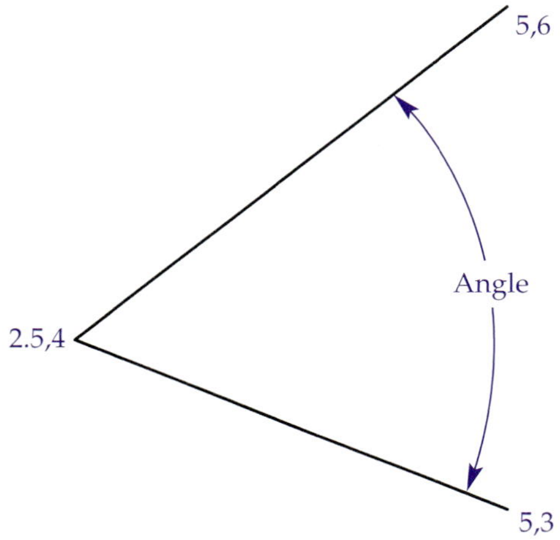

30. Draw a rectangle measuring 3.125 × 5.625. Use the **CAL** command to center a .75 diameter circle in the rectangle. Save the drawing as P7-30.

31. Draw the following object. Do not include dimensions. Then, use the **CAL** command to add another circle with a diameter that is 30% of the size of the existing circle. Center the new circle between the midpoints of Line 1 and Line 2. Save the drawing as P7-31.

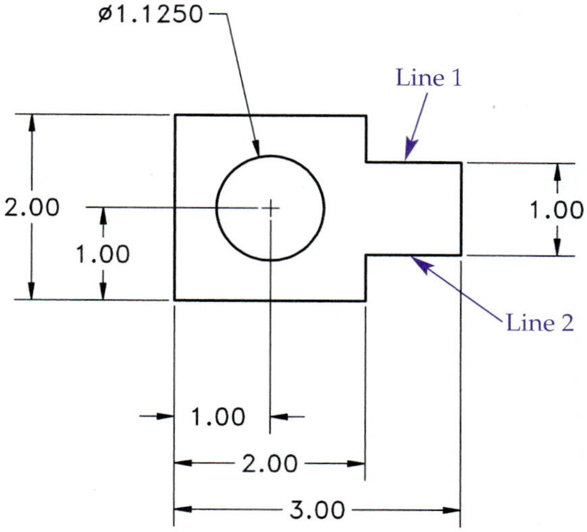

32. Draw the following object. Do not include dimensions. Then, use the **CAL** command to create another circle with the same diameter as the existing circle. Place the center of the new circle .5″ above a point that is midway between the center of the existing circle and the midpoint of the right-hand line of the object. Save the drawing as P7-32.

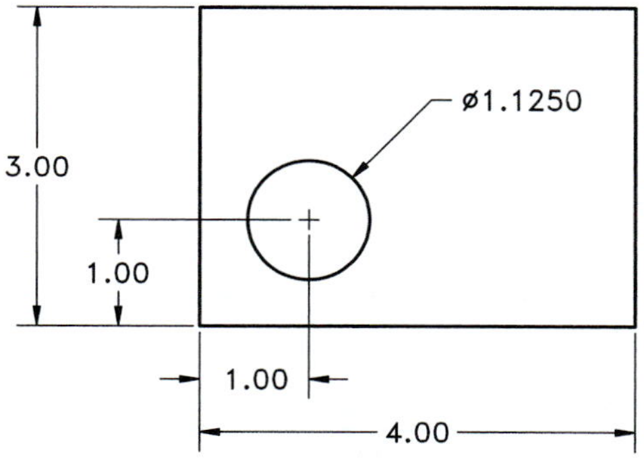

33. Draw the object shown below. Do not dimension the drawing. Then, use the **CAL** command to create another circle with a diameter that is 150 percent (1.5X) of the existing circle. Vertically center the new circle 3″ to the right of the existing circle. Save the drawing as P7-33.

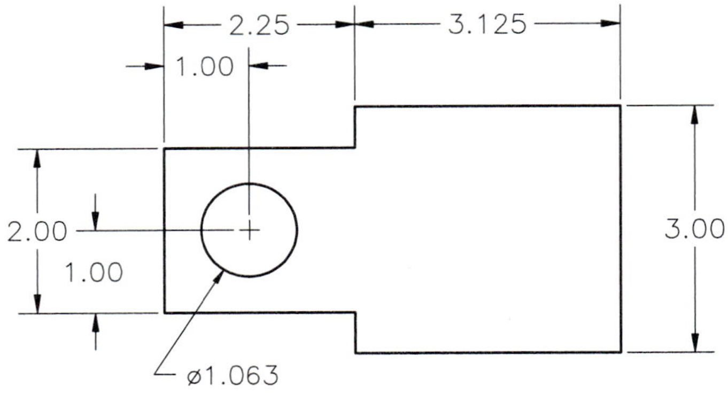

34. Use tracking, object snaps, and the geometric calculator to draw the object shown below based on these instructions:
    A. Draw the outline of the object first, followed by the 10 ∅.500 holes (A).
    B. The holes labeled B are located vertically halfway between the centers of the holes labeled A. They have a diameter one-quarter the size of the holes labeled A.
    C. The holes labeled C are located vertically halfway between the holes labeled A and B. Their diameter is three-quarters of the diameter of the holes labeled B.
    D. The holes labeled D are located horizontally halfway between the centers of the holes labeled A. These holes have the same diameter as the holes labeled B.
    E. Draw the rectangles around the circles as shown.
    F. Do not draw dimensions, notes, or labels.
    G. Save the drawing as P7-34.

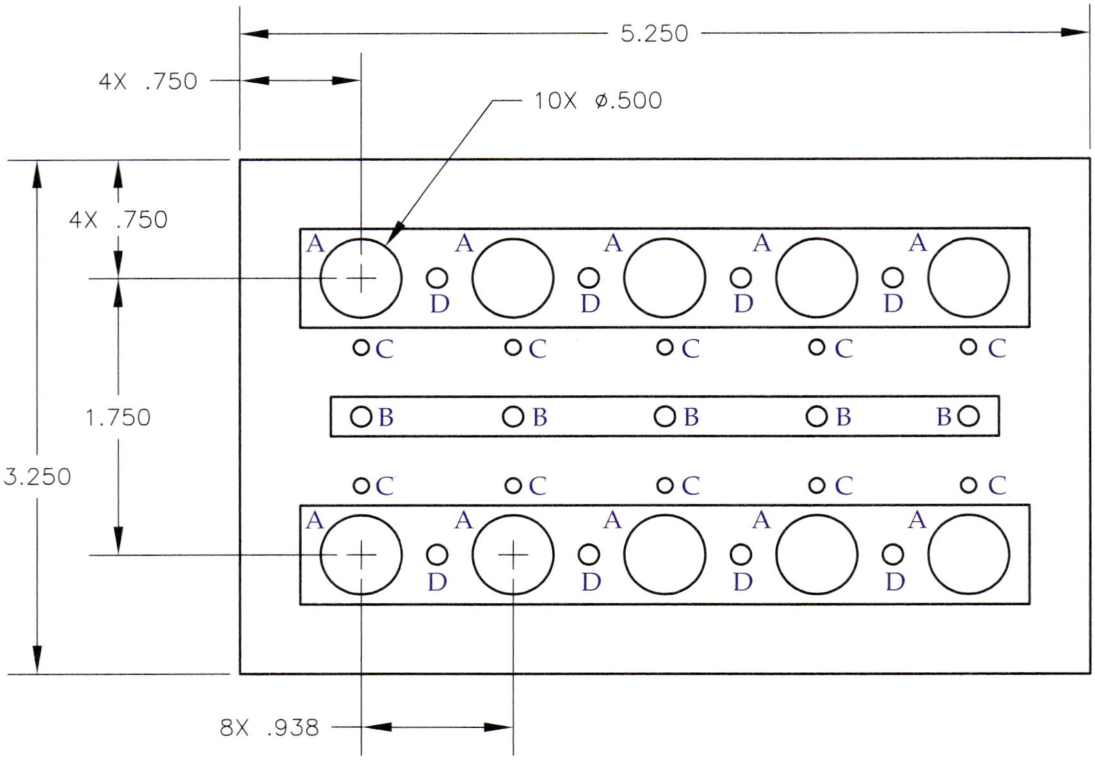

35. Open P7-34. Use a selection filter to erase all circles less than ∅.500. Name and save the filter set. Save the drawing as P7-35.

36. Draw the following roof plan. Do not dimension. Use the **CAL MEE** function to mirror the roof. Then, use the **FILTER** command to change the color of the roof and the linetype to CENTER. Finally, use the **FILTER** command to change the building outline to a continuous linetype. Save the drawing as P7-36.

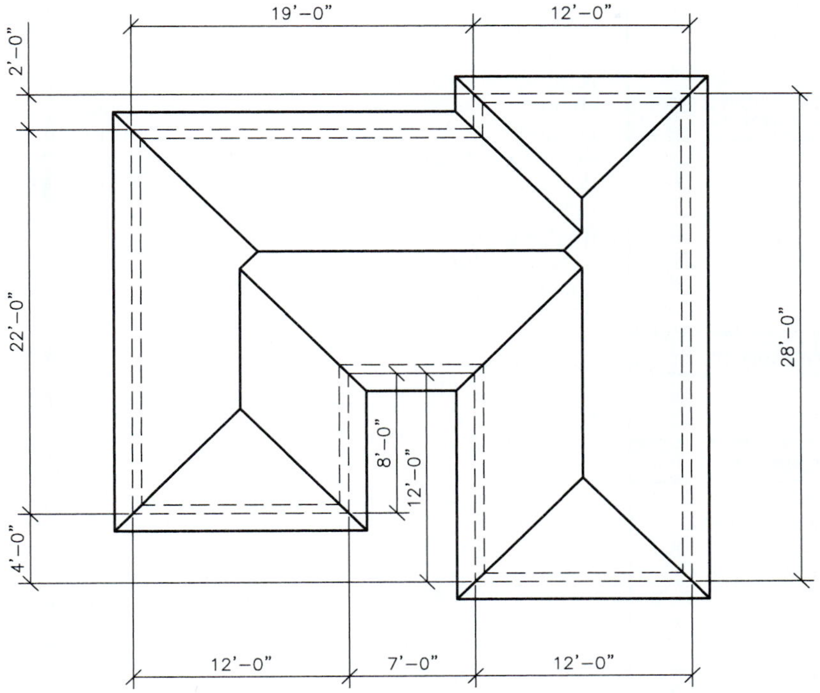

Drawing Problems - Chapter 7

This chart lists the units of measure (and acceptable abbreviations) that can be converted using the **CVUNIT** function. These units are defined in the acad.unt file. You can customize this file to have additional units of measure available for conversion.

Units Defined for Conversion with CVUNIT function

Basic SI Units

meter(s), metre(s), m
kilogram(s), kg
second(s), sec
ampere(s), amp(s)
kelvin, k
candela, cd

Derived SI Units

celsius, centigrade, c
rankine
fahrenheit
gram(s), gm, g
newton(s), n
pascal, pa
joule(s)

Exponent Synonyms

square, sq
cubic, cu

Units of Volume

barrel(s), bbl
board_f(oot.eet), fbm
bushel(s), bu
centiliter(s), cl
cord(s)
cc
decistere(s)
dekaliter(s), dal
dekastere(s)
dram(s)
dry_pint(s)
dry_quart(s)
firkin(s)
gallon(s), gal
gill(s)
hectoliter(s)
hogshead(s), hhd
kilderkin(s)
kiloliter(s)
liter(s)
milliliter(s), ml
minim(s)
fluid_ounce(s)
peck(s)
pint(s), fluid_pint(s)
pottle(s)
puncheon(s)
quart(s), qt, fluid_quart(s)
register_ton(s)
seam(s)
stere(s)
tun(s)

Circular Measure

circle(s)
radian(s)
degree(s)
grad(s)
quadrant(s)

Units of Length

Angstrom(s)
astronomical_unit(s), au
bolt(s)
cable(s)
caliber
centimeter(s), centimetre(s), cm(s)
chain(s)
cubit(s)
decimeter(s), decimetre(s), dm
dekameter(s), dekametre(s), dam
fathom(s), fath
f(oot.eet), ft, '
furlong(s), fur
gigameter(s), gigametre(s)
hand(s)
hectometer(s), hectometre(s), hm
inch(es), in(s), "
kilometer(s), kilometre(s), km
league_nautical
league_statute
light_year(s)
link(s)
microinch(es)
micron(s)
mil(s)
mile_nautical, inm
mile_statute, mile(s), mi
millimeter(s), millimetre(s), mm(s)
millimicron(s), nanometer(s), nanometre(s), nm(s)
pace(s)
palm(s)
parsec(s)
perch(es)
pica(s)
point(s)
rod(s), pole(s)
rope(s)
skein(s)
span(s)
survey_f(oot.eet)
yard(s), yd

Units of Time

centur(y.ies)
day(s)
decade(s)
fortnight(s)
hour(s), hr
milleni(um.a)
minute(s), min
sidereal_year(s)
tropical_year(s)
week(s), wk
year(s), yr

Solid Measure

sphere(s)
hemisphere(s)
steradian(s)

Units of Area

acre(s)
are(s)
barn(s)
centare(s)
hectare(s)
rood(s)
section(s)
township(s)

Units of Mass

dalton(s)
dyne(s)
grain(s)
hundredweight(s), cwt
long_ton(s)
ounce_weight, ounce(s), oz
ounce_troy
pennyweight(s), dwt, pwt
poundal(s)
pound(s), lb
scruple(s)
slug(s)
stone
ton(s)
tonn(e.es)

Units of Frequency

hertz, hz

Electromagnetic Units

coulomb(s)
farad(s)
henr(y.ies)
ohm(s)
siemens
tesla(s)
volt(s), v
watt(s), w
weber(s)

Dimensionless Prefixes

deca
hecto
kilo
mega
giga
tera
peta
exa

Fractions

deci
centi
milli
micro
nano
pico
femto
atto

CHAPTER 8

Placing Text on Drawings

Learning Objectives

After completing this chapter, you will be able to do the following:

- Use and discuss proper text standards.
- Use the **TEXT** command to create single-line text.
- Make multiple lines of text with the **MTEXT** command.
- Create text styles.
- Use **DesignCenter** to manage text styles.
- Draw special symbols using control characters.
- Underscore and overscore text.
- Explain the purpose of the Quick Text mode and use the **QTEXT** command.
- Insert fields into text.
- Edit existing text.
- Check your spelling.
- Search for and replace material automatically.
- Design title blocks for your drawing template.

Words and notes on drawings have traditionally been added by hand lettering. This is a slow, time-consuming task. Computer-aided drafting programs have reduced the tedious nature of adding notes to a drawing. In computer-aided drafting, lettering is referred to as *text*.

There are advantages of computer-generated text over hand-lettering techniques. When performed by computer, lettering is fast, easier to read, and more consistent. This chapter shows how text can be added to drawings. Also explained is the proper text presentation based on ASME Y14.2M, *Line Conventions and Lettering*.

Text Standards

Company standards often dictate how text appears on a drawing. The minimum recommended text height on engineering drawings is .125″ (3 mm). All dimension numbers, notes, and other text information should be the same height. Titles, subtitles, captions, revision information, and drawing numbers can be .188″ to .25″ (5 mm to 6.5 mm) high. Many companies specify a .188″, or 5/32″ (5 mm), lettering height for standard text. This text size is easy to read even after the drawing is reduced.

Figure 8-1.
Vertical and inclined text.

ABC.. abc.. 123..

ABC.. abc.. 123..

Vertical or inclined text may be used on a drawing, depending on company preference. See **Figure 8-1.** Do not use both text styles on the same drawing. The recommended slant for inclined text is 68° from horizontal. AutoCAD offers a variety of styles for specific purposes, such as titles or captions. Text on a drawing is normally uppercase, but lowercase letters are used in some instances.

Numbers in dimensions and notes are the same height as standard text. When fractions are used in dimensions, the fraction bar should be placed horizontally between the numerator and denominator using full-size numbers. Fractions can be stacked when using the **MTEXT** command. However, many notes placed on drawings have fractions displayed with a diagonal (/) fraction bar. A dash or space is usually placed between the whole number and the fraction. See **Figure 8-2.**

Scale Factors for Text Height

Scale factors and text heights should be determined before beginning a drawing. They are best incorporated as values within your template drawing files. Scale factors are important because this value is used to make sure the text is plotted at the proper height. The scale factor is multiplied by the desired plotted text height to get the AutoCAD text height.

The scale factor is always a reciprocal of the drawing scale. For example, if you wish to plot a drawing at a scale of 1/2″ = 1″, calculate the scale factor as follows:

1/2″ = 1″
.5″ = 1″
1/.5 = 2 The scale factor is 2.

An architectural drawing that is to be plotted at a scale of 1/4″ = 1′-0″ has a scale factor calculated as follows:

1/4″ = 1′-0″
.25″ = 12″
12/.25 = 48 The scale factor is 48.

The scale factor of a civil engineering drawing that has a scale of 1″ = 60′ is calculated as follows:

1″ = 60′
1″ = (60 × 12)″
720/1 = 720 The scale factor is 720.

If your drawing is in millimeters with a scale of 1:1, the drawing can be converted to inches with the formula 1″ = 25.4 mm. Therefore, the scale factor is 25.4. When the metric drawing scale is 1:2, the scale factor for converting to inches is 1″ = 25.4 × 2, or 1″ = 50.8. The scale factor is 50.8.

Figure 8-2.
Examples of numbers for different units of measure.

Decimal Inch	Fractional Inch	Millimeter
2.750 .25	$2\frac{3}{4}$ 2–3/4 2 3/4	2.5 3 0.7

After the scale factor has been determined, you should then calculate the height of the AutoCAD text. In a 1″ = 1″ scaled drawing, the scale factor equals 1. Therefore, the text height in the drawing will be 1/8″ high, because the text height multiplied by a scale factor of 1 equals 1/8″ high text. However, if you are working on a civil engineering drawing with a scale of 1″ = 60′, text drawn at 1/8″ high appears as a dot. Remember that the drawing you are working on is 720 times larger than it is when plotted at the proper scale. Therefore, you must multiply the text height by the 720 scale factor to have text in correct proportion on the screen:

text height × scale factor = model space scaled text height
.125″ × 720 = 90″ The proper text height in model space is 90″.

An architectural drawing with a scale of 1/4″ = 1′-0″ has a scale factor of 48. Text that is to be 1/8″ high when printed should be drawn 6″ high (1/8″ × 48 = 6″).

Text Composition

Composition refers to the spacing, layout, and appearance of the text. With manual lettering, it is necessary to space letters freehand. Spacing is performed automatically with computer-generated text.

Notes should be placed horizontally on the drawing. AutoCAD automatically sets lines of text apart at an equal distance. This helps maintain the identity of individual notes.

The term ***justify*** means to align the text to fit a given location. For example, left-justified text is aligned along an imaginary left border. Most lines of text are left-justified.

Using AutoCAD to Draw Text

AutoCAD provides two basic systems for creating text. There is line text for creating single-line text objects, and multiline text for preparing paragraphs of text. The **TEXT** command is used to create single-line text. This text is entered at the command line. The **MTEXT** command is used to create paragraph text. This text is entered in the ***multiline text editor.*** Each command is used differently, but the options are similar. Text styles allow you to make the text look the way you want.

Single-Line Text

The **TEXT** command allows you to see the text on the screen as you type. The **TEXT** command creates single-line text. This means that each line of text is a single text object. **TEXT** is most useful for text items that require only one line of text. Whenever the text has more than one line or requires mixed fonts, sizes, or colors, multiline text should be used.

The **TEXT** command can be issued by picking **Single Line Text** from the **Text** cascading menu in the **Draw** pull-down menu, picking the **Single Line Text** button in the **Text** toolbar, or entering TEXT at the Command: prompt as follows:

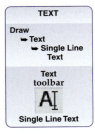

TEXT

Draw
➥ **Text**
➥ **Single Line Text**

Text toolbar

Single Line Text

Command: **TEXT**↵
Specify start point of text or [Justify/Style]: *(pick a starting point)*
Specify height <*current*>: *(enter the scaled text height value or press* [Enter]*)*
Specify rotation angle of text <0>: *(enter a value or press* [Enter]*)*
Enter text: *(type text and press* [Enter]*)*
Enter text: *(type the next line of text or press* [Enter] *to complete)*
Command:

When the Enter text: prompt appears, a text cursor equal in size to the text height appears on the screen at the text start point. **TEXT** can be used to enter multiple lines of text simply by pressing [Enter] at the end of each line. The Enter text: prompt is repeated for the next line of text. The text cursor automatically moves to the start point one line below the preceding line. Each line of text is a single object. Press [Enter] twice to exit the command and keep what you have typed. You can cancel the command at any time by pressing the [Esc] key. This action erases any incomplete lines of text.

While in the **TEXT** command, the screen crosshairs can be moved independently of the text cursor box. Selecting a new start point completes the line of text being entered and begins a new line at the selected point. Thus, multiple lines of text may be entered anywhere in the drawing without exiting the command. This saves a lot of drafting time. The following are a few aspects of the **TEXT** command to be aware of:

- ✓ When you end the **TEXT** command, the entered text is erased from the screen, and then regenerated.
- ✓ Regardless of the type of justification selected, the cursor box appears as if the text is left-justified. However, when you end the **TEXT** command, the text disappears and is then regenerated with the alignment you requested.
- ✓ When you use a control code sequence for a symbol, the control code, not the symbol, is displayed. When you complete the command, the text disappears and is then regenerated showing the proper symbol. Control codes are discussed later in this chapter.
- ✓ If you cancel the **TEXT** command, an incomplete line will be deleted.

TEXT and command line editing

When using the **TEXT** command, you can perform editing at the command line. The following keys are used to edit the entered material:

- **[↑].** The up arrow key moves backward through previously entered commands, allowing them to become a text entry. You might think of it as moving *up* the list of previous commands.
- **[↓].** After moving backward through any number of previous lines, the down arrow key moves forward again. You might think of this as moving back *down* the list of previously entered commands.
- **[←].** The left arrow key moves the cursor left through the text currently on the command line. Doing this allows you to reposition the cursor to insert text or words that were skipped when entering the text.
- **[→].** After using the left arrow key, the right arrow key moves the typing cursor back to the right.
- **[Home].** Moves the cursor to the home position, which is in front of the first character typed at the command line.
- **[End].** Moves the cursor back to the far right, at the very end of the text typed at the command line.
- **[Insert].** Toggles the command line between Insert mode and Overwrite mode. When in Insert mode, any new text is inserted at the cursor position, and any text existing to the right of the cursor is moved to the right. When in Overwrite mode, new text entered replaces the character at the cursor position.
- **[Delete].** Deletes the character to the right of the text cursor.
- **[Backspace].** Deletes the character to the left of the text cursor.

> **NOTE**
>
> In previous releases of AutoCAD, the **DTEXT** command was used to create single-line text. This command has been replaced by the **TEXT** command. If you enter DTEXT or its alias, DT, at the Command: prompt, the **TEXT** command is activated.

The Start point option

After entering the **TEXT** command, you are given the Specify start point of text or [Justify/Style]: prompt. The default option allows you to select a point on the screen where you want the text to begin. This point becomes the lower-left corner of the text. After you pick the start point, the prompt reads:

Specify Height <*current*>:

This prompt allows you to enter the text height. The default value is 0.2000. This is where the scaled text height needs to be entered. The previously selected letter height can be displayed as the current value. If you want letters that are .5 units high, then enter .5. The next prompt is:

Specify rotation angle of text <0>:

The default value for the rotation angle is 0, which places the text horizontally. The values rotate text in a counterclockwise direction. The text pivots about the starting point as shown in **Figure 8-3.** The last prompt is:

Enter text:

Type the desired text and press [Enter]. If no other justification is selected, the text is left-justified, as shown in **Figure 8-4.**

> **NOTE**
>
> If the default angle orientation or direction (**ANGBASE** and **ANGDIR** system variables) is changed, the text rotation is affected.

Figure 8-3. Different rotation angles for text. The starting point is indicated here with a plus sign.

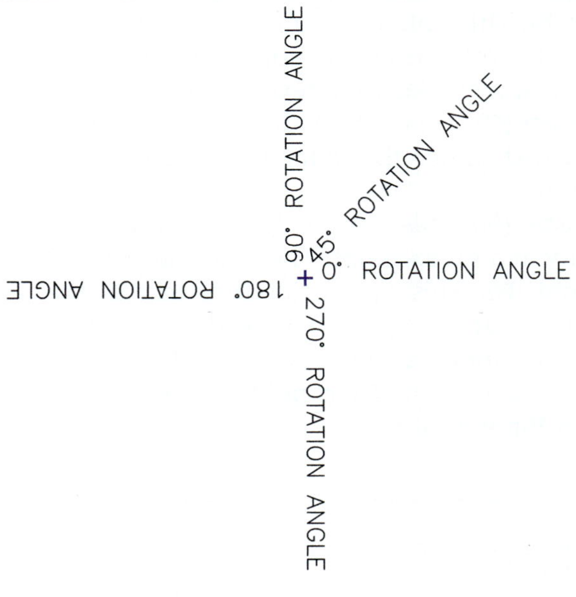

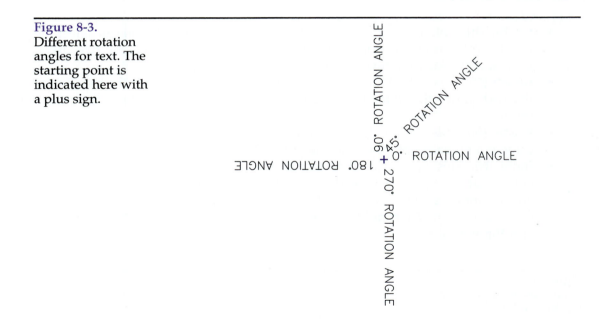

Figure 8-4.
Left-justified text with the start point shown.

The Justify option

The **TEXT** command offers a variety of justification options. Left-justification is the default. If you want another option, enter J at the Specify start point of text [Justify/Style]: prompt. When you select the **Justify** option, you can use one of several text alignment options. These options can be seen in the command sequence below, and are explained in the next sections.

Command: **TEXT**↵
Current text style: "Standard" Text height: 0.2000
Specify start point of text or [Justify/Style]: **J**↵
Enter an option [Align/Fit/Center/Middle/Right/TL/TC/TR/ML/MC/MR/BL/BC/BR]:

- **Align (A).** When this option is selected, you are prompted for two points between which the text string is confined. The beginning and endpoints can be placed horizontally or at an angle. AutoCAD automatically adjusts the text width to fit between the selected points. The text height is also changed with this option. The height varies according to the distance between the points and the number of characters. See Figure 8-5.

PROFESSIONAL TIP

TEXT is not recommended for aligned text because the text height for each line is adjusted according to the width. One line may run into another.

- **Fit (F).** This option is similar to the **Align** option, except that you can select the text height. AutoCAD adjusts the letter width to fit between the two given points, while keeping text height constant. See Figure 8-5.
- **Center (C).** This option allows you to select the center point for the baseline of the text. Enter the letter height and rotation angle after picking the center point.
- **Middle (M).** This option allows you to center text both horizontally and vertically at a given point. The letter height and rotation can also be changed.
- **Right (R).** This option justifies text at the lower-right corner. The point is entered at the Specify right endpoint of text baseline: prompt. The letter height and rotation can also be entered. The command sequence is similar to the sequence for the **Start point** option. Figure 8-6 compares the **Center, Middle,** and **Right** options.

Figure 8-5.
Examples of aligned and fit text. In aligned text, the text height is adjusted. In fit text, the text width is adjusted.

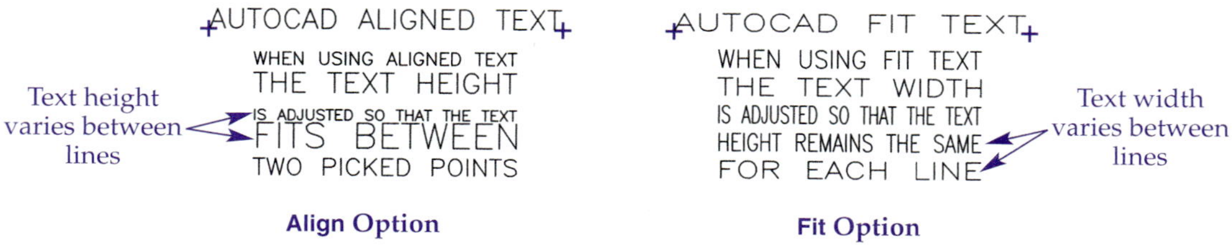

Figure 8-6.
Three justification options with start point shown.
A—Using the **Center** text option.
B—Using the **Middle** text option.
C—Using the **Right** text option.

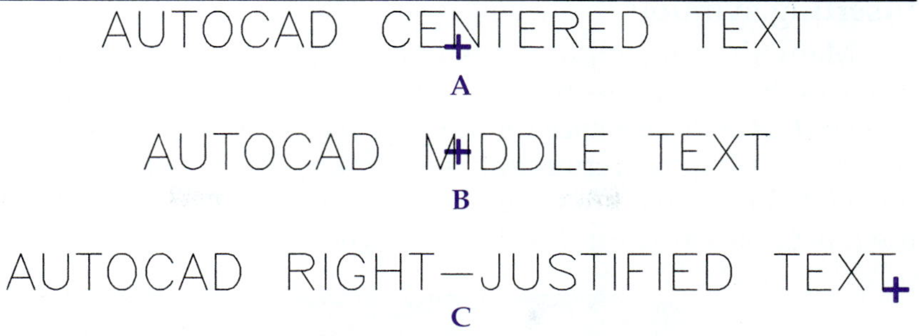

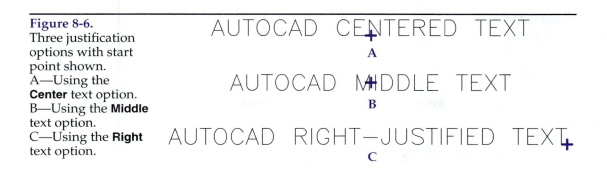

Other text alignment options

There are a number of text alignment options that allow you to place text on a drawing in relation to the top, bottom, middle, left side, or right side of the text. These alignment options are shown in **Figure 8-7.** These options are shown as abbreviations that correlate to the **TEXT** prompt line. To use one of these options, type the two letters for the desired option and press [Enter].

PROFESSIONAL TIP

If you already know which text alignment option you want to use in your drawing, you can enter it at the Specify start point of text or [Justify/Style]: prompt without entering J. Just type the letter or letters of the desired option and press [Enter].

Figure 8-7.
Using the **TL, TC, TR, ML, MC, MR, BL, BC,** and **BR** text alignment options. Notice what the abbreviations stand for.

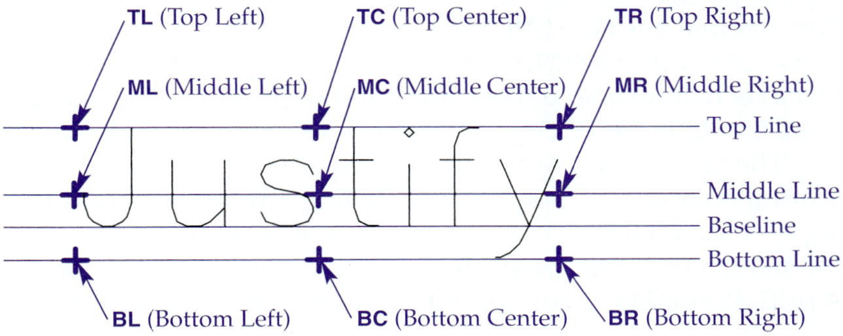

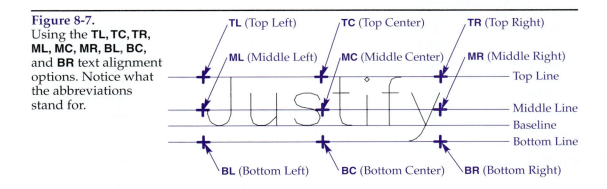

EXERCISE 8-1

Complete the Exercise on the Student CD.

Inserting symbols

Many drafting applications require special symbols for text and dimensions. In order to draw symbols with the **TEXT** command, AutoCAD requires a control code. The ***control code sequence*** for a symbol begins with two percent signs (%%). The next character you enter represents the symbol. These control codes are used for single-line text objects that are generated with the **TEXT** command. The following list gives the most popular control code sequences:

Control Code	Description	Symbol
%%D	Degrees symbol	°
%%P	Plus/minus sign	±
%%C	Diameter symbol	∅

For example, in order to add the note ∅2.75, the control sequence %%C2.75 is entered at the Enter text: prompt. See **Figure 8-8A.**

A single percent sign can be added normally. However, when a percent sign must precede another control sequence, %%% can be used to force a single percent sign. For example, suppose you want to type the note 25%±2%. You must enter 25%%%%%P2%.

Drawing underscored or overscored text

Text can be underscored (underlined) or overscored by typing a control sequence in front of the line of text. The control sequences are:

%%O = overscore
%%U = underscore

For example, the note UNDERSCORING TEXT must be entered at the Enter text: prompt as %%UUNDERSCORING TEXT. The resulting text is shown in **Figure 8-8B.** A line of text may require both underscoring and overscoring. For example, the control sequence %%O%%ULINE OF TEXT produces the note with both underscore and overscore.

The %%O and %%U control codes are toggles that turn overscoring and underscoring on and off. Type %%U preceding a word or phrase to turn underscoring on. Type %%U after the desired word or phrase to turn underscoring off. Any text following the second %%U then appears without underscoring. For example, DETAIL A HUB ASSEMBLY would be entered as %%UDETAIL A%%U HUB ASSEMBLY.

PROFESSIONAL TIP

Many drafters prefer to underline labels such as SECTION A-A or DETAIL B. Rather than draw line or polyline objects under the text, use **Middle** or **Center** justification modes and underscoring. The view labels are automatically underlined and centered under the views or details they identify.

∅2.75

A

UNDERSCORING TEXT

B

Figure 8-8.
A— The control sequence %%C creates the ∅ (diameter) symbol. B—The control sequence %%U underscores text.

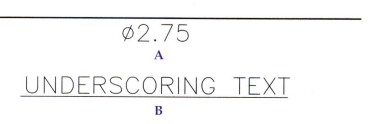

EXERCISE **8-2** Complete the Exercise on the Student CD.

Multiline Text

MTEXT
MT
T

Draw
➥ Text
➥ Multiline Text...

Draw toolbar
Text toolbar

A
Multiline Text

The **MTEXT** command is used to create multiline text objects. Instead of each line being an individual object, all the lines are part of the same object. The **MTEXT** command is accessed by picking the **Multiline Text** button in the **Draw** or **Text** toolbar, picking **Multiline Text...** in the **Text** cascading menu of the **Draw** pull-down, or entering T, MT, or MTEXT at the Command: prompt.

After entering the **MTEXT** command, AutoCAD asks you to specify the first and opposite corners of the text boundary. The ***text boundary*** is a box within which your text will be placed. When you pick the first corner of the text boundary, the cursor changes to a box with grayed-out letters that represent the current text height. Move the box until you have the desired size for your paragraph and pick the opposite corner. See **Figure 8-9.**

When drawing the text boundary, an arrow in the boundary shows the direction of text flow. While the width of the boundary provides a limit to the width of the text paragraphs, it does not affect the possible height. The boundary height is automatically resized to fit the actual text entered. The direction of the flow indicates where the boundary is expanded, if necessary. This is the command sequence:

Command: **T**, **MT**, *or* **MTEXT**↵
Current text style: "Standard" Text height: 0.2000
Specify first corner: *(pick the first corner)*
Specify opposite corner or [Height/Justify/Line spacing/Rotation/Style/Width]:
(pick the opposite corner)

After picking the text boundary, the multiline text editor appears. See **Figure 8-10.** The multiline text editor is divided into the **Text Formatting** toolbar and the ***text editor***. The **Text Formatting** toolbar controls the properties of text entered into the text editor. The text editor includes a paragraph ruler where indent stops and an indent marker are located. A cursor is located within the text editor. This cursor is the height set in the **Text Formatting** toolbar. This is where text is entered to create a paragraph.

As mentioned earlier, notes in drawings are often presented using uppercase text. Right-clicking inside the text editor displays a shortcut menu. The **AutoCAPS** option is found in this menu. Selecting this option turns on the caps lock on the keyboard each

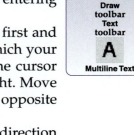

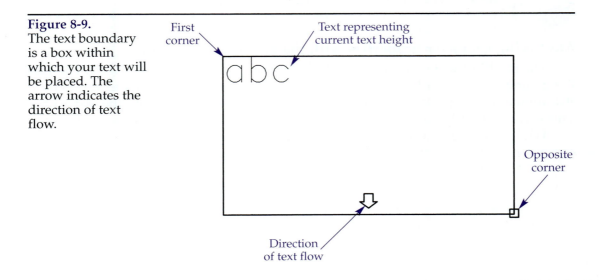

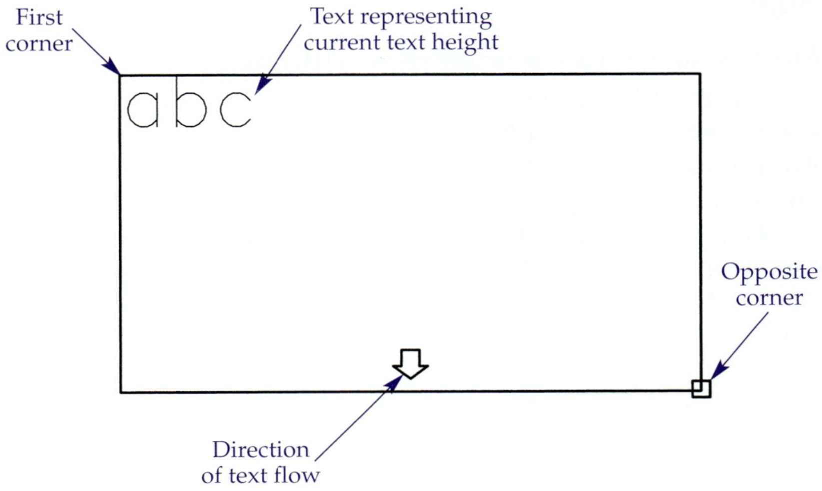

Figure 8-9.
The text boundary is a box within which your text will be placed. The arrow indicates the direction of text flow.

Figure 8-10.
The multiline text editor with the **AutoCAPS** shortcut menu deactivated.

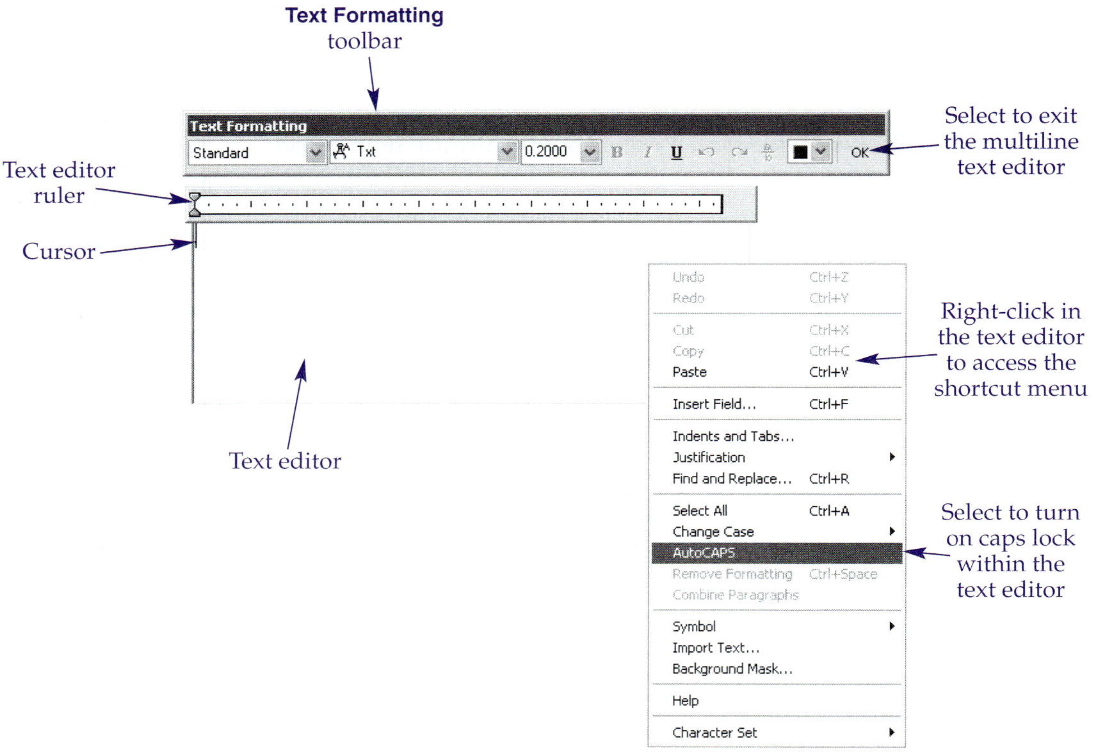

time the multiline text editor is accessed. The caps lock is turned off when you exit the multiline text editor so text in other programs is not all uppercase. Additional options are available in the text editor shortcut menu. These are discussed later.

When the text editor is filled with text and a new line is added, previous lines begin to be hidden and a scroll bar is displayed at the right. Use the scroll bar to move up and down to access lines in the text editor. Pressing the [Enter] key causes a new line to be entered. Pressing [Enter] twice creates a blank line between lines of text. Tabs can also be used to line up columns of text. When finished entering text in the editor, pick the **OK** button in the **Text Formatting** toolbar to exit the text editor.

EXERCISE 8-3 Complete the Exercise on the Student CD.

Modifying character properties with the multiline text editor

The multiline text editor is displayed after you define the text boundary. The **Text Formatting** toolbar controls the properties of the text entered in the text editor. Additional text controls can also be accessed by right-clicking within the text editor. This section describes all features within the toolbar, text editor, and shortcut menu.

While entering text in the multiline text editor, there are a number of keystroke combinations that are available. These combinations are as follows:

Keystroke	Function
[↑] [←] [↓] [→]	Arrow keys move the cursor through the text one position in the direction indicated by the arrow.
[Ctrl]+[→]	Moves the cursor one word in the direction indicated.
[Ctrl]+[←]	
[Home]	Moves the cursor to the start of the current line.
[End]	Moves the cursor to the end of the current line.
[Delete]	Deletes the character immediately to the right of the cursor.
[Backspace]	Deletes the character immediately to the left of the cursor.
[Ctrl]+[Backspace]	Deletes the word immediately to the left of the cursor.
[Ctrl]+[C]	Copy selection to Clipboard. The Clipboard is an internal storage area that temporarily stores information that you copy or cut from a document.
[Ctrl]+[V]	Paste Clipboard contents to the selection or current cursor location.
[Ctrl]+[X]	Cut selection to Clipboard.
[Ctrl]+[Z]	Undo.
[Enter]	Ends the current paragraph, starting a new one on the next line.
[Page Up]	These keys move the cursor up to 28 rows in the indicated direction.
[Page Down]	
[Ctrl]+[Page Up]	These keys move the cursor to the top or bottom of the currently
[Ctrl]+[Page Down]	visible page of text.
[Ctrl]+[Home]	Moves the cursor to Line 1, Column 1.
[Ctrl]+[End]	Moves the cursor to the last character position.
[Ctrl]+[A]	Selects all text in the current multiline text object.
[Shift]+[→]	Selects or deselects text. Increases or decreases the selection by one
[Shift]+[←]	character at a time, depending on the direction indicated.
[Shift]+[↑]	Selects or deselects text. Increases or decreases the selection by one
[Shift]+[↓]	line at a time, depending on the direction indicated.
[Ctrl]+[Shift]+[→]	Selects or deselects text. Increases or decreases the selection by one
[Ctrl]+[Shift]+[←]	word at a time, depending on the direction indicated.
[Esc]	Closes the multiline text editor and loses any changes made.

PROFESSIONAL TIP

Text can be pasted from any text-based application into the multiline text editor. For example, you can copy text from an application such as Microsoft® Word, and then paste it into the multiline text editor. The pasted text retains its properties. Likewise, text copied or cut from the multiline text editor can be pasted into another text-based application.

As you move the cursor into the editing window, it changes shape. If you have used other Windows text editors, this is a familiar text cursor shape. Pointing to a character position within the text and pressing the pick button causes the cursor to be placed at the selected location. You can then begin typing or editing as needed. If you begin typing where the text cursor is initially placed, your text begins in the upper-left corner of the text boundary.

Text is selected as it is with most standard Windows text editors. Place the cursor at one end of the desired selection, press and hold the pick button. Drag the cursor until the desired text is highlighted, then release the pick button. Now, any editing operations you perform affect the highlighted text. For example, a copy or cut operation places the highlighted text on the Clipboard. One other way to highlight text is to move your mouse to the word you would like to highlight and double-click it with the pick button. To entirely replace the highlighted text with new text, either paste the new text from the Clipboard or begin typing. The selection is erased and the new text appears in its place.

Figure 8-11 illustrates the features found in the **Text Formatting** toolbar. Keep in mind that ***selected text*** refers to text that you have highlighted in the text window:

- **Style.** This drop-down list includes a list of the different text styles available. A text style sets the font, size, obliquing angle, orientation, and other text characteristics. Selecting and creating text styles are covered in detail later in this chapter.
- **Font.** Pick the down arrow to open the drop-down list of available text fonts. Picking one of the options allows the selected text to have its font changed or newly entered text to use this font type. This overrides the font used in the current style. Txt is the default text font.
- **Text height.** This option allows selected text or new text to have its height changed. This overrides the current setting of the **TEXTSIZE** system variable and the text height set within the text style.
- **Bold.** Pick this button to have the selected text become bold. This only works with some TrueType fonts. The SHX fonts do not have this capability.
- **Italic.** Pick this button to have the selected text become italic. This only works with some TrueType fonts. The SHX style fonts do not have this capability.
- **Underline.** Picking this button underlines selected text.

> **NOTE**
>
> If you select text that is already bold, picking the **Bold** button returns the text to its normal appearance. This is also true for italic and underline.

- **Undo.** Pick this button to undo the previous activity.
- **Redo.** Redoes undone operations.

Figure 8-11.
The **Text Formatting** toolbar.

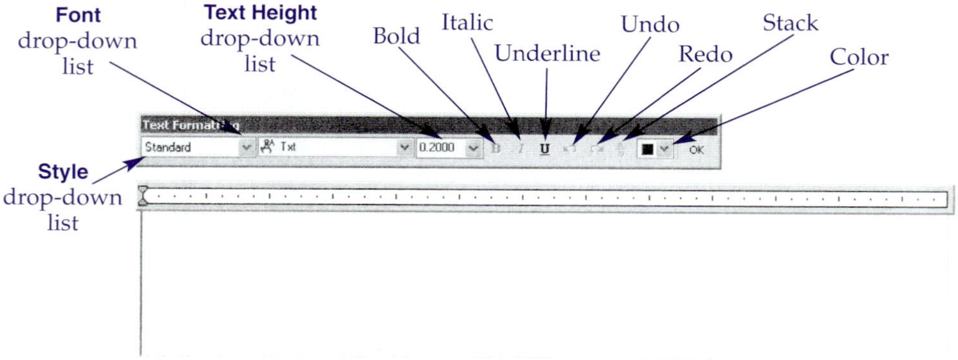

- **Stack.** This button allows selected text to be stacked vertically or diagonally. To use this feature for drawing a vertically stacked fraction, place a forward slash between the top and bottom items. Then select the text with your pointing device and pick the button. This button is also used for unstacking text that has been previously stacked. You can also use the caret (^) character between text if you want to stack the items without a fraction bar. This is called a ***tolerance stack.*** Typing a number sign (#) between selected numbers results in a diagonal fraction bar. See **Figure 8-12.**
- **Color.** The color is set ByLayer as default, but you can change the text color by picking one of the colors found in the **Color** drop-down list.

> **NOTE**
>
> The formatting of text within the multiline text editor may not always appear exactly as it does in the drawing. This is most commonly true when a substitute font is used for display in the editor. A substitute font may be wider or narrower than the font used in the drawing. AutoCAD automatically reformats the text to fit within the boundary defined in the drawing.

Using the text editor shortcut menu

The text editor shortcut menu was briefly introduced earlier in this section. This shortcut menu is accessed by right-clicking while the cursor is in the text editor. The menu and its options are displayed and explained in **Figure 8-13.**

The text editor shortcut menu has seven sections of options, plus a help section. The top section includes the **Undo** and **Redo** options also found in the **Text Formatting** toolbar. These commands undo changes made to text or redo your undo operations respectively. The second section includes Windows Clipboard functions that allow you to cut, copy, or paste text to or from the text editor. The next section includes the **Insert Field...** option. This opens the **Field** dialog box, which allows you to insert text that can be updated. There are many different preset fields, including formatting options. For example, you could insert the **Date** field into a title block. The field would then update automatically with the current date throughout the life of the drawing file. When a field is inserted into the multiline text editor, it is highlighted in gray to indicate the text is a field. Fields are discussed later in this chapter. The next three sections control multiline text and text content properties. The last section contains the **Character Set** option. This displays a menu of code pages. A code page provides support for character sets used in different languages. Select a code page to apply it to the selected text.

Figure 8-12.
Different types of stack characters.

	Selected Text	Stacked Text
Vertical Fraction	1/2	$\frac{1}{2}$
Tolerance Stack	1^2	$\genfrac{}{}{0pt}{}{1}{2}$
Diagonal Fraction	1#2	½

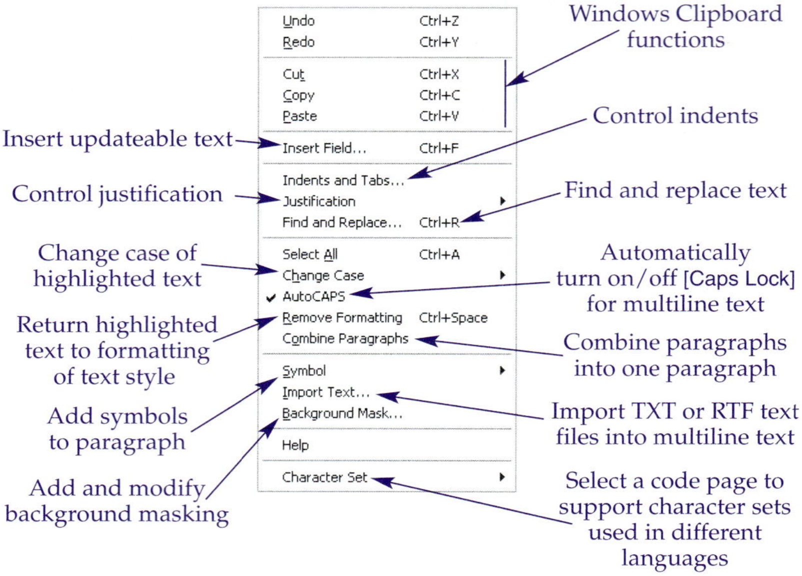

Figure 8-13. The text editor shortcut menu is accessed by right-clicking while the cursor is in the text editor.

Multiline text properties

The fourth section in the shortcut menu controls indentations and the justification of the multiline text object. Also included in this section is a find and replace tool to locate text in the paragraph and replace it with a different piece of text. Each of these commands is described as follows:

- **Indents and Tabs.** Selecting this option will open the **Indents and Tabs** dialog box, **Figure 8-14.** This dialog box allows you to set up the indentation for the first line of a paragraph of text as well as the remaining portion of a paragraph. Each time a new paragraph is started, the **First line** indent is used. As text is entered in the editor and is wrapped to the next line, the **Paragraph** indent is used. The **Tab stop position** allows you to set up a cursor stop position when the [Tab] key is pressed. Entering a new value and picking the **Set** button allows you to set up several additional tab locations in the paragraph. Picking the **Clear** button removes the highlighted tab location.
- **Justification.** Selecting this option produces a cascading menu of justification options. These options are similar to the text justification described earlier, except they apply to the entire paragraph of text. **Figure 8-15** displays the different justification options and how they relate to multiline text objects.

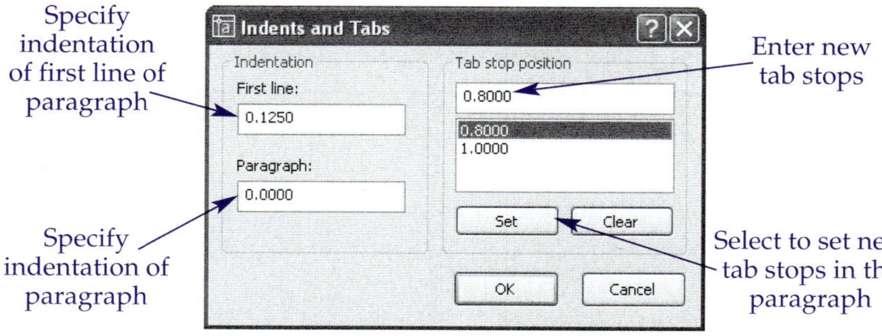

Figure 8-14. The **Indents and Tabs** dialog box is used to set up indentations within the multiline text object.

Figure 8-15.
The multiline text justification options.

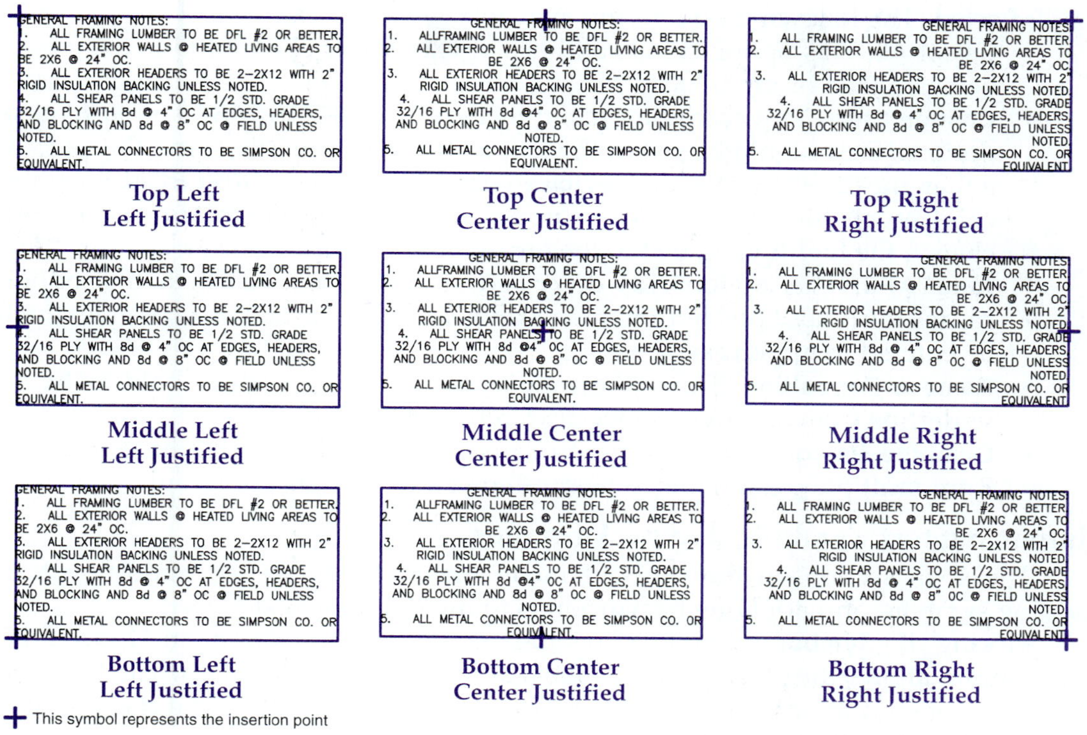

- **Find and Replace.** When this command is picked, the **Replace** dialog box is displayed. See **Figure 8-16.** Enter the text you are searching for in the **Find what:** text box. Then pick the **Find Next** button to highlight it. Next, enter the text that will be substituted in the **Replace with:** text box. You can then pick the **Replace** or the **Replace All** button to replace the highlighted text or all words that match your search criteria.

  The **Match whole word only** check box is used to specify a search for a whole word, and not part of another word. For example, if **Match whole word only** is not checked, a search for the word *the* would find those letters wherever they occur—including as part of other words, such as o<u>the</u>r or wea<u>the</u>r. You can also select the **Match case** check box if you are searching for words that are case specific.

Figure 8-16.
Using the **Find and Replace** option. A—Searching for a word. B—Replacing the text.

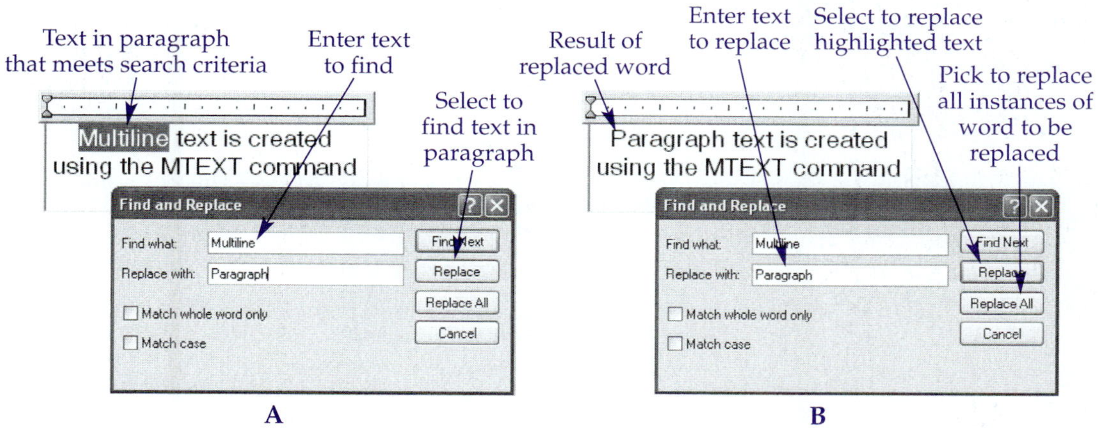

Controlling text properties

The fifth section within the shortcut menu controls how text is created, formatted, and selected. The following options are available:

- **Select All.** This option selects all lines of text within the multiline text object being created or modified.
- **Change Case.** This cascading menu includes the **UPPERCASE** and **lowercase** options. First highlight text in the text editor to be modified, and then access either the **UPPERCASE** or the **lowercase** options. The **UPPERCASE** option changes all highlighted text to uppercase, and the **lowercase** option will change the highlighted text to lowercase.
- **AutoCAPS.** This option was described earlier. When selected, this option causes the [Caps Lock] button on the keyboard to be turned on so that text will be entered in uppercase.
- **Remove Formatting.** This option removes formatting such as bold, italic, or underline from any highlighted text in the text editor.
- **Combine Paragraphs.** This option causes any lines of highlighted text that form multiple paragraphs to be combined into a single paragraph.

Importing text, symbols, and backgrounds

The sixth section on the shortcut menu includes options for importing text, adding symbols, and applying backgrounds to the multiline text object.

AutoCAD 2005 NEW FEATURE

Picking the **Symbol** option displays the cascading menu shown in **Figure 8-17.** This option allows the insertion of symbols at the text cursor location. The first two sections contain commonly used symbols. The third section contains the **Non-breaking Space** option, which keeps two separate words together. The **Other...** option opens the **Character Map** dialog box, **Figure 8-18.** To use this dialog box, pick the desired TrueType symbols from the **Font:** drop-down list. The following are the steps for using a symbol or symbols:

1. Pick the desired symbol and then pick the **Select** button. The selected symbol is displayed in the **Characters to copy:** box.
2. Pick the **Copy** button to have the selected symbol or symbols copied to the Clipboard.
3. Pick the **Close** button to close the dialog box.
4. Back in the multiline text editor, place the text cursor where you want the symbols displayed.
5. Move the screen cursor to anywhere inside the text editor and right-click to display the shortcut menu. Pick the **Paste** option to paste the symbol at the cursor location.

Import Text allows you to import text from an existing text file directly into the multiline text editor. The text file can be either a standard ASCII text file (TXT) or an

Figure 8-17.
The **Symbol** menu options.

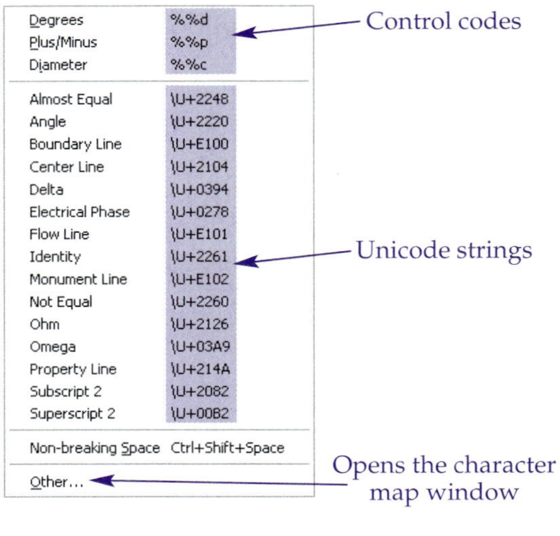

Figure 8-18.
The **Character Map** dialog box.

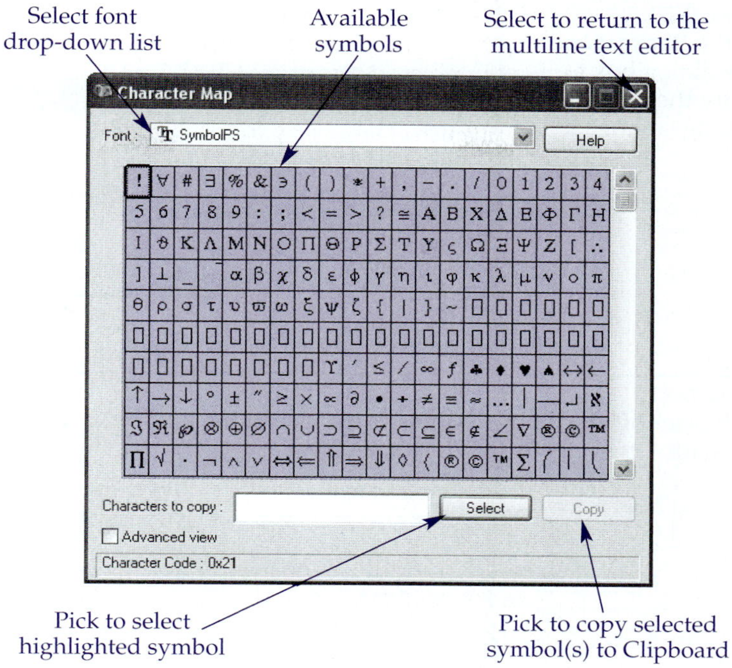

RTF (rich text format) file. The imported text becomes a part of the current multiline text object.

When this option is selected, the **Select File** dialog box is displayed. Select the text file to be imported and pick the **Open** button. If you import text while a portion of text is highlighted in the text editor, the **Inserting Text** dialog box shown in **Figure 8-19** appears. This dialog allows you to replace the highlighted text with the imported text, have the inserted text be placed after the highlighted text, or replace all of the text in the text editor with the text being inserted.

AutoCAD 2005 NEW FEATURE

Sometimes text has to be placed over existing objects, such as crosshatching, making the text hard to read. A **Background Mask** will hide the portion of the objects that are behind and around the text, so no objects are going through the text. Selecting **Background Mask...** from the text editor shortcut menu displays the **Background Mask** dialog box shown in **Figure 8-20.**

To apply the mask settings to the current multiline text object, check the **Use background mask** check box. The **Border offset factor:** text box is where you set how much of the underlying objects are masked out. This value, from 1 to 5, works with the text height value. If the border offset factor is set to 1, then the mask occurs directly within the boundary of the text. To offset the mask beyond the text boundary, use a value greater than 1. If the text height is 1/8″ and the border offset factor is set to 2, the text is masked along with the area 1/8th of an inch out from the text boundary. The calculation is border offset factor × text height = total masking distance from the bottom of the text. **Figure 8-21** shows text being masked with different border offset factor values.

Figure 8-19.
When importing text into the multiline text editor while text is highlighted, the **Inserting Text** dialog box provides insertion options.

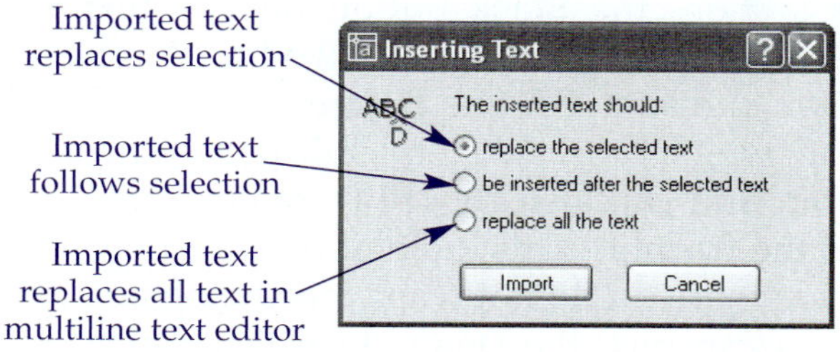

Figure 8-20.
Use the **Background Mask** dialog box to specify the text masking settings.

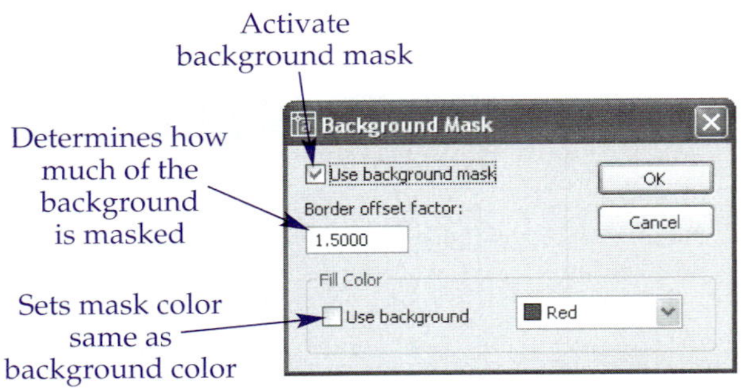

Figure 8-21.
The border offset factor determines the size of the background mask. The text in the figure is 1/8″ with different border offset factor values.

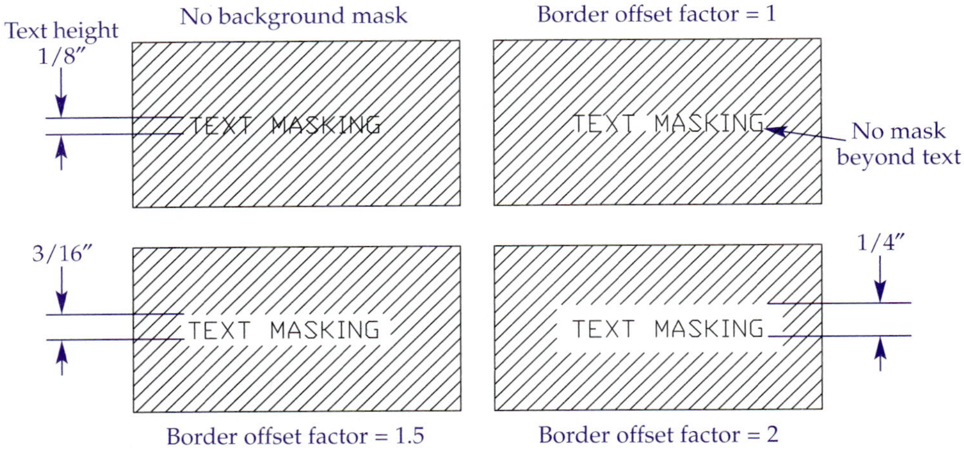

EXERCISE 8-4 Complete the Exercise on the Student CD.

Additional formatting

In addition to the shortcut menu items described previously, the multiline text editor includes other right-click shortcut items. When right-clicking on the text editor ruler, a shortcut menu appears with two options. See Figure 8-22. The **Indents and Tabs...** option accesses the **Indents and Tabs** dialog box described earlier. Picking the **Set Mtext Width...** option displays the **Set Mtext Width** dialog box where a new width for the paragraph can be specified. The width is set initially when you pick the two corners of the text boundary.

The width of the multiline text object can also be modified by moving the cursor to the right side of the ruler. The cursor changes to a double arrow cursor. Press and hold the pick button to stretch the text editor wider or narrower.

Earlier in this section, the **Stack** button on the **Text Formatting** toolbar was discussed. When you enter a fraction in the text editor for the first time, the **AutoStack Properties** dialog box is displayed. See Figure 8-23. This dialog box allows you to enable AutoStacking, which causes the entered fraction to stack with a horizontal or diagonal fraction bar. You can also choose to remove the leading space between a whole number and the fraction. This dialog box is displayed each time a fraction is entered. If you decide that you do not want this dialog box to pop up each time you create a fraction, you can pick the **Don't show this dialog again; always use these**

Figure 8-22.
Right-clicking on the text editor ruler yields a shortcut menu that controls the indents and width of the multiline text object.

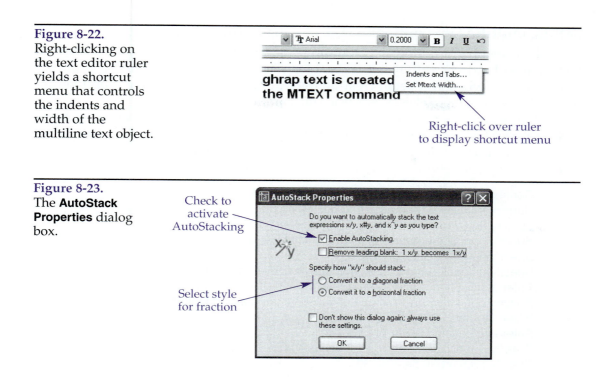

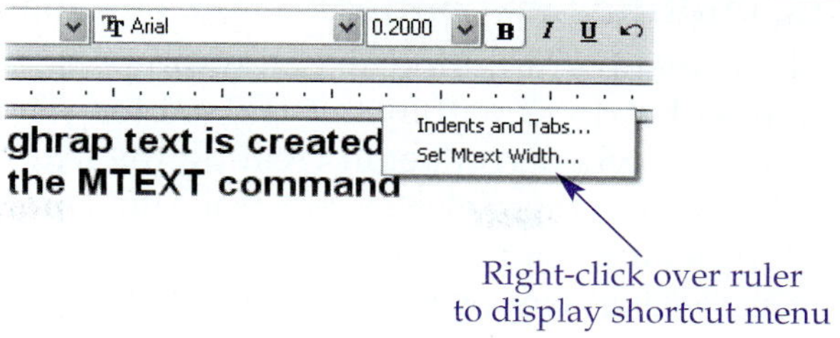

Figure 8-23.
The **AutoStack Properties** dialog box.

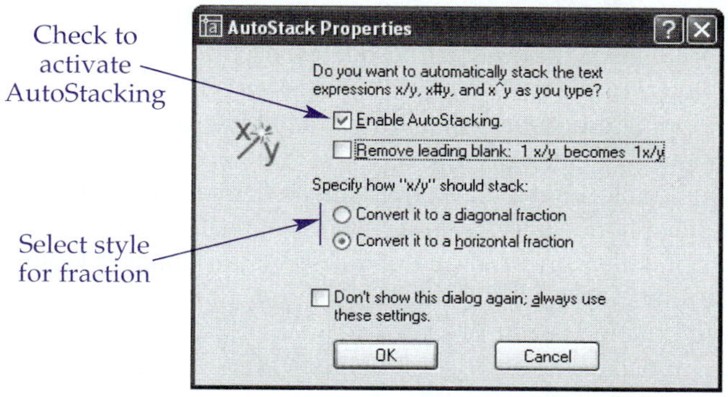

settings check box. Selecting this option causes new fractions to be created with the last settings you specified.

If you highlight a fraction and right-click, the shortcut menu appears with two additional options. The first option is **Unstack**, which causes the fraction to unstack. The upper and lower values are placed on a single line with the appropriate character (^, #, or /) displayed between the numbers. The second option is **Properties**, which displays the **Stack Properties** dialog box. The features of this dialog box are described in Figure 8-24.

Figure 8-24.
The **Stack Properties** dialog box.

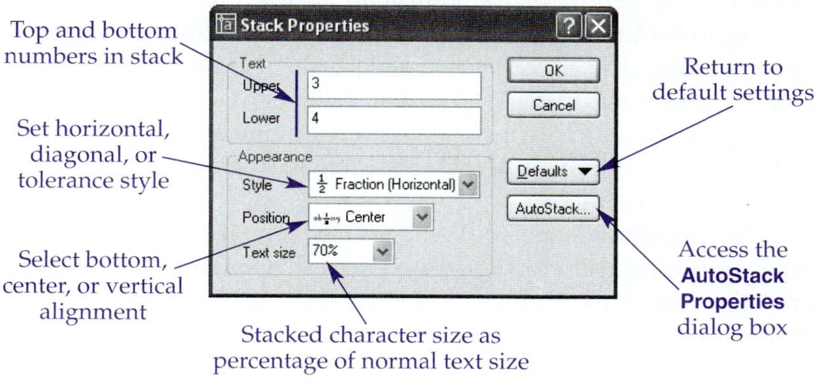

EXERCISE 8-5

Complete the Exercise on the Student CD.

Setting multiline text options at the command line

When creating multiline text, you can preset some of the settings so that they do not have to be done within the text editor. These options are available from the command line when you begin creating the text boundary. Two of these options are not available anywhere else except from the command line.

After picking the first boundary corner for the text, the Specify opposite corner or [Height/Justify/Line spacing/Rotation/Style/Width]: prompt is displayed. You can select any of the options by entering the appropriate letter at the prompt. The following command sequence shows an example:

Command: **T**, **MT**, *or* **MTEXT**↵
Current text style: Standard. Text height: 0.2000
Specify first corner: *(pick the first boundary corner)*
Specify opposite corner or [Height/Justify/Line spacing/Rotation/Style/Width]: **H**↵
Specify height <0.2000>: **.125**↵
Specify opposite corner or [Height/Justify/Line spacing/Rotation/Style/Width]: **J**↵
Enter justification [TL/TC/TR/ML/MC/MR/BL/BC/BR] <TL>: **MC**↵
Specify opposite corner or [Height/Justify/Line spacing/Rotation/Style/Width]: **L**↵
Enter line spacing type [At least/Exactly] <At least>: **E**↵
Enter line spacing factor or distance <1x>: **2X**↵
Specify opposite corner or [Height/Justify/Line spacing/Rotation/Style/Width]: **R**↵
Specify rotation angle <0>: **30**↵
Specify opposite corner or [Height/Justify/Line spacing/Rotation/Style/Width]: **S**↵
Enter style name or [?] <Standard>: ↵
Specify opposite corner or [Height/Justify/Line spacing/Rotation/Style/Width]: **W**↵
Specify width: **4**↵

A value specified in the **Width** option automatically sets the text boundary width and opens the multiline text editor.

The two options available at the Command: prompt are **Line spacing** and **Rotation**. The **Line spacing** option is used to control line spacing for newly created text. When the option is first entered, the Enter line spacing type [At least/Exactly] <At least>: prompt is displayed. Entering the **At least** option automatically adds spaces between lines based on the height of the character in the line. The **Exactly** option forces the line spacing to be the same for all lines of the multiline text object. After selecting one of these options, the Enter line spacing factor or distance <1x>: prompt is displayed. A number followed by an X specifies the spacing increment. This spacing increment is the vertical distance from the bottom of one line to the bottom of the next line of multiline text. For example, single-spaced lines are a value of 1X, and double spaced lines are a value of 2X.

The **Rotation** option allows you to specify a rotation angle for the text. After entering the rotation option the Specify rotation angle <0>: prompt is displayed. Enter a rotation value in degrees. After the text has been entered in the text editor and the **OK** button has been selected, the multiline text object is rotated at the desired angle.

NOTE

The **–MTEXT** command can be used to enter a multiline text object without using the multiline text editor. The options at the Command: prompt are identical to the options for the **MTEXT** command. Lines of text are entered at the Mtext: prompt, similar to the entry of single-line text.

AutoCAD Text Fonts

A ***font*** is a particular letter face design. Two of the standard AutoCAD text fonts are shown in **Figure 8-25.** The standard fonts have .shx file extensions.

The txt font is the AutoCAD default. The rough appearance of the txt font allows it to regenerate faster than other fonts. The Romans (roman simplex) font is smoother than txt. It closely duplicates the single-stroke lettering that has long been the standard for most drafting.

Several AutoCAD fonts provide special alphabets or symbols that are accessed from the ***character map***, as shown in **Figure 8-18**.

TrueType fonts are scaleable and have an outline. ***Scaleable*** means the font can be displayed on the screen or printed at any size and still maintain proportional letter thickness. TrueType fonts appear filled in the AutoCAD window, but the **TEXTFILL** system variable controls whether the plotted fonts will be filled. The **TEXTFILL** default is 1, which draws filled fonts. A setting of 0 draws the font outlines. A sample of a TrueType font, stylus BT, is shown in **Figure 8-26.** This is an excellent choice for the artistic appearance desired on architectural drawings.

NOTE

Additional standard fonts, characters, and TrueType fonts can be seen by experimenting within AutoCAD or reviewing the *AutoCAD Fonts* handout on the Student CD.

Figure 8-25.
Standard AutoCAD fonts.

Fast Fonts

Txt abcdABCD12345

Monotxt abcdABCD12345

Simplex Fonts

Romans abcdABCD12345

Italic *abcdABCD12345*

Triplex Fonts

Romant abcdABCD12345

Italict *abcdABCD12345*

Complex Fonts

Romanc abcdABCD12345

Italicc *abcdABCD12345*

Figure 8-26.
A few of the many TrueType fonts available.

Swiss 721

swiss (regular) abcdABCD12345

swissi (italic) *abcdABCD12345*

swissb (bold) **abcdABCD1234**

swissbi (bold italic) ***abcdABCD12345***

Architect's Hand Lettered

stylus BT abcdABCD12345

Vineta (shadow)

vinet (regular) abcdABCD12345

PROFESSIONAL TIP

TrueType fonts and other complex text fonts can be taxing on system resources. This can slow down display changes and increase drawing regeneration time significantly. Use these fonts only when necessary. When you must use complex fonts, set your system variables to speed-optimized settings.

AutoCAD Text Styles

Text styles are variations of fonts. A ***text style*** gives height, width, obliquing angle (slant), and other characteristics to a text font. You may have several text styles that use the same font, but with different characteristics. By default, the Standard text style uses the txt font, 0° rotation angle, width of 1, and 0° obliquing angle.

Selecting and Modifying Text Styles

STYLE
ST

Format
➥ Text Style...

Styles toolbar

Text Style Manager

Text styles are created, modified, and deleted using the **Text Style** dialog box, shown in Figure 8-27. Access this dialog box by picking **Text Style...** from the **Format** pull-down menu, selecting the **Text Style Manager** button in the **Styles** toolbar, or by entering ST or STYLE at the Command: prompt. The following describes the features found in this dialog box:

- **Style Name area.** Set a new current text style by making a selection from the drop-down list. Use the **New...** button to create a new text style and the **Rename...** button to rename a selected style. If you need to delete a style, use the **Delete** button.
- **Font area.** This area of the **Text Style** dialog box is where you select an available font, style of the selected font, and text height.

Figure 8-27.
The **Text Style** dialog box is used to set the characteristics of a text style.

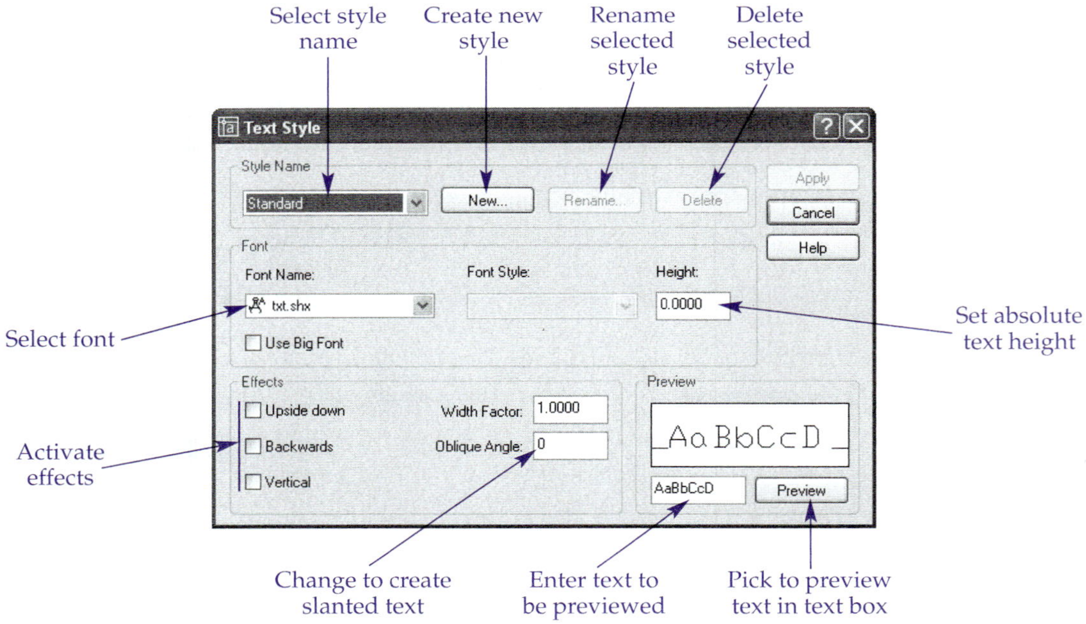

- **Font Name.** This drop-down list is used to access the available fonts. The default font is txt.shx. All SHX fonts are identified with an AutoCAD compass symbol, while the TrueType fonts have the TrueType symbol.
- **Font Style.** This drop-down list is inactive unless the selected font has options available, such as bold or italic. None of the SHX fonts have additional options, but some of the TrueType fonts may. For example, the SansSerif font has Regular, Bold, BoldOblique, and Oblique options. Each option provides the font with a different appearance.
- **Height.** This text box is used to set the text height. The default is 0.0000. This allows you to set the text height in the **TEXT** command. If you set a value such as .125, the text height becomes fixed for this text style and you are not prompted for the text height. Setting a text height value other than zero saves time during the command process, but also eliminates your flexibility. ASME-recommended text heights were discussed earlier in this chapter.

NOTE

The default text height is stored in the **TEXTSIZE** system variable. When a text style has a height other than 0, the style height overrides any default value stored in this variable.

PROFESSIONAL TIP

It is recommended that a text height value of 0 be used for text styles used in dimensions. Dimension styles allow you to specify a text height value for the annotation text. By specifying a text height in the text style, the dimension text height is overridden. Dimension styles are discussed later in this text.

- **Use Big Font.** Asian and other large format fonts (called ***Big Fonts***) are activated with this check box. The Big Font is used as a supplement to define many symbols not available in normal font files.

- **Effects area.** This area of the **Text Style** dialog box is used to set the text format. It contains the following options, which are shown in Figure 8-28:
  - **Upside down.** This check box is off by default. When it is checked, the text you draw is placed upside down.
  - **Backwards.** When the box is checked, text that you draw is placed backwards.

Figure 8-28.
Special effects for text styles can be set in the **Text Style** dialog box.

- **Vertical.** This check box is inactive for all TrueType fonts. A check in this box makes SHX font text vertical. Text on drawings is normally placed horizontally, but vertical text can be used for special effects and graphic designs. Vertical text works best when the rotation angle is 270°.

> **NOTE**
>
> The multiline text editor displays the text horizontally, right-side up, and forward. Any special effects such as vertical, backwards, or upside down take effect when you pick **OK** to exit the editor.

- **Width Factor.** This text box provides a value that defines the text character width relative to the height. A width factor of 1 is the default. A width factor greater than 1 expands the characters, and a factor less than 1 compresses the characters. See Figure 8-29.
- **Oblique Angle.** This text box allows you to set an angle at which text is slanted. The zero default draws characters vertically. A value greater than 0 slants the characters to the right, while a negative value slants characters to the left. See Figure 8-30. Some fonts, such as italic, are already slanted.

> **PROFESSIONAL TIP**
>
> Some companies, especially in structural drafting, like to slant text 15° to the right. Also, water features named on maps often use text that is slanted to the right.

- **Preview area.** The preview image allows you to see how the selected font or style will appear. This is a very convenient way to see what the font looks like before using it in a new style. Figure 8-31 shows previews of various fonts. Specific characters can also be previewed. Simply type the characters in the text box and then pick the **Preview** button.

Figure 8-29.
Text width factors are set in the **Text Style** dialog box.

Width Factor	Text
1	ABCDEFGHIJKLM
.5	ABCDEFGHIJKLMNOPQRSTUVWXY
1.5	ABCDEFGHI
2	ABCDEFG

Figure 8-30.
Text obliquing angles are set in the **Text Style** dialog box.

Obliquing Angle	Text
0	ABCDEFGHIJKLM
15	*ABCDEFGHIJKLM*
–15	ABCDEFGHIJKLM

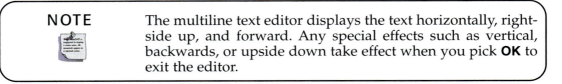

Figure 8-31.
The **Preview** image shows a sample of the font. A—The Scripts font. B—The Gothice font. C—The Italic font.

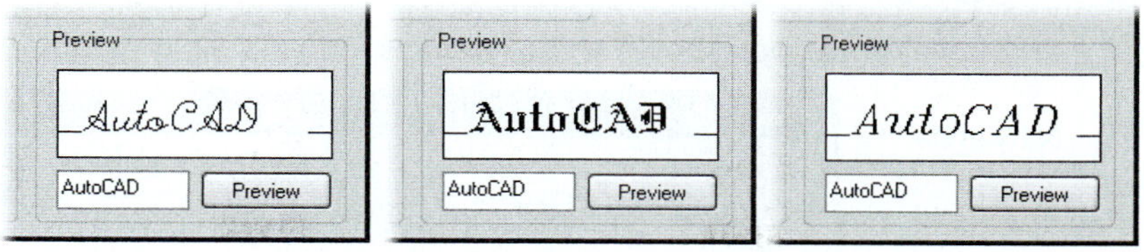

A B C

EXERCISE 8-6 Complete the Exercise on the Student CD.

Creating a New Text Style

If you start a new drawing with the AutoCAD default template, the only text style available is the Standard style. The Standard text style is based on the txt font.

What if you want to create a text style for mechanical drawings that uses the Romans font and characters .125″ high? You want to have this available as the most commonly used text on your drawings. Choose a style name that you can remember, such as ROMANS-125. It is still a good idea to record the name and details about the text styles you create and keep this information in a log for future reference.

Text style names can have up to 255 characters, including letters, numbers, dashes (–), underlines (_), and dollar signs ($). You can enter uppercase or lowercase letters. The following explains the steps to use to create this text style:

1. Open the **Text Style** dialog box. Standard is the current style with txt.shx as the font, and a zero text height.
2. Pick the **New...** button. This opens the **New Text Style** dialog box, Figure 8-32A. Notice style1 is in the **Style Name** text box. You can keep a text style name like style1 or style2, but this is not descriptive. Type ROMANS-125 in the box and then pick the **OK** button. See Figure 8-32B. ROMANS-125 is now displayed in the **Style Name** text box of the **Text Style** dialog box.
3. Go to the **Font Name** drop-down list, find romans.shx, and pick it. The font is now romans.shx.
4. Change the value in the **Height** text box to .125. Figure 8-33 shows the work done in Steps 2, 3, and 4.
5. Pick the **Apply** button and then the **Close** button. The new ROMANS-125 text style is now part of your drawing.

Now, ROMANS-125 is the default style when you use the **TEXT** or **MTEXT** commands. If you want to create a similar text style for your architectural drawings, you might consider a style name called ARCHITECTURAL-125. For this style, set the font name to Stylus BT and the height to .125.

Figure 8-32.
The **New Text Style** dialog box. A—The default entry. B—A new text style entered.

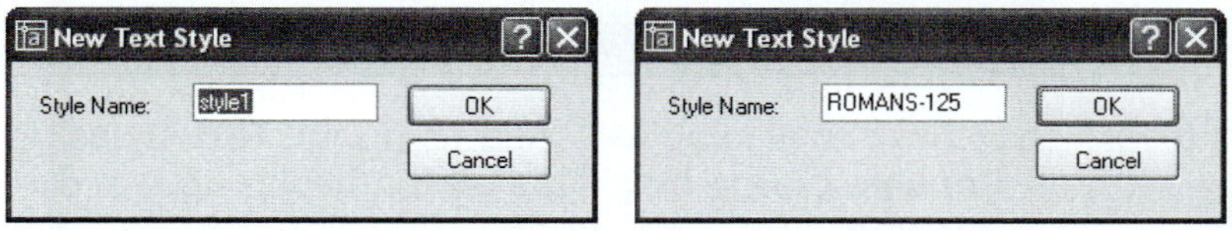

A B

Figure 8-33.
The **Text Style** dialog box showing the changes in the style, font, and height.

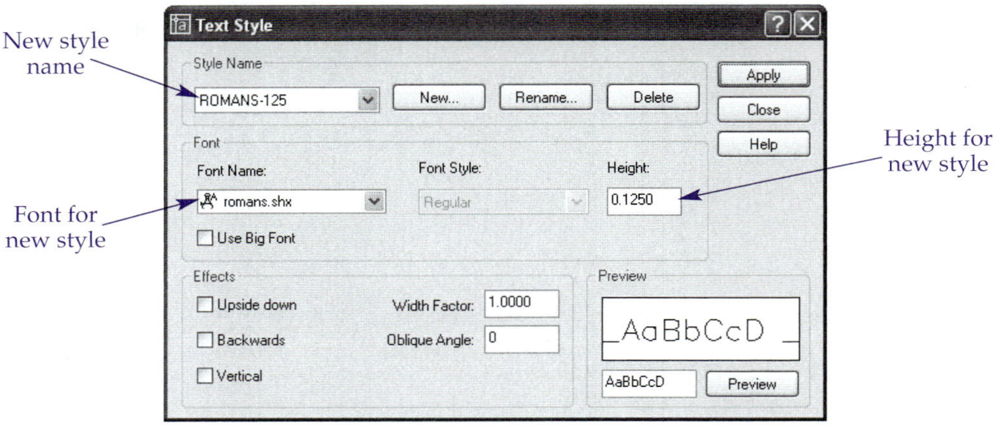

PROFESSIONAL TIP

You can make the text style name the same as the font name if you wish. In some cases, this is a clear and concise way of naming the style.

EXERCISE 8-7 Complete the Exercise on the Student CD.

PROFESSIONAL TIP

To save valuable drafting time, add text styles to your template drawings. If only a single text height is needed in the template, set the text height for the style. Do not forget to consider the scale factor when entering the text height. Enter the scaled text height for the style.

Changing, Renaming, and Deleting Text Styles

You can change the current text style without affecting existing text objects. The changes are applied only to text added using that style.

Existing text styles are easily renamed in the **Text Style** dialog box. Select the desired style name in the **Style Name** text box and pick the **Rename...** button. This opens the **Rename Text Style** dialog box, which is similar to the **New Text Style** dialog box. Change the text style name in the **Style Name** text box and pick the **OK** button.

NOTE

Styles can also be renamed using the **Text styles** option of the **Rename** dialog box. This dialog box is accessed by selecting **Rename...** from the **Format** pull-down menu or by entering RENAME at the Command: prompt.

You can also delete an existing text style in the **Text Style** dialog box by picking the desired style name in the **Style Name** drop-down list followed by picking the **Delete** button. If you try to delete a text style that has been used to create text objects in the drawing, AutoCAD gives you the following message:

Style is in use, can't be deleted.

This means that there are text objects in the drawing that reference this style. If you want to delete the style, change the text objects in the drawing to a different style. You cannot delete or rename the Standard style.

> NOTE
>
> If you change the font and orientation of an existing text style, all text items with that style are redrawn with the new values.

Importing Text Styles from Existing Drawings

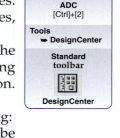

> **ADCENTER**
> **ADC**
> [Ctrl]+[2]
>
> **Tools**
> ➥ **DesignCenter**
>
> **Standard toolbar**
>
> **DesignCenter**

DesignCenter can be used to import text styles from existing drawing files. **DesignCenter** allows you to browse through drawing files to find desired text styles, and then add the needed style into your current drawing file.

DesignCenter can be accessed by picking the **DesignCenter** button on the **Standard** toolbar, selecting **DesignCenter** from the **Tools** pull-down menu, entering ADC or ADCENTER at the Command: prompt, or using the [Ctrl]+[2] key combination. See **Figure 8-34.**

The following procedure is used to import a text style into the current drawing:

1. In the tree view area, locate the existing drawing containing the text style to be copied.
2. Double-click on the file name or pick the plus (+) sign next to it to list the various types of content within the drawing.
3. Pick the Textstyles content in the tree view. This displays the text styles.
4. Select the text style or text styles to be copied into the drawing. You can then copy the text style in any of the following ways:
   - **Drag and drop.** Move the cursor over the top of the desired text style(s), press and hold the pick button on your pointing device, and drag the cursor to the drawing area of the opened drawing. Let go of the pick button and the text style(s) is added to your current drawing file.

Figure 8-34.
DesignCenter allows you to copy a text style from an existing drawing into the current drawing.

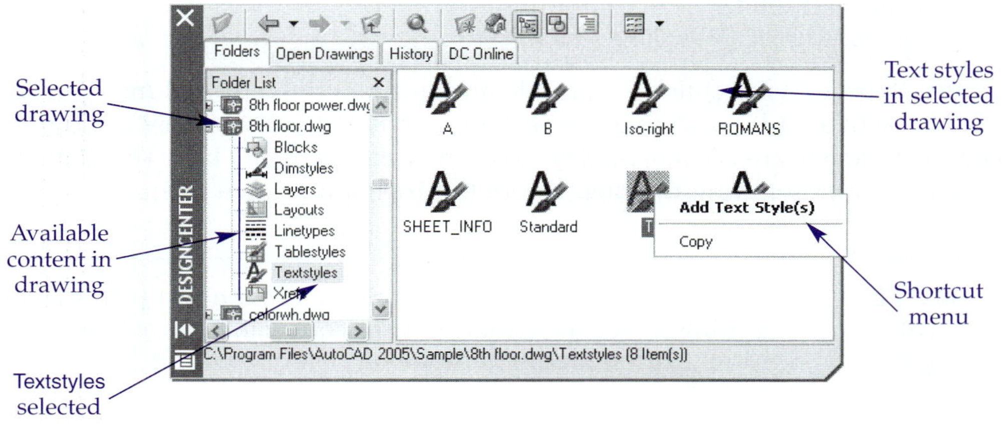

- **Shortcut menu.** Position the cursor over the desired text style and right-click to open the shortcut menu. See **Figure 8-34.** Pick the **Add Text Style(s)** option, and the text style is added to your current drawing.
- **Copy and paste.** Use the shortcut menu as described in the previous method, but select the **Copy** option. Move the cursor to the drawing where you want the text style added, then right-click your mouse button and select the **Paste** option from the shortcut menu. The copied text style is added to the current drawing.

PROFESSIONAL TIP

To select more than one text style at one time to import into your current drawing file, hold down the [Shift] key and pick the first and last text styles in a group of text styles, or hold down the [Ctrl] key to select multiple text styles individually.

NOTE

New text styles can be created at the Command: prompt with the **-STYLE** command. After entering the command, you are prompted to enter the new style name and properties (such as font, height, and obliquing angle).

EXERCISE 8-8 Complete the Exercise on the Student CD.

Redrawing Text Quickly

Text often requires a great deal of time to regenerate, redraw, and plot because each character is drawn with many individual vectors (line segments). The Quick Text mode makes text appear as rectangles equal to the height and length of each text string. This speeds regeneration and plotting time. The Quick Text mode is turned on and off with the **QTEXT** (quick text) command. **Figure 8-35** shows a comparison between displays when the Quick Text mode is on and off.

The **QTEXT** command is entered at the Command: prompt. If the last setting was off, the command line appears as follows:

Command: **QTEXT**↵
Enter mode [ON/OFF] <Off>:

Enter ON to activate Quick Text mode and quicken the redraw time. This mode can also be activated by selecting the **Show text boundary frame only** option in the **Display performance** area of the **Display** tab of the **Options** dialog box. This dialog box can be accessed by selecting **Options...** from the **Tools** pull-down menu.

NOTE

If you print with Quick Text mode on, the text prints as box outlines, not as actual text. If you want the actual text to print, turn Quick Text mode off before printing.

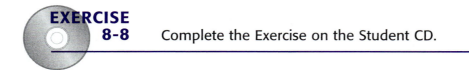

Figure 8-35. Comparison of Quick Text mode turned on and off.

Revising Text with DDEDIT

Text editing is accomplished using the **DDEDIT** command. **DDEDIT** is accessed by picking **Text** and then **Edit...** from the **Object** cascading menu in the **Modify** pull-down menu, entering ED or DDEDIT at the Command: prompt, or selecting the **Edit Text** button on the **Text** toolbar. The **DDEDIT** command can also be accessed by selecting the text object, right-clicking, and selecting **Mtext Edit...** or **Text Edit...** from the shortcut menu.

DDEDIT
ED

Modify
➥ **Object**
➥ **Text**
➥ **Edit...**

Text toolbar
Edit Text

If you pick single-line text, you get the **Edit Text** dialog box, **Figure 8-36.** Enter the new text string in the **Text:** text box. If you pick text that was drawn with the **MTEXT** command, you get the multiline text editor. Multiline text is also drawn with the **QLEADER** command, which is explained in Chapter 17.

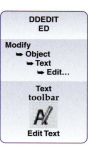

PROFESSIONAL TIP

You can double-click on a text object to edit it. Double-clicking on a single-line text object opens the **Edit Text** dialog box. Double-clicking on a multiline text object opens the multiline text editor.

Figure 8-36. The **DDEDIT** command activates the **Edit Text** dialog box if the selected text object was created with the **TEXT** command.

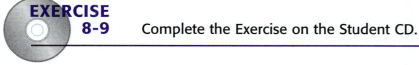

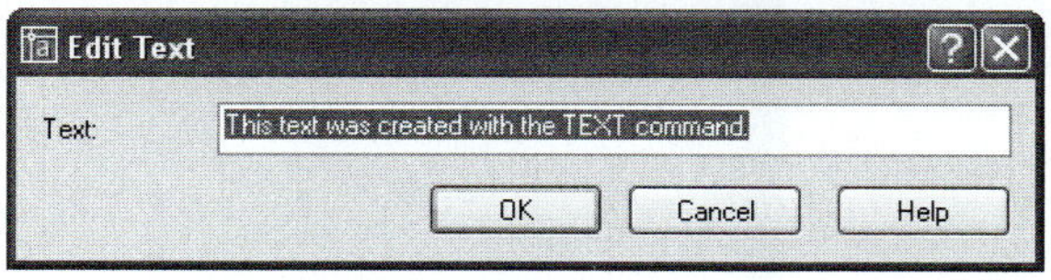

EXERCISE 8-9 Complete the Exercise on the Student CD.

Changing Text with the Properties Window

PROPERTIES
PROPS
CH
MO

Modify
➥ Properties

Standard toolbar

Properties

The **Properties** window can be used to change text. The **Properties** window can be opened by picking the **Properties** button on the **Standard** toolbar, selecting **Properties** from the **Modify** pull-down menu, or entering CH, MO, PROPS, or PROPERTIES at the Command: prompt. You can also open the **Properties** window by selecting the desired text and then right-clicking and selecting **Properties** from the shortcut menu.

You have two options for selecting text to change. You can select the desired text and then display the **Properties** window, or you can display the **Properties** window and then select the desired text. If you display the **Properties** window first, you may need to move the window before you can select the text (if the window covers the text you want to pick). Either way, the **Properties** window is opened, as shown in **Figure 8-37.**

Notice the top of the window displays Text in the box. This informs you that a text object has been selected. If multiple objects are selected, the drop-down list is used to select which object has its properties displayed.

The properties of the text object are displayed in different categories within the window. Picking on top of a property allows you to modify its value. The text properties are divided into the following categories:

- **General.** These general properties are found in nearly all AutoCAD object types. The general properties include color, layer, linetype, linetype scale, plot style, lineweight, hyperlink, and thickness.
- **Text.** Text properties are common to text and multiline text objects. These properties were explained earlier in this chapter and include items such as justification, rotation, and style.

Figure 8-37.
The **Properties** window shows the properties of the selected text. Note the properties of text created with the **TEXT** command are slightly different from the properties of text created with the **MTEXT** command.

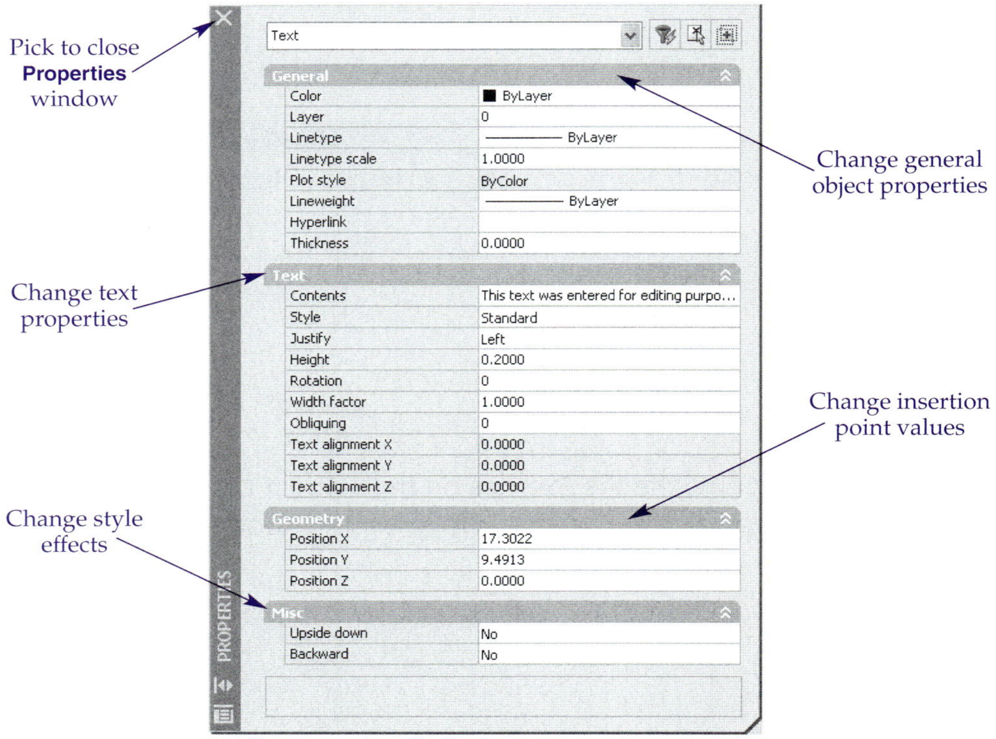

- **Geometry.** The geometry properties are the X, Y, and Z coordinate locations of the text insertion point.
- **Misc.** The miscellaneous settings are the Upside down and Backward properties. These properties are not listed for multiline text objects.

To change a property, pick the property or property setting with the cursor. The property setting can then be edited. For some properties, a pull-down can be used to select other settings. See **Figure 8-38.**

After you make the desired changes to your text, press [Enter] to apply the changes or pick the "X" in the **Properties** window title bar to close the **Properties** window. Then press the [Esc] key to deselect the text.

The **Properties** window can also be used to change multiline text. When you select the multiline text to change, the **Properties** window appears with MText identified as the selected object, as shown in **Figure 8-39.** The properties listed are similar to those listed for a text object. The properties that differ for the two objects are described below:

- **Contents.** Picking the button at the right opens the multiline text editor.
- **Direction.** Horizontal or vertical direction of the multiline text object is specified here.
- **Width.** Allows you to specify the width of the multiline text object.
- **Background mask.** Sets a background for the text.
- **Line space factor.** A line space factor of 1.0 is 1.66 times the text height.
- **Line space distance.** Use this setting if an absolute value, measured in drawing units, is needed.
- **Line space style.** Using At Least here will cause the line spacing to increase if the text overlaps.

Figure 8-38.
Modifying a property using the **Properties** window. When the **Justify** property is picked, the drop-down arrow appears next to the Left setting. Picking the arrow exposes the drop-down list shown.

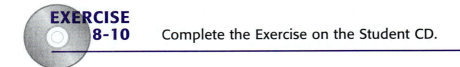

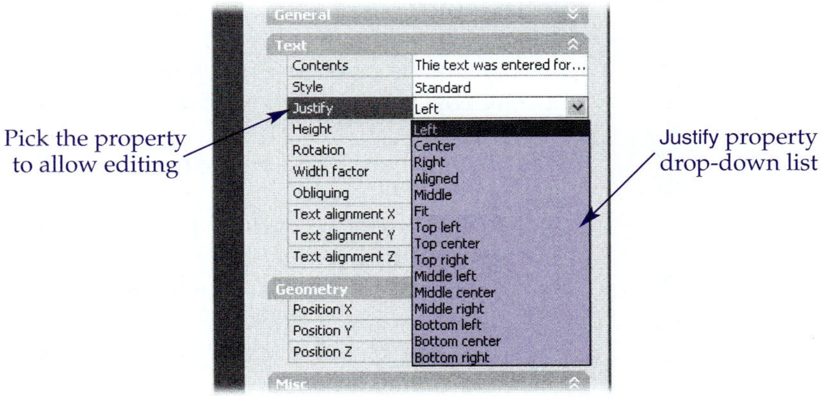

EXERCISE 8-10 Complete the Exercise on the Student CD.

Figure 8-39.
The **Properties** window with a multiline text object selected. Note the list of properties is slightly different from the list for a text object.

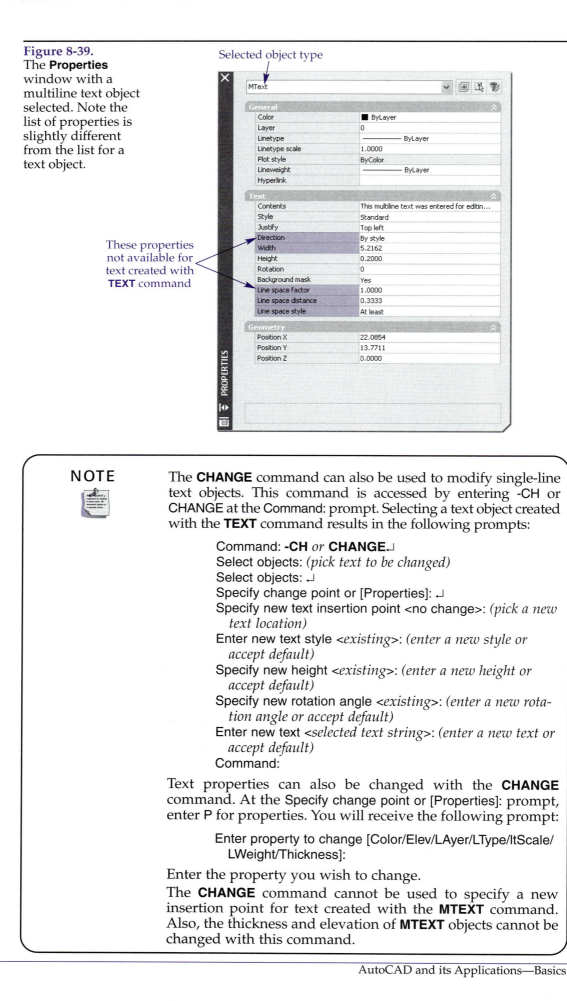

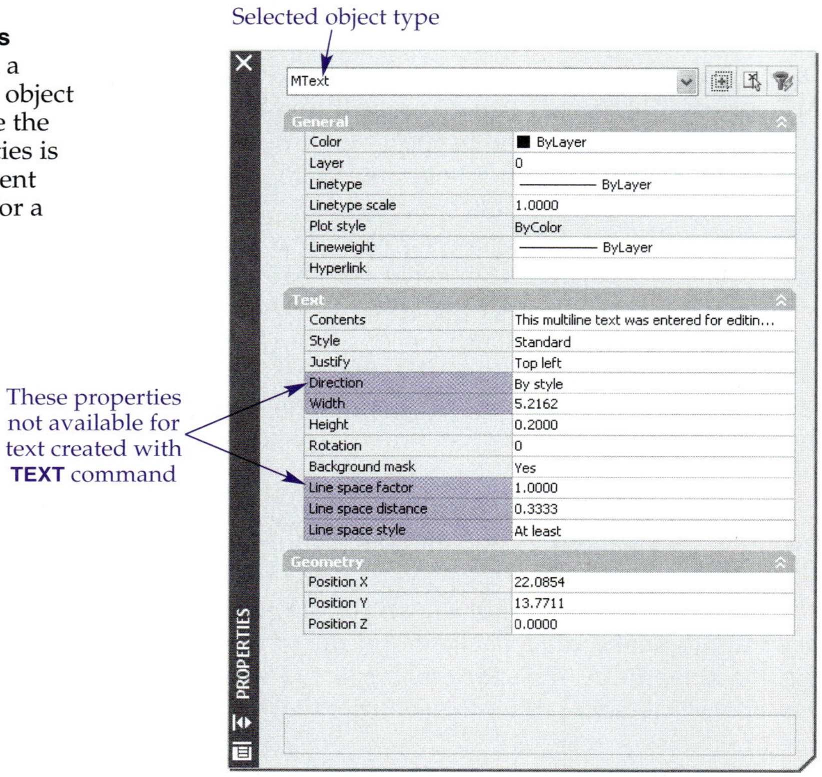

NOTE

The **CHANGE** command can also be used to modify single-line text objects. This command is accessed by entering -CH or CHANGE at the Command: prompt. Selecting a text object created with the **TEXT** command results in the following prompts:

Command: **-CH** *or* **CHANGE**↵
Select objects: *(pick text to be changed)*
Select objects: ↵
Specify change point or [Properties]: ↵
Specify new text insertion point <no change>: *(pick a new text location)*
Enter new text style <*existing*>: *(enter a new style or accept default)*
Specify new height <*existing*>: *(enter a new height or accept default)*
Specify new rotation angle <*existing*>: *(enter a new rotation angle or accept default)*
Enter new text <*selected text string*>: *(enter a new text or accept default)*
Command:

Text properties can also be changed with the **CHANGE** command. At the Specify change point or [Properties]: prompt, enter P for properties. You will receive the following prompt:

Enter property to change [Color/Elev/LAyer/LType/ltScale/LWeight/Thickness]:

Enter the property you wish to change.

The **CHANGE** command cannot be used to specify a new insertion point for text created with the **MTEXT** command. Also, the thickness and elevation of **MTEXT** objects cannot be changed with this command.

Scaling Text

Changing the height of text objects can be accomplished using the **SCALETEXT** command. The **SCALETEXT** command allows you to scale text objects in relation to their individual insertion points or in relation to a single base point. **SCALETEXT** is accessed by picking **Scale** from the **Text** cascading menu of the **Object** cascading menu in the **Modify** pull-down menu, entering SCALETEXT at the Command: prompt, or selecting the **Scale Text** button on the **Text** toolbar.

> **SCALETEXT**
> **Modify** → **Object** → **Text** → **Scale**
> **Text toolbar**: **Scale Text**

SCALETEXT works with single-line and multiline text objects. You can select both types of text objects simultaneously when using the **SCALETEXT** command. The prompts for the **SCALETEXT** command are as follows:

Command: **SCALETEXT**↵
Select objects: *(select the text object(s) to be scaled)*
Enter a base point option for scaling
[Existing/Left/Center/Middle/Right/TL/TC/TR/ML/MC/MR/BL/BC/BR] <Existing>: *(specify justification for base point)*
Specify new height or [Match object/Scale factor] <*default*>: *(specify scaling option)*
Command:

All the justification options except **Existing** and **Left** are shown in Figure 8-6 and Figure 8-7. Using the **Existing** option scales the text objects using their existing justification setting as the base point. Using the **Left** option scales the text objects using their lower-left point as the base point. Figure 8-40 shows text with different justification points being scaled using the **Existing** option. Notice how the text is scaled in relation to its own justification setting.

After specifying the justification to be used as the base point, AutoCAD prompts for the scaling type. The **Specify new height** option (default) is used to type a new value for the text height. All the selected text objects change to the new text height. The **Match object** option allows you to pick an existing text object. The selected text object's height adopts the text height from the picked text object. Use the **Scale factor** option to scale text objects that have different heights in relation to their current heights. Using a scale factor of 2 scales all the selected text objects to twice their current size.

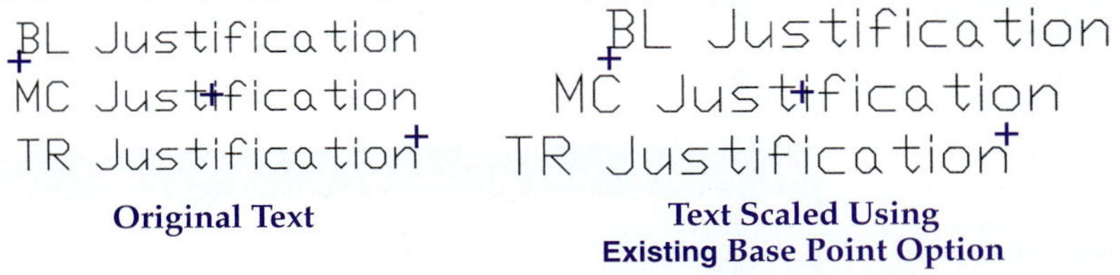

Figure 8-40. Using the **Existing** option of the **SCALETEXT** command, text objects are scaled using their individual justification settings.

Changing Text Justification

If you use the **Properties** window to change the justification setting of a text object, the text object(s) move to adjust to the new justification point. The justification point does not move. To change the justification point without moving the text, use the **JUSTIFYTEXT** command. **JUSTIFYTEXT** is accessed by picking **Justify** from the **Text** cascading menu of the **Object** cascading menu from the **Modify** pull-down menu, entering JUSTIFYTEXT at the Command: prompt, or by selecting the **Justify Text** button on the **Text** toolbar.

> **JUSTIFYTEXT**
> **Modify** → **Object** → **Text** → **Justify**
> **Text toolbar**: **Justify Text**

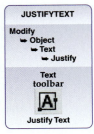

EXERCISE 8-11 Complete the Exercise on the Student CD.

Working with Fields

AutoCAD 2005 NEW FEATURE

A *field* is a special type of text object. A field displays a specific property value, setting, or characteristic. Fields can display information related to a specific object, general drawing properties, or information related to the current user or computer system.

The text displayed in the field can change if the value being displayed changes. AutoCAD can update the field information automatically. This makes fields useful tools for displaying information that may change throughout the course of a project.

Inserting Fields

AutoCAD 2005 NEW FEATURE

Fields can be inserted in both multiline and single-line text. To insert a field in multiline text, right-click in the text editor to display the text editor shortcut menu. Pick **Insert Field...** to display the **Field** dialog box. You can also use the [Ctrl]+[F] key combination to access this dialog box from the multiline text editor. To insert a field in single-line text, right-click and select **Insert Field...** from the shortcut menu while the Enter text: prompt is displayed. You can also insert a field without first accessing the **MTEXT** or **TEXT** commands by picking **Field...** from the **Insert** pull-down menu.

Regardless of the method used, the **Field** dialog box is displayed when you select to insert a field. See **Figure 8-41.** Many preset fields can be selected from the **Field** dialog box. To make it easier to locate a specific field, they are separated into categories, **Figure 8-42.** When you select a category from the **Field category** drop-down list, only the fields within the category are displayed in the **Field names** list box. This makes it much easier to locate a desired field.

Pick the field category, and then pick the field to be inserted from the **Field name** list box. The selected field and its current value are displayed in the center of the **Field** dialog box. You can also select from a list of formats to determine the display of the field. The **Format** list varies, depending on the selected field.

Figure 8-41.
Select fields using the **Field** dialog box.

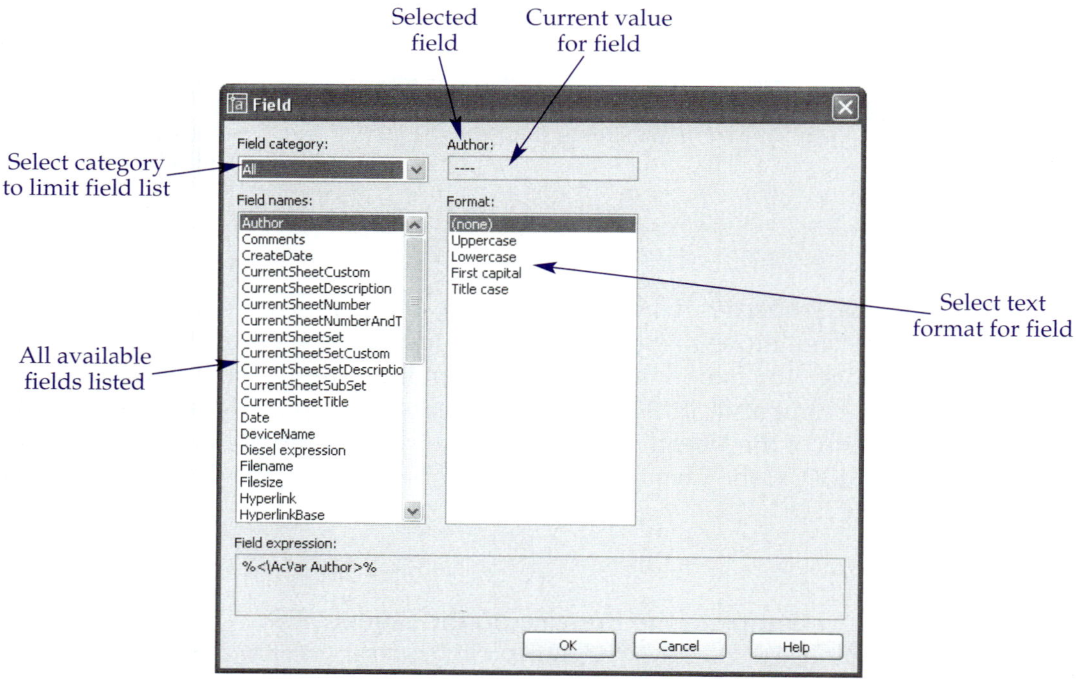

Figure 8-42.
Fields are separated into categories.

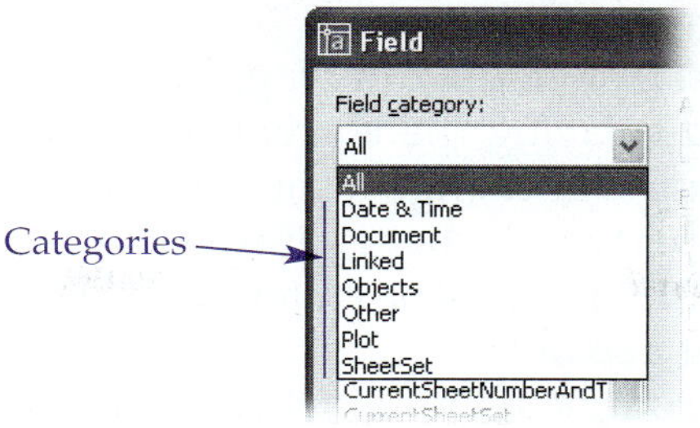

Once you have selected the field and format, pick the **OK** button to insert the field. The field assumes the current text style properties, such as font type and size. By default, the field text has a gray background. See Figure 8-43. This keeps you aware that the text is actually a field, so the value displayed may change. You can deactivate the background in the **Fields** area of the **User Preferences** tab of the **Options** dialog box, Figure 8-44. If you inserted the field from the **Insert** pull-down, the field is inserted as a multiline text object.

Figure 8-43.
A date and time field inserted into multiline text. The gray background identifies the text as a field.

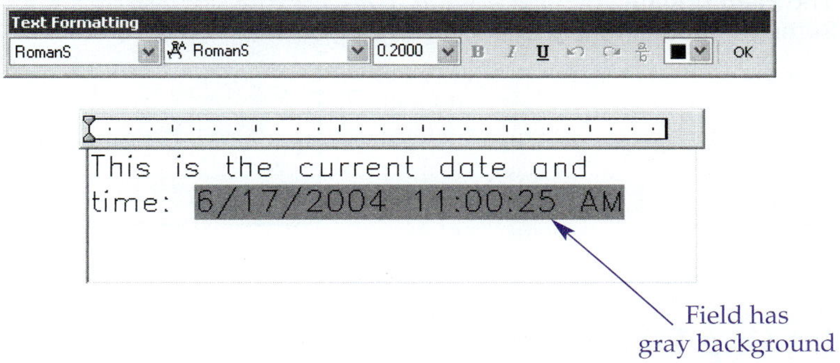

Figure 8-44.
The **Fields** area of the **Options** dialog box contains field settings.

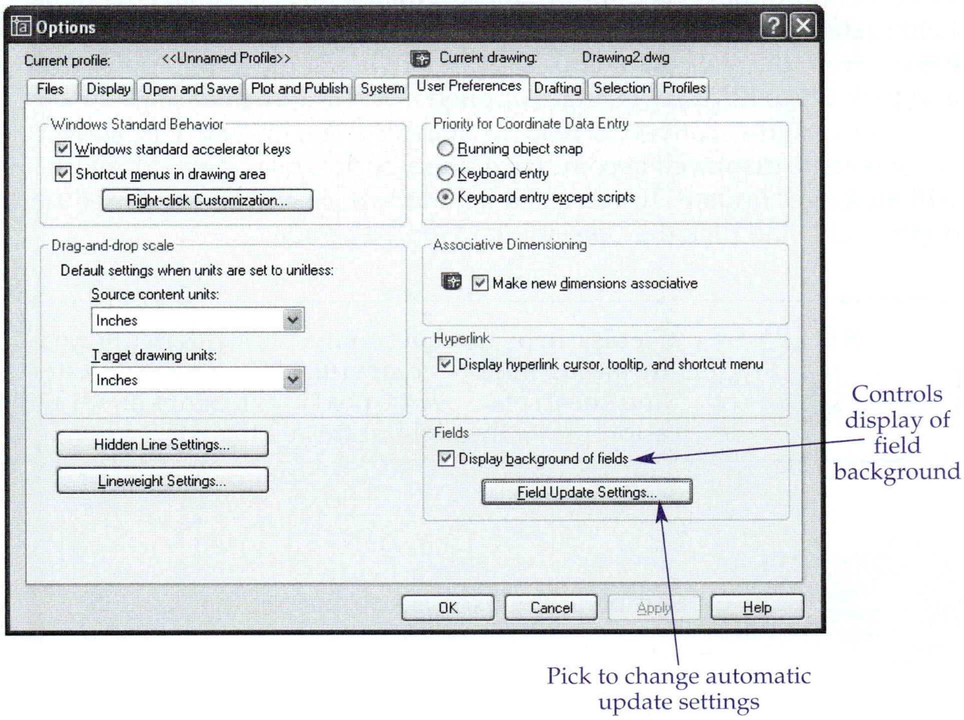

Updating Fields

AutoCAD 2005 NEW FEATURE

Once a field is inserted into a drawing, the value being displayed may change. For example, a field displaying the current date changes value every date. A field displaying the file name will change if the file name changes. A field displaying the value of an object property will change if the object is modified and the property is changed. ***Updating*** is the process of AutoCAD checking the value of the field and changing the display if needed.

Updating can be completed automatically or manually. Automatic updating is set using the **Field Update Settings** dialog box. To access this dialog box, pick the **Field Update Settings...** button in the **Fields** area of the **User Preferences** tab of the **Options** dialog box, Figure 8-45. Whenever a selected event (such as saving or regenerating) occurs, all fields are automatically updated.

You can also update fields manually by selecting **Update Fields** from the **Tools** pull-down menu (**UPDATEFIELD** command). After picking the command, select the fields to be updated. You can use the **All** selection option to quickly update all fields.

Figure 8-45.
The **Field Update Settings** dialog box.

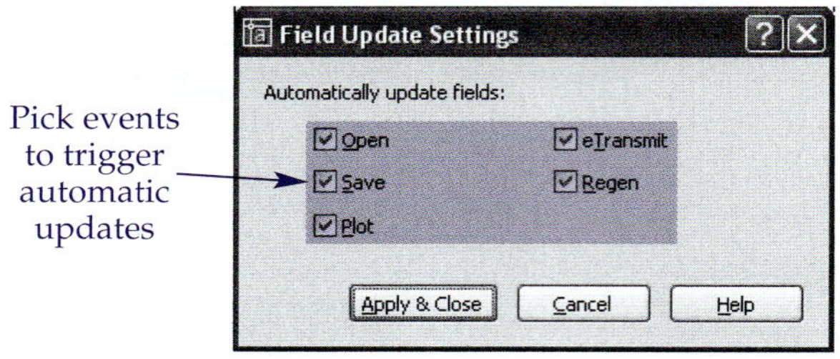

Editing Fields

AutoCAD 2005 NEW FEATURE

There may be instances in which you wish to edit a field. Typically, you would do so to select a different display format.

To edit a field, you must first select the text object containing the field for editing. Once the multiline text editor or **Edit Text** dialog box is displayed, double-click on the field to display the **Field** dialog box. You can also right-click on the field and pick **Edit Field...** from the shortcut menu. Use the **Field** dialog box to modify the field settings and pick **OK** to have the changes applied.

You can also convert a field to standard text. When you convert a field, the current value displayed becomes text, the association to the field is lost, and the value will no longer update. To convert a field to text, select the text for editing, right-click on the field, and pick the **Convert Field To Text** option.

NOTE

Fields can be used in conjunction with many AutoCAD tools, including inquiry commands, drawing properties, attributes, and sheet sets. Specific field applications are discussed where appropriate throughout this textbook.

EXERCISE 8-12

Complete the Exercise on the Student CD.

Checking Your Spelling

You have been introduced to editing text on the drawing using the **DDEDIT** command and the **Properties** window. You can use these methods to change lines of text and even correct spelling errors. However, AutoCAD has a powerful and convenient tool for checking the spelling on your drawing.

SPELL
SP

Tools
➥ Spelling...

To check spelling, enter SP or SPELL at the Command: prompt or pick **Spelling** from the **Tools** pull-down menu. After entering the command, you are asked to select the text to be checked. You need to pick each line of single-line text or make one pick on multiline text to select the entire paragraph. You can enter the **All** selection method to select all text in the drawing.

The **Check Spelling** dialog box is displayed. See **Figure 8-46.** The following describes the features found in the **Check Spelling** dialog box:

- **Current dictionary: American English.** The dictionary being used is identified at the top of the dialog box. You can change to a different dictionary by picking the **Change Dictionaries...** button.
- **Current word.** Displays a word that may be spelled incorrectly.
- **Suggestions.** Gives you a list of possible correct spellings for the current word. The highlighted word in the first box is AutoCAD's best guess. Following the highlighted word is a list of other choices. If there are many choices, a scroll bar is available for you to use. If you do not like the word that AutoCAD has highlighted, move the cursor arrow to another word and pick it. The word you pick then becomes highlighted in the list and is shown in the **Suggestions** text box. If none of the words in the **Suggestion** text box or list are correct and the current word is not correct either, you can enter the correct word in the **Suggestions** text box.
- **Ignore.** Pick this button to skip the current word. In **Figure 8-46,** ASME is not a misspelled word, it just is not recognized by the dictionary. You would select the **Ignore** button and the spell check goes on to the next word.
- **Ignore All.** Pick this button if you want AutoCAD to ignore all words that match the currently found misspelled word.
- **Change.** Pick this button to replace the current word with the word in the **Suggestions** text box.
- **Change All.** Pick this button if you want to replace the **Current word** with the word in the **Suggestions** text box throughout the entire selection set.
- **Add.** Pick this button to add the current word to the custom dictionary. You can add words with up to 63 characters.

Figure 8-46.
The **Check Spelling** dialog box.

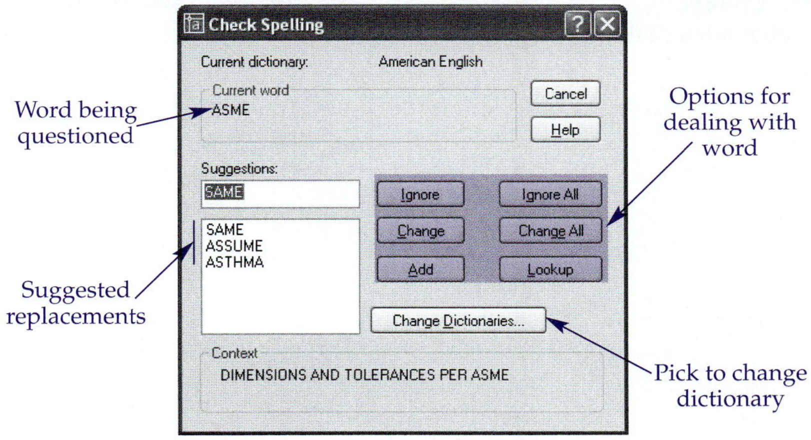

- **Lookup.** This button asks AutoCAD to check the spelling of the word you enter in the **Suggestions** text box.
- **Context.** At the bottom of the dialog box, AutoCAD displays the line of text where the current word was found.

Changing Dictionaries

AutoCAD provides you with several dictionaries: one American English, two British English, and two French. There are also dictionaries available for 24 different languages. Pick the **Change Dictionaries...** button to access the **Change Dictionary** dialog box. See Figure 8-47.

The areas of the **Change Dictionary** dialog box are as follows:

- **Main dictionary area.** This is where you can select one of the many language dictionaries to use as the current dictionary. To change the main dictionary, pick the down arrow to access the drop-down list. Next, pick the desired language dictionary from the list. The main dictionary is protected and cannot be added to.
- **Custom dictionary area.** This displays the name of the current custom dictionary, sample.cus by default. You can create your own custom dictionary by entering a new file name with a .cus extension. Words can be added or deleted and dictionaries can be combined using any standard text editor. If you use a word processor such as Microsoft Word, be sure to save the file as *text only*, with no special text formatting or printer codes.

PROFESSIONAL TIP

You can create custom dictionaries for various disciplines. For example, when in a mechanical drawing, common abbreviations and brand names might be added to a mech.cus file. A separate file named arch.cus might contain common architectural abbreviations and frequently used brand names.

- **Browse....** Pick this button to access the **Select Custom Dictionary** dialog box.
- **Custom dictionary words area.** Type a word in the text box that you either want to add or delete from the custom dictionary. For example, ASME Y14.5M is custom text used in engineering drafting. Pick the **Add** button to accept the custom word in the text box, or pick the **Delete** button to remove the word from the custom dictionary. Custom dictionary entries may be up to 32 characters in length.

Figure 8-47.
The **Change Dictionaries** dialog box.

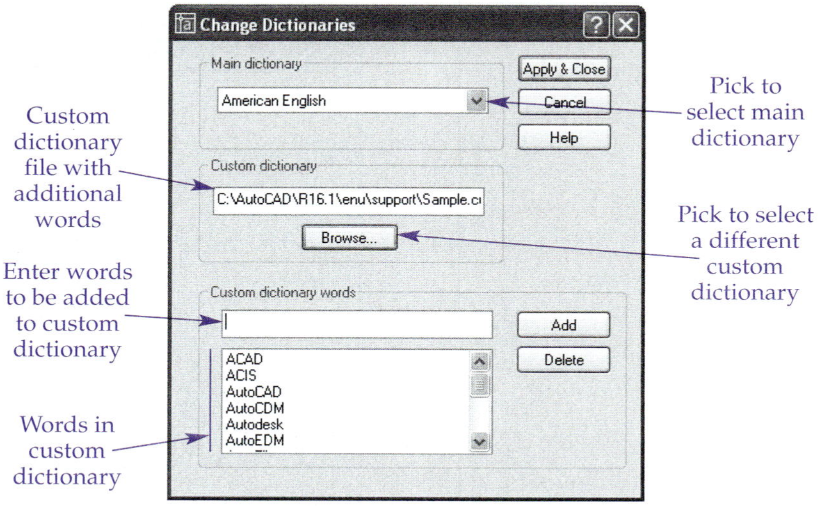

> **NOTE**
>
> The current main and custom dictionaries are stored in the **DCTMAIN** and **DCTCUST** system variables, respectively.

EXERCISE 8-13 Complete the Exercise on the Student CD.

Finding and Replacing Text

You can use the **SPELL** command to check and correct the spelling of text in a drawing. If you want to find a piece of text in your drawing and replace it with an alternative piece of text in a single instance or throughout your drawing, you should use the **FIND** command.

FIND
Edit
➥ **Find...**
Text toolbar
Find and Replace

To find a string of text in the drawing, enter FIND at the Command: prompt, pick **Find...** from the **Edit** pull-down menu, or pick the **Find and Replace** button on the **Text** toolbar. After you enter the command, AutoCAD displays the **Find and Replace** dialog box, shown in **Figure 8-48.**

The **Find and Replace** dialog box contains the following elements:

- **Find text string.** Specify the text string that you want to find in this text box. Enter a string, or choose one of the six most recently used strings from the drop-down list.
- **Replace with.** Specify the text string you want to replace in this text box. Enter a string, or choose one of the most recently used strings from the drop-down list.

Figure 8-48.
The **Find and Replace** dialog box.

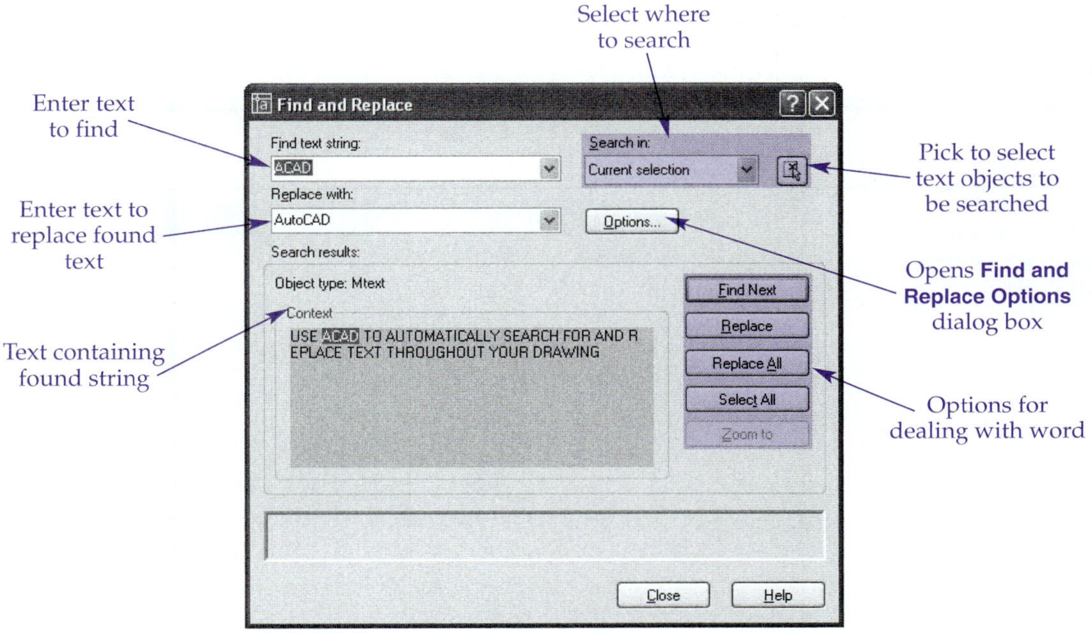

- **Search in.** Specify whether to search the entire drawing or only the current selection. If there is a current selection set, **Current selection** is the default value. If there is no current selection set, **Entire drawing** is the default value. Picking the **Select Objects** button closes the dialog box temporarily allowing you to select objects in your drawing. Press [Enter] to return to the dialog box.
- **Options....** This button displays the **Find and Replace Options** dialog box, in which you can define the type of objects and words that you want to find. See Figure 8-49. The following options are available:
  - **Include area.** This area contains the types of objects you want to include in the search. By default, all options are selected.
  - **Match case.** This check box allows you to include the case of the text in **Find text string** as part of the search criteria.
  - **Find whole words only.** This check box allows you to find only whole words that match the text in **Find text string**.
- **Context.** This area displays and highlights the currently found text string in its surrounding context. If you choose **Find Next**, AutoCAD refreshes the **Context** area and displays the next found text string in its surrounding context.
- **Find/Find Next.** This button allows you to find the text in **Find text string** text box. Once you find the first instance of the text, the **Find** button becomes a **Find Next** button, which you can use to find the next instance.
- **Replace.** Use this button to replace found text with the text entered in the **Replace with** text box.
- **Replace All.** This button allows you to find all instances of the text entered in the **Find text string** text box and replace all occurrences with the text in the **Replace with** text box.
- **Select All.** This button is used to find and select all loaded objects containing instances of the text in **Find text string** text box. This option is available only when searching the **Current selection**. When you choose this button, the dialog box closes and AutoCAD displays a message indicating the number of objects found and selected.
- **Zoom to.** Picking this button displays the area in the drawing that contains the found text.

NOTE

The find and replace strings are saved with the drawing file and may be reused.

Figure 8-49.
The **Find and Replace Options** dialog box.

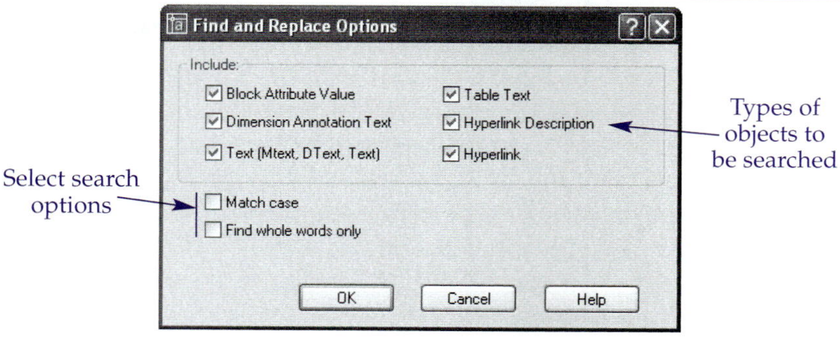

Additional Text Tips

Text presentation is important on any drawing. It is a good idea to plan your drawing using rough sketches to allow room for text and notes. Some things to consider when designing the drawing layout include:

- ✓ Arrange text to avoid crowding.
- ✓ Place related notes in groups to make the drawing easy to read.
- ✓ Place all general notes in a common location. Locate notes in the lower-left corner or above the title block when using ASME standards. Place notes in the upper-left corner when using military standards.
- ✓ Always use the spell checker.

EXPRESS TOOLS CHAPTER 8

The following Express Tools are related to topics discussed in this chapter. Refer to the Student CD for information on these tools:

Remote Text
Text Mask
Explode Text
Arc-Aligned Text
Enclose Text
Change Case
Text Fit
Unmask Text
Convert to MTEXT
Rotate Text
Automatic Numbering

Chapter Test

Answer the following questions on a separate sheet of paper.

1. Give the command and inputs required to use the **TEXT** command to display the following text string: IT IS FAST AND EASY TO DRAW TEXT USING AUTOCAD. The text must be .375 units high, have the default txt font, and fit between two points:
   A. Command: _____
   B. Specify start point of text or [Justify/Style]: _____
   C. Enter an option [Align/Fit/Center/Middle/Right/TL/TC/TR/ML/MC/MR/BL/BC/BR]: _____
   D. Specify first endpoint of text baseline: _____
   E. Specify second endpoint of text baseline: _____
   F. Specify height: _____
   G. Enter text: _____
2. How do you turn on the Quick Text mode if it is currently off using the Command: prompt?
3. List three ways to access the **TEXT** command.
4. Give the letter you must enter for the following justification options when using the **TEXT** command:
   A. Left-justified text.
   B. Right-justified text.
   C. Text between two points without regard for text height.
   D. Center the text horizontally and vertically.
   E. Text between two points with a fixed height.
   F. Center text along a baseline.
   G. Top and left horizontal.
   H. Middle and right horizontal.
   I. Bottom and center horizontal.

5. List the **TEXT** command **Justify** options.
6. How would you specify a text style with a double width factor?
7. How would you specify a text style with a 15° angle?
8. How would you specify vertical text?
9. Give the control sequence required to draw the following symbols when using the **TEXT** command:
   A. 30°
   B. 1.375 ±.005
   C. ∅24
   D. <u>NOT FOR CONSTRUCTION</u>
10. Why use the Quick Text mode rather than have the actual text displayed on the screen?
11. When setting text height in the **Text Style** dialog box, what value do you enter so text height can be altered each time the **TEXT** command is used?
12. List a command that lets you alter the location, style, height, and wording of existing single-line text.
13. Identify the command used to revise existing single-line text on the drawing by using the **Edit Text** dialog box.
14. When editing single-line text, how do you remove the character located in front of the text cursor?
15. When using the **Edit Text** dialog box, how do you move the text cursor to the left without removing text characters?
16. When using the **Edit Text** dialog box, how do you remove all of the text to the right of the text cursor?
17. When editing text in the **Text:** text box, the flashing vertical bar is called the ______.
18. Determine the AutoCAD text height for text to be plotted .188″ high using a half (1″ = 2″) scale. (Show your calculations.)
19. Determine the AutoCAD text height for text to be plotted .188″ high using a scale of 1/4″ = 1′-0″. (Show your calculations.)
20. What would you do if you just completed editing a line of text and discovered you made a mistake? Assume you are still in the **Edit Text** dialog box.
21. Identify two ways to move around inside the **Text:** box of the **Edit Text** dialog box.
22. What happens when you press the space bar or the [Backspace] key when the text inside the **Text:** text box is highlighted?
23. What happens when you press [Ctrl]+[X] when the text within the **Text:** text box is highlighted?
24. Name the command that lets you make multiline text objects.
25. How does the width of the multiline text boundary affect what you type?
26. What happens if the multiline text that you are entering exceeds or is not as long as the boundary length that you initially establish?
27. What happens when you pick the first corner followed by the other corner of the multiline text boundary?
28. What text feature allows you to hide parts of objects behind and around text?
29. Name two commands that allow you to edit multiline text.
30. How are fractions drawn when using the **TEXT** command?
31. How do you draw stacked fractions when using the **MTEXT** command?
32. What is the keyboard shortcut for the **TEXT** command?
33. What does a width factor of .5 do to the text when compared with the default width factor of 1?
34. What do you get when using the **DDEDIT** command on multiline text?
35. What is the keyboard shortcut for the **MTEXT** command?

36. How do you move the text cursor down one line at a time in the multiline text editor?
37. What happens when you pick the **Other...** option in the **Symbol** command of the text editor shortcut menu?
38. Name the internal storage area that temporarily stores information you copy or cut from a document.
39. When you are in the multiline text editor, how do you open the text editor shortcut menu?
40. What is the purpose of the **Set Mtext Width** option found in the shortcut menu when you right-click over the multiline text editor ruler?
41. Describe how to find a word or words in a text object and have the word or words replaced with another word or words.
42. Describe how you would create a text style that has the name ROMANS-125_15, uses the romans.shx font, has a fixed height of .125, a text width of 1.25, and an obliquing angle of 15.
43. Name the feature that allows you to move the cursor over the top of the desired text style in **DesignCenter**, hold down the pick button, and drag the cursor to the opened drawing.
44. Identify and briefly describe two methods that can be used to import an existing text style from **DesignCenter** to another drawing when you right-click over the desired text style.
45. Describe the two methods that can be used to select more than one text style at a time to import into your drawing from **DesignCenter**.
46. When using the **SCALETEXT** command, which base point option would you select to keep the text object(s) current justification point?
47. What is the difference between using the **JUSTIFYTEXT** command and using the **Properties** window to change the justification point of a text object?
48. What is a *field*?
49. What is different about the on-screen display of fields compared to that of text?
50. How can you access the **Field Update Settings** dialog box?
51. Identify three ways to access the AutoCAD spell checker.
52. What is the purpose of the word found in the **Current word** box of the **Check Spelling** dialog box?
53. How do you change the **Current word** if you do not think the word that is displayed in the **Suggestions:** text box of the **Check Spelling** dialog box is the correct word, but one of the words in the list of suggestions is the correct word?
54. What is the purpose of the **Add** button in the **Check Spelling** dialog box?
55. How do you change the main dictionary for use in the **Check Spelling** dialog box?
56. Outline at least five steps that are used to create a new text style with the **Text Style** dialog box.
57. Identify at least four different ways to open the **Properties** window, including all keyboard shortcuts.
58. Describe two ways to select text objects to change when using the **Properties** window.
59. How do you change the text layer in the **Properties** window?
60. Explain how to edit text in the **Properties** window.
61. Name the command that allows you to find a piece of text and replace it with an alternative piece of text in a single instance or for every instance in your drawing.

Drawing Problems

1. Start AutoCAD, use the setup option of your choice, and create text styles as needed. Use the **TEXT** command to type the following information. Change the text style to represent each of the four fonts named. Use a .25 unit text height and 0° rotation angle. Save the drawing as P8-1.

   TXT–AUTOCAD'S DEFAULT TEXT FONT WHICH IS AVAILABLE FOR USE WHEN YOU BEGIN A DRAWING.
   ROMANS–SMOOTHER THAN TXT FONT AND CLOSELY DUPLICATES THE SINGLE-STROKE LETTERING THAT HAS BEEN THE STANDARD FOR DRAFTING.
   ROMANC–A MULTISTROKE DECORATIVE FONT THAT IS GOOD FOR USE IN DRAWING TITLES
   ITALICC–AN ORNAMENTAL FONT SLANTED TO THE RIGHT AND HAVING THE SAME LETTER DESIGN AS THE COMPLEX FONT.

2. Start AutoCAD and use the setup option of your choice and create text styles as needed. Change the options as noted in each line of text. Then use the **TEXT** command to type the text, changing the text style to represent each of the four fonts named. Use a .25 unit text height. Save the drawing as P8-2.

   TXT–EXPAND THE WIDTH BY THREE.
   MONOTXT–SLANT TO THE LEFT –30°.
   ROMANS–SLANT TO THE RIGHT 30°.
   ROMAND–BACKWARDS.
   ROMANC–VERTICAL.
   ITALICC–UNDERSCORED AND OVERSCORED.
   ROMANS–USE 16d NAILS @ 10″ OC.
   ROMANT–∅32 (812.8).

3. Start AutoCAD and use the setup option of your choice. Create text styles with a .375 height with the following font: Arial, BankGothic LtBT, CityBlueprint, Stylus BT, Swis 721 BdOul BT, Vineta BT, and Wingdings. Use the **TEXT** command to type the complete alphabet and numbers 1–10 for the text fonts, all symbols available on the keyboard, and the diameter, degree, and plus/minus symbol. Save the drawing as P8-3.
4. Use the **MTEXT** command to type the following text using a text style with Romans font and .125 text height. The heading text height is .25. Check your spelling. Save the drawing as P8-4.

NOTES:
1. INTERPRET DIMENSIONS AND TOLERANCES PER ASME Y14.5M–1994.
2. REMOVE ALL BURRS AND SHARP EDGES.

CASTING NOTES UNLESS OTHERWISE SPECIFIED:
1. .31 WALL THICKNESS.
2. R.12 FILLETS.
3. R.06 ROUNDS.
4. 1.5°–3.0° DRAFT.
5. TOLERANCES:
   ±1° ANGULAR
   ±.03 TWO PLACE DIMENSIONS.
6. PROVIDE .12 THK MACHINING STOCK ON ALL MACHINE SURFACES.

5. Use the **MTEXT** command to type the following text using a text style with Stylus BT font and .125 text height. The heading text height is .188. After typing the text exactly as shown, edit the text with the following changes:
   A. Change the \ in item 7 to 1/2.
   B. Change the [in item 8 to 1.
   C. Change the 1/2 in item 8 to 3/4.
   D. Change the ^ in item 10 to a degree symbol.
   E. Check your spelling after making the changes.
   F. Save as drawing P8-5.

COMMON FRAMING NOTES:

1. ALL FRAMING LUMBER TO BE DFL #2 OR BETTER.
2. ALL HEATED WALLS @ HEATED LIVING AREAS TO BE 2 X 6 @ 24" OC.
3. ALL EXTERIOR HEADERS TO BE 2-2 X 12 UNLESS NOTED, W/ 2" RIGID INSULATION BACKING UNLESS NOTED.
4. ALL SHEAR PANELS TO BE 1/2" CDX PLY W/8d @ 4" OC @ EDGE, HDRS, & BLOCKING AND 8d @ 8" OC @ FIELD UNLESS NOTED.
5. ALL METAL CONNECTORS TO BE SIMPSON CO. OR EQUAL.
6. ALL TRUSSES TO BE 24" OC. SUBMIT TRUSS CALCS TO BUILDING DEPT. PRIOR TO ERECTION.
7. PLYWOOD ROOF SHEATHING TO BE \ STD GRADE 32/16 PLY LAID PERP TO RAFTERS. NAIL W/8d @ 6" OC @ EDGES AND 12" OC @ FIELD.
8. PROVIDE [1/2" STD GRADE T&G PLY FLOOR SHEATHING LAID PERP TO FLOOR JOISTS. NAIL W/10d @ 6" OC @ EDGES AND BLOCKING AND 12" OC @ FIELD.
9. BLOCK ALL WALLS OVER 10'-0" HIGH AT MID.
10. LET-IN BRACES TO BE 1 X 4 DIAG BRACES @ 45^ FOR ALL INTERIOR LOAD BEARING WALLS.

6. Open P4-4 and complete the window schedule by entering a text style with the Stylus BT font. Create a layer for the text. Draw the hexagonal symbols in the SYM column. Save the drawing as P8-6.

7. Open P4-2 and complete the door schedule by entering a text style with the Stylus BT font. Create a layer for the text. Draw the circle symbols in the SYM column. Save the drawing as P8-7.

8. Open P5-14 and complete the finish schedule by entering a text style with the Stylus BT font. Save the drawing as P8-8.

9. Open P4-6 and complete the block diagram by entering the text using a text style with the Romans font. Create a layer for the text. Save the drawing as P8-9.

10. Open P4-7 and complete the block diagram by entering a text style with the Romans font. Create a layer for the text. Save the drawing as P8-10.

11. Open P5-11 and add text to the circuit diagram. Use a text style with the Romans font. Create a layer for the text. Save the drawing as P8-11.

12. Add title blocks, borders, and text styles to the template drawings you created in earlier chapters. Create a Border layer for the borderlines and thick title block lines. Create a Title block layer for thin title block lines and text. Make three template drawings with borders and title blocks for your future drawings. Use the following guidelines:
    A. Prototype 1 for A-size, 8 1/2 × 11 drawings, named TITLEA–MECH.
    B. Prototype 2 for B-size, 11 × 17 drawings, named TITLEB–MECH.
    C. Prototype 3 for C-size, 17 × 22 drawings, named TITLEC–MECH.
    D. Set the following values for the drawing aids:
    Units = three-place decimal
    Grid = .500
    Snap = .250
    E. Draw a border 1/2″ from the drawing limits.
    F. Design a title block using created text styles. Place it in the lower-right corner of each drawing. The title block should contain the following information: company or school name, address, date (field), drawn by, approved by, scale, title, drawing number, material, revision number. See the example below.
    G. Record the information about each template in a log.

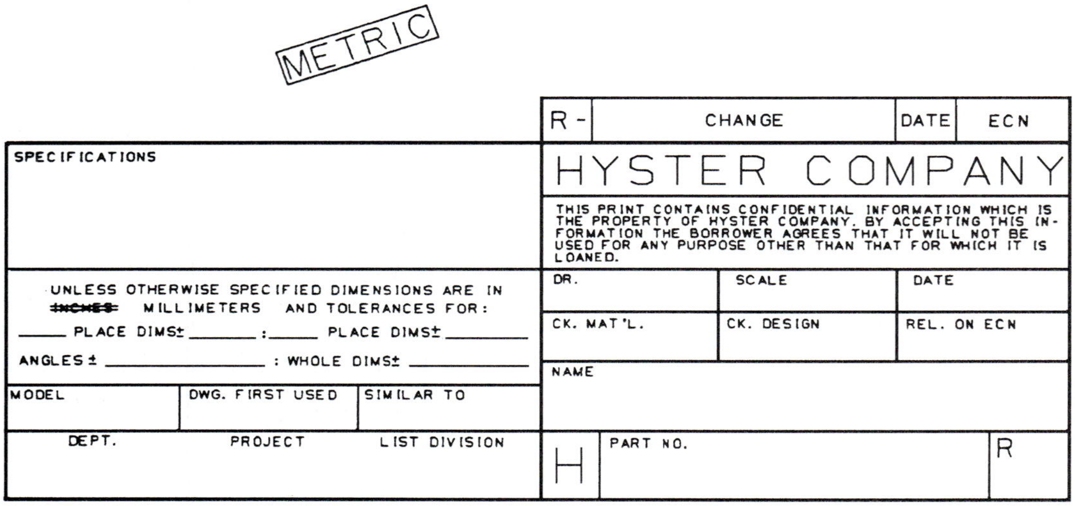

13. Draw a small parts list (similar to the one shown below) connected to your C-size prototype title block.
    A. Enter PARTS LIST with a style containing a complex font.
    B. Enter the other information using text and the **TEXT** command. Do not exit the **TEXT** command to start a new line of text.
    C. Save the drawing as TITLEC-PARTS.
    D. Record the information about the template in a log.

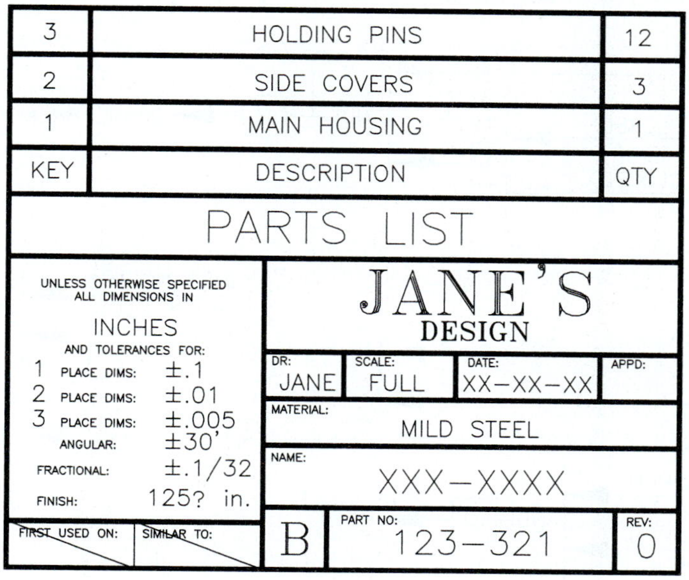

14. Draw an architectural template for a 17″ × 22″ or 22″ × 34″ sheet size with a title block along the right side similar to the one shown below. Use the same layout and layer instructions given for Problem 12. Save the drawing as ARCH. Record the information about the template in a log.

15. Draw title blocks with borders for your electrical, piping, and general drawings. Use the same instructions provided in Problem 12. The title block can be similar to the one displayed with Problem 12, but the area for mechanical drafting tolerances is not required. Research sample title blocks to come up with your design. Save the templates as **ELEC A**, **ELEC B**, **PIPE A**, **PIPE B**, or another name related to the drawing type and sheet size.

16. Draw the AND/OR schematic shown below. Save your drawing as **P8-16**.

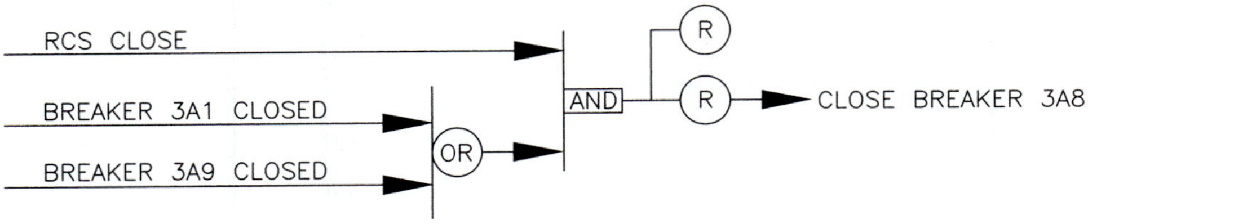

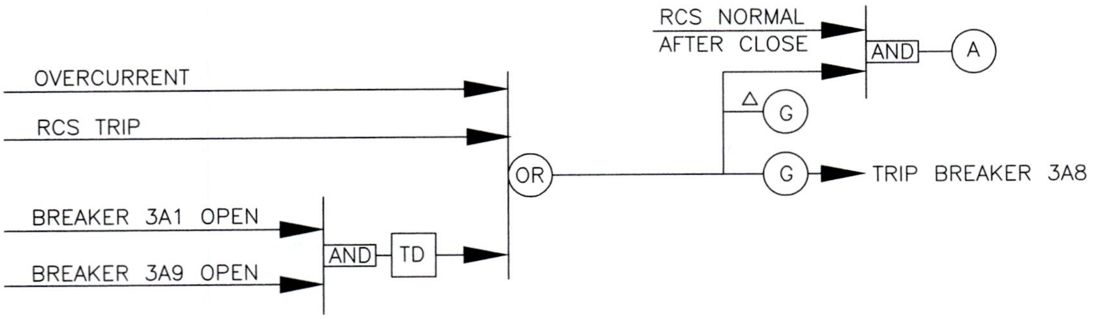

17. Draw the controller schematic shown below. Save your drawing as **P8-17**.

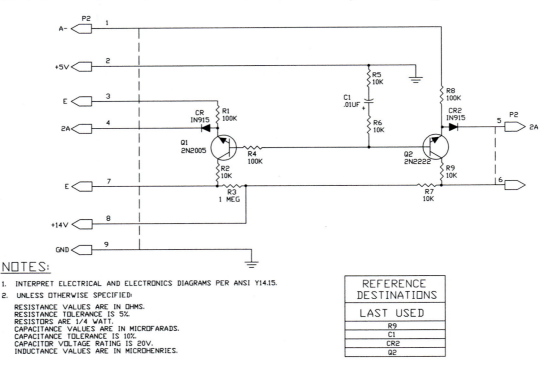

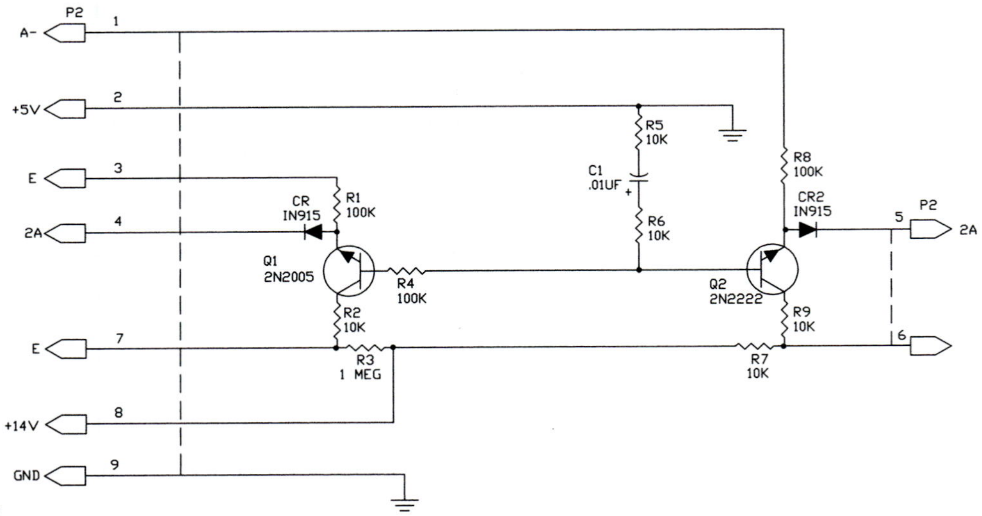

NOTES:

1. INTERPRET ELECTRICAL AND ELECTRONICS DIAGRAMS PER ANSI Y14.15.
2. UNLESS OTHERWISE SPECIFIED:

RESISTANCE VALUES ARE IN OHMS.
RESISTANCE TOLERANCE IS 5%.
RESISTORS ARE 1/4 WATT.
CAPACITANCE VALUES ARE IN MICROFARADS.
CAPACITANCE TOLERANCE IS 10%.
CAPACITOR VOLTAGE RATING IS 20V.
INDUCTANCE VALUES ARE IN MICROHENRIES.

REFERENCE DESTINATIONS
LAST USED
R9
C1
CR2
Q2

CHAPTER 9

Working with Tables

Learning Objectives

After completing this chapter, you will be able to do the following:

- Create a table with a style for use in a specific drafting discipline.
- Enter text into a table.
- Edit a table.
- Import table data from another source.

A *table* consists of rows and columns that organize data to make it easier to read. Tables are commonly used in drafting to show information such as bills of materials, door and window schedules, legends, and title block information.

Inserting Tables

AutoCAD 2005 NEW FEATURE

The **TABLE** command allows you to insert a table by specifying the number of rows and columns. Once the table is inserted, text can be typed into the table cells. You can also insert blocks and fields into table cells. Tables can contain specific format settings, then saved, and used in the same drawing or even other drawing files. This saves valuable drafting time and ensures that school or company standards are followed.

TABLE
TB
Draw
➥Table...
Draw toolbar
Table

To insert a table, pick **Table...** from the **Draw** pull-down menu, pick the **Table** button in the **Draw** toolbar, or enter TB or TABLE at the Command: prompt. This opens the **Insert Table** dialog box, Figure 9-1. In the **Table Style Settings** area, a table style can be selected from the **Table Style name** drop-down list, or the ellipsis (**...**) button can be selected to create or modify a style. Text height indicates the current text height setting for the table style and the preview area shows a preview of a table with the current table style settings. The preview area does not adjust to the column and row settings, but shows table style properties such as text font, text color, and background color.

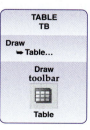

A table can be inserted by picking an insertion point or by windowing an area. This option is set in the **Insertion Behavior** area. If **Specify insertion point** is selected, picking the **OK** button prompts for an insertion point. When this option is used, the table is created by using the values in the **Column & Row Settings** area. The following

Figure 9-1.
The **Insert Table** dialog box.

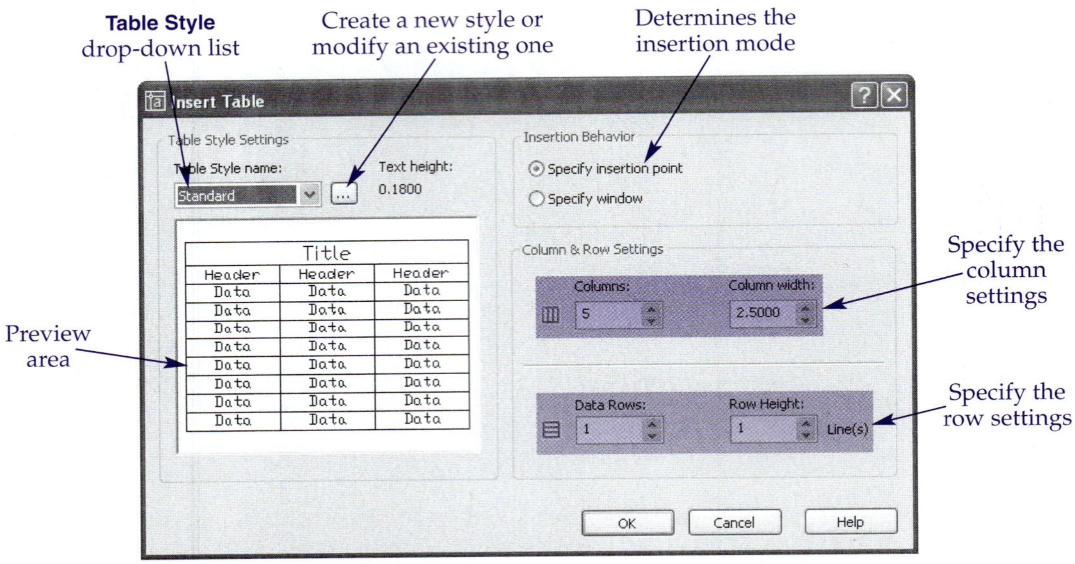

are the steps to create a table with three columns and five data rows using **Insertion point**:

1. Enter TABLE at the Command: prompt.
2. Pick the **Specify insertion point** radio button. See **Figure 9-2A.**
3. Enter the following settings:

   Columns: 3, Column width: 2.5, Data Rows: 5, and Row Height: 1

4. Pick **OK** to accept the settings.
5. Pick on the upper-left area of the drawing area to place the table.
6. Pick **OK** to finish.

If a table needs to be created to fit into a designated area, the **Specify window** option could be used. When this option is selected, only one of the column and row settings is available. This is because when the **OK** button is picked, you are prompted to select the upper-left and lower-right corners for the table. The fixed **Column & Row Settings** are used and the number of data rows is adjusted to fit the window. The following are the steps to create a table with three columns and five data rows using **Specify window**:

1. Enter TABLE at the Command: prompt.
2. Pick the **Specify window** radio button. See **Figure 9-2B.**
3. Enter the following settings:

   Columns: 3 and Row Height: 1

4. Pick **OK** to accept the settings.
5. Pick on the upper-left area of the drawing area to place the table.
6. Move the cursor to the lower-right until you see five data rows and three columns.
7. Pick on the drawing area to create the table.
8. Pick **OK** to finish.

The number of columns and rows and their width and height, are set in the **Column & Row Settings** area. After a table is inserted, these settings can be adjusted in other ways, so it is not crucial that the exact number of columns and rows are entered before the table is created. The following options are available in the **Column & Row Settings** area:

- **Columns.** The number of columns you want to start out with in the table.
- **Column width.** The width of each column in inches.

Figure 9-2.
There are two ways to insert a table. A—Single insertion point. B—Specify window.

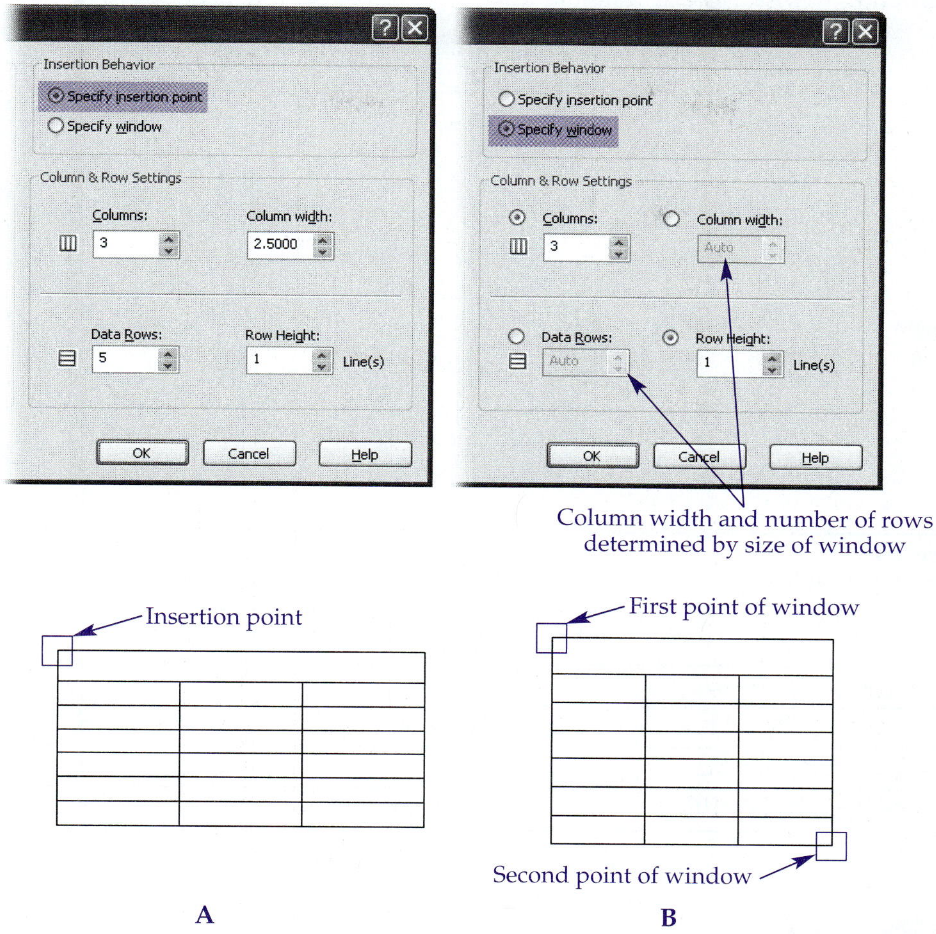

- **Data Rows.** The number of data rows you want to start out with in the table. This number does not include the Title and Header rows.
- **Row height.** This is the height of each row. This value is determined by the text height and cell margin in the current table style.

EXERCISE 9-1 Complete the Exercise on the Student CD.

Entering Text into a Table

AutoCAD 2005 NEW FEATURE

Once a table is inserted, the **Text Formatting** toolbar appears above the table and the text cursor is placed in the top cell ready for typing. The active cell is indicated by a dashed line around its border and a light gray background. Figure 9-3 shows a newly inserted table. Before typing, adjust the text settings in the **Text Formatting** toolbar if needed. When you are done entering the text in the active cell, press the [Tab] key to move to the next cell. Holding the [Shift] key and pressing the [Tab] key moves the active cell backwards (to the left and up). Pressing the [Enter] key makes the cell directly below the current one active. The arrow keys on the keyboard can also be used to navigate through the cells in a table. When you are done entering text in the table, pick the **OK** button on the **Text Formatting** toolbar or pick anywhere in the drawing area to exit the **TABLE** command. Figure 9-4 shows a completed table.

Figure 9-3.
The active cell is indicated by a blinking cursor, a dashed border, and a light gray background.

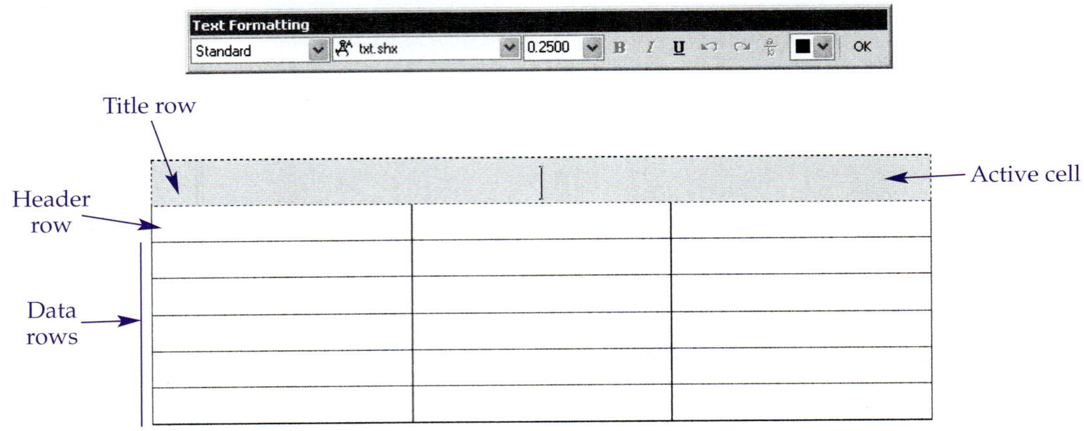

Figure 9-4.
A completed table.

Parts List		
Part Number	Part Type	Qty
100-SCR-45	Screw	18
202-BLT-32	Bolt	18
340-WSHR-06	Washer	18

EXERCISE 9-2 Complete the Exercise on the Student CD.

Editing Tables

AutoCAD 2005 NEW FEATURE

There are two levels of table editing: cell editing and table layout editing. Cell editing can include modifying the text content within a cell or changing the formatting (such as font type or text background) of the cell. Table layout editing can include changing the row heights and column width or changing the formatting of the entire table. These topics are discussed in the following sections.

Editing Table Cells

A table cell can be edited by double-clicking inside the cell, typing TABLEDIT at the Command: prompt and then selecting the cell, or by picking inside the cell, right-clicking, and selecting **Edit Cell Text** from the selected cell shortcut menu. This makes the selected cell active and the **Text Formatting** toolbar appear.

Right-clicking in an active cell displays the active cell shortcut menu. See Figure 9-5. This menu is nearly identical to the text editor shortcut menu. Refer to Chapter 8 for a discussion of the options. The active cell shortcut menu does not include the **Background Mask** and **Indents and Tabs** options. The only additional

Figure 9-5.
The cell shortcut menu is displayed when right-clicking in the active cell.

Undo	Ctrl+Z
Redo	Ctrl+Y
Cut	Ctrl+X
Copy	Ctrl+C
Paste	Ctrl+V
✔ Show Toolbar	
Insert Field...	Ctrl+F
Symbol	▶
Import Text...	
Justification	▶
Find and Replace...	Ctrl+R
Select All	Ctrl+A
Change Case	▶
AutoCAPS	
Remove Formatting	Ctrl+Space
Combine Paragraphs	
Character Set	▶
Help	F1

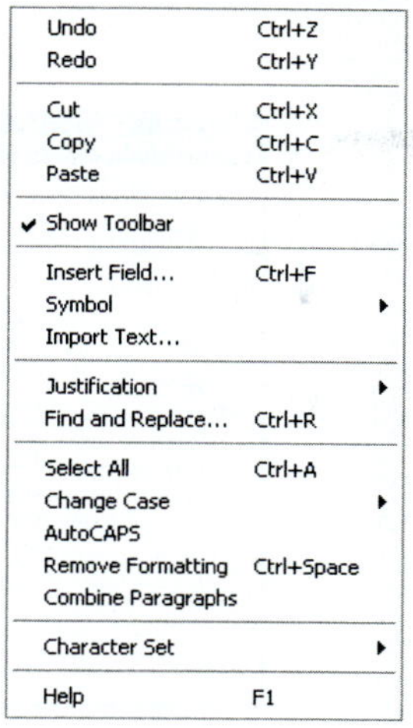

option in the active cell shortcut menu is the **Show Toolbar** option, which is active by default. If you do not want AutoCAD to display the **Text Formatting** toolbar when you work with tables, pick this option to deactivate it.

EXERCISE 9-3 Complete the Exercise on the Student CD.

Editing the Table Layout

With almost every table you work with, at some point new columns or rows need to hold more data. The size of the table may also need to be adjusted so all of the content fits into a certain area. These settings and others can be edited after a table has been created. The selected cell shortcut menu offers many of the options. To display this menu, pick inside a cell to activate grips, and then right-click. This is different from double-clicking inside of a cell to make it active. Also, make sure you pick completely inside of the cell with the pick box. If one of the cell borders is selected, then the entire table becomes the selected object. The selected cell shortcut menu is displayed as in **Figure 9-6.**

AutoCAD 2005
NEW FEATURE

Figure 9-6.
The selected cell shortcut menu gives options for editing cell properties, cell content, column settings, and row settings.

Controls border lineweight and color

Copy formatting settings from one cell to another

Available when multiple columns are selected

Available when multiple rows are selected

Same as selecting a cell and pressing [Delete] key

Windows Clipboard functions

Justification for entire cell contents

Inserts a block into the cell

Opens the **Text Formatting** toolbar

Remove or add columns

Remove or add rows

Returns properties to default settings

Combines multiple cells into one cell

Opens the **Property** window for the selected cell

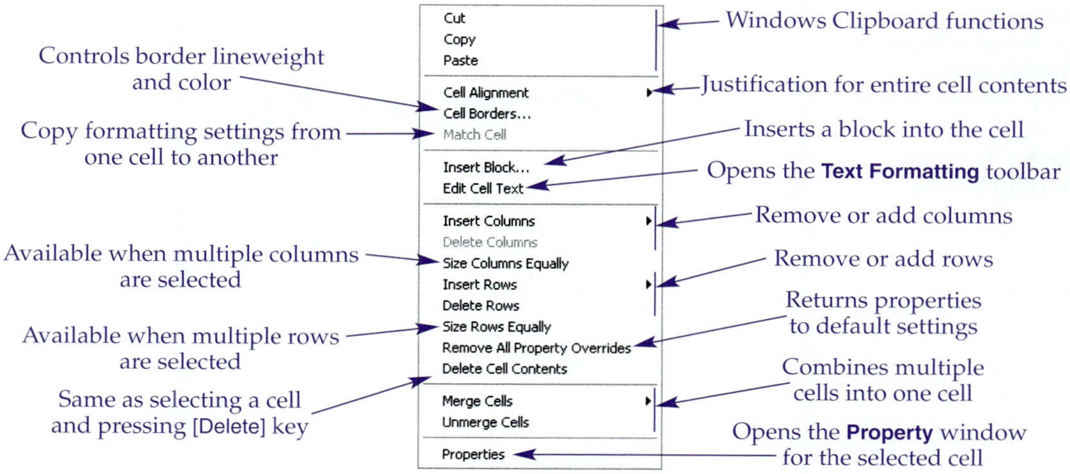

Figure 9-7.
The **Cell Border Properties** dialog box allows each cell border to have its own settings.

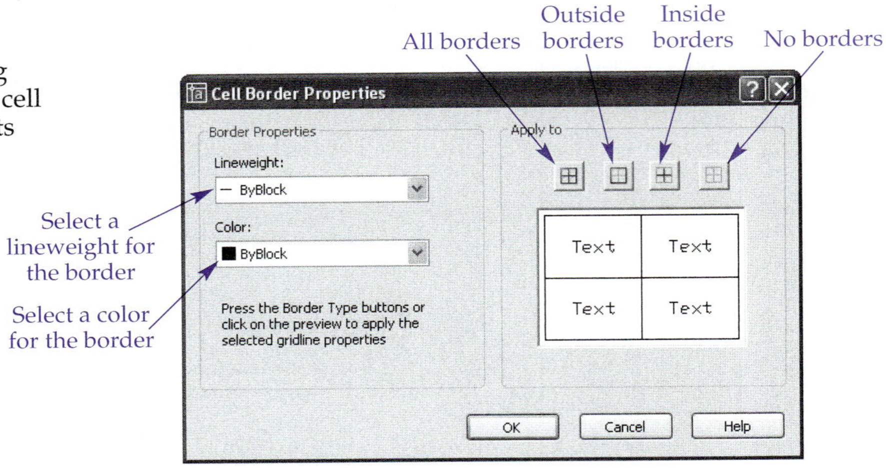

The first section of the shortcut menu offers the Windows Clipboard functions: **Cut**, **Copy**, and **Paste**. When one of these options is used, it affects the entire contents of the cell. The second section of the menu includes cell options. Each of these commands is described as follows:

- **Cell Alignment.** Selecting this option displays a cascading menu of alignment options. These work the same as justification settings seen earlier in the chapter, except they work on all the contents of a cell, not just text.
- **Cell Borders.** This opens the **Cell Border Properties** dialog box. See Figure 9-7. In the **Border Properties** area, the lineweight and border color can be set. The **Apply to** area allows you to apply the properties to all borders, outside borders, inside borders, or no borders.
- **Match Cell.** This option allows you to quickly copy formatting settings from one cell to another. To use this, select the cell that has the settings you wish to copy. Right-click and select **Match Cell** from the shortcut menu. You are then prompted to select a destination cell. Pick the cell in which you want to copy the settings to. Select another cell or right-click to exit.
- **Insert Block.** A block can be inserted into a cell using the **Insert Block...** option of the selected cell shortcut menu. This is useful when creating a legend, or to show the images of parts in a column. Blocks are discussed in detail in Chapter 22. Selecting **Insert Block...** from the shortcut menu opens the **Insert a Block in a Table Cell** dialog box as shown in Figure 9-8. The following options are available:

Figure 9-8.
The **Insert a Block in a Table cell** dialog box is opened when selecting **Insert Block...** from the shortcut menu.

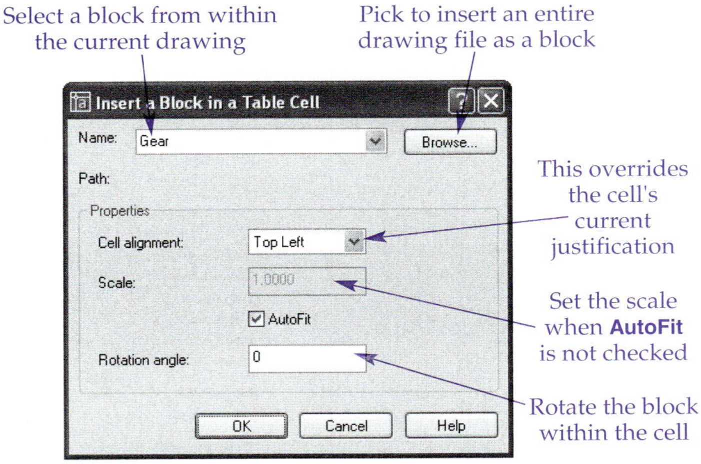

- **Name.** A block that is stored in the current drawing can be selected from the **Name** drop-down list.
- **Browse.** Picking this button displays the **Select Drawing File** dialog box, where a drawing file can be selected and inserted into the table cell as a block.
- **Cell alignment.** This determines the justification of the block in the cell. This setting overrides the current cell alignment setting.
- **Scale.** Enter a block insertion scale. A value of 2 inserts the block twice its original size. A value of 0.5 inserts the block half of its created size. If **AutoFit** is checked, the **Scale** option is not available.
- **AutoFit.** Scales the block automatically to fit inside of the cell.
- **Rotation angle.** Rotates the block the specified amount.

NOTE

Text and a block cannot reside in the same cell. If a block is inserted into a cell that contains text, the text is erased and the block is inserted. Double-clicking in a cell that contains a block opens the **Insert a Block in a Table Cell** dialog box.

- **Edit Cell Text.** This opens the **Text Formatting** toolbar and makes the current cell active. It is the same as double-clicking in a cell as discussed earlier.
- **Insert Columns.** Places a new column to the left or right of the selected cell.
- **Delete Columns.** Deletes the column that the selected cell is in.
- **Size Columns Equally.** Automatically adjusts the selected columns to be the same width. This option is only available when cells belonging to multiple columns are selected.
- **Insert Rows.** Creates a new row in the table. The options from the cascading menu are **Below** and **Above**.
- **Delete Rows.** Deletes the row that the selected cell is in.
- **Size Rows Equally.** Automatically sizes the selected rows to be the same height. This option is only available when cells belonging to multiple rows are selected.
- **Remove All Property Overrides.** Picking this option returns all property settings of the selected cell to the default settings.
- **Delete Cell Contents.** Deletes the contents in the selected cell. It is the same as selecting a cell and pressing the [Delete] key.
- **Merge Cells.** To use this option, multiple cells need to be selected. You can select multiple cells by picking in a cell and dragging the window over the other cells. When the pick button is released, all of the cells touching the window become selected. An example of this is shown in **Figure 9-9A.** Multiple cells can also be selected by picking a cell, holding the [Shift] key, and then picking another cell. The picked cells and the cells in between the picked cells are then selected. See **Figure 9-9B.** To merge cells together, select the cells to be merged and then pick **Merge Cells** from the selected cell shortcut menu.
- **Unmerge Cells.** This option separates merged cells back into individual cells.
- **Properties.** Selecting this option opens the **Properties** window of the selected cell. These properties are shown in **Figure 9-10** and are explained here:
  - **Cell width.** Type a value to adjust the cell width. This also affects the other cells in the column.
  - **Cell height.** Type a value to adjust the cell height. This also affects the other cells in the row.
  - **Background fill.** Select a color from the drop-down list to change the cell background color.
  - **Text rotation.** Rotates the text in the current cell.

Figure 9-9.
Selecting multiple cells in a table for editing. A—Using the pick and drag method. B—Picking a range of cells using the [Shift] key.

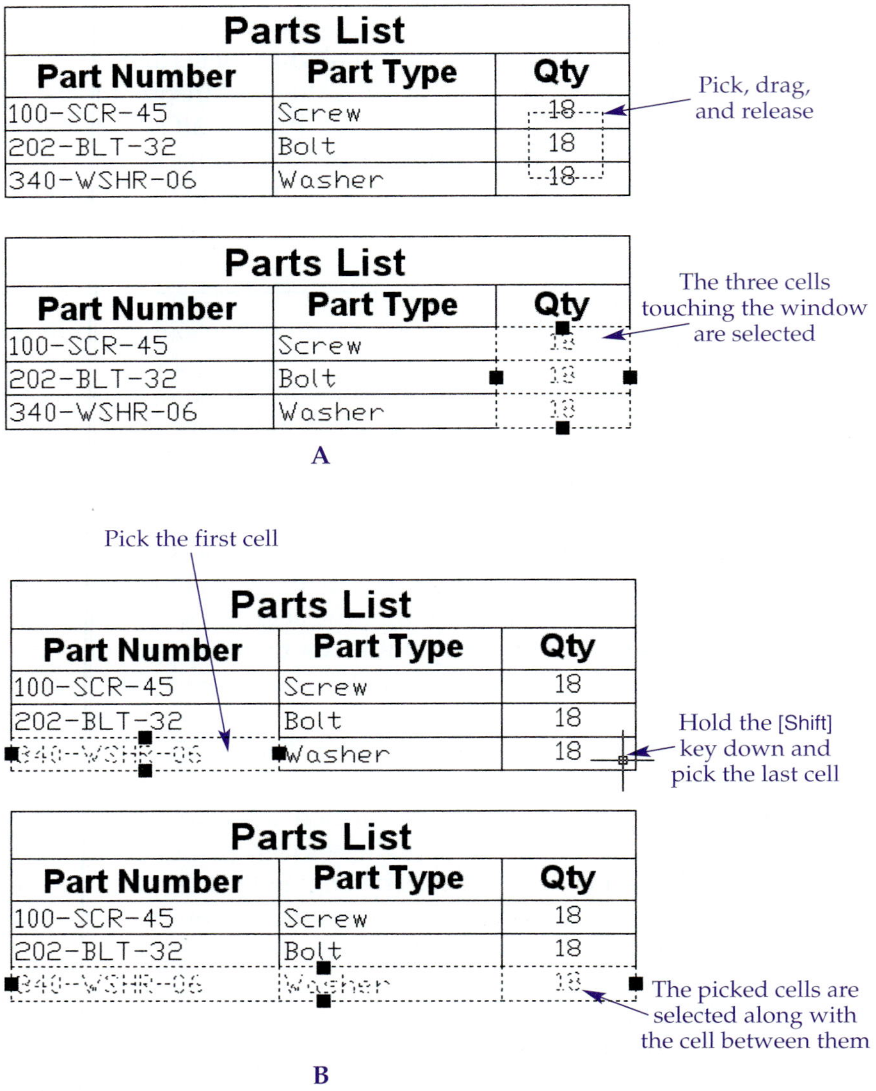
Parts List
Part Number
Part Type
Qty
100-SCR-45
Screw
18
202-BLT-32
Bolt
18
340-WSHR-06
Washer
18
Pick, drag, and release
The three cells touching the window are selected
A
Pick the first cell
Hold the [Shift] key down and pick the last cell
The picked cells are selected along with the cell between them
B

EXERCISE 9-4

Complete the Exercise on the Student CD.

PROFESSIONAL TIP

The size of the columns and rows can also be adjusted using grips. Selecting any of the cell borders activates the grips. To resize a column or row, select a grip and then move the mouse and pick. Grips are discussed in detail in Chapter 13.

Figure 9-10.
The **Properties** window displayed while a cell is selected. Some of the cell settings can only be modified in the **Properties** window.

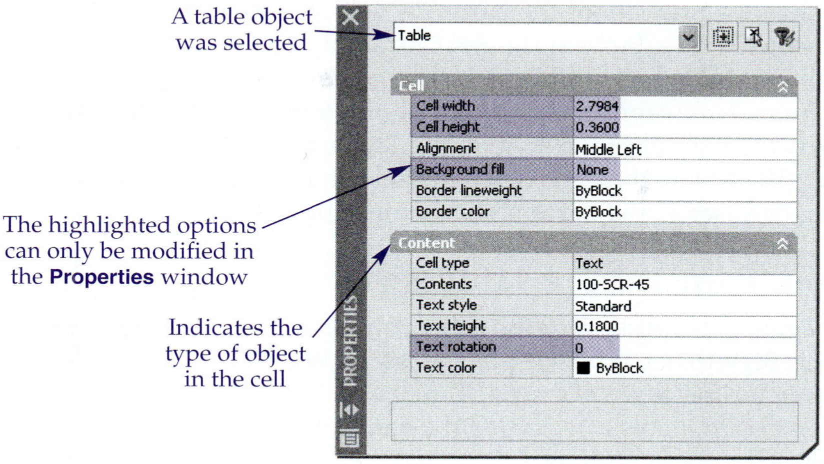

Table Styles

When working for a company, drafting standards are used to create a consistent appearance of the drawings. Other desired standards can also be used on a project for special purposes. Formatting standards are used in tables and can include settings such as the text height, text font, spacing, and alignment. These settings and others can be preset in tables by using table styles.

AutoCAD 2005
NEW FEATURE

Working with Table Styles

TABLESTYLE
TS
Format
➥ Table Style...
Styles toolbar
Table Style Manager

The **Table Style** dialog box allows you to create, modify, and delete table styles. To open the **Table Style** dialog box, select **Table Style...** from the **Format** pull-down menu, select the **Table Style Manager** button in the **Styles** toolbar, or enter TS or TABLESTYLE at the Command: prompt. The **Table Style** dialog box can also be opened from the **Insert Table** dialog box by picking the ellipsis (**...**) button (shown in **Figure 9-1**). The **Table Style** dialog box is displayed in **Figure 9-11.**

Figure 9-11.
The **Table Style** dialog box.

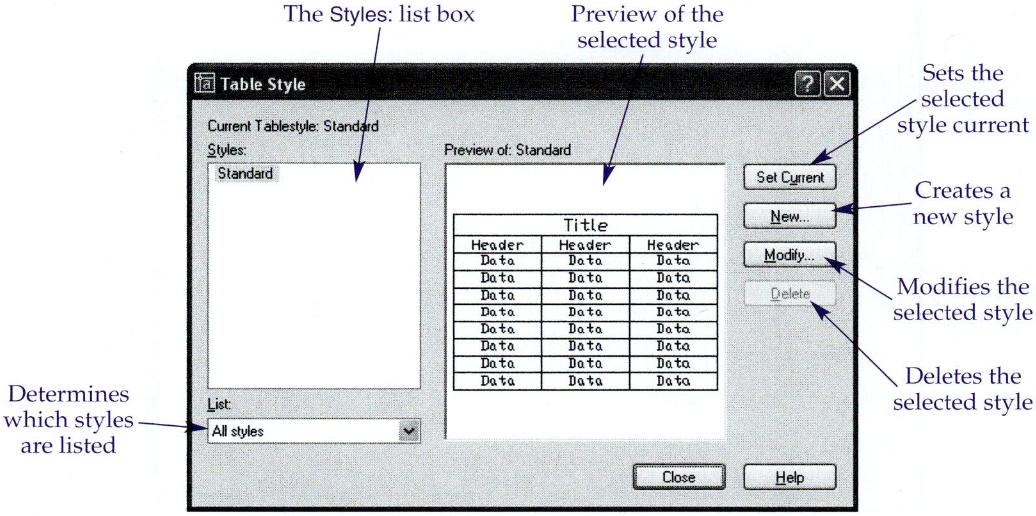

The **Styles** list box displays all of the table styles available in the current drawing when the **List** drop-down list is set to All styles. When the **List** drop-down list is set to Styles in use, only the table styles used in the drawing appear in the list box. The **Preview** area shows a preview of the currently selected style. To select a style, pick it once in the **Styles** list box. Picking the **Set Current** button sets the selected style to be the current table style. When a table is inserted into the drawing, it uses the formatting settings from the current table style. Use the **New** button to create a new table style. To modify a style, select the style in the **Styles** list box and then pick the **Modify** button. Picking the **Delete** button deletes the selected style. A style that is being used in the drawing or is set as the current style cannot be deleted.

Creating and Formatting a Table Style

AutoCAD 2005 NEW FEATURE

To create a new table style, pick the **New...** button in the **Table Style** dialog box. The **Create New Table Style** dialog box is displayed. See **Figure 9-12.** In the **New Style Name** text box, type a name for the new table style. The new table can be based on the formatting settings from an existing table by selecting the name of the table style from the **Start With** drop-down list. After these settings are specified, pick the **Continue** button to open the **New Table Style** dialog box. This dialog box is shown in **Figure 9-13.**

Figure 9-12.
In the **Create New Table Style** dialog box, specify the new table style's name and the existing style that will be copied.

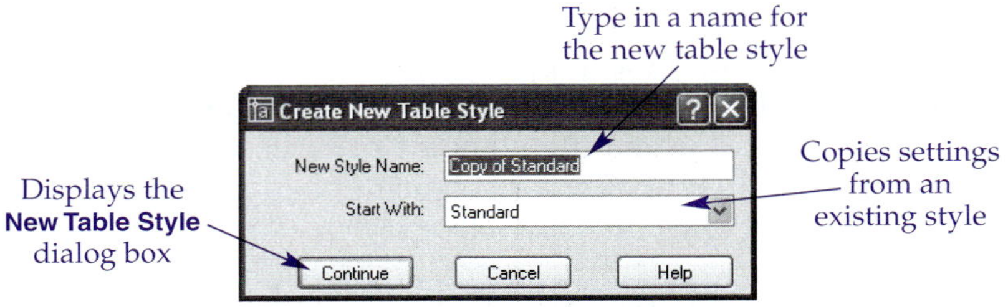

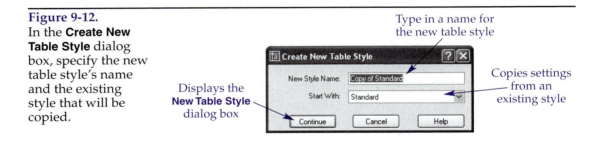

Figure 9-13.
When creating a new table style, the formatting properties are specified in the **New Table Style** dialog box.

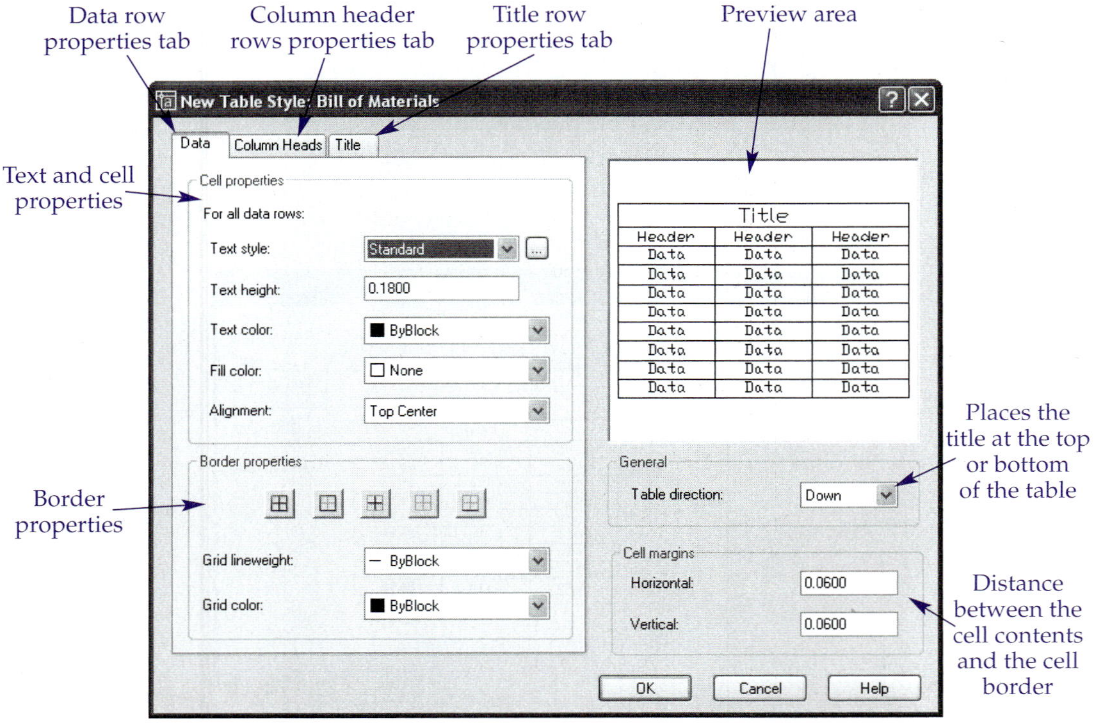

The tabs at the top left of the **New Table Style** dialog box allow for the data rows, columns header rows, and the title row to have their own formatting properties. Picking the tabs displays the properties for each row type. In Figure 9-13 the **Data** tab is selected.

The text and cell formatting properties are set in the **Cell properties** area. The following options are available:

- **Text style.** This is a drop-down list that displays all of the text styles that are in the current drawing. If you want a cell to use text settings such as bold or italicized, these can be preset in a text style. If a new text style needs to be created or an existing one needs to be modified, picking the ellipsis (**...**) button to the right of the drop-down list opens the **Text Style** dialog box. Text styles were discussed in Chapter 8.
- **Text height.** Specify the height of the text. This field uses the unit setting specified in the **Drawing Units** dialog box. If a text height of other then 0 has been set in the text style, this field is grayed out.
- **Text color.** Used to set the color of the text.
- **Fill color.** This is the background color of the cells. The default setting is None. This forces the cells to use the background color of the current drawing. If you want the cell background color to be different from the drawing background, select the color from the drop-down list.
- **Alignment.** This drop-down list shows the different cell justification options.

Cell borders can be set to different lineweights and colors. There are options for different border styles available in the **Border properties** area of each data row specification. The five buttons at the top of this area are the different border styles that are available. Figure 9-14 shows an example of each border style. The **Border style option** buttons from left to right are as follows:

- **All Borders**
- **Outside Borders**
- **Inside Borders**
- **No Borders**
- **Bottom Borders**

Select a preset value from the **Grid lineweight** drop-down list to assign a lineweight to the cell borders. The color of the cell borders is set with the **Grid color** drop-down list.

> **NOTE** AutoCAD displays border lineweights only if lineweights are being displayed. Pick the **LWT** button to display lineweights.

Figure 9-14.
There are five different border options to choose from. Changes shown were applied to the table's data area only.

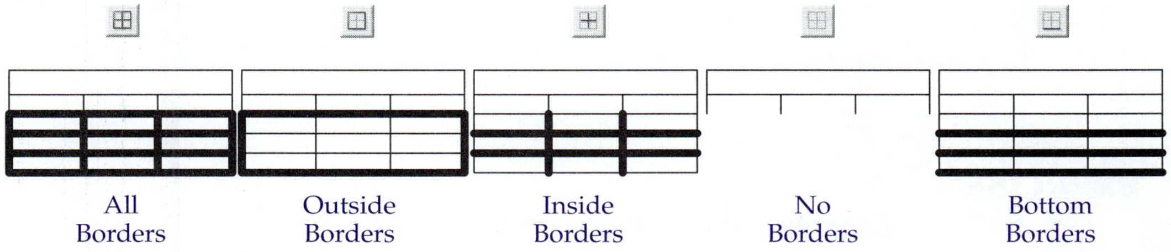

The **Table direction** setting in the **General** area determines the placement of the data rows. The two options are **Down** and **Up**. When set to **Down**, the data rows are below the title and header rows. When set to **Up**, the data rows are above the title and header rows. The difference can be viewed in the preview window by selecting the different options.

The spacing between the cell content (text or block) and the borders is set in the **Cell margins** area. The values in the **Horizontal** and **Vertical** text boxes determine the spacing between the content and the cell border. The default setting for US Customary is 0.06 and for metric is 1.5.

The **Column Heads** and **Title** tabs have the same format settings that are found in the **Data** tab. They do have one additional setting that allows you to turn off these rows if they are not needed. If the **Include Header row** check box in the **Column Heads** tab is checked, the header row is used. If unchecked, the header row is hidden. See **Figure 9-15.** The **Title** tab has a similar option called **Include Title row.**

> **NOTE**
>
> If a cell's formatting properties have been specified in the **Text Formatting** toolbar, the active cell shortcut menu, or the **Properties** window, these settings override the table style settings.

Figure 9-15.
The **Include Header row** option is found on the **Column Heads** tab and the **Include Title row** option is located on the **Title** tab.

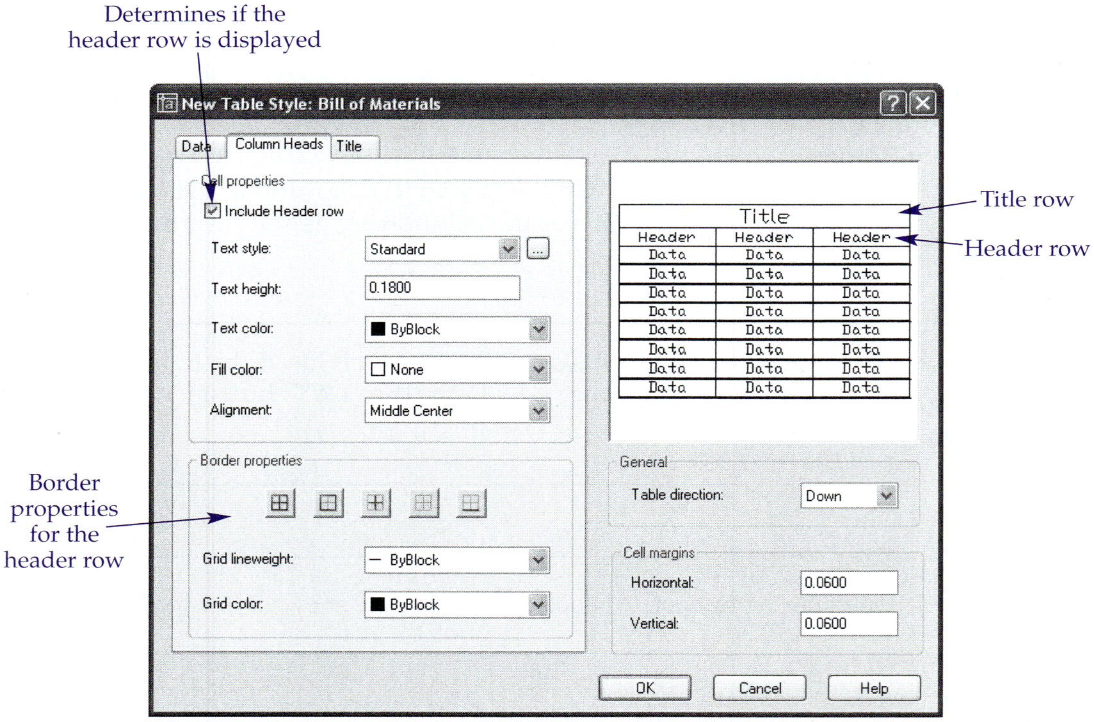

EXERCISE 9-5 Complete the Exercise on the Student CD.

PROFESSIONAL TIP

If table data has already been created in Microsoft® Excel, this table can be imported into AutoCAD. This process is discussed in ***AutoCAD and its Applications—Advanced.***

Chapter Test

Answer the following questions on a separate sheet of paper.

1. List three ways to open the **Insert Table** dialog box.
2. Name the two options for inserting a table and explain the difference.
3. By default, what toolbar opens after the table has been inserted?
4. If you are done typing in one cell and want to move to the next cell in the same row, what two keyboard keys will allow you to do this?
5. List two ways to make a cell active for editing.
6. Name the three types of rows that can be used in a table.
7. Which of these options can be inserted into a cell: block, hatch pattern, text, raster image?
8. How would you insert a new row at the bottom of the table?
9. Why would you create a table style?
10. Does the preview window in the **Table Style** dialog box show: a preview of the current style or of the selected style?
11. What does the **Alignment** setting in the **New Table Style** dialog box do?
12. Which setting would you adjust in the **New Table Style** dialog box to increase the spacing between the text and the top of the cell?
13. How would you hide the Title row?
14. In which type of table row would the following information be found: Title, column header, or data?
    A. Door Number
    B. 3′6″× 6′8″
    C. Wood
    D. Door Size
    E. Door Schedule
    F. Quantity

Drawing Problems

Load AutoCAD for each of the following problems, and use one of your templates or start a new drawing using your own variables.

1. Create a bill of materials for a mechanical drawing with the content of your choice, or locate a drawing with a bill of materials and duplicate your findings.
2. Create a door and window schedule for an architectural drawing with the content of your choice, or locate a drawing with a door and window schedule and duplicate your findings.
3. Create a legend for a civil drawing with the content of your choice, or locate a drawing with a legend and duplicate your findings.
4. Create a parts list for a mechanical drawing with the content of your choice, or locate a drawing with a parts list and duplicate your findings.

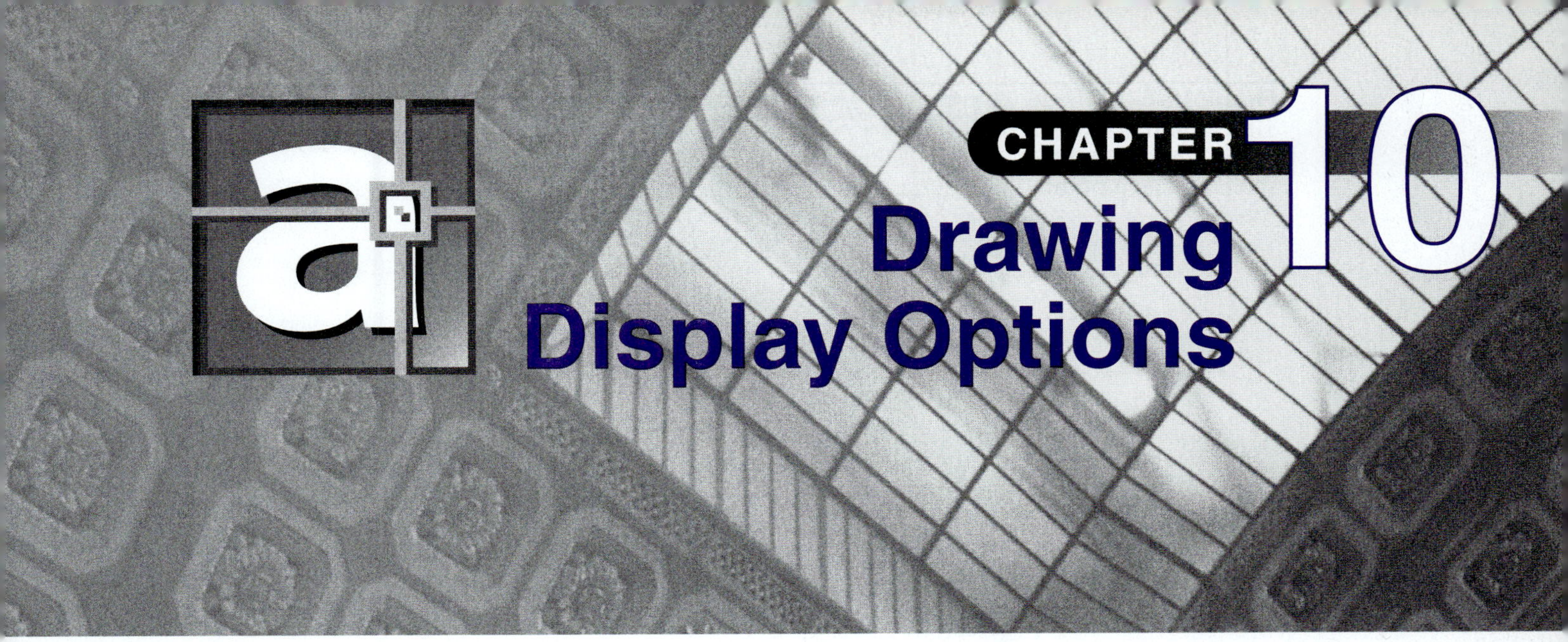

CHAPTER 10

Drawing Display Options

Learning Objectives

After completing this chapter, you will be able to do the following:

- Explain the differences between the **REDRAW** command and the **REGEN** command.
- Magnify a small part of the drawing to work on details.
- Move the display window to reveal portions of the drawing outside the boundaries of the monitor.
- Create named views that can be recalled instantly.
- Use the **Aerial View** window.
- Define the terms *model space* and *paper space.*
- Create multiple viewports in the graphics window.
- Create 3D viewpoints with the **3DORBIT** command and preset viewpoints.
- Control display order.

You can view a specific portion of a drawing using the AutoCAD display commands. The **ZOOM** command is used to enlarge or reduce the amount of the drawing displayed. The portion displayed can also be moved using the **PAN** command. *Panning* is like looking through a camera and moving the camera across the drawing. Using the **Aerial View** window, you can locate a particular area of the drawing to view. Use the **VIEW** command to create and name specific views of the drawing. When further drawing or editing operations are required, the view can be quickly and easily recalled.

Display functions allow you to work in model space or paper space. *Model space* is used for drawing and designing, while *paper space* is used for plotting. Detailed information on the use of model space and paper space to prepare multiview drawings is provided in Chapter 11.

This chapter also discusses the differences between the **REDRAW** and **REGEN** commands. Additionally, using the **REGENAUTO** and **VIEWRES** commands to achieve optimum display speeds and quality is discussed.

Redrawing and Regenerating the Screen

REDRAW
R
View
➥ Redraw

A *blip* is a small cross that is displayed when a point is picked on the screen. See Figure 10-1. These blips are not part of your drawing; they are visual indicators of pick positions that stay on the screen until it is redrawn. The **REDRAW** command is used to clean the blips from the screen and refresh the display of objects after editing operations.

Figure 10-1.
Tiny crosshairs, or blips, appear on the screen when a point is selected.

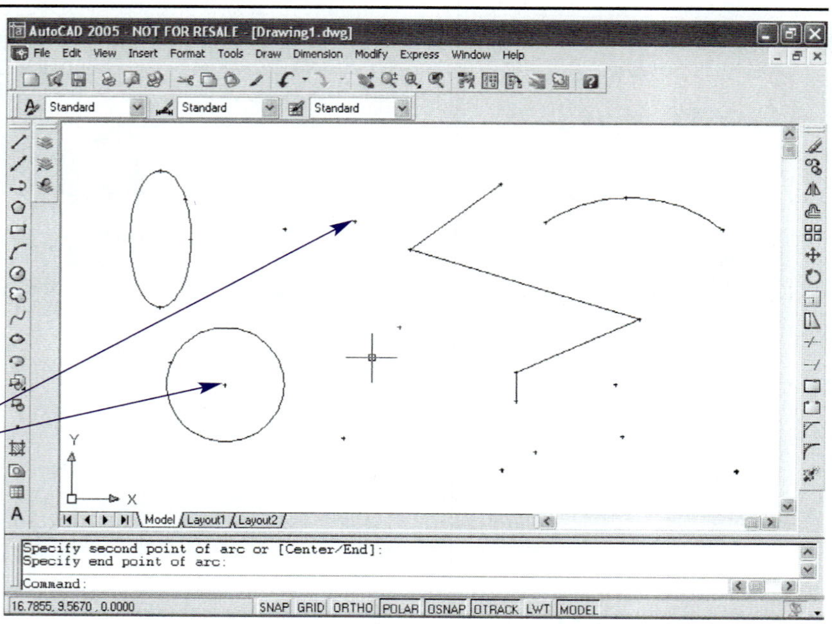

Redraw the screen by selecting **Redraw** from the **View** pull-down menu or by entering R or REDRAW at the Command: prompt.

> **PROFESSIONAL TIP**
>
> Using **REDRAW** every time blips appear slows your drawing sessions. Redraw the screen only when the blips interfere with the drawing process.

The **REDRAW** command simply refreshes the current screen. To regenerate the screen, the **REGEN** command is used. This command recalculates all drawing object coordinates and regenerates the display based on the current zoom magnification. For example, if you have zoomed in on objects in your drawing and curved edges appear to be straight segments, using **REGEN** will smooth the curves.

> **REGEN**
> **RE**
>
> **View**
> ➥ **Regen**

To access the **REGEN** command, pick **Regen** from the **View** pull-down menu or enter RE or REGEN at the Command: prompt. The screen is immediately regenerated.

Blips are often turned off to eliminate the need for redraws. Blips can be turned on or off by entering the **BLIPMODE** command at the Command: prompt and then entering either ON or OFF as desired.

> **PROFESSIONAL TIP**
>
> Turning **BLIPMODE** off affects the current drawing only. If you want blips to be off in new drawings, turn **BLIPMODE** off in the template drawing.

Getting Close to Your Work

Zooming in (magnifying) on a drawing gives designers the ability to create extremely small items, such as the electronic circuits found in a computer. The **ZOOM** command is a helpful tool that you will use often. The different options of the **ZOOM** command are discussed in the next sections.

The ZOOM Options

ZOOM
Z

View
➥ **Zoom**

Each of the **ZOOM** options can be accessed by its corresponding button in the **Standard** toolbar, or by selecting the option in the **Zoom** cascading menu from the **View** pull-down menu. All the buttons in the **Zoom** flyout are also found in the **Zoom** toolbar. See **Figure 10-2.** All **ZOOM** options except **In** and **Out** are available at the Command: prompt:

Command: **Z** *or* **ZOOM**↵
Specify corner of window, enter a scale factor (nX or nXP), or
[All/Center/Dynamic/Extents/Previous/Scale/Window/Object] <real time>:

The **ZOOM** options are as follows:

- **real time.** The default option allows you to perform realtime zooming. This interactive zooming is discussed later in this chapter.
- **All.** Zooms to the edge of the drawing limits. If objects are drawn beyond the limits, the **All** option zooms to the edges of your geometry. Always use this option after you change the drawing limits.
- **Center.** Zoom the center of the display screen to a picked point. If you want to zoom to the center of an area of the drawing and want to magnify the view as well, then pick the center and height of the area in the drawing. Rather than a height, a magnification factor can be entered by typing a number followed by

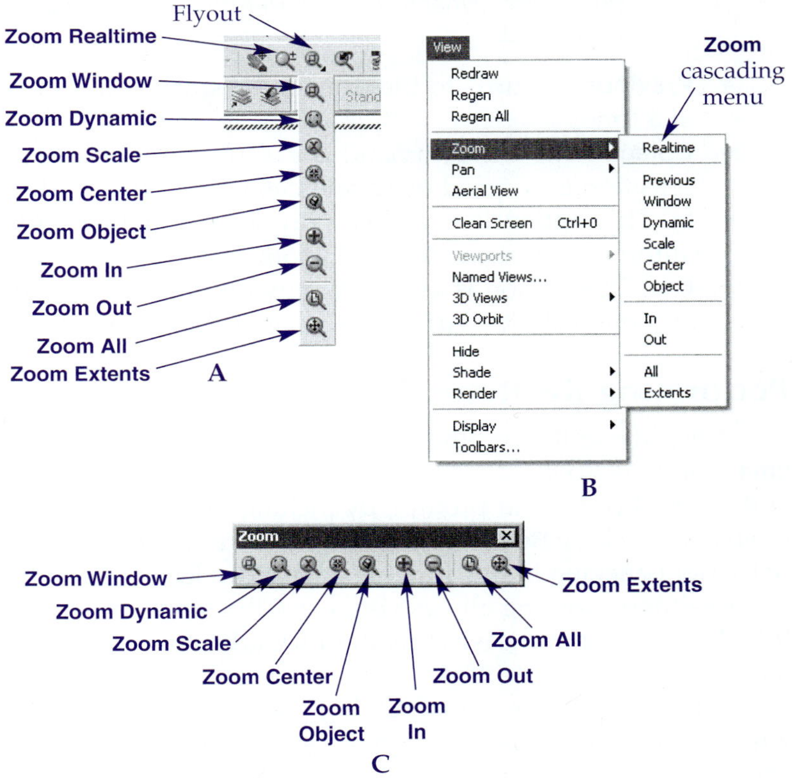

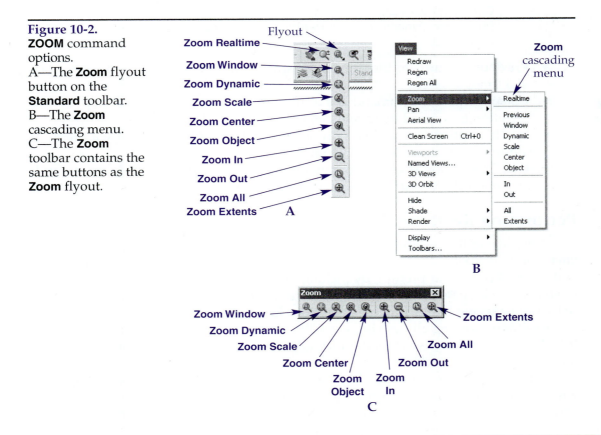

Figure 10-2.
ZOOM command options.
A—The **Zoom** flyout button on the **Standard** toolbar.
B—The **Zoom** cascading menu.
C—The **Zoom** toolbar contains the same buttons as the **Zoom** flyout.

an X, such as 4X. The current value represents the height of the screen in drawing units. Entering a smaller number enlarges the image size, while a larger number reduces it. The command sequence is as follows:

> [All/Center/Dynamic/Extents/Previous/Scale/Window/Object] <real time>: **C**↵
> Specify center point: (*pick a center point*)
> Enter magnification or height <*current*>: **4X**↵
> Command:

- **Dynamic.** Allows for a graphic pan and zoom with the use of a view box that represents the screen. This option is discussed in detail later in the chapter.
- **Extents.** Zooms to the extents (or edges) of the geometry in a drawing. This is the portion of the drawing area that contains drawing objects.
- **Window.** Pick opposite corners of a box. Objects in the box enlarge to fill the display. The **Window** option is the default if you pick a point on the screen upon entering the **ZOOM** command.
- **Scale.** The following prompt appears when you select the **Scale** option:

  > Enter a scale factor (nX or nXP):

  There are two options, **nX** or **nXP**. The **nX** option scales the display relative to the current display. To use this option, type a positive number, then X, and then press [Enter]. For example, enter 2X to magnify the current display "two times." To reduce the display, enter a number less than 1. For example, if you enter .5X, objects appear half as large as they did in the previous display.

  The **nXP** option is used in conjunction with model space and paper space. It scales a drawing in model space relative to paper space and is used primarily in the layout of scaled multiview drawings.

  Both of the **Scale** options can be entered at the initial **ZOOM** command prompt. For example, enter the following to enlarge the current display by a factor of three:

  > Command: **Z** *or* **ZOOM**↵
  > [All/Center/Dynamic/Extents/Previous/Scale/Window/Object] <real time>: **3X**↵
  > Command:

- **Previous.** Returns to the previous display. You can go back ten displays, one at a time.
- **Object.** After the command is executed, select an object or set of objects. The selection is zoomed in on and centered to fill the display area.

AutoCAD 2005 NEW FEATURE

- **In.** This option is available only on the toolbar and the pull-down menu. It automatically executes a 2X zoom scale factor.
- **Out**. This option is available only on the toolbar and the pull-down menu. It automatically executes a .5X zoom scale factor.

Performing Realtime Zoom

When using the command line, the default option of the **ZOOM** command is **real time**. A *realtime* zoom can be viewed as it is performed. It is activated by pressing [Enter] at the **ZOOM** command prompt, by picking the **Zoom Realtime** button in the **Standard** toolbar, by picking **Realtime** in the **Zoom** cascading menu in the **View** pull-down menu, or by right-clicking in the drawing area and selecting **Zoom** in the shortcut menu.

Realtime zooming allows you to see the model move on the screen as you zoom. It is the quickest and easiest method for adjusting the magnification of drawings on the screen.

The Zoom cursor (a magnifying glass icon with a plus and minus) is displayed when realtime zoom is executed. Press and hold the left mouse button (pick button) and move the pointer up to zoom in (enlarge) and down to zoom out (reduce). When you have achieved the display you want, release the button. If the display needs further adjustment after the initial zoom, press and hold the left mouse button again and move the pointer to get the desired display. To exit once you are done, press the [Esc] key, the [Enter] key, or right-click to get the shortcut menu and pick **Exit**.

If you right-click while the Zoom cursor is active, a shortcut menu is displayed. See Figure 10-3. This menu appears at the Zoom cursor location and contains six viewing options.

- **Pan.** Activates the **PAN Realtime** option. This allows you to adjust the placement of the drawing on the screen. If additional zooming is required, right-click again to display the shortcut menu and pick **Zoom**. In this manner you can toggle back and forth between **PAN** and **ZOOM Realtime** to accurately adjust the view. A detailed explanation of the **PAN** command is given later in the chapter.
- **Zoom.** Activates the **ZOOM Realtime** option. A check appears to the left of this option if it is active.
- **3D Orbit.** When this is selected, your point of view around your drawing can change. Similar to **ZOOM**, this option is used to move around a 3D object. A detailed explanation of **3D Orbit** is provided later in this chapter.
- **Zoom Window.** Activates the **ZOOM Window** option and changes the cursor display. See Figure 10-4. You can pick opposite corners of a window but, unlike the typical zoom window, you must press and hold the pick button while dragging the window box to the opposite corner, then release the pick button.
- **Zoom Original.** Restores the previous display before any realtime zooming or panning had occurred. This is a handy function if the current display is not to your liking, and it would be easier to start over rather than to make further adjustments.
- **Zoom Extents.** Zooms to the extents of the drawing geometry.

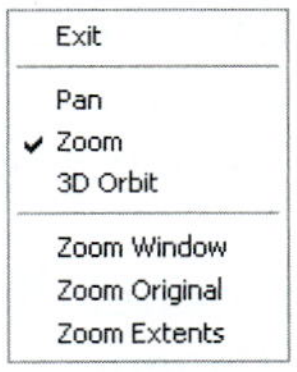

Figure 10-3.
The shortcut menu appears at the Zoom cursor location and contains six viewing options.

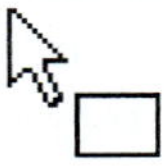

Figure 10-4.
The cursor changes when **Zoom Window** is selected from the shortcut menu.

Enlarging with a Window

The **ZOOM Window** option requires that you pick opposite corners of a rectangular window enclosing the area to be zoomed. The first point you pick is automatically accepted as the first corner of the zoom window. After this corner is picked, move the mouse, and a box appears showing the area that will be displayed or zoomed into once the second corner is picked. The box grows and shrinks as you move the pointing device. When the second corner is picked, the center of the window becomes the center of the new screen display. Figure 10-5 shows **ZOOM Window** used on a drawing.

Figure 10-5.
Using the **ZOOM Window** option. A—Select the corners of a window (highlighted area). B—The selected window fills the drawing screen. To return to the original view, use the **ZOOM Previous** option.

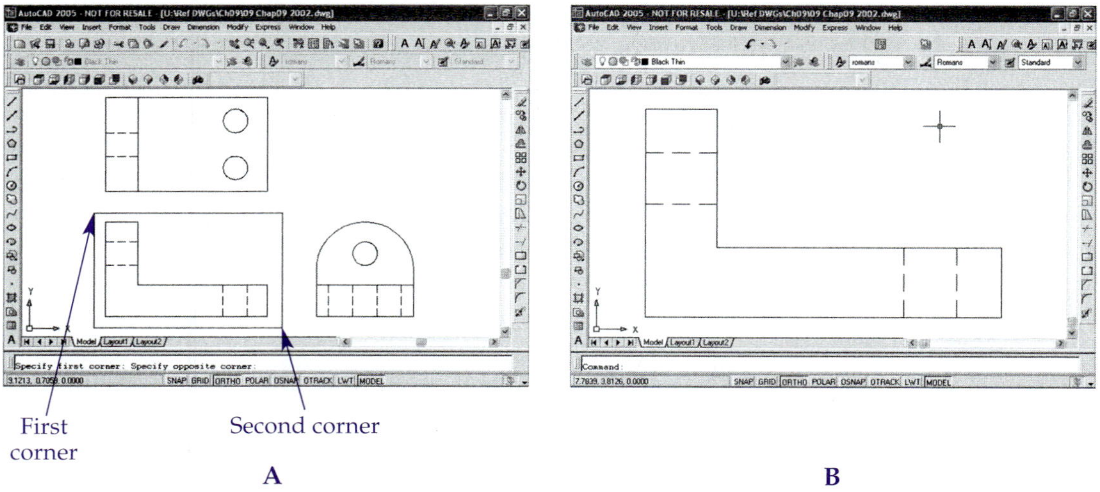

Accurate Displays with a Dynamic Zoom

The **ZOOM Dynamic** option allows you to accurately specify the portion of the drawing you want displayed. This is done by constructing a *view box*. This view box is proportional to the size of the display area of your screen. If you are looking at a zoomed-in view when **ZOOM Dynamic** is selected, the entire drawing is displayed on the screen. To practice using this command, load any drawing into AutoCAD. Then, select the **ZOOM Dynamic** option.

The screen is now occupied by three boxes. See Figure 10-6. A fourth box is displayed later. Each box has a specific function:

- **Drawing extents.** (blue dotted line) This box shows the area of the drawing that is occupied by drawing objects. It is the same area that is displayed with **ZOOM Extents**.
- **Current view.** (green dotted line) This is the view that was displayed before you selected **ZOOM Dynamic**.
- **Panning view box.** (X in the center) Move the pointing device to find the center point of the desired zoomed display. When you press the pick button, the zooming view box appears.
- **Zooming view box.** (arrow on right side) This box allows you to decrease or increase the area that you wish to zoom. Move the pointer to the right and the box increases in size. Move the pointer to the left and the box shrinks. You can also pan up or down with the zooming view box. The only restriction is that you cannot move the box to the left.

The **ZOOM Dynamic** command is not complete until you press [Enter]. If you press the pick button to select the zooming view box, you can resize the viewing area. Press the pick button again and the panning view box reappears. The panning view box can then be repositioned over the area desired. In this manner, you can fine-tune the exact display needed. This is also helpful in defining permanent views, which is discussed later in this chapter.

Figure 10-6.
Features of the **ZOOM Dynamic** option.

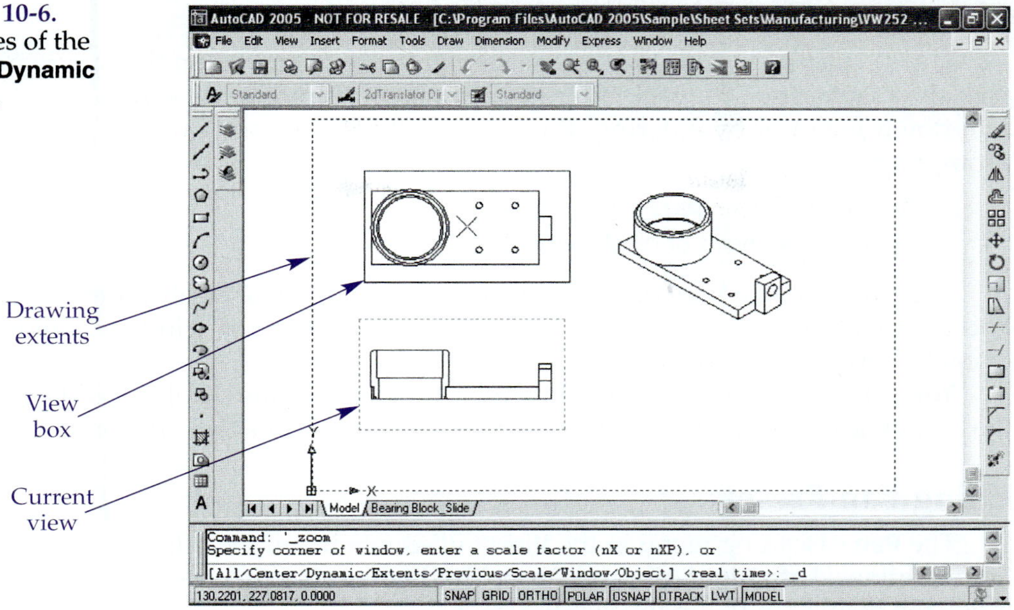

EXERCISE 10-1 Complete the Exercise on the Student CD.

Moving around the Display Screen

The **PAN** command is used to move your viewpoint around the drawing without changing the magnification factor.

Performing Realtime Pan

PAN
P

View
➥ **Pan**
➥ **Realtime**

Standard toolbar
Pan Realtime

A *realtime pan* allows you to see the drawing move on the screen as you pan. It is the quickest and easiest method for adjusting the view around the drawings on the screen. To activate realtime panning, pick **Realtime** from the **Pan** cascading menu in the **View** pull-down menu, pick the **Pan Realtime** button on the **Standard** toolbar, or enter P or PAN at the Command: prompt.

After starting the command, press and hold the pick button and move the pointing device in the direction you wish to pan. The pan icon of the hand is displayed when a realtime pan is used. A right-click displays the shortcut menu shown in **Figure 10-3.**

If you pan to the edge of your drawing, a bar is displayed on one side of the hand cursor. The bar correlates to the side of the drawing. For example, if you reach the left side of the drawing, a bar and arrow appear on the left side of the hand. These icons are shown in **Figure 10-7.**

Figure 10-7.
A bar and arrow appear by the hand cursor when you pan to the edge of the drawing.

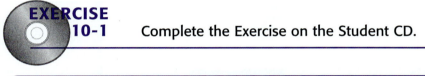

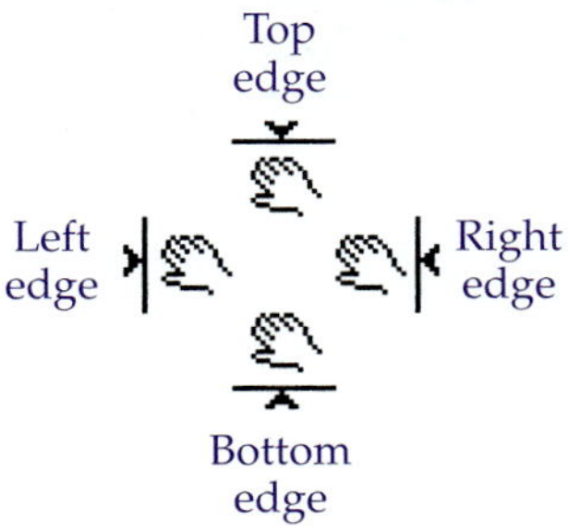

Picking the Pan Displacement

The *pan displacement* is the distance the drawing is moved on the screen. You can pick the displacement by selecting **Point** from the **Pan** cascading menu in the **View** pull-down menu or by entering -P or -PAN at the Command: prompt. The following prompt appears:

Command: **-P** *or* **-PAN**↵
Specify base point or displacement:

You can specify a base point by picking a point or entering absolute coordinates. You are then prompted to select a second point. The display window is moved the distance between the points.

You can also enter the displacement, or the distance the display window is to be moved, by giving coordinates. The coordinates can be either relative or absolute.

Using Pan Presets

The **Pan** cascading menu in the **View** pull-down menu includes four preset directional options: **Left**, **Right**, **Up**, and **Down**. See Figure 10-8. Select one of the options to move the display in the indicated direction.

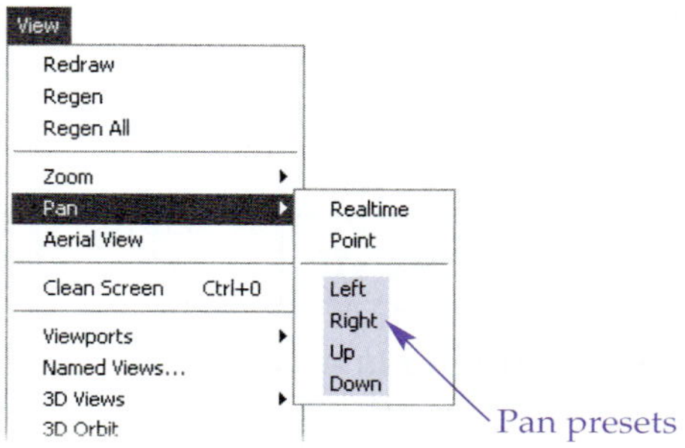

Figure 10-8.
The **Pan** options can be found in the **Pan** cascading menu of the **View** pull-down menu.

Using Scroll Bars to Pan

The scroll bars found at the bottom and to the right of the drawing area can also be used to pan the display. See Figure 10-9. Pick the arrows at the end of the scroll bar to pan in small increments. Select the scroll bar itself to pan in larger increments. Position the cursor over the box in the scroll bar, pick and hold the left mouse button, and then move the mouse to see realtime panning in the horizontal or vertical direction.

> **NOTE**
>
> The drawing area scroll bars can be activated and deactivated by selecting the **Display scroll bars in drawing window** option in the **Window Elements** area of the **Display** tab of the **Options** dialog box. To access this dialog box, select **Options...** from the **Tools** pull-down menu or right-click in the drawing area and select **Options...** from the shortcut menu.

Figure 10-9.
The drawing area scroll bars can be used for panning operations.

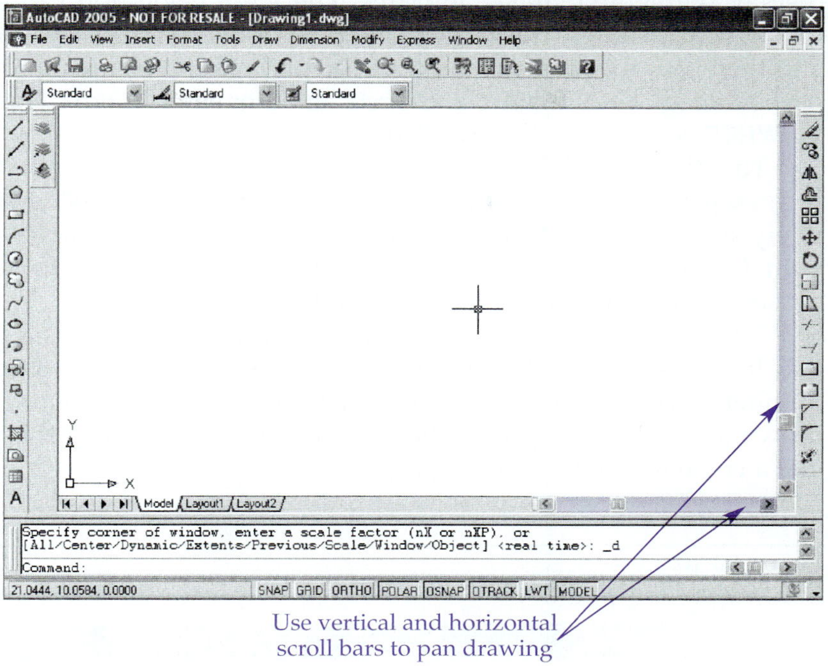

> **PROFESSIONAL TIP**
>
> AutoCAD supports most mice that have a scroll wheel. This is a wheel between the two normally functioning mouse buttons that usually scrolls the display up or down. Within AutoCAD the scroll wheel mouse has these basic functions in addition to the standard operation of the two buttons:
>
> - Roll the wheel forward or away from you to zoom in.
> - Roll the wheel backward or toward you to zoom out.
> - Press and hold the wheel button down and move the mouse to pan.
> - Double-click on the wheel to zoom to the drawing extents.
>
> The **ZOOMFACTOR** system variable controls the incremental movement of the wheel. By default, the zoom factor is set to 10 percent. Thus, each increment in the wheel rotation changes the zoom level by 10 percent.
>
> The **MBUTTONPAN** system variable controls the behavior of the third button or wheel to support the **PAN** command or the **Object Snap** shortcut menu. A 0 supports the action defined in the menu (MNU) file and 1 supports panning when you hold and drag the button or wheel.

Setting View Resolution for Quick Displays

AutoCAD can save you time on zooming and panning at the expense of display accuracy. AutoCAD can also provide a highly accurate display at the expense of zoom and pan speed. The main factor is the view resolution.

The *view resolution* refers to the number of lines used to draw circles and arcs. High resolution values display smooth circles and arcs. Low resolution values display segmented circles and arcs. The view resolution can be set in the **Options** dialog box. To access this dialog box, pick **Options...** from the **Tools** pull-down menu, and then pick the **Display** tab. In the **Display resolution** area in the upper-right corner of the dialog box is the **Arc and circle smoothness** text box. This contains the current **VIEWRES** setting. See Figure 10-10.

The display smoothness of circles and arcs is controlled by the **VIEWRES** setting. It can vary between 1 and 20000. The default setting is 1000, which produces a relatively smooth circle. A number smaller than 1000 causes circles and arcs to be drawn with fewer vectors (straight lines). See Figure 10-11. A number larger than 1000 causes more vectors to be included in the circles.

It is important to remember that the **VIEWRES** setting is a display function only and has no effect on the plotted drawing. A drawing is plotted using an optimum number of vectors for the size of circles and arcs. In other words, even if a circle you draw looks like a polygon in the drawing area before **REGEN** is used, it will still look like a circle when the drawing is plotted.

Figure 10-10.
The view resolution (**VIEWRES**) variable can be set in the **Options** dialog box.

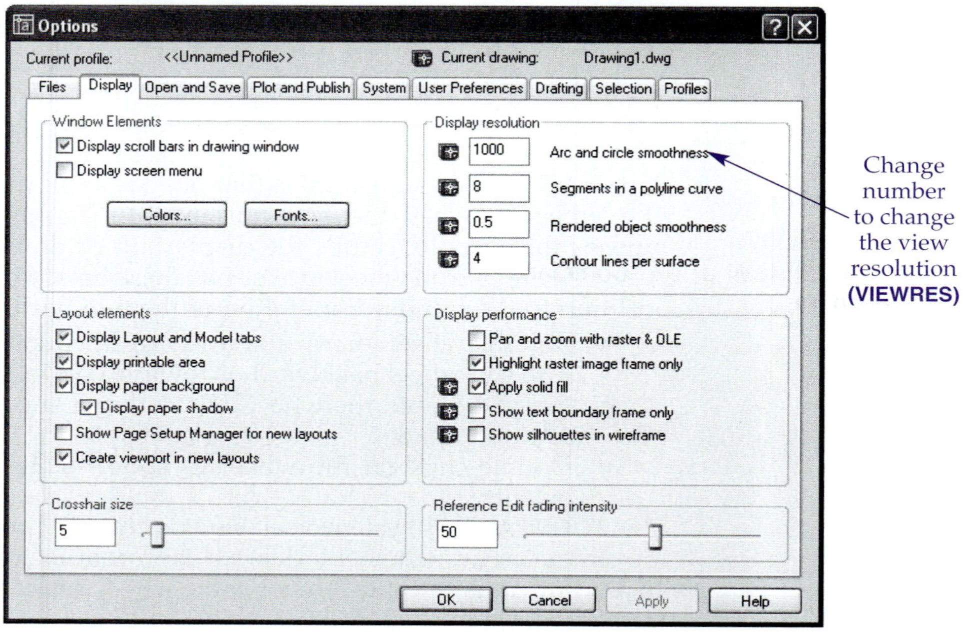

Figure 10-11.
The higher the **VIEWRES** value, the smoother a circle will appear.

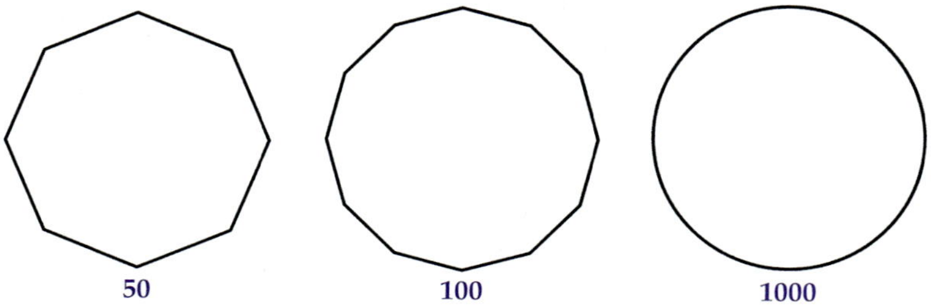

NOTE

You can change the **VIEWRES** setting by entering VIEWRES at the Command: prompt. A Do you want fast zooms? prompt appears. This prompt is no longer useful, but remains in AutoCAD so programs written for earlier versions will still function properly.

EXERCISE 10-2 Complete the Exercise on the Student CD.

Creating Your Own Working Views

On a large drawing with a number of separate details, using the **ZOOM** and **PAN** commands can be time-consuming. Being able to quickly specify a certain part of the drawing is much easier. This is possible with the **VIEW** command. It allows you to create named views of any area of the drawing. A view can be a portion of the drawing, such as the upper-left quadrant, or it can represent an enlarged portion. After the view is created, you can instruct AutoCAD to display it at any time.

Creating Views

VIEW
V
DDVIEW

View
➥ Named Views...

View toolbar
Named Views

The **VIEW** command can be accessed by picking the **Named Views** button in the **View** toolbar, selecting **Named Views...** from the **View** pull-down menu, or entering V, VIEW, or DDVIEW at the Command: prompt. This activates the **View** dialog box. See Figure 10-12.

The **View** dialog box contains the **Named Views** and the **Orthographic & Isometric Views** tabs. The **Named Views** tab is where new views are defined. The **Orthographic & Isometric Views** tab provides preset views around the drawing in AutoCAD.

A list of currently defined views is shown in the **Named Views** tab. If you want to save the current display as a view, pick the **New...** button to access the **New View** dialog box, Figure 10-13. Now, type the desired view name in the **View name:** edit box. The **Current Display** option button is the default. Click **OK** and the view name is

Figure 10-12.
Select a different view in the **View** dialog box. Create a new view by selecting the **New...** button.

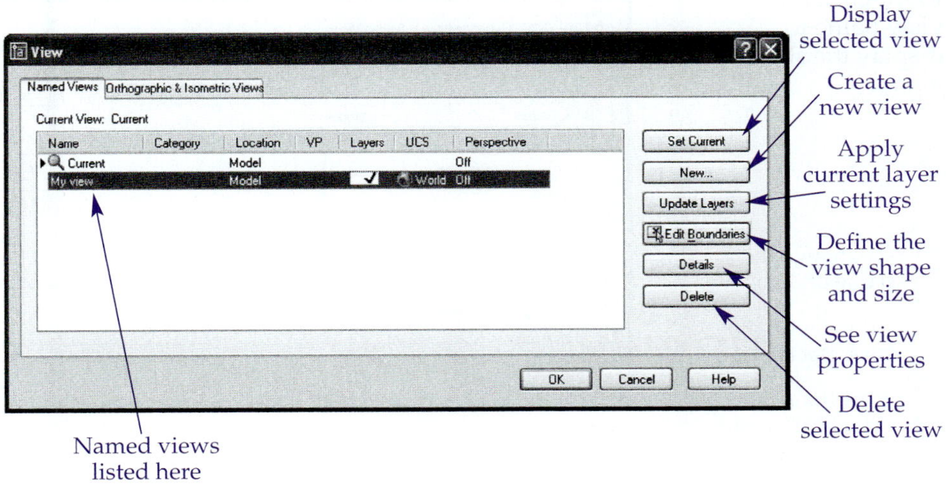

Figure 10-13.
In the **New View** dialog box, name the new view and define the window.

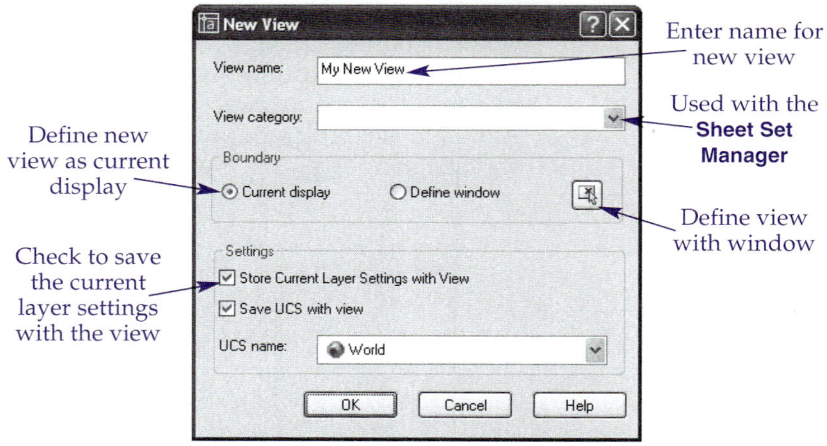

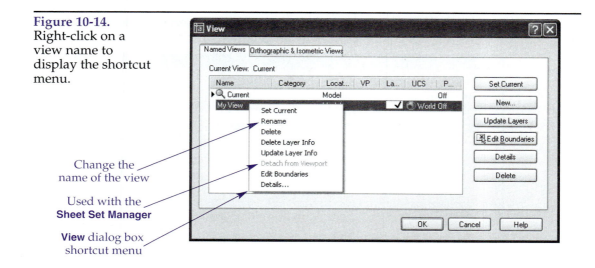

added to the list. AutoCAD creates a view from what is currently being displayed in the graphics window.

If you want to use a window to define the view, pick the **Define Window** radio button in the **New View** dialog box, and then pick the **Define View Window** button. You are prompted to Specify first corner. Pick two points to define a window. After the second corner is selected, the **New View** dialog box reappears. Pick the **OK** button and the **View** dialog box is updated to reflect the new view.

AutoCAD 2005 NEW FEATURE

If the named view is associated with a category in the **Sheet Set Manager**, the category can be selected from the **View category** drop-down list. The **Sheet Set Manager** is discussed in Chapter 25.

AutoCAD 2005 NEW FEATURE

When a view is saved, the current layer settings can also be saved with the view. These layer settings will be recalled each time the view is set current. To do this, check the **Store Current Layer Settings with View** check box.

NOTE

When creating a view, it is possible to save a named UCS (User Coordinate System) to the particular view being created. The World Coordinate System is the default system in AutoCAD. It determines where the 0,0,0 point is for the X, Y, and Z axes. The **UCS** command is introduced in Chapter 6 of this text and covered in depth in *AutoCAD and its Applications—Advanced.*

Figure 10-14.
Right-click on a view name to display the shortcut menu.

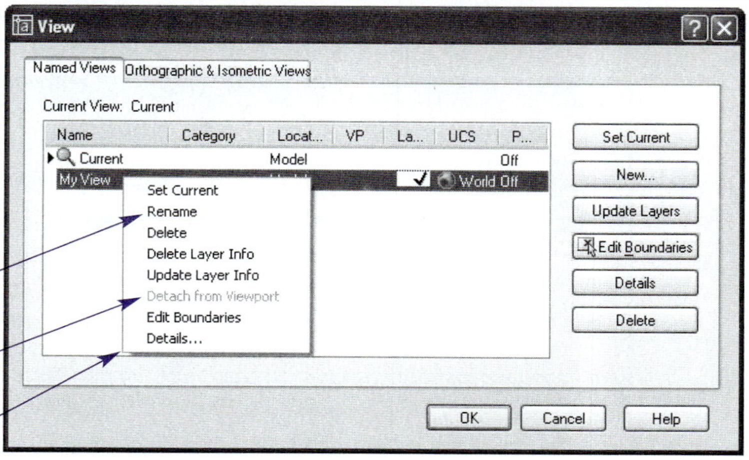

To display one of the listed views, pick its name from the list in the **Named Views** tab and pick the **Set Current** button. The name of the current view appears in the **Current View:** label below the **Named Views** tab. Now, pick the **OK** button and the screen displays the selected view.

When you right-click on a view name in the **View** dialog box, a shortcut menu appears, **Figure 10-14**. The following options are available in this shortcut menu:

- **Set Current.** Set the selected view current.
- **Rename.** Change the name of the selected view.
- **Delete.** The selected view will be deleted.
- **Delete Layer Info.** If the layer settings were saved with the view, this can be undone
- **Update Layer Info.** If the layer settings were changed after the view was created, this option will update them to the current layer settings.
- **Detach from Viewport.** Pick this to disassociate the selected name view and its viewport in the **Sheet Set Manager.** The **Sheet Set Manager** is discussed in detail in Chapter 25.
- **Edit Boundaries.** When this option is picked, the **View** dialog box hides temporarily so a window can be defined to set the new view shape and size.
- **Details...** This will present a detailed description of the selected view. A discussion of these values related to 3D drawings is given in ***AutoCAD and its Applications—Advanced.***

AutoCAD 2005 NEW FEATURE

The **Orthographic & Isometric Views** tab in the **View** dialog box is used to quickly choose a preset view around the drawing. See **Figure 10-15.** Notice that the icons display the side of the drawing that will be viewed. There are orthogonal views such as Top, Bottom, Front, Back, Left, and Right. Picking any of these icons, then pressing the **Set Current** button changes the view in AutoCAD so you are looking at your drawing from the selected direction. There are isometric views such as Southwest, Southeast, Northeast, and Northwest. These views can also be selected from the **3D Views** cascading menu in the **View** pull-down menu or from the **View** toolbar. See **Figure 10-16.** Selecting any of these icons displays a 3D (isometric) view of the drawing. Orthogonal and isometric views are covered in greater depth in ***AutoCAD and its Applications—Advanced.***

Figure 10-15.
The **Orthographic & Isometric Views** tab contains six orthographic views and four isometric views.

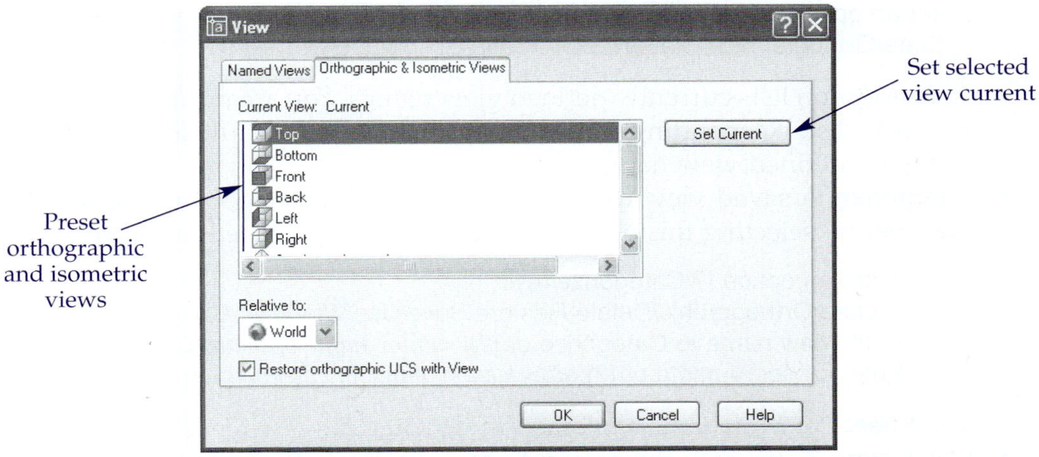

Figure 10-16.
Preset orthographic and isometric views can also be selected in the **3D Views** cascading menu in the **View** pull-down menu or from the **View** toolbar.

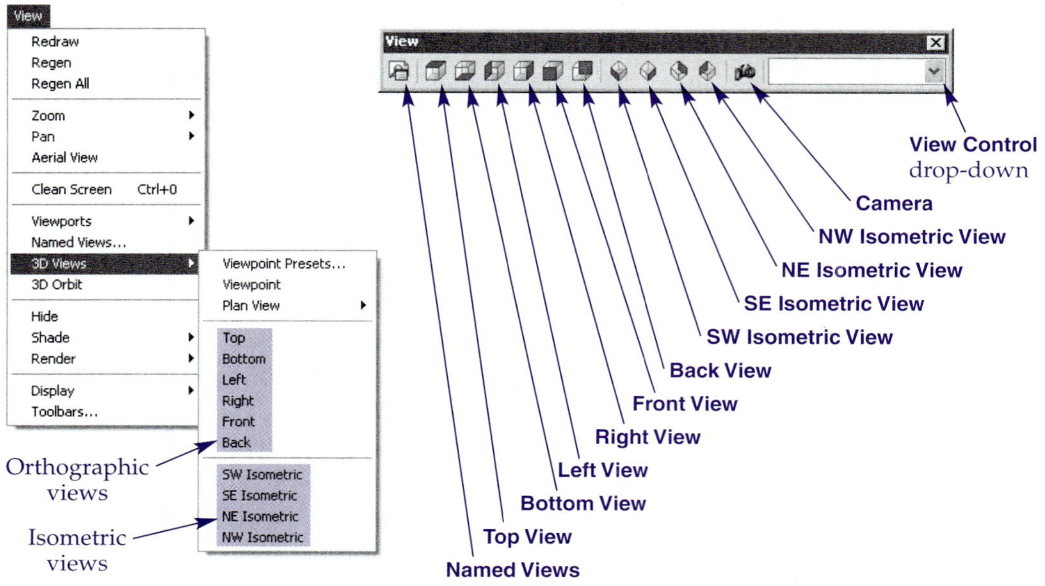

PROFESSIONAL TIP

Part of your project planning should include view names. A consistent naming system guarantees that all users know the view names without having to list them. The views can be set as part of the template drawings. Then, view names can be placed in a custom screen, or pull-down menu as discussed in ***AutoCAD and its Applications—Advanced.***

Working with Views at the Command: Prompt

-VIEW
-V

The **-VIEW** command is used to create and set views at the Command: prompt. When -V or -VIEW is entered at the Command: prompt, you are presented with the following options:

Enter an option [?/Categorize/Layer
State/Orthographic/Delete/Restore/Save/Ucs/Window]:

- **?.** This option lists currently defined view names. You are prompted for which views to list. Responding with [Enter] accepts the default and displays all currently defined view names.

AutoCAD 2005 NEW FEATURE

- **Categorize.** A saved view can be associated with a category in the **Sheet Set Manager** by selecting this option. The command sequence is as follows:

Enter an option [?/Categorize/lAyer
state/Orthographic/Delete/Restore/Save/Ucs/Window]: **C**↵
Enter view name to Categorize or [?]: *<enter name of view>*↵
Enter category name or [?]: <""> *<enter name of category>*↵

The **Sheet Set Manager** is explained in Chapter 25.

AutoCAD 2005 NEW FEATURE

- **Layer state.** Gives you the option to save or delete the current layer settings with a named view.
- **Orthographic.** This option changes the view to one of the orthographic views that you choose. You are prompted to choose an orthographic view to display.

- **Delete.** This option removes unneeded views. After selecting this option, you are prompted to enter the name of the view to be deleted. Type the name and press [Enter].
- **Restore.** A saved view can be displayed on the screen using this option. Simply enter the name of the view you want to display at the Enter view name to restore: prompt. The view is then immediately displayed.
- **Save.** This option creates a new view. Enter the new view name at the Enter view name to save: prompt. The current display becomes the new view.
- **UCS.** This option allows you to save the current UCS with any new views you create. You are prompted with Save current UCS with named views? [Yes/No].
- **Window.** This option also creates a new view and prompts for a window selection.

Using Transparent Display Commands

To begin a new command, you usually need to complete or cancel the current command. Most menu picks automatically cancel the command in progress before initiating the new one. However, some commands function without canceling an active command.

A *transparent command* temporarily interrupts the active command. After the transparent command is completed, the command that was interrupted is resumed. Therefore, it is not necessary to cancel the initial command. Many display commands can be used transparently, including **REDRAW**, **PAN**, and **ZOOM**.

Suppose that while drawing a line, you need to place one end somewhere off the screen. One option is to cancel the **LINE** command, zoom out to see more of the drawing, and select **LINE** again. A more efficient method is to use **PAN** or **ZOOM** while still in the **LINE** command. An example of drawing a line to a point off the screen is as follows:

Command: **L** *or* **LINE**↵
Specify first point: (*pick a point*)
Specify next point or [Undo]: (*pick the* **Pan** *button or enter* 'PAN)
>>Press Esc or Enter to exit, or right-click to display shortcut menu. (*pan to the location desired then press* [Enter])
Resuming LINE command.
Specify next point or [Undo]: (*pick a point*)
Specify next point or [Undo]: ↵
Command:

The double prompt (>>) indicates that a command has been put "on hold" while you use a transparent command. The transparent command must be completed before the original command is returned. At that time, the double prompt disappears.

The above procedure is similar when using the **ZOOM** command. When typed at the keyboard, an apostrophe (') is used before the command. To connect a line to a small feature, enter **'Z** or **'ZOOM**.

PROFESSIONAL TIP

The **Pan**, **Zoom**, and **View** buttons activate commands transparently.

PROFESSIONAL TIP

A transparent redraw is executed when **Redraw** is picked from the **View** pull-down menu. Commands such as **GRID**, **SNAP**, and **ORTHO** can be used transparently, but it is quicker to activate these modes with the appropriate function keys or from the status bar.

EXERCISE 10-3 Complete the Exercise on the Student CD.

Using the Aerial View

When working on a large drawing, you can spend a lot of time zooming and panning the graphics window while trying to locate a particular detail or feature. One of the most powerful display features in AutoCAD is the **Aerial View** window. **Aerial View** is a navigation tool that lets you see the entire drawing in a separate window, locate the detail or feature you want, and move to it quickly. You can zoom in on an area, change the magnification, and match the view in the graphics window to the one in the **Aerial View** window (or vice versa).

AV
DSVIEWER
View
➥ Aerial View

To open the **Aerial View** window, pick **Aerial View** from the **View** pull-down menu or enter AV or DSVIEWER at the Command: prompt. The entire drawing is then displayed in the **Aerial View** window. See Figure 10-17.

The **Aerial View** window initially appears at the lower right of the drawing area, but can be moved to any convenient location on the screen. To do so, pick the title bar of the **Aerial View** window, hold down the left mouse button, and drag the window to a new location.

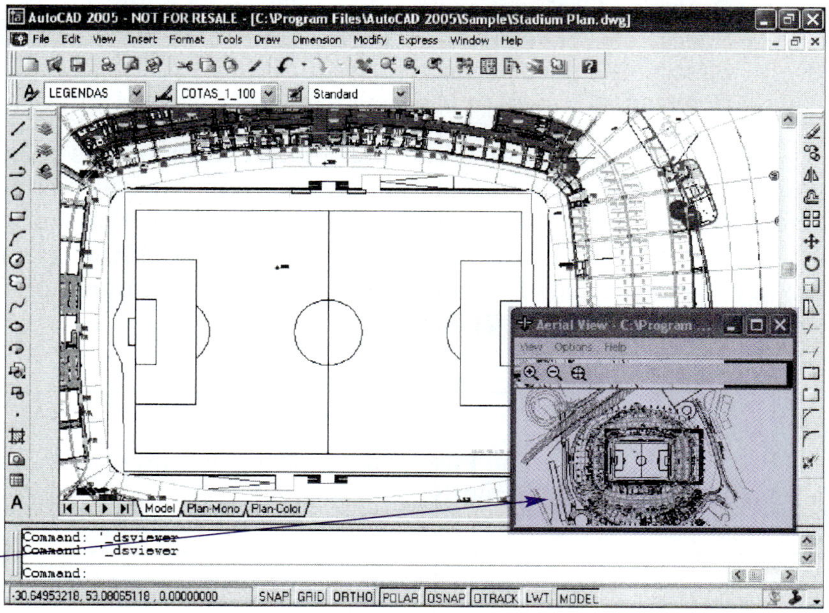

Aerial View window

Figure 10-17. The **Aerial View** window (highlighted window) is initially in the lower-right corner of the screen.

The menu bar in the **Aerial View** window contains three pull-down menus and three buttons. See Figure 10-18. The buttons provide the same options found in the **View** pull-down menu:

- **Zoom In.** Increases the magnification of the image in the **Aerial View** window by a factor of 2.
- **Zoom Out.** Decreases the magnification of the image in the **Aerial View** window by a factor of 2.
- **Global.** Displays the entire generated drawing area (the extents of the drawing) in the **Aerial View** window.

The **Options** pull-down menu contains the following **Aerial View** window options:

- **Auto Viewport.** When on, switching to a different tiled viewport automatically causes the new viewport to be displayed in the **Aerial View** window. When off, AutoCAD will not update the **Aerial View** window to match the active viewport.
- **Dynamic Update.** This causes the **Aerial View** window to update its display after each change in the drawing. Disable this if the display updates are too slow.
- **Realtime Zoom.** Activating this will update the drawing view area as you zoom and pan in the **Aerial View** window.

Selecting **Aerial View Help** from the **Help** pull-down menu opens the **AutoCAD 2005 Help** window to the **Aerial View Window** section. The **Aerial View** window is similar to the **ZOOM Dynamic** command. When using the **Aerial View**, the overall drawing can be viewed. There is a current view box that can be resized by pressing the pick button. Moving the pointing device right or left shrinks or enlarges the current view. Press the pick button again and by moving the pointing device around you can pan around in the window. When the desired view has been obtained, right-click and AutoCAD will set that as the current view.

NOTE

You can also right-click inside the **Aerial View** window to get a shortcut menu that accesses the functions described earlier. Best of all, you can use the **Aerial View** zoom and pan functions transparently while a drawing or editing command is in progress.

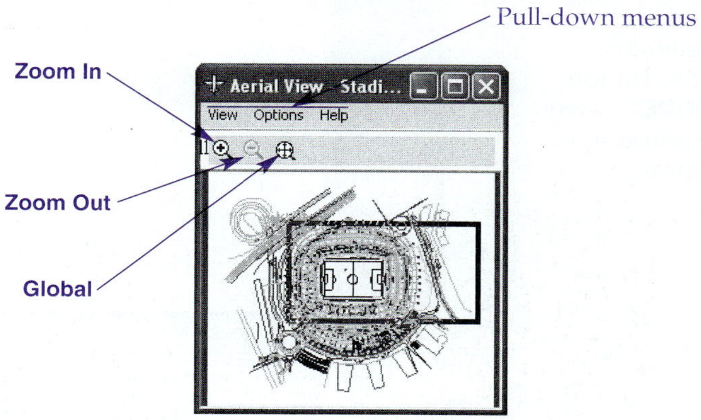

Figure 10-18.
The **Aerial View** window has pull-down menus and a toolbar. These contain options for working with the window.

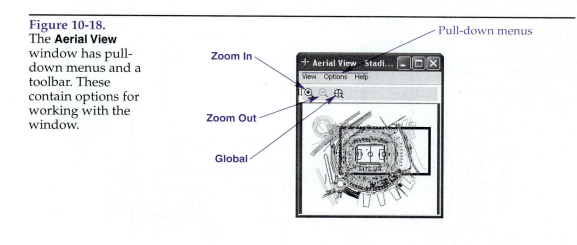

EXERCISE 10-4

Complete the Exercise on the Student CD.

Model Space and Paper Space

Model space can be thought of as the space where you draw and design in AutoCAD. The term *model* has more meaning when working in 3D, but you can consider any drawing or design as a model, even if it is two-dimensional. An introduction of User Coordinate Systems and the UCS icon is given in Chapter 6 of this text, and a detailed discussion is in ***AutoCAD and its Applications—Advanced.***

Paper space is a *space* you use to lay out a drawing or model to be plotted. Basically, it is as if you place a sheet of paper on the screen, then insert, or *reference*, one or more drawings to the paper. In order to enter paper space, you can pick one of the layout tabs at the bottom of the screen. See **Figure 10-19.** You can also use the **MODEL** or **PAPER** button on the status bar to switch between model space and paper space. The button displays the current environment, and picking it switches to the other environment.

Remember that you should create all your drawings and designs in the **Model** tab, not in the **Layout** tab. Only paper layouts for plotting purposes should be created in the **Layout** tab. To return to model space, pick the **Model** tab.

Do not be confused by model space and paper space. The discussion in Chapter 11 provides you with additional understanding. Right now, think of these terms in the following manner:

Tab	Environment	Status Bar Button	Activity
Model	Model space	**MODEL**	Drawing and design
Layout	Paper space	**PAPER**	Plotting and printing

Figure 10-19.
The layout tabs are located at the bottom of the drawing area window. The **PAPER** button indicates the paper space environment is active. The button reads **MODEL** when you are working in model space.

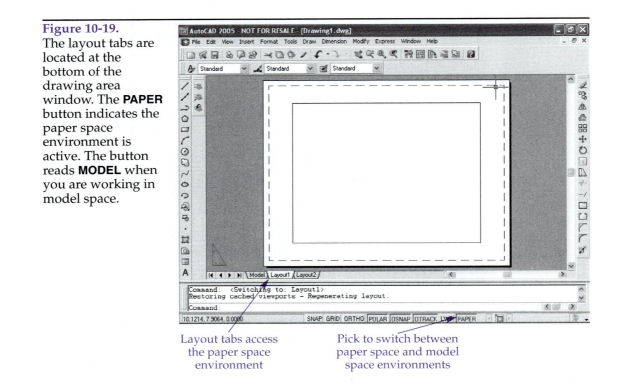

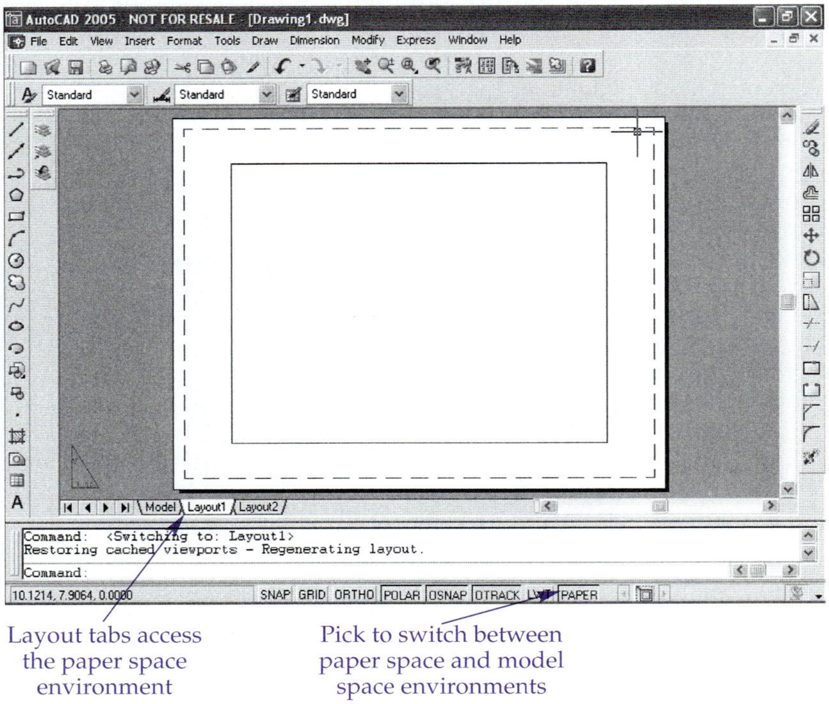

Tiled Viewports

The **Model** tab drawing area can be divided into various viewports. These viewports are called *tiled viewports*. Another type of viewport, *floating viewport*, can be created in the **Layout** tab. Tiled viewports are created in model space, floating viewports are created in paper space.

By default, there is only one viewport in the drawing area. Additional viewports can be added. The edges of tiled viewports butt against one another like floor tile. The tiled viewports cannot overlap.

Viewports are different views in the same drawing. Only one viewport can be active at any given time. The active viewport has a bold outline around its edges. See **Figure 10-20.**

Figure 10-20.
An example of three tiled viewports in model space. All viewports contain the same objects, but the display in each viewport can be unique.

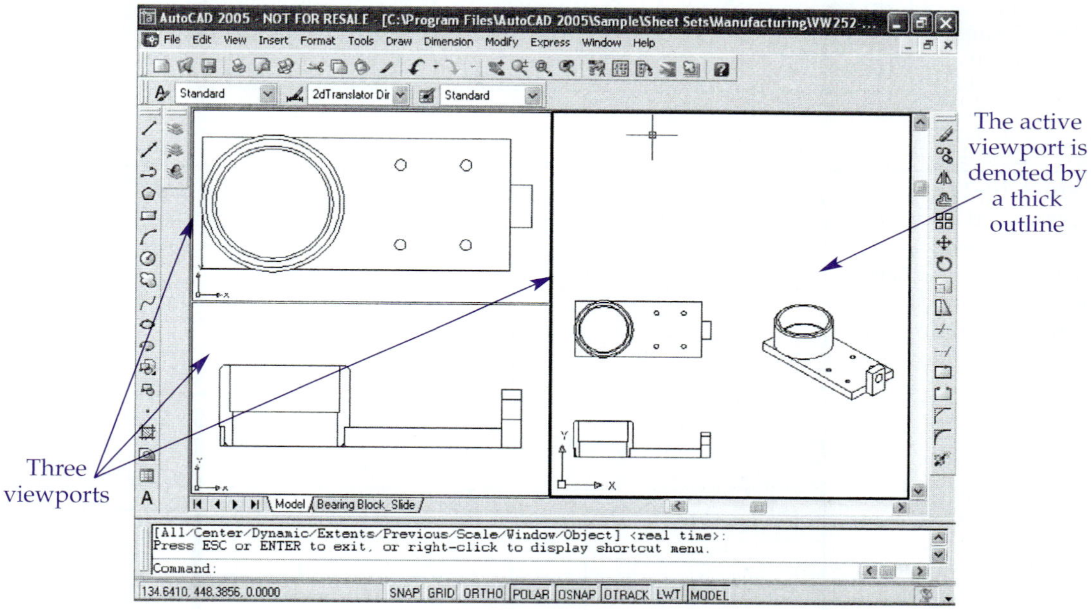

Creating Tiled Viewports

Viewports can be created using the **Viewports** dialog box, **Figure 10-21.** Picking the **Display Viewports Dialog** button from either the **Layouts** or **Viewports** toolbar can access this dialog box. You can also enter VPORTS at the Command: prompt, or select **New Viewports...** from the **Viewports** cascading menu in the **View** pull-down menu.

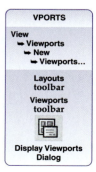

VPORTS

View
➥ Viewports
➥ New
➥ Viewports...

Layouts toolbar

Viewports toolbar

Display Viewports Dialog

The **New Viewports** tab is shown in **Figure 10-21.** The **Standard viewports:** list contains many preset viewport configurations. The configuration name identifies the number of viewports and the arrangement or location of the largest viewport. These configurations are shown in **Figure 10-22.** Select one, and a preview appears in the **Preview** area. Select *Active Model Configuration* to preview the current configuration.

You can name and save a configuration. Enter a name in the **New name:** text box. When you pick the **OK** button, the new named viewport configuration is recorded in the **Named Viewports** tab. Use a descriptive name. For example, if you are going to configure four viewports, you might name this as Four Viewports.

Figure 10-21.
Specify the number and arrangement of tiled viewports in the **New Viewports** tab of the **Viewports** dialog box.

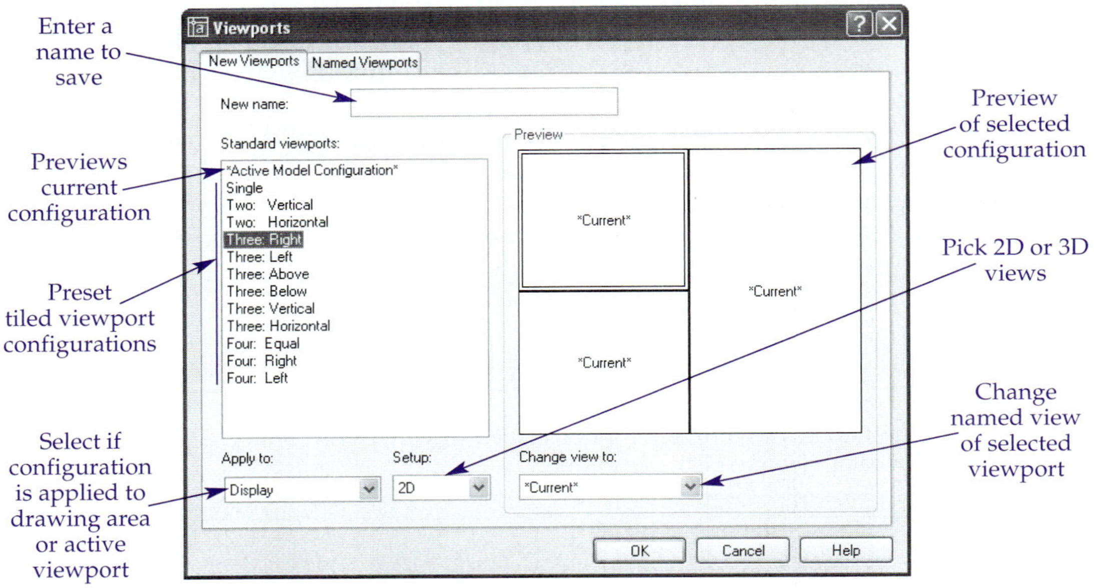

Figure 10-22.
Preset tiled viewport configurations are available in the **New Viewports** tab of the **Viewports** dialog box.

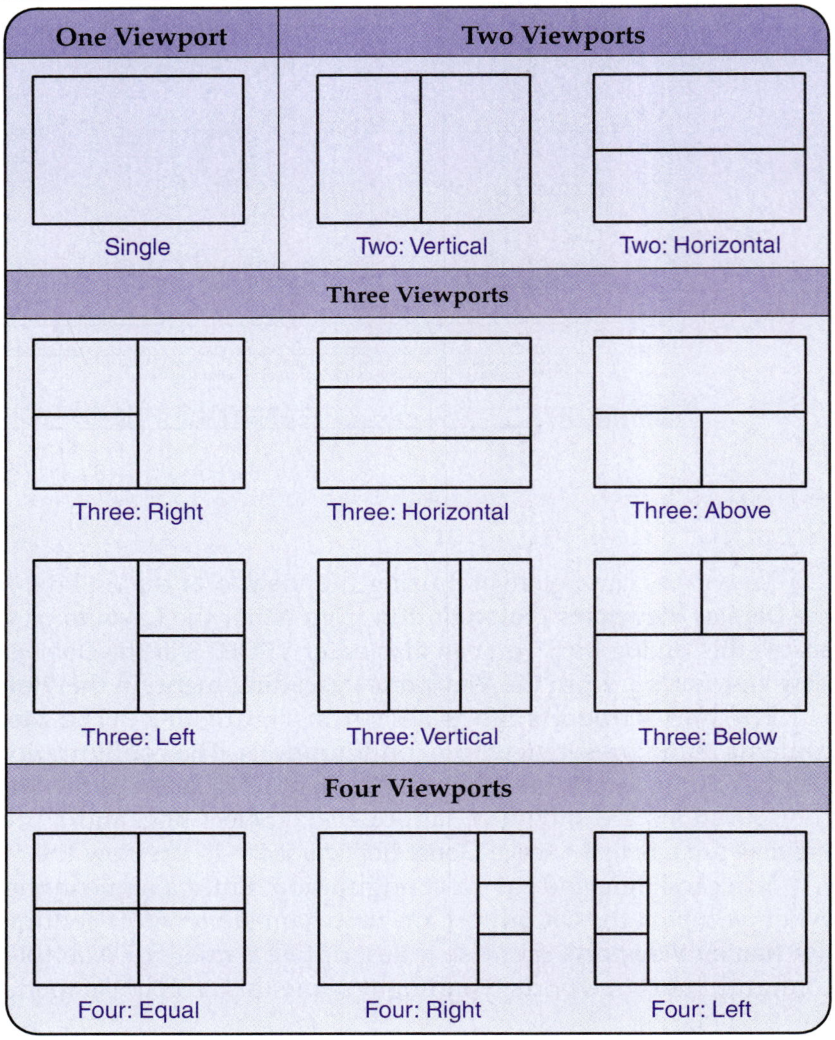

The **Apply to:** drop-down list allows you to specify if the viewport configuration is applied to the graphics window or to the active viewport. Select **Display** to have the configuration applied to the entire drawing area. Select **Current Viewport** to have the new configuration in the active viewport only. See **Figure 10-23.**

The default setting in the **Setup:** drop-down list is **2D**. When this is selected, all viewports show the top view of the drawing. If the **3D** option is selected, the different viewports display various 3D views of the drawing. At least one viewport is set up with an isometric view. The other viewports have different views, such as a top view or side view. The viewpoint is displayed within the viewport in the **Preview** image. To change a view in a viewport, pick the viewport in the **Preview** image and then select the new viewpoint from the **Change view to:** drop-down list.

The **Named Viewports** tab displays the names of saved viewport configurations and gives you a preview of each. See **Figure 10-24.** Select the named viewport configuration and pick **OK** to apply it to the drawing area. Named viewport configurations cannot be applied to the active viewport.

You can also select a viewport configuration from the **Viewports** cascading menu in the **View** pull-down menu, shown in **Figure 10-25.** The following configuration options are available:

- **1 Viewport.** This option replaces the current viewport configuration with a single viewport.
- **2 Viewports.** When you select this option, you are prompted to select a vertical or horizontal arrangement:

  Enter a configuration option [Horizontal/Vertical] <Vertical>:

  The arrangement you choose is then applied to the active viewport. This configuration does not replace the current viewport configuration.
- **3 Viewports.** The following prompt appears when you select this option:

  Enter a configuration option [Horizontal/Vertical/Above/Below/Left/Right] <Right>:

  The arrangement you choose is then applied to the active viewport. This configuration does not replace the current viewport configuration.
- **4 Viewports.** This option creates four equal viewports within the active viewport.

Figure 10-23.
Viewport configurations can be applied to the drawing area or the active viewport. A—Original configuration (Three: Right). B—Use the **Current Viewport** option to create additional viewports within the active viewport. Here, the Two: Vertical configuration is specified for the active viewport.

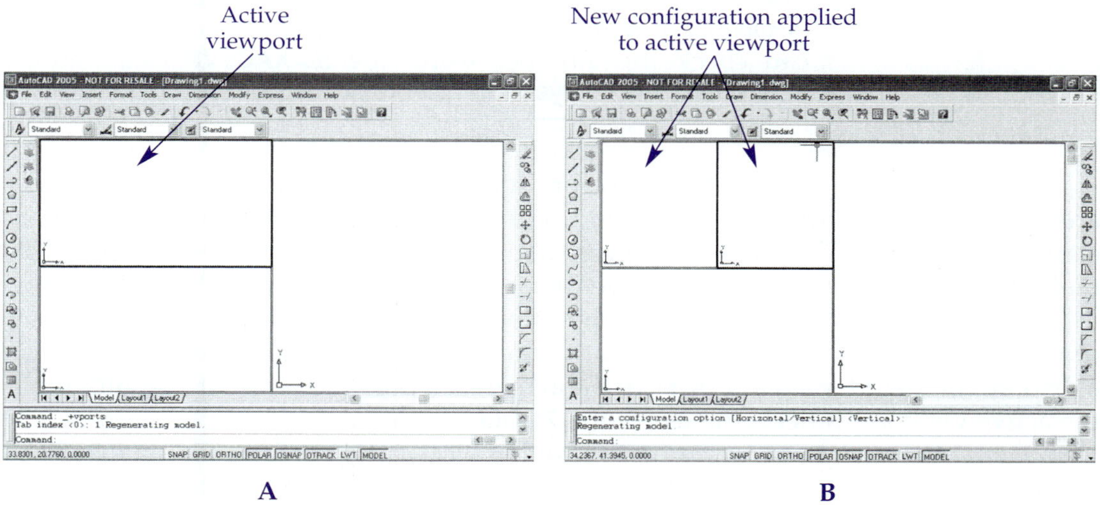

Figure 10-24.
The **Named Viewports** tab.

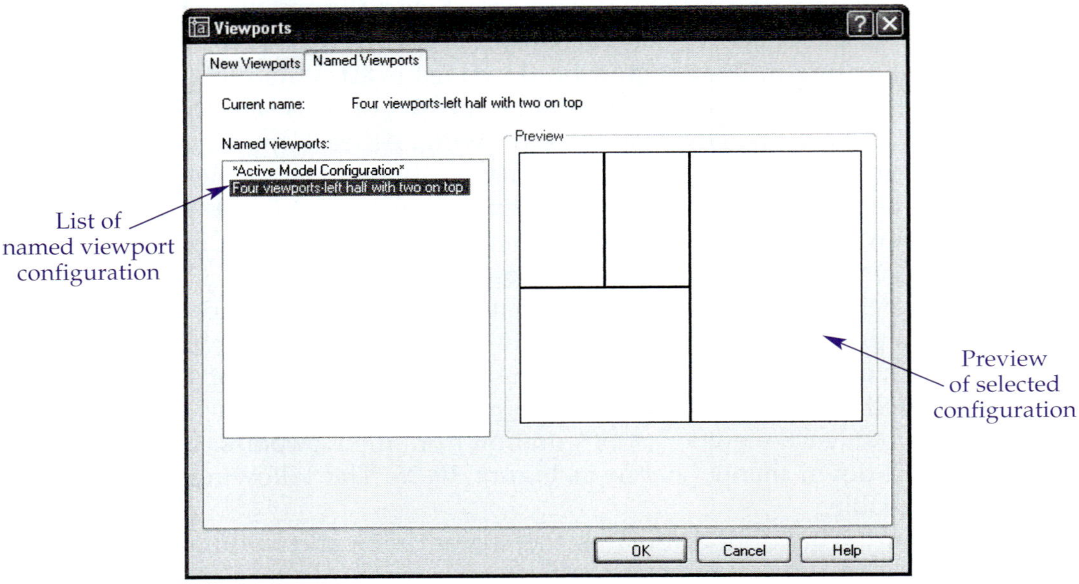

Figure 10-25.
The **Viewports** cascading menu in the **View** pull-down menu.

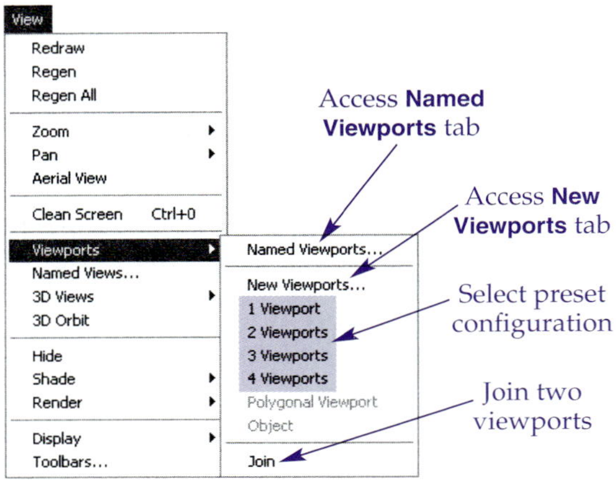

NOTE

The AutoCAD graphics window can be divided into *tiled viewports*, of which only 64 can be available at one time. You can check this number using the **MAXACTVP** (maximum active viewports) system variable at the Command: prompt.

Once you have selected the viewport configuration and returned to drawing area, move the pointing device around and notice that only the active viewport contains crosshairs. The pointer is represented by an arrow in the other viewports. To make a different viewport active, move the pointer into it and press the pick button.

As you draw in one viewport, the image is displayed in all viewports. Try drawing lines and other shapes and notice how the viewports are affected. Then use a display command, such as **ZOOM**, in the active viewport and notice the results. Only the active viewport reflects the use of the **ZOOM** command.

If you want to join two viewports together, you can do so by picking **Join** from the **Viewports** cascading menu in the **View** pull-down menu. Once **Join** is selected, you are prompted to Select dominant viewport. Select the viewport that has the view you want to keep in the joined viewport.

Once the dominant viewport is selected, you are prompted to Select viewport to join. Select the viewport that you want to join with the active viewport. Once you select a viewport to join, AutoCAD "glues" the two viewports together and retains the dominant view. The two viewports you are joining cannot create an L-shape viewport. In other words, the two edges of the viewports must be the same size in order to join them.

NOTE

The **-VPORTS** command can be used to create viewports at the Command: prompt. Enter -VPORTS and the following prompt appears:

Command: **-VPORTS**↵
Enter an option [Save/Restore/Delete/Join/SIngle/?/2/
<3>/4] <3>:

The options are similar to those already discussed.

Uses of Tiled Viewports

Viewports in model space can be used for both 2D and 3D drawings. They are limited only by your imagination and need. See ***AutoCAD and its Applications—Advanced*** for examples of the tiled viewports in 3D. The nature of 2D drawings, whether mechanical multiview, architectural construction details, or unscaled schematic drawings, lend themselves well to viewports.

NOTE

Several sample drawings are included with the AutoCAD software. If AutoCAD was installed using default settings, the sample drawings should be located in the AutoCAD Sample folder. Check with your instructor or supervisor to locate these drawings, or browse through the folders to determine their locations. The sample drawings include a variety of drawing and design disciplines and are excellent for testing and practice. You should use these drawings, especially when learning the display commands.

EXERCISE 10-5 Complete the Exercise on the Student CD.

Floating Viewports

The layout tabs are used to set up a page to be printed or plotted. The paper space environment is activated when you switch from the **Model** tab to a layout tab. Viewports created in paper space are called floating viewports. These *floating viewports* are actually holes cut into the paper in the layout tab so that the model space drawing can be seen. These viewports are separate objects and can overlap, thus the term "floating viewports," as they can be moved around.

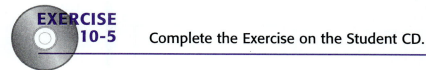

After floating viewports are created, display commands are used to modify the model space "showing through" the viewport. Editing commands such as **MOVE**, **ERASE**, and **COPY** can be used in paper space to modify the viewports.

As you work through the following sections describing floating viewports, be sure a layout tab is selected on your AutoCAD screen.

> **NOTE** The first time you select a layout tab, the **Page Setup** dialog box may appear. This dialog box will be discussed in Chapter 11. For the time being, simply pick the **OK** button to access the layout tab.

Creating Floating Viewports

The process of creating floating viewports in paper space is nearly identical to the process of creating tiled viewports in model space. A viewport configuration can be selected from the **Viewports** dialog box, which was discussed earlier in this chapter. Also, the **MVIEW** command options can be used to create single or multiple viewports.

MVIEW
MV

As discussed earlier, when model space is active, the **Viewports** dialog box creates tiled viewports. When paper space is active, it creates floating viewports. This dialog box differs slightly depending on the current environment—model space or paper space. The **Apply to:** drop-down list found in model space becomes the **Viewport spacing:** text box in paper space. Use this setting to specify the space around the edges of the floating viewports. See **Figure 10-26.**

Floating viewports can also be created using the **MVIEW** command.

Command: **MV** *or* **MVIEW**↵
Specify corner of viewport or [ON/OFF/Fit/Shadeplot/Lock/Object/Polygonal/
Restore/2/3/4] <Fit>:

The default option is to define a rectangular floating viewport by selecting opposite corners. See **Figure 10-27.**

Figure 10-26.
When paper space is active, the **New Viewports** tab in the **Viewports** dialog box contains the **Viewport Spacing:** setting.

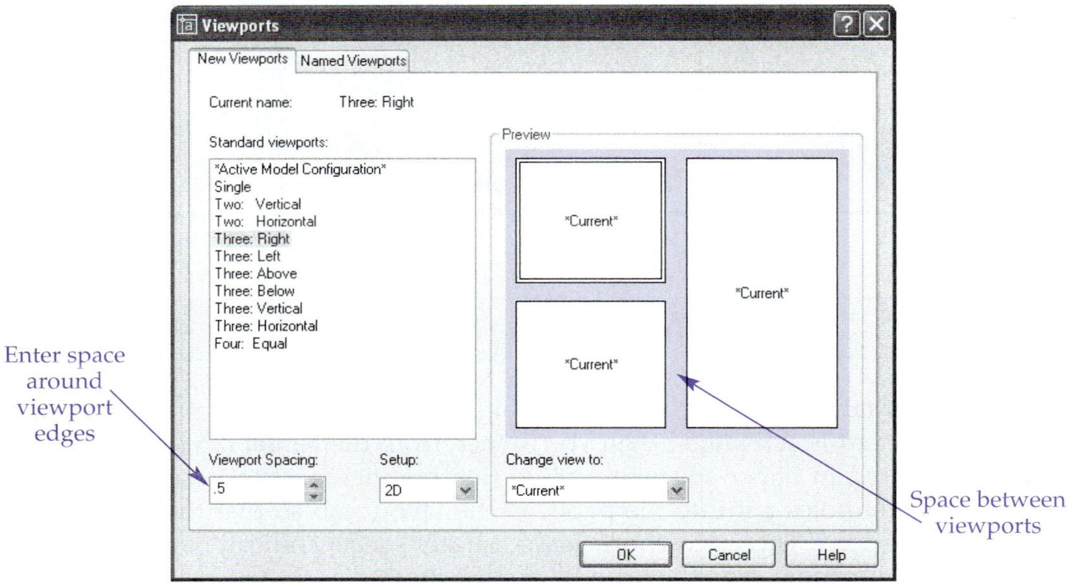

Figure 10-27.
Creating a rectangular floating viewport using the **MVIEW** command.

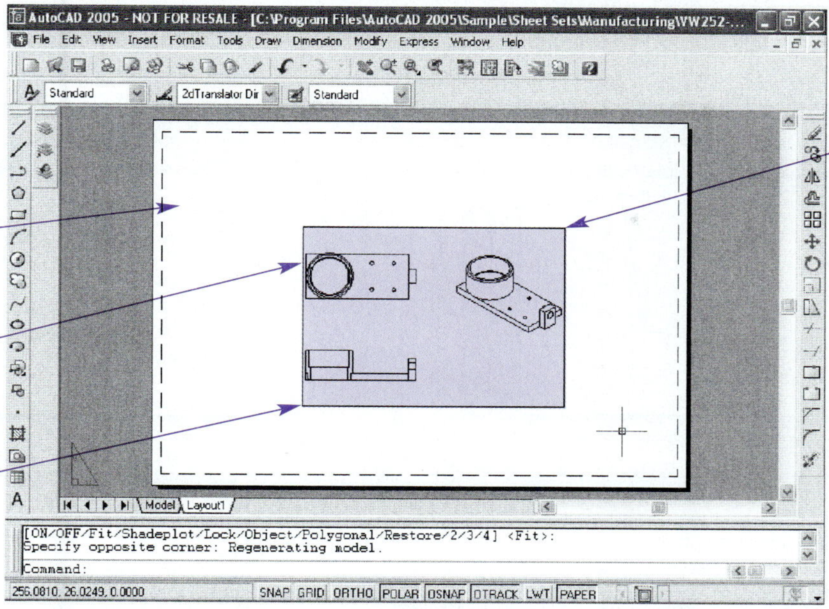

The **2**, **3**, and **4** options provide preset viewport configurations similar to the **Viewports** dialog box. These options can also be selected from the **Viewports** cascading menu in the **View** pull-down menu, as was discussed for tiled viewports.

The remaining options are described as follows:

- **ON and OFF.** These options activate and deactivate the model space display within a viewport. When you enter the **OFF** option, you are prompted to select the viewports to be affected. Use the **ON** option to reactivate the viewport.
- **Fit.** This default option creates a single rectangular floating viewport that fills the entire printable area on the sheet.
- **Shadeplot.** Specifies how viewports in layouts appear when plotted. This option is covered in greater detail in *AutoCAD and its Applications—Advanced.*
- **Lock.** This option allows you to lock the view in one or more viewports. When a viewport is locked, objects within the viewport can still be edited and new objects can be added, but you are unable to use display commands such as **ZOOM** and **PAN**. This option is also used to unlock a locked viewport.
- **Restore.** Converts saved viewport configurations into individual floating viewports.
- **Object.** Use this option to change a closed object drawn in paper space into a floating viewport. Circles, ellipses, polygons, and other closed shapes can be used as floating viewport outlines. See Figure 10-28. This option can also be accessed by picking the **Convert Object to Viewport** button in the **Viewports** toolbar or by selecting **Object** from the **Viewports** cascading menu in the **View** pull-down menu.

View
➡ Viewports
➡ Object

Viewports toolbar

Convert Object to Viewport

- **Polygonal.** Use this option to draw a floating viewport outline using a polyline. Polylines are discussed in Chapter 14. The viewport shape can be any closed shape composed of lines and arcs. This option can also be accessed by picking the **Polygonal Viewport** button in the **Viewports** toolbar or by selecting **Polygonal Viewport** from the **Viewports** cascading menu in the **View** pull-down menu.

View
➡ Viewports
➡ Polygonal Viewports

Viewports toolbar

Polygonal Viewport

Figure 10-28.
Viewports can be created from closed objects. A—Draw the objects in paper space. B—Objects converted to viewports.

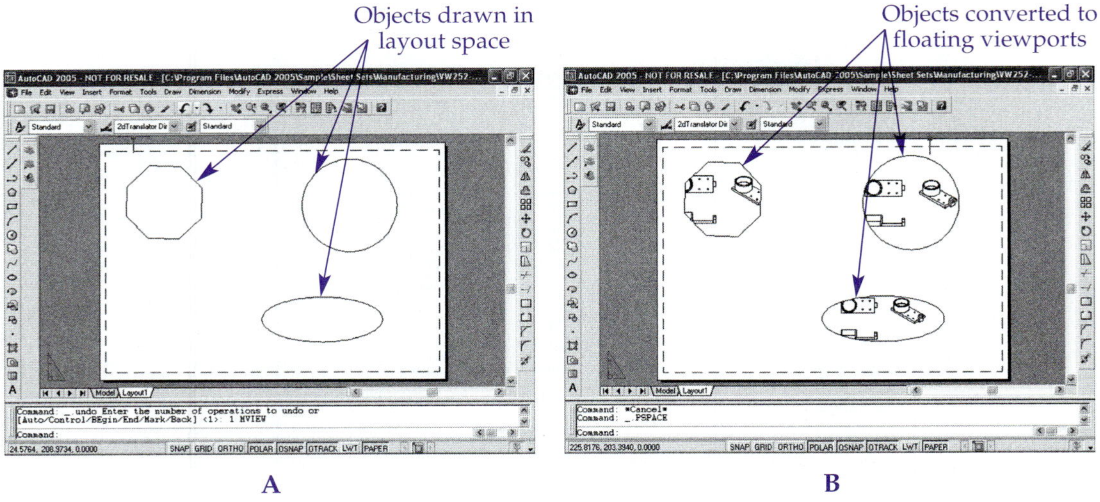

Introduction to 3D Display Commands

AutoCAD provides several tools for creating 3D views. The following sections describe two of these methods: the **3DORBIT** command and viewpoint presets found in the **View** pull-down menu. An introduction to the basics of 3D drawing can be found in Chapter 27.

Using 3DOrbit to Obtain a View

3DORBIT
3DO

View
➥ 3D Orbit

3D Orbit toolbar

3D Orbit

The **3DORBIT** command is a viewing tool that dynamically obtains a new 3D view of your drawing. To access the **3DORBIT** command, pick the **3D Orbit** button from the **3D Orbit** toolbar, select **3D Orbit** from the **View** pull-down menu, or enter 3DO or 3DORBIT at the Command: prompt. If you are realtime zooming or realtime panning, you can right-click and select **3D Orbit** from the shortcut menu.

Once the **3DORBIT** command is accessed, a 3D view appears in the active viewport. The UCS (User Coordinate System) is changed to a shaded 3D icon, and an arcball, which is a circle divided into four quadrants by smaller circles, appears in the middle of the viewport. See Figure 10-29.

The drawing crosshairs also change to a sphere encircled with two lines. By holding down the pick button and moving your pointing device, a 3D view can be obtained. By dragging the pointing device you can see your new viewpoint adjust. It is like walking around your drawing and moving your eye position up, down, and around.

If the cursor is moved over the top of one of the quadrant circles on the arcball, it changes shape, showing you the direction the view can be rotated. If the right mouse button is pressed, a shortcut menu appears so you can use realtime zoom or realtime pan. There are several other options and possibilities with the **3DORBIT** command. The **3DORBIT** command is covered in greater detail in ***AutoCAD and its Applications—Advanced.***

Figure 10-29.
When you activate the **3DORBIT** command, the arcball, shaded UCS icon, and 3D Orbit cursor appear. You can then rotate the objects in 3D space.

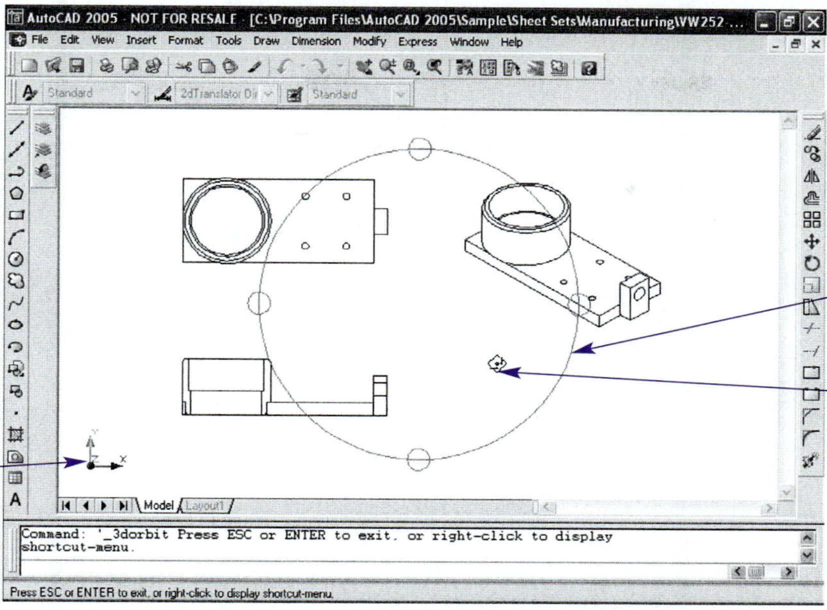

Using Preset Isometric and Orthographic Views

When creating 3D drawings, viewports can be used to display different 3D views of the object or structure. The **3DORBIT** command can be used to specify the viewpoint in each viewport. Another method of specifying viewpoints is using the preset isometric and orthographic viewpoints available in the **View** pull-down menu.

The following example provides an introduction to using the preset 3D viewpoints using the Oil Module.dwg drawing in the AutoCAD \Sample folder. First, open the Oil Module.dwg drawing. The drawing that appears is a 3D model of oil piping. It is displayed in a model tab from a northwest isometric view.

Select **Top** from the **3D Views** cascading menu in the **View** pull-down menu. This sets the viewpoint for an orthographic top view, which is the same as a plan view. Your display should look like Figure 10-30.

Access the **Viewports** dialog box and select the Three: Right configuration. Next, make the large viewport active by picking anywhere inside it. Then, select **2D Wireframe** from the **Shade** cascading menu in the **View** pull-down menu. This allows viewing of the model in a wireframe view.

Select the **NE Isometric** option from the **3D Views** cascading menu in the **View** pull-down menu. The model is now displayed as if you were viewing it from an elevated location from the northeast. Use the **ZOOM** command to display the "nearest" corner of the model, as shown in Figure 10-31.

Pick a point within the upper-left viewport to make it active. Select the **Right** option from the **3D Views** cascading menu in the **View** pull-down menu to create a right elevation view. Use the **ZOOM** command to display the corner shown in the large viewport. Repeat the process in the lower-left viewport using the **Back** option instead of the **Right** option. Finally, activate each viewport and enter HIDE at the Command: prompt to remove hidden lines. The **HIDE** command affects only the active viewport, so you will need to enter the command three times. The finished drawing is shown in Figure 10-32.

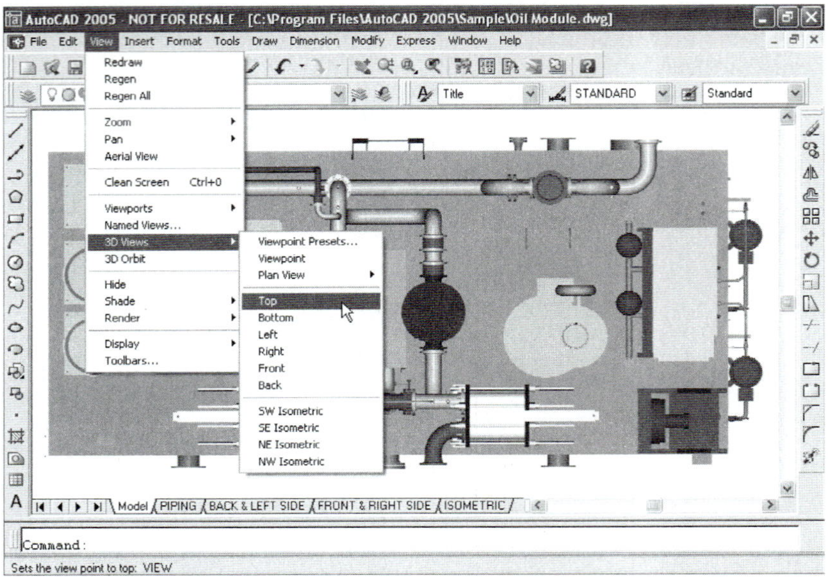

Figure 10-30.
Plan (top) view of the Oil Module drawing.

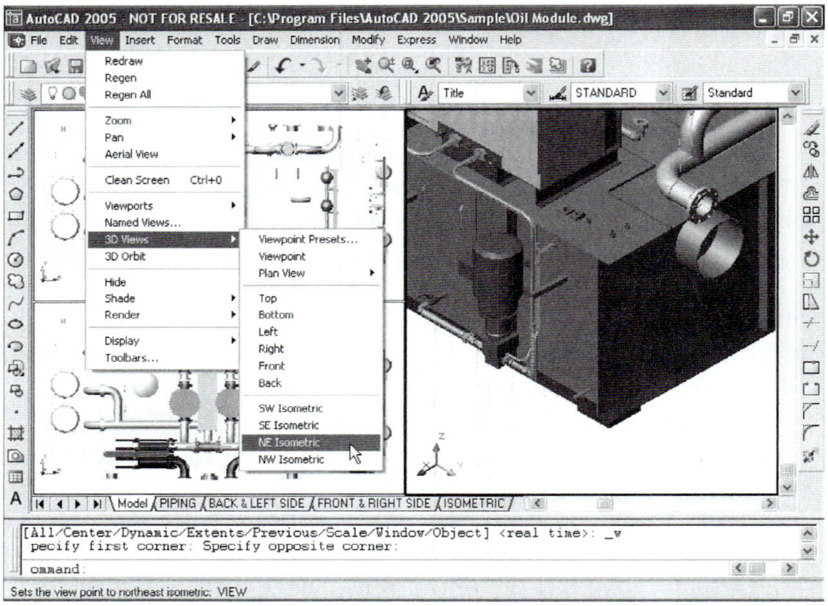

Figure 10-31.
The large viewport is set to the NE isometric viewpoint and shaded.

NOTE

In addition to the **3DORBIT** command and the preset 3D viewpoints, there are several other tools available in AutoCAD to establish 3D views. The **DVIEW** command defines a viewing "camera" and "target" for precise control of the view. The **VPOINT** or **DDVPOINT** command allows you to define a viewing direction by entering coordinates at the Command: prompt or by dynamically positioning a compass and tripod. The tool you choose to use to establish a 3D view depends on the subject and requirements of the view. All of the 3D viewing tools are discussed thoroughly in ***AutoCAD and its Applications—Advanced.***

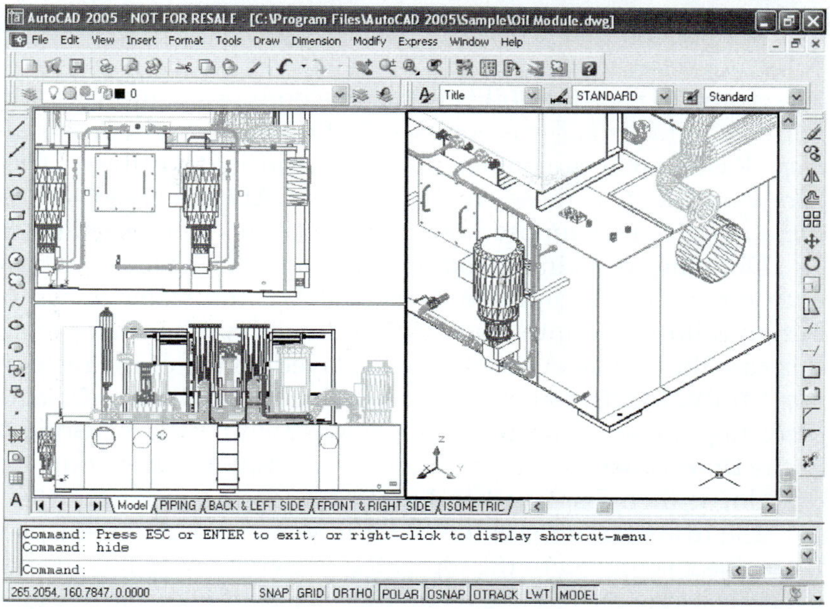

Figure 10-32.
Three different 3D views of the Oil Module drawing.

EXERCISE 10-6 Complete the Exercise on the Student CD.

Redrawing and Regenerating Viewports

Since each viewport is a separate screen, you can redraw or regenerate a single viewport at a time without affecting the others. The **REGEN** (regenerate) command instructs AutoCAD to recalculate all objects in the drawing. This takes considerably longer than a **REDRAW**, especially if the drawing is large. However, **REGEN** can clarify a drawing by smoothing out circles, arcs, ellipses, and splines.

REDRAWALL
RA
View
➥ Redraw

To redraw all viewports, use the **REDRAWALL** command or pick **Redraw** from the **View** pull-down menu. If you need to regenerate all viewports, use the **REGENALL** command or pick **Regen All** from the **View** pull-down menu.

REGENALL
REA
View
➥ Regen All

Controlling Automatic Regeneration

When developing a drawing, you may use a command that changes certain aspects of the entities. When this occurs, AutoCAD does an automatic regeneration to update the objects. This may not be of concern to you when working on small drawings, but this regeneration may take considerable time on large and complex drawings. In addition, it may not be necessary to have a regeneration of the drawing at all times. If this is the case, set the **REGENAUTO** command to off.

Command: **REGENAUTO**↵
Enter mode [ON/OFF] <*current*>: **OFF**↵
Command:

Some of the commands that may automatically cause a regeneration are **PLAN**, **HIDE**, and **VIEW Restore**.

Controlling the Order of Display

AutoCAD has the ability to display both raster and vector images in the graphics window. A *raster image* is composed of dots, or pixels, and is also referred to as a *bit map*. Raster images contain no XYZ coordinate values. Objects in a *vector image* (drawing), such as those created in AutoCAD, are given XYZ coordinate values. All these objects are composed of points, or *vectors*, connected by straight lines.

DRAWORDER
DR

Tools
➥ **Draw Order**
➥ **Bring Above Objects**

Draw Order toolbar

Bring Above Objects

Drawings containing both raster and vector images can have objects that overlap each other. For example, in Figure 10-33A the raster image of the **Zoom Previous** button is imported into AutoCAD and overlays the vector image of the text label. In this case the text label should be displayed on top of the raster image. To do this, use the **DRAWORDER** command by picking **Bring Above Objects** in the **Draw Order** cascading menu of the **Tools** pull-down menu, pick the **Bring Above Objects** button in the **Draw Order** toolbar, or enter DR or DRAWORDER at the Command: prompt. The drawing is then displayed and plotted as shown in Figure 10-33B.

The drawing order is the order in which objects are displayed, plotted, or both. If an object is moved to the top of the drawing order, it is displayed and plotted first. If one object is moved above another object, it is displayed on top—such as the text in Figure 10-33B. These order and arrangement functions are handled by the following **DRAWORDER** options:

AutoCAD 2005
NEW FEATURE

- **Above objects.** The selected object is moved above the reference object.
- **Under objects.** The selected object is moved below the reference object.
- **Front.** The selected object is placed to the front of the drawing.
- **Back.** The selected object is placed to the back of the drawing.

These options can also be accessed from the selected object shortcut menu.

NOTE

See *AutoCAD and its Applications—Advanced* for more detailed information on the use of raster drawings in AutoCAD.

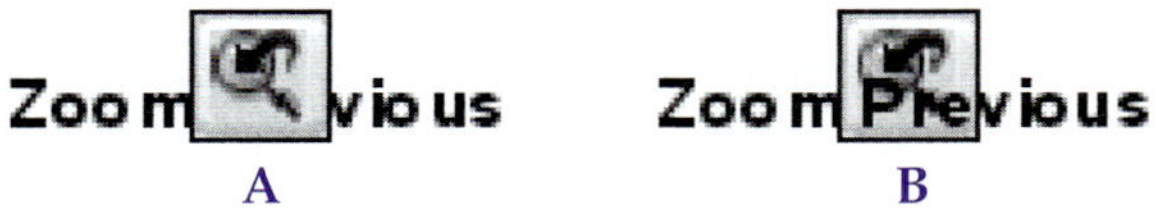

Figure 10-33.
A—An imported raster image obscures part of a vector drawing.
B—The **DRAWORDER** command is used to bring the vector drawing above the raster image.

Clearing the Screen

The AutoCAD window can become crowded in the course of a drawing session. Each toolbar and modeless dialog box displayed on-screen reduces the size of the drawing area. As the drawing area gets smaller, less of the drawing is visible. This can make drafting difficult. You can quickly maximize the size of the drawing area using the **Clean Screen** tool.

This tool clears the AutoCAD window of all toolbars, modeless dialog boxes, and title bars. See **Figure 10-34.** The **Clean Screen** tool is accessed by picking **Clean Screen** from the **View** pull-down menu or using the [Ctrl]+[0] (zero) key combination. To return to the normal display, use the [Ctrl]+[0] (zero) key combination.

[Ctrl]+[0]

View
➥ **Clean Screen**

PROFESSIONAL TIP

The **Clean Screen** tool can be helpful when you have multiple drawings displayed. Only the active drawing is displayed when the **Clean Screen** tool is used. This allows you to work more efficiently within one of the drawings. You can use the **Window** pull-down menu options to switch between drawings.

Figure 10-34.
Using the **Clean Screen** tool. A—Initial display with default toolbars displayed. B—Display after using the **Clean Screen** tool.

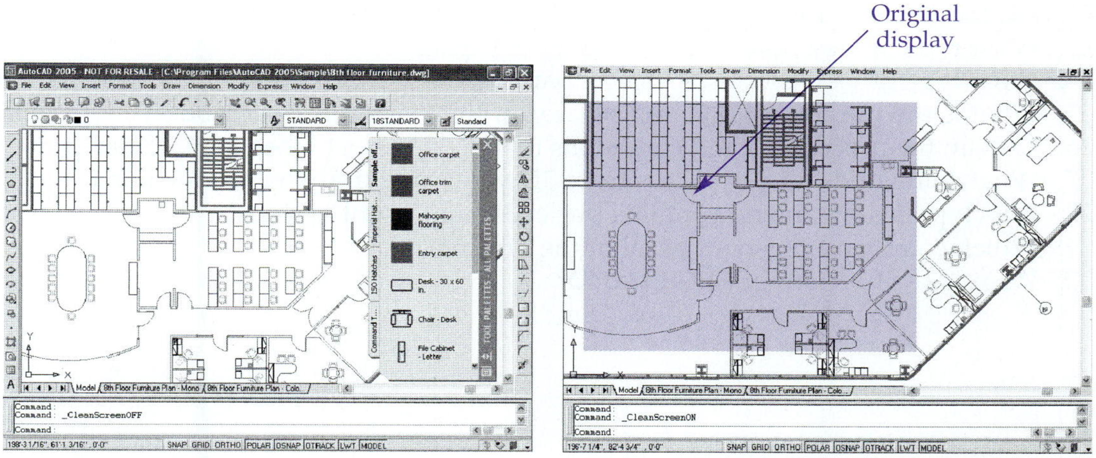

A B

Chapter Test

Answer the following questions on a separate sheet of paper.

1. What is the difference between the **REDRAW** and **'REDRAW** commands?
2. What are *blips* and how does **REDRAW** affect them?
3. Which command allows you to change the display of blips?
4. Give the proper command option and value to automatically zoom to a 2X scale factor.
5. What is the difference between **ZOOM Extents** and **ZOOM All**?
6. During the drawing process, when should you use **ZOOM**?
7. How many different boxes are displayed during the **ZOOM Dynamic** command?
8. What is a *pan displacement*?
9. When using the **ZOOM Dynamic** option, what represents the current view?
10. What is the purpose of the **PAN** command?
11. Explain how scroll bars can be used to pan the drawing display.
12. How do you access the **PAN** command presets?
13. What is *view resolution*?
14. In which dialog box is circle and arc smoothness set?
15. How do you create a named view of the current screen display?
16. How do you display an existing view?
17. How would you obtain a listing of existing views?
18. How is a transparent display command entered at the keyboard?
19. What is the effect of picking **Global** from the **View** pull-down menu in the **Aerial View** window?
20. What is the function of the **Auto Viewport** option of the **Aerial View** window?
21. Cite several advantages of **Aerial View** over other display commands.
22. Explain the difference between model space and paper space.
23. What type of viewport is created in model space?
24. What type of viewport is created in paper space?
25. What is the purpose of the **Preview** area of the **Viewports** dialog box?
26. Explain the procedures and conditions that need to exist when joining viewports.
27. What commands allow you to create 3D views in a drawing or viewport?
28. Which pull-down menu contains preset 3D viewpoint options?
29. Which command regenerates all of the viewports?
30. What is the function of **REGENAUTO**?

Drawing Problems

1. Open the drawing named wilhome.dwg found in the AutoCAD \Sample folder. Perform the following display functions on the drawing:
   A. Select the **Model** tab.
   B. **ZOOM Extents**.
   C. Create a view named All.
   D. Zoom in to display the right side of the building.
   E. Create a view of this new window named Grand Entrance.
   F. **ZOOM Previous**.
   G. Use realtime pan and realtime zoom to create a display of the lower-left staircase.
   H. Create a view of this display named Kitchen Elevations.
   I. Display the view named All.
   J. Save the drawing as P10-1.

2. Load one of your own mechanical template drawings that contains a border and title block. Do the following:
   A. Zoom into the title block area. Create and save a view named Title.
   B. Zoom to the extents of the drawing and create and save a view named All.
   C. Determine the area of the drawing that will contain notes, parts list, or revisions. Zoom into these areas and create views with appropriate names such as Notes, Partlist, and Revisions.
   D. Divide the drawing area into commonly used multiview sections. Save the views with descriptive names such as Top, Front, Rightside, and Leftside.
   E. Restore the view named All.
   F. Save the drawing as P10-2, or as a template.

3. Load one of your own template drawings used for architectural layout that contains a border and title block. Do the following:
   A. Zoom into the title block area. Create and save a view named Title.
   B. Zoom to the extents of the drawing and create and save a view named All.
   C. Determine the area of the drawing that will contain notes, schedules, or revisions. Zoom into these areas and create views with appropriate names such as Notes, Schedules, and Revisions.
   D. Restore the view named All.
   E. Save the drawing as P10-3, or as a template.

4. Open the drawing named Oil Module.dwg. This drawing should be in the AutoCAD \Sample folder. Perform the following:
   A. Make sure the **Model** tab is active. Set the named view FRONT as the current view.
   B. Pick **4 Viewports** from the **Viewports** cascading menu in the **View** pull-down menu. In each viewport, zoom to a different quadrant of the drawing. Pick **2D Wireframe** from the **Shade** cascading menu in the **View** pull-down menu in each viewport.
   C. Create named views of different parts of the module, such as LowerRight, LowerLeft, UpperRight, and UpperLeft.
   D. In the upper-right viewport, **ZOOM All** and create a view named All.
   E. Use **3DORBIT** to obtain a 3D view in the upper-right viewport and use the **HIDE** command to remove the hidden lines.
   F. Make the upper-left viewport active and split it into four equal viewports.
   G. In each of the new viewports, restore your named views from step C.
   H. Pick **Join** from the **Viewports** cascading menu in the **View** pull-down menu to join the two far-right viewports together. Make the 3D view the dominant view.
   I. In the lower-left viewport, restore the **All** view.
   J. Save the drawing as P10-4 only if required by your instructor.

CHAPTER 11

Layouts, Plotting, and Printing

Learning Objectives

After completing this chapter, you will be able to do the following:

- Print and plot a drawing.
- Set up layouts using title blocks and viewports.
- Create new layouts.
- Manage layouts.
- Select a plotting device and modify a plotting device configuration.
- Explain plot styles, plot style tables, and plot style modes.
- Create and modify plot styles and plot style tables.
- Attach plot style tables to drawings and layouts.
- Assign plot styles to drawings, layers, and objects.
- Select plot settings.
- Calculate scale factors based on drawing scale.
- Create a plot file.
- Plot a group of drawings using the Batch Plot utility.
- Explain keys to efficient plotting.

Often, the end result of your AutoCAD work will be a plotted drawing. It is far easier for a construction crew in the field to use a printed copy of the drawing rather than use a computer to view the DWG file. Therefore, it is important that you understand the various plotting options available in AutoCAD.

Paper space, model space, the **Model** tab, and layout tabs were discussed in Chapter 10. Each layout tab can be set to plot different views of the objects using different plotting settings. This allows you to create several different plots using a single drawing.

Plotting Procedure

You can create plots from the **Model** tab (model space) and from the layout tabs (paper space). The general procedures for both cases are similar. The following steps are explained later in this chapter:

1. Create the drawing objects in the **Model** tab (model space). If you are creating a layout, create the floating viewports, title block, and other desired items in a layout tab (paper space).

2. Configure the plotting device if it is not already configured.
3. Access the **Page Setup Manager** or **Plot** dialog box and specify values for the plotting settings. Each tab (**Model** and layout) can have its own settings, so each layout can produce a different plot.
4. Plot the drawing.

Layout and Plotting Terms

It is important to understand the terminology used when discussing model space, paper space, layouts, and plotting. Therefore, this section provides you with a quick overview of the commands and functions that enable you to lay out and plot a drawing. These terms are described in greater detail later in this chapter.

- **Model space.** This is the drawing environment in which the drawing objects are constructed. Model space is active when the **Model** tab is selected. Model space is also activated when you double-click inside a floating viewport in a layout tab.
- **Paper space.** This is the drawing environment used to create plotting layouts, which are arrangements of various objects (such as floating viewports, title blocks, and annotations) on the page to be plotted. Paper space is active by default when a layout tab is selected. If you double-click inside a floating viewport in a layout tab, the viewport becomes active and model space is entered. To switch back to paper space, double-click in an area outside the floating viewport.
- **Layouts.** A layout is the manner in which a drawing is arranged in paper space. A layout may contain a title block, one or more viewports, and annotations. Each drawing can have multiple layouts, and each layout is shown as a tab along the bottom of the drawing area. Each layout can have different page setups and plotting settings.
- **Page setups.** A page setup is the manner in which the drawing is displayed on a sheet of paper in order to create a layout. Most of the aspects of how the drawing is plotted can be established in a page setup, from the plot device to pen settings to scales. Other included settings are paper size and drawing units, paper orientation, plot area, plot scale, plot offset, and plot options. These settings can even be saved in the drawing file as a named page setup, which can be recalled each time the drawing is plotted.
- **Plotters window.** The **Plotters** window allows you to add, delete, configure, and reconfigure plotters. It can be accessed by selecting **Plotter Manager...** from the **File** pull-down menu. When a device is configured, the settings are saved in a PC3 file.
- **Plot styles.** Plot styles contain settings that are applied to objects when they are plotted. A *color-dependent plot style* is applied to all objects with a specific color. A *named plot style* can be assigned to an object or layer.
- **Plot style tables.** A plot style table is a collection of plot styles. There are two types of plot style tables: color-dependent and named. A plot style table can only contain plot styles of a single *plot style mode* (either color-dependent or named). The **Model** tab and each layout tab can have a unique plot style table attached. Only plot styles in the attached plot style table can be used within a tab.
- **Plot Styles window.** The **Plot Styles** window allows you to manage all your plot style table files. From here you can open and edit the plot styles within a plot style table. You can also create new plot style tables.

- **Plot settings.** These settings are created in the **Plot** dialog box and include many of the same items found in the **Page Setup** dialog box. They control how the drawing is printed on paper. Although this may seem like the last step in the process, plot settings can be created at the beginning of a project and then saved to be used again.

Layout Settings

A ***layout*** shows the arrangement of objects on a sheet of paper for plotting purposes. A layout may include a title block, floating viewports showing your model space drawing, and annotation.

A single drawing can have multiple layouts. Named layouts are displayed as tabs along the bottom of the drawing area. Each layout tab represents a different paper space configuration.

When you start AutoCAD, a new drawing is started automatically. This drawing is based on a template file containing default settings and has two layouts by default. These layouts are identified by the **Layout1** and **Layout2** tabs below the drawing area. When you pick a layout tab for the first time, the layout will be displayed using default settings primarily based on an 8.5″ × 11″ sheet of paper in a landscape orientation.

When a layout tab is selected, an image showing a preview of the final printed drawing is shown. See **Figure 11-1.** The dashed line around the edge of the paper represents the page margins. The solid lines show the outline of a floating viewport. By default, a single viewport is created.

Figure 11-1. A layout is displayed when a layout tab is selected. The layout provides a preview of how the plotted drawing will appear.

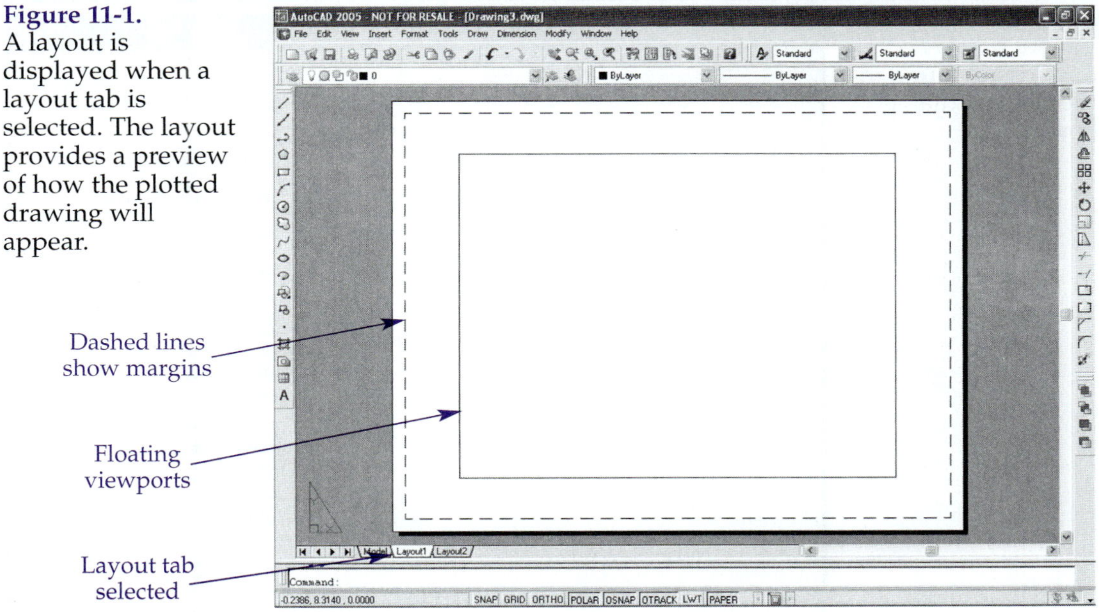

Working in Layout Tabs

A layout can contain many types of objects, including floating viewports, a title block, and various types of annotation such as, general notes, revision levels and descriptions, and a bill of material. Assembling these items in a layout allows you to see exactly what the final plot will look like.

Several settings that affect the display of layouts are contained in the **Layout elements** area of the **Display** tab in the **Options** dialog box. See Figure 11-2. Access this dialog box by selecting **Options...** from the **Tools** pull-down menu. Use the default settings until you are comfortable working with layouts.

Inserting a title block

Most layouts contain a title block. Title blocks are generally saved in a template file and then inserted as a block when needed. A block is a single object comprising multiple individual objects. See Chapter 22 for a complete discussion on blocks.

It is best to insert a title block into the layout and then save it as a template file. You can then start a new drawing based on the template, and the layout with the title block will already be created.

To insert a title block, select **Block...** from the **Insert** pull-down menu to access the **Insert** dialog box. Pick the **Browse...** button and select the title block drawing to be inserted. Figure 11-3 shows the ANSI A title block inserted into a layout.

> **NOTE**
>
> You can also copy a layout containing the title block from an existing drawing using **DesignCenter**. This is discussed later in this chapter.

Figure 11-2.
Layout display options are found in the **Options** dialog box.

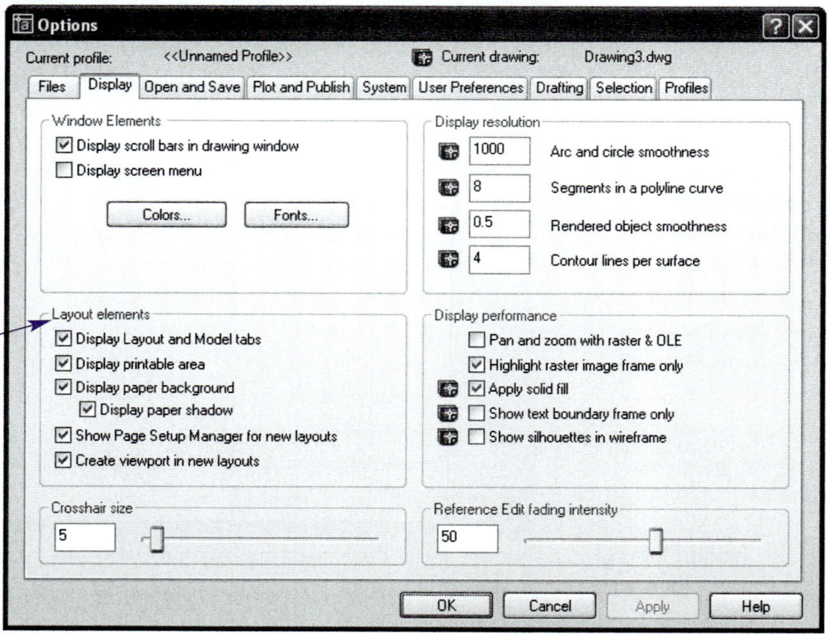

Layout display options

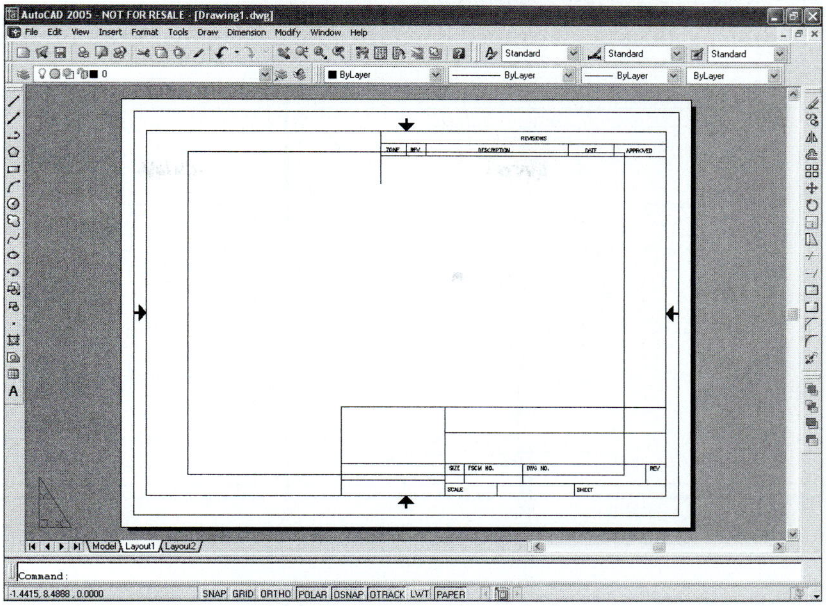

Figure 11-3.
The ANSI A title block inserted into the layout. Note the viewport created by default has been deleted.

Working with floating viewports

Chapter 10 explained how to create floating viewports in a layout. Once the viewports are created, the display within the viewport must be set to show the correct part of the model space drawing.

Create the floating viewports after the title block has been inserted. This will allow you to position the viewports so they do not interfere with the title block. Floating viewports are created using the **Viewports** dialog box or the **MVIEW** command.

Figure 11-4 illustrates the following procedure for establishing the display in two floating viewports:

1. Create the first viewport using the **Viewports** dialog box. The model space drawing is visible in the viewport.
2. Create a second viewport.
3. Double-click in the new viewport to enter model space.
4. Use the **XP** option of the **ZOOM** command or the scale drop-down list on the **Viewports** toolbar to scale the drawing. Use realtime panning to display the part of interest in the drawing.
5. Double-click outside of the viewports to activate paper space. Use grips or the **STRETCH** command to resize the viewport.

Using multiple viewports in a layout allows you to illustrate different aspects of the drawing. Using multiple layouts, various types of drawings can be created from a single drawing model. This is a very simple example of the use of floating viewports within a layout. Figure 11-5 shows the viewports created by the **Std. 3D Engineering Views** option available in the **Create Layout** wizard. The viewports show the three primary orthographic views and an isometric view. The **Create Layout** wizard is discussed later in this chapter.

> **CAUTION**
>
> If you use zoom to adjust the drawing inside the viewport, the drawing may no longer be to scale. Always use the **ZOOM XP** option or the scale drop-down list on the **Viewports** toolbar as the final step prior to plotting to be certain the drawing is scaled inside the viewport.

Figure 11-4.
These steps illustrate the procedure for adding viewports to a simple layout outlined in the text.

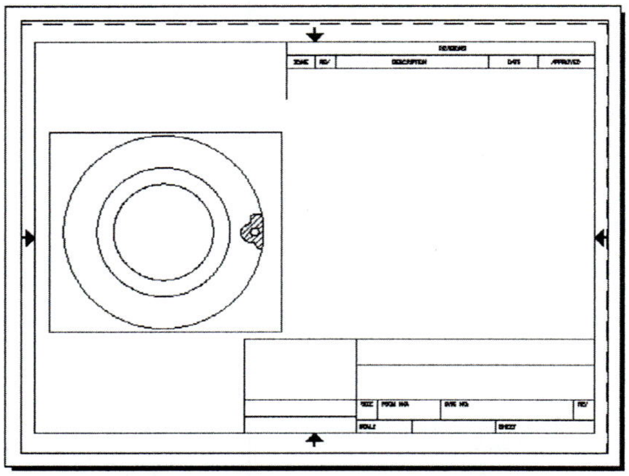

Step 1—Create viewport.

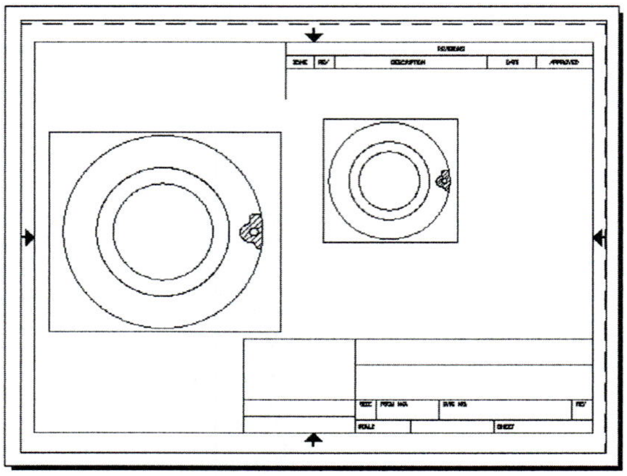

Step 2—Create second viewport.

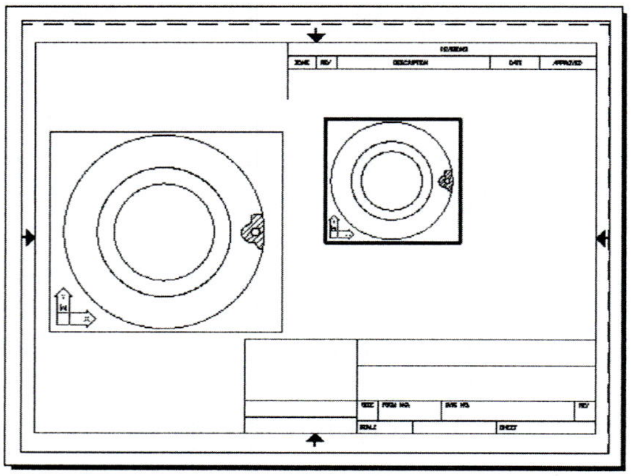

Step 3—Make second viewport active.

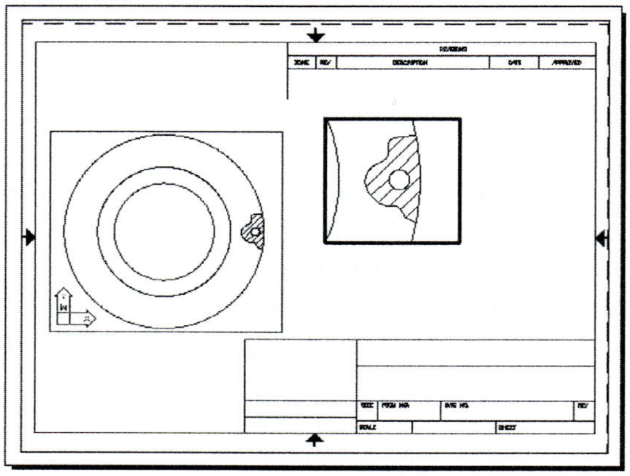

Step 4—Zoom and pan display in second viewport.

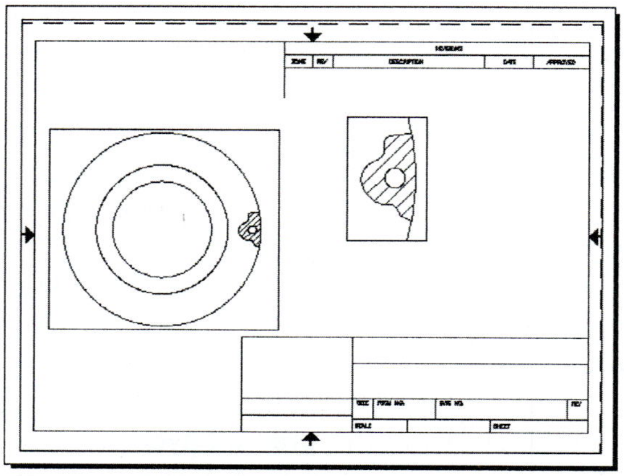

Step 5—Resize viewport.

EXERCISE 11-1 Complete the Exercise on the Student CD.

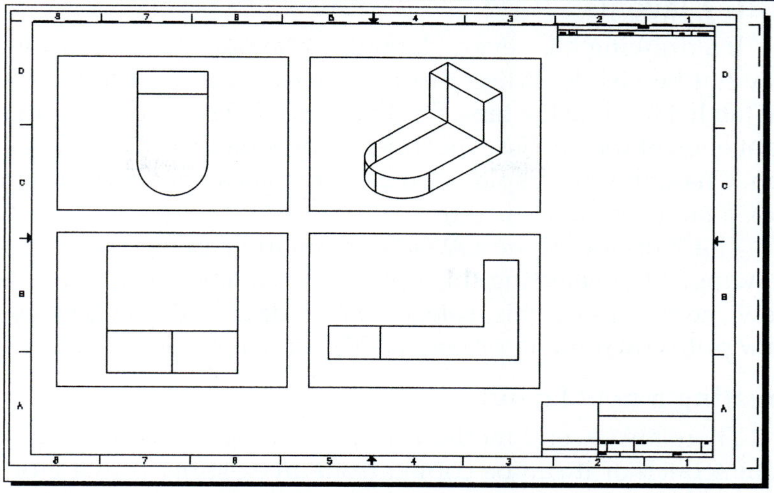

Figure 11-5.
This example shows the ANSI D title block and the **Std. 3D Engineering Views** viewport configuration. This configuration is available in the **Create Layout** wizard.

Managing Layouts

The **LAYOUT** command allows you to manage layouts. To access this command, type LO or LAYOUT at the Command: prompt:

Command: **LO** *or* **LAYOUT**↵
Enter layout option [Copy/Delete/New/Template/Rename/SAveas/Set/?] <set>:

You are prompted to select a **LAYOUT** command option. Some of these options are also available in the **Layouts** toolbars or the **Layout** cascading menu of the **Insert** pull-down menu. You can also position the cursor over a layout tab and right-click to display the layout shortcut menu, Figure 11-6. This shortcut menu also contains many **LAYOUT** command options.

Setting the current layout

The current layout is identified by the highlighted tab at the bottom of the drawing area. To set the current layout, pick the layout tab using the cursor. You can also use the **Set** option of the **LAYOUT** command to specify the current layout.

PROFESSIONAL TIP

If you are selecting options from the layout shortcut menu, you must have the appropriate layout set as current before selecting the command. For example, if you select **Delete** from the layout shortcut menu, the current layout is deleted. If you work at the Command: prompt, the current layout is the default but you can specify a different layout.

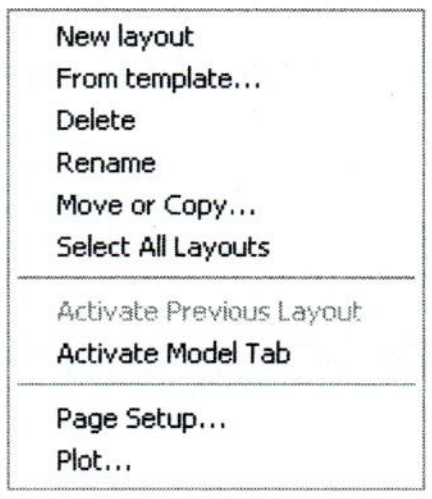

Figure 11-6.
Right-click on a layout tab to display the layout shortcut menu. Many options for managing layouts are available.

Listing layouts

If a drawing has several layouts or layouts with fairly long names, all layout tabs may not be visible. When this is the case, you can use the four buttons to the left of the tab list to view the tabs. See **Figure 11-7.** The two outer arrows display the left and right ends of the tab list. The inner arrows move the list one tab in the indicated direction. Changing the display of the tab list does not affect the current tab. You still must pick a tab to set it as current.

The **?** option of the **LAYOUT** command can be used to list all layouts within the drawing. After selecting this option, you must switch to the **AutoCAD Text Window** to view the list. To do this, select **Text Window** from the **Display** cascading menu in the **View** pull-down menu or use the [F2] function key.

Creating a new layout

There are several methods of creating new layouts. A new layout can be created from scratch or it can be copied from an existing drawing or template file. Finally, a layout within the drawing can be copied to create a new layout. These methods are described as follows:

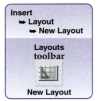

Insert
➥ Layout
➥ New Layout

Layouts toolbar

New Layout

- **New layout from scratch.** Use the **New** option of the **LAYOUT** command to create a new layout. You can also create a new layout by selecting **New Layout** from the **Layout** cascading menu in the **Insert** pull-down menu, picking the **New Layout** button in the **Layouts** toolbar, or by right-clicking on a layout tab and selecting **New layout** from the layout shortcut menu. If you select the option from the command line, toolbar, or pull-down menu, the following prompt appears:

  Enter new Layout name <Layout3>: *(type a name or accept default name)*

  The layout name appears on the layout tab. If you use the **New layout** option in the layout shortcut menu, the new layout is created with the default name. You can then use the **Rename** option to change the name.

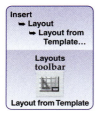

Insert
➥ Layout
➥ Layout from Template...

Layouts toolbar

Layout from Template

- **New layout from template.** This option creates a new layout based on a layout stored in an existing drawing or template file. Select this option by using the **Template** option of the **LAYOUT** command, selecting **Layout from Template...** from the **Layout** cascading menu in the **Insert** pull-down menu, or picking the **Layout from Template** button in the **Layouts** toolbar. You can also right-click on a layout tab and select **From template...** in the layout shortcut menu.

  When you select this option, the **Select Template From File** dialog box is displayed, **Figure 11-8A.** The Template folder in the path set by the AutoCAD Drawing Template File Location is selected by default. To verify the location of AutoCAD template files, access the **Files** tab in the **Options** dialog box, expand the **Template Settings** selection, and check the path listed under the Drawing Template File Location. After verifying the files location, close the **Options** dialog box and reopen the **Select Template From File** dialog box.

Figure 11-7.
Use the arrows to select which layout tabs are displayed.

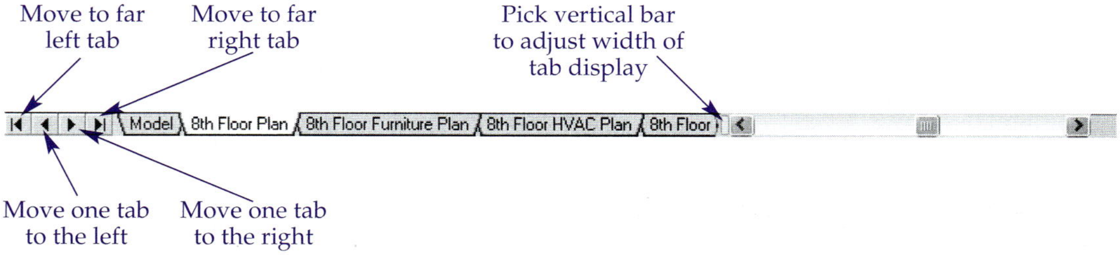

Select the drawing file or template file containing the layout to be copied and pick the **Open** button. If you selected the command option from the shortcut menu, toolbar, or pull-down menu, the **Insert Layout(s)** dialog box appears. See **Figure 11-8B.** This dialog box lists all layouts in the selected file. Highlight the layout(s) you want to copy and pick the **OK** button.

If you select this option from the command line, the **Insert Layout(s)** dialog box does not appear. Instead, you are prompted to enter the name of the layout to copy.

PROFESSIONAL TIP

It is much easier to select layouts to copy using the **Insert Layout(s)** dialog box than it is to enter the name at the Command: prompt. Therefore, use the shortcut menu, toolbar, or pull-down menu to select this **LAYOUT** command option.

Figure 11-8.
Creating a new layout from another drawing or template. A—Select the drawing or template containing the layout. B—Highlight the layout(s) to be added to the current drawing.

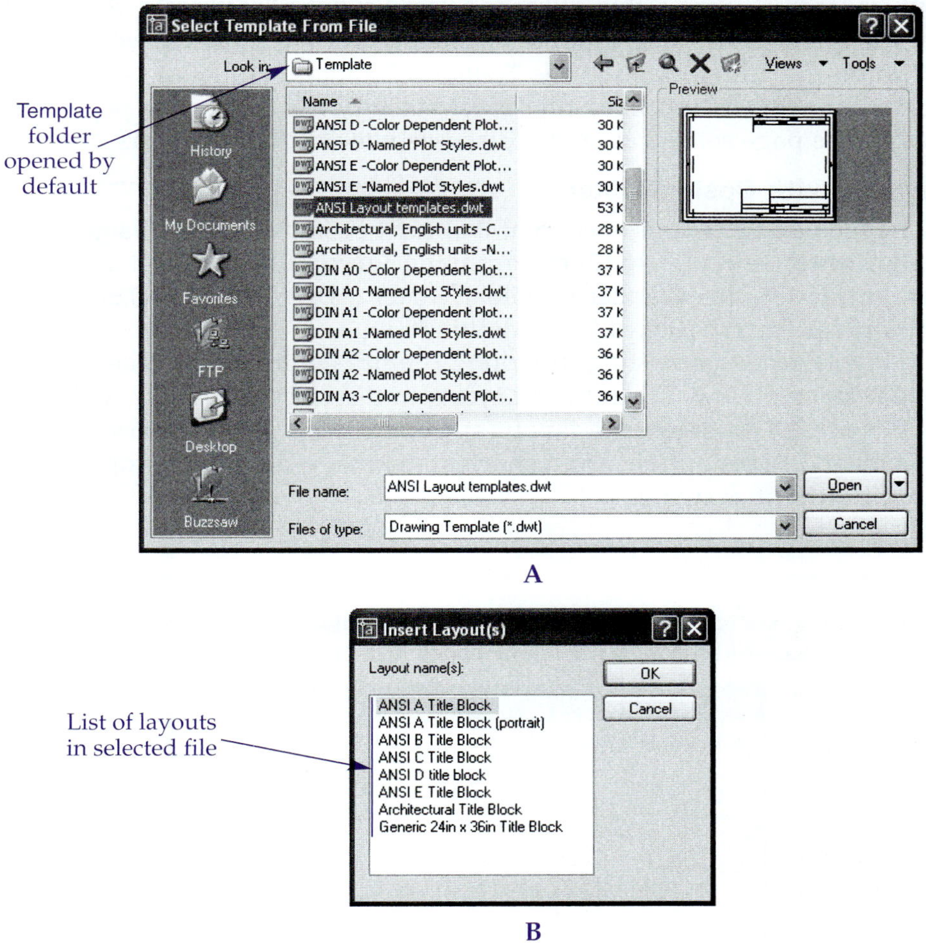

- **Copy layout in drawing.** You can create a new layout by copying an existing layout. If you use the **Copy** option of the **LAYOUT** command, enter the name of the layout to copy, and then enter the name for the new copy. The current layout is the default layout to copy. If a name for the copy is not entered, AutoCAD uses the current layout name plus a number in parentheses. For example, if the current layout is named **Layout3**, the following prompts appear:

  Command: **LO** *or* **LAYOUT**↵
  Enter layout option [Copy/Delete/New/Template/Rename/SAveas/Set/?]
  <set>: **C**↵
  Enter name of layout to copy <Layout3>: ↵
  Enter layout name for copy <Layout3 (2)>: ↵
  Layout "Layout3" copied to "Layout3 (2)".

  You can also copy an existing layout by selecting **Move or Copy...** from the layout shortcut menu. This option provides no opportunity to change the layout to be copied; the current layout tab is copied. When you select this option, the **Move or Copy** dialog box appears, **Figure 11-9.** Activate the **Create a copy** check box, and then select which layout the new layout tab should be to the left of. The default name is automatically assigned to the new layout. Use the **Rename** option to change it.
- **Using the Create Layout wizard.** You can create a new layout using the **Create Layout** wizard. To access this wizard, select **Layout Wizard** from the **Layout** cascading menu in the **Insert** pull-down menu or select **Create Layout...** from the **Wizards** cascading menu in the **Tools** pull-down menu. The pages of the wizard allow you to specify a title block, viewports, and many page setup values. These page setup values are discussed later in this chapter.

ADCENTER
ADC
[Ctrl]+[2]

Tools
➥ **DesignCenter**

Standard
toolbar

DesignCenter

Copying layouts with DesignCenter

Layouts are included as a type of content that can be viewed using **DesignCenter**. To access **DesignCenter**, select **DesignCenter** from the **Tools** pull-down menu, pick the **DesignCenter** button in the **Standard** toolbar, enter ADC or ADCENTER at the Command: prompt, or use the [Ctrl]+[2] key combination.

To copy a layout from an existing drawing or template, first locate the drawing in the **DesignCenter** tree view. Then select Layouts to display the layouts within the drawing. See **Figure 11-10.** Select the layout(s) to be copied and then use the **Add Layout(s)** or **Copy** and **Paste** options from shortcut menus or drag-and-drop to insert the layouts in the current drawing.

Figure 11-9.
The **Move or Copy** dialog box is used to reorganize the layout tabs and to copy layout tabs within a drawing. It is accessed through the layout shortcut menu.

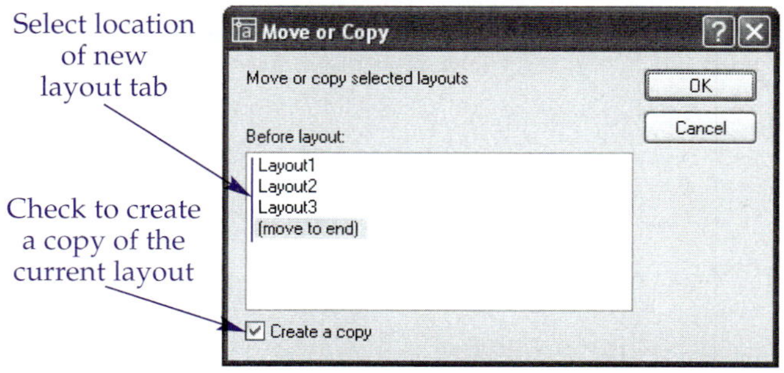

Figure 11-10.
Layouts can be shared between drawings using **DesignCenter**.

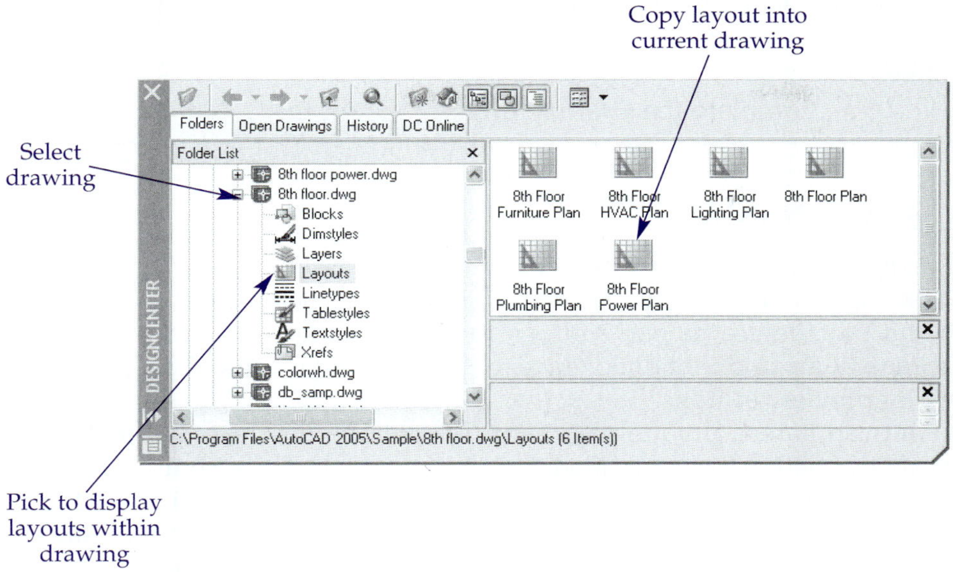

Renaming a layout

The name of the layout appears on its tab. Layouts created by default are named **Layout***n*, where *n* is a number. A layout created by copying another layout has the same name as the initial layout, followed by a number in parentheses. For example, the first copy of **Layout2** is named **Layout2 (1)**.

Layouts are easier to work with when they have a descriptive name. Layouts can be renamed using the **Rename** option of the **LAYOUT** command. When you select the **Rename** option of the **LAYOUT** command, you are prompted to enter the name of the layout to be renamed. The current layout is provided as a default. Once you have entered the layout to be renamed, you are prompted to enter the new layout name.

You can also rename a layout by right-clicking on the layout tab and selecting **Rename** from the layout shortcut menu. This accesses the **Rename Layout** dialog box. If you select this option, you can rename only the current layout. Enter the new name in the text box and pick the **OK** button. After the layout has been renamed, the new name is displayed on the tab.

Deleting a layout

When a layout is no longer useful, it can be deleted. You can delete a layout using the **Delete** option of the **LAYOUT** command. You can also delete the active layout by right-clicking on the layout tab and selecting **Delete** from the layout shortcut menu.

When you use the **Delete** option of the **LAYOUT** command, you are prompted to enter the name of the layout to be deleted. The current layout is provided as the default.

If you select **Delete** from the layout shortcut menu, an alert box warns you that the layout will be permanently deleted. Pick the **OK** button to delete the layout.

Saving a layout

The **Saveas** option of the **LAYOUT** command is used to save a single layout as a drawing template or drawing file. The following is the command sequence:

Command: **LO** *or* **LAYOUT**↵
Enter layout option [Copy/Delete/New/Template/Rename/SAveas/Set/?] <set>: **SA**↵
Enter layout to save to template <*current layout*>: *(enter name of layout or accept default)*

After you specify the layout to save, the **Create Drawing File** dialog box appears. You can save the layout in a DWT, DWG, or DXF file. Enter the file name and pick the **SAVE** button. The layout is now saved in the new file.

EXERCISE 11-2 Complete the Exercise on the Student CD.

Page Setups for Plotting

AutoCAD 2005 NEW FEATURE

A *page setup* contains the settings required to create a finished plot of the drawing. Most aspects of how the drawing is plotted can be established in a page setup, from the plot device to pen settings to scales. In fact, the only difference between the **Page Setup** and **Plot** dialog boxes is that the **Page Setup** dialog box does not provide plot preview buttons.

Each layout can have a unique page setup. Therefore, the **Page Setup Manager** dialog box is always tied to the active **Model** tab or layout tab. These settings can even be saved in the drawing file as a named page setup, which can be recalled each time the drawing is plotted. Therefore, the setup becomes a productivity tool since it decreases the amount of time required to prepare a drawing for plotting.

PAGESETUP
File
➥ **Page Setup...**
Layouts toolbar
Page Setup Manager

The settings that compose the page setup are set in the **Page Setup** dialog box. This dialog box is accessed by selecting **Page Setup Manager...** from the **File** pull-down menu, picking the **Page Setup Manager** button in the **Layouts** toolbar, typing PAGESETUP at the Command: prompt, or right-clicking on a layout tab and selecting **Page Setup Manager...** from the layout shortcut menu. The **Page Setup Manager** dialog box is shown in Figure 11-11A.

The initial dialog box of **Page Setup Manager** is divided into two areas: **Page setups** in the upper area and **Selected page setup details** below. The **Page setups** area shows a list of the available page setups on the left. On the right are buttons labeled **Set Current**, **New...**, **Modify...**, and **Import...**.

The **Set Current** button attaches the highlighted page setup from the list of available page setups to the current layout. The **New...** button allows you to create a new page setup. The **New Page Setup** dialog box will be displayed as shown in Figure 11-11B. The **Modify...** button allows you to change the settings of an existing page setup. The **Page Setup** dialog box will be displayed after picking the **Modify...** button and after picking **OK** from the **New Page Setup** dialog box. See Figure 11-11C. The **Import...** button allows you to bring in previously created page setups from an existing drawing.

The page setup consists of many settings including printer selection, plot style (pen settings) choices, paper size and orientation, scale, and other settings that define how the model is going to appear on the final plotted output. All of these settings will be discussed later in this chapter.

PROFESSIONAL TIP

In the planning stages of your work, create one or more page setups for the drawing and save them in a template drawing.

Figure 11-11.
Creating a new layout in the **Page Setup** dialog box.

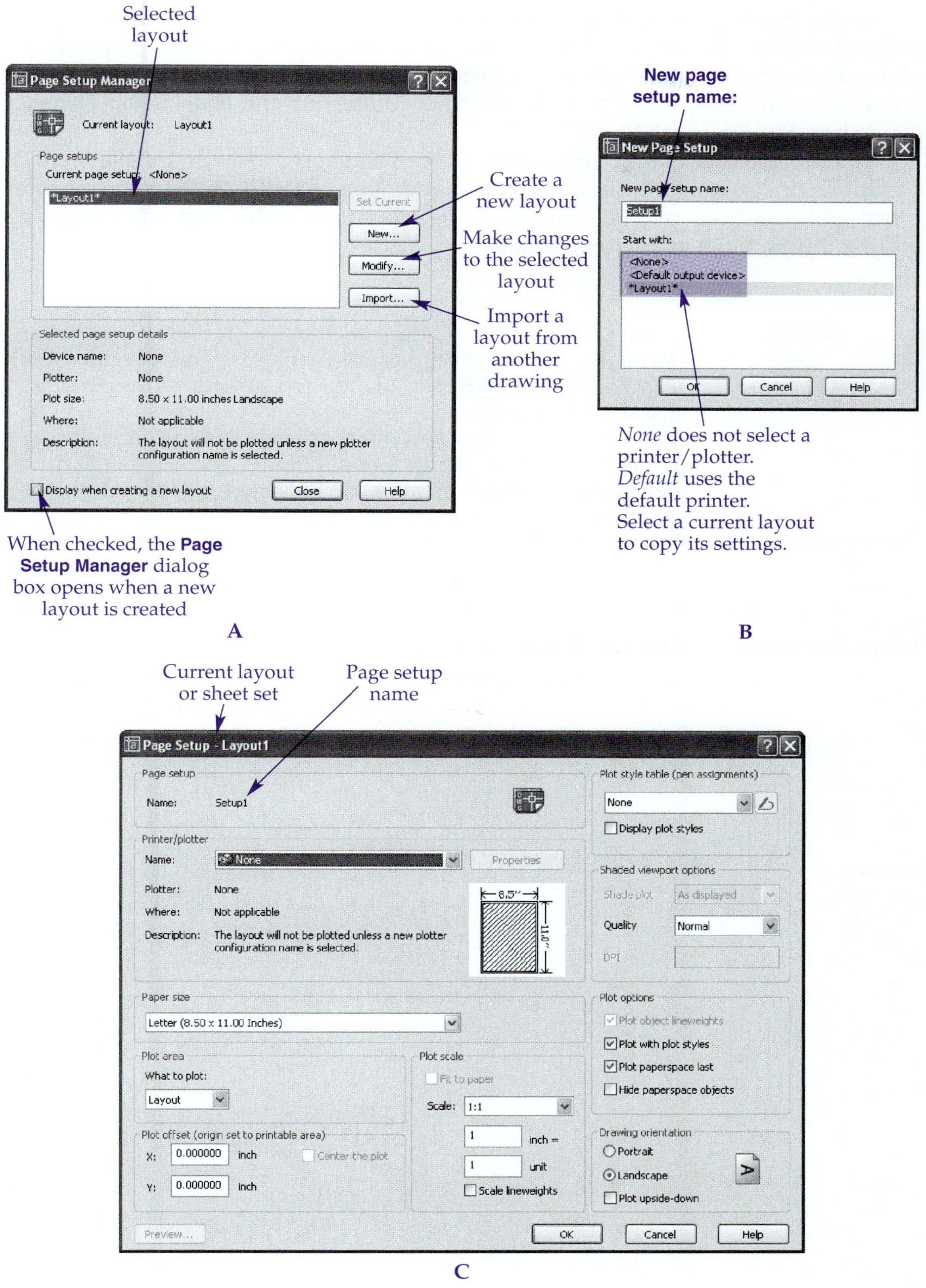

Plot Device Selection and Management

Before printing or plotting, make sure that your output device is configured properly. AutoCAD displays information about the currently configured printer or plotter in the **Printer/plotter** area of the **Page Setup** dialog box that appears when you press either the **New...** button or the **Modify...** button on the **Page Setup Manager** dialog box. See Figure 11-12.

You can use this tab to change many of the printer or plotter specifications. The current device is displayed in the **Printer/plotter** area of the **Page Setup** dialog box. When additional devices are configured, you can make a different one current by picking it from the **Name:** drop-down list.

> **NOTE**
>
> Add printers and plotters to the list by selecting **Plotter Manager...** in the **File** pull-down menu. This executes the **PLOTTERMANAGER** command and displays the **Plotters** window. Select the Add-A-Plotter Wizard icon to add, modify, and remove printing and plotting devices. When a plotter or printer is installed using the **Add Plotter** wizard, a PC3 (plot configuration) file is created. This file contains all the settings required for the plotter to function.

Figure 11-12.
The **Printer/Plotter** area of the **Page Setup** dialog box.

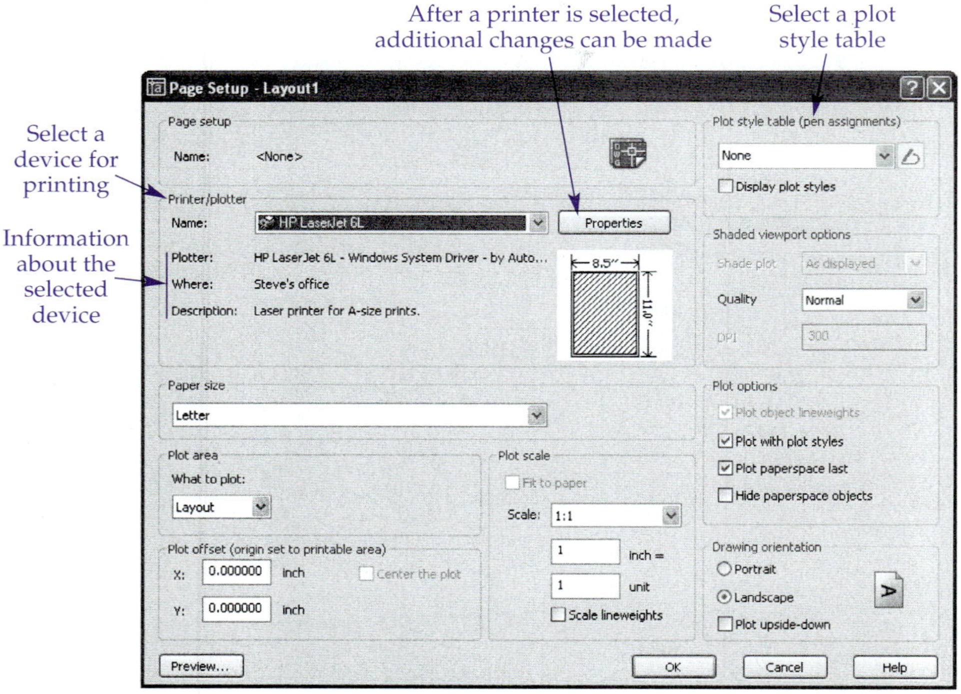

Modifying the Plotter Configuration

To change the properties of the current plot device, pick the **Properties...** button in the **Plotter configuration** area. This opens the **Plotter Configuration Editor** dialog box. See **Figure 11-13.** Three tabs provide access to the plotting device property settings:

- **General tab.** General information about the current plotter is displayed in this tab. The only item you can change is the description.
- **Ports tab.** Use this tab to pick a port to send the plot to, plot to a file, or select **AutoSpool**. Using **AutoSpool**, plot files can be sent to a ***plot spooler*** file, which automatically plots the drawing in the background while you continue to work.
- **Device and Document Settings tab.** This tab displays a tree list of all the settings applicable to the current plotting device. Clicking on the desired icon enables you to modify specific settings. Items in this list that are displayed in brackets (< >) can be changed. The **Custom Properties** item is highlighted by default because it contains the properties most often changed. Pick the **Custom Properties...** button to display the properties dialog box specific to your plotter. Pick the **Save As...** button to save your changes to a PC3 file.

> **CAUTION**
>
> Avoid editing and saving modified PC3 files unless you have been instructed to do so. These files are critical to the proper functioning of your plotter.

Figure 11-13.
The **Plotter Configuration Editor** dialog box. The **Device and Document Settings** tab is shown here.

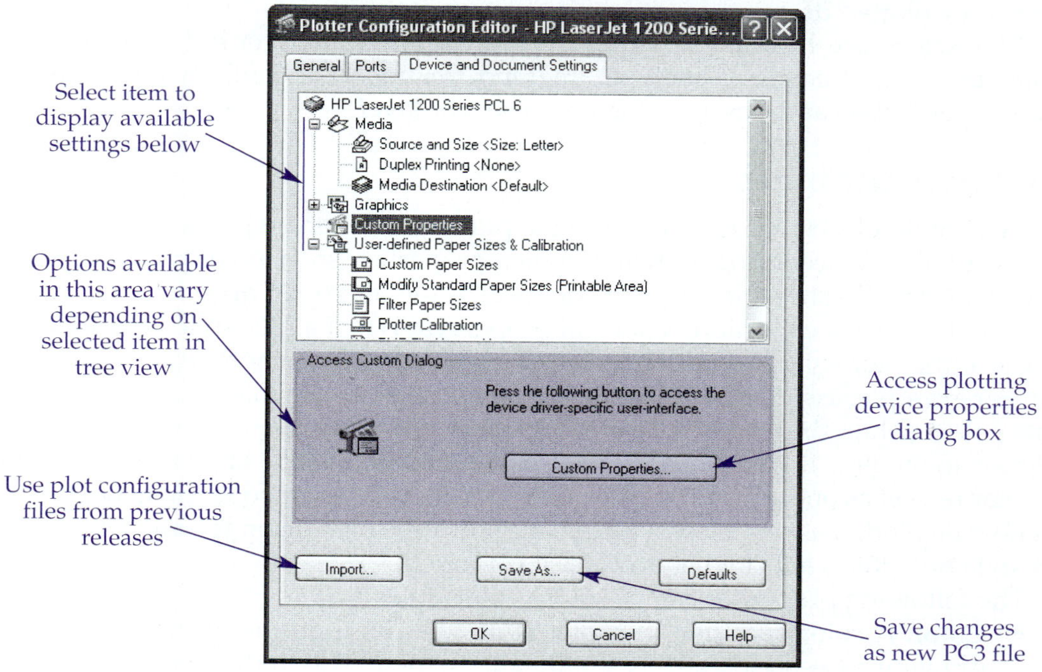

Specifying a Plot Style Table

The **Plot style table** area is located in the upper right of the **Page Setup** dialog box. This area allows you to list and select customized pen assignment files for specialized plotting purposes. Use the default of **None** until you possess a good understanding of plot style tables. Plot style tables are discussed in the following section.

NOTE

If you want to plot a drawing without using a plot style, pick **None** in the **Plot style table** area of the **Page Setup** dialog box.

EXERCISE 11-3 Complete the Exercise on the Student CD.

Plot Styles

The properties of objects in an AutoCAD drawing, such as color, layer, linetype, and lineweight, are used as defaults for plotting. This means that all colors, linetypes, and lineweights will be plotted exactly as they appear in the drawing. You also have the ability to create multiple plots of the same drawing using different plot style tables. A ***plot style table*** is a named file that provides complete control over pen settings for plotted drawings.

Plot styles are basically a variety of pen settings that control, among other things, the color, thickness, linetype, line end treatment, and fill style of drawing objects. Plot styles can be assigned to any object or layer.

Plot Style Attributes

By default, objects are drawn without a plot style. When no plot style is applied, objects are plotted according to their assigned properties, such as color, linetype, and lineweight. The finished plot appears identical to the on-screen display.

A plot style is a collection of several properties. When a plot style is assigned to an object, the plot style properties replace the object's properties *for plotting purposes only*. For example, assume a drawing has a layer named Blue, which has blue selected as its color. A line drawn on this layer appears blue on screen. If no plot style is assigned to the line, it will plot as blue also. Now assume a plot style is created with the color red set as one of its properties. This plot style is assigned to the line. The line will now be plotted as red. However, the line still appears blue on screen, because the plot style only takes effect when the object is plotted.

The following properties can be set in a plot style:

- **Color.** A color specified in a plot style will override the object color in the drawing. Use object color is the default setting. This setting plots the object with the same color shown on screen. The following options related to color could also be specified:
  - **Dithering.** *Dithering* is the intermingling of dots of various colors to produce what appears to be a new color. Dithering is either enabled or disabled. It is ignored if the plotter does not support it. Dithering may create incorrect linetypes when plotting pale colors or thin lines. It is best

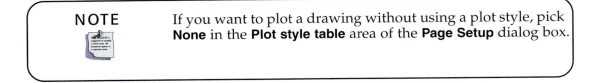

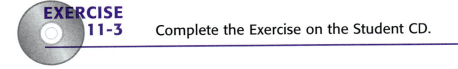

Figure 11-14.
The effects of the Convert to grayscale plot style setting.

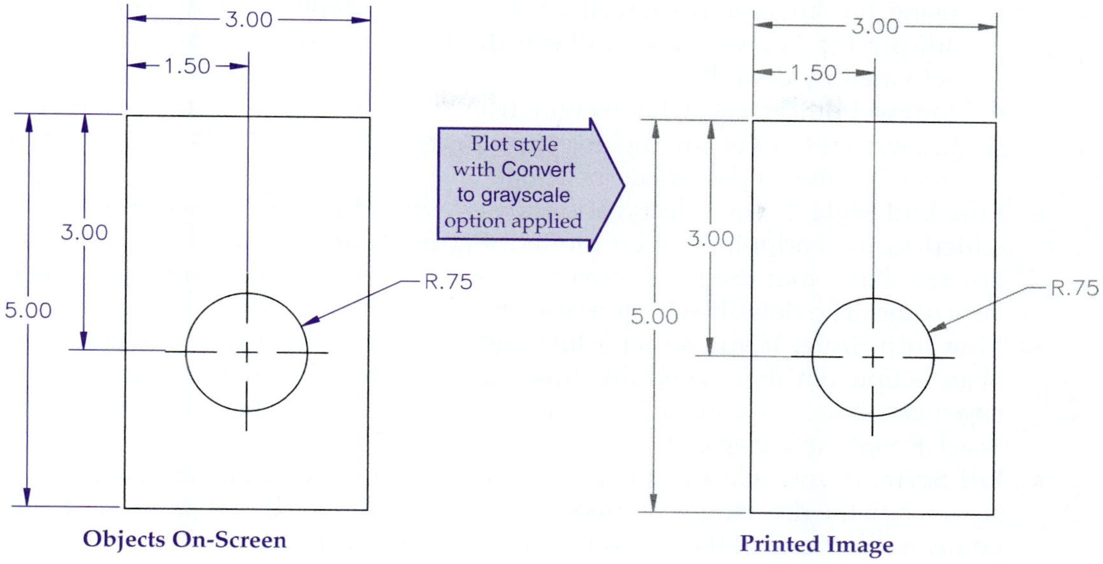

to test dithering to see if it produces the expected results. Dithering can be used regardless of the object color selected.

- **Convert to Grayscale.** If this option is selected, the object's colors are converted to grayscale if the plotter supports it. If this is not selected, the object colors are used. This option is illustrated in Figure 11-14.
- **Use Assigned Pen Number.** This setting only applies to pen plotters. Available pens range from 1 to 32. The assigned pen number cannot be changed if the plot style color is set to Use object color, or if you are editing a plot style in a color-dependent plot style table. In this case, the value is set to Automatic. If you enter 0 for pen number, the field reads Automatic. AutoCAD selects a pen based on the plotter configuration.
- **Virtual Pen Number.** Pen numbers between 1 and 255 allow non-pen plotters to simulate pen plotters using virtual pens. A 0 or Automatic setting instructs AutoCAD to assign a virtual pen from the AutoCAD Color Index (ACI).
- **Screening.** This affects the amount of ink placed on the paper while plotting. A value of 0 produces the color white, and 100 plots the color's full intensity. The effects of screening are shown in Figure 11-15.

Figure 11-15.
Using the screening plot style settings.

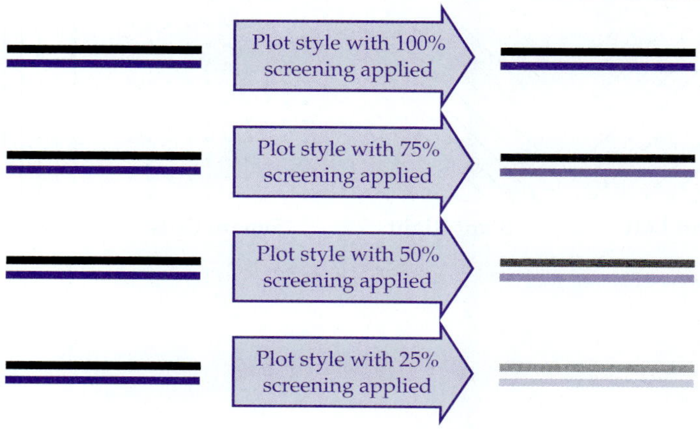

- **Linetype.** If you select a plot style linetype, it overrides the object's linetype when plotted. The default value (Use object linetype) plots the object using the linetype displayed on screen. An adaptive adjustment setting adjusts the linetype scale to keep the linetype pattern complete. This is activated by default.
- **Lineweight.** Select a lineweight from this list if you want the plotted lineweight to override the object property in the AutoCAD drawing. The default value is Use object lineweight.

- **Line End Style.** If you select a line end style from this list, the line end style is added to the endpoints when plotted. **Figure 11-16** illustrates the end style options. Note that the lines must be relatively thick for the end styles to be noticeable. The default setting is Use object end style.
- **Line Join Style.** If you select a line join style from this list, it overrides the object's line join style when the drawing is plotted. The default setting is Use object join style, but you can select one of the following line end styles: Miter, Bevel, Round, and Diamond.
- **Fill Style.** If you select a fill style from this list, it overrides the object's fill style when the drawing is plotted. The default setting is Use object fill style, but you can select one of the fill styles shown in **Figure 11-17.**

Figure 11-16.
End line style options can be specified within a plot style.

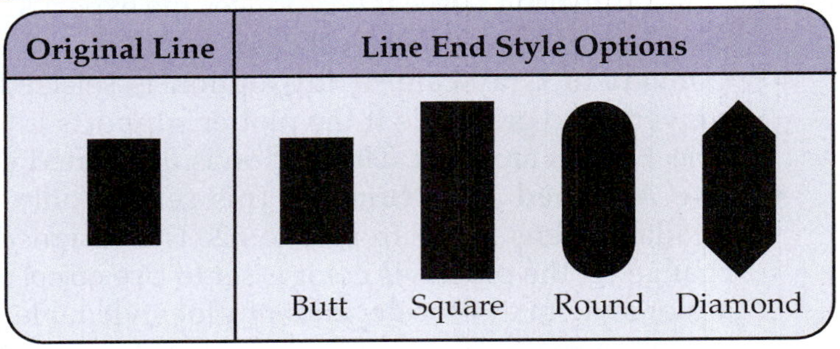

Figure 11-17.
These fill styles can be set for a plot style.

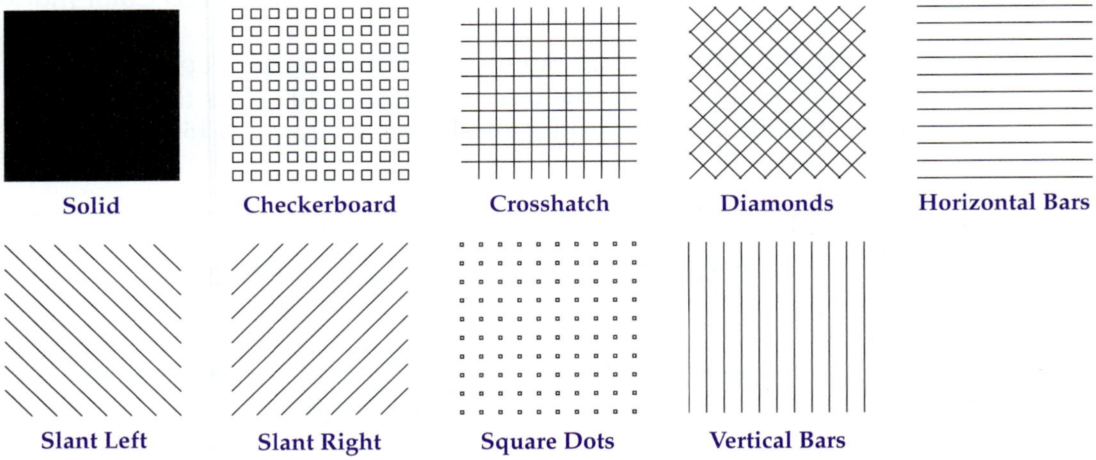

Plot Style Modes

There are two plot style modes: color-dependent and named. You can create a ***color-dependent plot style*** in which each color can be assigned values for the various plotting properties. These settings are saved in a ***color-dependent plot style table*** file with a CTB extension.

A ***named plot style*** is assigned to objects. The settings in the named plot style override the object properties when the object is plotted. ***Named plot style tables*** are saved in a file with an STB extension. These tables allow you to use color properties in the drawing without having the object's color tied to its plotting characteristics. These tables are useful if, for example, you are working on a multiphase project in which different components of the drawing must be highlighted, subdued, or plotted in a specific lineweight or linetype.

Plot Style Tables

AutoCAD is supplied with several plot style tables. You can also create and save your own customized tables. Plot style tables are given file names with CTB or STB extensions. These files are saved in the path set by the AutoCAD Plot Style Table Search Path. To verify the location of AutoCAD plot style table, access the **Files** tab in the **Options** dialog box and check the path listed under the Plot Style Table Search Path, after expanding the **Printer support File Path** selection.

To view the available plot style tables, select **Plot Style Manager...** from the **File** pull-down menu or enter STYLESMANAGER at the Command: prompt. The **Plot Styles** window is displayed. See Figure 11-18.

The **Plot Styles** window displays icons for each of the saved plot style tables. There is also an icon to access the **Add Plot Style Table** wizard. You can double-click on an icon to access the **Plot Style Table Editor** dialog box. This dialog box, which is discussed later in the chapter, is used to edit the plot style table.

Creating a plot style table

Create a named plot style table if you know that components of the drawing or project, such as layouts, layers, and objects, will be plotted at different times using different colors, linetypes, lineweights, or area fills.

Figure 11-18.
Double-click on an icon to edit the plot style table. Select the Add-A-Plot Style Table Wizard icon to create a new table.

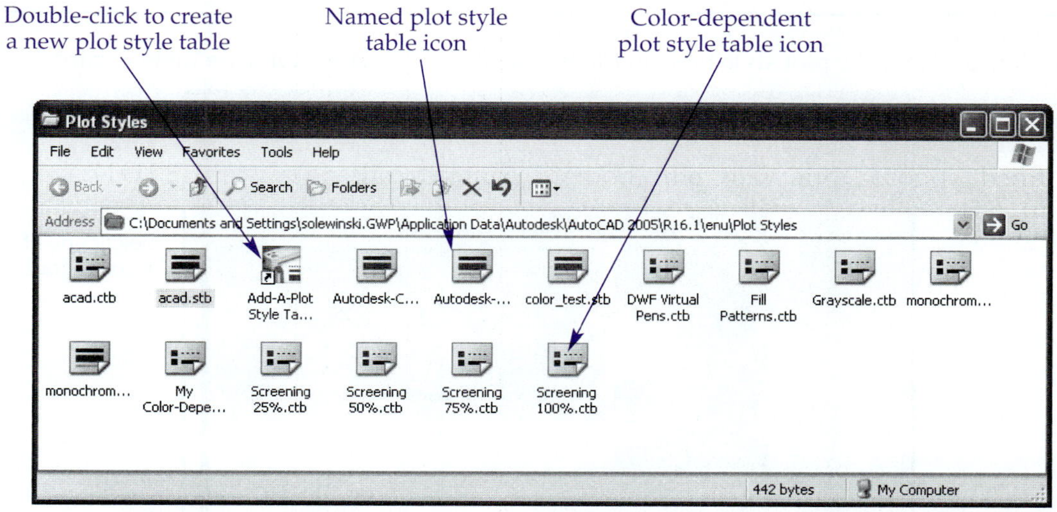

Plot style tables are created using the **Add Plot Style Table** wizard. To access this wizard, select **Add Plot Style Table...** from the **Wizards** cascading menu of the **Tools** pull-down menu. You can also select the Add-A-Plot Style Table Wizard icon in the **Plot Styles** window, which is discussed later in the chapter. The **Add Plot Style Table** wizard is displayed. Read the introductory page and pick **Next** to access the **Begin** page. See Figure 11-19. Four options are available:

- **Start from scratch.** Constructs a new plot style table. The **Browse File** page is skipped with this option because the new plot style table is not based on any existing settings.
- **Use an existing plot style table.** Copies an existing plot style table to be used as a template for a new one. The **Table Type** page is skipped when this option is selected because the plot style mode is determined by the file selected as the template.
- **Use My R14 Plotter Configuration (CFG).** Copies the pen assignments from the acad14.cfg file to be used as a template for a new one. This option should be used if you did not save either a PCP or PC2 file in Release 14.
- **Use a PCP or PC2 file.** Pen assignments saved previously in a Release 14 PCP or PC2 file are used to make a new plot style table.

After you have selected the beginning plot style table option, press **Next** to go to the **Table Type** page. See Figure 11-20. This page is not displayed if the **Use an existing plot style table** option was selected. Select the **Named Plot Style Table** option to use the named plot style mode, and then pick **Next**.

Select the file on which the plot style table is to be based in the **Browse File** page. This page is not displayed if the **Start from scratch** option was selected. Enter the file name in the text box or pick the **Browse...** button to display a **Select File** dialog box. The type of file you select depends on the selected beginning plot style table option. If you are using a CFG file, you must also select the plotter or printer to use.

After selecting the appropriate file, pick the **Next** button to access the **File name** page. See Figure 11-21. Enter a name for the new plot style table. A CTB extension is added to color-dependent plot style tables, and an STB extension is added to named plot style tables.

Once you have entered the plot style table name, pick **Next** to display the **Finish** page. See Figure 11-22. Pick the check box at the bottom of the page to attach this plot style table to all new drawings by default. That is, the plot style table will be listed in the **Plot style table area** of the **Page Setup** dialog box. This check box is only available if you are creating a plot style using the mode (color-dependent or named) specified

Figure 11-19.
Select the basis for the plot style table in the **Begin** page of the **Add Plot Style Table** wizard.

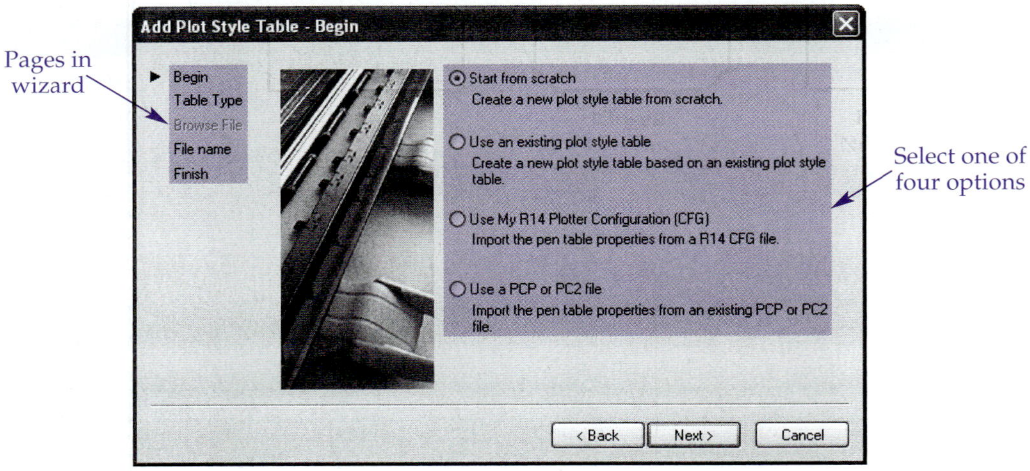

Figure 11-20.
Select the plot style mode in the **Table Type** page. This page does not appear if the new table is based on an existing plot style table.

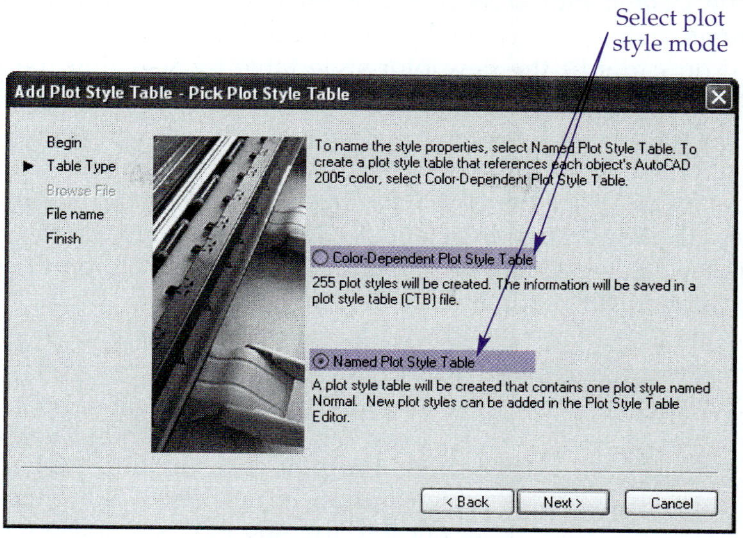

Figure 11-21.
Enter the name for the plot style table in the **File name** page.

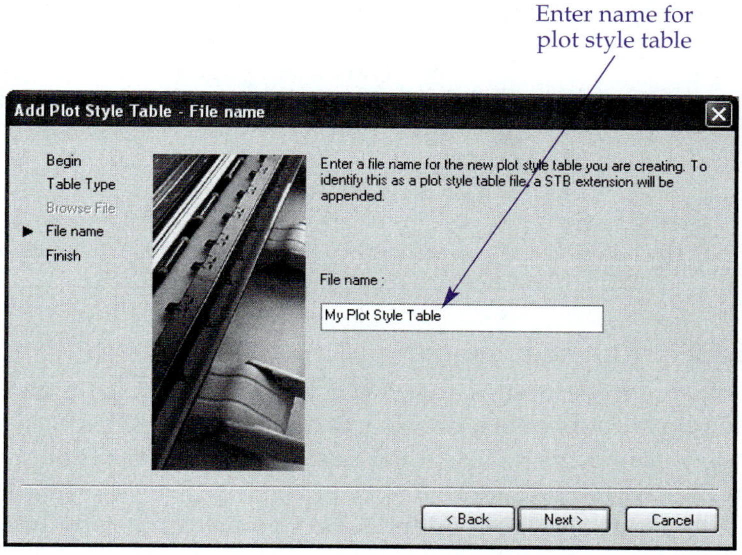

Figure 11-22.
The **Finish** page allows you to edit the new plot style table immediately and to attach the new table to all new drawings (if the plot style mode matches the setting in the **Options** dialog box).

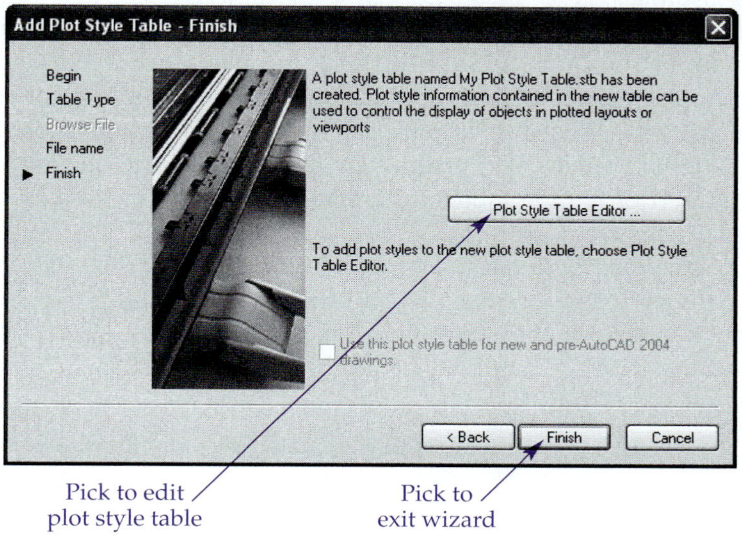

in the **Default plot style behavior for new drawings** area of the **Plotting** tab in the **Options** dialog box. This tab is discussed later in the chapter.

You can edit the new plot style table by selecting the **Plot Style Table Editor...** button, which accesses the **Plot Style Table Editor** dialog box. This is discussed later in the chapter.

Pick **Finish** and the new plot style table is created. The new file is saved in the folder path set by the Plot Style Table Search Path. To verify the location of this file, access the **Files** tab in the **Options** dialog box and check the path listed under the Plot Style Table Search Path after expanding the **Printer Support File Path** selection. A corresponding icon is added to the **Plot Styles** window.

NOTE

The **Wizards** cascading menu also contains an **Add Named Plot Style Table...** or **Add Color-Dependent Plot Style Table...** option. The plot style mode set for the drawing determines which option is available. The pages in these wizards are identical to the **Add Plot Style Table** wizard with the following exceptions:

- On the **Begin** page, the **Use an existing plot style table** option is not available.
- There is no **Table Type** page.
- The **Finish** page includes an option to attach the new plot style table to the current drawing.

EXERCISE 11-4 Complete the Exercise on the Student CD.

Editing a plot style table

Plot style properties are set in the **Plot Style Table Editor** dialog box. To access this dialog box, double-click on the icon for the desired plot style table in the **Plot Styles** window. You can also select the **Edit...** button in the **Plot style table** area in the **Page Setup** dialog box.

The **Plot Style Table Editor** dialog box is used to edit both color-dependent and named plot style tables. Color-dependent plot style tables contain 255 preset plot styles—one for each ACI color. A new named plot style table contains one preset plot style, Normal.

The **Plot Style Table Editor** contains three tabs. The **General** tab contains information about the plot style table. See Figure 11-23. Enter a description in the text box. The **Apply global scale factor to non-ISO linetypes and fill patterns** option scales all non-ISO linetypes and fill patterns by the value entered in the **Scale factor** text box.

The **Table View** and **Form View** tabs are used to set the plot style attributes and, for named plot style tables, to create and delete plot styles. These tabs are shown in Figure 11-24.

When editing a named plot style table, the Normal plot style is created automatically. This plot style cannot be modified, and is assigned to all layers by default. To create a new plot style, pick the **Add Style** button. In the **Table View** tab, this inserts a new table with the name Style *n* highlighted at the top. Enter a new name. In the **Form View** tab, the **Add Plot Style** dialog box appears. Enter a new name and pick the **OK** button.

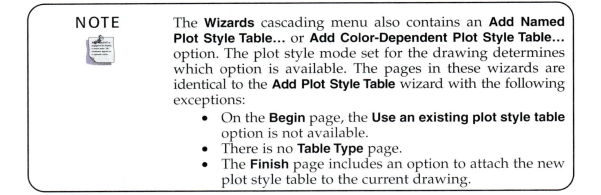

Figure 11-23.
Information about a plot style table is contained in the **General** tab of the **Plot Style Table Editor** dialog box.

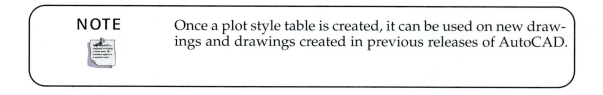

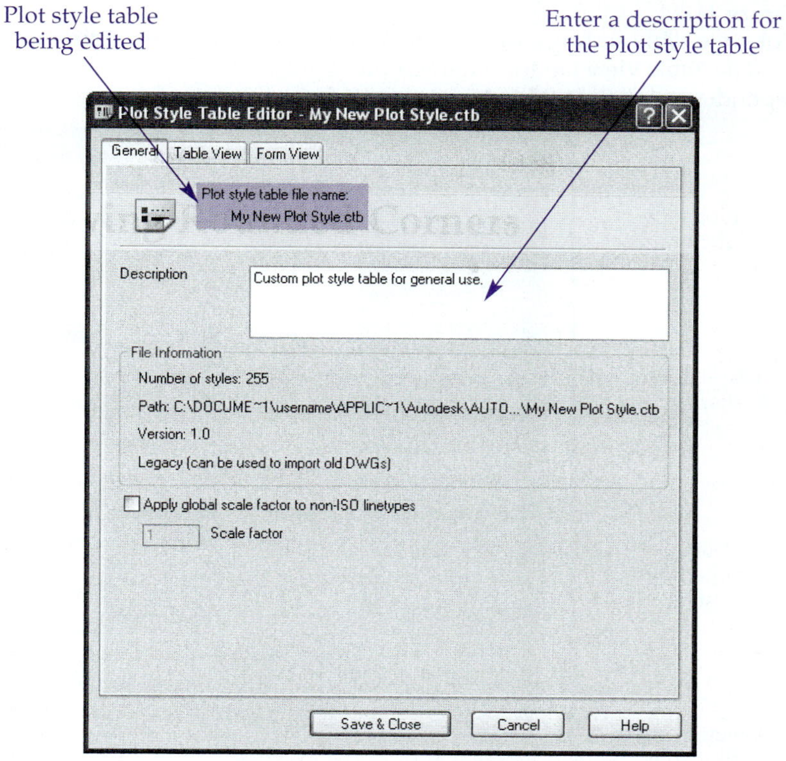

If you wish to delete a named plot style, pick the **Delete Style** button in either tab. If the **Form View** tab is displayed, the current style is deleted. If the **Table View** tab is displayed, first pick in the gray bar above the name of the plot style to be deleted, then pick the **Delete Style** button.

To modify plot style attributes in the **Table View** tab, first use the scroll bar to display the plot style to be edited. Pick the value to be changed and you can modify it with a text box or drop-down list. This editing procedure is similar to changing object properties in the **Properties** window.

The **Form View** tab lists all the attributes in a different format. To view all of the settings for a specific plot style, simply pick the plot style in the **Plot styles:** list box. The properties of the selected plot style are listed in the **Properties** area. Modify the properties using the drop-down lists provided.

Pick the **Save As...** button to change the table name, or pick the **Save & Close** button to save the current file and exit.

> **NOTE**
>
> Once a plot style table is created, it can be used on new drawings and drawings created in previous releases of AutoCAD.

EXERCISE 11-5 Complete the Exercise on the Student CD.

Figure 11-24.
Plot style table settings are modified in the **Plot Style Table Editor** dialog box. A—The **Table View** tab for a named plot style table. B—The **Form View** tab for a color-dependent plot style table.

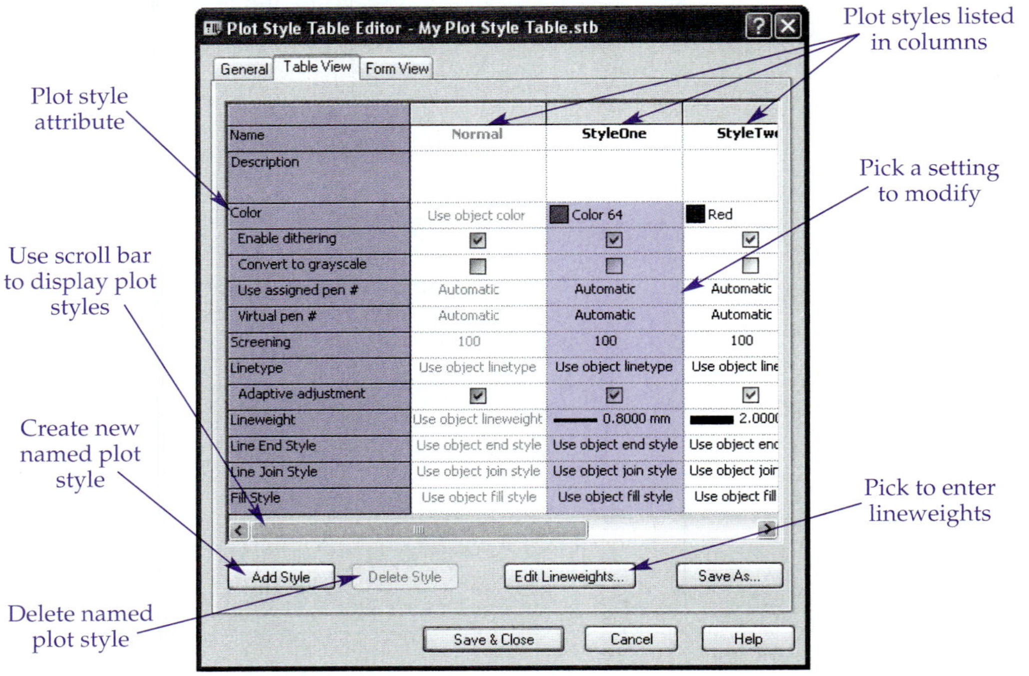

A

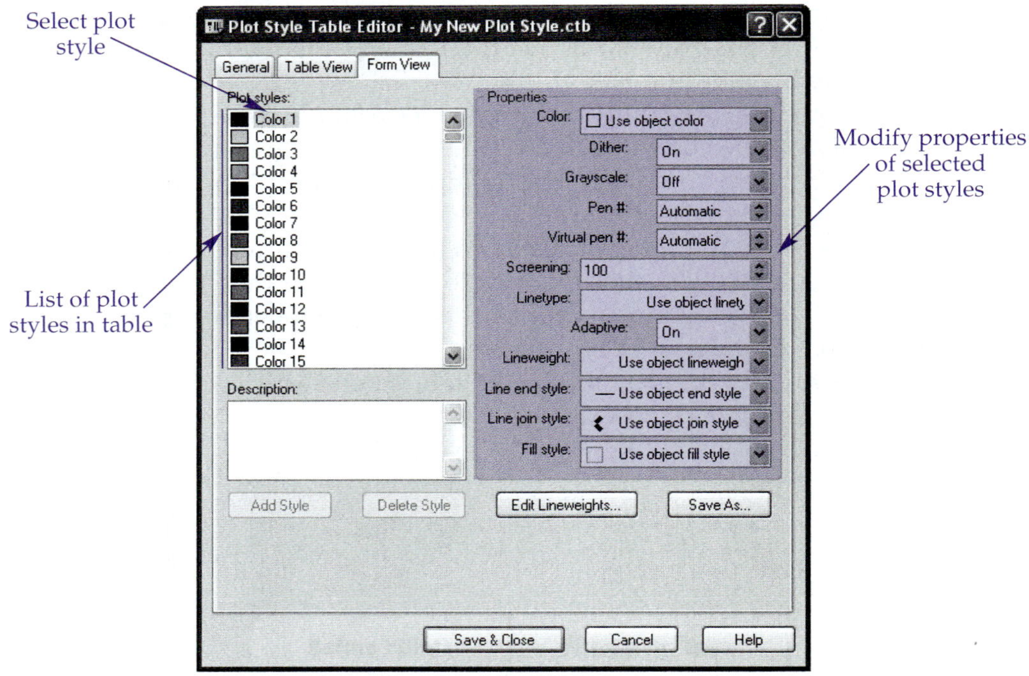

B

Applying Plot Styles

In order to assign plot styles, plot style tables must be specified in the drawing. The **Model** tab and each individual layout tab can be assigned one plot style table each. Only the styles within the attached plot style table can be applied within the layout.

The plot style mode (color-dependent or named) for a drawing is determined when the drawing is first created. The setting is found in the **Plot and Publish** tab of the **Options** dialog box. To access the **Options** dialog box, select **Options...** from the **Tools** pull-down menu or enter OP or OPTIONS at the Command: prompt. You can also right-click in the drawing area and select **Options...** from the shortcut menu.

The **Plot and Publish** tab of the **Options** dialog box is shown in Figure 11-25A. Options having to do with plot styles are accessed by picking the **Plot Style Table Settings...** button at the lower right of the **Plot and Publish** tab. The **Plot Style Table Settings** dialog box is displayed in Figure 11-25B. The plot style mode for new drawings is determined by the setting in the **Default plot style behavior for new drawings** area. By default, the **Use color dependent plot styles** option is selected. When this

Figure 11-25.
Use the **Plot and Publish** tab of the **Options** dialog box to set default plot style modes and tables for new drawings.

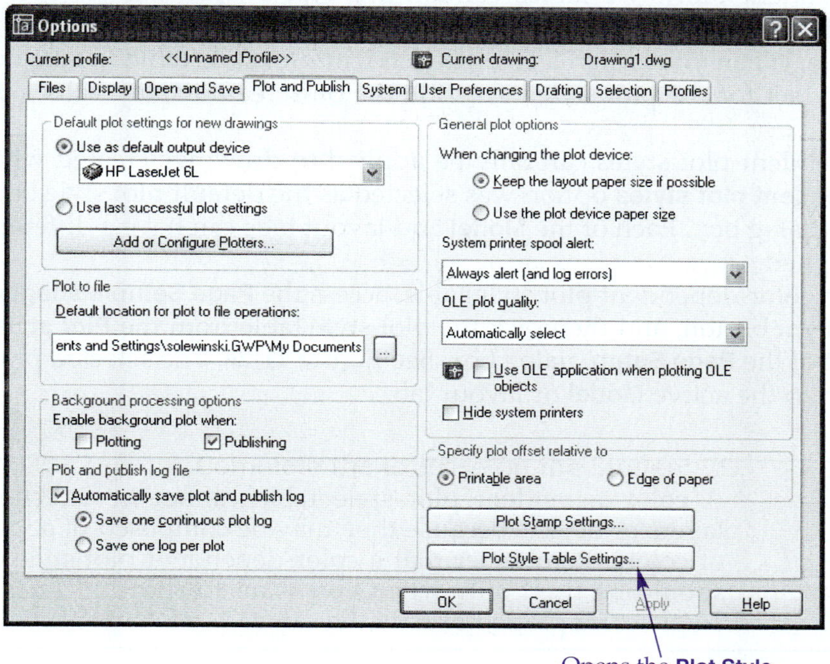

Opens the **Plot Style Table Settings** dialog box

A

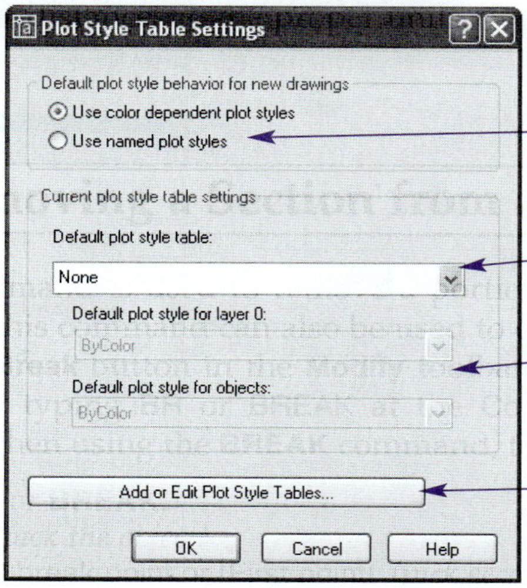

Select default plot style mode for new drawings

Select default plot style table for new drawings

Select default plot styles for named plot style tables

Go to the **Plot Styles** window

B

option is selected, new drawings are set to use only color-dependent plot styles. The default plot style behavior setting can also be set using the **PSTYLEPOLICY** system variable (0 for named plot style mode and 1 for color-dependent mode).

The **Default plot style table** drop-down list can be used to set a default plot style table. When None is selected, objects in the new drawing are plotted based on their on-screen properties. The default plot style table is applied to the **Model** tab and layout tabs in new drawings. However, the plot style table can be changed at any time in the **Page Setup** dialog box.

If you select the **Use named plot styles** option, the drop-down lists below the default plot style table are activated. You can select the default plot styles for layer 0 and for objects. You can select any plot styles from the default plot style table.

The **Add or Edit Plot Style Tables…** button accesses the **Plot Styles** window. This window is where you edit existing plot style tables and create new plot style tables.

Applying color-dependent plot styles

Color-dependent plot style tables contain 255 plot styles—one for each color available for display in AutoCAD. You cannot add or delete plot styles in a color-dependent table. When you assign a color-dependent plot style table to a layout, the property values set for the plot styles override the on-screen display values during plotting.

Color-dependent plot styles can only be applied to drawings created while the **Use color dependent plot styles** option was selected as the default plot style behavior in the **Options** dialog box. Each of the **Model** and layout tabs can have a different plot style table assigned.

To assign a color-dependent plot style table, access the **Page Setup Manager**, then select the **Modify…** button, and then pick the plot style table from the **Plot style table** drop-down list of the **Page Setup** dialog box. See Figure 11-26. The selected plot style table is applied to the active **Model** or layout tab.

NOTE A color-dependent plot style table cannot be attached to layers or objects because they may be composed of a variety of colors. Remember that a color-dependent plot style table should be used only when you want to show all lines of a single color plotted exactly the same.

Figure 11-26.
Selecting a plot style table for a layout.

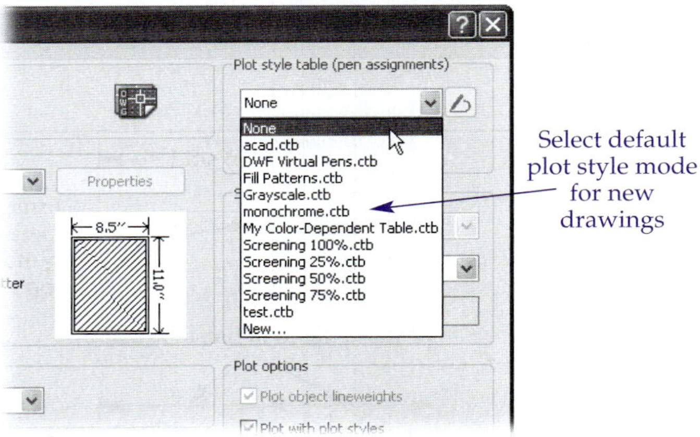

EXERCISE 11-6 Complete the Exercise on the Student CD.

Applying named plot styles

In order for named plot styles to be used in a drawing, the drawing must have been created with the **Use named plot styles** option selected as the default plot style behavior in the **Options** dialog box. The drawing could also be based on a template with named plot styles.

The **Model** tab and each layout tab can have a named plot style table attached. When you select a plot style table for the **Model** tab, you are also presented the option of selecting the plot style table for all layout tabs. However, each layout tab can have a different plot style table.

Once the named plot style tables have been assigned to the **Model** tab and layout tabs, plot styles can be assigned to objects and layers. A plot style assigned to an object overrides a plot style assigned to a layer, just as a color or linetype assigned to an object overrides the layer setting.

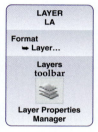

> **LAYER**
> **LA**
>
> **Format**
> ➥ **Layer...**
>
> **Layers toolbar**
>
> **Layer Properties Manager**

Plot styles can be assigned to layers in the **Layer Properties Manager** dialog box only when the drawing was created with a named plot style. See **Figure 11-27.** To access this dialog box, pick the **Layer Properties Manager** button from the **Layers** toolbar, select **Layer...** from the **Format** pull-down menu, or type LA or LAYER at the Command: prompt.

To modify the plot style, pick the current plot style listed for the layer. The **Select Plot Style** dialog box is displayed, **Figure 11-28.** This dialog box lists the plot styles available in the plot style table attached to the current tab. You can select a different plot style table from the **Active plot style table:** drop-down list. If you cannot select another plot style, the drawing was created with a color-dependent plot style. Changing the **PSTYLEPOLICY** system variable to 0 (zero) will not change the current drawing, only new drawings. If you select another plot style table, the change is reflected in the **Plot style table** area of the **Page Setup** dialog box. Pick the **Editor...** button to access the **Plot Style Table Editor** dialog box.

Named plot styles can also be applied to objects. When a plot style is applied to an object, the plot style remains attached to the object in all layout tabs. If the plot style attached to the object is contained in the plot style table attached to the layout tab, the object will be plotted with the plot style settings. However, if the plot style assigned to the object is not found within the plot style table attached to the layout tab, the object is plotted according to its on-screen display settings.

Figure 11-27.
Named plot styles can be assigned to layers using the **Layer Properties Manager** dialog box.

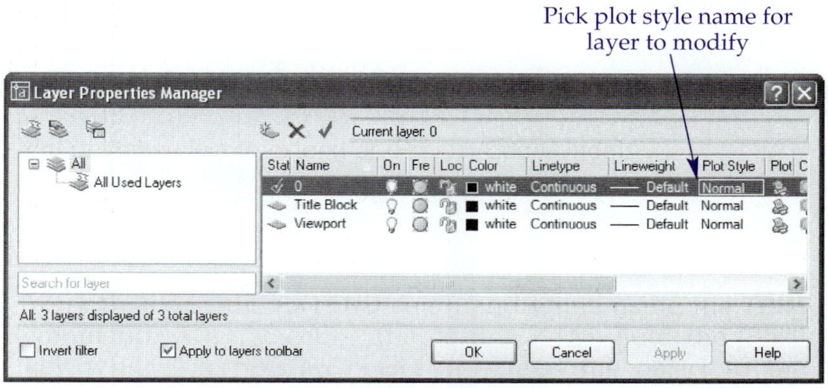

Figure 11-28.
Use the **Select Plot Style** dialog box to select a plot style for a layer.

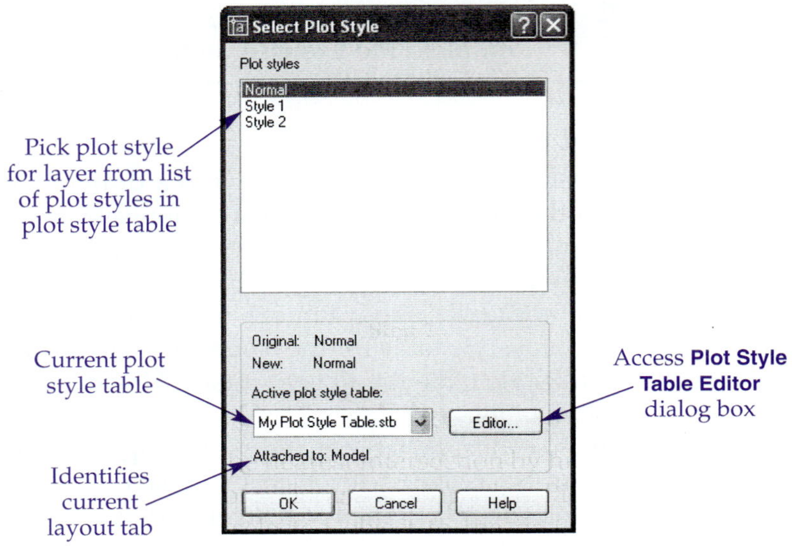

Modifying an object's plot style is similar to modifying an object's layer, color, or linetype. You can select the new plot style from the **Plot Style Control** drop-down list in the **Properties** toolbar, Figure 11-29A, or you can use the **Properties** window to change the plot style, Figure 11-29B. Selecting the **Other...** option accesses the **Select Plot Style** dialog box.

> **NOTE**
>
> Every AutoCAD object and layer is automatically assigned a plot style. If the current drawing is set to use a named plot style table, the default plot style for objects in the drawing is ByLayer. This means that objects retain the properties of their layer. The default plot style for a layer is Normal. Objects plotted with these settings keep their original properties.

Figure 11-29.
Assigning a new plot style to an object. A—Using the **Plot Style Control** drop-down list in the **Properties** toolbar. B—Using the **Properties** window.

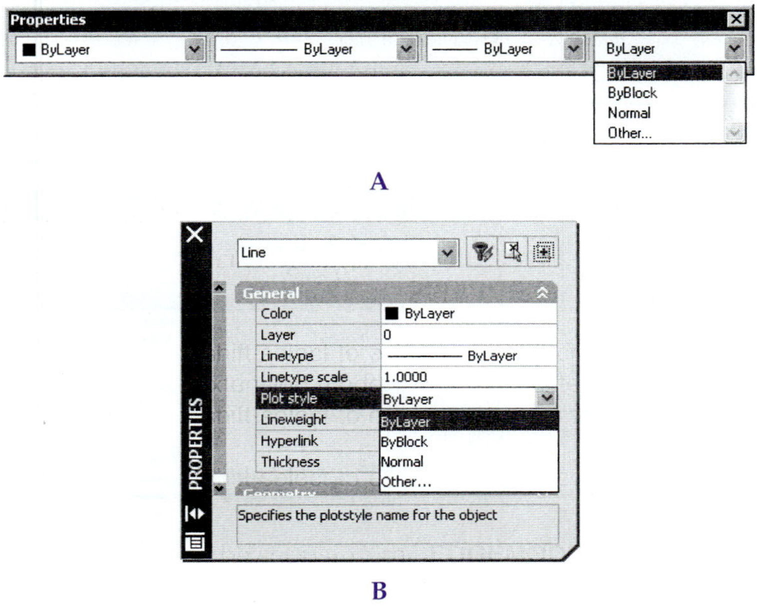

EXERCISE 11-7 Complete the Exercise on the Student CD.

Viewing Plot Style Effects before You Plot

The display of lineweights in an AutoCAD drawing is controlled by the **LWDISPLAY** system variable. If **LWDISPLAY** is on, lineweights are displayed on-screen. Similarly, it is possible to display plot style effects on-screen to see how they will appear. To do so, pick the **Display plot styles** check box in the **Plot style table** area in the **Page Setup** dialog box. Keep in mind that these two display features can increase the time required to regenerate drawings, and may decrease the performance of AutoCAD.

A quicker method is to use the print preview option, which is discussed later in the text. This displays all lineweights and plot styles exactly as they will appear on the plotted drawing.

Plot Settings

A majority of the settings that must be considered prior to plotting can be established and saved in layouts, viewports, layers, plot style tables, and template drawings. If you plan your work well, there should be very few settings, if any, you will have to adjust prior to plotting. Take a look at some of the items required for plotting, and where they can be saved.

Item	Location
Border and title block	Layout
View scales	Viewport (**Zoom XP**)
Text height	Drawing
Object color, lineweight, and end style	Layers and plot style tables
Plot device	Page setup
Plot style table	Page setup
Paper size and drawing orientation	Page setup
Plot scale, area, offset, and options	Page setup

If you prepare for plotting as soon as you begin a new drawing, the act of plotting may mean just a few clicks of your pointing device.

Selecting the desired output device and plot style table was discussed earlier in this chapter. Once these settings are complete, you can elaborate on the plot settings in the **Plot** dialog box or in the **Page Setup** dialog box of the **Page Setup Manager**. See Figure 11-30.

Figure 11-30.
A—The **Plot** dialog box. B—The **Page Setup** dialog box of the **Page Setup Manager**.

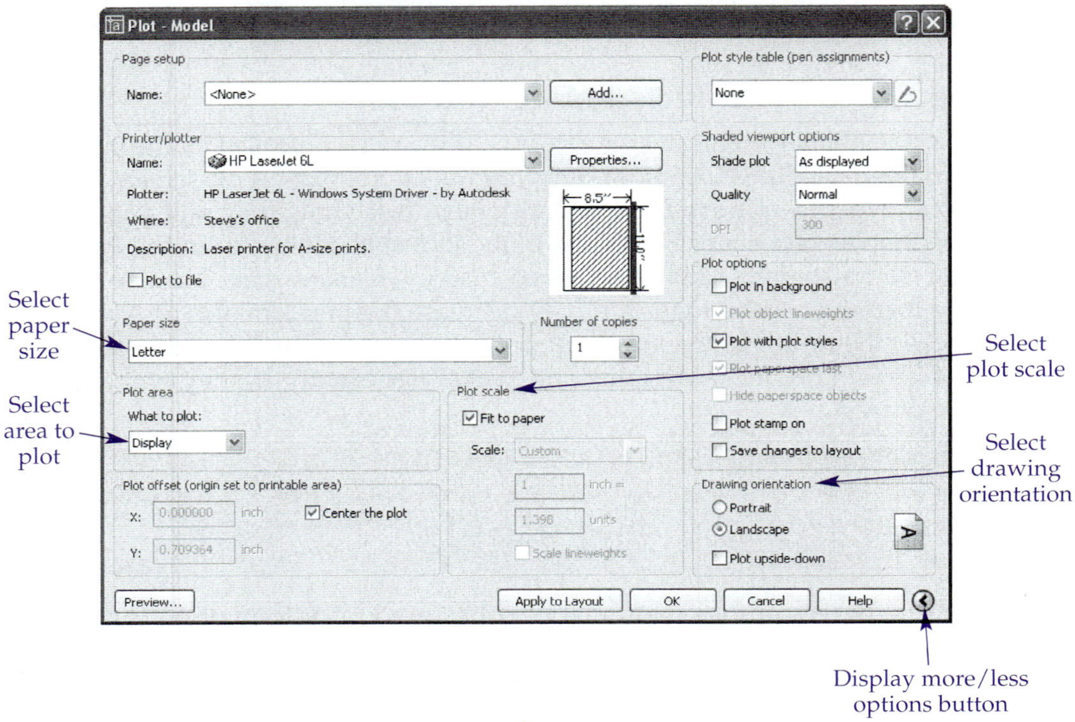

A

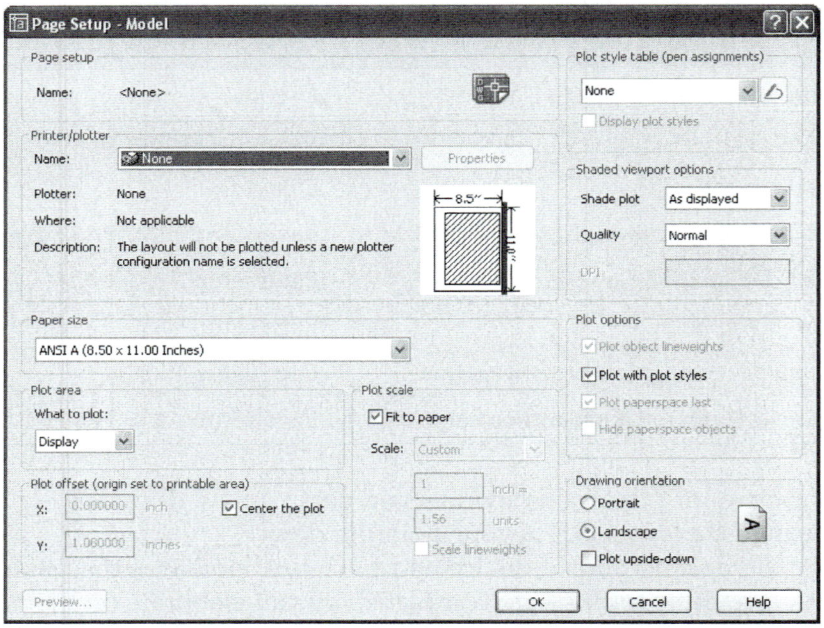

B

Paper Size, Units, and Drawing Orientation

The **Paper size** area of the **Plot** dialog box controls the paper size. Select the appropriate paper size from the drop-down list. Paper sizes are listed in inches or millimeters.

The **Drawing orientation** area of the **Plot** dialog box controls the plot rotation. You may need to select the ">" (more options) button in the lower right of the **Plot** dialog box to see this area. ***Portrait*** orients the long side of the paper vertically, and is the standard orientation for most written documents printed on 8.5 × 11 paper. ***Landscape*** orients the long side of the paper horizontally, and is the default for AutoCAD drawings. If you consider landscape format to be a rotation angle of 0°, the following table should help you determine how to use the **Plot upside-down button** option to achieve several rotation angles.

Orientation Buttons	Rotation Angle
Landscape	0°
Portrait	90°
Upside-down landscape	180°
Upside-down portrait	270°

In AutoCAD, the horizontal screen measurement relates to the long side of the paper (landscape format). However, you might create a drawing, form, or chart in portrait format. This format orients the long side of the plot vertically. AutoCAD rotates plots in 90° increments, as shown in the previous table. Figure 11-31 illustrates the result of a 90° portrait rotation.

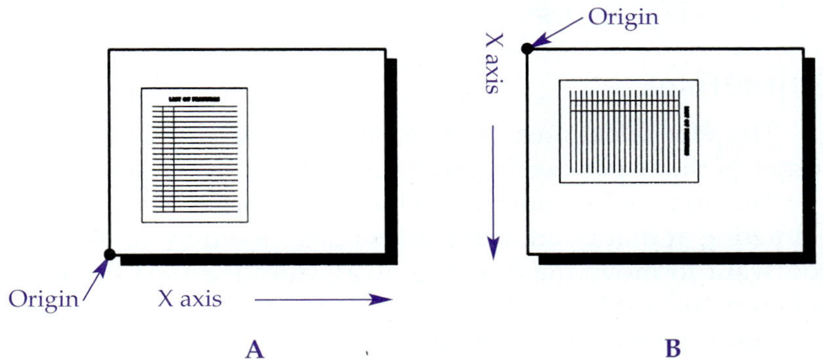

Figure 11-31.
The long side of the plot is oriented vertically in a 90° portrait rotation.

Plotting Area

The **Plot area** region of the **Plot** dialog box allows you to choose the portion of the drawing to be plotted, and how it is to be plotted. The options contained in the drop-down list are described as follows:

- **Layout/Limits.** The **Layout** option is displayed when plotting a layout. Everything inside the margins of the layout is plotted. The **Limits** option is displayed when plotting from the **Model** tab. This option plots everything inside the defined drawing limits.
- **Extents.** The **Extents** option plots only the area of the drawing in which objects are drawn. Before using this option, zoom the extents to include all drawn objects to verify exactly what will be plotted. Be aware that border lines around your drawing (like the title block) may be clipped off if they are at the extreme edge of the screen. This often happens because you are requesting the plotter to plot at the extreme edge of its active area.

- **Display.** This option plots the current screen display.
- **View.** Use this option to plot named views, which were discussed in Chapter 10. This option is not shown if no views have been saved in the drawing. Select the name of the view from the drop-down list. This option is available only when the **Model** tab is current.
- **Window.** When this option is selected, the dialog will disappear so that you can pick two opposite corners to define a window around the area to be plotted. After doing so, the dialog will reappear. A **Window...** button will now be displayed in the **Plot area** region. This button can be used to redefine the opposite corners of a window around the portion of the drawing to be plotted.

NOTE

If the window you define is too close to an object, some portion of that object may be clipped off in your plot. If this happens, simply adjust the window size the next time you plot. You can prevent these errors by using the plot preview option to see what exactly will be plotted.

Shaded Viewport Options

AutoCAD allows viewports to be plotted in shaded modes. You may need to select the "**>**" button in the lower right of the **Plot** dialog box to see this area. If a viewport has been designated to be plotted in **Wireframe** or **Hidden** mode, no options from this area of the **Plot** dialog box are editable. If a viewport is designated to be plotted in **As Displayed** or **Rendered** mode, you have the option of setting the quality of the shading for the viewports. Each predefined quality setting has a certain dots-per-inch (dpi) setting associated with it. If you choose **Custom** in the **Quality:** drop-down list, enter a value in the **DPI:** text box.

Plot Offset

The **Plot offset** area controls how far the drawing is offset from the lower-left corner of the paper. See Figure 11-32.

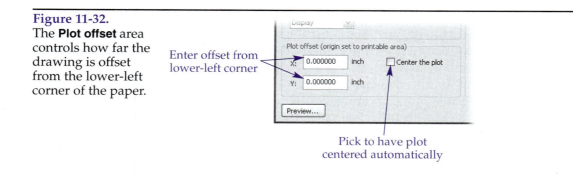

The origin of a plotter is the lower-left corner of the plot media. To begin plotting a drawing at that point, leave the values shown in the **X:** and **Y:** text boxes at 0.00. If you want to move the drawing away from the default origin, change the required values in the text boxes. For example, to move the drawing four units to the right and three units above the plotter origin, enter 4 in the **X:** text box, and 3 in the **Y:** text box.

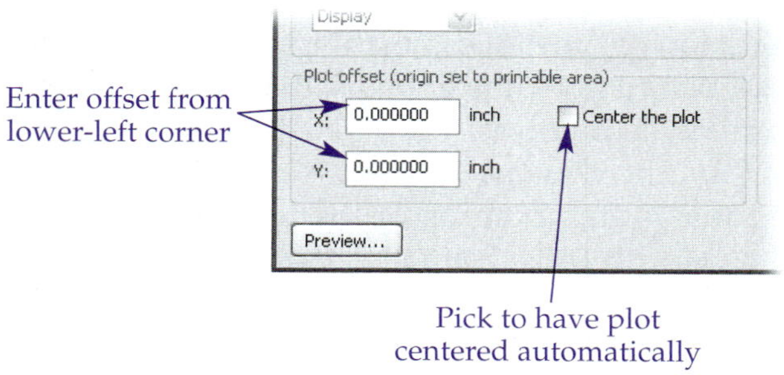

Figure 11-32. The **Plot offset** area controls how far the drawing is offset from the lower-left corner of the paper.

Other Plotting Options

The **Plot options** area of the **Plot** dialog box contains a list of items that can affect how, and if, objects appear on your plots, especially relating to paper space and model space objects. You may need to select the ">" button in the lower right of the **Plot** dialog box to see this area. Apply these options only when required for the plot by picking the appropriate check box. The following options are available:

AutoCAD 2005
NEW FEATURE

- **Plot in background.** This option allows you to continue working in AutoCAD while your computer processes the plot.
- **Plot object lineweights.** Lines having a lineweight other than 0 are plotted using the appropriate thickness. This box is checked by default.
- **Plot with plot styles.** All plot styles attached to the drawing and its components are plotted.
- **Plot paperspace last.** Paper space objects are plotted first by default. If this box is checked, paper space objects are plotted last. Since there are no paper space objects present in the **Model** tab, this option is available only when plotting from a layout tab.
- **Hide paperspace objects.** This option removes hidden lines from 3D objects that have been created in paper space. This option is only available when you are plotting from a layout tab. This option affects only objects drawn in paper space. It does not affect any 3D objects within a viewport. To plot objects within viewports with hidden lines removed, you must change the Shade plot property of the viewport. To do this, select the layout tab, pick the viewport, and open the **Properties** window. Pick the Shade plot property and change the setting to Hidden. See Figure 11-33.
- **Plot stamp on.** Checking this option will attach a plot stamp along the edge of the plot. See the "Adding a Plot Stamp" section later in this chapter.
- **Save changes to layout.** This option allows any changes that are made to the settings in the **Plot** dialog box to be saved to the layout as the default page setup for the layout.

Figure 11-33.
In order to plot objects in a floating viewport with hidden lines removed, the Shade plot setting for the viewport must be Hidden.

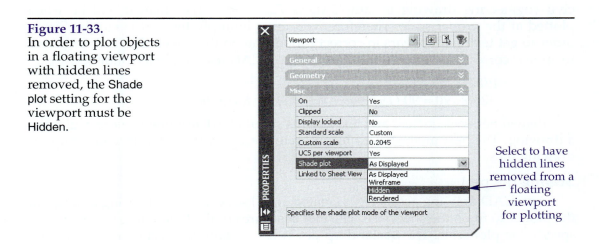

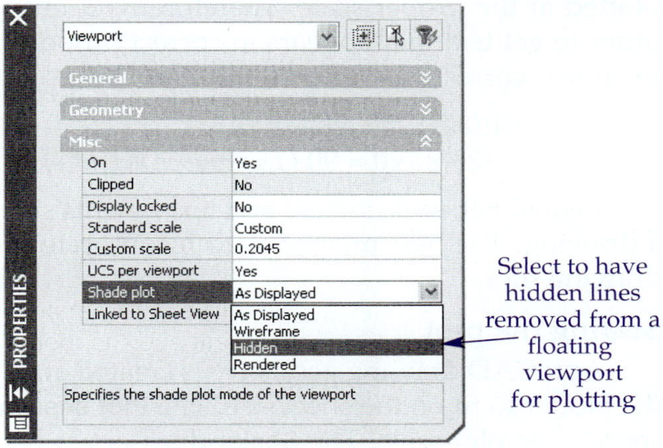

Determining Drawing Scale Factors

The proper scale factor is vitally important because it ensures that text, dimension values, and dimensioning entities (such as arrowheads and tick marks) are plotted at the proper size. The scale factor of the drawing should already be established by the time you are ready to plot and should be an integral part of your template drawings. To obtain the correct text height, the desired plotted text height is multiplied by the scale factor. The scale factor is also used in scaling dimensions.

NOTE Determine the plot scale and scale factor when you begin the drawing. If you find the drawing scale factor does not correspond to the plotting scale, you will need to update dimensions and text.

The scale factor is always the reciprocal of the drawing scale. For example, if you wish to plot a mechanical drawing at a scale of 1/2″ = 1″, calculate the scale factor as follows:

1/2″ = 1″
.5″ = 1″
1 ÷ .5 = 2 *(The scale factor is 2)*

An architectural drawing to be plotted at a scale of 1/4″ = 1′-0″ has a scale factor calculated as follows:

1/4″ = 1′-0″
.25″ = 12″
12 ÷ .25 = 48 *(The scale factor is 48)*

The scale factor of a civil engineering drawing that has a scale of 1″ = 60′ is calculated as follows:

1″ = 60′
1″ = 60 × 12 = 720″ *(The scale factor is 720)*

Once the scale factor of the drawing has been determined, calculate the height of the text in AutoCAD. If text height is to be plotted at 1/8″, it should not be drawn at that height unless the drawing will be plotted at full scale. Remember, all geometry created in AutoCAD should be drawn at full scale.

For example, if you are working on a civil engineering drawing with a scale of 1″ = 60′, the scale factor equals 720. Text drawn 1/8″ high appears as a dot. The full-size civil engineering drawing in AutoCAD is 720 times larger than it will be when plotted at the proper scale. Therefore, you must multiply the text height by 720 in order to get text that appears in correct proportion on the screen. For 1/8″ high text to appear correctly on screen, calculate the AutoCAD text height as follows:

1/8″ × 720
.125 × 720 = 90 *(The proper height of the text is 90)*

Remember, scale factors and text heights should be determined before beginning a drawing. The best method is to incorporate these as values within your template drawing files.

Scaling the plot

AutoCAD drawing geometry is created at full scale, and the drawing is scaled at the plotter to fit on the sheet size. The **Plot scale** area of the **Plot** dialog box is used to specify the plot scale. The **Scale:** drop-down list contains a selection of 32 different decimal and architectural scales. See **Figure 11-34.** The text boxes below the predefined scales drop-down list allow you to specify the plot scale as a ratio of plotted units to drawing units. An architectural drawing to be plotted at 1/4″ = 1′-0″ can be entered in the text boxes as:

1/4″ = 1′ *or* .25 = 12 *or* 1 = 48

A mechanical drawing to be plotted at a scale of 1/2″ = 1″ can be entered in the text boxes as:

1/2″ = 1″ *or* .5 = 1 *or* 1 = 2

Figure 11-34.
The **Scale:** drop-down list contains a selection of 34 different decimal and architectural scales, including Custom.

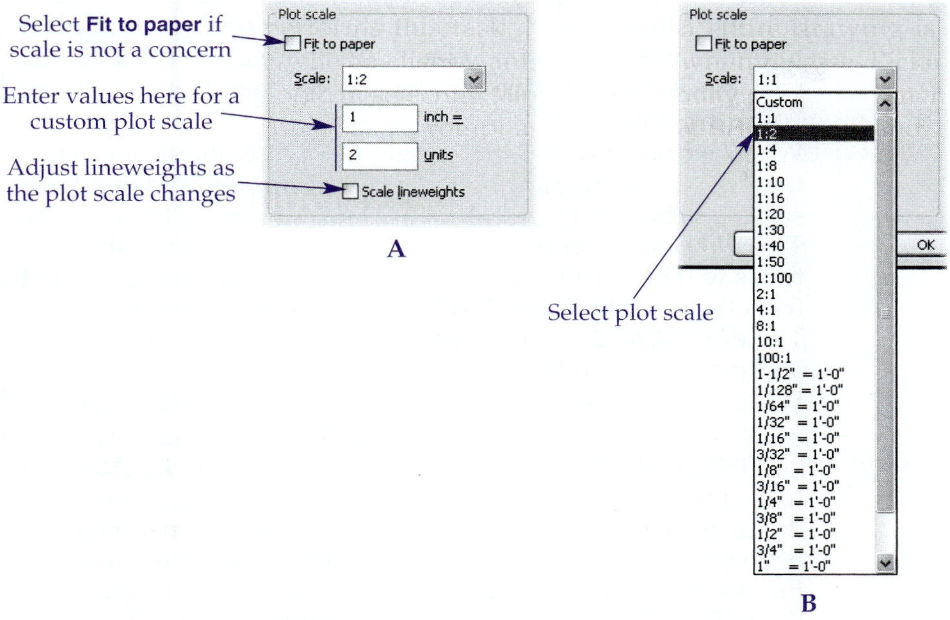

Pick the **Fit to paper** check box above the predefined scales drop-down list if you want AutoCAD to automatically adjust your drawing to fit on the paper. This is useful if you have a C-size pen plotter but need to plot a D-size or E-size drawing. However, keep in mind that you may have considerable blank space left on the paper, depending on the size and proportions of your drawing. AutoCAD 2005 NEW FEATURE

The **Fit to paper** option is also useful if you are printing a large drawing on a printer that can only use A-size sheets. The drawing is automatically scaled down to fit the size of the printer paper.

Calculating the drawing area and limits

To calculate the available area on a sheet of paper at a specific scale, use this formula:

Scale factor × Media size = Limits

For example, the limits of a B-size (17″ × 11″) sheet of paper at 1/2″ = 1″ scale (scale factor = 2) can be calculated as follows:

2 × 17 = 34 (X distance)
2 × 11 = 22 (Y distance)

Thus, the limits of a B-size sheet at the scale of 1/2″ = 1″ are 34,22. The same formula applies to architectural scales. The limits of a C-size architectural sheet (24″ × 18″) at a scale of 1/4″ = 1′-0″ (scale factor = 48) can be determined as follows:

48 × 24 = 1152″ = 96′ (X distance)

Use the same formula to calculate the Y distance for the 18″ side of the paper. Refer to the charts on the Student CD to find the limits for common scales on various paper sizes for each drafting field.

CAUTION

Before you plot a drawing, always check the **LTSCALE** and **PSLTSCALE** system variables. These variables control model space and paper space linetype scaling. The **LTSCALE** variable is set to a value representing the scale factor to be applied to linetypes that contain dashes and spaces. The **PSLTSCALE** variable is a toggle that can be set to either 1 or 0, "on" or "off" respectively.

When working in the model tab, **LTSCALE** should be set to the inverse of the plotting scale. For example, if the plotting scale is to be 1/48 (1/4"=1′-0"), **LTSCALE** should be set to 48. This way, unless you are zoomed in extremely close, the linetypes will be readily apparent. If the drawing is to be plotted from the model tab, **LTSCALE** should remain set to this value. The **PSLTSCALE** variable setting has no effect when working and plotting from the model tab.

When plotting from a layout tab, especially with viewports of two or more differing scales, the **LTSCALE** should be set to 1, and **PSLTSCALE** should be set to 1 ("on"). Setting **PSLTSCALE** to 1 allows the zoom scale factor of the viewport to control the scale factor of the linetypes. In this case the linetypes will be displayed through the viewports at a scale factor based on the product of the viewport zoom scale factor multiplied by the **LTSCALE** setting (which should be 1). Differently scaled viewports will display and plot linetypes at the same size, relative to paper space.

When plotting from a layout tab with a single viewport, or multiple viewports zoomed to the same scale, the **LTSCALE** can be set to the inverse of the zoom scale factor of the viewport(s) and the **PSLTSCALE** variable can be set to 0 ("off"). For the sake of consistency, if your school or company is using layouts, it might be a good idea to standardize on the linetype scaling method outlined in the previous paragraph.

Previewing the Plot

Depending on their size and complexity, drawings can require long plotting times. By previewing a plot before it is sent to the output device, you can catch errors, saving material and valuable plot time. This feature is controlled by the **Preview...** button at the lower-left corner of the **Plot** dialog box.

Pick the **Preview...** button to display the drawing as it will actually appear on the plotted hard copy. The display reflects any plot style tables that have been attached to the drawing if the **Plot with plot styles** button is checked in the **Plot options** area. Displaying the preview takes the same amount of time as a drawing regeneration. Therefore, the drawing size determines how quickly the image is produced.

The drawing is displayed inside a paper outline. The Zoom cursor appears. Press and hold the pick button as you move the cursor up to enlarge and down to reduce. Right-click to display the shortcut menu shown in Figure 11-35. It provides several display options, a **Plot** option, and an **Exit** option. The shortcut menu is handy because it allows you to closely examine the drawing before you commit to plotting. When you are finished previewing, press [Esc] or [Enter] to return to the **Plot** dialog box.

A preview is also displayed by picking **Plot Preview** in the **File** pull-down menu. This selection bypasses the **Plot** dialog box.

Figure 11-35.
Right-click to display the shortcut menu when a plot preview is displayed.

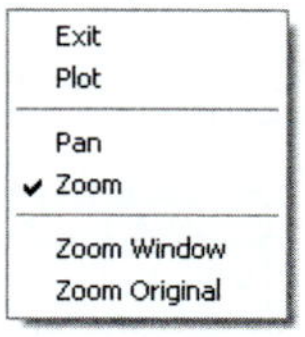

Before you pick **OK** in the **Plot** dialog box, there are several items you should check:

✓ The printer or plotter is plugged in and turned on.
✓ The printer's data cable is secure.
✓ The paper and ink/toner are loaded correctly.
✓ The printer or plotter area is clear for unblocked paper movement.

Once you are satisfied with all plotter parameters and are ready to plot, pick the **OK** button to exit the **Plot** dialog box. AutoCAD then displays the following message on the command line:

Effective plotting area: *(xx)* wide by *(yy)* high
Plotting viewport *n*
Plotting viewport *n*

These are the actual dimensions of the current plotting area. Depending on the type of plotter or printer you are using, one or more dialog boxes may be displayed, showing the drawing name and a meter showing the percentage of the file that has been regenerated and sent to the printer.

Adding a Plot Stamp

A plot stamp is specific text information included on a printed or plotted drawing. A plot stamp may include information such as the drawing name or the date and time the drawing was printed.

In the **Plot** dialog box, the **Plot stamp on** area in the **Plot options** area allows you to activate and modify the plot stamp. See Figure 11-36. If the **On** check box is activated, a **Plot Stamp Settings** button appears next to the check box and a plot stamp will be printed on the drawing. You can also specify the items to be included in the plot stamp by picking the **Plot Stamp Settings...** button. This accesses the **Plot Stamp** dialog box, which is shown in Figure 11-37.

Figure 11-36.
Activate the plot stamp in the **Plot options** area of the **Plot** dialog box. Pick the **Plot Stamp Settings...** button to access the **Plot Stamp** dialog box.

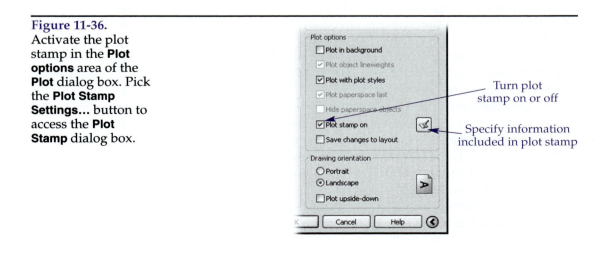

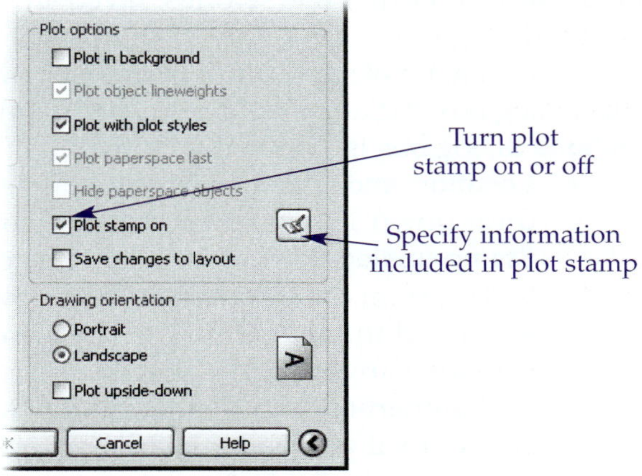

Figure 11-37.
Use the **Plot Stamp** dialog box to specify the information included in the plot stamp. You can save plot stamp settings as PSS files.

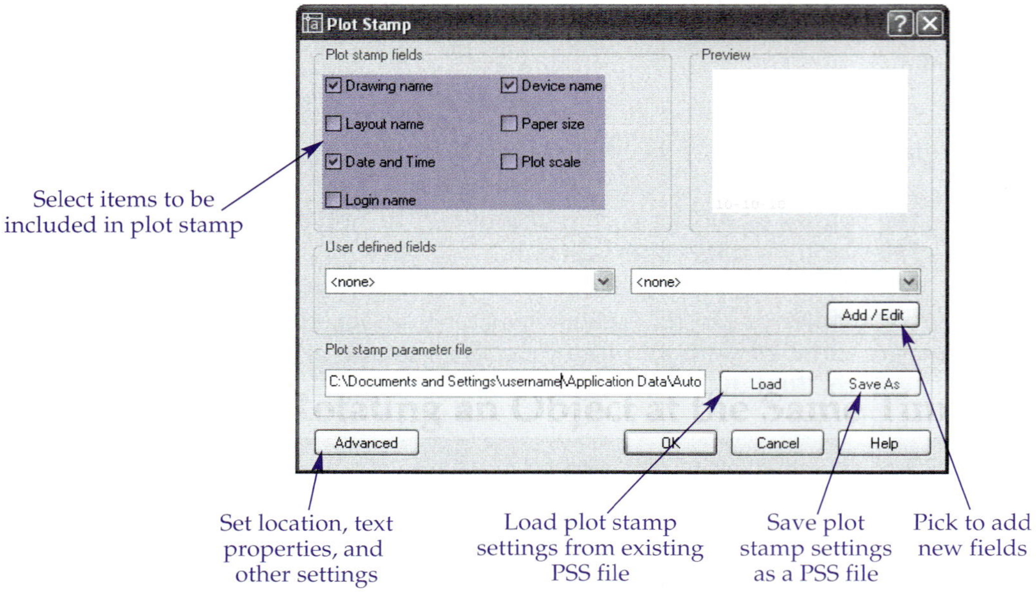

Specify the information to be included in the plot stamp in the **Plot stamp fields** area of the **Plot Stamp** dialog box. The following items can be included:

- Drawing name
- Layout name
- Date and time
- Login name
- Device name
- Paper size
- Plot scale

You can create additional plot stamp items in the **User defined fields** area. For example, you could add a field for the client name, the project name, or the contractor who will be using the drawing.

The **Preview** area provides a preview of the location and orientation of the plot stamp. The preview does not show the actual plot stamp text.

Plot stamp settings can be saved in a PSS (plot stamp parameter) file. If you load an existing PSS file, the settings saved in the file are automatically set in the **Plot Stamp** dialog box.

Additional plot stamp options are set in the **Advanced Options** dialog box. To access this dialog box, pick the **Advanced...** button in the **Plot Stamp** dialog box. The **Advanced Options** dialog box is shown in Figure 11-38. The following options are available:

- **Location and offset.** Pick the corner where the plot stamp begins from the drop-down list. If you want the plot stamp to print upside-down, pick the **Stamp upside-down** check box. The orientation is set by picking Horizontal or Vertical from the **Orientation** drop-down list. The X offset and Y offset distance is entered in the text boxes. The offset distances are measured relative to the printable area or paper border.
- **Text properties.** Specify the text font and height. Pick the **Single line plot stamp** check box if you want the plot stamp constrained to a single line. If this check box is not checked, the plot stamp will be printed in two lines.
- **Plot stamp units.** Select the plot stamp units. The plot stamp units can be different from the drawing units.

Figure 11-38.
Specify the plot stamp location, orientation, text font and size, and units in the **Advanced Options** dialog box.

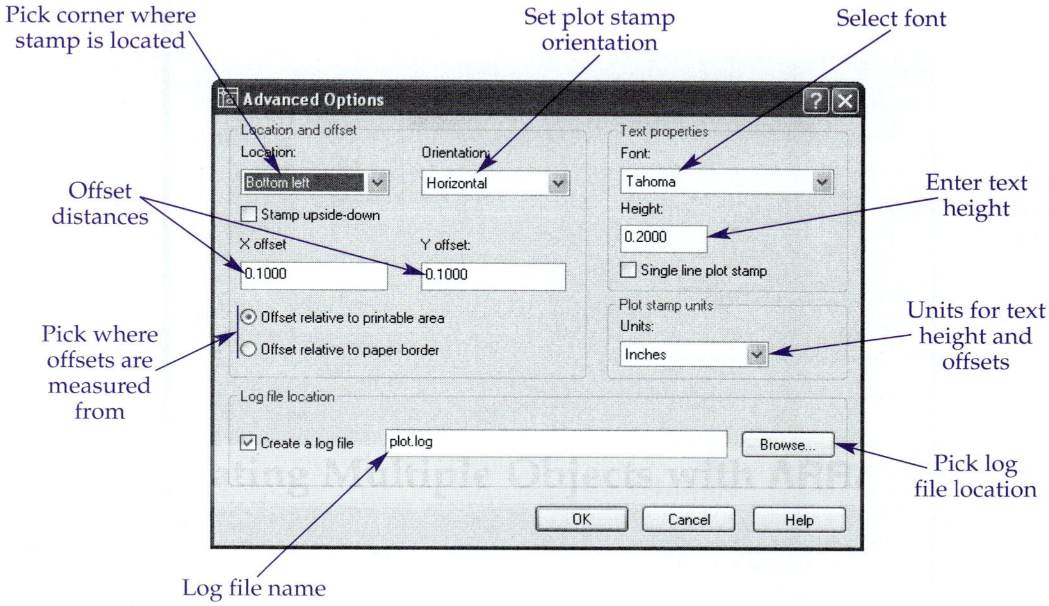

- **Log file location.** Pick the **Create a log file** check box to create a log file of plotted items. Specify the name of the log file in the text box. Pick **Browse...** to specify the location of the log file.

> **NOTE**
> The log file settings are independent of the plot stamp settings. Thus, you can produce a log file without creating a plot stamp or have a plot stamp without producing a log file.

Additional Plotting Options

The **Plot and Publish** tab of the **Options** dialog box contains general plotting settings, some of which will seldom have to be changed. See **Figure 11-39.** To access this dialog box, select **Options...** from the **Tools** pull-down menu. The **Plot and Publish** tab provides several general plotting options. The areas are discussed briefly here.

- **Default plot settings for new drawings.** The default setting is **Use as default output device**. The device can be selected from the drop-down list. The **Use last successful plot settings** option retains the previous plot settings. Picking the **Add or Configure Plotters** button displays the **Plotters** window.
- **General plot options.** This area allows you to use either the **Keep the layout paper size if possible** option, regardless of the plotter selected, or the **Use the plot device paper size** option. If you choose to keep the layout size, AutoCAD will use the paper size specified in the **Page Setup** dialog box. If this size cannot be plotted, AutoCAD defaults to the size listed in the plotter's PC3 file. These radio buttons reflect the setting of the **PAPERUPDATE** system variable.
  - **System printer spool alert.** If a port conflict occurs during plotting and a drawing is spooled to a system printer, AutoCAD can display an alert and log the error. This drop-down list gives four options for alerting and logging errors.

Figure 11-39.
General plotting settings are found in the **Plot and Publish** tab of the **Options** dialog box.

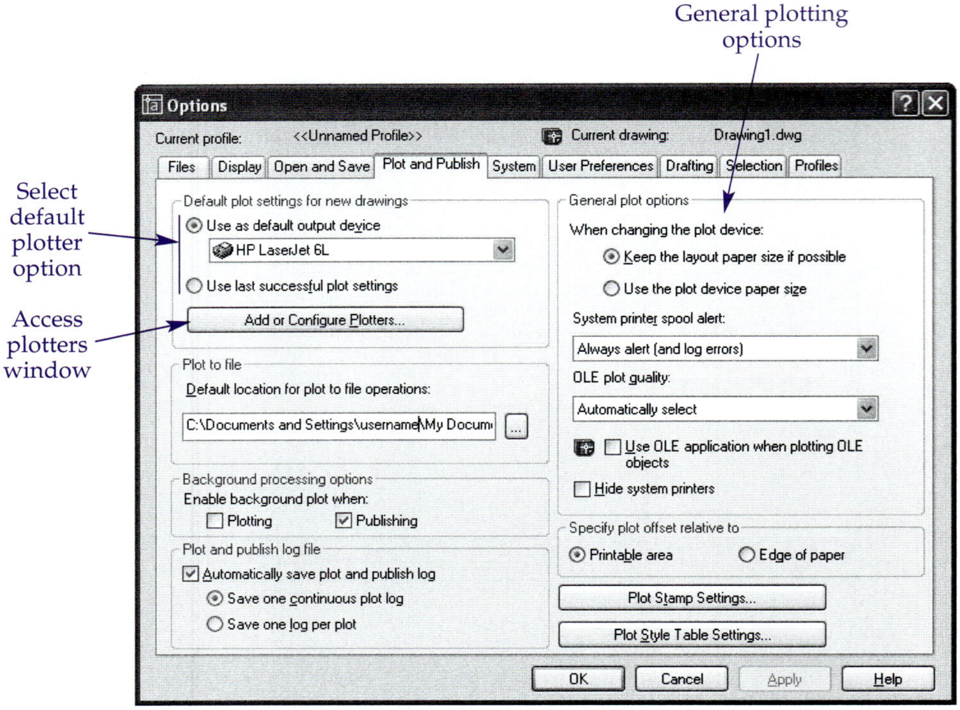

- **OLE plot quality.** *OLE* is an acronym for ***object linking and embedding*** and refers to any text or graphic object that is imported from another software application. This drop-down list allows you to select the type of OLE objects that will be plotted. The **OLEQUALITY** system variable also controls this option.
- **Use OLE application when plotting OLE objects.** If this check box is activated, applications used to create OLE objects are launched. This may be desirable if you wish to use the OLE software to adjust the quality of the object. This option is also controlled by the **OLESTARTUP** system variable.

Alternative Plotting

Typically, the end result of executing the plotting procedures is a paper drawing, also known as a hardcopy. Largely because of the growth of the Internet, many drawings are being exchanged as electronic files instead of paper drawings. AutoCAD can generate two types of electronic files: design web format (DWF) and plot (PLT). The DWF file may be e-mailed, uploaded to the Internet, or posted on a company's internal Web site. The file is viewed using Autodesk's free application, *DWF Viewer*®. The other electronic file, PLT, is eventually sent to a printer or plotter. The reason for creating this file instead of plotting directly to paper is to save time. PLT's can be created during the workday and sent to the plotter at night, when the plotter is not busy. Sometimes the PLT files are sent to a plot spooler so your computer is not waiting for the plotter to finish. There is additional information regarding these files in ***AutoCAD and its Applications—Advanced***.

Using Publish to Create a DWF File

A DWF file is created from the **Publish** dialog box. You can also send the drawings to a plotter from the **Publish** dialog box. This technique will be presented along with the DWF procedure. You can access this dialog box by picking the **Publish** button on the **Standard** toolbar, picking **Publish** from the **File** pull-down menu, or typing PUBLISH at the Command: prompt. The listing of sheets to publish will be empty unless the **Model** or layout tabs have been initialized. If open, close the **Publish** dialog box and create some geometry and text in the **Model** view. Pick each layout tab to initialize them. Open the **Publish** dialog box again and notice the three sheets listed in the Sheets to publish area. It should say No errors under the status title for each sheet. See **Figure 11-40.**

The eight buttons below the **Sheets to publish** area are:

- **Preview.** Same as **Plot Preview**.
- **Add Sheets.** Add a sheet from another drawing.
- **Remove Sheets.** Remove the selected sheet from the list.
- **Move Sheet Up.** The published sheets are viewed or plotted in the order shown in the list.
- **Move Sheet Down.** Used with the button above to reorder the sheets.
- **Load Sheet List...** Loads a previously saved list of sheets to publish.
- **Save Sheet List...** This button is available after the current drawing is saved.
- **Plot Stamp Settings.** Same as the **Plot Stamp Settings** in the **Plot** dialog box.

Below these buttons is the **Publish to** area containing two destinations. The first, **Plotter named in page setup**, sends each sheet directly to the plotter designated in its page setup. Each sheet plots using the page setup named in the **Sheets to Publish** area. The second, **DWF File**, creates a design web format file that can be used as described in the first paragraph of this chapter. The location of this file, along with other options, can be found by picking the **Publish Options** button.

Other features to note are the **Number of copies** text box and the **Include when adding sheets** area. The number of copies only applies when the destination is a plotter and the page setup is not plotting to a file. The type of sheets, model or layout, to include when publishing is controlled in the second area mentioned. A detailed description of the publishing options and methods of delivering the DWF files

Figure 11-40.
The DWF files and paper copies can be created from the **Publish** dialog box.

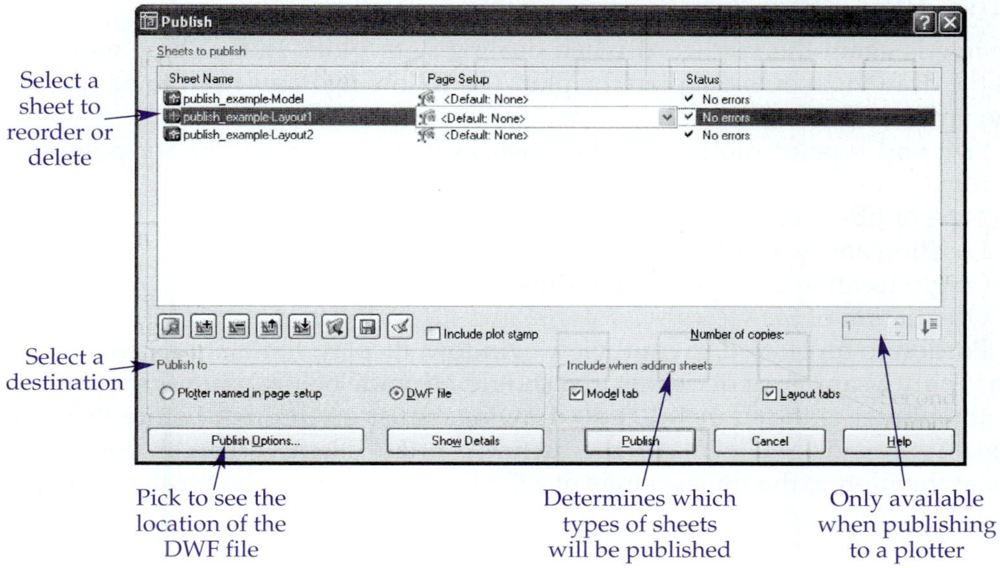

through e-mail and the Internet can be found in ***AutoCAD and its Applications—Advanced***. After configuring the necessary options, pick **Publish** to create the DWF file or send the sheets to a plotter.

Creating a PLT File

The PLT file is generated within the **Plot** dialog box. All of the options that you would configure for a paper plot have to be considered when creating the PLT file. Even the plotter has to be selected for a file to be created. Open the **Plot** dialog box, as described in the previous sections, and prepare all of the options as you would when making a hardcopy. Make sure that you have chosen a plotter. Now, put a check in the **Plot to file** checkbox located in the **Printer/plotter** area. See Figure 11-41. Pick the **OK** button and the **Browse for Plot File** dialog box will pop up. If necessary, you can change the file name and location before saving the file.

Figure 11-41.
PLT files are created from the **Plot** dialog box.

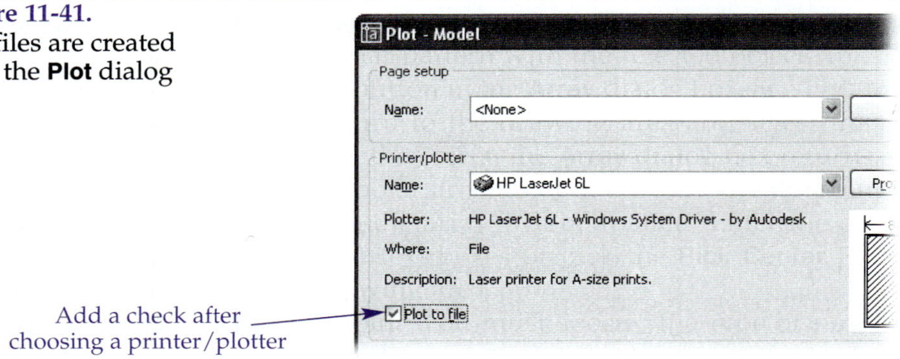

Plotting Hints

Plotting can slow down productivity in an office or a classroom if not done efficiently. Establish and follow a procedure for using the plotter, and instruct all drafters, engineers, and other plotter users of the proper operating procedures. Post these in strategic locations.

Planning Your Plots

Planning is again the key word when dealing with plots. In the same way you planned the drawing, you must plan the plot. The following items need to be considered when planning:

- ✓ Size and type of plotting media, such as bond paper, vellum, or polyester film.
- ✓ Type of title block.
- ✓ Location and scale of multiple views.
- ✓ Origin location and scale of the drawing.
- ✓ Orientation of 3D views.
- ✓ Portion to be plotted: layout, view, window, display, limits, or extents.

This is only a sample of decisions that should be made before you begin plotting. Usually, the plotter is the funnel that all drawings must go through before they are evaluated, approved, and sent to production or the client. When a bottleneck develops at the plotter, the time savings of a CAD system can be drastically reduced.

Eliminate Unnecessary Plots

The easiest way to eliminate the problems associated with plotting is to eliminate plotting. Make plots *only* when absolutely necessary. This results in time and money savings. A few additional suggestions include the following:

- ✓ Obtain approvals of designs while the drawings are on screen.
- ✓ Transfer files for the checker's comments.
- ✓ Create a special layer with a unique color for markups. Freeze or erase this layer when finally making a plot.
- ✓ Use a "redlining" software package that enables the checker to review the drawing and apply markups to it without using AutoCAD.
- ✓ Check drawings on disk. Use a special layer for comments.
- ✓ Use a printer when check prints are sufficient.
- ✓ Avoid making plots for backups. Rather, establish a reliable backup procedure. This may be accomplished using tape cartridges, optical disks, or other external storage devices.

If You Must Plot...

Industry still exists on a paper-based system. Therefore, it is important that plotters are used efficiently. This means using the plotter only for what is required. Here are a few hints for doing just that.

- ✓ Ask yourself, "Do I *really* need a plot?" If the answer is an unqualified *yes*, then proceed.
- ✓ Plan your plot!
- ✓ Pick the least busy time to make the plot.
- ✓ Select the smallest piece of paper possible.
- ✓ Use the lowest quality paper possible.
- ✓ Create batch plot files and use batch plotting at times when plotter and printer use is light.

Producing Quality Plots

When you must plot the highest quality drawing for reproduction, evaluation, or presentation, use your plotter in a manner that does the job right the first time. Keep in mind these points before making that final plot.

- ✓ Choose the device that will produce the quality of print needed. Select the right tool for the job.
- ✓ Choose the paper type and size appropriate for the project.
- ✓ If using wet ink pens, select the proper ink for your climate.
- ✓ Apply the appropriate plot style table for color plotting.

Chapter Test

Answer the following questions on a separate sheet of paper.

1. What is paper space?
2. Which drawing environment (space) is active when the **Model** tab is selected?
3. What is a layout?
4. How do you create floating viewports in a layout?
5. When working in a layout tab, how do you activate a viewport in order to zoom or pan the viewport display?
6. List three methods used to create a new layout tab.
7. When creating a new layout by copying an existing layout, why is it better to select the command option from the shortcut menu rather than using the toolbar button?
8. How can you rename a layout?
9. If all layout tabs are not visible on screen, how do you select a tab that is not currently visible?
10. List the types of files a layout can be saved as.
11. How do you access the **Plotter Configuration Editor** from the **Page Setup Manager** dialog box?
12. List five properties that can be set within a plot style.
13. Name the two plot style modes and the file extensions for their plot style tables.
14. What is a plot style table?
15. How do you access the **Plot Styles** window?
16. How do you create a new plot style table?
17. When you create a new color-dependent plot style table, how many plot styles does it contain?
18. When you create a new named plot style table, how many plot styles does it contain?
19. List two ways to access the **Plot Style Table Editor**.
20. What determines the plot style mode for a drawing?
21. Explain how you can specify a plot style table to be attached to all new drawings by default.
22. How does a color-dependent plot style table attached to a layout affect the plotting of the layout?
23. Plot styles of which plot style mode can be attached to layers and objects?
24. Explain how to assign a plot style to a layer.
25. Name two methods of assigning a plot style to an object.
26. What setting is used to have the effect of plot styles displayed in a layout?
27. Calculate the scale factors for drawings with the following scales:
    A. 1/4″ = 1″
    B. 1/8″ = 1′-0″
    C. 1″ = 30′
28. Calculate the drawing limits for the following scales and sheet sizes:
    A. 2″ = 1″ scale, 17 × 11 sheet size
    B. 1/2″ = 1′-0″ scale, 48 × 36 sheet size
    C. 1″= 10′ scale, 36 × 24 sheet size
29. Define *plot file* and explain how it is used.
30. Define *plot queue*.
31. What do you enter in the **Plot** dialog box to make the plotted drawing twice the size of the soft copy drawing?
32. What do you enter to specify a plot scale of 1/4″ = 1′-0″?
33. What system variable controls paper space linetype scaling?
34. Name the pull-down menu where the **Plot...** command is found.

35. How do you add a printer or plotter to the **Printer/Plotter** area of the **Plot** dialog box?
36. What is the difference between a PC2 file and a PC3 file?
37. How do you save a plot file named PLOT1 to a specific folder?
38. Identify the two types of paper orientation.
39. Cite two advantages of the preview format.
40. Can you zoom while viewing a preview?
41. Explain why you should plan your plots.
42. Provide the best method to speed up the plotting process in a classroom or company.
43. What type of paper and pens should be used for a check plot?
44. What type of paper and pens should be used for a final plot?

For Questions 46–50, specify if the statement is true or false.

45. Plot styles can be added to and deleted from color-dependent plot style tables.
46. Plot styles can be added to and deleted from named plot style tables.
47. The plot style mode of a drawing cannot be changed.
48. A plot style assigned to a layer will override a plot style assigned to an object on the layer when the drawing is plotted.
49. If a drawing has multiple layouts, all layouts must use the same plot style table.

Drawing Problems

1. Create a new B-size decimal template drawing for use with mechanical (machine) parts. Use the following guidelines:
   A. Create a layout with the border and title block.
   B. Establish the appropriate settings to make this a half-scale (1″= 2″) drawing.
   C. Create three different text styles: one to plot at 1/8″ high, another at 3/16″ high, and a third at 1/4″ high. Set the text heights and linetype scale according to the values given in the chart on the Student CD.
   D. Save the drawing template as MECH-B-HALF.DWT.

2. Create a new C-size architectural template drawing. Use the following guidelines:
   A. Create a layout with the border and title block. Set units to architectural and set the area to 160′ × 120′. Select to work on the drawing without the layout visible.
   B. Establish the appropriate settings to make this a 1/8″= 1′-0″ scale drawing.
   C. Create three different text styles: one to plot at 1/8″ high, another at 3/16″ high, and a third at 1/4″ high. Set the text heights and linetype scale according to the values given in the chart on the Student CD.
   D. Save the drawing as ARCH-C-EIGHTH.DWT.

3. Create a new C-size civil engineering template drawing. Use the following guidelines:
   A. Create a layout with the border and title block. Set units to engineering, angle to surveyor, angle measure to east, angle direction to counterclockwise, and set the area to 1000′ × 750′. Select to work on the drawing while viewing the layout.
   B. Establish the appropriate settings to make this a 1″ = 50′ scale drawing.
   C. Create three different text styles: one to plot at 1/8″ high, another at 3/16″ high, and a third at 1/4″ high. Set the text heights and linetype scale according to the values given in the chart on the Student CD.
   D. Save the drawing as CIVIL-C-1=50.DWT.

4. Open one of your drawings from Chapter 8. Plot the drawing on B-size paper using the **Limits** option. Use different color pens for each color in the drawing.

5. Zoom in on a portion of the drawing used for Problem 4 and select the **Display** plotting option. Rotate the plot 90° and fit it on the paper.

6. Using the same drawing used in Problem 4, use the **Window** option. Window a detailed area of the drawing. Plot the drawing to fit the paper size chosen.

7. Draw the views needed to describe the object completely. Set up appropriate layers, colors, and linetypes. Do not dimension the drawing. Plot from a layout tab using a scale of 1:1. Save the problem as P11-7.

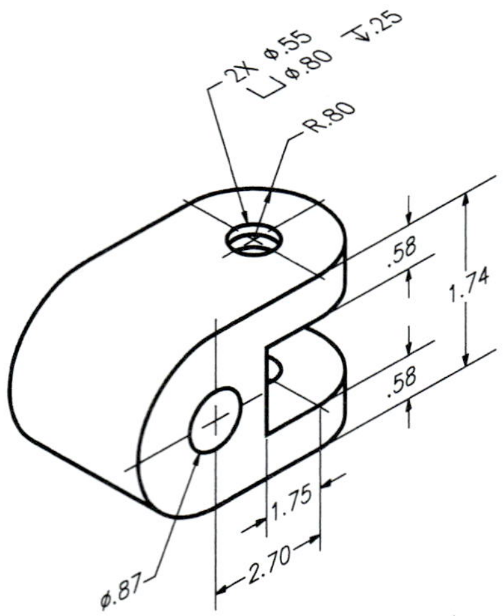

8. Draw the shown stainless steel stud on a B-size sheet at a scale of 2:1 (2 times actual size). Use a template drawing with a single floating model space viewport. Do not dimension the drawing. Be sure that paper space is active before using the **PLOT** command. Set the plot scale at 1:1. Save the drawing as P11-8.

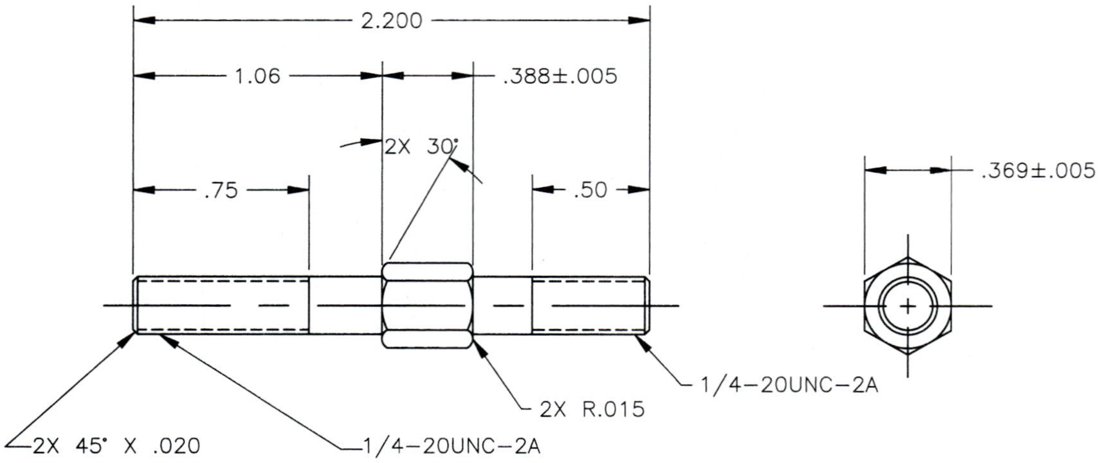

9. On an A-size sheet draw, at full scale, the schematic shown. Keep the proportions of each component and the entire drawing as shown. Using color-dependent plot styles, have the equipment (shown in color in the diagram) plot with a lineweight of 0.8 mm and 80% screening. Plotted text height should be 1/8″. Plot in paper space at 1:1. Save the drawing as P11-9.

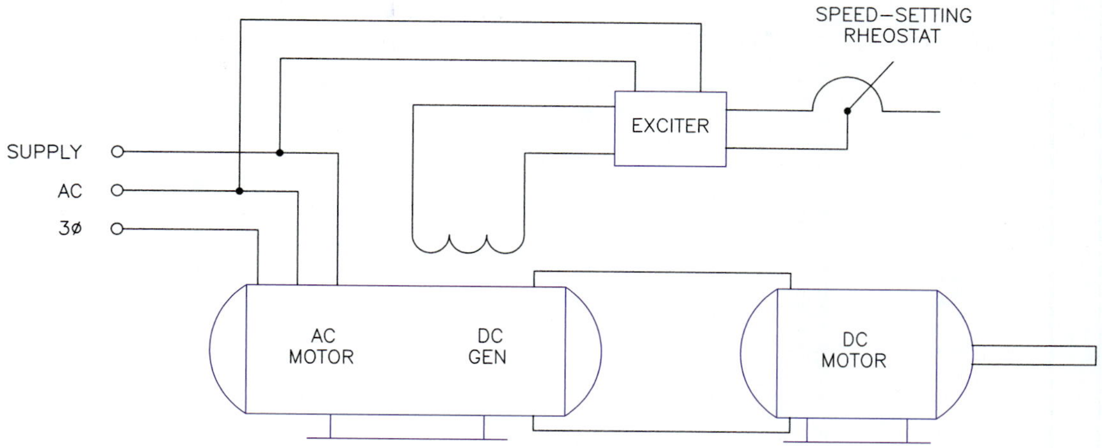

10. On a B-size sheet draw, at full scale, the schematic shown. Keep the proportions of each component and the entire drawing as shown. Plotted text height should be 1/8″. Create four layouts with the names and displays as follows:
   A. The **Entire Schematic** layout plots the entire schematic.
   B. The **3 Wire Control** layout plots only the 3 Wire Control diagram.
   C. The **Motor** layout plots the motor symbol and connections in the lower-center of the schematic.
   D. The **Schematic** layout plots schematic without the 3 Wire Control and motor components.

   Plot in paper space at 1:1. Save the drawing as P11-10.

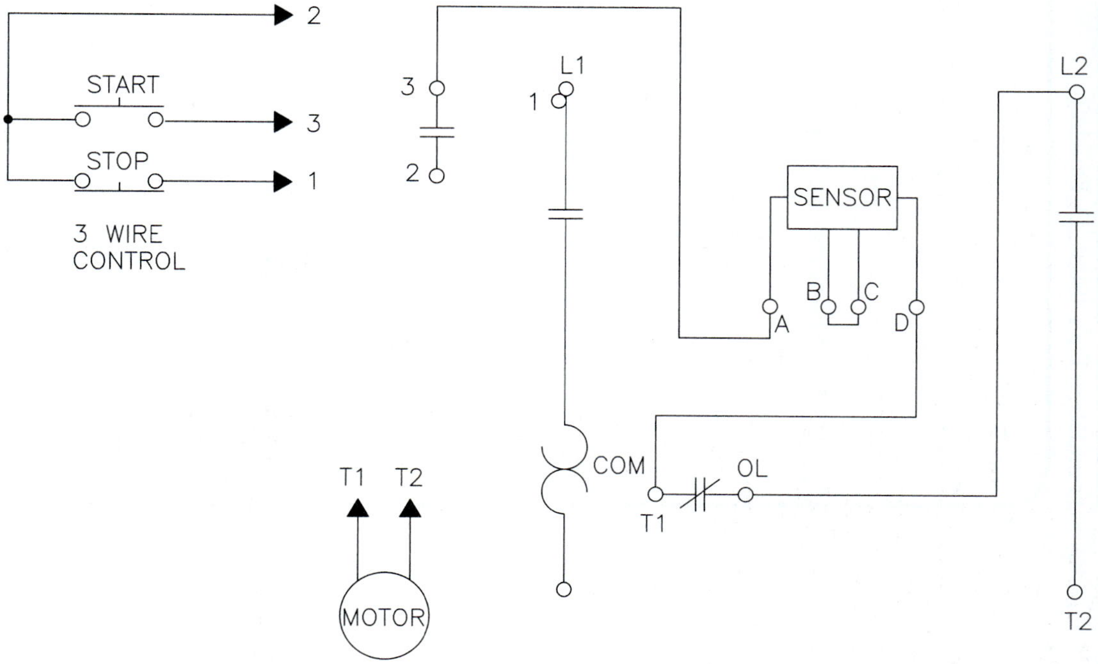

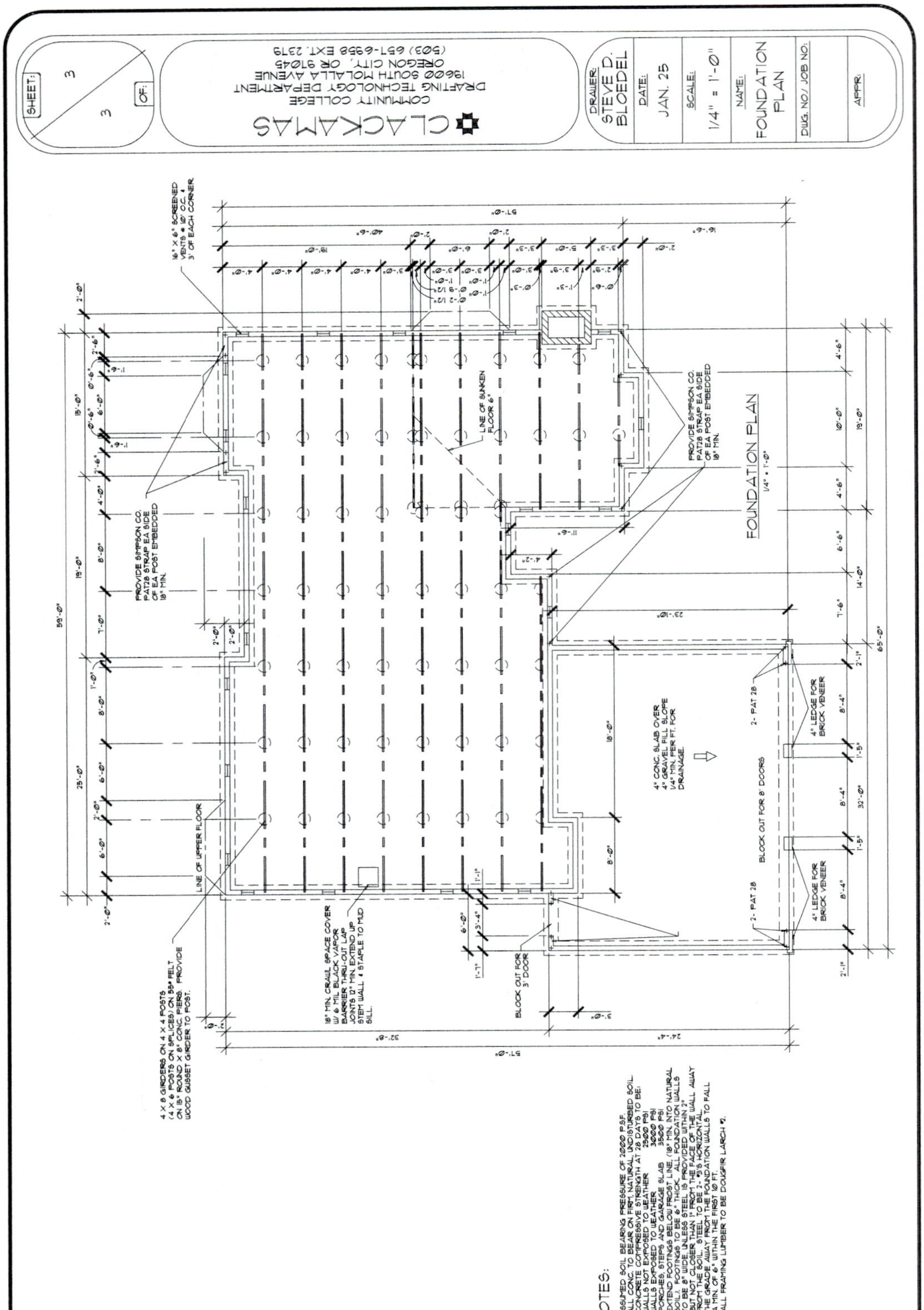

Foundation Plan. (Steve D. Bloedel)

CHAPTER 12

Basic Editing Commands

Learning Objectives

After completing this chapter, you will be able to do the following:

- Draw chamfers and angled corners with the **CHAMFER** command.
- Use the **FILLET** command to draw fillets, rounds, and other rounded corners.
- Remove portions of lines, circles, and arcs using the **BREAK** command.
- Use the **TRIM** and **EXTEND** commands to edit objects.
- Relocate objects using the **MOVE** command.
- Make single and multiple copies of existing objects using the **COPY** command.
- Draw mirror images of objects using the **MIRROR** command.
- Change the angular position of objects using the **ROTATE** command.
- Create arrangements of objects using the **ARRAY** command.
- Use the **ALIGN** command to simultaneously move and rotate objects.
- Change the size of objects using the **SCALE** command.
- Modify the lengths and heights of objects using the **STRETCH** and **LENGTHEN** commands.
- Create selection sets and object groups using the **GROUP** command.

This chapter explains commands and methods for changing a drawing. With manual drafting techniques, editing and modifying a drawing can take hours or even days. AutoCAD, however, makes the same editing tasks simpler and quicker. In Chapter 3, you learned how to draw and erase lines. The **ERASE** command is one of the most commonly used editing commands. You also learned how to select objects by picking with the cursor or using a window box, crossing box, window polygon, crossing polygon, or fence. The items selected are referred to as a *selection set*.

Many of the same selection methods and techniques can be used for the editing commands discussed in this chapter. You will learn how to draw angled and rounded corners and how to move, copy, rotate, scale, and create mirror images of existing objects. These features are found in the **Modify** toolbar and the **Modify** pull-down menu. The editing commands discussed in this chapter are basically divided into two general groups—editing individual features of a drawing and editing major portions of a drawing. Commands typically used to edit individual features of a drawing include the following:

- **CHAMFER**
- **FILLET**
- **BREAK**

- **TRIM**
- **EXTEND**
- **LENGTHEN**

The following commands are used to edit entire drawings or major portions of a drawing, though they can also be used to edit individual features:

- **MOVE**
- **COPY**
- **ROTATE**
- **ARRAY**
- **MIRROR**
- **SCALE**
- **STRETCH**
- **CHANGE**
- **GROUP**

Drawing Chamfers

A *chamfer* in mechanical drafting is a small angled surface used to relieve a sharp corner. AutoCAD defines a *chamfer* as "any angled corner on the drawing." A chamfer's distance from the corner determines the chamfer's size. A 45° chamfer is the same distance from the corner in each direction. See **Figure 12-1.** Chamfers were introduced in Chapter 5.

CHAMFER
CHA

Modify
➡ Chamfer

Modify
toolbar

Chamfer

Chamfers are drawn between two lines that may or may not intersect. They can also connect polylines, xlines, and rays. Selecting the **Chamfer** button in the **Modify** toolbar, picking **Chamfer** from the **Modify** pull-down menu, or typing CHA or CHAMFER at the Command: prompt accesses the **CHAMFER** command. The following shows the default values and available options when you enter the **CHAMFER** command:

Command: **CHA** *or* **CHAMFER**↵
(TRIM mode) Current chamfer Dist1 = *current*, Dist2 = *current*
Select first line or [Polyline/Distance/Angle/Trim/Method/mUltiple]:

The current settings are displayed for your reference. Chamfers are established with two distances or one distance and an angle. A value of 0.5 for both distances produces a 45° × 0.5 chamfered corner. The following is a brief description of each **CHAMFER** option:

- **Polyline.** Use this option if you want to chamfer all the eligible corners on a polyline. The term *eligible* means the chamfer distance is small enough to work on the corner.
- **Distance.** This option lets you set the chamfer distance for each line from the corner.

Figure 12-1.
Examples of different chamfers.

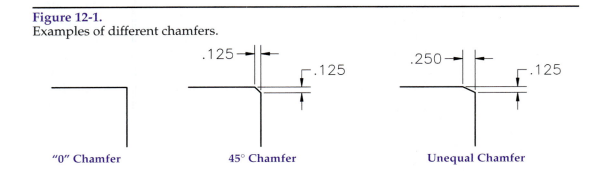

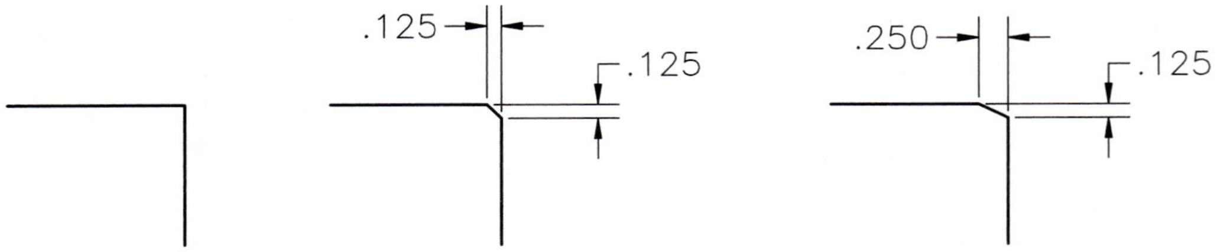

"0" Chamfer   45° Chamfer   Unequal Chamfer

- **Angle.** This option uses a chamfer distance on the first selected line and applies a chamfer angle to determine the second line chamfer.
- **Trim.** Enter this to set the Trim mode. If **Trim** is on, the selected lines are trimmed or extended as required from the corner, before the chamfer line is created. If **No trim** is active, the Trim mode is off. In this case, the selected lines are not trimmed or extended, and only the chamfer line is added.
- **Method.** This is a toggle that sets the chamfer method to either **Distance** or **Angle. Distance** and **Angle** values can be set without affecting each other.
- **Multiple.** Using this option repeats the chamfer command until you press the [Enter] key. After successfully chamfering two objects, you are prompted to Select first line or [Polyline/Distance/Angle/Trim/Method/mUltiple]: again, which is basically restarting the command, using the last settings.

Setting the Chamfer Distance

The chamfer distance must be set before you can draw chamfers. The distances you set remain in effect until changed. Most drafters set the chamfer distance as exact values, but you can pick two points to set the distance. The following procedure is used to set the chamfer distance:

> Command: **CHA** *or* **CHAMFER**↵
> (TRIM mode) Current chamfer Dist1 = *current*, Dist2 = *current*
> Select first line or [Polyline/Distance/Angle/Trim/Method/mUltiple]: **D**↵
> Specify first chamfer distance <*current*>: *(specify a distance, such as* .25*)*
> Specify second chamfer distance <*current*>: *(press* [Enter] *for the current distance or type a new value)*
> Select first line or [Polyline/Distance/Angle/Trim/Method/mUltiple]:

Now you are ready to draw chamfers. Select the first and second lines:

> Select first line or [Polyline/Distance/Angle/Trim/Method/mUltiple]: *(pick the first line)*
> Select second line: *(pick the second line)*

After the lines are picked, AutoCAD automatically chamfers the corner. Objects can be chamfered even when the corners do not meet. AutoCAD extends the lines as required to generate the specified chamfer and complete the corner if Trim mode is on. If Trim mode is off, AutoCAD does not extend the lines to complete the corner. This is discussed later.

If the specified chamfer distance is so large that the chamfered objects disappear, AutoCAD does not perform the chamfer. Instead, a message, such as Distance is too large *Invalid*, is given. If you want to chamfer additional corners, press [Enter] to repeat the **CHAMFER** command. The results of several chamfering operations are shown in Figure 12-2.

NOTE

For the distance method, the first and second chamfer distance values are stored in system variables. The first distance is stored in the **CHAMFERA** system variable, and the second distance is stored in the **CHAMFERB** system variable.

Figure 12-2.
Using the **CHAMFER** command.

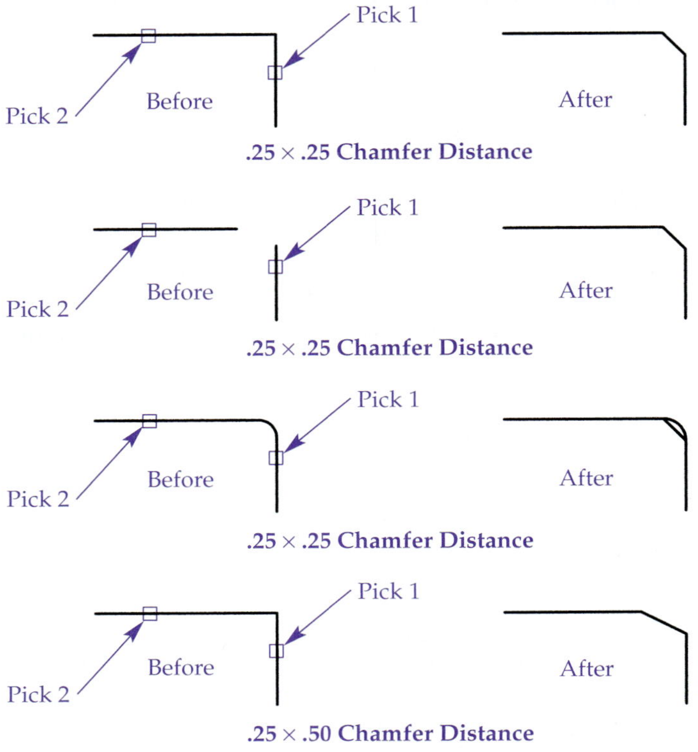

Chamfering the Corners of a Polyline

Polylines are objects that can be made up of many different widths and shapes. Drawing and editing polylines is discussed further in Chapter 14 and Chapter 15. All corners of a closed polyline can be chamfered at one time. Enter the **CHAMFER** command, select the **Polyline** option, and then select the polyline. The corners of the polyline are chamfered to the distance values set. If the polyline was drawn without using the **Close** option, the beginning corner is not chamfered, as shown in Figure 12-3.

Figure 12-3.
Using the **Polyline** option of the **CHAMFER** command.

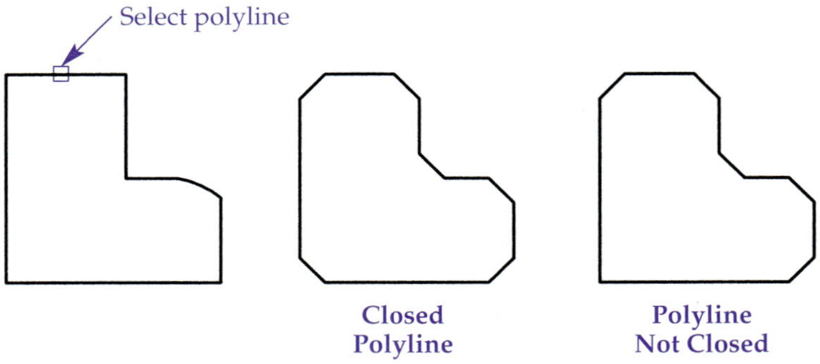

Setting the Chamfer Angle

Instead of setting two chamfer distances, you can set the chamfer distance for one line and set an angle to determine the chamfer to the second line. To do this, use the **Angle** option. See Figure 12-4.

> Command: **CHA** *or* **CHAMFER**↵
> (TRIM mode) Current chamfer Dist1 = <*current*>, Dist2 = <*current*>
> Select first line or [Polyline/Distance/Angle/Trim/Method/mUltiple]: **A**↵
> Specify chamfer length on the first line <*current*>: *(enter a chamfer distance—*.5*, for example)*
> Specify chamfer angle from the first line <*current*>: *(enter an angle—*45*, for example)*
> Select first line or [Polyline/Distance/Angle/Trim/Method/mUltiple]: *(pick the first line)*
> Select second line: *(pick the second line)*
> Command:

NOTE For the angle method, the chamfer distance and angle values are stored in system variables. The chamfer distance is stored in the **CHAMFERC** system variable, and the chamfer angle is stored in the **CHAMFERD** system variable.

EXERCISE 12-1 Complete the Exercise on the Student CD.

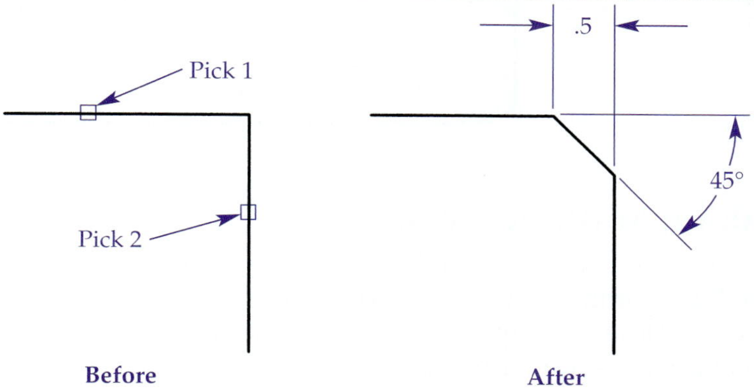

Figure 12-4.
Using the **Angle** option of the **CHAMFER** command with the chamfer length set at .5 and the angle set at 45°.

Setting the Chamfer Method

When you set chamfer distances or a distance and an angle, AutoCAD maintains the setting until you change it. You can set the values for each method without affecting the other. Use the **Method** option if you want to toggle between drawing chamfers by **Distance** and **Angle**. The default option contains the values you previously set:

> Command: **CHA** *or* **CHAMFER**↵
> (TRIM mode) Current chamfer Length = *current*, Angle = *current*
> Select first line or [Polyline/Distance/Angle/Trim/Method/mUltiple]: **M**↵
> Enter trim method [Distance/Angle] <Angle>: **D**↵
> Select first line or [Polyline/Distance/Angle/Trim/Method/mUltiple]: *(pick the first line)*
> Select second line: *(pick the second line)*
> Command:

Setting the Chamfer Trim Mode

You can have the selected lines automatically trimmed with the chamfer, or you can have the selected lines remain in the drawing after the chamfer, as shown in Figure 12-5. To set this, enter the **Trim** option, and then select either T for **Trim** or N for **No trim**:

Command: **CHA** *or* **CHAMFER**↵
(TRIM mode) Current chamfer Dist1 = *current*, Dist2 = *current*
Select first line or [Polyline/Distance/Angle/Trim/Method/mUltiple]: **T**↵
Enter Trim mode option [Trim/No trim] <Trim>: **N**↵
Select first line or [Polyline/Distance/Angle/Trim/Method/mUltiple]: *(pick the first line)*
Select second line: *(pick the second line)*
Command:

You can also use the **TRIMMODE** system variable to set **Trim** or **No trim** by typing TRIMMODE at the Command: prompt. A 1 setting trims the lines before chamfering, while a 0 setting does not trim the lines.

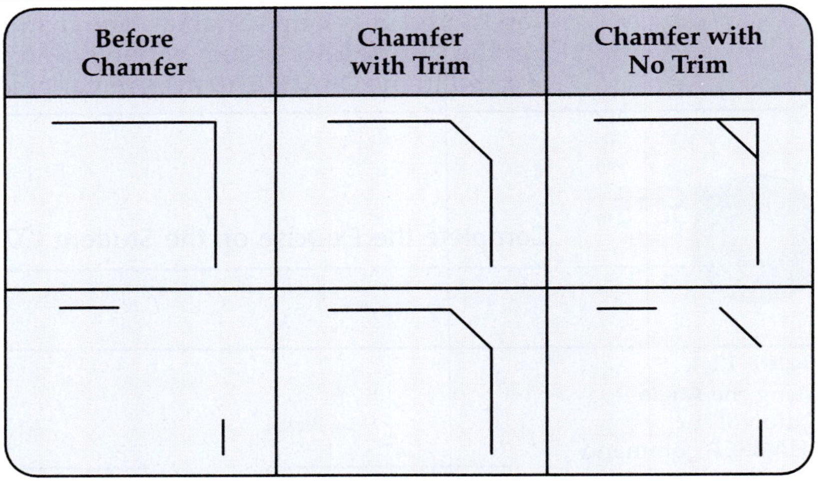

Figure 12-5. Comparison of the **Trim** and **No trim** options with the **CHAMFER** command.

Making Multiple Chamfers

To make several chamfers on the same object, select the **Multiple** option of the **CHAMFER** command by typing U at the Select first line or [Polyline/Distance/Angle/Trim/Method/mUltiple]: prompt. The prompt for a first line repeats. When you have made all the chamfers needed, press [Enter].

NOTE

The **TRIMMODE** system variable affects both the **FILLET** and **CHAMFER** commands. If the **Polyline** option is used with the **No trim** option active, any chamfer lines created are not part of the polyline.

PROFESSIONAL TIP

When the **CHAMFER** or **FILLET** command is set to **Trim**, lines not connecting at a corner are automatically extended, and the chamfer or fillet is applied. When the **No trim** option is used, however, these lines are not extended, but the chamfer or fillet is drawn anyway. If you have lines drawn short of a corner, and you want them to connect to the chamfer or fillet, you need to extend them when you draw with the **No trim** option active.

EXERCISE 12-2 Complete the Exercise on the Student CD.

Drawing Rounded Corners

In mechanical drafting, an inside rounded corner is called a *fillet*. An outside rounded corner is called a *round*. AutoCAD refers to all rounded corners as *fillets*.

Fillets were introduced in Chapter 5, when drawing filleted corners on rectangles with the **RECTANG** command. The **FILLET** command draws a rounded corner between intersecting and nonintersecting lines, circles, and arcs. To access the **FILLET** command, pick the **Fillet** button on the **Modify** toolbar, select **Fillet** from the **Modify** pull-down menu, or type F or FILLET at the Command: prompt.

FILLET
F

Modify
➥ Fillet

Modify toolbar
Fillet

Fillets are sized by radius. A new radius is specified first by typing R on the prompt line for the **Radius** option, as follows. See Figure 12-6.

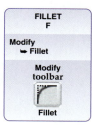

Command: **F** *or* **FILLET**↵
Current settings: Mode = *current*, Radius = *current*
Select first object or [Polyline/Radius/Trim/mUltiple]: **R**↵
Specify fillet radius <*current*>: *(type the fillet radius—*.25, *for example—and press* [Enter]*; you can also press* [Enter] *to accept the current value)*
Select first object or [Polyline/Radius/Trim/mUltiple]: *(pick the first object to be filleted)*
Select second object: *(pick the other object to be filleted)*
Command:

NOTE The value of the radius for fillets is stored in the **FILLETRAD** system variable. This variable is changed when you enter a new value using the **Radius** option of the **FILLET** command. You can also change **FILLETRAD** at the Command: prompt.

EXERCISE 12-3 Complete the Exercise on the Student CD.

Figure 12-6.
Using the **FILLET** command.

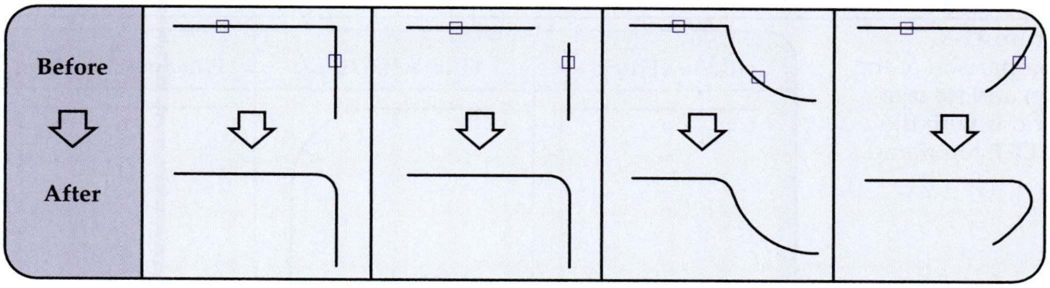

Rounding the Corners of a Polyline

Fillets can be drawn at all corners of a closed polyline by selecting the **Polyline** option. The current fillet radius is used with this option. Polylines are fully explained in Chapter 14 and Chapter 15. The command sequence used to draw the objects in Figure 12-7 is as follows:

Command: **F** *or* **FILLET**↵
Current settings: Mode = *current*, Radius = *current*
Select first object or [Polyline/Radius/Trim/mUltiple]: **P**↵
Select 2D polyline: *(pick the polyline)*
n lines were filleted
Command:

AutoCAD tells you how many lines were filleted. The Command: prompt returns. If the polyline was drawn without using the **Close** option, the beginning corner is not filleted.

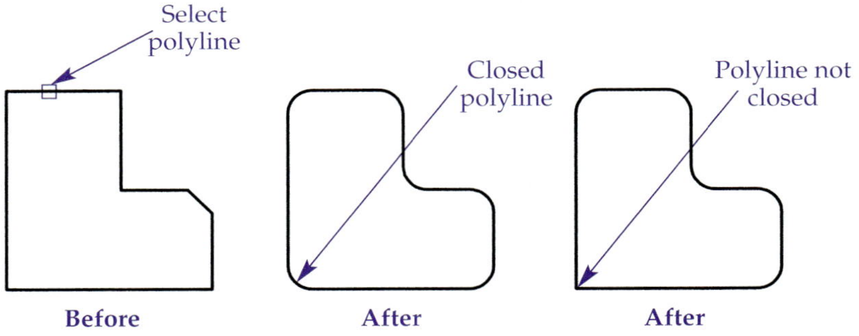

Figure 12-7.
Using the **Polyline** option of the **FILLET** command.

Setting the Fillet Trim Mode

The **TRIMMODE** system variable and the **Trim** option control whether or not the **FILLET** command trims object segments extending beyond the fillet radius point. When the Trim mode is active, objects are trimmed. When the Trim mode is inactive, the filleted objects are not changed after the fillet is inserted, as shown in Figure 12-8. Use the **Trim** option like this:

Command: **F** *or* **FILLET**↵
Current settings: Mode = *current*, Radius = *current*
Select first object or [Polyline/Radius/Trim/mUltiple]: **T**↵
Enter Trim mode option [Trim/No trim] <Trim>: **N**↵
Select first object or [Polyline/Radius/Trim/mUltiple]: *(pick the first object)*
Select second object: *(pick the second object)*
Command:

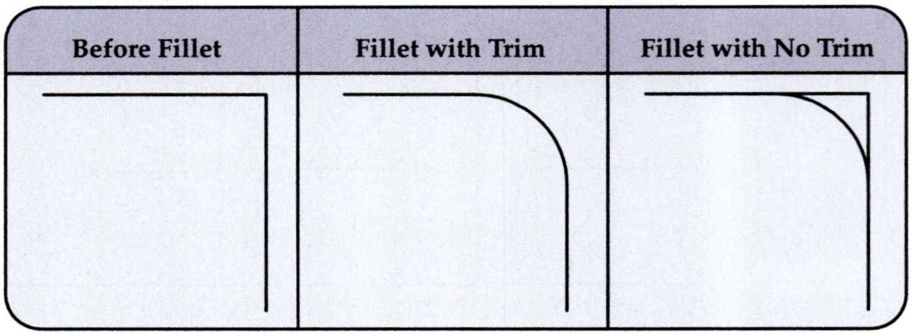

Figure 12-8.
Comparison of the **Trim** and **No trim** options with the **FILLET** command.

If the lines to be filleted do not connect at the corner, they are automatically extended when the Trim mode is on. They are not extended, however, when using the **No trim** option. If you do not want a separation between the line and the filleted corner, extend the lines to the corner before filleting.

Filleting Parallel Lines

You can also draw a fillet between parallel lines. When parallel lines are selected, a radius is placed between the two lines. In Trim mode, a longer line is trimmed to match the length of a shorter line. The radius of a fillet between parallel lines is always half the distance between the two lines, regardless of the radius setting for the **FILLET** command.

Making Multiple Fillets

To make several fillets on the same object, select the **Multiple** option of the **FILLET** command by typing U at the Select first object or [Polyline/Radius/Trim/mUltiple]: prompt. The prompt for a first object repeats. When you have made all the fillets needed, press [Enter].

PROFESSIONAL TIP

Using the **FILLET** or **CHAMFER** command with a 0 fillet radius or 0 chamfer distances is a quick and convenient way to create square corners.

EXERCISE 12-4

Complete the Exercise on the Student CD.

PROFESSIONAL TIP

The **CHAMFER** and **FILLET** commands can be used in any drafting field. For example, angled or rounded corners are frequently used in architectural drafting. If you are working in architectural drafting, be sure to set the chamfer or fillet distances in the proper units.

Removing a Section from an Object

BREAK
BR

Modify
➥ Break

Modify toolbar

Break

The **BREAK** command is used to remove a portion of a line, a circle, an arc, a trace, or a polyline. This command can also be used to divide a single object into two objects. Picking the **Break** button in the **Modify** toolbar, picking **Break** in the **Modify** pull-down menu, or typing BR or BREAK at the Command: prompt accesses the **BREAK** command. When using the **BREAK** command, the following prompts appear:

Command: **BR** *or* **BREAK**↵
Select object: *(pick the object)*
Specify second break point or [First point]: *(pick second break point or type* F *to select first break point)*

The **BREAK** command requires you to select the object to be broken, the first break point, and the second break point. When you select the object, the point you pick is also used as the first break point by default. If you wish to select a different first break point, type F at the Specify second break point or [First point]: prompt to select the **First point** option. After both break points are specified, the part of the object between the two points is deleted. See **Figure 12-9.**

Modify toolbar

Break at Point

The **BREAK** command can also be used to split an object in two without removing a portion. Selecting the same point for both the first and second break points does this. This can be accomplished by entering @ at the Specify second break point or [First point]: prompt. The @ symbol repeats the coordinates of the previously selected point. Using the **BREAK** command without removing a portion of the object is shown in **Figure 12-10.**

When breaking arcs or circles, always work in a counterclockwise direction. Otherwise, you may break the portion of the arc or circle you want to keep. If you want to break off the end of a line or an arc, pick the first point on the object. Pick the second point slightly beyond the end to be cut off. See **Figure 12-11.** When you pick a second point not on the object, AutoCAD selects the point on the object nearest the point you picked.

PROFESSIONAL TIP

You may want to turn running object snaps off if they conflict with the points you are trying to pick when using the **BREAK** command. Picking the **OSNAP** button on the status bar is an easy way to temporarily override the running object snaps.

Figure 12-9.
Using the **BREAK** command to break an object. The first pick can be used to select both the object and the first break point.

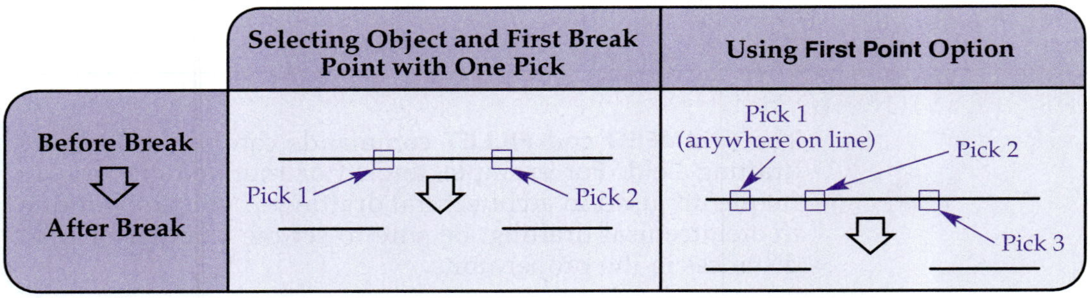

Figure 12-10.
Using the **BREAK** command to break an object at a single point, without removing any of the object. Select the same point as the first and second break points.

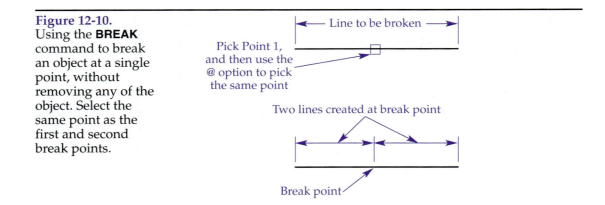

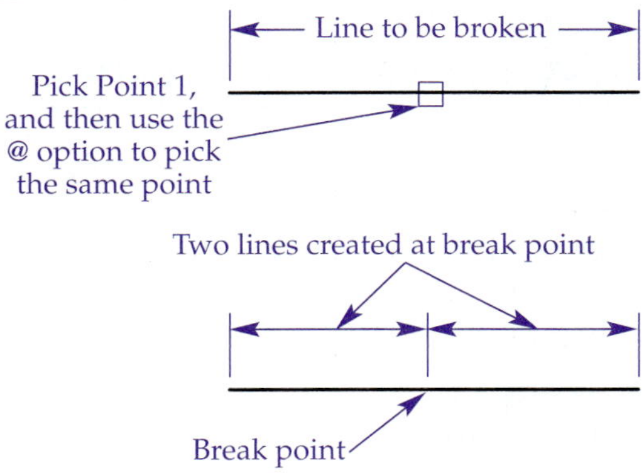

Figure 12-11.
Using the **BREAK** command on circles and arcs.

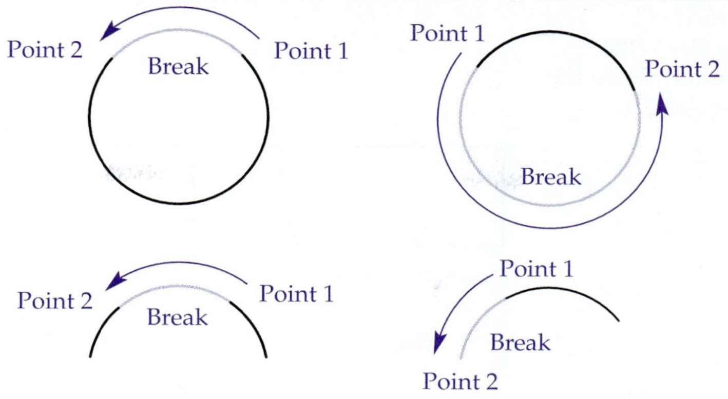

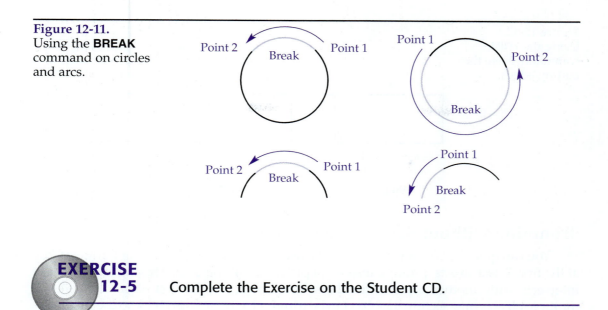

EXERCISE 12-5

Complete the Exercise on the Student CD.

Trimming Sections of Lines, Circles, and Arcs

The **TRIM** command cuts lines, polylines, circles, arcs, ellipses, splines, xlines, and rays extending beyond a desired point of intersection. To access the **TRIM** command, pick the **Trim** button in the **Modify** toolbar, pick **Trim** from the **Modify** pull-down menu, or type TR or TRIM at the Command: prompt. The command requires you to pick a "cutting edge" and the object(s) to trim. The *cutting edge* can be an object defining the point where the object you are trimming will be cut. A cutting edge can be an object such as a line, an arc, or text. If two corners of an object overrun, select two cutting edges and two objects. Refer to **Figure 12-12** as you go through the following sequence:

TRIM
TR

Modify
➥ Trim

Modify toolbar

Trim

Command: **TR** *or* **TRIM**↵
Current settings: Projection=UCS, Edge=*current*
Select cutting edges ...
Select objects: *(pick first cutting edge)*
1 found
Select objects: *(pick second cutting edge)*
1 found, 2 total
Select objects: ↵
Select object to trim or shift-select to extend or [Project/Edge/Undo]: *(pick the first object to trim)*
Select object to trim or shift-select to extend or [Project/Edge/Undo]: *(pick the second object to trim)*
Select object to trim or shift-select to extend or [Project/Edge/Undo]: ↵
Command:

NOTE

You can access the **EXTEND** command while using the **TRIM** command. After selecting the cutting edge, hold the [Shift] key while selecting an object to extend the object to the cutting edge. The **EXTEND** command is discussed later in this chapter.

Figure 12-12.
Using the **TRIM** command. Note the cutting edges.

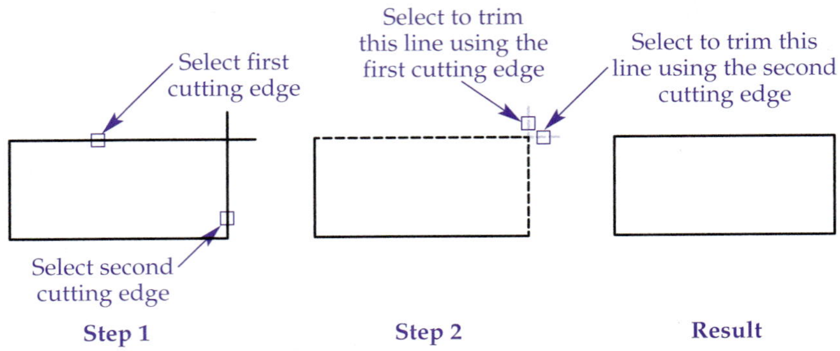

Trimming without Selecting a Cutting Edge

You can quickly trim objects back to the nearest intersection by hitting the [Enter] key at the first Select objects: prompt, instead of picking a cutting edge. Picking an object that intersects with another object trims the selected object to the first object. If there are multiple objects intersecting the object to be trimmed, it is trimmed back to the first intersection. After trimming an object, you can select other objects to be trimmed without having to restart the command. When you are done trimming, press the [Enter] key to exit the command. The command sequence for this **TRIM** method is as follows:

Command: **TR** *or* **TRIM**↵
Current settings: Projection=UCS, Edge=*current*
Select cutting edges ...
Select objects: ↵
Select object to trim or shift-select to extend or [Project/Edge/Undo]: *(pick the object to trim)*
Select object to trim or shift-select to extend or [Project/Edge/Undo]: *(pick the object to trim)*
Select object to trim or shift-select to extend or [Project/Edge/Undo]: ↵
Command:

Trimming to an Implied Intersection

An *implied intersection* is the point where two or more objects would meet if they were extended. Trimming to an implied intersection is possible using the **Edge** option of the **TRIM** command. When you enter the **Edge** option, the choices are **Extend** and **No extend**. When **Extend** is active, AutoCAD checks to see if the cutting edge object will extend to intersect the object to be trimmed. If so, the implied intersection point can be used to trim the object. This does not change the cutting edge object at all. The command sequence for the **TRIM** operation shown in Figure 12-13 is as follows:

Command: **TR** *or* **TRIM**↵
Current settings: Projection=UCS, Edge=*current*
Select cutting edges ...
Select objects: *(pick the cutting edge)*
1 found
Select objects: ↵
Select object to trim or shift-select to extend or [Project/Edge/Undo]: **E**↵
Enter an implied edge extension mode [Extend/No extend] <*current*>: **E**↵
Select object to trim or shift-select to extend or [Project/Edge/Undo]: *(pick the object to trim)*
Select object to trim or shift-select to extend or [Project/Edge/Undo]: ↵
Command:

The **Edge** option can also be set using the **EDGEMODE** system variable. **Extend** is active when the **EDGEMODE** is 1. With this setting, the cutting edge object is checked

Figure 12-13. Trimming to an implied intersection.

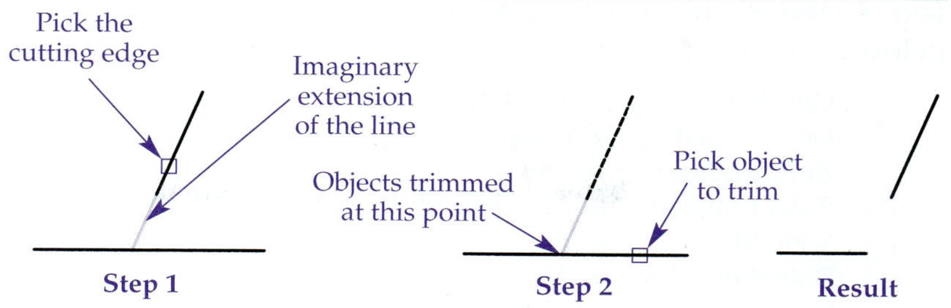

to see if it will extend to intersect the object to be trimmed. The **No extend** option is set when **EDGEMODE** is set to 0. Set the **EDGEMODE** system variable by typing EDGEMODE at the Command: prompt and entering the new value.

Using the Undo Option

The **TRIM** command has an **Undo** option that allows you to cancel the previous trimming without leaving the command. This is useful when the result of a trim is not what you expected. To undo the previous trim, simply type U immediately after performing an unwanted trim. The trimmed portion returns, and you can continue trimming other objects:

Command: **TR** *or* **TRIM**↵
Current settings: Projection=UCS, Edge=Extend
Select cutting edges ...
Select objects: *(pick the first cutting edge)*
1 found
Select objects: ↵
Select object to trim or shift-select to extend or [Project/Edge/Undo]: *(pick the object to trim)*
Select object to trim or shift-select to extend or [Project/Edge/Undo]: **U**↵
Command has been completely undone.
Select object to trim or shift-select to extend or [Project/Edge/Undo]: *(pick the object to trim)*
Select object to trim or shift-select to extend or [Project/Edge/Undo]: ↵
Command:

Introduction to the Project Mode

In a 3D drawing environment, some lines may appear to intersect, but not actually intersect. In such a case, using the **Project** option of the **TRIM** command can allow trimming operations. The **PROJMODE** system variable also controls this option. Using AutoCAD for 3D drawing is explained in ***AutoCAD and its Applications—Advanced***.

Extending Lines

The **EXTEND** command is the opposite of the **TRIM** command. It is used to lengthen lines, elliptical arcs, rays, open polylines, and arcs to meet other objects. **EXTEND** does not work on closed polylines because an unconnected endpoint does not exist.

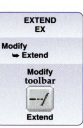

EXTEND
EX
Modify
➥ Extend
Modify toolbar
Extend

To use the **EXTEND** command, pick the **Extend** button in the **Modify** toolbar, select **Extend** from the **Modify** pull-down menu, or type EX or EXTEND at the Command: prompt. The command format is similar to **TRIM**. You are asked to select boundary edges, as opposed to cutting edges. *Boundary edges* are objects, such as lines, arcs, or text, to which the selected objects are extended. The command sequence is shown below and illustrated in **Figure 12-14:**

Command: **EX** *or* **EXTEND**↵
Current settings: Projection=UCS, Edge=*current*
Select boundary edges ...
Select objects: *(pick the boundary edge)*
1 found
Select objects: ↵
Select object to extend or shift-select to trim or [Project/Edge/Undo]: *(pick the object to extend)*
Select object to extend or shift-select to trim or [Project/Edge/Undo]: ↵
Command:

If there is nothing for the selected line to meet, AutoCAD gives the message Object does not intersect an edge.

NOTE

You can access the **TRIM** command while using the **EXTEND** command. After selecting the boundary edge, hold the [Shift] key while selecting an object to trim the object at the boundary edge.

Figure 12-14.
Using the **EXTEND** command. Note the boundary edges.

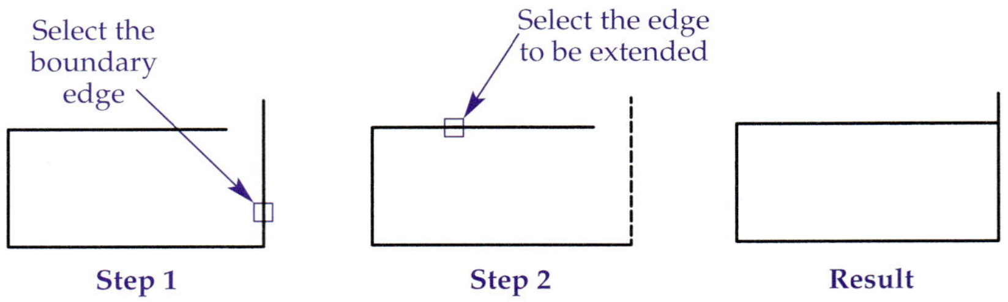

Extending without Selecting a Boundary Edge

You can quickly extend objects to the nearest object by hitting the [Enter] key at the first Select objects: prompt, instead of picking a boundary edge. Using this method, the selected object automatically extends it to the nearest object in its path. If there is no object to which to extend it, a message on the command line reads Object does not intersect an edge. After extending an object, you can select other objects to be extended or press the [Enter] key to exit the command. The command sequence for this **EXTEND** method is as follows:

Command: **EX** *or* **EXTEND**↵
Current settings: Projection=UCS, Edge=*current*
Select boundary edges ...
Select objects: ↵
Select object to extend or shift-select to trim or [Project/Edge/Undo]: *(pick the object to extend)*
Select object to extend or shift-select to trim or [Project/Edge/Undo]: ↵
Command:

Extending to an Implied Intersection

You can extend an object to an implied intersection using the **Edge** option in the **EXTEND** command. When you enter the **Edge** option, the choices are **Extend** and **No extend**, the same as the choices for the **TRIM** command. When **Extend** is active, the boundary edge object is checked to see if it intersects an object when it is extended. If so, the implied intersection point can be used as the boundary for the object to be extended, as shown in **Figure 12-15.** This does not change the boundary edge object at all.

Command: **EX** *or* **EXTEND**↵
Current settings: Projection=UCS, Edge=*current*
Select boundary edges ...
Select objects: *(pick the boundary edge)*
Select objects: ↵
Select object to extend or shift-select to trim or [Project/Edge/Undo]: **E**↵
Enter an implied edge extension mode [Extend/No extend] <*current*>: **E**↵
Select object to extend or shift-select to trim or [Project/Edge/Undo]: *(pick the object to extend)*
Select object to extend or shift-select to trim or [Project/Edge/Undo]: ↵
Command:

The **Edge** option can also be set using the **EDGEMODE** system variable, as previously discussed with the **TRIM** command.

Figure 12-15.
Extending to an implied intersection.

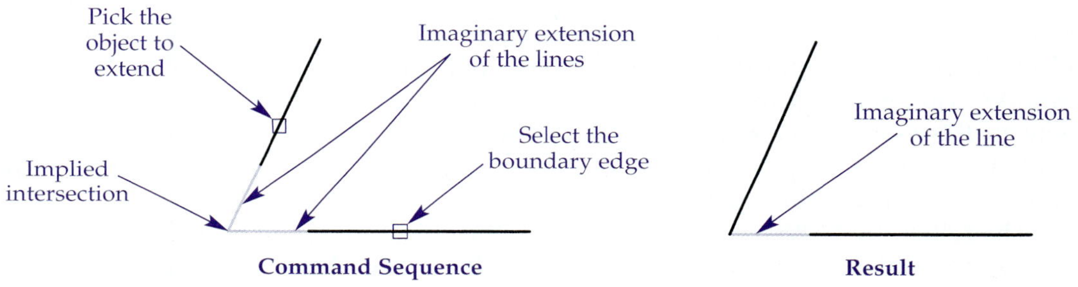

Using the Undo Option

The **Undo** option in the **Extend** command can be used to reverse the previous operation without leaving the **EXTEND** command. The command sequence is the same as discussed for the **TRIM** command.

The Project Mode of the EXTEND Command

In a 3D drawing, some lines may appear to intersect in a given view, but not actually intersect. In such a case, you can use the **Project** option or the **PROJMODE** system variable as explained for the **TRIM** command.

Changing Lines and Circles

CHANGE
-CH

The endpoint location of a line or the radius of a circle can be altered using the **CHANGE** command. To access the **CHANGE** command, type -CH or CHANGE at the Command: prompt. The keyboard shortcut is a hyphen (-) typed before CH. You are then prompted to select the objects to change. After the objects are selected, AutoCAD prompts for the change point. The *change point* is the new endpoint or radius location. The **CHANGE** command also has a **Properties** option. This option can be used to change several properties of the selected object.

PROFESSIONAL TIP

The **CHANGE** command is normally an inefficient command to use. It is easier to relocate line endpoints using grip editing (discussed in Chapter 13). You can modify object properties more easily using the **Properties** window or the **Properties** toolbar.

EXERCISE 12-6 Complete the Exercise on the Student CD.

Moving an Object

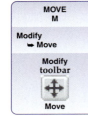

MOVE
M

Modify
➥ Move

Modify toolbar
Move

In many situations, you may find that the location of a view or feature is not where you want it. This problem is easy to fix using the **MOVE** command. Picking the **Move** button in the **Modify** toolbar, picking **Move** from the **Modify** pull-down menu, or typing M or MOVE at the Command: prompt accesses the **MOVE** command.

After the **MOVE** command is accessed, AutoCAD asks you to select the objects to be moved. Use any of the selection set options to select the objects. Once the items are selected, the next prompt requests the base point or displacement. The *base point* provides a reference point. Most drafters select a point on an object, the corner of a view, or the center of a circle. The next prompt asks for the second point of displacement. This is the new position. All selected entities are moved the distance from the base point to the displacement point.

The following **MOVE** operation relates to the object shown in **Figure 12-16.** As the base point is picked, the object is automatically dragged into position. This is the command sequence:

Command: **M** *or* **MOVE**↵
Select objects: *(select the object or objects to be moved)*
n found
Select objects: ↵
Specify base point or displacement: *(enter coordinates or pick a point on screen)*
Specify second point of displacement or <use first point as displacement>: *(establish the new position by typing coordinates or picking a second point on screen)*
Command:

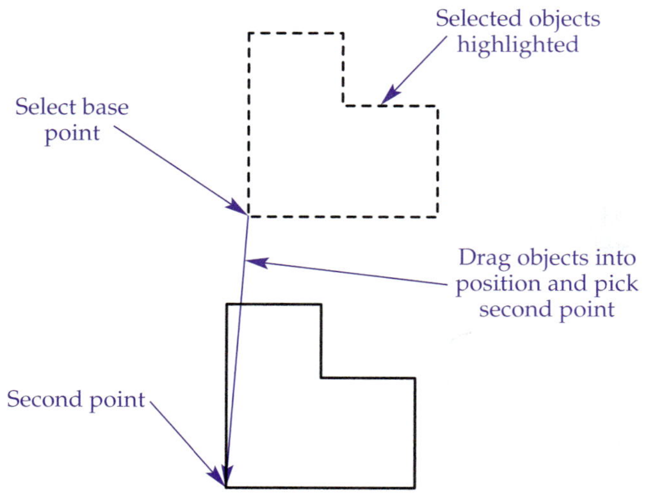

Figure 12-16. Using the **MOVE** command. When you select the object to be moved, it becomes highlighted.

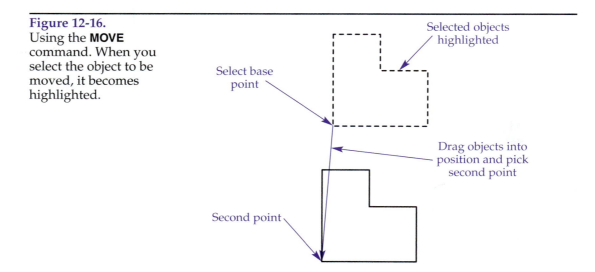

Using the First Point As Displacement

In the previous **MOVE** command, you selected a base point and then selected a second point of displacement. The object moved the distance and direction you specified. You can also move the object relative to the first point. This means the coordinates you use to select the base point are automatically used as the coordinates for the direction and distance for moving the object. Follow this command sequence to do this:

Command: **M** *or* **MOVE**↵
Select objects: *(select the objects to move)*
Select objects: ↵
Specify base point or displacement: **2,4**↵
Specify second point of displacement or <use first point as displacement>: ↵ *(the object moves a distance and direction equal to the coordinates specified for the base point, which is 2 units in the X direction and 4 units in the Y direction, for this example)*
Command:

PROFESSIONAL TIP

Always use object snap modes to your best advantage with editing commands. For example, suppose you want to move an object to the center point of a circle. Use the **Center** object snap mode to select the center of the circle as the base point.

Copying Objects

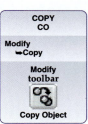

COPY
CO
Modify ➥Copy
Modify toolbar
Copy Object

The **COPY** command is used to make a copy of an existing object or objects. To access the **COPY** command, pick the **Copy** button in the **Modify** toolbar, select **Copy** from the **Modify** pull-down menu, or type CO or COPY at the Command: prompt. The command prompts are the same as the **MOVE** command. When a second point of displacement is picked, however, the original object remains, and a copy is drawn. The following command sequence is illustrated in **Figure 12-17:**

Command: **CO** *or* **COPY**↵
Select objects: *(select the objects to be copied)*
n found
Select objects: ↵
Specify base point or displacement: *(select base point)*
Specify second point of displacement or <use first point as displacement>: *(pick second point)*
Specify second point of displacement: ↵
Command:

The **COPY** command is similar to the **MOVE** command. You can either specify a base point and a second point of displacement or simply specify a displacement. If you specify a displacement, a copy of the object is made at the specified location.

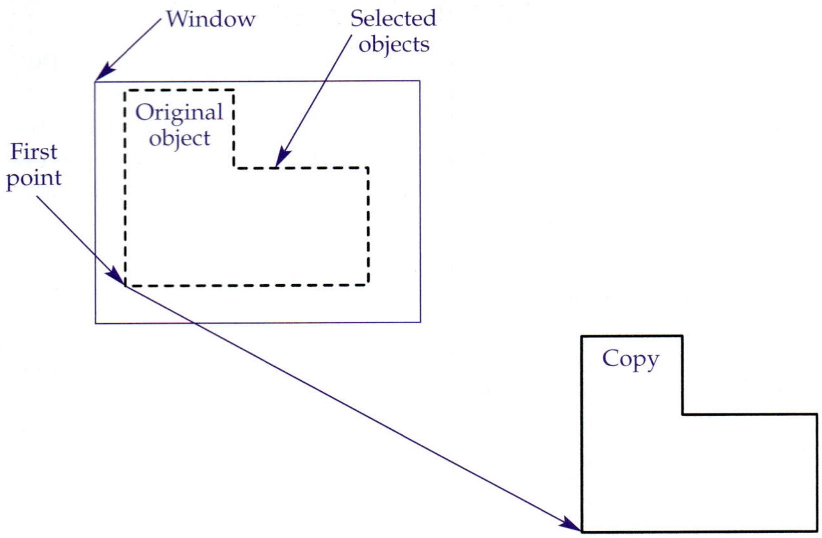

Figure 12-17.
Using the **COPY** command.

Making Multiple Copies

To make several copies of the same object, specify a point of displacement at the Specify second point of displacement or <use first point as displacement>: prompt. The prompt for a second point of displacement repeats until you end the command. When you have made all the copies needed, press [Enter]. The results are shown in **Figure 12-18.**

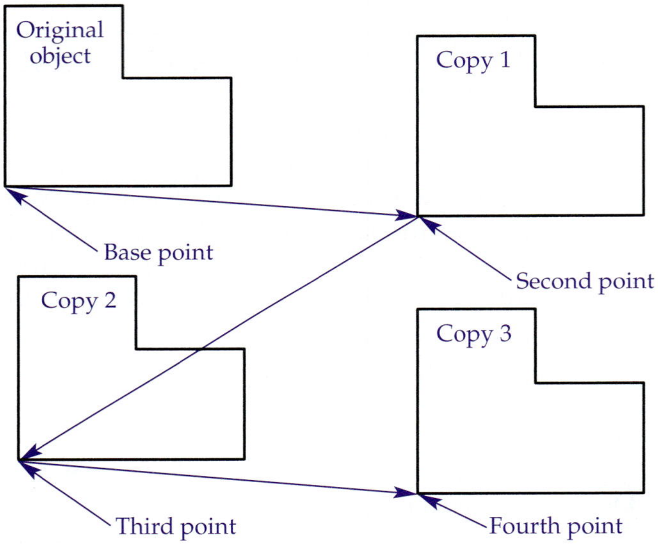

Figure 12-18.
Using the **COPY** command to make multiple copies.

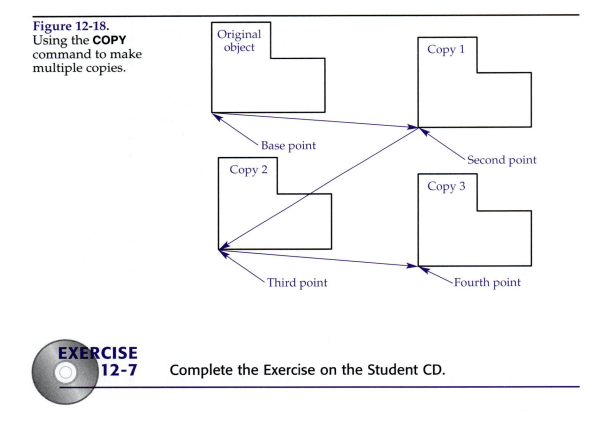

EXERCISE 12-7 Complete the Exercise on the Student CD.

Drawing a Mirror Image of an Object

MIRROR
MI

Modify
➥ Mirror

Modify
toolbar

Mirror

It is often necessary to draw an object in a reflected, or mirrored, position. The **MIRROR** command performs this task. Mirroring an entire drawing is common in architectural drafting when a client wants a plan drawn in reverse. Picking the **Mirror** button in the **Modify** toolbar, selecting **Mirror** in the **Modify** pull-down menu, or typing MI or MIRROR at the Command: prompt accesses the **MIRROR** command.

Selecting the Mirror Line

When you enter the **MIRROR** command, you select the objects to mirror and then select a mirror line. The *mirror line* is the hinge about which objects are reflected. The objects and any space between the objects and the mirror line are reflected. See **Figure 12-19.**

The mirror line can be placed at any angle. Once you pick the first endpoint, a mirrored image appears and moves with the cursor. Once you select the second mirror line endpoint, you have the option to delete the original objects. Refer to **Figure 12-20** and the following command sequence:

Command: **MI** *or* **MIRROR**↵
Select objects: *(select objects to be mirrored)*
n found
Select objects: ↵
Specify first point of mirror line: *(pick the first point on the mirror line)*
Specify second point of mirror line: *(pick the second point on the mirror line)*
Delete source objects? [Yes/No] <N>: *(type* Y *and press* [Enter] *to delete the original objects; you can also press* [Enter] *to accept the default and keep the original objects)*
Command:

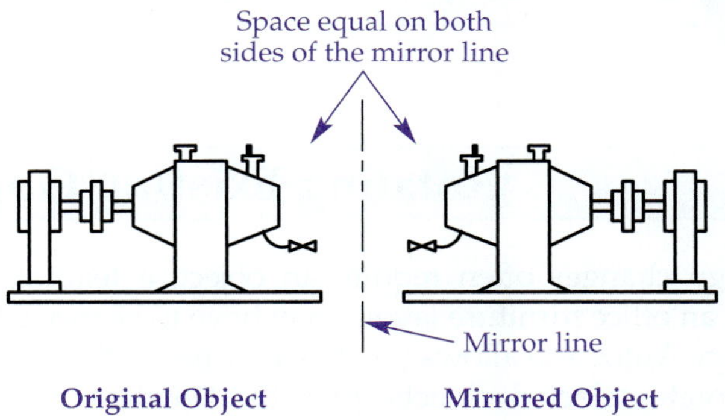

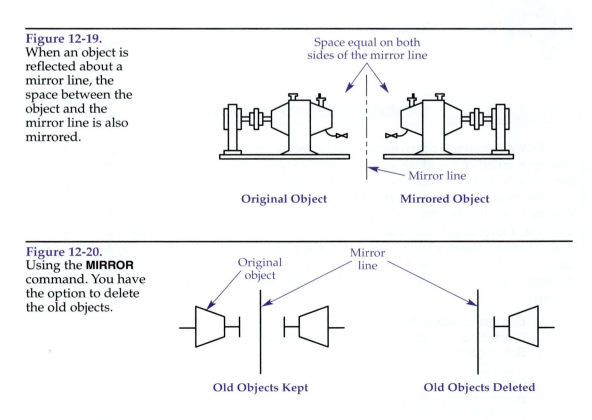

Figure 12-19.
When an object is reflected about a mirror line, the space between the object and the mirror line is also mirrored.

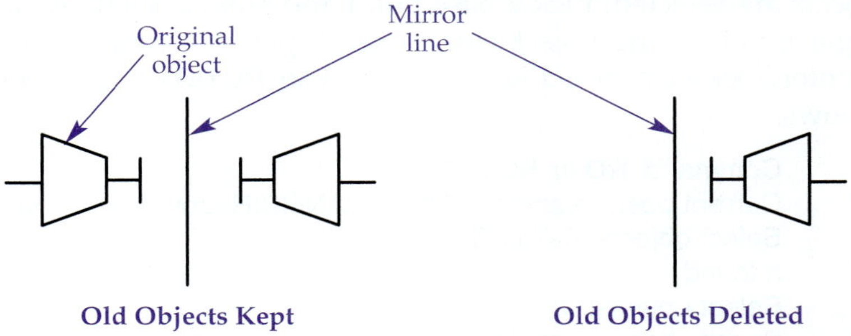

Figure 12-20.
Using the **MIRROR** command. You have the option to delete the old objects.

EXERCISE 12-8 Complete the Exercise on the Student CD.

Mirroring Text

The **MIRROR** command can reverse any text associated with the selected object. Backward text is generally not acceptable, although it is used for reverse imaging. To keep the text readable, the **MIRRTEXT** system variable must be 0. This is the default value. There are two values for **MIRRTEXT**, as shown in Figure 12-21:

- 1. Text is mirrored in relation to the original object. This is the default value.
- 0. Prevents text from being reversed.

To draw a mirror image of an existing object and reverse the text, set the **MIRRTEXT** variable to 1 by typing MIRRTEXT at the Command: prompt and entering 1. Proceed to the **MIRROR** command.

Figure 12-21.
The **MIRRTEXT** system variable options.

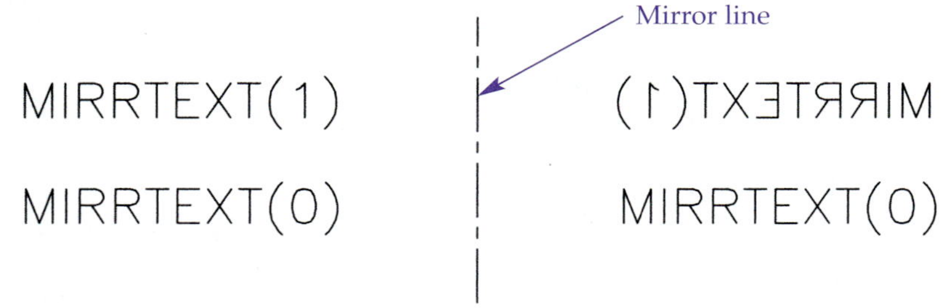

EXERCISE 12-9 Complete the Exercise on the Student CD.

Rotating Existing Objects

ROTATE
RO

Modify
➥ Rotate

Modify toolbar

Rotate

Design changes often require an object, a feature, or a view to be rotated. For example, an office furniture layout may have to be moved, copied, or rotated for an interior design. AutoCAD allows you to easily revise the layout to obtain the final design.

To rotate selected objects, pick the **Rotate** button on the **Modify** toolbar, pick **Rotate** from the **Modify** pull-down menu, or type RO or ROTATE at the Command: prompt. Objects can be selected using any of the selection set options. Once the objects are selected, pick a base point and enter a rotation angle. A negative rotation angle revolves the object clockwise. A positive rotation angle revolves the object counterclockwise. See Figure 12-22. The **ROTATE** command sequence appears as follows:

Command: **RO** *or* **ROTATE**↵
Current positive angle in UCS: ANGDIR=counterclockwise ANGBASE=0
Select objects: *(select the objects)*
n found
Select objects: ↵
Specify base point: *(pick the base point or enter coordinates; press* [Enter]*)*
Specify rotation angle or [Reference]: *(type a positive or negative rotation angle and press* [Enter]*; you can also pick a point on screen)*
Command:

Figure 12-22.
Rotation angles.

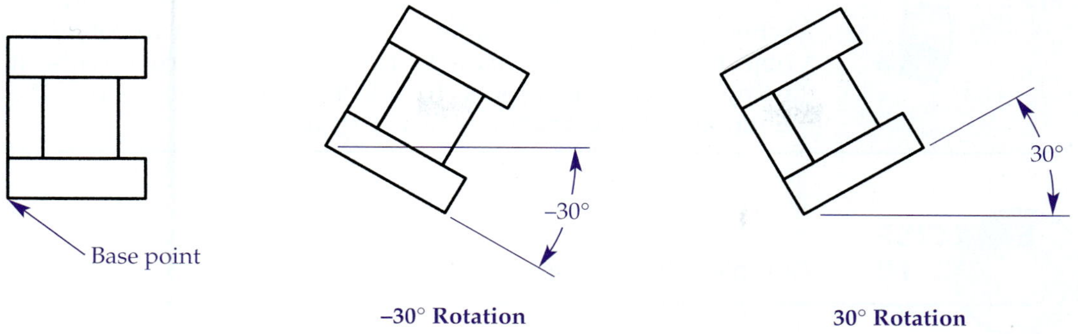

If an object is already rotated, and you want a different angle, you can change the angle in two ways. Both ways involve using the **Reference** option after selecting the object for rotation. The first way is to specify the existing angle and then the new angle. See **Figure 12-23A:**

> Specify rotation angle or [Reference]: **R**↵
> Specify the reference angle <0>: **135**↵
> Specify the new angle: **180**↵
> Command:

The other method is to pick a reference line on the object and rotate the object in relationship to the reference line. See **Figure 12-23B:**

> Specify rotation angle or [Reference]: **R**↵
> Specify the reference angle <0>: *(pick an endpoint of a reference line that forms the existing angle)*
> Specify second point: *(pick the other point of the reference line that forms the existing angle)*
> Specify the new angle: *(specify a new angle, such as* 180*, and press* [Enter]*)*
> Command:

Figure 12-23.
Using the **Reference** option of the **ROTATE** command.
A—Entering reference angles.
B—Selecting points on a reference line.

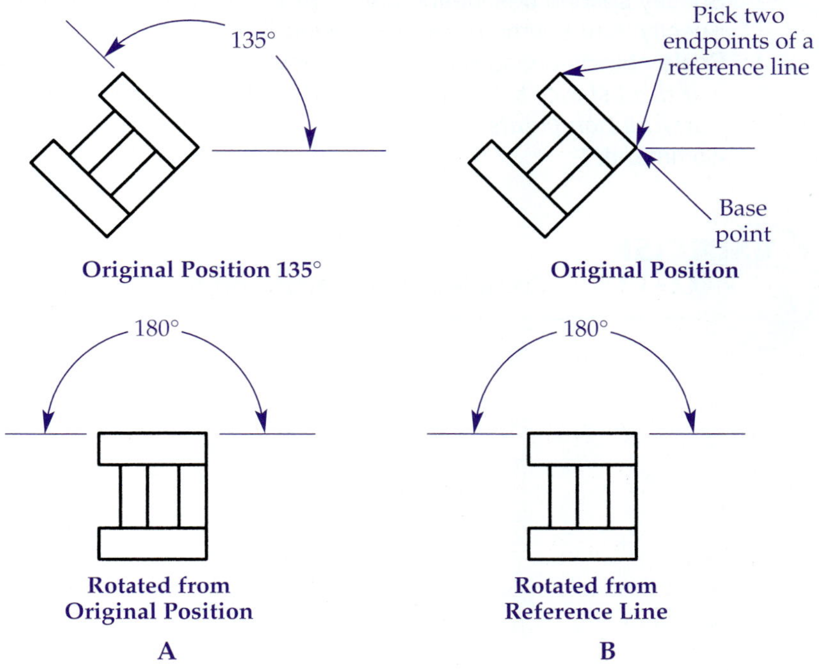

PROFESSIONAL TIP

Always use the object snap mode to your best advantage when editing. For example, suppose you want to rotate an object. It may be difficult to find an exact corner without using object snap mode. To select the base point, use the **Endpoint** or **Intersection** object snap mode.

EXERCISE 12-10 Complete the Exercise on the Student CD.

Moving and Rotating an Object at the Same Time

The **ALIGN** command is primarily used for 3D applications, but it has 2D applications when you want to move and rotate an object. The command sequence asks you to select objects and then asks for three source points and three destination points. For 2D applications, you only need two source points and two destination points. Press [Enter] when the prompt requests the third source and destination points. The *source points* define a line related to the object's original position. The *destination points* define the location of this line relative to the object's new location.

ALIGN
AL
Modify
➥ **3D Operation**
➥ **Align**

To access the **ALIGN** command, pick **Align** in the **3D Operation** cascading menu of the **Modify** pull-down menu or type AL or ALIGN at the Command: prompt. The command sequence is as follows. Refer to Figure 12-24:

Command: **AL** *or* **ALIGN**↵
Select objects: *(select the objects)*
Select objects: ↵
Specify first source point: *(pick the first source point)*
Specify first destination point: *(pick the first destination point)*
Specify second source point: *(pick the second source point)*
Specify second destination point: *(pick the second destination point)*
Specify third source point or <continue>: ↵
Scale objects based on alignment points? [Yes/No] <N>: *(enter* Y *to scale the object if the distance between the source points is different than the distance between the destination points)*
Command:

EXERCISE 12-11 Complete the Exercise on the Student CD.

Figure 12-24.
Using the **ALIGN** command to move and rotate a kitchen cabinet layout against a wall.

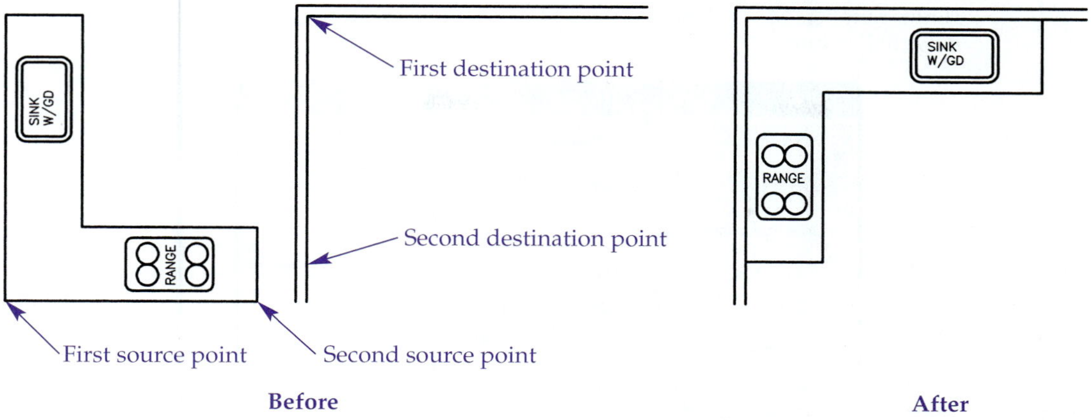

Creating Multiple Objects with ARRAY

Some designs require a rectangular or circular pattern of the same object. For example, office desks are often arranged in rows. Suppose your design calls for five rows, each having four desks. You can create this design by drawing one desk and copying it nineteen times. This operation, however, is time-consuming. A quicker method is to create an array.

There are two types of arrays: rectangular and polar. A *rectangular array* creates rows and columns of the selected items, and you must provide the spacing. A *polar array* constructs a circular arrangement. For a circular array, you must specify the number of items to array, the angle between items, and the center point of the array. Some examples are shown in Figure 12-25.

ARRAY
AR

Modify
➡ Array...

Modify toolbar

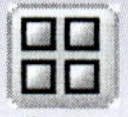

Array

Arrays are specified using the **Array** dialog box. To access this dialog box, pick the **Array** button in the **Modify** toolbar, select **Array...** from the **Modify** pull-down menu, or enter AR or ARRAY at the Command: prompt. All input needed to create the array is specified in the **Array** dialog box. See Figure 12-26. Use the **Rectangular Array** and **Polar Array** radio buttons to specify the type of array. Pick the **Select objects** button to return to the AutoCAD window and pick the objects to be included in the array.

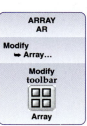

Figure 12-25.
Examples of arrays created with the **ARRAY** command.

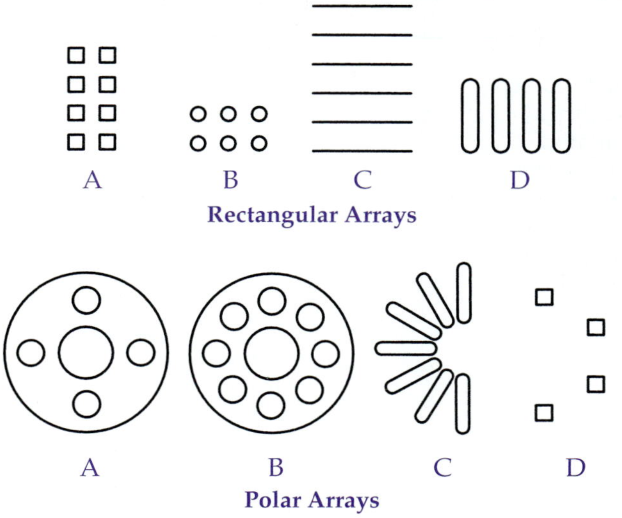

Figure 12-26.
The **Array** dialog box options for a rectangular array.

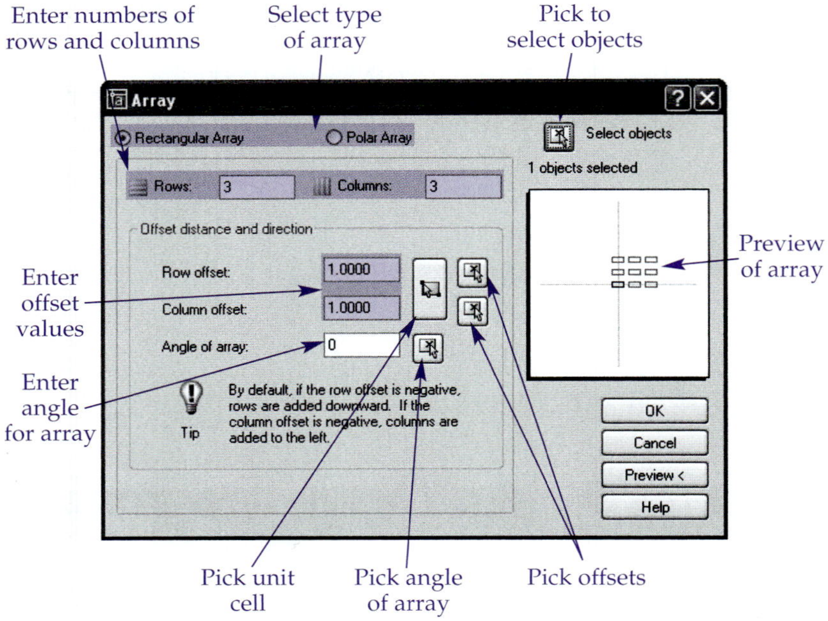

Arranging Objects in a Rectangular Pattern

A rectangular array places objects in line along the X and Y axes. You can specify a single row, a single column, or multiple rows and columns. *Rows* are horizontal, and *columns* are vertical.

To create a rectangular pattern for a .5 unit square having three rows, three columns, and a .5 spacing between objects, enter 3 in the **Rows:** and **Columns:** text boxes and 1.0000 in the **Row offset:** and **Column offset:** text boxes. This is shown in Figure 12-26. You can also use the **Pick Row Offset** and **Pick Column Offset** buttons in the **Array** dialog box to specify the row and column distances.

The original object and resulting array are shown in Figure 12-27. When giving the distance between rows and columns, be sure to include the width and height of the object. Figure 12-27 shows how to calculate the distance between objects in a rectangular array.

Figure 12-27.
The original object (in dashed lines) and the created rectangular array. Note how the distance between rows and columns is determined.

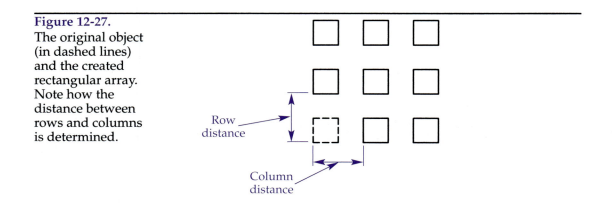

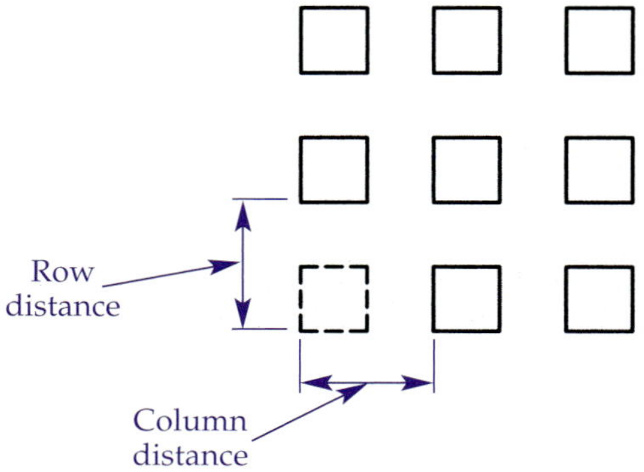

Figure 12-28.
You can specify a unit cell distance for a rectangular array by using your pointing device. The unit cell spacing is the same as the distance between rows and columns.

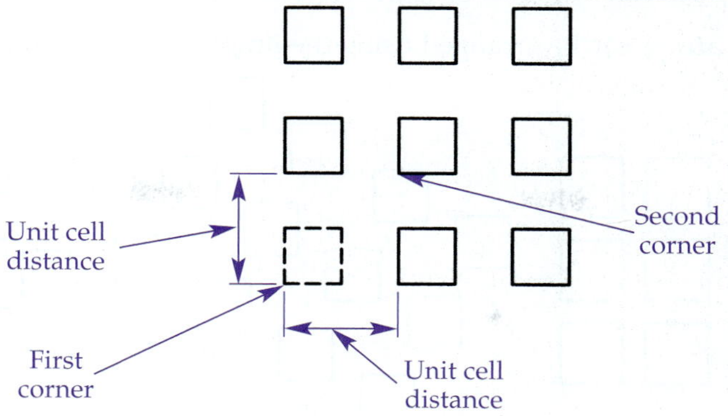

AutoCAD allows you to specify the distance separating objects with your pointing device. This distance is called the *unit cell*. The unit cell distance is the same as the distance between rows and columns. It is entered with the pointing device, however, just like selecting a window. See Figure 12-28. The second point's distance and direction from the first point determines the X and Y spacing for the array. To specify a unit cell, pick the **Pick Both Offsets** button in the **Array** dialog box.

Figure 12-29 shows how you can place arrays in four directions by entering either positive or negative row and column distance values. The dashed box is the original object. The row and column distance is 1 unit, and the box is .5 units square. Specifying the unit cell distance can create a quick row and column arrangement in any direction. For example, in Figure 12-30, the second unit cell corner is picked below and to the left of the first corner.

You can also create an angled rectangular array. Enter the angle in the **Angle of array:** text box or pick the **Pick Angle of Array** button to specify the angle with the crosshairs. The column and row alignments are rotated, not the objects. See Figure 12-31.

Figure 12-29.
By entering positive or negative row and column distance values, you can place an array in one of four directions. The original object is shown dashed.

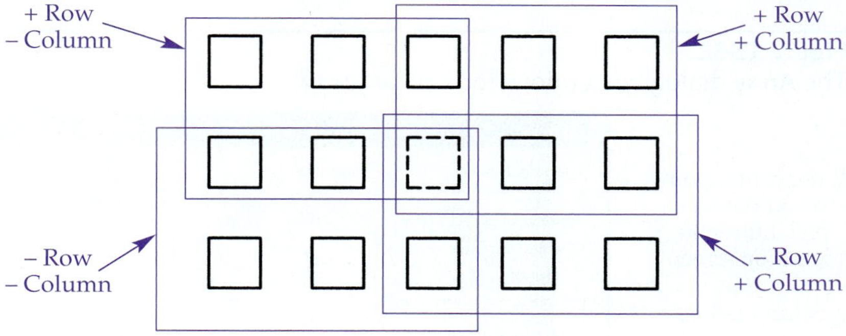

Figure 12-30.
Creating a rectangular array by specifying a negative unit cell distance.

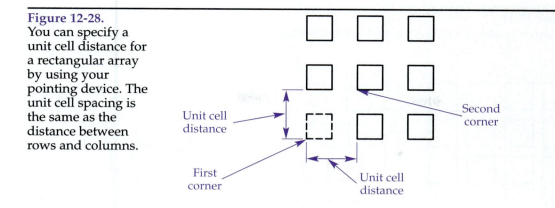

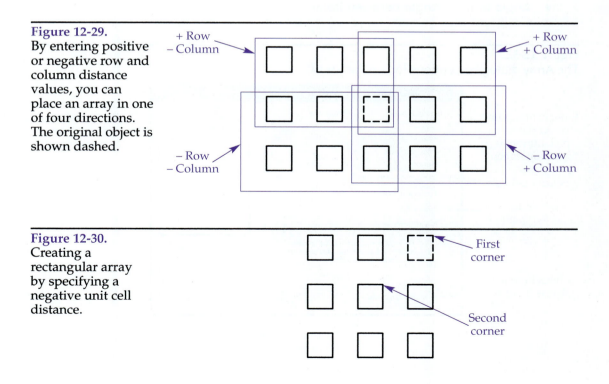

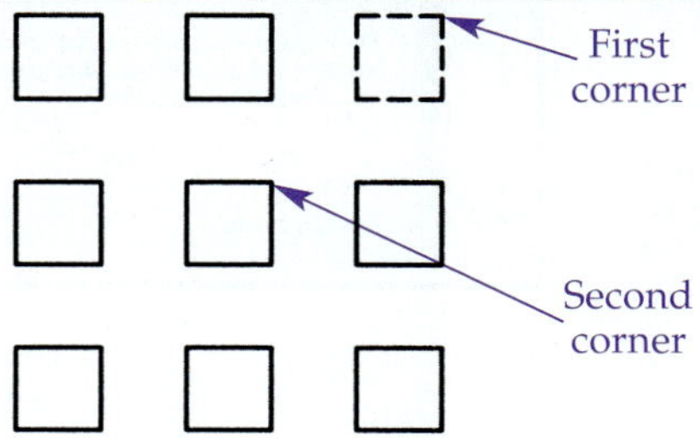

Figure 12-31.
Rectangular arrays can be arranged using the **Angle of array:** setting.

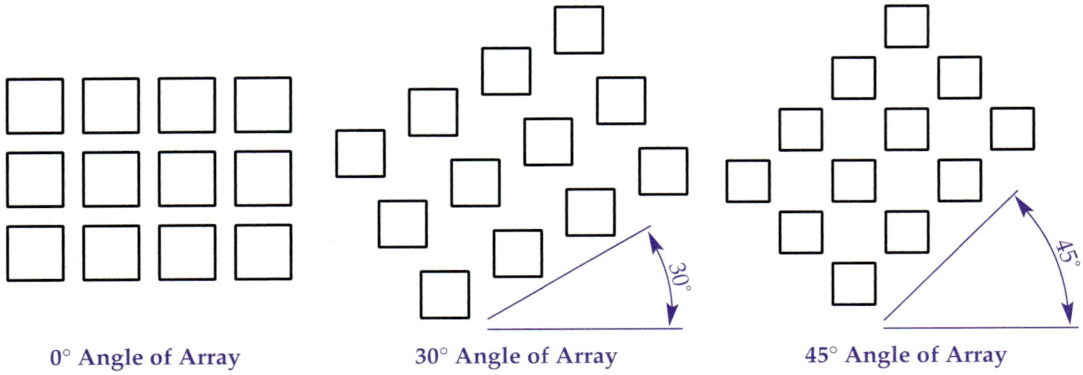

Arranging Objects around a Center Point

A polar array creates a circular pattern with the selected object. To create a polar array, pick the **Polar Array** radio button in the **Array** dialog box. See Figure 12-32. Pick the **Select objects** button to return to the drawing area and select the object to be arrayed. Once you have selected the object, the **Array** dialog box returns.

The next step in creating a polar array is to specify the center point. This is the point about which the objects in the array will be rotated. Enter the coordinates for the center point in the **X:** and **Y:** text boxes or pick the **Pick Center Point** button to select the center point in the drawing area.

After selecting the center point, you must specify the type of polar array to be created, using the **Method:** drop-down list. The selected method determines which settings in the dialog box are available. Three methods are available:

- **Total number of items & Angle to fill.**
- **Total number of items & Angle between items.**
- **Angle to fill & Angle between items.**

Figure 12-32.
The **Array** dialog box options for a polar array.

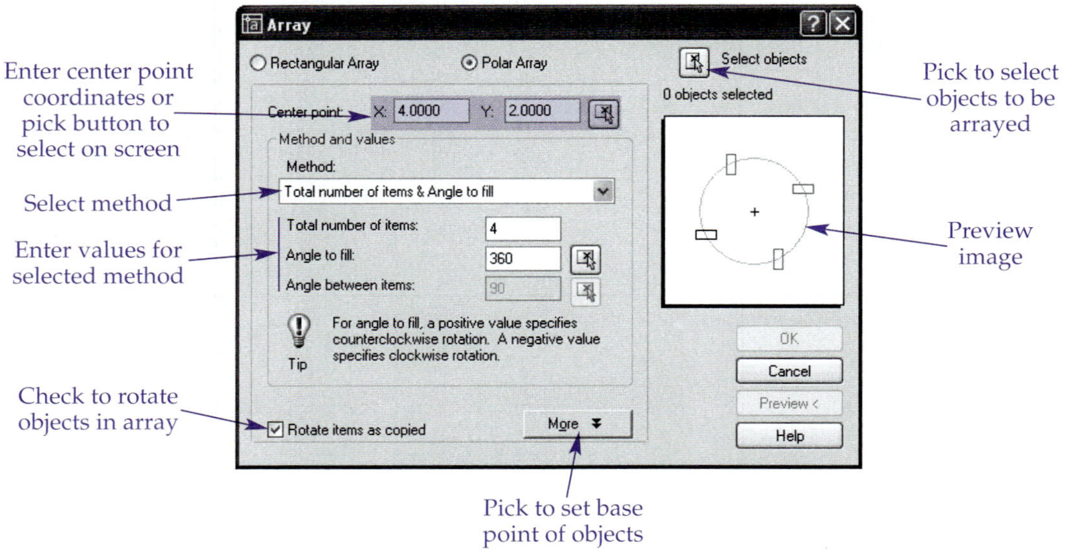

The **Total number of items:** setting is the total number of objects to be in the array, including the originally selected object. If you do not know how many items will be in the array, use the **Angle to fill & Angle between items** method. **The Angle to fill:** setting can be positive or negative. To array the object in a counterclockwise direction, enter a positive angle. To array the object in a clockwise direction, enter a negative angle. Enter 360 to create a complete circular array. The **Angle between items:** setting specifies the angular distance between adjacent objects in the array. For example, if you were creating a circular pattern of five items spaced 18° apart, you would enter 5 in the **Total number of items:** text box and 18 in the **Angle between items:** text box.

You can have the objects rotated as they are copied around the center point by checking the **Rotate items as copied** check box. This keeps the same face of the object always pointing toward the center point. If objects are not rotated as they are copied, they remain in the same orientation as the original object. See Figure 12-33.

When AutoCAD creates a polar array, the base point of the object is rotated and remains at a constant distance from the center point. The default base point varies for different types of objects, as shown in the following table:

Object Type	Default Base Point
Arc, circle, ellipse	Center
Rectangle, polygon	First corner
Line, polyline, donut	Starting point
Block, text	Insertion point

If the default base point does not produce the desired array, you can select a different base point for the selected object. Pick the **More** button in the **Array** dialog box to display the **Object base point** area. Deactivate the **Set to object's default** check box. Enter a new base point in the text boxes or pick the button to select a base point on screen.

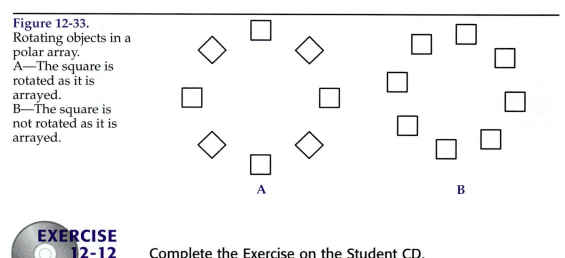

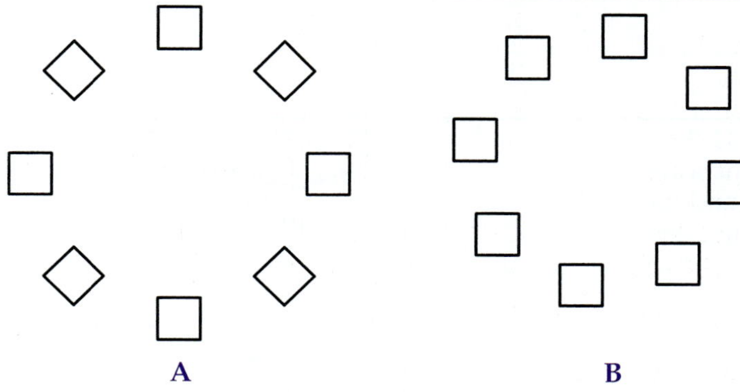

Figure 12-33.
Rotating objects in a polar array.
A—The square is rotated as it is arrayed.
B—The square is not rotated as it is arrayed.

EXERCISE 12-12 Complete the Exercise on the Student CD.

Changing the Size of an Object

A convenient editing command that saves hours of drafting time is the **SCALE** command. This command lets you change the size of an object or of the complete drawing. The **SCALE** command enlarges or reduces the entire object proportionately. If associative dimensioning is used, the dimensions also change to reflect the new size. This is discussed in Chapter 19.

SCALE
SC

Modify
➥ Scale

Modify toolbar

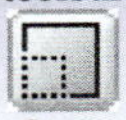

Scale

To scale objects, pick the **Scale** button in the **Modify** toolbar, pick **Scale** from the **Modify** pull-down menu, or type SC or SCALE at the Command: prompt. The command sequence is as follows:

Command: **SC** *or* **SCALE**↵
Select objects: *(select objects to be scaled)*
n found
Select objects: ↵
Specify base point: *(select the base point)*
Specify scale factor or [Reference]:

Specifying the scale factor is the default option. Enter a number to indicate the amount of enlargement or reduction. For example, if you want to double the scale, type 2 at the Specify scale factor or [Reference]: prompt, as shown in **Figure 12-34.** The chart in **Figure 12-35** shows sample scale factors.

Figure 12-34.
Using the **SCALE** command. The base point does not move, but every other point in the object does.

Figure 12-35.
Different scale factors and the resulting sizes.

Scale Factor	Resulting Size
10	10 × bigger
5	5 × bigger
2	2 × bigger
1	Equal to existing size
.75	3/4 of original size
.50	1/2 of original size
.25	1/4 of original size

Using the Reference Option

An object can also be scaled by specifying a new size in relation to an existing dimension. For example, suppose you have a shaft that is 2.50″ long, and you want to make it 3.00″ long. To do so, use the **Reference** option as follows, as shown in **Figure 12-36:**

Specify scale factor or [Reference]: **R**↵
Specify reference length <1>: **2.5**↵
Specify new length: **3**↵
Command:

> **NOTE** The **SCALE** command changes all dimensions of an object proportionately. If you want to change only the width or length of an object, use the **STRETCH** or **LENGTHEN** command.

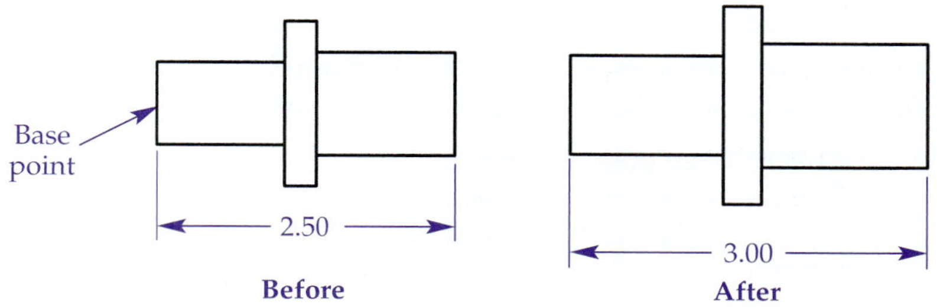

Figure 12-36. Using the **Reference** option of the **SCALE** command.

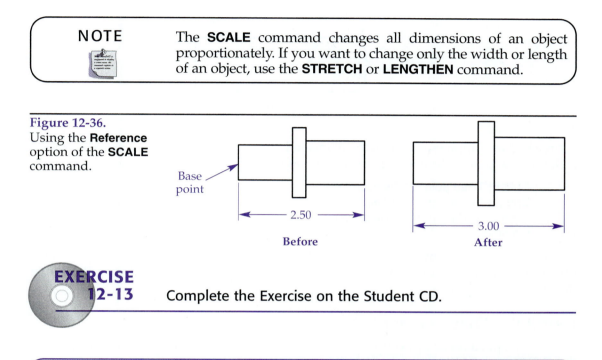

EXERCISE 12-13 Complete the Exercise on the Student CD.

Stretching an Object

The **SCALE** command changes the length and width of an object proportionately. The **STRETCH** command changes only one dimension of an object. In manual drafting, it is common to increase the length of a part, while leaving the diameter or width the same. In architectural design, room sizes may be stretched to increase the square footage.

When using the **STRETCH** command, you can select objects with a crossing window or crossing polygon. To use a crossing window, type C at the Select objects: prompt or drag your selection window from right to left. To access the **STRETCH** command, pick the **Stretch** button in the **Modify** toolbar, pick **Stretch** from the **Modify** pull-down menu, or type S or STRETCH at the Command: prompt. The command sequence is as follows:

> **STRETCH**
> **S**
> **Modify ➡ Stretch**
> **Modify toolbar**
> **Stretch**

Command: **S** *or* **STRETCH**↵
Select objects to stretch by crossing-window or crossing-polygon...
Select objects: *(select the first corner of a crossing window)*
Specify opposite corner: *(pick the second corner)*
Select objects: *(pick additional objects or press* [Enter]*)*

Select only the portion of the object to be stretched, as shown in **Figure 12-37.** If you select the entire object, the **STRETCH** command works like the **MOVE** command. Next, you are asked to pick the base point. This is the point from which the object will be stretched. Pick a new position for the base point. As you move the screen cursor, the object

Figure 12-37.
Using the **STRETCH** command.

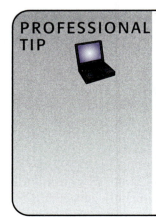

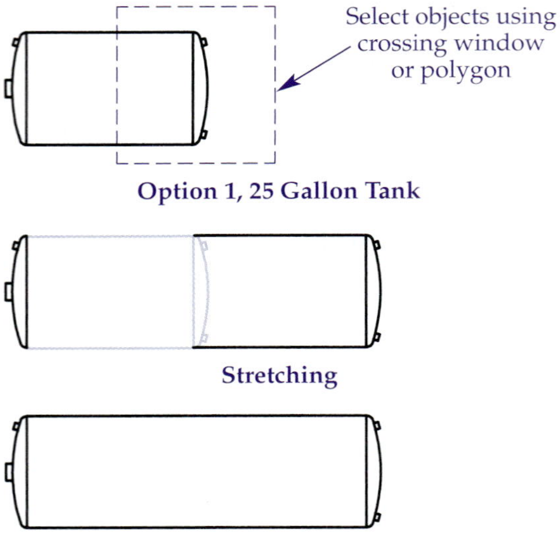

is stretched or compressed. When the displayed object is stretched to the desired position, pick the new point. The command sequence after selecting objects is as follows:

Specify base point or displacement: *(pick the base point for the stretch to begin)*
Specify second point of displacement or <use first point as displacement>: *(pick the final location of the base point)*
Command:

The example in Figure 12-37 shows the object being stretched. This is a common use of the **STRETCH** command. You can also use the **STRETCH** command to reduce the size of an object.

Using the Displacement Option

The displacement option works the same with the **STRETCH** command as with the **MOVE** and **COPY** commands. After selecting the objects to be stretched, enter a displacement, as shown in the following:

Specify base point or displacement: *(enter an X and Y displacement, such as* 2,3*)*
Specify second point of displacement or <use first point as displacement>: ↵
Command:

When you press [Enter] at the Specify second point of displacement: prompt, the object is automatically stretched as you specified with the X and Y coordinates. In this case, the object is stretched two units in the X direction and three units in the Y direction.

PROFESSIONAL TIP

It may not be common to have objects lined up in a convenient manner for using the crossing box selection method with the **STRETCH** command. You should consider using the crossing polygon selection method to make selecting the objects easier. Also, make sure the **DRAGMODE** variable is turned on so you can watch the object stretch to its new size. If the stretched object is not what you expected, cancel the command with the [Esc] key. The **STRETCH** command and other editing commands discussed in this chapter work well with the Ortho mode on. This restricts the object movement to only horizontal and vertical directions.

EXERCISE 12-14 Complete the Exercise on the Student CD.

Changing the Length of an Object

The **LENGTHEN** command can be used to change the length of objects and the included angle of an arc. Only one object can be lengthened at a time. The **LENGTHEN** command does not affect closed objects. For example, you can lengthen a line, a polyline, an arc, an elliptical arc, or a spline, but you cannot lengthen a closed polygon or circle.

To access the **LENGTHEN** command, pick **Lengthen** from the **Modify** pull-down menu or type LEN or LENGTHEN at the Command: prompt. When you select an object, AutoCAD gives you the current length, if the object is linear, or the included angle, if the object is an arc:

> **LENGTHEN**
> **LEN**
>
> **Modify**
> ➥ **Lengthen**

Command: **LEN** *or* **LENGTHEN**↵
Select an object or [DElta/Percent/Total/DYnamic]: *(pick an object)*
Current length: *current*
Select an object or [DElta/Percent/Total/DYnamic]:

Each option is described below:

- **Delta.** The **Delta** option allows you to specify a positive or negative change in length, measured from the endpoint of the selected object. The lengthening or shortening happens closest to the selection point and changes the length by the amount entered. See **Figure 12-38.**

  Command: **LEN** *or* **LENGTHEN**↵
  Select an object or [DElta/Percent/Total/DYnamic]: **DE**↵
  Enter delta length or [Angle] <*current*>: *(enter the desired length—*.75*, for example)*
  Select an object to change or [Undo]: *(pick the object)*
  Select an object to change or [Undo]: *(select another object to lengthen or press* [Enter] *to exit the command)*
  Command:

  The **Delta** option has an **Angle** suboption that lets you change the included angle of an arc by a specified angle. The command sequence is as follows, as shown in **Figure 12-39:**

Figure 12-38.
Using the **Delta** option of the **LENGTHEN** command.

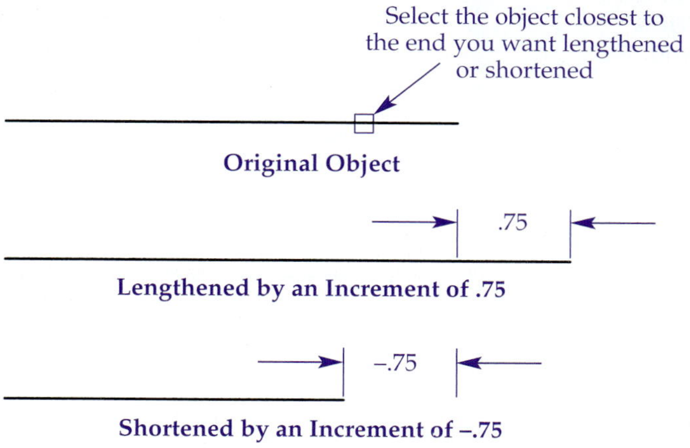

Figure 12-39.
Using the **Angle** suboption of the **LENGTHEN** command's **Delta** option.

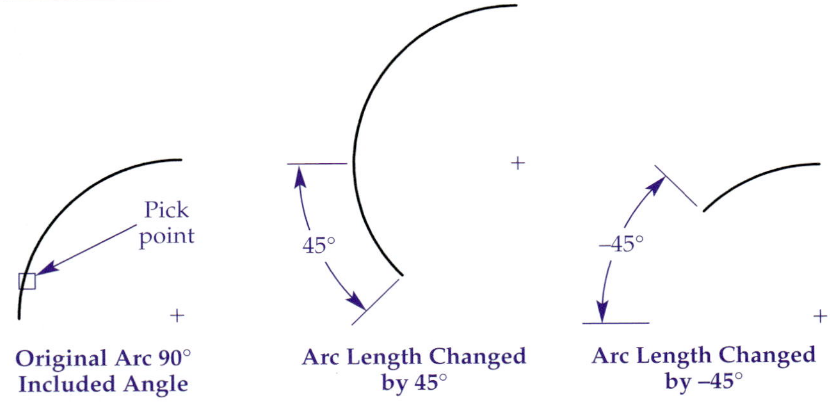

Command: **LEN** *or* **LENGTHEN**↵
Select an object or [DElta/Percent/Total/DYnamic]: **DE**↵
Enter delta length or [Angle] <*current*>: **A**↵
Enter delta angle <*current*>: *(enter an angle, such as* 45*)*
Select an object to change or [Undo]: *(pick the arc)*
Select an object to change or [Undo]: ↵
Command:

- **Percent.** The **Percent** option allows you to change the length of an object or the angle of an arc by a specified percentage. If you consider the original length to be 100 percent, you can make the object shorter by specifying less than 100 percent or longer by specifying more than 100 percent. Look at Figure 12-40 and follow this command sequence:

Command: **LEN** *or* **LENGTHEN**↵
Select an object or [DElta/Percent/Total/DYnamic]: **P**↵
Enter percentage length <*current*>: **125**↵
Select an object to change or [Undo]: *(pick the object)*
Select an object to change or [Undo]: ↵
Command:

- **Total.** The **Total** option allows you to set the total length or angle to the value you specify. You do not have to select the object before entering one of the options, but doing so lets you know the current length and, if it is an arc, the angle of the object. See Figure 12-41.

Figure 12-40.
Using the **Percent** option of the **LENGTHEN** command.

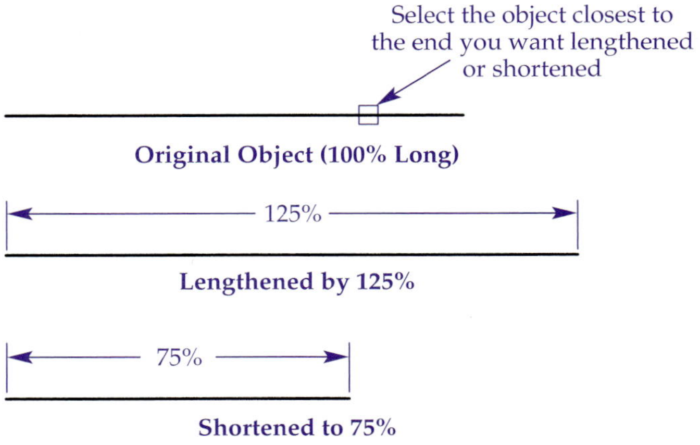

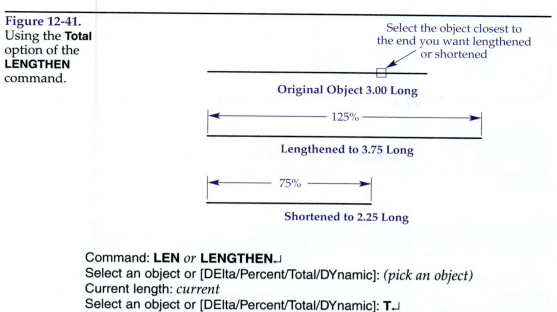

Figure 12-41.
Using the **Total** option of the **LENGTHEN** command.

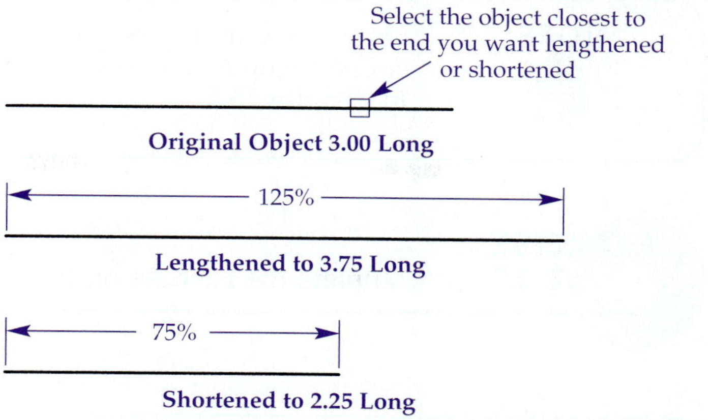

Command: **LEN** *or* **LENGTHEN**↵
Select an object or [DElta/Percent/Total/DYnamic]: *(pick an object)*
Current length: *current*
Select an object or [DElta/Percent/Total/DYnamic]: **T**↵
Specify total length or [Angle] <*current*>: *(enter a new length, such as* 3.75*, or* A*, if it is an angle)*
Select an object to change or [Undo]: *(pick the object)*
Select an object to change or [Undo]: ↵
Command:

- **Dynamic.** This option lets you drag the endpoint of the object to the desired length or angle with the screen cursor. See Figure 12-42. It is helpful to have the grid and snap set to usable increments when using this option. This is the command sequence:

Command: **LEN** *or* **LENGTHEN**↵
Select an object or [DElta/Percent/Total/DYnamic]: **DY**↵
Select an object to change or [Undo]: *(pick the object)*
Specify new end point: *(move the cursor to the desired length and pick)*
Select an object to change or [Undo]: ↵
Command:

Figure 12-42.
Using the **Dynamic** option of the **LENGTHEN** command.

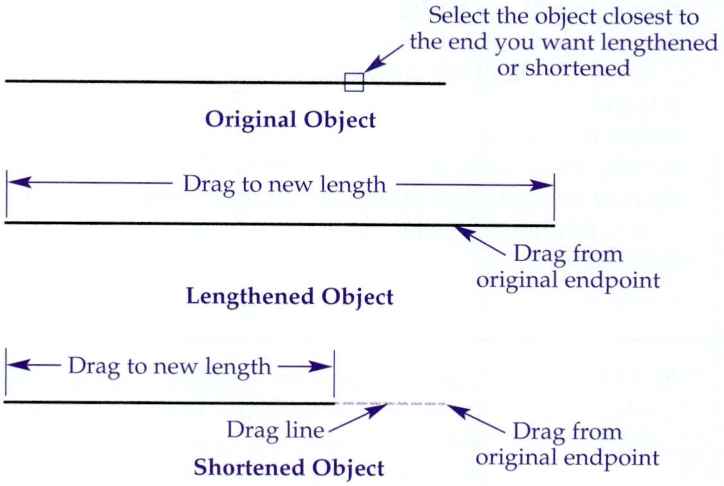

NOTE

Only lines and arcs can be lengthened dynamically. A spline's length can only be decreased. Splines are discussed in Chapter 15.

EXERCISE 12-15 Complete the Exercise on the Student CD.

Selecting Objects for Future Editing

Throughout this chapter, you have worked with the basic editing commands by entering the command and then selecting the object to be edited. You can also set up AutoCAD to let you select the object first and then enter the desired editing command. The settings controlling object selection are found in the **Selection** tab of the **Options** dialog box. These settings are discussed in Chapter 13.

The **SELECT** command is used to preselect an object or group of objects for future editing. It is designed to increase your productivity. Often, you are working with the same set of objects—moving, copying, or scaling them. Set these aside as a selection set with the **SELECT** command. Continue to perform another drawing task. To return to those objects set aside, enter P for **Previous** at the Select objects: prompt. Only the last selection set you make can be modified. The command sequences for creating a selection set and then moving it are as follows:

Command: **SELECT**↵
Select objects: *(use any method to select an individual object or group of objects)*
n found
Select objects: *(select additional objects or press* [Enter]*)*
Command:

This creates a selection set. Later, when you want to move these objects, use the **Previous** option as follows:

Command: **M** *or* **MOVE**↵
Select objects: **P**↵ *(this selects the object or group of objects previously selected using the* **SELECT** *command)*
n found
Select objects: ↵
Specify base point or displacement: *(pick the base point)*
Specify second point of displacement or <use first point as displacement>: *(pick the new location of the base point)*
Command:

NOTE

The selection set created with the **SELECT** command cannot be accessed with the **Previous** option after another selection set is defined. For example, you use the **SELECT** command and select three circles as a selection set. You then use the **MOVE** command to move a line. The line you moved would now be selected by the **Previous** option, rather than the circles defined with the **SELECT** command.

EXERCISE 12-16 Complete the Exercise on the Student CD.

Creating Object Groups

A *group* is a named selection set. These selection sets are saved with the drawing and, therefore, exist between multiple drawing sessions. Objects can be members of more than one group, and groups can be nested. *Nesting* means placing one group inside another group.

An object existing in multiple groups creates an interesting situation. For example, if a line and an arc are grouped, and then the arc is grouped with a circle, moving the first group moves the line and arc, and moving the second group moves the arc and circle. Nesting can be used to place smaller groups into larger groups for easier editing.

By default, selecting one object within a group causes the entire group to be selected. This setting can be changed in the **Selection** tab of the **Options** dialog box, with the **Object grouping** check box in the **Selection Modes** area. Typing G or GROUP at the Command: prompt accesses the **GROUP** command. Either of these entry methods displays the **Object Grouping** dialog box, shown in Figure 12-43.

GROUP
G

There are many elements found in the **Object Grouping** dialog box. The text box displays the **Group Name** and lists whether or not the group is selectable. If a group is selectable, picking any object in it selects the entire group. Making a group nonselectable allows individual objects within the group to be edited.

The **Group Identification** area has several components:

- **Find Name.** This button displays a dialog list of all groups with which an object is associated. When you pick this button, a Pick a member of a group prompt appears. Once you pick an object, the **Group Member List** dialog box lists any groups with which the object is associated.
- **Highlight.** This button allows a group name to be specified and then highlights all its members in the drawing editor. This allows you to see the parts of the drawing identified as the members of that group. Pick the **Continue** button or press [Enter] to return to the **Object Grouping** dialog box.

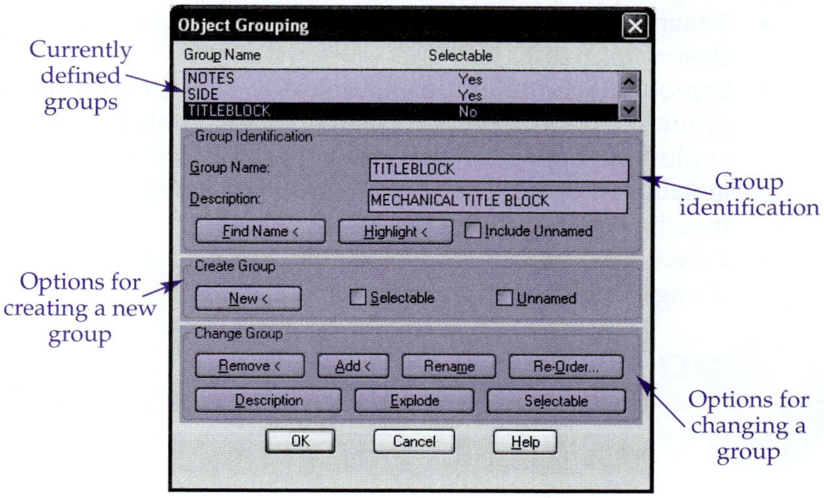

Figure 12-43.
The **Object Grouping** dialog box. The different elements are shown here highlighted.

- **Include Unnamed.** This check box causes unnamed groups to be listed with named groups. Unnamed groups are given a default name by AutoCAD in the format of *A*x*, where *x* is an integer value that increases with each new group, such as *A6. Unnamed groups can be named later using the **Rename** option.

The **Create Group** area contains the options for creating a new group:

- **New.** This button creates a new group from the selected objects using the name entered in the **Group Name:** text box. AutoCAD issues a Select objects for grouping: Select objects: prompt after you enter a new name in the **Group Name:** text box.
- **Selectable.** A check in this box sets the initial status of the **Selectable** value as Yes for the new group. This is indicated in the **Selectable** list described earlier. No check here specifies No in the **Selectable** list. This can be changed later.
- **Unnamed.** This indicates whether or not the new group will be named. If this box is checked, AutoCAD assigns its own default name as detailed previously.

The **Change Group** area of the **Object Grouping** dialog box shows the options for changing a group:

- **Remove.** Pick this button to remove objects from a group definition.
- **Add.** This button allows objects to be added to a group definition.
- **Rename.** Pick this button to change the name of an existing group. Unnamed groups can be renamed.
- **Re-Order.** Objects are numbered in the order they are selected when defining the group. The first object is numbered 0, not 1. This button allows objects to be reordered within the group. For example, if a group contains a set of instructions, you can reorder the instructions to suit the typical steps used. The **Order Group** dialog box is displayed when you pick this button. The elements of this dialog box are briefly described as follows:
    - **Group Name.** Displays the name of the selected group.
    - **Description.** Displays the description for the selected group.
    - **Remove from position (0-*n*).** Position number of the object to reorder, where *n* is one less than the total number of objects found in the group. You place the desired order in the text boxes to the right of this feature and the next two features.
    - **Replace at position (0-*n*).** Position to which the number is being moved.
    - **Number of objects (1-*n*).** Displays the number of objects or the range to reorder.
    - **Reverse Order.** Pick this button to have the order of all members in the group reversed.
- **Description.** Updates the group with the new description entered in the **Description:** text box.
- **Explode.** Pick this button to delete the selected group definition, but not the group's objects. The group name is removed, and the original group is exploded. Copies of the group become unnamed groups. By selecting the **Include Unnamed** check box, these unnamed groups are displayed and can then be exploded, if needed.
- **Selectable.** Toggles the selectable value of a group. This is where you can change the value in the **Selectable** list.

EXERCISE 12-17 Complete the Exercise on the Student CD.

Chapter Test

Answer the following questions on a separate sheet of paper.

1. Give the command and entries used to draw a .125 × .125 chamfer:
   A. Command: _____
   B. Select first line or [Polyline/Distance/Angle/Trim/Method/mUltiple]: _____
   C. Specify first chamfer distance <*current*>: _____
   D. Specify second chamfer distance <*current*>: _____
   E. Select first line or [Polyline/Distance/Angle/Trim/Method/mUltiple]: _____
   F. Select second line: _____
2. Give the command and entries required to produce .50 radius fillets on all corners of a closed polyline:
   A. Command: _____
   B. Select first object or [Polyline/Radius/Trim/mUltiple]: _____
   C. Specify fillet radius <*current*>: _____
   D. Select first object or [Polyline/Radius/Trim/mUltiple]: _____
   E. Select second object: _____
3. Give the command, entries, and actions required to move an object from Position A to Position B:
   A. Command: _____
   B. Select objects: _____
   C. Select objects: _____
   D. Specify base point or displacement: _____
   E. Specify second point of displacement or <use first point as displacement>: _____
4. Give the command and entries needed to make two copies of the same object:
   A. Command: _____
   B. Select objects: _____
   C. Select objects: _____
   D. Specify base point or displacement, or [Multiple]: _____
   E. Specify base point: _____
   F. Specify second point of displacement or <use first point as displacement>: _____
   G. Specify second point of displacement or <use first point as displacement>: _____
5. Give the command and entries necessary to draw a reverse image of an existing object and remove the existing object:
   A. Command: _____
   B. Select objects: _____
   C. Select objects: _____
   D. Specify first point of mirror line: _____
   E. Specify second point of mirror line: _____
   F. Delete source objects? [Yes/No] <N>: _____
6. Give the command and entries needed to rotate an object 45° clockwise:
   A. Command: _____
   B. Select objects: _____
   C. Select objects: ____
   D. Specify base point: _____
   E. Specify rotation angle or [Reference]: _____
7. Give the command and entries required to reduce the size of an entire drawing by one-half:
   A. Command: _____
   B. Select objects: _____
   C. Select objects: _____
   D. Specify base point: _____
   E. Specify scale factor or [Reference]: _____

8. What is the purpose of the **Method** option in the **CHAMFER** command?
9. How is the size of a fillet specified?
10. Name the system variable used to preset the fillet radius.
11. Describe the difference between the **Trim** and **No trim** options when using the **CHAMFER** and **FILLET** commands.
12. How can you split an object in two without removing a portion?
13. In what direction should you pick points to break a portion out of a circle or an arc?
14. Name the command that trims an object to a cutting edge.
15. The **EXTEND** command is the opposite of the _____ command.
16. Name the command associated with boundary edges.
17. How do you use the Smart mode with the **TRIM** and **EXTEND** commands?
18. Name the option in the **TRIM** and **EXTEND** commands allowing you to trim or extend to an implied intersection.
19. List two locations drafters normally choose as the base point when using the **MOVE** or **COPY** commands.
20. Define the term *displacement*, as it relates to the **MOVE** and **COPY** commands.
21. Explain the difference between the **MOVE** and **COPY** commands.
22. Name the command that can be used to move and rotate an object simultaneously.
23. What is the difference between polar and rectangular arrays?
24. What four values should you know before you create a rectangular array?
25. Suppose an object is 1.5″ (38 mm) wide, and you want to create a rectangular array with .75″ (19 mm) spacing between objects. What should you specify for the distance between columns?
26. Define the term *unit cell*.
27. How do you create a rotated rectangular array?
28. How do you specify a clockwise polar array rotation?
29. What values should you know before you create a polar array?
30. The **MOVE**, **COPY**, **TRIM**, **EXTEND**, and **STRETCH** commands are located in the _____ pull-down menu.
31. Identify the selection method or methods issued by AutoCAD when using the **STRETCH** command.
32. How do you cancel the **STRETCH** command?
33. Give the keyboard shortcuts for the following commands:
    A. **CHAMFER**
    B. **FILLET**
    C. **BREAK**
    D. **TRIM**
    E. **EXTEND**
    F. **CHANGE**
    G. **MOVE**
    H. **COPY**
    I. **MIRROR**
    J. **ROTATE**
    K. **ALIGN**
    L. **ARRAY**
    M. **SCALE**
    N. **LENGTHEN**
34. Identify the **LENGTHEN** command option corresponding to each of the following descriptions:
    A. Allows a positive or negative change in length from the endpoint.
    B. Changes a length or an arc angle by a percentage of the total.
    C. Sets the total length or angle to the value specified.
    D. Drags the endpoint of the object to the desired length or angle.
35. Describe the purpose of the **SELECT** command.
36. What is a *selection set*?
37. How do you select objects for editing that have previously been picked using the **SELECT** command?
38. Define a *group*.
39. How do you access the **Object Grouping** dialog box?
40. Describe how you create a new group.

Drawing Problems

Use your templates as appropriate for each of the following problems. Start a new drawing for each problem, unless indicated otherwise.

1. Draw Object A using the **LINE** and **ARC** commands. Make sure the corners overrun and the arc is centered, but does not touch the lines. Use the **TRIM**, **EXTEND**, and **MOVE** commands to make Object B. Save the drawing as P12-1.

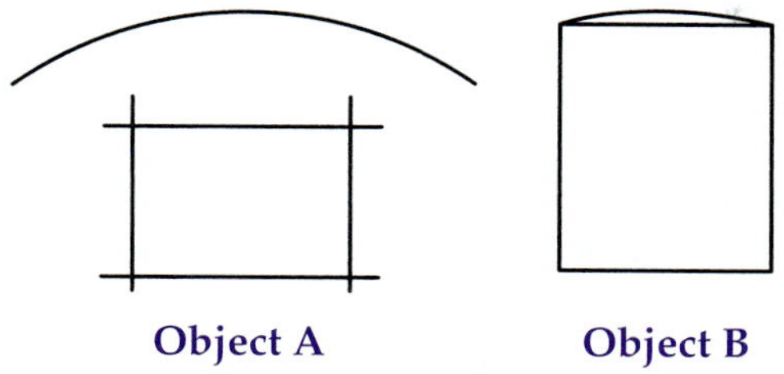

2. Open drawing P12-1 for further editing (Object A). Using the **STRETCH** command, change the shape to Object B. Make a copy of the new revision. Change the copy to represent Object C. Save the drawing as P12-2.

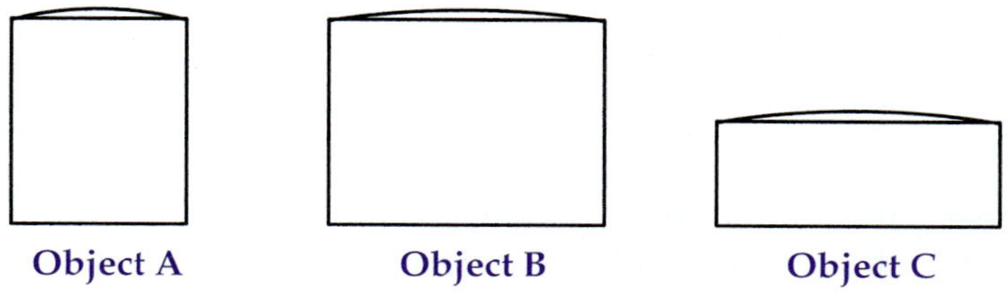

3. Refer to **Figure 12-37** in this chapter. Draw and make three copies of the object shown in Option 1. Stretch the first copy to twice its length, as shown in Option 2. Stretch the second copy to twice its height. Double the size of the third copy using the **SCALE** command. Save the drawing as P12-3.
4. Draw Objects A, B, and C, shown below, without dimensions. Move Objects A, B, and C to new positions. Select a corner of Object A and the centers of Objects B and C as the base points. Save the drawing as P12-4.

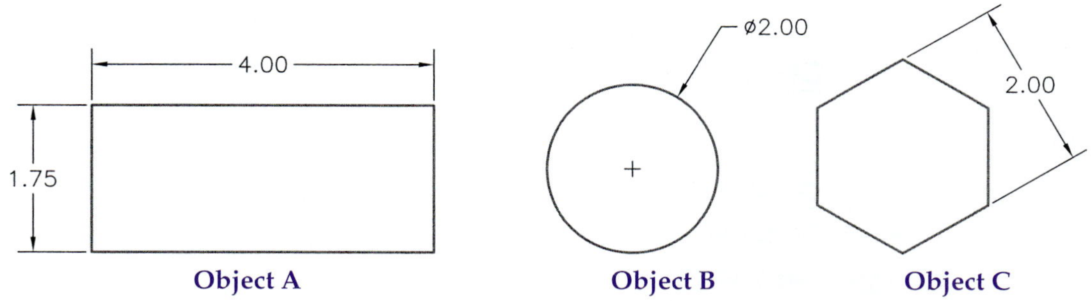

5. Draw Objects A, B, and C, shown in Problem 12-4, on the left side of the screen. Make a copy of Object A, 2 units to the right. Make four copies of Object B, 3 units, center-to-center, to the right, using the **Multiple** option. Make three copies of Object C, 3 units, center-to-center, to the right. Save the drawing as P12-5.

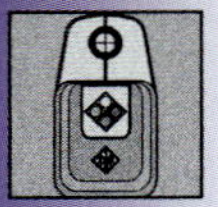

6. Draw the object shown using the **ELLIPSE**, **COPY**, and **LINE** commands. The rotation angle of the ellipse is 60°. Use the **BREAK** or **TRIM** command when drawing and editing the lower ellipse. Save the drawing as P12-6.

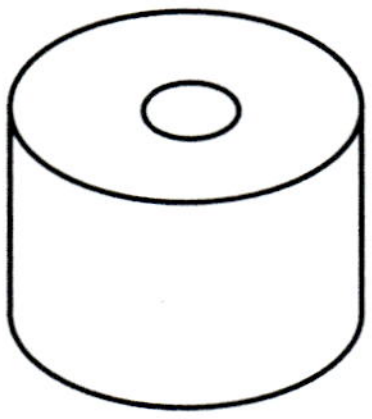

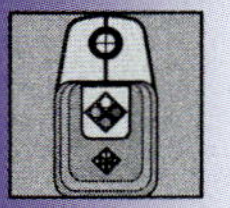

7. Open drawing P12-6 for further editing. Shorten the height of the object using the **STRETCH** command, as shown below. Next, add to the object as indicated. Save the drawing as P12-7.

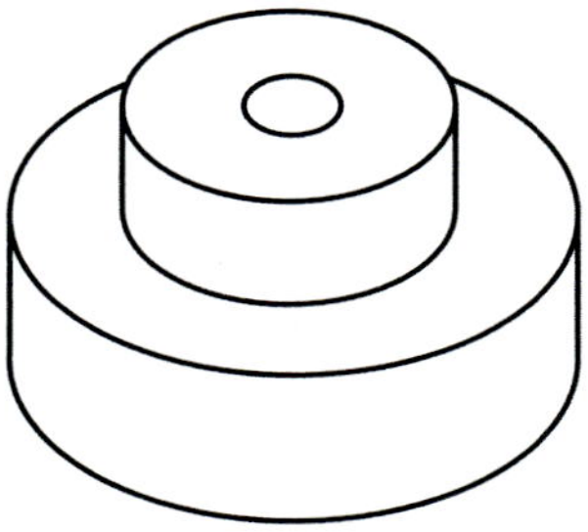

8. You have been given an engineer's sketches and notes to construct a drawing of a sprocket. Create a front and side view of the sprocket using the **ARRAY** command. Place the drawing on one of your templates. Do not add dimensions. Save the drawing as P12-8.

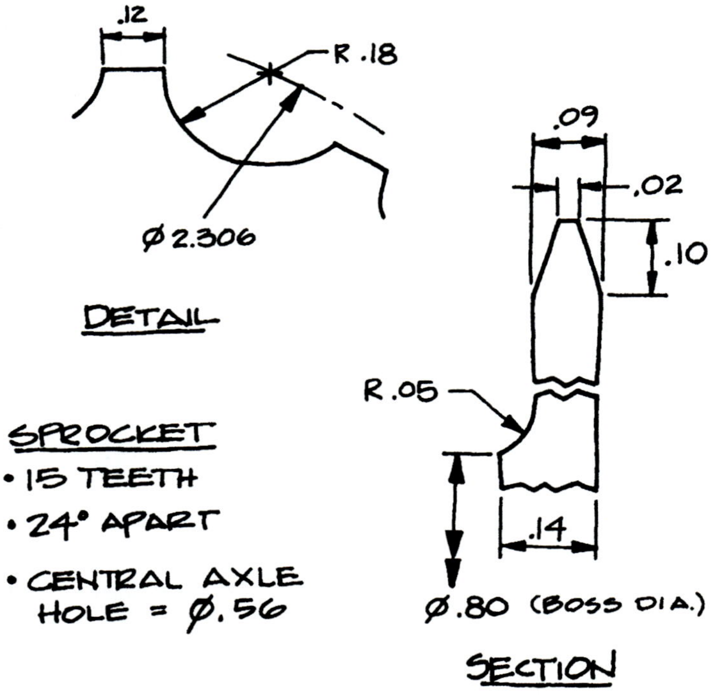

9. Draw Object A without dimensions. Use the **CHAMFER** and **FILLET** commands to your best advantage. Draw a mirror image as Object B. Now, remove the original view and move the new view so Point 2 is at the original Point 1 location. Save the drawing as P12-9.

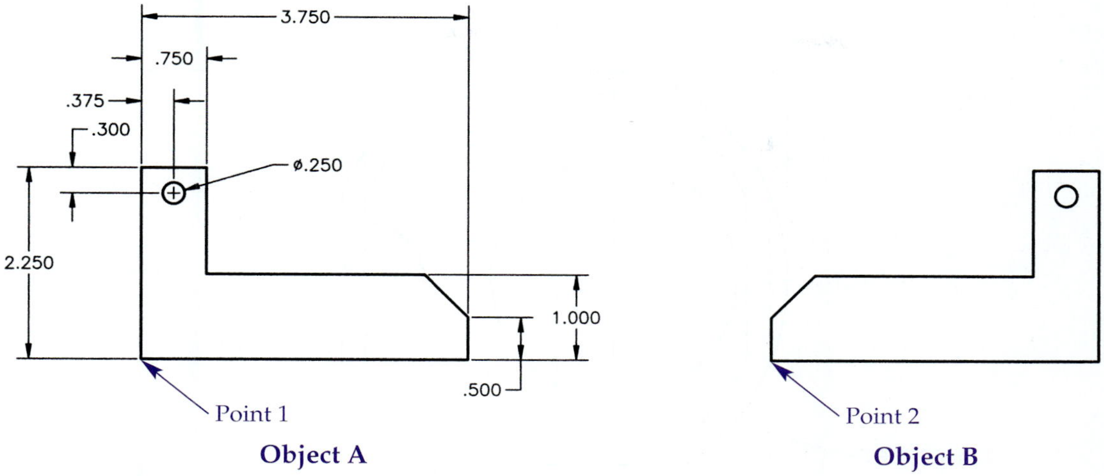

10. Draw the object shown below without dimensions. The object is symmetrical; therefore, draw only one half. Mirror the other half into place. Use the **CHAMFER** and **FILLET** commands to your best advantage. All fillets and rounds are .125. Save the drawing as P12-10.

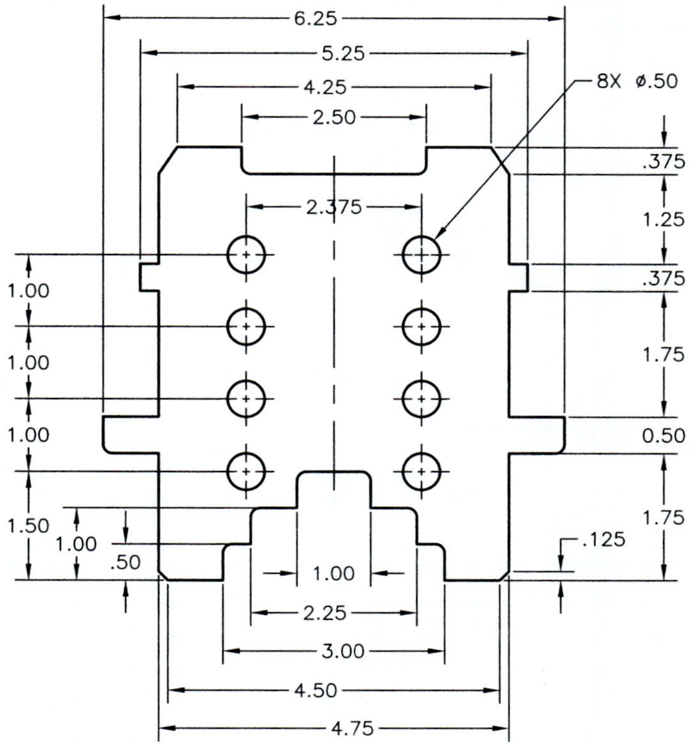

11. Use the **TRIM**, **OSNAP**, and **OFFSET** commands to assist you in drawing this object. Do not draw centerlines or dimensions. Save the completed drawing as P12-11.

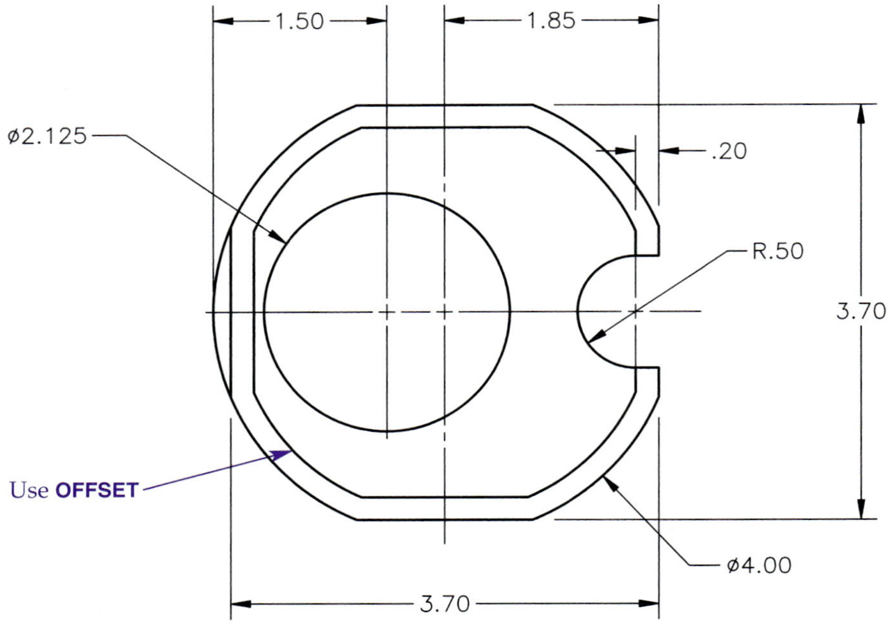

12. Draw the object shown below without dimensions. Mirror the right half into place. Use the **CHAMFER** and **FILLET** commands to your best advantage. Save the drawing as P12-12.

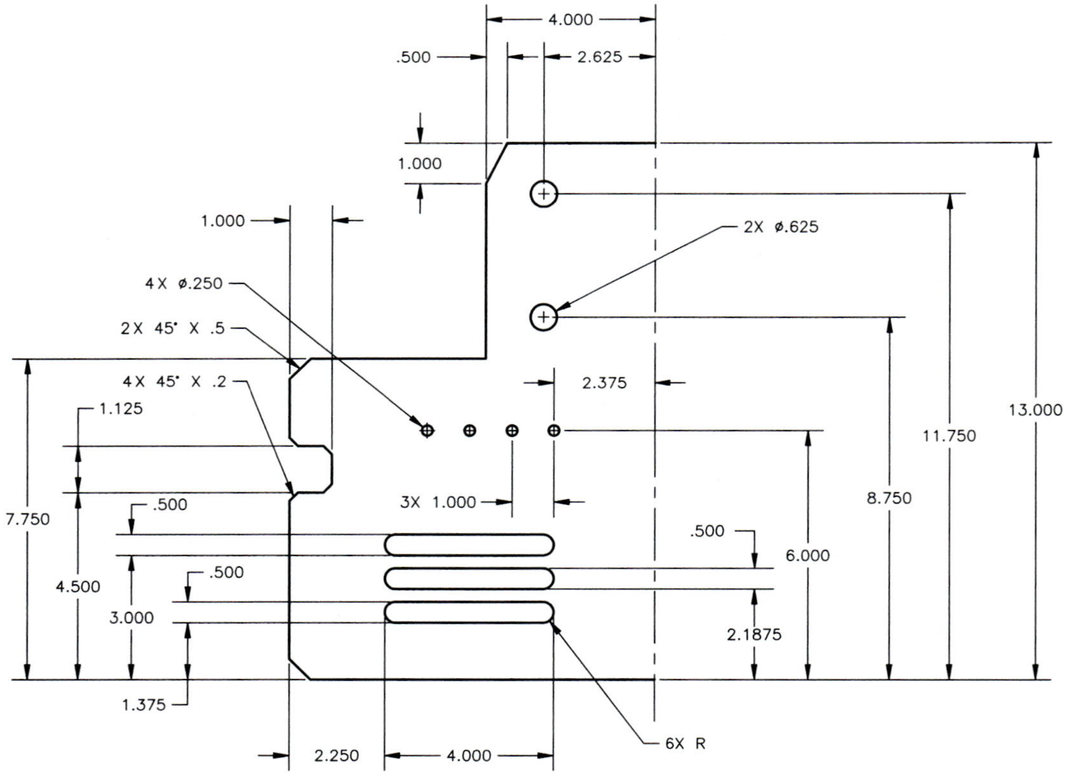

13. Redraw the objects shown below. Mirror the drawing, but have the text remain readable. Delete the original image during the mirroring process. Save the drawing as P12-13.

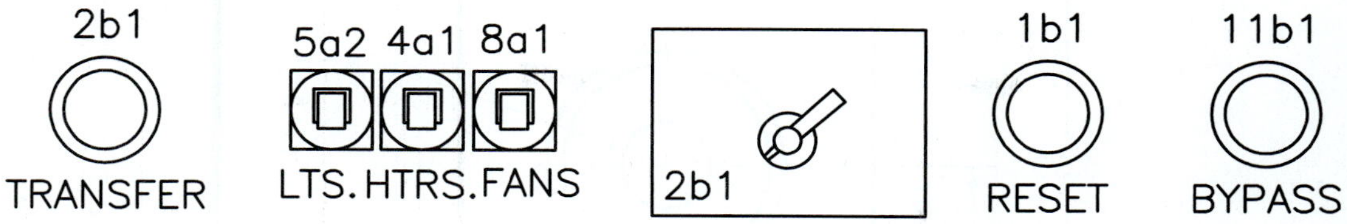

14. Draw the following object views using the dimensions given. Use **ARRAY** to construct the hole and tooth arrangements. Use one of your templates for the drawing. Do not add dimensions. Save the drawing as P12-14.

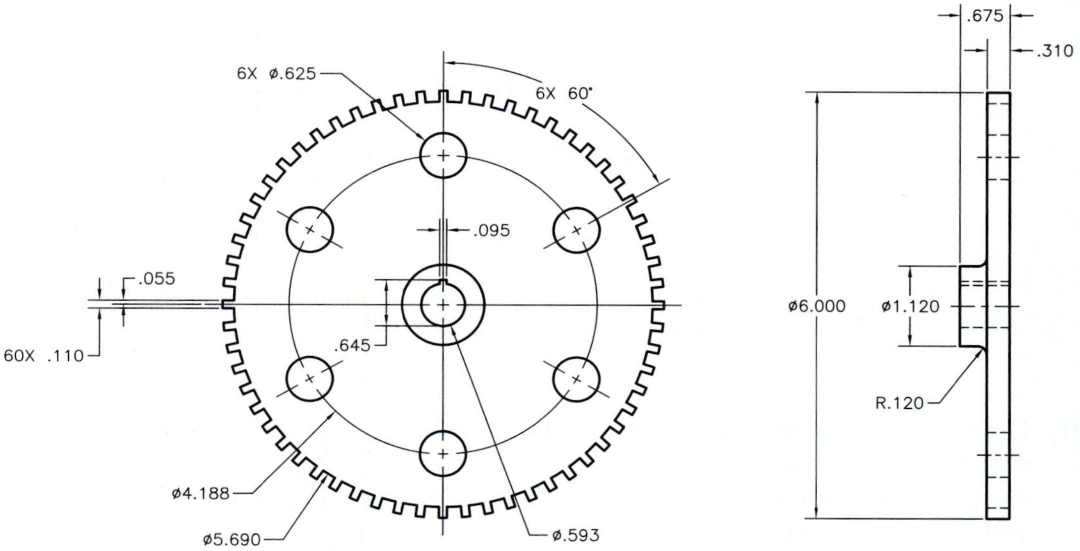

Drawing Problems - Chapter 12

15. Draw the following object without dimensions. Use the **TRIMMODE** setting to your advantage. Save the drawing as P12-15.

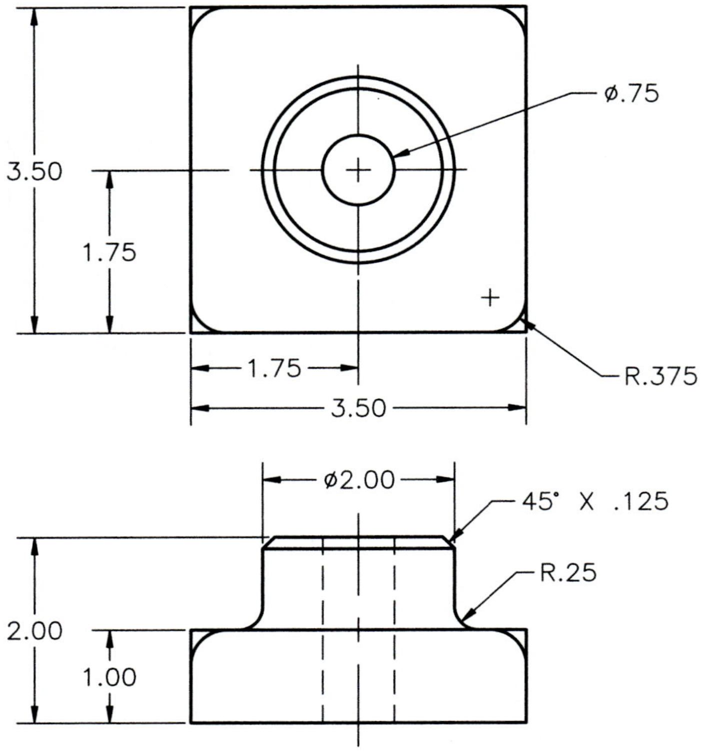

16. Draw the objects shown below. Use the **GROUP** command to name each of the objects with the names below them. Use the object groups to draw the one-line electrical diagram shown below. Use the **Explode** option to edit the symbols at 1 and 2 in the diagram, as shown. Save the drawing as P12-16.

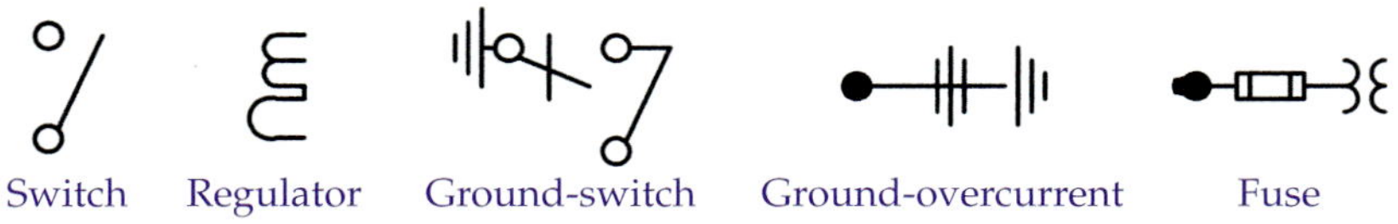

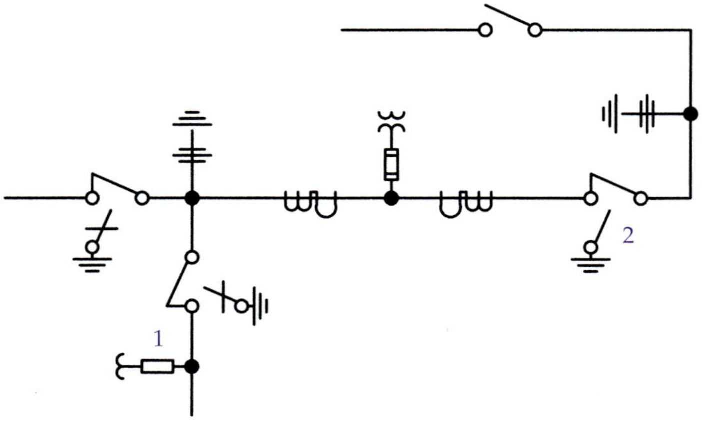

17. Draw the following bracket. Do not include dimensions in your drawing. Use the **FILLET** command where appropriate. Save the drawing as P12-17.

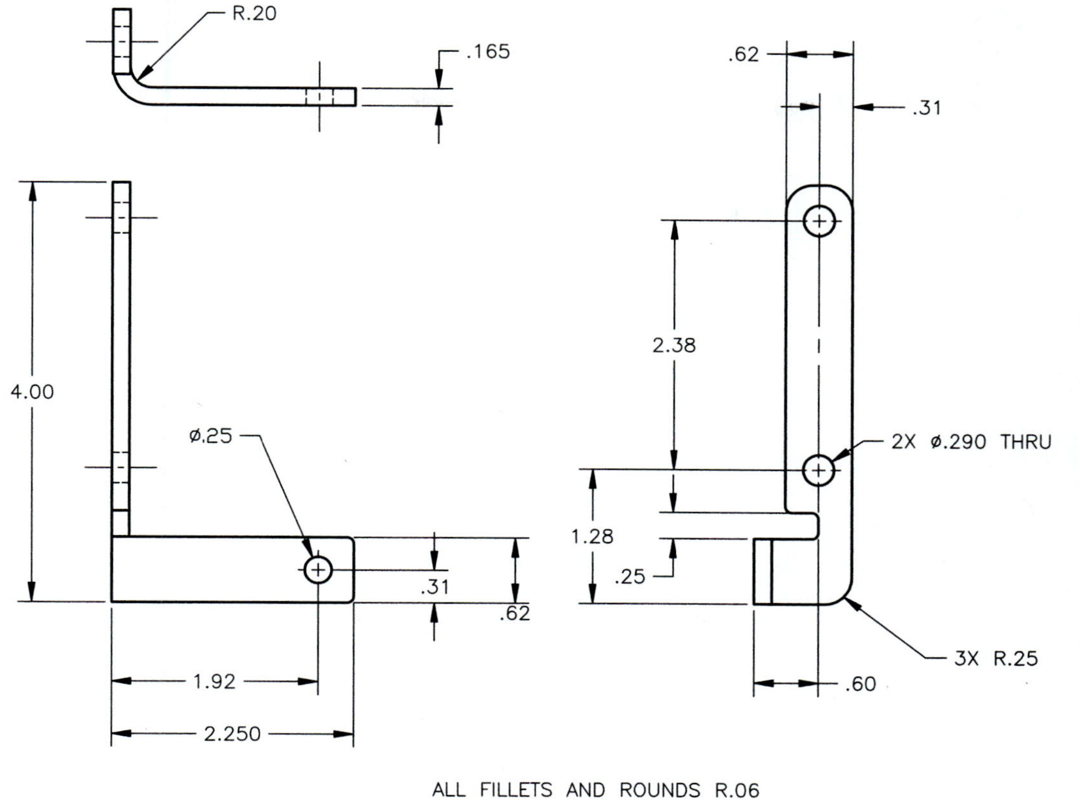

18. Draw this refrigeration system schematic. Save the drawing as P12-18.

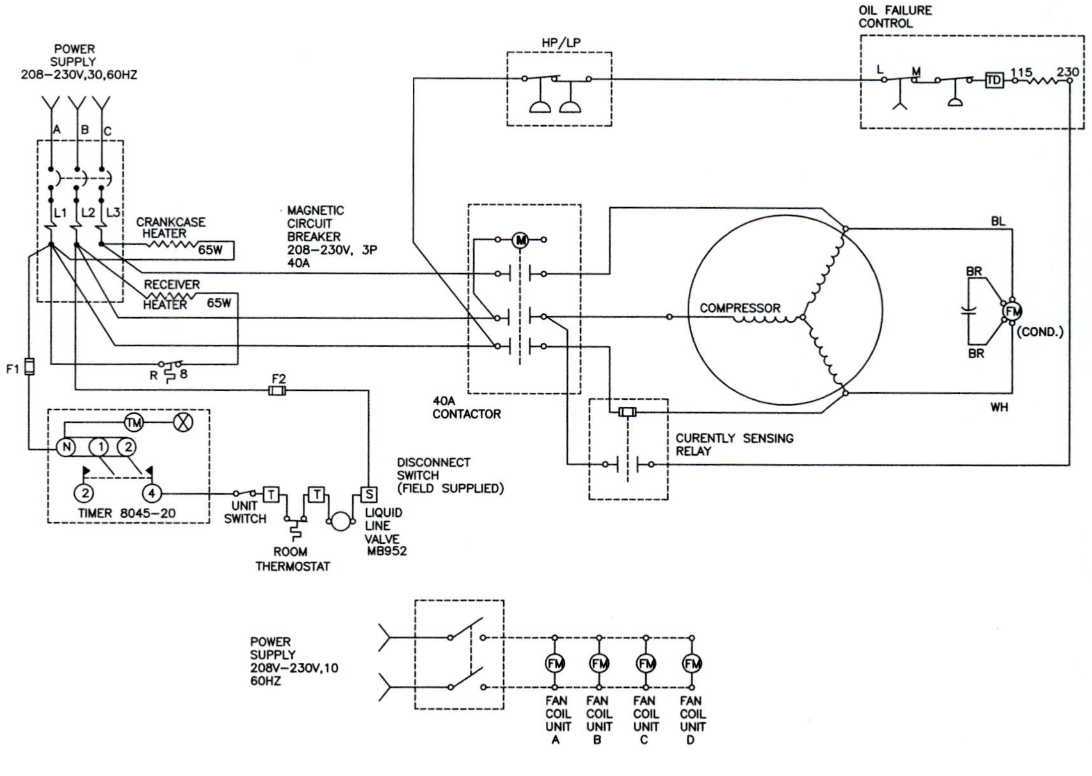

19. Draw this timer schematic. Save the drawing as P12-19.

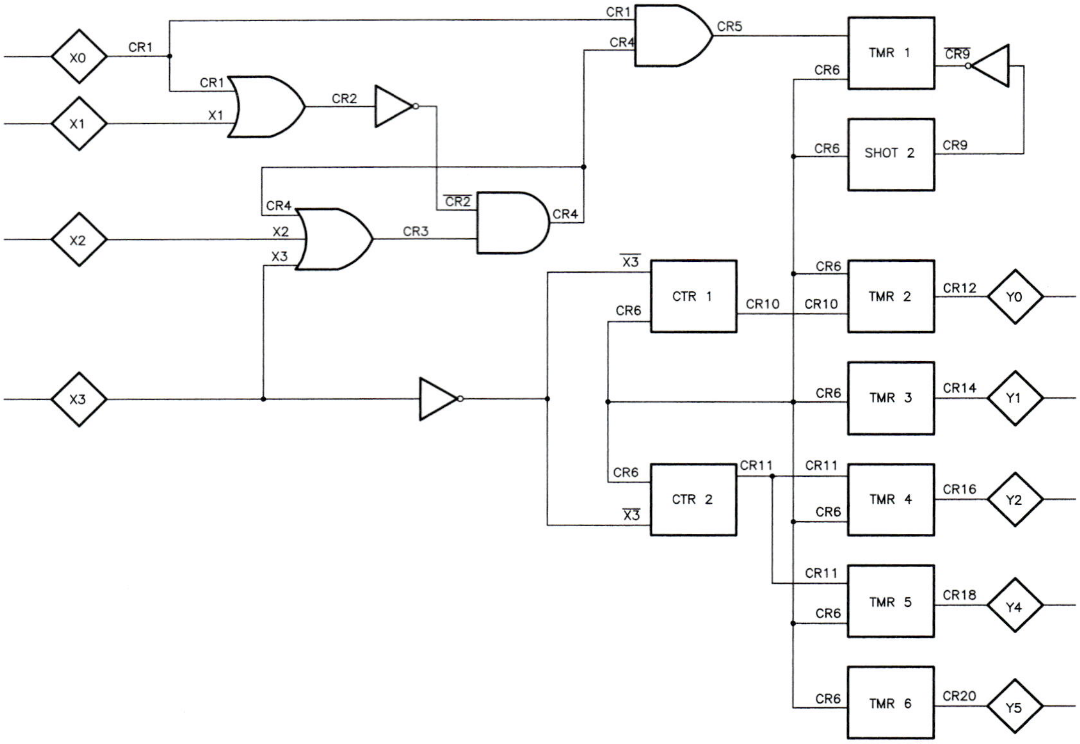

20. The following engineering sketch shows a steel column arrangement on a concrete floor slab for a new building. The *I*-shaped symbols represent the steel columns. The columns are arranged in "bay lines" and "column lines." The column lines are numbered *1*, *2*, and *3*. The bay lines are labeled *A* through *G*. The width of a bay is 24′-0″. Line balloons, or tags, identify the bay and column lines. Draw the arrangement, using **ARRAY** for the steel column symbols and the tags. Do not dimension the drawing. The following guidelines will help you.
   A. Begin a new drawing, named P12-20, or use an architectural template.
   B. Select architectural units and specify a 36 × 24 sheet size. Determine the scale required for the floor plan to fit on this sheet size and specify your limits accordingly.
   C. Draw the steel column symbol to the dimensions given.
   D. Set the grid spacing at 2′-0″ (24″).
   E. Set the snap spacing at 12″.
   F. Draw all other objects.
   G. Place text inside the balloon tags. Set the running object snap mode to **Center** and **Justify** the text to **Middle**. Make the text height 6″.
   H. Place a title block on the drawing.
   I. Save the drawing as P12-20..

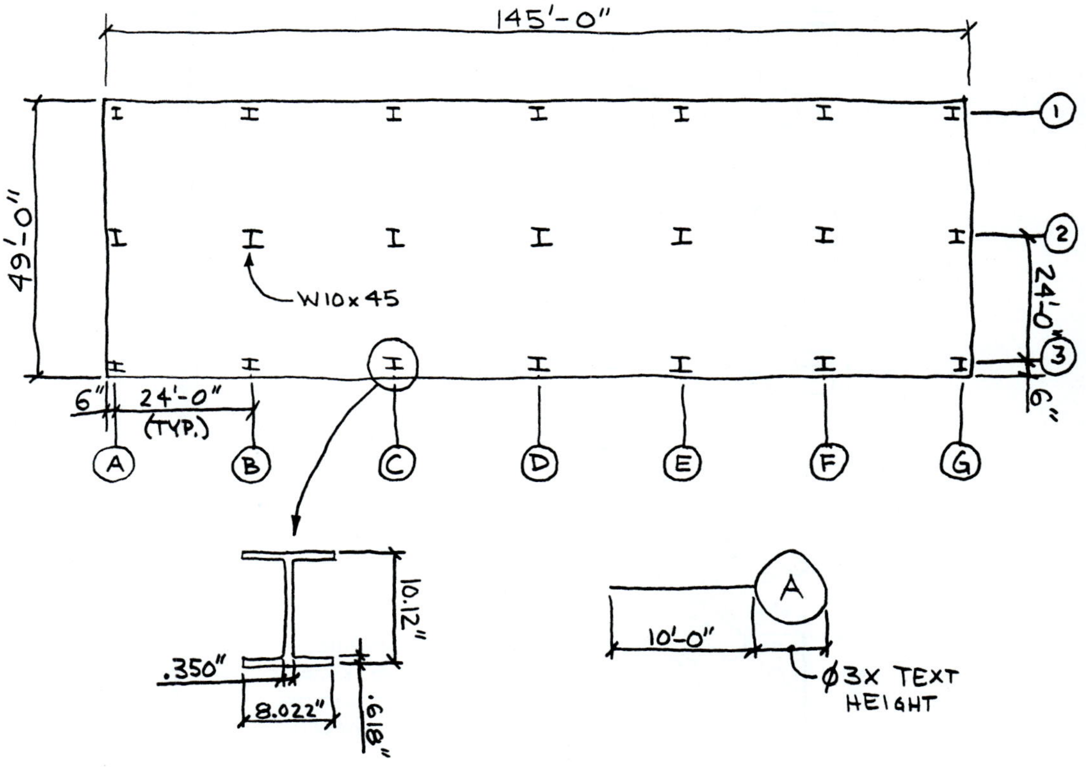

21. The engineering sketch given is a proposed office layout of desks and chairs. One desk is shown with the layout of a chair, keyboard, monitor, and tower-mounted computer (drawn with dotted lines). All the desk workstations should have the same configuration. The exact sizes and locations of the doors and windows are not important for this problem. Use the following guidelines to complete this problem.
    A. Begin a new drawing, called P12-21.
    B. Choose architectural units.
    C. Select a C-size template drawing and be sure to create the drawing in model space. Use the **ZOOM nXP** option to display the drawing at a scale fitting the C-size layout.
    D. Use the appropriate drawing and editing commands to complete this problem quickly and efficiently.
    E. Draw the desk and computer hardware to the dimensions given.
    F. Do not dimension the drawing. Plot a paper space layout tab at a one-to-one scale.
    G. Save the drawing as P12-21.

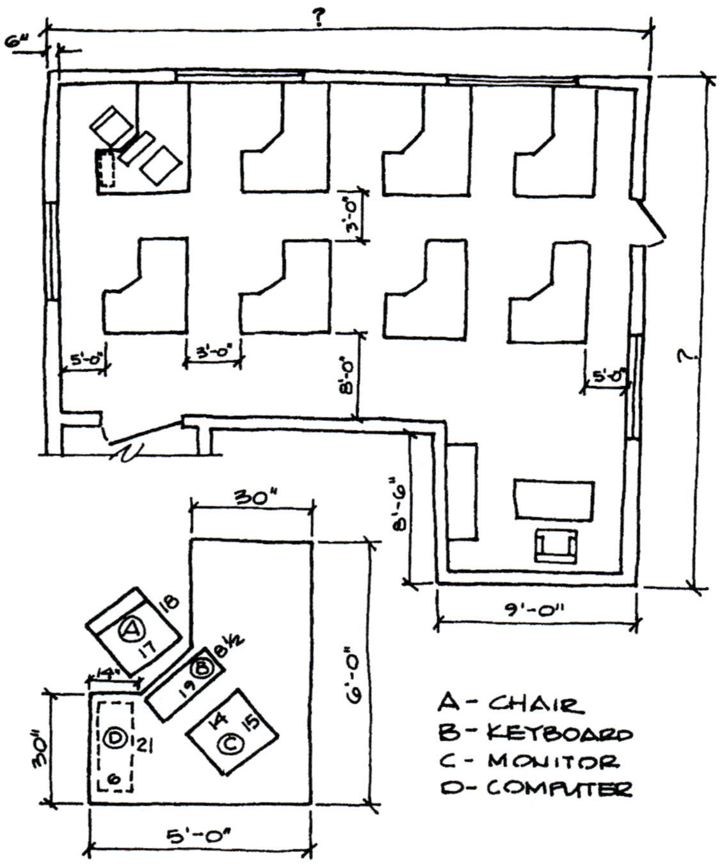

CHAPTER 13

Automatic Editing

Learning Objectives

After completing this chapter, you will be able to do the following:

- Use grips to do automatic editing with the **STRETCH**, **COPY**, **MOVE**, **ROTATE**, **SCALE**, and **MIRROR** commands.
- Identify the system variables used for automatic editing.
- Perform automatic editing with the **Properties** window.
- Use the **MATCHPROP** command to match object properties.

In Chapter 12, you learned how to use commands that let you do a variety of drawing and editing activities with AutoCAD. These editing commands give you maximum flexibility and increase productivity. This chapter takes editing a step further, however, by allowing you to first select an object and then automatically perform editing operations.

Automatic Editing with Grips

Hold, *grab*, and *grasp* are all words synonymous with *grip*. In AutoCAD, ***grips*** are features on an object that are highlighted with small boxes. For example, the grips on a straight line are the endpoints and midpoint. When grips are used for editing, you can select an object to automatically activate the grips. Pick any of the small boxes to perform **STRETCH**, **COPY**, **MOVE**, **ROTATE**, **SCALE**, or **MIRROR** operations.

When grips are enabled and there is no command active, a pick box is located at the intersection of the screen crosshairs. You can pick any object to activate the grips. Figure 13-1 shows what grips look like on several different objects. For text, the grip box is located at the insertion point.

You can control grip settings in the **Selection** tab of the **Options** dialog box. The **Options** dialog box is opened by picking **Options...** in the **Tools** pull-down menu or by right-clicking and selecting **Options...** from the shortcut menu. You can access the **Selection** tab of the **Options** dialog box directly by typing GR or DDGRIPS at the Command: prompt. The **Selection** tab in the **Options** dialog box is shown in Figure 13-2.

DDGRIPS
GR
Tools
➥ **Options...**

Figure 13-1.
Grips are placed at strategic locations on objects.

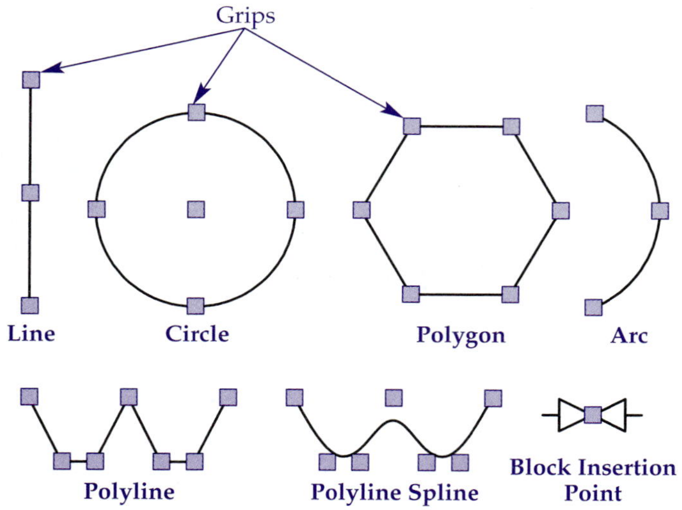

Figure 13-2.
The **Selection** tab of the **Options** dialog box contains grip control settings.

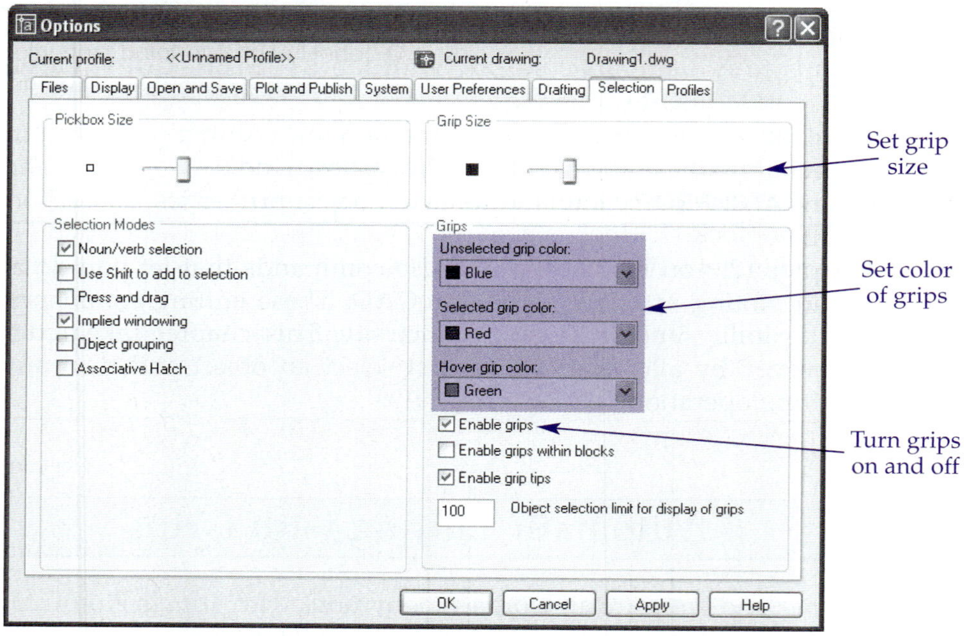

The **Pickbox Size** scroll bar lets you adjust the size of the pick box. The sample in the image tile gets smaller or larger as you move the scroll bar. Stop when you have the desired size. The pick box size is also controlled by the **PICKBOX** system variable, where the desired size is set in pixels.

The **Grip Size** scroll bar in the **Selection** tab of the **Options** dialog box lets you graphically change the size of the grip box. The sample in the image tile gets smaller or larger as you move the scroll bar. Change the grip size to whatever works best for your drawing. Very small grip boxes may be difficult to pick. The grips may overlap, however, if they are too large. The grip size can be given a numerical value at the Command: prompt using the **GRIPSIZE** system variable. To change the default setting of 5, enter GRIPSIZE at the Command: prompt, and then type a desired size in pixels.

The three color drop-down lists allow you to change the color of grips. The grips displayed when you first pick an object are referred to as ***unselected grips*** because you have not yet picked a grip to perform an operation. An unselected grip is a filled-in square using the color of the **Unselected grip color:** setting. Unselected grips are blue (Color 160) by default and are called *warm*.

After you pick a grip, it is called a ***selected grip***. A selected grip appears as a filled-in square using the **Selected grip color:** setting. Selected grips are Red by default and are called *hot*. If more than one object is selected and has warm grips, what you do with the hot grips affects all the selected objects. Objects having warm and hot grips are highlighted and are part of the selection set.

You can remove highlighted objects from a selection set by holding down the [Shift] key and picking the objects to be removed. The [Shift] key can also be used to add or remove hot grips. If you want to make more than one grip hot, hold the [Shift] key down, and then select the grip. To add more grips to the hot grip selection set, continue to hold the [Shift] key down and select the other grips. With the [Shift] key held down, selecting a hot (red) grip returns it to the warm (blue) stage. Figure 13-3 shows two different circles being modified by using hot grips. Moving the crosshairs over a warm grip and pausing changes the color of the grip to the **Hover grip color:** setting found in the **Selection** tab of the **Options** dialog box. By default, this color is set to Green. This is useful when multiple grips are close together. Pausing over the warm grip and letting it change color ensures that you select the correct grip.

You can also control grip color with the **GRIPCOLOR**, **GRIPHOT**, and **GRIPHOVER** system variables. **GRIPCOLOR** controls the color of warm grips, and **GRIPHOT** regulates the color of hot grips. The hover grip color can be changed by using the **GRIPHOVER** system variable. When you enter one of these variables, simply set the color number as desired.

Notice the three check boxes in the **Grips** area. Pick the **Enable grips** check box to turn grips on or off. This setting can also be set using the **GRIPS** system variable.

Pick the **Enable grips within blocks** check box to have grips displayed on every subobject of a block. A ***block*** is a special symbol designed for multiple uses. Blocks are discussed in detail in Chapter 22. When this check box is off, the grip location for a block is at the insertion point, as shown in Figure 13-1. Grips in blocks can also be controlled with the **GRIPBLOCK** system variable.

When the **Enable grip tips** box is checked, a tip displays relating to the selected object. This option only works on custom objects supporting grip tips. Standard AutoCAD objects do not have grip tips. The **GRIPTIPS** system variable also controls this option.

Figure 13-3.
You can modify multiple objects by using the [Shift] key to select grips to make them hot.

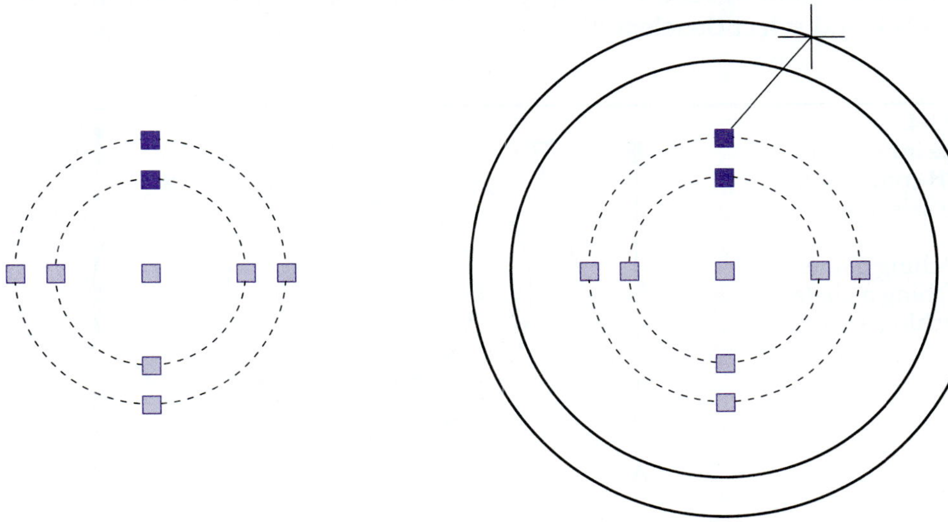

Using Grips

To activate grips, move the pick box to the desired object and pick. The object is highlighted, and the warm grips are displayed. To select a grip, move the pick box to the desired grip and pick it. Notice the crosshairs snap to a grip. When you pick a grip, the command line shows the following prompt:

** STRETCH **
Specify stretch point or [Base point/Copy/Undo/eXit]:

This activates the **STRETCH** command. All you have to do is move the cursor to make the selected object stretch, as shown in Figure 13-4. If you pick the middle grip of a line or an arc or the center grip of a circle, the object moves. These are the other options:

- **Base point.** Type B and press [Enter] to select a new base point.
- **Copy.** Type C and press [Enter] if you want to make one or more copies of the selected object.
- **Undo.** Type U and press [Enter] to undo the previous operation.
- **Exit.** Type X and press [Enter] to exit the command. The hot grip is gone, but the warm grips remain. You can also use the [Esc] key to cancel the command. Canceling twice removes the selected and unselected grips and returns to the Command: prompt.

You can pick objects individually or use a window or crossing box. Figure 13-5 shows how you can stretch features of an object after selecting all the objects. Step 1 in Figure 13-5A stretches the first corner, and Step 2 stretches the second corner. You can also make more than one grip hot at the same time by holding down the [Shift] key as you pick the grips, as shown in Figure 13-5B. Here are some general rules and guidelines that can help make grips work for you:

✓ Be sure the **GRIPS** system variable is on.
✓ Pick an object or group of objects to activate grips. Objects in the selection set are highlighted.
✓ Pick a warm grip to make it hot.
✓ Make multiple grips hot by holding the [Shift] key while picking warm grips.
✓ If more than one object has hot grips, they are all affected by the editing commands.
✓ Remove objects from the selection set by holding down the [Shift] key and picking them, thus making the grips warm.
✓ Return objects to the selection set by picking them again.
✓ Remove hot grips from the selection set by pressing the [Esc] key to cancel. Cancel again to remove all grips from the selection set. You can also right-click and select **Deselect All** from the shortcut menu to remove all grips.

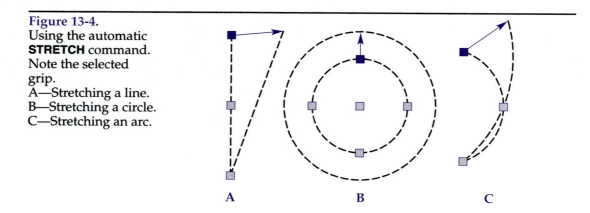

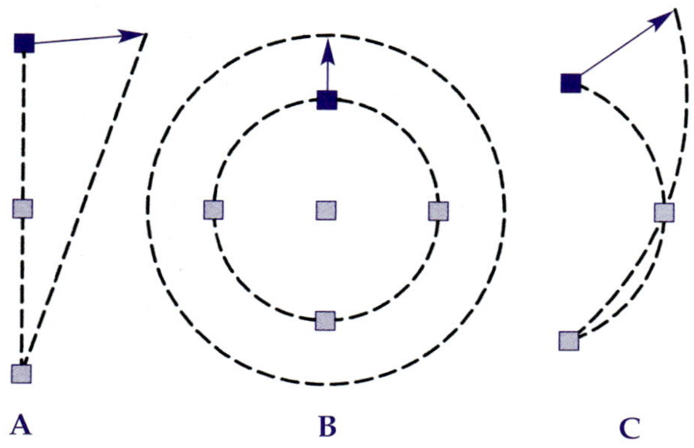

Figure 13-4.
Using the automatic **STRETCH** command. Note the selected grip.
A—Stretching a line.
B—Stretching a circle.
C—Stretching an arc.

Figure 13-5.
Stretching an object. A—Select corners to stretch individually. B—Select several hot grips by holding down the [Shift] key.

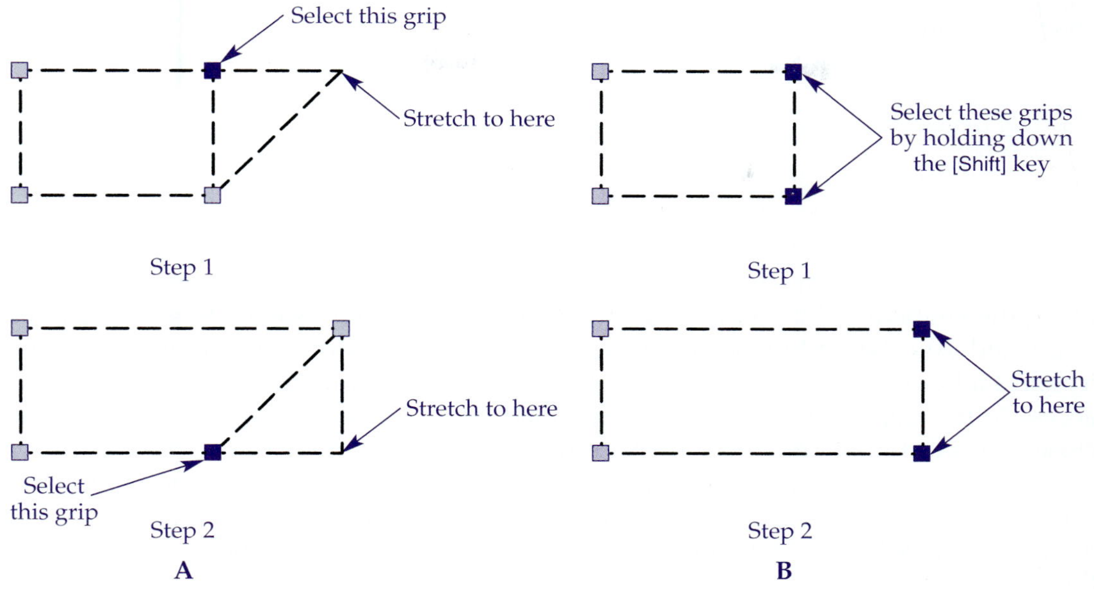

PROFESSIONAL TIP

When editing with grips, you can enter coordinates to help improve your accuracy. Remember that any of the coordinate entry methods work.

EXERCISE 13-1 Complete the Exercise on the Student CD.

You can also use the **MOVE**, **ROTATE**, **SCALE**, and **MIRROR** commands to automatically edit objects. All you have to do is pick the object, and then select one of the grips. When you see the ** STRETCH ** command, press [Enter] to cycle through the command options:

```
** STRETCH **
Specify stretch point or [Base point/Copy/Undo/eXit]: ↵
** MOVE **
Specify move point or [Base point/Copy/Undo/eXit]: ↵
** ROTATE **
Specify rotation angle or [Base point/Copy/Undo/Reference/eXit]: ↵
** SCALE **
Specify scale factor or [Base point/Copy/Undo/Reference/eXit]: ↵
** MIRROR **
Specify second point or [Base point/Copy/Undo/eXit]: ↵
** STRETCH **
Specify stretch point or [Base point/Copy/Undo/eXit]:
```

As an alternative to pressing [Enter], you can enter the first two characters of the desired command from the keyboard. Type MO for **MOVE**, MI for **MIRROR**, RO for **ROTATE**, SC for **SCALE**, and ST for **STRETCH**.

AutoCAD also allows you to right-click and access a grips shortcut menu, as shown in Figure 13-6. This menu is only available after a grip has been turned into a

Figure 13-6.
The grips shortcut menu appears when a grip is selected and you right-click.

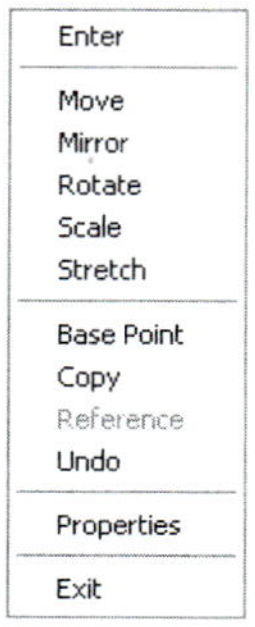

hot grip. The shortcut menu allows you to access the five grip editing options without using the keyboard. All you have to do is pick **Move**, **Mirror**, **Rotate**, **Scale**, or **Stretch** as needed. Another option in the shortcut menu is **Base Point**. This option allows you to select a base point other than the hot grip. The shortcut menu also provides direct access to the **Copy** option, which is explained later in this chapter. The **Undo** option closes the shortcut menu and returns to the current grip activity.

An added bonus in the grips shortcut menu is the **Properties** option. Selecting this opens the **Properties** window, where you can change properties of the objects being edited. Selecting the **Exit** option closes the grips shortcut menu and removes the hot grip.

NOTE

When AutoCAD is configured to display a screen menu, the **Move**, **Mirror**, **Rotate**, **Scale**, and **Stretch** automatic editing commands appear in a separate screen menu whenever a grip is selected.

PROFESSIONAL TIP

Many of the conventional AutoCAD editing operations can be performed when warm grips are displayed on screen and the **PICKFIRST** variable is set to 1 (its default value). The editing commands can be selected from the pull-down menus, selected from the toolbars, or entered at the Command: prompt. For example, the **ERASE** command can be used to clear the screen of all objects displayed with warm grips by first picking the objects and then selecting the **ERASE** command.

Moving an Object Automatically

If you want to move an object with grips, select the object, pick a grip to use as the base point, and then press [Enter] to cycle through the commands until you get to this prompt:

```
** MOVE **
Specify move point or [Base point/Copy/Undo/eXit]:
```

The selected grip becomes the base point. Move the object to a new point by picking the new location. You may want to use object snap mode or coordinates to place it in a new location. The **MOVE** operation is complete, as shown in Figure 13-7. If you accidentally pick the wrong grip or want to have a base point other than the selected grip, type B and press [Enter] for the **Base point** option. Pick a new base point.

Figure 13-7.
The automatic **MOVE** command. The selected grip becomes the base point for the move.

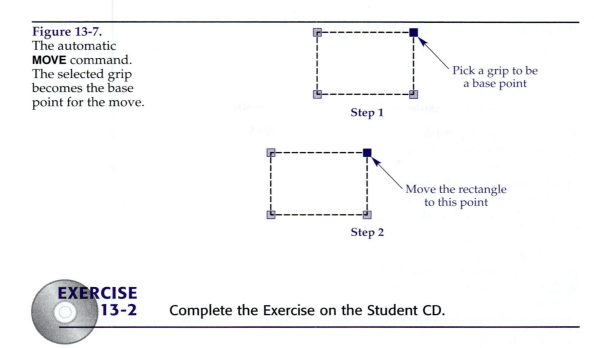

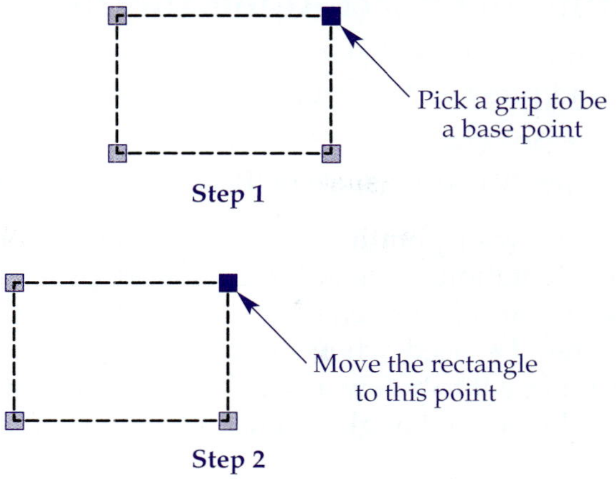
Pick a grip to be a base point
Step 1
Move the rectangle to this point
Step 2

EXERCISE 13-2 Complete the Exercise on the Student CD.

Copying an Object Automatically

The **Copy** option is found in each of the editing commands. When using the **STRETCH** command, the **Copy** option allows you to make multiple copies of the object you are stretching. Holding down the [Shift] key while performing the first **STRETCH** operation accesses the **Multiple** option. The prompt looks like this:

```
** STRETCH (multiple) **
Specify stretch point or [Base point/Copy/Undo/eXit]: ↵
Command:
```

The **Copy** option in the **MOVE** command is the true form of the **COPY** command. You can activate the **Copy** option by typing C, as follows:

** MOVE **
Specify move point or [Base point/Copy/Undo/eXit]: **C**↵
** MOVE (multiple) **
Specify move point or [Base point/Copy/Undo/eXit]: *(make as many copies as desired and enter* X*, press* [Esc]*, or select* **Exit** *from the grips shortcut menu to exit)*

Holding down the [Shift] key while performing the first **MOVE** operation also accesses the **Copy** option. The **Copy** option works similarly in each of the editing commands. Try it with each to see what happens. When you are in the **STRETCH** or **MOVE** command, you can also access the **Copy** option directly by picking the right mouse button to open the grips shortcut menu.

PROFESSIONAL TIP

When in the **Copy** option of the **MOVE** command, if you make the first copy and then hold the [Shift] key, the distance of the first copy automatically becomes the snap spacing for additional copies.

EXERCISE 13-3 Complete the Exercise on the Student CD.

Rotating an Object Automatically

To automatically rotate an object, select the object, pick a grip to use as the base point, and press [Enter] until you see this prompt:

** ROTATE **
Specify rotation angle or [Base point/Copy/Undo/Reference/eXit]:

Now, move your pointing device to rotate the object. Pick the desired rotation point or enter a rotation angle at the Command: prompt.

Type R and press [Enter] if you want to use the **Reference** option. The **Reference** option may be used when the object is already rotated at a known angle and you want to rotate it to a new angle. The reference angle is the current angle, and the new angle is the desired angle. Figure 13-8 shows the **ROTATE** options.

EXERCISE 13-4 Complete the Exercise on the Student CD.

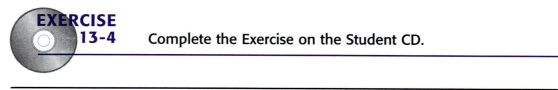

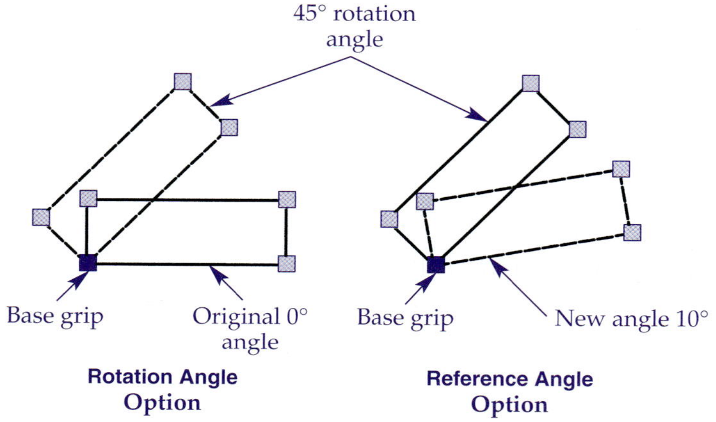

Figure 13-8. The rotation angle and **Reference** option of the **ROTATE** command.

Scaling an Object Automatically

If you want to scale an object with grips, cycle through the editing options until you get this prompt:

** SCALE **
Specify scale factor or [Base point/Copy/Undo/Reference/eXit]:

Move the screen cursor and pick when the object is dragged to the desired size. You can also enter a scale factor to automatically increase or decrease the scale of the original object. You can use the **Reference** option if you know a current length and a desired length. The selected base point remains in the same place when the object is scaled. Figure 13-9 shows the two **SCALE** options.

EXERCISE 13-5 Complete the Exercise on the Student CD.

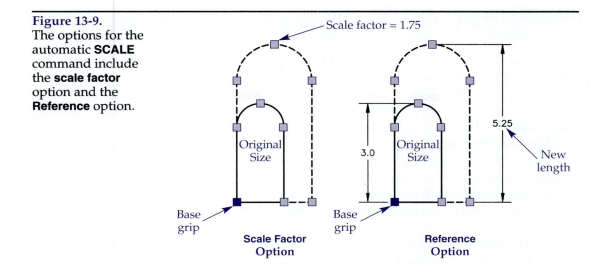

Figure 13-9.
The options for the automatic **SCALE** command include the **scale factor** option and the **Reference** option.

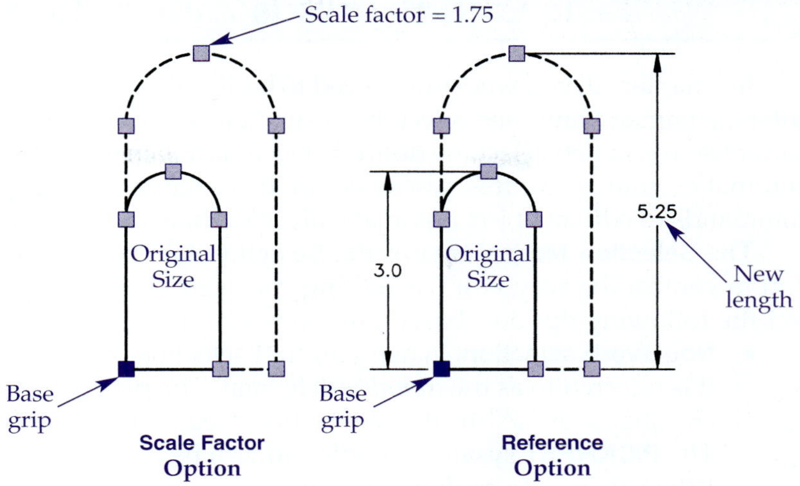

Mirroring an Object Automatically

If you want to mirror an object using grips, the selected grip becomes the first point of the mirror line. Press [Enter] to cycle through the editing commands until you get this prompt:

** MIRROR **
Specify second point or [Base point/Copy/Undo/eXit]:

Use the **Base point** option to reselect the first point of the mirror line. Pick another grip or any point on the screen as the second point of the mirror line. See Figure 13-10. Unlike the standard **MIRROR** command, the automatic **MIRROR** command does not give you the option to delete the old objects. The old objects are deleted automatically. If you want to keep the original object while mirroring, use the **Copy** option in the **MIRROR** command.

Figure 13-10.
When using the automatic **MIRROR** command, the selected grip becomes the first point of the mirror line, and the original object is automatically deleted.

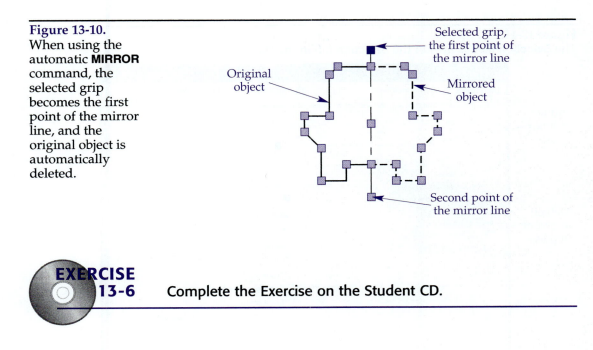

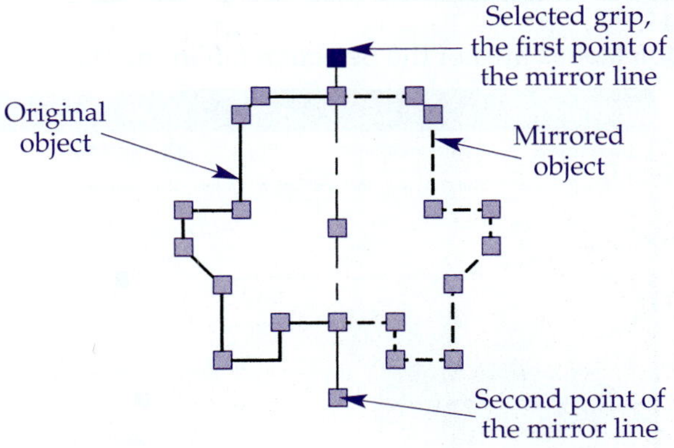

EXERCISE 13-6 Complete the Exercise on the Student CD.

Basic Editing versus Automatic Editing

In Chapter 12, you were introduced to basic editing. Basic editing allows you to first enter a command and then select the desired object to be edited. You can also set system variables so you first select the desired objects and then enter the desired command. The automatic editing features discussed in this chapter use grips and related editing commands to edit an object automatically, after first selecting the object.

The **Selection Modes** area of the **Selection** tab in the **Options** dialog box allows you to control the way you use editing commands. See Figure 13-11. Select or deselect the following options, based on your own preferences:

- **Noun/verb selection.** When you first select objects and then enter a command, it is referred to as the ***noun/verb*** format. The pick box is displayed at the screen crosshairs. A "✓" in this check box means the noun/verb method is active. The **PICKFIRST** system variable can also be used to set the **Noun/verb selection**. When using the ***verb/noun*** format, you enter the command before selecting the object. Remove the "✓" from the **Noun/verb selection** check box to enter the command before making a selection.

> **NOTE**
> Some editing commands, such as **FILLET**, **CHAMFER**, **DIVIDE**, **MEASURE**, **OFFSET**, **EXTEND**, **TRIM**, and **BREAK**, require you to enter the command before you select the object.

- **Use Shift to add to selection.** When this check box is off, every object or group of objects you select is highlighted and added to the selection set. If you pick this check box, it changes the way AutoCAD accepts objects you pick. For example, if you pick an object, it is highlighted and added to the selection set. If you pick another object, however, it is highlighted, and the first one is removed from the

Figure 13-11.
The **Selection Modes** area of the **Selection** tab in the **Options** dialog box.

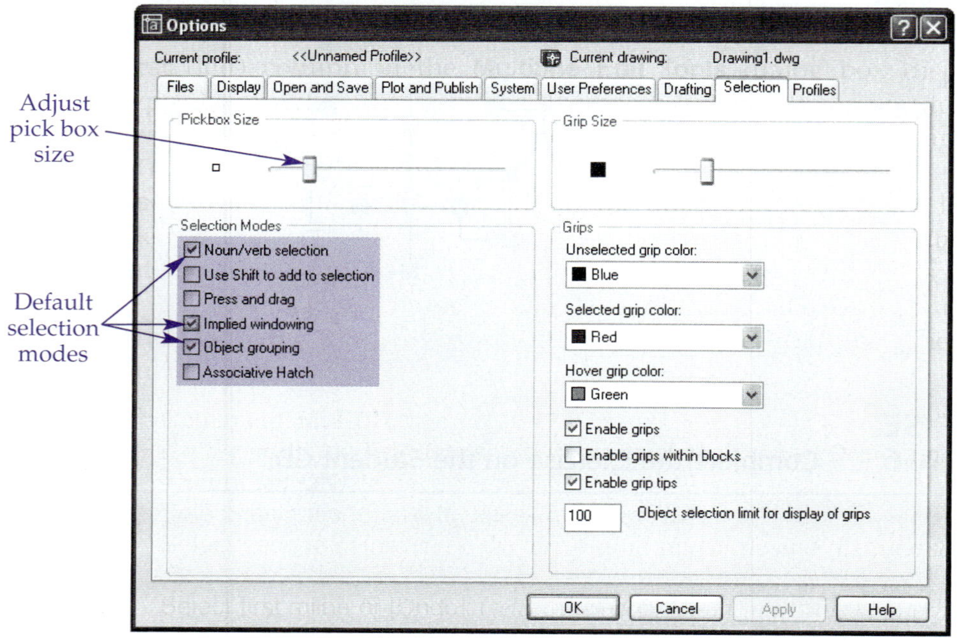

selection set. This means you can only select one object by picking or one group of objects with a selection window. If you want to add more items to the selection set, you must hold down the [Shift] key as you pick them. Turning off the **PICKADD** system variable does the same thing as turning on this feature.

- **Press and drag.** This is the same as turning on the **PICKDRAG** system variable. With **Press and drag** on, you create a selection window by picking the first corner and moving the cursor while holding down the pick button. Release the pick button when you have the desired selection window. By default, this option is off. This means you need to pick both the first and second corners of the desired selection window.
- **Implied windowing.** By default, this option is on. This means you can automatically create a window by picking the first point and moving the cursor to the right to pick the second point, or you can make a crossing box by picking the first point and moving the cursor to the left to pick the second point. This is the same as turning on the **PICKAUTO** system variable. This does not work if **PICKDRAG** is on.
- **Object grouping.** This option controls whether or not AutoCAD recognizes grouped objects as singular objects. When it is off, the individual elements of a group can be selected for separate editing without having to first explode the group.
- **Associative Hatch.** The default is off, which means, if an associative hatch is moved, the hatch boundary does not move with it. Select this toggle if you want the boundary of an associative hatch to move when you move the hatch pattern. It is a good idea to have this on for most applications. Hatches and hatch boundaries are fully explained in Chapter 21.

Using the Properties Window

PROPERTIES
PROPS
CH
MO
[Ctrl]+[1]

Modify
➥ Properties

Standard toolbar

Properties

An object can be edited automatically using the **Properties** window. To edit an object using the **Properties** window, pick the **Properties** button from the **Standard** toolbar; pick **Properties** from the **Modify** pull-down menu; or type MO, CH, PROPS, or PROPERTIES at the Command: prompt. You can also toggle the **Properties** window on and off using the [Ctrl]+[1] key combination. If an object has already been selected, you can also access the **Properties** window by right-clicking and selecting **Properties** from the shortcut menu.

The **Properties** window appears, as shown in **Figure 13-12.** The **Properties** window can be docked in the drawing area, similar to a toolbar. This was discussed in Chapter 1. While the **Properties** window is displayed, you can enter commands and continue to work in AutoCAD. You can close the box by picking the **X** in the top left corner, picking the **Properties** button on the **Modify** toolbar, or using the [Ctrl]+[1] key combination.

When you access the **Properties** window without first selecting an object, No selection can be seen in the top drop-down list. This means AutoCAD does not have any objects selected to modify. The four categories—**General**, **Plot style**, **View**, and **Misc**—list the current settings for the drawing.

Underneath each category is a list of object properties. For example, in **Figure 13-12,** the current color is ByLayer. To change a property, pick the property or its current value. Once the property is highlighted, one of the following methods is used to set the new value:

- A drop-down arrow with a list of values.
- A pick point button, which allows you to pick a new coordinate location.
- A text box, which is opened when you select certain properties, such as the radius of an arc. Entering a new value in this box allows you to change the radius.

Figure 13-12.
The **Properties** window can be used to modify different properties of an object.

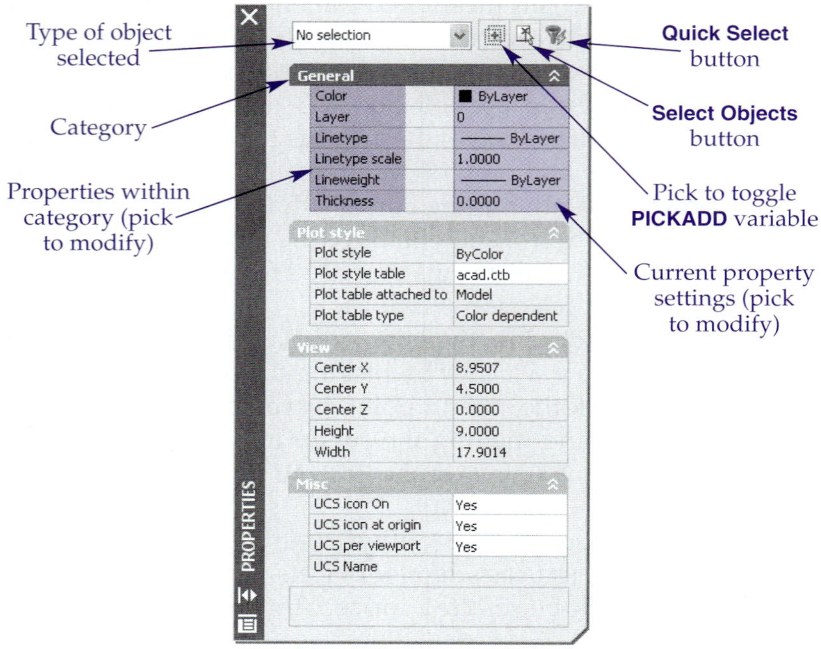

Once a property to be modified has been selected, a description of what that property does is shown at the bottom of the dialog box.

In the upper-right portion of the **Properties** window are three buttons. Pick the **Quick Select** button to access the **Quick Select** dialog box, where you can create object selection sets. This dialog box is discussed in Chapter 7. Picking the **Select Objects** button deselects the currently selected objects and changes the crosshairs to a pick box. The third button toggles the value of the **PICKADD** system variable, which determines whether or not you need to hold the [Shift] key when adding objects to a selection set.

Modifying an Object Using the Properties Window

The previous discussion introduced you to the **Properties** window. The following explains how to change object properties in the **Properties** window. In order to modify an object, the **Properties** window must be open, and an object must be selected. For example, if a circle and a line are drawn and you need to modify the circle, first pick on the circle to make the grips appear, and then use one of the methods to open the **Properties** window.

The **Properties** window displays the categories that can be modified for the circle. All objects have a **General** category. The **General** category allows you to modify properties such as color, layer, linetype, linetype scale, plot style, lineweight, hyperlink, and thickness. For example, do the following to change the color of the circle:

1. Select the **Color** property in the window by picking on the word **Color**. A drop-down arrow appears to the right of the current color.
2. Select the drop-down arrow, and a list of available colors appears.
3. Select the new color. If the desired color is not on the list, select **Select color...** from the bottom of the list. This displays the **Select Color** dialog box, from which a color can be selected.

Once a color has been selected, the **Properties** window displays the current color for the circle.

A description of each of the properties in the **General** category follows:

- **Color.** Pick this property to display a drop-down arrow from which a color can be selected. At the bottom of the drop-down list is the **Select Color...** option, which displays the **Select Color** dialog box showing all the colors available.

- **Layer.** Select the desired layer for the object here. Layers are discussed in Chapter 4.
- **Linetype.** Select the desired linetype for the object.
- **Linetype scale.** To change the individual object's linetype, highlight the value and type a new scale value. The linetype scale for an individual object is a multiplier of the **LTSCALE** system variable. This was discussed in Chapter 4.
- **Plot style.** Picking on this property displays a drop-down arrow with various plot styles. Initially, only one style is available: ByColor. In order to create a list of plot styles, you must create a plot style table. Plotting and plot styles are discussed in Chapter 11.
- **Lineweight.** Select the desired lineweight for the object. Lineweights are discussed in Chapter 4.
- **Hyperlink.** Picking on this property displays a **...** (ellipsis) button. By selecting this button, you can access the **Insert Hyperlink** dialog box. Use this dialog box to add a hyperlink to a graphical object or a description or URL address to an object.
- **Thickness.** This property allows you to change the thickness of a 3D object in a text box.

As stated earlier, all objects have a **General** category. Depending on the type of object that has been selected to modify, other categories are also displayed. See **Figure 13-13.** One of the most common categories is **Geometry**. Although most objects have a **Geometry** category, the properties within the categories vary, depending on the type of object. Typically, there are three properties that allow you to change the absolute coordinates for the object by specifying the X, Y, and Z coordinates. Pick one of these properties, and a pick button is displayed. The button allows you to pick a point in your drawing for the new location. In addition to the pick button, the value for the coordinate can also be changed in a text box.

When multiple objects are selected, you can use the **Properties** window to modify all the objects, or you can pick only one of the selected objects to be modified. The drop-down list displays the types of objects selected. See **Figure 13-14.** Select All to change the properties of all selected objects. Only properties shared by all selected objects are displayed when All is selected. To modify only one object, select the appropriate object type.

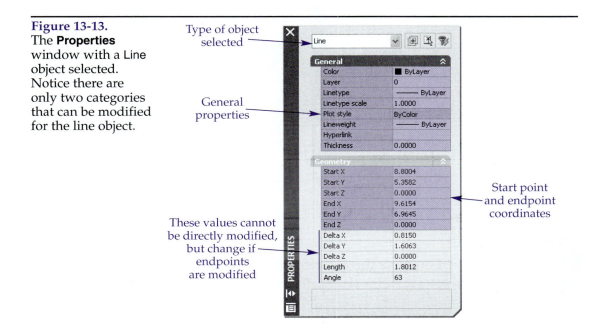

Figure 13-13.
The **Properties** window with a Line object selected. Notice there are only two categories that can be modified for the line object.

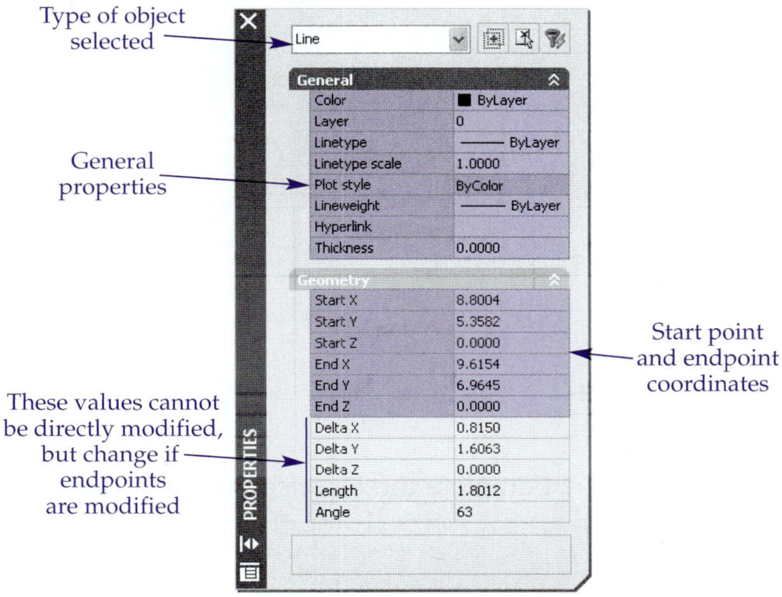

Figure 13-14.
The **Properties** window with three objects selected. You can edit the objects individually or all together by selecting All (3).

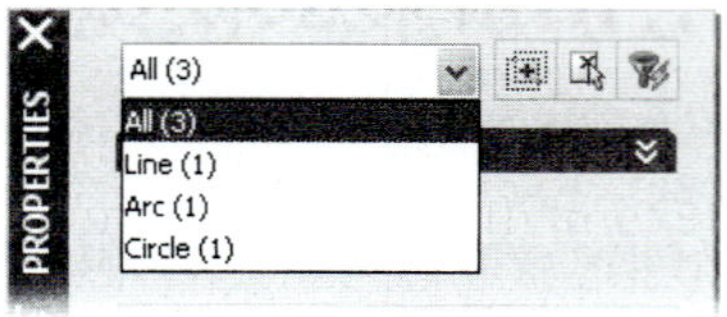

When all the changes to the object have been made, press the [Esc] button on the keyboard to clear the grips and remove the object from the **Properties** window. The object is now displayed in the drawing window with the desired changes. For example, if you select a circle, two categories appear in the **Properties** window—**General** and **Geometry**. See Figure 13-15. The **Geometry** category displays the current location of the center of the circle by showing three properties: **Center X**, **Center Y**, and **Center Z**. To choose a new center location for the circle, select the appropriate property. Pick a new point or type the coordinate values. There are also other properties that can be modified for the circle, such as the **Radius**, **Diameter**, **Circumference**, and **Area**. By changing any of these values, you are modifying the size of the circle.

> **NOTE**
>
> The **Properties** window is discussed where appropriate throughout this text.

Figure 13-15.
The **Properties** window with a Circle object selected for editing.

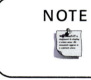

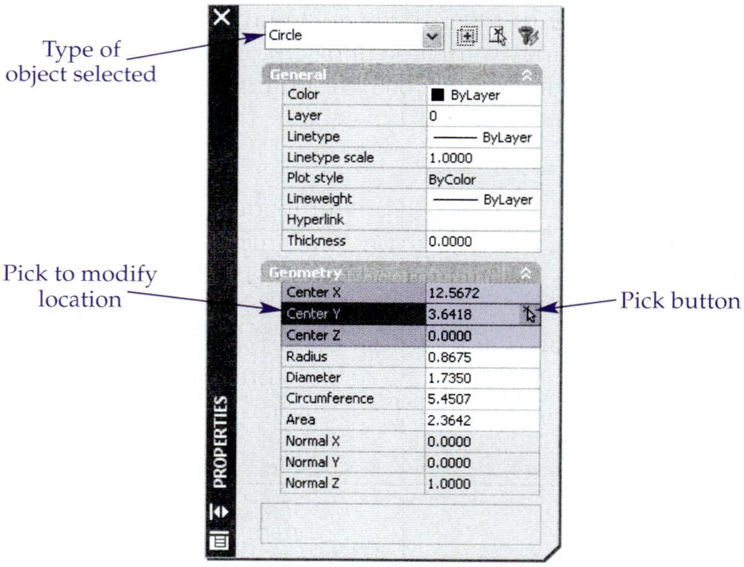

EXERCISE 13-7 Complete the Exercise on the Student CD.

Changing the Properties of an Object at the Command: Prompt

Object properties can be changed at the Command: prompt using the **CHANGE** and **CHPROP** commands. Select the **Properties** option of the **CHANGE** command, as follows:

Command: **-CH** *or* **CHANGE**↵
Select objects: *(pick the object)*
n found
Select objects: ↵
Specify change point or [Properties]: **P**↵
Enter property to change
  [Color/Elev/LAyer/LType/ltScale/LWeight/Thickness/Plotstyle]:

The following properties can be changed with the **CHANGE** command:

- **Color.** Changes the color of the selected object.
- **Elevation.** Changes the elevation in 3D drawings.
- **Layer.** Changes the layer designation.
- **Linetype.** Changes the current linetype of a selected object to a linetype that has been loaded using the **LINETYPE** command.
- **Linetype scale.** Changes the individual object's linetype scale.
- **Lineweight.** Changes the individual object's lineweight.
- **Thickness.** Changes the thickness in 3D drawings.
- **Plot style.** Changes the named plot style for the object. This option is not available in drawings using color-dependent plot styles.

The **CHPROP** (change property) command lets you change only properties of an object. It does not allow for a point change, as does the **CHANGE** command. This is the command sequence for **CHPROP**:

Command: **CHPROP**↵
Select objects: *(pick the object)*
n found
Select objects: ↵
Enter property to change [Color/LAyer/LType/ltScale/LWeight/Thickness/Plotstyle]:

Except for **Elevation**, the **CHPROP** options are the same as those discussed for the **CHANGE** command.

EXERCISE 13-8 Complete the Exercise on the Student CD.

Editing between Multiple Drawings

One of the advantages of AutoCAD is the capability of editing in more than one drawing at a time. This allows you to copy objects from one drawing to another drawing. You can also refer to another drawing to obtain information (such as a distance) while working in a different drawing.

To take a look at how this works, use the **OPEN** command to first open EX13-7. Use the **OPEN** command again to open EX13-8. Two drawings have now been opened in AutoCAD. In the **Window** pull-down menu, pick **Tile Horizontally**. This "tiles" the two open drawings. See **Figure 13-16.**

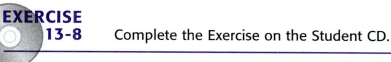

Figure 13-16.
Multiple drawings can be tiled to make editing easier.

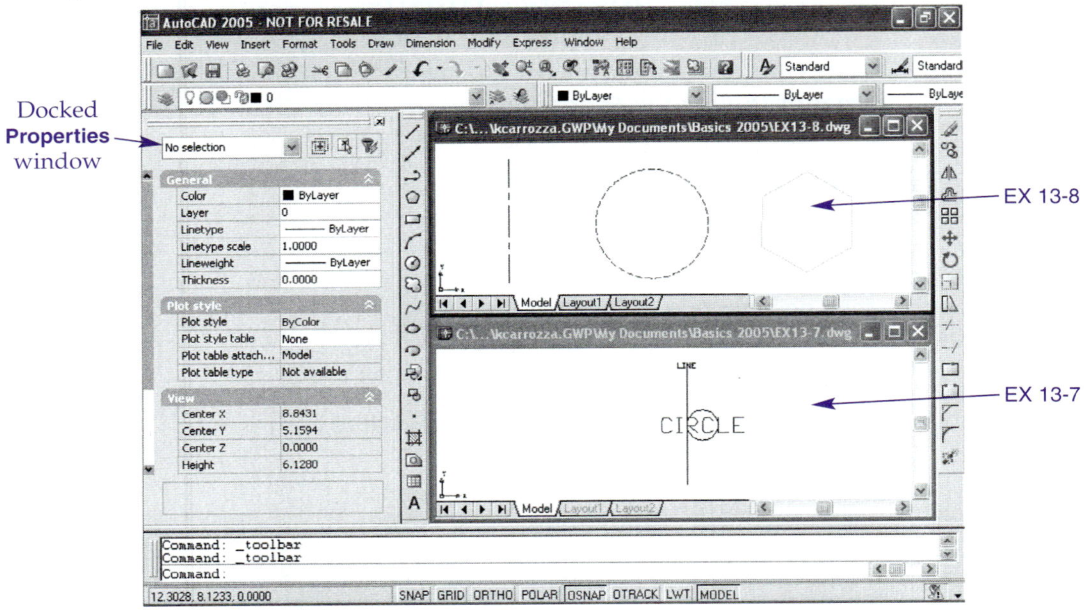

NOTE The Multiple Design Environment (MDE) is discussed in more detail in Chapter 2.

Copying Objects between Drawings

The Windows function ***copy and paste*** is used to copy an object from one drawing to another. To use this feature in AutoCAD, the object you intend to copy must be selected with grips. For example, if you want to copy the circle from drawing EX13-8 to drawing EX13-7, you would first select the circle. Once the circle is selected, right-click to get the shortcut menu shown in Figure 13-17. The shortcut menu has two options allowing you to copy to the Windows Clipboard:

- **Copy.** This option takes selected objects from AutoCAD and places them on the Windows Clipboard to be used in another application or AutoCAD drawing.

Figure 13-17.
Right-click to access this shortcut menu to select one of the copy options.

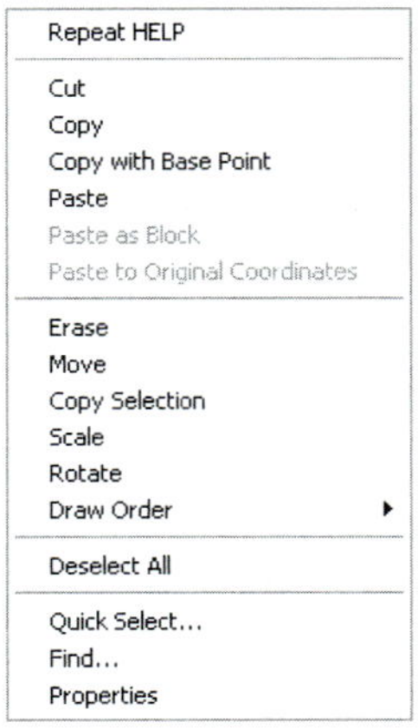

- **Copy with Base Point.** This option also copies the selected objects to the Clipboard, but it allows you to specify a base point to position the copied object when it is pasted. When using this option, AutoCAD prompts you to select a base point. Select a logical base point, such as a corner or center point of the object.

Once you have selected one of the two copy options, make the second drawing active by picking inside of it. Right-click, and a shortcut menu is displayed, as shown in Figure 13-18. Notice the copy options remain available, but three paste options are now available below the copy options. The paste options are only available if there is something on the Clipboard. The three options are described below:

- **Paste.** This option pastes any information from the Clipboard into the current drawing. If the **Copy with Base Point** option was used to place objects in the Clipboard, the objects being pasted are attached to the crosshairs at the specified base point.
- **Paste as Block.** This option "joins" all objects in the Clipboard when they are pasted into the drawing. The pasted objects act like a block in that they are single objects joined together to form one object. Blocks are covered in Chapter 22. Use the **EXPLODE** command to get the objects to act individually again.
- **Paste to Original Coordinates.** This option pastes the objects from the Clipboard to the same coordinates at which they were located in the original drawing.

You can also copy objects between drawings using a drag-and-drop operation. To do so, first open both drawings and arrange their windows so they are both visible in the drawing area. Select the object to be copied, and then press and hold the pick button. Move the cursor into the other drawing and release the pick button. The object is automatically copied into the second drawing.

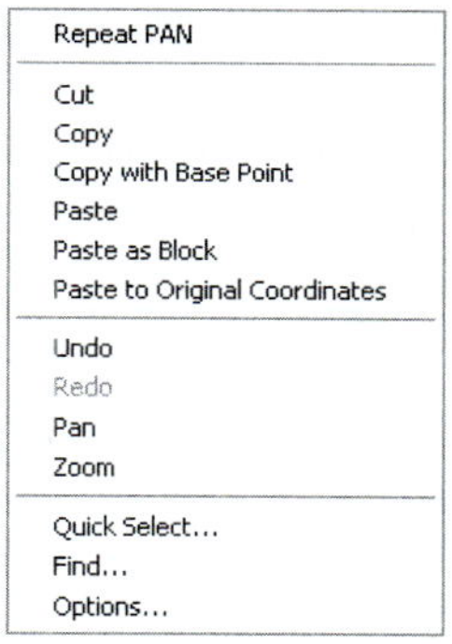

Figure 13-18.
Right-click to access this shortcut menu and select one of the paste options to paste an object from the Clipboard to a drawing.

EXERCISE 13-9 Complete the Exercise on the Student CD.

Matching Properties

MATCHPROP
MA
PAINTER

Modify
➥ Match Properties

Standard toolbar

Match Properties

The **MATCHPROP** command allows you to copy properties from one object to one or more objects. This can be done in the same drawing or between drawings. To access the **MATCHPROP** command, select the **Match Properties** button from the **Standard** toolbar; select **Match Properties** from the **Modify** pull-down menu; or enter MA, MATCHPROP, or PAINTER at the Command: prompt. The following is the prompt sequence:

Command: **MA**, **MATCHPROP**, *or* **PAINTER**↲
Select source object: *(pick the object with the properties you want to paint)*

When you first access the **MATCHPROP** command, AutoCAD prompts you for the source object. The source object is the object with all the properties you would like to copy to another object or series of objects. Once the source object has been selected, AutoCAD displays the properties it will paint to the destination object. The next prompt reads:

Select destination object(s) or [Settings]:

This allows you to pick the objects you want to receive the properties of the source object. If you want the properties painted to all objects in the drawing, type ALL at this prompt.

To change the properties to be painted, access the **Settings** option by typing S and pressing [Enter], as follows:

Select destination object(s) or [Settings]: **S**↲

The **Property Settings** dialog box now appears, showing the types of properties that can be painted. See **Figure 13-19.** The following describes the major areas of the **Property Settings** dialog box:

- **Basic Properties.** This area lists the general properties of the selected object. If you do not want the property to be copied, deselect the appropriate check box. All active properties will be transferred to the destination objects.
- **Special Properties.** In addition to general properties, you can also paint over dimension styles, text styles, and hatch patterns. These properties are replaced in the destination object if these check boxes are active.

For example, if you want to paint only the color property and text style of one text object to another text object, uncheck all boxes except the **Color** and **Text** property check boxes.

NOTE

To use the **MATCHPROP** command between drawings, select the source object from one drawing and the destination object from another.

PROFESSIONAL TIP

Use the **Partial Open** option in the **OPEN** command to partially open existing drawings to be used as source objects for copying or property matching. **Partial Open** is discussed in Chapter 2.

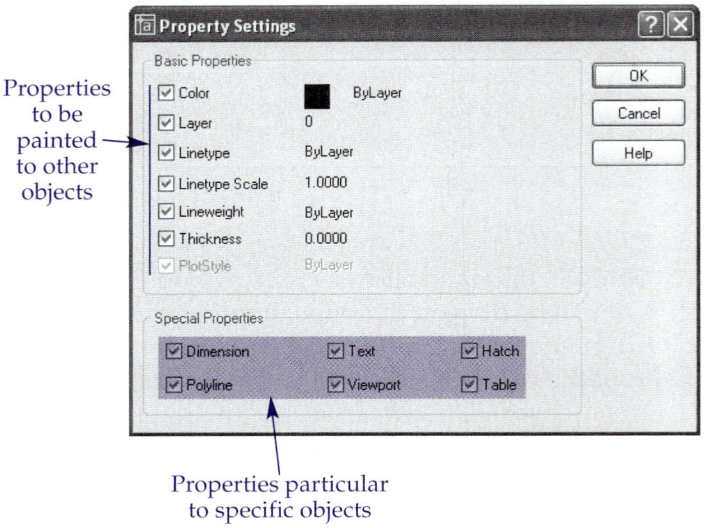

Figure 13-19. The **Property Settings** dialog box for the **MATCHPROP** command. Select the properties to paint onto a new object.

EXERCISE 13-10 Complete the Exercise on the Student CD.

Chapter Test

Answer the following questions on a separate sheet of paper.

1. Name the editing commands that can be accessed automatically using grips.
2. Identify two ways to access the **Options** dialog box.
3. Explain two ways to change the pick box size.
4. What is the purpose of the **Selection** tab found in the **Options** dialog box?
5. Name the three system variables controlling the color of grips.
6. How do you turn grips on and off?
7. When grips are active, how do you cycle through the available automatic commands?
8. How do you access the grips shortcut menu?
9. What is the purpose of the **Base Point** option in the grips shortcut menu?
10. Explain the function of the **Undo** option in the grips shortcut menu.
11. Describe the purpose of the **Properties** option in the grips shortcut menu.
12. What happens when you choose the **Exit** option from the grips shortcut menu?
13. Which option of the automatic **ROTATE** command would you use to rotate an object from an existing 60° angle to a new 25° angle?
14. What scale factor is used to scale an object to become three-quarters of its original size?
15. Name the system variable allowing you to set the "noun/verb" selection.
16. Explain the difference between "noun/verb" selection and "verb/noun" selection.
17. What does **Use Shift to add to selection** mean?
18. Describe how the **Press and drag** option works.
19. Name the system variable used to turn on the **Press and drag** option.
20. Name the system variable that turns on the **Implied windowing** option.
21. Identify the pull-down menu and the item you pick from this menu to access the **Properties** window.
22. How do you change the color of an object using the **Properties** window?
23. How would you change the linetype of an object using the **Properties** window?
24. How do you change existing text reading AutoCAD to read AutoCAD 2005 by using the **Properties** window?
25. Explain how you would change the radius of a circle from 1.375 to 1.875 using the **Properties** window.
26. Name the command used at the Command: prompt to change only the properties of an object.
27. Name the command allowing you to change the location of an object or object properties at the Command: prompt.
28. Name the option used to have a group of objects joined as a block when they are pasted.
29. When you use the option described in Question 28, how do you separate the objects back into individual objects?
30. What command is used to quickly change the properties of objects to match the properties of a different object?

Drawing Problems

Use templates as appropriate for each of the following problems. Use grips and the associated editing commands or other editing techniques discussed in this chapter.

1. Draw the objects labeled *A*, below, and then use the **STRETCH** command to make them look like the objects labeled *B*. Do not include dimensions. Save the drawing as P13-1.

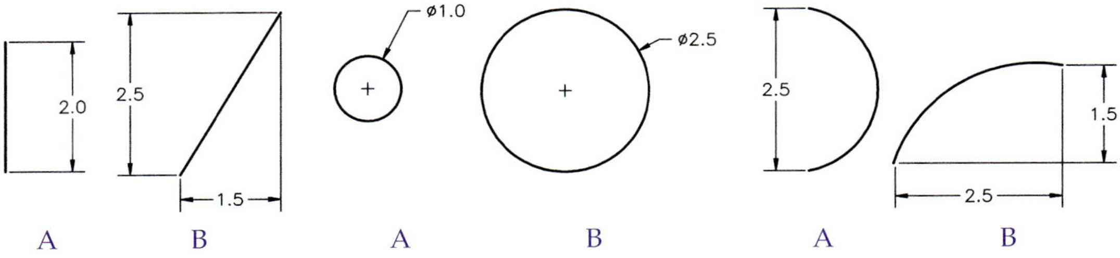

2. Draw the object labeled *A*, below. Using the **Copy** option of the **MOVE** command, copy the object to the position labeled *B*. Edit Object A so it resembles Object C. Edit Object B so it looks like Object D. Do not include dimensions. Save the drawing as P13-2.

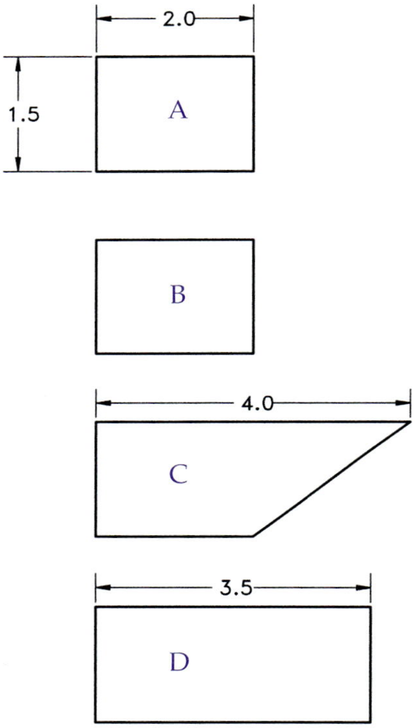

3. Draw the object labeled *A*, below. Copy the object, without rotating it, to a position below, as indicated by the dashed lines. Rotate the object 45°. Copy the rotated object labeled *B* to a position below, as indicated by the dashed lines. Use the **Reference** option to rotate the object labeled *C* to 25°, as shown. Do not include dimensions. Save the drawing as P13-3.

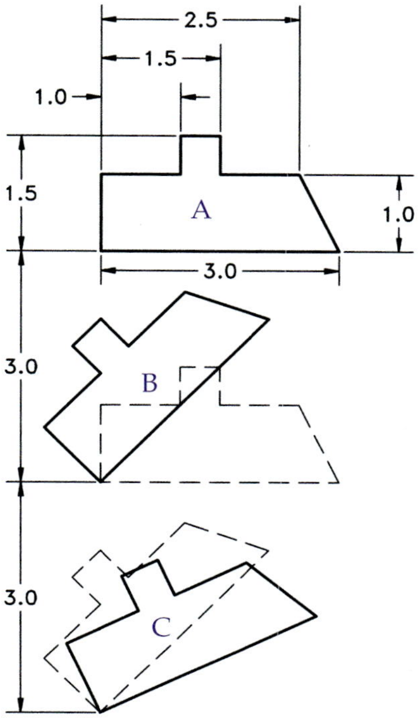

4. Draw the individual objects (vertical line, horizontal line, circle, arc, and C shape) in A, below, using the dimensions given. Use grips and the editing commands to create the object shown in B. Do not include dimensions. Save the drawing as P13-4.

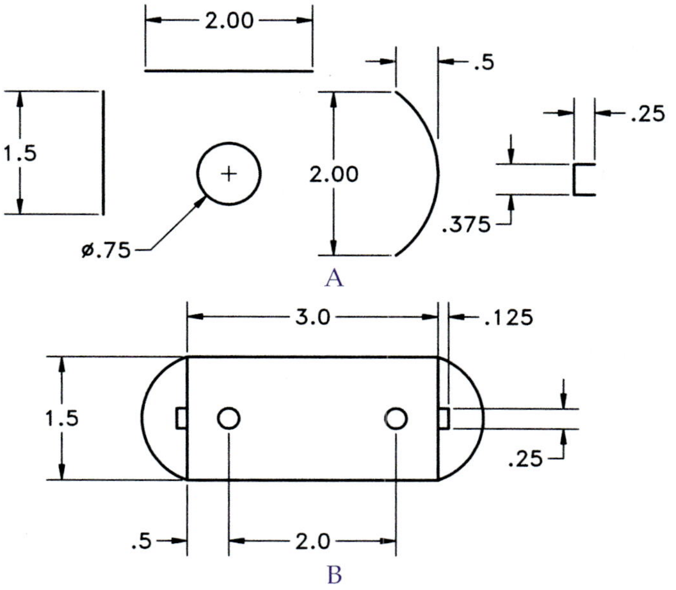

Drawing Problems - Chapter 13

5. Use the completed drawing from Problem 13-4. Erase everything except the completed object and move it to a position similar to A, below. Copy the object two times to positions B and C. Use the automatic **SCALE** command to scale the object in position B to 50 percent of its original size. Use the **Reference** option of the **SCALE** command to enlarge the object in position C from the existing 3.0 length to a 4.5 length, as shown in C. Do not include dimensions. Save as P13-5.

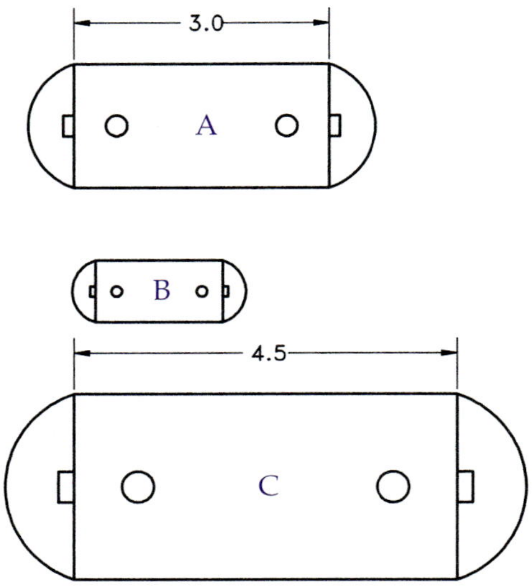

6. Draw the dimensioned partial object shown in A. Do not include dimensions. Mirror the drawing to complete the four quadrants, as shown in B. Change the color of the horizontal and vertical parting lines to red and the linetype to CENTER. Save the drawing as P13-6.

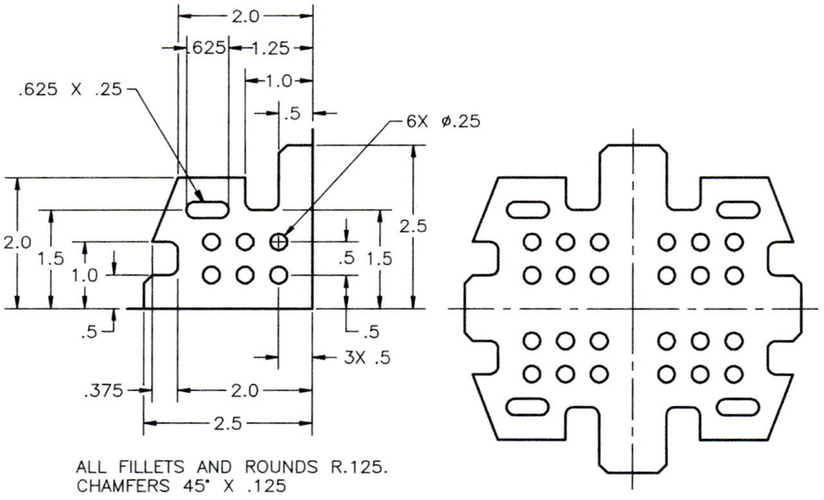

A B

7. Load the final drawing you created in Problem 13-6. Use the **Properties** window to change the diameters of the circles from .25 to .125. Change the linetype of the slots to PHANTOM. Be sure the linetype scale allows the linetypes to be displayed. Save the drawing as P13-7.

8. Use the editing commands discussed in this chapter to assist you in drawing the following object. Draw the object within the boundaries of the given dimensions. All other dimensions are flexible. Do not include dimensions in the drawing. Save the drawing as P13-8.

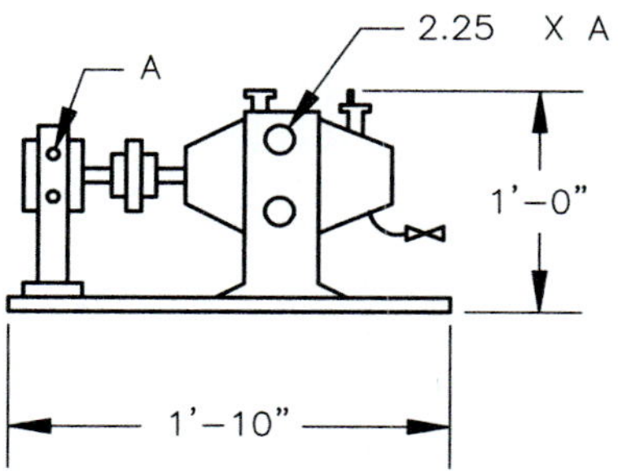

9. Draw the following object within the boundaries of the given dimensions. All other dimensions are flexible. Do not include dimensions. After drawing the object, create a page for a vendor catalog, as follows:
   - All labels should be ROMAND text, centered directly below the view. Use a text height of .125″.
   - Label the drawing ONE-GALLON TANK WITH HORIZONTAL VALVE.
   - Keep the valve the same scale as the original drawing in each copy.
   - Copy the original tank to a new location and scale it so it is 2 times its original size. Rotate the valve 45°. Label this tank TWO-GALLON TANK WITH 45° VALVE.
   - Copy the original tank to another location and scale it so it is 2.5 times the size of the original. Rotate the valve 90°. Label this tank TWO- AND ONE-HALF GALLON TANK WITH 90° VALVE.
   - Copy the two-gallon tank to a new position and scale it so it is 2 times this size. Rotate the valve to 22°30′. Label this tank FOUR-GALLON TANK WITH 22°30′ VALVE.
   - Left-justify this note at the bottom of the page: Combinations of tank size and valve orientation are available upon request.
   - Use the **Properties** window to change all tank labels to ROMANC, .25″ high.
   - Change the note at the bottom of the sheet to ROMANS, centered on the sheet, using uppercase letters.
   - Save the drawing as P13-9.

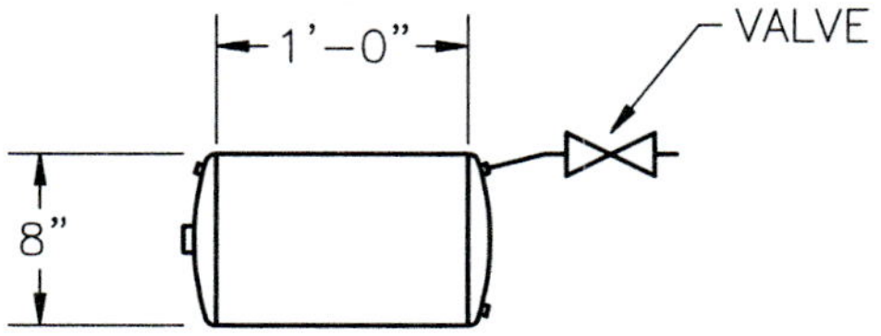

Drawing Problems - Chapter 13

Elevation section. (Steve D. Bloedel)

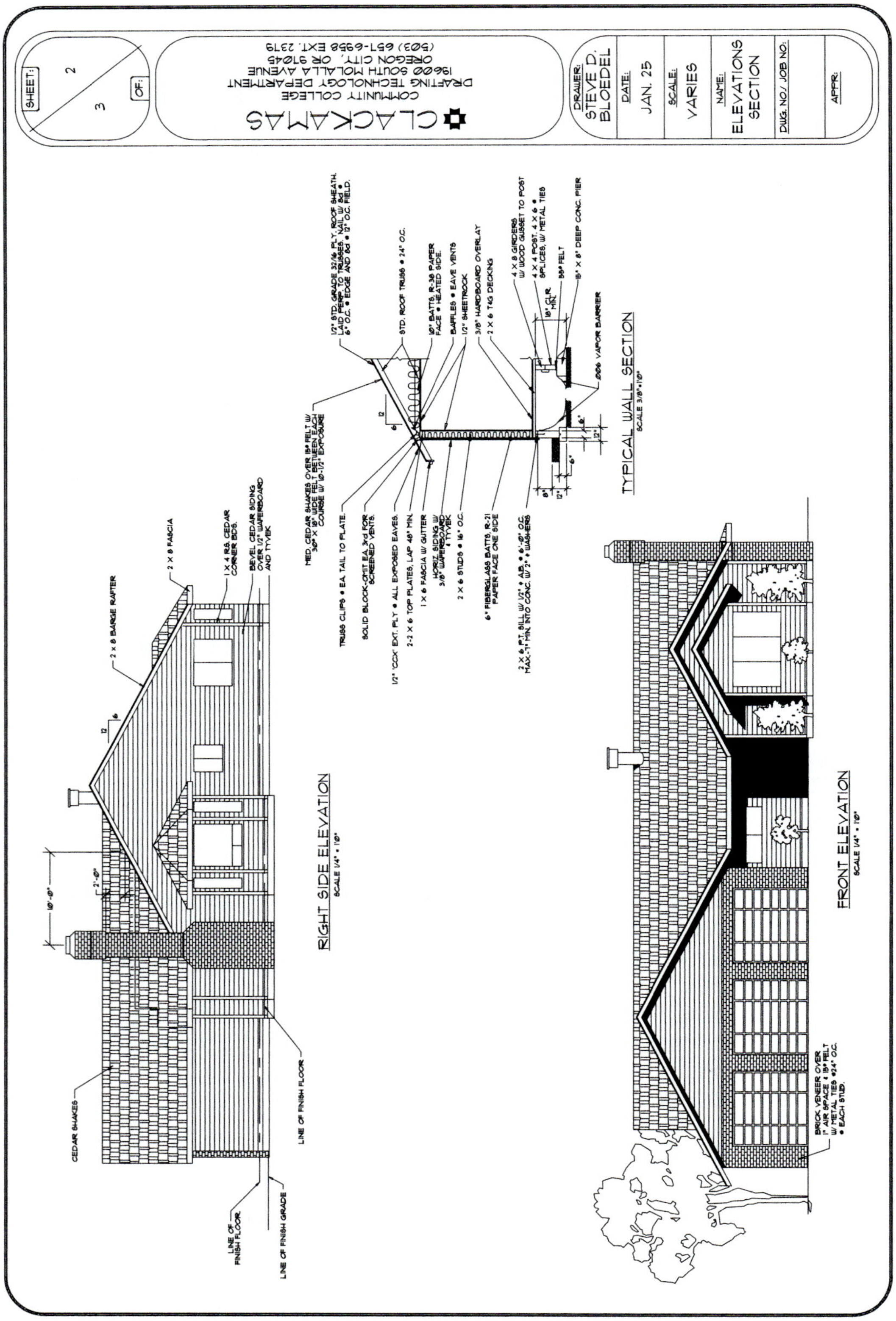

CHAPTER 14

Introduction to Polylines and Multilines

Learning Objectives

After completing this chapter, you will be able to do the following:

- Use the **PLINE** command to draw polyline objects.
- Draw objects with the **TRACE** command.
- Explain the functions of the **UNDO** and **REDO** commands.
- Compare the results of using the **FILL** mode on and off.
- Use the **MLINE** command to draw multilines.
- Create your own multiline styles with the **MLSTYLE** command.
- Edit multiline intersections, corners, and vertices.
- Perform drawing tasks with the **SKETCH** command.

Polylines and multilines are two AutoCAD features that provide you with special line creation abilities. This chapter introduces you to the use of polylines and fully explains how to create drawing features with multilines. You will also learn how to sketch freehand with AutoCAD. A complete discussion of drawing polyline arcs and editing polylines is provided in Chapter 15.

The term *polyline* is composed of the words "poly" and "line." ***Poly*** means *many.* A ***polyline*** is a single object that can be made up of one or more line segments. Each line segment can vary in width. Polylines are drawn with the **PLINE** command and its various options. The **TRACE** command is similar to the **PLINE** command and also introduced in this chapter.

Multilines are combinations of parallel lines consisting of individual lines called ***elements.*** Multilines can have up to 16 individual line elements. You can offset the elements as needed to create a desired pattern for any field of drafting (for example, architectural, schematic, or mechanical drafting). Multilines are drawn using the **MLINE** command and its options.

Introduction to Drawing Polylines

The **PLINE** command is used to draw polylines and any related objects made up of line segments. Polylines have advantages over normal lines because they:

- Can be drawn as thick or tapered lines.
- Have much more flexibility than lines drawn with the **TRACE** command.

- Can be used with any linetype.
- Can be edited using advanced editing features.
- Can be drawn as closed polygons.
- Have an area and perimeter that can be determined easily.
- Can be used to draw a single object comprised of arcs and straight lines of varying thickness.

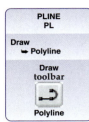

PLINE
PL

Draw
➥ Polyline

Draw toolbar

Polyline

The function of the **PLINE** command is similar to the function of the **LINE** command. However, there are additional command options. Also, all segments of a polyline are treated as a single object. To draw a polyline, you can pick the **Polyline** button on the **Draw** toolbar, pick **Polyline** from the **Draw** pull-down menu, or type PL or PLINE at the Command: prompt:

> Command: **PL** *or* **PLINE**↵
> Specify start point: *(select a point)*
> Current line-width is 0.0000
> Specify next point or [Arc/Halfwidth/Length/Undo/Width]: *(select the next point)*

A line width of 0.0000 produces a line of minimum width. If this is acceptable, select the endpoint of the line segment. If additional line segments are drawn, the endpoint of the first line segment automatically becomes the starting point of the next line segment. When you are done drawing line segments, press [Enter] or [Esc] to end the **PLINE** command and return to the Command: prompt.

Setting the Polyline Width

If it is necessary to change the width of a line segment, enter the **PLINE** command and select the first point. Then, use the Width option:

> Command: **PL** *or* **PLINE**↵
> Specify start point: *(select a point)*
> Current line-width is 0.0000
> Specify next point or [Arc/Halfwidth/Length/Undo/Width]: **W**↵

When the **Width** option is selected, you are asked to specify the starting and ending widths of the line. The starting width value becomes the default setting for the ending width. Therefore, to draw a line segment with one width, press [Enter] at the second prompt. If a tapered line segment is desired, enter different values for the starting and ending widths. After the widths are specified, the rubberband line from the first point reflects the width settings.

The following command sequence draws the line segment shown in **Figure 14-1.** Notice that the starting and ending points of the line are located at the center of the line segment's width.

> Command: **PL** *or* **PLINE**↵
> Specify start point: **4,4**↵
> Current line-width is 0.0000
> Specify next point or [Arc/Halfwidth/Length/Undo/Width]: **W**↵
> Specify starting width <0.0000>: **.25**↵
> Specify ending width <0.2500>: ↵
> Specify next point or [Arc/Halfwidth/Length/Undo/Width]: **8,4**↵
> Specify next point or [Arc/Close/Halfwidth/Length/Undo/Width]: ↵
> Command:

Figure 14-1.
A thick polyline drawn using the **Width** option of the **PLINE** command.

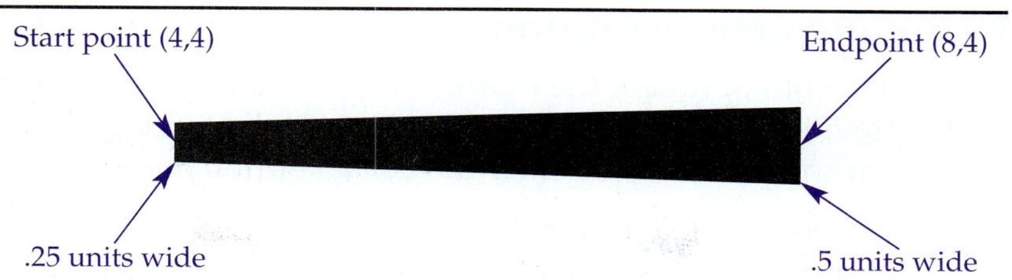

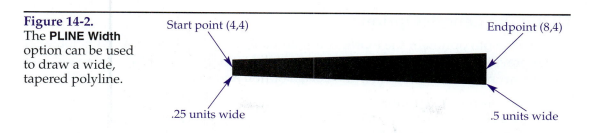

Figure 14-2.
The **PLINE Width** option can be used to draw a wide, tapered polyline.

Drawing a Tapered Polyline

By entering different starting and ending width values, a tapered polyline is drawn, **Figure 14-2.** In the following example, the starting width is .25 units, and the ending width is .5 units:

Command: **PL** *or* **PLINE**↵
Specify start point: **4,4**↵
Current line-width is 0.0000
Specify next point or [Arc/Halfwidth/Length/Undo/Width]: **W**↵
Specify starting width <0.0000>: **.25**↵
Specify ending width <0.2500>: **.5**↵
Specify next point or [Arc/Halfwidth/Length/Undo/Width]: **8,4**↵
Specify next point or [Arc/Close/Halfwidth/Length/Undo/Width]: ↵
Command:

The **Width** option of the **PLINE** command can be used to draw an arrowhead. To do so, specify 0 as the starting width and then use any desired ending width.

Using the Halfwidth Option

The **Halfwidth** option of the **PLINE** command allows you to specify the width of the polyline from the center to one side. After picking the first point of the polyline, enter the Halfwidth option. Then, specify starting and ending values. Notice that the polyline in **Figure 14-3** is twice as wide as the polyline in **Figure 14-2** even though the same width values are entered.

Specify next point or [Arc/Halfwidth/Length/Undo/Width]: **H**↵
Specify starting half-width <0.0000>: **.25**↵
Specify ending half-width <0.2500>: **.5**↵

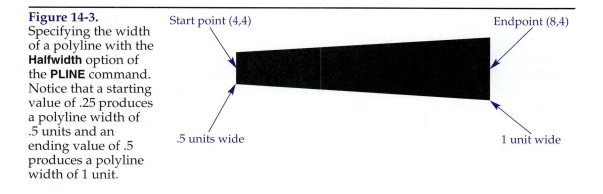

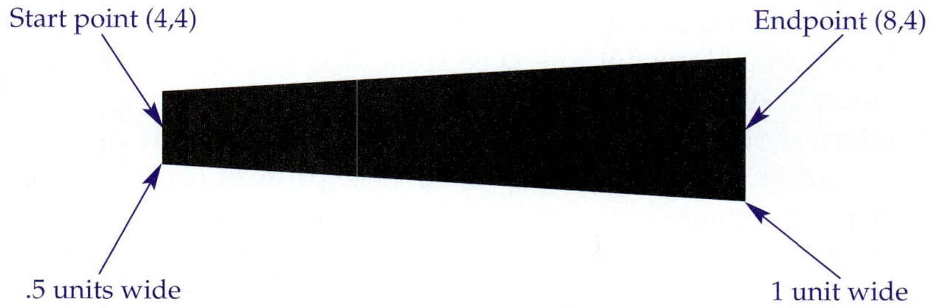

Figure 14-3.
Specifying the width of a polyline with the **Halfwidth** option of the **PLINE** command. Notice that a starting value of .25 produces a polyline width of .5 units and an ending value of .5 produces a polyline width of 1 unit.

Using the Length Option

The **Length** option of the **PLINE** command allows you to draw a polyline parallel to the previous polyline. After drawing a polyline, reissue the **PLINE** command and pick a starting point. Then, enter the Length option and give the desired length:

Command: **PL** *or* **PLINE**↵
Specify start point: *(pick the starting point for the first polyline)*
Current line-width is 0.0000
Specify next point or [Arc/Halfwidth/Length/Undo/Width]: *(pick the endpoint for the first polyline)*
Specify next point or [Arc/Close/Halfwidth/Length/Undo/Width]: ↵
Command: ↵
PLINE
Specify start point: *(pick a starting point for the second polyline)*
Current line-width is 0.0000
Specify next point or [Arc/Halfwidth/Length/Undo/Width]: **L**↵
Specify length of line: *(enter or pick any desired length for the second polyline)*
Specify next point or [Arc/Close/Halfwidth/Length/Undo/Width]: ↵
Command:

The second polyline is drawn parallel to the previous polyline with the length you specified.

Undoing Previously Drawn Polylines

While inside the **PLINE** command, you can use the **Undo** option of the command to erase the last line segment. To do so, type U on the prompt line and press [Enter]. Each time you use the **Undo** option, another line segment is erased. The segments are removed in reverse order (from the order in which they were drawn). This is a quick way to go back and correct the polyline while remaining in the **PLINE** command.

Specify next point or [Arc/Close/Halfwidth/Length/Undo/Width]: **U**↵
Specify next point or [Arc/Close/Halfwidth/Length/Undo/Width]:

After you press [Enter], the last polyline segment drawn is automatically removed. The rubberband is attached to the end of the line segment that was drawn before the undone segment. You can now continue to draw additional line segments or undo another segment. You can use the **Undo** option to remove all of the polyline segments up to the first point of the polyline. You cannot, however, specify a new first point for the polyline.

The **U** command (*not* the **Undo** option of the **PLINE** command) is also used to undo actions. However, the **U** command is used to undo the actions of the previous command. After a command has been completed, pick the **Undo** button on the **Standard** toolbar, pick **Undo** from the **Edit** pull-down menu, press the [Ctrl]+[Z] key combination, or type U at the Command: prompt and press [Enter]. The **U** command can also be activated by right-clicking in the drawing area and selecting **Undo** from the shortcut menu. AutoCAD indicates which command was undone on the prompt line:

U
[Ctrl]+[Z]

Edit
➥ **Undo**

Standard
toolbar

Undo

Command: **U**↵
PLINE
Command:

In this example, the **PLINE** command was the last command. Therefore, it was the command whose actions were undone. You can reissue the **U** command to continue undoing commands. However, you can only undo one command at a time and they must be undone in the order in which they were used. The **UNDO** command has a number of options not available with the **U** command, including the ability to undo more than one command. The **UNDO** command is discussed later in this chapter.

EXERCISE 14-1 Complete the Exercise on the Student CD.

Drawing Thick Lines Using the TRACE Command

TRACE

When it is necessary to draw wide lines, the **TRACE** command can be used instead of the **PLINE** command. To use the **TRACE** command, type TRACE at the Command: prompt. Then, specify the trace width and select points as you would with the **LINE** command. The current trace width is stored in the **TRACEWID** system variable.

Command: **TRACE**↵
Specify trace width <*current*>: *(enter width)*
Specify start point: *(select start point)*
Specify next point: *(select second point)*
Specify next point: *(select additional points or press* [Enter] *to complete)*
Command:

When you use the **TRACE** command, objects are made up of ***trace segments.*** Trace segment ends are mitered to fit the next segment. Therefore, the previous trace segment is not drawn on screen until the next endpoint is specified. There is no close option with the **TRACE** command. Also, all segments drawn with the command must be the same width. However, you can reissue the command and draw new trace segments with a different width. Also, you can edit with grips to create a single segment of varying width.

EXERCISE 14-2 Complete the Exercise on the Student CD.

Using the UNDO Command

UNDO

As mentioned earlier in this chapter, the **UNDO** command is different from the **U** command. The **UNDO** command offers several options that allow you to undo a single command or a number of commands at once. The command sequence is:

Command: **UNDO**↵
Enter the number of operations to undo or [Auto/Control/BEgin/End/Mark/Back] <1>:

The default option allows you to designate the number of previous command sequences you wish to remove. For example, if you enter 1, the previous command sequence is undone. If you enter 2, the previous two command sequences are undone. AutoCAD tells you which commands were undone with a message on the prompt line:

Command: **UNDO**↵
Enter the number of operations to undo or [Auto/Control/BEgin/End/Mark/Back]: **2**↵
PLINE LINE
Command:

UNDO Options

There are several other options for the **UNDO** command. When the **Auto** option is on, any commands that are part of a group and used to perform a single operation are removed together. For example, when a command contains other commands, all of the commands in that group are removed as one single command. The **Auto** option is active by default. If it is turned off, each command in a group of commands is treated individually.

The **Control** option allows you to specify how many of the **UNDO** command options you want active. You can even disable the **UNDO** command altogether. To use the **Control** option, type C after issuing the **UNDO** command:

> Enter the number of operations to undo or [Auto/Control/BEgin/End/Mark/Back]: **C↵**
> Enter an UNDO control option [All/None/One] <All>: *(enter a control option and press* [Enter]*)*

Selecting the **All** suboption keeps the full range of **UNDO** command options active. This is the default setting. The **None** suboption disables the **U** and **UNDO** commands. When the **U** command is entered, the following prompt appears:

> Command: **U↵**
> U command disabled. Use UNDO command to turn it on

This prompt indicates how to reactivate the **U** and **UNDO** commands. If you type UNDO at the Command: prompt, the following appears:

> Command: **UNDO↵**
> Enter an UNDO control option [All/None/One] <All>:

To reactivate all of the **UNDO** options, press [Enter] to accept the default **All**.

The **One** suboption limits **UNDO** to one operation only. When this suboption is active and you issue the **UNDO** command, the following prompt appears:

> Command: **UNDO↵**
> Control/<1>: ↵
> LINE
> Everything has been undone
> Command:

If you attempt to enter a number higher than one, you get an error message. You can type C at the Control/<1>: prompt to display the **Control** suboptions.

PROFESSIONAL TIP

When you use the **UNDO** command, AutoCAD maintains an "undo" file. This file saves previously used **UNDO** commands. All **UNDO** entries saved before disabling **UNDO** with the **Control None** suboption are discarded. This frees up some disk space and may be valuable information for you to keep in mind if you ever get close to having a full disk. If you want to continue using the **U** and **UNDO** commands to some extent, then you might consider using the **UNDO Control One** suboption. This allows you to keep using the **U** and **UNDO** commands to a limited extent while freeing up disk space holding current information about **UNDO**.

The **BEgin** and **End** options of the **UNDO** command are used together to perform several undo operations at once. They allow you to group a series of commands and treat them as a single command. Once the group is defined, the **U** command is then used to remove the commands that follow the **BEgin** option, but precede the **End** option. These options are useful if you can anticipate the possible removal of several commands that are entered consecutively. For example, if you think you may want to undo the next three commands altogether, do the following:

Command: **UNDO**↵
Enter the number of operations to undo or [Auto/Control/BEgin/End/Mark/Back]:
BE↵
Command: **L** *or* **LINE**↵ *(this is the first command in the group)*
Specify first point: *(pick a point)*
Specify next point or [Undo]: *(pick an endpoint)*
Specify next point or [Undo]: ↵
Command: **PL** *or* **PLINE**↵
Specify start point: *(pick a point)*
Current line-width is 0.0000
Specify next point or [Arc/Halfwidth/Length/Undo/Width]: *(pick an endpoint)*
Specify next point or [Arc/Halfwidth/Length/Undo/Width]: ↵
Command: **L** *or* **LINE**↵
Specify first point: *(pick a point)*
Specify next point or [Undo]: *(pick an endpoint)*
Specify next point or [Undo]: ↵ *(this completes the last command in the group)*
Command: **UNDO**↵
Enter the number of operations to undo or [Auto/Control/BEgin/End/Mark/Back]: **E**↵
Command: **U**↵
GROUP
Command:

Since the three commands that were executed between the **BEgin** and **End** options, the **U** command treats them as one command and undoes all three. Note that the **BEgin** option must precede the command sequence and the **End** option must immediately follow the last command in the group to be undone.

The **UNDO Mark** option allows you to insert a marker in the undo file. Then, the **UNDO Back** option undoes all commands issued after the marker was inserted. For example, if you do not want certain work to be undone by the **Back** option, enter the **Mark** option after completing the work:

Command: **UNDO**↵
Enter the number of operations to undo or [Auto/Control/BEgin/End/Mark/Back]: **M**↵
Command:

Now, continue working. To undo all work since the marker was inserted, reissue the **UNDO** command and enter the **Back** option.

Command: **UNDO**↵
Enter the number of operations to undo or [Auto/Control/BEgin/End/Mark/Back]: **B**↵

If no marker has been inserted, everything in the entire drawing is undone. AutoCAD questions your choice:

This will undo everything. OK? <Y>:

If you want everything that you have drawn and edited to be undone, press [Enter]. If not, type N or NO and press [Enter], or press the [Esc] key.

PROFESSIONAL TIP

The **UNDO Mark** option can be used to assist in the design process. For example, if you are working on a project and have completed a portion of the design, you can mark the spot with the **Mark** option and then begin work on the next design phase. If anything goes wrong with this part of the design, you can simply use the **UNDO Back** option to remove everything back to the mark.

CAUTION

Be very careful when using the **UNDO Back** option. Entering this option can undo everything in the entire drawing. You can bring back what you have undone if you use the **REDO** command immediately after using the **UNDO Back** option. If you use any other command, even **REDRAW**, after using **UNDO Back**, the drawing is lost forever. The **REDO** command is explained later in this chapter.

Using the UNDO List

The **UNDO** list allows you to graphically select a number of commands to undo. Using this feature performs the same function as using the **UNDO** command and entering a number. Access the **UNDO** list by picking the down arrow to the right of the **Undo** button on the **Standard** toolbar. A small window containing a sequential list of commands is displayed below the button, Figure 14-4. The first (top) command in the list is the most recent command. Commands must be undone in reverse order. To select a number of commands, move the cursor down. The commands that will be undone are highlighted. To execute the undo operation, pick the last command to undo. All commands executed after the one selected will be undone along with the selected command. Using this list is an easy way to undo back to an exact command without having to figure out how many commands have been issued since.

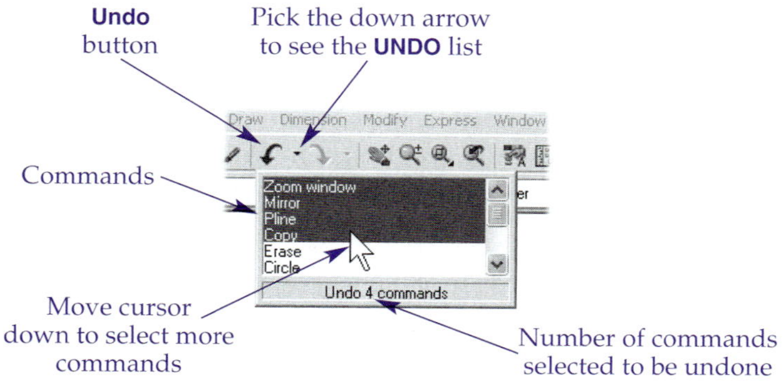

Figure 14-4. The **UNDO** list accessed from the **Standard** toolbar.

Redoing the Undone

REDO
[Ctrl]+[Y]
Edit
➥ Redo
Standard toolbar
Redo

The **REDO** command is used to reverse the action of the **UNDO** and **U** commands. Type REDO at the Command: prompt, pick **Redo** from the **Edit** pull-down menu, press the [Ctrl]+[Y] key combination, or pick the **Redo** button from the **Standard** toolbar to activate the command.

The **REDO** command works only *immediately* after undoing something. **REDO** does *not* bring back polyline segments that were removed using the **Undo** option of the **PLINE** command.

If multiple undos are performed, any or all of the commands that were undone can be redone using the **REDO** list. Pick the down arrow next to the **Redo** button on the **Standard** toolbar. The list window is displayed, which shows the commands that were undone and can be redone. This list functions in the same way as the **UNDO** list discussed earlier.

EXERCISE 14-3 Complete the Exercise on the Student CD.

Filling Polylines and Traces

FILL

In the discussion of the **PLINE** and **TRACE** commands earlier in this chapter, the results were shown as if the objects were solid, or filled in. You can have traces and polylines filled in or you can show them as an outline, Figure 14-5. These functions are controlled by the **FILL** command, which can be either **ON** or **OFF**.

Command: **FILL**↵
Enter mode [ON/OFF] <*current*>:

The current setting is shown in brackets. When **FILL** is on, traces and polylines appear filled after they are drawn. When **FILL** is off, traces and polylines appear as outlines and the corners are mitered. The **REGEN** command is used to display traces and polylines with the new setting.

OPTIONS
OP
Tools
➥ Options...

The **FILL** mode can also be set with the **Apply solid fill** check box in the **Options** dialog box. The check box is located in the **Display performance** area of the **Display** tab. When checked, **FILL** is on.

PROFESSIONAL TIP

When there are many wide polylines or traces in a drawing, it is best to have **FILL** turned off. This saves time when redrawing, regenerating, or plotting a check copy of the drawing. Turn **FILL** on for the final plotting.

Figure 14-5.
Examples of **FILL** mode on and off.

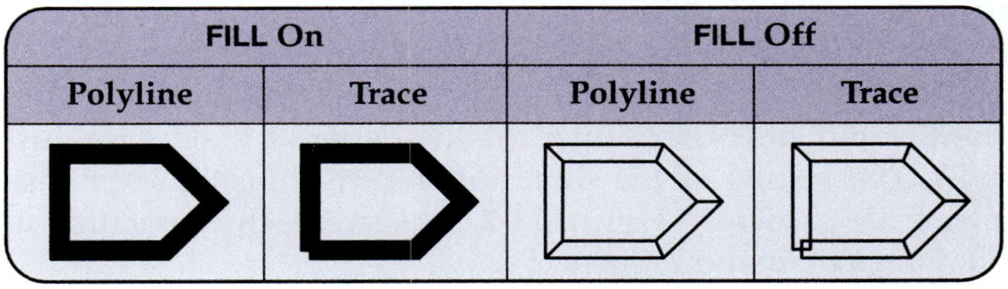

EXERCISE 14-4 Complete the Exercise on the Student CD.

Drawing Multilines

MLINE
ML

Draw
➥ Multiline

Multilines are objects that can consist of up to 16 parallel lines. The lines in a multiline are called ***elements.*** The **MLINE** command is used to draw multilines. A multiline configuration, or style, can be set using the **MLSTYLE** command. The default AutoCAD multiline style has two elements and is called STANDARD.

The **MLINE** command is accessed by picking **Multiline** from the **Draw** pull-down menu or by typing ML or MLINE at the Command: prompt:

Command: **ML** *or* **MLINE**↵
Current settings: Justification = Top, Scale = 1.00, Style = STANDARD
Specify start point or [Justification/Scale/STyle]: **2,2**↵
Specify next point: **6,2**↵
Specify next point or [Undo]: **6,6**↵
Specify next point or [Close/Undo]: **2,6**↵
Specify next point or [Close/Undo]: **C**↵
Command:

The prompts and options for the **MLINE** command are similar to those for the **LINE** command. As shown in the previous command sequence, you can use the **Close** option at the last prompt to close a polygon. Enter U during the command sequence to undo the previously drawn multiline segment. The object created in the previous command sequence is shown in **Figure 14-6.** You can see AutoCAD's STANDARD multiline style consists of two parallel lines. If you pick on the line to display grips, you can see that the entered coordinates correspond to the inner square.

Figure 14-6.
A multiline object created with AutoCAD's STANDARD multiline style.

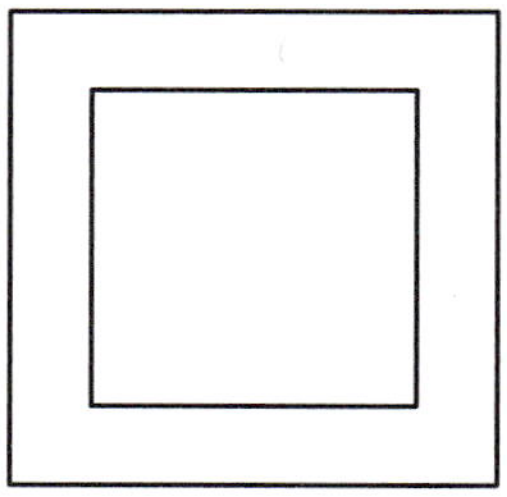

Multiline Justification

Multiline justification determines how the resulting lines are offset from the definition points provided. ***Definition points*** are the points you pick or coordinates you enter when drawing multilines. The justification is based on counterclockwise movement and can be specified only once during a single **MLINE** command sequence. The justification options are **Top** (default), **Zero**, and **Bottom**.

To change the justification, type J at the first prompt displayed after entering the **MLINE** command. Then, enter the first letter of the desired justification format (T, Z, or B). The results of the three different justification options using identical point entries are shown in **Figure 14-7.** Observe each orientation as you go through the following command sequence:

Figure 14-7.
Multilines drawn using each of the three justification options. The definition points (represented by plus symbols) are picked in a counterclockwise rotation.

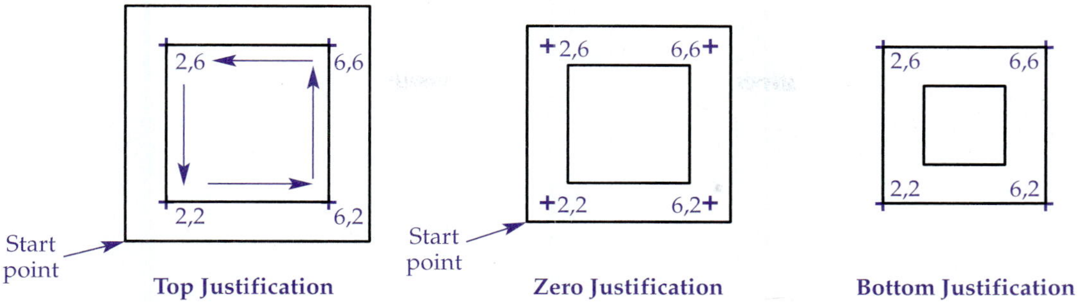

Command: **ML** *or* **MLINE**↵
Current settings: Justification = Top, Scale = 1.00, Style = STANDARD
Specify start point or [Justification/Scale/STyle]: **J**↵
Enter justification type [Top/Zero/Bottom] <*current*>: (*type* T, Z, *or* B, *and press* [Enter])
Current settings: Justification = *specified value*, Scale = 1.00, Style = STANDARD
Specify start point or [Justification/Scale/STyle]: **2,2**↵
Specify next point: **6,2**↵
Specify next point or [Undo]: **6,6**↵
Specify next point or [Close/Undo]: **2,6**↵
Specify next point or [Close/Undo]: **C**↵
Command:

The current multiline justification setting is stored in the **CMLJUST** system variable. You can change the setting by entering 0 for the **Top** option, 1 for the **Zero** option, or 2 for the **Bottom** option.

PROFESSIONAL TIP

As shown in **Figure 14-7,** the multiline justification options control the direction of the offsets for elements of the current style. The multiline segments in these examples are drawn in a counterclockwise direction. Unexpected results can sometimes occur when using the **MLINE** command, depending on the justification and drawing direction.

EXERCISE 14-5 Complete the Exercise on the Student CD.

Adjusting the Multiline Scale

The **MLINE Scale** option is a multiplier applied to the offset distance specified in the multiline style. The multiline style is defined with the **MLSTYLE** command. The multiplier is stored in the **CMLSCALE** system variable. The example in the previous section used a scale setting of 1 (default). With this setting, the distance between multiline elements is equal to 1 times the offset distance. For example, if the offset distance is 0.5, the distance between multiline elements is 0.5 when the multiline scale is 1. However, if the multiline scale is specified as 2, the distance between multiline elements is 1 (0.5×2).

The multiline scale is set to 2 in the next example. Multilines drawn with different scale settings are shown in **Figure 14-8.**

Figure 14-8.
Multiline scale settings.

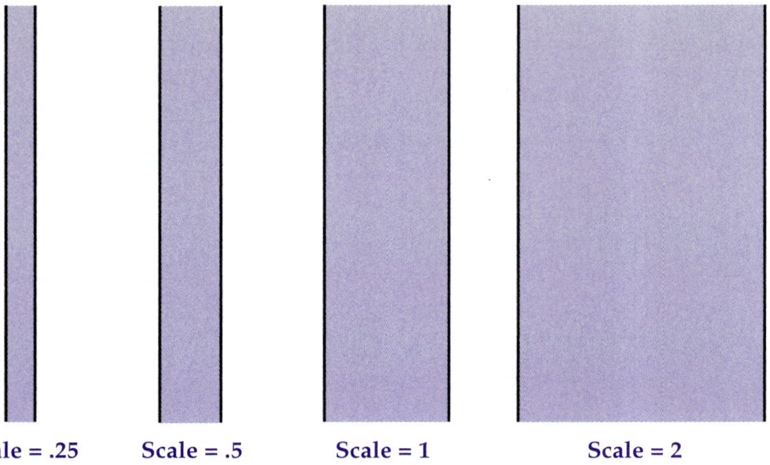

Command: **ML** *or* **MLINE**↵
Current settings: Justification = Top, Scale = 1.00, Style = STANDARD
Specify start point or [Justification/Scale/STyle]: **S**↵
Enter mline scale <1.00>: **2**↵
Current settings: Justification = Top, Scale = 2.00, Style = STANDARD
Specify start point or [Justification/Scale/STyle]:

EXERCISE 14-6 Complete the Exercise on the Student CD.

Changing the Multiline Style

You can specify the current multiline style by using the **STyle** option of the **MLINE** command. However, before a new multiline style can be accessed, it must be created and saved using the **MLSTYLE** command. To use a saved multiline style, enter ST to access the **STyle** option and then enter the style name:

Command: **ML** *or* **MLINE**↵
Current settings: Justification = Top, Scale = 1.00, Style = STANDARD
Specify start point or [Justification/Scale/STyle]: **ST**↵
Enter mline style name or [?]: **ROAD1**↵
Justification = Top, Scale = 1.00, Style = ROAD1
Specify start point or [Justification/Scale/STyle]:

If you forget the name of the desired multiline style, you can enter ? at the Enter mline style name or [?]: prompt. The text window is opened and the currently loaded multiline styles are listed, Figure 14-9. Then, type the name of the style you want to use.

If you try to specify a multiline style that is not loaded, the **Load multiline style from file** dialog box is displayed. You can look for the desired multiline style in the acad.mln file library. You can also pick the **Tools** button and then **Find...** to open the **Find:** dialog box. This dialog box allows you to search other files for the multiline style. The **Find** dialog box is discussed in Chapter 2. If the desired multiline style does not exist in the file you select, AutoCAD displays the message:

Multiline style *style name* not found in *path and file selected.*
You can use the "MLSTYLE" command to load it from another file.

Figure 14-9.
A list of loaded multiline styles can be displayed in the text window.

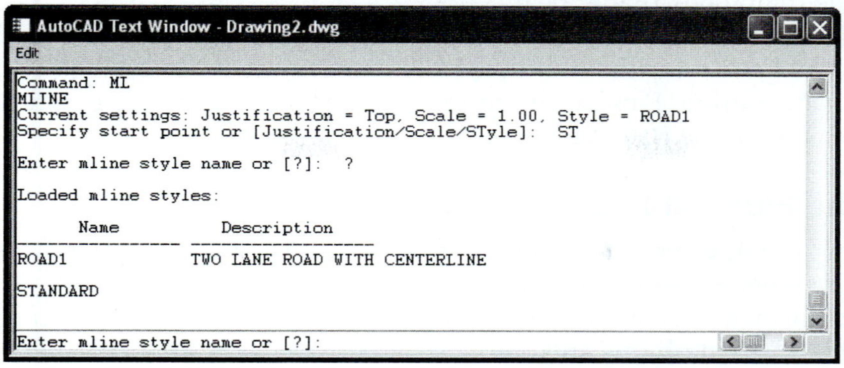

Creating Multiline Styles

MLSTYLE
Format
➥ **Multiline Style...**

Multiline styles are defined using the **MLSTYLE** command. The current style is stored in the **CMLSTYLE** system variable. The **MLSTYLE** command can be accessed by picking **Multiline Style...** from the **Format** pull-down menu. You can also type MLSTYLE at the Command: prompt.

The **MLSTYLE** command displays the **Multiline Styles** dialog box, Figure 14-10. This is where multiline styles can be defined, edited, and saved. Styles can be saved to an external file so they can be used in other drawings. The image tile in the center of the **Multiline Styles** dialog box displays a representation of the current multiline style. The options provided in the **Multiline Style** area of the **Multiline Styles** dialog box are described as follows:

- **Current: drop-down list.** The **Current:** drop-down list allows you to set a different style as the current style. Pick the arrow and select the style from the list. Specifying a different style changes the setting of the **CMLSTYLE** system variable. Until you create or load a multiline style, the only style available is STANDARD.
- **Name: text box.** This text box is used to enter the name for a new style. It is also for renaming an existing style.
- **Description: text box.** An optional description of your multiline style may be entered in this text box. This is discussed later in this chapter.
- **Load... button.** This button allows you to load a multiline style from an external multiline definition file.

Figure 14-10.
The **Multiline Styles** dialog box is used to define, edit, and save multiline styles.

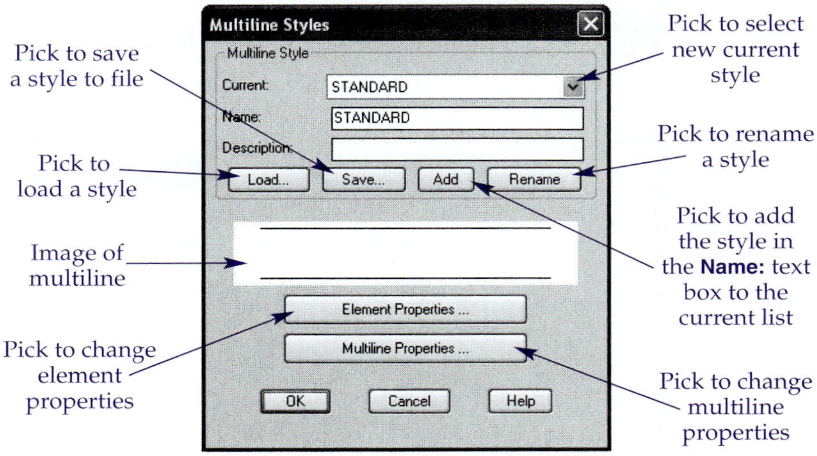

- **Save... button.** This button is used to save a style to a file. To add the style to an existing definition file, specify the existing file name in the **Save Multiline Style** dialog box that appears.
- **Add button.** This button saves the style under the name specified in the **Name:** text box and adds the multiline style name to the list of defined styles.
- **Rename button.** Pick this button to rename the multiline style under the name specified in the **Name:** text box.

Using the Element Properties Dialog Box

Picking the **Element Properties...** button in the **Multiline Styles** dialog box displays the **Element Properties** dialog box, Figure 14-11. This dialog box is where you define the elements of the current multiline style. It is also where you define the elements for a new multiline style.

- **Elements: area.** This area displays the current offset, color, and linetype settings for each multiline element. Picking one of the elements in this area allows it to be modified.
- **Add button.** A multiline style definition can have from one to 16 different elements. Pick this button to add a new element to the multiline style definition. The new element has the settings **Offset** = 0.0, **Color** = BYLAYER, and **Ltype** = ByLayer. See Figure 14-12. Once a new element is added, its properties can be changed.
- **Delete button.** Pick this button to delete the element highlighted in the **Elements:** area.
- **Offset text box.** The value in this text box is the offset from 0 justification. This value can be positive, negative, or zero. This offset value is the value on which the **MLINE Scale** option operates.
- **Color... button.** Used to change the display color of the element highlighted in the **Elements:** area. Pick the button or the color swatch to open the **Select Color** dialog box. Then, pick the color you wish to assign to the element. Pick the **OK** button to close the **Select Color** dialog box. The new color is displayed

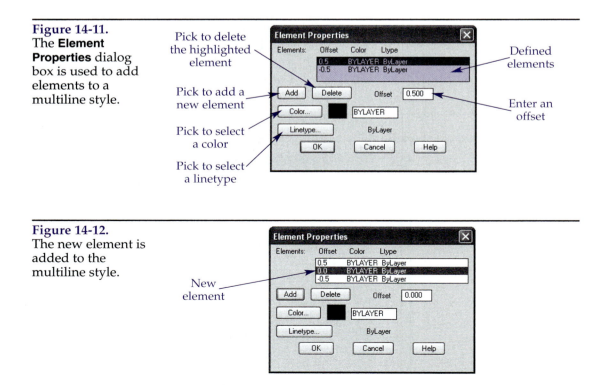

Figure 14-11.
The **Element Properties** dialog box is used to add elements to a multiline style.

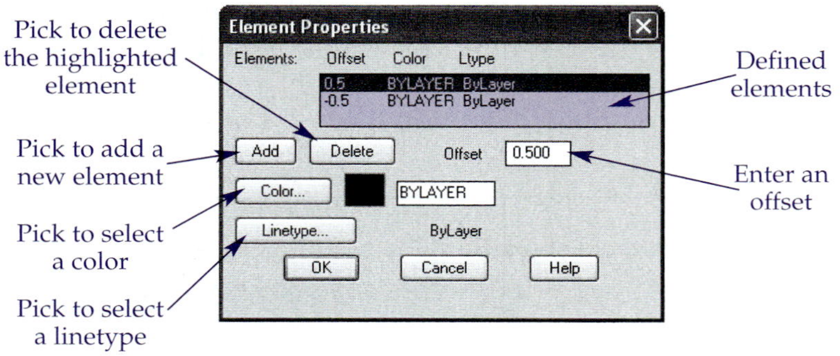

Figure 14-12.
The new element is added to the multiline style.

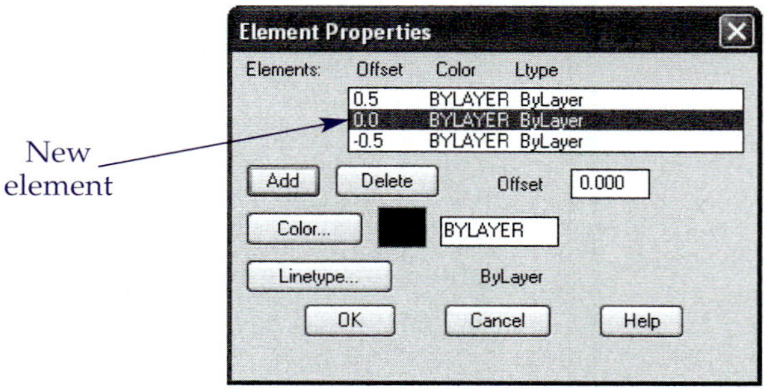

in the color swatch and its name appears in the text box to the right of the color swatch. You can also change the color by typing the name of a color in the text box.

- **Linetype... button.** Used to change the linetype of the element highlighted in the **Elements:** area. Picking the button displays the **Select Linetype** dialog box. Then, pick the desired linetype from the list. Linetypes must be loaded before they can be used (see Chapter 4). Pick **OK** to close the **Select Linetype** dialog box. The new linetype is assigned to the highlighted element.

Once the elements have been modified, pick **OK** to exit the **Element Properties** dialog box. The changes to the multiline style definition are displayed in the image tile in the **Multiline Styles** dialog box.

Using the Multiline Properties Dialog Box

Picking the **Multiline Properties...** button in the **Multiline Styles** dialog box opens the **Multiline Properties** dialog box. See **Figure 14-13.** This dialog box offers additional options for customizing multiline styles. You can add caps and segment joints to multiline elements. You can also add a background color, or fill, to the multiline. When done making changes, pick **OK** to return to the **Multiline Styles** dialog box.

- **Display joints check box.** When checked, joints are displayed on the multiline. ***Joints*** are lines that connect the vertices of adjacent multiline elements. Joints are also referred to as ***miters.*** Multilines drawn with and without joints are shown in **Figure 14-14.**
- **Caps area.** The settings in this area control the placement of caps on multilines. ***Caps*** are lines connecting the corresponding vertices of the beginning or ending points of the multiline elements. Using the check boxes, caps can be set at the start points, endpoints, or both. Several examples of different cap options are shown in **Figure 14-15.**

Figure 14-13.
The **Multiline Properties** dialog box is used to customize a multiline style.

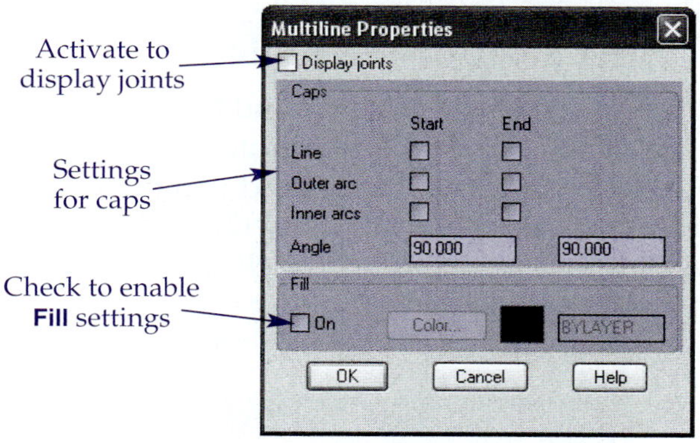

Figure 14-14.
Multilines can be drawn with or without displayed joints.

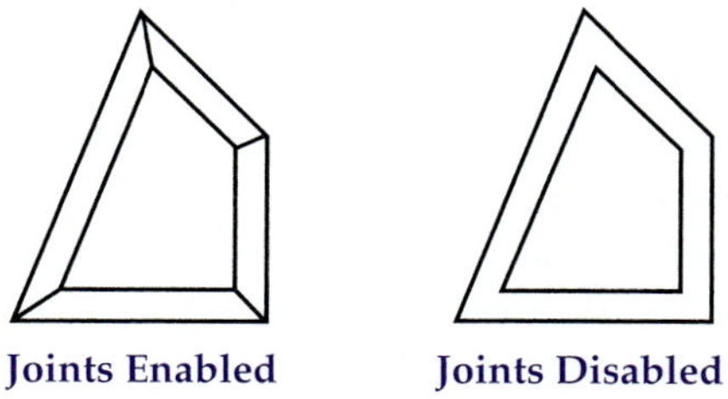

Figure 14-15.
Various cap options used with multilines.

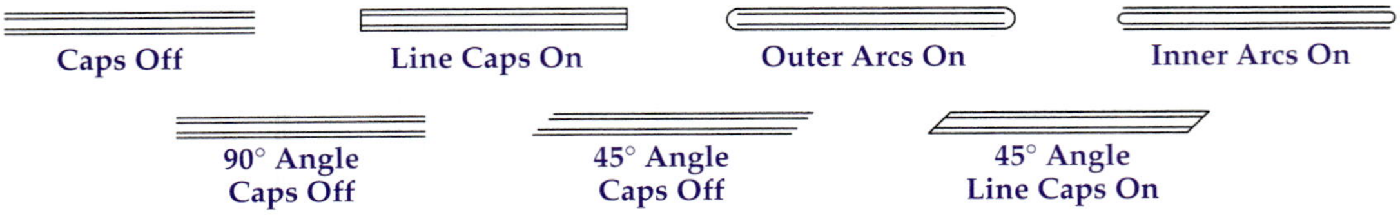
Caps Off
Line Caps On
Outer Arcs On
Inner Arcs On
90° Angle
Caps Off
45° Angle
Caps Off
45° Angle
Line Caps On

The caps can be drawn as arcs. Arcs can be set to connect the ends of the outermost elements only, pairs of inner elements, or both the outer and inner elements. There must be at least two multiline elements for outer arcs to be drawn. Arcs are drawn tangent to the elements they connect.

You can change the angle of the caps relative to the direction of the multiline elements. To do so, enter values in the **Angle** text boxes. There is a text box for the start points and one for the endpoints.

- **Fill area.** If the **On** check box is checked, the multiline is filled with a solid pattern. The color of the pattern is shown in the color swatch. To change the color, pick the **Color...** button or the color swatch. Then, choose a new color in the **Select Color** dialog box. You can also change the color by typing the color name in the text box to the right of the color swatch. Multilines drawn with the **Fill** setting on and off are shown in Figure 14-16.

Figure 14-16.
The multiline **Fill** setting allows you to draw multilines with a solid fill pattern.

Fill Setting On
Fill Setting Off

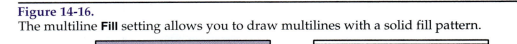

Creating and Using a Multiline Style

Now that you have seen how the **MLINE** and **MLSTYLE** commands work, you can create your own multiline style and draw multilines with it. Suppose you need to draw a multiline for a two-lane road to be used in a mapping project. The following procedure is used to create the style and draw the multiline.

1. Open the **Multiline Styles** dialog box. Pick the **Element Properties...** button to open the **Element Properties** dialog box.
2. Add one new element. Then, set the following elements properties.

Offset	Color	Ltype
0.25	BYLAYER	ByLayer
0.0	YELLOW	CENTER2
–0.25	BYLAYER	ByLayer

3. Pick **OK** to close the **Element Properties** dialog box.
4. Pick the **Multiline Properties...** button in the **Multiline Styles** dialog box to display the **Multiline Properties** dialog box.
5. Be sure the **Display joints**, **Fill**, and all check boxes in the **Caps** area are not checked. Also, make sure 90 appears in both **Angle** text boxes.
6. Pick **OK** to close the **Multiline Properties** dialog box.
7. Type ROAD1 in the **Name:** text box in the **Multiline Style** area of the **Multiline Styles** dialog box.

8. In the **Description:** text box, enter the description TWO LANE ROAD WITH CENTERLINE.
9. Pick the **Save...** button to display the **Save Multiline Style** dialog box.
10. Select the file acad.mln so its name appears in the **File name:** text box, as shown in Figure 14-17. Then, pick the **Save** button to add the multiline style definition to the acad.mln file.
11. Pick the **Load...** button in the **Multiline Styles** dialog box to access the **Load Multiline Styles** dialog box.
12. Highlight the ROAD1 multiline style, as shown in Figure 14-18. Then, pick **OK** to load the style and set it current.
13. Pick **OK** to exit the **Multiline Styles** dialog box.
14. Using the **MLINE** command, draw the multiline shown in Figure 14-19:

Command: **ML** *or* **MLINE**↵
Current settings: Justification = Top, Scale = 1.00, Style = ROAD1
Specify start point or [Justification/Scale/STyle]: *(enter start point)*
Specify next point: *(enter endpoint)*
Specify next point or [Undo]: ↵
Command:

Figure 14-17.
Use the **Save Multiline Style** dialog box to save the ROAD1 style to the acad.mln file.

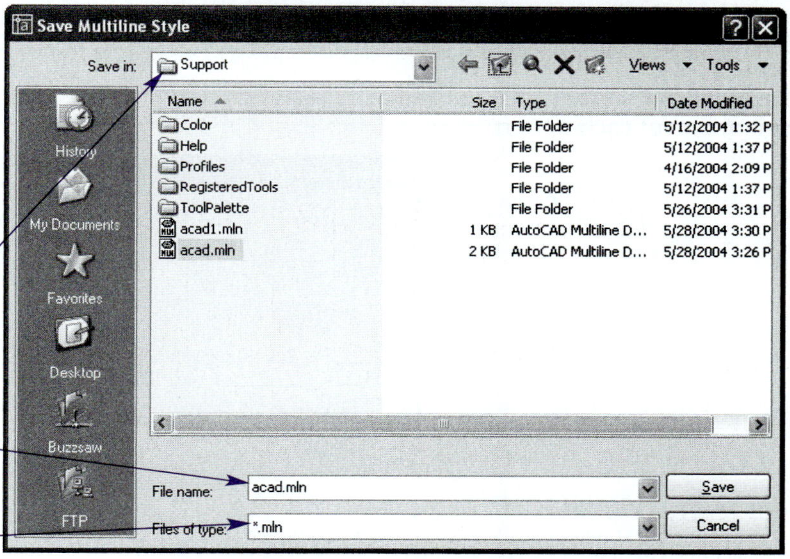

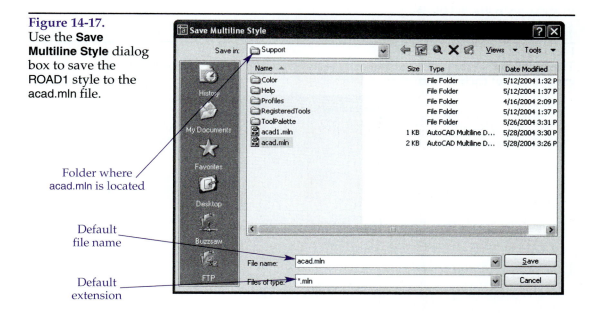

Figure 14-18.
The **Load Multiline Styles** dialog box.

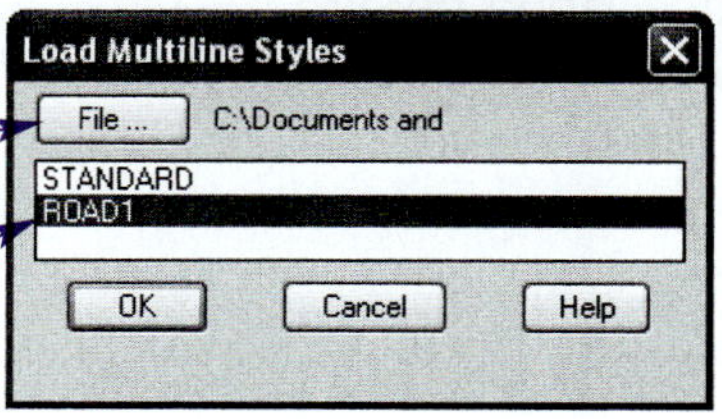

Figure 14-19.
A multiline drawn with the ROAD1 style.

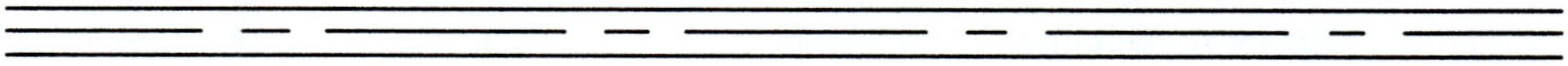

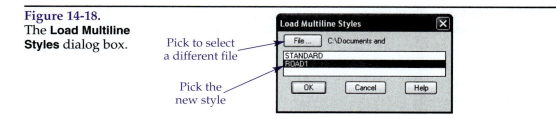

EXERCISE
14-7
Complete the Exercise on the Student CD.

Editing Multilines

MLEDIT
Modify
➥ **Object**
➥ **Multiline...**

The **MLEDIT** command permits limited editing operations for multiline objects. Access this command by picking **Multiline...** from the **Object** cascading menu in the **Modify** pull-down menu or by typing MLEDIT at the Command: prompt. This displays the **Multiline Edit Tools** dialog box, Figure 14-20. This dialog box contains four columns of image buttons. Each column contains three image buttons of related command options. The image on each button gives you an example of what to expect when using the editing option. The name of the **MLEDIT** option is displayed in the lower-left corner of the dialog box when you pick an image button.

Once you pick the **OK** button, the dialog box is closed. You are prompted on the Command: line to continue with the command. The command options are described in the following sections.

Figure 14-20.
The **Multiline Edit Tools** dialog box has 12 different options. Refer to the text for an explanation of each option.

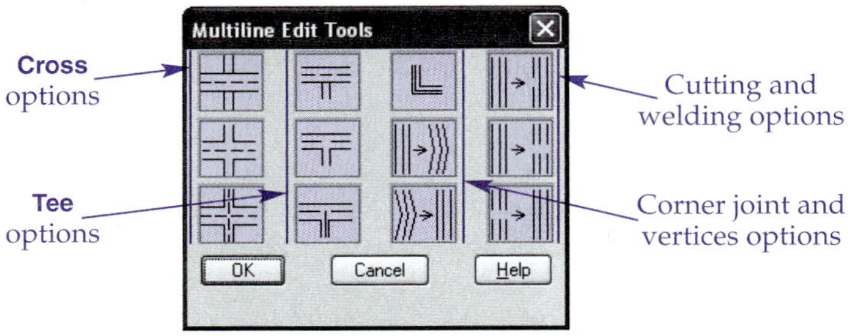

Editing Intersections

The first (left) column in the **Multiline Edit Tools** dialog box displays three different types of multiline intersections. Picking a button allows you to create the type of intersection shown. The effect of the buttons in the first column are shown in Figure 14-21 and described below.

- **Closed Cross.** When using this option, the first multiline selected is called the background and the second multiline is called the foreground. A ***closed cross*** is created by trimming the background while the foreground remains unchanged. The trimming is apparent, not actual. This means the line visibility of the background multiline is changed, but it is still a single multiline. The command sequence is:

  Command: **MLEDIT**↵
  (In the **Multiline Edit Tools** *dialog box, pick the* **Closed Cross** *image button and then* **OK***)*
  Select first mline: *(pick the background multiline)*
  Select second mline: *(pick the foreground multiline and the intersection is created)*
  Select first mline or [Undo]: *(select the background multiline of another intersection, type* U *to undo the intersection, or press* [Enter] *to end the command)*

Figure 14-21.
Creating a **Closed Cross**, **Open Cross**, and **Merged Cross** intersection with the **MLEDIT** command.

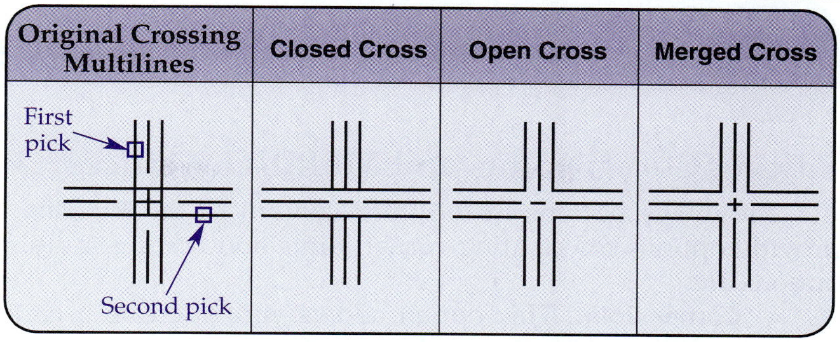

- **Open Cross.** Select the **Open Cross** image button to trim all of the elements of the first multiline and only the outer elements of the second multiline, as shown in Figure 14-21. The command sequence is the same as that used for the **Closed Cross** option.
- **Merged Cross.** The **Merged Cross** image button allows you to trim the outer elements of both multilines. The inner elements are not changed. See Figure 14-21.

EXERCISE 14-8 Complete the Exercise on the Student CD.

Editing Tees

The image buttons in the second column of the **Multiline Edit Tools** dialog box are used for editing multiline tees. The results of using the tee options are illustrated in Figure 14-22. The three options are:

- **Closed Tee.** Pick the **Closed Tee** option to have AutoCAD trim or extend the first selected multiline to its intersection with the second multiline.
- **Open Tee.** The **Open Tee** option is similar to the **Closed Tee** option. It allows you to trim the elements where a trimmed or extended multiline intersects with another multiline. The first pick specifies the multiline to trim or extend and the second pick specifies the intersecting multiline. The intersecting multiline is trimmed and left open where the two multilines join.
- **Merged Tee.** The **Merged Tee** option is similar to the **Open Tee** option. It trims the intersecting multiline after the first multiline is trimmed or extended. However, the inner elements are joined. This creates an open appearance with the outer elements while merging the inner elements.

Figure 14-22.
Using the **MLEDIT Tee** options to edit multiline tees.

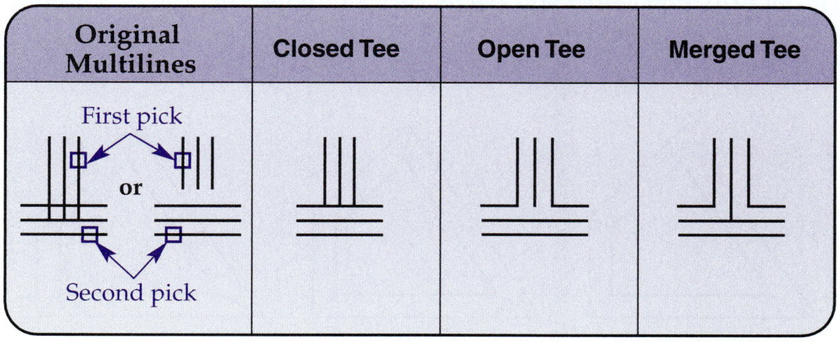

EXERCISE 14-9 Complete the Exercise on the Student CD.

Editing Corner Joints and Multiline Vertices

The image buttons in the third column of the **Multiline Edit Tools** dialog box provide options for creating corner joints and editing multiline vertices. The three options are:

- **Corner Joint.** This option allows you to create a corner joint between two multilines. The first multiline is trimmed or extended to its intersection with the second multiline, as shown in **Figure 14-23.**
- **Add Vertex.** This option adds a vertex to an existing multiline at the location you pick, **Figure 14-24.** The command sequence differs slightly from the sequences used with the other **MLEDIT** options. After you select the **Add Vertex** option and pick **OK**, you are prompted with:

  Select mline: *(pick a location on the multiline for the new vertex)*
  Select mline or [Undo]: ↵
  Command:

- **Delete Vertex.** This option allows you to remove a vertex from an existing multiline. The vertex closest to the location you pick is deleted, **Figure 14-24.** The command sequence is the same as for the **Add Vertex** option.

Figure 14-23.
A corner joint can be created between two multilines using the **MLEDIT Corner Joint** option.

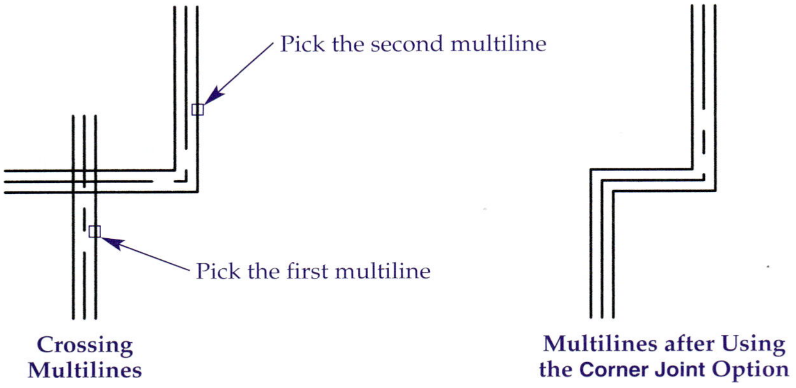

Figure 14-24.
The **MLEDIT Add Vertex** and **Delete Vertex** options are used to edit multiline vertices.

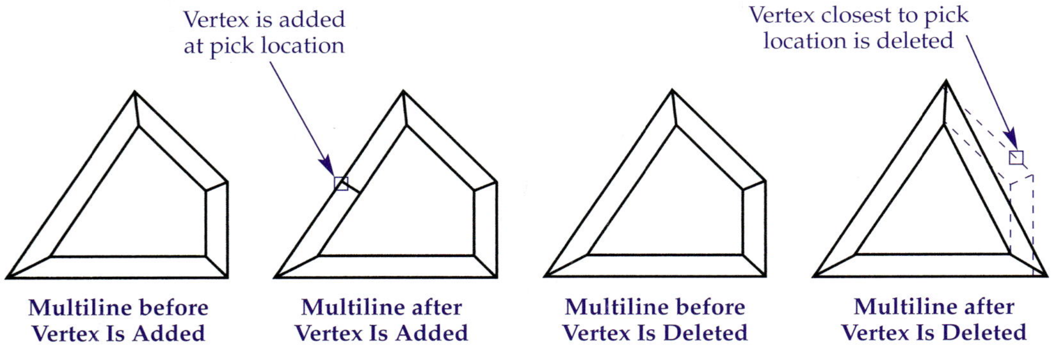

EXERCISE 14-10 Complete the Exercise on the Student CD.

Cutting and Welding Multilines

The fourth column of image buttons in the **Multiline Edit Tools** dialog box is used for ***cutting*** a portion out of a single multiline element or the entire multiline. The spaces between multiline elements can also be connected. AutoCAD refers to the connecting operation as ***welding***. The **MLEDIT** cutting and welding options are:

- **Cut Single.** This option allows you to cut a single multiline element between two specified points, as shown in Figure 14-25. Cutting only affects the visibility of elements and does not separate a multiline object. The multiline is still a single object. After selecting the **Cut Single** option and picking **OK**, you are prompted with:

  Select mline: *(pick a location for the first cutting point on the multiline)*
  Select second point: *(pick a location for the second cutting point)*
  Select mline or [Undo]: ↵
  Command:

- **Cut All.** This option cuts all elements of a multiline between specified points. See Figure 14-25. The multiline is still a single object even though it appears to be separated.
- **Weld All.** This option allows you to repair all cuts in a multiline. Select the **Weld All** button, pick **OK**, and select a point on each side of the cut multiline. The multiline is restored to its precut condition.

PROFESSIONAL TIP

Multiline objects can be converted to individual line segments with the **EXPLODE** command. This command is explained in Chapter 22. The following is a brief look at the **EXPLODE** command sequence:

Command: **X** *or* **EXPLODE**↵
Select objects: *(pick the object to explode)*
x found
Select objects: ↵
Command:

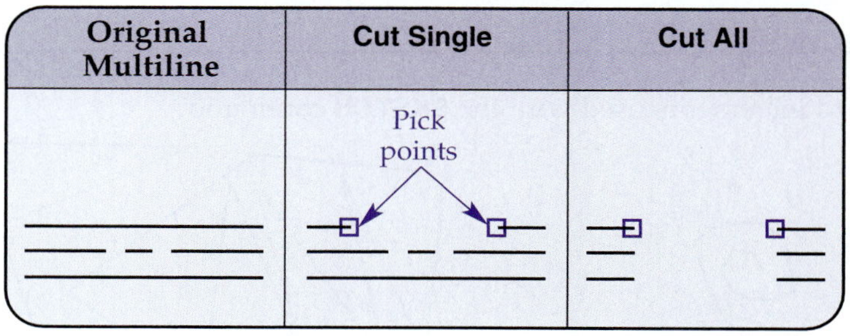

Figure 14-25.
The **MLEDIT** cutting options allow you to cut single multiline elements or entire multilines between two specified points.

EXERCISE 14-11 Complete the Exercise on the Student CD.

Sketching with AutoCAD

Sketching is a feature of AutoCAD that allows you to draw objects as if you were sketching with pencil and paper. Sketching is done with the **SKETCH** command. While this command is not commonly used, it does have value for certain applications. It is sometimes used when it is necessary to draw a contour that is not defined by geometric shapes or lines. Other examples of applications for freehand sketching in AutoCAD include:

- Contour lines on topographic maps.
- Maps of countries and states.
- Architectural landscape symbols such as trees, bushes, and plants.
- Graphs and charts.
- Graphic designs, such as those found on a greeting card.
- Short breaks, such as those used in mechanical drafting.

Before using the **SKETCH** command, it is best to turn the **Snap** and **Ortho** modes off because they limit the cursor's movement. Normally, you want total control over the cursor when sketching. Then use the **SKETCH** command:

Command: **SKETCH**↵
Record increment <0.1000>:

The ***record increment*** is the length of each sketch line element generated as you move the cursor. For example, if the record increment is set to 0.1000 (the default value), sketched images consist of lines that are 0.1 units in length. An increment setting of 1 creates sketched line segments one unit long. Reducing the increment setting increases the accuracy of your sketched image. However, record increments less than 0.1 greatly increase the drawing file size. To view the chosen record increment, turn **ORTHO** on and draw a set of stair steps. The smallest horizontal and vertical elements represent the length of the record increment. If **SNAP** is turned on, the record increment then becomes equal to the snap spacing. A comparison of record increments is shown in **Figure 14-26.** After the record increment is entered, the command continues:

Pen eXit Quit Record Erase Connect .

This prompt displays the **SKETCH** subcommands. Once you see this prompt, a subcommand can be accessed by entering its corresponding capitalized letter. Pressing the left mouse button activates the **Pen** subcommand.

The buttons on a multibutton puck can also be used to activate the **SKETCH** subcommands. The normal puck buttons for the **Snap** (4) and **Ortho** (5) modes remain disabled as long as the **SKETCH** command is active. The following table lists the keyboard entries and puck buttons used to access each subcommand.

Figure 14-26.
Record increments used with the **SKETCH** command.

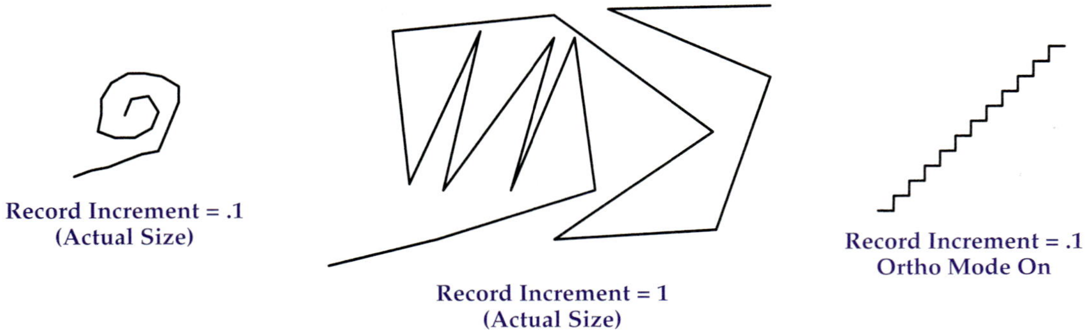

Subcommand	Keyboard Entry	Puck Button	Subcommand Function
Pen	P	0	Toggles pen up and down.
Period	.	1	Draws a line from the endpoint of a sketched line.
Record	R	2	Records sketched lines as permanent.
eXit	X, spacebar, or [Enter]	3	Records sketched lines and exits the **SKETCH** command.
Quit	Q or [Esc]	4	Removes all unrecorded objects.
Erase	E	5	Erases all unrecorded objects.
Connect	C	6	Allows connection to the endpoint of a sketched line when pen is up.

Sketch segments are, by default, line objects. You can use the **SKPOLY** system variable to create sketched lines that are defined as polyline objects. An **SKPOLY** system variable setting of 0 is for line objects and 1 for polyline objects.

Drawing Sketched Lines

After entering the **SKETCH** command, actual sketching is done with the **Pen** subcommand. Using this subcommand is similar to sketching with paper and pencil. When the pencil is "down," you are ready to draw. When the pencil is "up," you are thinking about what to draw next or moving to the next location. After issuing the **SKETCH** command, enter P to toggle the pen down and begin sketching. You can also press your left mouse button to move the pen up and down. Move the cursor around to create a line. Enter P again or press your left mouse button to toggle the pen up and stop sketching.

PROFESSIONAL TIP

If you do not consider yourself an artist, trace an existing design. Tape the design to a digitizer and move the cursor along the outline of the shape with the pen down. Move the pen up when you want to specify a new sketching location.

Using the Period (.) Subcommand

The **Period** subcommand allows you to draw a straight line from the endpoint of the last sketched line to a selected point. This subcommand is accessed by entering a period (.) at the prompt displayed by the **SKETCH** command. Use the following procedure.

1. Complete the segment you are working on and make sure the pen is up.
2. Move the cursor to the desired endpoint.
3. Enter a period (.) or press puck button 1. A straight line is automatically drawn. If **ORTHO** is turned on, only vertical or horizontal segments are drawn to connect the points.

Using the Connect Subcommand

It is common to toggle the pen up to pause from sketching or to make a menu selection. When the pen is up, you can return to the last sketched point and resume sketching by using the **Connect** subcommand. To do so, enter C or press puck button 6. AutoCAD responds with this message:

Connect: Move to endpoint of line.

Move the cursor to the end of the previously sketched line. As soon as the crosshairs touch the previously drawn line, the pen automatically moves down and you can resume sketching.

Using the Erase Subcommand

You can erase line segments while sketching. If you make a mistake, enter E for the Erase subcommand or press puck button 5. The pen may be up or down. If the pen is down, it is automatically raised. AutoCAD responds with the message:

Erase: Select end of delete. <Pen up>

Move the cursor to erase any portion of the sketch. Every part of the sketch from the last point to the portion you select will be erased. When finished, enter P or press puck button 0. If you decide not to erase anything, enter E or press puck button 5. AutoCAD returns to the **SKETCH** command prompt after issuing the message Erase aborted.

Recording Sketched Lines

Sketched lines are displayed in color when you first begin to sketch. These lines are referred to as ***temporary lines.*** Temporary lines become ***permanent lines*** and are displayed in their final color after they are ***recorded.*** You can record lines and remain in the **SKETCH** command by entering R or pressing puck button 2. You can also record lines and exit the **SKETCH** command by entering X or pressing the spacebar, [Enter], or puck button 3. AutoCAD responds with a message indicating the number of lines recorded. For example, if you created 32 lines, the message reads 32 lines recorded.

Quitting the SKETCH Command

To quit the **SKETCH** command without recording any lines, enter Q or press the [Esc] key or puck button 4. This removes all temporary lines and returns you to the Command: prompt.

Managing Storage Space with the SKETCH Command

Sketching rapidly consumes computer storage space. For example, the sketch of a rose shown in Figure 14-27 may be less than 50KB as a JPEG file. However, created using the **SKETCH** command and saved as an AutoCAD drawing file, this drawing is nearly 1.5MB. Therefore, the **SKETCH** command should be used only when necessary.

Figure 14-27.
A rose drawn using the **SKETCH** command. (Courtesy of Susan Waterman)

The record increment should be set as large as possible, but low enough that the results are pleasing.

EXERCISE 14-12 Complete the Exercise on the Student CD.

Chapter Test

Answer the following questions on a separate sheet of paper.

1. Give the command and entries required to draw a polyline from Point A to Point B with a beginning width of .500 and an ending width of 0.
   A. Command: _____
   B. Specify start point: _____
   Current line-width is 0.0000
   C. Specify next point or [Arc/Halfwidth/Length/Undo/Width]: _____
   D. Specify starting width <0.0000>: _____
   E. Specify ending width <.500>: _____
   F. Specify next point or [Arc/Halfwidth/Length/Undo/Width]: _____
   G. Specify next point or [Arc/Close/Halfwidth/Length/Undo/Width]: _____
2. Give the command and entries needed to draw a multiline with zero justification and the saved style ROAD1.
   A. Command: _____
   B. Current settings: Justification = Top, Scale = 1.00, Style = STANDARD
   C. Specify start point or [Justification/Scale/STyle]: _____
   D. Enter mline style name or [?]: _____
   Current settings: Justification = Top, Scale = 1.00, Style = ROAD1
   E. Specify start point or [Justification/Scale/STyle]: _____
   F. Enter justification type [Top/Zero/Bottom] <top>: _____
   Current settings: Justification = Zero, Scale = 1.00, Style = ROAD1
   G. Specify start point or [Justification/Scale/STyle]: _____
   H. Specify next point: _____
   I. Specify next point or [Undo]: _____
3. How do you draw a filled arrow using the **PLINE** command?
4. Name two commands that can be used to draw wide lines.
5. Which **PLINE** command option allows you to specify the width from the center to one side?
6. What is an advantage of leaving the **FILL** mode turned off?
7. What is the difference between picking **Undo** from the **Edit** pull-down menu and entering the **UNDO** command?
8. Name the command that is used to bring back an object that was previously removed using **UNDO**.
9. Name the **MLINE** command option that establishes how the resulting lines are offset based on the definition points provided.
10. Name the option that controls the multiplier value for the offset distances specified with the **MLINE** command.
11. How do you access the **Multiline Styles** dialog box?
12. Describe the function of the **Add** button in the **Element Properties** dialog box.
13. Describe the function of the **Linetype...** button in the **Element Properties** dialog box.
14. Define *caps.*
15. List the settings in the **Multiline Properties** dialog box that control the options for placing end caps on multilines.

16. Define *joints.*
17. What is displayed when you enter the **MLEDIT** command?
18. How do you access one of the **MLEDIT** options?
19. List the three options that are used for editing multiline intersections with the **MLEDIT** command.
20. Name the **MLEDIT** option in which the intersecting multiline is trimmed and left open after the first multiline is trimmed or extended to its intersection with the intersecting multiline.
21. Name the **MLEDIT** option that allows you to remove a vertex from an existing multiline.
22. Name the **MLEDIT** option that lets you remove a portion from an individual multiline element.
23. Name the **MLEDIT** option that removes all of the elements of a multiline between two specified points.
24. Name the **MLEDIT** option that repairs all cuts in a multiline between two selected points.
25. Explain why the **Snap** and **Ortho** modes should be turned off for most sketching applications.

Drawing Problems

1. Use the **PLINE** command to draw the following object with a .032 line width. Do not draw dimensions. Save the drawing as P14-1.

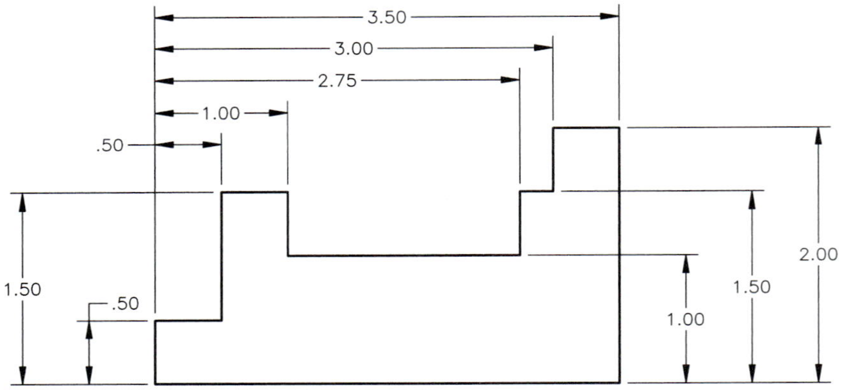

2. Use the **PLINE** command to draw the following object with a .032 line width. Do not draw dimensions. Save the drawing as P14-2.

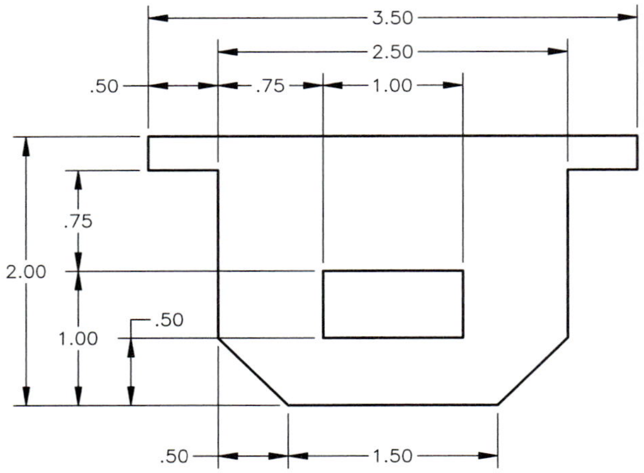

3. Use the **TRACE** command to draw the following object with a .032 line width. Do not draw dimensions.
   A. Turn off the **FILL** mode and use the **REGEN** command. Then, turn on **FILL** and reissue the **REGEN** command.
   B. Observe the difference with **FILL** mode on and off.
   C. Save the drawing as P14-3.

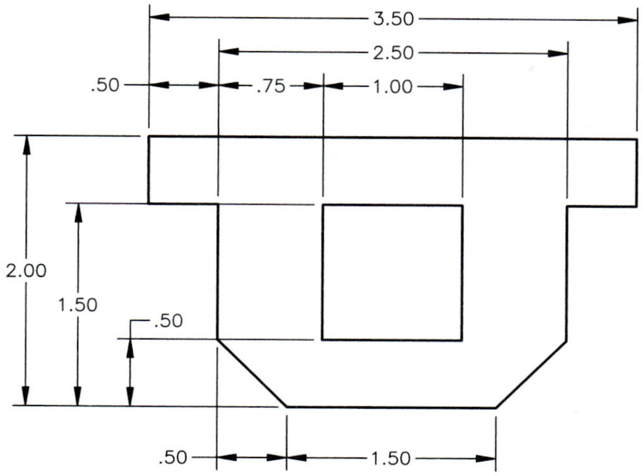

4. Use the **PLINE** command to draw the filled rectangle shown below. Do not draw dimensions. Save the drawing as P14-4.

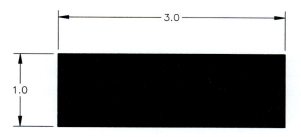

5. Draw the objects shown below. Do not draw dimensions. Then, use the **UNDO** command to remove Object B. Use the **REDO** command to bring Object B back. Save the drawing as P14-5.

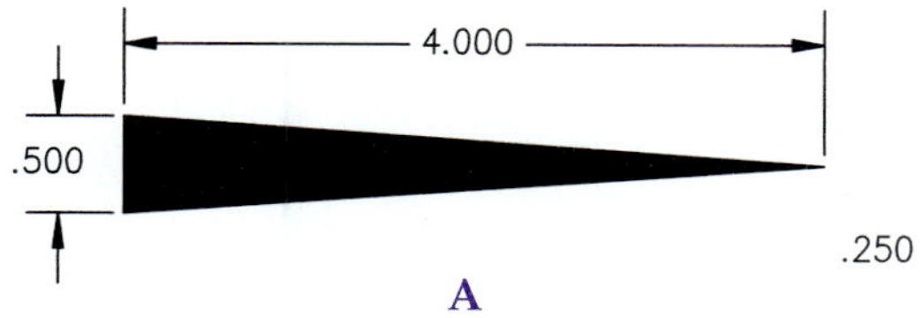

A

B

6. Draw the object shown below. Do not draw dimensions. Set decimal units, .25 grid spacing, and .0625 snap spacing. Set the limits to 11,8.5. Save the drawing as P14-6.

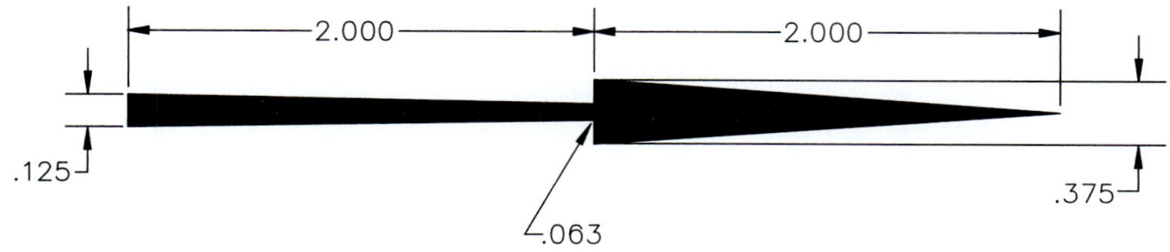

7. Open P4-7 and add the arrowheads. Draw one arrowhead using the **PLINE** command and then use the necessary editing commands to place the rest. Refer to the original problem. Save the drawing as P14-7.

8. Draw the objects shown using the **MLINE** command. Use the justification options indicated with each illustration. Set the limits to 11,8.5, grid spacing to .50, and snap spacing to .25. Set the offset for the multiline elements to .125. Do not add text or dimensions. Save the drawing as P14-8.

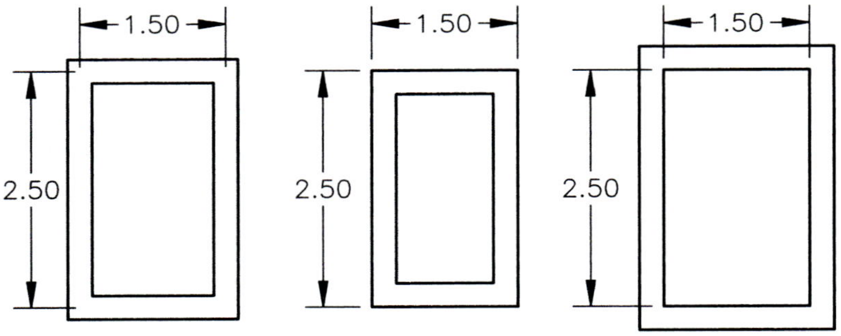

Zero Justification   **Bottom** Justification   **Top** Justification

9. Draw the partial floor plan shown using the multiline commands. Carefully observe how the dimensions correlate with the multiline elements to determine your justification settings. Also, use the appropriate cap and multiline editing options. Use architectural units. Set the limits to 88′,68′, grid spacing to 24″, and snap spacing to 12″. Make all walls 6″ thick. Do not add text or dimensions. Save the drawing as P14-9.

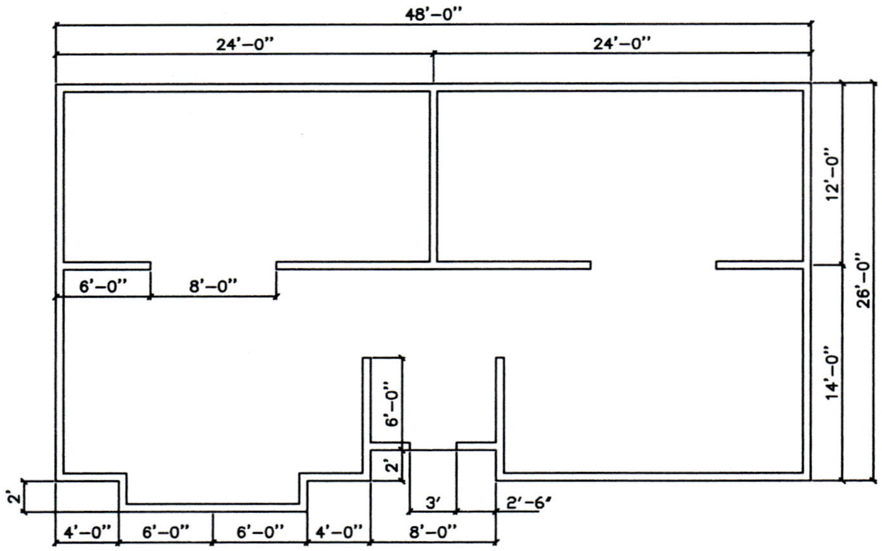

10. Draw the proposed subdivision map using the multiline commands. The roads are 30′ wide. Use a centerline linetype for the center of each road. Adjust the linetype scale as needed. Do not include dimensions. Save the drawing as P14-10.

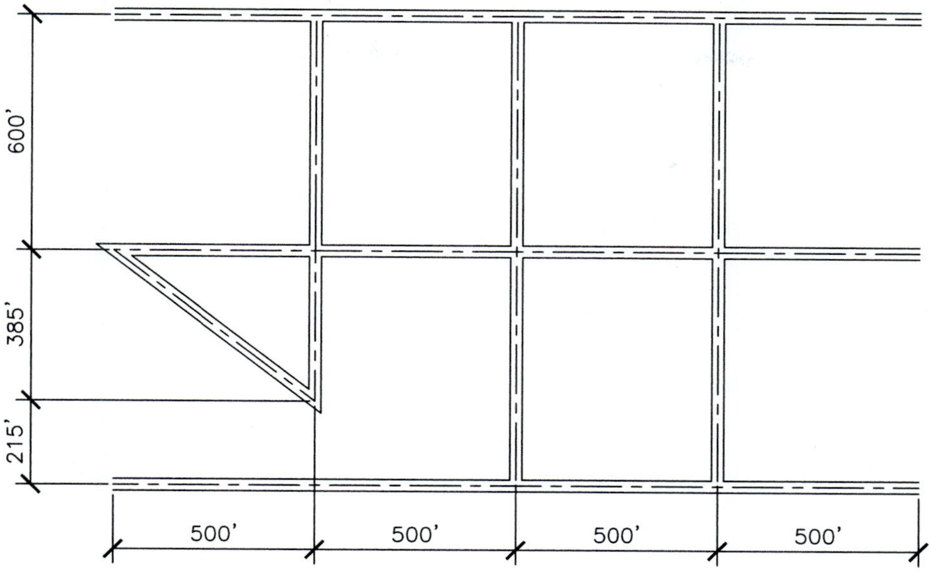

11. Draw the partial floor plan shown below using multilines for the walls. Do not dimension the floor plan. Save the drawing as P14-11.

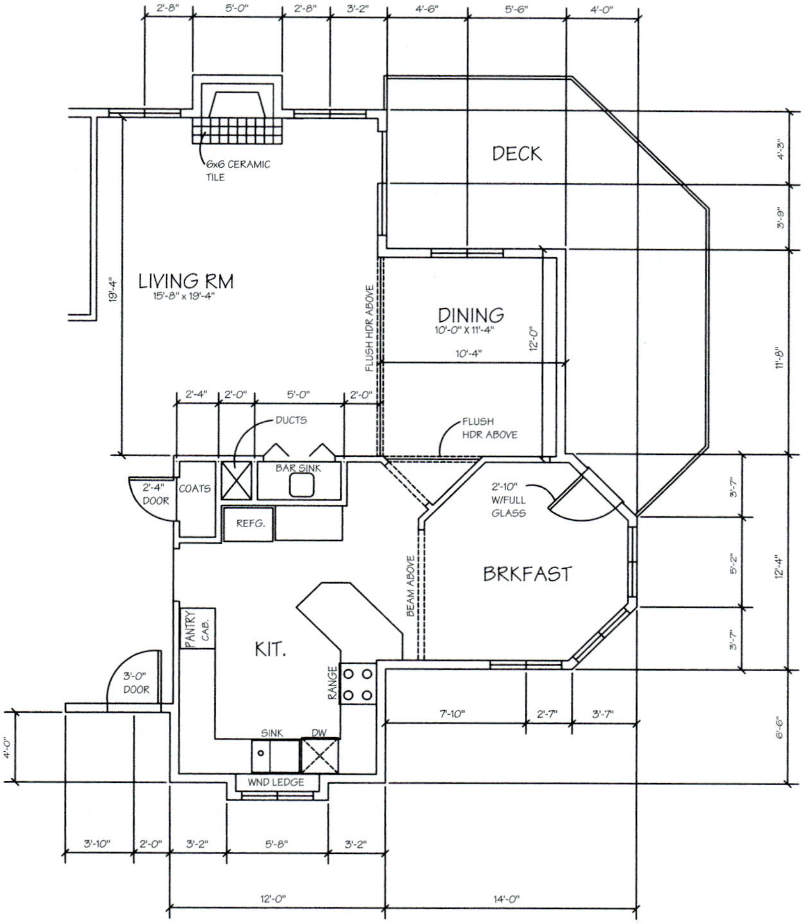

12. Draw the proposed electrical circuit using the multiline commands. Establish a line offset that is proportional to the given layout. Use a phantom linetype for the center of each run. Do not draw the grid, which is provided as a drawing aid. Save the drawing as P14-12.

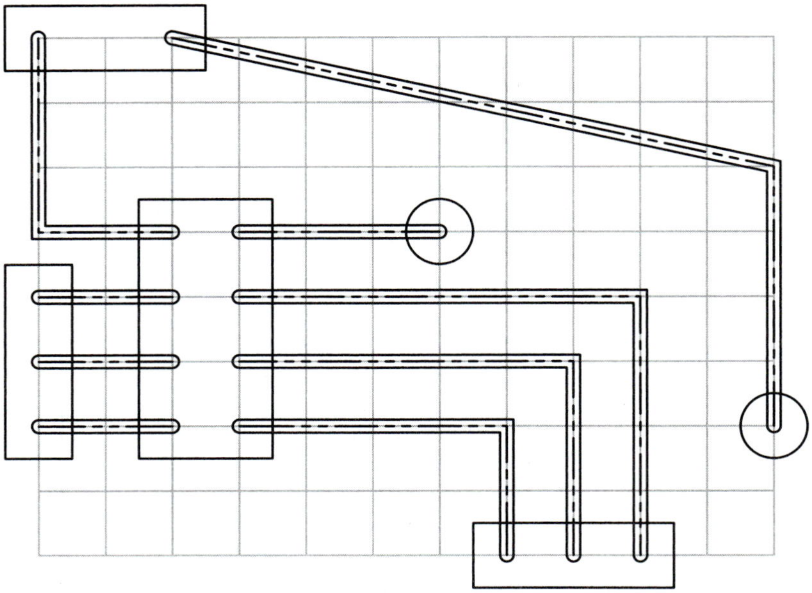

13. Use the **SKETCH** command to sign your name. Save the drawing as P14-13.

14. Use the **SKETCH** command to design the cover of a greeting card. Save the drawing as P14-14.

15. Locate a map of your state. Using the **SKETCH** command:
    A. Sketch the outline of the map.
    B. Include all major rivers and lakes.
    C. Save the drawing as P14-15.

CHAPTER 15

Drawing and Editing Polylines and Splines

Learning Objectives

After completing this chapter, you will be able to do the following:

- Use the **PLINE** command to draw straight and curved polylines.
- Edit existing polylines with the **PEDIT** command.
- Describe the function of each **PEDIT** command option.
- Use the **EXPLODE** command to change polylines into individual line and arc segments.
- Draw and edit spline curves.
- Create a polyline boundary.

The **PLINE** command was introduced in Chapter 14 as a way to draw thick and tapered lines. The discussion focused on line-related options, such as **Width**, **Halfwidth**, and **Length**. The editing functions were limited to the **ERASE** and **UNDO** commands. As you will find in this chapter, the **PLINE** command can also be used to draw a variety of special shapes, limited only by your imagination. This chapter explains how to use the **PLINE** command to create polyline arcs and introduces advanced editing commands for polylines. This chapter also discusses how to convert polylines into smooth curves and how to create and edit true spline curves.

The **PLINE** command can be accessed by picking the **Polyline** button in the **Draw** toolbar or selecting **Polyline** from the **Draw** pull-down menu. You can also type PL or PLINE at the Command: prompt.

PLINE
PL

Draw
➥ Polyline

Draw toolbar
Polyline

Drawing Polyline Arcs

The **Arc** option of the **PLINE** command is similar to the **ARC** command except that the **PLINE Width** and **Halfwidth** options can be used to set an arc width. The arc width can range from 0 up to the radius of the arc. A polyline arc can also be drawn with different starting and ending widths using the **Width** option. The arc shown in Figure 15-1 was drawn with the following command sequence:

Figure 15-1.
A polyline arc with different starting and ending widths.

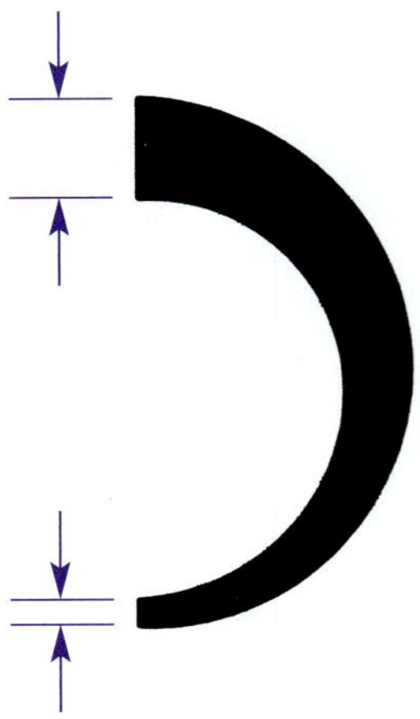

Command: **PL** *or* **PLINE**↵
Specify start point: *(pick the first point)*
Current line-width is 0.0000
Specify next point or [Arc/Halfwidth/Length/Undo/Width]: **W**↵
Specify starting width <*current*>: **.1**↵
Specify ending width <*current*>: **.4**↵
Specify next point or [Arc/Halfwidth/Length/Undo/Width]: **A**↵
Specify endpoint of arc or
[Angle/CEnter/Direction/Halfwidth/Line/Radius/ Second pt/Undo/Width]: *(pick the arc endpoint)*
Specify endpoint of arc or
[Angle/CEnter/CLose/Direction/Halfwidth/Line/Radius/ Second pt/Undo/Width]: ↵
Command:

Drawing a Continuous Polyline Arc

A polyline arc continued from a previous line or polyline is tangent to the last object drawn. The arc's center is determined automatically, but you can pick a new center. If a straight polyline is continued from a polyline arc, the arc's tangent direction remains the same as that of the previous line, arc, or polyline. This may not be what you want. In this case, it may be necessary to specify a setting with one of the **PLINE Arc** options. These options are **Angle, CEnter, CLose, Direction, Radius,** and **Second pt** (second point). The options are very similar to the **ARC** command options and are explained in the following sections.

Specifying the Included Angle

The following is an example of using the **Angle** option inside the **PLINE Arc** command sequence to specify an angle for a polyline arc. The angle value is based on the number of degrees in a circle. Therefore, a value of 180 draws a half circle, 270 draws 3/4 of a circle, and so on. The values 0 and 360 cannot be entered. A negative value draws the arc in a clockwise direction. The object drawn in the following sequence is illustrated in Figure 15-2.

Figure 15-2.
Drawing a polyline arc with a specified angle.

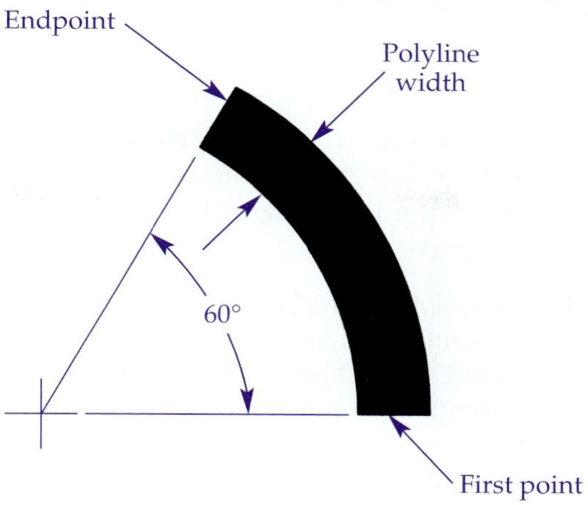

Command: **PL** *or* **PLINE**↵
Specify start point: *(pick the first point)*
Current line-width is 0.4000
Specify next point or [Arc/Halfwidth/Length/Undo/Width]: **A**↵
Specify endpoint of arc or
[Angle/CEnter/Direction/Halfwidth/Line/Radius/ Second pt/Undo/Width]: **A**↵
Specify included angle: *(specify the included angle,* 60 *in this case, and press* [Enter]*)*
Specify endpoint of arc or [CEnter/Radius]: *(pick the arc endpoint)*
Specify endpoint of arc or
[Angle/CEnter/CLose/Direction/Halfwidth/Line/Radius/ Second pt/Undo/Width]: ↵
Command:

Using the CEnter Option

When a polyline arc is drawn as a continuation of a polyline segment, the center point of the arc is automatically calculated. You may want to pick a new center point if the polyline arc does not continue from another object or if the center point calculated is not suitable. The **CEnter** option allows you to specify a new center point for the arc. It is used as follows:

Command: **PL** *or* **PLINE**↵
Specify start point: *(pick the first point)*
Current line-width is 0.4000
Specify next point or [Arc/Halfwidth/Length/Undo/Width]: *(pick the endpoint of the first segment)*
Specify next point or [Arc/Close/Halfwidth/Length/Undo/Width]: **A**↵
Specify endpoint of arc or
[Angle/CEnter/CLose/Direction/Halfwidth/Line/Radius/ Second pt/Undo/Width]: **CE**↵ *(notice that two letters,* CE*, are required for this option)*
Specify center point of arc: *(pick the desired arc center point)*
Specify endpoint of arc or [Angle/Length]: *(select the arc endpoint, or type* A *or* L*, and press* [Enter]*)*

If the endpoint is picked, the polyline arc is drawn. If A is entered, the next prompt is:

Specify included angle: *(enter an included angle and press* [Enter]*)*

If L is entered at the Specify endpoint of arc or [Angle/Length]: prompt, the next prompt is:

Specify length of chord: *(enter a chord length and press* [Enter]*)*

Using the Direction Option

The **Direction** option alters the bearing of the arc. The default option places a polyline arc tangent to the last polyline, arc, or line. The **Direction** option is used to change this and can also be entered when you are drawing an unconnected polyline arc. The **Direction** option functions much like the **Direction** option of the **ARC** command. The following is an example of using the **Direction** option inside the **PLINE Arc** command sequence.

Specify next point or [Arc/Close/Halfwidth/Length/Undo/Width]: **A**↵
Specify endpoint of arc or
[Angle/CEnter/CLose/Direction/Halfwidth/Line/Radius/ Second pt/Undo/Width]: **D**↵
Specify the tangent direction for the start point of arc: *(enter a direction in positive or negative degrees, or pick a point on either side of the start point)*
Specify endpoint of the arc: *(select an endpoint)*

Drawing a Polyline Arc by Radius

Polyline arcs can be drawn by giving the arc's radius. Enter the **Radius** option inside the **PLINE Arc** command sequence as follows:

Specify next point or [Arc/Close/Halfwidth/Length/Undo/Width]: **A**↵
Specify endpoint of arc or
[Angle/CEnter/Direction/Halfwidth/Line/Radius/ Second pt/Undo/Width]: **R**↵
Specify radius of arc: *(enter the arc radius and press* [Enter]*)*
Specify endpoint of arc or [Angle]: *(pick the arc endpoint or enter* A *to specify an included angle)*

Specifying a Three-Point Polyline Arc

A three-point polyline arc can be drawn using the **Second pt** option. The command sequence after entering the **Arc** option is:

Specify endpoint of arc or
[Angle/CEnter/Direction/Halfwidth/Line/Radius/ Second pt/Undo/Width]: **S**↵
Specify second point on arc: *(pick the second point on the arc)*
Specify end point of arc: *(pick the endpoint to complete the arc)*

Using the CLose Option

The **CLose** option saves drafting time by automatically adding the last segment to close a polygonal shape. Using this option inside the **PLINE Arc** command sequence closes the shape with a polyline arc segment, rather than a straight polyline. See Figure 15-3. Notice that CL is entered at the prompt line to distinguish this option from the **CEnter** option:

Specify endpoint of arc or
[Angle/CEnter/CLose/Direction/Halfwidth/Line/Radius/ Second pt/Undo/Width]: **CL**↵

EXERCISE 15-1 Complete the Exercise on the Student CD.

Figure 15-3.
Using the **CLose** option inside the **PLINE Arc** command sequence to close a polygonal shape.

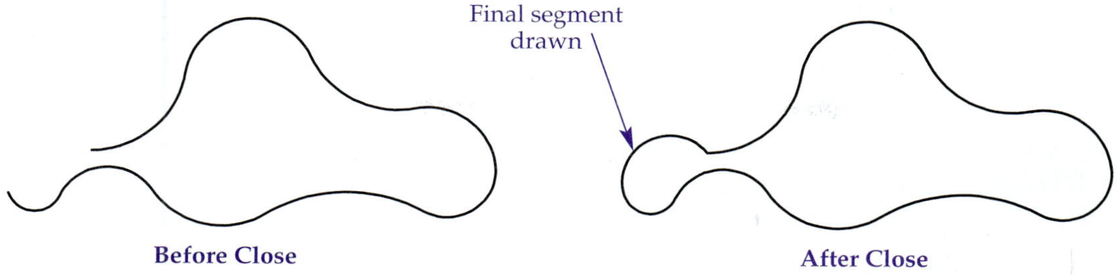

Presetting Polyline Widths

You can preset a constant width for polylines with the **PLINEWID** system variable. This can save you valuable drafting time if you are drawing many wide lines of the same thickness. To specify a setting, type PLINEWID at the Command: prompt. Then, enter a new value. When you are done drawing wide polylines, be sure to set the value of **PLINEWID** to 0.

Objects drawn with the **POLYGON** command are constructed with polylines. However, the width of these objects is not affected by the **PLINEWID** system variable.

Revising Polylines Using the PEDIT Command

Polylines are drawn as multiple segments. A single polyline may be drawn as a straight segment joined to an arc segment and completed with another straight segment. Even though you have drawn separate segments, AutoCAD puts them all together. The result is one polyline treated as a single object. When editing a polyline, you must edit it as one object or divide it into its individual segments. These changes are made with the **PEDIT** and **EXPLODE** commands. The **EXPLODE** command is discussed later in this chapter.

PEDIT
PE

Modify
➥ **Object**
➥ **Polyline**

Modify II toolbar

Edit Polyline

The **PEDIT** command is accessed by picking the **Edit Polyline** button on the **Modify II** toolbar, typing PE or PEDIT at the Command: prompt, or selecting **Polyline** from the **Object** cascading menu in the **Modify** pull-down menu. You can also select a polyline, right-click in the drawing area, and choose **Polyline Edit** from the shortcut menu. The **PEDIT** command is initiated as follows:

Command: **PE** *or* **PEDIT**↵
Select polyline or [Multiple]: *(select the polyline)*

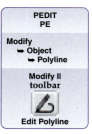

When selecting a wide polyline, you must pick on the edge of a polyline segment rather than in the center. If you want to edit more than one polyline, type M to select the **Multiple** option. If the polyline you want to change was the last object drawn, simply type L for **Last** at the Select polyline: prompt. If the object you select is a line or arc object, the following message is displayed:

Object selected is not a polyline
Do you want to turn it into one? <Y>

Entering Y or pressing [Enter] turns the selected object into a polyline. Type N and press [Enter] to leave the object as is. The command then continues. The command options are explained later in this chapter.

You can have AutoCAD automatically turn lines and arcs into polylines without displaying the previous prompt. The value of the **PEDITACCEPT** system variable controls this feature. When set to 0, you are prompted when a line or arc is selected.

When the system variable is set to 1, AutoCAD automatically turns selected lines and arcs into polylines. The command then continues normally.

Circles drawn with the **CIRCLE** command cannot be changed to polylines for editing purposes. Polyline circles can be created by using the **PLINE Arc** option and drawing two 180° arcs, or by using the **DONUT** command.

PROFESSIONAL TIP

A group of connected lines and arcs can be turned into a continuous polyline by using the **PEDIT Join** option. This option is discussed later in this chapter.

Revising a Polyline As One Unit

A polyline can be edited as a single object or it can be divided into individual segments. The segments can then be revised individually. This section discusses the options for changing the entire polyline. The command sequence is:

> Command: **PE** *or* **PEDIT**↵
> Select polyline or [Multiple]: *(pick a polyline)*
> Enter an option [Close/Join/Width/Edit vertex/Fit/Spline/Decurve/Ltype gen/Undo]:

There is no default option for the **PEDIT** command; you must select one of the options. Pressing [Enter] returns you to the Command: prompt.

Opening and Closing a Polyline

You may decide that you need to close an open polyline or open a closed polyline. These functions are performed with the **Open** and **Close** options of the **PEDIT** command. Open and closed polylines are shown in Figure 15-4.

If you select a closed polyline, AutoCAD displays the **Open** option along with the other **PEDIT** command options. Enter this option to open the polyline by removing the last segment.

The **Open** option is only available if the polygon was closed using the **Close** option of the **PLINE** command. It is not displayed if the polyline was closed by manually drawing the final segment. Instead, the **Close** option is displayed.

If you select an open polyline, the **Close** option is displayed instead of the **Open** option. Enter this option to close the polyline.

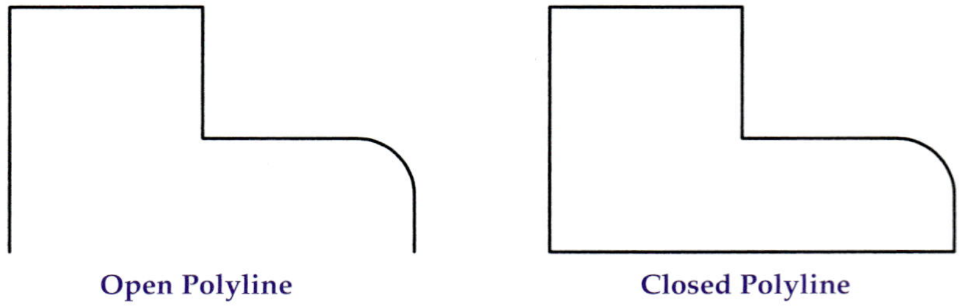

Figure 15-4.
Open and closed polylines.

Joining Polylines to Other Polylines, Lines, and Arcs

Connected polylines, lines, and arcs can be joined to create a single polyline. This is done with the **Join** option of the **PEDIT** command. This option works only if the polyline and other existing objects meet *exactly*. They cannot cross, nor can there be any spaces or breaks between the objects. See **Figure 15-5.** The command sequence to join objects to a polyline is:

Command: **PE** *or* **PEDIT**↵
Select polyline or [Multiple]: *(select the original polyline)*
Enter an option [Close/Join/Width/Edit vertex/Fit/Spline/Decurve/Ltype gen/Undo]: **J**↵
Select objects: *(select all of the objects to be joined)*
Select objects: ↵
n segments added to polyline
Enter an option [Close/Join/Width/Edit vertex/Fit/Spline/Decurve/Ltype gen/Undo]: ↵
Command:

Select each object to be joined or group the objects with one of the selection set options. The original polyline can be included in the selection set, but it does not need to be. See **Figure 15-6.** If you select lines and arcs to join, AutoCAD automatically converts these objects to polylines, regardless of the **PEDITACCEPT** setting.

PROFESSIONAL TIP

Once items have been joined into a continuous polyline, the polyline can be closed using the **PEDIT Close** option.

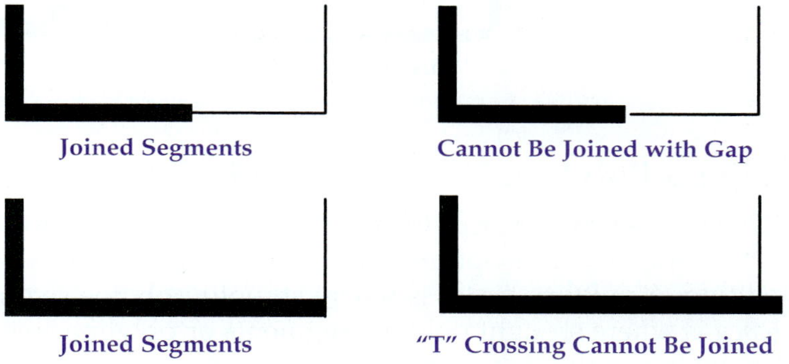

Figure 15-5. Features that can and cannot be joined using the **PEDIT Join** option.

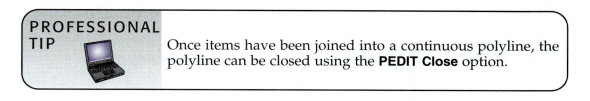

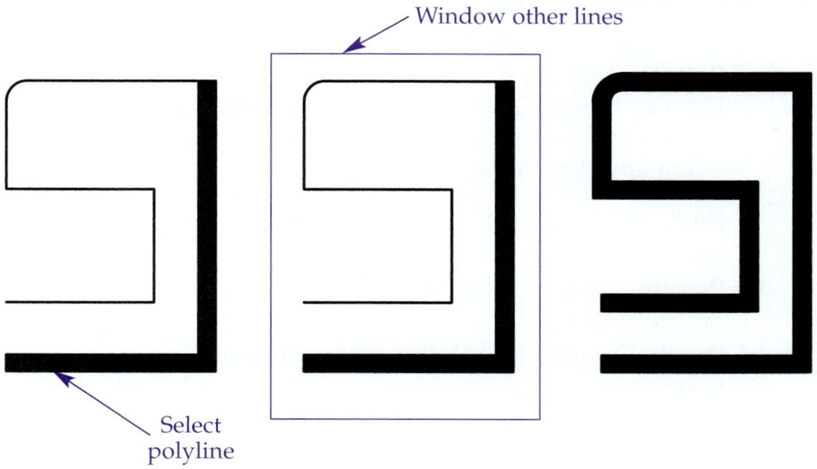

Figure 15-6. Joining a polyline to other connected lines and arcs.

Changing the Width of a Polyline

The **Width** option of the **PEDIT** command allows you to change a polyline width to a new width. The width of the original polyline can be constant or it can vary. However, *all* segments will be changed to the constant width you specify. To change a polyline from a .06 width to a .1 width, follow these steps:

Command: **PE** *or* **PEDIT**↵
Select polyline or [Multiple]: *(pick the polyline)*
Enter an option [Close/Join/Width/Edit vertex/Fit/Spline/Decurve/Ltype gen/Undo]: **W**↵
Specify new width for all segments: **.1**↵
Enter an option [Close/Join/Width/Edit vertex/Fit/Spline/Decurve/Ltype gen/Undo]: ↵
Command:

An unedited polyline and a new polyline after using the **PEDIT Width** option are shown in Figure 15-7. The width of donuts can be changed using this procedure as well.

EXERCISE 15-2 Complete the Exercise on the Student CD.

Figure 15-7.
Changing the width of a polyline.

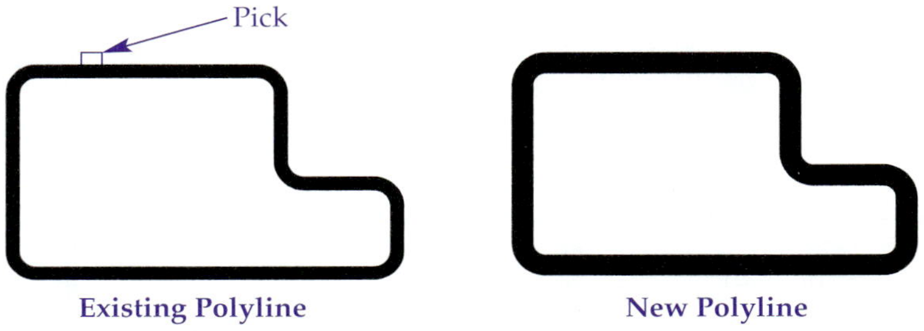

Editing a Polyline Vertex or Point of Tangency

The **Edit vertex** option of the **PEDIT** command is used to edit polyline vertices and points of tangency. This option is not available if you have selected multiple polylines for editing. A polyline *vertex* is where straight polyline segments meet and a *point of tangency* is where straight polyline segments or polyline arcs join other polyline arcs. When you enter the **Edit vertex** option, an "X" marker appears on screen at the first polyline vertex or point of tangency. The **Edit vertex** option has 10 suboptions, as shown in the following command sequence and explained below.

Command: **PE** *or* **PEDIT**↵
Select polyline or [Multiple]: *(pick the polyline)*
Enter an option [Close/Join/Width/Edit vertex/Fit/Spline/Decurve/Ltype gen/Undo]: **E**↵
Enter a vertex editing option [Next/Previous/Break/Insert/Move/Regen/Straighten/
Tangent/Width/eXit] <N>:

- **Next.** Moves the "X" marker on screen to the next vertex or point of tangency on the polyline.
- **Previous.** Moves the "X" marker to the previous vertex or point of tangency on the polyline.
- **Break.** Breaks the polyline between two vertices or points of tangency.
- **Insert.** Adds a new polyline vertex at a selected point.
- **Move.** Moves a polyline vertex to a new location.
- **Regen.** Generates the revised version of the polyline.

- **Straighten.** Straightens polyline arc segments or multiple segments between two points.
- **Tangent.** Specifies a tangent direction for curve fitting when using the **PEDIT Fit** option.
- **Width.** Changes the width of a polyline segment.
- **eXit.** Returns the **PEDIT** command prompt.

Only the current point identified by the "X" marker is affected by editing functions. In Figure 15-8, the marker is moved clockwise through the points using the **Next** option and counterclockwise using the **Previous** option. If you edit the vertices of a polyline and nothing appears to happen, use the **Regen** suboption to regenerate the polyline.

Making Breaks in a Polyline

You can break a polyline into two separate polylines with the **Break** suboption of the **Edit vertex** option of the **PEDIT** command. Once the **Edit vertex** option is entered, use the **Next** or **Previous** suboption to move the "X" marker to the first vertex where the polyline is to be broken. Then, enter the **Break** suboption:

Enter an option [Close/Join/Width/Edit vertex/Fit/Spline/Decurve/Ltype gen/Undo]: **E**↵
Enter a vertex editing option
[Next/Previous/Break/Insert/Move/Regen/Straighten/Tangent/Width/eXit] <N>: *(use* **Next** *and* **Previous** *to move the "X" marker to the position where you want the break to begin)*
Enter a vertex editing option
[Next/Previous/Break/Insert/Move/Regen/Straighten/Tangent/Width/eXit] <N>: **B**↵

A marker is placed at the first break point. The command sequence continues:

Enter an option [Next/Previous/Go/eXit] <N>: *(move the "X" marker to the second vertex of the break using* Next *or* Previous*)*
Enter an option [Next/Previous/Go/eXit] <N>: **G**↵

The **Go** suboption instructs AutoCAD to remove the portion of the polyline between the two points. You can also break the polyline without removing a segment by specifying **Go** without moving to a second vertex. The results of the following command sequence are illustrated in Figure 15-9. The polyline was drawn clockwise.

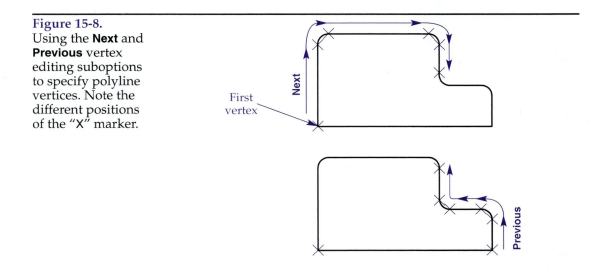

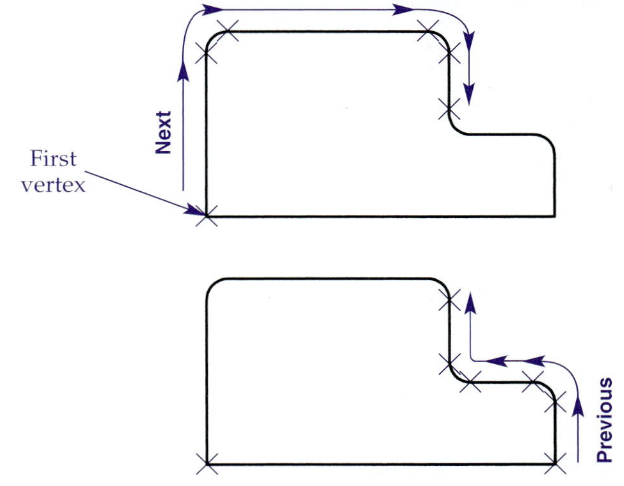

Figure 15-8.
Using the **Next** and **Previous** vertex editing suboptions to specify polyline vertices. Note the different positions of the "X" marker.

Figure 15-9.
Using the **Break** vertex editing suboption to break a polyline and remove a portion.

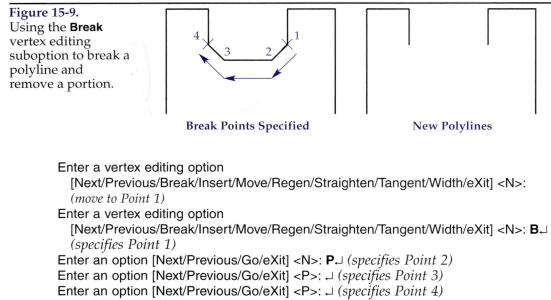

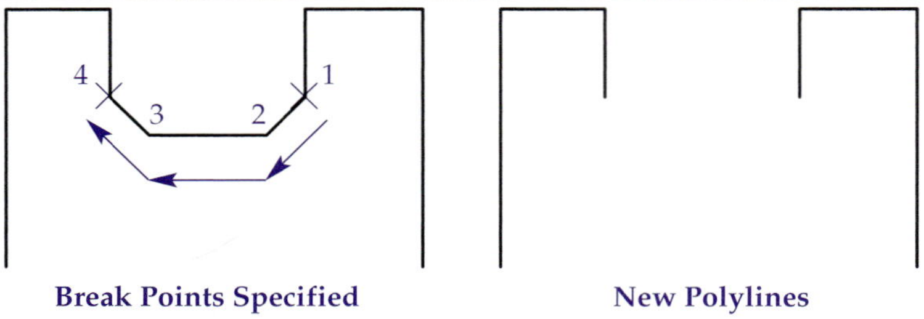

Enter a vertex editing option
[Next/Previous/Break/Insert/Move/Regen/Straighten/Tangent/Width/eXit] <N>: *(move to Point 1)*
Enter a vertex editing option
[Next/Previous/Break/Insert/Move/Regen/Straighten/Tangent/Width/eXit] <N>: **B**↵ *(specifies Point 1)*
Enter an option [Next/Previous/Go/eXit] <N>: **P**↵ *(specifies Point 2)*
Enter an option [Next/Previous/Go/eXit] <P>: ↵ *(specifies Point 3)*
Enter an option [Next/Previous/Go/eXit] <P>: ↵ *(specifies Point 4)*
Enter an option [Next/Previous/Go/eXit] <P>: **G**↵ *(breaks the polyline between Points 1 and 4)*

Inserting a New Vertex in a Polyline

A new vertex can be added to a polyline using the **Insert** vertex editing suboption. The new vertex can be inserted on an existing polyline segment, but does not need to be. First, use the **Next** or **Previous** suboption to locate the vertex next to where you want the new vertex. Refer to **Figure 15-10** as you go through the following command sequence:

Enter an option [Close/Join/Width/Edit vertex/Fit/Spline/Decurve/Ltype gen/Undo]: **E**↵
Enter a vertex editing option [Next/Previous/Break/Insert/Move/Regen/Straighten/Tangent/Width/eXit] <N>: *(move the "X" marker to the desired location)*
Enter a vertex editing option [Next/Previous/Break/Insert/Move/Regen/Straighten/Tangent/Width/eXit] <N>: **I**↵
Specify location for new vertex: *(pick the new vertex location using your pointing device or enter the coordinates)*
Enter a vertex editing option [Next/Previous/Break/Insert/Move/Regen/Straighten/Tangent/Width/eXit] <N>: **X**↵

Figure 15-10.
Using the **Insert** vertex editing suboption to add a new vertex to a polyline.

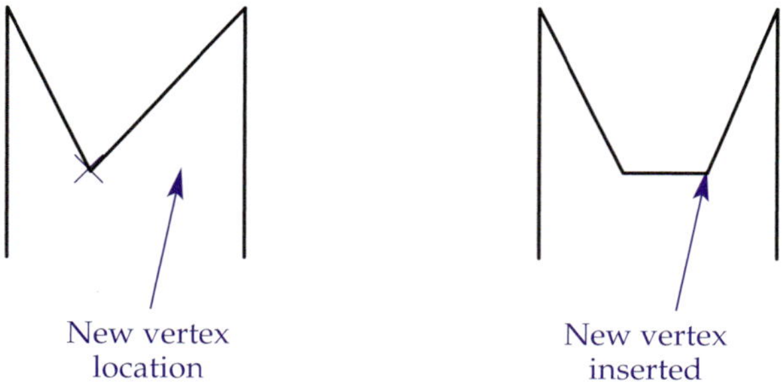

Moving a Polyline Vertex

The **Move** vertex editing suboption enables you to move a polyline vertex to a new location. The "X" marker must first be placed on the vertex you want to move. Then, enter the **Move** suboption and specify the new vertex location. The results of the following sequence are shown in **Figure 15-11:**

Figure 15-11.
Using the **Move** vertex editing suboption to place a polyline vertex at a new location.

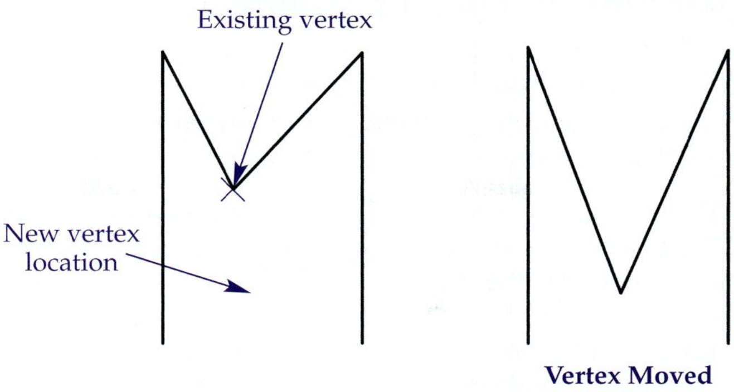

Enter an option [Close/Join/Width/Edit vertex/Fit/Spline/Decurve/Ltype gen/Undo]: **E**↵
Enter a vertex editing option [Next/Previous/Break/Insert/Move/Regen/Straighten/ Tangent/Width/eXit] <N>: *(move the "X" marker to the vertex to be moved)*
Enter a vertex editing option [Next/Previous/Break/Insert/Move/Regen/Straighten/ Tangent/Width/eXit] <N>: **M**↵
Specify new location for marked vertex: *(pick the desired location with your pointing device or enter the coordinates)*
Enter a vertex editing option [Next/Previous/Break/Insert/Move/Regen/Straighten/ Tangent/Width/eXit] <N>: **X**↵

Straightening Polyline Segments or Arcs

The **Straighten** vertex editing suboption allows you to straighten polyline segments or arcs between two points. The command sequence is:

Enter an option [Close/Join/Width/Edit vertex/Fit/Spline/Decurve/Ltype gen/Undo]: **E**↵
Enter a vertex editing option [Next/Previous/Break/Insert/Move/Regen/Straighten/ Tangent/Width/eXit] <N>: *(move the "X" marker to the first point of the segments to be straightened)*
Enter a vertex editing option [Next/Previous/Break/Insert/Move/Regen/Straighten/ Tangent/Width/eXit] <N>: **S**↵
Enter an option [Next/Previous/Go/eXit] <N>: *(move the "X" marker to the last point of the segments to be straightened)*
Enter an option [Next/Previous/Go/eXit] <N>: **G**↵

If the "X" marker is not moved before G is entered, AutoCAD straightens the segment from the first marked point to the next vertex. This provides a quick way to straighten an arc. See **Figure 15-12.**

Figure 15-12.
The **Straighten** vertex editing suboption is used to straighten polyline segments.

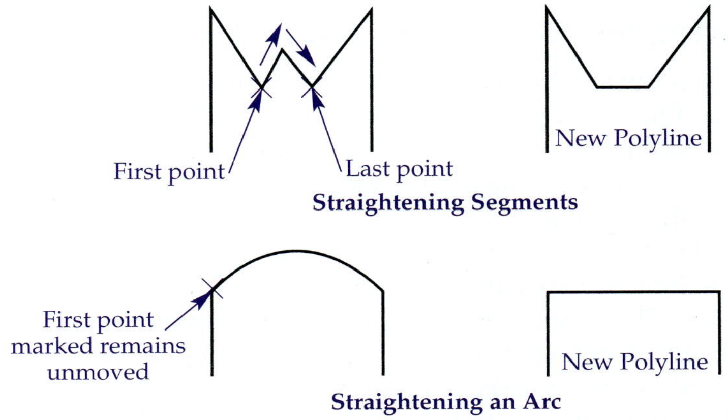

Changing Polyline Segment Widths

The **Width** vertex editing suboption is used to change the starting and ending widths of an individual polyline segment. To change a segment width, move the "X" marker to the beginning vertex of the segment to be altered. Then, enter the **Width** option and specify the new width. The command sequence is:

> Enter an option [Close/Join/Width/Edit vertex/Fit/Spline/Decurve/Ltype gen/Undo]: **E**↵
> Enter a vertex editing option [Next/Previous/Break/Insert/Move/Regen/Straighten/Tangent/Width/eXit] <N>: *(move the "X" marker to the beginning vertex of the segment to be changed)*
> Enter a vertex editing option [Next/Previous/Break/Insert/Move/Regen/Straighten/Tangent/Width/eXit] <N>: **W**↵
> Specify starting width for next segment <*current width of segment*>: *(enter the revised starting width and press* [Enter]*)*
> Specify ending width for next segment <*revised starting width*>: *(enter the revised ending width and press* [Enter]*, or press* [Enter] *to keep the width the same as the starting width)*
> Enter a vertex editing option [Next/Previous/Break/Insert/Move/Regen/Straighten/Tangent/Width/eXit] <N>: **R**↵

Notice the default starting width value is the current width of the segment to be changed. The default ending width value is the same as the revised starting width. If nothing appears to happen to the segment when you specify the ending width and press [Enter], enter the **Regen** option to have AutoCAD draw the revised polyline. See **Figure 15-13.**

EXERCISE 15-3 Complete the Exercise on the Student CD.

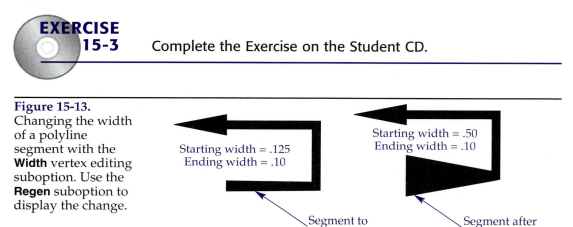

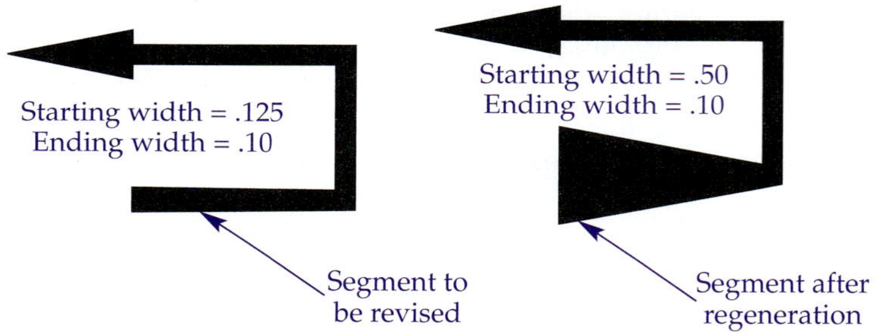

Figure 15-13. Changing the width of a polyline segment with the **Width** vertex editing suboption. Use the **Regen** suboption to display the change.

Making Smooth Curves out of Polylines

In some situations, you may need to convert a polyline into a series of smooth curves. One example of this is a graph. A graph may show a series of plotted points as a smooth curve rather than straight segments. This process is called ***curve fitting*** and is accomplished using the **Fit** option and the **Tangent** vertex editing suboption of the **PEDIT** command.

The **Fit** option allows you to construct pairs of arcs passing through control points. You can specify the control points or you can simply use the vertices of the polyline. The more closely spaced the control points, the smoother the curve.

Prior to curve fitting, each vertex can be given a tangent direction. AutoCAD then fits the curve based on the tangent directions that you set. However, you do not need to enter tangent directions. Specifying tangent directions is a way to edit vertices when the **PEDIT Fit** option does not produce the best results.

The **Tangent** vertex editing suboption is used to edit tangent directions. After entering the **PEDIT** command and the **Edit vertex** option, move the "X" marker to each vertex to be changed. Enter the **Tangent** suboption for each specified vertex and enter a tangent direction in degrees or pick a point in the expected direction. The direction you choose is then indicated by an arrow placed at the vertex. The command sequence is:

Enter an option [Close/Join/Width/Edit vertex/Fit/Spline/Decurve/Ltype gen/Undo]: **E**↵
Enter a vertex editing option
[Next/Previous/Break/Insert/Move/Regen/Straighten/Tangent/Width/eXit] <N>: *(move the "X" marker to the desired vertex)*
Enter a vertex editing option
[Next/Previous/Break/Insert/Move/Regen/Straighten/Tangent/Width/eXit] <N>: **T**↵
Specify direction of vertex tangent: *(specify a direction in positive or negative degrees and press* [Enter] *or pick a point in the desired direction)*

Continue by moving the marker to each vertex that you want to change, entering the **Tangent** suboption for each vertex, and selecting a tangent direction. Once the tangent directions are given for all vertices to be changed, enter the **PEDIT Fit** option.

You can also enter the **PEDIT** command, select a polyline, and then enter the **Fit** option without adjusting tangencies if desired. The polyline shown in Figure 15-14 was made into a smooth curve using the following steps:

Command: **PE** *or* **PEDIT**↵
Select polyline or [Multiple]: *(pick the polyline to be edited)*
Enter an option [Close/Join/Width/Edit vertex/Fit/Spline/Decurve/Ltype gen/Undo]: **F**↵

If the resulting curve does not look like what you had anticipated, enter the **Edit vertex** option. Then, make changes using the various vertex editing suboptions as necessary.

Figure 15-14.
Using the **PEDIT Fit** option to turn a polyline into a smooth curve.

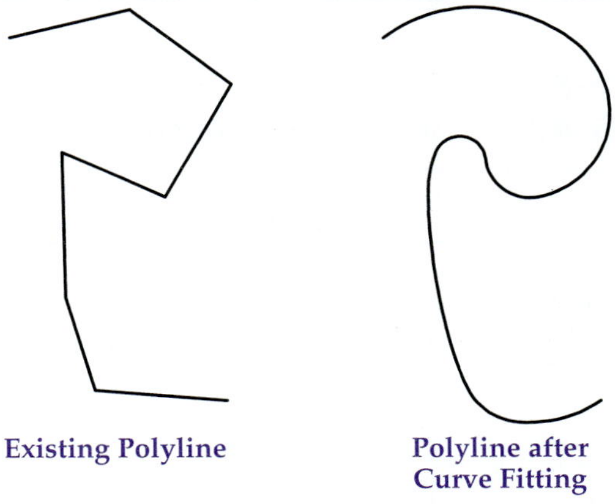

Using the PEDIT Spline Option

When a polyline is edited with the **PEDIT Fit** option, the resulting curve passes through each of the polyline's vertices. The **PEDIT Spline** option also smoothes the corners of a straight-segment polyline. However, this option produces different results. The resulting curve passes through the first and last control points or vertices only. The curve *pulls* toward the other vertices, but does not pass through them. The **Spline** option is used as follows:

Command: **PE** *or* **PEDIT**↵
Select polyline or [Multiple]: *(pick the polyline to be edited)*
Enter an option [Close/Join/Width/Edit vertex/Fit/Spline/Decurve/Ltype gen/Undo]: **S**↵

The results of using the **Fit** and **Spline** options on a polyline are illustrated in Figure 15-15.

Figure 15-15.
A comparison of polylines edited with the **PEDIT Fit** and **Spline** options.

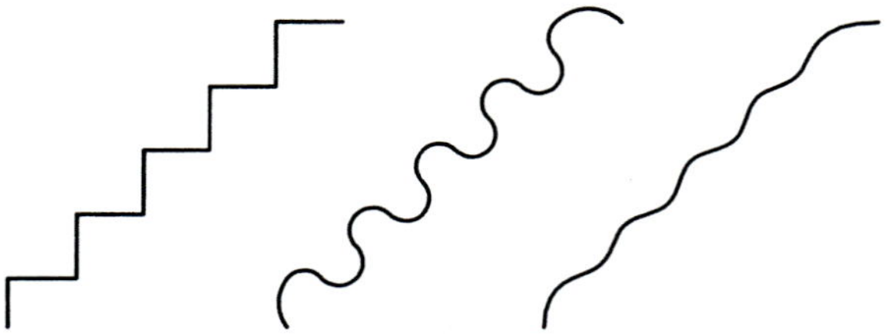

Straightening All Segments of a Polyline

The **PEDIT Decurve** option returns a polyline edited with the **Fit** or **Spline** options to its original form. However, the information entered for tangent directions is kept for future reference. You can also use the **Decurve** option to straighten the curved segments of a polyline. See Figure 15-16.

Command: **PE** *or* **PEDIT**↵
Select polyline: *(pick the polyline to be edited)*
Enter an option [Close/Join/Width/Edit vertex/Fit/Spline/Decurve/Ltype gen/Undo]: **D**↵

PROFESSIONAL TIP

If you make a mistake while editing a polyline, remember that the **Undo** option is available inside the **PEDIT** command. Using the **Undo** option more than once allows you to step backward through each operation. The **UNDO** command can also be used at the Command: prompt to undo all of the effects of the last **PEDIT** command.

EXERCISE 15-4 Complete the Exercise on the Student CD.

Figure 15-16.
The **PEDIT Decurve** option is used to straighten the curved segments of a polyline.

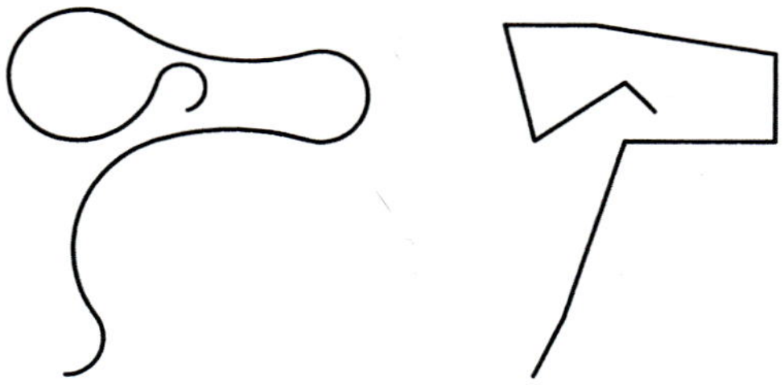

Changing the Appearance of Polyline Linetypes

The **PEDIT Ltype gen** (linetype generation) option determines how linetypes other than Continuous appear in relation to the vertices of a polyline. For example, when a Center linetype is used and the **Ltype gen** option is disabled, the polyline has a long dash at each vertex. When the **Ltype gen** option is activated, the polyline is generated with a constant pattern in relation to the polyline as a whole. The difference between using the **Ltype gen** option off and on is illustrated in Figure 15-17. Also shown are the effects these settings have on spline curves. To turn the **Ltype gen** option on:

Figure 15-17.
A comparison of polylines with the **PEDIT Ltype gen** option on and off.

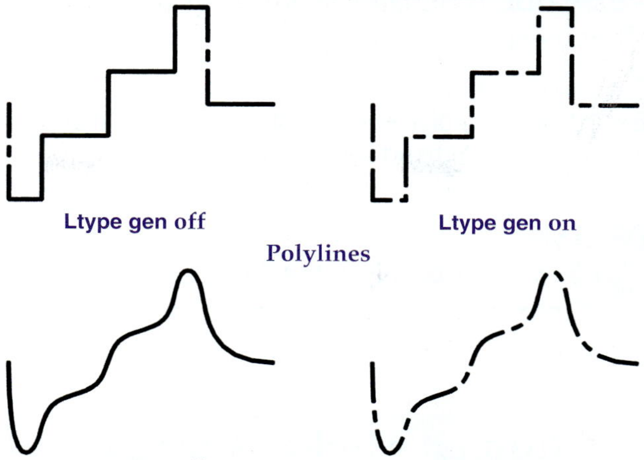

Command: **PE** *or* **PEDIT**↵
Select polyline or [Multiple]: *(pick the polyline)*
Enter an option [Close/Join/Width/Edit vertex/Fit/Spline/Decurve/Ltype gen/Undo]: **L**↵
Enter polyline linetype generation option [ON/OFF] <Off>: **ON**↵

You can also change the **Ltype gen** option setting for new polylines with the **PLINEGEN** system variable. This variable must be set before the polyline is drawn. Changing the setting does not affect existing polylines. The settings for the **PLINEGEN** system variable are 0 (off) and 1 (on).

Converting a Polyline into Individual Line and Arc Segments

A polyline is a single object composed of line and arc segments. The **EXPLODE** command allows you to change a polyline into a series of individual lines and arcs. You can then edit each segment individually. The resulting segments are not, however, polylines. When a wide polyline is exploded, the resulting line or arc is redrawn along the centerline of the original polyline. See Figure 15-18.

EXPLODE
X
Modify
➡ Explode
Modify toolbar

Explode

To explode an object, pick the **Explode** button on the **Modify** toolbar, select **Explode** from the **Modify** pull-down menu, or type X or EXPLODE at the Command: prompt. You are then asked to select objects:

Command: **X** *or* **EXPLODE**↵
Select objects: *(pick the polyline to be exploded)*
Select objects: ↵

Figure 15-18.
Exploding a wide polyline.

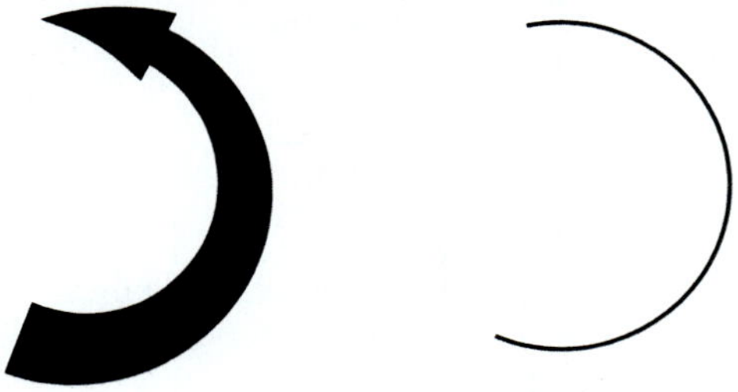

The **EXPLODE** command removes all width characteristics and tangency information. If you explode a wide polyline, AutoCAD reminds you of this fact with the message:

Exploding this polyline has lost width information.
The UNDO command will restore it.

EXERCISE 15-5 Complete the Exercise on the Student CD.

Additional Methods for Smoothing Polylines

The methods for smoothing polylines that were introduced earlier in this chapter focused on using the **Fit** and **Spline** options of the **PEDIT** command. With the **Fit** option, the resulting *fit curve* passes through the polyline vertices. The **Spline** option creates a *spline curve* that passes through the first and last control points or vertices. The resulting curve *pulls* toward the other vertices but does not pass through them.

The **Spline** option creates a curve that approximates a true B-spline. AutoCAD's **SPLINE** command creates a true B-spline curve. You can choose between one of two types of calculations used by the **Spline** option to create the curve—cubic and quadratic. A ***cubic curve*** is extremely smooth. A ***quadratic curve*** is not as smooth as a cubic curve, but it is smoother than a curve produced with the **Fit** option. Like a cubic curve, a quadratic curve passes through the first and last control points. The remainder of the curve is tangent to the polyline segments between the intermediate control points, as shown in Figure 15-19.

The **SPLINETYPE** system variable determines whether AutoCAD draws cubic or quadratic curves. The default setting is 6. At this setting, a cubic curve is drawn when using the **Spline** option of the **PEDIT** command. If the **SPLINETYPE** system variable is set to 5, a quadratic curve is generated. The only valid values for **SPLINETYPE** are 5 and 6.

EXERCISE 15-6 Complete the Exercise on the Student CD.

Figure 15-19.
A comparison of curves drawn with the **PEDIT Fit** and **Spline** options. The **SPLINETYPE** system variable controls whether a quadratic or cubic curve is drawn with the **Spline** option.

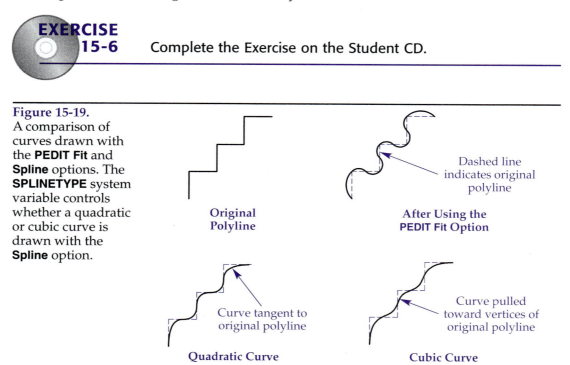

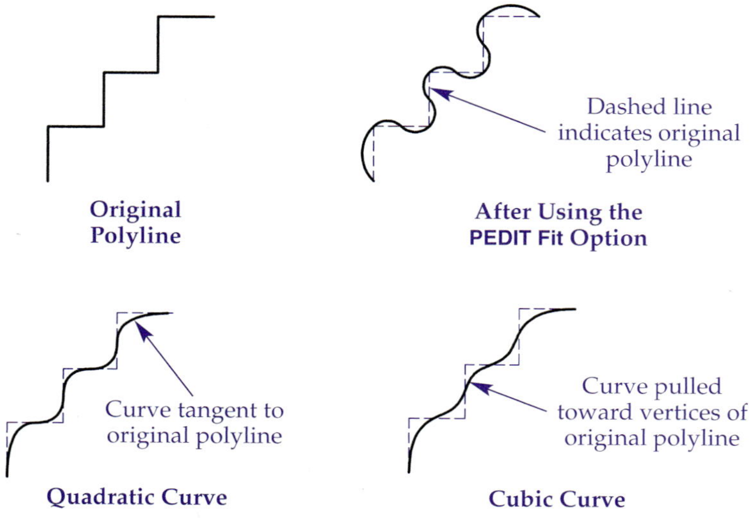

The **SPLINESEGS** system variable controls the number of line segments used to construct spline curves. It can be set at the Command: prompt or in the **Segments in a polyline curve** text box in the **Display resolution** area of the **Display** tab of the **Options** dialog box. The **SPLINESEGS** default value is 8, which creates a fairly smooth spline curve with moderate regeneration time. If you decrease the value, the resulting spline curve is less smooth. If you increase the value, the resulting spline curve is smoother but the regeneration time and drawing file size is increased. The relationship between **SPLINESEGS** values and spline curves is shown in **Figure 15-20.**

EXERCISE 15-7 Complete the Exercise on the Student CD.

Figure 15-20.
A comparison of curves drawn with different settings for the **SPLINESEGS** system variable.

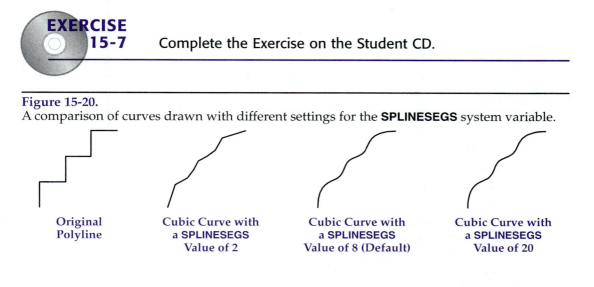

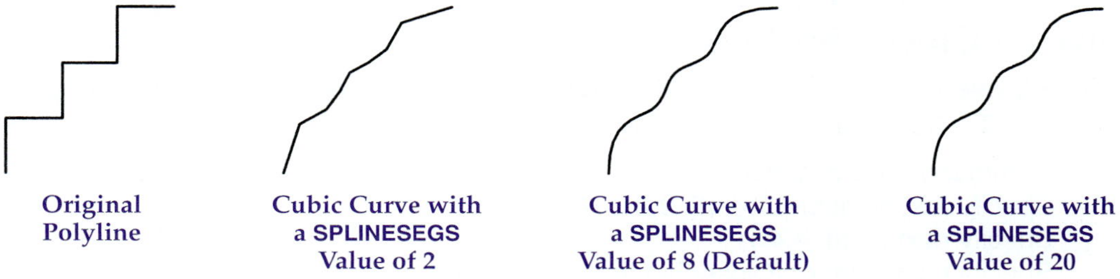

Drawing Curves Using the SPLINE Command

The **SPLINE** command is used to create a special type of curve called a nonuniform rational B-spline (NURBS). A *NURBS* curve is considered to be a true spline. A spline created by fitting a spline curve to a polyline is merely a linear approximation of a true spline and is not as accurate. An additional advantage of spline objects over smoothed polylines is that splines use less disk space.

SPLINE
SPL
Draw
➡ Spline
Draw toolbar
Spline

To access the **SPLINE** command, pick the **Spline** button on the **Draw** toolbar, pick **Spline** from the **Draw** pull-down menu, or type SPL or SPLINE at the Command: prompt. A spline is created by specifying the control points using any standard coordinate entry method.

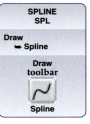

Command: **SPL** *or* **SPLINE**↵
Specify first point or [Object]: **2,2**↵
Specify next point: **4,4**↵
Specify next point or [Close/Fit tolerance] <start tangent>: **6,2**↵
Specify next point or [Close/Fit tolerance] <start tangent>: ↵
Specify start tangent: ↵
Specify end tangent: ↵
Command:

When you have given all of the necessary points along the spline, pressing [Enter] ends the point specification process and allows the start tangency and end tangency to be entered. Specifying the tangents changes the direction in which the spline curve begins and ends. Pressing [Enter] at these prompts accepts the default direction, as calculated by AutoCAD, for the specified curve. The results of the previous command sequence are shown in **Figure 15-21.**

Figure 15-21.
A spline drawn with the **SPLINE** command using the AutoCAD defaults for the start and end tangents.

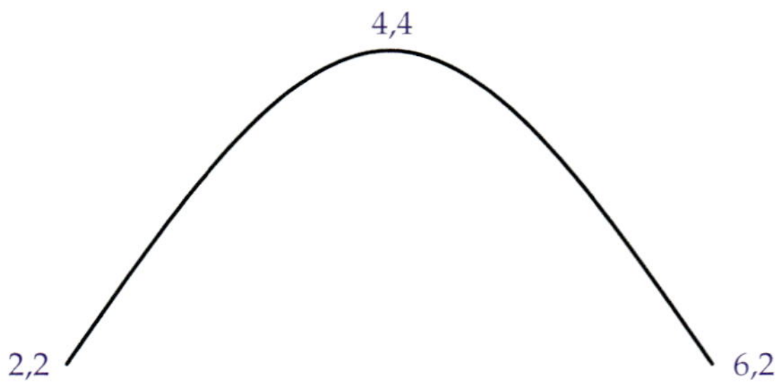

> **NOTE**
>
> If only two points are specified along the spline curve, an object that looks like a line is created, but the object is a spline.

Drawing Closed Splines

The **Close** option of the **SPLINE** command enables you to draw closed splines, Figure 15-22. The command sequence is:

Command: **SPL** *or* **SPLINE**↵
Specify first point or [Object]: **2,2**↵
Specify next point: **4,4**↵
Specify next point or [Close/Fit tolerance] <start tangent>: **6,2**↵
Specify next point or [Close/Fit tolerance] <start tangent>: **C**↵
Specify tangent: ↵
Command:

After closing a spline, you are prompted to specify a tangent direction for the start/end point of the spline. Pressing [Enter] accepts the default calculated by AutoCAD.

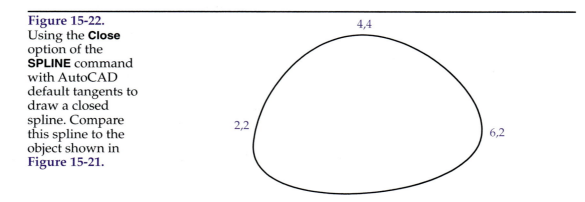

Figure 15-22.
Using the **Close** option of the **SPLINE** command with AutoCAD default tangents to draw a closed spline. Compare this spline to the object shown in Figure 15-21.

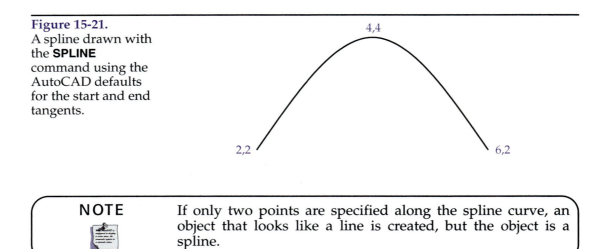

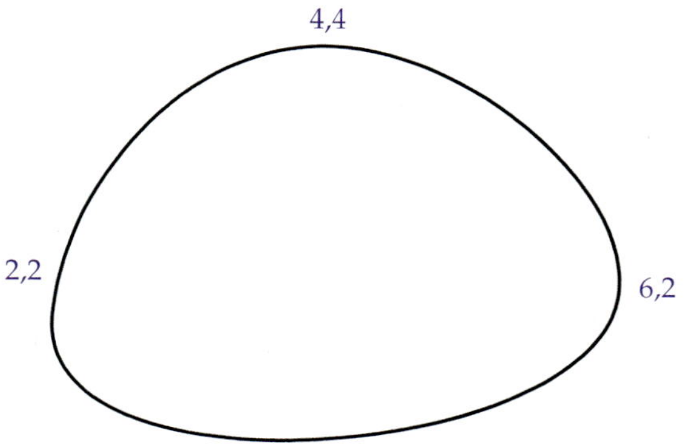

Altering the **Fit Tolerance** Specifications

When drawing splines, different results can be achieved by altering the specifications used with the **Fit Tolerance** option. The outcomes of different settings vary, depending on the configuration of the individual spline object. The setting specifies a *tolerance* within which the spline curve falls as it passes through the control points.

Specifying the Start and End Tangents

The previous **SPLINE** command examples used AutoCAD's default start and end tangents. You can set start and end tangent directions by entering values at the prompts that appear after you pick the points of the spline. The tangency is based on

Figure 15-23.
These splines were drawn through the same points but have different start and end tangent directions. The tangent directions are indicated by the arrows.

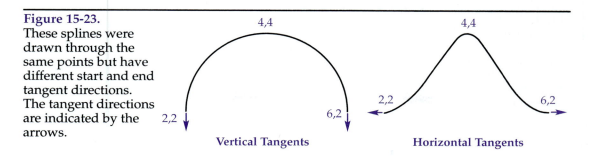

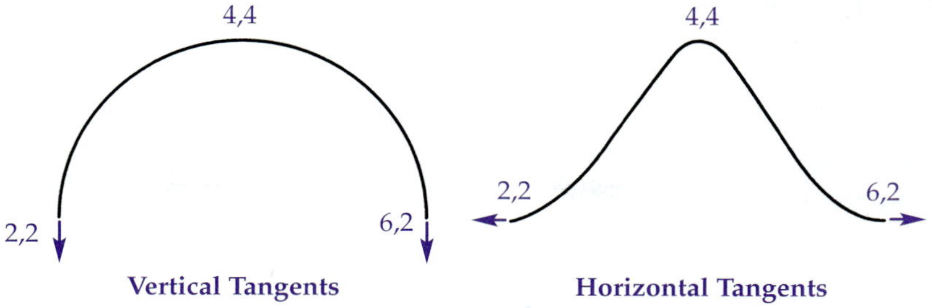

the tangent direction of the selected point. The results of using the horizontal and vertical tangent directions using **Ortho** mode are shown in Figure 15-23. The command sequence is:

Command: **SPL** *or* **SPLINE**↵
Specify first point or [Object]: **2,2**↵
Specify next point: **4,4**↵
Specify next point or [Close/Fit tolerance] <start tangent>: **6,2**↵
Specify next point or [Close/Fit tolerance] <start tangent>: ↵
Specify start tangent: *(move cursor in tangent direction and press* [Enter]*)*
Specify end tangent: *(move cursor in tangent direction and press* [Enter]*)*
Command:

Converting a Spline-Fitted Polyline to a Spline

A spline-fitted polyline object can be converted to a spline object using the **Object** option of the **SPLINE** command. This option works for either 2D or 3D objects. The command sequence is as follows:

Command: **SPL** *or* **SPLINE**↵
Specify first point or [Object]: **O**↵
Select objects to convert to splines...
Select objects: *(pick the spline-fitted polyline)*
Select objects: ↵
Command:

EXERCISE 15-8 Complete the Exercise on the Student CD.

Editing Splines

The **SPLINEDIT** command allows you to edit spline objects. Several editing options are available. Control points can be added, moved, or deleted to alter the shape of an existing curve. A spline can also be opened or closed. In addition, you can change the start and end tangents.

SPE
SPLINEDIT
Modify
➥ Object
➥ Spline
Modify II toolbar
Edit Spline

To access the **SPLINEDIT** command, pick the **Edit Spline** button on the **Modify II** toolbar, pick **Spline** from the **Object** cascading menu in the **Modify** pull-down menu, or enter SPE or SPLINEDIT at the Command: prompt. The command sequence is:

Command: **SPE** *or* **SPLINEDIT**↵
Select spline: *(pick a spline)*

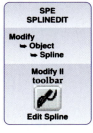

When you pick a spline, the control points are identified by grips, as shown in Figure 15-24. The command sequence continues:

Enter an option [Fit data/Close/Move vertex/Refine/rEverse/Undo]:

The **SPLINEDIT** command options are described in the following sections.

Figure 15-24.
The control points on a spline are displayed as grips when using the **SPLINEDIT** command.

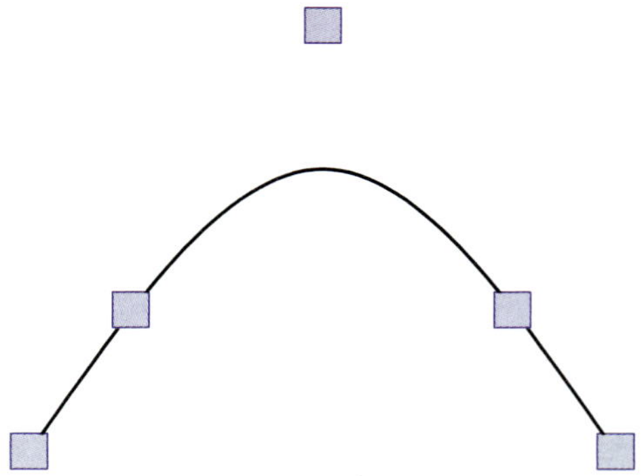

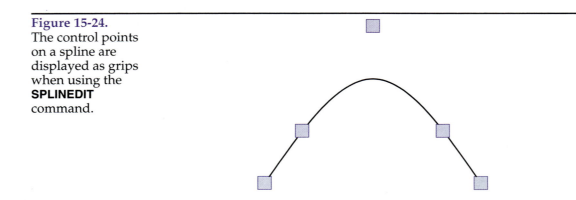

Editing Fit Data

The **Fit data** option of the **SPLINEDIT** command allows spline control points to be edited. Spline control points are called ***fit points***. The **Fit data** option has several suboptions:

Command: **SPE** *or* **SPLINEDIT**↵
Select spline: *(pick a spline)*
Enter an option [Fit data/Close/Move vertex/Refine/rEverse/Undo]: **F**↵
Enter a fit data option
[Add/Close/Delete/Move/Purge/Tangents/toLerance/eXit] <eXit>:

Each of the **Fit data** suboptions is explained next. See Figure 15-25 for examples of using these options.

- **Add.** This suboption allows you to add new fit points to a spline definition. When adding, a fit point can be located by picking a point or entering coordinates. Fit points appear as unselected grips. When one is selected, it becomes highlighted along with the next fit point on the spline. You can then add a fit point between the two highlighted points. If the endpoint of the spline is selected, only the endpoint becomes highlighted. If the start point of the spline is selected, the following prompt is issued:

  Specify new point or [After/Before]: <exit>:

  This prompt asks whether to insert the new fit point before or after the existing one. Respond by entering A or B accordingly. When a fit point is added, the spline curve is refit through the added point. See Figure 15-25.

  The **Add** option functions in a running mode. This means that you can continue to add points as needed. By pressing [Enter] at a Specify new point <exit>: prompt, you can select other existing fit points. Therefore, points can be added anywhere on the spline.
- **Close/Open.** If the selected spline is open, the **Close** suboption is displayed. If the spline is closed, the **Open** suboption is displayed. These options allow you to open a closed spline or close an open spline.
- **Delete.** The **Delete** suboption allows you to delete fit points as needed. However, at least two fit points must remain. Even when only two points remain, the object is still defined as a spline although it looks like a line. Like the **Add** option, the **Delete** option operates in a running mode, allowing as many deletions as needed. The spline is recurved through the remaining fit points.

Figure 15-25.
Examples of using the **SPLINEDIT Fit Data** suboptions to edit a spline. Compare the original spline to each of the edited objects.

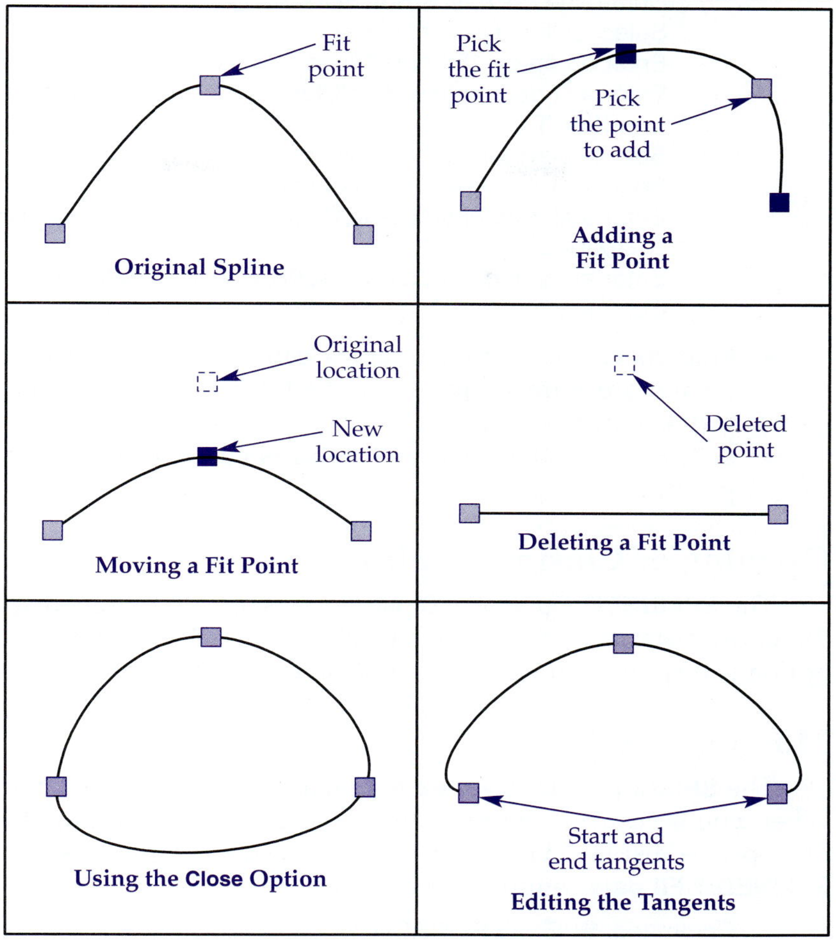

- **Move.** This suboption allows fit points to be moved as necessary. When the **Move** option is entered, the start point of the spline is highlighted. You can specify a different location simply by picking a new point with your left mouse button. You can also specify other fit points to move. The options are explained as follows:
  - **Specify new location.** This suboption allows you to move the currently highlighted point to a specified location.
  - **Next.** This suboption highlights the next fit point. It is activated by pressing [Enter].
  - **Previous.** Entering this suboption highlights the previous fit point.
  - **Select point.** This suboption allows you to pick a different fit point to move rather than using the **Next** or **Previous** options.
  - **eXit.** This suboption returns you to the **Fit Data** suboption prompt.
- **Purge.** This suboption lets you remove fit point data from a spline. After using this option, the resulting spline is not as easy to edit. In very large drawings where many complex splines are created, such as Geographical Information Systems (GIS) drawings, purging fit point data reduces the file size by simplifying the definition. Once a spline is purged, the **Fit Data** option is no longer displayed by the **SPLINEDIT** command for the purged spline.
- **Tangents.** This suboption allows editing of the start and end tangents for an open spline and editing of the start tangent for a closed spline. The tangency is based on the direction of the selected point. You can also use the **System default** option to set the tangency values to the AutoCAD defaults:

Command: **SPE** *or* **SPLINEDIT**↵
Select spline: *(pick a spline)*
Enter an option [Fit data/Close/Move vertex/Refine/rEverse/Undo]: **F**↵
Enter a fit data option [Add/Close/Delete/Move/Purge/Tangents/toLerance/eXit]
<eXit>: **T**↵
Specify start tangent or [System default]: **S**↵
Specify end tangent or [System default]: **S**↵
Enter a fit data option [Add/Close/Delete/Move/Purge/Tangents/toLerance/eXit]
<eXit>: ↵
Enter an option [Fit data/Close/Move vertex/Refine/rEverse/Undo]: ↵
Command:

- **toLerance.** Fit tolerance values can be adjusted using this suboption. The results are immediate, so the fit tolerance can be adjusted as necessary to produce different results.
- **eXit.** Entering this suboption returns you to the **SPLINEDIT** command option prompt.

Opening or Closing a Spline

The **SPLINEDIT Open** and **Close** options are alternately displayed, depending on the current status of the spline object being edited. If the spline is open, the **Close** option is displayed. If the spline is closed, the **Open** option is displayed.

Moving a Vertex

The **SPLINEDIT Move vertex** option allows you to move the fit points of a spline. When you access this option, you can specify a new location for a selected fit point. The options displayed are identical to those used with the **Move** suboption inside the **SPLINEDIT Fit data** command sequence.

Command: **SPE** *or* **SPLINEDIT**↵
Select spline: *(pick a spline)*
Enter an option [Fit data/Close/Move vertex/Refine/rEverse/Undo]: **M**↵
Specify new location or [Next/Previous/Select point/eXit] <N>:

You can pick a new location for the highlighted fit point using your left mouse button or you can enter a suboption. The **Move vertex** suboptions are explained below:

- **Specify new location.** Move the currently highlighted point to a specified location.
- **Next.** Highlight the next fit point.
- **Previous.** Highlight the previous fit point.
- **Select point.** Pick a different fit point to move, rather than cycling through points with the **Next** or **Previous** suboptions.
- **eXit.** Return to the **SPLINEDIT** command prompt.

EXERCISE 15-9 Complete the Exercise on the Student CD.

Smoothing or Reshaping a Section of the Spline

The **SPLINEDIT Refine** option allows fine tuning of the spline curve. Fit points can be added to help smooth or reshape a section of the spline. When you use this option, the fit point data is removed from the spline. The command sequence is:

Command: **SPE** *or* **SPLINEDIT**↵
Select spline: *(pick a spline)*
Enter an option [Fit data/Close/Move vertex/Refine/rEverse/Undo]: **R**↵
Enter a refine option [Add control point/Elevate order/Weight/eXit] <eXit>:

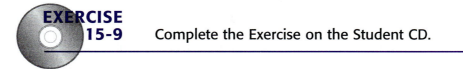

- **Add control point.** Specify new fit points on a spline as needed.
- **Elevate order.** The *order* of a spline is the degree of the spline polynomial +1. In simple terms, it is the degree of refinement of the spline. For example, a cubic spline has an order of 4. Elevating the order of a spline causes more control points to appear on the curve for greater control. In **Figure 15-26,** the order of the spline is elevated from 4 to 6. The order setting can be from 4 to 26, but it cannot be adjusted downward. For example, if the order is set to 24, the only remaining settings are 25 and 26.
- **Weight.** When all control points have the same weight, they exert the same amount of pull on the spline. When a weight value is lessened for a control point, the spline is not pulled as close to the point as before. Likewise, when a weight value is increased, the control point exerts more pull on the spline. See **Figure 15-26.** The default setting of 1.0000 can be adjusted to a higher or lower value. The weight setting must be positive. The control point selection suboptions of the **Weight** option are the same as those used with the **SPLINEDIT Move vertex** option. You can specify a new weight for the highlighted control point by using the **Enter new weight** option:

Enter a refine option [Add control point/Elevate order/Weight/eXit] <eXit>: **W**↵
Enter new weight (current = 1.0000) or [Next/Previous/Select point/eXit] <N>:
(enter a positive number)

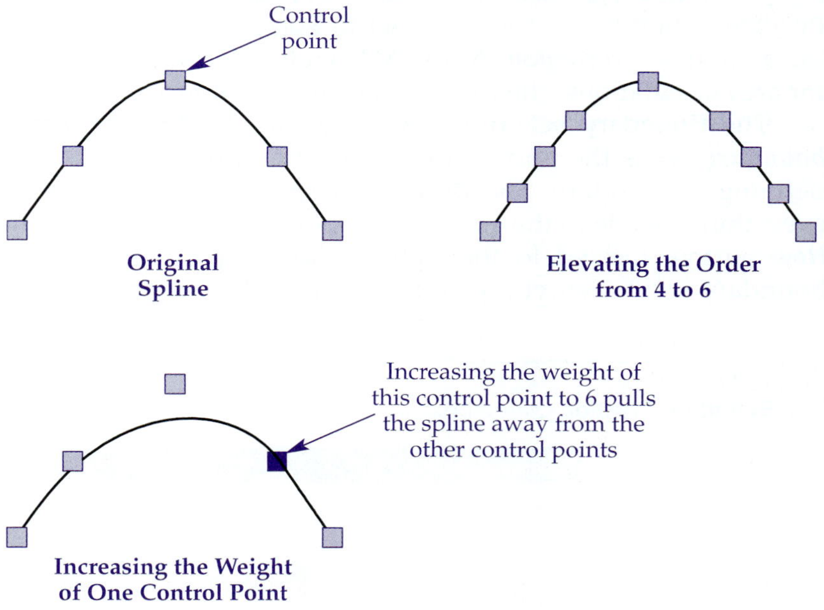

Figure 15-26. The effects of elevating the order of a spline and increasing the weight of an individual control point.

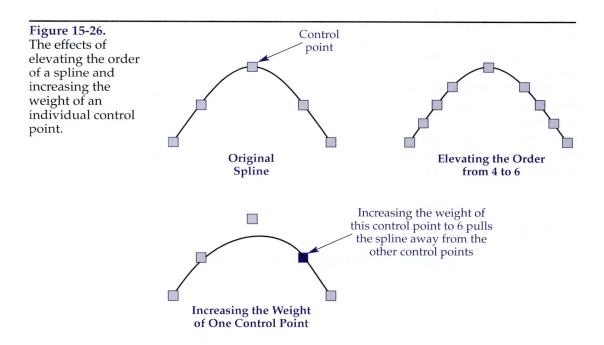

Reversing the Order of Spline Control Points

The **rEverse** option of the **SPLINEDIT** command allows you to reverse the listed order of the spline control points. This makes the previous start point the new endpoint and the previous endpoint the new start point. Using this option affects the various control point selection options as a result.

Undoing SPLINEDIT Changes

The **SPLINEDIT Undo** option undoes the previous change made to the spline. You can also use this option to undo changes back to the beginning of the current **SPLINEDIT** command sequence.

Exiting the SPLINEDIT Command

To exit the **SPLINEDIT** command, press [Enter] or type X and press [Enter] at the following prompt after making changes:

```
Enter an option [Close/Move vertex/Refine/rEverse/Undo/eXit] <eXit>: ↵
Command:
```

EXERCISE 15-10 Complete the Exercise on the Student CD.

Creating a Polyline Boundary

BOUNDRY
BO
Draw
➥ Boundary...

When you draw an object with the **LINE** command, each line segment is a single object. You can create a polyline boundary of an area made up of closed line segments using the **BOUNDARY** command. To do so, pick **Boundary...** from the **Draw** pull-down menu or type BO or BOUNDARY at the Command: prompt. This displays the **Boundary Creation** dialog box, Figure 15-27. Many of the features in this dialog box are inactive because they are used for hatching operations with the **BHATCH** command. This command is covered in Chapter 21.

The **Object type** drop-down list contains two options—**Polyline** and **Region**. The **Polyline** option is the default. If set to **Polyline**, AutoCAD creates a polyline around the area. If set to **Region**, AutoCAD creates a closed 2D area. A region may be used for area calculations, shading, extruding a solid model, or other purposes.

The **Boundary set** drop-down list has the **Current viewport** setting active. A ***boundary set*** is the portion or area of the drawing that AutoCAD evaluates when defining a boundary. The **Current viewport** option defines the boundary set from everything visible in the current viewport, even if it is not in the current display. The **New** button, located to the right of the drop-down list, allows you to define a boundary set. When you pick this button, the **Boundary Creation** dialog box closes

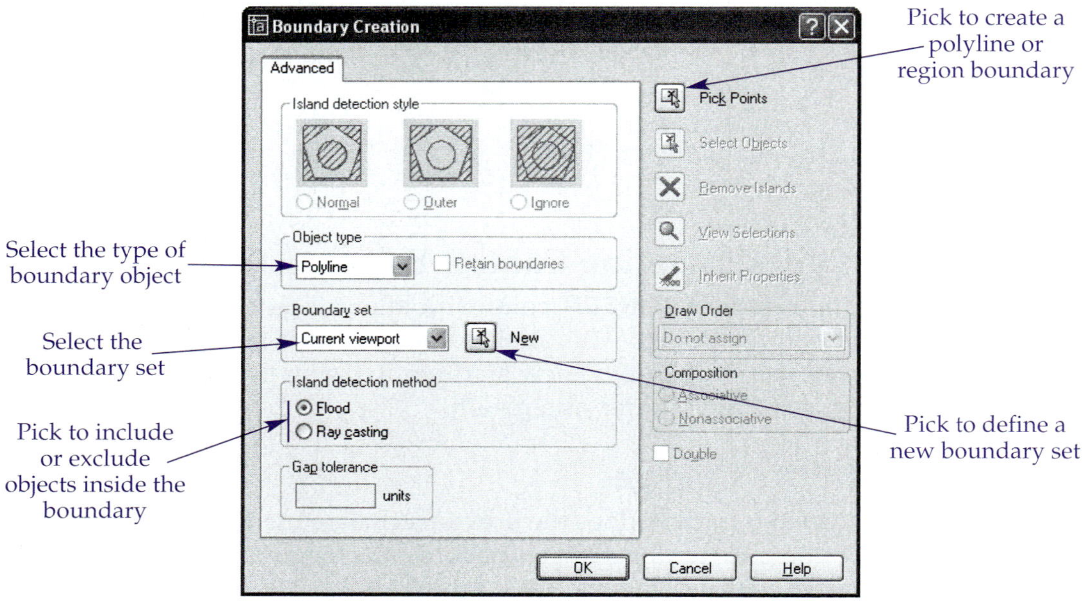

Figure 15-27.
The **Boundary Creation** dialog box.

and the Select objects: prompt appears. You can then select the objects you want to use to create a boundary set. After you are done, press [Enter]. The **Boundary Creation** dialog box returns with **Existing set** active in the **Boundary set** drop-down list. This means that the boundary set is defined from the objects that you selected.

The **Island detection method** area is used to specify whether objects within the boundary are used as boundary objects. Objects inside a boundary are called ***islands,*** Figure 15-28. There are two options in the **Island detection method** area. Activate the **Flood** radio button if you want islands to be included as boundary objects. Activate the **Ray casting** radio button if you do not want to include islands as boundary objects.

The only other active feature in the **Boundary Creation** dialog box is the **Pick Points** button, which is located in the upper-right corner. When you pick this button, the **Boundary Creation** dialog box closes and the Select internal point: prompt appears. If the point you pick is inside a closed polygon, the boundary is highlighted, as shown in Figure 15-29. If the point you pick is not within a closed polygon, the **Boundary Definition Error** alert box appears. Pick **OK**, close the area in which you want to pick, and try again.

Unlike an object created with the **PEDIT Join** option, a polyline boundary created with the **BOUNDARY** command does not replace the original objects from which it was created. The polyline simply *traces* over the defining objects with a polyline. Thus, the separate objects still exist and are *underneath* the newly created boundary. To avoid

Figure 15-28.
Objects within a boundary, called islands, can be included or excluded when defining a boundary set.

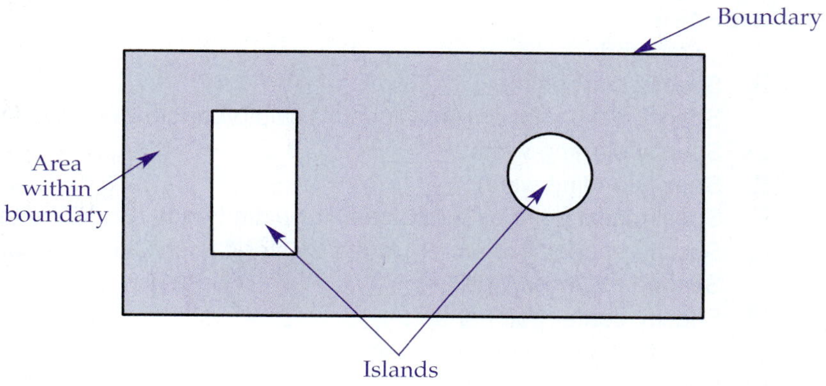

Figure 15-29.
When you select a point inside a closed polygon, the boundary is highlighted. Boundaries must be defined by closed objects.

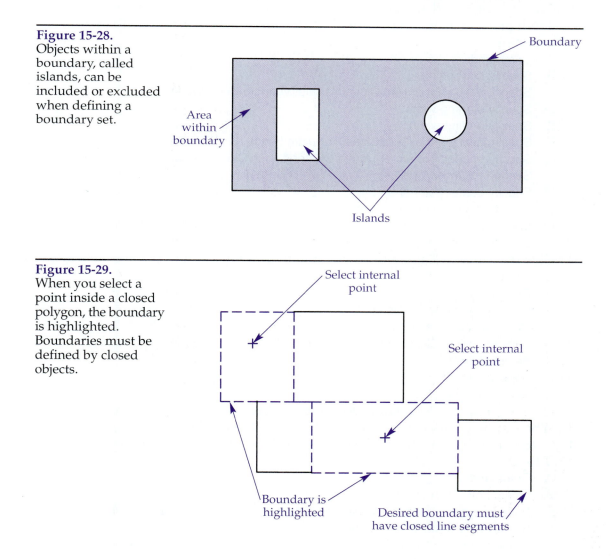

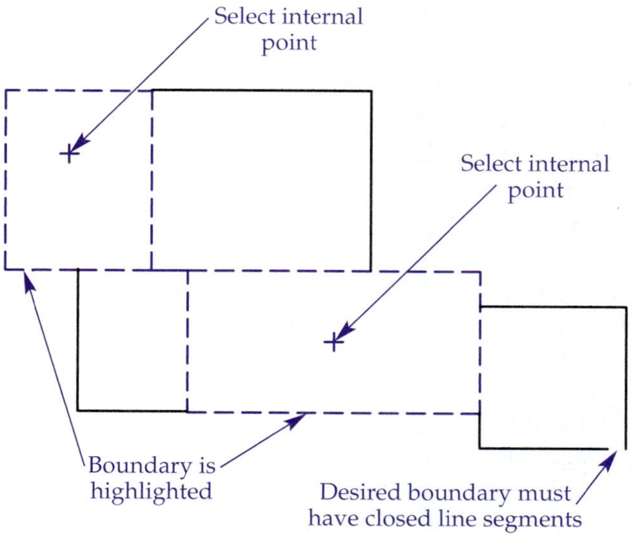

duplicate geometry, move the boundary to another location on screen, erase the original defining objects, and then move the boundary back to its original position.

PROFESSIONAL TIP

Area calculations can be simplified by first using the **BOUNDARY** command, or by joining objects with the **PEDIT Join** option, before issuing the **AREA** command. Then, use the **AREA Object** option to perform the area calculation. The **AREA** command is covered in Chapter 16. If you want to retain the original separate objects and the **PEDIT Join** option was used, explode the joined polyline after the area calculation. If the **BOUNDARY** command was used, simply erase the polyline boundary after the calculation.

Chapter Test

Answer the following questions on a separate sheet of paper.

1. Give the command and entries required to create a polyline arc with a starting width of 0 and an ending width of .25. Draw the arc from a known center to an endpoint.
   A. Command: _____
   B. Specify start point: _____
   C. Specify next point or [Arc/Close/Halfwidth/Length/Undo/Width]: _____
   D. Specify starting width: _____
   E. Specify ending width: _____
   F. Specify next point or [Arc/Close/Halfwidth/Length/Undo/Width]: _____
   G. Specify endpoint of arc or [Angle/CEnter/CLose/Direction/Halfwidth/Line/Radius/Second pt/Undo/Width]: _____
   H. Specify center point of arc: _____
   I. Specify endpoint of arc or [Angle/Length]: _____
   J. Specify endpoint of arc or [Angle/CEnter/CLose/Direction/Halfwidth/Line/Radius/Second pt/Undo/Width]: _____
2. Give the command and entries required to turn three connected lines into a single polyline.
   A. Command: _____
   B. Select polyline or [Multiple]: _____
   C. Object selected is not a polyline. Do you want to turn it into one? <Y>: _____
   D. Enter an option [Close/Join/Width/Edit vertex/Fit/Spline/Decurve/Ltype gen/Undo]: _____
   E. Select objects: _____
   F. Select objects: _____
   G. Select objects: _____
   H. Enter an option [Close/Join/Width/Edit vertex/Fit/Spline/ Decurve/Ltype gen/Undo]: _____
3. Which system variable controls the display of the prompt in 2C?
4. Give the command and entries needed to change the width of a polyline from .1 to .25.
   A. Command: _____
   B. Select polyline or [Multiple]: _____
   C. Enter an option [Close/Join/Width/Edit vertex/Fit/Spline/Decurve/Ltype gen/Undo]: _____
   D. Specify new width for all segments: _____
   E. Enter an option [Close/Join/Width/Edit vertex/Fit/Spline/Decurve/Ltype gen/Undo]: _____

For Questions 5 through 11, give the **PEDIT Edit vertex** *option that relates to the definition given.*

5. Moves the "X" marker to the next position.
6. Moves a polyline vertex to a new location.
7. Breaks a polyline at a point or between two points.
8. Generates the revised version of a polyline.
9. Specifies a tangent direction.
10. Adds a new polyline vertex.
11. Returns you to the **PEDIT** command prompt.
12. Which **PEDIT** command option and suboption allow you to change the starting and ending widths of a polyline?
13. Why may it appear that nothing happens after you change the starting and ending widths of a polyline?
14. Name the **PEDIT** command option and the **Edit vertex** suboption used for curve fitting.
15. Which command will remove all width characteristics and tangency information from a polyline?
16. Which two **PEDIT** command options allow you to open a closed polyline and close an open polyline?
17. When you enter the **Edit vertex** option of the **PEDIT** command, where is the "X" marker placed by AutoCAD?
18. How do you move the "X" marker to edit a different polyline vertex?
19. Can you use the **Fit** option of the **PEDIT** command without using the **Tangent** vertex editing suboption first?
20. Explain the difference between a fit curve and a spline curve.
21. Compare a quadratic curve, cubic curve, and fit curve.
22. Discuss the appearance of a quadratic curve.
23. Which **SPLINETYPE** system variable setting allows you to draw a quadratic curve?
24. Which **SPLINETYPE** setting allows you to draw a cubic curve?
25. Name the system variable that can be set to adjust the smoothness of a spline curve.
26. Name the pull-down menu and menu selections used to access the polyline editing options.
27. Explain how you can adjust the way polyline linetypes are generated using the **PEDIT** command.
28. Name the system variable that allows you to alter the way polyline linetypes are generated.
29. Name the command used to create a polyline boundary.
30. Name the command that can be used to create a true spline.
31. How do you accept the AutoCAD defaults for the start and end tangents of a spline?
32. Name the **SPLINE** command option that allows you to turn a spline-fitted polyline into a true spline.
33. Name the command that allows you to edit splines.
34. What is the purpose of the **Add** suboption of the **SPLINEDIT Fit data** option?
35. What is the minimum number of fit points for spline?
36. Name the **SPLINEDIT** option that allows you to move the fit points in a spline.
37. What is the purpose of the **SPLINEDIT Refine** option?
38. Identify the **SPLINEDIT Refine** suboption that lets you increase, but not decrease, the number of control points appearing on a spline curve.
39. Name the **SPLINEDIT Refine** option that controls the pull exerted by a control point on a spline.
40. How many operations can you undo inside the **SPLINEDIT** command with the **Undo** option?

Drawing Problems

Start a new drawing for each of the following problems. Specify your own units, limits, and other settings to suit each problem.

1. Draw the single polyline shown below. Use the **PLINE Arc**, **Width**, and **Close** options to complete the shape. Set the polyline width to 0, except at the points indicated. Save the drawing as P15-1.

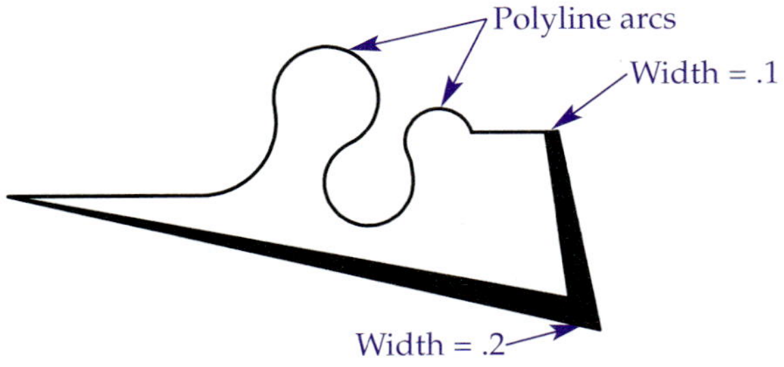

2. Draw the two curved arrows shown below using the **PLINE Arc** and **Width** options. The arrowheads should have a starting width of 1.4 and an ending width of 0. The body of each arrow should have a beginning width of .8 and an ending width of .4. Save the drawing as P15-2.

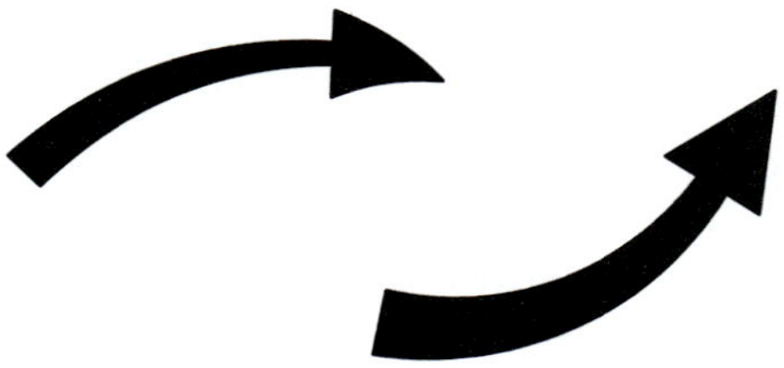

3. Open drawing P15-1 and make a copy of the original object to edit. Use the **PEDIT** command to change the object drawn into a rectangle. Use the **PEDIT Decurve** and **Width** options and the **Straighten**, **Insert**, and **Move** vertex editing suboptions. Save the completed drawing as P15-3.

4. Open drawing P15-2 and make the following changes. Then, save the drawing as P15-4.
   A. Combine the two polylines using the **PEDIT Join** option.
   B. Change the beginning width of the left arrow to 1.0 and the ending width to .2.
   C. Draw a polyline .062 wide similar to Line A as shown.

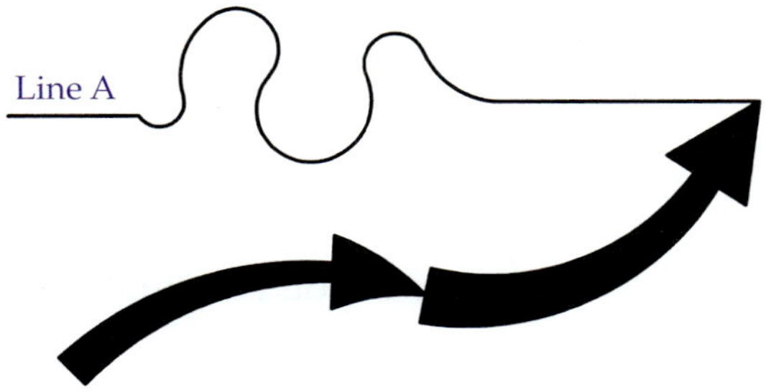

5. Draw a polyline .032 wide using the following absolute coordinates.

Point	Coordinates	Point	Coordinates	Point	Coordinates
1	1,1	5	3,3	9	5,5
2	2,1	6	4,3	10	6,5
3	2,2	7	4,4	11	6,6
4	3,2	8	5,4	12	7,6

Copy the polyline three times so there are four polylines. Use the **PEDIT Fit** option to smooth the first copy. Use the **PEDIT Spline** option to turn the second copy into a quadratic curve. Make the third copy into a cubic curve. Use the **PEDIT Decurve** option to return one of the three copies to its original form. Save the drawing as P15-5.

6. Use the **PLINE** command to draw a patio plan similar to the one shown in Example A below. Draw the house walls 6″ wide. Copy the drawing three times and use the **PEDIT** command to create the remaining designs shown. Use the **Fit** option for Example B, a quadratic spline for Example C, and a cubic spline for Example D. Change the **SPLINETYPE** system variable as required. Save the drawing as P15-6.

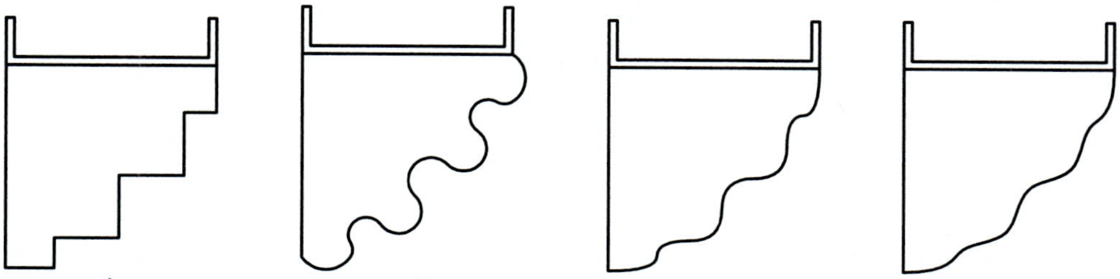

A B C D

7. Open drawing P15-6 and create four new patio designs. This time, use grips to edit the polylines and create designs similar to Examples A, B, C, and D below. Save the drawing as P15-7.

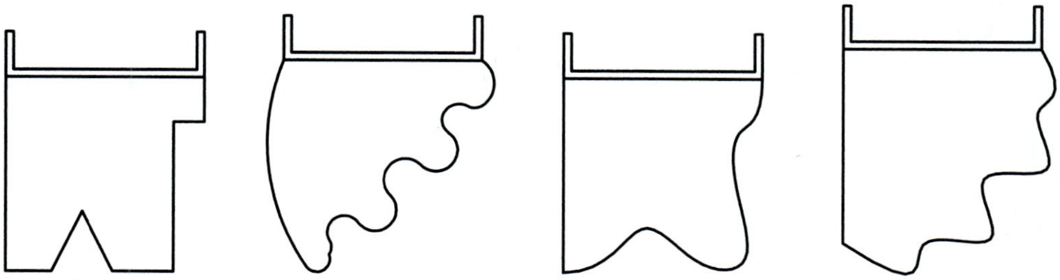

A B C D

8. Use **SPLINE** and other commands, such as **ELLIPSE**, **MIRROR**, **OFFSET**, and **PLINE**, to design an architectural door knocker similar to the one shown. Use an appropriate text command and font to place your initials in the center. Save the drawing as P15-8.

9. Use the **SPLINE** command to draw the curve for the cam displacement diagram below. Use the following guidelines and the given drawing to complete this problem.
   A. The total rise equals 2.000.
   B. The total displacement can be any length.
   C. Divide the total displacement into 30° increments.
   D. Draw a half circle divided into 6 equal parts on one end.
   E. Draw a horizontal line from each division of the half circle to the other end of the diagram.
   F. Draw the displacement curve with the **SPLINE** command by picking points where the horizontal and vertical lines cross.
   G. Label the displacement increments along the horizontal scale as shown. Save the drawing as P15-9.

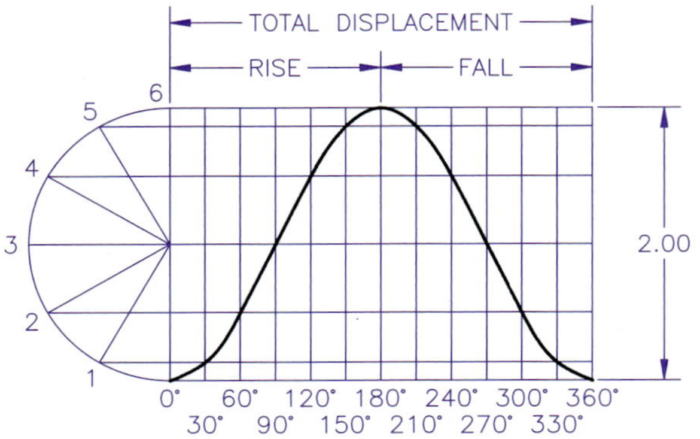

10. Draw a spline similar to the original spline shown below. Copy the spline seven times to create a layout similar to the one given. Perform the **SPLINEDIT** operations identified under each of the seven copies. Save the drawing as P15-10.

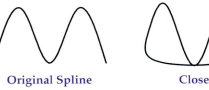

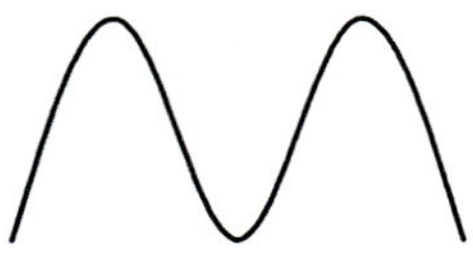
Original Spline

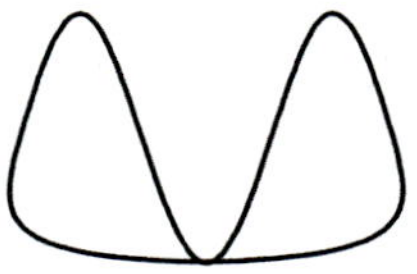
Close

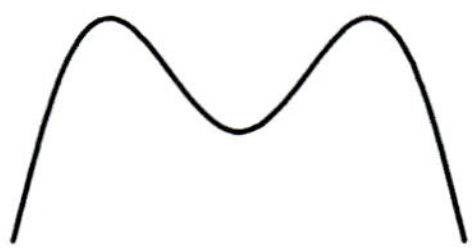
Move a Control Point

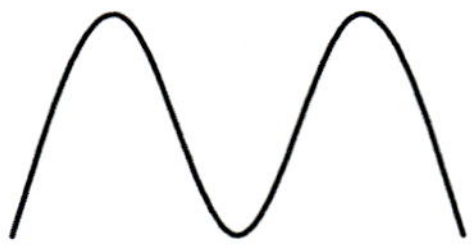
Elevate the Order to 10

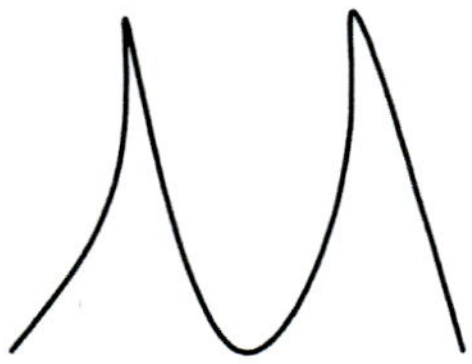
Add Two Control Points

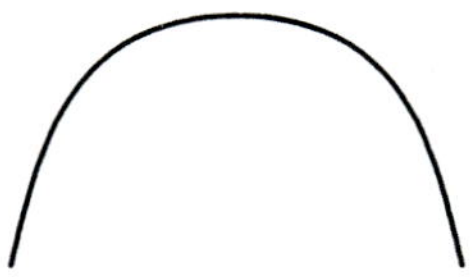
Delete a Control Point

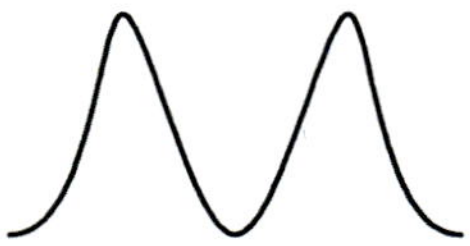
Edit the Tangents

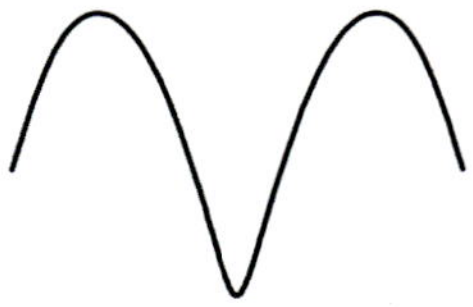
Increase the Weight of a Control Point to 4

CHAPTER 16

Obtaining Information about the Drawing

Learning Objectives

After completing this chapter, you will be able to do the following:

- Use the **AREA** command to calculate the area of an object by adding and subtracting objects.
- Display object properties in a drawing using fields.
- List data related to a single point, object, group of objects, or an entire drawing.
- Find the distance between two points.
- Identify a point location.
- Determine the amount of time spent in a drawing session.
- Determine the status of drawing parameters.

When working on a drawing, you may need to ask AutoCAD for information about the drawing, such as object distances and areas. You can also ask AutoCAD to tell you how much time you have spent on a drawing. The commands to do this include **AREA**, **DBLIST** (database list), **DIST** (distance), **ID** (identification), **LIST**, **STATUS**, and **TIME**.

These commands are accessed from the **Inquiry** cascading menu in the **Tools** pull-down menu. You can also access these commands from the **Inquiry** toolbar. See Figure 16-1. To display this toolbar, pick **Toolbars...** from the **View** pull-down menu. Then, place a check in the box next to **Inquiry** in the **Toolbars** tab and pick **Close**. You can also display the toolbar by right-clicking on any visible toolbar and selecting **Inquiry** from the shortcut menu.

NOTE

The **Region/Mass Properties** button or pull-down menu entry provides data related to the properties of a 2D region or 3D solid. This topic is discussed in *AutoCAD and its Applications—Advanced.*

Figure 16-1.
The inquiry commands are grouped in the **Inquiry** cascading menu in the **Tools** pull-down menu and on the **Inquiry** toolbar.

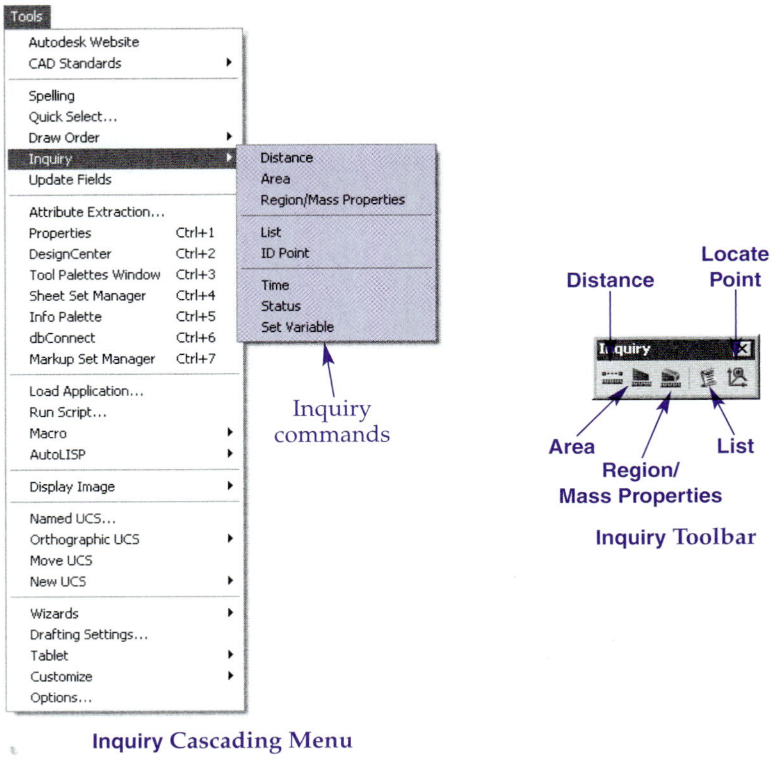

Finding the Area of Shapes and Objects

AREA
AA

Tools
➥ Inquiry
➥ Area

Inquiry toolbar

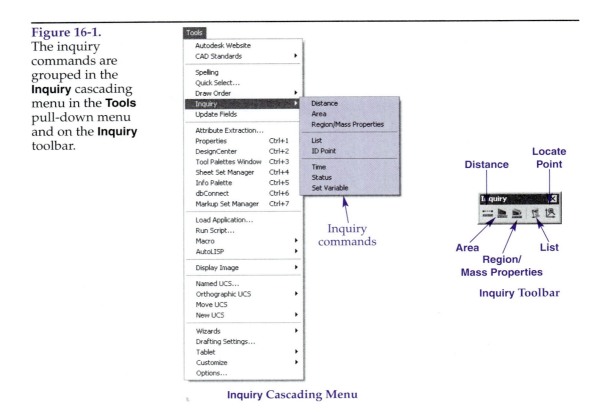

Area

The most basic function of the **AREA** command is to find the area of any object, circle, polygon, polyline, or spline. The command sequence is:

Command: **AA** *or* **AREA**↵
Specify first corner point or [Object/Add/Subtract]: **O**↵
Select objects: *(pick the object)*
Area = *n.nn*, Circumference = *n.nn*
Command:

The two numeric values represented by *n.nn* indicate the area and circumference of the object. The second value returned by the **AREA** command varies depending on the type of object selected, as shown in the following table:

Object	Value returned
Line	Does not have an area (no value given)
Polyline	Length or perimeter
Circle	Circumference
Spline	Length or perimeter
Rectangle	Perimeter

PROFESSIONAL TIP

AutoCAD gives you the area between three or more points picked on the screen, even if the three points are not connected by lines. The perimeter of the selected points is also given.

Shapes drawn with polylines do not need to be closed for AutoCAD to calculate their area. AutoCAD calculates the area as if a line segment connects the first and last points.

To find the area of a shape created with the **LINE** command, pick all the vertices of that shape. This is the default mode of the **AREA** command. Setting a running object snap mode such as **Endpoint** or **Intersection** will help you pick the vertices. See **Figure 16-2.**

Command: **AREA**↵
Specify first corner point or [Object/Add/Subtract]: *(pick point 1)*
Specify next corner point or press ENTER for total: *(pick point 2)*
Specify next corner point or press ENTER for total: *(continue picking points until all corners of the object have been selected; then press* [Enter]*)*
Area = *n.nn*, Perimeter = *n.nn*
Command:

Figure 16-2.
Pick all vertices to find the area of an object drawn with the **LINE** command.

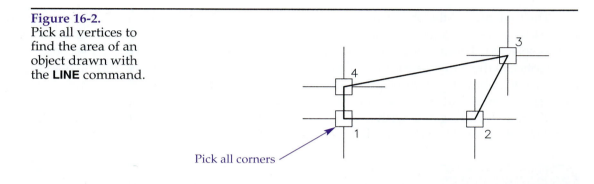

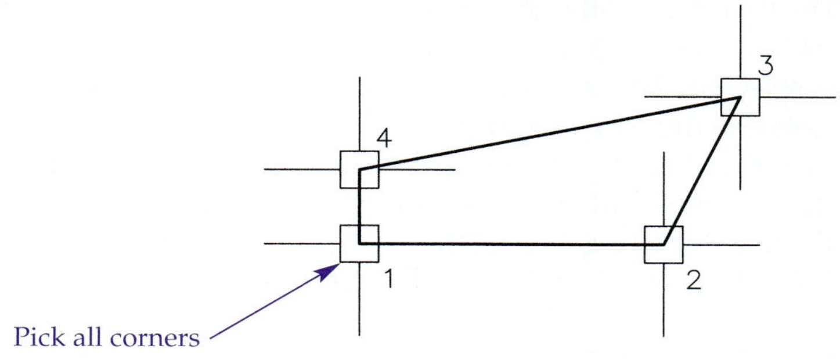

Adding and Subtracting Areas

If you use the **Add** option of the **AREA** command, you can pick multiple objects or areas. As you add objects or areas, a running total of the area is automatically calculated. The **Subtract** option allows you to remove objects or areas from the selection set. Once either of these options is entered, the **AREA** command remains in effect until canceled.

The next example shows how to use these two options in the same operation. Polyline-based objects are selected in the operation. Refer to **Figure 16-3** as you go through the following command sequence:

Command: **AREA**↵
Specify first corner point or [Object/Add/Subtract]: **A**↵
Specify first corner point or [Object/Subtract]: **O**↵
(ADD mode) Select objects: *(pick the polyline)*
Area = 13.7854, Length = 20.1416
Total area = 13.7854
(ADD mode) Select objects: ↵
Specify first corner point or [Object/Subtract]: **S**↵
Specify first corner point or [Object/Add]: **O**↵
(SUBTRACT mode) Select objects: *(pick the first circle)*
Area = 0.7854, Circumference = 3.1416
Total area = 13.0000
(SUBTRACT mode) Select objects: *(pick the second circle)*
Area = 0.7854, Circumference = 3.1416
Total area = 12.2146
(SUBTRACT mode) Select objects: ↵
Specify first corner point or [Object/Add]: ↵
Command:

Figure 16-3.
To calculate the area of an object drawn with the **PLINE** command, first select the outer boundary of the object using the **AREA** command **Add** option. Then, select the inner boundaries (the circles) using the **AREA** command **Subtract** option. This will calculate the area of the object.

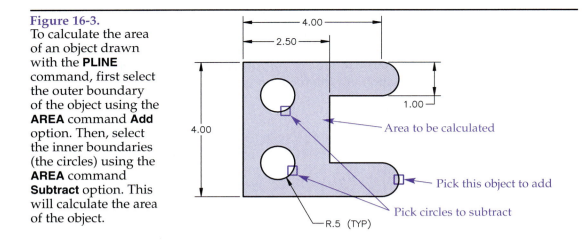

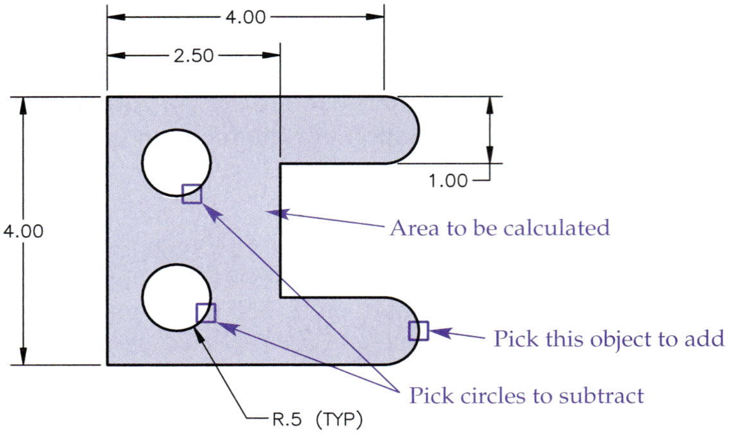

The total area of the object in Figure 16-3 after subtracting the areas of the two holes is 12.2146. An area value and a length or circumference value are given for each object as it is selected. These values are not affected by the adding or subtracting functions.

Notice in the previous command sequence that when you are finished adding objects and wish to subtract, you must press [Enter] at the (ADD mode) Select objects: prompt. You can also right-click the mouse and then type S to enter subtract mode. If you have completed subtracting and wish to add, you must press [Enter] at the (SUBTRACT mode) Select objects: prompt or right-click the mouse and then, type A to enter Add mode.

PROFESSIONAL TIP

Calculating area, circumference, and perimeter values of shapes drawn with the **LINE** command can be time-consuming. You must pick each vertex on the object. If you need to calculate areas, it is best to create lines and arcs with the **PLINE** or **SPLINE** command. Then use the **AREA** command **Object** option when adding or subtracting objects.

EXERCISE 16-1

Complete the Exercise on the Student CD.

AutoCAD 2005 NEW FEATURE

Displaying Information with Fields

You can list some object properties and drawing information using fields. A *field* is a text object that displays a set property, setting, or value for an object, a drawing, or a computer system. If the value of the field setting changes, the text is updated automatically to reflect the change. Fields were introduced in Chapter 8.

Each object type, such as lines, circles, and polylines, has different properties that can be displayed in a field. For example, using fields, you can place text next to a circle listing the circle's area and circumference.

To display an object property value using a field, access the **Field** dialog box from the **MTEXT** command, **TEXT** command, or by selecting **Field...** from the **Insert** pull-down menu. In the **Field** dialog box, pick **Objects** from the **Field category** drop-down list, and then pick **Object** in the **Field names** list box. See Figure 16-4. Pick the **Select object** button to return to the drawing window and pick the object.

Figure 16-4.
Pick the **Object** field to add a property for a specific object to a field. Pick the **Select object** button to select the object.

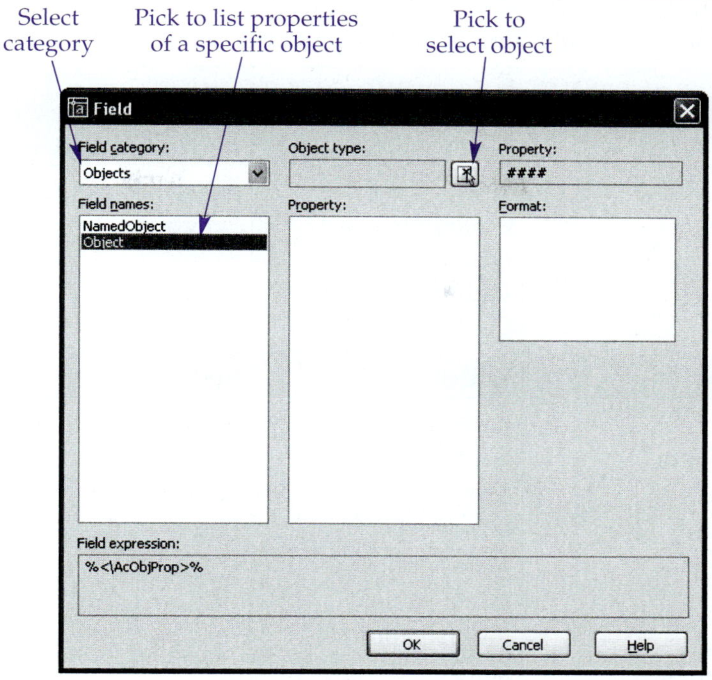

When you select the object, the **Field** dialog box reappears with the available properties listed. See Figure 16-5. Pick the property, select the format, and pick **OK** to have the field inserted in the text object. Once the field is created, whenever the object is modified, the value displayed in the field automatically updates.

In addition to the object property settings, such as layer, linetype, lineweight, and plot style, many inquiry properties can be included in a field. The table in Figure 16-6 lists some of the inquiry data that can be displayed in fields for various object types.

Figure 16-5.
After picking the object, properties specific to the object type are listed. Pick the property and format for the field.

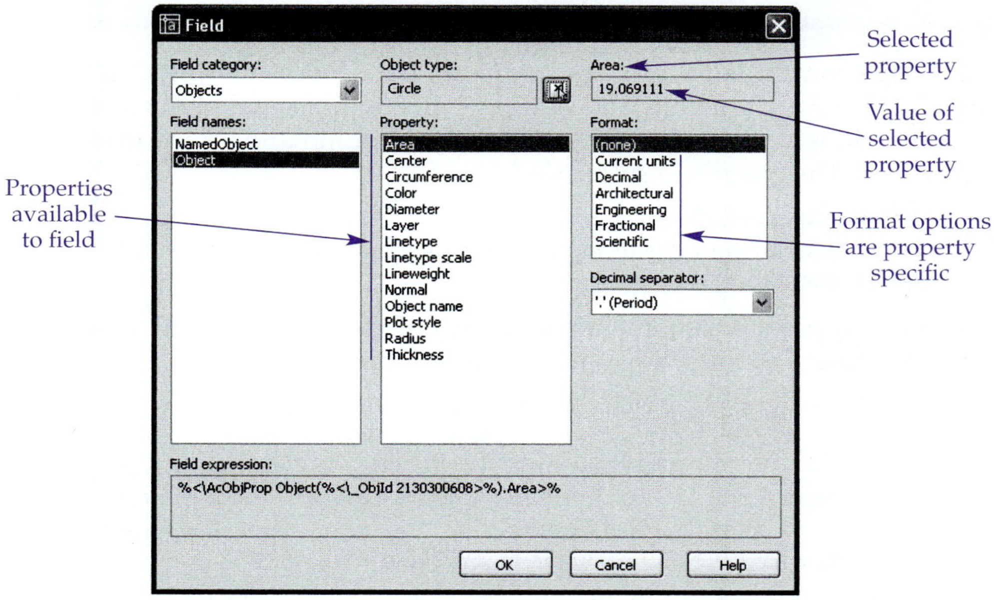

Figure 16-6.
This table is a partial listing of inquiry properties available for various object types.

Object Properties Available for Display in Fields			
Line Object	**Circle Object**	**Polyline Object**	**Rectangle Object**
Length Angle Delta Start End	Area Circumference Diameter Radius Center	Area Length	Area Length
Arc Object	**Ellipse Object**	**Spline Object**	**Region Object**
Area Arc length Radius Center Total angle Start End Start angle End angle	Area Center Major axis Minor axis Major radius Minor radius Radius ratio Start End Start angle End angle	Area Degree Start tangent End tangent	Area Perimeter

EXERCISE 16-2 Complete the Exercise on the Student CD.

Listing Drawing Data

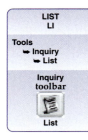

LIST
LI

Tools
➥ Inquiry
➥ List

Inquiry toolbar
List

The **LIST** command enables you to display data about any AutoCAD object. Line lengths, circle or arc locations and radii, polyline widths, and object layers are just a few of the items you can identify with the **LIST** command. You can select several objects to list. The command sequence is:

Command: **LI** *or* **LIST**↵
Select objects: *(pick one or more objects using any selection method)*
Select objects: ↵

When you press [Enter], the data for each of the objects picked are displayed in the text window. The following data are given for a line:

```
                 LINE      Layer:   layer name
                           Space:   Model space
                 Handle = nn
      from point,  X = nn.nn      Y = nn.nn      Z = nn.nn
        to point,  X = nn.nn      Y = nn.nn      Z = nn.nn
  Length = nn.nn,        Angle in XY Plane = nn.nn
         Delta X = nn.nn,     Delta Y = nn.nn, Delta Z = nn.nn
```

The delta X and delta Y values indicate the horizontal and vertical distances between the *from point* and *to point* of the line. These two values, along with the length and angle, provide you with four measurements for a single line. An example of the data and measurements provided for two-dimensional lines is shown in **Figure 16-7.** If a line is three-dimensional, the **LIST** command displays an additional line of information:

3D Length = *nn.nn*, Angle from XY Plane = *nn.nn*

The **LIST** command can also be used to determine information about text and multiline text. The data given for text, multiline text, circles, and splines are:

TEXT	Layer: *layer name*		
	Space: *Model or Paper space*		
	Layout: *Only in paper space*		
Handle = *nn*			
Style = *name*			
Font file = *name*			
start point, X = *n.nn*	Y = *n.nn*	Z = *n.nn*	
height *n.nn*			
text *text contents*			
rotation angle	*nn*		
width scale factor	*n.nn*		
obliquing angle	*nn*		
generation normal			

	MTEXT	Layer: *layer name*	
		Space: Model space	
	Handle = *nn*		
Location:	X = *n.nn*	Y = *n.nn*	Z = *n.nn*
Width:	*n.nn*		
Normal:	X = *n.nn*	Y = *n.nn*	Z = *n.nn*
Rotation:	*nn*		
Text style:	*style name*		
Text height:	*n.nn*		
Line spacing:	Multiple *n.nn* = *n.nn*		
Attachment:	*corner of multiline text insertion point*		
Flow direction:	*direction text is read based on language*		
Contents:	*multiline text contents*		

CIRCLE		Layer: *layer name*		
		Space: Model space		
Handle = *nn*				
center point,		X = *n.nn*	Y = *n.nn*	Z = *n.nn*
radius	*n.nn*			
circumference	*n.nn*			
area	*n.nn*			

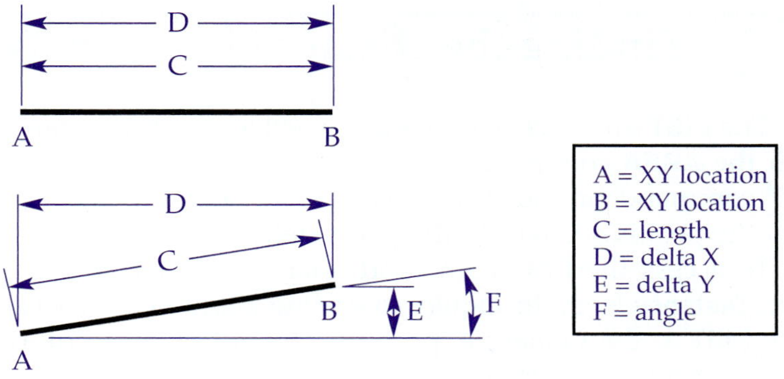

Figure 16-7. The various data and measurements of a line provided by the **LIST** command.

SPLINE	Layer:	*layer name*		
	Space:	Model space		
Handle = *nn*				
Length:	*n.nn*			
Order:	*n.nn*			
Properties:	Planar, Non-Rational, Non-Periodic			
Parametric Range:	Start *n.nn*			
	End *n.nn*			
Number of control points:	*n*			
Control Points:	X = *n.nn*,	Y = *n.nn*,	Z = *n.nn*	
	(the XYZ of all control points are listed)			
Number of fit points:	*n*			
User Data:	Fit Points			
	X = *n.nn*,	Y = *n.nn*,	Z = *n.nn*	
	(the XYZ of all fit points are listed)			
Fit point tolerance:	*n.nn*			

PROFESSIONAL TIP

The **LIST** command is the most powerful inquiry command in AutoCAD. It provides all the information you need to know about an object. Also, when selecting an object from the polyline family, the **LIST** command reports the area and perimeter of the object so you do not need to use the **AREA** command. The **LIST** command also reports an object's color and linetype, unless both are "by layer."

Listing Drawing Data for All Objects

The **DBLIST** (database list) command lists all data for every object in the current drawing. This command is initiated by typing DBLIST at the Command: prompt. The information is provided in the same format used by the **LIST** command. As soon as you enter the **DBLIST** command, the data begin to quickly scroll up the screen in the text window. The scrolling stops when a complete page (or screen) is filled with database information. Press [Enter] to scroll to the end of the next page. Use the scroll buttons to move forward and backward through the listing.

If you find the data you need, press the [Esc] key to exit the **DBLIST** command. You can exit the text window by pressing the [F2] function key.

Finding the Distance between Two Points

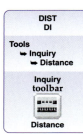

DIST
DI

Tools
➥ **Inquiry**
➥ **Distance**

Inquiry toolbar

Distance

The **DIST** (distance) command is used to find the distance between two points. As with the **AREA** command, use object snap modes to accurately pick locations. The **DIST** command provides the distance between the points and the angle of the line from the positive X axis. It also gives delta X, Y, and Z dimensions.

To access the **DIST** command, pick the **Distance** button in the **Inquiry** toolbar, select **Distance** from the **Inquiry** cascading menu in the **Tools** pull-down menu, or type DI or DIST at the Command: prompt. The button and pull-down selections issue the command transparently and can be used within other commands.

Command: **DI** *or* **DIST**↵
Specify first point: *(select point)*
Specify second point: *(select point)*
Distance = *n.nn*, Angle in XY Plane = *n*, Angle from XY Plane = *n*
Delta X = *n.nn*, Delta Y = *n.nn*, Delta Z = *n.nn*
Command:

Identifying Point Locations

ID
Tools
➥ Inquiry
➥ ID Point
Inquiry toolbar
Locate Point

The **ID** command gives the coordinate location of a single point on screen. This command can be used to find the coordinates of a line endpoint or the center of a circle. Simply pick the point to be identified when the Specify point: prompt appears. Use the object snap modes for accuracy.

Command: **ID**↵
Specify point: *(select the point)*
X = *nn.nn*   Y = *nn.nn*   Z = *nn.nn*
Command:

In conjunction with "blip" mode, the **ID** command can help you identify where a coordinate is on the screen. Suppose you want to see where the point (X = 8.75, Y = 6.44) is located. Enter these numbers at the Specify point: prompt. AutoCAD responds by placing a blip (marker) at that exact location. In order to use this feature, the **BLIPMODE** system variable must be on.

Command: **BLIPMODE**↵
Enter mode [ON/OFF] <ON>: **ON**↵
Command: **ID**↵
Specify point: **8.75,6.44**↵
X = 8.75   Y = 6.44   Z = 0.00
Command:

EXERCISE 16-3 Complete the Exercise on the Student CD.

Checking the Time

TIME
Tools
➥ Inquiry
➥ Time

The **TIME** command allows you to display the current time, time related to your drawing, and time related to the current drawing session. The following information is displayed in the text window when the **TIME** command is entered:

Command: **TIME**↵
Current time: Wednesday, February 14, 2004 at 13:39:22:210 PM
Times for this drawing:
  Created: Monday, February 12, 2004 at 10:24:48:130 AM
  Last updated: Monday, February 12, 2004 at 14:36:23:46 PM
  Total editing time: 0 days 01:23:57:930
  Elapsed timer (on): 0 days 00:35:28:650
  Next automatic save in: 0 days 01:35:26:680
Enter option [Display/ON/OFF/Reset]:

There are a few things to keep in mind when checking the text window display after issuing the **TIME** command. First, the drawing creation time starts when you begin a new drawing, not when a new drawing is first saved. Second, the **SAVE** command affects the Last updated: time. However, if you exit AutoCAD and do not save the drawing, all time in that session is discarded. Finally, you can time a specific drawing task by using the **TIME** command **Reset** option to reset the elapsed timer.

When the **TIME** command is issued, the times shown in the text window are static. This means that none of the times are being updated. You can request an update by using the **Display** option:

Enter option [Display/ON/OFF/Reset]: **D**↵

When you enter the drawing area, the timer is on by default. If you want to stop the timer, simply enter OFF at the Enter option [Display/ON/OFF/Reset]: prompt. If the timer is off, enter ON to start it again.

NOTE

The Windows operating system maintains the date and time settings for the computer. You can change these settings in the Windows Control Panel. To access the Control Panel, pick **Settings** and then **Control Panel** from the **Start** menu.

EXERCISE 16-4 Complete the Exercise on the Student CD.

Determining the Drawing Status

STATUS
Tools
➥ Inquiry
➥ Status

While working on a drawing, you may forget some of the drawing parameters, such as the limits, grid spacing, or snap values. All the information about a drawing can be displayed using the **STATUS** command. Access this command by typing STATUS at the Command: prompt or selecting **Status** from the **Inquiry** cascading menu in the **Tools** pull-down menu. The drawing information is displayed in the text window. See **Figure 16-8.**

The number of objects in a drawing refers to the total number of objects—both erased and existing. Drawing aid settings are shown along with the current settings for layer, linetype, and color. These topics are discussed in later chapters of this text. Free drawing (dwg) disk space represents the space left on the drive containing your drawing file.

When you have completed reviewing the information, press [F2] to close the text window. You can also switch to the graphics window without closing the text window by picking anywhere inside the graphics window or using the Windows [Alt]+[Tab] feature.

NOTE

Another way to move between the graphics window and the text window is provided with the AutoCAD commands **GRAPHSCR** and **TEXTSCR**. Typing TEXTSCR at the Command: prompt displays the text window. Typing GRAPHSCR closes the text window. You can also open to the text window by selecting **Text Window** from the **Display** cascading menu in the **View** pull-down menu.

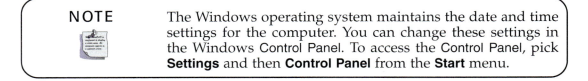

Figure 16-8.
The drawing information listed by the **STATUS** command is shown in the text window.

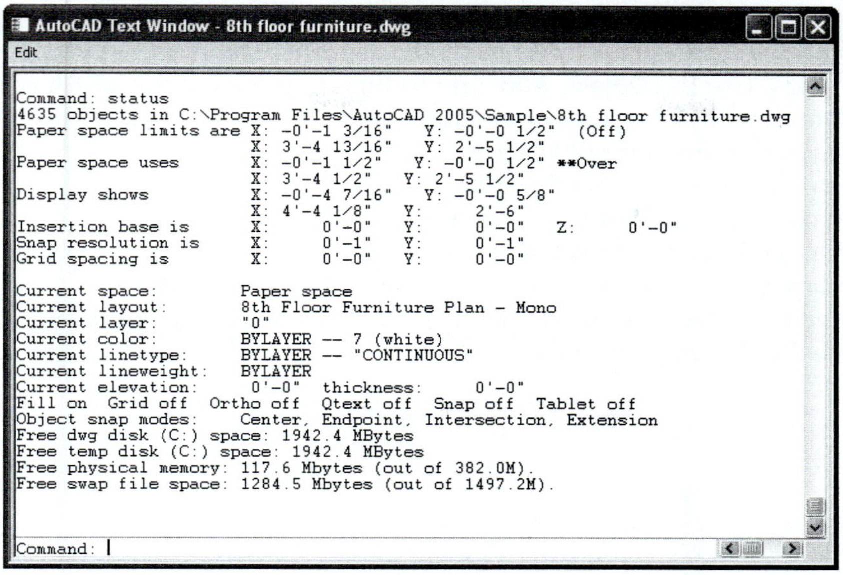
AutoCAD Text Window - 8th floor furniture.dwg
Edit
Command: status
4635 objects in C:\Program Files\AutoCAD 2005\Sample\8th floor furniture.dwg
Paper space limits are X: -0'-1 3/16" Y: -0'-0 1/2" (Off)
X: 3'-4 13/16" Y: 2'-5 1/2"
Paper space uses X: -0'-1 1/2" Y: -0'-0 1/2" **Over
X: 3'-4 1/2" Y: 2'-5 1/2"
Display shows X: -0'-4 7/16" Y: -0'-0 5/8"
X: 4'-4 1/8" Y: 2'-6"
Insertion base is X: 0'-0" Y: 0'-0" Z: 0'-0"
Snap resolution is X: 0'-1" Y: 0'-1"
Grid spacing is X: 0'-0" Y: 0'-0"
Current space: Paper space
Current layout: 8th Floor Furniture Plan - Mono
Current layer: "0"
Current color: BYLAYER -- 7 (white)
Current linetype: BYLAYER -- "CONTINUOUS"
Current lineweight: BYLAYER
Current elevation: 0'-0" thickness: 0'-0"
Fill on Grid off Ortho off Qtext off Snap off Tablet off
Object snap modes: Center, Endpoint, Intersection, Extension
Free dwg disk (C:) space: 1942.4 MBytes
Free temp disk (C:) space: 1942.4 MBytes
Free physical memory: 117.6 Mbytes (out of 382.0M).
Free swap file space: 1284.5 Mbytes (out of 1497.2M).
Command:

Chapter Test

Answer the following questions on a separate sheet of paper.

1. To add the areas of several objects when using the **AREA** command, when do you select the **Add** option?
2. When using the **AREA** command, explain how picking a polyline is different from picking an object drawn with the **LINE** command.
3. What information is provided by the **AREA** command?
4. What is the **LIST** command used for?
5. Describe the meaning of delta X and delta Y.
6. What is the function of the **DBLIST** command?
7. How do you cancel the **DBLIST** command?
8. What are the two purposes of the **ID** command?
9. What information is provided by the **TIME** command?
10. When does the drawing creation time start?

Drawing Problems

1. Draw the object shown below using the dimensions given. Check the time when you start the drawing. Draw all of the features using the **PLINE** and **CIRCLE** commands. Use the **Object**, **Add**, and **Subtract** options of the **AREA** command to calculate the following measurements:
   A. Area and perimeter of Object A.
   B. Area and perimeter of Object B.
   C. Area and circumference of one of the circles.
   D. Area of Object A minus the area of Object B.
   E. Area of Object A minus the areas of the other three features.
   F. Enter the **TIME** command and note the editing time spent on your drawing. Save the drawing as P16-1.

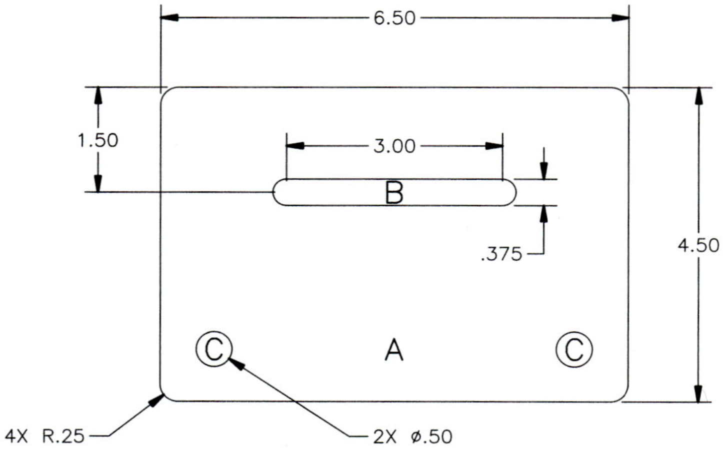

2. Draw the deck shown below using the **PLINE** command. Draw the hexagon using the **POLYGON** command. Use the following guidelines to complete this problem:
   A. Specify architectural units for your drawing. Use 1/2″ fractions and decimal degrees. Leave the remaining settings for the drawing units at the default values.
   B. Set the limits to 100′,80′ and perform a **ZOOM All**.
   C. Set the grid spacing to 2′ and the snap spacing to 1′.
   D. Calculate the measurements listed below.
      a. Area and perimeter of Object A.
      b. Area and perimeter of Object B.
      c. Area of Object A minus the area of Object B.
      d. Distance between Point C and Point D.
      e. Distance between Point E and Point C.
      f. Coordinates of Points C, D, and F.
   E. Enter the **DBLIST** command and check the information listed for your drawing.
   F. Enter the **TIME** command and note the total editing time spent on your drawing.
   G. Save the drawing as P16-2.

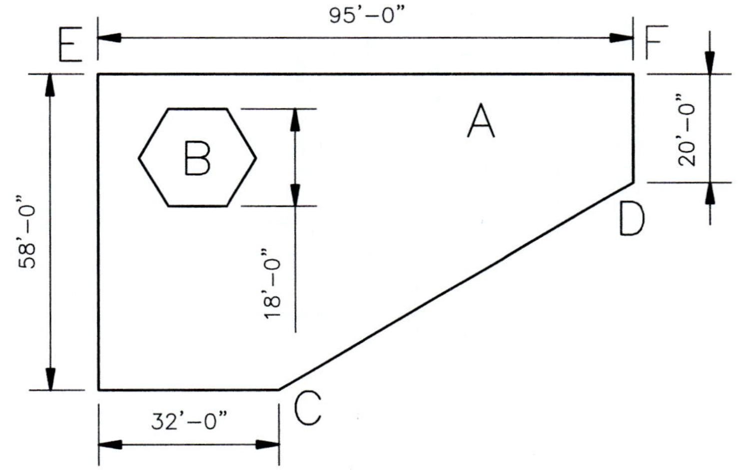

3. The drawing below is a view of the gable end of a house. Draw the house using the dimensions given. Draw the windows as single lines only (the location of the windows is not important). The spacing between the second-floor windows is 3″. The width of this end of the house is 16′-6″. The length of the roof is 40′. You may want to use the **PLINE** command to assist in creating specific shapes in this drawing, except as noted above. Save the drawing as P16-3. Then, calculate the following:
   A. Total area of the roof.
   B. Diagonal distance from one corner of the roof to the other.
   C. Area of the first-floor window.
   D. Total area of all second-floor windows, including the 3″ space between them.
   E. Siding will cover the house. What is the total area of siding for this end?

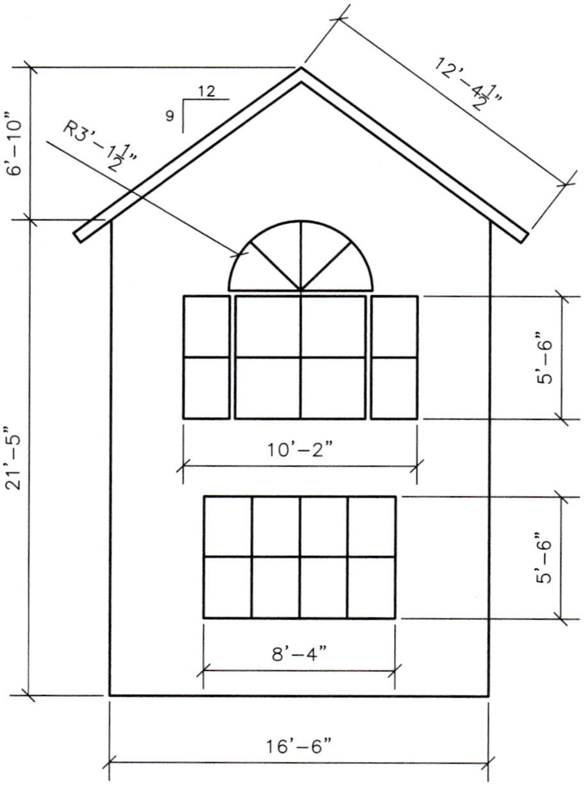

Drawing Problems - Chapter 16

4. The drawing shown below is a side view of a pyramid. The pyramid has four sides. Create an auxiliary view showing the true size of a pyramid face. Save the drawing as **P16-4**. Using inquiry techniques, calculate:
   A. Area of one side.
   B. Perimeter of one side.
   C. Area of all four sides.
   D. Area of the base.
   E. True length (distance) from the midpoint of the base on one side to the apex.

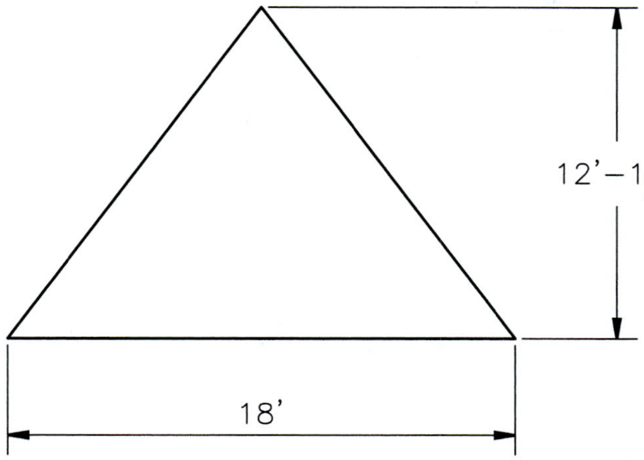

5. Draw the property plat shown below. Label property line bearings and distances only if required by your instructor. Calculate the area of the property plat in square feet and convert to acres. Save the drawing as **P16-5**.

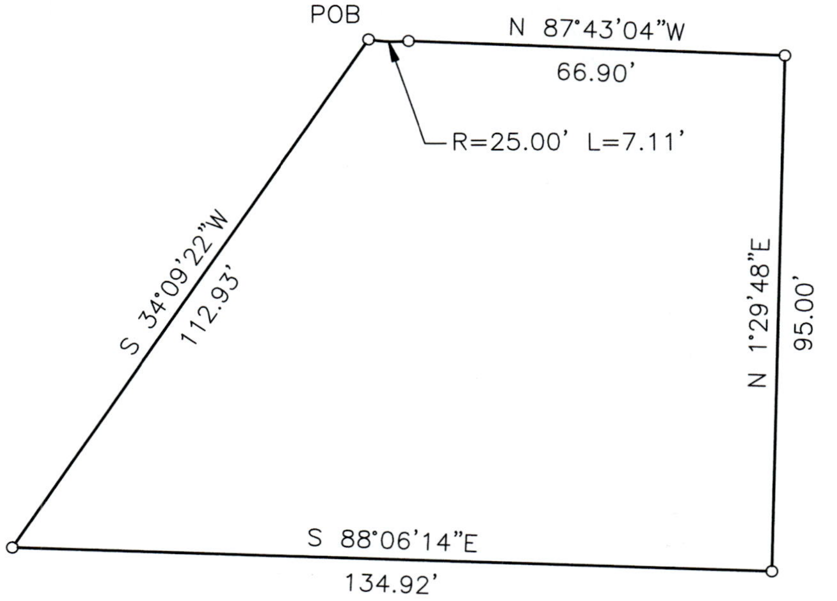

Drawing Problems - Chapter 16

6. Draw the subdivision plat shown below. Label the drawing as shown. Calculate the acreage of each lot and record each value as a label inside the corresponding lot (for example, .249 AC). Save the drawing as P16-6.

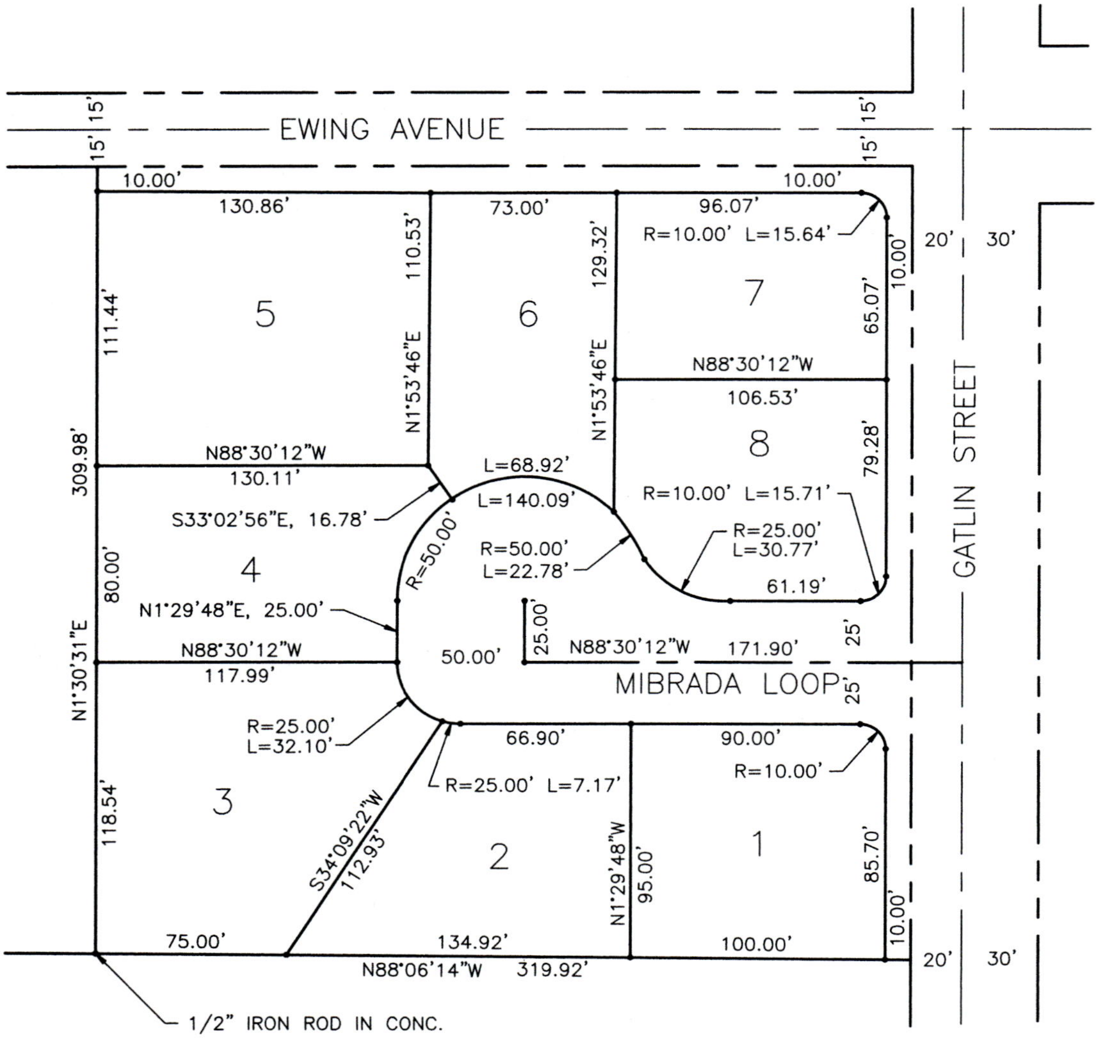

CHAPTER 17

Basic Dimensioning Practices

Learning Objectives

After completing this chapter, you will be able to do the following:

- Use the dimensioning commands to dimension given objects to ASME and other drafting standards.
- Control the appearance of dimensions.
- Add linear, angular, diameter, and radius dimensions to a drawing.
- Set the appropriate units and decimal places for dimension numbers.
- Use text size and style consistent with ASME and other professional standards.
- Use the proper character codes to display symbols within dimension text.
- Add dimensions to a separate layer.
- Place general notes on drawings.
- Draw datum and chain dimensions.
- Add dimensions for multiple items using the **QDIM** command.
- Dimension curves.
- Draw oblique dimensions.
- Use the **QLEADER** command to draw specific notes with linked leader lines.
- Dimension objects with arrowless tabular dimensions.
- Prepare thread symbols and notes.
- Create and use dimension styles.
- Create dimension style overrides.

Dimensions are given to describe the size, shape, and location of features on an object or structure. The dimension may consist of numerical values, lines, symbols, and notes. Typical AutoCAD dimensioning features and characteristics are shown in **Figure 17-1.**

Each drafting field (such as mechanical, architectural, civil, and electronics) uses a different type of dimensioning technique. It is important for a drafter to place dimensions in accordance with company and industry standards. The standard emphasized in this text is ASME Y14.5M-1994, *Dimensioning and Tolerancing*. The *M* in Y14.5M means the standard is written with metric numeric values. ASME Y14.5M-1994 is published by The American Society of Mechanical Engineers (ASME). This text discusses the correct application of both inch and metric dimensioning.

AutoCAD's dimensioning functions provide you with unlimited flexibility. Commands allow you to dimension linear distances, circles, and arcs. You can also

Figure 17-1.
Dimensions describe size and location. Follow accepted conventions when dimensioning.

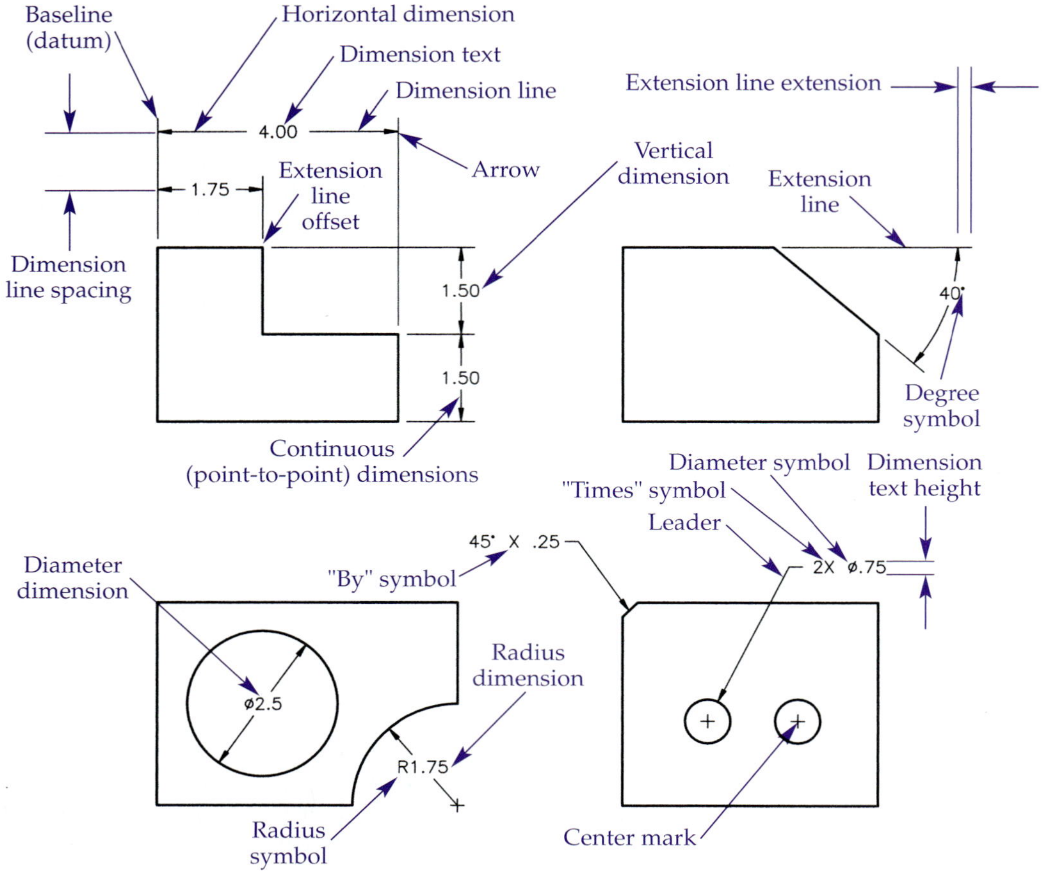

place a note with an arrow and leader line pointing to the feature. In addition to these commands, dimension styles allow you to control the height, width, style, and spacing of individual components of a dimension.

This text covers the comprehensive elements of AutoCAD dimensioning in four chapters. This chapter covers fundamental standards and practices for dimensioning. Chapter 18 covers editing procedures for dimensions. Chapter 19 covers dimensioning applications with tolerances. Chapter 20 covers geometric dimensioning and tolerancing practices. If you use AutoCAD for mechanical drafting in the manufacturing industry, you may want to study all four dimensioning chapters. If your business is in another field, such as architectural design, you may want to learn the basics covered in Chapters 17 and 18 and skip Chapters 19 and 20.

This chapter will get you started dimensioning immediately with AutoCAD. As you progress, you will learn about dimension settings that can be used to control the way dimensions are presented. You can control things such as the space between dimension lines; arrowhead size and type; and text style, height, and position. You will also learn how to create dimension styles that have settings used on the types of drawings done at your company or school.

When you dimension objects with AutoCAD, the objects are automatically measured exactly as you have them drawn. This makes it important for you to draw accurate original objects and features. Use the object snaps to your best advantage when dimensioning.

Dimension Arrangement

Dimensions are meant to communicate information about the drawing. Different industries and companies apply similar techniques for presenting dimensions. The two most accepted arrangements of text are unidirectional and aligned.

Unidirectional Dimensioning

Unidirectional dimensioning is typically used in the mechanical drafting field. The term ***unidirectional*** means *one direction*. This system has all dimension numbers and notes placed horizontally on the drawing. They are read from the bottom of the sheet.

Unidirectional dimensions normally have arrowheads on the ends of dimension lines. The dimension number is usually centered in a break near the center of the dimension line. See **Figure 17-2.**

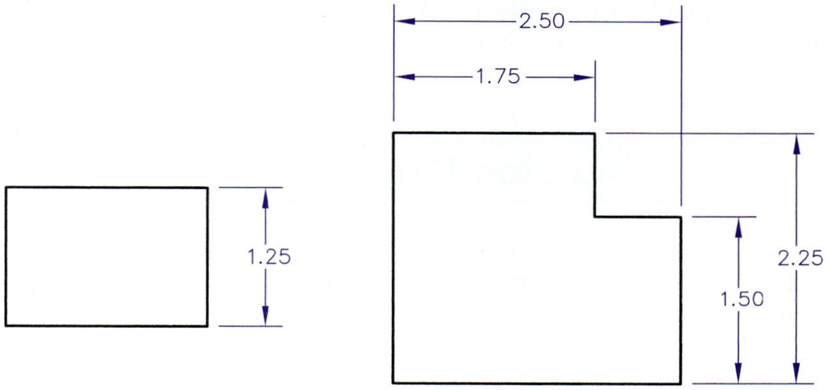

Figure 17-2.
When applying unidirectional dimensions, all dimension numbers and notes are placed horizontally on the drawing.

Aligned Dimensioning

Aligned dimensions are typically placed on architectural or structural drawings. The term ***aligned*** means the dimension numbers are lined up with the dimension lines. The dimension numbers for horizontal dimensions read horizontally. Dimension numbers for vertical dimensions are placed so they are read from the right side of the sheet. See **Figure 17-3.** Numbers for dimensions placed at an angle read at the same angle as the dimension line. Notes are usually placed so they read horizontally.

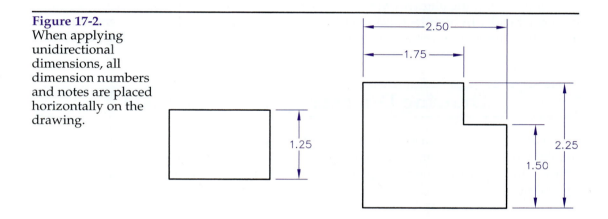

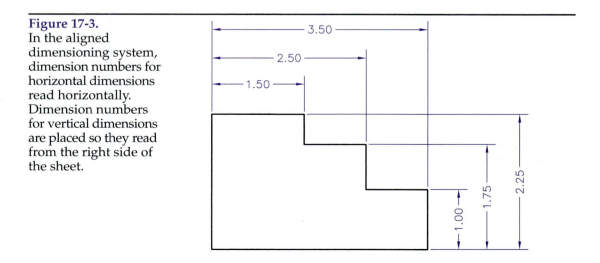

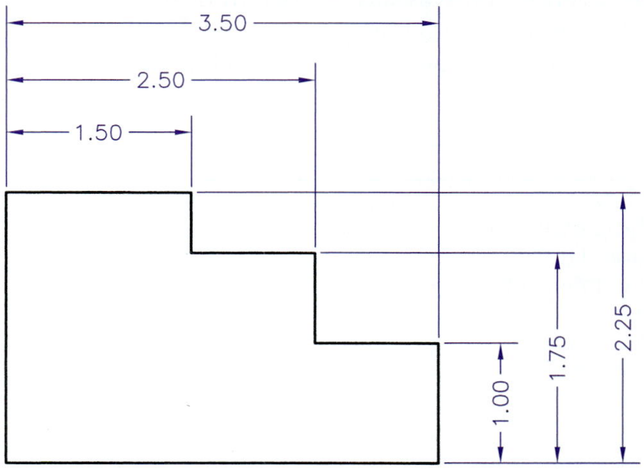

Figure 17-3.
In the aligned dimensioning system, dimension numbers for horizontal dimensions read horizontally. Dimension numbers for vertical dimensions are placed so they read from the right side of the sheet.

Figure 17-4.
An example of aligned dimensioning in architectural drafting. Notice the tick marks used in place of the arrowheads and the placement of the dimensions above the dimension line.

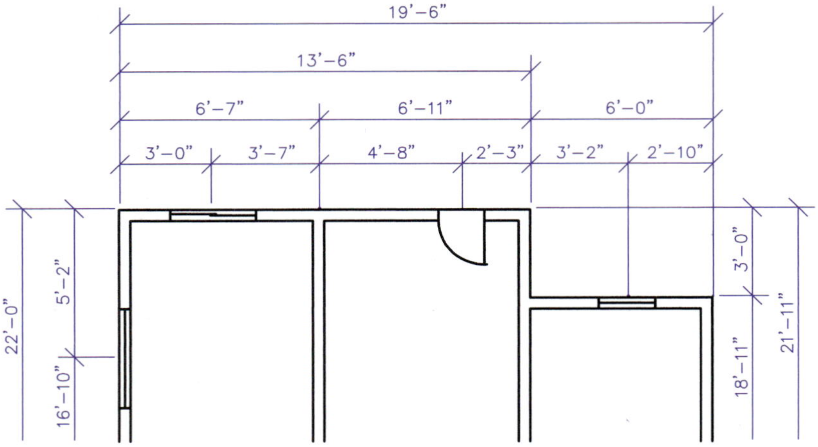

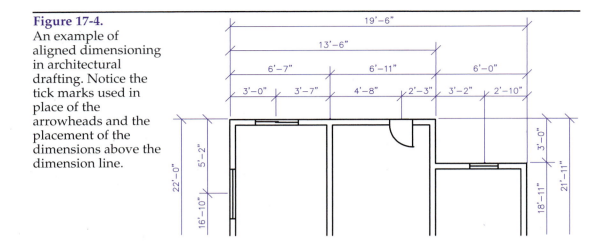

When using the aligned system, terminate dimension lines with tick marks, dots, or arrowheads. In architectural drafting, the dimension number is generally placed above the dimension line and tick marks are used as terminators. See **Figure 17-4.**

Drawing Dimensions with AutoCAD

AutoCAD has a variety of dimensioning applications that fall into five fundamental categories: linear, angular, diameter, radius, and ordinate. These applications allow you to perform nearly every type of dimensioning practice needed for your discipline.

Drawing Linear Dimensions

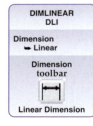

DIMLINEAR
DLI

Dimension
➡ Linear

Dimension toolbar

Linear Dimension

Linear means straight. In most cases, dimensions measure straight distances, such as horizontal, vertical, or slanted surfaces. The **DIMLINEAR** command allows you to measure the length of an object and place extension lines, dimension lines, dimension text, and arrowheads automatically. To do this, pick the **Linear Dimension** button in the **Dimension** toolbar, select **Linear** from the **Dimension** pull-down menu, or enter DLI or DIMLINEAR at the Command: prompt.

Once the command is initiated, you are asked to pick the origin of the first extension line. Then you are asked the origin of the second extension line. The points you pick are the extension line origins. See **Figure 17-5.** Place the crosshairs directly on the corners of the object where the extension lines begin. Use object snap modes for accuracy.

Figure 17-5.
Establishing extension line origins. The **Endpoint** or **Intersection** object snap modes are useful in accurately locating the origins.

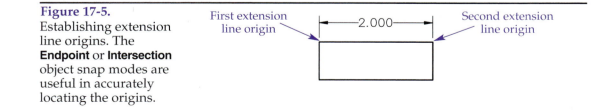

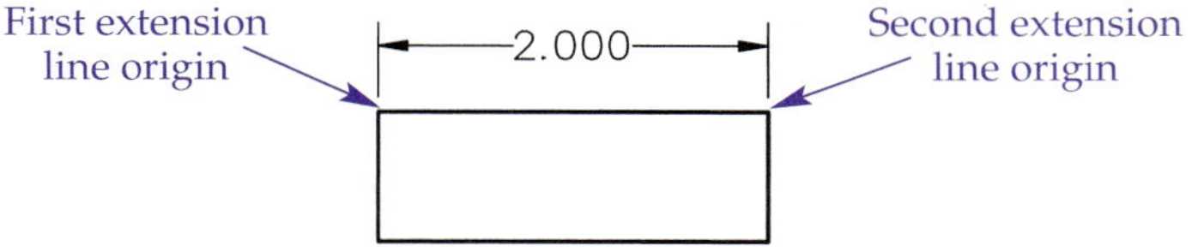

The **DIMLINEAR** command allows you to generate horizontal, vertical, or rotated dimensions. After selecting the object or points of origin for dimensioning, you are given the Specify dimension line location or [Mtext/Text/Angle/Horizontal/Vertical/Rotated] prompt. The options are as follows:

- **Specify dimension line location.** This is the default. Simply drag the dimension line to a desired location and pick. See Figure 17-6. This is where preliminary plan sheets and sketches help you determine proper distances to avoid crowding. The extension lines, dimension line, dimension text, and arrowheads are automatically drawn after the location is picked.
- **Mtext.** Accesses the multiline text editor and the **Text Formatting** toolbar, Figure 17-7. Here you can provide a specific measurement or text format for the dimension. See Chapter 8 for a complete description of the multiline text editor and the **Text Formatting** toolbar. The chevrons (< >) represent the current dimension value. Edit the dimension text and pick **OK**. For example, the ASME standard recommends that a reference dimension be displayed enclosed in parentheses. Type an open and closed parenthesis around the chevrons to create a reference dimension. If you want the current dimension value changed, delete the chevrons and type the new value. If you want the chevrons to be part of the dimension text, type the new value inside or next to the chevrons. While this is not an ASME standard, it may be needed for some applications.

Figure 17-6.
Establishing the dimension line's location.

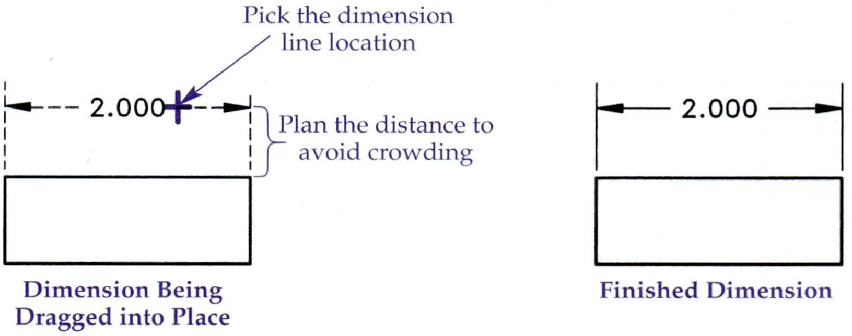

Figure 17-7.
When you use the **Mtext** option, the multiline text editor appears. The chevrons (< >) represent the dimension value AutoCAD has calculated.

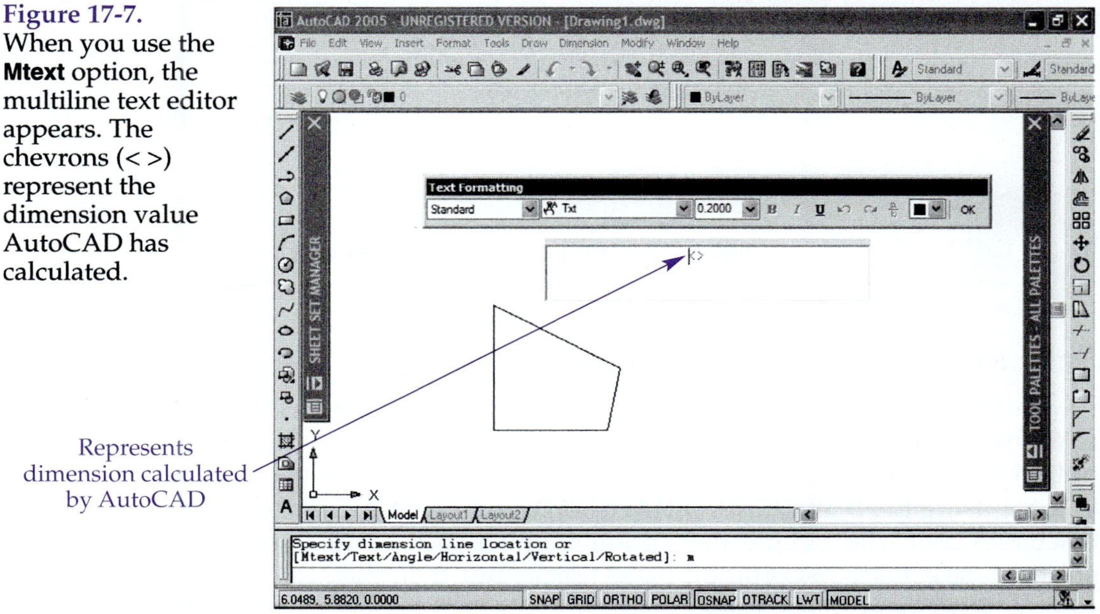

- **Text.** Uses the command line to change dimension text. This is convenient if you prefer to type the desired text rather than using the multiline text editor. The **Text** and **Mtext** options both create multiline text objects. The **Text** option displays the current dimension value in brackets. Pressing [Enter] accepts the current value. Type a new value, such as placing the chevrons inside parentheses to create a reference dimension.
- **Angle.** Allows you to change the dimension text angle. This option can be used when creating rotated dimensions or for adjusting the dimension text to a desired angle. The desired angle is entered at the Specify angle of dimension text: prompt.
- **Horizontal.** Sets the dimension to a horizontal distance only. This may be helpful when dimensioning the horizontal distance of a slanted surface. The **Mtext**, **Text**, and **Angle** options are available again in case you want to change the dimension text value or angle.
- **Vertical.** Sets the dimension being created to a vertical distance only. This option may be helpful when dimensioning the vertical distance of a slanted surface. Like the **Horizontal** option, the **Mtext**, **Text**, and **Angle** options are available.
- **Rotated.** Allows an angle to be specified for the dimension line. A practical application is dimensioning to angled surfaces and auxiliary views. This technique is different from other dimensioning commands because you are asked to provide a dimension line angle. See Figure 17-8. At the Specify angle of dimension line <0>: prompt, enter a value, such as 45, or pick two points on the line to be dimensioned.

Figure 17-8.
Rotating a dimension for an angled view.

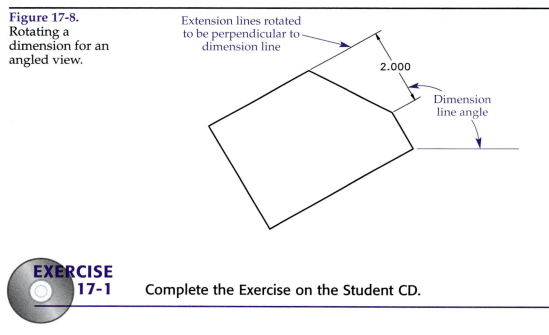

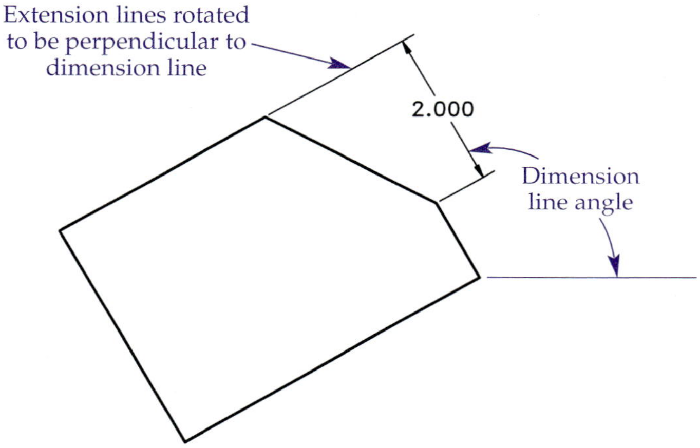

EXERCISE 17-1 Complete the Exercise on the Student CD.

Selecting an Object to Dimension

In the previous discussion, the extension line origins were picked in order to establish the extents of the dimension. Another powerful AutoCAD dimensioning option allows you to pick a single line, circle, or arc to dimension. This works when you are using the **DIMLINEAR, DIMALIGNED**, and **QDIM** commands; the latter two are discussed later. You can use this option anytime you see the Specify first extension line origin or <select object>: prompt. Press [Enter] and then pick the object being dimensioned. When you select a line or arc, AutoCAD automatically begins the extension lines from the endpoints. If you pick a circle, the extension lines are drawn from the closest quadrant and its opposite quadrant. See **Figure 17-9.**

PROFESSIONAL TIP

Dimensioning in AutoCAD should be performed as accurately and neatly as possible. You can achieve consistently professional results by using the following guidelines:

- Always construct drawing geometry accurately. Never truncate, or round off, decimal values when entering locations, distances, or angles. For example, enter .4375 for 7/16 rather than .44.
- Set the desired precision level before beginning your dimensioning. Most drawings have varying levels of precision for specific drawing features, so select the most common precision level to start with and adjust the precision as needed for each dimension. Setting the dimension precision is explained later in this chapter.
- Always use the precision drawing aids to ensure the accuracy of dimensions. If the point being dimensioned does not coincide with a snap point or a known coordinate, use an appropriate object snap override.
- *Never* type a different dimension value than what appears in the brackets. If a dimension needs to change, revise the drawing or dimensioning variables accordingly. The ability to change the dimension in the brackets is provided by AutoCAD so that a different text format can be specified for the dimension. Prefixes and suffixes can also be added to the dimension in the brackets. A typical example of a prefix might be to specify the number of times a dimension occurs, such as 4X 1.750. Other examples of this capability appear later in this chapter.

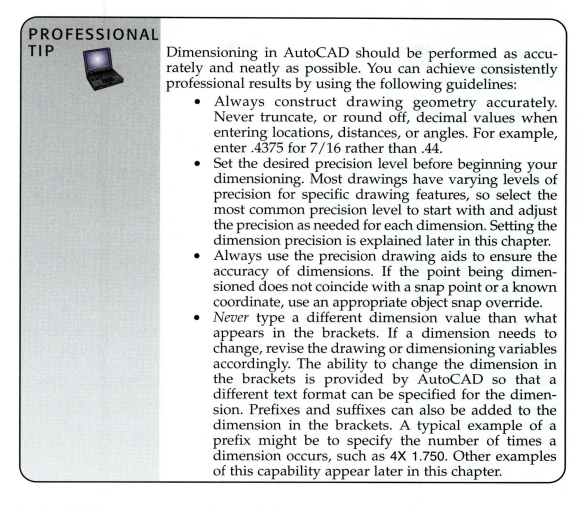

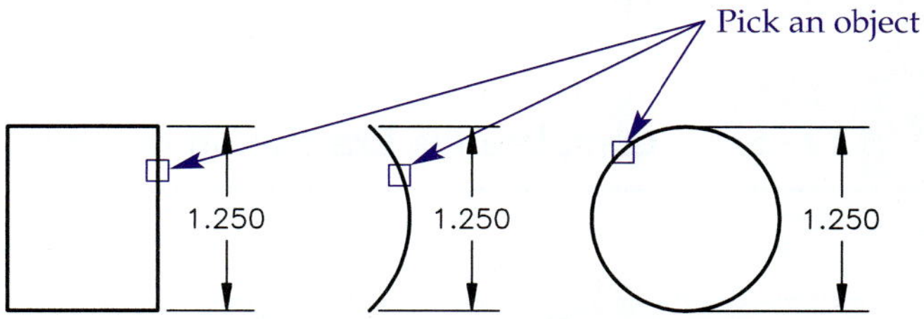

Figure 17-9.
AutoCAD can automatically determine the extension line origins if you select a line, arc, or circle.

EXERCISE 17-2

Complete the Exercise on the Student CD.

Dimensioning Angled Surfaces and Auxiliary Views

When dimensioning a surface drawn at an angle it may be necessary to align the dimension line with the surface. For example, auxiliary views are normally placed at an angle. In order to properly dimension these features, the **DIMALIGNED** command or the **Rotated** option of the **DIMLINEAR** command can be used.

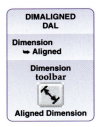

DIMALIGNED
DAL

Dimension
➥ Aligned

Dimension toolbar

Aligned Dimension

Using the DIMALIGNED Command

The **DIMALIGNED** command can be accessed by picking the **Aligned Dimension** button on the **Dimension** toolbar, picking **Aligned** in the **Dimension** pull-down menu, or entering DAL or DIMALIGNED at the Command: prompt. The results of the **DIMALIGNED** command are displayed in Figure 17-10. The command sequence is:

Command: **DAL** *or* **DIMALIGNED**↵
Specify first extension line origin or <select object>: *(pick first extension line origin)*
Specify second extension line origin: *(pick second extension line origin)*
Specify dimension line location or
[Mtext/Text/Angle]: *(pick the dimension line location)*
Dimension text = 2.250
Command:

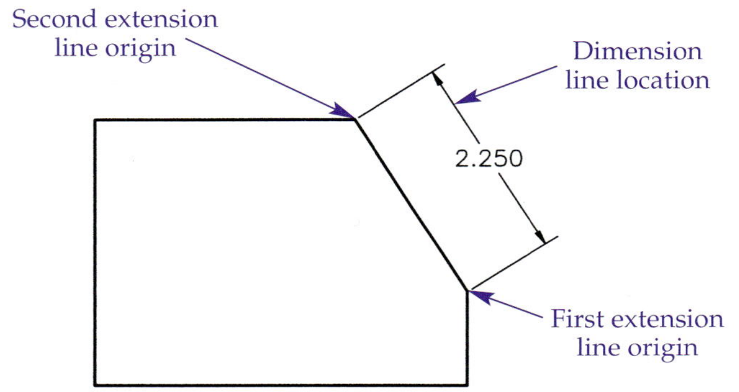

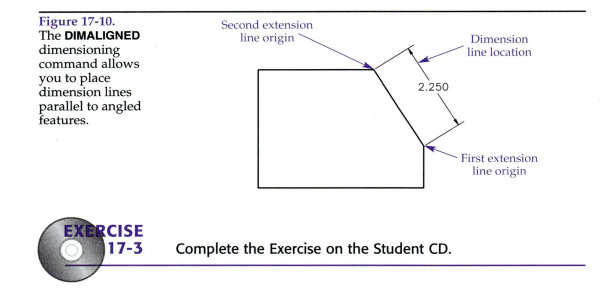

Figure 17-10.
The **DIMALIGNED** dimensioning command allows you to place dimension lines parallel to angled features.

EXERCISE 17-3 Complete the Exercise on the Student CD.

Dimensioning Angles

Coordinate and angular dimensioning are both accepted for dimensioning angles. In ***coordinate dimensioning*** of angles, dimensions locate the corner of the angle, as shown in Figure 17-11. This can be accomplished with the **DIMLINEAR** command.

Angular dimensioning locates one corner with a dimension and provides the value of the angle in degrees. See Figure 17-12. You can dimension the angle between any two nonparallel lines. The intersection of the lines is the angle's vertex. AutoCAD automatically draws extension lines if they are needed. The angular unit of measure is set in the dimension style, which is discussed later in this chapter.

DIMANGULAR
DAN

Dimension
➥ Angular

Dimension toolbar

Angular Dimension

The **DIMANGULAR** command is used for the angular method. It is accessed by picking the **Angular Dimension** button on the **Dimension** toolbar, picking **Angular** in the **Dimension** pull-down menu, or by entering DAN or DIMANGULAR at the Command: prompt. The dimension in Figure 17-12A was drawn with the following sequence:

Figure 17-11.
Coordinate dimensioning of angles.

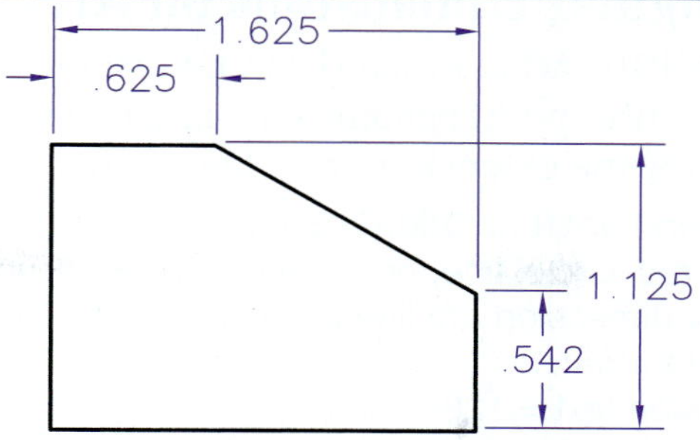

Command: **DAN** *or* **DIMANGULAR**↵
Select arc, circle, line, or <specify vertex>: *(pick the first leg of the angle to be dimensioned)*
Select second line: *(pick the second leg of the angle to be dimensioned)*
Specify dimension arc line location or [Mtext/Text/Angle]: *(pick the desired location of the dimension line arc)*
Dimension text = 30
Command:

The last prompt asks you to pick the dimension line arc location. If there is enough space, AutoCAD places the dimension text, dimension line arc, and arrowheads inside the extension lines. If there is not enough room between extension lines for the arrowheads and numbers, AutoCAD automatically places the arrowheads outside and the number inside the extension lines. If space is very tight, AutoCAD may place the dimension line arc and arrowheads inside and the text outside, or place everything outside of the extension lines. See **Figure 17-13.**

Figure 17-12.
Two examples of drawing angular dimensions.

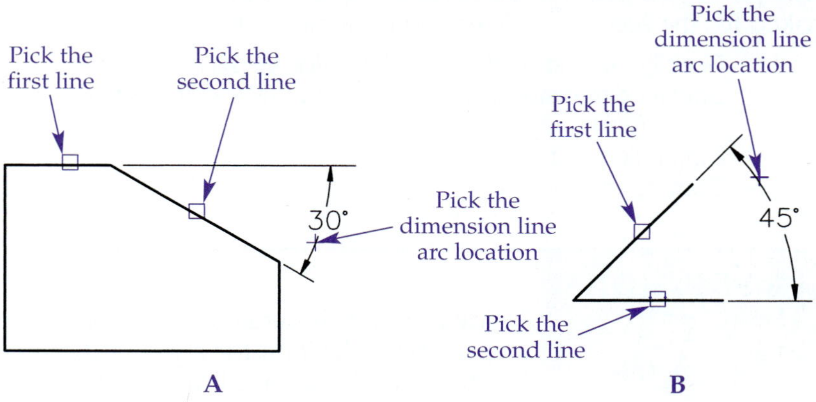

Figure 17-13.
The dimension line arc location determines where the dimension line arc, text, and arrows are displayed.

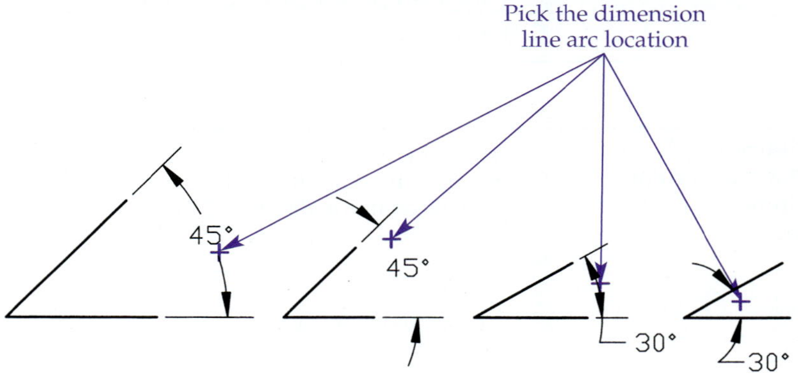

Placing Angular Dimensions on Arcs

The **DIMANGULAR** command can be used to dimension the included angle of an arc. The arc's center point becomes the angle vertex and the two arc endpoints are the origin points for the extension lines. See **Figure 17-14.** The command sequence is:

Command: **DAN** *or* **DIMANGULAR**↵
Select arc, circle, line, or <specify vertex>: *(pick the arc)*
Specify dimension arc line location or [Mtext/Text/Angle]: *(pick the desired dimension line location)*
Dimension text = 128
Command:

Figure 17-14.
Placing angular dimensions on arcs.

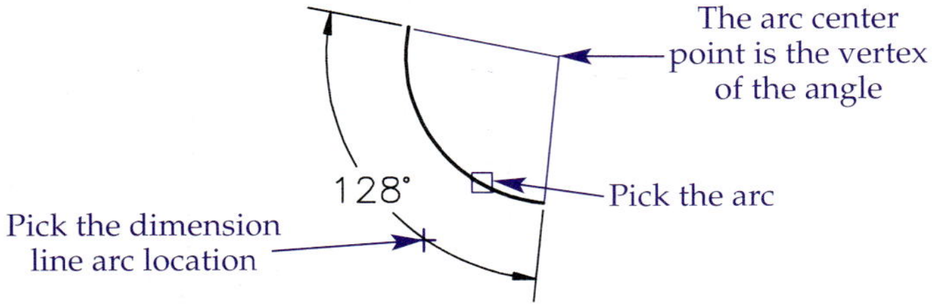
The arc center point is the vertex of the angle
128°
Pick the arc
Pick the dimension line arc location

Placing Angular Dimensions on Circles

The **DIMANGULAR** command can also be used to dimension a portion of a circle. The circle's center point becomes the angle vertex and two picked points are the origin points for the extension lines. See **Figure 17-15.** The command sequence is:

Command: **DAN** *or* **DIMANGULAR**↵
Select arc, circle, line, or <specify vertex>: *(pick the circle)*

The point you pick on the circle is the endpoint of the first extension line. You are then asked for the second angle endpoint, which is the endpoint of the second extension line:

Specify second angle endpoint: *(pick the second point)*
Specify dimension arc line location or [Mtext/Text/Angle]: *(pick the desired dimension line location)*
Dimension text = 85
Command:

PROFESSIONAL TIP

Using angular dimensioning for circles increases the number of possible solutions for a given dimensioning requirement, but the actual uses are limited. One professional application is dimensioning an angle from a quadrant point to a particular feature without having to first draw a line to dimension. Another benefit of this option is the ability to specify angles that exceed 180°.

Figure 17-15.
Placing angular dimensions on circles.

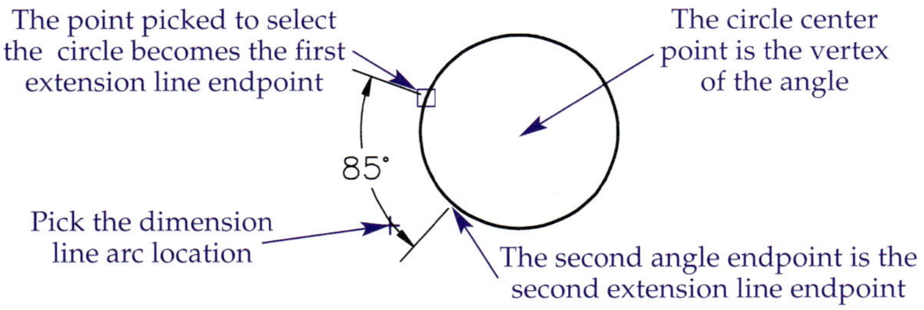
The point picked to select the circle becomes the first extension line endpoint
The circle center point is the vertex of the angle
85°
Pick the dimension line arc location
The second angle endpoint is the second extension line endpoint

Angular Dimensioning through Three Points

You can also establish an angular dimension through three points. The points are the angle vertex and two angle line endpoints. See **Figure 17-16.** To do this, press [Enter] after the first prompt:

Command: **DAN** *or* **DIMANGULAR**↵
Select arc, circle, line, or <specify vertex>: ↵
Specify angle vertex: *(pick a vertex point; a rubberband connects the vertex and the cursor to help locate the endpoints)*
Specify first angle endpoint: *(pick the first endpoint)*
Specify second angle endpoint: *(pick the second endpoint)*
Non-associative dimension created.
Specify dimension arc line location or [Mtext/Text/Angle]: *(pick the desired dimension line location)*
Dimension text = 60

This method also dimensions angles over 180°.

Figure 17-16.
Angular dimensions using three points.

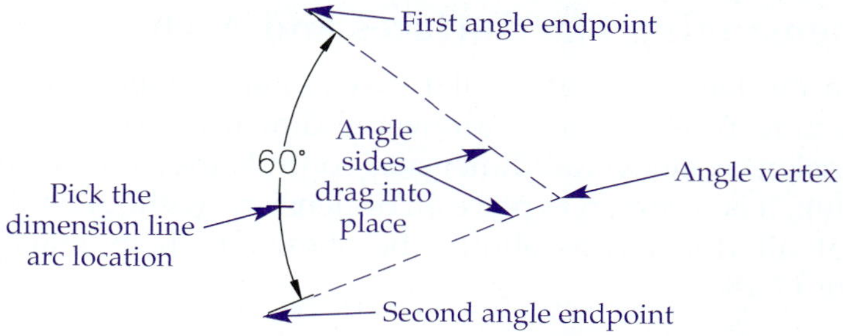

EXERCISE 17-4 Complete the Exercise on the Student CD.

Dimensioning Practices

Dimensioning practices often depend on product requirements, manufacturing accuracy, standards, and tradition. Dimensional information includes size dimensions, location dimensions, and notes. Two techniques that identify size and location are chain and datum dimensioning. Which method is used depends on the accuracy of the product and the drafting field. Both methods are covered later in this chapter.

Size Dimensions and Notes

Size dimensions provide the size of physical features. They include lines, notes, or dimension lines and numbers. Size dimensioning practices depend on the techniques used to dimension different geometric features. See **Figure 17-17.** A ***feature*** is considered any physical portion of a part or object, such as a surface, hole, window, or door. Dimensioning standards are used so an object designed in one place can be manufactured or built somewhere else.

Specific notes and general notes are the two types of notes on a drawing. ***Specific notes*** relate to individual or specific features on the drawing. They are attached to the feature being dimensioned using a leader line. ***General notes*** apply to the entire drawing and are placed in the lower-left corner, upper-left corner, or above or next to the title block. Where they are placed depends on company or school practice.

Figure 17-17.
Size dimensions and specific notes.

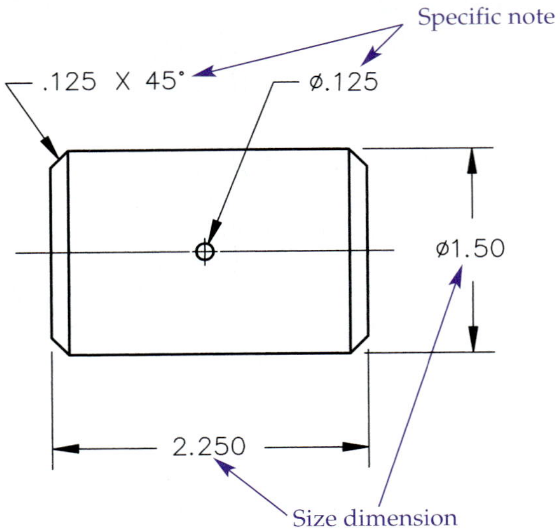

Dimensioning Flat Surfaces and Architectural Features

In mechanical drafting, flat surfaces are dimensioned by giving measurements for each feature. If there is an overall dimension provided, you can omit one of the dimensions. The overall dimension controls the omitted dimension. In architectural drafting, it is common to place all dimensions without omitting any of them. The idea is that all dimensions should be shown to help make construction easier. See **Figure 17-18.**

Figure 17-18.
Dimensioning flat surfaces and architectural features.

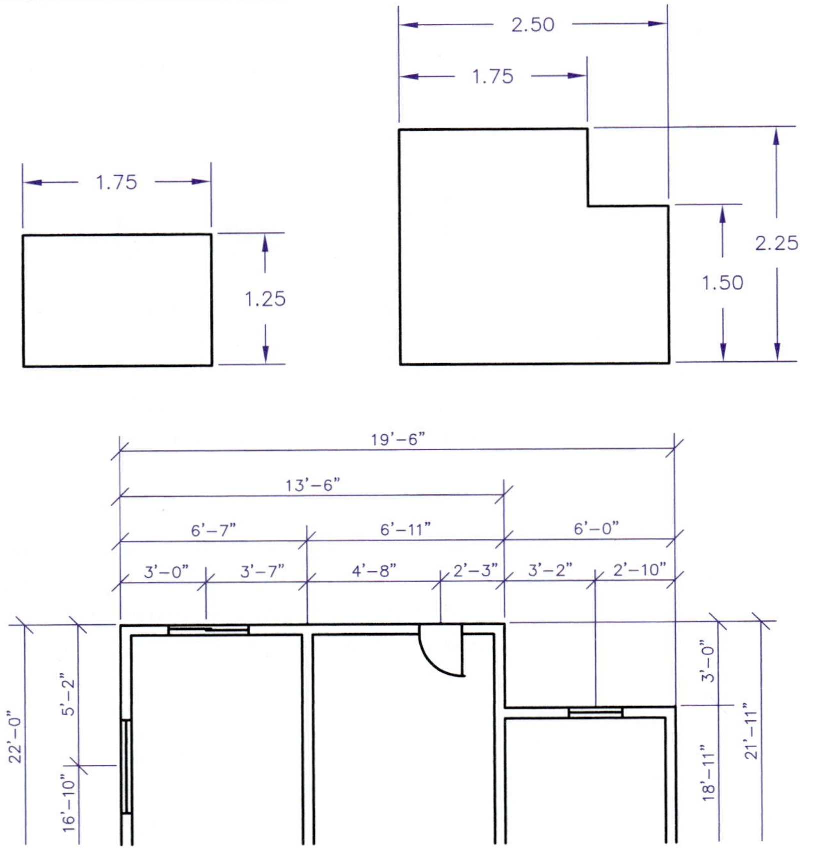

Dimensioning Cylindrical Shapes

Both the diameter and length of a cylindrical shape can be dimensioned in the view in which the cylinder appears rectangular. See **Figure 17-19.** This allows the view in which the cylinder appears as a circle to be omitted.

Figure 17-19.
Dimensioning cylindrical shapes.

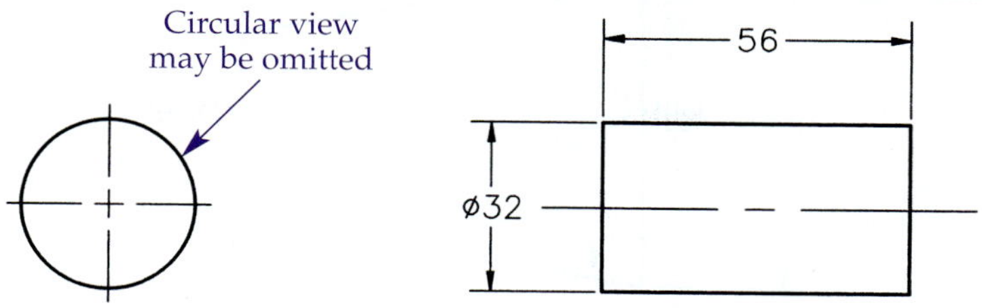

Dimensioning Square and Rectangular Features

Square and rectangular features are usually dimensioned in the views in which the length and height are shown. The square symbol can be used preceding the dimension for the square feature. See **Figure 17-20.** The square symbol must be created as a block and inserted. Blocks are discussed in Chapter 22 of this text.

Figure 17-20.
Dimensioning square and rectangular features.

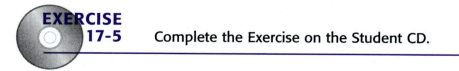

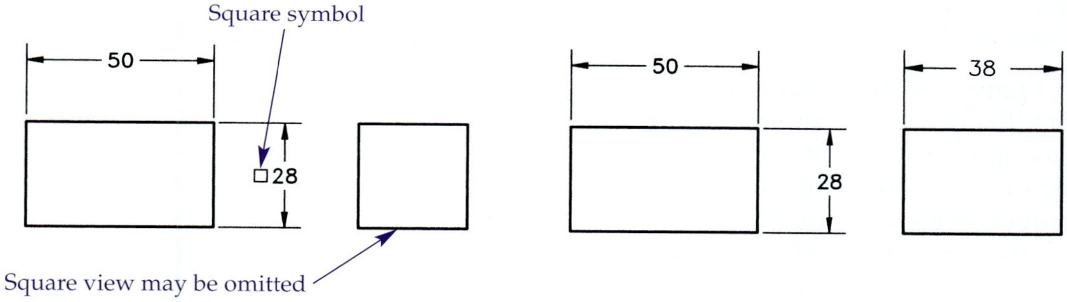

Dimensioning Cones and Hexagonal Shapes

There are two ways to dimension a conical shape. One method is to dimension the diameters at both ends and the length. See **Figure 17-21.** Another method is to dimension the taper angle and the length. Hexagonal shapes are dimensioned by giving the distance across the flats and the length.

EXERCISE 17-5 Complete the Exercise on the Student CD.

Figure 17-21.
A—Dimensioning conical shapes. These shapes can also be dimensioned with an angle and length. B—Hexagons are dimensioned across their flats with a length given.

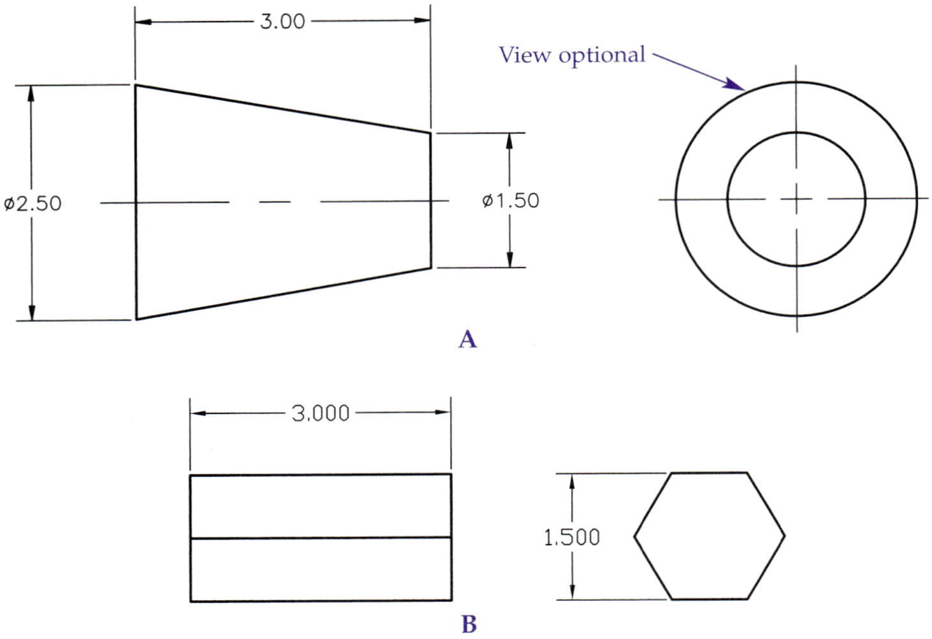

Location Dimensions

Location dimensions are used to locate features on an object. They do not provide the size. Holes and arcs are dimensioned to their centers in the view in which they appear circular. Rectangular features are dimensioned to their edges. See Figure 17-22. In architectural drafting, windows and doors are dimensioned to their centers on the floor plan.

Rectangular coordinates and polar coordinates are the two basic location dimensioning systems. ***Rectangular coordinates*** are linear dimensions used to locate features from surfaces, centerlines, or center planes. AutoCAD performs this type of dimensioning using a variety of dimensioning commands. The most frequently used dimensioning command is **DIMLINEAR** and its options. See Figure 17-23. The ***polar coordinate system*** uses angular dimensions to locate features from surfaces, centerlines, or center

Figure 17-22.
Locating circular and rectangular features.

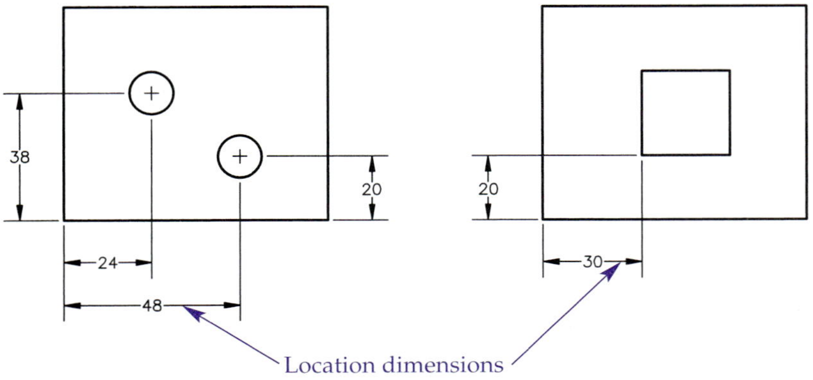

Figure 17-23.
A—Rectangular coordinate location dimensions. B—Polar coordinate location dimensions.

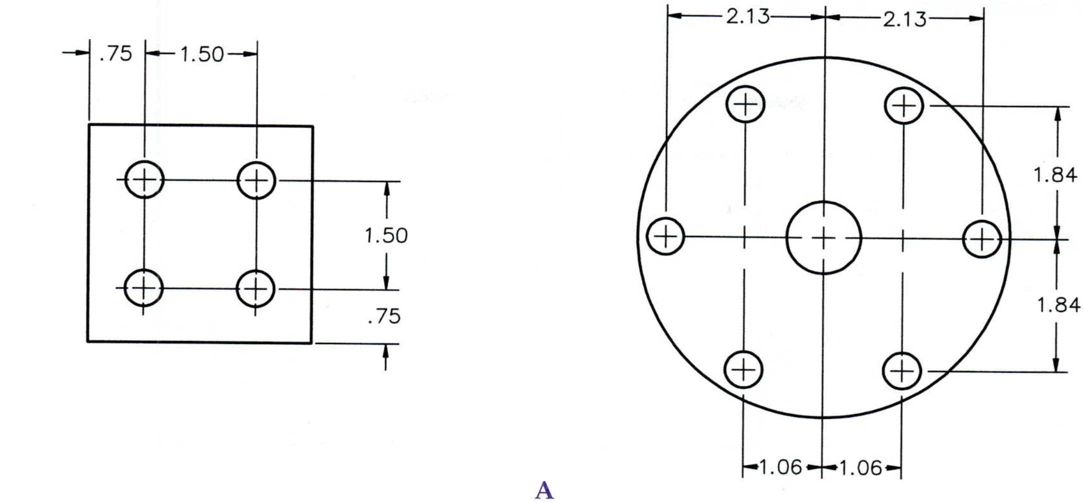

A

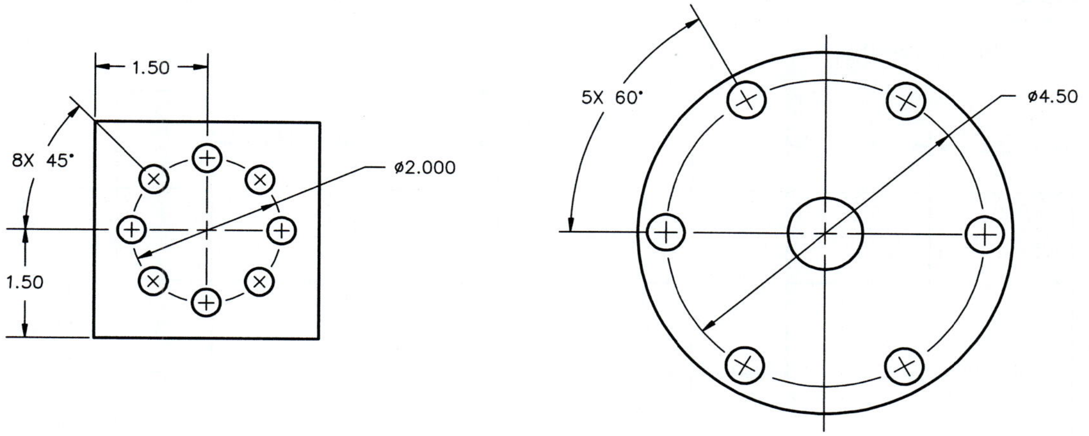

B

planes. The angular dimensions in the polar coordinate system are drawn using AutoCAD's **DIMANGULAR** command.

Datum and Chain Dimensioning

With ***datum dimensioning,*** or ***baseline dimensioning,*** dimensions on an object originate from common surfaces, centerlines, or center planes. Datum dimensioning is commonly used in mechanical drafting because each dimension is independent of the others. This achieves more accuracy in manufacturing. Figure 17-24 shows an object dimensioned with surface datums.

Chain dimensioning, also called ***point-to-point dimensioning,*** places dimensions in a line from one feature to the next. Chain dimensioning is sometimes used in mechanical drafting. However, there is less accuracy than with datum dimensioning since each dimension is dependent on other dimensions in the chain. Architectural drafting uses chain dimensioning in most applications. Figure 17-25 shows two examples of chain dimensioning. In mechanical drafting, it is common to leave one dimension blank and provide an overall dimension. Architectural drafting practices usually show dimensions all the way across plus an overall dimension.

Figure 17-24.
Datum dimensioning.

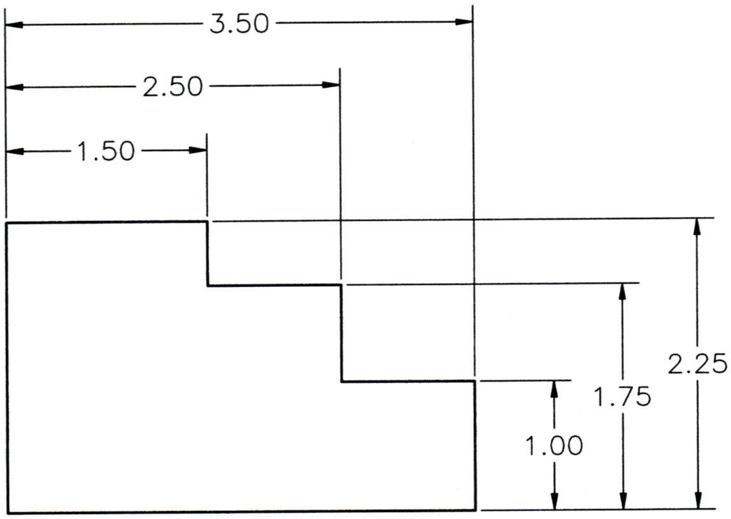

Figure 17-25.
Chain dimensioning.

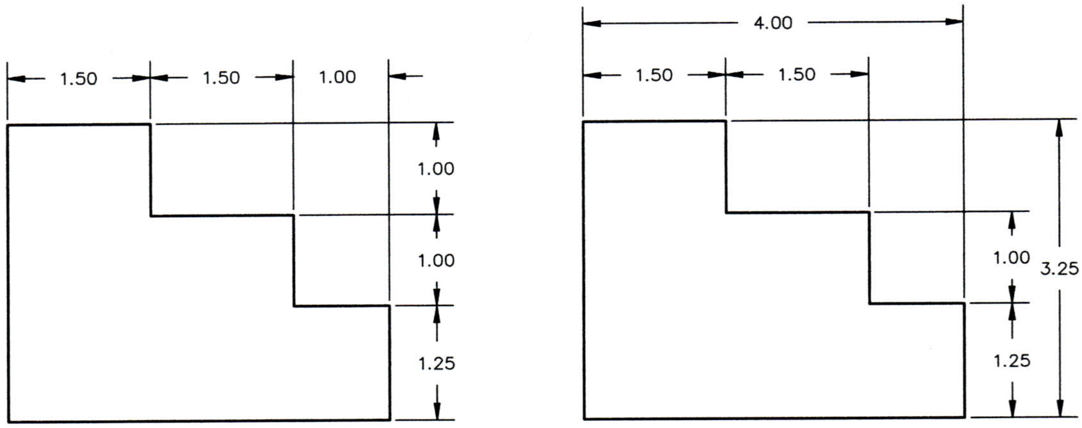

Making Datum and Chain Dimensioning Easy

AutoCAD refers to datum dimensioning as ***baseline*** and chain dimensioning as ***continue***. Datum dimensioning is controlled by the **DIMBASELINE** command. Chain dimensioning is controlled by the **DIMCONTINUE** command. The **DIMBASELINE** and **DIMCONTINUE** commands are used in the same manner. The prompts and options are the same. Use the **Undo** option in the **DIMBASELINE** or **DIMCONTINUE** commands to undo previously drawn dimensions.

DIMBASELINE
DBA

Dimension
➥ Baseline

Dimension toolbar

Baseline Dimension

Datum Dimensions

Datum dimensions are created by picking the **Baseline Dimension** button in the **Dimension** toolbar, picking **Baseline** in the **Dimension** pull-down menu, or by entering either DBA or DIMBASELINE at the Command: prompt. Baseline dimensions can be created with linear, ordinate, and angular dimensions. Ordinate dimensions are discussed later in this chapter.

When you enter the **DIMBASELINE** command, AutoCAD asks you to Specify a second extension line origin. This is because a baseline dimension is a continuation of an existing dimension. Therefore, a dimension must exist before using the command. AutoCAD automatically selects the most recently drawn dimension as the base dimension unless you specify a different one. As you add datum dimensions, AutoCAD automatically places the extension lines, dimension lines, arrowheads, and numbers. For example, use the following procedure to dimension the series of horizontal baseline dimensions shown in **Figure 17-26.**

> Command: **DLI** *or* **DIMLINEAR**↵
> Specify first extension line origin or <select object>: *(pick the first extension line origin)*
> Specify second extension line origin: *(pick the second extension line origin)*
> Specify dimension line location or
> [Mtext/Text/Angle/Horizontal/Vertical/Rotated]: *(pick the dimension line location)*
> Dimension text = 2.000
> Command: **DBA** *or* **DIMBASELINE**↵
> Specify a second extension line origin or [Undo/Select] <Select>: *(pick the next second extension line origin)*
> Dimension text = 3.250
> Specify a second extension line origin or [Undo/Select] <Select>: *(pick the next second extension line origin)*
> Dimension text = 4.375
> Specify a second extension line origin or [Undo/Select] <Select>: ↵
> Select base dimension: ↵
> Command:

You can continue to add baseline dimensions until you press [Enter] twice to return to the Command: prompt. Notice as additional dimension extension line origins are picked, AutoCAD automatically places the dimension text; you do not specify a location.

If you want to add datum dimensions to an existing dimension other than the most recently drawn one, use the **Select** option by pressing [Enter] at the first prompt. At the Select base dimension: prompt, pick the dimension to serve as the base. When picking a dimension to use as the baseline, the extension line nearest the point where you select the dimension is used as the baseline point. Then, select the new second extension line origins as described earlier.

You can also draw baseline dimensions to angular features. First, draw an angular dimension. Then, enter the **DIMBASELINE** command. You can also pick an existing angular dimension other than the one most recently drawn. **Figure 17-27** shows angular baseline dimensions.

Figure 17-26.
Using the **DIMBASELINE** command. AutoCAD automatically places the extension lines, dimension lines, arrowheads, and numbers.

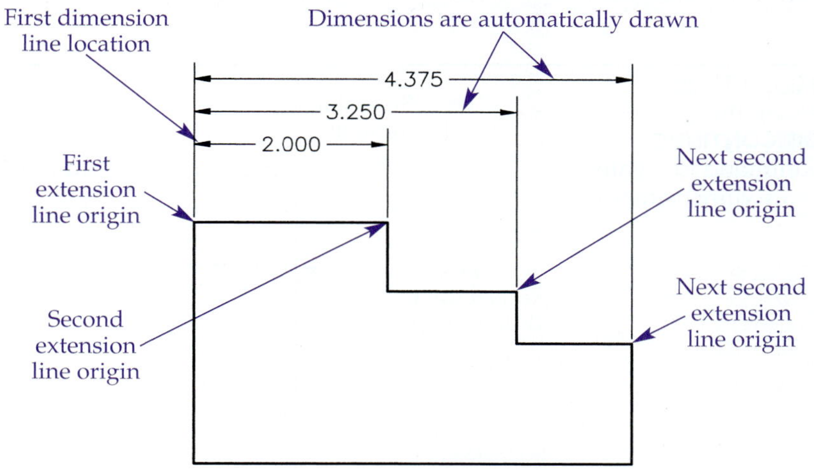

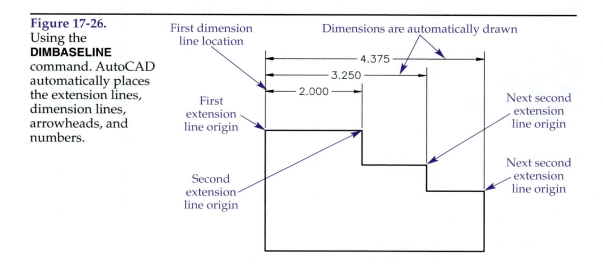

Figure 17-27.
Using the **DIMBASELINE** command to datum dimension angular features.

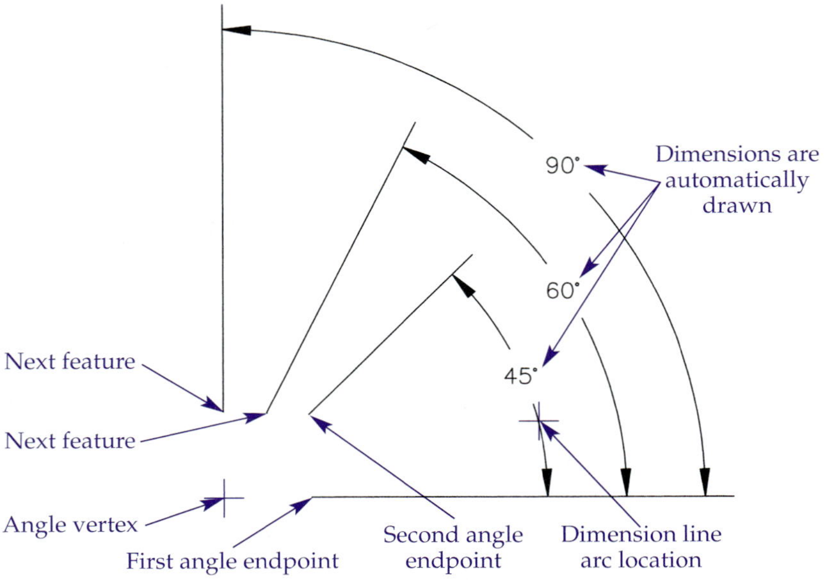

Chain Dimensions

DIMCONTINUE
DCO

Dimension
➡ Continue

Dimension toolbar

Continue Dimension

As previously mentioned, when creating chain dimensions you will receive the same prompts and options received while creating datum dimensions. Chain dimensioning is shown in **Figure 17-28.** Chain dimensions (continue dimensions) are created by picking the **Continue Dimension** button on the **Dimension** toolbar, picking **Continue** in the **Dimension** pull-down menu, or by entering DCO or DIMCONTINUE at the Command: prompt. Continue dimensions can be created with linear, ordinate, and angular dimensions. Ordinate dimensions are discussed later in this chapter.

PROFESSIONAL TIP

You do not have to use **DIMBASELINE** or **DIMCONTINUE** immediately after a dimension that is to be used as a base or chain. You can come back later and use the **Select** option as previously discussed. Then, select the dimension you want to use and draw the datum or chain dimensions that you need.

Figure 17-28.
Using the **DIMCONTINUE** command to create chain dimensions.

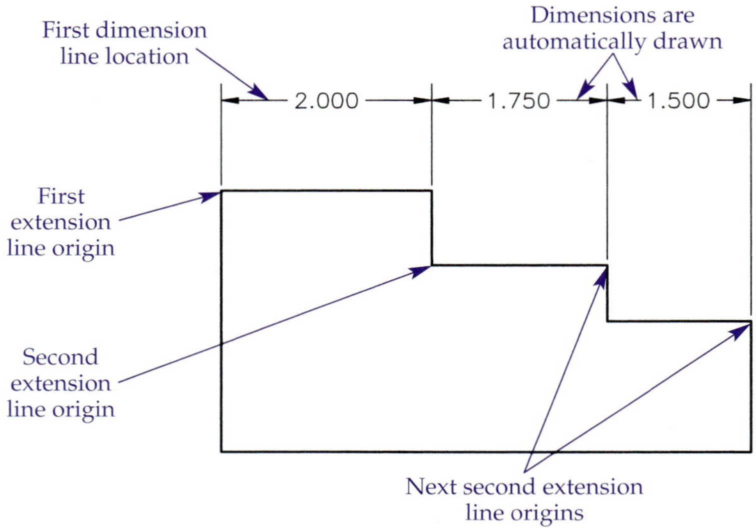

EXERCISE 17-6 Complete the Exercise on the Student CD.

Using QDIM to Dimension

The **QDIM**, or quick dimension, command makes chain and datum dimensioning easy by eliminating the need to define the exact points being dimensioned. Often, the points that need to be selected for dimensioning are the endpoint of a line or the center of an arc. AutoCAD automates the process of point selection in the **QDIM** command by finding those points for you. The **QDIM** command can be accessed by selecting **Quick Dimension** from the **Dimension** pull-down menu, picking the **Quick Dimension** button on the **Dimension** toolbar, or entering QDIM at the Command: prompt.

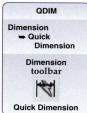

> **QDIM**
> **Dimension** ➥ **Quick Dimension**
> **Dimension** toolbar
> **Quick Dimension**

The type of geometry selected affects the **QDIM** output. If a single polyline is selected, **QDIM** attempts to draw linear dimensions to every vertex of the polyline. If a single arc or circle is selected, then **QDIM** draws a radius or diameter dimension. If multiple objects are selected, linear dimensions are drawn to the vertex of every line or polyline and to the center of every arc or circle. In each case, AutoCAD finds the points automatically. The command line sequence is:

Command: **QDIM**↵
Associative dimension priority = Endpoint
Select geometry to dimension: *(pick several lines, polylines, arcs and/or circles)*
Select geometry to dimension: ↵
Specify dimension line position, or
[Continuous/Staggered/Baseline/Ordinate/Radius/Diameter/datumPoint/Edit/seTtings]
<current>: *(pick a position for the dimension lines)*
Command:

Figure 17-29 shows examples of different types of objects being dimensioned with the **QDIM** command. The upper dimensions are created by selecting each object separately. The lower dimensions are created by selecting all objects at once.

Figure 17-29.
The **QDIM** command can dimension multiple features or objects at the same time.

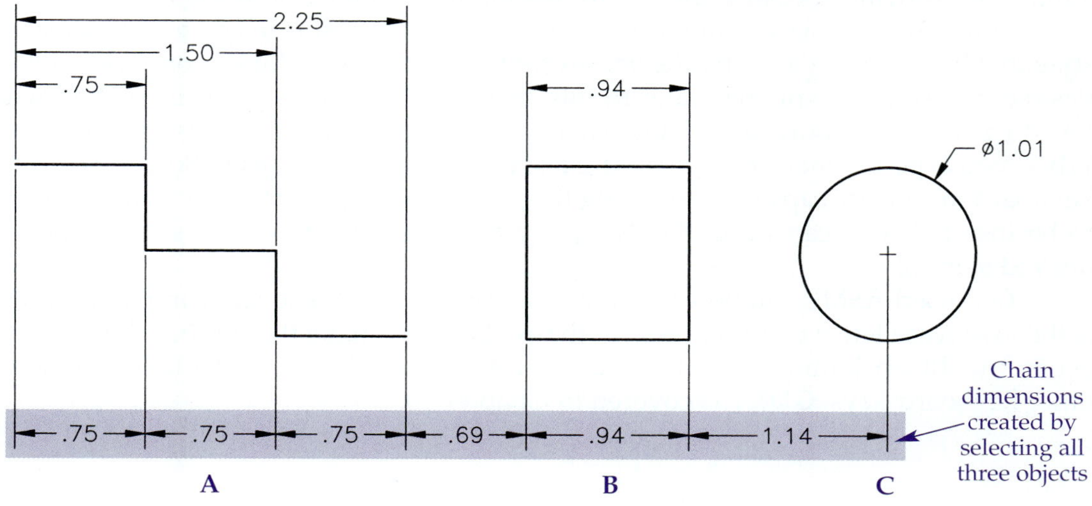

The **Continuous**, **Staggered**, **Baseline**, **Ordinate**, **Radius**, and **Diameter** options relate to the different modes of dimensioning discussed earlier in this chapter. In Figure 17-29, Object A was dimensioned with the **Baseline** option of the **QDIM** command. The command sequence is:

Command: **QDIM**↵
Select geometry to dimension: *(pick polyline shown in Figure 17-29A)*
Specify dimension line position, or
[Continuous/Staggered/Baseline/Ordinate/Radius/Diameter/datumPoint/Edit/seTtings]
<Continuous>: **B**↵
Specify dimension line position, or
[Continuous/Staggered/Baseline/Ordinate/Radius/Diameter/datumPoint/Edit/seTtings]
<Baseline>: *(pick a vertical or horizontal position for the dimension line)*
Command:

The dimensions at the bottom of Figure 17-29 are created using the **Continuous** option of the **QDIM** command and selecting all three objects.

The **QDIM** command can also be used as a way to edit any existing associative dimension. Editing dimensions and a description of the **datum Point, Edit,** and **Setting** options of the **QDIM** command are discussed in Chapter 18.

Including Symbols with Dimension Text

After you select a feature to dimension, AutoCAD responds with the measurement (dimension number). In some cases, such as dimensioning radii and diameters, AutoCAD automatically places the radius (R) or diameter (∅) symbol before the dimension number. However, in other cases related to linear dimensioning, this is not automatic. The recommended ASME standard for a diameter dimension is to place the diameter symbol (∅) before the number. This can be done using the **Mtext** option of the dimensioning commands. When the multiline text editor appears, place the cursor in the location where you want the symbol, such as in front of the chevrons. Then, right-click to display the shortcut menu and select **Diameter** from the **Symbol** cascading menu. After you pick **OK** in the text editor, the command continues and you are asked to pick the dimension line location.

Other symbols are also available from the **Symbol** cascading menu. You can also use the character codes or the Unicode entries to place symbols. The multiline text editor and drawing special symbols are covered in Chapter 8 of this text.

Another way to place symbols with your dimension text is to create a dimension style that has a text style using the gdt.shx font. Establishing a dimension style with a desired text style is explained later in this chapter. A text style with this font allows you to place commonly used dimension symbols with the lowercase letter keys. When you type a dimension containing a symbol, press the [Caps Lock] key on your keyboard to activate caps lock. By doing this, text is uppercase. When a symbol needs to be inserted, you can press the [Shift] key and the letter that corresponds to the desired symbol.

Often-used ASME symbols are shown in Figure 17-30. The letter in parentheses is the lowercase letter that you press at the keyboard to make the symbol. Additional geometric dimensioning and tolerancing (GD&T) symbols are available by pressing other keyboard keys. GD&T is covered in Chapter 20.

Figure 17-30.
Common dimensioning symbols and how to draw them. The lowercase letter displayed in parentheses with some symbol names is the keystroke for placing the symbol with the **gdt.shx** font.

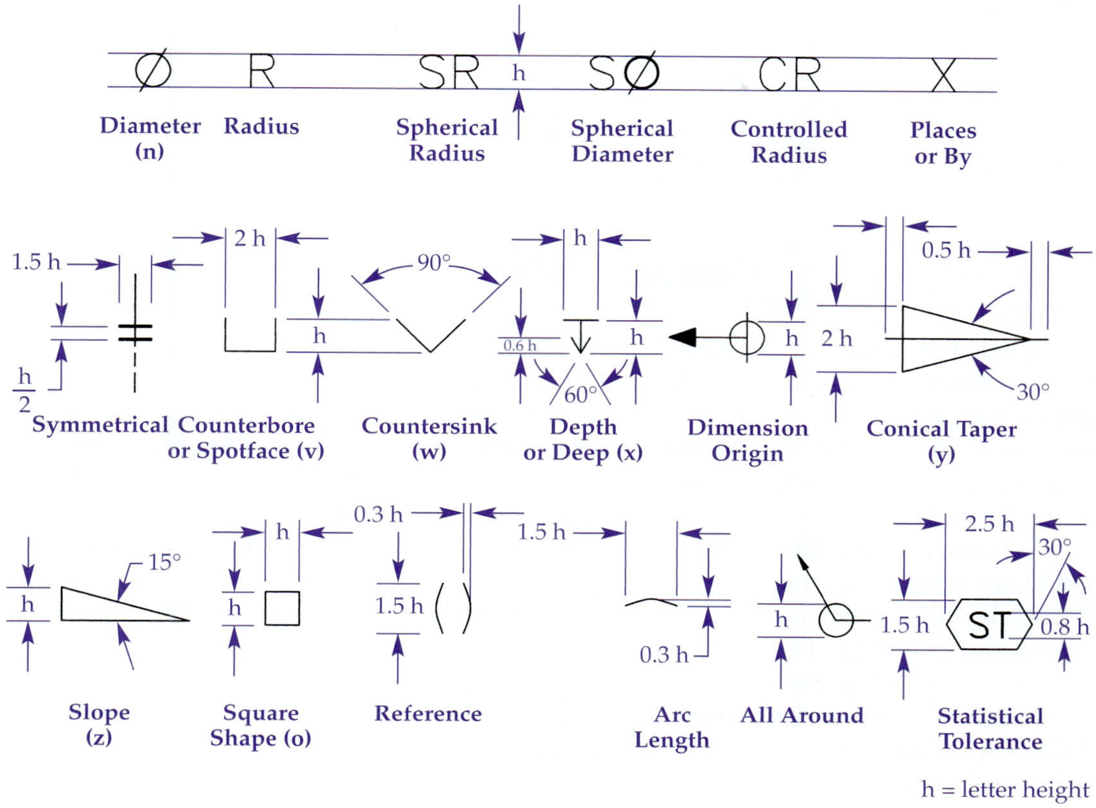

Drawing Center Dashes or Centerlines in a Circle or Arc

DIMCENTER
DCE

Dimension
➥ Center Mark

Dimension toolbar

Center Mark

When small circles or arcs are dimensioned, the **DIMDIAMETER** and **DIMRADIUS** commands leave center dashes. If the dimension of a large circle crosses through the center, the dashes are left out. However, you can manually add center dashes and centerlines with the **DIMCENTER** command. The command is accessed by picking the **Center Mark** button on the **Dimension** toolbar, picking **Center Mark** in the **Dimension** pull-down menu, or entering DCE or DIMCENTER at the Command: prompt. Once the command is entered, you are prompted to pick an arc or circle.

When the circle or arc is picked, center marks are automatically drawn. The size of the center marks or the amount that the centerlines extend outside the circle or arc is controlled by the **Center Mark for Circles** area in the **Lines and Arrows** tab of the **Modify Dimension Style** dialog box. Later in this chapter you will see how to control all settings for the display of dimensions using dimension styles. Figure 17-31 shows the difference between drawing center marks and centerlines in arcs and circles.

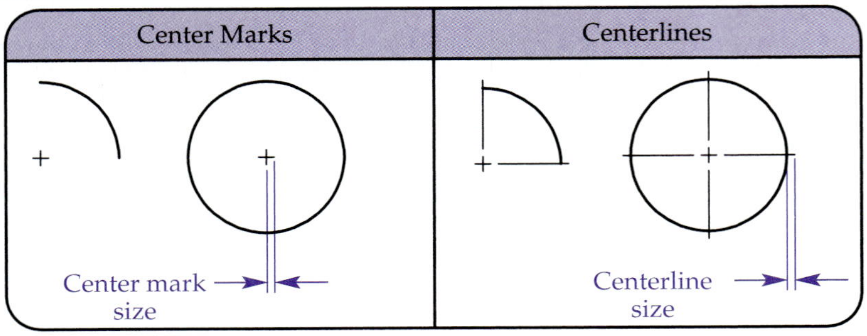

Figure 17-31. Arcs and circles displayed with center marks and centerlines.

Dimensioning Circles

DIMDIAMETER
DDI
Dimension ➥ Diameter
Dimension toolbar
Diameter Dimension

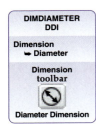

Circles are normally dimensioned by giving the diameter. The ASME standard for dimensioning arcs is to give the radius. However, AutoCAD allows you to dimension either a circle or an arc with a diameter dimension. Diameter dimensions are produced by picking the **Diameter Dimension** button on the **Dimension** toolbar, picking **Diameter** in the **Dimension** pull-down menu, or entering DDI or DIMDIAMETER at the Command: prompt. You are then prompted to select the arc or circle.

When using the **DIMDIAMETER** command, a leader line and diameter dimension value are attached to the cursor when you pick the desired circle or arc. You can drag the leader to any desired location and length. Pick the location and length and the dimension is placed. The resulting leader points to the center of the circle or arc just as recommended by the ASME standard. See Figure 17-32.

You also have the **Mtext, Text,** and **Angle** options that were introduced earlier. Use the **Mtext** or **Text** option if you want to change the text value or the **Angle** option if you want to change the angle of the text.

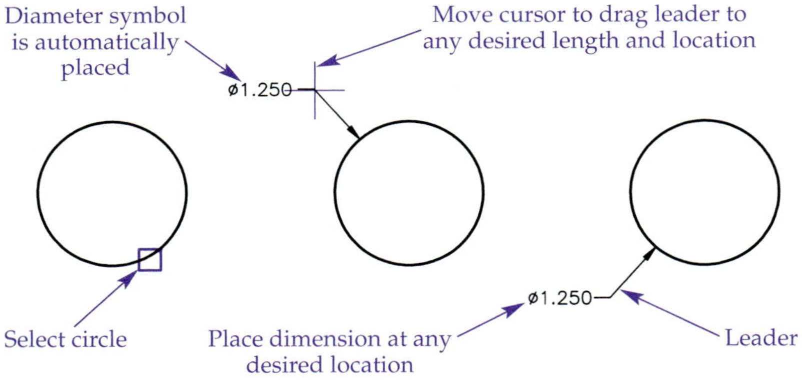

Figure 17-32. Using the **DIMDIAMETER** command with the AutoCAD dimensioning variable defaults.

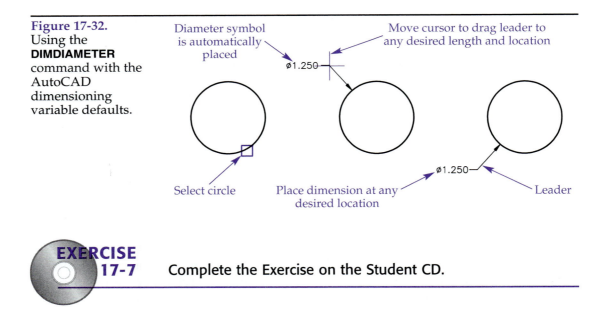

EXERCISE 17-7 Complete the Exercise on the Student CD.

Dimensioning Holes

Holes are dimensioned in the view in which they appear as circles. Give location dimensions to the center and a leader showing the diameter. Leader lines can be drawn using the **DIMDIAMETER** command, as previously discussed. The center mark type and size are controlled in the dimension style, which is discussed later. Multiple holes of the same size can be noted with one hole dimension, such as 2X ∅.50. See Figure 17-33. Use the **Mtext** or **Text** option to create this dimension. The **Angle** option can be used to change the angle of the text numbers, but it is not commonly done.

PROFESSIONAL TIP

The ASME standard recommends a small space between the object and the extension line. This happens when the **Offset from Origin** setting within the dimension style is set to its default or some other desired positive value. This is very useful *except* when providing dimensions to centerlines for the location of holes. When the endpoint of the centerline is picked, a positive value leaves a space between the centerline and the beginning of the extension line. This is not a preferred practice. Change the **Offset from Origin** setting to 0 to remove the gap. Be sure to change back to its positive setting when dimensioning other objects.

Use of the **Dimension Style Manager** dialog box to set this and other dimensioning settings is fully explained later in this chapter.

Figure 17-33.
Dimensioning holes.

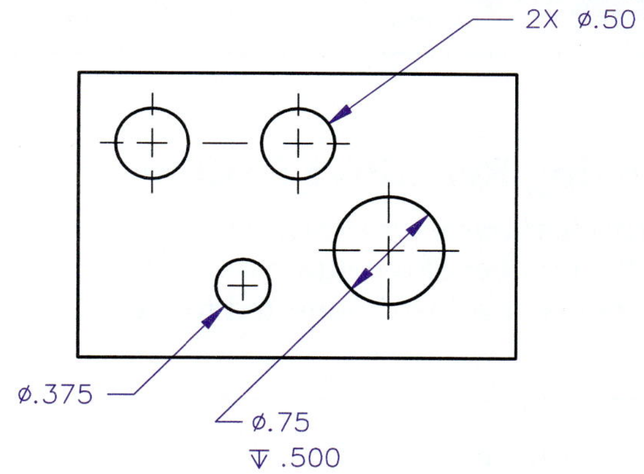

Dimensioning for Manufacturing Processes

A ***counterbore*** is a larger-diameter hole machined at one end of a smaller hole. It provides a place for the head of a bolt. A ***spotface*** is similar to a counterbore except that it is not as deep. The spotface provides a smooth, recessed surface for a washer. A ***countersink*** is a cone-shaped recess at one end of a hole. It provides a mating surface for a screw head of the same shape. A note for these features is provided using symbols. First, locate the centers in the circular view. Then, place a leader providing machining information in a note. See Figure 17-34.

Symbols for this type of application can be customized, as discussed in Chapter 22. These symbols can also be drawn by creating a dimension style with a text style using the gdt.shx font, as explained earlier in this chapter. The symbols and related gdt.shx keyboard letter used to make the symbol are displayed in Figure 17-30.

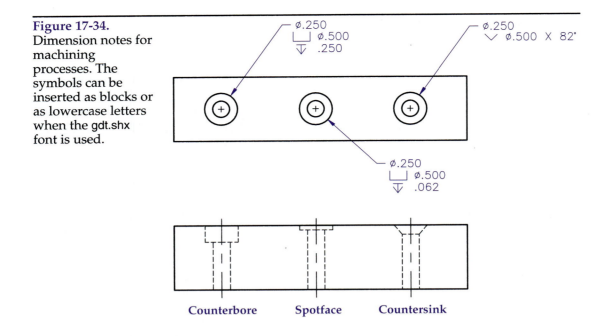

Figure 17-34.
Dimension notes for machining processes. The symbols can be inserted as blocks or as lowercase letters when the gdt.shx font is used.

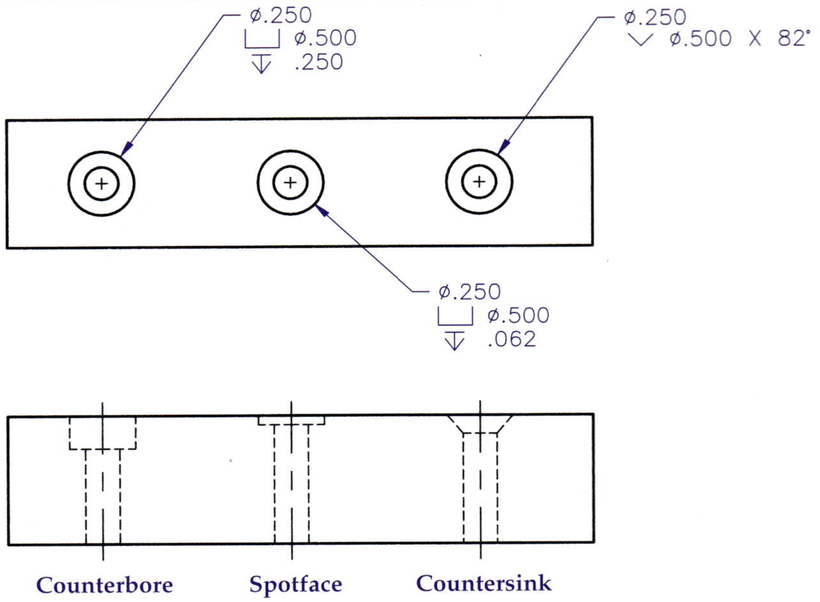

The **DIMDIAMETER** command gives you multiline text to use during the creation of the dimension. Additional text can be added by editing the dimension text, since it is actually an mtext object.

PROFESSIONAL TIP

After creating any dimension, the dimension text can be directly edited using the **Properties** window. Editing dimensions is covered in Chapter 18 of this text.

Dimensioning Repetitive Features

Repetitive features refer to many features having the same shape and size. When this occurs, the number of repetitions is followed by an X, a space, and the size dimension. The dimension is then connected to the feature with a leader. See **Figure 17-35.**

Figure 17-35.
Dimensioning repetitive features (shown in color).

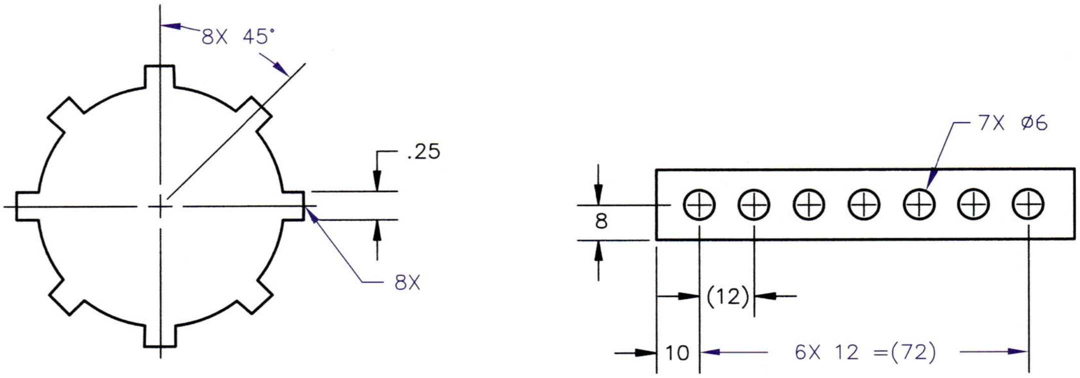

EXERCISE 17-8 Complete the Exercise on the Student CD.

Dimensioning Arcs

DIMRADIUS
DRA

Dimension
➥ Radius

Dimension
toolbar

Radius Dimension

The standard for dimensioning arcs is a radius dimension. A radius dimension is placed with the **DIMRADIUS** command. Access this command by picking the **Radius Dimension** button on the **Dimension** toolbar, picking **Radius** in the **Dimension** pull-down menu, or entering either DRA or DIMRADIUS at the Command: prompt.

When you pick the desired arc or circle to dimension, a leader line and radius dimension value are attached to the cursor. You can drag the leader to any desired location and length. Pick the location and length and the dimension is placed. The resulting leader points to the center of the arc or circle as recommended by the ASME standard. See Figure 17-36.

As with the previous dimensioning commands, you can use the **Mtext** or **Text** option to change the dimension text. You can also use the **Angle** option to change the angle of the text value.

Figure 17-36. Using the **DIMRADIUS** command to dimension arcs with AutoCAD dimensioning defaults.

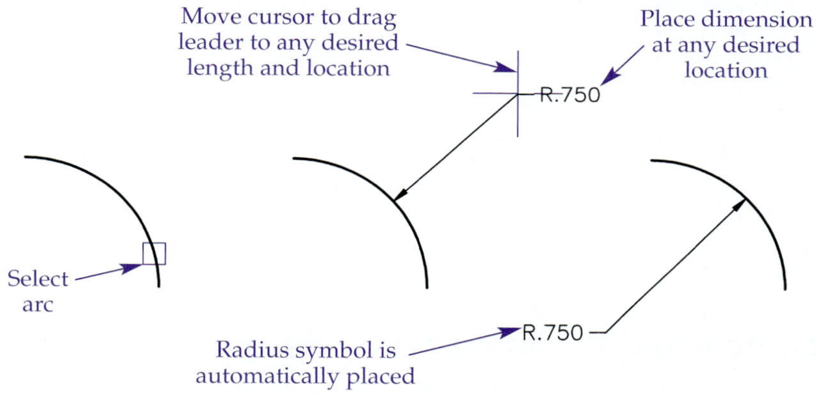
Move cursor to drag leader to any desired length and location
Place dimension at any desired location
R.750
Select arc
Radius symbol is automatically placed
R.750

Dimensioning Fillets and Rounds

Small inside arcs are called ***fillets***. Small arcs on outside corners are called ***rounds***. Fillets are designed to strengthen inside corners. Rounds are used to relieve sharp corners. Fillets and rounds can be dimensioned individually as arcs or in a general note. The general note such as ALL FILLETS AND ROUNDS R.125 UNLESS OTHERWISE SPECIFIED is usually placed near the title block. See Figure 17-37.

EXERCISE 17-9 Complete the Exercise on the Student CD.

Figure 17-37.
Dimensioning fillets and rounds.

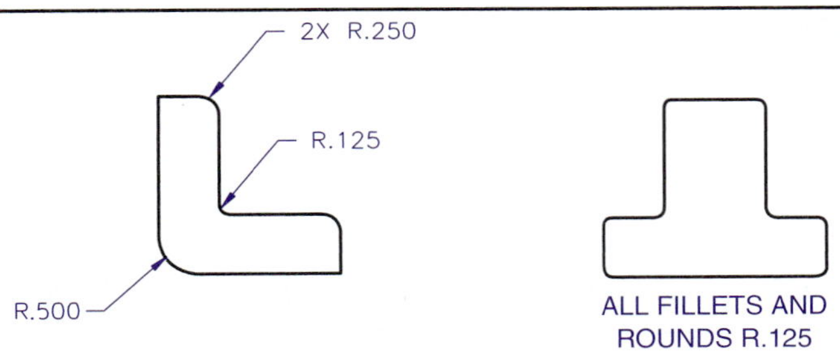

Dimensioning Curves

When possible, curves are dimensioned as arcs. When they are not in the shape of a constant-radius arc, they should be dimensioned to points along the curve using the **DIMLINEAR** command. See **Figure 17-38.**

Figure 17-38.
Dimensioning curves that do not have a constant radius.

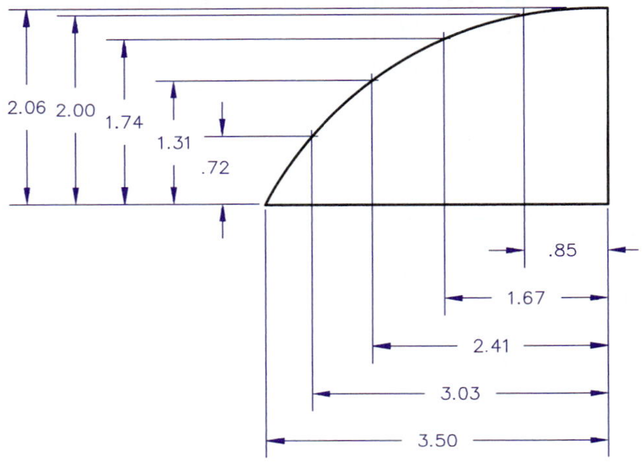

Dimensioning Curves with Oblique Extension Lines

The curve shown in **Figure 17-38** is dimensioned using the normal practice, but, in some cases, spaces may be limited and oblique extension lines are used. First, dimension the object using the **DIMLINEAR** command as appropriate, even if dimensions are crowded or overlap. See **Figure 17-39A.**

DIMEDIT
Dimension ➥ Oblique

The .150 and .340 dimensions are to be placed at an oblique angle above the view. The **Oblique** option of the **DIMEDIT** command is used to draw oblique dimensions. The **DIMEDIT** command is explained in detail in Chapter 19. The command option is accessed by picking **Oblique** in the **Dimension** pull-down menu. After selecting the command, you are asked to select the objects. Pick the dimensions to be redrawn at an oblique angle. In this case, the .150 and .340 dimensions are selected.

Next, you are asked for the obliquing angle. Careful planning is needed to make sure the correct obliquing angle is selected. Obliquing angles originate from 0° East and revolve counterclockwise. Enter 135 for the obliquing angle. The result is shown in **Figure 17-39B.**

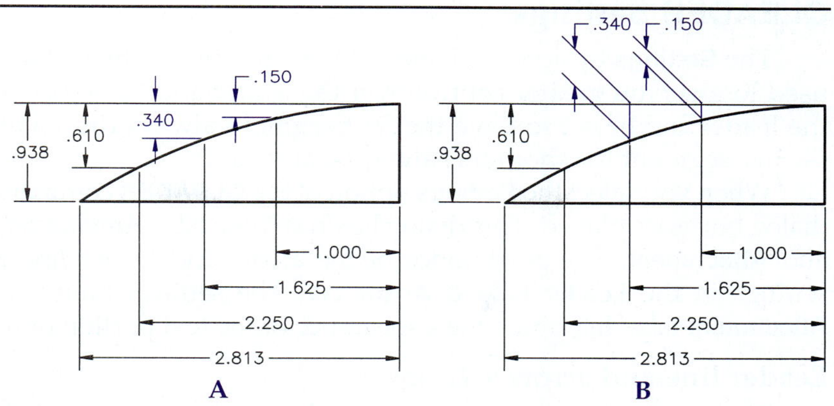

Figure 17-39. Drawing dimensions with oblique extension lines.

Drawing Leader Lines

The **DIMDIAMETER** and **DIMRADIUS** commands automatically place leaders on the drawing. The **QLEADER** command allows you to begin and end a leader line where you desire. You can also place single or multiple lines of text with the leader. This command is ideal for:

- Adding specific notes to the drawing.
- Staggering a leader line to go around other drawing features. Keep in mind that staggering leader lines is not a recommended ASME standard.
- Drawing a double leader. Drawing two leaders from one note is not a recommended ASME standard.
- Making custom leader lines.
- Drawing curved leaders for architectural applications.

The **QLEADER** command creates leader lines and related notes that are considered complex objects. This command provides you with the flexibility to place tolerances and multiple lines of text with the leader. Some of the leader line characteristics, such as arrowhead size, are controlled by the dimension style settings. Other features, such as the leader format and annotation style, are controlled by the **Settings** option within the **QLEADER** command. An ***annotation*** is text such as notes and dimensions on a drawing.

QLEADER
LE

Dimension
➡ Leader

Dimension toolbar

Quick Leader

The **QLEADER** command is accessed by picking the **Quick Leader** button in the **Dimension** toolbar, selecting **Leader** in the **Dimension** pull-down menu, or entering LE or QLEADER at the Command: prompt. The first two prompts look like the **LINE** command, with the Specify from point: and Specify to point: prompts. This allows you to pick where the leader begins and ends.

Command: **LE** *or* **QLEADER**↵
Specify first leader point, or [Settings] <Settings>: *(pick the leader start point)*
Specify next point: *(pick the second leader point, which is the start of the leader shoulder)*
Specify next point: *(press* [Enter] *and the shoulder is drawn automatically)*
Specify text width <0.0000>: ↵
Enter first line of annotation text <Mtext>: *(enter text)*
Enter next line of annotation text: ↵
Command:

In this example, AutoCAD automatically draws a leader shoulder in front of the text.

In mechanical drafting, properly drawn leaders have one straight segment extending from the feature to a horizontal shoulder that is 1/4″ (6 mm) long. While most other fields also use straight leaders, AutoCAD provides the option of drawing curved leaders, which are commonly used in architectural drafting. This is done with the **Settings** option of the command.

QLEADER Settings

The **Settings** option available at the beginning of the **QLEADER** command can be used to give you greater control over the leader and its associated text. For example, the leader can be set to have the first segment always drawn at a 45° angle and the second segment (or shoulder) always drawn at 0°.

When you select the **Settings** option of the **QLEADER** command, the **Leader Settings** dialog box is displayed. This dialog box has three tabs: **Annotation**, **Leader Line & Arrow**, and **Attachment**. The appearance of the arrow and leader line is determined by the settings in the **Leader Line & Arrow** tab. The settings found in the **Annotation** and **Attachment** tabs determine the appearance of the text portion of the leader.

Leader line and arrow settings

The **Leader Line & Arrow** tab of the **Leader Settings** dialog box is shown in Figure 17-40. The settings in this tab determine the type of arrowhead, type of leader line, angles for leader line and shoulder, and number of requested points.

The **Leader Line** area is used to specify the shape of the leader line. A leader with straight-line segments is drawn by picking the **Straight** radio button. A curved leader is drawn by picking the **Spline** radio button. The spline leader is commonly used in architectural drafting. Figure 17-41 shows examples of the spline and straight leader lines.

Figure 17-40.
The **Leader Line & Arrow** tab of the **Leader Settings** dialog box.

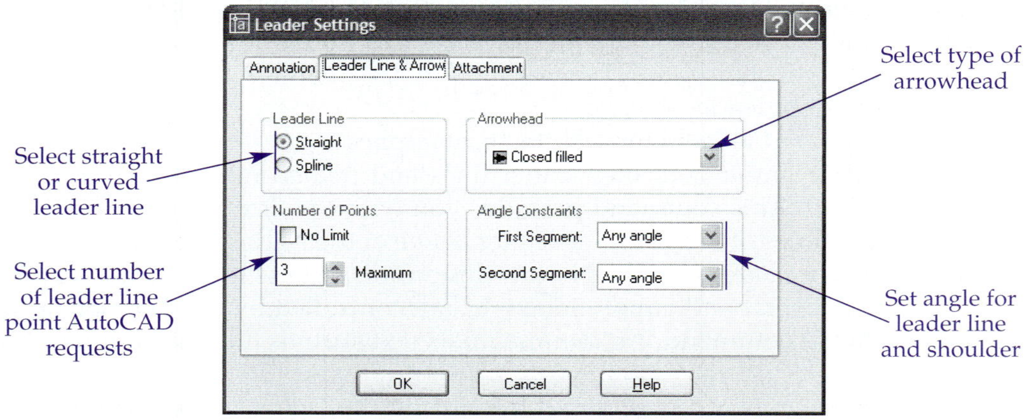

Figure 17-41.
The type of leader line (straight or spline) is set in the **Leader Line & Arrow** tab of the **Leader Settings** dialog box.

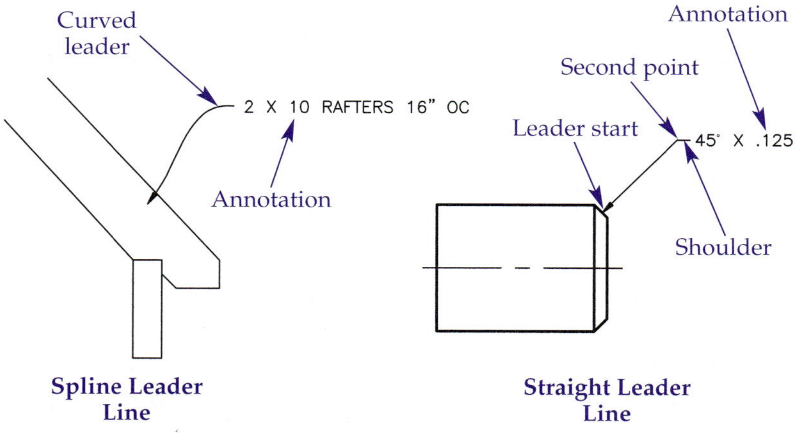

You can also set the maximum number of vertices on the leader line. This is set in the **Number of Points** area. Set a maximum number of vertices in the **Maximum** text box or select the **No Limit** check box to have an unlimited number. After the maximum number is reached, the **QLEADER** command automatically stops drawing the leader and asks for text information. To use less than the maximum number of points, press the [Enter] key at the Specify next point prompt. If the leader is a line object, a value of three for the maximum number of points defines a maximum total of two line segments.

The **Arrowhead** area uses the default value assigned to leaders within the current dimension style. To change the appearance of the arrowhead, pick the drop-down list and select a terminator from the full range of choices. Changing the **Arrowhead** setting creates a dimension style override, which is discussed later in this chapter.

The first two segments of the leader line can be restricted to certain angles. These angles are set in the **Angle Constraints** area. The options for each segment are **Any angle**, **Horizontal**, **90**, **45**, **30**, or **15**. The **Ortho** mode setting overrides the angle constraints so it is advisable to turn **Ortho** mode off while using this command.

PROFESSIONAL TIP

The ASME standard for leaders does not recommend a leader line that is less than 15° or greater than 75° from horizontal. Use the **Angle Constraints** settings in the **Leader Settings** dialog box to help maintain these standards.

Leader text settings

The **Annotation** and **Attachment** tabs of the **Leader Settings** dialog box control the way text is used with the leader line. The **Annotation** tab contains settings that specify the type of object used for annotation, additional options for mtext objects, and tools that automatically repeat annotations. The **Attachment** tab has options for specifying the point where the leader line shoulder meets an mtext annotation object.

The **Annotation** tab is shown in **Figure 17-42.** The **Annotation Type** area determines which type of entity is inserted and attached to the end of the leader line. The following options are available.

- **MText.** This is the default setting, causing a multiline text object to be inserted after the leader lines are drawn. See **Figure 17-43A.**

Figure 17-42.
The **Annotation** tab of the **Leader Settings** dialog box.

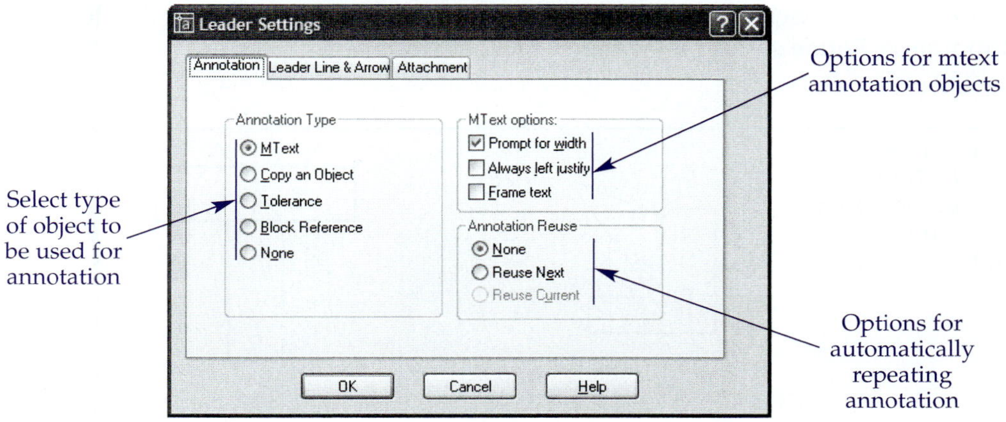

Figure 17-43.
The annotation type is selected in the **Annotation** tab of the **Leader Settings** dialog box.

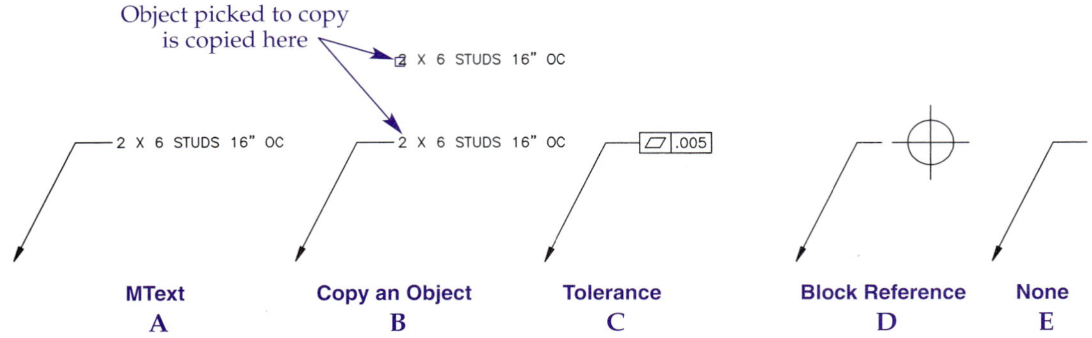

- **Copy an Object.** This option allows an mtext, text, block, or tolerance object to be copied from the current drawing and inserted at the end of the current leader line. This is useful when the same note or symbol is required in many places throughout a drawing. After drawing the leader line, the Select an object to copy: prompt appears. The selected object is placed at the end of the shoulder. See **Figure 17-43B.**
- **Tolerance.** This displays the **Geometric Tolerance** dialog box for creation of a feature control frame after the leader line is drawn. See **Figure 17-43C.** Geometric tolerancing is explained in detail in Chapter 20 of this text.
- **Block Reference.** This option inserts a specified block at the end of the leader. A ***block*** is a symbol that was previously created and saved. Blocks can be inserted into other drawings. These multiple-use symbols are explained in detail in Chapter 22 of this text. Blocks can be scaled during the insertion process. A special symbol block named Target is inserted in **Figure 17-43D.**
- **None.** This option ends the leader with no annotation of any kind. See **Figure 17-43E.** The **None** option can be used as a way to create multiple leaders for a single leader annotation, as shown in **Figure 17-44.** Multiple leaders are not a recommended ASME standard, but they are used for some applications, such as the leader for welding symbols. The welding symbol shown in **Figure 17-44B** was created as a block and then inserted using the **Block Reference** annotation option.

You can automatically repeat the previous leader annotation using the options in the **Annotation Reuse** area. The default option is **None**. This allows you to specify the annotation when creating a leader. If you wish to use an annotation repeatedly, select the **Reuse Next** option and then create the first leader and annotation. When you create another leader, the setting automatically changes to **Reuse Current** and the annotation is inserted. The annotation is repeated for all new leaders until the **Annotation Reuse** setting is changed back to **None**.

Figure 17-44.
Use the **None** annotation option when drawing multiple leaders.

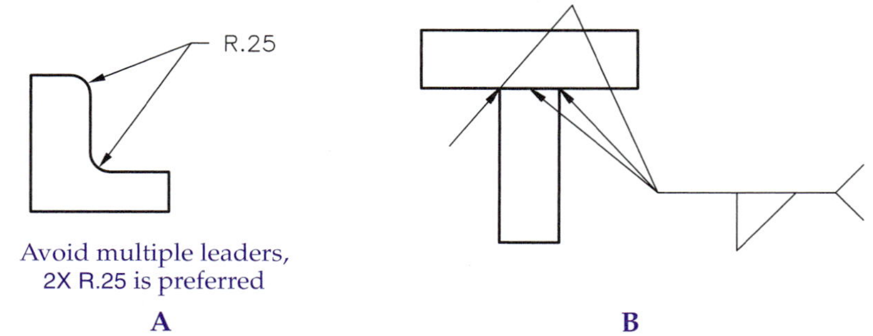

The **MText options** area of the **Annotation** tab is only available if **MText** is selected as the annotation type. These settings can be overridden by selecting the **MText** option during the **QLEADER** command. The following options are available.

- **Prompt for width.** If checked, you are prompted to define the size of the mtext box. If this option is not checked, a value of 0 (no text wrapping) is assigned to the mtext box.
- **Always left justify.** Forces the mtext to be left justified, regardless of the direction of the leader line.
- **Frame text.** Creates a box around the mtext text box. The default properties of the frame are controlled by the dimension line settings of the current dimension style.

The **Attachment** tab is only available when the **MText** option is selected in the **Annotation Type** area of the **Annotation** tab. This tab contains options that determine how the mtext object is positioned relative to the endpoint of the leader line shoulder. See Figure 17-45. Different options can be specified for mtext to the right of the leader line and mtext to the left of the leader line. These options are shown in Figure 17-46.

The **Underline bottom line** option causes a line to be drawn along the bottom of the mtext box. When this check box is selected, the choices for text on left and right side become grayed-out.

PROFESSIONAL TIP

Common drafting practice is to use the **Middle of bottom line** option for left-sided text and the **Middle of top line** option for right-sided text. These are the default settings.

NOTE

The **LEADER** command can also be used to draw leaders. This command does not provide the convenience, flexibility, and ability to easily comply with drafting standards as does the **QLEADER** command.

Figure 17-45.
The **Attachment** tab of the **Leader Settings** dialog box determines the location of the mtext annotation relative to the leader line shoulder.

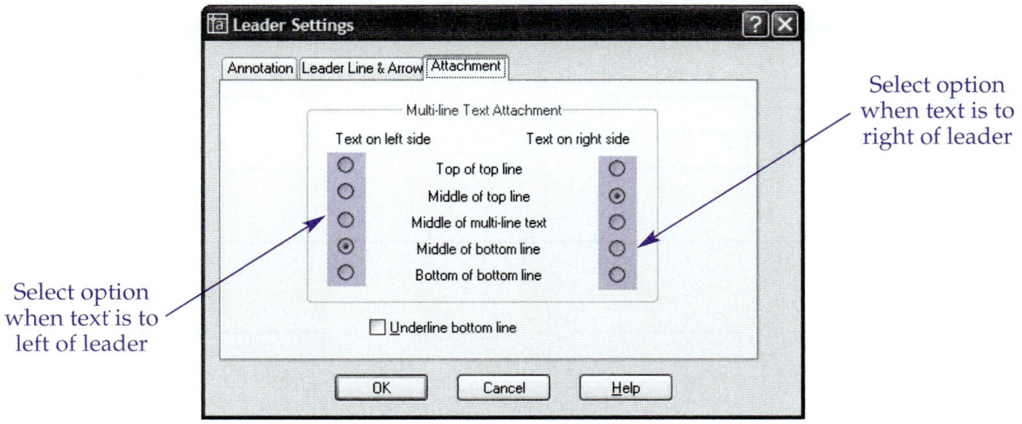

Figure 17-46.
Placement of mtext is controlled by the options in the **Attachment** tab of the **Leader Settings** dialog box. Shaded examples are the recommended ASME standard.

	Top of Top Line	Middle of Top Line	Middle of Multiline Text	Middle of Bottom Line	Bottom of Bottom Line
Text on Left Side	⌀.250 ⌴⌀.500 ↧.062	⌀.250 ⌴⌀.500 ↧.062	⌀.250 ⌴⌀.500 ↧.062	⌀.250 ⌴⌀.500 ↧.062	⌀.250 ⌴⌀.500 ↧.062
Text on Right Side	⌀.250 ⌴⌀.500 ↧.062	⌀.250 ⌴⌀.500 ↧.062	⌀.250 ⌴⌀.500 ↧.062	⌀.250 ⌴⌀.500 ↧.062	⌀.250 ⌴⌀.500 ↧.062

EXERCISE 17-10 Complete the Exercise on the Student CD.

Dimensioning Chamfers

A ***chamfer*** is an angled surface used to relieve sharp corners. The ends of bolts are commonly chamfered to allow them to engage the threaded hole better. Chamfers of 45° are dimensioned with a leader giving the angle and linear dimension, or with two linear dimensions. This can be accomplished using the **QLEADER** command. See Figure 17-47.

Chamfers other than 45° must have either the angle and a linear dimension or two linear dimensions placed on the view. See Figure 17-48. The **DIMLINEAR** and **DIMANGULAR** commands are used for this purpose.

EXERCISE 17-11 Complete the Exercise on the Student CD.

Figure 17-47.
Dimensioning 45° chamfers.

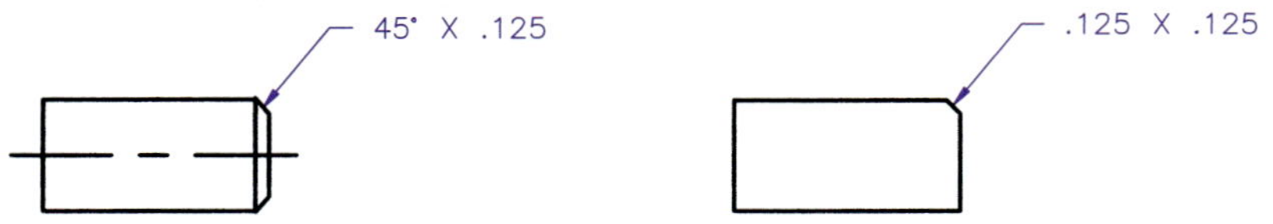

Figure 17-48.
Dimensioning chamfers that are not 45°.

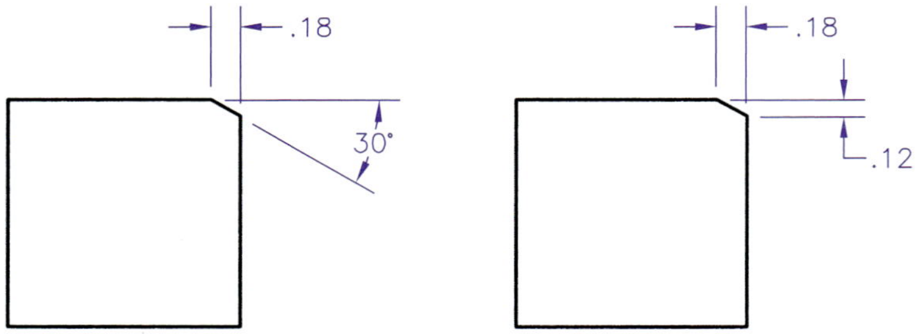

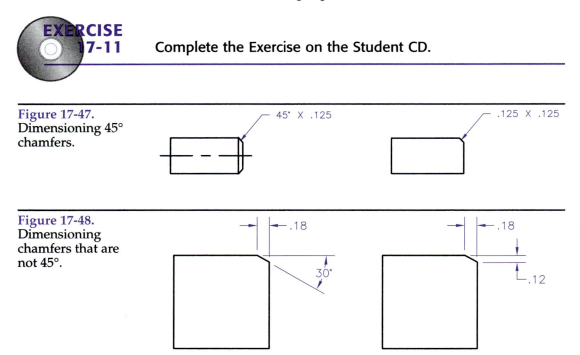

Alternate Dimensioning Practices

It is becoming common to omit dimension lines in industries where computer-controlled machining processes are used. Arrowless, tabular, and chart dimensioning are three types of dimensioning that omit dimension lines.

Arrowless Dimensioning

Arrowless dimensioning is becoming popular in mechanical drafting. It is also used in electronics drafting, especially for chassis layout. This type of dimensioning has only extension lines and numbers. Dimension lines and arrowheads are omitted. Dimension numbers are aligned with the extension lines. Each dimension number represents a dimension originating from a common point. This starting, or 0, dimension is typically known as a ***datum***, or ***baseline***. Holes or other features are labeled with identification letters. Sizes for these features are given in a table placed on the drawing. See **Figure 17-49.**

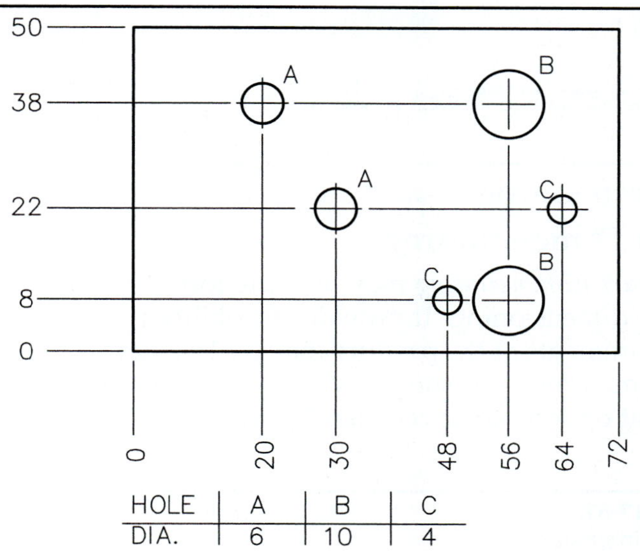

Figure 17-49. Arrowless dimensioning.

Tabular Dimensioning

Tabular dimensioning is a form of arrowless dimensioning where dimensions to features are shown in a table. Each feature is labeled with a letter or number that correlates to the table. The table gives the location of features from the X and Y axes. It also provides the depth of features from a Z axis, when appropriate. See **Figure 17-50.**

Figure 17-50.
Tabular dimensioning. (Doug Major)

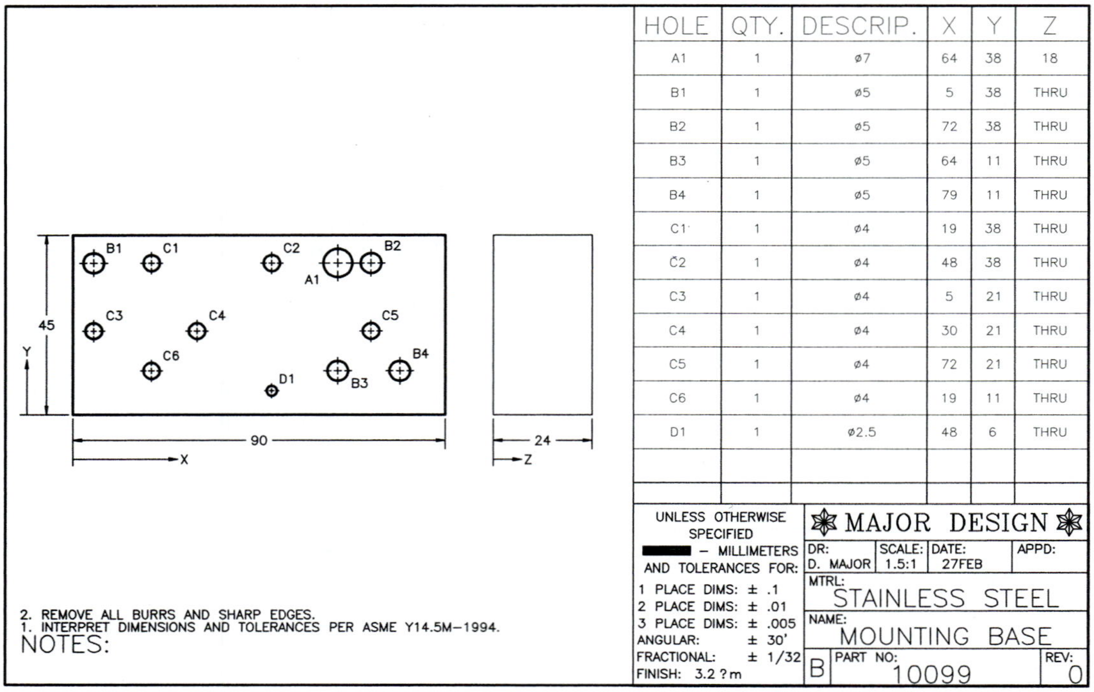

HOLE	QTY.	DESCRIP.	X	Y	Z
A1	1	ø7	64	38	18
B1	1	ø5	5	38	THRU
B2	1	ø5	72	38	THRU
B3	1	ø5	64	11	THRU
B4	1	ø5	79	11	THRU
C1	1	ø4	19	38	THRU
C2	1	ø4	48	38	THRU
C3	1	ø4	5	21	THRU
C4	1	ø4	30	21	THRU
C5	1	ø4	72	21	THRU
C6	1	ø4	19	11	THRU
D1	1	ø2.5	48	6	THRU

Chart Dimensioning

Chart dimensioning may take the form of unidirectional, aligned, arrowless, or tabular dimensioning. It provides flexibility in situations where dimensions change as requirements of the product change. The views of the product are drawn and variable dimensions are shown with letters. The letters correlate to a chart where the different options are given. See **Figure 17-51.**

Figure 17-51.
Chart dimensioning.

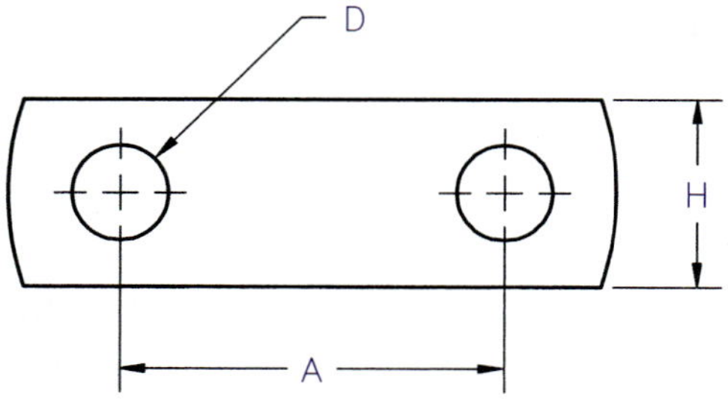

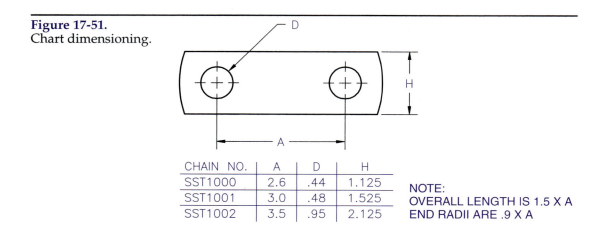

CHAIN NO.	A	D	H
SST1000	2.6	.44	1.125
SST1001	3.0	.48	1.525
SST1002	3.5	.95	2.125

NOTE:
OVERALL LENGTH IS 1.5 X A
END RADII ARE .9 X A

WCS and UCS

The world coordinate system (WCS) origin, the 0,0,0 coordinate, has been in the lower-left corner of the screen for the drawings you have already completed. In most cases, this is fine. However, when doing arrowless dimensioning, it is best to have the dimensions originate from a primary datum, which is often a corner of the object. Depending on how the object is drawn, this point may or may not align with the WCS origin.

The WCS is fixed; the user coordinate system (UCS), on the other hand, can be moved to any orientation desired. The UCS is discussed in detail in ***AutoCAD and its Applications—Advanced.*** In general, the UCS allows you to set your own coordinate system.

All arrowless dimensions drawn in AutoCAD originate from the current UCS origin. Move the UCS origin to the corner of the object or the appropriate datum feature by selecting **Move UCS** from the **Tools** pull-down menu. You are then prompted to specify a new origin point. Use an object snap mode to select the corner of the object or appropriate datum feature. In **Figure 17-52A,** the UCS is moved to an appropriate location.

Tools
➥ Move UCS

When done drawing arrowless dimensions from a datum, you can leave the UCS origin at the datum or move it back to the WCS origin. To return to the WCS, select **World** from the **New UCS** cascading menu in the **Tools** pull-down menu.

Tools
➥ New UCS
➥ World

Drawing Arrowless Dimensions

DIMORDINATE
DOR

Dimension
➥ Ordinate

Dimension toolbar

Ordinate Dimension

AutoCAD refers to arrowless dimensioning as ***ordinate dimensioning.*** These dimensions are drawn using the **DIMORDINATE** command, which is accessed by picking the **Ordinate Dimension** button on the **Dimension** toolbar, picking **Ordinate** in the **Dimension** pull-down menu, or entering DOR or DIMORDINATE at the Command: prompt. When using this command, AutoCAD automatically places an extension line and number along X and Y coordinates.

Since you are working in the XY plane, it is often best to have **Ortho** mode on. Also, if there are circles on your drawing, use the **DIMCENTER** command to place center marks in the circles, as shown in **Figure 17-52B.** This makes your drawing conform to ASME standards and provides something to pick when dimensioning the circle locations.

Now, you are ready to start placing the ordinate dimensions. Enter the **DIMORDINATE** command. When the Specify feature location: prompt appears, move the screen cursor to the point or feature to be dimensioned. If the feature is the corner of the object, pick the corner. If the feature is a circle, pick the end of the center mark. This leaves the required space between the center mark and the extension line. Zoom in if needed and use the object snap modes. The next prompt asks for the leader endpoint. This actually refers to the extension line endpoint, so pick the endpoint of the extension line.

If the X axis or Y axis distance between the feature and the extension line endpoint is large, the default axis may not be the desired axis for the dimension. When this happens, use the **Xdatum** or **Ydatum** option to tell AutoCAD from which axis the dimension originates. The **Mtext**, **Text**, and **Angle** options are identical to the options available with other dimensioning commands. Pick the leader endpoint to complete the command.

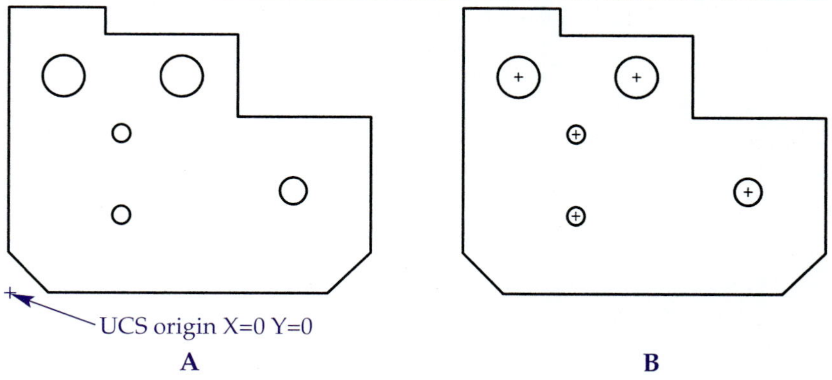

Figure 17-52. A—Draw the object and move the UCS origin to the appropriate location. B—Add the center marks to the circular features using the **DIMCENTER** command.

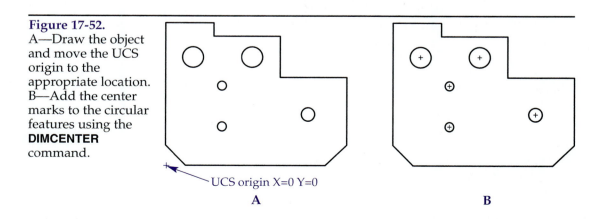

Figure 17-53A shows the ordinate dimensions placed on the object. Notice the dimension text is aligned with the extension lines. Aligned dimensioning is standard with ordinate dimensioning. Finally, complete the drawing by adding any missing lines, such as centerlines or fold lines. Identify the holes with letters and correlate a dimensioning table. See **Figure 17-53B.**

Figure 17-53.
A—Placing ordinate dimensions.
B—Completing the drawing.

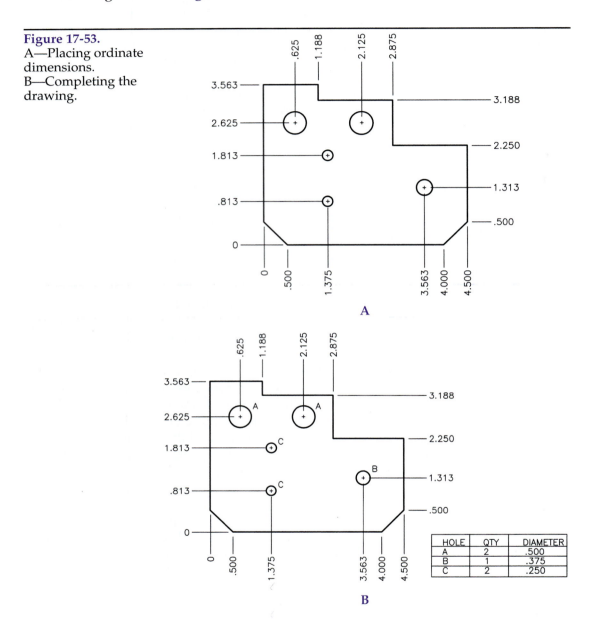

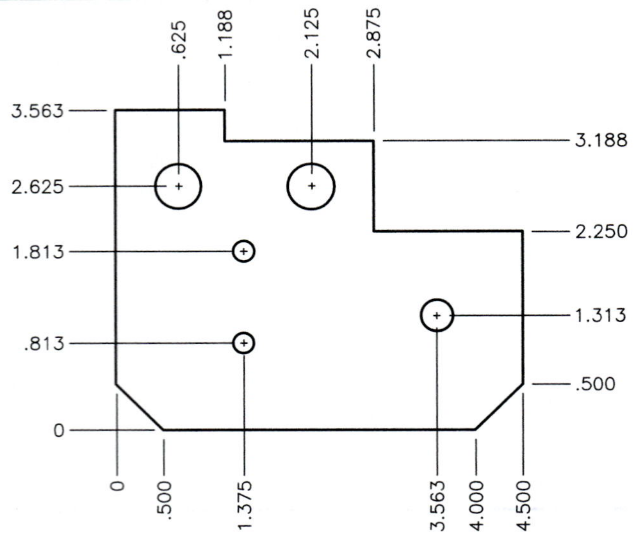

A

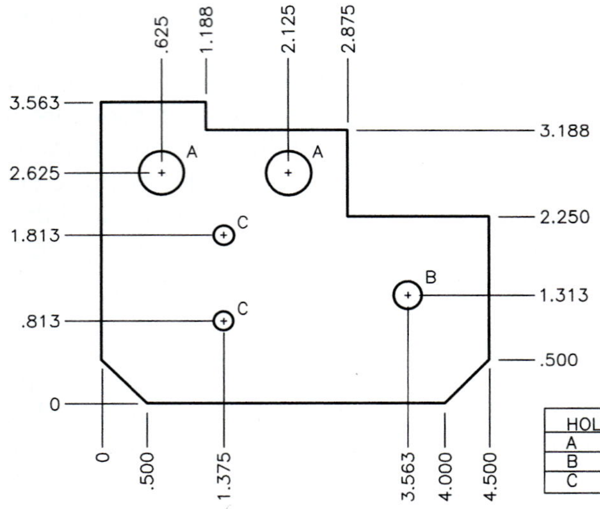

HOLE	QTY	DIAMETER
A	2	.500
B	1	.375
C	2	.250

B

PROFESSIONAL TIP

Most ordinate dimensioning tasks work best with **Ortho** mode on. However, when the extension line is too close to an adjacent dimension number, it is best to stagger the extension line as shown in the following illustration. With **Ortho** mode off, the extension line is automatically staggered when you pick the offset second extension line point as demonstrated.

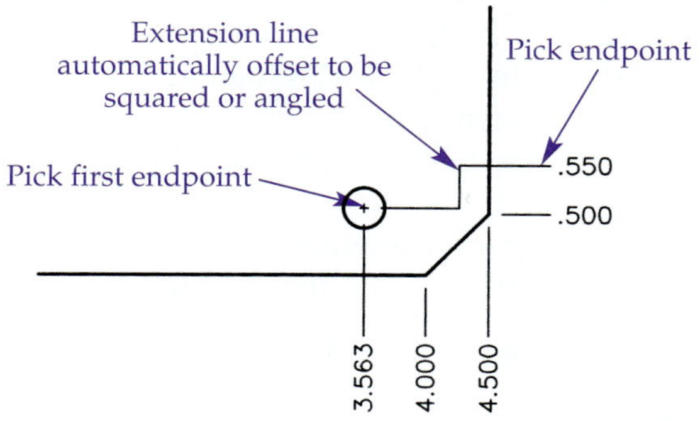

EXERCISE 17-12 Complete the Exercise on the Student CD.

Thread Drawings and Notes

There are many different thread forms. The most common forms are the Unified and metric screw threads. The parts of a screw thread are shown in **Figure 17-54.**

Threads are commonly shown on a drawing with a simplified representation. Thread depth is shown with a hidden line. This method is used for both external and internal threads. See **Figure 17-55.**

Figure 17-54. Parts of a screw thread.

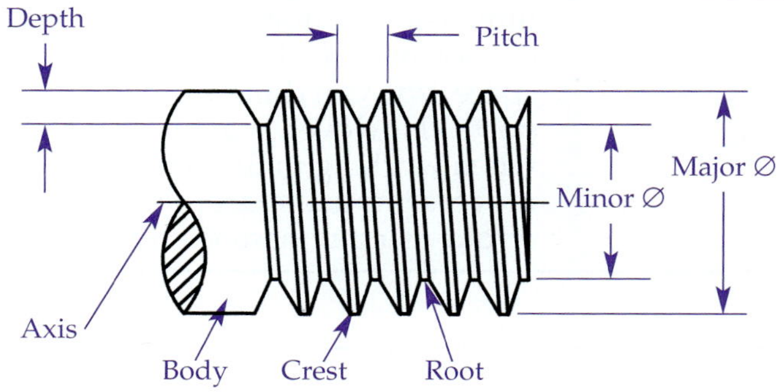

Figure 17-55. Simplified thread representations.

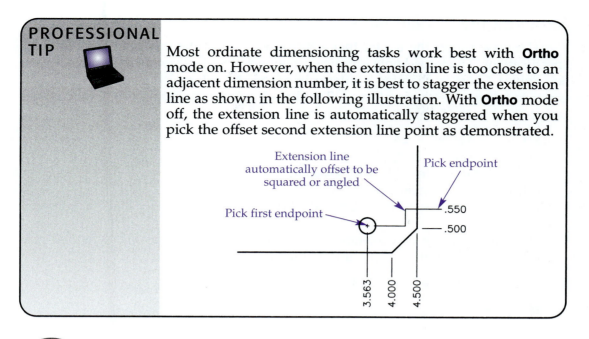

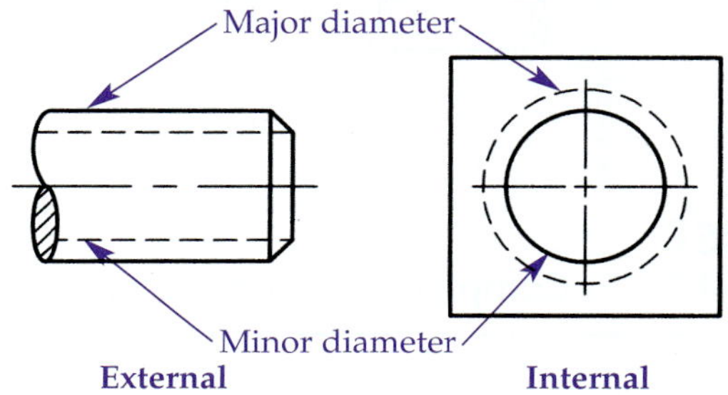

Showing the Thread Note

The view shows the reader that a thread exists, but the thread note gives exact specifications. The thread note is typically connected to the thread view with a leader. See **Figure 17-56.** A chamfer is often placed on the external thread. This makes it easier to engage the mating thread. The thread note for Unified screw threads must be specified in the format:

3/4 - 10UNC - 2A
(1) (2) (3) (4) (5)

(1) Major diameter of thread, given as fraction or number.
(2) Number of threads per inch.
(3) Thread series. UNC = Unified National Coarse. UNF = Unified National Fine.
(4) Class of fit. 1 = large tolerance. 2 = general purpose tolerance. 3 = tight tolerance.
(5) A = external thread. B = internal thread.

The thread note for metric threads is specified in the format:

M 14 X 2
(1) (2) (3)

(1) M = metric thread.
(2) Major diameter in millimeters.
(3) Pitch in millimeters.

There are too many Unified and metric screw threads to discuss here. Refer to the *Machinery's Handbook,* available from Goodheart-Willcox Publisher, or a comprehensive drafting text for more information.

PROFESSIONAL TIP

Dimensions can be drawn in either model space or layout (paper) space. Model space and layout space are discussed in Chapters 10 and 11. Model space dimensions must be scaled by the drawing scale factor to achieve the correct feature size, such as text height and arrow size. Associative paper space dimensions automatically adjust to model modifications and do not need to be scaled. Also, if you dimension in paper space, you can dimension the model differently in two viewports. However, paper space dimensions are not visible when working in the **Model** tab, so you must be careful not to move a model space object into a paper space dimension. Avoid using nonassociative paper space dimensions.

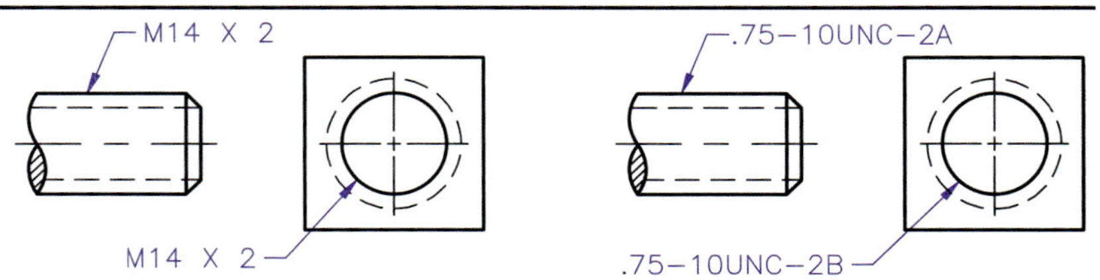

Figure 17-56. Displaying the thread note with a leader.

EXERCISE 17-13 Complete the Exercise on the Student CD.

Dimension Styles

The appearance of dimensions, from the size and the style of the text to the color of the dimension line, is controlled by over 70 different settings. ***Dimension styles*** are saved configurations of these settings. So far in this chapter, you have used only a few of these settings. The dimension settings that you used were introduced to help you perform specific tasks.

A dimension style is created by changing the dimension settings as needed to achieve the desired dimension appearance for your drafting application. For example, the dimension style for mechanical drafting probably has Romans text font placed in a break in the dimension line and the dimension lines are terminated with arrowheads. See **Figure 17-3.** The dimension style for architectural drafting may use CityBlueprint or Stylus BT text font placed above the dimension line and dimension lines are terminated with slashes. See **Figure 17-4.**

The dimension style can have dimensions based on national or international standards, or may be set up to match company or school applications and standards. The dimensioning that you have been doing in this chapter is based on the AutoCAD Standard dimension style. This dimension style uses the AutoCAD default settings and variables.

Creating Dimension Styles

You might think of dimension styles as the dimensioning standards you use. Dimension styles are usually established for a specific type of drafting field or application. You can customize dimension styles to correspond to drafting standards such as ASME/ANSI, International Organization for Standardization (ISO), military (MIL), architectural, structural, civil, or your own school or company standards.

DIMSTYLE
D
DST
DDIM
DIMSTY

Dimension
➥ Style...
Format
➥ Dimension Style...

Dimension toolbar

Dimension Style

Dimension styles are created using the **Dimension Style Manager** dialog box. See **Figure 17-57.** This dialog box is accessed by picking the **Dimension Styles** button on the **Dimension** toolbar, **Dimension Style...** in the **Format** pull-down menu, or **Style...** in the **Dimension** pull-down menu. You can also enter D, DST, DDIM, DIMSTY, or DIMSTYLE at the Command: prompt.

The current dimension style, which is initially Standard, is noted at the top of the **Dimension Style Manager** dialog box. The **Styles:** box displays the dimension styles found within the current drawing. The selection in the **List:** drop-down list controls whether all styles or only the styles in use are displayed in the **Styles:** box.

If there are external reference drawings (xrefs) within the current drawing, the **Don't list styles in Xrefs** box can be checked to eliminate xref-dependent dimension styles from the **Styles:** box. This is often valuable because xref dimension styles cannot be used to create new dimensions. External references are discussed in Chapter 23.

The **Description** area and **Preview of:** image provide information about the selected dimension style. The Standard dimension style is the AutoCAD default. If you change any of the AutoCAD default dimension settings without first creating a new dimension style, the changes are automatically stored in a dimension style override.

There are additional options found in the **Dimension Style Manager** dialog box. These include:

- **Set Current.** This button makes the dimension style selected in the **Styles:** box current. When a dimension style is current, all new dimensions are created in that style. Existing dimensions are not affected by a change to the current style. Xref-dependent dimension styles cannot be set current.

Figure 17-57.
The **Dimension Style Manager** dialog box. The Standard dimension style is the AutoCAD default.

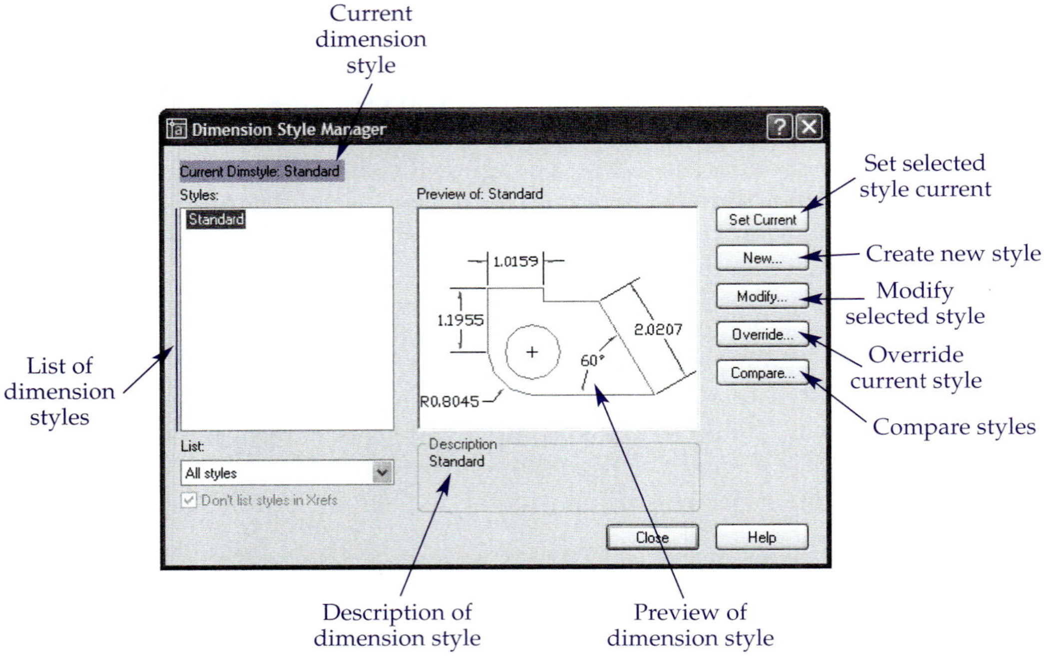

- **New.** Use this button to create a new dimension style. When you pick this button, the **Create New Dimension Style** dialog box is displayed. See **Figure 17-58.** The following options are available in this dialog box:
  - **New Style Name.** Give your new dimension style a descriptive name, such as Architectural or Mechanical.
  - **Start With.** This option helps you save time by basing the settings for a new style on an existing dimension style. Xref dimension styles can be selected from this dialog box only if they were displayed in the **Dimension Style Manager** dialog box.
  - **Use for.** The choices in this drop-down list are **All dimensions**, **Linear dimensions**, **Angular dimensions**, **Radius dimensions**, **Diameter dimensions**, **Ordinate dimensions**, and **Leaders and Tolerances**. Use the **All dimensions** option to create a new dimension style. If you select one of the other options, you create a "substyle" of the dimension style specified in the **Start With:** text box. The settings in the new style are applied to the dimension type selected in this drop-down list.
  - Pick the **Continue** button to access the **New Dimension Style** dialog box.

Figure 17-58.
The **Create New Dimension Style** dialog box.

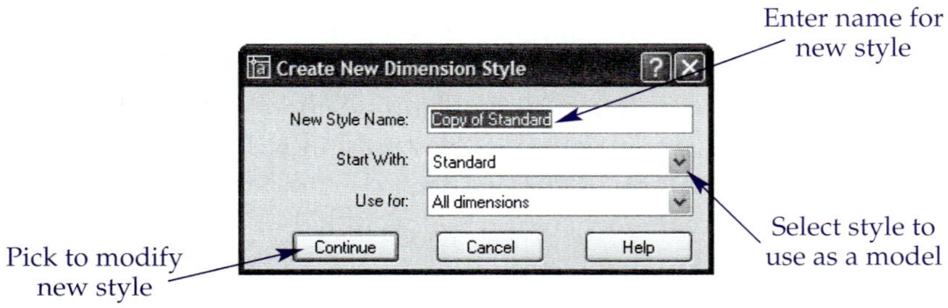

- **Modify.** Selecting this button opens the **Modify Dimension Style** dialog box, which allows you to make changes to the style highlighted in the **Styles** list. Xref styles cannot be modified.
- **Override.** An *override* is a temporary change to the current style settings. Including a text prefix for just a few of the dimensions on a drawing is an example of an override. Picking this button opens the **Override Current Style** dialog box. This button is only available for the current style. Once an override is created it is made current and is displayed as a branch, called the *child,* of the style from which it is created. The dimension style from which the child is created is called the *parent.* The override settings are lost when any other style, including the parent, is set current.
- **Compare.** Sometimes it is useful to view the details of two styles to determine the differences. When the **Compare...** button is selected, the **Compare Dimension Styles** dialog box is opened. You can compare two styles by entering the name of one style in the **Compare:** drop-down list and the name of the other in the **With:** drop-down list. The differences between the selected styles are displayed in the dialog box.

The **New Dimension Style**, **Modify Dimension Style**, and **Override Current Style** dialog boxes have the same tabs. See Figure 17-59. The **Lines and Arrows**, **Text**, **Fit**, **Primary Units**, **Alternate Units**, and **Tolerances** tabs access the settings used for changing the way dimensions are displayed. These are discussed in the next sections.

After completing the information on all tabs, pick the **OK** button to return to the **Dimension Style Manager** dialog box. Select **Set Current** to have all new dimensions take on the qualities of your newly created or modified style.

Figure 17-59.
The **Lines and Arrows** tab of the **Modify Dimension Style** dialog box.

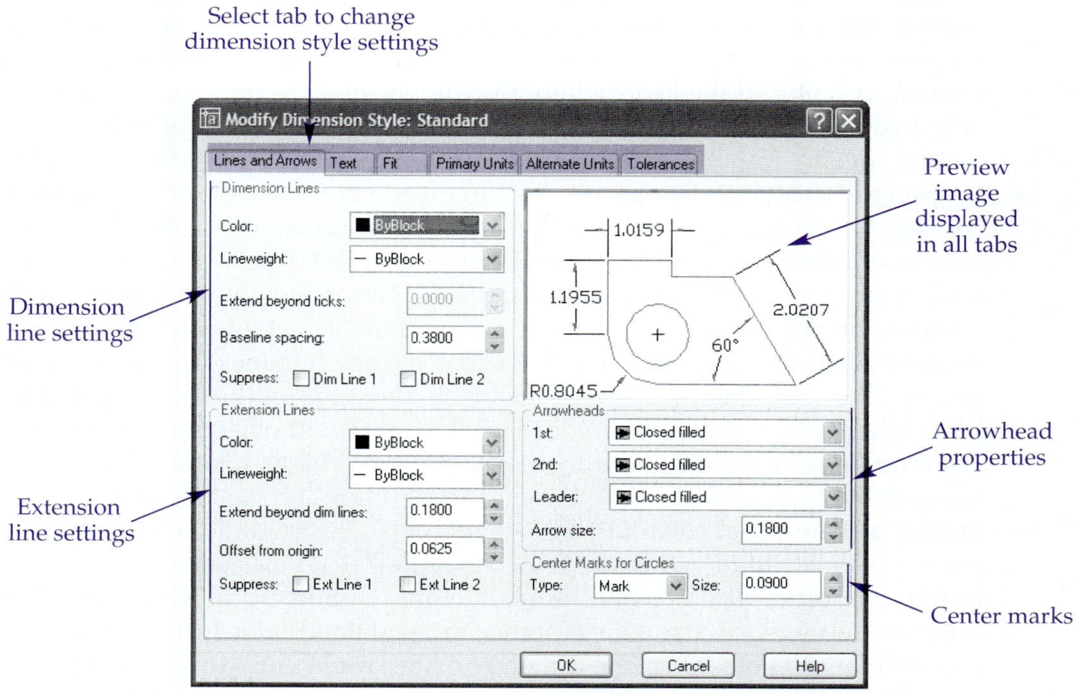

System Variables

An alternative method of setting the dimension variables is to access the variables directly at the Command: prompt. For example, **DIMSCALE** is a system variable that can be used to change the **Use overall scale of:** setting on the **Fit** tab. The following shows an example of setting the dimension variable for overall scale at the command line.

Command: **DIMSCALE**↵
Enter new value for DIMSCALE <*current*>: *(enter a new value)*

In this book, the system variables are noted in parenthesis where applicable.

Using the Lines and Arrows Tab

When the **New** (or **Modify**) button is selected from the **Dimension Style Manager** dialog box, the **New** (or **Modify**) **Dimension Style** dialog box is displayed with six tabs: **Lines and Arrows, Text, Fit, Primary Units, Alternate Units,** and **Tolerances.** As adjustments are made to the current dimension style, an image on each tab updates to graphically reflect those changes. The **Lines and Arrows** tab controls all settings for the display of the lines, arrowheads, leaders, and center marks of dimension strings. See **Figure 17-59.**

The **Dimension Lines** area is used to change the format of the dimension line with the following settings.

- **Color.** (**DIMCLRD**) By default, the dimension line color is assigned ByBlock, which indicates that the line assumes the currently active color setting of all elements within the dimension object. The ByBlock color setting means that the color assigned to the created block is used for the component objects of the block. All associative dimensions are created as block objects. Blocks are symbols designed for multiple use and are explained in Chapter 22. Associative dimensions are discussed in this chapter and in Chapter 18. If the current entity color is set to ByLayer when the dimension block is created, then it comes in with a ByLayer setting. The component objects of the block then take on the color of the layer where the dimensions are created. If the current object color is an absolute color, then the component objects of the block take on that specific color regardless of the layer where the dimension was created.
- **Lineweight.** (**DIMLWD**) By default, the dimension line lineweight is assigned to ByBlock, which indicates that the line assumes the currently active lineweight setting of all elements within the dimension object. The ByBlock lineweight setting means that the lineweight assigned to the created block is used for the component objects of the block. If the current object lineweight is set to ByLayer when the dimension block is created, then it comes in with a ByLayer setting. The component objects of the block then take on the lineweight of the layer where the dimensions are created. If the current object lineweight is an absolute lineweight, the component objects of the block take on that specific lineweight regardless of the layer where the dimension was created.
- **Extend beyond ticks.** (**DIMDLE**) This text box is inactive unless you are using tick marks instead of arrowheads. Architectural tick marks or oblique arrowheads are often used when dimensioning architectural drawings. The different settings for arrowhead styles are explained later in this chapter. In this style of dimensioning, the dimension lines often cross over the extension lines. The extension represents how far the dimension line extends beyond the extension line. See **Figure 17-60.** The 0.00 default is used to draw dimensions that are not extended past the extension lines.

Figure 17-60.
Using the **Extend beyond ticks** settings to allow the dimension line to extend past the extension line. With the default value of 0, the dimension line does not extend.

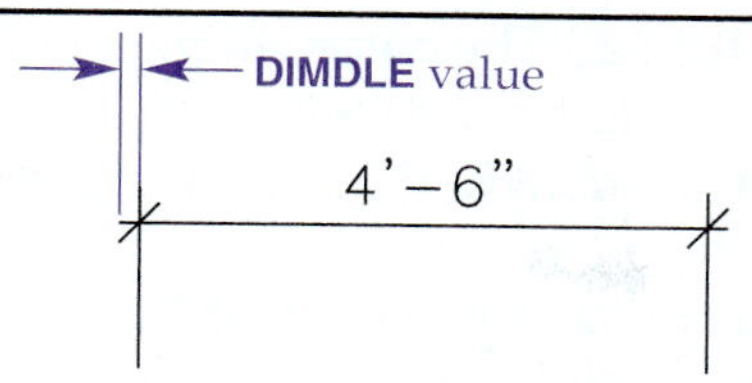

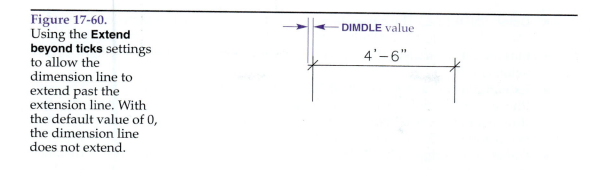

- **Baseline spacing.** (**DIMDLI**) This text box allows you to change the spacing between the dimension lines of baseline dimensions created with the **DIMBASELINE** command. The default spacing is .38 units, which is generally too close for most drawings. Try other values to help make the drawing easy to read. Figure 17-61 shows the dimension line spacing.
- **Suppress.** (**DIMSD1** and **DIMSD2**) This option has two toggles that prevent the display of the first, second, or both dimensions lines and their arrowheads. The **Dim Line 1** and **Dim Line 2** check boxes refer to the first and second points picked when the dimension is created. Both dimension lines are displayed by default. The results of using these options are shown in Figure 17-62.

The **Extension Lines** area of the **Lines and Arrows** tab is used to change the format of the extension lines with the following dimension settings.

Figure 17-61.
The **Baseline spacing** setting controls the spacing between dimension lines.

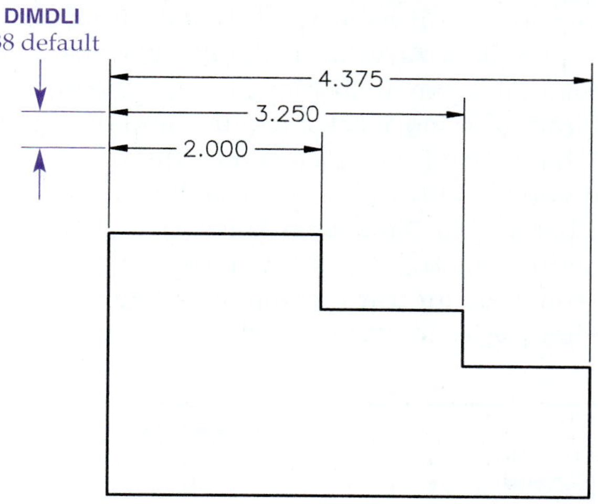

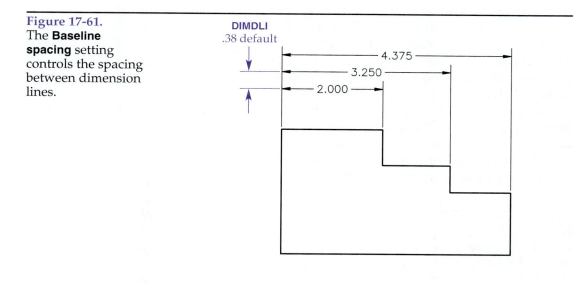

Figure 17-62.
Using the **Dim Line 1** and **Dim Line 2** dimensioning settings. "Off" is equivalent to an unchecked **Suppress** check box in the "dimension style" dialog box.

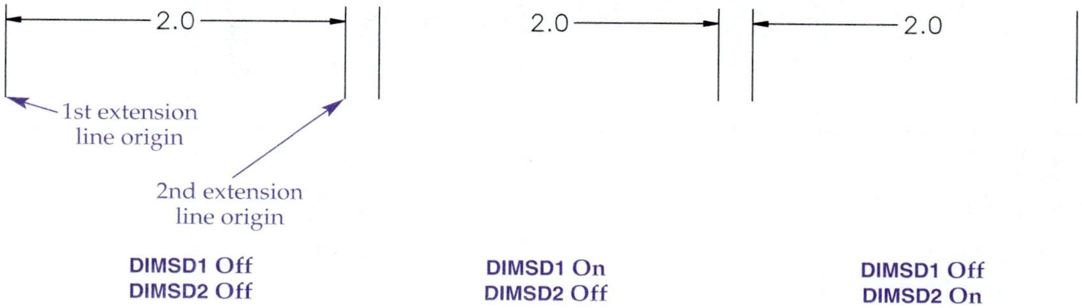

- **Color.** (**DIMCLRE**) The color choice made here controls the extension line color. The default value is ByBlock.
- **Lineweight.** (**DIMLWE**) The lineweight setting controls the lineweight of the extension lines.
- **Extend beyond dim lines.** (**DIMEXE**) This text box is used to set the extension line extension, which is the distance the extension line runs past the last dimension line. See **Figure 17-63.** The default value is 0.18; an extension line extension of .125 is common on most drawings.
- **Offset from origin.** (**DIMEXO**) This text box is used to change the distance between the object and the beginning of the extension line. See **Figure 17-63.** Most applications require this small offset. The default is .0625. When an extension line meets a centerline, use a setting of 0.0 to prevent a gap.
- **Suppress.** (**DIMSE1** and **DIMSE2**) This option is used to suppress the first, second, or both extension lines using the **Ext Line 1** and **Ext Line 2** check boxes. Extension lines are displayed by default. An extension line might be suppressed, for example, if it coincides with an object line. See **Figure 17-64.**

The **Arrowheads** area provides several different arrowhead options and controls the arrowhead size. Use the appropriate drop-down list to select the arrowhead used for the **1st** arrowhead (**DIMBLK1**), **2nd** arrowhead (**DIMBLK2**), and **Leader** arrowhead (**DIMDRBLK**). The default arrowhead is closed filled; other options are shown in **Figure 17-65.** If you pick a new arrowhead in the **1st:** drop-down list, AutoCAD automatically makes the same selection for the **2nd:** drop-down list. Check your drafting standards and then select the appropriate arrowhead.

Notice in **Figure 17-65** there is no example of a user arrow. This option is used to access an arrowhead of your own design. For this to work, you must first design an arrowhead and save it as a block. Blocks are discussed in Chapter 22 of this text. When you pick **User Arrow...** in the **Arrowheads** drop-down list, the **Select Custom Arrow Block** dialog box is displayed. Type the name of your custom arrow block in the **Select from Drawing Blocks:** text box and then pick **OK** to have the arrow used for the style. The name of the block is then displayed in the **Arrowheads** drop-down list.

When you select the oblique or architectural tick arrowhead, the **Extend beyond ticks:** text box in the **Dimension Lines** area is activated. This allows you to enter a value for a dimension line projection beyond the extension line. The default value is zero, but some architectural companies like to project the dimension line past the extension line. Refer to **Figure 17-60.**

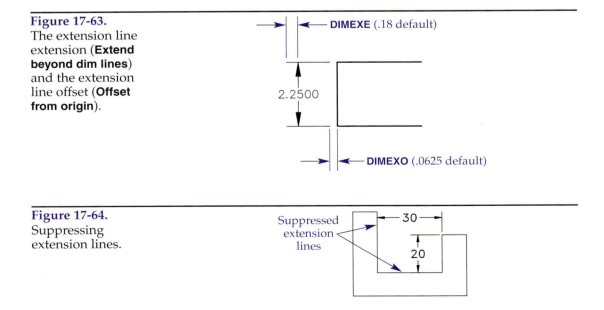

Figure 17-63.
The extension line extension (**Extend beyond dim lines**) and the extension line offset (**Offset from origin**).

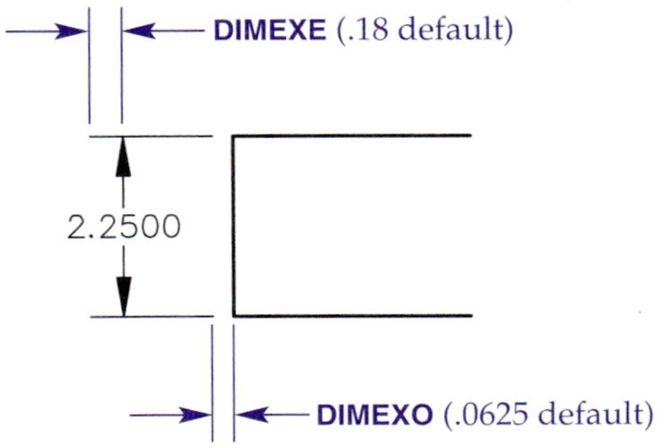

Figure 17-64.
Suppressing extension lines.

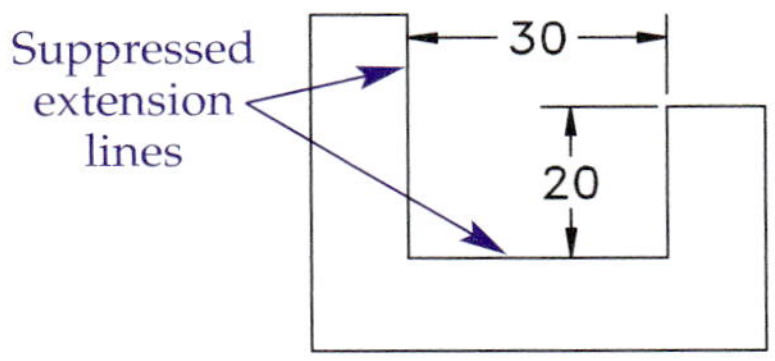

Figure 17-65.
Examples of dimensions drawn using the options found in the **Arrowhead** drop-down list.

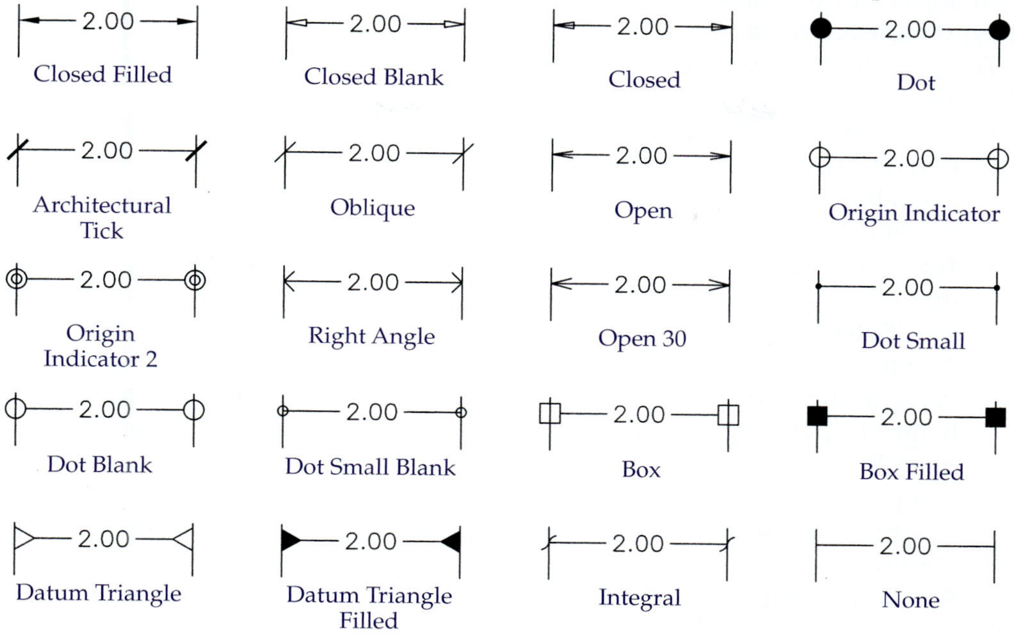

The **Arrow Size:** text box (**DIMASZ**) allows you to change the size of arrowheads. The default value is .18. An arrowhead size of .125″ is common on mechanical drawings. Figure 17-66 shows the arrowhead size value.

The **Center Marks for Circles** area (**DIMCEN**) of the **Lines and Arrows** tab allows you to select the way center marks are placed in circles and arcs. The **Type:** drop-down list contains the following options.

- **None.** Provides for no center marks to be placed in circles and arcs.
- **Mark.** Used to place only center marks without centerlines.
- **Line.** Places center marks and centerlines.

After selecting either the **Mark** or **Line** option, you can place center marks on circles and arcs by using the **DIMCENTER** command. The results of drawing center marks and centerlines are shown in Figure 17-31.

The **Size:** text box in the **Center Marks for Circles** area is used to change the size of the center mark and centerline. The default size is .09. The size specification controls the **Mark** and **Line** options in different ways, as shown in Figure 17-31.

Figure 17-66.
The default arrow size is .18.

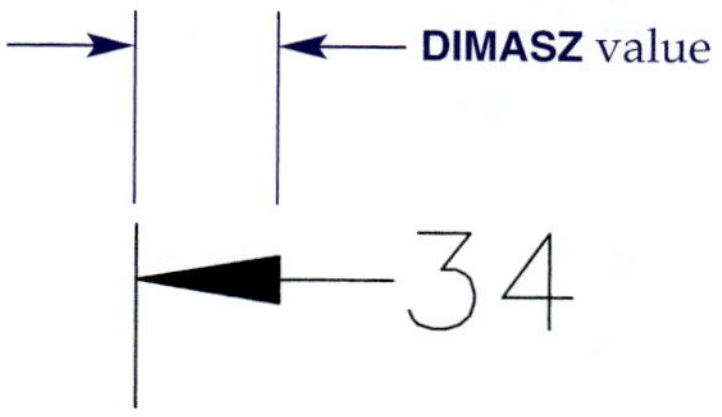

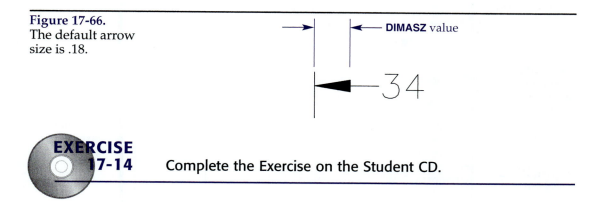

EXERCISE 17-14 Complete the Exercise on the Student CD.

Using the Text Tab

Changes can be made to dimension text by picking the **Text** tab in the **New** (or **Modify**) **Dimension Style** dialog box. See **Figure 17-67.**

The **Text Appearance** area is used to set the dimension text style, color, height, and frame. The options in this area are:

- **Text style.** (**DIMTXSTY**) The dimension text style uses the Standard text style by default. Text styles must be loaded in the current drawing before they are available for use in dimension text. Pick the desired text style from the drop-down list.
- **Text color.** (**DIMCLRT**) The dimension color default is ByBlock. Use the drop-down list to select a color for the text. If the color is not in the drop-down list, pick **Select Color...** to select a color from the **Select Color** dialog box.
- **Text height.** (**DIMTXT**) The dimension text height is set by entering the desired value in this text box. Dimension text height is commonly the same as the text height found on the rest of the drawing except for titles, which are larger. The default dimension text height is .18, which is an acceptable standard. Many companies use a text height of .125. The ASME standard recommends text height between .125 and .188. The text height for titles and labels is usually between .18 and .25.
- **Fraction height scale.** (**DIMTFAC**) This setting controls the height of fractions for architectural or fractional unit dimensions. The value in this box is multiplied by the text height value to determine the height of the fraction. A value of 1.0 creates fractions that are the same text height as regular (nonfractional) text, which is the normally accepted standard. A value less than 1.0 makes the fraction smaller than the regular text height.
- **Draw frame around text.** (**DIMGAP**) If checked, AutoCAD draws a rectangle around the text. The distance between the text and the frame is determined by the setting for the **Offset from dim line** value, which is explained later in this chapter.

The **Text Placement** area of the **Text** tab is used to place the text relative to the dimension line. See **Figure 17-68.** The preview image changes to represent the selections you make. The **Vertical:** (**DIMTAD**) drop-down list has the following options for the vertical justification.

Figure 17-67.
The **Text** tab of the **Modify Dimension Style** dialog box.

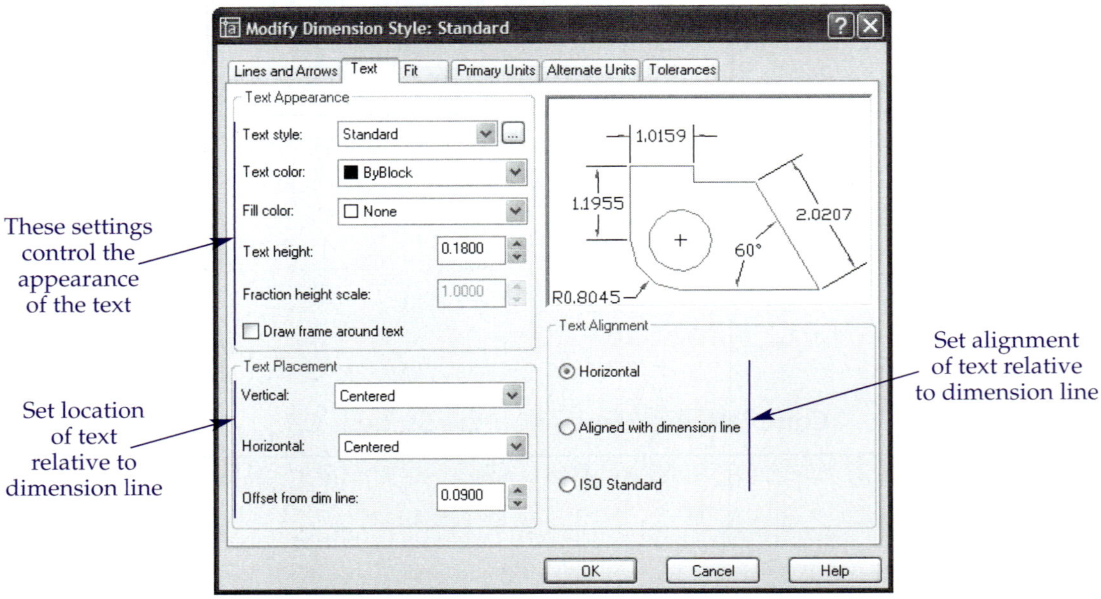

Figure 17-68.
Dimension text justification options. A—Vertical justification options, with the horizontal **Centered** justification. B—Horizontal justification options, with the vertical **Centered** justification.

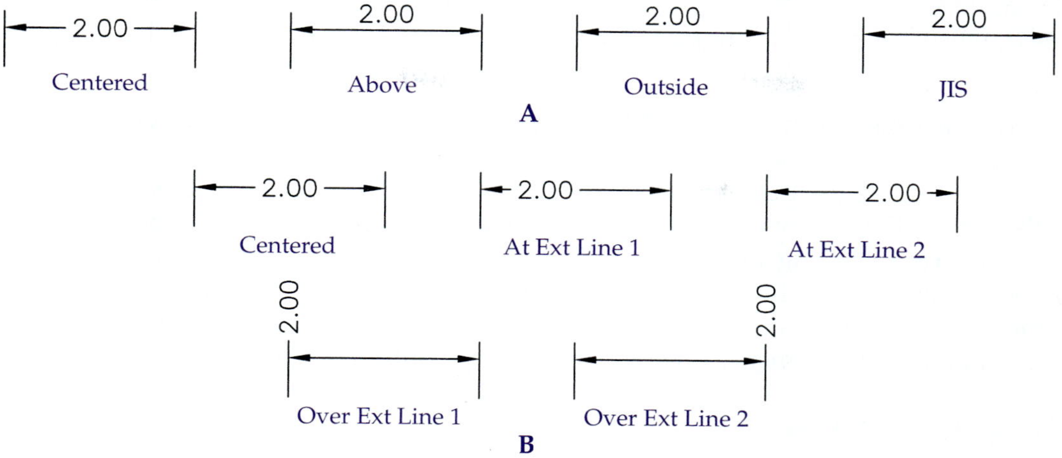

- **Centered.** This option is the default. It places dimension text centered in a gap provided in the dimension line. This is the dimensioning practice commonly used in mechanical drafting and many other fields.
- **Above.** This option is generally used for architectural drafting and building construction. The dimension text is placed horizontally and above horizontal dimension lines. For vertical and angled dimension lines, the text is placed in a gap provided in dimension line. Architectural drafting commonly uses ***aligned dimensioning*** in which the dimension text is aligned with the dimension lines and all text reads from either the bottom or right side of the sheet. An additional setting to provide this is discussed later.
- **Outside.** This option places the dimension text outside the dimension line and either above or below a horizontal dimension line or to the right or left of a vertical dimension line. The direction you move the cursor determines the above/below and left/right placement.
- **JIS.** This is the option to use when dimensioning for the Japanese Industrial Standards.

In addition to the vertical placement of the dimension text, you can control the horizontal placement. The **Horizontal:** (**DIMJUST**) drop-down list has the following options for the horizontal justification.

- **Centered.** This option is the AutoCAD default. It places dimension text centered between the extension lines.
- **At Ext Line 1.** This option locates the text next to the extension line placed first.
- **At Ext Line 2.** This option locates the text next to the extension line placed second.
- **Over Ext Line 1.** This option places the text aligned with and over the first extension line. This practice is not commonly used.
- **Over Ext Line 2.** This option places the text aligned with and over the second extension line. This practice is also not commonly used.

The **Offset from dim line:** (**DIMGAP**) text box is used to set the gap between the dimension line and the dimension text. This setting also controls the distance between the leader shoulder and the text, and the space between the basic dimension box and the text. Basic dimensions are used in geometric tolerancing and explained in Chapter 20. The default gap is .09. The gap should be set to half the text height. **Figure 17-69** shows the gap in linear and leader dimensions.

Figure 17-69.
The gap displayed in a linear dimension and a leader dimension.

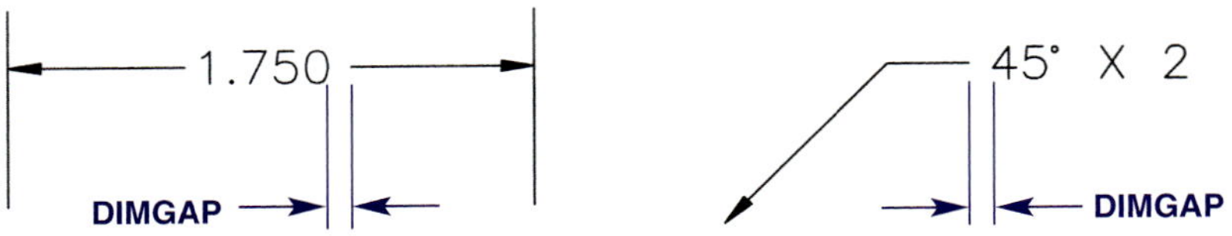

The **Text Alignment** area (**DIMTOH** and **DIMTIH**) of the **Text** tab allows you to control the alignment of dimension text. This area is used when you want to draw unidirectional dimensions or aligned dimensions, which were discussed earlier in this chapter. The **Horizontal** option draws unidirectional dimensions commonly used for mechanical manufacturing drafting applications. The **Aligned with dimension line** option creates aligned dimensions, which are typically used for architectural dimensioning. The **ISO Standard** option creates aligned dimensions when the text falls between the extension lines and horizontal dimensions when the text falls outside the extension lines.

Using the Fit Tab

The **Fit** tab in the **New** (or **Modify**) **Dimension Style** dialog box is used to establish the way in which dimension text appears on the drawing and arrowheads are placed. The **Fit** tab is shown in Figure 17-70 with default settings.

The **Fit Options** area (**DIMATFIT**) of the **Fit** tab controls how text and arrows should behave if they do not fit within the given area between two extension lines. These effects are most obvious on dimensions where space is limited. Watch the preview image change as you try each of the following options. This should help you understand how each option acts. Notice that these options are radio buttons, which means only one option can be active at any given time.

- **Either the text or the arrows, whichever fits best.** (**DIMATFIT** = 3) This is the default setting and allows AutoCAD to place text and dimension lines with arrowheads inside extension lines if space is available. Dimension lines with arrowheads are placed outside of extension lines if space is limited. Everything is placed outside of extension lines if there is not enough space between extension lines.

Figure 17-70.
The **Fit** tab of the **Modify Dimension Style** dialog box.

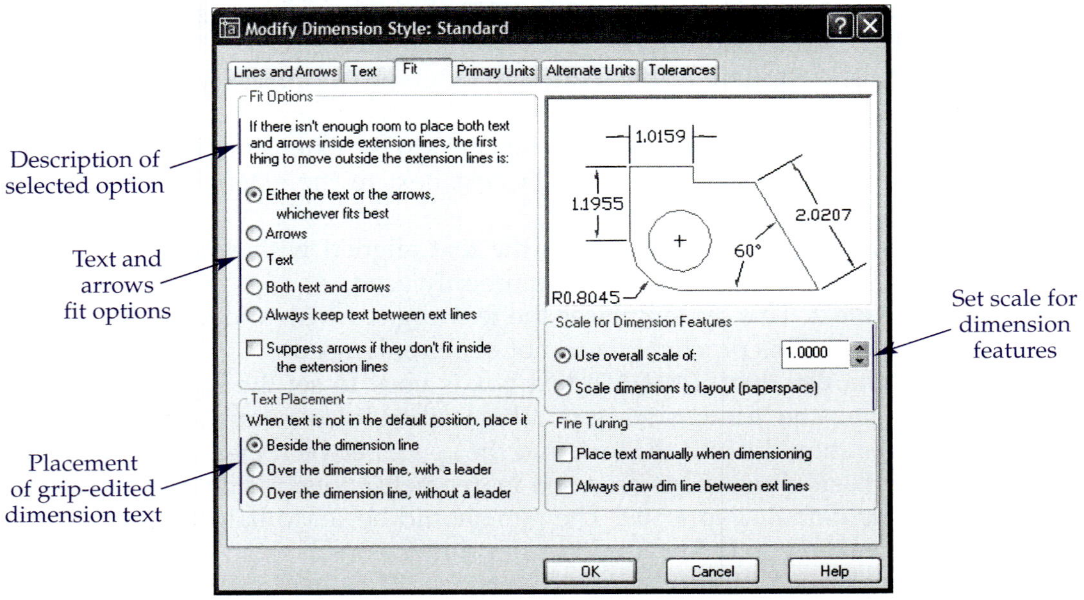

- **Arrows.** (**DIMATFIT** = 1) The text, dimension line, and arrowheads are placed inside the extension lines if there is enough space. The text is placed outside if there is enough space for only the arrowheads and dimension line inside the extension lines. Everything is outside if there is not enough room for anything inside.
- **Text.** (**DIMATFIT** = 2) The text, dimension line, and arrowheads are placed inside the extension lines if there is enough space for everything. If there is enough space for only the text inside the extension lines, then the dimension lines and arrowheads are placed outside. Everything is outside if there is not enough room for the text inside.
- **Both text and arrows.** (**DIMATFIT** = 0) When this option is used, AutoCAD places the text, dimension line, and arrowheads inside the extension lines if there is enough space, or everything is placed outside the extensions if there is not enough space.
- **Always keep text between ext lines.** (**DIMTIX**) This option always places the dimension text between the extension lines. This may cause problems when there is limited space between extension lines.
- **Suppress arrows if they don't fit inside the extension lines.** (**DIMSOXD**) This option removes the arrowheads if they do not fit inside the extension lines. Use this with caution because it can create dimensions that violate standards.

Sometimes it becomes necessary to move the dimension text from its default position. The text can be moved by grip editing the text portion of the dimension. The options in the **Text Placement** area (**DIMTMOVE**) of the **Fit** tab instruct AutoCAD how to handle these grip editing situations. The following options are available.

- **Beside the dimension line.** (**DIMTMOVE** = 0) When the dimension text is grip edited and moved, the text is constrained to move with the dimension line and can only be placed within the same plane as the dimension line.
- **Over the dimension line, with a leader.** (**DIMTMOVE** = 1) When the dimension text is grip edited and moved, the text can be moved in any direction away from the dimension line. A leader line is created that connects the text to the dimension line.
- **Over the dimension line, without a leader.** (**DIMTMOVE** = 2) When the dimension text is grip edited and moved, the text can be moved in any direction away from the dimension line without a connecting leader.

PROFESSIONAL TIP

To return the dimension text to its default position, select the dimension, right-click to display the shortcut menu, and select **Home text** from the **Dim Text position** cascading menu.

The **Scale for Dimension Features** area of the **Fit** tab is used to set the scale factor for all dimension features in the drawing. The **Use overall scale of:** (**DIMSCALE** > 0) sets a multiplier for dimension settings, such as text height and the offset from origin. For example, if the height of the dimensioning text is set to .125 and the value for the overall scale is set to 100, then the dimension text can be measured within the drawing to be 12.5 units (100 × .125). If the drawing is plotted with a plot scale of 1 = 100, the size of the dimension text on the paper measures .125 units.

Select the **Scale dimensions to layout (paperspace)** (**DIMSCALE** = 0) option if you are dimensioning in a floating viewport in a layout (paper space) tab. It allows the overall scale to adjust according to the active floating viewport by setting the overall scale equal to the viewport scale factor.

The **Fine Tuning** area of the **Fit** tab provides you with maximum flexibility in controlling where you want to place dimension text. The **Place text manually when dimensioning** (**DIMUPT**) option gives you control over text placement and dimension line length outside extension lines. The text can be placed where you want it, such as moved to the side within the extension lines, or placed outside of the extension lines.

The **Always draw dim line between ext lines** (**DIMTOFL**) option forces AutoCAD to place the dimension line inside the extension lines, even when the text and arrowheads are outside. The default application is with the dimension line and arrowheads outside the extension lines. Figure 17-71 shows the difference between checked (**DIMTOFL** on) and unchecked (**DIMTOFL** off). Forcing the dimension line inside the extension lines is not an ASME standard, but it may be preferred by some companies.

PROFESSIONAL TIP

When dimensioning mechanical drawings, it is common to have **Place text manually when dimensioning** on, centered horizontal and vertical justification, and horizontal text alignment.

For architectural drafting, it is typical to have **Place text manually when dimensioning** on, **Always draw dimension line** on, centered horizontal justification, above vertical justification, and text aligned with dimension lines.

Figure 17-71.
The effects of the **Always draw dim line between ext lines** option of the **Fine Tuning** area of the **Fit** tab.

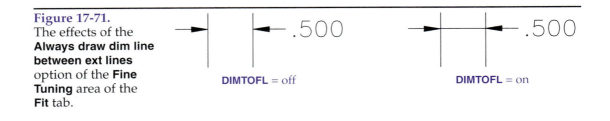

EXERCISE 17-15 Complete the Exercise on the Student CD.

Using the Primary Units Tab

The **Linear Dimensions** area of the **Primary Units** tab of the **New** (or **Modify**) **Dimension Style** dialog box is used to set units for linear dimensions. See Figure 17-72. This area has the following setting options.

- **Unit format.** (**DIMLUNIT**/**DIMALTU**) Select the type of units for dimension text from this drop-down list. The default selection is **Decimal** units. A definition and examples of the different units are provided in Chapter 2 of this text.
- **Precision.** (**DIMDEC**/**DIMALTD**) This drop-down list allows you to decide how many zeros follow the decimal place when decimal-related units are selected. The default is 0.0000; 0.00 and 0.000 settings are also common in mechanical drafting. When fractional units are selected, the precision values are related to the smallest desired fractional denominator. The default is 1/16″ but you can choose other options ranging from 1/256″ to 1/2″; 0″ displays no fractional values. A variety of dimension precision may be found on the same drawing.
- **Fraction format.** (**DIMFRAC**) The options for controlling the display of fractions are **Diagonal**, **Horizontal**, and **Not Stacked**. The **Fraction format** option is only available if the **Architectural** or **Fractional** style is selected for the unit format.

Figure 17-72.
The **Primary Units** tab of the **Modify Dimension Style** dialog box.

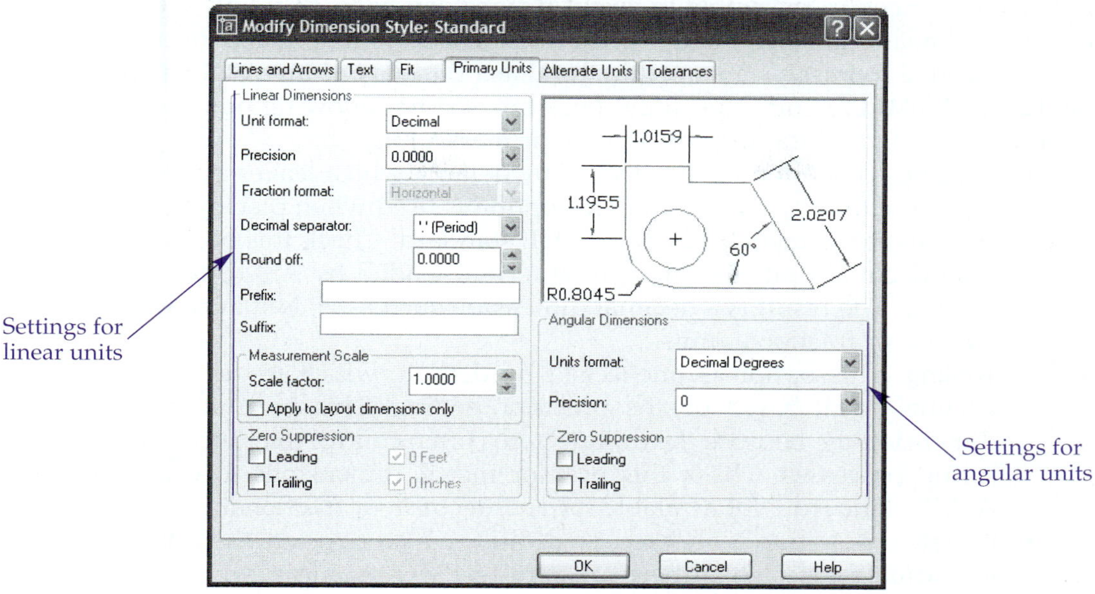

- **Decimal separator.** (**DIMDSEP**) Decimal numbers may use commas, periods, or spaces as separators. The **'.' (Period)** option is the default. The **Decimal separator** option is not available if the **Architectural** or **Fraction** style is selected for the unit format.
- **Round off.** (**DIMRND/DIMALTRND**) This text box specifies the accuracy of rounding for dimension numbers. The default is zero, which means that no rounding takes place and all dimensions are placed exactly as measured. If you enter a value of .1, all dimensions are rounded to the closest .1 unit. For example, an actual measurement of 1.188 is rounded to 1.2.
- **Prefix.** (**DIMPOST/DIMAPOST**) *Prefixes* are special notes or applications placed in front of the dimension text. A typical prefix might be SR3.5 where SR means spherical radius. When a prefix is used on a diameter or radius dimension, the prefix replaces the ∅ or R symbol.
- **Suffix.** (**DIMPOST/DIMAPOST**) *Suffixes* are special notes or applications placed after the dimension text. A typical suffix might be 3.5 MAX, where MAX is the abbreviation for maximum. The abbreviation IN can also be used when one or more inch dimensions are placed on a metric dimensioned drawing or a suffix of MM on one or more millimeter dimensions are placed on an inch drawing.

PROFESSIONAL TIP

Usually, a prefix or suffix is not used on every dimension in the drawing. A prefix or suffix is normally a special specification and might be used in only a few cases. Because of this, you might set up a special dimension style for these applications or enter them when needed by using the **MText** or **Text** option of the related dimensioning command.

The **Measurement Scale** area within the **Linear Dimensions** area of the **Primary Units** tab is used to set the scale factor of linear dimensions. Set the value in the **Scale factor:** text box (**DIMLFAC**). If a value of 1 is set, dimension values are displayed the same as they are measured. If the setting is 2, dimension values are twice as much as the measured amount. For example, an actual measurement of 2 inches is displayed as 2 with a scale factor of 1, but the same measurement is displayed as 4 when the scale factor is 2. Placing a check in the **Apply to layout dimensions only** (**DIMLFAC** < 0) check box makes the linear scale factor active only when dimensioning in a layout tab.

This **Zero Suppression** area within the **Linear Dimensions** area of the **Primary Units** tab (**DIMZIN/DIMALTZ**) provides four check boxes. The following options are used to suppress leading and trailing zeros in the primary units.

- **Leading.** This option is unchecked by default, which leaves a zero on decimal units less than 1, such as 0.5. This option is used when placing metric dimensions as recommended by the ASME standard. Check this box to remove the 0 on decimal units less than 1, as recommended by ASME for inch dimensioning. The result is a decimal dimension such as .5. Not available for architectural or fractional units.
- **Trailing.** This option is unchecked by default, which leaves zeros after the decimal point based on the precision setting. This is usually off for inch dimensioning, because the trailing zeros often control tolerances for manufacturing processes. Check this box for metric dimensions to conform to the ASME standard. Not available for architectural or fractional units.
- **0 Feet.** This option is checked by default, which removes the zero in feet and inch dimensions when there are zero feet. For example, when unchecked, a dimension may read 0′-11″. When checked, however, the dimension reads 11″. Only available for architectural or fractional units.
- **0 Inches.** This option is checked by default, which removes the zero when the inch part of feet and inch dimensions is less than one inch, such as 12′-7/8″. If checked, the same dimension reads 12′-0 7/8″. Also, it removes the zero from a dimension with no inch value; 12′ rather than 12′-0″. Only available for architectural or fractional units.

The **Angular Dimensions** area of the **Primary Units** tab is used to set the desired type of angular units for dimensioning. Angular units are discussed in the section in Chapter 2 on AutoCAD setup and with the **UNITS** command. The setup options and **UNITS** command do not control the type of units used for dimensioning. The following settings are found in this area.

- **Units format.** (**DIMAUNIT**) The default setting is **Decimal Degrees**. The other options are **Degrees Minutes Seconds**, **Gradians**, and **Radians**. Select the desired option from the drop-down list.
- **Precision.** (**DIMADEC**) Sets the desired precision of the angular dimension number. Select an option from the drop-down list.
- **Zero Suppression.** (**DIMAZIN**) This area of the **Angular Dimensions** area is used to keep or remove leading or trailing zeros on the angular dimension.

Using the Alternate Units Tab

The **Alternate Units** tab of the **Dimension Style** dialog box is used to set alternate units. See Figure 17-73. ***Alternate units***, or ***dual dimensioning***, have inch measurements followed by millimeters in brackets, or millimeters followed by inches in brackets. Dual dimensioning practices are no longer a recommended ASME standard. ASME recommends that drawings be dimensioned using inch or metric units only. However, the use of alternate units can be used in many other applications.

The **Display alternate units** (**DIMALT**) check box must be checked in order to activate the settings. The tab has many of the same settings found in the **Primary Units** tab. The **Multiplier for alt units** (**DIMALTF**) setting is multiplied by the primary unit to establish the value for the alternate unit. The default is 25.4 because an inch value is multiplied by 25.4 to convert it to millimeters. The **Placement** area controls the location of the alternate-unit dimension. The two options are **After primary value** and **Below primary value**.

Figure 17-73.
The **Alternate Units** tab of the **Modify Dimension Style** dialog box.

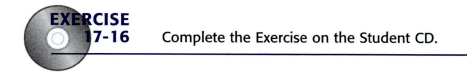

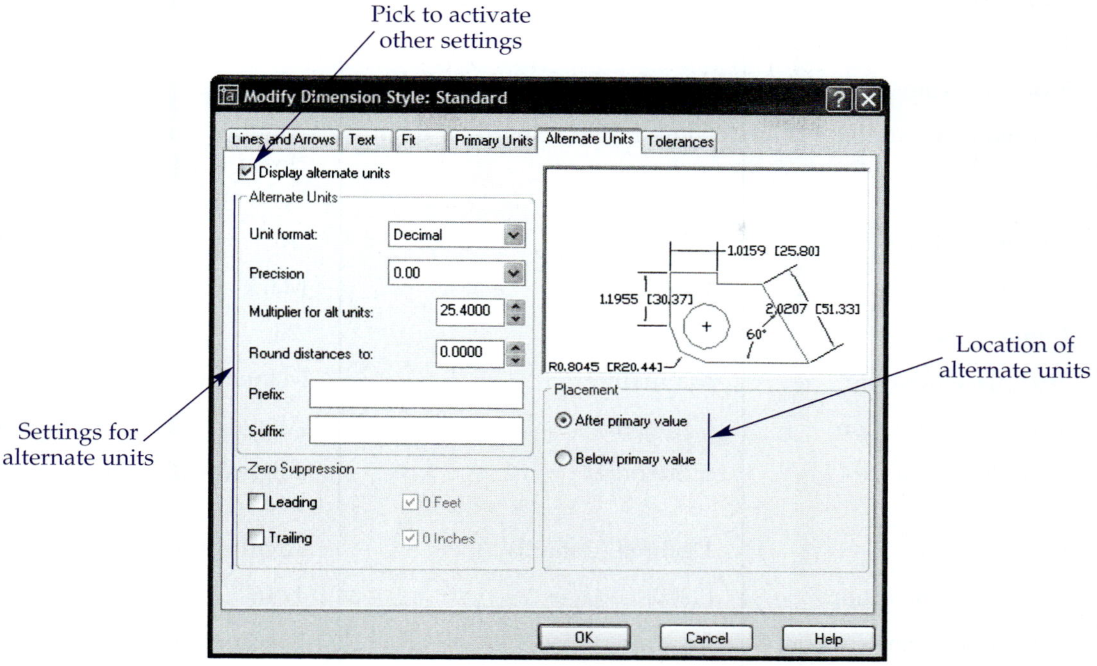

NOTE The final tab in the **Modify Dimension Style** dialog box, **Tolerances**, is discussed in Chapter 19.

EXERCISE 17-16 Complete the Exercise on the Student CD.

Making Your Own Dimension Styles

Creating and recording dimension styles is part of your AutoCAD management responsibility. You should carefully evaluate the items contained in the dimensions for the type of drawings you do. During this process, be sure to carefully check school, company, or national standards to verify the accuracy of your plan. Then, make a list of features and values for the dimensioning settings you use based on what you have learned in this chapter. When you are ready, use the **Dimension Style Manager** dialog box options to establish dimension styles named to suit your drafting practices.

The following chart provides possible settings for two dimension style. One list is for mechanical manufacturing and the other is for architectural drafting applications. For settings not listed here, use the AutoCAD defaults.

Setting	Mechanical (Inch)	Architectural
Dimension line spacing	.50	.75
Extension line extension	.125	.18
Extension line offset	.0625	.08
Arrowhead options	Closed filled, closed, or open	Architectural tick, dot, closed filled, oblique, or right angle
Arrowhead size	.125	.18
Center	Line	Mark
Center size	.25	.25
Text placement	Manually	Manually
Vertical justification	Centered	Above
Text alignment	Horizontal	Aligned with dimension line
Primary units	Decimal (default)	Architectural
Dimension precision	0.000	1/16″
Zero suppression (metric)	Leading off	Leading off
	Trailing on	Trailing on
Zero suppression (inch)	Leading on	Leading on
	Trailing off	Trailing off
Angles	Decimal degrees (default)	Deg/min/sec
Tolerances	By application	None
Text style	gdt	Stylus BT
Text height	.125	.125
Text gap	.05	.1

EXERCISE 17-17 Complete the Exercise on the Student CD.

Overriding Existing Dimensioning Variables

Generally, it is appropriate to have one or more dimension styles set to perform specific tasks that relate to your dimensioning practices. However, there are situations where a few dimensions require settings that are not covered by your basic styles. These situations may be too few and far between to warrant creating a new style. For example, assume you have the value for **Offset from origin** set at .0625, which conforms to ASME standards. However, in your final drawing there are three dimensions that require a 0 **Offset from origin** setting. For these dimensions, you can perform a ***dimension style override*** and temporarily alter the settings for the dimension style without actually modifying the style.

Dimension Style Override for Existing Dimensions

PROPERTIES
PROPS
CH
MO
[Ctrl]+[1]

Modify
➥ Properties

Standard toolbar

Properties

To override the dimension style of an existing dimension, first select the dimension. Then, open the **Properties** window by picking the **Properties** button on the **Standard** toolbar, selecting **Properties** from the **Modify** pull-down menu, or typing PROPERTIES at the Command: prompt. You can also right-click in the viewport and select **Properties** from the shortcut menu or double-click on the selected dimension.

The dimension properties listed in the **Properties** window are broken down into eight categories. See **Figure 17-74.** To change an existing property or value, access the proper category and pick the property to highlight it. You can then change the corresponding value. Refer to Chapter 13 for a discussion on how to make changes in the **Properties** window.

The changes made in the **Properties** window are overrides to the dimension style for the selected dimension. The changes do not alter the original dimension style. Also, the changes are not applied to new dimensions.

Figure 17-74.
The **Properties** window can be used to edit dimension properties and create a dimension style override.

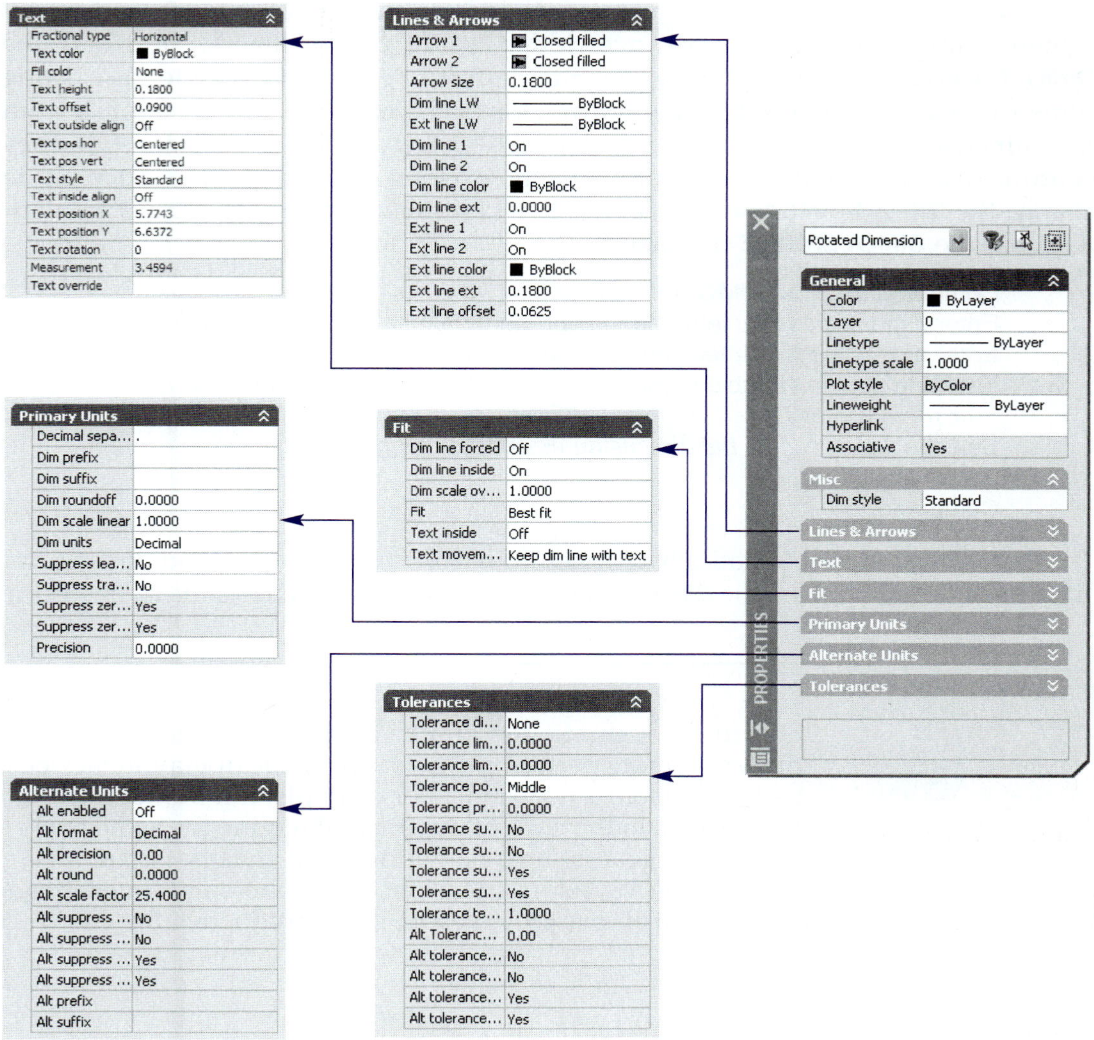

Dimension Style Override for New Dimensions

To override the dimension style for dimensions you are about to draw, open the **Dimensions Style Manager.** Then, select the dimension style that you are going to override from the **Styles** list. Finally, pick the **Override...** button to display the **Override Current Style** dialog box. This dialog box has the same features as the **New** (or **Modify**) **Dimensioning Style** dialog box. Make any changes to the style and pick the **OK** button. The style you overrode now has a branch under it labeled **<style overrides>,** which is set as the current style. Close the **Dimension Style Manager** and draw the needed dimensions.

To clear the overrides, return to the **Dimension Style Manager** and set any other style current. However, this will discard the overrides. If you want to incorporate the overrides into the style that was overridden, right-click on the **<style overrides>** name and select **Save to current style** from the shortcut menu. To save the changes to a new style, pick the **New...** button. Then, select **<style overrides>** in the **Start With** drop-down list in the **Create New Dimension Style** dialog box. Finally, in the **New Dimension Style** dialog box, simply pick **OK** to save the overrides as a new style.

Dimension Style Override on the Command Line

DIMOVERRIDE
DOV

A dimension style is really a set of dimensioning variable values. Individual dimensioning variables can be overridden using the command line and the **DIMOVERRIDE** command. This has a similar effect to overriding a style for existing dimensions using the **Properties** window. However, you must be very familiar with the dimensioning variable names and which aspect of the dimension style they control. Also, the command can only change existing dimensions. For example, to change the **Offset from origin** setting, which is controlled by the **DIMEXO** system variable, use the **DIMOVERRIDE** command:

Command: **DOV** *or* **DIMOVERRIDE**↵
Enter dimension variable name to override or [Clear overrides]: **DIMEXO**↵
Enter new value for dimension variable <0.0625>: **0**↵
Enter dimension variable name to override: *(type another variable name to override or press* [Enter]*)*
Select objects: *(select the dimension or dimensions to override)*
Select objects: ↵
Command:

The **DIMEXO** variable automatically changes from .0625 to 0 on the selected dimensions. To clear any overrides, use the **Clear** option. Exiting the command discards all overrides.

PROFESSIONAL TIP

Carefully evaluate the dimensioning requirements in a drawing before performing a style override. It may, in fact, be better to create a new style. For example, if a number of the dimensions in the current drawing all require the same overrides, then generating a new dimension style is a good idea. If only one or two dimensions need the same overrides, performing an override may be more productive.

EXERCISE 17-18 Complete the Exercise on the Student CD.

NOTE

Dimensions can also be created in dimensioning mode. To access dimensioning mode, enter DIM at the Command: prompt. The Command: prompt becomes the Dim: prompt and you can enter dimensioning commands. To exit dimensioning mode, press the [Esc] key and the Command: prompt is displayed. This method was common in earlier releases of AutoCAD, but has become a relatively inefficient method of command entry. Newer dimensioning commands, such as **QLEADER** and **QDIM**, cannot be accessed from the Dim: prompt.

Chapter Test

Answer the following questions on a separate sheet of paper.

1. What are the recommended standard units of measure for mechanical drawings?
2. Name the units of measure commonly used in architectural and structural drafting. Show an example.
3. What is the recommended height for dimension numbers and notes on drawings?
4. Name the pull-down menu where the **Linear**, **Aligned**, and **Radius** dimensioning commands are found.
5. Name the two dimensioning commands that provide linear dimensions for angled surfaces.
6. Name the **DIMLINEAR** option that opens the multiline text editor for changing the dimension text.
7. Name the **DIMLINEAR** option that allows you to change dimension text at the prompt line.
8. What is the keyboard shortcut (command alias) for the **DIMBASELINE** command?
9. Which command other than **DIMBASELINE** can be used to create baseline dimensions?
10. Name at least three modes of dimensioning available through the **QDIM** command.
11. Name the command used to dimension angles in degrees.
12. AutoCAD refers to chain dimensioning as _____.
13. AutoCAD refers to datum dimensioning as _____.
14. The command used to provide diameter dimensions for circles is _____.
15. The command used to provide radius dimensions for arcs is _____.
16. What does the *M* mean in the title of the standard ASME Y14.5M-1994?
17. Does a text style have to be loaded before it can be accessed for use in dimension text?
18. How do you access the **DIMRADIUS** and **DIMDIAMETER** commands from a pull-down menu?
19. How do you place a datum dimension from the origin of the previously drawn dimension?
20. How do you place a datum dimension from the origin of a dimension that was drawn during a previous drawing session?
21. Which type of dimensions are created when you select multiple objects in the **QDIM** command?
22. Oblique extension lines are drawn using the _____ command and by accessing the _____ option.
23. Define *annotation.*

24. Identify how to access the **QLEADER** command using:
    A. Toolbar.
    B. Pull-down menu.
    C. Command: prompt.
25. Text placed using the **QLEADER** command is a _____ text object.
26. Describe the purpose of the **Copy an object** option in the **Leader Settings** dialog box.
27. Define *arrowless dimensioning.*
28. AutoCAD refers to arrowless dimensioning as _____ dimensioning.
29. Name the pull-down menu selection that allows you to draw arrowless dimensions.
30. What is the importance of the user coordinate system (UCS) when drawing arrowless dimensions?
31. Identify the elements of this Unified screw thread note: 1/2-13 UNC-2B.
    A. 1/2.
    B. 13.
    C. UNC.
    D. 2.
    E. B.
32. Identify the elements of this metric screw thread note: M 14 X 2.
    A. M.
    B. 14.
    C. 2.
33. How does the arrowhead specified for the dimension style affect the arrowhead used with the **QLEADER** command?
34. Name the dialog box that is used to create dimension styles.
35. Identify at least three ways to access the dialog box identified in Question 34.
36. Define an AutoCAD *dimension style.*
37. Name the dialog box tab used to control the appearance of dimension lines, extension lines, arrowheads, and center marks.
38. Name the dialog box tab used to control dimensioning settings that adjust the location of dimension lines, dimension text, arrowheads, and leader lines.
39. Name the dialog box tab used to control the dimensioning settings that display the dimension text.
40. Name at least four arrowhead types that are available in the **Lines and Arrows** tab for common use on architectural drawings.
41. Identify the dialog box tab used to control the dimension text location as you place the dimension.
42. Name the area in the **Modify Dimension Style** dialog box in which vertical justification of text can be set.
43. Which option for the vertical justification mentioned in Question 42 is commonly used in mechanical drafting?
44. Define *primary units.*
45. Given the following dimension text examples, identify if the application is for inch decimal drawings, metric decimal drawings, or architectural drawings.
    A. 12′-6″
    B. 0.5
    C. .500

Drawing Problems

Use the startup option of your choice or use one of your templates. Set limits, units, dimension styles, and other parameters as needed. Use the following general guidelines.

A. Use dimension styles and text fonts that match the type of drawing as discussed in this chapter.
B. Use grids and object snap modes to your best advantage.
C. Apply dimensions accurately using ASME or other related industry/architectural standards. Dimensions are in inches, or feet and inches, unless otherwise specified.
D. Set separate layers for dimensions and other features.
E. Plot drawings with proper line weights.
F. For mechanical drawings, place general notes 1/2″ from lower-left corner:
   3.UNLESS OTHERWISE SPECIFIED, ALL DIMENSIONS ARE IN INCHES *(or* MILLIMETERS *as applicable).*
   2.REMOVE ALL BURRS AND SHARP EDGES.
   1.INTERPRET DIMENSIONS AND TOLERANCES PER ASME Y14.5M-1994.
   NOTES:
G. Save each drawing as P17-(*problem number*).

1.

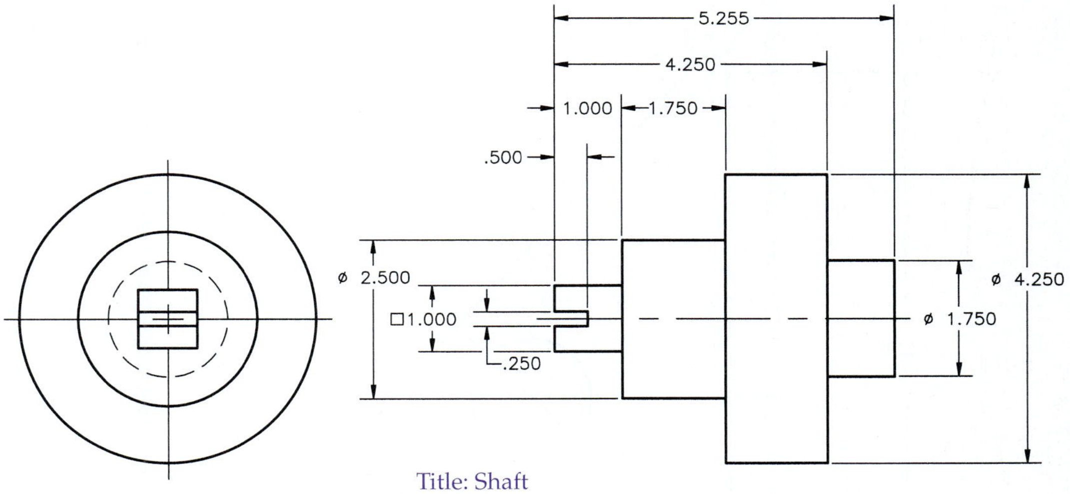

Title: Shaft
Material: SAE 1030

2.

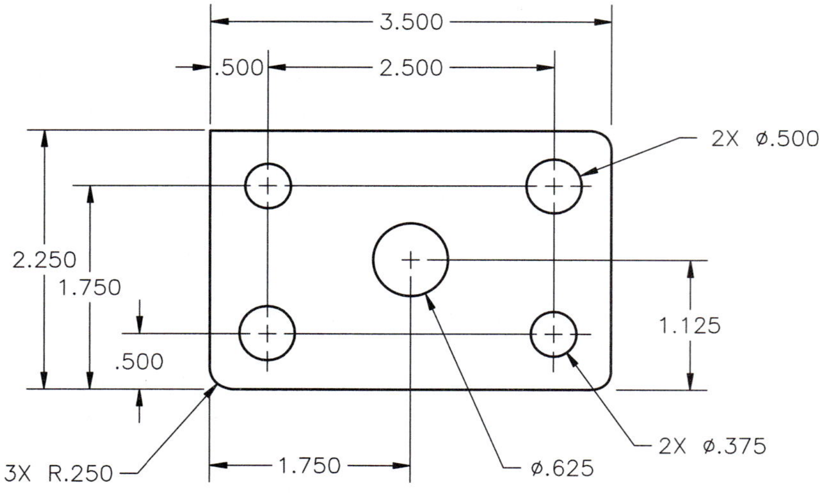

Title: Gasket

3.

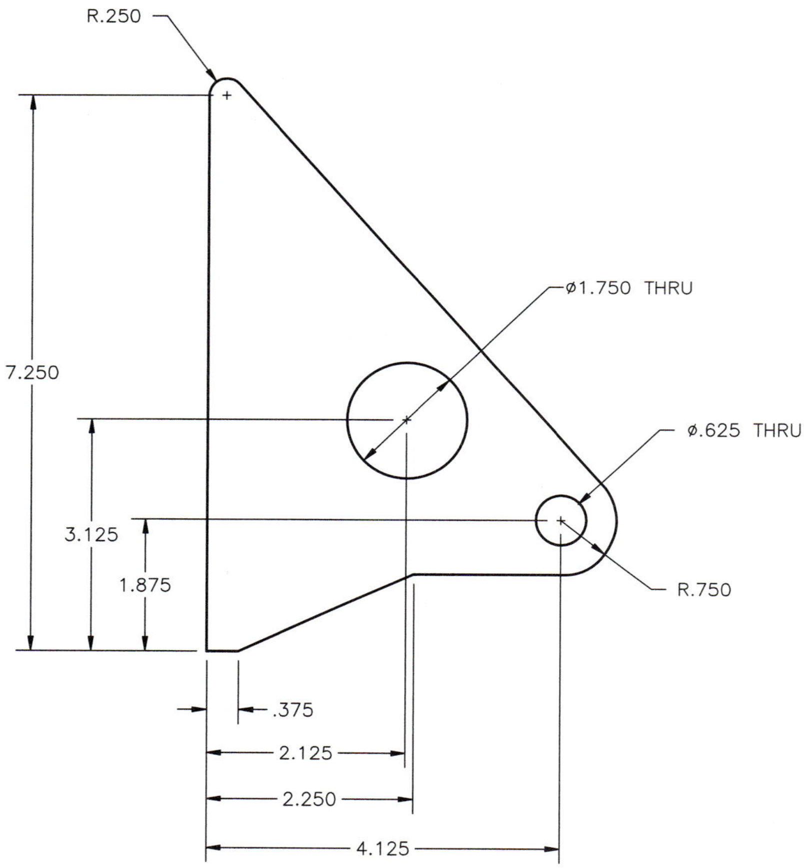

Title: Gasket

4.

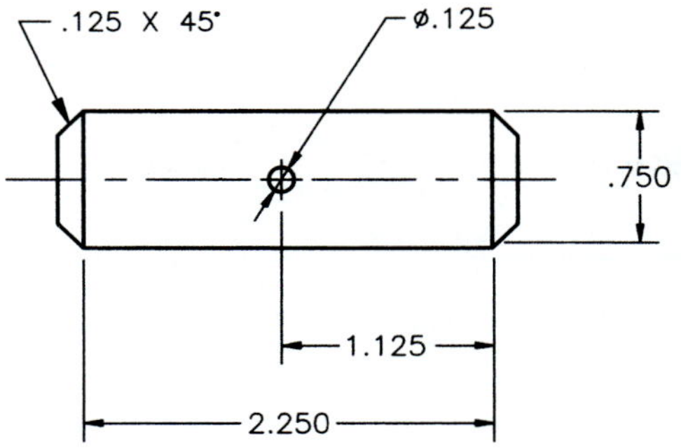

Title: Pin
Material: SAE 4320

5.

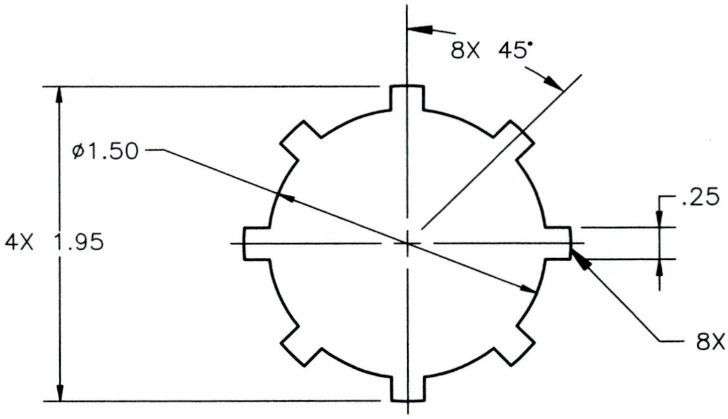

Title: Spline
Material: MS .125 THK

6.

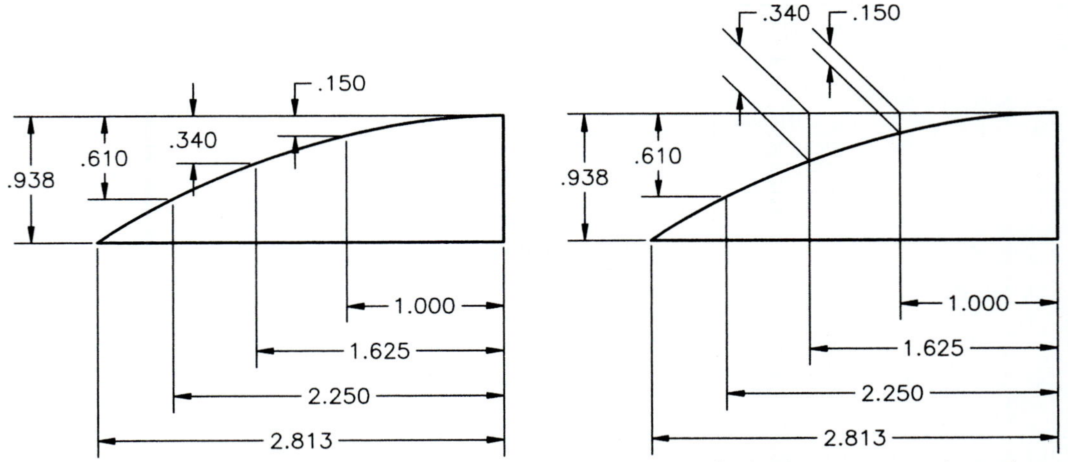

Draw this object.
A

Modify the dimensions as shown here.
B

Title: Shim

Drawing Problems - Chapter 17

7.

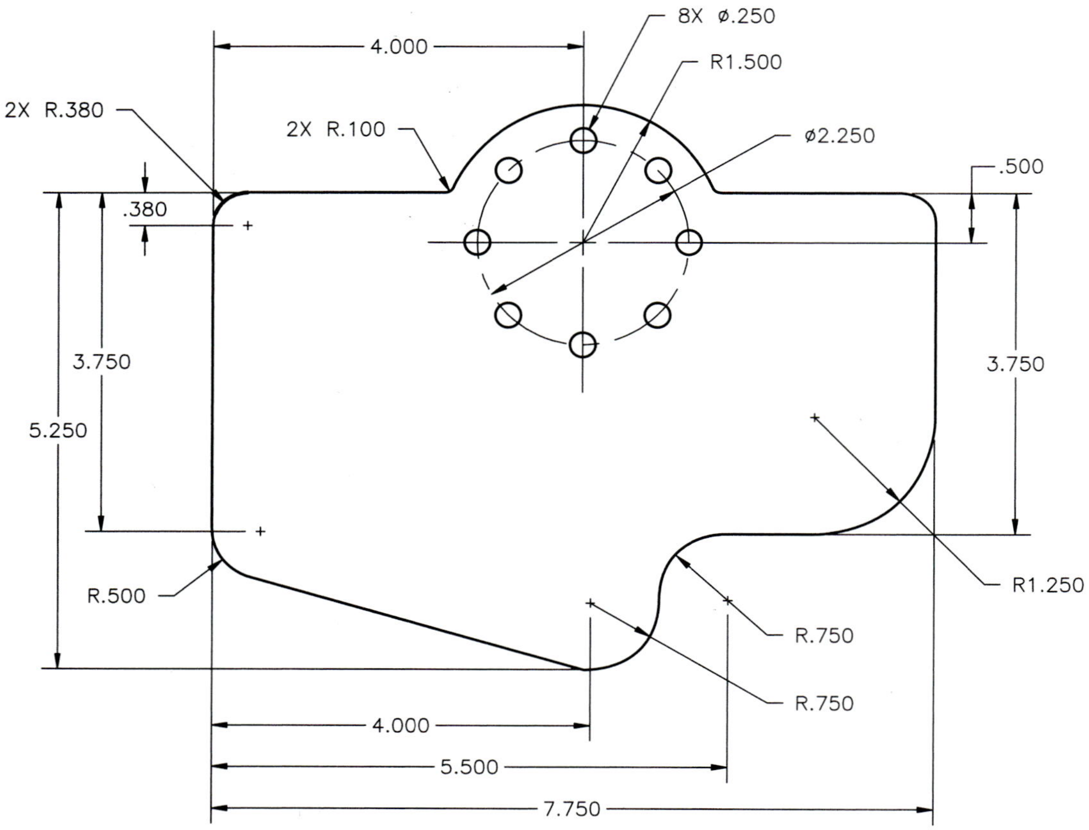

8.

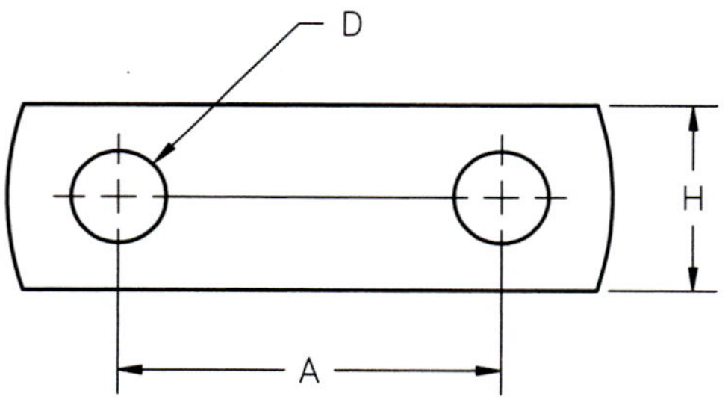

CHAIN NO.	A	D	H
SST1000	2.6	.44	1.125
SST1001	3.0	.48	1.525
SST1002	3.5	.95	2.125

Note:
Overall Length is 1.5xA
end radii are .9xA

Title: Chain Link
Material: Steel

Drawing Problems - Chapter 17

9. Convert the given drawing to a drawing with the holes located using arrowless dimensioning based on the X and Y coordinates given in the table. Place a table above your title block with Hole (identification), Quantity, Description, and Depth (Z-axis).

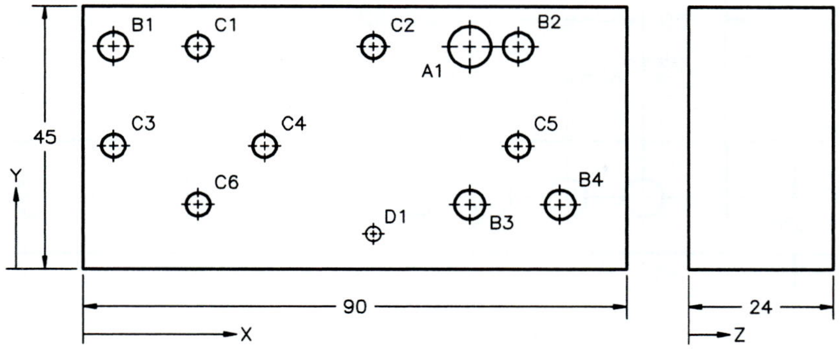

HOLE	QTY	DESC	X	Y	Z
A1	1	⌀7	64	38	18
B1	1	⌀5	5	38	THRU
B2	1	⌀5	72	38	THRU
B3	1	⌀5	64	11	THRU
B4	1	⌀5	79	11	THRU
C1	1	⌀4	19	38	THRU
C2	1	⌀4	48	38	THRU
C3	1	⌀4	5	21	THRU
C4	1	⌀4	30	21	THRU
C5	1	⌀4	72	21	THRU
C6	1	⌀4	19	11	THRU
D1	1	⌀2.5	48	6	THRU

Title: Base
Material: Bronze

10.

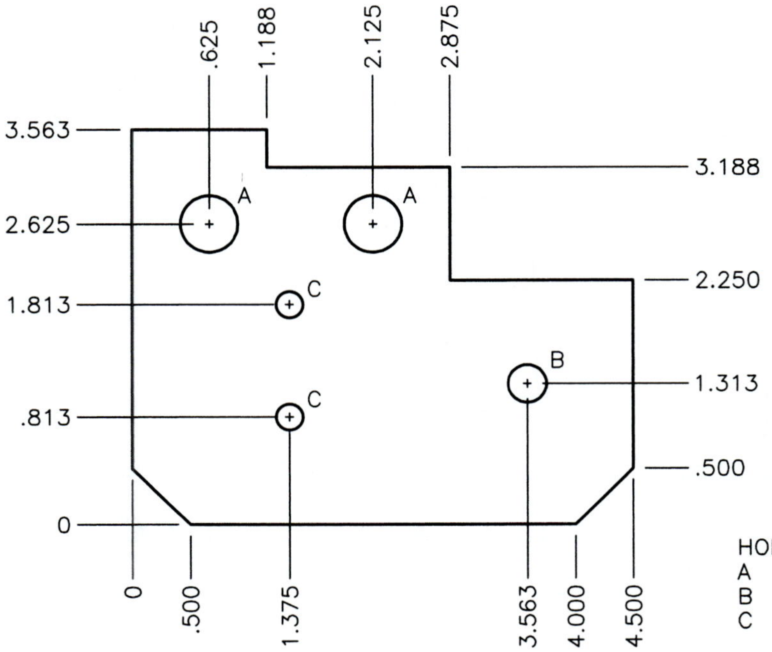

HOLE	QTY	DIAMETER
A	2	.500
B	1	.375
C	2	.250

Title: Chassis
Material: Aluminum .100 THK

11.

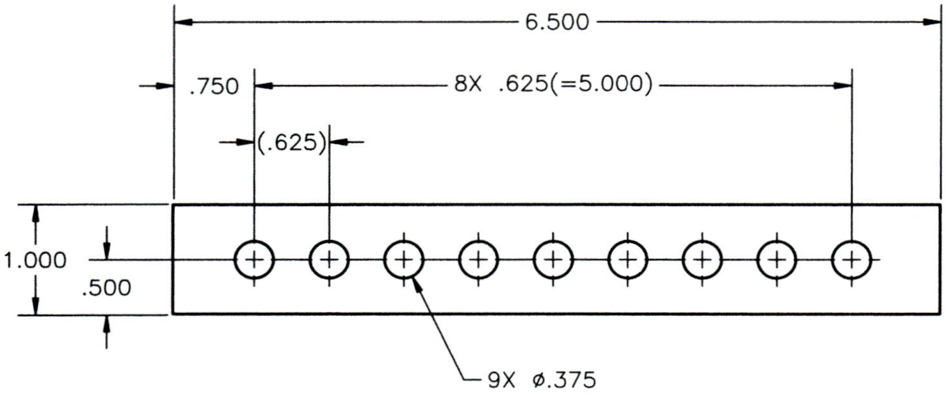

12.

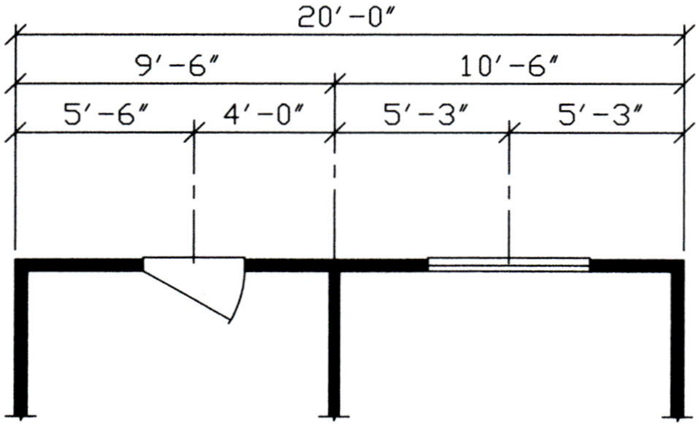

Door and Window

13.

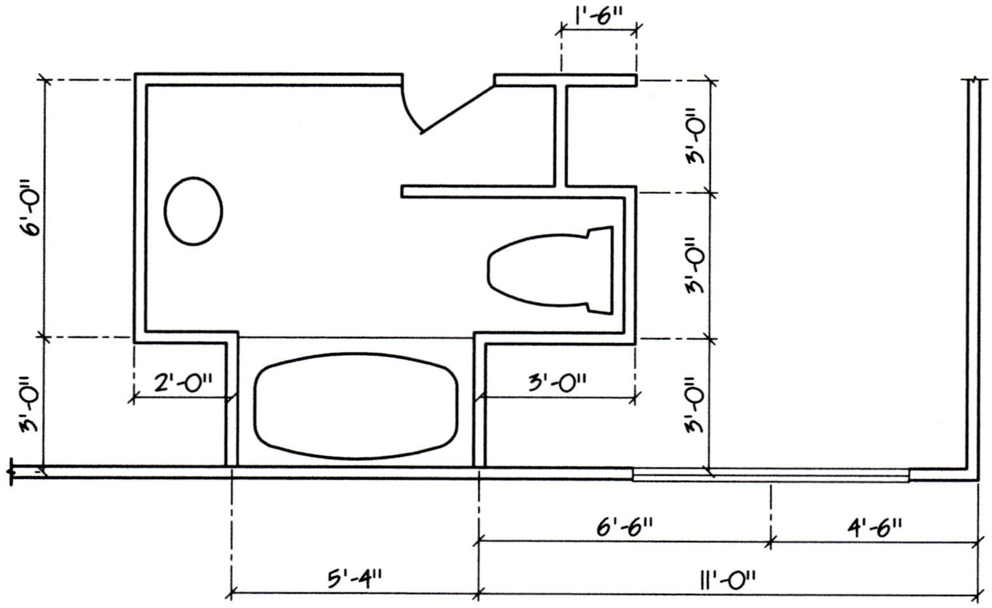

Title: Bathroom Area

For Problems 14–16, use the isometric drawing provided to create a multiview drawing for the part. Include only the views necessary to fully describe the object. Dimension according to the ASME standards discussed in this chapter using a dimension style appropriate for mechanical drafting.

14.

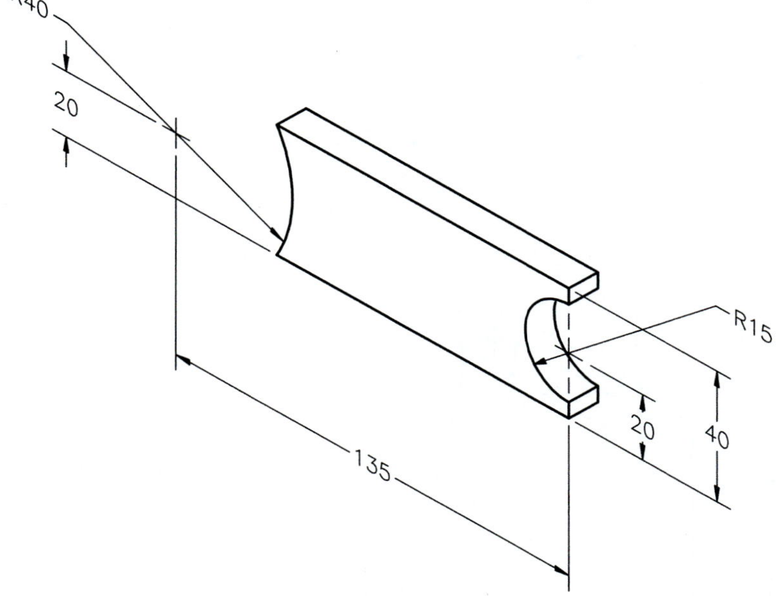

Title: Shim MS
Metric 10 THK

15. Half of the object is removed for clarity. The entire object should be drawn.

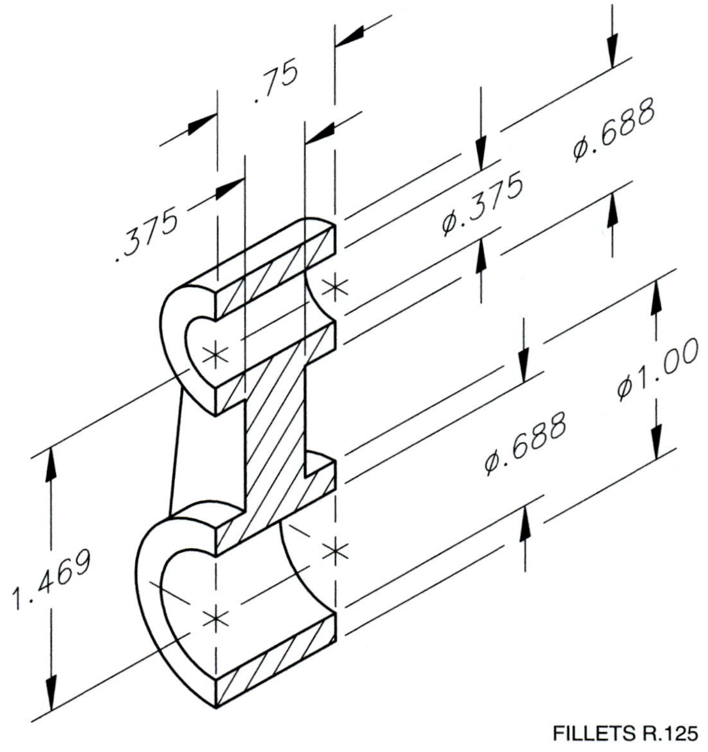

Title: Shaft Support
Material: Cast Iron (CI)

Drawing Problems - Chapter 17

16. Half of the object is removed for clarity. The entire object should be drawn.

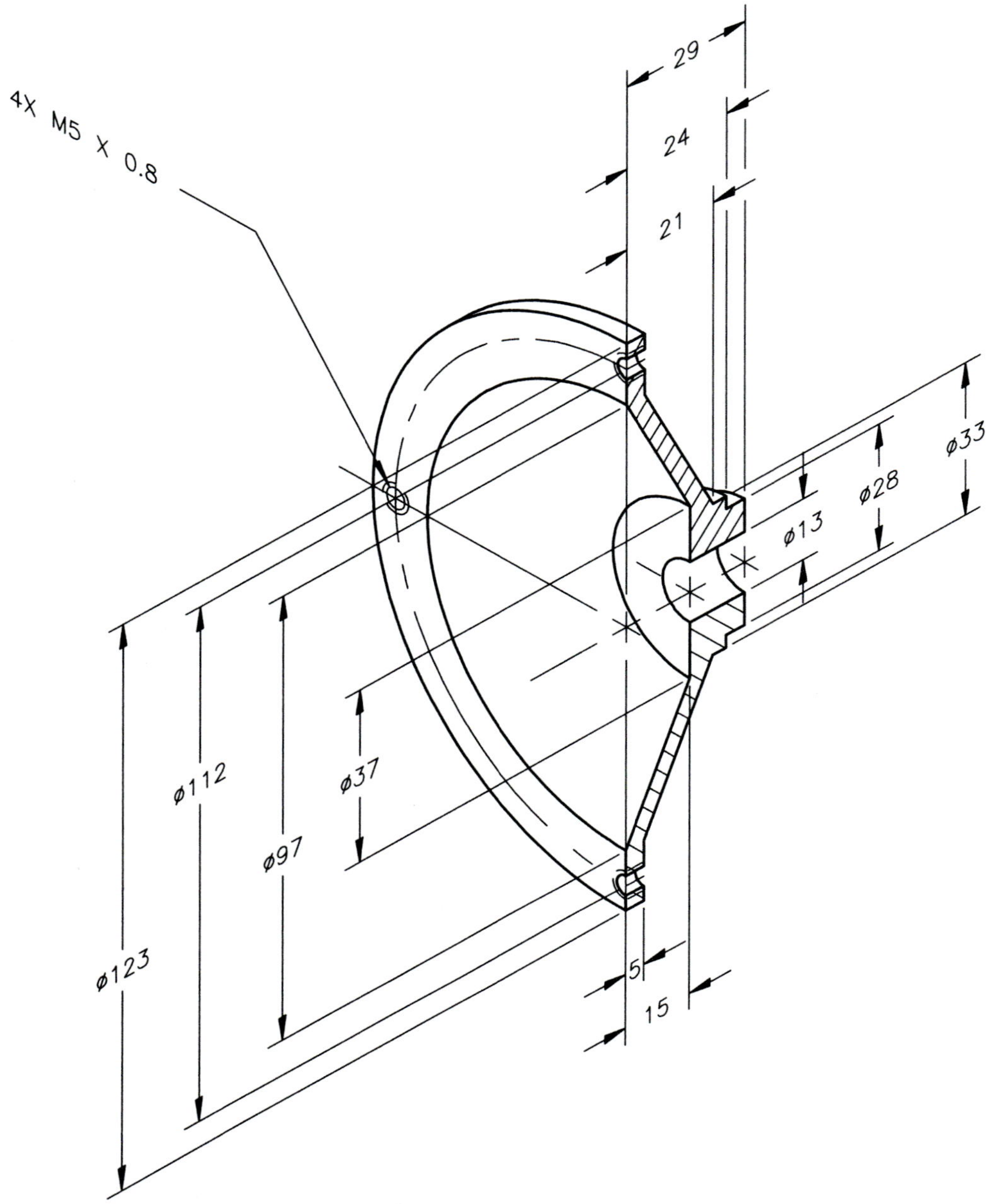

Title: Transmission Cover
Material: Cast Iron (CI)
Metric

17. Draw this floor plan. Size the windows and the doors to your own specifications.

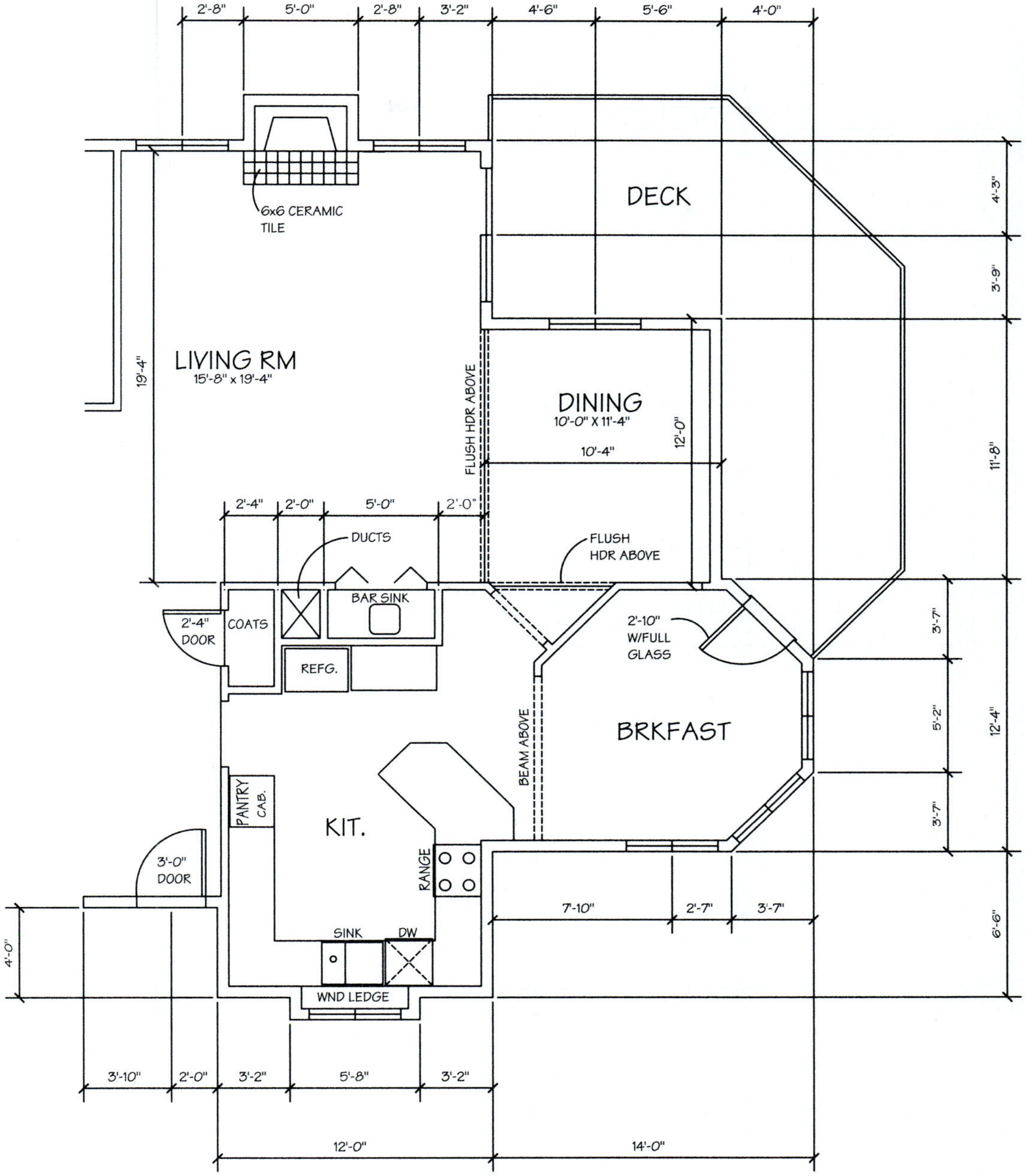

18.

HOLE LAYOUT			
KEY	SIZE	DEPTH	NO. REQD
A	⌀.250	THRU	6
B	⌀.125	THRU	4
C	⌀.375	THRU	4
D	R.125	THRU	2

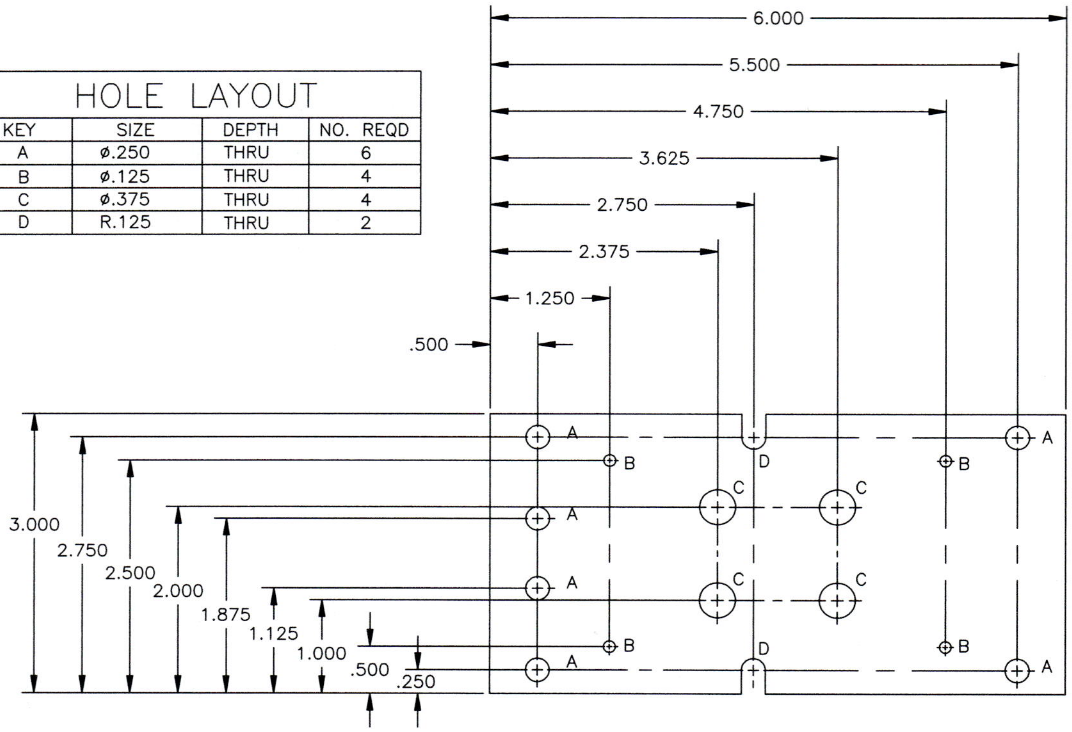

Title: Chassis Base (datum dimensioning)
Material: 12 gage Aluminum

19.

HOLE LAYOUT			
KEY	SIZE	DEPTH	NO. REQD
A	⌀.250	THRU	6
B	⌀.125	THRU	4
C	⌀.375	THRU	4
D	R.125	THRU	2

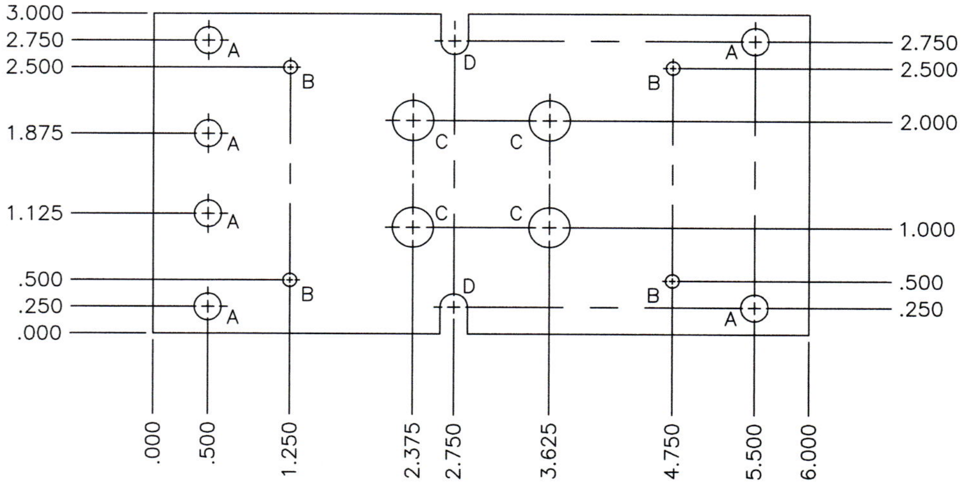

Title: Chassis Base (arrowless dimensioning)
Material: 12 gage Aluminum

20.

HOLE LAYOUT				
KEY	X	Y	SIZE	TOL
A1	.500	2.750	⌀.250	±.002
A2	.500	1.875	⌀.250	±.002
A3	.500	1.125	⌀.250	±.002
A4	.500	.250	⌀.250	±.002
A5	5.500	2.750	⌀.250	±.002
A6	5.500	.250	⌀.250	±.002
B1	1.250	2.500	⌀.125	±.001
B2	1.250	.500	⌀.125	±.001
B3	4.750	2.500	⌀.125	±.001
B4	4.750	.500	⌀.125	±.001
C1	2.375	2.000	⌀.375	±.005
C2	2.375	1.000	⌀.375	±.005
C3	3.625	2.000	⌀.375	±.005
C4	3.625	1.000	⌀.375	±.005
D1	2.750	2.750	R.125	±.002
D2	2.750	.250	R.125	±.002

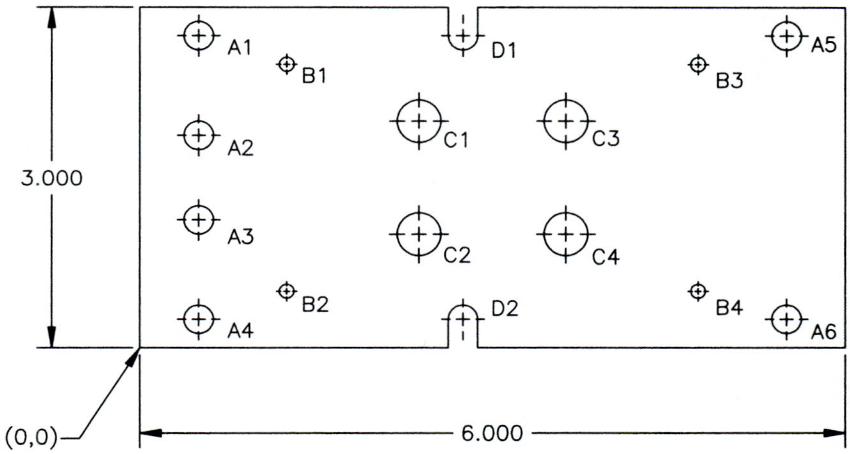

Title: Chassis Base (arrowless tabular dimensioning)
Material: 12 gage Aluminum

21.

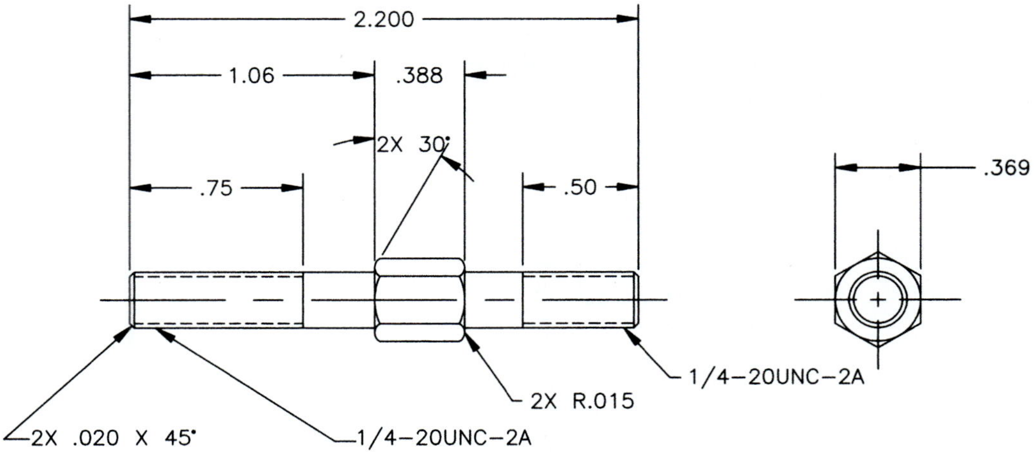

Title: Stud
Material: Stainless Steel

22.

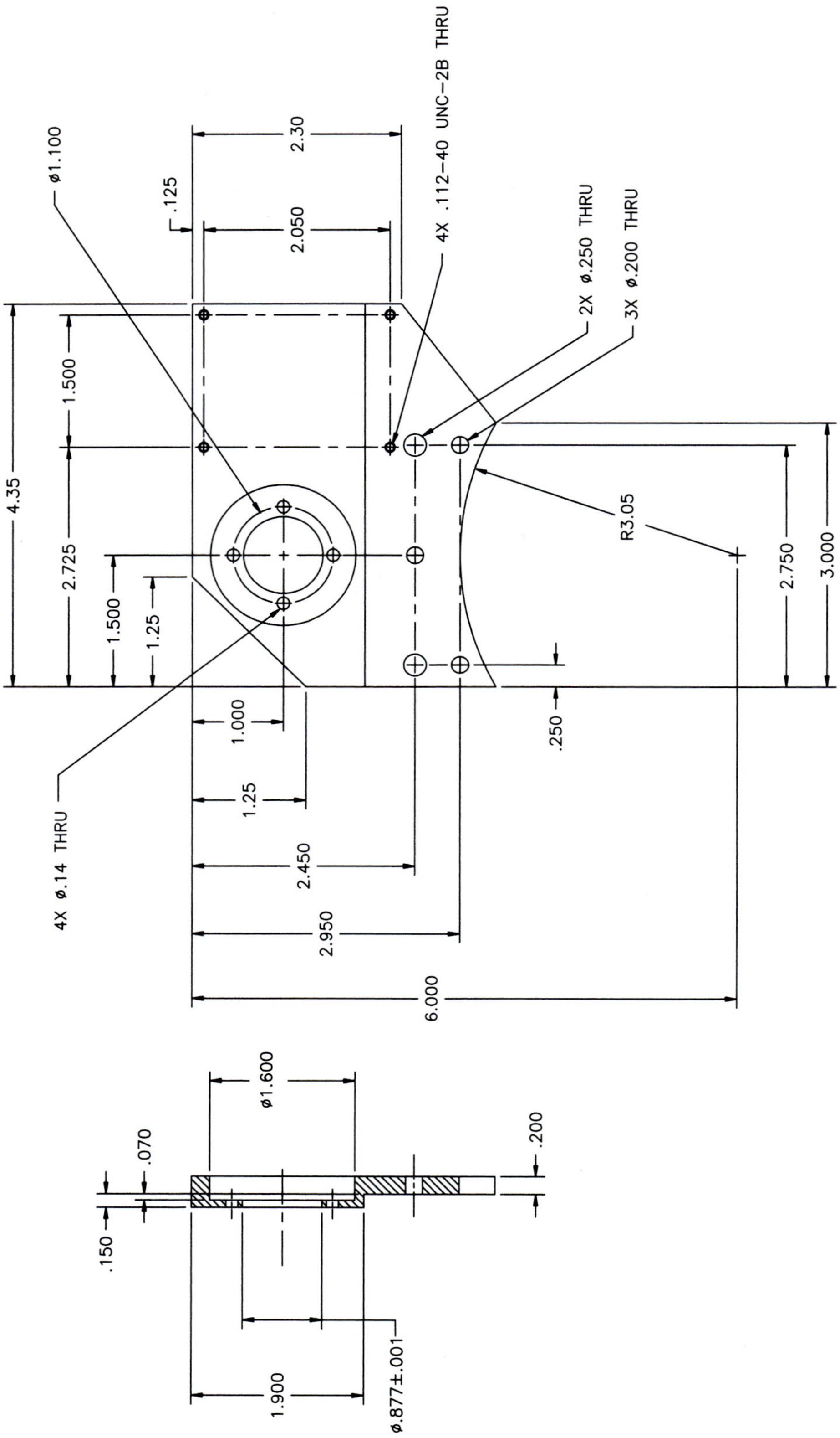

Title: Bracket
Material: SAE 1040

23.

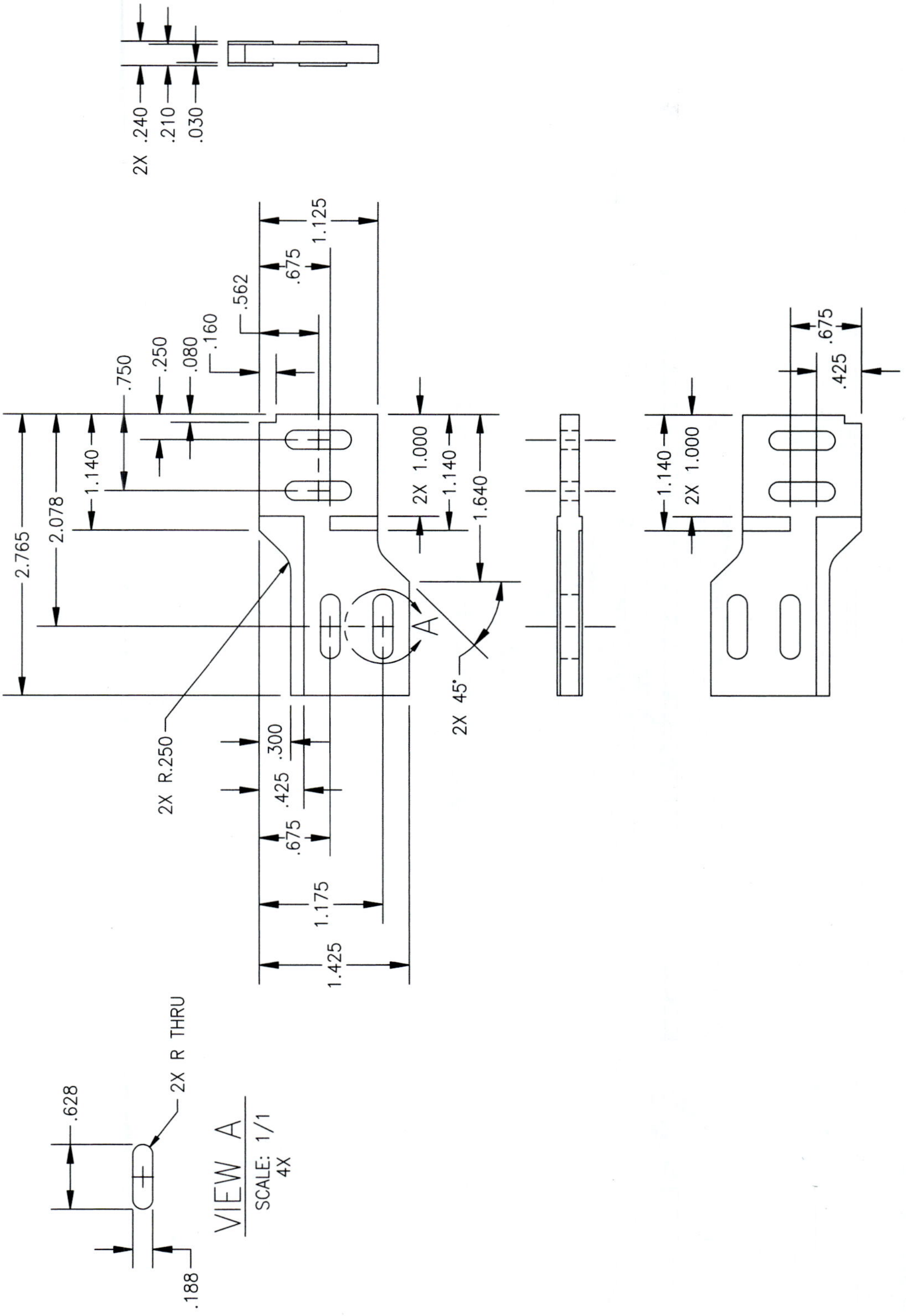

Title: Support
Material: Aluminum

Roof framing details. (Mark Hartman)

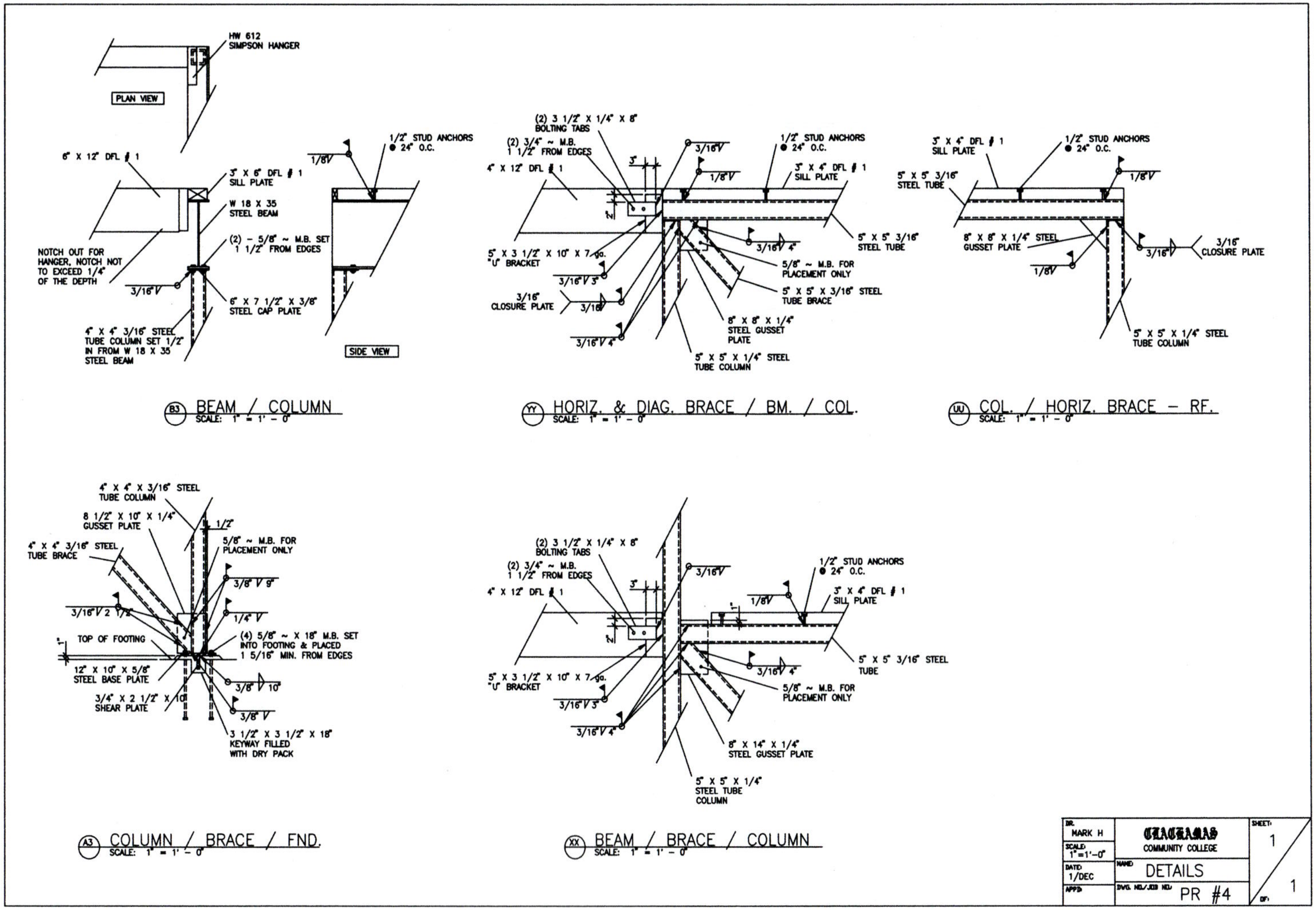

CHAPTER 18

Editing Dimensions

Learning Objectives

After completing this chapter, you will be able to do the following:

- Make changes to existing dimensions.
- Update a dimension to reflect the current dimension style.
- Import dimension styles from another drawing.
- Use the **Properties** window to edit individual dimension properties.
- Edit individual elements of associative dimensions.

The tools used to edit dimensions vary from simple erasing techniques to object editing commands. Often, the dimensioned object is edited and the dimensions are automatically updated to reflect the changes. This chapter provides you with a variety of useful techniques for editing dimensions.

Erasing Dimensions

In Chapter 3, you were introduced to the **ERASE** command. Among the many selection options used with this command are **Last**, **Previous**, **Window**, **Crossing**, **WPolygon**, **CPolygon**, and **Fence**.

Erasing existing features such as large groups of dimensions often becomes difficult. For example, the objects may be very close to other parts of the drawing. When there are many objects, it is usually time-consuming to erase each one individually. When this situation occurs, the **Crossing**, **CPolygon**, and **Fence** selection options of the **ERASE** command are useful. A comparison of using the **Window** and **Crossing** selection options with the **ERASE** command on a group of dimensions is shown in **Figure 18-1.** For a review of these techniques, refer to Chapter 3.

PROFESSIONAL TIP

Dimensions are block objects inside of AutoCAD. After erasing dimensions, use the **PURGE** command to purge the erased dimension blocks. The **PURGE** command is discussed in Chapter 22.

Figure 18-1.
Using the **Window** and **Crossing** selection options of the **ERASE** command to erase dimensions.

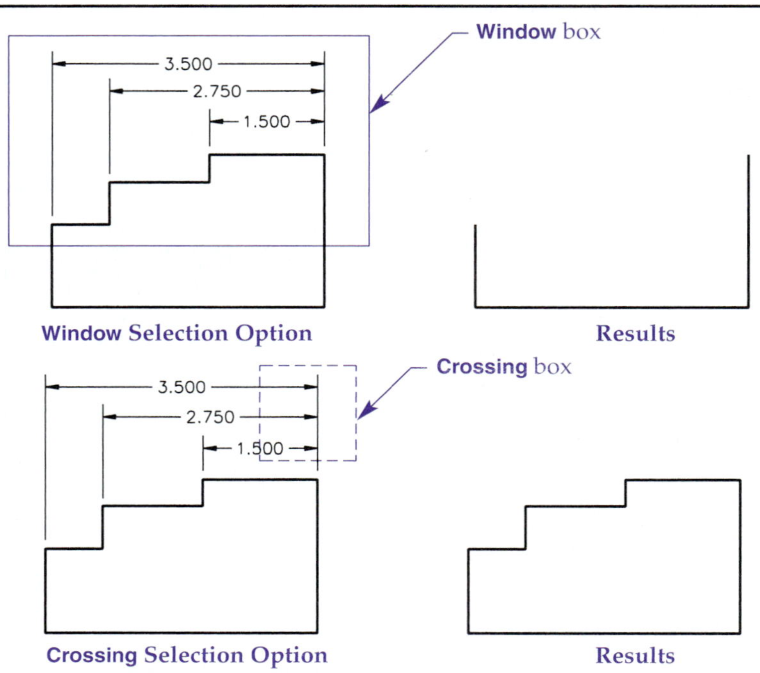

Editing Dimension Text Values

DDEDIT
ED

Modify
➥ **Object**
➥ **Text**
➥ **Edit...**

Text toolbar

Edit Text

The **DDEDIT** command can be used to edit existing dimension text. You can add a prefix or suffix to the text, or edit the dimension text format. This is useful when you wish to alter dimension text without creating a new dimension. For example, a linear dimension does not automatically place a diameter symbol with the text value. Using the **DDEDIT** command is one way to place this symbol on the dimension once it has already been placed in the drawing.

You can access the **DDEDIT** command by picking **Text** and then **Edit...** from the **Object** cascading menu in the **Modify** pull-down menu. You can also enter ED or DDEDIT at the Command: prompt. When this command is issued, the Select an annotation object or [Undo]: prompt is displayed.

After you select a dimension to edit, the multiline text editor and **Text Formatting** toolbar are displayed. See Figure 18-2. The two chevrons (< >) represent the existing dimension text. To add a diameter symbol to the text, place the cursor at the position that you want to add the symbol and right-click. Then, select **Diameter** from the **Symbol** cascading menu. This adds the %%c control code, which displays the diameter symbol in the text object. Pick the **OK** button on the **Text Formatting** toolbar to close the multiline text editor. The result of changing an existing dimension in this manner is shown in Figure 18-3.

Figure 18-2.
The multiline text editor can be used to edit existing dimension text.

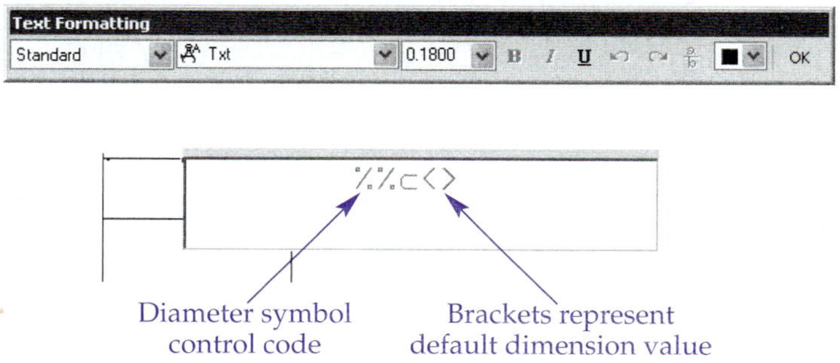

Figure 18-3.
Using the **DDEDIT** command to add a diameter symbol to an existing dimension. A—Original dimension. B—Diameter symbol added.

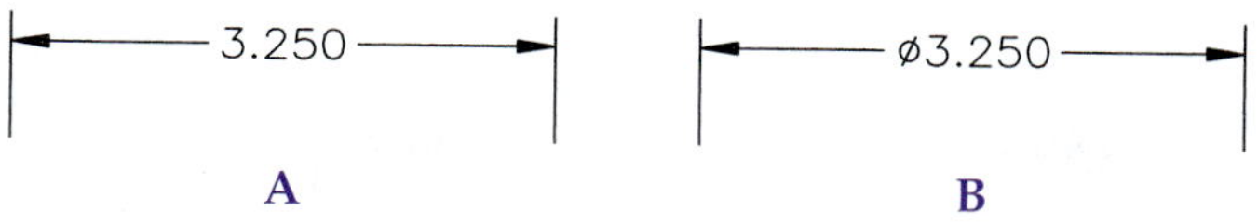

PROFESSIONAL TIP

You can replace the brackets representing the dimension value with numeric values. However, if the dimension is subsequently stretched, trimmed, or extended, the dimension text value will not change. Therefore, try to leave the default value.

EXERCISE 18-1 Complete the Exercise on the Student CD.

Editing Dimensions with the QDIM Command

The **QDIM** command can be used to place a new dimension in a drawing. This was discussed in Chapter 17. The **QDIM** command can also be used to perform several dimension editing operations. You can change the arrangement of an existing dimension, add an additional dimension, or remove an existing dimension. The **QDIM** command can be accessed by picking the **Quick Dimension** button on the **Dimension** toolbar, picking **Quick Dimension** from the **Dimension** pull-down menu, or entering QDIM at the Command: prompt. The **QDIM** command sequence is:

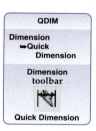

> **QDIM**
> **Dimension**
> **➥Quick Dimension**
> **Dimension toolbar**
> **Quick Dimension**

Command: **QDIM**↵
Associative dimension priority = Endpoint
Select geometry to dimension: *(pick the dimension to edit)*
Select geometry to dimension: ↵
Specify dimension line position, or
[Continuous/Staggered/Baseline/Ordinate/Radius/Diameter/datumPoint/Edit/seTtings]
<Continuous>:

The **Continuous** option allows you to change the arrangement of a selected group of dimensions to chain dimensions. In chain, or continuous, dimensioning the dimensions are placed next to each other in a line, or end to end. This is discussed in Chapter 17. An example of this type of dimensioning is shown in Figure 18-4A.

The **Baseline** option allows you to create a series of baseline dimensions from an existing dimension arrangement. In baseline dimensioning, all dimensions originate from common features. Baseline dimensions are drawn in Figure 18-4B. In the example shown, the **Baseline** option has been used to change the dimensioning arrangement from continuous in Figure 18-4A to baseline.

The **Edit** option allows you to add dimensions to, or remove dimensions from, a selected group and then automatically reorder the group. You can use the **Add** suboption of the **Edit** option to add a dimension. The **Remove** option is used to remove a dimension. The command sequence to add the dimension shown in Figure 18-4C to the baseline dimensions is:

Figure 18-4.
The **QDIM** command can be used to change existing dimension arrangements and add or remove dimensions.

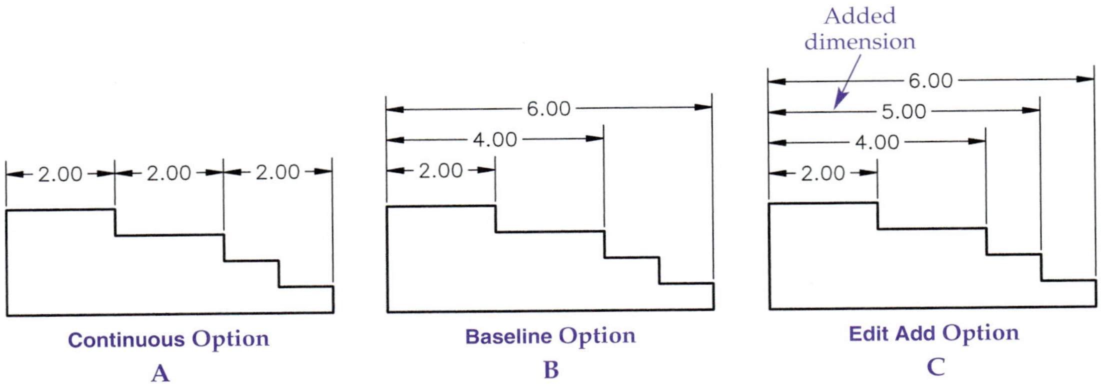

Command: **QDIM**↵
Associative dimensions priority = Endpoint
Select geometry to dimension: *(select all dimensions in the group to change)*
Select geometry to dimension: ↵
Specify dimension line position, or
[Continuous/Staggered/Baseline/Ordinate/Radius/Diameter/datumPoint/Edit/seTtings]
<Baseline>: **E**↵
Indicate dimension point to remove, or [Add/eXit] <eXit>: **A**↵
Indicate dimension point to add, or [Remove/eXit] <eXit>: *(pick the location or feature for which the dimension is to be added)*
One dimension point added.
Indicate dimension point to add, or [Remove/eXit] <eXit>: ↵
Specify dimension line position, or
[Continuous/Staggered/Baseline/Ordinate/Radius/Diameter/datumPoint/Edit/seTtings]
<Baseline>: *(pick a location for the baseline dimension arrangement)*

The dimensions are then automatically realigned after you pick a location for the arrangement. You do not have to pick all of the dimensions in the group. However, if you do not pick the entire group you must select the location carefully. The spacing for the edited dimension and the dimensions in the group that were not selected may not be consistent.

EXERCISE 18-2 Complete the Exercise on the Student CD.

Editing Dimension Text Placement

Good dimensioning practice requires that adjacent dimension text be *staggered,* rather than stacked. As an example, in Figure 18-5, one of the dimensions has been moved to a new location to separate the text elements. The **DIMTEDIT** command allows you to change the placement and orientation of an existing associative dimension text value. An ***associative dimension*** is one in which all elements of the dimension (including the dimension line, extension lines, arrowheads, and text) are connected to the object being dimensioned. Thus, if the object is modified, the dimension updates automatically. Associative dimensioning is controlled by the **DIMASSOC** system variable and is active by default.

Figure 18-5.
Using the **DIMTEDIT** command to stagger dimension text. A—Original dimension. B—Dimension text moved.

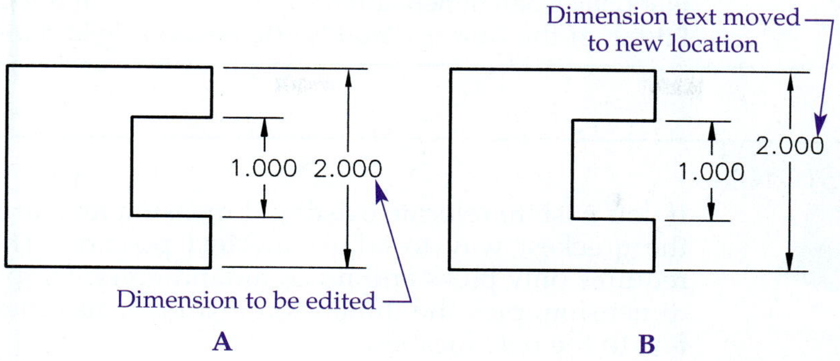

DIMTEDIT

Dimension
➥Align Text

Dimension toolbar

Dimension Text Edit

To access the **DIMTEDIT** command, pick the **Dimension Text Edit** button on the **Dimension** toolbar, pick one of the options from the **Align Text** cascading menu in the **Dimension** pull-down menu, or enter DIMTEDIT at the Command: prompt. After entering the command, select the dimension to be altered.

If the **DIMASSOC** system variable was on when the dimension was created, the text of the selected dimension automatically drags with the screen cursor. This allows you to relocate the text with your pointing device. If you pick a point, AutoCAD automatically moves the text and reestablishes the break in the dimension line. You can also select from the options offered at the Specify new location for dimension text or [Left/Right/Center/Home/Angle]: prompt.

- **Left.** Moves horizontal text to the left and vertical text down.
- **Right.** Moves horizontal text to the right and vertical text up.
- **Center.** Centers the dimension text on the dimension line.
- **Home.** Moves relocated text back to its original position.
- **Angle.** Allows you to place dimension text at an angle. When the **Angle** option is entered, you are asked to specify a rotation angle. The text is then rotated about its middle point.

The result after using each of the **DIMTEDIT** command options is shown in **Figure 18-6.**

Figure 18-6.
A comparison of the options used with the **DIMTEDIT** command.

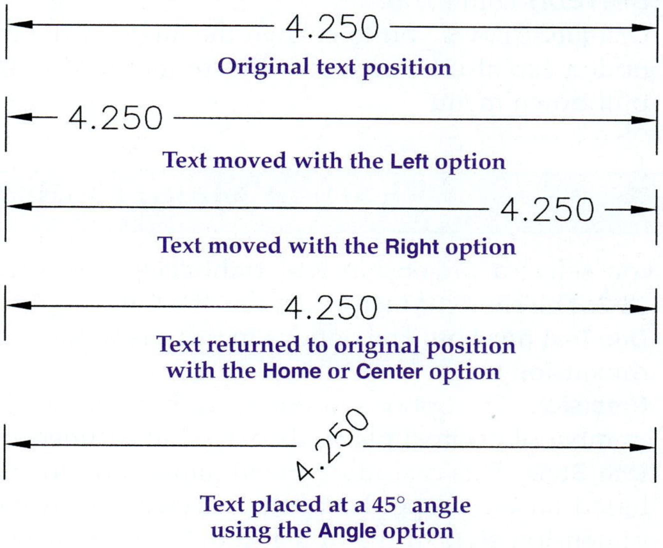

NOTE

You can locate dimension text as desired without using automatic horizontal justification by activating the **Place text manually when dimensioning** check box, which is located in the **Fit** tab of the **New** (or **Modify**) **Dimension Style** dialog box.

PROFESSIONAL TIP

If you wish to relocate existing dimension text, using grips is the quickest way to adjust the text position. This method requires only picks and no command entry. Simply pick the dimension, pick the dimension text grip, and then drag the text to the new location.

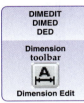

EXERCISE 18-3 Complete the Exercise on the Student CD.

Using the DIMEDIT Command

DIMEDIT
DIMED
DED
Dimension toolbar
Dimension Edit

The **DIMEDIT** command can be used to change the text value, text placement, or extension lines of an existing dimension. You can access the **DIMEDIT** command by picking the **Dimension Edit** button on the **Dimension** toolbar or by entering DED, DIMED, or DIMEDIT at the Command: prompt. You are prompted to enter the type of dimensioning editing. You have four options that can be used to edit individual or multiple dimensions.

- **Home.** The default option; identical to the **Home** option of the **DIMTEDIT** command.
- **New.** Allows you to specify new dimension text and is similar to the **DDEDIT** command. After entering this option, the multiline text editor is displayed. Enter a prefix or suffix for the text and pick **OK**. The Select objects: prompt then appears. Any dimensions that are selected assume the new text.
- **Rotate.** Used to rotate dimension text; similar to the **Angle** option of the **DIMTEDIT** command.
- **Oblique.** Allows you to change the angle of the extension lines. The **Oblique** option can also be accessed directly by picking **Oblique** from the **Dimension** pull-down menu.

Shortcut Menu Options

If you select a dimension and right-click, a shortcut menu is displayed. See Figure 18-7. The shortcut menu contains the following dimension-specific options:

- **Dim Text position.** The options in this cascading menu automatically move the dimension text.
- **Precision.** The options in this cascading menu allow you to easily adjust the number of decimal places displayed in a dimension text value.
- **Dim Style.** This cascading menu allows you to create a new dimension style based on the properties of the selected dimension. You can also change the dimension style of the dimension. In addition to the **Dim Style** option in the shortcut menu, there are other methods of changing the dimension style of an existing dimension. These are discussed in the next sections.

Figure 18-7.
Select a dimension and then right-click to access this shortcut menu.

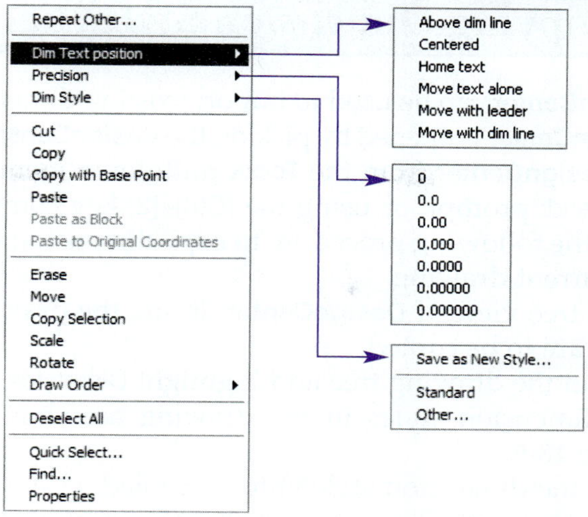

Changing the Dimension Style

So far you have learned how to edit dimension text, text placement, dimension group arrangements, and other elements of existing dimensions. In addition to these operations, you will often find it necessary to change the dimension style of a dimension. You can also import dimension styles from a separate drawing for use in the current drawing. These methods are discussed in the following sections.

As discussed in Chapter 17, you can create dimension styles by specifying settings for text styles, positioning elements, and other properties in the **Dimension Style Manager** dialog box. When there are a number of dimension styles used in your drawing, you may need to change the style of an existing dimension to a different style. A dimension's style can be changed using any of the following methods:

- **Dim Style cascading menu in the shortcut menu.** Select the dimension and right-click to display the shortcut menu. Select a new dimension style from the cascading menu.
- **Dim Style Control drop-down list in the Dimension toolbar.** Select the dimension and then select the new dimension style from this drop-down list. See Figure 18-8.
- **Dim Style Control drop-down list in the Styles toolbar.** Select the dimension and then select the new dimension style from this drop-down list.
- **Properties window.** Select a new dimension style in the **Misc** category. Refer to Chapter 13 for a discussion on how to change settings in the **Properties** window.
- **Update option.** The **Update** dimension command changes the style of the selected dimension to the current dimension style. This command can be accessed by picking the **Dimension Update** button on the **Dimension** toolbar or by selecting **Update** from the **Dimension** pull-down menu.

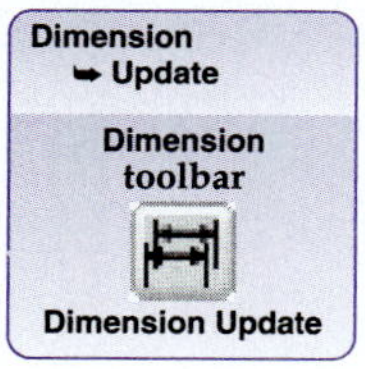

Figure 18-8.
The **Dim Style Control** drop-down list on the **Dimension** toolbar can be used to change the style of an existing dimension.

Copying Dimension Styles between Drawings

ADCENTER
ADC
[Ctrl]+[2]

Tools
➥ **DesignCenter**

Standard toolbar

DesignCenter

DesignCenter can be used to import existing dimension styles from other drawing files. **DesignCenter** is opened by picking the **DesignCenter** button on the **Standard** toolbar, picking **DesignCenter** from the **Tools** pull-down menu, typing ADC or ADCENTER at the Command: prompt, or using the [Ctrl]+[2] key combination. Once **DesignCenter** is open, use the following procedure to copy dimension styles from an existing drawing into the current drawing.

1. In the tree view of **DesignCenter**, locate the drawing from which the dimension styles are to be copied.
2. Expand the drawing tree and highlight Dimstyles.
3. The dimension styles in the drawing are shown in the preview palette. See **Figure 18-9.**
4. Select the dimension style(s) to be copied. Use the [Ctrl] and [Shift] keys to select multiple items. Then, right-click and select **Add Dimstyle(s)** from the shortcut menu to copy the styles to the current drawing. You can also use the **Cut** and **Paste** options from the shortcut menus or simply drag the dimension style icon and drop it into the drawing area.

Figure 18-9.
Copying dimension styles using **DesignCenter**.

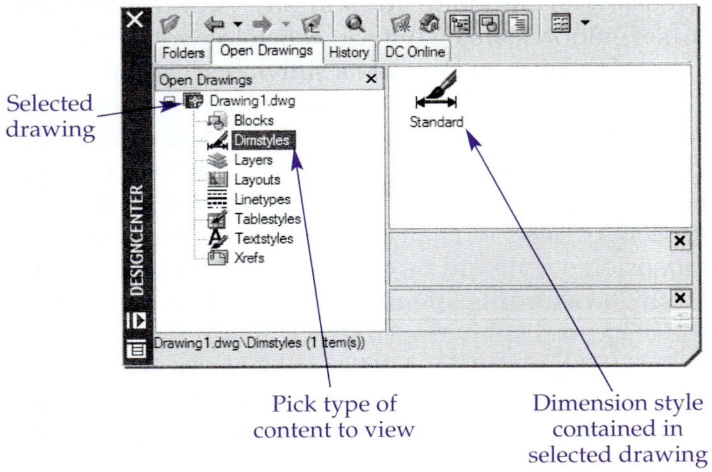

EXERCISE 18-4 Complete the Exercise on the Student CD.

Using the Properties Window to Edit Dimensions

The **Properties** window can be used to change the various text, justification, and formatting properties of selected dimensions. However, as discussed in Chapter 17, doing so creates a dimension style override for the edited dimensions. Also, as discussed earlier in this chapter, you can assign a different style to the selected dimension using the **Properties** window.

EXERCISE 18-5 Complete the Exercise on the Student CD.

Using the MATCHPROP Command

The dimension editing methods presented in this chapter have focused on updating individual dimension properties and changing dimensions to a different dimension style. You can also edit dimensions by matching the properties of one dimension to another. The **MATCHPROP** command allows you to select the properties of one dimension and apply those properties to one or more existing dimensions.

MATCHPROP
MA
Modify
➥ Match Properties
Standard toolbar
Match Properties

The **MATCHPROP** command can be accessed by picking the **Match Properties** button on the **Standard** toolbar, selecting **Match Properties** from the **Modify** pull-down menu, or entering MA or MATCHPROP at the Command: prompt. This command is covered more completely in Chapter 13. The command sequence is:

Command: **MA** *or* **MATCHPROP**↵
Select source object: *(pick the dimension from which to copy the style)*
Current active settings: Color Layer Ltype Ltscale Lineweight Thickness PlotStyle Text Dim Hatch
Select destination object(s) or [Settings]: *(pick one or more dimensions to which the style is to be applied)*
Select destination object(s) or [Settings]: ↵
Command:

After you select the dimensions to change, press [Enter] and all of the destination dimensions are updated to reflect the properties of the source dimension.

For the **MATCHPROP** command to work with dimensions, the **Dimension** setting must be active. You can check this after you have selected the source object. When the Current active settings: prompt line appears, Dim should appear with the other settings. (Notice that the **Dimension** setting is active in the previous command sequence.) If this setting does not appear when you are prompted to select a destination object, enter S for the **Settings** option. This displays the **Property Settings** dialog box. Activate the **Dimension** check box in the **Special Properties** area and pick **OK**. Then, select the destination dimensions.

PROFESSIONAL TIP

The style of the source dimension is applied to the destination dimensions. If the dimension style of the source dimension has been overridden, the "base" style is applied along with the dimension style override. Reapplying the "base" style will remove the overrides.

EXERCISE 18-6 Complete the Exercise on the Student CD.

Editing Associative Dimensions

As discussed earlier in this chapter, an associative dimension is made up of a group of individual elements and treated as a single object. When an associative dimension is selected for editing, the entire group of elements is highlighted. If you use the **ERASE** command, for example, you can pick the dimension as a single object and erase all the elements at once.

One benefit of associative dimensioning is that it permits existing dimensions to be updated as an object is edited. This means that when a dimensioned object is edited the dimension value automatically changes to match the edit. The automatic update is only applied if you accepted the default text value during the original dimension placement, or if you kept the value represented by chevrons (< >) in the multiline text editor. This provides you with an important advantage when editing an associative-dimensioned drawing. Any changes to objects are automatically transferred to the dimensions.

Associative dimensioning is controlled by the **DIMASSOC** dimension variable. **DIMASSOC** is set by entering DIMASSOC at the Command: prompt. You can also open the **Options** dialog box and select the **User Preferences** tab. Then, check or uncheck the **Make new dimensions associative** option in the **Associative Dimensioning** area.

There are three settings for the **DIMASSOC** dimension variable: 0, 1, and 2. A setting of 0 turns off associative dimensioning. In this case, elements of the dimension are created separately, as if the dimension is exploded. The dimension is not updated when the object is edited. With a setting of 1, the components that make up a dimension are grouped together, but the dimension is not associated with an object. If you edit the object, you also have to edit the dimension.

If **DIMASSOC** is set to 2, the components that make up a dimension are grouped and the dimension is associated with the object. If the object is stretched, trimmed, or extended, the dimension updates automatically. See Figure 18-10. An associative dimension also updates when using grips or the **MOVE**, **MIRROR**, **ROTATE**, or **SCALE** commands.

In the **Options** dialog box, checking the **Make new dimensions associative** check box sets **DIMASSOC** to 2. If you uncheck the check box, the **DIMASSOC** value changes its previous value other than 2 (either 1 or 0).

Figure 18-10.
The original drawing was created with associative dimensions. The drawing was revised using grips to change the rectangle dimensions, the **Properties** window to modify the circle diameter, and the **MOVE** command to relocate the circle. The dimensions automatically updated to the new object geometry.

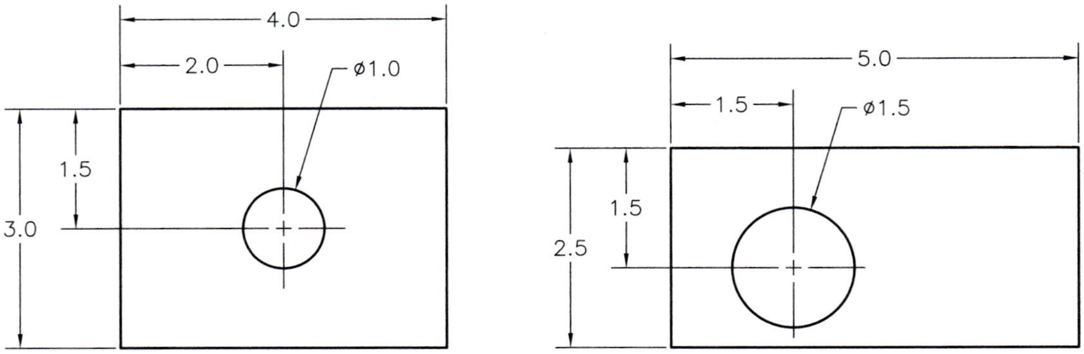

Original Object

Revised Drawing

NOTE

Associative dimensions in paper space attached to model space objects also automatically update when the object is edited.

Nonassociative dimensions can be converted to associative dimensions using the **DIMREASSOCIATE** command. To access this command, select **Reassociate Dimensions** from the **Dimension** pull-down menu or enter DRE or DIMREASSOCIATE at the Command: prompt. You are prompted to select the dimensions to be associated. After selecting the dimensions, an X marker appears at the first extension line endpoint. Select the point on an object with which to associate this extension line. Then, select the associated point for the second extension line.

DIMREASSOCIATE
DRE
Dimension
➡ Reassociate Dimensions

Use the **Next** option to advance to the next definition point. You can also use the **Select object** option to select an object with which to associate the dimension. The extension line endpoints are then automatically associated with the object endpoints.

To disassociate a dimension from an object, enter DDA or DISASSOCIATE at the Command: prompt and then select the dimension. The dimension objects will still be grouped together, but the dimension will not be associated with an object.

DISASSOCIATE
DDA

EXERCISE 18-7 Complete the Exercise on the Student CD.

Exploding an Associative Dimension

As previously discussed, the component parts of an associative dimension cannot be edited separately. An associative dimension is treated as one object even though it consists of extension lines, a dimension line, arrowheads, and text. At times, you may find it necessary to edit the individual parts. For example, you may want to erase the text without erasing the dimension line, arrowheads, or extension lines. To do this, you must first explode the dimension using the **EXPLODE** command.

Always be careful when exploding dimensions because they may lose their layer assignment. Also, an exploded dimension loses its association with the related feature.

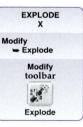

EXPLODE
X
Modify
➡ Explode
Modify toolbar
Explode

PROFESSIONAL TIP

One way to edit individual dimension properties without removing the associative dimensioning feature is to use the **Properties** window to create a dimension style override.

Dimension Definition Points

When you draw an associative dimension, the points used to specify the dimension location and the center point of the dimension text are called the ***definition points***, or ***defpoints***. When a dimension location is redefined, the revised position is based on the definition points. The definition points are located on the Defpoints layer. This layer is automatically created by AutoCAD. The definition points are displayed with the dimension.

Normally, the Defpoints layer does not plot. The definition points are plotted only if the Defpoints layer is renamed and the layer is set to plot. The definition points are displayed when the dimensioning layer is on, even if the Defpoints layer is turned off.

If you select an object for editing and wish to include the dimensions in the edit, then you must include the definition points of the dimension in the selection set. If you need to snap to a definition point only, use the **Node** object snap.

Chapter Test

Answer the following questions on a separate sheet of paper.

1. Name at least three selection options that can be used to easily erase a group of dimensions surrounding an object without erasing any part of the object.
2. Explain how you would add a diameter symbol to a dimension text value using the **DDEDIT** command.
3. Which command and option can you use to add a new baseline dimension to an existing set of baseline dimensions?
4. Define *associative dimension.*
5. Name the command that allows you to control the placement and orientation of an existing associative dimension text value.
6. What happens when you use the **New** option of the **DIMEDIT** command?
7. Name the **DIMEDIT** option that is used to change extension lines to an angle of your choice.
8. Which three command options related to dimension editing are available in the shortcut menu accessed when a dimension is selected?
9. Name three methods of changing the dimension style of a dimension.
10. How does the **Dimension Update** command affect selected dimensions?
11. Name three methods of copying dimension styles from the preview palette of the **DesignCenter** into the current drawing.
12. When using the **Properties** window to edit a dimension, what is the effect on the dimension style?
13. How do you access the **Property Settings** dialog box?
14. Why is it important to have associative dimensions for editing objects?
15. Describe the differences between the dimensions created using the three **DIMASSOC** settings.
16. Which **Options** dialog box setting controls associative dimensioning?
17. Which command is used to convert nonassociative dimensions to associative dimensions?
18. Which command is used to convert associative dimensions to nonassociative dimensions?
19. What are definition points?
20. On which layer are definition points automatically located by AutoCAD?

Drawing Problems

1. Open P17-1 and edit as follows.
   A. Erase the left side view.
   B. Stretch the vertical dimensions to provide more space between dimension lines. Be sure the space you create is the same between all vertical dimensions.
   C. Stagger the existing vertical dimension numbers if they are not staggered as shown in the original problem.
   D. Erase the 1.750 horizontal dimension and then stretch the 5.255 and 4.250 dimensions to make room for a new datum dimension from the baseline to where the 1.750 dimension was located. This should result in a new baseline dimension that equals 2.750. Be sure all horizontal dimension lines are equally spaced.
   E. Save the drawing as P18-1.
2. Open P17-2 and edit as follows.
   A. Stretch the total length from 3.500 to 4.000, leaving the holes the same distance from the edges.
   B. Fillet the upper-left corner. Modify the 3X R.250 dimension accordingly.
   C. Save the drawing as P18-2.
3. Open P17-4 and edit as follows.
   A. Use the existing drawing as the model and make four copies.
   B. Leave the original drawing as it is and edit the other four pins in the following manner, keeping the ∅.125 hole exactly in the center of each pin.
   C. Make one pin have a total length of 1.500.
   D. Create the next pin with a total length of 2.000.
   E. Edit the third pin to a length of 2.500.
   F. Change the last pin to a length of 3.000.
   G. Organize the pins on your drawing in a vertical row ranging in length from the smallest to the largest. You may need to change the drawing limits.
   H. Save the drawing as P18-3.
4. Open P17-5 and edit as follows.
   A. Modify the spline to have 12 projections, rather than eight.
   B. Change the angular dimension, linear dimension, and 8X dimension to reflect the modification.
   C. Save the drawing as P18-4.
5. Open P17-11 and edit as follows.
   A. Stretch the total length from 6.500 to 7.750.
   B. Add two more holes that continue the equally spaced pattern of .625 apart.
   C. Change the 8X .625(=5.00) dimension to read 10X .625(=6.250).
   D. Save the drawing as P18-5.
6. Open P17-13 and edit as follows.
   A. Make the bathroom 8′-0″ wide by stretching the walls and vanity that are currently 6′-0″ wide to 8′-0″. Do this without increasing the size of the water closet compartment. Provide two equally spaced oval sinks where there is currently one.
   B. Save the drawing as P18-6.

7. Open P17-19 and edit as follows.
   A. Lengthen the part .250 on each side for a new overall dimension of 6.500.
   B. Change the width of the part from 3.000 to 3.500 by widening an equal amount on each side.
   C. Save the drawing as P18-7.
8. Open P17-21 and edit as follows.
   A. Shorten the .75 thread on the left side to .50.
   B. Shorten the .388 hexagon length to .300.
   C. Save the drawing as P18-8.

CHAPTER 19

Dimensioning with Tolerances

Learning Objectives

After completing this chapter, you will be able to do the following:

- Define and use dimensioning and tolerancing terminology.
- Identify different types of tolerance dimensions.
- Create dimension styles with specified tolerance settings.
- Prepare drawings with dimensions and tolerances from engineering designs, sketches, and layouts.

This chapter discusses the basics of tolerancing and explains how to prepare dimensions with tolerances for mechanical manufacturing drawings. Chapter 17 introduced you to the creation of dimension styles and explained how to set the specifications for dimension geometry, fit format, primary units, alternate units, and text. Dimensioning for mechanical drafting usually uses the following AutoCAD settings, depending on company practices.

Lines and Arrows

- The dimension line spacing for baseline dimensioning is usually more than the .38 default.
- The extension line extension is .125 and the extension line offset is .0625.
- Arrowheads are closed filled, closed blank, closed, or open.
- A small dot is used on a leader pointing to a surface.
- The centerline option is used for center marks for circles and located arcs. Fillets and rounds generally have no center marks.

Fit Format

- The manually defined format is convenient for flexible text placement.
- The best fit option for text and arrows is common, but other format options work better for some applications.
- Horizontal and vertical justification is usually in centered format.
- Text placement is normally inside and outside horizontal for unidirectional dimensioning.

Primary Units, Text, and Tolerances

- Objects are dimensioned in inches or millimeters.
- The primary units are typically decimal with the number of decimal places controlled by the feature tolerance.
- Using alternate units for dual dimensioning is not a recommended ASME practice.
- The text is usually placed using the Romans font, a height of .125, and a gap of .0625.
- The tolerance method depends on the application.

Tolerancing Fundamentals

A ***tolerance*** is the total amount that a specific dimension is permitted to vary. A tolerance is not given to values identified as reference, maximum, minimum, or stock sizes. The tolerance may be applied directly to the dimension, indicated by a general note, or identified in the drawing title block. See **Figure 19-1.**

The ***limits*** of a dimension are the largest and smallest numerical values that the feature can be. In **Figure 19-2A,** the dimension is stated as 12.50±0.25. This is referred to as ***plus-minus dimensioning***. The tolerance of this dimension is the difference between the maximum and minimum limits. The upper limit is 12.75 (12.50 + 0.25), and the lower limit is 12.25 (12.50 – 0.25). If you take the upper limit and subtract the lower limit, the tolerance is .50.

The specified dimension is the part of the dimension from where the limits are calculated. The specified dimension of the feature shown in **Figure 19-2** is 12.50. A tolerance on a drawing may be displayed with plus-minus dimensioning, or the limits may be calculated and shown as in **Figure 19-2B.** Many schools and companies prefer the second method, which is called ***limits dimensioning***. This is because the limits are given and calculations are not required.

Figure 19-1.
Tolerances can be specified on the dimension, in a general note, or in the drawing title block.

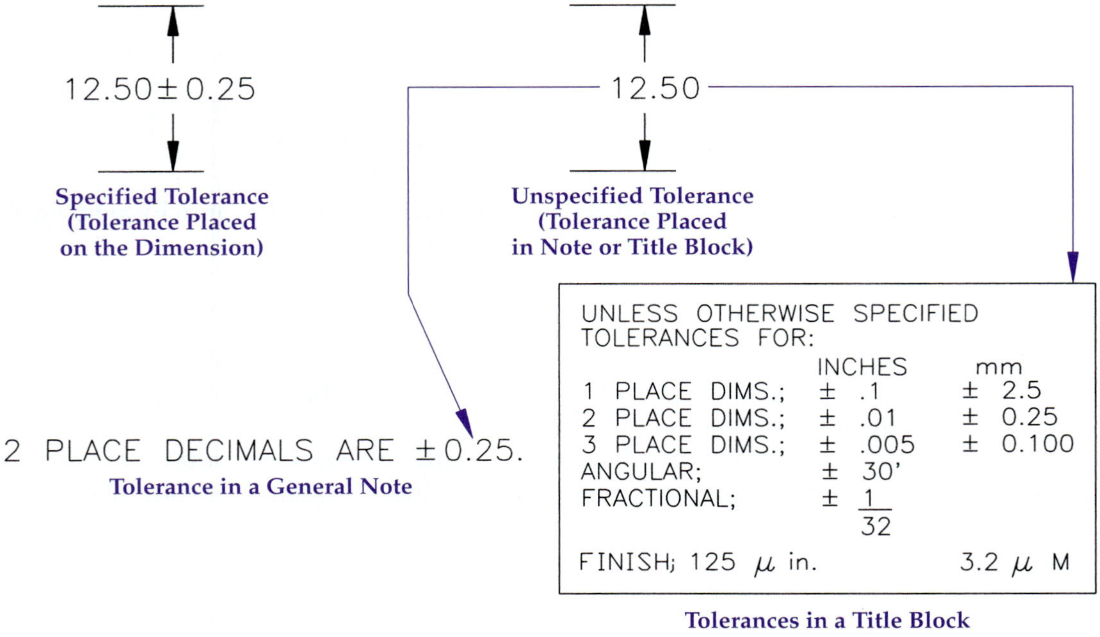

Figure 19-2.
Examples of plus-minus dimensioning and limits dimensioning.

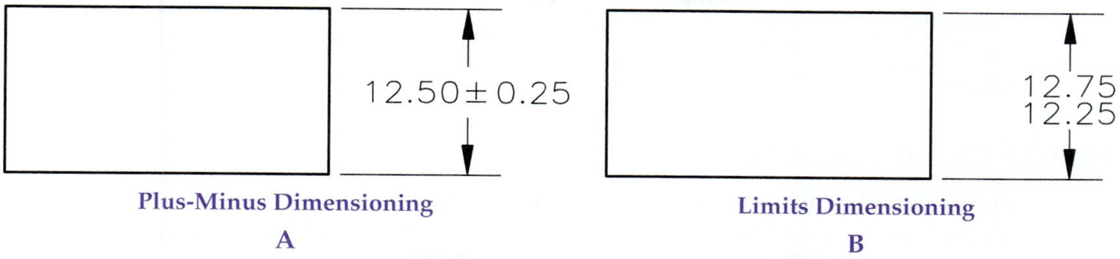

A ***bilateral tolerance*** permits variance in both the positive and negative directions from the specified dimension. An ***equal bilateral tolerance*** has the same variance in both directions. In an ***unequal bilateral tolerance***, the variance from the specified dimension is not the same in both directions. See **Figure 19-3.**

A ***unilateral tolerance*** is permitted to increase or decrease in only one direction from the specified dimension. See **Figure 19-4.**

Figure 19-3.
Examples of bilateral tolerances.

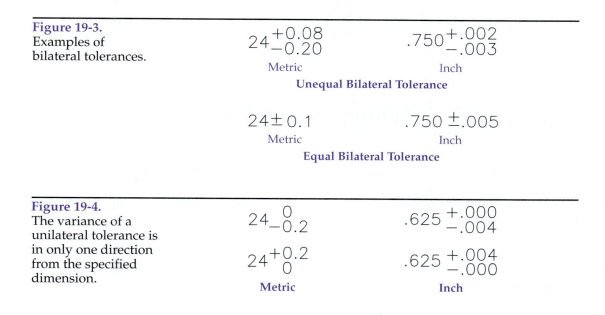

$24^{+0.08}_{-0.20}$ (Metric) $.750^{+.002}_{-.003}$ (Inch)

Unequal Bilateral Tolerance

24 ± 0.1 (Metric) $.750 \pm .005$ (Inch)

Equal Bilateral Tolerance

Figure 19-4.
The variance of a unilateral tolerance is in only one direction from the specified dimension.

Metric	Inch
$24^{0}_{-0.2}$	$.625^{+.000}_{-.004}$
$24^{+0.2}_{0}$	$.625^{+.004}_{-.000}$

Assigning Decimal Places to Dimensions and Tolerances

The standard, ASME Y14.5M—*Dimensioning and Tolerancing*, has separate recommendations for the way the number of decimal places is displayed for inch and metric dimensions. Examples of decimal dimension values in inches and metric units are shown in **Figure 19-3** and **Figure 19-4.** The following are some general rules.

Inch Dimensioning

- A specified inch dimension is expressed to the same number of decimal places as its tolerance. Zeros are added to the right of the decimal point if needed. For example, the inch dimension .250±.005 has an additional zero added to the .25 to match the three-decimal tolerance. Similarly, the dimensions 2.000±.005 and 2.500±.005 both have zeros added to match the tolerance.

- Both values in a plus and minus tolerance for an inch dimension have the same number of decimal places. Zeros are added to fill in where needed. For example:

  +.005 *not* +.005
  –.010 –.01

Metric Dimensioning

- The decimal point and zeros are omitted from the dimension when the metric dimension is a whole number. For example, the metric dimension 12 has no decimal point followed by a zero. This rule is true unless tolerance values are displayed.
- When a metric dimension includes a decimal portion, the last digit to the right of the decimal point is not followed by a zero. For example, the metric dimension 12.5 has no zero to the right of the 5. This rule is true unless tolerance values are displayed.
- Both values in a plus and minus tolerance for a metric dimension have the same number of decimal places. Zeros are added to fill in where needed.
- Zeros are not added after the specified dimension to match the tolerance. For example, both 24±0.25 and 24.5±0.25 are correct. However, some companies prefer to add zeros after the specified dimension to match the tolerance, in which case 24.00±0.25 and 24.50±0.25 are both correct.

Setting Primary Units

DDIM
D

Format
➥ Dimension Style

Dimension toolbar

Dimension Style

As discussed in Chapter 17, a dimension style can be created with specific formatting, justification, and text settings. The **Dimension Style Manager** dialog box is used to create dimension styles. See Figure 19-5. This dialog box is accessed by picking the **Dimension Style** button on the **Dimension** toolbar, picking **Dimension Style...** from the **Format** pull-down menu, or entering D or DDIM at the Command: prompt.

In the **Dimension Style Manager** dialog box, highlight the style you want to modify and pick the **Modify...** button to access the **Modify Dimension Style** dialog box. The **Primary Units** tab is used to set the type of units and precision of the dimension. See Figure 19-6A. The **Tolerances** tab allows you to set the tolerance format values. See Figure 19-6B.

Figure 19-5.
The **Dimension Style Manager** dialog box.

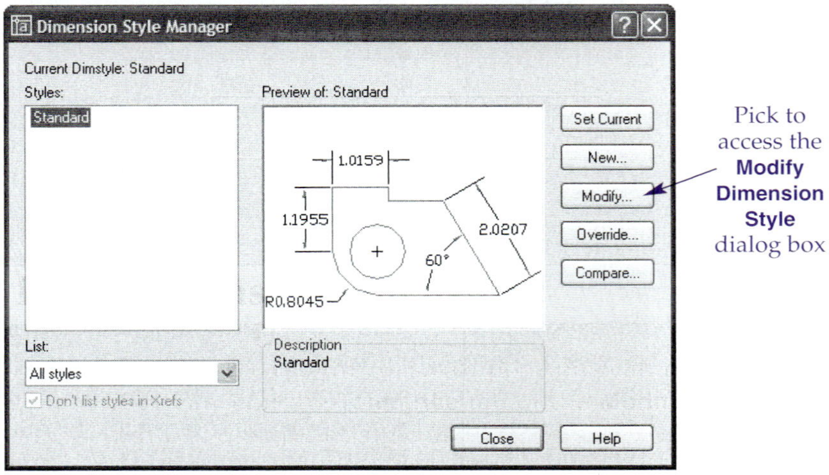

Figure 19-6.
A—Settings for the unit format and precision of linear dimensions are located in the **Primary Units** tab. B—The **Tolerances** tab contains formatting settings for tolerance dimensions.

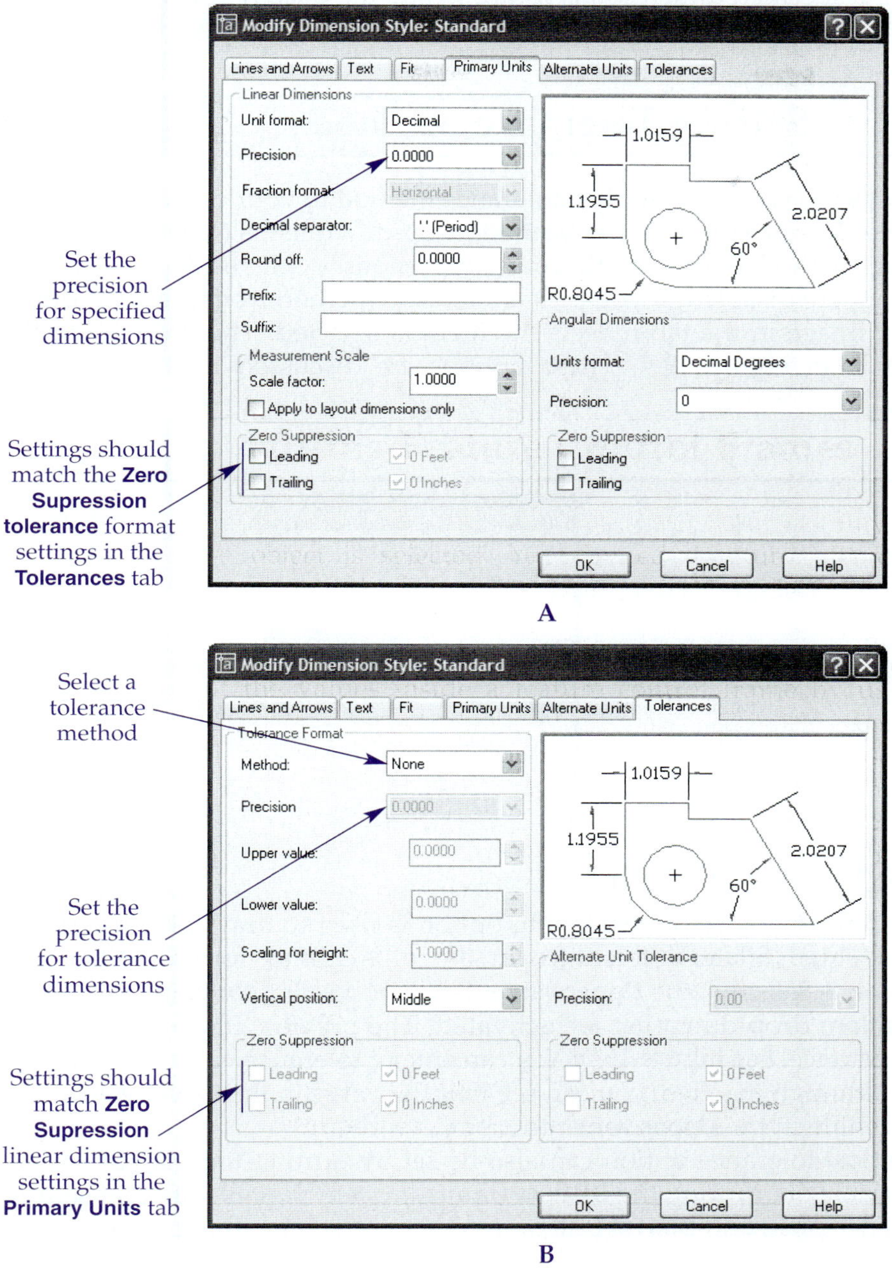

Set the precision for specified dimensions
Settings should match the Zero Supression tolerance format settings in the Tolerances tab
A
Select a tolerance method
Set the precision for tolerance dimensions
Settings should match Zero Supression linear dimension settings in the Primary Units tab
B

In the **Linear Dimensions** area of the **Primary Units** tab, the **Precision** drop-down list allows you to specify the number of zeros displayed after the decimal point of the specified dimension. The ASME standard recommends that the precision for the dimension and the tolerance be the same for inch dimensions, but it may be different for metric values, as previously discussed. After setting the primary unit precision, AutoCAD will automatically make the default for the tolerance precision in the **Tolerances** tab the same.

The **Zero Suppression** settings were explained in Chapter 17. The suppression settings for linear dimensions in the **Primary Units** tab should be the same as the **Zero Suppression** tolerance format settings in the **Tolerances** tab. For example, the **Leading** options should be off and the **Trailing** options should be on for metric dimensions. For inch dimensions, the **Leading** options should be on and the **Trailing** options should be off. AutoCAD does not automatically match the tolerance setting to the primary units setting. Changing the tolerance zero suppression is discussed later in this chapter. Zero suppression for the specified dimension is controlled by the **DIMZIN** system variable.

Setting Tolerance Methods

The **Tolerances** tab is used to apply a tolerance method to your drawing. Refer to Figure 19-6B. The default option in the **Method:** drop-down list is None. This means that no tolerance method is used with your dimensions. As a result, most of the options in this area are disabled. If you pick a tolerance method from the drop-down list, the resulting image in the tab reflects the method selected. The drop-down list options are shown in Figure 19-7. These options are discussed in the following sections.

Figure 19-7.
A tolerance dimensioning method can be selected from the options in the **Method:** drop-down list, located in the **Tolerance Format** area of the **Tolerances** tab.

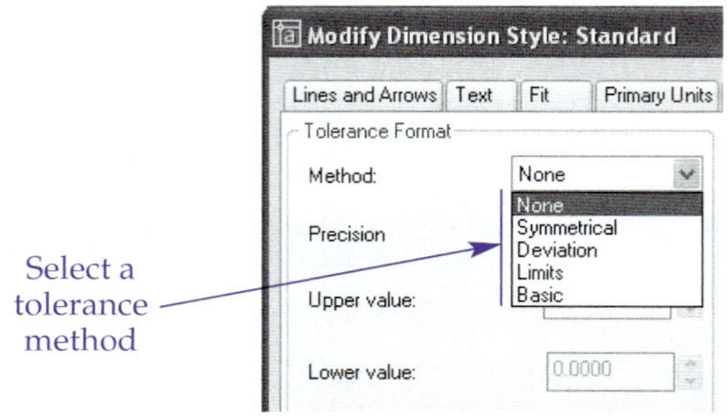

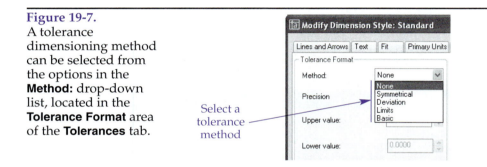

Symmetrical Tolerance Method

The **Symmetrical** tolerance dimensioning option is used to draw dimension text that displays an equal bilateral tolerance in the plus/minus format. When the **Symmetrical** option is selected, the **Upper value:** text box, **Scaling for height:** text box, and **Vertical position:** drop-down list are activated. The preview image displays an equal bilateral tolerance. See Figure 19-8. You can enter a tolerance value in the **Upper value:** text box. Although inactive, you can see that the value in the **Lower value:** text box matches the value in the **Upper value:** text box.

The **Symmetrical** tolerance option can also be set by turning the **DIMTOL** (tolerance) system variable on, turning the **DIMLIM** (limits) system variable off, and setting the **DIMTP** (tolerance plus) and **DIMTM** (tolerance minus) system variables to the same numerical value.

NOTE When you turn the **DIMTOL** system variable on, **DIMLIM** is automatically turned off. When you turn **DIMLIM** on, **DIMTOL** is automatically turned off.

EXERCISE 19-1 Complete the Exercise on the Student CD.

Figure 19-8.
Setting the **Symmetrical** tolerance method option current with an equal bilateral tolerance value of 0.005.

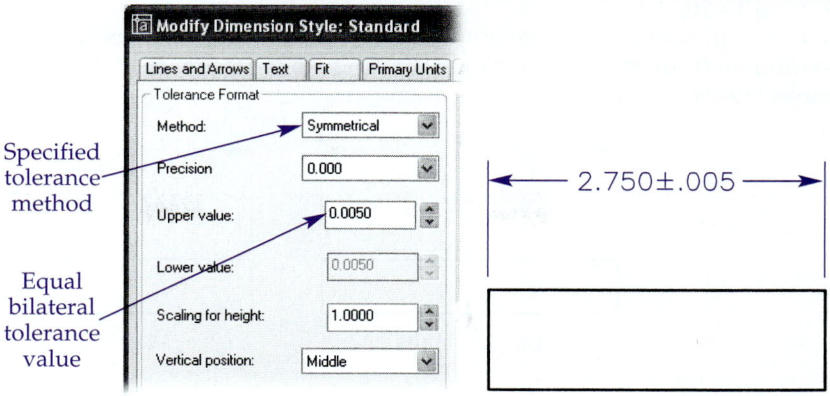

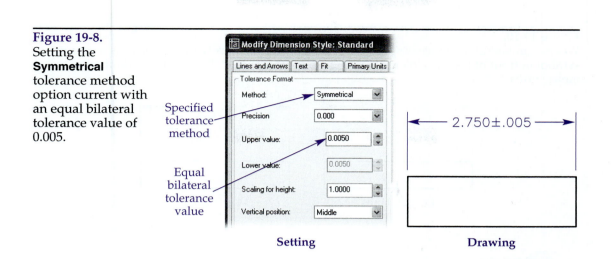

Setting   Drawing

Deviation Tolerance Method

AutoCAD refers to an unequal bilateral tolerance as a ***deviation.*** This means that the tolerance deviates (departs) from the specified dimension with two different values. The deviation tolerance method can be set by selecting **Deviation** in **Method:** drop-down list of the **Tolerances** tab. After selecting this option, the **Upper value:** and **Lower value:** text boxes are activated so that you can enter the desired upper and lower tolerance values. See Figure 19-9. The preview image in the tab changes to match a representation of an unequal bilateral tolerance.

The **Deviation** option can also be used to draw a unilateral tolerance by entering zero for either the **Upper value:** or **Lower value:** setting. If you are using inch units, AutoCAD includes the plus or minus sign before the zero tolerance. When metric units are used, the sign is omitted for the zero tolerance. See Figure 19-10.

The **Deviation** tolerance method option can also be set by turning the **DIMTOL** system variable on or the **DIMLIM** system variable off and setting the **DIMTP** and **DIMTM** system variables to different numerical values.

> NOTE
>
> The **MEASUREMENT** system variable is used to change between English (inch) units and metric units. If the variable is set to 0, English units are active. A setting of 1 corresponds to metric units.

Figure 19-9.
Setting the **Deviation** tolerance method option current with unequal bilateral tolerance values.

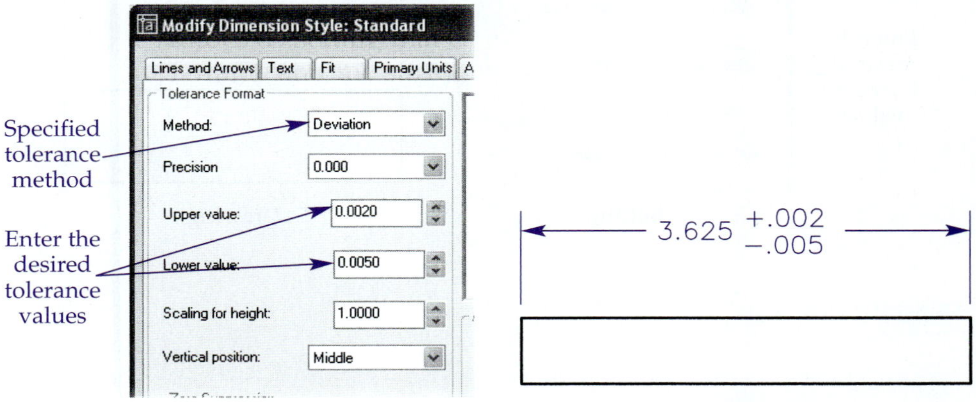

Setting   Drawing

Figure 19-10.
When a unilateral tolerance is specified, AutoCAD automatically places the plus or minus symbol in front of the zero tolerance if English units are used. The symbol is omitted with metric units.

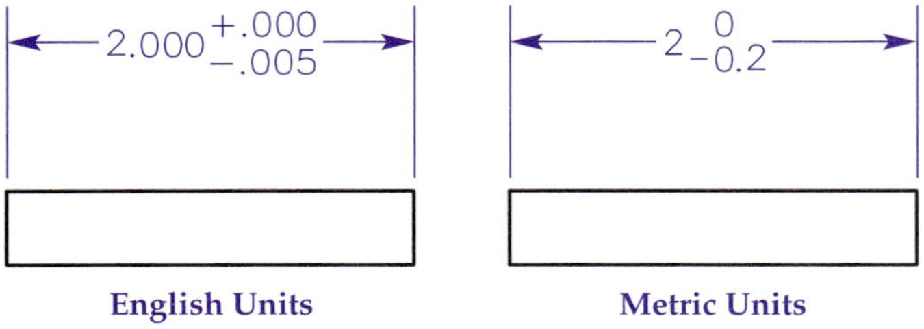

EXERCISE 19-2 Complete the Exercise on the Student CD.

Limits Tolerance Method

In limits dimensioning, the tolerance limits are given and no calculations from the specified dimension are required (unlike plus-minus dimensioning). The limits tolerance method can be set by picking **Limits** in the **Method:** drop-down list in the **Tolerances** tab. When this option is set, the **Upper value:** and **Lower value:** text boxes are activated. You can then enter the desired upper and lower tolerance values that are added and subtracted from the specified dimension. The values you enter can be the same or different. See Figure 19-11.

EXERCISE 19-3 Complete the Exercise on the Student CD.

Figure 19-11.
Selecting the **Limits** tolerance method and setting limit values.

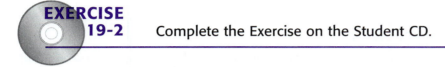

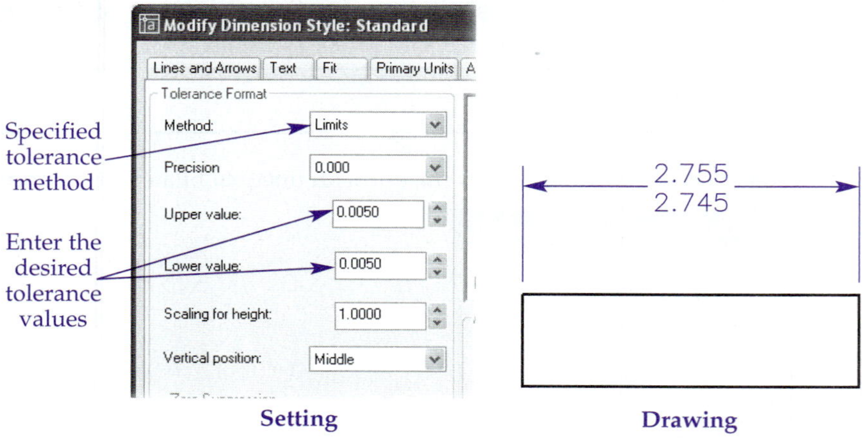

Basic Tolerance Method

The basic tolerance method is used to draw basic dimensions. A ***basic dimension*** is considered to be a theoretically perfect dimension and is used in geometric dimensioning and tolerancing, which is covered in Chapter 20. The basic tolerance method can be set by picking **Basic** in the **Method:** drop-down list in the **Tolerances** tab. With this setting, the **Upper value:** and **Lower value:** options in the **Tolerance Format** area are disabled because a basic dimension has no tolerance. A basic dimension is distinguished from other dimensions by a rectangle placed around the dimension number, as shown in Figure 19-12.

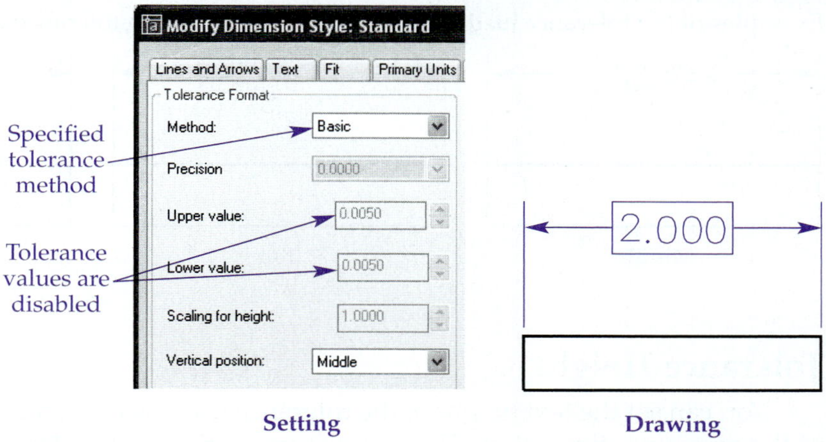

Figure 19-12. The **Basic** tolerance method is used for basic dimensioning. The dimension text for a basic dimension is placed inside a rectangle.

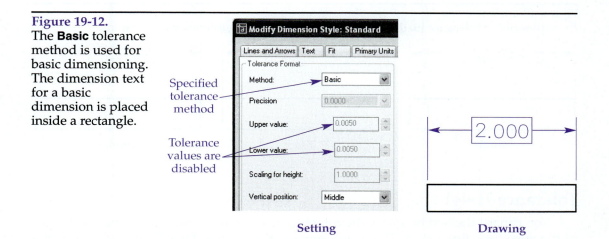

Tolerance Precision and Zero Suppression

After a tolerance method is specified in the **Method:** drop-down list of the **Tolerances** tab, you can set the precision of the tolerance. By default, this setting matches the precision in the **Primary Units** tab. If the setting does not reflect the level of precision you want, change it using the **Precision** drop-down list in the **Tolerance Format** area. The tolerance precision setting is stored in the **DIMTDEC** system variable.

As is the case with the precision settings, a tolerance method must be selected before the **Zero Suppression** tolerance format options can be specified. AutoCAD does not automatically match the tolerance setting to the primary units setting. Zero suppression for the tolerance dimension is controlled by the **DIMTZIN** system variable.

Tolerance Method Review

- ✓ Each tolerance method option you pick is represented by an image preview in the **Modify Dimension Style** dialog box.
- ✓ When drawing inch tolerance dimensions, you should activate the **Leading Zero Suppression** tolerance format option in the **Tolerances** tab. The same option should be activated for linear dimensions in the **Primary Units** tab. You can then properly draw inch tolerance dimensions without placing the zero before the decimal point, as recommended by ASME standards. These settings would allow you to draw a tolerance dimension such as .625±.005.
- ✓ When drawing metric tolerance dimensions, deactivate the **Leading Zero Suppression** tolerance format option in the **Tolerances** tab. Deactivate the same option for linear dimensions in the **Primary Units** tab. This allows you to place a metric tolerance dimension with the zero before the decimal point, as recommended by ASME standards (for example, a dimension such as 12±0.2).

Tolerance Justification

You can control the alignment, or justification, of deviation tolerance dimensions using the options in the **Vertical position:** drop-down list in the **Tolerance Format** area of the **Tolerances** tab. The **Middle** option centers the tolerance with the specified dimension and is the default. This is also the recommended ASME practice. The other justification options are **Top** and **Bottom**. Deviation tolerance dimensions displaying each of the justification options are shown in **Figure 19-13.** The justification for deviation tolerance dimensions is controlled by the **DIMTOLJ** system variable.

Figure 19-13.
Examples of the tolerance justification options for deviation tolerance dimensions.

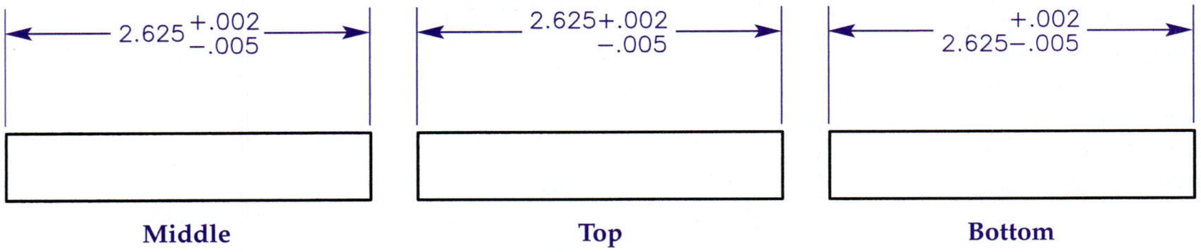

Tolerance Height

You can set the text height of the tolerance dimension in relation to the text height of the specified dimension. This is done using the **Scaling for height:** text box in the **Tolerance Format** area of the **Tolerances** tab. The default of 1.0000 makes the tolerance dimension text the same height as the specified dimension text. This is the recommended ASME standard. If you want the tolerance dimension height to be three-quarters as high as the specified dimension height, enter .75 in the **Scaling for height:** text box. Some companies prefer this practice to keep the tolerance part of the dimension from taking up additional space. Examples of tolerance dimensions with different text heights are shown in **Figure 19-14.** The tolerance text height is controlled by the **DIMTFAC** system variable.

Figure 19-14.
Using different scale settings for the text height of tolerance dimensions.

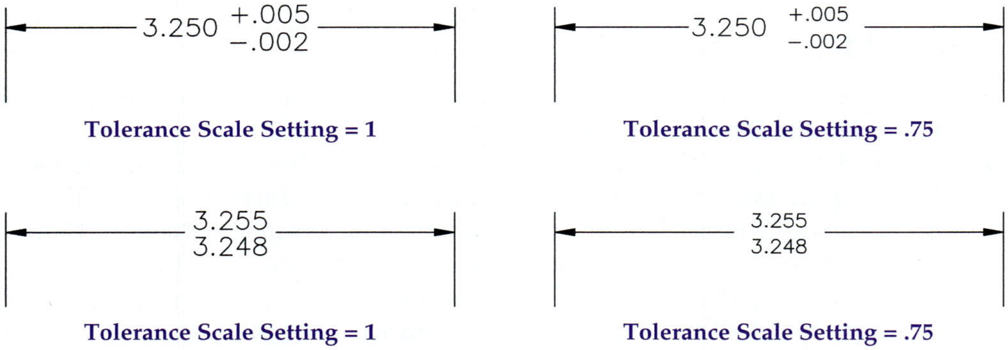

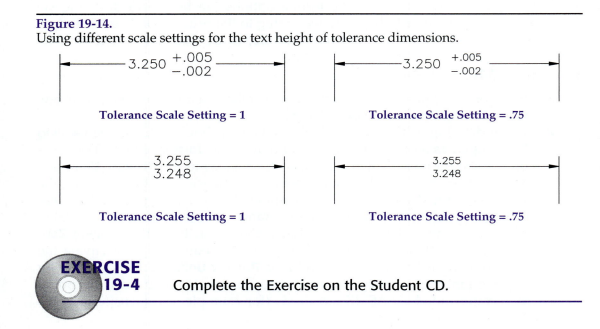

EXERCISE 19-4 Complete the Exercise on the Student CD.

Chapter Test

Answer the following questions on a separate sheet of paper.

1. Define the term *tolerance.*
2. Give an example of an equal bilateral tolerance in inches and in metric units.
3. Give an example of an unequal bilateral tolerance in inches and in metric units.
4. What are the limits of the tolerance dimension 3.625±.005?
5. Give an example of a unilateral tolerance in inches and in metric units.
6. Which dialog box is used to create dimension styles? How is it accessed?
7. How do you open the **Tolerances** tab?
8. How do you set the number of zeros displayed after the decimal point for a tolerance dimension?
9. Which zero suppression settings should be specified for linear and tolerance dimensions when using metric units?
10. Which zero suppression settings should be specified for linear and tolerance dimensions when using inch units?
11. What is the purpose of the **Symmetrical** tolerance method option?
12. What is the purpose of the **Deviation** tolerance method option?
13. What is the purpose of the **Limits** tolerance method option?
14. What happens to the preview image in the **Tolerances** tab when a tolerance method option is picked from the **Method:** drop-down list?
15. Name the tolerance dimension justification option recommended by the ASME standard.
16. Explain the results of setting the **Scaling for height:** option to 1 in the **Tolerances** tab.
17. What setting would you use for the **Scaling for height:** option if you wanted the tolerance dimension height to be three-quarters of the specified dimension height?

Drawing Problems

Set the limits, units, dimension style options, and other parameters as needed for the following problems. Use the guidelines given below.

A. Draw and dimension the necessary views for the following drawings to exact size. These problems are presented in 3D; draw the proper 2D views for each.

B. Apply dimensions accurately using ASME standards. Create dimension styles that suit the specific needs of each drawing. For example, save different dimension styles for metric and inch dimensions.

C. Create separate layers for the views and dimensions.

D. Plot the drawings with 0.6 mm object lines and 0.3 mm thin lines.

E. Place the following general notes in the lower-left corner of each drawing.

3. UNLESS OTHERWISE SPECIFIED, ALL DIMENSIONS ARE IN MILLIMETERS. *(or* INCHES *as applicable)*
2. REMOVE ALL BURRS AND SHARP EDGES.
1. INTERPRET PER ASME Y14.5M-1994.

NOTES:

F. Save the drawings as P19-1, P19-2, and so on.

1.

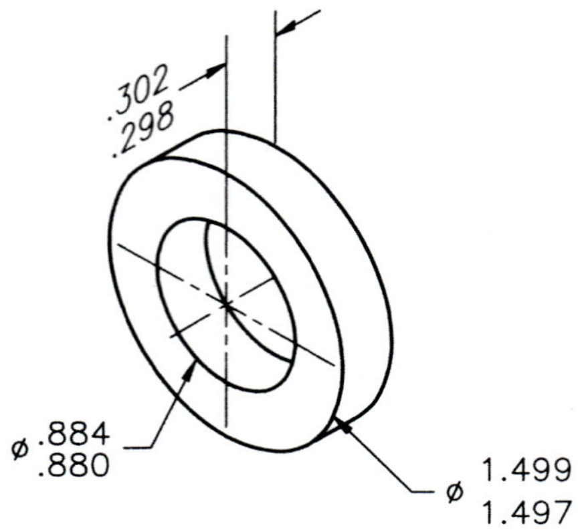

Title: Washer
Material: SAE 1020
Inch

2.

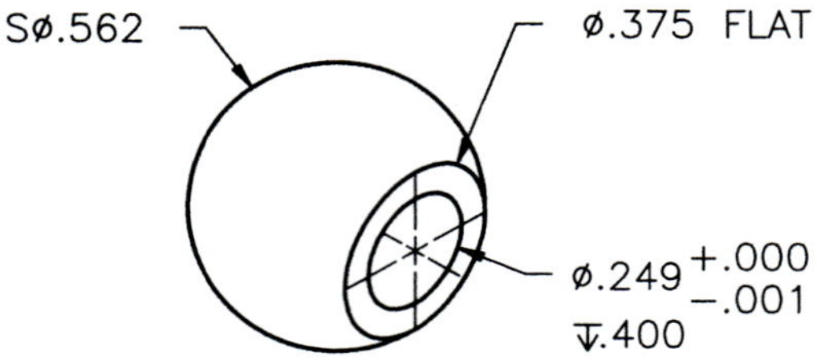

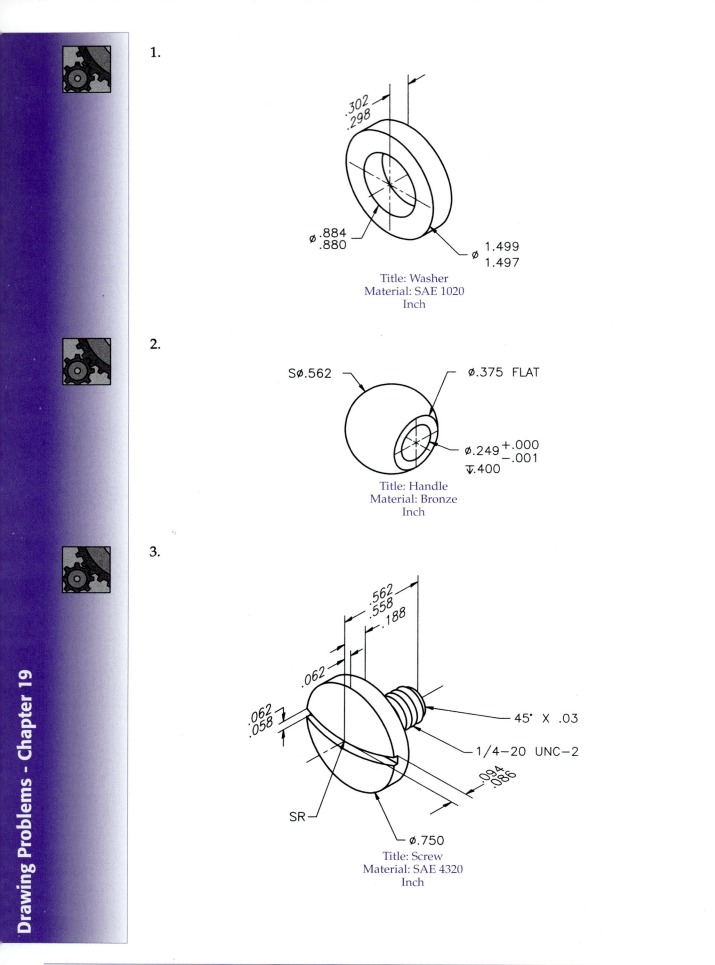

Title: Handle
Material: Bronze
Inch

3.

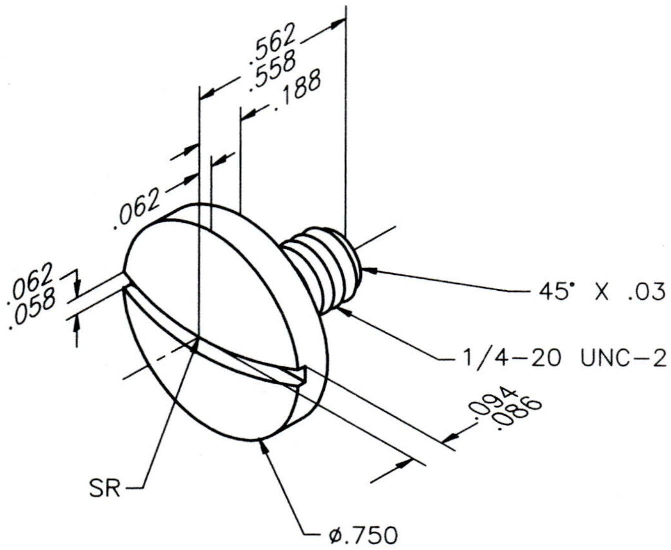

Title: Screw
Material: SAE 4320
Inch

4.

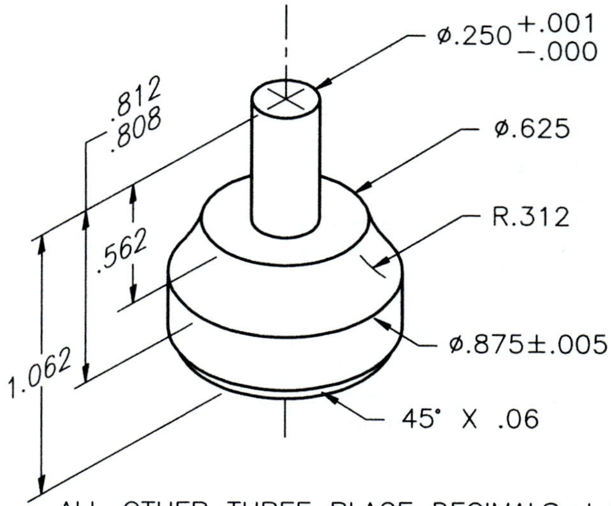

ALL OTHER THREE PLACE DECIMALS ±.010

Title: Pin
Material: Mild Steel
Inch

5. This object is shown as a section for clarity. Do not draw a section.

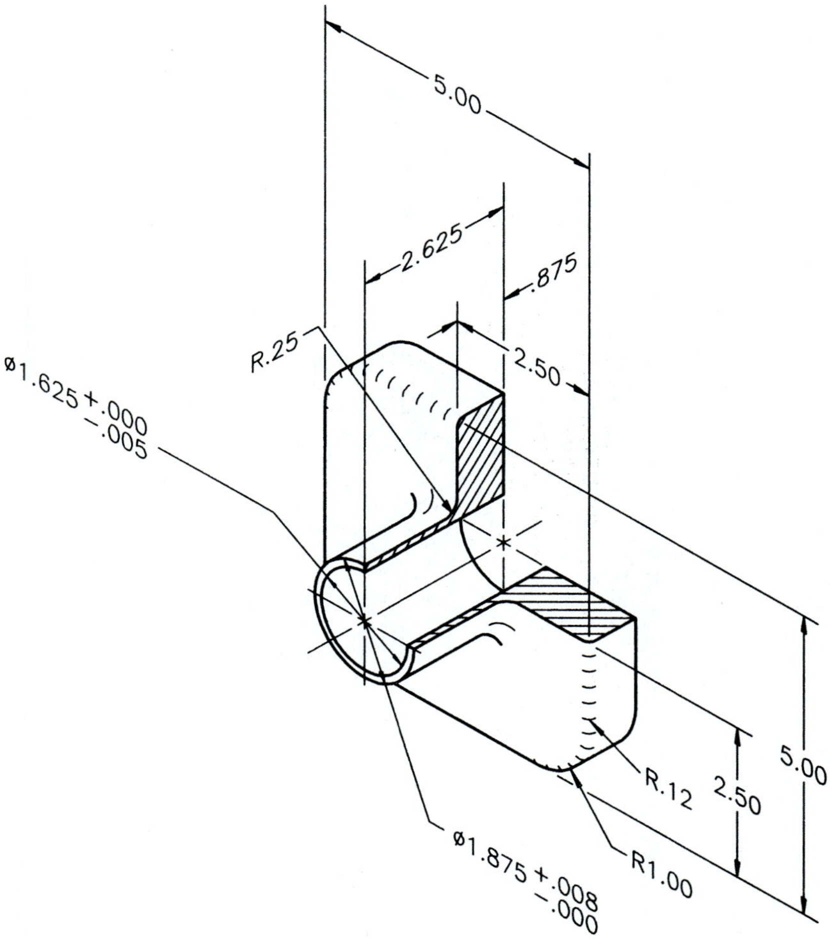

Title: Thrust Washer
Material: SAE 5150
Inch

6.

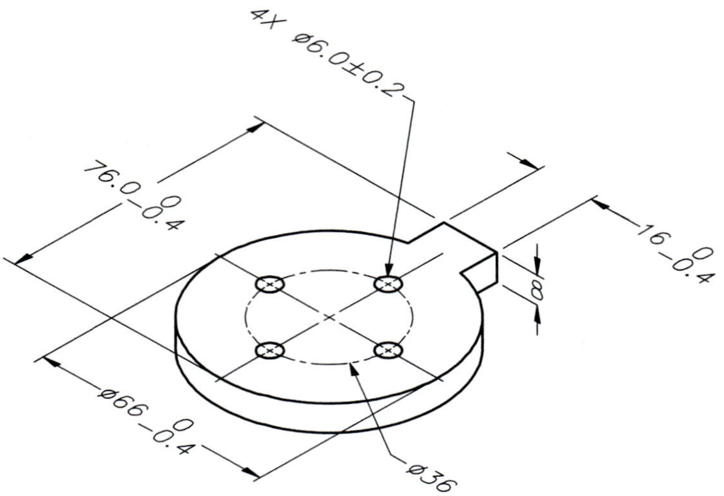

Title: Spacer
Material: Cold Rolled Steel
Metric

7.

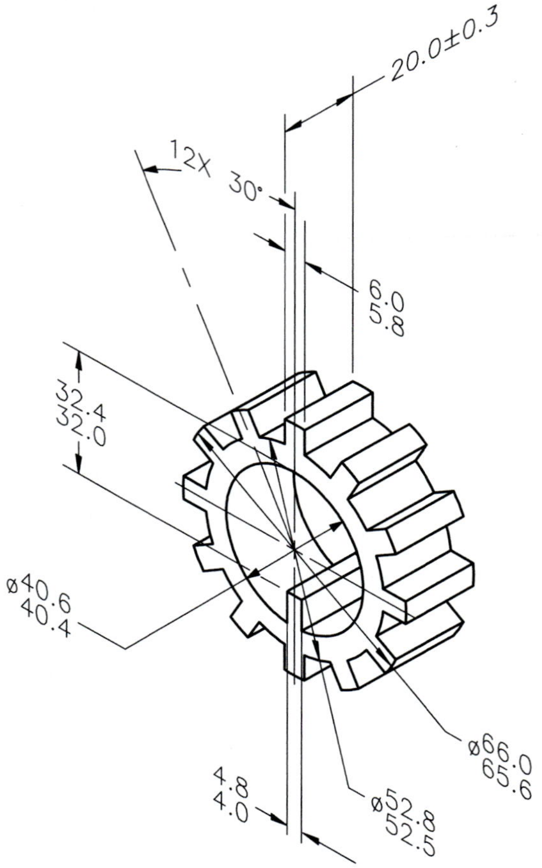

Title: Locking Collar
Material: SAE 1080
Metric

CHAPTER 20

Geometric Dimensioning and Tolerancing

Learning Objectives

After completing this chapter, you will be able to do the following:

- Identify symbols used in geometric dimensioning and tolerancing.
- Use the **TOLERANCE**, **QLEADER**, and **LEADER** commands to create geometric tolerancing symbols.
- Draw and edit feature control frames.
- Draw datum feature symbols.
- Place basic dimensions on a drawing.

This chapter is an introduction to geometric dimensioning and tolerancing (GD&T) principles as adopted by the American National Standards Institute (ANSI) and published by the American Society of Mechanical Engineers (ASME) for engineering and related document practices. The standard is ASME Y14.5M-1994, *Dimensioning and Tolerancing*. ***Geometric tolerancing*** is a general term that refers to tolerances used to control the form, profile, orientation, runout, and location of features on an object.

The drafting applications covered in this chapter use the AutoCAD geometric tolerancing capabilities and additional recommendations to comply with the ASME Y14.5M-1994 standard. This chapter is only an introduction to geometric dimensioning and tolerancing. For complete coverage of GD&T, refer to *Geometric Dimensioning and Tolerancing* published by Goodheart-Willcox Publisher. Before beginning this chapter, it is recommended that you have a solid understanding of dimensioning and tolerancing standards and AutoCAD applications. This introductory material is presented in Chapters 17, 18, and 19 of this text.

The discussion in this chapter divides the dimensioning and geometric tolerancing symbols into five basic types:

- Dimensioning symbols.
- Geometric characteristic symbols.
- Material condition symbols.
- Feature control frames.
- Datum feature symbols.

When you draw GD&T symbols, it is recommended that you place them on a dimensioning layer so the symbols and text can be plotted as lines that have the same thickness as extension and dimension lines (.01″ or .3 mm). The suggested text font is Romans. These practices correspond with the standard ASME Y14.2M-1992, *Line Conventions and Lettering*.

Dimensioning Symbols

Symbols represent specific information that would be difficult and time-consuming to duplicate in note form. Symbols must be clearly drawn to the required size and shape so they communicate the desired information uniformly. Symbols are recommended by ASME Y14.5M because they are an international language; they are read the same way in any country. In an international economy, it is important to have effective communication on engineering drawings. Symbols make this communication process uniform. ASME Y14.5M also states that the adoption of dimensioning symbols does not prevent the use of equivalent terms or abbreviations in situations where symbols are considered inappropriate.

Symbols aid in clarity, presentation of the drawing, and reduction of drawing time. Creating and using AutoCAD symbols is covered later in this chapter and in Chapter 22. A sample group of recommended dimensioning symbols is shown in **Figure 20-1.**

Figure 20-1.
Dimensioning symbols recommended by ASME Y14.5M-1994.

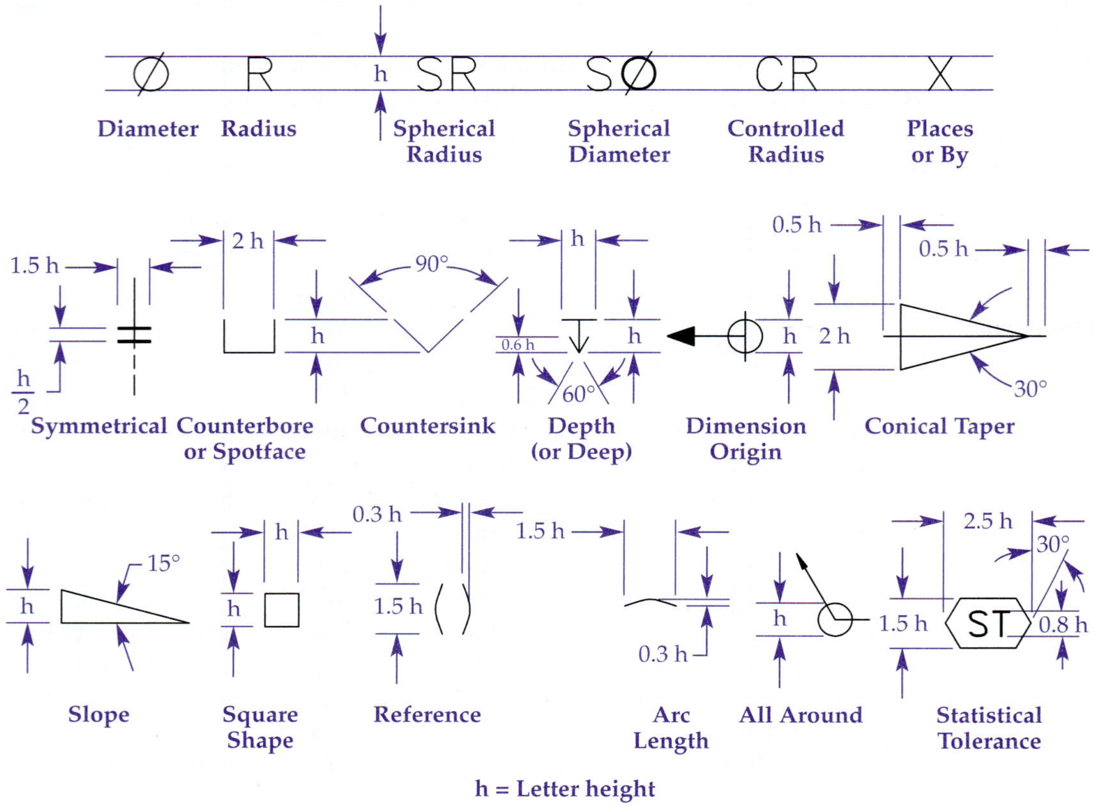

Geometric Characteristic Symbols

In GD&T, symbols are used to provide specific controls related to the form of an object, orientation of features, outlines of features, relationship of features to an axis, or location of features. These symbols are known as ***geometric characteristic*** symbols. Geometric characteristic symbols are separated into five types: form, profile, location, orientation, and runout. See **Figure 20-2.**

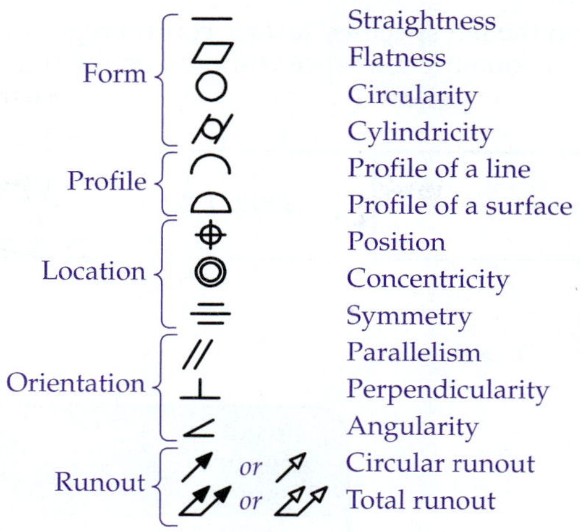

Figure 20-2. Geometric characteristic symbols recommended by ASME Y14.5M-1994.

Material Condition Symbols

Material condition symbols are often referred to as *modifying symbols* because they modify the geometric tolerance in relation to the produced size or location of the feature. Material condition symbols are only used in geometric dimensioning applications. The symbols used in a feature control frame to indicate maximum material condition (MMC) or least material condition (LMC) are shown in **Figure 20-3.** Regardless of feature size (RFS) is also a material condition. However, there is no symbol for RFS because it is assumed for all geometric tolerances and datum references unless MMC or LMC is specified.

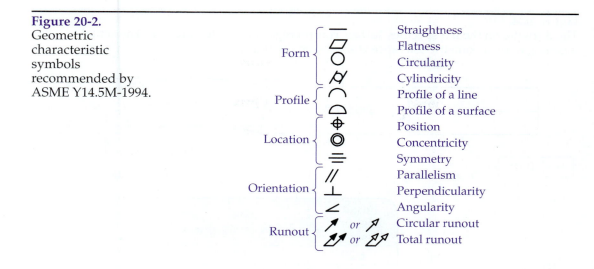

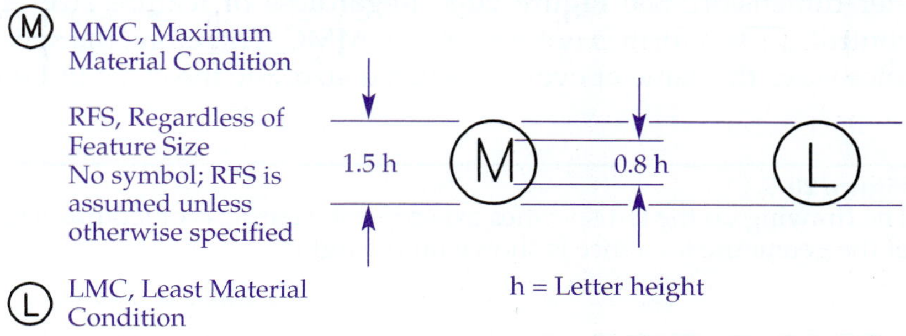

Figure 20-3. Material condition symbols. In ASME Y14.5M-1994, there is no symbol for RFS since it is assumed unless otherwise specified.

Surface Control, Regardless of Feature Size

Regardless of feature size is assumed as the material condition when there is no material condition symbol following the geometric tolerance in a feature control frame. ***Regardless of feature size (RFS)*** means the geometric tolerances remain the same regardless of the actual produced size. The term ***produced size,*** when used here, means the actual size of the feature when measured after manufacture.

When a feature control frame is connected to a feature surface with a leader or an extension line, it is referred to as ***surface control.*** See **Figure 20-4.** The geometric characteristic symbol shown is straightness, but the application is the same for any characteristic.

Look at the chart in **Figure 20-4** and notice how the possible sizes range from 6.20 (MMC) to 5.80 (LMC). With surface control, perfect form is required at MMC. ***Perfect form*** means the object cannot exceed a true geometric form boundary established at

Figure 20-4.
The drawing on the left specifies surface control regardless of feature size. The actual meaning of the geometric tolerance is shown on the right.

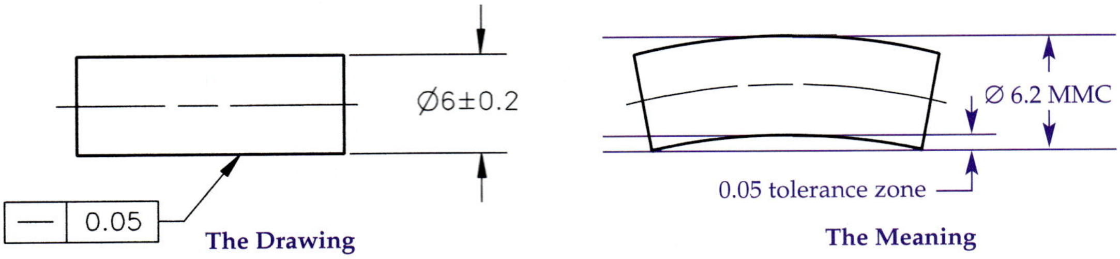

	Possible produced sizes	Maximum out-of-straightness
MMC	6.20	* 0
	6.10	0.05
	6.00	0.05
	5.90	0.05
LMC	5.80	0.05

* Perfect form required

maximum material condition. The geometric tolerance at MMC is zero, as shown in the chart. As the produced size varies from MMC in the chart, the geometric tolerance increases until it equals the amount specified in the feature control frame.

Axis Control, Regardless of Feature Size

Axis control is indicated when the feature control frame is shown with a diameter dimension. See **Figure 20-5.** Regardless of feature size is assumed. With axis control, perfect form is not required at MMC. Therefore, the specified geometric tolerance stays the same at every produced size. See the chart in **Figure 20-5.**

Figure 20-5.
The drawing on the left specifies axis control regardless of feature size. The actual meaning of the geometric tolerance is shown on the right.

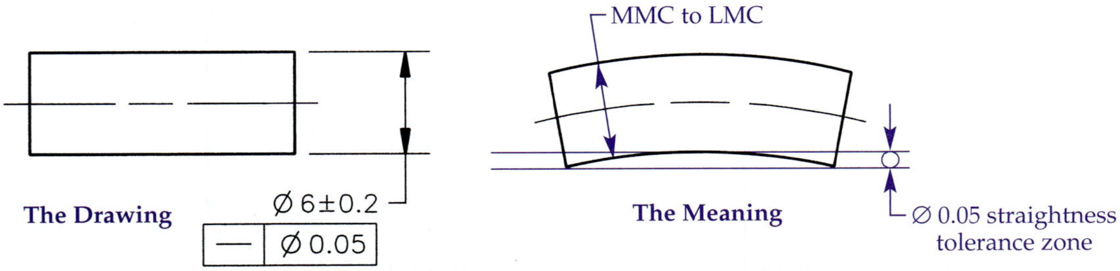

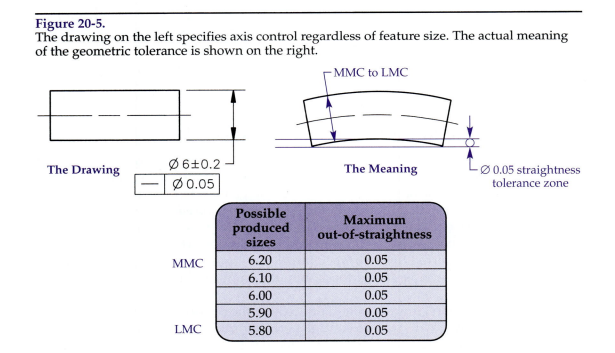

	Possible produced sizes	Maximum out-of-straightness
MMC	6.20	0.05
	6.10	0.05
	6.00	0.05
	5.90	0.05
LMC	5.80	0.05

Maximum Material Condition Control

If the material condition control is ***maximum material condition (MMC)***, the symbol for MMC must be placed in the feature control frame. See **Figure 20-6.** When this application is used, the specified geometric tolerance is held at the maximum material condition produced size. See the chart in **Figure 20-6.** Then, as the produced size varies from MMC, the geometric tolerance increases equal to the change. The maximum geometric tolerance is at the LMC produced size.

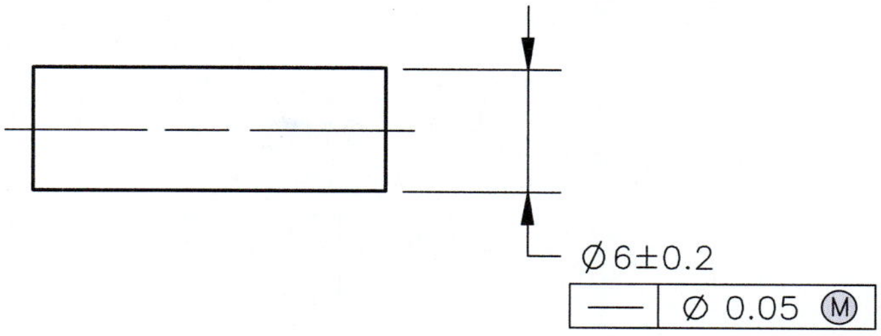

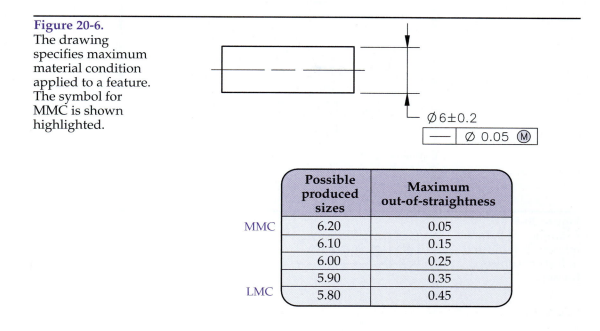

Figure 20-6.
The drawing specifies maximum material condition applied to a feature. The symbol for MMC is shown highlighted.

	Possible produced sizes	Maximum out-of-straightness
MMC	6.20	0.05
	6.10	0.15
	6.00	0.25
	5.90	0.35
LMC	5.80	0.45

Least Material Condition Control

If the material condition control is ***least material condition (LMC)***, the symbol for LMC must be placed in the feature control frame. When this application is used, the specified geometric tolerance is held at the least material condition produced size. Then, as the produced size varies from LMC, the geometric tolerance increases equal to the change. The maximum geometric tolerance is at the MMC produced size.

Feature Control Frame

The geometric characteristic, geometric tolerance, material condition, and datum reference (if any) for an individual feature are specified by means of a feature control frame. The ***feature control frame*** is divided into compartments containing the geometric characteristic symbol in the first compartment, followed by the geometric tolerance. Where applicable, the geometric tolerance is preceded by the diameter symbol, which describes the shape of the tolerance zone, and is followed by a material condition symbol (if other than RFS). See **Figure 20-7.**

When a geometric tolerance is related to one or more datums, the datum reference letters are placed in compartments following the geometric tolerance. ***Datums*** are considered theoretically perfect surfaces, planes, points, or axes. When there is a multiple datum reference, both datum reference letters are separated by a dash and placed in a single compartment after the geometric tolerance. A ***multiple datum reference*** is established by two datum features, such as an axis established by two datum diameters. Several feature control frames with datum references are shown in **Figure 20-8.**

Figure 20-7.
Feature control frames containing the geometric characteristic symbol, geometric tolerance, and diameter symbol (as applicable). There is no material condition symbol for RFS since it is assumed. Note that the geometric tolerance is expressed as a total, not a plus-minus value.

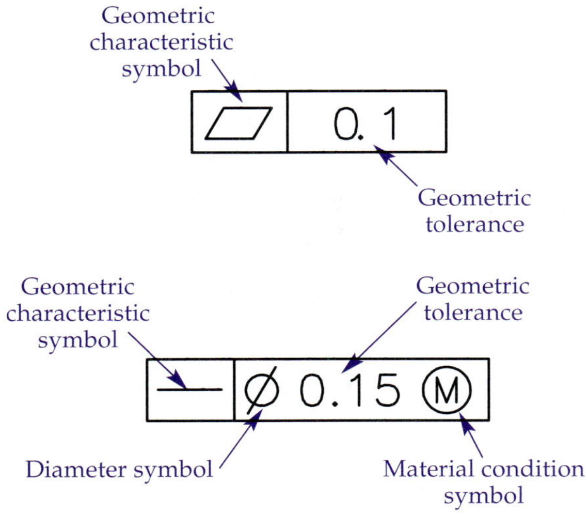

Figure 20-8.
Examples of datum references indicated in feature control frames.

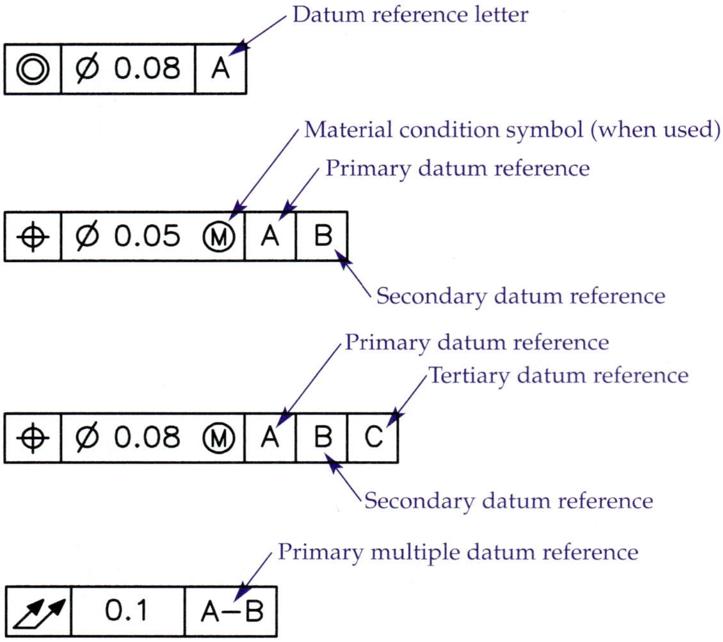

There is a specific order used to display elements in a feature control frame. See **Figure 20-9.** Notice the datum reference letters can be followed by a material condition symbol where applicable.

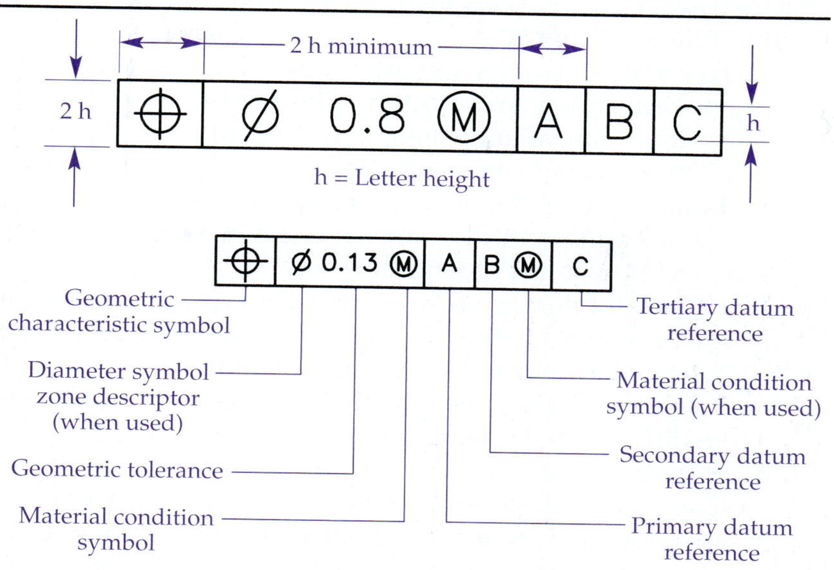

Figure 20-9. The order of elements in a feature control frame.

Basic Dimensions

A ***basic dimension*** is considered a theoretically perfect dimension. Basic dimensions are used to describe the theoretically exact size, profile, orientation, and location of a feature. These dimensions provide the basis from which permissible variations are established by tolerances on other dimensions, in notes, or in feature control frames. In simple terms, a basic dimension tells you where the geometric tolerance zone or datum target is located.

Basic dimensions are shown on a drawing with a rectangle placed around the dimension text, as shown in **Figure 20-10.** A general note can also be used to identify basic dimensions in some applications. For example, the note UNTOLERANCED DIMENSIONS LOCATING TRUE POSITION ARE BASIC indicates the dimensions that are basic. The basic dimension rectangle is a signal to the reader to look for a geometric tolerance in a feature control frame related to the features being dimensioned.

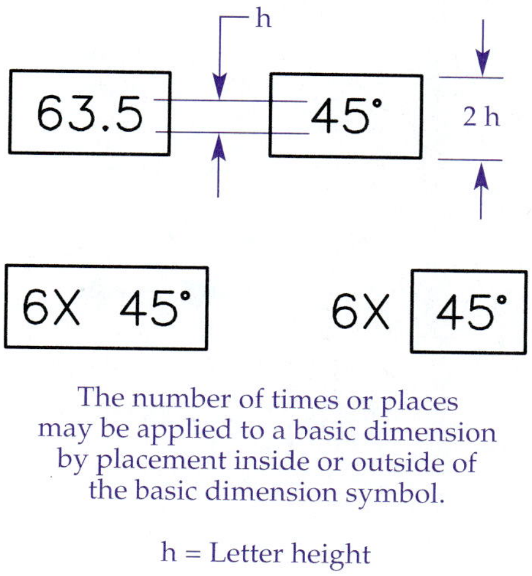

Figure 20-10. Basic dimensions are identified with a rectangle drawn around the text.

Additional Symbols

Other symbols commonly used in geometric dimensioning and tolerancing are shown in Figure 20-11. These symbols are used for specific applications, and are identified as follows:

- **Free state.** Free state describes distortion of a part after the removal of forces applied during manufacture. The free state symbol is placed in the feature control frame after the geometric tolerance and the material condition (if any) if the feature must meet the tolerance specified while in free state.
- **Tangent plane.** A tangent plane symbol is placed after the geometric tolerance in the feature control frame when it is necessary to control a feature surface by contacting points of tangency.
- **Projected tolerance zone.** A projected tolerance zone symbol is placed in the feature control frame to inform the reader that the geometric tolerance zone is projected away from the primary datum.
- **Between.** The between symbol is used with profile geometric tolerances to identify where the profile tolerance is applied.
- **Statistical tolerance.** The statistical tolerance symbol is used to indicate that a tolerance is based on statistical tolerancing. ***Statistical tolerancing*** is the assigning of tolerances to related dimensions based on the requirements of statistical process control. ***Statistical process control (SPC)*** is a method of monitoring and adjusting a manufacturing process based on statistical signals. The statistical tolerancing symbol is placed after the dimension or geometric tolerance that requires SPC. See Figure 20-12. When the feature can be manufactured by either SPC or conventional means, both the statistical tolerance with the statistical tolerance symbol and the conventional tolerance must be shown. An appropriate general note should accompany the drawing. Either of the two following notes is acceptable:
  - FEATURES IDENTIFIED AS STATISTICAL TOLERANCED SHALL BE PRODUCED WITH STATISTICAL PROCESS CONTROL.
  - FEATURES IDENTIFIED AS STATISTICAL TOLERANCED SHALL BE PRODUCED WITH STATISTICAL PROCESS CONTROL, OR THE MORE RESTRICTIVE ARITHMETIC LIMITS.

Figure 20-11. Additional recommended dimensioning symbols.

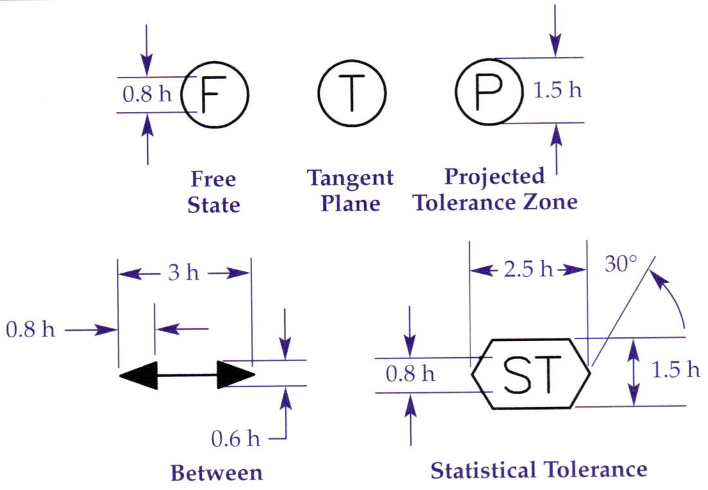

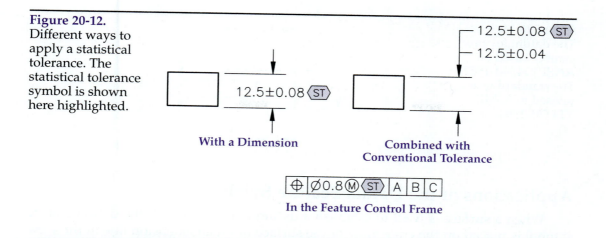

Figure 20-12.
Different ways to apply a statistical tolerance. The statistical tolerance symbol is shown here highlighted.

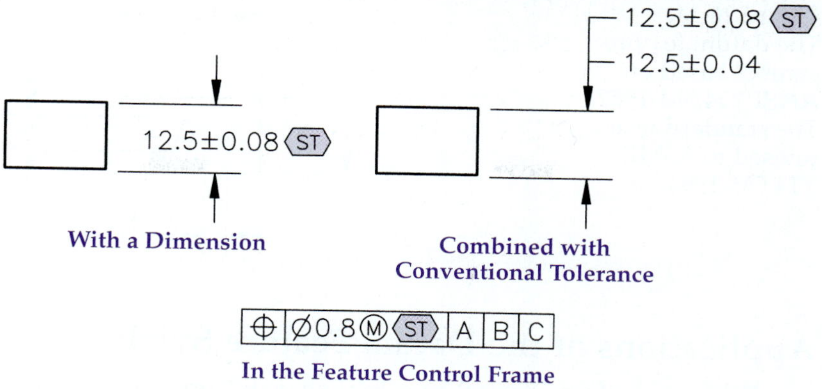

Datum Feature Symbols

As discussed previously, datums refer to theoretically perfect surfaces, planes, points, or axes. In this introduction to datum-related symbols, the datum is assumed. In geometric dimensioning and tolerancing, the datums are identified with a ***datum feature symbol***.

Each datum feature requiring identification must have its own identification letter. Any letter of the alphabet can be used to identify a datum except *I*, *O*, or *Q*. These letters can be confused with the numbers 1 or 0. On drawings where the number of datums exceeds 23, double letters are used, starting with *AA* through *AZ*, and then *BA* through *BZ*. Datum feature symbols can be repeated only as necessary for clarity.

In **Figure 20-13,** the datum feature symbol recommended by ASME Y14.5M-1994 is shown. The datum feature symbol used in drawings prior to the release of ASME Y14.5M-1994 is distinctively different. The previously used datum feature symbol is shown in **Figure 20-14.**

Figure 20-13.
The datum feature symbol based on ASME Y14.5M-1994.

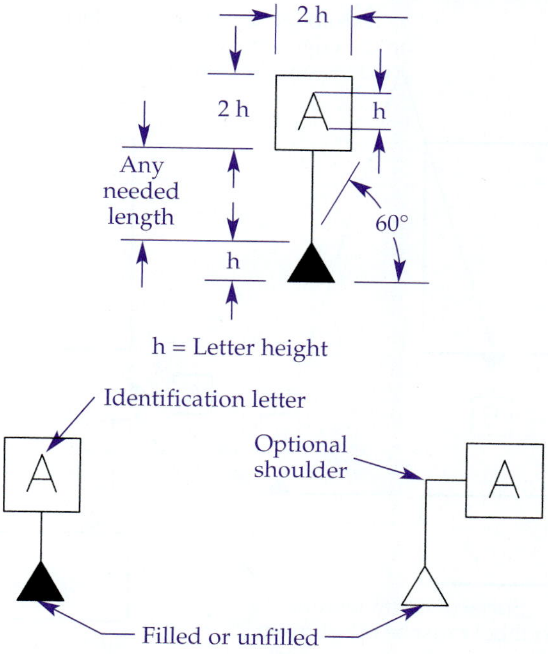

Figure 20-14.
The datum feature symbol based on ANSI Y14.5M-1982. The standard was revised to ASME Y14.5M-1994.

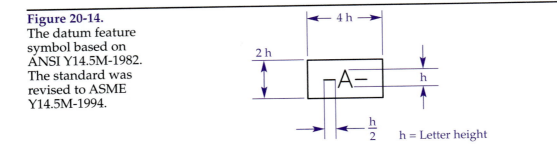

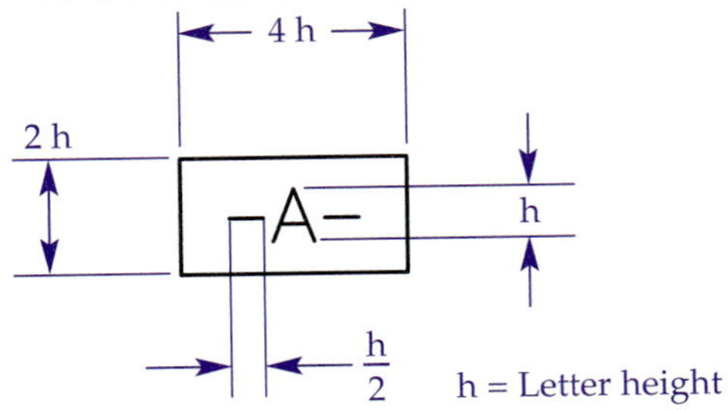

Applications of the Datum Feature Symbol

When a surface is used to establish a datum plane on a part, the datum feature symbol is placed on the edge view of the surface or on an extension line in the view where the surface appears as a line. See **Figure 20-15.** A leader line can also be used to connect the datum feature symbol to the view.

When the datum is an axis, the datum feature symbol can be placed on the drawing using one of the following methods. See **Figure 20-16.**

- The symbol can be placed on the outside surface of a cylindrical feature.
- The symbol can be centered on the opposite side of the dimension line arrowhead.
- The symbol can replace the dimension line and arrowhead when the dimension line is placed outside the extension lines.
- The symbol can be placed on a leader line shoulder.
- The symbol can be placed below, and attached to, the center of a feature control frame.

Elements on a rectangular symmetrical part or feature can be located and dimensioned in relationship to a datum center plane. Datum center plane symbols are shown in **Figure 20-17.**

Figure 20-15.
Datum feature symbols used to identify datum planes.

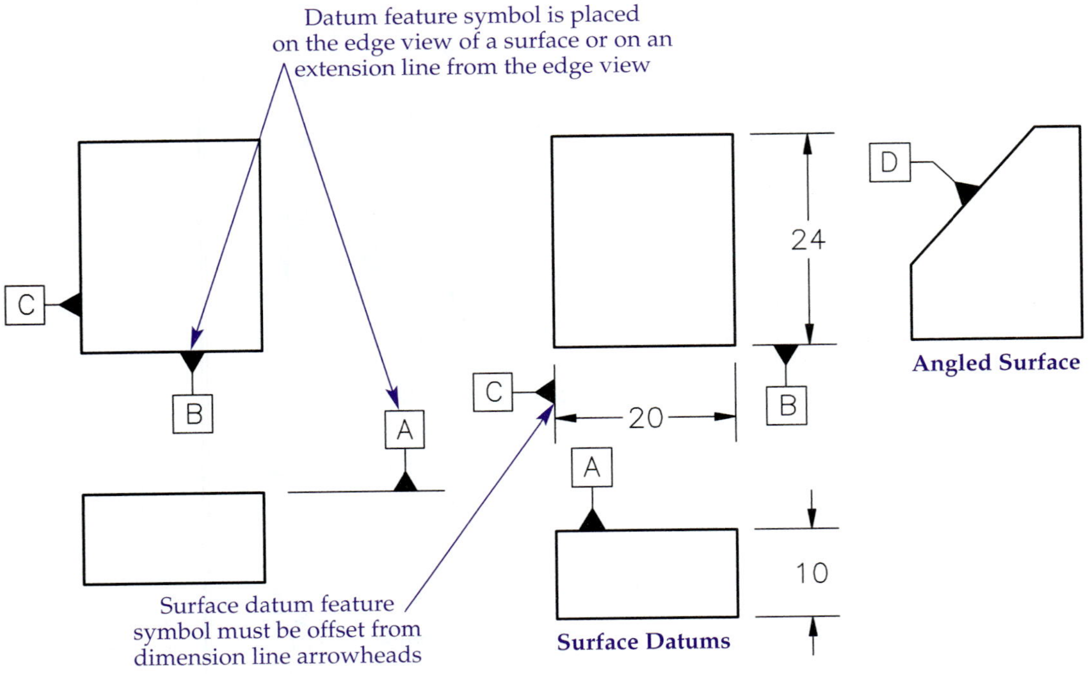

Figure 20-16. Different methods of using the datum feature symbol to represent a datum axis.

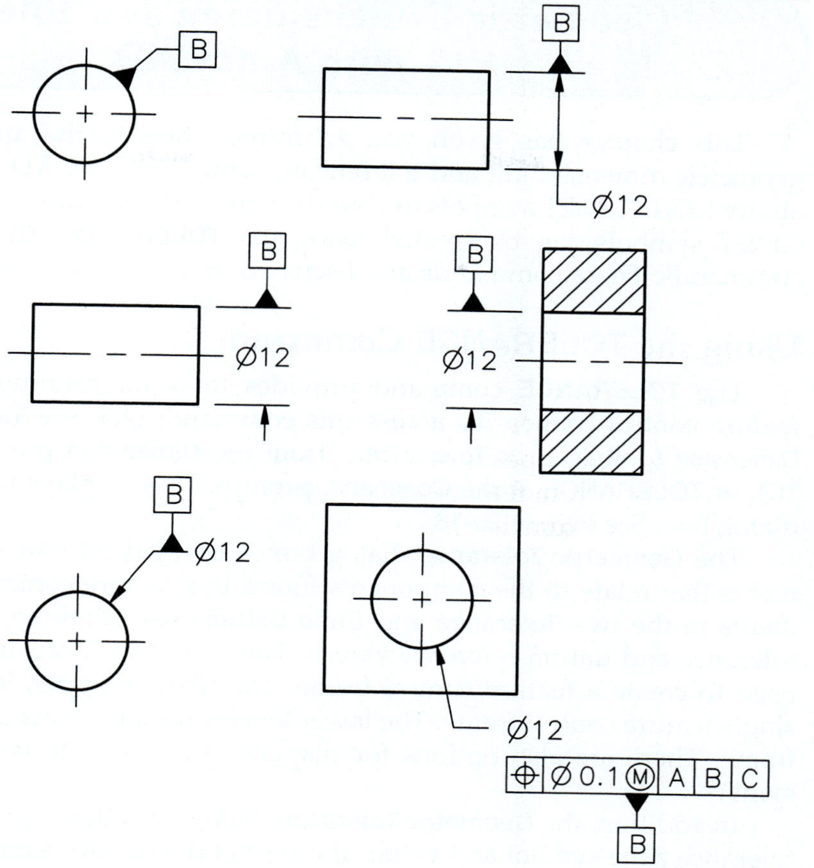

Figure 20-17. Placing datum center plane symbols. Axis and center plane datum feature symbols must align with, or replace, the dimension line arrowhead. Or, the datum feature symbol must be placed on the feature, leader shoulder, or feature control frame.

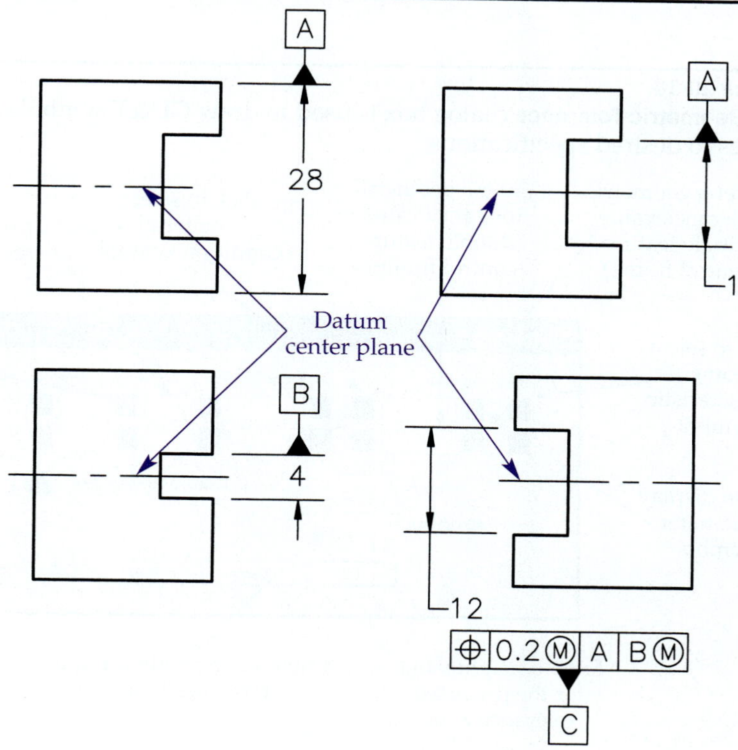

Geometric Dimensioning and Tolerancing with AutoCAD

This chapter has given you an introduction to the appearance and use of geometric dimensioning and tolerancing symbols. AutoCAD provides you with the ability to add GD&T symbols to your drawings. The feature control frame and related GD&T symbols can be created using the **TOLERANCE**, **QLEADER**, and **LEADER** commands. These commands are discussed in the following sections.

Using the TOLERANCE Command

TOLERANCE
TOL

Dimension
➥ Tolerance

Dimension toolbar

Tolerance

The **TOLERANCE** command provides tools for creating GD&T symbols and feature control frames. To access this command, pick the **Tolerance** button on the Dimension toolbar, pick **Tolerance...** from the **Dimension** pull-down menu, or enter TOL or TOLERANCE at the Command: prompt. This displays the **Geometric Tolerance** dialog box. See Figure 20-18.

The **Geometric Tolerance** dialog box is divided into areas containing compartments that relate to the components found in a feature control frame. The compartments in the two **Tolerance** and three **Datum** areas allow you to specify geometric tolerance and datum reference values. There are two levels in each area that can be used to create a feature control frame. The first, or upper, level is used to make a single feature control frame. The lower level is used to create a double feature control frame. There are also options for displaying a diameter symbol and a modifying symbol.

In addition, the **Geometric Tolerance** dialog box allows you to display a projected tolerance zone symbol and value, and part of the datum feature symbol. The options and features in the **Geometric Tolerance** dialog box are explained in the following sections.

Figure 20-18.
The **Geometric Tolerance** dialog box is used to draw GD&T symbols and feature control frames to desired specifications.

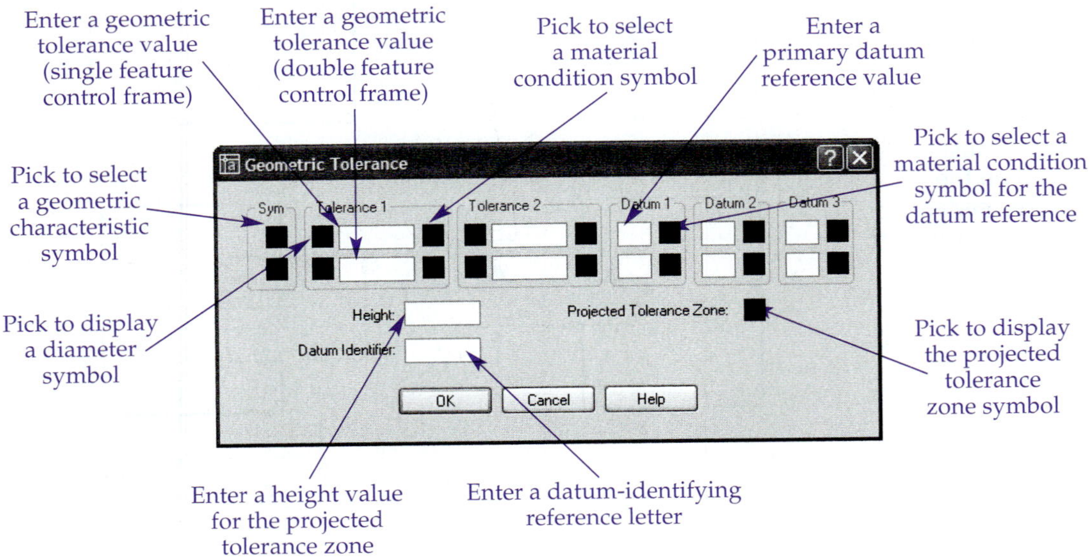

Selecting a geometric characteristic symbol

Geometric characteristic symbols can be accessed in the **Sym** area located at the far left of the **Geometric Tolerance** dialog box. This area has two image tile buttons that can be used to display one or two geometric characteristic symbols. Keep in mind that the corresponding text boxes along the upper row in each area are used for a single feature control frame. The text boxes in the lower row are used to create a double feature control frame.

Picking one of the image tile buttons in the **Sym** area opens the **Symbol** dialog box, Figure 20-19. Pick a symbol to have it displayed in the **Sym** image tile that you selected. After making a selection, the **Geometric Tolerance** dialog box returns. You can pick the same image tile again to select a different symbol, if you wish. To remove a previously selected symbol, pick the blank image tile in the lower-right corner of the **Symbol** dialog box.

Figure 20-19.
The **Symbol** dialog box is used to select a geometric characteristic symbol for use in a feature control frame.

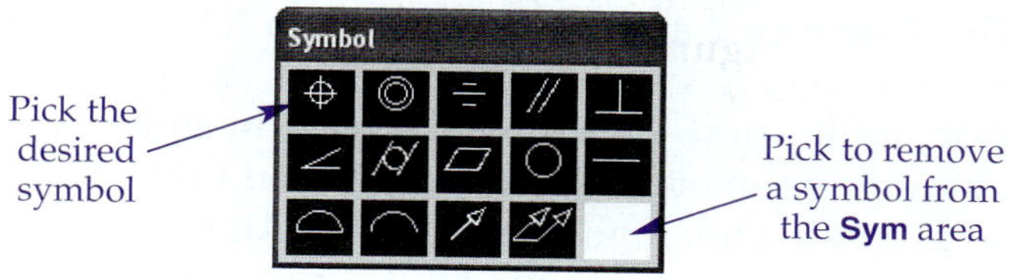

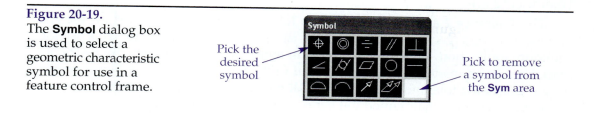

Tolerance 1 area

The **Tolerance 1** area of the **Geometric Tolerance** dialog box allows you to enter the first geometric tolerance value used in the feature control frame. If you are drawing a single feature control frame, enter the desired value in the upper text box. If you are drawing a double feature control frame, also enter a value in the lower text box. Double feature control frames, discussed later in this chapter, are used for applications such as unit straightness, unit flatness, composite profile tolerance, composite positional tolerance, and coaxial positional tolerance. You can add a diameter symbol by picking the image tile to the left of the text box. Pick the diameter image tile again to remove the diameter symbol.

The image tile to the right of the text box is used to place a material condition symbol. When you pick this image tile, the **Material Condition** dialog box appears. See Figure 20-20. Pick the desired symbol to have it displayed in the image tile you selected. In the example given, an MMC symbol is selected. To remove a material condition symbol, pick the blank tile in the **Material Condition** image tile menu. The RFS symbol in Figure 20-20 was used in ANSI Y14.5M-1982. The symbol is not used in ASME Y14.5M-1994 because RFS is assumed unless otherwise specified.

In Figure 20-21, a position symbol is shown in the **Sym** image tile and 0.5 is entered as the tolerance value in the upper text box in the **Tolerance 1** area. The tolerance value is preceded by a diameter symbol and followed by an MMC symbol. Remember that a zero precedes metric decimals but not inch decimals.

Figure 20-20.
The **Material Condition** dialog box. Pick the desired material condition symbol for the geometric tolerance and datum reference as needed. Notice the symbol for RFS is available. This symbol is not used in ASME Y14.5M-1994, but it may be needed when editing older drawings.

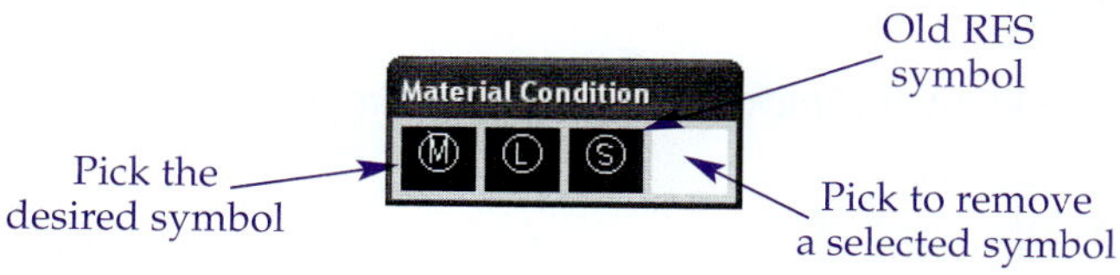

Figure 20-21.
The **Geometric Tolerance** dialog box with a diameter symbol, geometric tolerance value, and MMC material condition symbol added to the **Tolerance 1** area.

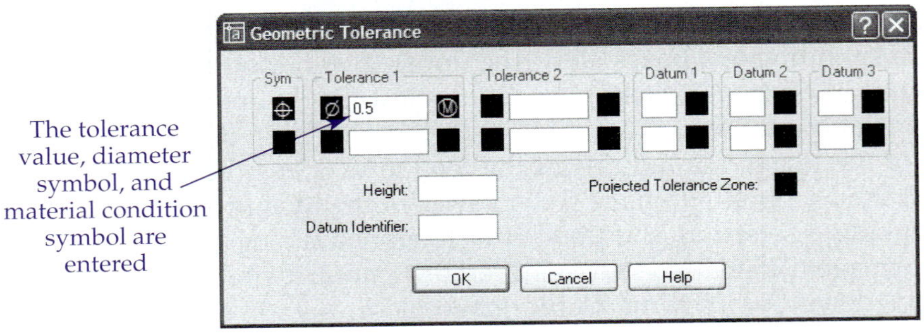

Tolerance 2 area

The **Tolerance 2** area of the **Geometric Tolerance** dialog box is used for the addition of a second geometric tolerance to the feature control frame. This is not a common application, but it may be used in some cases where there are restrictions placed on the geometric tolerance specified in the first compartment. For example, a second geometric tolerance value of 0.8 MAX means that the specification given in the first compartment is maintained but cannot exceed 0.8 maximum.

Datum areas

The **Datum 1** area of the **Geometric Tolerance** dialog box is used to establish the information needed for the primary datum reference compartment. Like the **Tolerance** areas, this area offers two levels of text boxes to create single or double feature control frames. You can also specify a material condition symbol for the datum reference by picking the image tile next to the corresponding text box to open the **Material Condition** dialog box.

The **Datum 2** and **Datum 3** areas are used to specify the secondary and tertiary datum reference information. Refer to Figure 20-9 to see how the datum reference and related material condition symbols are placed in the feature control frame.

Projected Tolerance Zone: image tile and Height: text box

The **Projected Tolerance Zone:** image tile can be picked to display a projected tolerance zone symbol in the feature control frame. The **Height:** text box is used to specify the height of a projected tolerance zone. The projected tolerance zone symbol and the **Height:** value are used together when a projected tolerance zone is applied to the drawing. The use of a projected tolerance zone in a drawing is discussed later in this chapter.

Datum Identifier: text box

The **Datum Identifier:** text box is used to enter a datum-identifying reference letter to be used as part of the datum feature symbol. An uppercase letter should be entered. However, if you want to comply with ASME Y14.5M-1994, you need to design a datum feature symbol and save it as a block. Creating your own dimensioning symbols is discussed later in this chapter and blocks are discussed in Chapter 22.

Completing the command

After you have entered all the desired information in the **Geometric Tolerance** dialog box, pick **OK**. See Figure 20-22A. The following prompt is then displayed on the command line.

> Enter tolerance location: *(pick the location for the feature control frame to be drawn)*
> Command:

The feature control frame for the given example is shown in Figure 20-22B.

Figure 20-22.
A—When the desired values have been specified in the **Geometric Tolerance** dialog box, pick **OK**. In this example, primary, secondary, and tertiary datum reference values have been added and are shown highlighted along with the geometric tolerance value. B—The feature control frame created by the values specified in the dialog box.

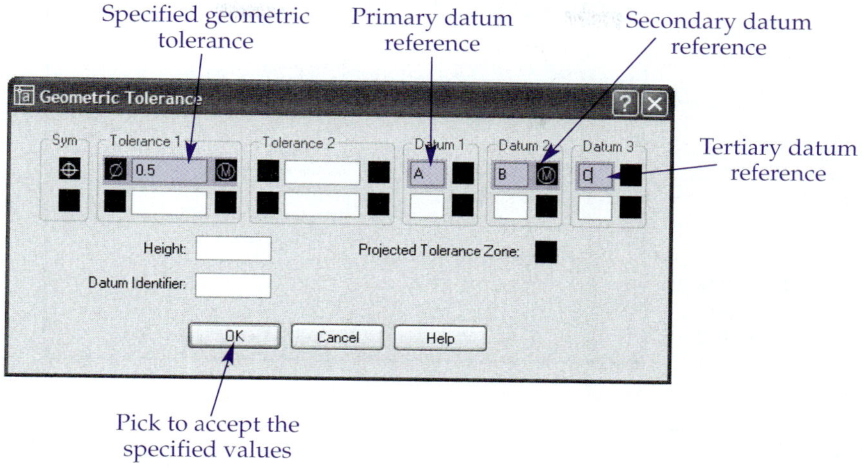

A

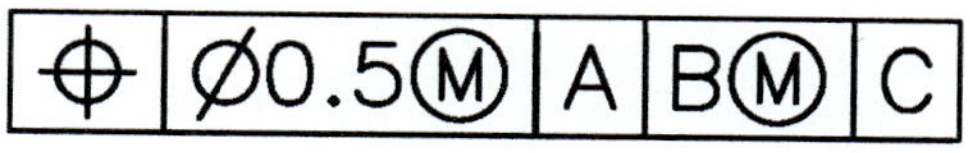

B

EXERCISE 20-1 Complete the Exercise on the Student CD.

Using the QLEADER and LEADER Commands to Place GD&T Symbols

In many cases, leader lines are connected to feature control frames or other GD&T symbols in order to identify toleranced features. The **QLEADER** and **LEADER** commands enable you to draw leader lines and access the dialog boxes used to create feature control frames in one operation. Refer to Chapter 17 for a complete discussion of the **QLEADER** command.

The **QLEADER** command can be accessed by picking the **Quick Leader** button on the **Dimension** toolbar, picking **Leader** from the **Dimension** pull-down menu, or by entering LE or QLEADER at the Command: prompt. When you enter this command, use the **Settings** option to open the **Leader Settings** dialog box. See **Figure 20-23.** Then, pick the **Tolerance** radio button in the **Annotation** tab to connect a feature control frame or datum feature symbol to a leader line. When asked to specify the first leader point, pick the leader start point. Now, pick the next leader point. Press [Enter] to end the leader line. After pressing [Enter], the **Geometric Tolerance** dialog box is displayed. Specify the desired settings and values for the feature control frame. Then, pick the **OK** button. The feature control frame is connected to the leader line in your drawing, as shown in **Figure 20-24.**

QLEADER
LE

Dimension ➡ Leader

Dimension toolbar

Quick Leader

Figure 20-23.
The **Leader Settings** dialog box. Activate the **Tolerance** radio button when placing a feature control frame with the **QLEADER** command.

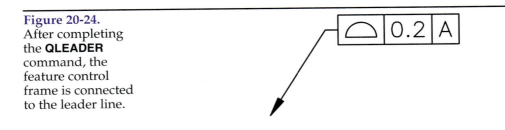

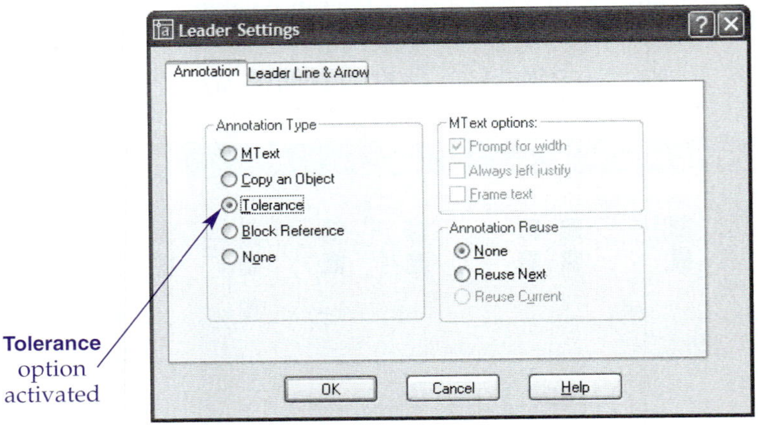

Figure 20-24.
After completing the **QLEADER** command, the feature control frame is connected to the leader line.

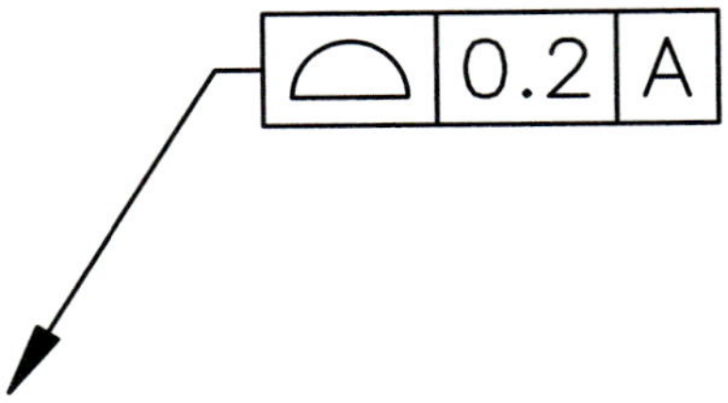

LEADER
LEAD

The **LEADER** command can also be used to connect a feature control frame to a leader line. After picking a start point and a second leader point, enter the **Annotation** option. The command sequence is:

Command: **LEAD** *or* **LEADER**
Specify leader start point: *(pick the leader start point)*
Specify next point: *(pick the next point of the leader)*
Specify next point or [Annotation/Format/Undo] <Annotation>: ↵
Enter first line of annotation text or <options>: ↵
Enter an annotation option [Tolerance/Copy/Block/None/Mtext] <Mtext>: **T**

Entering the **Tolerance** annotation option displays the **Geometric Tolerance** dialog box. You can then establish the feature control frame information. When you pick **OK**, the feature control frame is connected to the leader shoulder.

EXERCISE 20-2 Complete the Exercise on the Student CD.

Introduction to Projected Tolerance Zones

In some situations where positional tolerance is used entirely in out-of-squareness, it may be necessary to control perpendicularity and position next to the part. The use of a ***projected tolerance zone*** is recommended when variations in perpendicularity of threaded or press-fit holes may cause the fastener to interfere with the mating part. A projected tolerance zone is usually specified for a fixed fastener, such as the threaded hole for a bolt or the press-fit hole for a pin. The length of a projected tolerance zone can be specified as the distance the fastener extends into the mating part, the thickness of the part, or the height of a press-fit stud. The normal positional tolerance extends through the thickness of the part.

However, this application can cause an interference between the location of a thread or press-fit object and its mating part. This is because the attitude of a fixed fastener is controlled by the actual angle of the threaded hole. There is no clearance available to provide flexibility. For this reason, the projected tolerance zone is established at true position and extends away from the primary datum at the threaded feature. The projected tolerance zone provides a larger tolerance because it is projected away from the primary datum, rather than within the thread. A projected tolerance is also easier to inspect than the tolerance applied to the pitch diameter of the thread. This is because a thread gauge with a post projecting above the threaded hole can be used to easily verify the projected tolerance zone with a coordinate measuring machine (CMM).

Representing a Projected Tolerance Zone

One method for displaying the projected tolerance zone is to place the projected tolerance zone symbol and height in the feature control frame after the geometric tolerance and related material condition symbol. The related thread specification is then connected to the section view of the thread symbol. With this method, the projected tolerance zone is assumed to extend away from the threaded hole at the primary datum. See **Figure 20-25.**

To provide additional clarification, the projected tolerance zone can be shown using a chain line in the view where the related datum appears as an edge and the minimum height of the projection is dimensioned. See **Figure 20-26.** The projected tolerance zone symbol is shown alone in the feature control frame after the geometric tolerance and material condition symbol (if any). The meaning is the same as previously discussed.

Figure 20-25. A projected tolerance zone representation with the length of the projected tolerance zone given in the feature control frame. The projected tolerance zone symbol is shown highlighted.

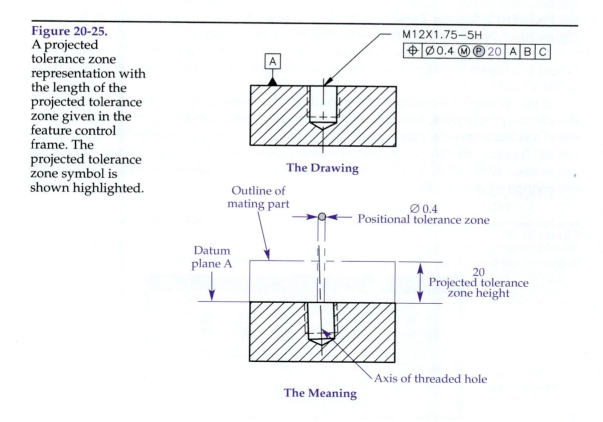

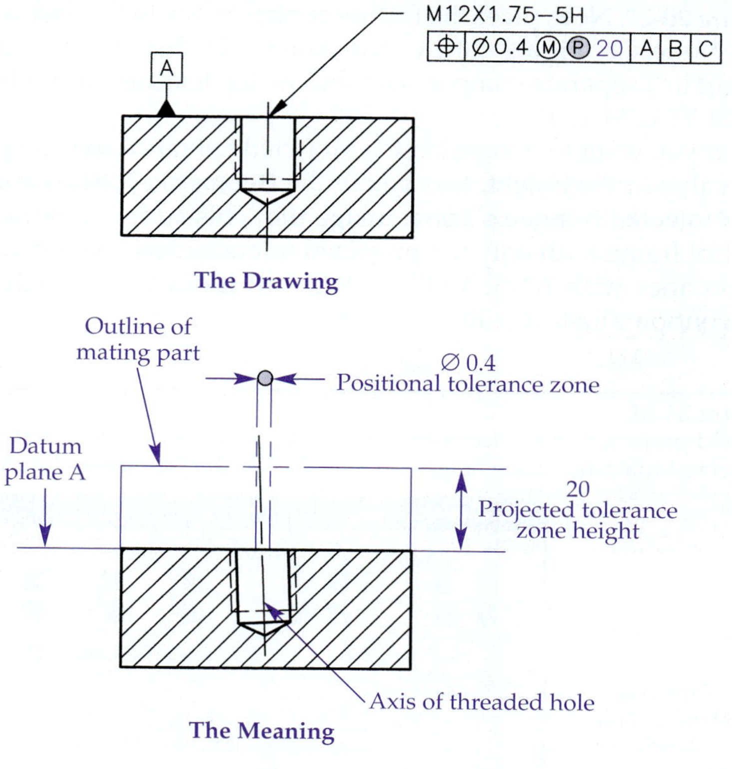

Figure 20-26.
A projected tolerance zone representation with the length of the projected tolerance zone shown with a chain line and a minimum dimension in the adjacent view.

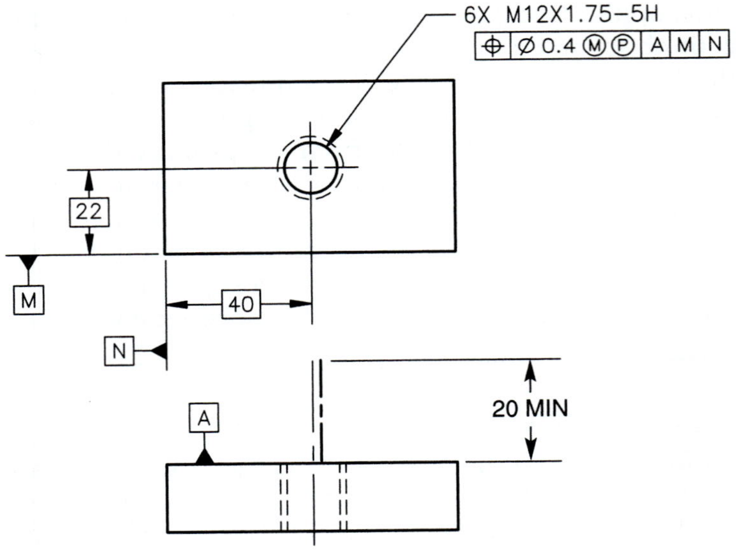

Drawing the Projected Tolerance Zone

AutoCAD specifies projected tolerance zones according to the 1982 standard. To specify a projected tolerance zone according to the 1994 standard, create a feature control frame without modifiers in the **Tolerance 1** area and add space and the letter P after the tolerance value. When completed, use the **CIRCLE** command to draw a circle around the letter P. You can group the feature control frame and the circle so they stay together.

When following the 1982 standard, enter the desired geometric tolerance, diameter symbol, material condition symbol, and datum reference as previously discussed. Pick the **Projected Tolerance Zone:** image tile and enter the height in the **Height:** text box, Figure 20-27. Now, place the feature control frame in the desired location in the drawing.

Notice in Figure 20-28 that AutoCAD displays the projected tolerance zone height in a separate compartment below the feature control frame, in accordance with ANSI Y14.5M-1982.

If you want to dimension the projected tolerance zone height with a chain line, omit the value in the **Height:** text box in the **Geometric Tolerance** dialog box and pick only the **Projected Tolerance Zone:** image tile. This adds a compartment below the feature control frame with only the projected tolerance zone symbol. This representation is in accordance with ANSI Y14.5M-1982, but it does not match the ASME Y14.5M-1994 convention illustrated in Figure 20-26.

Figure 20-27.
To add projected tolerance zone specifications to the feature control frame, enter the projected tolerance zone height and symbol in the **Geometric Tolerance** dialog box.

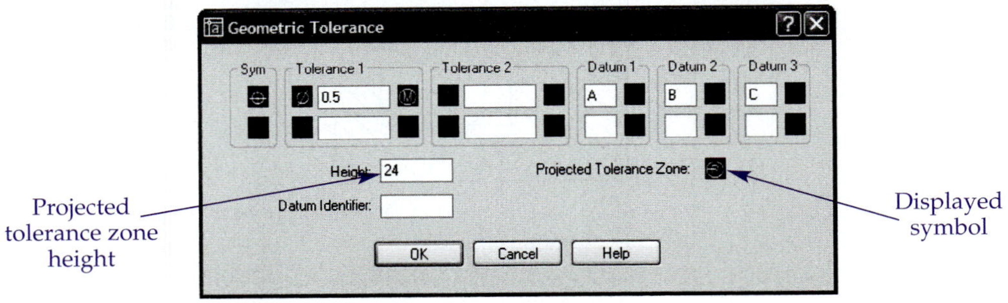

Figure 20-28.
The feature control frame created by the values specified in Figure 20-27. The AutoCAD projected tolerance zone compartment conforms to ANSI Y14.5M-1982 standards. See Figure 20-25 and Figure 20-26 for applications of the projected tolerance zone as recommended by ASME Y14.5M-1994.

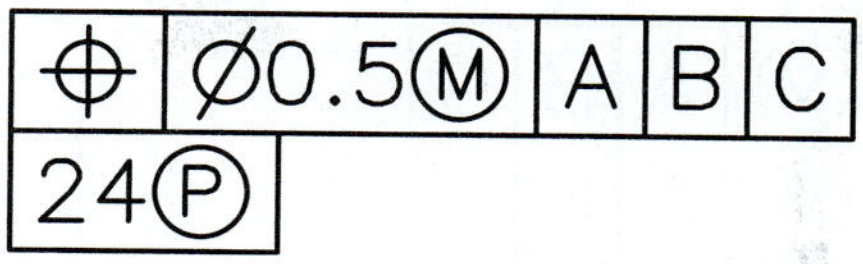

EXERCISE 20-3 Complete the Exercise on the Student CD.

Drawing a Double Feature Control Frame

Several GD&T applications require that the feature control frame be doubled in height, with two sets of geometric tolerancing values provided. These applications include unit straightness and flatness, composite positional tolerance, and coaxial positional tolerance.

To draw a double feature control frame, first use the **TOLERANCE** command and create the desired first level of the feature control frame in the **Geometric Tolerance** dialog box as previously discussed. You can also use the **QLEADER** or **LEADER** command if you are connecting the feature control frame to a leader line. Next, pick the lower image tile in the **Sym** area. When the **Symbol** dialog box is displayed again, pick another geometric characteristic symbol. This results in two symbols displayed in the **Sym** area. Continue specifying the needed information in the lower-level **Tolerance** and **Datum** compartments. Sample entries for a double feature control frame are shown in Figure 20-29.

If the two symbols in the **Sym** image tiles are the same, then the double feature control frame is drawn with one geometric characteristic symbol displayed in a single compartment. See Figure 20-30A. This is acceptable if only one geometric characteristic symbol is required for the feature-relating control, but it is inappropriate if you need to display the same geometric characteristic symbol twice. If you are drawing a double feature control frame with different geometric characteristic symbols for a combination control, then the feature control frame must have two separate compartments. See Figure 20-30B.

Figure 20-29.
Specifying information for a double feature control frame in the **Geometric Tolerance** dialog box.

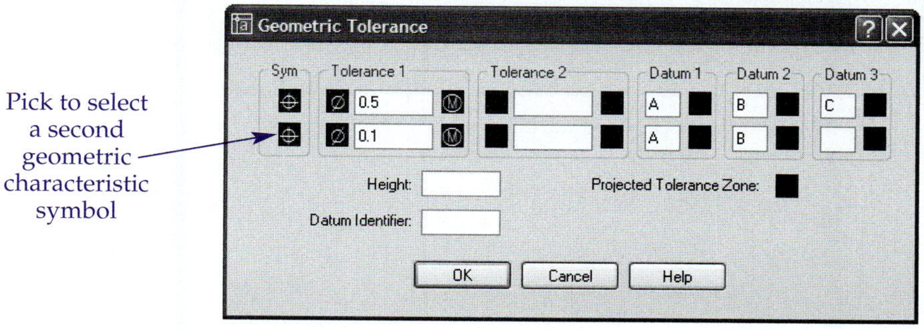

Figure 20-30.
A—If the same geometric characteristic symbol is entered in both **Symbol** boxes of the **Geometric Tolerance** dialog box, only one symbol is shown in the first compartment of the double feature control frame. B—If two different symbols are used, they are displayed in separate compartments.

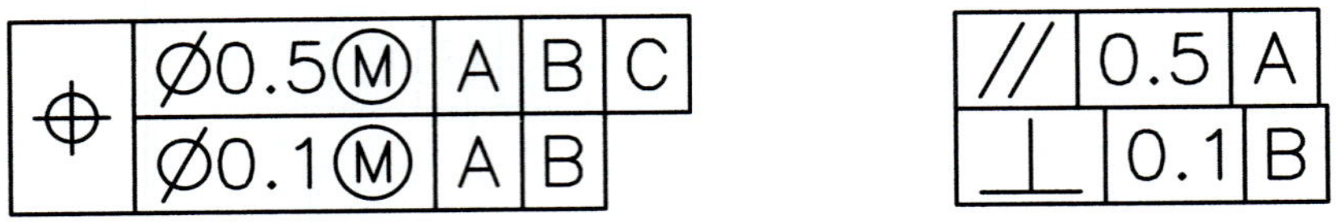

A B

EXERCISE 20-4 Complete the Exercise on the Student CD.

Drawing Datum Feature Symbols

As discussed earlier in this chapter, datums in a drawing are identified by datum feature symbols. You can draw datum feature symbols using the **TOLERANCE**, **QLEADER**, or **LEADER** commands. When you access the **Geometric Tolerance** dialog box, enter the desired datum reference letter in the **Datum Identifier:** text box. See Figure 20-31.

After picking **OK**, place the datum feature symbol at the desired location in your drawing. You can also draw a datum feature symbol connected to a feature control frame by selecting the desired geometric characteristic symbol and entering the necessary information in the **Geometric Tolerance** dialog box. In Figure 20-32, datum feature symbols are shown with and without a feature control frame. Notice the symbols are placed inside squares. This complies with the ANSI Y14.5M-1982 standard, rather than ASME Y14.5M-1994. In order to match the ASME Y14.5M-1994 standard, the symbols need to be drawn as shown in Figure 20-13. One way to do this is to create your own symbols that you can insert as needed. Creating and saving your own symbols are discussed in Chapter 22.

Figure 20-31.
Using the **Geometric Tolerance** dialog box to enter a datum-identifying reference letter. This letter is used to create the datum feature symbol.

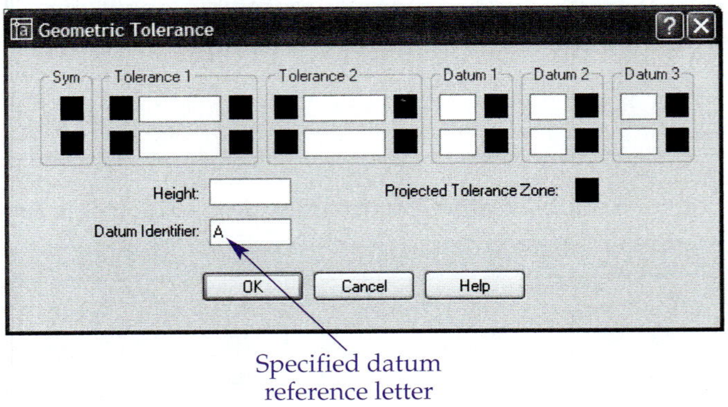

Figure 20-32.
A—A datum feature symbol drawn without a feature control frame. B—A datum feature symbol drawn with a feature control frame. Note the symbols in A and B do not comply with the ASME Y14.5M-1994 standard.

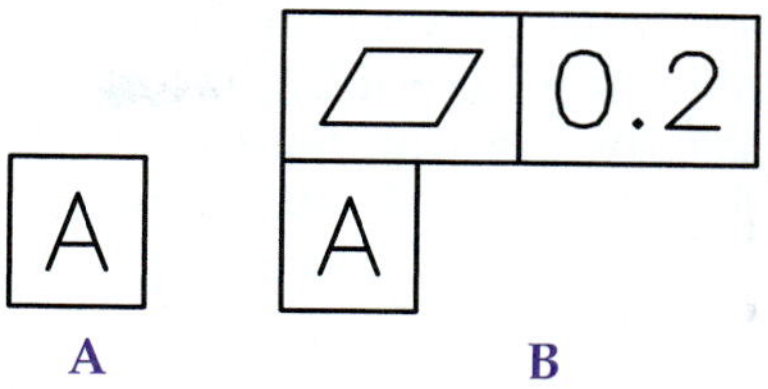

Before you learn how to create your own symbols, you can modify the symbols shown in Figure 20-32 by establishing a dimension style with leader line terminators set to **Datum triangle** or **Datum triangle filled**. These leader options are available in the **Leader:** drop-down list in the **Arrowheads** area of the **Lines and Arrows** tab in the **Modify Dimension Style** dialog box. Creating dimension styles with the **Dimension Style Manager** and the **Modify Dimension Style** dialog boxes are discussed in Chapter 17.

After creating a dimension style that uses datum triangles for leader arrowheads, enter the **QLEADER** or **LEADER** command to draw a leader segment that connects to the datum feature symbol as shown in Figure 20-33A. This modifies the symbol in Figure 20-32A. Use the object snap modes to help you properly position the leader with the symbol. If you use the **QLEADER** command, make sure the annotation setting is set to **Mtext**. Then, pick the leader start point and endpoint, and then press [Enter]. When prompted for the text width, press the [Esc] key. If you use the **LEADER** command, pick the leader line points, and then use the **None** suboption of the **Annotation** option to specify no annotation text.

To modify the datum feature symbol shown in Figure 20-32B, you must draw the datum feature symbol, the feature control frame, and the leader line separately. First, draw the datum feature symbol as previously discussed. Then, use the **QLEADER** or **LEADER** command to draw a connecting leader segment as shown in Figure 20-33B. Finally, draw the feature control frame and connect it to the datum triangle as shown. The datum feature symbol and the feature control frame can be moved as needed to allow for proper positioning.

Figure 20-33.
A—To draw a datum feature symbol in accordance with ASME Y14.5M-1994, create a dimension style that uses the **Datum triangle** or **Datum triangle filled** leader arrowhead option. Then, use the **QLEADER** or **LEADER** command to connect a leader arrow to the existing symbol. B—If a feature control frame is to be used, the datum feature symbol, leader line, and feature control frame must be drawn separately.

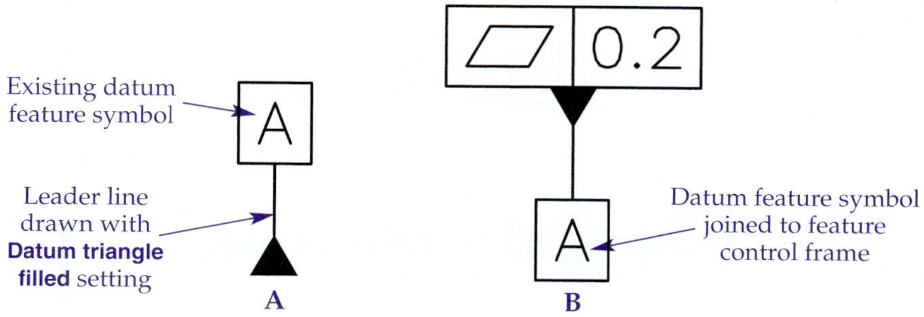

PROFESSIONAL TIP

Chapter 22 of this text provides a detailed discussion on how to create your own symbol libraries. A ***symbol library*** is a related group of symbols. It is recommended that you design dimensioning symbols that are not available in AutoCAD, such as the datum feature symbol that is recognized by ASME Y14.5M-1994. This symbol is shown in Figure 20-13.

Your symbol library might include the counterbore, countersink, depth, and other dimensioning symbols illustrated in Figure 20-1. These symbols are easily drawn if you establish a dimension style that uses the gdt.shx font. Chapter 17 explains how to create such a dimension style to help you draw these symbols when needed.

EXERCISE 20-5 Complete the Exercise on the Student CD.

Controlling the Height of the Feature Control Frame

Referring to Figure 20-9, the height of the feature control frame is twice the height of the text. Text on engineering drawings is generally drawn at a height of .125″ (3 mm), which makes the feature control frame height .25″ (6 mm). As a result, the distance from the text to the feature control frame should be equal to half the text height. For example, if the height of the drawing text is .125″, the space between the text and the feature control frame should be .0625″ to result in a .25″ high frame.

The distance from the text to the feature control frame is controlled by the **DIMGAP** dimension variable. See Figure 20-34. The default value is .09″. You can change this setting at the command line or by entering a new value in the **Offset from dim line:** text box in the **Text Placement** area of the **Text** tab in the **Modify Dimension Style** dialog box. The setting also controls the gap between the dimension line and the dimension text for linear dimensions and the space between the dimension text and the rectangle for basic dimensions. Basic dimensions are discussed in the next section.

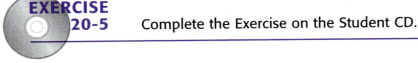

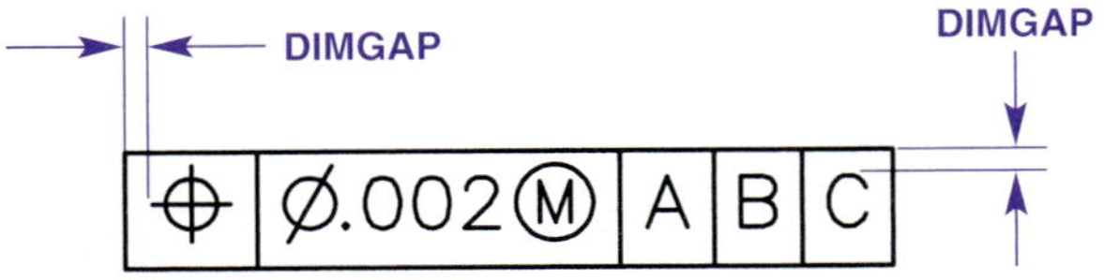

Figure 20-34.
The **DIMGAP** dimension variable setting controls the distance from the text to the feature control frame.

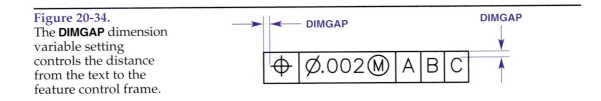

Drawing Basic Dimensions

A basic dimension is shown in Figure 20-35. Basic dimensions can be automatically drawn by setting a basic tolerance in the **Tolerance** tab of the **Modify Dimension Style** dialog box, as discussed in Chapter 19. It is recommended that you establish a separate dimension style for basic dimensions because not all of your dimensions on

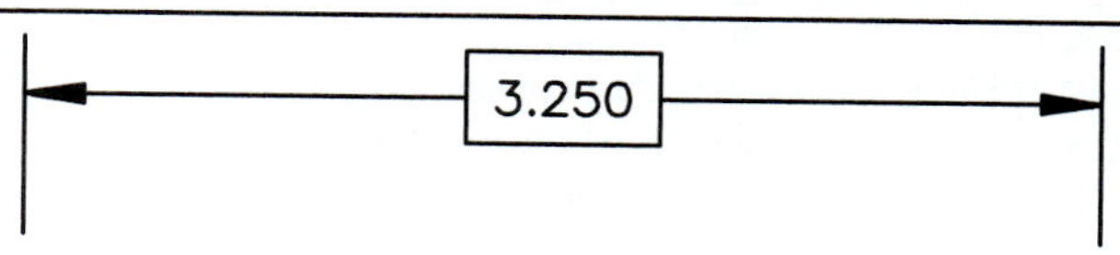

Figure 20-35.
An AutoCAD basic dimension.

a drawing will be basic. The **Offset from dim line:** setting (**DIMGAP**) in the **Text** tab of the **Modify Dimension Style** dialog box controls the space between the basic dimension text and the rectangle around the dimension.

EXERCISE 20-6 Complete the Exercise on the Student CD.

Editing Feature Control Frames

A feature control frame acts as one object. When you pick any location on the frame, the entire object is selected. You can edit feature control frames using AutoCAD editing commands such as **ERASE, COPY, MOVE, ROTATE,** and **SCALE.** The **STRETCH** command only allows you to move a feature control frame. This effect is similar to the results of using the **STRETCH** command with text objects.

DDEDIT
ED
Modify
➥ Object
➥ Text
➥ Edit...

You can edit the values inside a feature control frame by using the **DDEDIT** command. To access the command, double-click on the feature control frame you wish to edit, select **Edit...** from the **Modify** pull-down **Object** cascading and **Text** cascading menu, or enter ED or DDEDIT at the Command: prompt. When you enter this command and select the desired frame, the **Geometric Tolerance** dialog box is displayed with all the current values listed. After you make the desired changes and pick **OK**, the feature control frame is updated.

You can also use the **DDEDIT** command to edit basic dimensions. When you select a basic dimension for editing, the multiline text editor is displayed. You can then edit the basic dimension as you would any other dimension.

> **NOTE** If you double-click on a dimension, AutoCAD opens the **Properties** dialog box instead of the multiline text editor.

Sample GD&T Applications

This chapter is intended to give you a general overview of GD&T applications and basic instructions on how to draw GD&T symbols using AutoCAD. If you are in the manufacturing industry, you may have considerable use for geometric dimensioning and tolerancing. The support information presented in this chapter may be a review or it may inspire you to learn more about this topic. The drawings in Figure 20-36 are intended to show you some common GD&T applications using the available dimensioning and geometric characteristic symbols.

Figure 20-36.
Examples of typical geometric dimensioning and tolerancing applications using various dimensioning and geometric characteristic symbols.

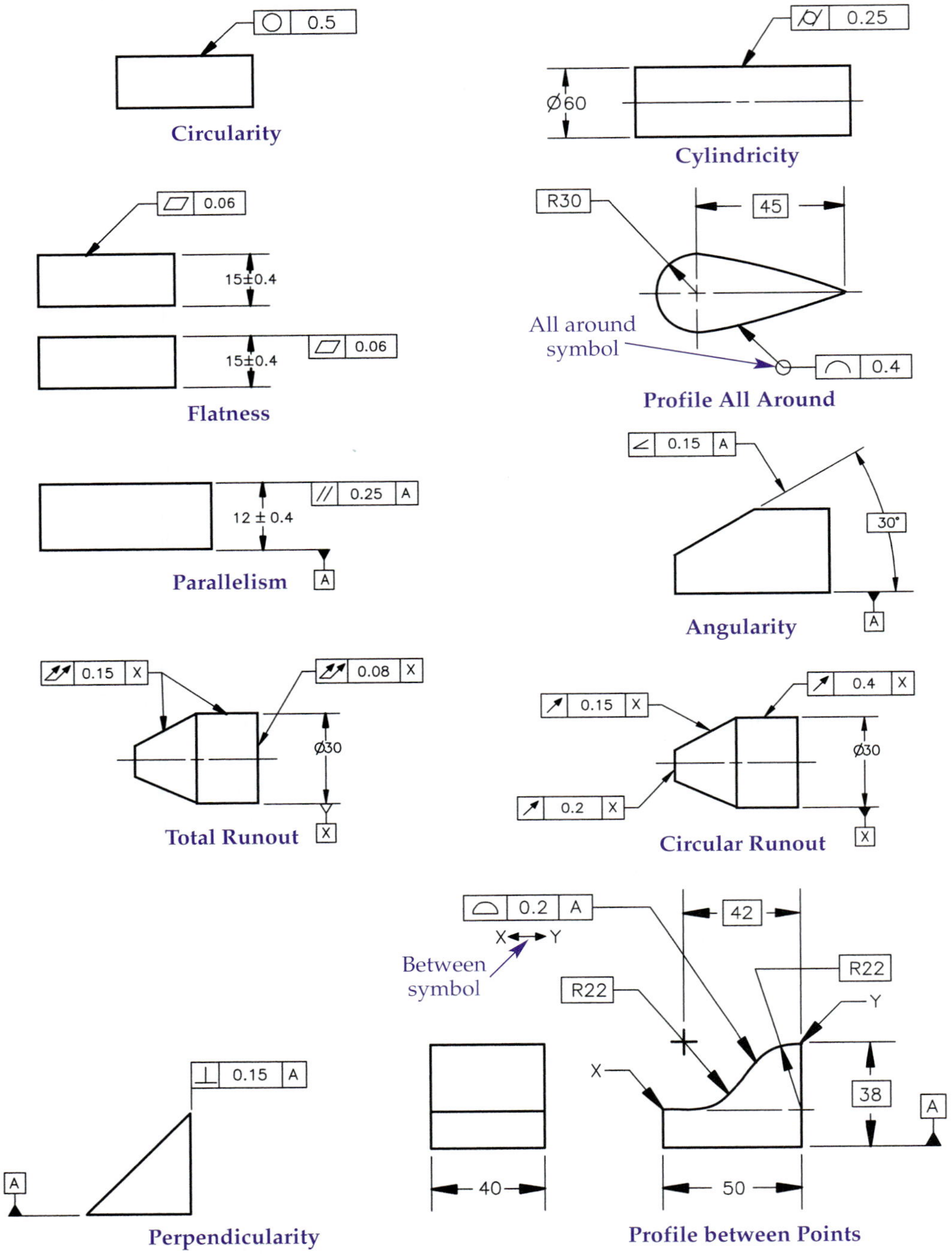

Chapter Test

Answer the following questions on a separate sheet of paper.

1. Identify each of the following geometric characteristic symbols.

 A. — H. ◎

 B. ▱ I. ☰

 C. ○ J. //

 D. ⌀ K. ⊥

 E. ⌒ L. ∠

 F. ⌓ M. ⤢

 G. ⊕ N. ⤢⤢

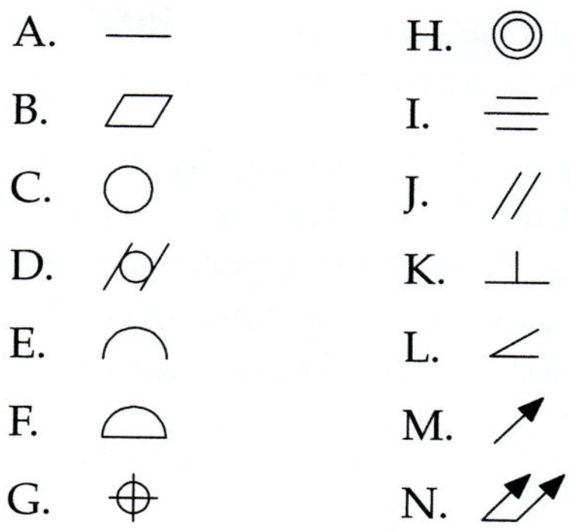

2. Identify the parts of the feature control frame shown below.

 | ⊕ | ⌀ 0.05 Ⓜ | A | B Ⓜ | C |

 A. B. C. D. E. F. G.

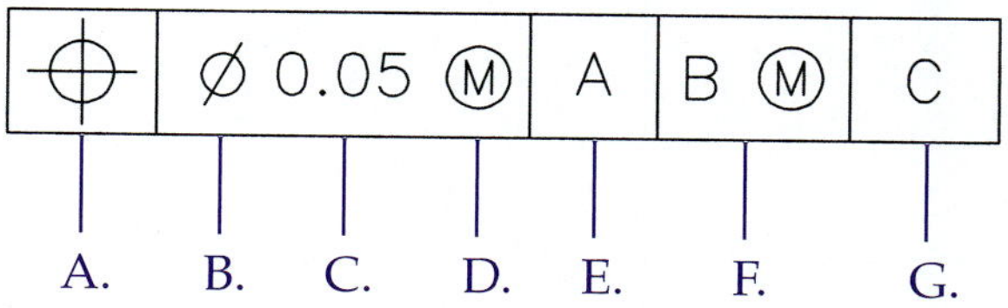

3. Name the current standard for dimensioning and tolerancing that is adopted by the American National Standards Institute and published by the American Society of Mechanical Engineers.

4. Name three commands that can be used to draw a feature control frame.

5. Identify the dialog box that contains settings used to create a feature control frame.

6. How do you access the **Symbol** dialog box in which a geometric characteristic symbol can be selected?

7. How do you remove a geometric characteristic symbol from one of the image tiles in the **Sym** area of the **Geometric Tolerance** dialog box?

8. Describe the procedure used to draw a feature control frame connected to a leader line.

9. Describe how to place a projected tolerance zone symbol and height value with the feature control frame.

10. Explain how to create a double feature control frame.

11. Which AutoCAD setting allows you to draw basic dimensions? How is it accessed?

12. Identify the AutoCAD setting that controls the space between the text in a feature control frame and the surrounding frame.

13. Describe how to draw a datum feature symbol without an attached feature control frame. How do you add a leader line with a filled datum triangle to the symbol?

14. Name the command that can be used to edit the existing values in a feature control frame.

Drawing Problems

Create dimension styles that will assist you with the following problems. Draw fully dimensioned multiview drawings. The required number of views depends on the problem and is to be determined by you. Apply geometric tolerancing as discussed in this chapter. Modify the available AutoCAD drawing applications to comply with ASME Y14.5M-1994 standards. The problems are presented in accordance with ASME Y14.5M-1994.

1. Open drawing P19-5. Edit the drawing by adding the geometric tolerancing applications shown below. Untoleranced dimensions are ±.02 for two-place decimal precision and ±.005 for three-place decimal precision. If you did not draw P20-5, then start a new drawing and draw the problem now. The problem is shown as a cutaway for clarity. You do not need to draw a section. Save the drawing as P20-1.

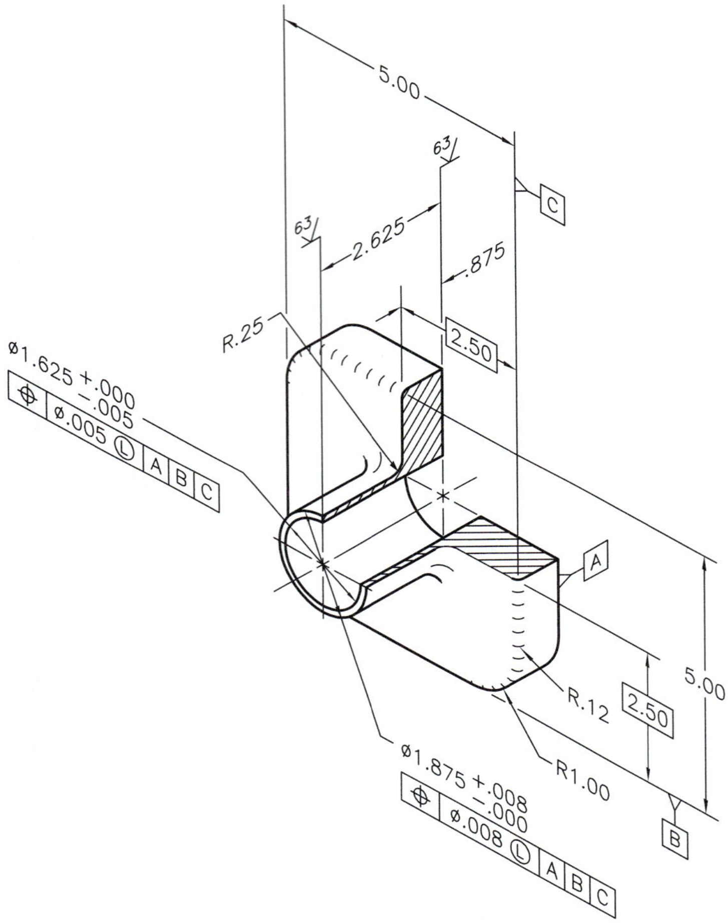

2. Open drawing P19-6. Edit the drawing by adding the geometric tolerancing applications shown below. Untoleranced dimensions are ±0.5. If you did not draw P20-6, then start a new drawing and draw the problem now. Save the drawing as P20-2.

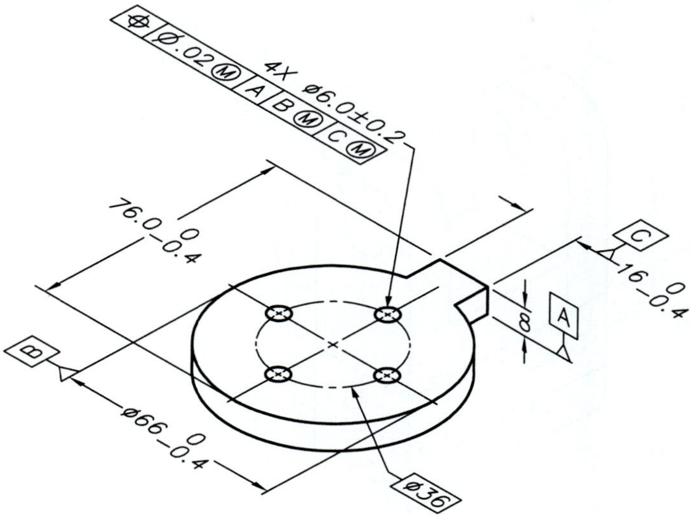

3. Open drawing P19-7. Edit the drawing by adding the geometric tolerancing applications shown below. If you did not draw P20-7, start a new drawing and draw the problem now. Save the drawing as P20-3.

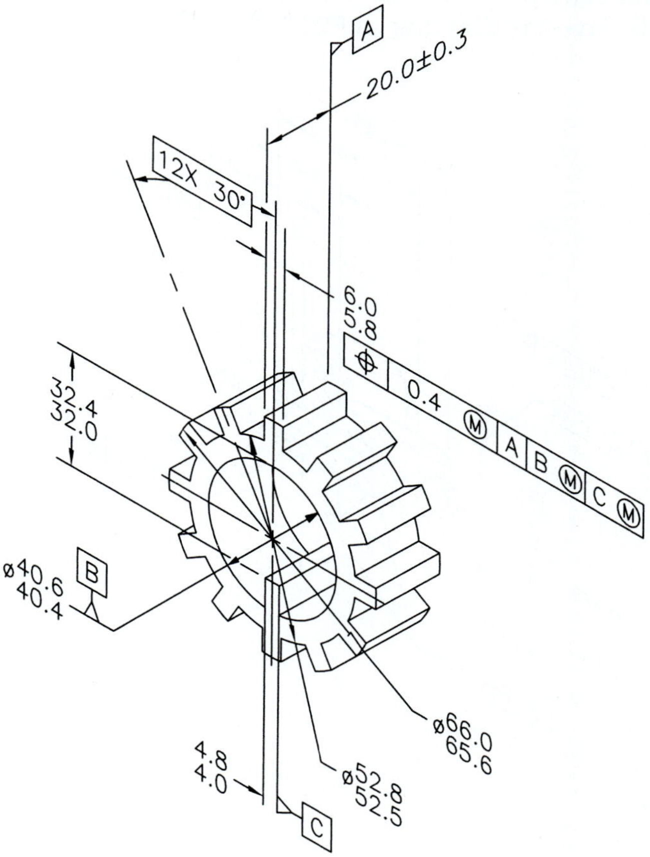

4. Draw the following object as previously instructed. Untoleranced dimensions are ±0.3. Save the drawing as P20-4.

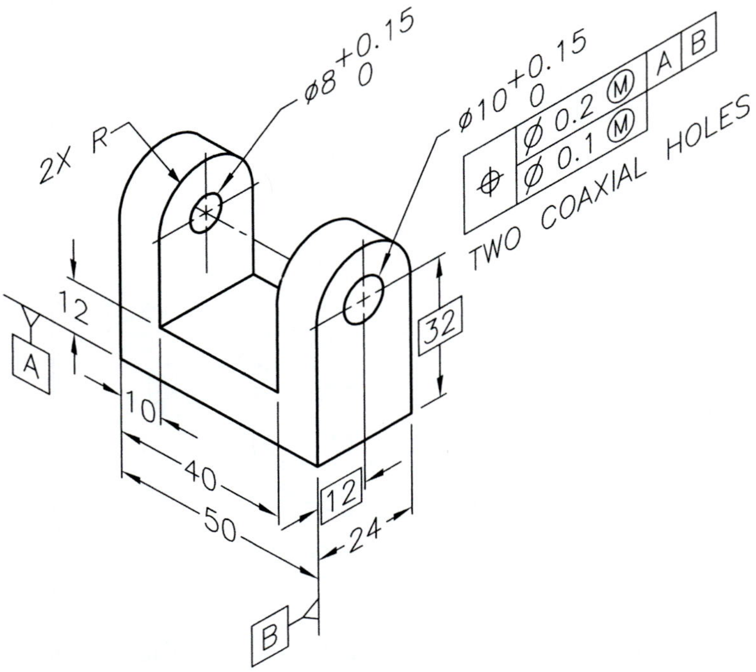

5. Draw the following object as previously instructed. The problem is shown with a full section for clarity. You do not need to draw a section. Untoleranced dimensions are ±.010. Save the drawing as P20-5.

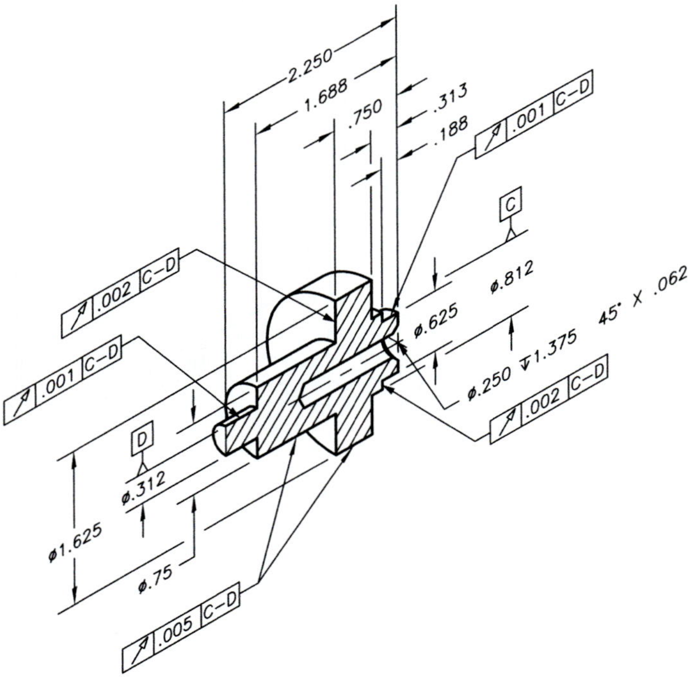

6. Open drawing P17-22. Edit the drawing by adding the geometric tolerancing applications shown below. If you did not draw P17-22, start a new drawing and draw the problem now. Save the drawing as P20-6.

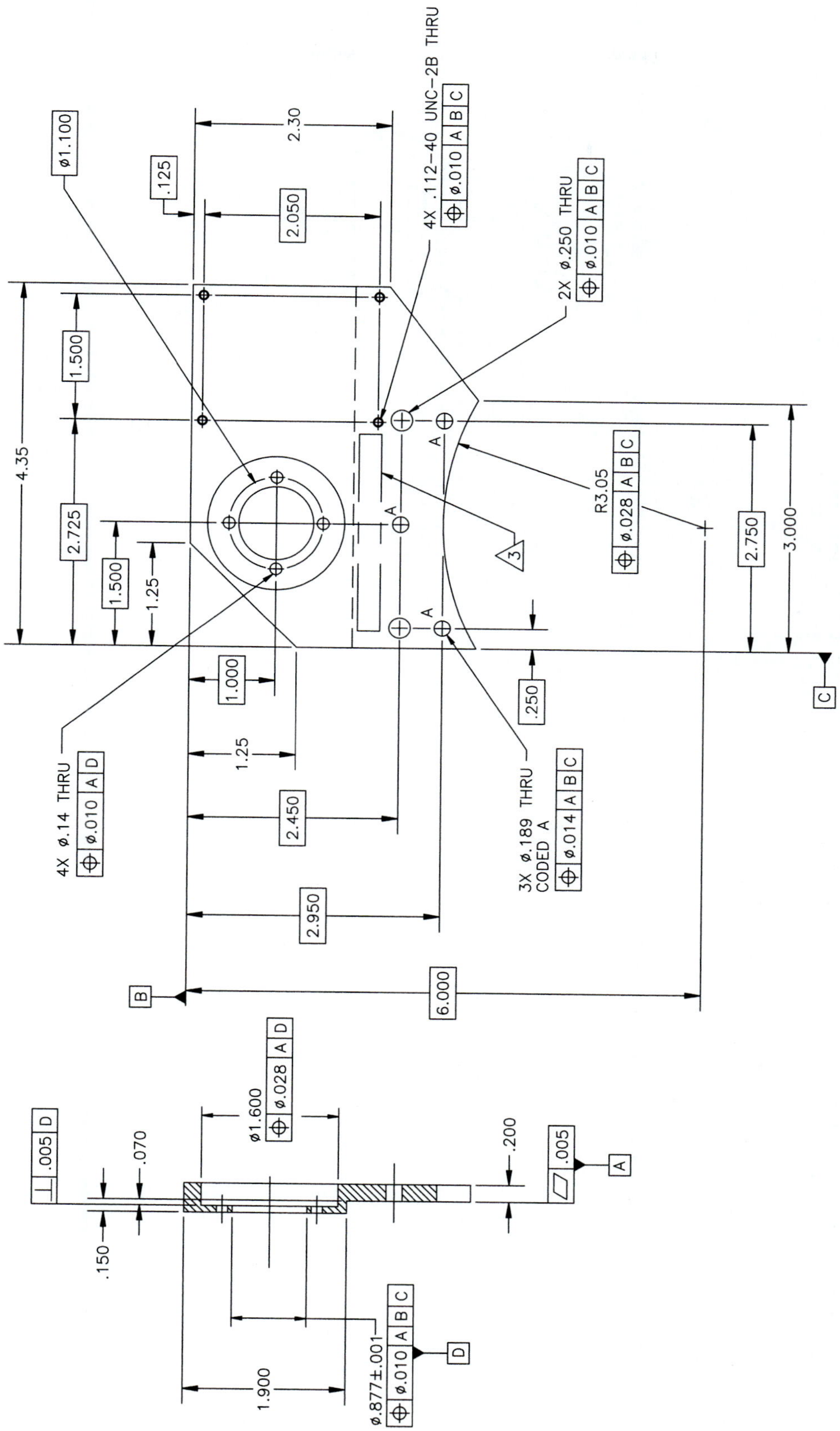

7. Draw the following object as previously instructed. The problem is shown with a half section for clarity. You do not need to draw a section. Untoleranced dimensions are ±.010. Save the drawing as P20-7.

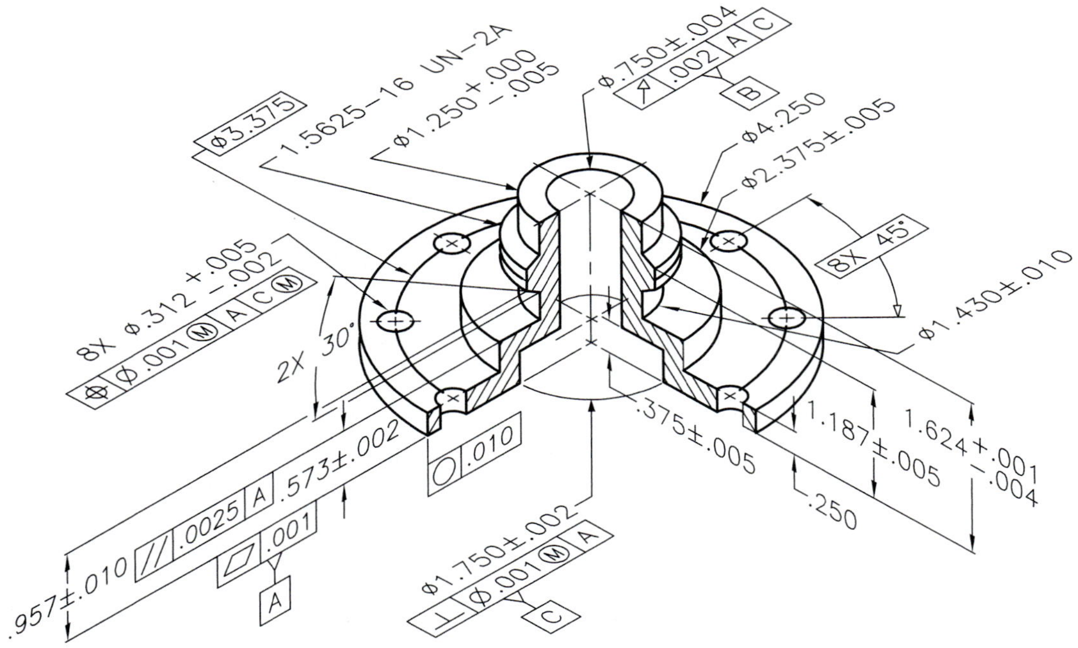

CHAPTER 21

Drawing Section Views and Graphic Patterns

Learning Objectives

After completing this chapter, you will be able to do the following:

- Identify sectioning techniques.
- Use sections and dimensioning practices to draw objects given in engineering sketches.
- Draw section material using the **BHATCH** and **SOLID** commands.
- Insert hatch patterns into drawings using **DesignCenter** and tool palettes.
- Edit existing hatch patterns with the **HATCHEDIT** command.

In mechanical drafting, internal features in drawings appear as hidden lines. It is poor practice to dimension to hidden lines, but these features must be dimensioned. Therefore, section views are used to clarify the hidden features.

Section views show internal features as if a portion of the object is cut away. They are used in conjunction with multiview drawings to completely describe the exterior and interior features of an object.

When sections are drawn, a ***cutting-plane line*** is placed in one of the views to show where the cut was made. The cutting-plane line is the *saw* that cuts through the object to expose internal features. It is drawn with a thick dashed or phantom line in accordance with ASME Y14.2M, *Line Conventions and Lettering*. The arrows on the cutting-plane line indicate the line of sight when looking at the section view.

The cutting-plane lines are often labeled with letters that relate to the proper section view. A title, such as SECTION A-A, is placed under the view. When more than one section view is drawn, labels continue with B-B through Z-Z. The letters *I*, *O*, and *Q* are not used because they may be confused with numbers.

Labeling multiple section views is necessary for drawings with multiple sections. When only one section view is present and its location is obvious, a label is not needed. Section lines are used in the section view to show where the material has been cut away. See **Figure 21-1.**

Sectioning is also used in other drafting fields, such as architectural and structural drafting. Cross sections through buildings show the construction methods and materials. See **Figure 21-2.** The cutting-plane lines used in these fields are often composed of letter and number symbols. This helps coordinate the large number of sections found in a set of architectural drawings.

Figure 21-1.
A three-view multiview drawing with a full section view.

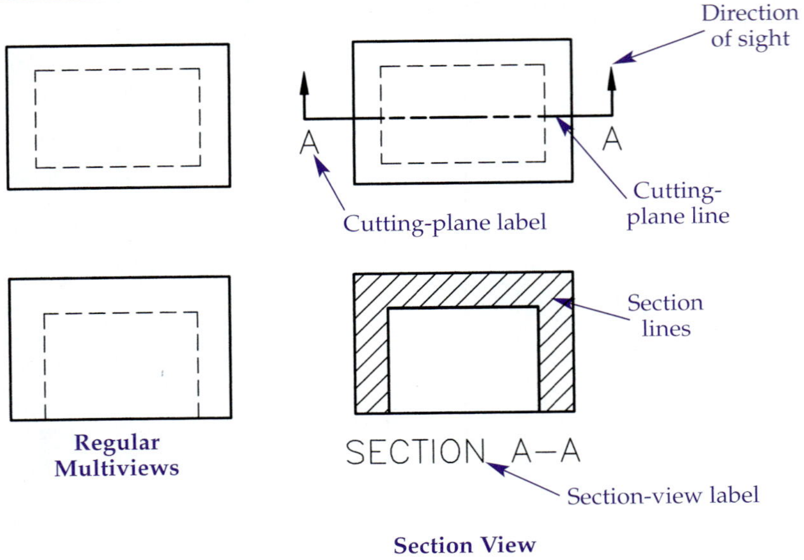

Figure 21-2.
An architectural section view. (Alan Mascord Design Associates)

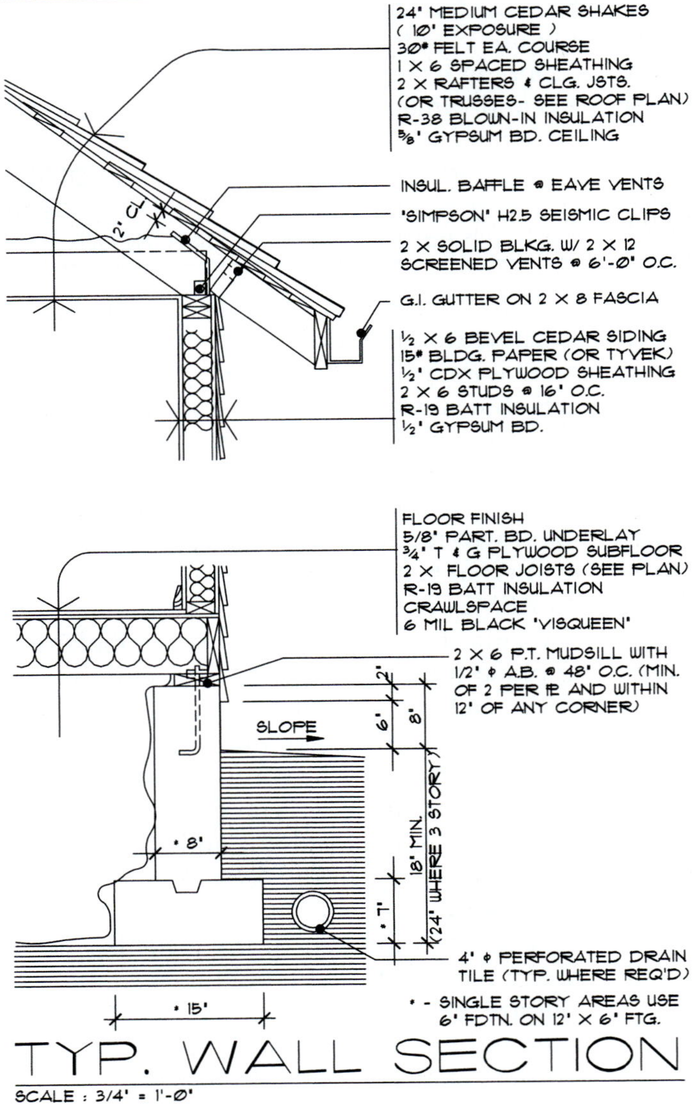

Types of Sections

There are many types of sections available for the drafter to use. The section used depends on the detail to be sectioned. For example, one object may require the section be taken completely through the object. Another may only need to remove a small portion to expose the interior features.

Full sections remove half the object. Refer to **Figure 21-1.** In this type of section, the cutting-plane line passes completely through the object along a center plane.

Offset sections are the same as full sections, except the cutting-plane line is staggered. This allows you to cut through features that are not in a straight line. See **Figure 21-3.**

Half sections show one-quarter of the object removed. The term *half* is used because half of the view appears in section and the other half is shown as an exterior view. Half sections are commonly used on symmetrical objects. A centerline is used to separate the sectioned part of the view from the unsectioned portion. Hidden lines are normally omitted from the unsectioned side. See **Figure 21-4.**

Aligned sections are used when a feature is out of alignment with the center plane. In this case, an offset section will distort the image. The cutting-plane line cuts through the feature to be sectioned. It is then rotated to align with the center plane before projecting into the section view. See **Figure 21-5.**

Revolved sections clarify the contour of objects that have the same shape throughout their length. The section is revolved in place within the object, or part of the view may be broken away. See **Figure 21-6.** This type of section makes dimensioning easier.

Removed sections serve much the same function as revolved sections. The section view is removed from the regular view. A cutting-plane line shows where the section has been taken. When multiple removed sections are taken, the cutting planes and related views are labeled. Drawing only the ends of the cutting-plane lines simplifies the views. See **Figure 21-7.**

Broken-out sections show only a small portion of the object removed. This type of section is used to clarify a hidden feature. See **Figure 21-8.**

Figure 21-3.
An offset section.

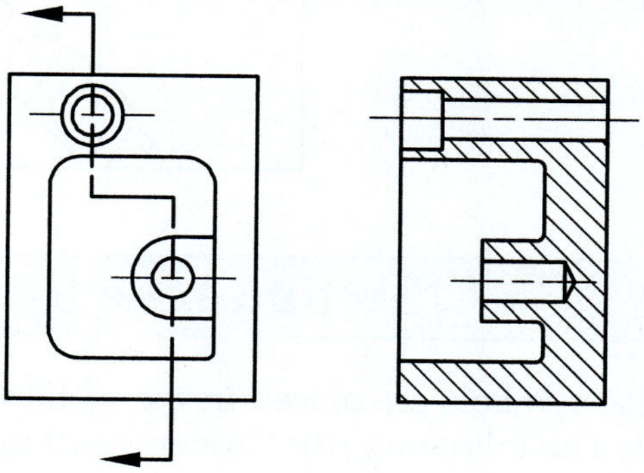

Figure 21-4.
A half section.

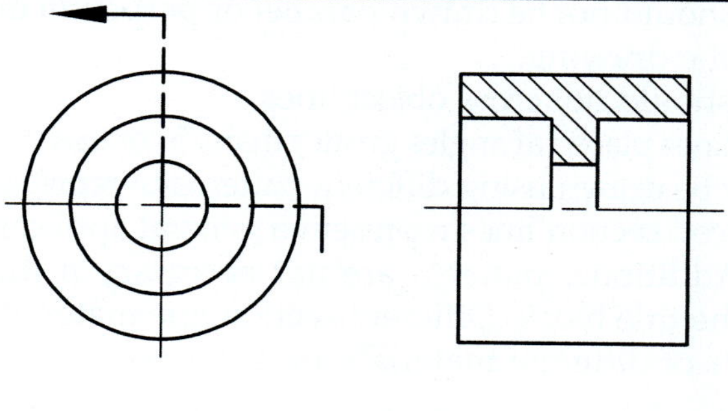

Figure 21-5.
An aligned section.

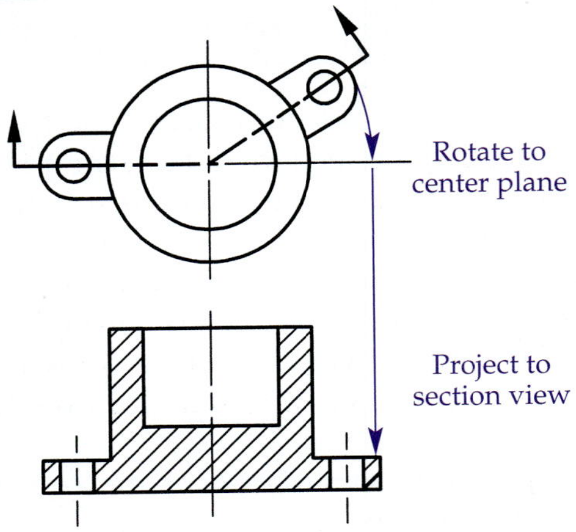

Figure 21-6.
A revolved section.

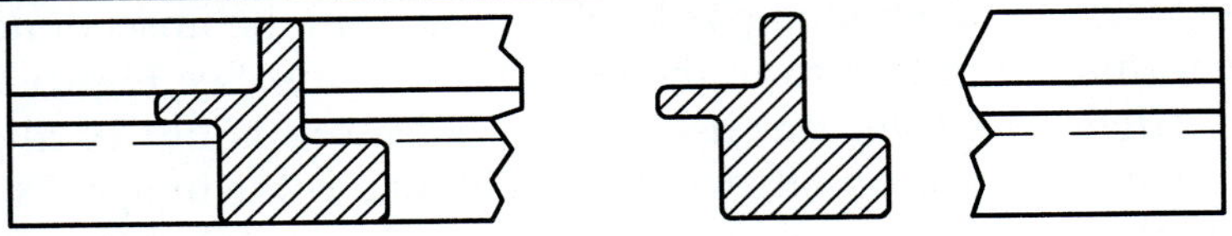

Figure 21-7.
Removed sections.

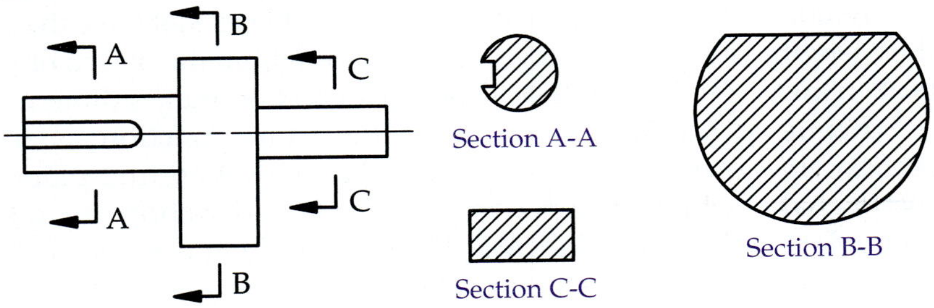

Figure 21-8.
A broken-out section.

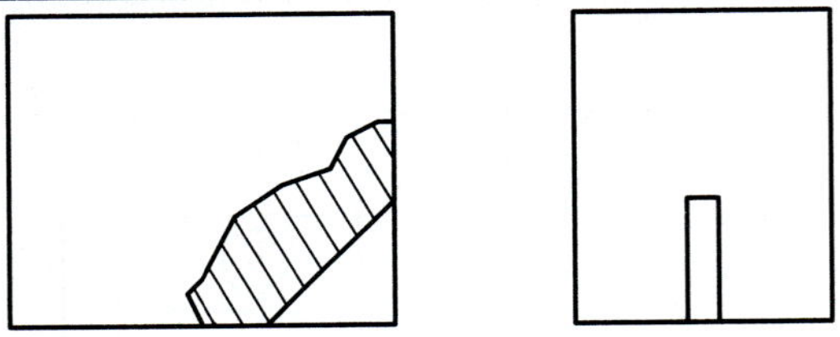

Section Line Symbols

Section line symbols are placed in the section view to show where material has been cut away. The following rules govern section line symbol usage:

- Section lines are placed at 45° unless another angle is required to satisfy the next two rules.
- Section lines should not be drawn parallel or perpendicular to any other adjacent lines on the drawing.
- Section lines should not cross object lines.
- Avoid section lines placed at angles greater than 75° or less than 15° from horizontal.

Section lines may be drawn using different patterns to represent the specific type of material. Equally spaced section lines represent a general application. This is adequate in most situations. Additional patterns are not necessary if the type of material is clearly indicated in the title block. Different section line material symbols are needed when connected parts of different materials are sectioned.

AutoCAD has standard section line symbols available. These are referred to as ***hatch patterns***. These symbols are defined in the acad.pat file. The AutoCAD pattern labeled ANSI31 is the general section line symbol and is the default pattern in a new drawing. It is also used when representing cast iron in a section. When you change to a different hatch pattern, the new pattern becomes the default in the current drawing until it is changed.

The ANSI32 symbol is used for sectioning steel. A sampling of other standard AutoCAD hatch patterns is shown in **Figure 21-9.**

Figure 21-9.
Standard AutoCAD hatch patterns. (Autodesk, Inc.)

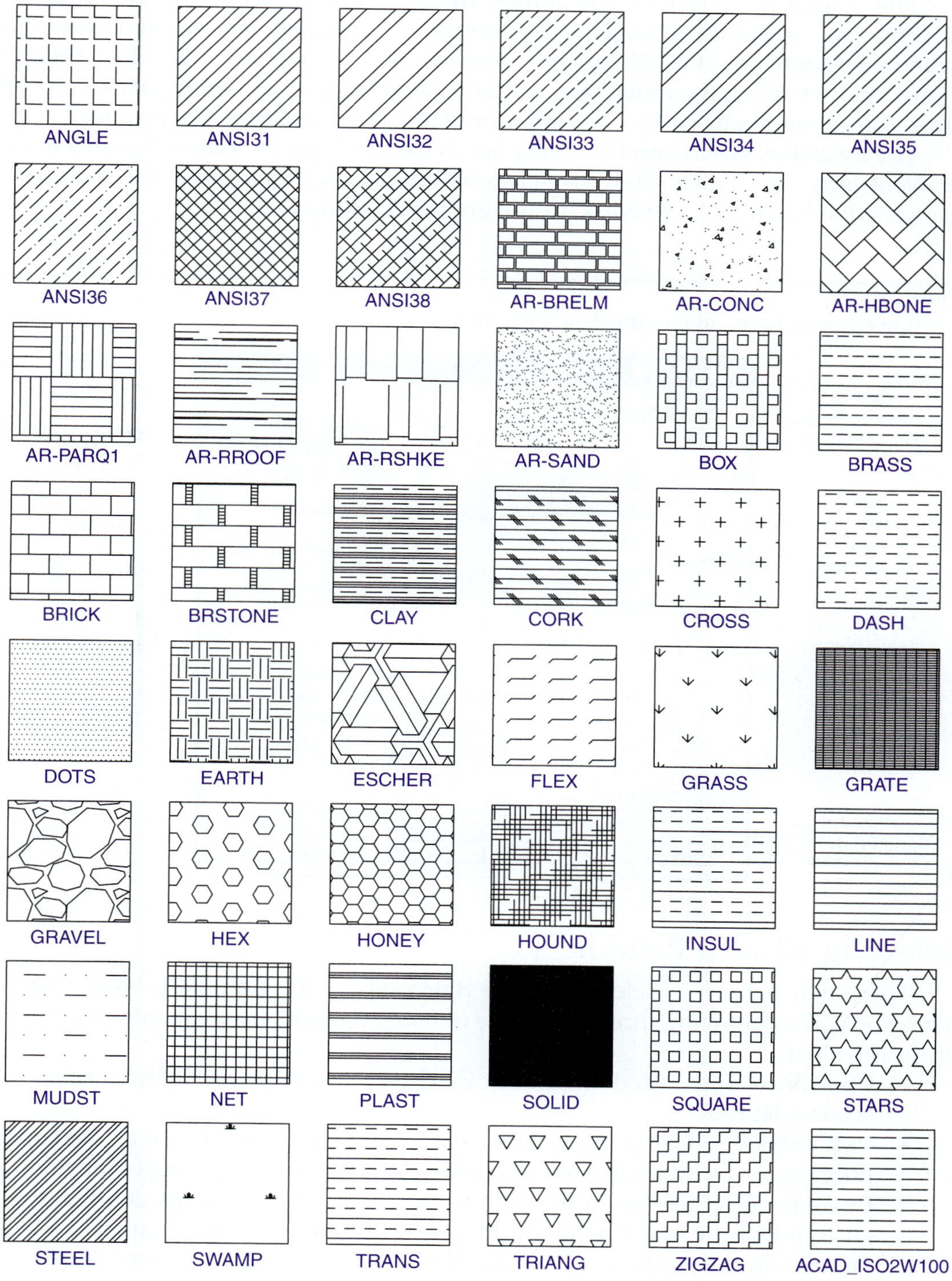

When very thin objects are sectioned, the material may be completely blackened or filled in to clarify features. AutoCAD refers to this as *solid*. The ASME Y14.2M standard recommends that very thin sections be drawn without section lines or solid fill.

Drawing Section Lines and Hatch Patterns

AutoCAD hatch patterns are not limited to sectioning. They can be used as artistic patterns in a graphic layout for an advertisement or promotion. They might also be added as shading on an architectural elevation or technical illustration.

BHATCH
H

Draw
➥ Hatch...

Draw toolbar
Hatch

The **BHATCH** command simplifies the hatching process by automatically hatching any enclosed area. Hatch patterns are selected and applied using the **Boundary Hatch and Fill** dialog box. Access this dialog box with the **BHATCH** command by picking the **Hatch** button on the **Draw** toolbar, by picking **Hatch...** in the **Draw** pull-down menu, or by entering H or BHATCH at the Command: prompt.

The **Boundary Hatch and Fill** dialog box is divided into the **Hatch**, **Advanced**, and **Gradient** tabs. See **Figure 21-10.** A series of buttons that determine the method of applying the hatch and a **Preview** button are also included.

Figure 21-10.
The **Hatch** tab of the **Boundary Hatch and Fill** dialog box.

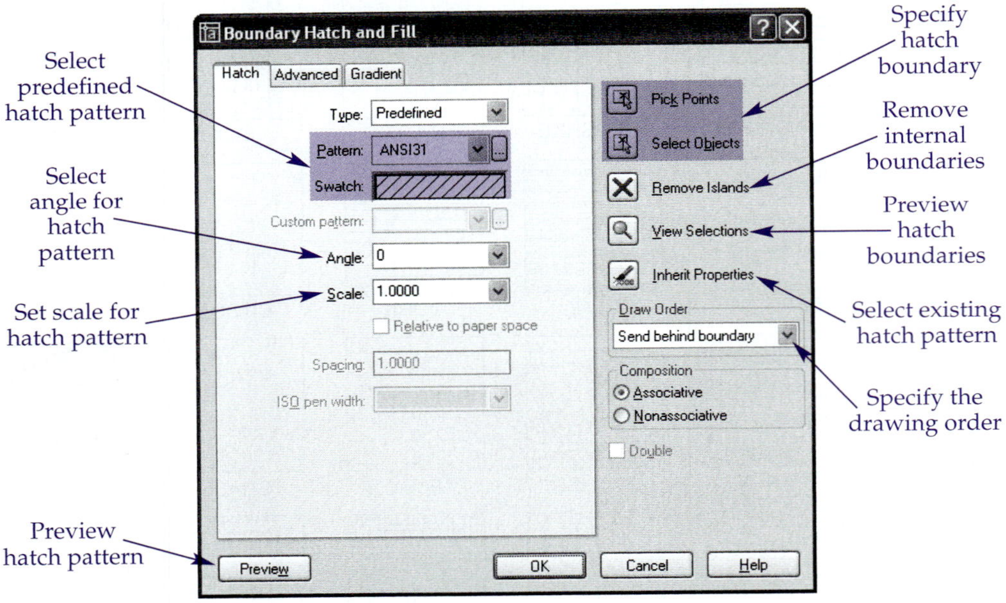

Selecting a Hatch Pattern

The hatch pattern is selected in the **Hatch** tab of the **Boundary Hatch and Fill** dialog box. The following three categories of hatch patterns are available in the **Type:** drop-down list:

- **Predefined.** These predefined AutoCAD patterns are stored in the acad.pat and acadiso.pat files.
- **User defined.** Selecting this option creates a pattern of lines based on the current linetype in your drawing. You can control the angle and spacing of the lines.
- **Custom.** Selecting this option allows you to specify a pattern defined in any custom PAT file that you have added to the AutoCAD search path. (To use the patterns in the supplied acad.pat and acadiso.pat files, choose Predefined.)

Predefined hatch patterns

AutoCAD has many predefined hatch patterns. These patterns are contained in the acad.pat and acadiso.pat files. To select a predefined hatch pattern, select **Predefined** in the **Type:** drop-down list and then select the predefined pattern. You can select the pattern from the **Pattern:** drop-down list, or you can pick the ellipsis (...) button next to the **Pattern:** drop-down arrow to display the **Hatch Pattern Palette** dialog box. See Figure 21-11.

The **Hatch Pattern Palette** dialog box provides sample images of the predefined hatch patterns. The hatch patterns are divided among the four tabs: **ANSI**, **ISO**, **Other Predefined**, and **Custom**. Select the desired pattern from the appropriate tab, and pick the **OK** button to return to the **Boundary Hatch and Fill** dialog box. The selected pattern is displayed in the **Swatch:** tile and listed in the **Pattern:** text box. You can also access the **Hatch Pattern Palette** dialog box by picking the image displayed in the **Swatch:** tile.

You can control the angle and scale of any predefined pattern using the **Angle:** and **Scale:** drop-down lists. For predefined ISO patterns, you can also control the ISO pen width using the **ISO pen width:** drop-down list.

An object can be hatched solid by selecting the Solid predefined pattern or selecting an option from the **Gradient** tab. This is discussed later in this chapter.

User defined hatch patterns

A user defined hatch pattern is a pattern of lines drawn using the current linetype. The angle for the pattern relative to the X axis is set in the **Angle:** text box, and the spacing between the lines is set in the **Spacing:** text box.

You can also specify double hatch lines by selecting the **Double** check box on the right side of the **Boundary Hatch and Fill** dialog box. This check box is only available when User defined is selected in the **Type:** drop-down list. Figure 21-12 shows examples of user defined hatch patterns.

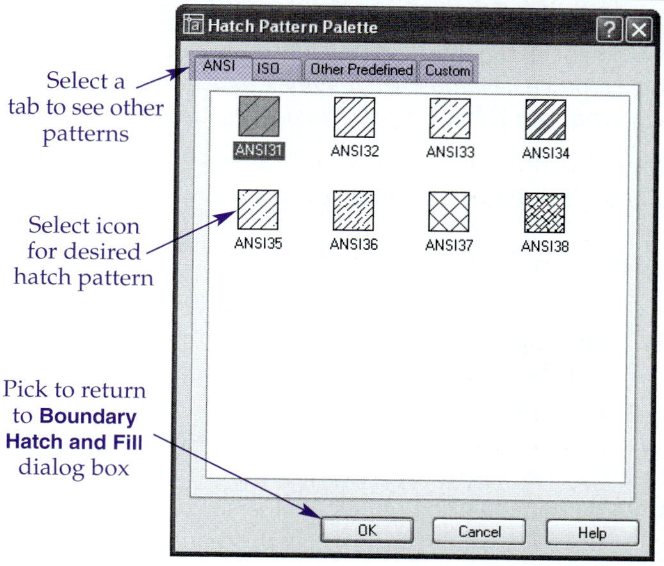

Figure 21-11.
The **Hatch Pattern Palette** dialog box can be used to select a predefined or custom hatch pattern.

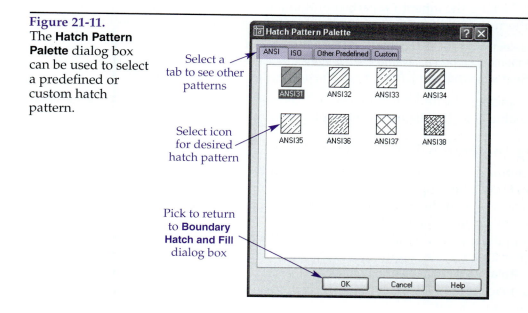

Figure 21-12.
Examples of user defined hatch patterns with different hatch angles and spacing.

Angle	0°	45°	0°	45°
Spacing	.125	.125	.250	.250

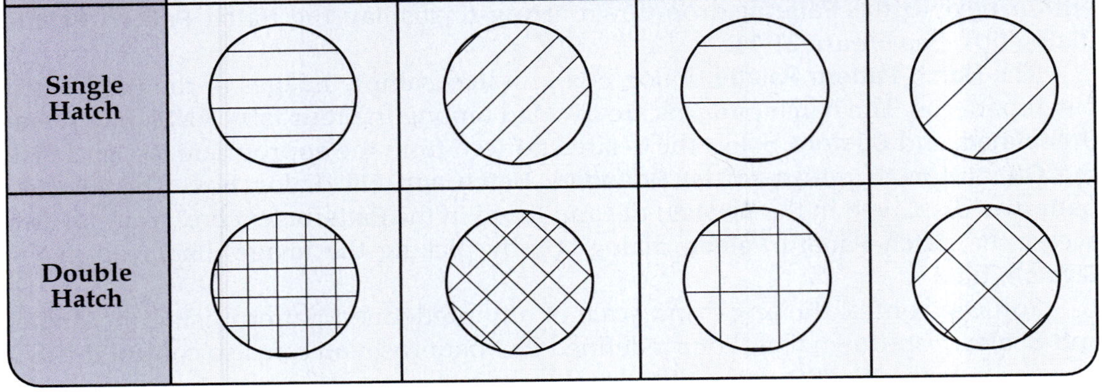

Custom hatch patterns

You can create custom hatch patterns and save them in PAT files. When you select **Custom** in the **Type:** drop-down list, the **Custom pattern:** drop-down list is enabled. You can select a custom pattern from this drop-down list, or pick the ellipsis (...) button to select the pattern from the **Custom** tab of the **Hatch Pattern Palette** dialog box. You can set the angle and scale of custom hatch patterns, just as you can with predefined hatch patterns.

Selecting an existing pattern

You can specify the hatch pattern by selecting an identical hatch pattern from the drawing. Picking the **Inherit Properties** button allows you to select a previously drawn hatch pattern and use it for the current hatch pattern settings. The prompts look like this:

Select associative hatch object: *(pick the desired hatch pattern)*
Inherited Properties: Name <*hatch name*>, Scale <*hatch scale*>, Angle <*hatch angle*>
Select internal point: *(pick a point inside the new area to be hatched)*

After picking the internal point desired, press [Enter] to return to the **Boundary Hatch and Fill** dialog box. The dialog box is displayed with the settings of the selected pattern.

Setting the Hatch Pattern Scale

Predefined and custom hatch patterns can be scaled by entering a value in the **Scale:** text box. The drop-down list contains common scales broken down in .25 increments. The scales in this list start with .25 and progress to a scale of 2, although you can type any scale in the text box.

The pattern scale default is 1 (full scale). If the drawn pattern is too tight or too wide, enter a new scale. Figure 21-13 shows examples of different scales.

The **Relative to paper space** check box is used to scale the hatch pattern relative to paper space units. Use this option to easily display hatch patterns at a scale appropriate for your layout.

Figure 21-13.
Hatch pattern scale factors.

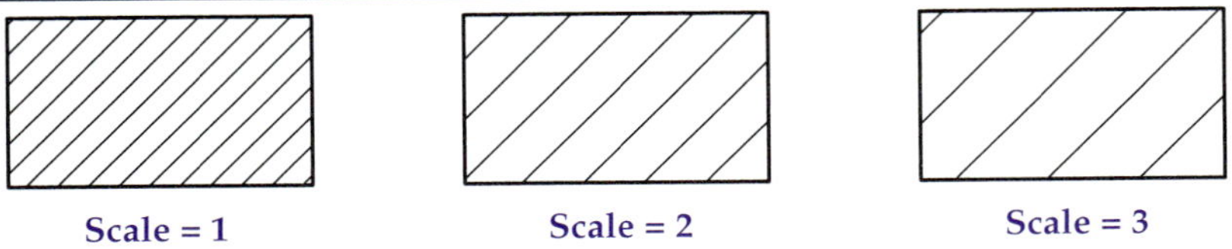

PROFESSIONAL TIP

When hatching large areas, enter a larger scale factor. This makes your section lines look neater and saves regeneration and plot time. For metric drawings, set the hatch scale to 25.4, because 1″ = 25.4 mm.

Selecting Areas to Be Hatched

Areas to be hatched can be selected by one of two methods: picking points or selecting objects. Both of these selection methods are accessed by picking a button in the **Boundary Hatch and Fill** dialog box.

Using the **Pick Points** button is the easiest method of defining an area to be hatched. When you pick the button, the drawing returns. Pick a point within the region to be hatched, and AutoCAD automatically defines the boundary around the selected point.

More than one internal point can be selected. When you are finished selecting points, press [Enter] and the **Boundary Hatch and Fill** dialog box returns. Then pick the **OK** button, and the feature is automatically hatched. See **Figure 21-14.**

NOTE

When you are at the Select internal point: prompt, you can enter U or UNDO to undo the last selection, in case you picked the wrong area. You can also undo the hatch pattern by entering U at the Command: prompt after the pattern is drawn. However, you can preview the hatch before applying it to save time.

The **Select Objects** button is used to define the hatch boundary if you have items that you want to hatch by picking the object, rather than picking inside the object. See **Figure 21-15.** These items can be circles, polygons, or closed polylines. This method

Figure 21-14.
Defining the hatch boundary by picking a point.

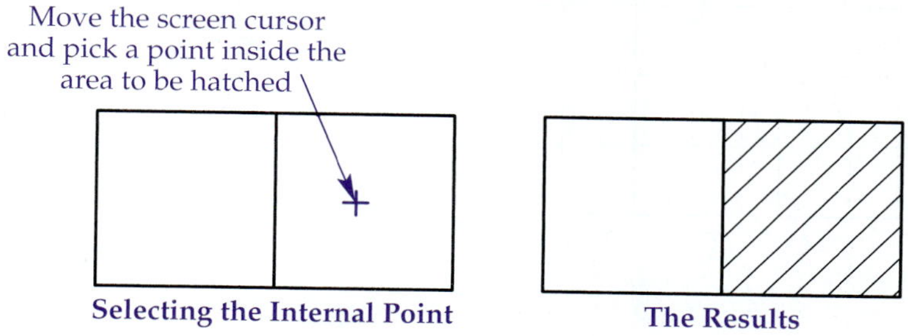

Figure 21-15.
Selecting objects to be hatched.

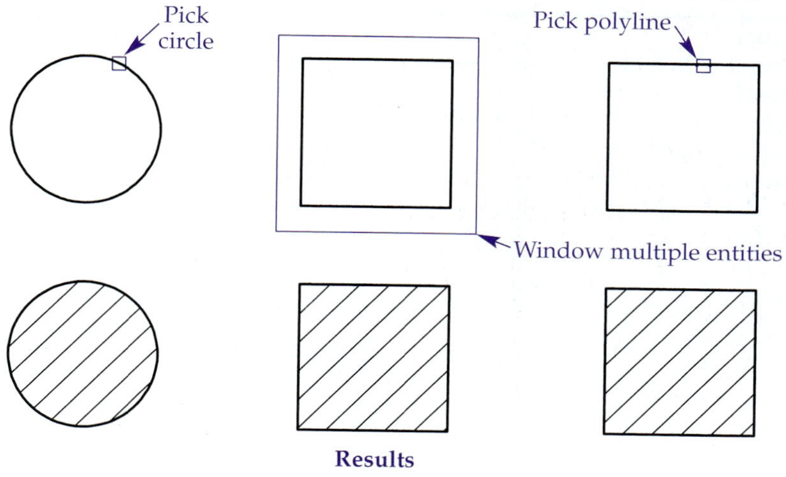

works especially well if the object to be hatched is crossed by other objects, such as the graph lines that cross the bars in **Figure 21-16.** Picking a point inside the bar results in the hatch displayed in **Figure 21-16A.** You can pick inside each individual area of each bar, but this can be time-consuming. If the bars were drawn using a closed polyline, all you have to do is use the **Select Objects** button to pick each bar. See **Figure 21-16B.**

The **Select Objects** button can also be used to pick an object inside an area to be hatched to exclude it from the hatch pattern. An example of this is the text shown inside the hatch area of **Figure 21-17.**

Figure 21-16.
A—Applying a hatch pattern to objects that cross each other using the **Pick Points** button.
B—Applying a hatch pattern to a closed polygon using the **Select Objects** button.

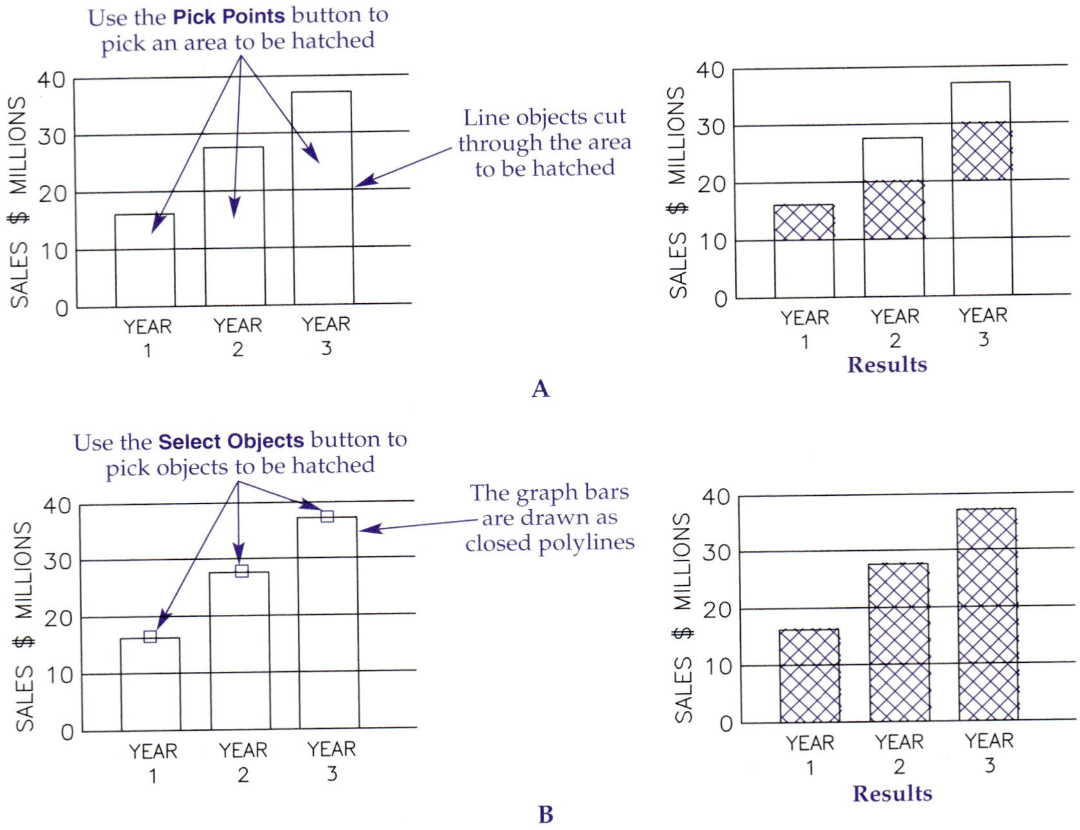

Figure 21-17.
Using the **Select Objects** button to exclude an object from the hatch pattern.

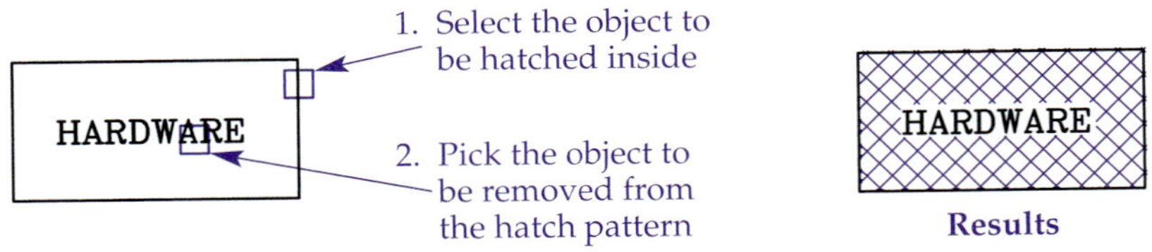

Hatching Objects with Islands

Boundaries inside another boundary are known as ***islands***. AutoCAD can either ignore these internal boundary objects and hatch through them or consider them as islands and hatch around them. See **Figure 21-18.**

When you use the **Pick Points** button to hatch an internal area, islands are left unhatched by default, as shown in **Figure 21-18B.** However, if you want islands to be hatched, pick the **Remove Islands** button in the **Boundary Hatch and Fill** dialog box after selecting the internal point. The drawing window returns with the following prompts:

Select island to remove: *(pick the islands to remove)*
<Select island to remove>/Undo: ↵

Select the islands to remove and press [Enter] to return to the dialog box. The island objects are now hatched. See **Figure 21-18C.**

The **Advanced** tab of the **Boundary Hatch and Fill** dialog box allows you to set the island detection style and the island detection method. See **Figure 21-19.**

The **Island detection style** area is used to specify the method for hatching islands. If no islands exist, specifying an island detection style has no effect. There are three options that allow you to choose the features to be hatched. These options are illustrated by the image tiles in the dialog box. The three style options are:

- **Normal.** This option hatches inward from the outer boundary. If AutoCAD encounters an island, it turns off hatching until it encounters another island. Then the hatching is reactivated. Every other closed boundary is hatched with this option.
- **Outer.** This option hatches inward from the outer boundary. AutoCAD turns hatching off when it encounters an island and does not turn it back on. AutoCAD hatches only the outermost level of the structure and leaves the internal structure blank.
- **Ignore.** This option ignores all islands and hatches everything within the selected boundary.

The **Island detection method** area has two options: **Flood** and **Ray casting**. These options determine whether internal boundaries are defined as islands when hatching. The **Flood** option is selected by default. This setting allows you to leave internal objects unhatched. Pick the **Ray casting** option if you want to ignore island boundaries and hatch through the islands.

Figure 21-18.
A—Original objects. B—Using the **Pick Points** button to hatch an internal area leaves islands unhatched. C—After picking an internal point, use the **Remove Islands** button and pick the islands. This allows the islands to be hatched.

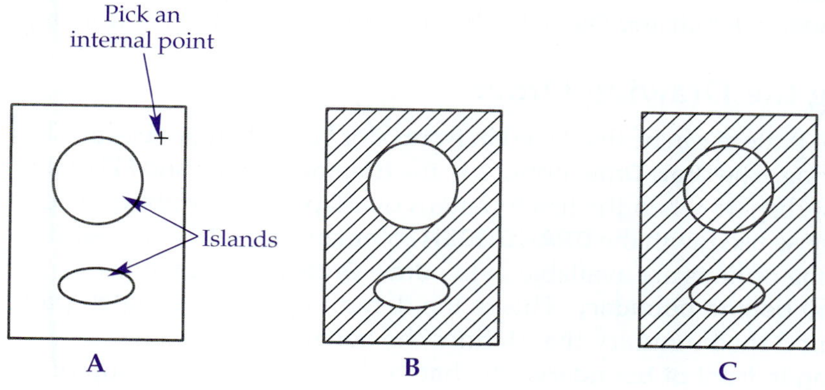

Figure 21-19.
The **Advanced** tab of the **Boundary Hatch and Fill** dialog box contains options for island detection and boundary object creation.

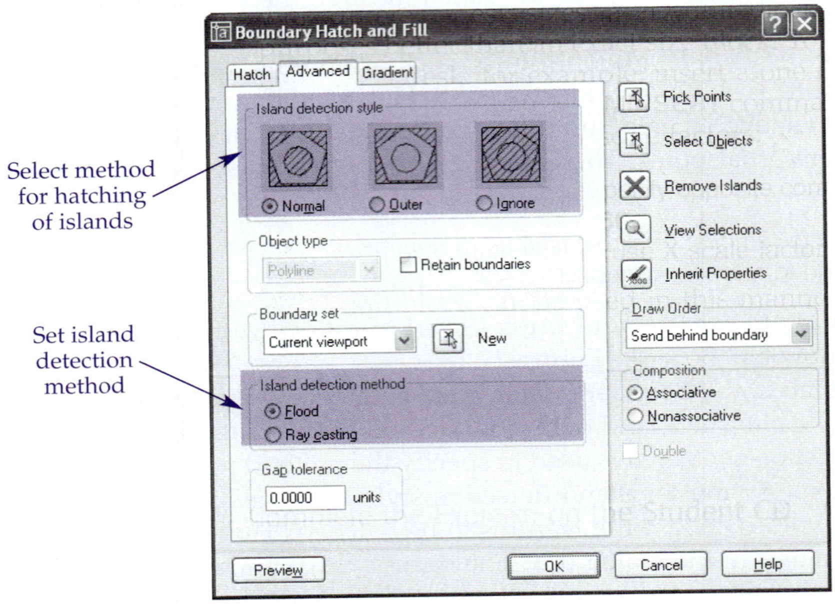

Previewing the Hatch

Before applying a hatch pattern to the selected area, you can use preview tools to be sure the hatch pattern and hatch boundary settings are correct. The following buttons, which are found in the **Boundary Hatch and Fill** dialog box, can be used to preview the boundary and hatch pattern:

- **View Selections button.** You can instruct AutoCAD to let you see the boundaries of selected objects. The **View Selections** button is available after picking objects to be hatched. Pick this button and the drawing is displayed with the hatch boundaries highlighted. When you are finished, press [Enter] or right-click to return to the **Boundary Hatch and Fill** dialog box.
- **Preview button.** Pick the **Preview** button if you want to look at the hatch pattern before you apply it to the drawing. This allows you to see if any changes need to be made before the hatch is drawn. When using this option, AutoCAD temporarily places the hatch pattern on your drawing. You can press [Enter] or right-click to accept the results. If you want to make changes after previewing the hatch, press [Esc] to return to the **Boundary Hatch and Fill** dialog box. Change the hatch pattern, scale, or rotation angle as needed and preview the hatch again. When you are satisfied with the preview of the hatch, pick the **OK** button in the **Boundary Hatch and Fill** dialog box to have it applied to the drawing.

AutoCAD 2005 NEW FEATURE

Defining the Drawing Order

A hatch pattern can be displayed in front of or behind other objects when it is placed in the drawing. The **Draw Order** options in the **Boundary Hatch and Fill** dialog box control the order of display when the hatch pattern overlaps another object. These options are similar to those used with the **DRAWORDER** command, which is discussed in Chapter 10. The following options are available in the **Draw Order** drop-down list:

- **Send behind boundary.** This is the default option. The hatch pattern appears behind the boundary that defines the hatch pattern area.
- **Bring in front of boundary.** The hatch pattern appears on top of the boundary that defines the hatch pattern area.

- **Do not assign.** No drawing order setting is assigned to the hatch pattern.
- **Send to back.** The hatch pattern is sent behind all other objects in the drawing. Any objects that are in the hatching area appear as if they are on top of the hatch pattern.
- **Bring to front.** The hatch pattern is in front, or on top of, all other objects in the drawing. Any objects that are in the hatching area appear as if they are behind the hatch pattern.

If the draw order setting needs to be changed after the hatch pattern is created, use the **DRAWORDER** command. You can also select the hatch pattern, right-click, and then select the appropriate shortcut menu option from the **Draw Order** cascading menu.

Specifying the Hatch Pattern Composition

The **BHATCH** command creates associative hatch patterns by default, but can be set to create nonassociative patterns. ***Associative hatch patterns*** update automatically when the boundary is edited. If the boundary is stretched, scaled, or otherwise edited, the hatch pattern automatically fills the new area with the original hatch pattern. Associative hatch patterns can be edited using the **HATCHEDIT** command, which is discussed later in this chapter.

The **Composition** area of the **Boundary Hatch and Fill** dialog box has the **Associative** and **Nonassociative** options. The **Associative** option is on by default. When selected, the **Nonassociative** option creates a nonassociative hatch that is independent of its boundaries. This means that if you pick only the hatch boundary to edit, the hatch pattern does not change with it. For example, if you pick a hatch boundary to scale, only the boundary is scaled while the pattern remains the same. You need to select both the boundary and the pattern before editing if you want to modify both.

EXERCISE 21-1 Complete the Exercise on the Student CD.

Creating Solid Hatch Patterns

As discussed earlier in this chapter, solid hatches can be created with the Solid predefined hatch pattern. See Figure 21-20. This pattern can be accessed from the **Pattern:** drop-down list in the **Boundary Hatch and Fill** dialog box or the **Other Predefined** tab in the **Hatch Pattern Palette** dialog box. The pattern can be assigned a color. However, the hatching options used with other predefined hatches are not available. This is a quick way to fill a closed object solid. Filled objects can also be created with the **SOLID** command. This command is discussed later in this chapter.

More advanced types of fills can be applied to closed objects by using the gradient fill hatching options available with the **BHATCH** command. A ***gradient fill*** is a shading transition between the tones of one color or two separate colors. Gradient

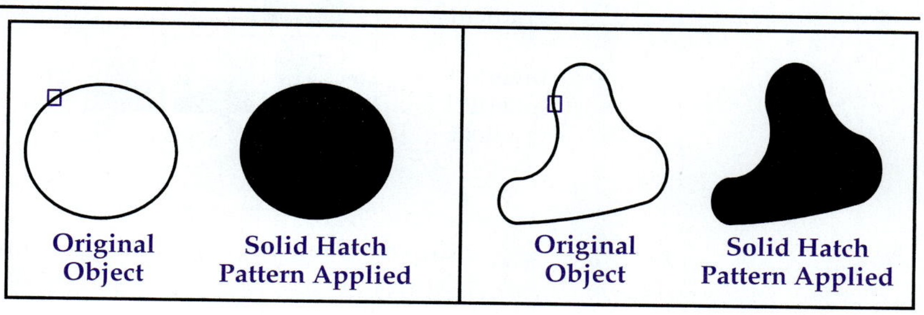

Figure 21-20. Using the Solid hatch pattern to make a basic solid hatch object.

fills can be used to simulate color-shaded objects. There are nine different gradient fill patterns available. They are accessed in the **Gradient** tab of the **Boundary Hatch and Fill** dialog box. See **Figure 21-21.**

The fills are based on linear sweep, spherical, radial, and curved shading. They create the appearance of a lit surface with a gradual transition from an area of highlight to a filled area. When two colors are used, a transition from light to dark between the colors is simulated.

As with other types of hatch patterns, gradient fills are associative when applied by default. They can also be edited in the same way as other hatch patterns with the **HATCHEDIT** command.

The options in the **Gradient** tab of the **Boundary Hatch and Fill** dialog box include settings for one or two fill colors, gradient configuration, and fill angle. The options are as follows:

- **One Color.** This is the default option. It specifies a fill that has a smooth transition between the darker shades and lighter tints of one color. To select a color, pick the ellipsis (...) button next to the color swatch to access the **Select Color** dialog box. When the **One color** option is active, the **Shade** and **Tint** slider bar appears.
- **Two Color.** This option allows you to specify a fill using a smooth transition between two colors. A color swatch with an ellipsis (...) button is displayed for each color.
- **Shade and Tint.** This slider bar allows you to specify the tint or shade of a color used for a one-color gradient fill. A *shade* is a specific color mixed with gray or black. A *tint* is a specific color mixed with white.
- **Centered.** This option is used to specify the gradient configuration. Picking the check box applies a symmetrical configuration. If this option is not selected, the gradient fill is shifted to simulate the projection of a light source from the left of the object.
- **Angle.** This option is used to specify the angle of the gradient fill. The default angle is 0°. The fill can be rotated by selecting a different angle from the drop-down list. The specified angle is relative to the current UCS and is independent of the angle setting for hatch patterns.

Figure 21-21.
The **Gradient** tab of the **Boundary Hatch and Fill** dialog box contains options for creating gradient fill hatch patterns. There are nine types of gradient patterns available.

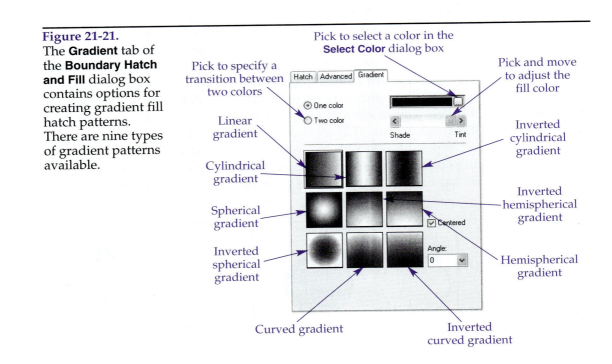

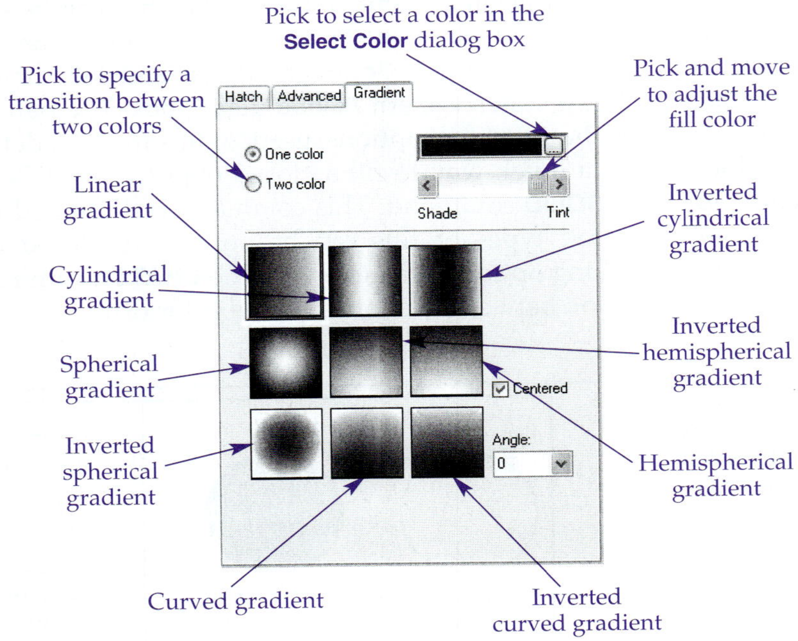

Using DesignCenter to Insert Hatch Patterns

Hatch patterns can be readily located and previewed before they are inserted using **DesignCenter**. To insert a hatch pattern into the current drawing, you can use a drag-and-drop operation. To access **DesignCenter**, pick the **DesignCenter** button on the **Standard** toolbar, select **DesignCenter** from the **Tools** pull-down menu, enter ADC or ADCENTER at the Command: prompt, or use the [Ctrl]+[2] key combination. To drag and drop a hatch pattern from **DesignCenter**, you need to select a PAT file. Once the PAT file is selected, the hatch patterns it contains are displayed in the preview palette. See **Figure 21-22.**

NOTE

AutoCAD includes two PAT files: acad.pat and acadiso.pat. Both are AutoCAD support files located in the Documents and Settings folder path set by the AutoCAD 2005 Support File Search Path. To verify the location of AutoCAD 2005 support files, access the **Files** tab in the **Options** dialog box and check the path listed under the Support File Search Path.

Pick a hatch pattern in the preview palette to display a preview of the pattern. Use one of the following three methods to transfer a hatch pattern from **DesignCenter** into the active drawing:

- **Drag and drop.** Pick the hatch pattern from **DesignCenter** and hold the mouse button. Move the cursor into the active drawing, and a hatch pattern symbol is displayed under the cursor, **Figure 21-23A.** Place the cursor within the area to be hatched, and then release the pick button. The hatch is applied automatically. See **Figure 21-23B.**
- **Boundary Hatch and Fill dialog box.** Right-click on a hatch pattern in **DesignCenter** and select **BHATCH...** from the shortcut menu to access the **Boundary Hatch and Fill** dialog box. The selected hatch pattern is displayed automatically.

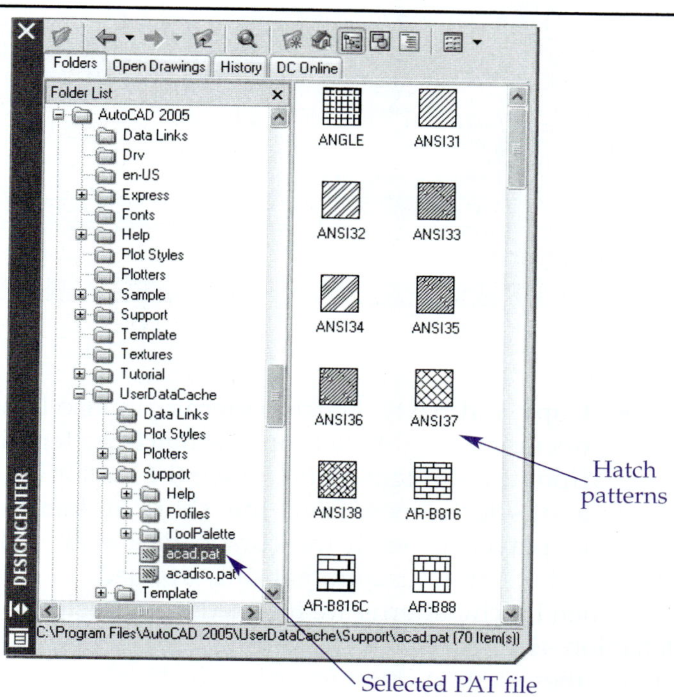

Figure 21-22.
Pick a PAT file in **DesignCenter** to display the available hatch patterns in the preview palette.

Figure 21-23.
When a hatch pattern is selected in the preview palette, a preview image appears. A—The hatch pattern symbol appears under the cursor during the drag-and-drop and paste operations. B—The hatch pattern added to the drawing.

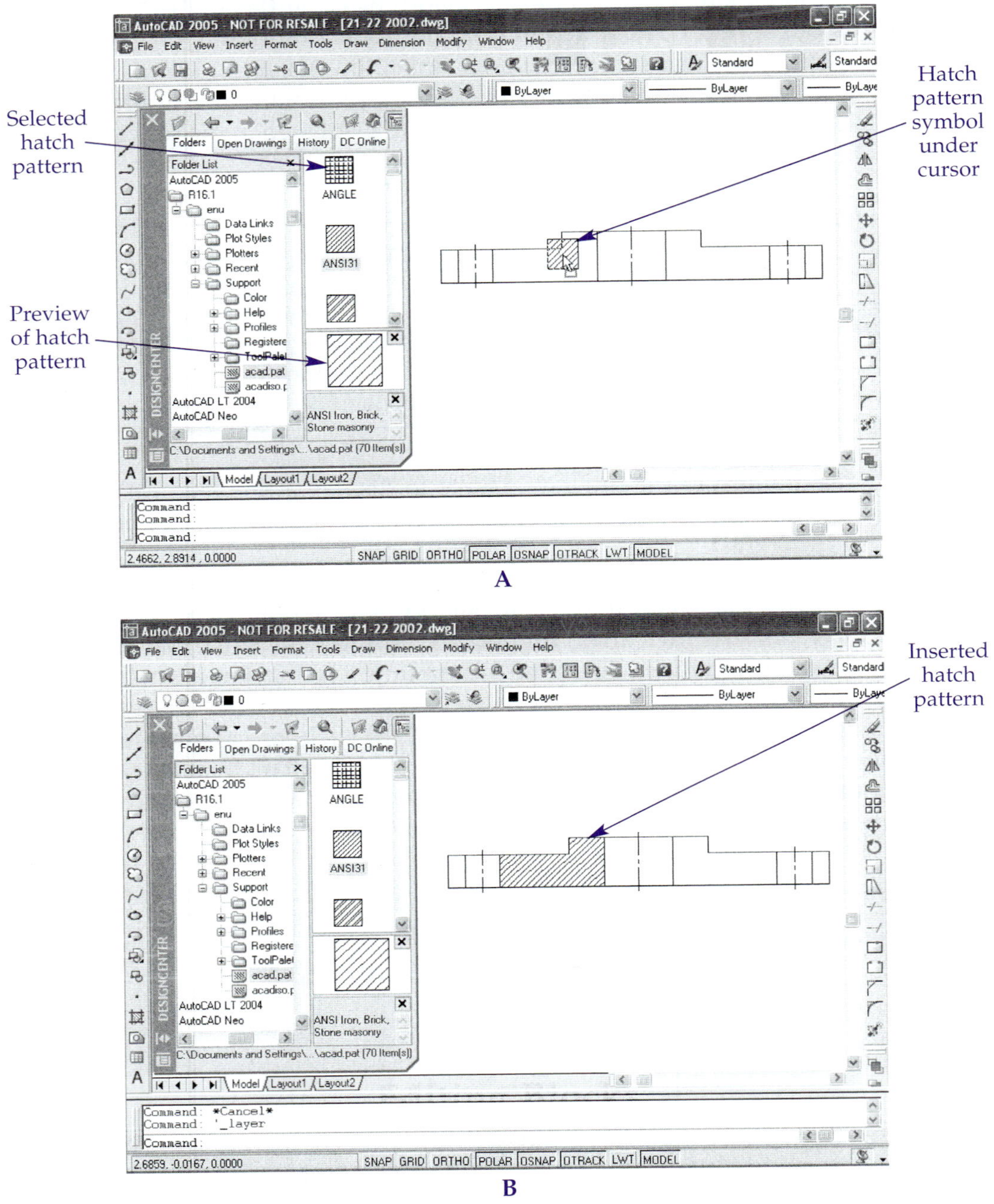

- **Copy and paste.** Hatch patterns can also be inserted using a copy and paste operation. Right-click on the hatch pattern in **DesignCenter** and pick **Copy** from the shortcut menu. Move the cursor into the active drawing, right-click, and select **Paste** from the shortcut menu. The hatch pattern symbol is displayed beneath the cursor. Pick within the area to be hatched, and the hatch pattern is automatically applied.

When hatch patterns are inserted from **DesignCenter**, the angle, scale, and island detection settings match the settings of the previous hatch pattern. If you wish to change these settings after inserting the hatch pattern, use the **HATCHEDIT** command.

NOTE	If you drag and drop or paste a hatch pattern into an area that is not a closed boundary, AutoCAD displays the Valid hatch boundary not found message at the Command: prompt.

EXERCISE 21-2 Complete the Exercise on the Student CD.

Using Tool Palettes to Insert Hatch Patterns

TOOLPALETTES
TP
[Ctrl]+[3]

Tools
➥ **Tool Palettes Window**

Standard toolbar

Tool Palettes

Inserting hatch patterns with the **Tool Palettes** window is similar to inserting them with **DesignCenter**. As with **DesignCenter**, a pattern can be previewed in a window before it is applied. To open the **Tool Palettes** window, pick the **Tool Palettes** button on the **Standard** toolbar, select **Tool Palettes Window** from the **Tools** pull-down menu, enter TP or TOOLPALETTES at the Command: prompt, or use the [Ctrl]+[3] key combination. The **Tool Palettes** window is shown in Figure 21-24.

To drag and drop a hatch pattern from the **Tool Palettes** window, access the palette in which the pattern resides. There are two ways to drag the pattern for insertion into the drawing. You can pick the pattern and drag the image into the drawing while holding down the mouse button, or you can place the cursor over the hatch pattern image and pick once. When you then move the cursor into the drawing area, the hatch pattern is attached to the crosshairs automatically. The location where the crosshairs and the hatch pattern are connected is defined by the insertion point of the hatch pattern. Drag the pattern image to the desired boundary area and pick.

Once the hatch pattern is inserted, you can make modifications with the **HATCHEDIT** command. Hatch editing is discussed later in this chapter.

NOTE	Hatch patterns can be added to the **Tool Palettes** window from **DesignCenter**. There are a variety of customization options available. Using the **Tool Palettes** window is discussed in greater detail in Chapter 22.

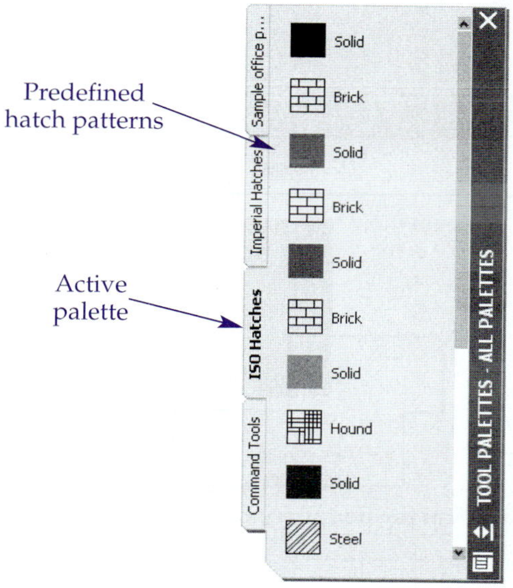

Figure 21-24.
The **Tool Palettes** window can be used to access and insert hatch patterns.

EXERCISE 21-3 Complete the Exercise on the Student CD.

Hatching Unenclosed Areas and Correcting Boundary Errors

AutoCAD 2005 NEW FEATURE

The **BHATCH** command works well unless you have an error in the hatch boundary or pick a point outside a boundary area to be hatched. The most common error is a gap in the boundary. This can be very small and difficult to detect, and happens when you do not close the geometry. However, AutoCAD is quick to let you know by displaying the **Boundary Definition Error** alert box. See Figure 21-25. This alert notifies you that the area cannot be hatched unless you close the boundary or specify a gap tolerance value. The ***gap tolerance*** controls the amount of gap allowed for the opening in the boundary when hatching. The gap tolerance can be set near the bottom of the **Advanced** tab of the **Boundary Hatch and Fill** dialog box. See Figure 21-26. The value in the **Gap tolerance** text box is set to 0 by default. Setting a different value allows you to hatch an unenclosed boundary. Any gaps in the boundary equal to or smaller than the gap tolerance are ignored when applying the hatch. Before the hatch is generated, AutoCAD issues a warning to remind you that the boundary is not closed.

If you encounter the **Boundary Definition Error** alert box and decide you want to find and correct the problem, pick **OK** and return to the drawing. Figure 21-27 shows an object where the corner does not close. The error is too small to see on the screen, but using the **ZOOM** command reveals the problem. Fix the error and use the **BHATCH** command again.

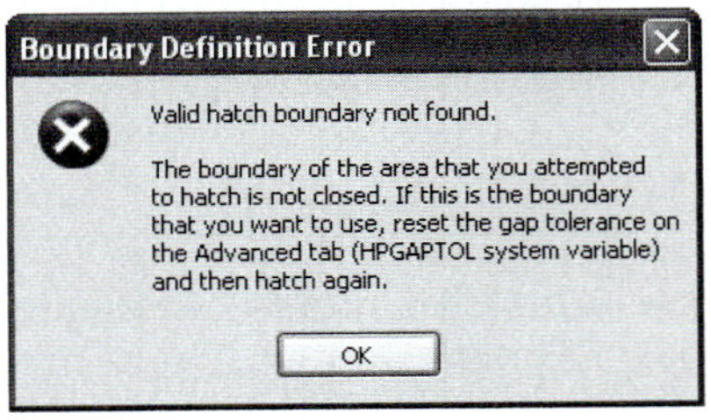
Boundary Definition Error
Valid hatch boundary not found.
The boundary of the area that you attempted to hatch is not closed. If this is the boundary that you want to use, reset the gap tolerance on the Advanced tab (HPGAPTOL system variable) and then hatch again.
OK

Figure 21-25. The **Boundary Definition Error** alert box is displayed if problems occur in your hatching operation.

Gap tolerance
1.0000
units

Figure 21-26. The **Gap tolerance** setting controls whether hatching can be applied to open boundaries.

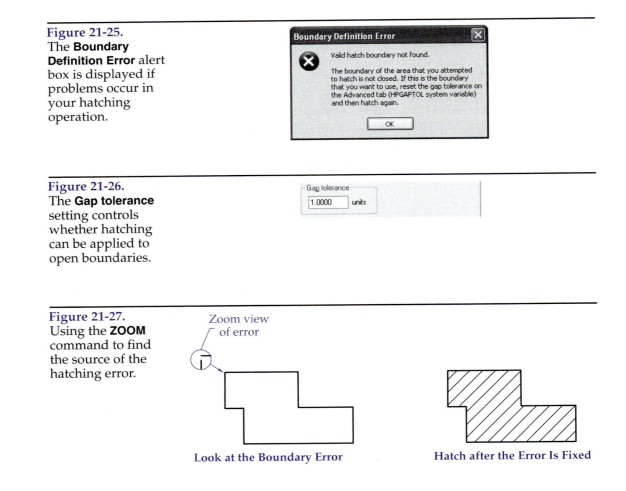

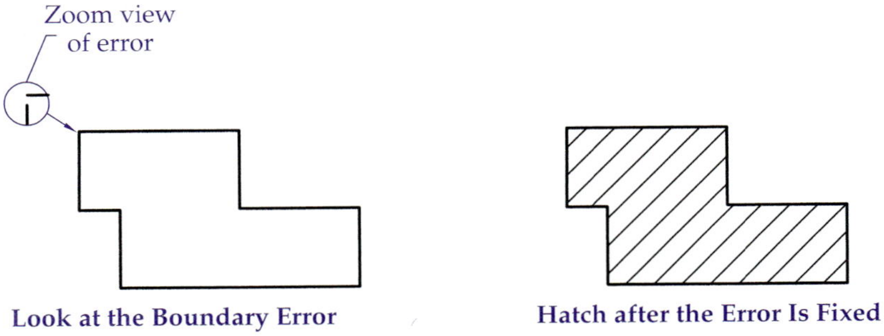
Zoom view of error
Look at the Boundary Error
Hatch after the Error Is Fixed

Figure 21-27. Using the **ZOOM** command to find the source of the hatching error.

PROFESSIONAL TIP

When creating an associative hatch, it is best to specify only one internal point per hatch block placement. If you specify more than one internal point in the same operation, AutoCAD creates one hatch object from all points picked. This can cause unexpected results when trying to edit what appears to be a separate hatch object.

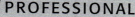

Improving Boundary Hatching Speed

In most situations, boundary hatching works with satisfactory speed. Normally, the **BHATCH** command evaluates the entire drawing visible on screen to establish the boundary. This process can take some time on a large drawing.

You can improve the hatching speed and resolve other problems using options found in the **Advanced** tab in the **Boundary Hatch and Fill** dialog box. See Figure 21-28.

The drop-down list in the **Boundary set** area specifies what is evaluated when hatching. The default setting is Current viewport. If you want to limit what AutoCAD evaluates when hatching, you can define the boundary area so the **BHATCH** command only considers a specified portion of the drawing. To do this, pick the **New** button. Then at the Select objects: prompt, use a window to select the features of the object to be hatched. This is demonstrated in Figure 21-29.

After selecting the object(s), the **Boundary Hatch and Fill** dialog box returns, displaying the **Advanced** tab. Notice in the **Boundary set** area that the drop-down list now displays Existing set as shown in Figure 21-30. The drawing with hatch patterns applied is shown in Figure 21-31.

You can make as many boundary sets as you wish. However, the last one made remains current until another is created. The **Retain boundaries** check box in the **Object type** area can be selected as soon as a boundary set is made. Checking this box allows you to keep the boundary of a hatched area as a polyline, and new boundaries

Figure 21-28.
The **Advanced** tab of the **Boundary Hatch and Fill** dialog box provides options to improve hatching efficiency.

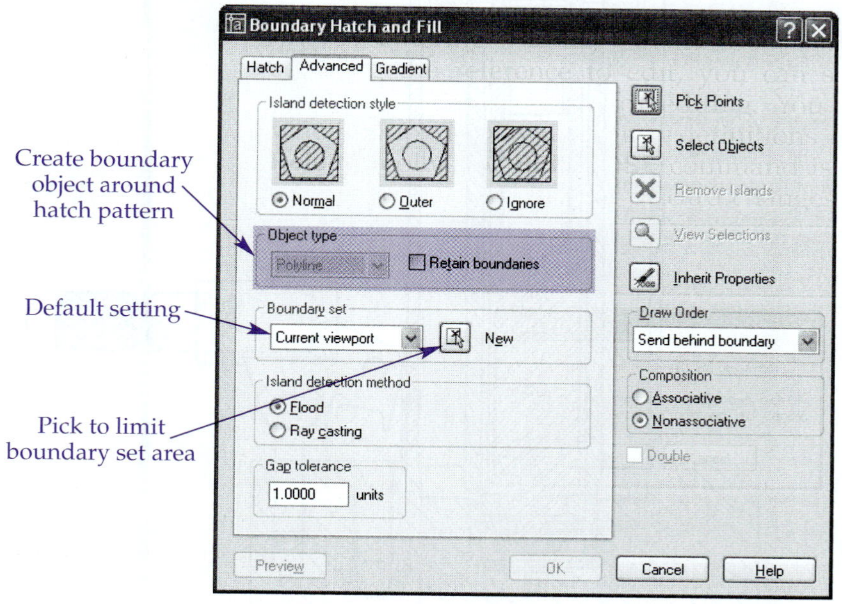

Figure 21-29.
The boundary set limits the area that AutoCAD evaluates during a boundary hatching operation.

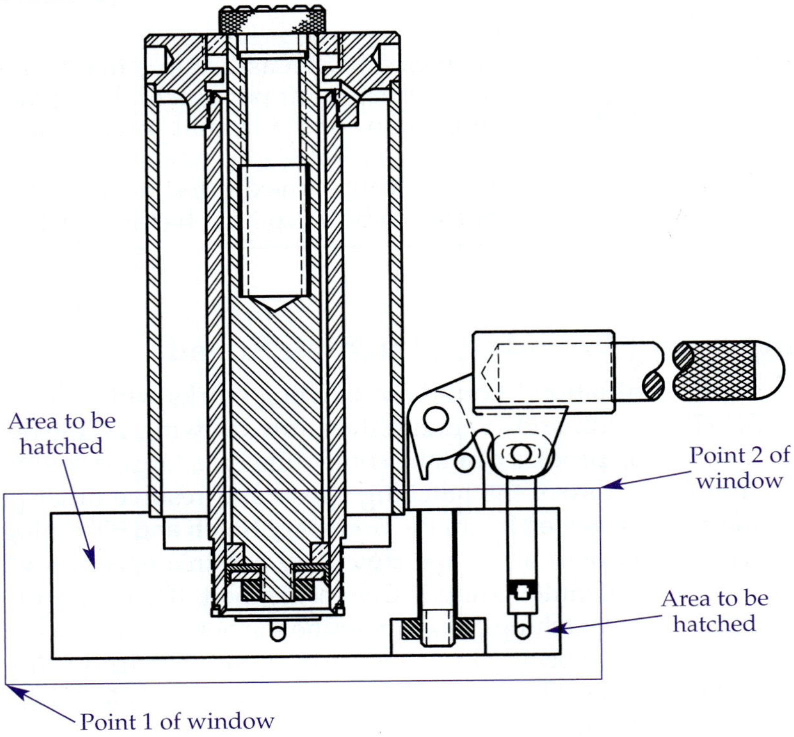

Figure 21-30.
When the **Boundary set** area displays Existing set in the drop-down list, AutoCAD only evaluates objects in the boundary for the hatch.

Figure 21-31.
Results of hatching the drawing in Figure 21-29 after selecting a boundary set.

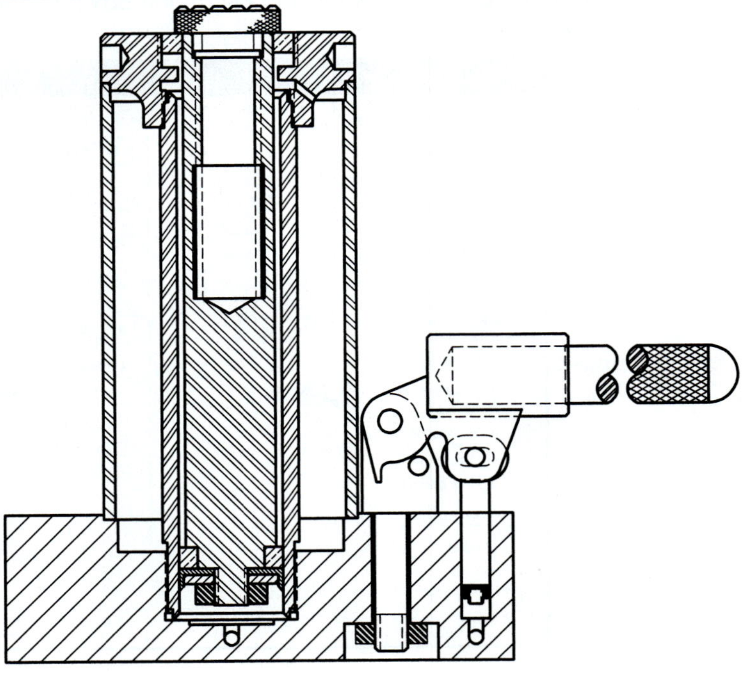

will continue to be saved as polylines whenever you create a boundary area. The default is no check in this box, so the hatched boundaries are not saved as polylines.

When you use the **BHATCH** command and pick an internal area to be hatched, AutoCAD automatically creates a temporary boundary around the area. If the **Retain boundaries** check box is unchecked, the temporary boundaries are automatically removed when the hatch is complete. However, if you check the **Retain boundaries** check box, the hatch boundaries are kept when the hatch is completed.

When the **Retain boundaries** check box is checked, the **Object type** drop-down list is activated. See Figure 21-32. Notice that the drop-down list has two options: Polyline (the default) and Region. If Polyline is selected, the boundary is a polyline object around the hatch area. If Region is selected, then the hatch boundary is the hatched region. A ***region*** is a closed two-dimensional area.

PROFESSIONAL TIP

There are a number of techniques that can help you save time when hatching, especially with large and complex drawings. These include the following:

- Zoom in on the area to be hatched to make it easier for you to define the boundary. When you zoom into an area to be hatched, the hatch process is much faster because AutoCAD does not have to search the entire drawing to find the hatch boundaries.
- Preview the hatch before you apply it. This allows you to easily make last-minute adjustments.
- Turn off layers where there are lines or text that might interfere with your ability to accurately define hatch boundaries.
- Create boundary sets of small areas within a complex drawing to help save time.

NOTE

The **HATCH** command can also be used to hatch objects using entries at the Command: prompt. This command provides prompts for most of the options available in the **Boundary Hatch and Fill** dialog box. The **HATCH** command creates nonassociative hatch patterns, so it is recommended that you use the **Boundary Hatch and Fill** dialog box to hatch objects. For more information on the **HATCH** command, refer to the AutoCAD help system.

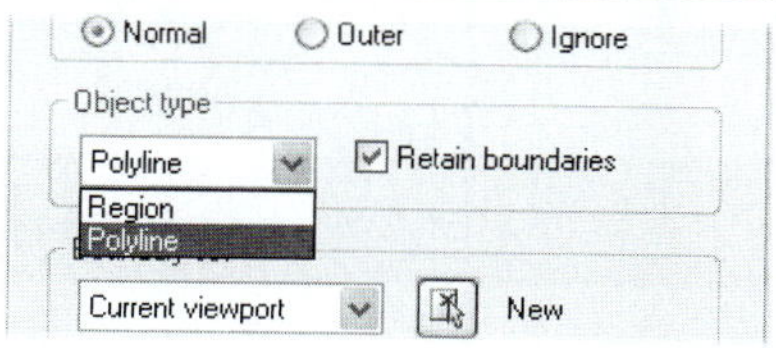

Figure 21-32.
There are two object type options for saving a boundary. These options are only available if the **Retain boundaries** option is checked.

Editing Hatch Patterns

You can edit hatch boundaries and hatch patterns with grips and editing commands such as **ERASE**, **COPY**, **MOVE**, **ROTATE**, **SCALE**, and **TRIM**. If a hatch pattern is associative, whatever you do to the hatch boundary is automatically done to the associated hatch pattern. As explained earlier, a hatch pattern is associative if the **Associative** option in the **Boundary Hatch and Fill** dialog box is active.

HATCHEDIT
HE

Modify
➥ **Object**
➥ **Hatch...**

Modify II toolbar

Edit Hatch

A convenient way to edit a hatch pattern is by using the **HATCHEDIT** command. You can access this command by picking **Hatch...** from the **Object** cascading menu in the **Modify** pull-down menu, picking the **Edit Hatch** button on the **Modify II** toolbar, or entering HE or HATCHEDIT at the Command: prompt. You can also double-click on the hatch pattern you wish to edit. The command sequence is as follows:

Command: **HE** *or* **HATCHEDIT**↵
Select associative hatch object: *(pick the hatch pattern to edit)*

When you select a hatch pattern or patterns to edit, the **Hatch Edit** dialog box is displayed. See **Figure 21-33.** The **Hatch Edit** dialog box has the same features as the **Boundary Hatch and Fill** dialog box, except that only the items that control hatch pattern characteristics are available.

The available features work just like they do in the **Boundary Hatch and Fill** dialog box. You can change the pattern type, scale, or angle; remove the associative qualities; set the inherit properties of an existing hatch pattern; or use the **Advanced** or **Gradient** tab options to edit the hatch pattern. You can also preview the edited hatch before applying it to your drawing.

PROFESSIONAL TIP

The **MATCHPROP** command can also be used to inherit the properties of an existing hatch pattern and apply it to the hatch pattern you wish to edit. This command can be used to apply existing hatch patterns to objects in the current drawing file or to objects in other drawing files that are open in AutoCAD.

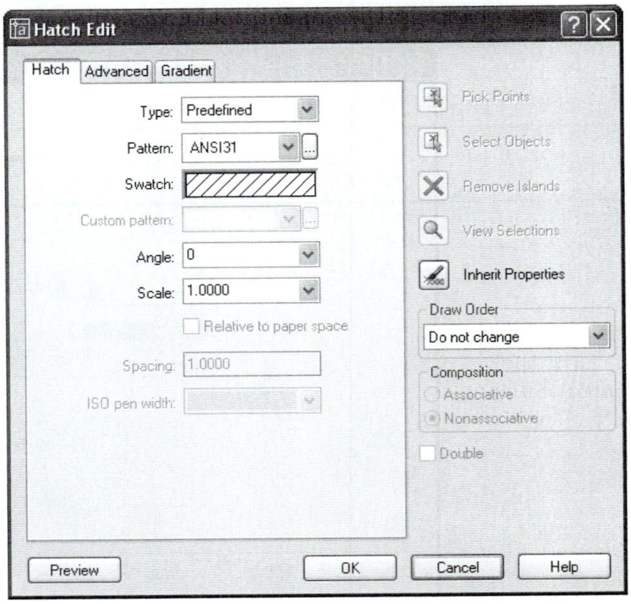

Figure 21-33.
The **Hatch Edit** dialog box is used to edit hatch patterns. Notice that only the options related to hatch characteristics are available.

EXERCISE 21-4 Complete the Exercise on the Student CD.

Editing Associative Hatch Patterns

When you edit an object with an associative hatch pattern, the hatch pattern changes to match the edit. For example, the object in **Figure 21-34A** is stretched and the hatch pattern matches the new object. When the island in **Figure 21-34B** is erased, the hatch pattern is automatically revised to fill the area where the island was located. As long as the original boundary is being edited, the associative hatch will update. After you erase the island in **Figure 21-34B,** a new island cannot be added, because it was not originally calculated to be a part of the hatch boundary.

Figure 21-34.
Editing objects with associative hatch patterns. The hatch pattern changes to match the edit.

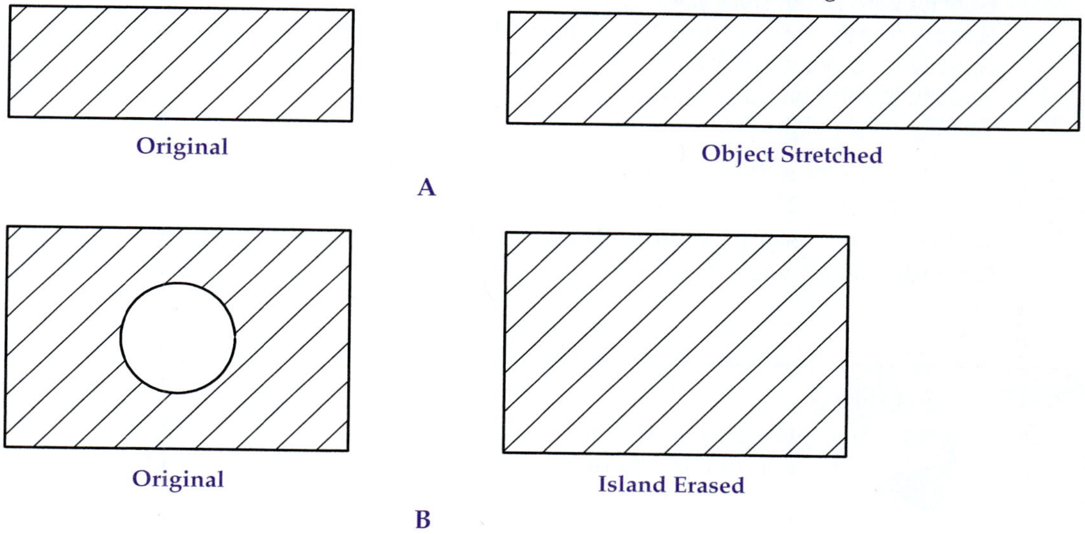

EXERCISE 21-5 Complete the Exercise on the Student CD.

Drawing Objects with Solid Fills

In previous chapters, you have learned that polylines, polyarcs, trace segments, and donuts may be filled in solid when **FILL** mode is on. When **FILL** is off, these objects are drawn as outlines only. The **SOLID** command works in much the same manner except that it fills objects or shapes that are already drawn and fills areas that are simply defined by picking points.

The **SOLID** command is accessed by picking the **2D Solid** button from the **Surfaces** toolbar, picking **2D Solid** from the **Surfaces** cascading menu in the **Draw** pull-down menu, or entering SO or SOLID at the Command: prompt. You are then prompted to select points. If the object to fill solid is rectangular, pick the corners in the numbered sequence shown in **Figure 21-35.**

SOLID
SO

Draw
➥ **Surfaces**
➥ **2D Solid**

Surfaces toolbar

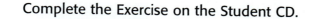

2D Solid

Figure 21-35.
Using the **SOLID** command. Select the points in the order shown.

Notice that AutoCAD prompts you for another third point after the first four. This prompt allows you to fill in additional parts of the same object, if needed. AutoCAD assumes that the third and fourth points of the previous solid are now points one and two for the next solid. The subsequent points you select fill in the object in a triangular fashion. Continue picking points, or press [Enter] to stop. The following sequence draws the object shown in **Figure 21-36:**

Command: **SO** *or* **SOLID**↵
Specify first point: *(pick point 1)*
Specify second point: *(pick point 2)*
Specify third point: *(pick point 3)*
Specify fourth point or <exit>: *(pick point 4 and the rectangular portion is drawn)*
Specify third point: *(pick point 5)*
Specify fourth point or <exit>: ↵
Specify third point: ↵

Different types of solid arrangements can be drawn by altering the numbering sequence. See **Figure 21-37.** Also, the **SOLID** command can be used to draw filled shapes without prior use of the **LINE**, **PLINE**, or **RECTANG** commands; simply pick the points. Consider using various object snap modes when picking the points of existing geometry.

PROFESSIONAL TIP

Keep in mind that many solids and dense hatches require extensive regeneration. On a complex drawing, create filled solids and hatching on a separate layer and keep the layer frozen until you are ready to plot the drawing. Many solids and dense hatch patterns also adversely affect plot time. Save plotting time by making check plots with **FILL** mode off.

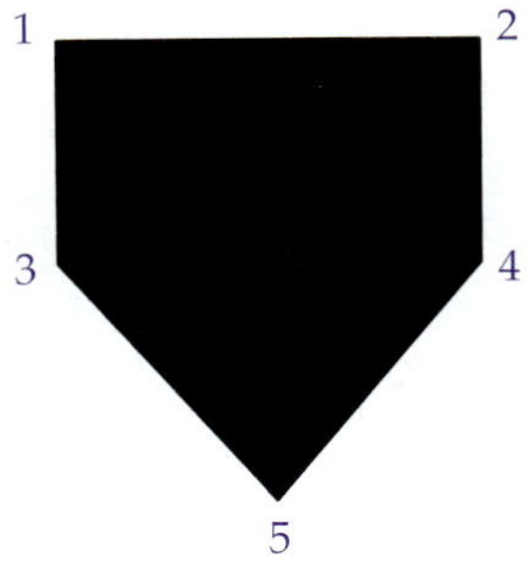

Figure 21-36.
The **SOLID** command allows you to enter a second "third point" (point 5 here) after entering the fourth point.

Figure 21-37.
Using a different numbering sequence for the **SOLID** command will give you different results.

EXERCISE 21-6 Complete the Exercise on the Student CD.

EXPRESS TOOLS CHAPTER 21 The following Express Tool is related to topics discussed in this chapter. Refer to the Student CD for information on this tool:
Super Hatch

Chapter Test

Answer the following questions on a separate sheet of paper.

For Questions 1–6, name the type of section identified in each of the following statements:

1. Half of the object is removed, the cutting-plane line generally cuts completely through along the center plane.
2. Used primarily on symmetrical objects, the cutting-plane line cuts through one-quarter of the object.
3. The cutting-plane line is staggered through features that do not lie in a straight line.
4. The section is turned in place to clarify the contour of the object.
5. The section is rotated and located from the object. The location of the section is normally identified with a cutting-plane line.
6. A small portion of the view is removed to clarify an internal feature.

7. AutoCAD's standard section line symbols are called _____.
8. In which pull-down menu can you select **Hatch...** to display the **Boundary Hatch and Fill** dialog box?
9. Name the two files that contain hatch patterns that can be copied from **DesignCenter**.
10. Explain the purpose and function of the ellipsis (...) buttons in the **Boundary Hatch and Fill** dialog box.
11. Identify two ways to select a predefined hatch pattern in the **Boundary Hatch and Fill** dialog box.
12. Explain how you set a hatch scale in the **Boundary Hatch and Fill** dialog box.
13. Explain how to use an existing hatch pattern on a drawing as the current pattern for your next hatch.
14. Describe the purpose of the **Preview** button found in the **Boundary Hatch and Fill** dialog box.
15. What is the purpose of the **Gap tolerance** setting in the **Boundary Hatch and Fill** dialog box?
16. How do you limit AutoCAD hatch evaluation to a specific area of the drawing?
17. Define *associative hatch pattern*.
18. How do you change the hatch angle in the **Boundary Hatch and Fill** dialog box?
19. Describe the fundamental difference between using the **Pick Points** and the **Select Objects** buttons in the **Boundary Hatch and Fill** dialog box.
20. If you use the **Pick Points** button inside the **Boundary Hatch and Fill** dialog box to hatch an area, how do you hatch around an island inside the area to be hatched?

21. How do you use the **BHATCH** command to hatch an object with text inside without hatching the text?
22. Name the command that may be used to edit existing associative hatch patterns.
23. How does the **Hatch Edit** dialog box compare to the **Boundary Hatch and Fill** dialog box?
24. Explain the three island detection style options.
25. What happens if you erase an island inside an associative hatch pattern?
26. What is the result of stretching an object that is hatched with an associative hatch pattern?
27. In addition to the **BHATCH** command, what command can be used to fill an object solid?
28. What are gradient fill hatch patterns? How are they created with the **BHATCH** command?
29. Explain how to use drag-and-drop to insert a hatch pattern from **DesignCenter** into an active drawing.
30. Explain two ways to use drag-and-drop for inserting a hatch pattern from a tool palette into the drawing.

Drawing Problems

For Problems 1–4, use the following guidelines:

A. Use an appropriate template with a mechanical drawing title block.

B. Create separate layers for views, dimensions, and section lines.

C. Place the following general notes 1/2″ from the lower-left corner.

2. REMOVE ALL BURRS AND SHARP EDGES
1. INTERPRET DIMENSIONS AND TOLERANCES PER ASME Y14.5M-1994
NOTES:

1. Draw the full section shown on the right. Save the drawing as P21-1.

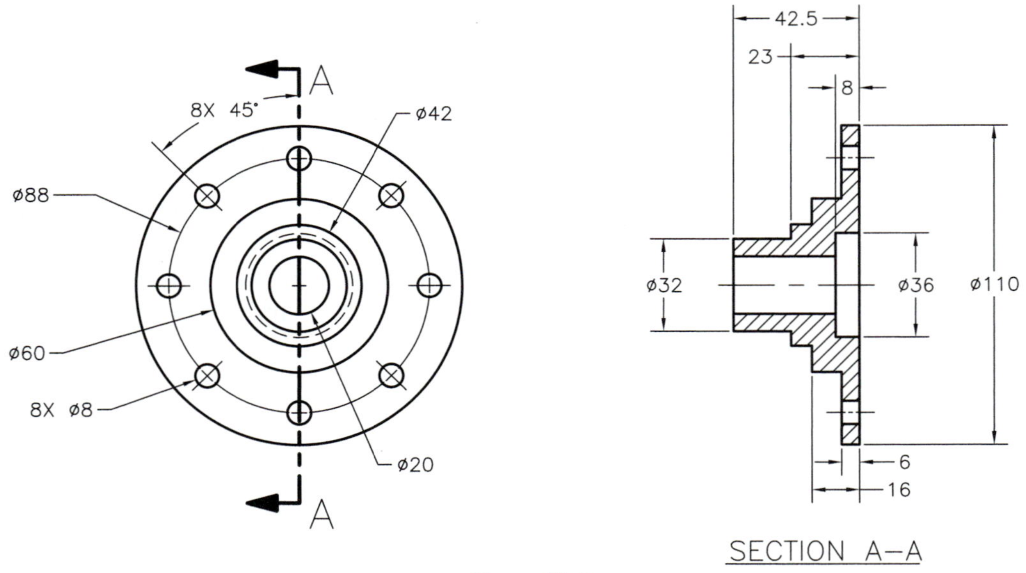

Name: Hub
Material: Cast Iron

2. Draw the half section shown in the center. Add the following notes: OIL QUENCH 40-45C, CASE HARDEN .020 DEEP, and 59-60 ROCKWELL C SCALE. Save the drawing as P21-2.

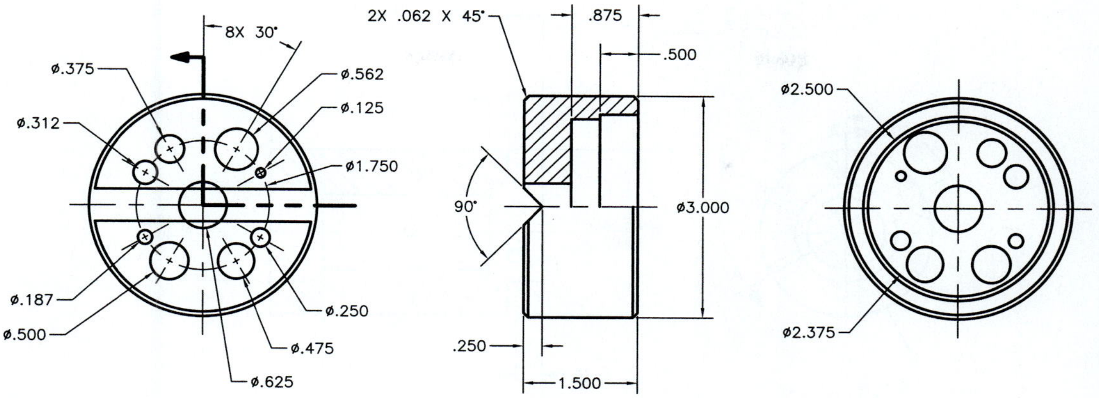

Name: Diffuser
Material: AISI 1018

3. Draw the aligned section shown on the right. Add the following notes: FINISH ALL OVER 1.63 mm UNLESS OTHERWISE SPECIFIED and ALL DIMENSIONS ARE IN MILLIMETERS. Save the drawing as P21-3.

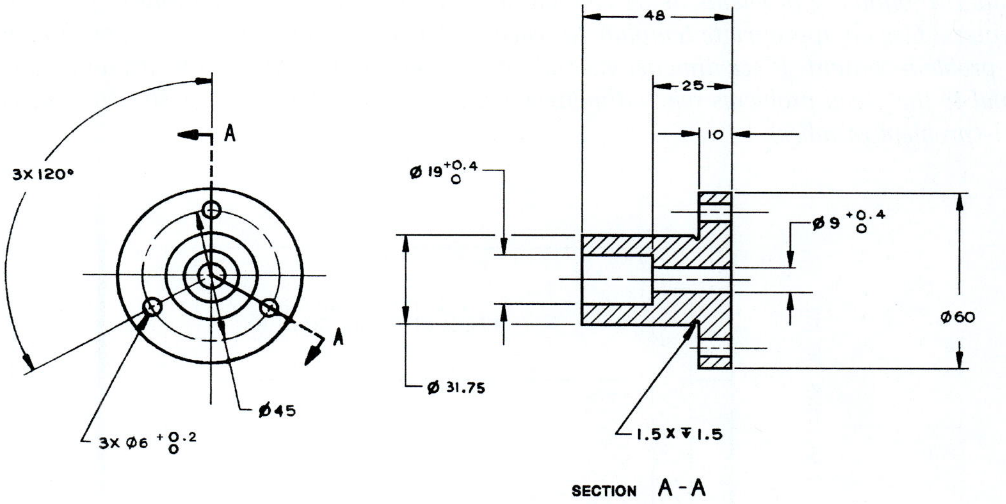

Name: Bushing
Material: SAE 1030

4. Draw the aligned section shown on the right. Add the following notes: FINISH ALL OVER 1.63 mm UNLESS OTHERWISE SPECIFIED and ALL DIMENSIONS ARE IN MILLIMETERS. Save the drawing as P21-4.

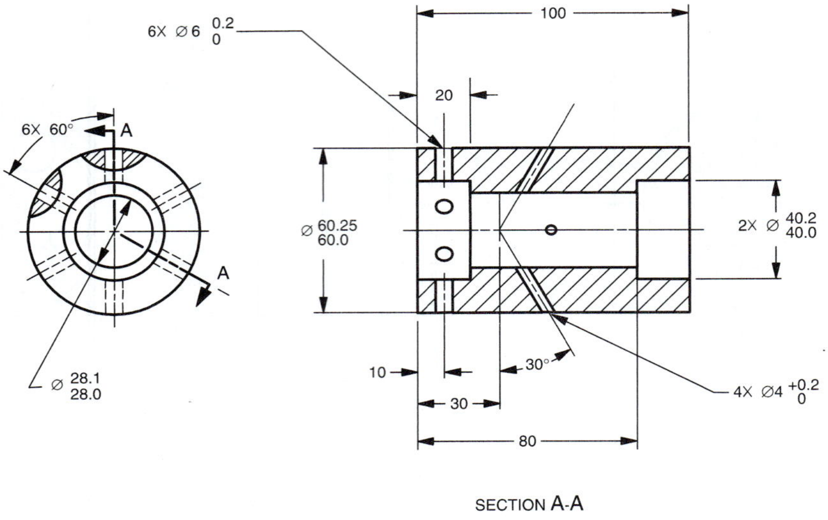

Name: Nozzle
Material: Phosphor Bronze

Draw the following problems using commands discussed in this chapter and in previous chapters. Use an appropriate template for each problem. Use text styles that correlate with the problem content. Place dimensions and notes when needed. Make your drawings proportional to the given problems when dimensions are not given. Save each of the drawings as P21-(problem number).

5.

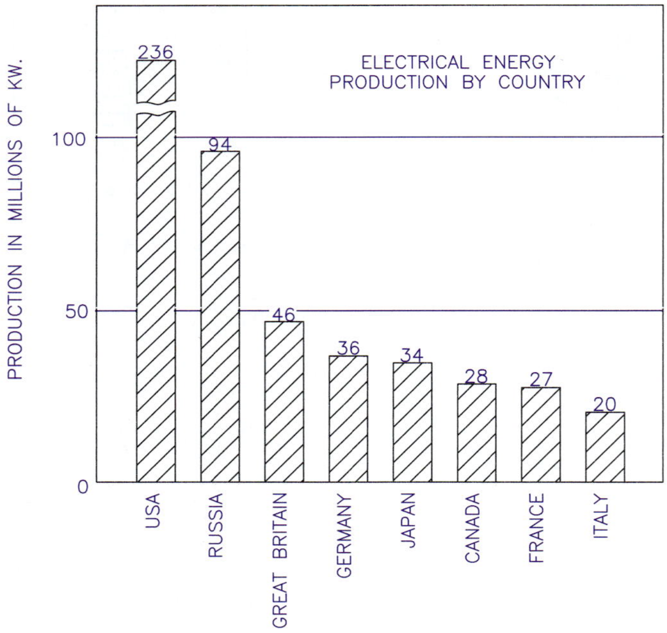

6.

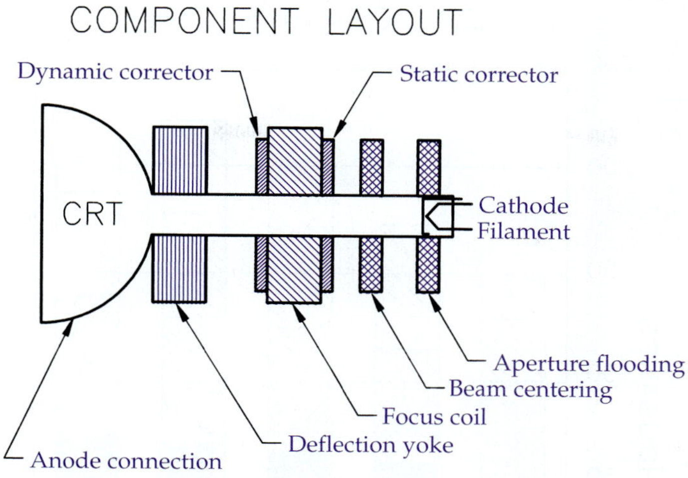
COMPONENT LAYOUT
Dynamic corrector
Static corrector
CRT
Cathode
Filament
Aperture flooding
Beam centering
Focus coil
Deflection yoke
Anode connection

7.

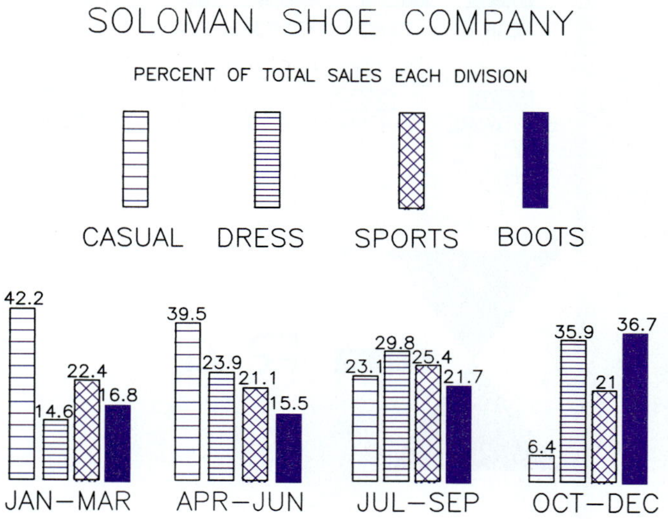
SOLOMAN SHOE COMPANY
PERCENT OF TOTAL SALES EACH DIVISION
CASUAL
DRESS
SPORTS
BOOTS
42.2
14.6
22.4
16.8
39.5
23.9
21.1
15.5
23.1
29.8
25.4
21.7
6.4
35.9
21
36.7
JAN–MAR
APR–JUN
JUL–SEP
OCT–DEC

8.

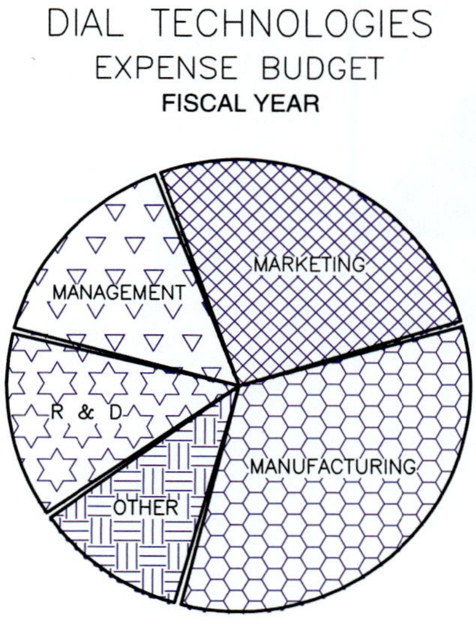
DIAL TECHNOLOGIES
EXPENSE BUDGET
FISCAL YEAR
MARKETING
MANAGEMENT
R & D
OTHER
MANUFACTURING

9.

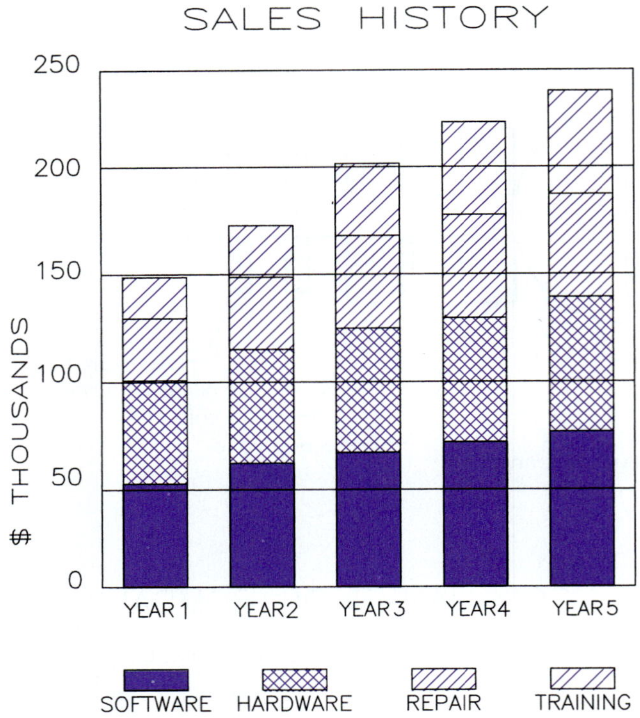
SALES HISTORY
250
200
150
100
50
0
$ THOUSANDS
YEAR 1
YEAR2
YEAR 3
YEAR4
YEAR 5
SOFTWARE
HARDWARE
REPAIR
TRAINING

10.

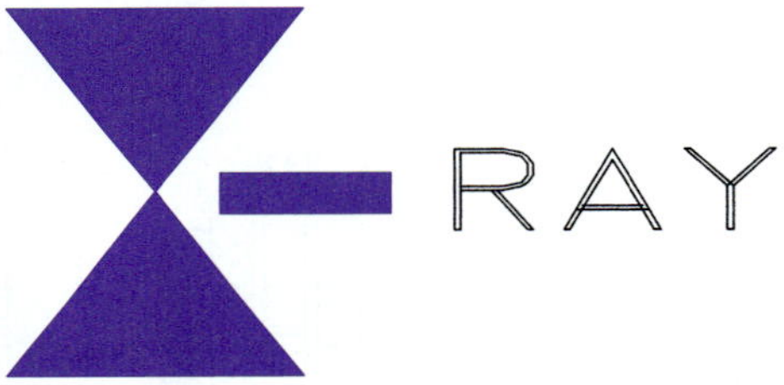
RAY

11.

Architectural
Design
Consultants

12.

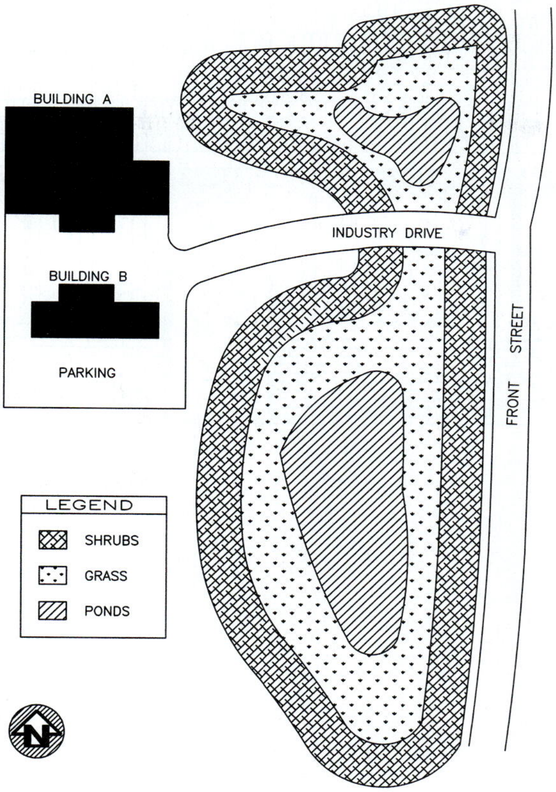
BUILDING A
INDUSTRY DRIVE
BUILDING B
PARKING
FRONT STREET
LEGEND
SHRUBS
GRASS
PONDS
N

13.

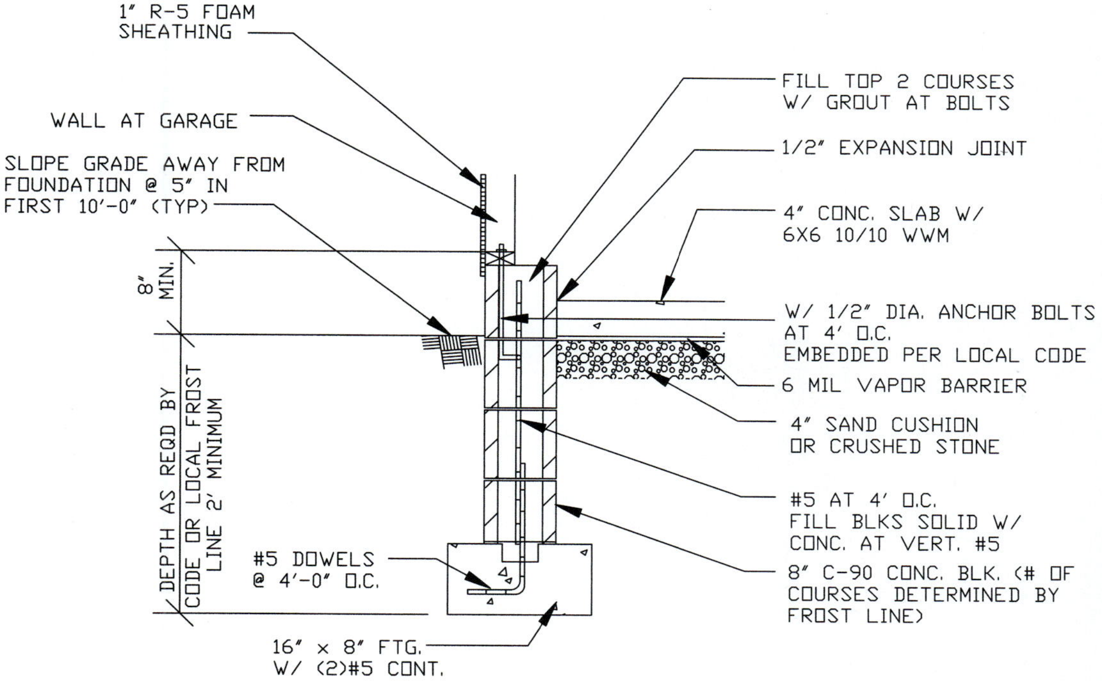
1" R-5 FOAM SHEATHING
WALL AT GARAGE
SLOPE GRADE AWAY FROM FOUNDATION @ 5" IN FIRST 10'-0" (TYP)
8" MIN.
DEPTH AS REQD BY CODE OR LOCAL FROST LINE 2' MINIMUM
#5 DOWELS @ 4'-0" O.C.
16" x 8" FTG. W/ (2)#5 CONT.
FILL TOP 2 COURSES W/ GROUT AT BOLTS
1/2" EXPANSION JOINT
4" CONC. SLAB W/ 6X6 10/10 WWM
W/ 1/2" DIA. ANCHOR BOLTS AT 4' O.C. EMBEDDED PER LOCAL CODE
6 MIL VAPOR BARRIER
4" SAND CUSHION OR CRUSHED STONE
#5 AT 4' O.C. FILL BLKS SOLID W/ CONC. AT VERT. #5
8" C-90 CONC. BLK. (# OF COURSES DETERMINED BY FROST LINE)

14.

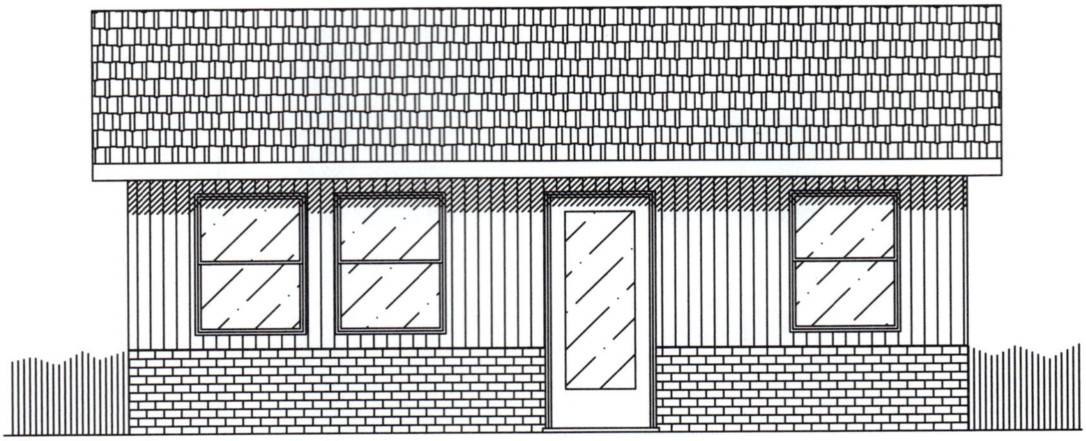

CHAPTER 22

Creating Symbols for Multiple Use

Learning Objectives

After completing this chapter, you will be able to do the following:

- Create and save blocks.
- Insert blocks into a drawing.
- Edit a block and update it in a drawing.
- Insert drawings and blocks into drawings using **DesignCenter**.
- Insert blocks and other objects into drawings using tool palettes.
- Create blocks that are saved independent of the drawing.
- Construct and use a symbol library of blocks.
- Customize tool palettes.

One of the greatest benefits of AutoCAD is its ability to store symbols for future use. These symbols, or ***blocks***, can be inserted into a drawing and scaled and rotated in one operation. If a block is edited, drawings containing the block can be updated to include the new version.

There are two types of blocks used in AutoCAD. A ***block*** created with the **BLOCK** command is stored within a drawing. A ***wblock*** created with the **WBLOCK** command is saved as a separate drawing file. Both types of blocks can be shared between drawings. Blocks can be copied between drawings using **DesignCenter** or the **Tool Palettes** window, and wblocks can be inserted into drawings using **DesignCenter**, the **Tool Palettes** window, and the **INSERT** command. Both types of blocks can be used to create a ***symbol library***, which is a related group of symbols.

When a drawing is inserted or referenced, it becomes part of the drawing on screen, but its content is not added to the current drawing file. Any named objects, such as blocks and layers, are referred to as ***dependent symbols***. When a dependent symbol is revised, a drawing that references it is automatically updated by AutoCAD the next time it is opened.

Creating Symbols As Blocks

The ability to draw and store symbols is one of the greatest time-saving features of AutoCAD. The **BLOCK** command is used to create a symbol within a specific drawing file. The block can then be inserted as many times as needed into the drawing in which it was defined with the **INSERT** command. It can also be copied into other drawings using **DesignCenter** or tool palettes. A predrawn block created with the **WBLOCK** command can be inserted as many times as needed into *any* drawing with the **INSERT** command. Upon insertion, both types of blocks can be scaled and rotated to meet the drawing requirements.

There are advantages to creating and storing symbols as blocks rather than as individual drawing files. However, the best method for block usage depends on the needs of the user and the project. This chapter discusses the construction and management of blocks, wblocks, and symbol libraries. Blocks are discussed in the following sections.

Constructing Blocks

A block can be any shape, symbol, view, or drawing that you use more than once. Before constructing a block, review the drawing you are working on. This is where a sketch of your drawing can be useful. Look for any shapes, components, notes, and assemblies that are used more than once. These can be drawn once and then saved as blocks.

PROFESSIONAL TIP

Blocks that vary in size from one drawing to the next should be drawn to fit inside a one-unit square. It does not matter if the object is measured in feet, inches, or millimeters. This makes it easy to scale the symbol later when you insert it into a drawing.

Drawing the Block Components

Draw a block as you would any other drawing geometry. If you want the block to have the color and linetype of the layer it will be inserted on, be sure to set layer 0 current before you begin drawing the block. If you forget to do this and draw the objects on another layer, simply use the **Properties** window or **Properties** toolbar to place all the objects on layer 0 before using the **BLOCK** command.

When you finish drawing the object, determine the best location on the symbol to use as an insertion point. When you insert the block into a drawing, the symbol is placed with its insertion point on the screen cursor. Several examples of commonly used blocks with their insertion points highlighted are shown in **Figure 22-1.**

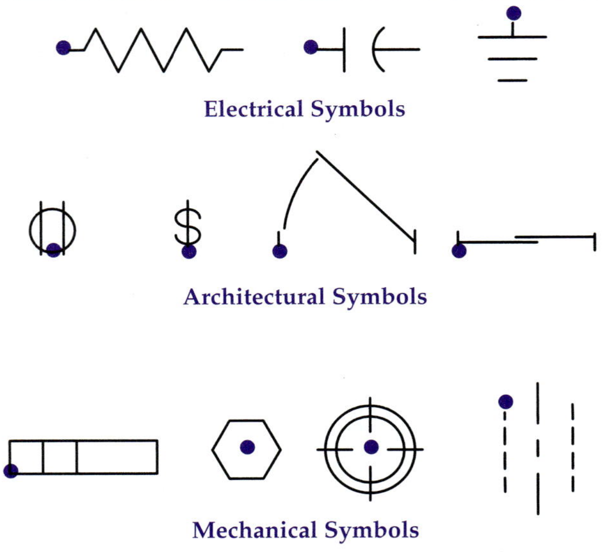

Figure 22-1. Common drafting symbols and their insertion points for placement on drawings. The insertion points are shown as colored dots.

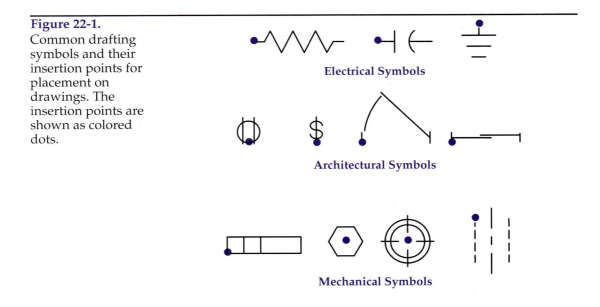

If it is important that the block maintains a specific color and linetype regardless of the layer it is to be used on, be sure to set the color and linetype before drawing the objects. On the other hand, if the block can assume the current color and linetype when the block is inserted into a drawing, set the current object color and linetype to ByBlock.

To set the color to ByBlock, pick ByBlock in the **Color Control** drop-down list of the **Properties** toolbar. You can also pick **Color...** from the **Format** pull-down menu to access the **Select Color** dialog box. Pick the **ByBlock** button as shown in Figure 22-2.

To set the linetype to ByBlock, pick ByBlock in the **Linetype Control** drop-down list of the **Properties** toolbar. Or, pick **Linetype...** from the **Format** pull-down menu to display the **Linetype Manager** dialog box. Pick ByBlock in the **Linetype** list and then pick the **Current** button. See Figure 22-3.

Once the current color and linetype are both set to ByBlock, you can create blocks. A block created with these settings assumes the current color and linetype when it is inserted into a drawing, regardless of the current layer setting.

Figure 22-2.
After picking **Color...** from the **Format** pull-down menu to display the **Select Color** dialog box, pick the **ByBlock** button to have the block assume the current color when it is inserted into a drawing.

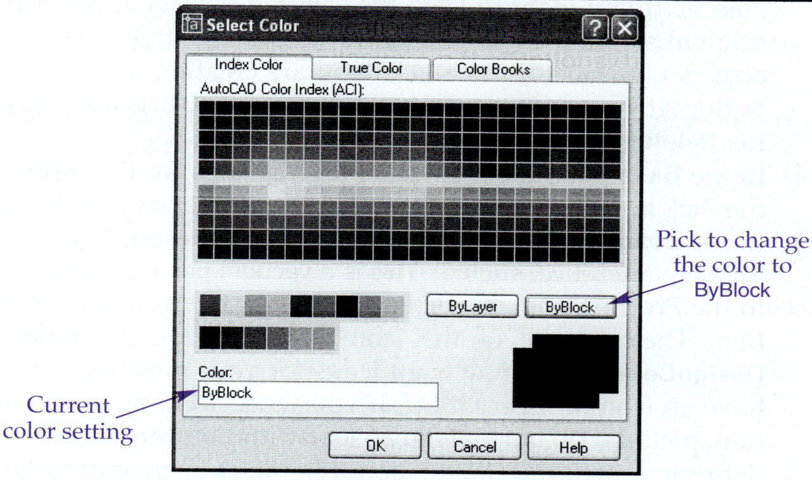

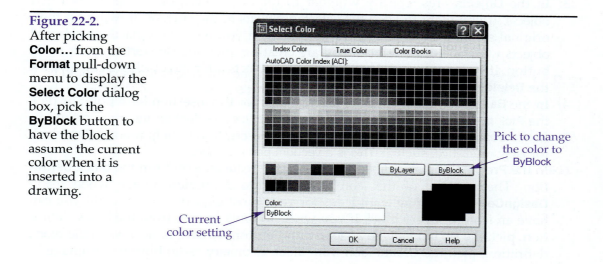

Figure 22-3.
To set the ByBlock linetype current, pick ByBlock in the **Linetype** list of the **Linetype Manager** dialog box and then pick the **Current** button.

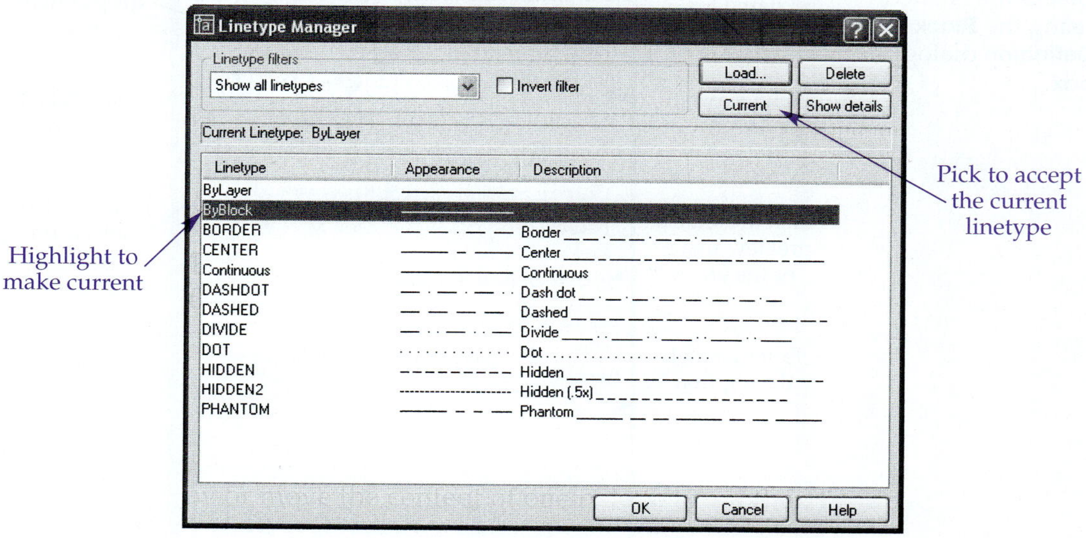

BLOCK
B
BMAKE

Draw
➥ Block
➥ Make...

Draw toolbar

Make Block

Creating Blocks

When you draw a shape or symbol, you have not yet created a block. To save your object as a block, pick the **Make Block** button on the **Draw** toolbar, pick **Make...** from the **Block** cascading menu in the **Draw** pull-down menu, or enter B, BLOCK, or BMAKE at the Command: prompt. Any one of these methods displays the **Block Definition** dialog box, **Figure 22-4.** The process for creating a block is as follows:

1. In the **Name:** text box, enter a name for the block, such as PUMP. The name cannot exceed 255 characters. It can include numbers, letters, and spaces, as well as the dollar sign ($), hyphen (-), and underscore (_).
2. In the **Objects** area, pick the **Select objects** button to use your pointing device to select objects for the block definition. The drawing area returns and you are prompted to select objects. Select all the objects that will make up the block. Press [Enter] when you are done. The **Block Definition** dialog box reopens, and the number of objects selected is shown in the **Objects** area. If you want to create a selection set, use the **Quick Select** button to define a filter for your selection set.
3. In the **Objects** area, specify whether to retain, convert, or delete the selected objects. If you want to keep the selected objects in the current drawing (in their original state), pick the **Retain** radio button. If you want to replace the selected objects with one of the blocks you are creating, pick the **Convert to block** radio button. If you want to remove the selected objects after the block is defined, pick the **Delete** radio button.
4. In the **Base point** area, enter the coordinates for the insertion base point or pick the **Pick point** button to use your pointing device to select an insertion point.
5. In the **Description:** text box, enter a textual description to help identify the block for easy reference, such as This is a vacuum pump symbol.
6. In the **Preview icon** area, specify whether to create an icon from the block definition. The purpose of the icon is to provide a preview image when using **DesignCenter**. You may want icons for your most important blocks, but you can have an icon for every block if you wish. To omit an icon from the block definition, pick the **Do not include an icon** radio button. To save an icon with the block definition, pick the **Create icon from block geometry** radio button. An image of the icon is then displayed to the right.

Figure 22-4.
Blocks are created using the **Block Definition** dialog box.

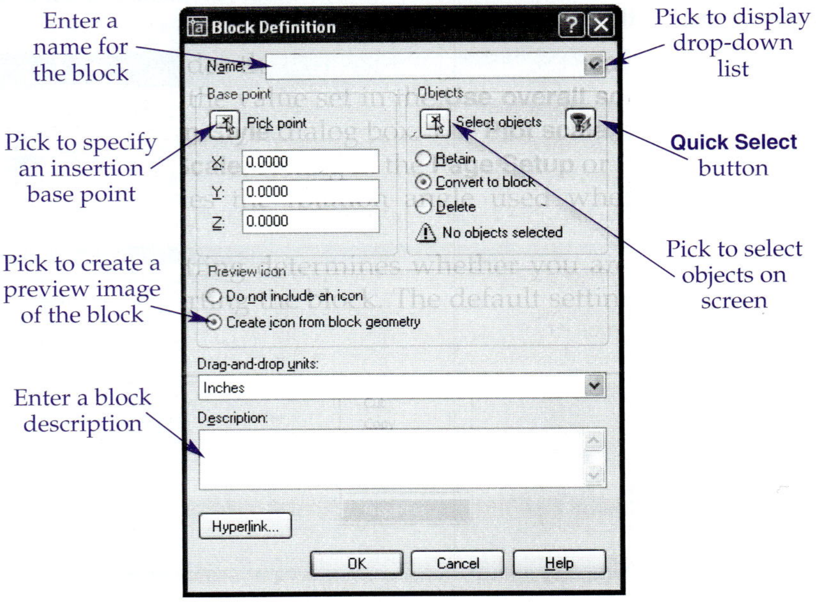

7. Use the **Drag-and-drop units:** drop-down list to specify the type of units **DesignCenter** will use when inserting the block.
8. After you have finished defining the block, pick **OK**.

The **Convert to block** radio button is active by default. If you select the **Delete** option and then decide that you want to keep the original geometry in the drawing after you have defined the block, you can enter the **OOPS** command. This returns the original objects to the screen, whereas entering U at the Command: prompt or picking the **Undo** button from the **Standard** toolbar removes the block from the drawing.

> **NOTE**
> The **Block Definition** dialog box contains a **Hyperlink...** button. Pick this button to access the **Insert Hyperlink** dialog box to insert a hyperlink in the block. Hyperlinks and other Internet features for AutoCAD are discussed in ***AutoCAD and Its Applications—Advanced.***

To verify that the block was saved properly, access the **Block Definition** dialog box. Pick the **Name:** drop-down list button to display a list of all blocks in the current drawing. The block names are organized in numerical and alphabetical order. If there are more than six blocks in your drawing, a scroll bar appears to the right of the list so that you can access the remaining blocks.

-BLOCK
-B

The **-BLOCK** command can also be used to create new blocks and list existing blocks. Access this command by entering **-B** or **-BLOCK** at the Command: prompt. When the **-BLOCK** command is entered, the options in the **Block Definition** dialog box are presented as prompts on the command line. To display a list of block names, use the **?** option as follows:

Command: **-B** *or* **-BLOCK**↵
Enter block name or [?]: **?**↵
Enter block(s) to list <*>

Press [Enter] to list all of the blocks in the current drawing. The following information is then displayed in the **AutoCAD Text Window:**

Defined blocks.
"PUMP"

User Blocks	External References	Dependent Blocks	Unnamed Blocks
1	0	0	0

This listing reports each block name, as well as the different types of blocks and the number of each type in the drawing. When you create a block, you have actually created a ***block definition***. Therefore, the first entry in the block listing is that of *defined* blocks. ***User blocks*** are those created by you. ***External references*** are drawings referenced with the **XREF** command. (External references are discussed in Chapter 24.) Blocks that reside in a referenced drawing are called ***dependent blocks***. ***Unnamed blocks*** are objects such as associative and nonassociative dimensions.

Try stepping through the process of creating a block again. Draw a one-unit square and name it PLATE. See **Figure 22-5.** After creating the block, be sure to confirm that the PLATE block was saved by using the **-BLOCK** command.

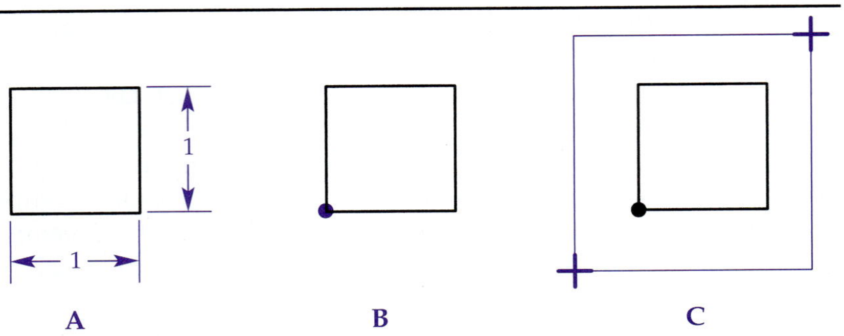

Figure 22-5.
The procedure for drawing a one-unit square and defining it as a block. A—Draw the block. B—Pick the insertion base point. C—Select the square using the **Window** selection option or any other suitable option.

PROFESSIONAL TIP

Blocks can be used when creating other blocks. Suppose you design a complex part or view that will be used repeatedly. You can insert existing blocks into the view and then save the entire object as a block. This is called ***nesting***, where larger blocks contain smaller blocks. The larger block must be given a different name. Proper planning and knowledge of all existing blocks can speed up the drawing process and the creation of complex parts.

EXERCISE 22-1

Complete the Exercise on the Student CD.

Using Blocks in a Drawing

Once a block has been created, it is easy to insert it into a drawing. First, determine a proper size and rotation angle for the block. Blocks are normally inserted on specific layers, so set the proper layer *before* inserting the block. Once a block has been inserted into a drawing, it is referred to as a *block reference*.

INSERT
I
DDINSERT

Insert
➥ Block...

Draw toolbar

Insert Block

Inserting Blocks

Blocks are placed in a drawing with the **INSERT** command. Enter I, INSERT, or DDINSERT at the Command: prompt, pick the **Insert Block** button from the **Draw** toolbar, or pick **Block...** from the **Insert** pull-down menu. This accesses the **Insert** dialog box, Figure 22-6.

Pick the **Name:** drop-down list button to access the defined blocks in the current drawing. Highlight the name of the block you wish to insert. If the list of block names is long, use the scroll bar to display additional blocks. You may also enter the name of the block in the **Name:** text box. Once the desired block has been chosen, you must specify the insertion location, scale, and rotation angle. You can also specify whether to explode the block upon inserting it. The option buttons and other features in the **Insert** dialog box are described as follows:

- **Browse... button.** Pick this button to display the **Select Drawing File** dialog box and select a drawing file for insertion into the current drawing.
- **Insertion point area.** If the **Specify On-screen** check box is activated, you can pick an insertion point on screen and insert the block dynamically. If you wish to insert the block using absolute coordinates, disable the check box and enter the coordinates in the **X:**, **Y:**, and **Z:** text boxes.

Figure 22-6.
The **Insert** dialog box allows you to select and prepare a block for insertion. Select the block you wish to insert from the drop-down list or enter the block name in the **Name:** text box.

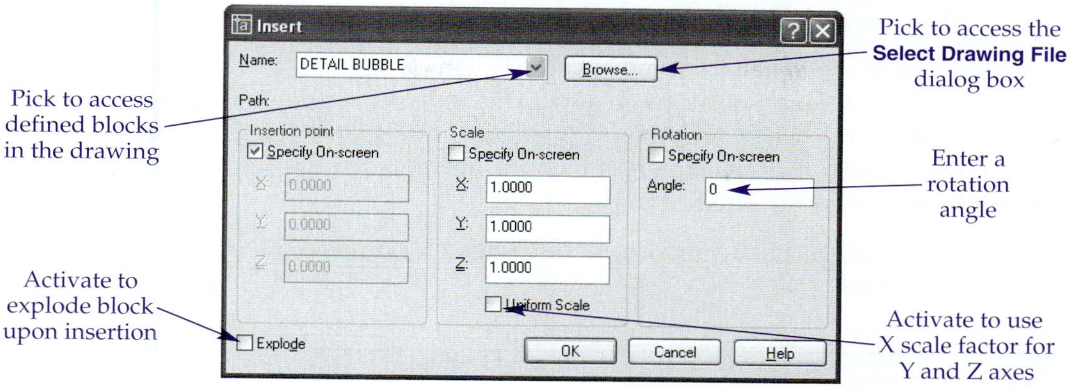

- **Scale area.** The **Scale** area allows you to specify scale values for the block in relation to the X, Y, and Z axes. By default, the **Specify On-screen** check box is inactive. This causes the block to be inserted at a one-to-one scale once the insertion point has been selected. If you want to be prompted for the scale at the command line when inserting the block, activate the **Specify On-screen** check box. If the check box is inactive, you can enter scale values in the **X:**, **Y:**, and **Z:** text boxes. If you activate the **Uniform Scale** check box, you can simply specify a scale value for the X axis. The same value is then used for the Y and Z axes when the block is inserted.
- **Rotation area.** The **Rotation** area allows you to insert the block at a specified angle. By default, the **Specify On-screen** check box is inactive and the block is inserted at an angle of zero. If you want to use a different angle, enter a value in the **Angle:** text box. If you want to be prompted for the rotation angle at the command line when inserting the block, activate the **Specify On-screen** check box.
- **Explode check box.** When a block is created, it is saved as a single object. Therefore, it is defined as a single object when inserted in the drawing, no matter how many objects were used to create the block. Activate the **Explode** check box if you wish to explode the block into its original objects for editing purposes. If you explode the block upon insertion, it will assume its original properties, such as its original layer, color, and linetype.

When you pick the **OK** button, prompts appear for any values defined as **Specify On-screen** in the **Insert** dialog box. If you are specifying the insertion point on screen, the following prompt appears:

Specify insertion point or [Scale/X/Y/Z/Rotate/PScale/PX/PY/PZ/PRotate]: *(pick the point to insert the block)*

If you select one of the options, the new value will override any setting in the **Insert** dialog box. The options allow you to enter a value for the overall scale, enter independent scale factors for the X, Y, and Z axes, enter a rotation angle, and preview the scale of the X, Y, and Z axes or the rotation angle before entering actual values. The following prompt appears if you are specifying the X scale factor on screen:

Enter X scale factor, specify opposite corner, or [Corner/XYZ] <1>: *(pick a point, or enter a value for the scale)*

Moving the cursor scales the block dynamically as it is dragged. If you want to scale the block visually, pick a point when the object appears correct. You can also use the **Corner** option to scale the block dynamically.

If you enter an X scale factor or press [Enter] to accept the default scale value, you are then prompted with the following:

Enter Y scale factor <use X scale factor>: *(enter a value or press* [Enter] *to accept the same scale specified for the X axis)*

The X and Y scale factors allow you to stretch or compress the block to suit your needs, **Figure 22-7.** This is why it is a good idea to draw blocks to fit inside a one-unit square. It makes the block easy to scale because you can enter the exact number of units for the X and Y dimensions. If you want the block to be three units long and two units high, respond with the following:

Enter X scale factor, specify opposite corner, or [Corner/XYZ] <1>: **3**↵
Enter Y scale factor <use X scale factor>: **2**↵

PROFESSIONAL TIP

A block's rotation angle can be based on the current UCS. If you want to insert a block at a specific angle based on the current UCS or an existing UCS, be sure the proper UCS is active. Then insert the block and use a rotation angle of zero. If you decide to change the UCS later, any inserted blocks retain their original angle.

Figure 22-7.
A comparison of different X and Y scale factors used for inserting the PLATE block.

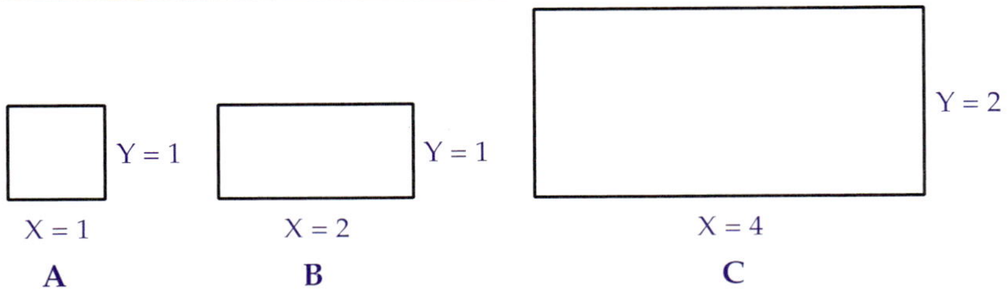

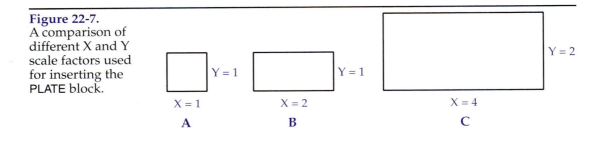

Block Scaling Options

It is possible to create a mirror image of a block by simply entering a negative value for the scale factor. For example, entering -1 for both the X scale factor and the Y scale factor mirrors the block to the opposite quadrant of the original orientation specified and retains the original size. Different mirroring techniques are shown in **Figure 22-8.** The insertion point is indicated by a dot.

In addition to the scaling options previously discussed, a block that is scaled during insertion can be classified as a *real block*, a *schematic block*, or a *unit block*. A ***real block*** is one that is drawn at a one-to-one scale. It is then inserted into the drawing using 1 for both the X and Y scale factors. Examples of real blocks could include a car design, a bolt, or a pipe fitting. See **Figure 22-9A.**

A ***schematic block*** is a block that is originally drawn at a one-to-one scale. It is then inserted into the drawing using the scale factor of the drawing for both the X and Y scale values. Examples of schematic blocks could include notes, detail bubbles, or section symbols. See **Figure 22-9B.**

A ***unit block*** is also originally drawn at a one-to-one scale. There are three different types of unit blocks. One example of a *1D unit block* is a 1″ line object that is turned into a block. A *2D unit block* is any object that can fit inside a 1″ × 1″ square. A *3D unit block* is any object that can fit inside a 1″ cube. To use a unit block, insert the block and determine the individual scale factors for each axis. For example, a 1D unit block could be inserted at a scale of 4, which would turn the line into a 4″ line. A 2D

Figure 22-8.
Negative and positive scale factors have different effects when used to insert a block.

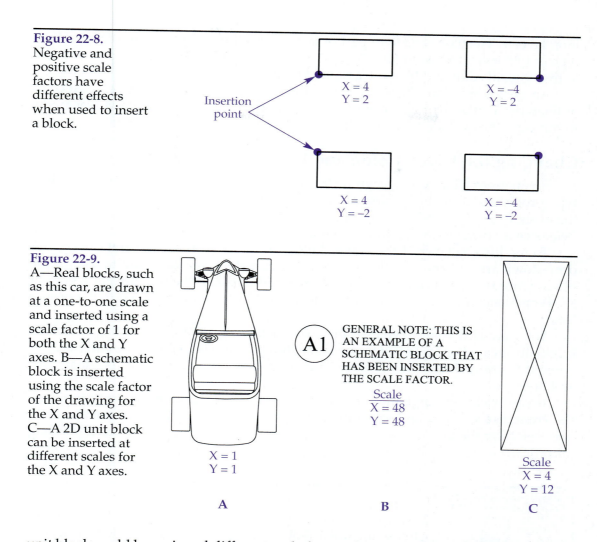

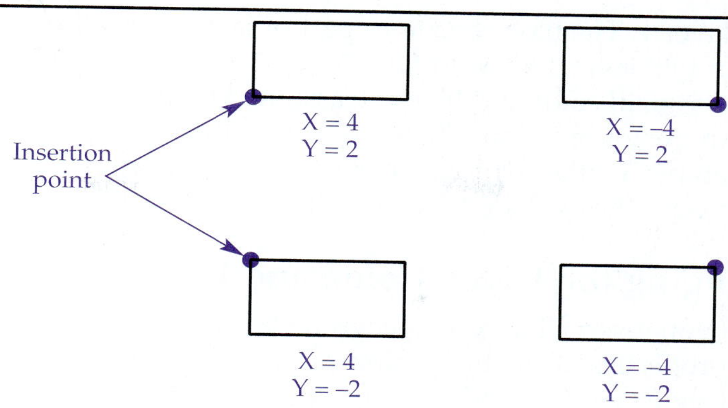

Figure 22-9.
A—Real blocks, such as this car, are drawn at a one-to-one scale and inserted using a scale factor of 1 for both the X and Y axes. B—A schematic block is inserted using the scale factor of the drawing for the X and Y axes. C—A 2D unit block can be inserted at different scales for the X and Y axes.

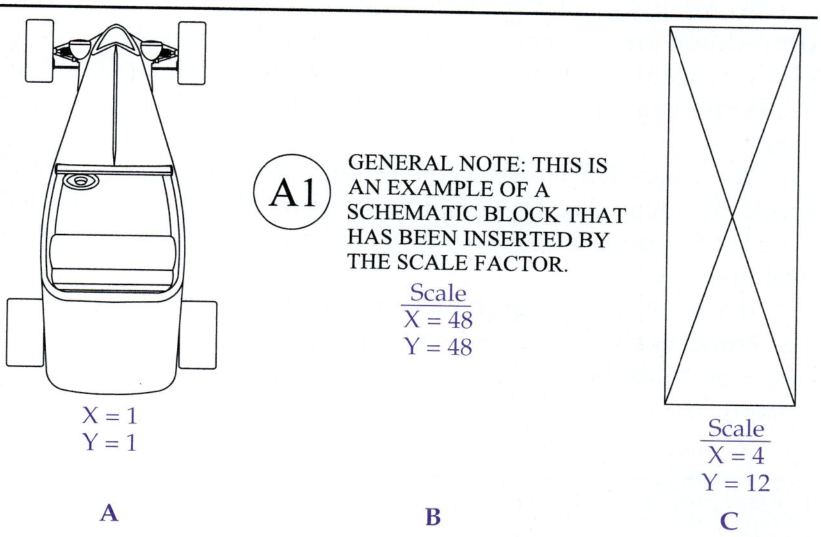

unit block could be assigned different scale factors for the X and Y axes, such as 48 for the X axis and 72 for the Y axis. See **Figure 22-9C.** A 3D unit block could be inserted at different scales for the X, Y, and Z axes.

EXERCISE 22-2 Complete the Exercise on the Student CD.

The Effects of Layers on Blocks

Blocks retain the property characteristics of the layer(s) on which they were drawn. In Chapter 4, you learned that all objects in AutoCAD are created in ByLayer mode by default. This means the object color and linetype properties are dictated by the layer on which objects are created. For example, suppose the CIRCLE block was drawn on layer 1 with the color red and a dashed linetype. When inserted, the block appears red and dashed, no matter what layer it is inserted on. If different colors, linetypes, or even layers are used in a block, they also remain the same when the block is inserted on a different layer. Therefore, a block defined in ByLayer mode retains its properties when inserted into a drawing (or another drawing, if the block was saved as a drawing file). If the layers included in the inserted block do not exist in the drawing, AutoCAD automatically creates them.

For a block to assume the property characteristics of the layer it is inserted on, it must be created on layer 0. Suppose you create the CIRCLE block on layer 0 and insert it on layer 1. The block becomes part of layer 1 and thus assumes the color and linetype of that layer. Exploding the CIRCLE block returns the objects back to layer 0 and to the original color and linetype assigned to layer 0.

An exception occurs if objects within the block are drawn using an explicit color or linetype; in other words, the objects are not drawn using the default ByLayer mode. In this case, the exploded CIRCLE block objects would retain their original properties.

Changing the Layer, Color, and Linetype of a Block

If you insert a block on the wrong layer, or if you wish to change the color or linetype properties of the block, you can use the **Properties** window to modify it. Select the block to modify, and its properties are listed. See Figure 22-10. Notice that Block Reference is specified in the drop-down list. You can now modify the selected block.

To modify the layer of the selected block, pick **Layer** in the **General** category. A drop-down arrow appears, allowing you to access the layer you want to use for the block. Once the new layer has been selected, pick the X at the upper-right corner of the **Properties** window to close the window. The block is now changed to the proper layer.

You may also want to change the color or linetype of a block. If the block was originally created on layer 0, it will assume the color and linetype of the current layer when it is inserted. If it was created on another layer, it will retain its original color and linetype.

If you wish to change the color or linetype of an inserted block, you can access the **Properties** window and select the corresponding property in the **General** section after selecting the block. Select the desired color or linetype from the corresponding drop-down list.

PROFESSIONAL TIP

If you want to change the properties of several blocks, you can use the **Quick Select** dialog box to create a selection set of block reference objects. Once the blocks are selected, change the properties using the **Properties** window or **Object Properties** toolbar. The **Quick Select** dialog box is discussed in Chapter 7.

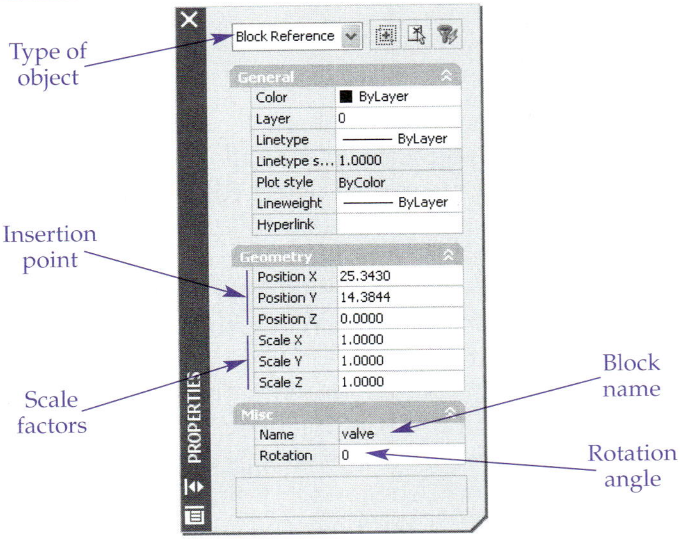

Figure 22-10.
The **Properties** window allows you to change the layer, color, linetype, and other properties of a block.

Inserting Multiple Copies of a Block

The features of the **INSERT** and **ARRAY** commands are combined using the **MINSERT** (multiple insert) command. This method of inserting and arraying blocks saves time and disk space. To access the **MINSERT** command, enter MINSERT at the Command: prompt.

An example of an application using the **MINSERT** command is the arrangement of desks on a drawing. Suppose you want to draw the layout shown in Figure 22-11. First, specify architectural units and set the limits to 30′,22′. Draw a 4′ × 3′ rectangle and save it as a block named DESK. The arrangement is to be three rows and four columns. Make the horizontal spacing between desks 2′, and the vertical spacing 4′. Use the following command sequence:

Command: **MINSERT**↵
Enter block name or [?]: <*current*>: **DESK**↵
Specify insertion point or [Scale/X/Y/Z/Rotate/PScale/PX/PY/PZ/PRotate]: *(pick a point)*
Enter X scale factor, specify opposite corner, or [Corner/XYZ] <1>: ↵
Enter Y scale factor <use X scale factor>: ↵
Specify rotation angle <0>: ↵
Enter number of rows (---) <1>: **3**↵
Enter number of columns (|||) <1>: **4**↵
Enter distance between rows or specify unit cell (---): **7′**↵
Specify distance between columns (|||): **6′**↵

The resulting arrangement is shown in Figure 22-11. The complete pattern takes on the characteristics of a block, except that an array created with the **MINSERT** command cannot be exploded. Since the array cannot be exploded, you can use the **Properties** window to modify the number of rows and columns, change the spacing between objects, or change the layer, color, or linetype properties. If the initial block is rotated, all arrayed objects are also rotated about their insertion points. If the arrayed objects are rotated about the insertion point while using the **MINSERT** command, all objects are aligned on that point.

Figure 22-11. Creating an arrangement of desks using the **MINSERT** command.

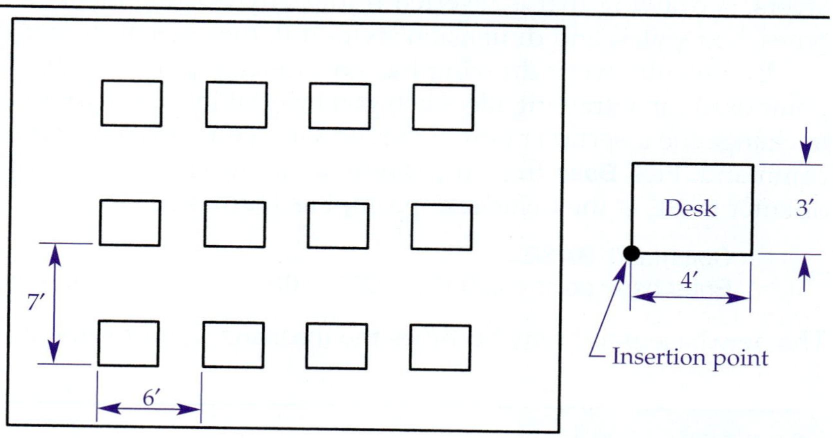

PROFESSIONAL TIP

As an alternative to the previous example, if you were working with different desk sizes, a 2D unit block may serve your purposes better than an exact size block. To create a 5′ × 3′-6″ (60″ × 42″) desk, for example, insert a one-unit square block using either the **INSERT** or **MINSERT** command, and enter the following for the X and Y scale factors:

Enter X scale factor, specify opposite corner, or
  [Corner/XYZ] <1>: **60**↵
Enter Y scale factor <use X scale factor>: **42**↵

A 2D unit block can be used in this manner for a variety of objects.

EXERCISE 22-3 Complete the Exercise on the Student CD.

Inserting Entire Drawings

The **INSERT** command can be used to insert an entire drawing file into the current drawing. To do so, enter the **INSERT** command and pick the **Browse...** button in the **Insert** dialog box to access the **Select Drawing File** dialog box. You can then select a drawing file to insert, as discussed earlier in this chapter.

When one drawing is inserted into another, the inserted drawing becomes a block reference. As a block, it may be moved to a new location with a single pick. The drawing is inserted on the current layer, but it does not inherit the color, linetype, or thickness properties of that layer. You can explode the inserted drawing back to its original objects if desired. Once exploded, the drawing objects revert to their original layers. A drawing that is inserted brings any existing block definitions, layers, linetypes, text styles, and dimension styles into the current drawing.

BASE
Draw
➥ Block
➥ Base

By default, every drawing has an insertion point of 0,0,0. (This is the insertion point used for a drawing file when you insert it into the current drawing.) If you want to change the insertion point of the drawing you need to insert, you can use the **BASE** command. Pick **Base** from the **Block** cascading menu in the **Draw** pull-down menu, or enter BASE at the Command: prompt as follows:

Command: **BASE**↵
Enter base point <0.0000, 0.0000, 0.0000>: *(pick a point or enter new coordinates)*

The new base point now becomes the insertion point for the drawing.

PROFESSIONAL TIP

When working on a drawing, it is common practice in industry to refer to other drawings to check features or dimensions. When you need to reference another drawing, you can insert it into your current drawing with the **INSERT** command. When you are done checking the features or dimensions you need, simply use the **UNDO** command to undo the **INSERT** operation or erase the inserted drawing.

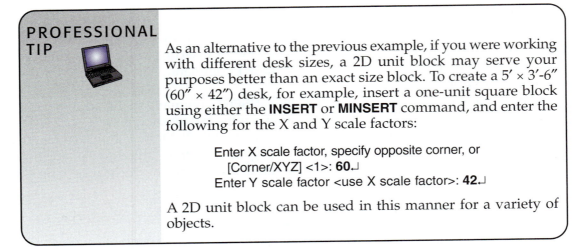

EXERCISE 22-4 Complete the Exercise on the Student CD.

Using DesignCenter to Insert Blocks

Blocks or drawing files can be readily located and previewed before they are inserted using **DesignCenter**. You can insert blocks or entire drawings into your current drawing using the drag-and-drop capability of **DesignCenter**. You can also browse through existing drawings for blocks, show images of blocks and drawings, and display other information about saved blocks or files.

> **ADCENTER**
> **ADC**
> [Ctrl]+[2]
>
> **Tools**
> ➥ **DesignCenter**
>
> **Standard toolbar**
> **DesignCenter**

To access **DesignCenter**, pick the **DesignCenter** button on the **Standard** toolbar, select **DesignCenter** from the **Tools** pull-down menu, enter ADC or ADCENTER at the Command: prompt, or use the [Ctrl]+[2] key combination. When **DesignCenter** opens, it displays the content that was last selected in it. **DesignCenter** is able to do this because it keeps a history of the drawing files and the content that had been previously accessed. The **Tree View** area, located on the left side of the **DesignCenter** window, is used to navigate to drawing files. The right side of **DesignCenter** is called the **Content** area. This area displays the available content from what is selected in the **Tree View** area. See **Figure 22-12.** If a folder is selected on the **Tree View** side, the **Content** area displays all the drawing files within that folder. If a named object category is selected within a drawing file, such as Blocks, then the **Content** area displays all the objects of the specified type in the drawing file.

The **DesignCenter** toolbar buttons and tabs contain features for navigating to drawing file content and viewing options. **Figure 22-13** shows the button options available on the **DesignCenter** toolbar. The following features are used for navigation:

- **Load.** Displays the **Load** dialog box. Selecting a file and picking **Open** makes the drawing file active in **DesignCenter**.
- **Back.** Shows the last drawing file content that was selected. Picking the **Back** pull-down arrow shows a list of the previous drawing file content.
- **Forward.** If the **Back** button has been used, the **Forward** button is available. Picking it shows the last drawing file content that was selected. Picking the **Forward** pull-down arrow shows a list of the previous drawing file content.

Figure 22-12.
DesignCenter is used to search for existing blocks and drawing files for insertion into the current drawing.

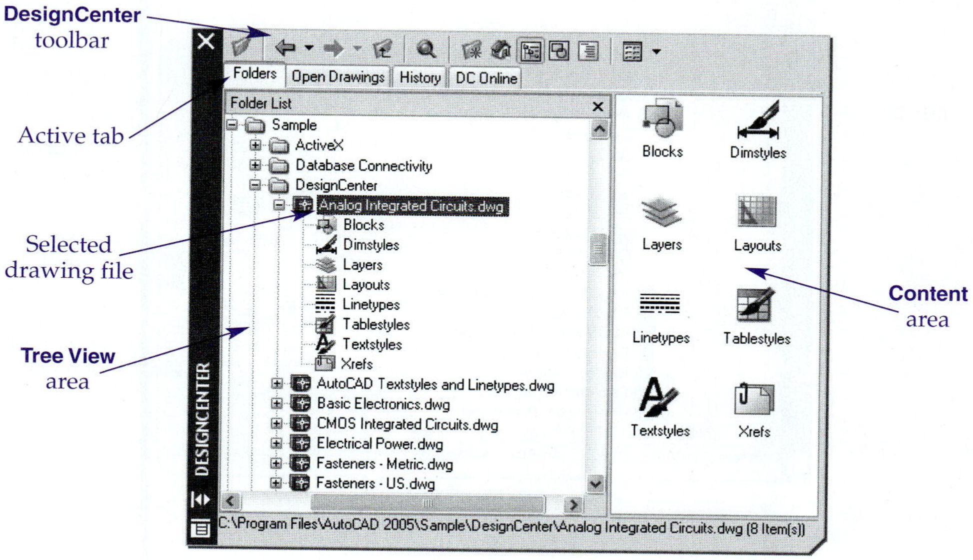

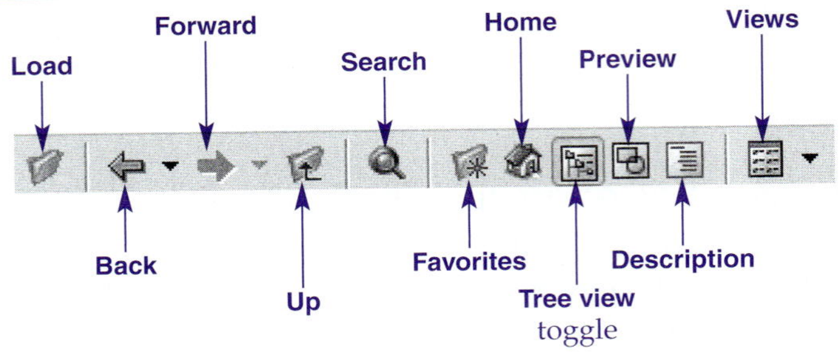

Figure 22-13.
The **DesignCenter** toolbar.

- **Up.** Moves up one folder from the current one in the folder hierarchy.
- **Search.** Opens the **Search** dialog box, which allows you to search for drawings by specifying various criteria.
- **Favorites.** Displays the content of the **Favorites** folder. Content can be added to the **Favorites** folder by right-clicking over an item in the **Tree View** area or the **Content** area and selecting **Add to Favorites** from the right-click menu. This could be a drive letter, a folder, a drawing file, or any named objects within a drawing file, such as Blocks or Layers.
- **Home.** Selecting the **Home** button moves to the *home* content in **DesignCenter**. By default, *home* is the DesignCenter folder located in the AutoCAD 2005\Sample folder. To change this, right-click over an item in the **Tree View** area and select **Set as Home** from the right-click menu. This could be a drive letter, folder, or drawing file. The home location should be your most commonly accessed item in **DesignCenter**.

The last four buttons on the **DesignCenter** toolbar control viewing options within the **DesignCenter** window. The areas controlled by these options are shown in Figure 22-14. The following features are available:

- **Tree View Toggle.** This button controls whether the **Tree View** area is hidden. The toggle only works when the **Folders** or **Open Drawings** tab is current.
- **Preview.** This is a toggle that displays or hides the **Preview** area. If no preview was saved for the selected content, the area is empty.

Figure 22-14.
Viewing options on the **DesignCenter** toolbar control how the selected content is displayed.

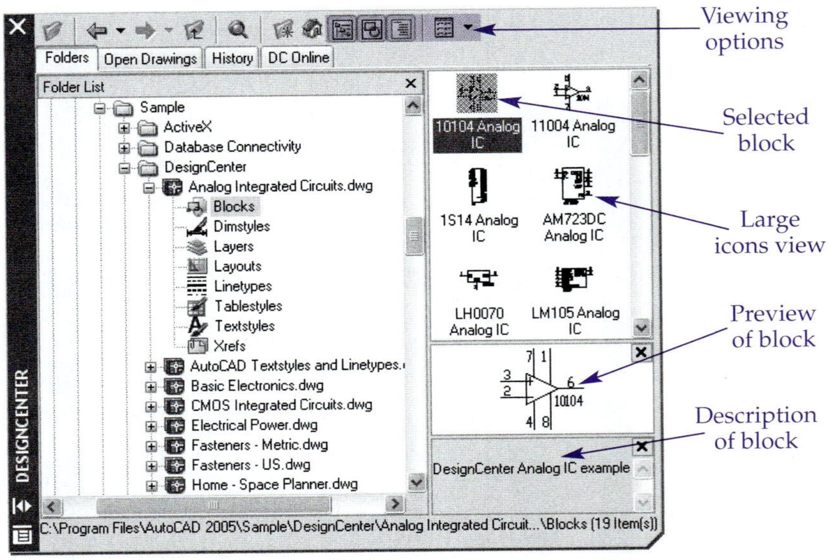

- **Description.** This is a toggle that displays or hides the **Description** area. If a description was given when a block was created, the related text is displayed in this area. If no description was given, the area displays *No description found*.
- **Views.** This button is used to control how the display appears in the **Content** area. Content can be displayed using large icons, small icons, a list view, or a detailed view.

When **DesignCenter** is opened, the active tab is set to **Folders**. This shows the hierarchy of files and folders on your computer, including network drives. Navigating in the **Folder List** view is similar to using Windows Explorer. The **Open Drawings** tab displays all the open drawing files in the current AutoCAD session. The **History** tab displays the most recently accessed files in **DesignCenter**. The **DC Online** tab gives you access to drawing content that can be downloaded from the Internet on the DesignCenter Online Web page.

To view the blocks that belong to a drawing, click on the Blocks icon in the **Tree View** area or double-click on the Blocks icon in the **Content** area. Once the desired block has been found, you can use a drag-and-drop operation or the **Insert** dialog box to insert it into the current drawing.

To use drag-and-drop, move the cursor over the top of the block in the **Content** area, press and hold down the pick button on your pointing device, and drag the cursor to the opened drawing. Release the pick button and the block is inserted into the drawing. The block is inserted based on the type of drag-and-drop units specified when creating the block. For example, if the original block was a 1″ × 1″ square, and the drag-and-drop units specified were feet when the block was created, then the block will be a 12″ × 12″ square when it is inserted from **DesignCenter**.

You can access the **Insert** dialog box while inserting a block from **DesignCenter** by right-clicking on the block icon in the **Content** area. When the shortcut menu appears, select **Insert Block...** to activate the **INSERT** command. This allows you to scale, rotate, or explode the block during insertion.

To insert an entire drawing using **DesignCenter**, select the folder in which the drawing resides in the **Tree View** area. Any drawings in the selected folder appear in the **Content** area. Use drag-and-drop to insert them into the current drawing. You can also right-click on a drawing icon and select **Insert as Block...** from the shortcut menu. In addition to blocks and drawings, **DesignCenter** can be used to insert dimension styles, layers, layouts, linetypes, table styles, text styles, and external references.

Using the Tool Palettes to Insert Blocks

TOOLPALETTES
TP
[Ctrl]+[3]

Tools
➥ Tool Palettes Window

Standard toolbar
Tool Palettes

Tool palettes provide another quick way to access blocks for insertion into a drawing. This feature is similar to **DesignCenter** in the way that blocks can be previewed before inserting them. To open the **Tool Palettes** window, pick the **Tool Palettes** button on the **Standard** toolbar, select **Tool Palettes Window** from the **Tools** pull-down menu, enter TP or TOOLPALETTES at the Command: prompt, or use the [Ctrl]+[3] key combination. The **Tool Palettes** window is shown in Figure 22-15. The window is divided into tool palettes, each with a tab. The tool palettes are used to store blocks and hatch patterns.

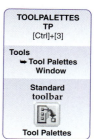

To insert a block from the **Tool Palettes** window, select the tool palette tab in which the block resides and locate the block. Use the scroll bar on the side of the window to move up or down in the tool palette. When the block is located, place the cursor over the block icon. You can use the drag-and-drop method, or you can pick once on the block icon. Then, move the cursor into the drawing area and pick again to place the block. When a block is selected in the tool palette with a single pick, the block is attached to the crosshairs once the cursor is moved into the drawing area. The location where the crosshairs and the block are connected is defined by the insertion point of the block.

Figure 22-15.
The **Tool Palettes** window. Blocks may be inserted into the current drawing from a selected tab.

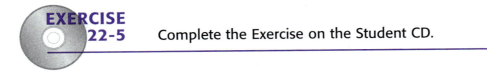

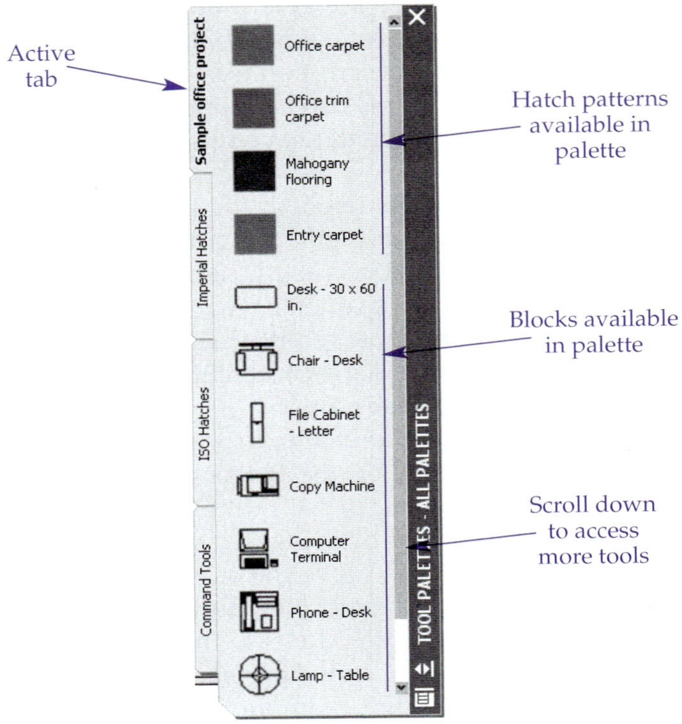

When inserting a block in this manner, you can access scaling and rotation options for the block at the command line before picking an insertion point. Enter S to scale the block along the XYZ axes or R to specify a rotation angle for the block. Blocks inserted from tool palettes are automatically scaled based on a ratio of the current drawing scale to the scale used in the original block definition.

Blocks can be added to tool palettes from **DesignCenter**. A number of customization options are available for storing blocks and arranging palettes. The **Tool Palettes** window is discussed in greater detail later in this chapter.

EXERCISE 22-5 Complete the Exercise on the Student CD.

Editing Blocks

AutoCAD gives you the ability to edit blocks in the current drawing. This is referred to as *in-place reference editing*. This allows you to make minor changes to blocks, wblocks, or drawings that have been inserted in the current drawing. This type of editing can be used to modify the selected block reference as well as the original block definition. When editing blocks within a drawing, changes made to one block reference can be automatically applied to all instances of the same block in the drawing. When editing wblocks and inserted drawings, changes can be made without the need to open the original file. In-place editing cannot be used on blocks that have been inserted into a drawing with the **MINSERT** command.

If you do not use in-place reference editing, blocks must first be broken into their original components before they can be edited. Two methods can be used to break blocks apart. One involves the **INSERT** command and the **Explode** option in the **Insert** dialog box. As previously discussed, this method is used at the time of insertion. The other method involves the **EXPLODE** command and can be done at any time. This method is discussed later in this chapter.

Editing Blocks in Place

> **REFEDIT**
> **Modify** ➥ **Xref and Block Editing** ➥ **Edit Reference In-Place**
> **Refedit toolbar**
> **Edit Block or Xref**

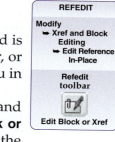

You can edit a block in-place by using the **REFEDIT** command. This command is accessed by entering REFEDIT at the Command: prompt, using the **Refedit** toolbar, or by picking **Edit Reference In-Place** from the **Xref and Block Editing** cascading menu in the **Modify** pull-down menu.

To display the **Refedit** toolbar, right-click on any displayed toolbar button and pick **Refedit**. See Figure 22-16. The button on the left of the toolbar is **Edit block or Xref**. You can use this button to access the **REFEDIT** command. When you enter the **REFEDIT** command, you get this prompt:

Command: **REFEDIT**↵
Select reference: *(select the block to edit)*

Now the **Reference Edit** dialog box is displayed. See Figure 22-17. The features and options in the **Identify Reference** tab are explained as follows:

- **Reference name: area.** This area displays the name of the selected block and any references nested within the selected block. Figure 22-18 shows a block nested within the selected block.
- **Preview area.** An image of the selected block is displayed here. You can cycle through nested blocks by picking the reference name. The preview image changes to display the currently selected block.
- **Automatically select all nested objects**. This option in the **Path:** area makes all of the block objects available for editing, including nested blocks.
- **Prompt to select nested objects.** If this option is used, AutoCAD prompts you to select nested objects. Individual objects can then be selected for editing.

Figure 22-16.
The **Refedit** toolbar.

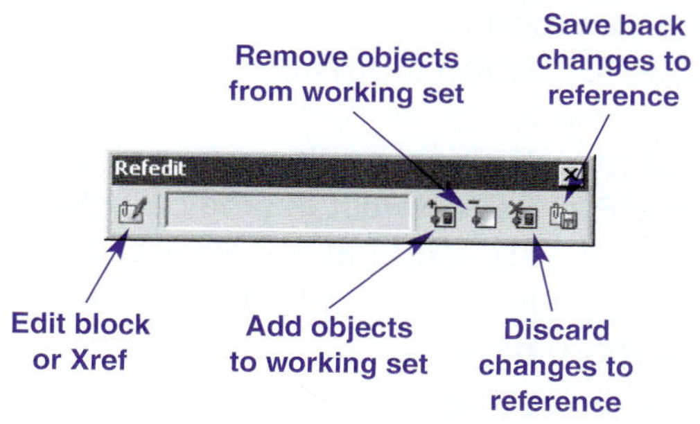

Figure 22-17.
The **Reference Edit** dialog box.

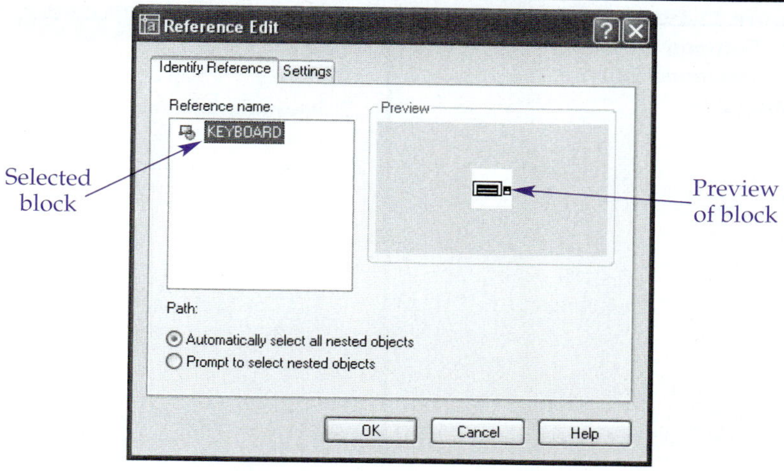

Figure 22-18.
Nested blocks are shown in the tree view of the **Reference Edit** dialog box.

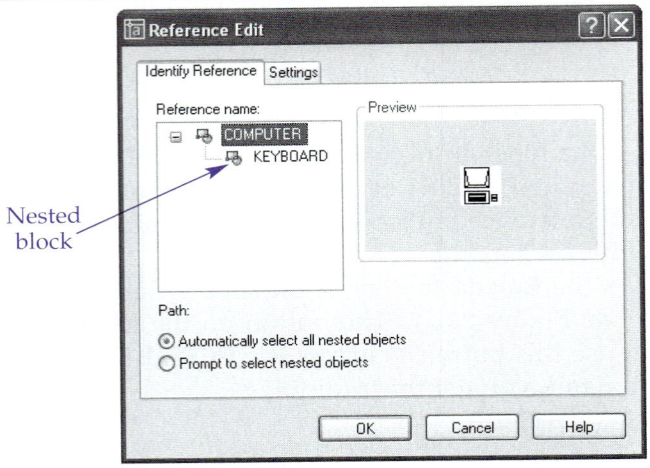

The **Reference Edit** dialog box also contains the **Settings** tab. See Figure 22-19. The options in this tab are explained as follows:

- **Create unique layer, style, and block names.** This option controls the naming of layers and other named objects extracted from the reference. If this option is active, named objects are given a prefix such as $#$.
- **Display attribute definitions for editing.** If this option is checked, the block attributes and attribute definitions in the reference are available for editing. The attributes of the original block reference are unchanged when your changes are saved to the block being edited. The edited attribute definitions only take effect in future insertions of the edited block. Attributes are explained in detail in Chapter 23.
- **Lock objects not in working set.** When this option is checked, all objects that are not a part of the working set are locked. This means they cannot be selected and modified. The *working set* consists of all of the objects in the block available for editing during the reference editing sequence. If the block contains nested objects, they are only available for editing if the **Automatically select all nested objects** option is used, or if they are selected when prompted using the **Prompt to select nested objects** option.

Once all settings are made in the **Reference Edit** dialog box, pick the **OK** button to begin editing the block. If the **Prompt to select nested objects** option is used, you get the following prompts:

Select nested objects: *(select the objects in the block to edit)*

Figure 22-19.
The **Settings** tab of the **Reference Edit** dialog box.

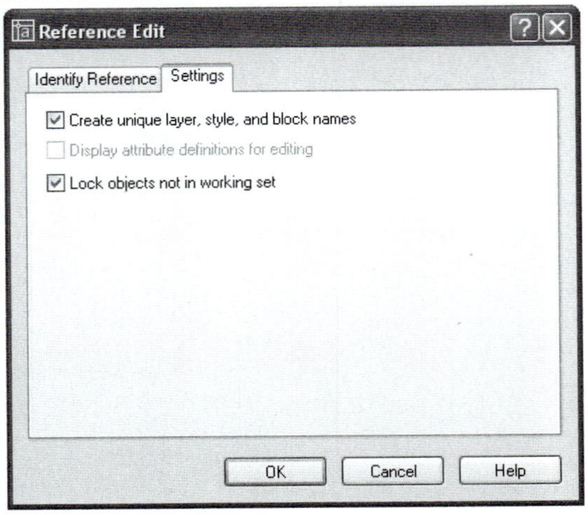

Pick all objects in the block to be edited, then press [Enter].

Select nested objects: ↵
n items selected
Use REFCLOSE or the Refedit toolbar to end reference editing session.
Command:

If multiple insertions of the same block are displayed, be sure to pick from the one you originally selected.

When the Command: prompt is available, all the objects in the drawing are grayed out, except the objects you selected. Now use any drawing or editing commands to alter the object as desired. Pick the **Save back changes to reference** button on the **Refedit** toolbar. Pick **OK** at the AutoCAD alert shown in Figure 22-20 if you want to continue with the save. Changes to the edited block are displayed immediately. The changes also affect other insertions of the same block and future insertions of the block.

Objects that are selected for the working set appear brighter than other objects. Objects that are not a part of the working set are faded. The percent of fading is controlled in the **Display** tab of the **Options** dialog box. A maximum of 90% fading is allowed, and the default is 50%.

Objects that are added to the drawing during the edit can be removed from the working set. The additional buttons on the **Refedit** toolbar are described below.

- **Add objects to working set.** Any object that is drawn during the in-place edit is automatically added to the working set. Additional existing objects can be added with this feature. If an object is added to the working set, it is removed from the host drawing. The **REFSET** command allows you to add to or remove objects from the working set.
- **Remove objects from working set.** Use this feature to remove objects from the working set. When an object is removed from the set, it appears faded. If an object is removed from the working set, it is added to the host drawing.
- **Discard changes to reference.** Pick this button if you want to exit the reference edit function without saving changes to the object. The **REFCLOSE** command allows you to save or discard changes to the working set, and closes reference editing.

NOTE

The **REFEDIT** command can also be used on the command line by entering -REFEDIT at the Command: prompt. After selecting the reference to edit, you can select any nested objects or nested blocks for editing. You can also specify whether to display attribute definitions for editing. The **Refedit** toolbar or **REFCLOSE** command is used to end the editing session and save or discard changes.

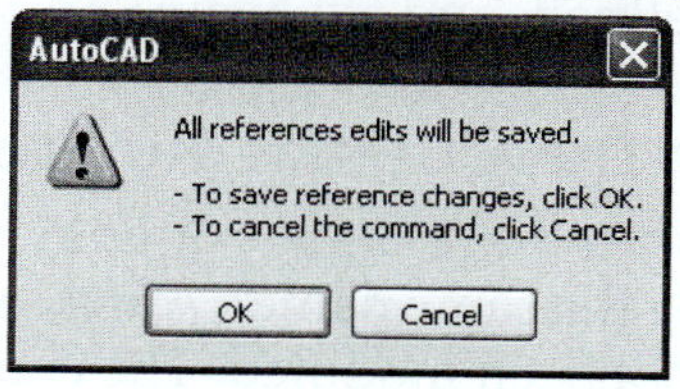

Figure 22-20.
This dialog box appears after editing the selected objects within the block and picking the **Save back changes to reference** button.

EXERCISE 22-6 Complete the Exercise on the Student CD.

Exploding a Block

EXPLODE
X

Modify
➥ Explode

Modify
toolbar

Explode

As previously discussed, you can insert a block and explode it in a single operation using the **Insert** dialog box. This is useful when you want to edit the individual objects of the block. You can also use the **EXPLODE** command to break apart a block into its individual objects.

The **EXPLODE** command is used to break apart any existing block, polyline, or dimension. To access this command, pick the **Explode** button on the **Modify** toolbar, select **Explode** from the **Modify** pull-down menu, or enter X or EXPLODE at the Command: prompt as follows:

Command: **X** *or* **EXPLODE**↵
Select objects: *(pick the block)*
Select objects: ↵

When the block is exploded, the component objects are quickly redrawn. The individual objects can then be edited individually. To see if the **EXPLODE** command worked properly, select any object that was formerly part of the block. Only that object should be highlighted. If so, the block was exploded properly.

Redefining Existing Blocks

One way to edit a block is to use the **REFEDIT** command. Once the block is modified and the changes are saved, all instances of that block in the drawing are also updated. This can also be accomplished by what is referred to as *redefining* a block by using the **EXPLODE** and **BLOCK** commands together. To redefine an existing block, follow this procedure:

1. Insert the block to be redefined anywhere in your drawing.
2. Make sure you know where the insertion point of the block is located.
3. Explode the inserted block using the **EXPLODE** command.
4. Edit the block as needed.
5. Recreate the block definition using the **BLOCK** command.
6. Give the block the same name and the same insertion point it originally had.
7. Select the objects to be included in the block.
8. Pick **OK**. When a message from AutoCAD appears and asks if you want to redefine the block, pick **Yes**.
9. When the **BLOCK** command is complete, all insertions of the block are updated.

A common mistake is to forget to use the **EXPLODE** command before redefining the block. When you try to create the block again with the same name, an alert box indicating the block references itself is displayed. This means you are trying to create a block that already exists. Once you press the **OK** button, the alert box disappears and the **Block Definition** dialog box is redisplayed. Press the **Cancel** button, explode the block to be redefined, and try again.

Understanding the Circular Reference Error

As described in the previous example, when you try to redefine a block that already exists (using the same name), AutoCAD informs you that the block references itself or that it has not been modified. The concept of a block *referencing itself* may be a little difficult to grasp at first without fully understanding how AutoCAD works with blocks. A block can be composed of any objects, including other blocks. When using the **BLOCK** command to incorporate an existing block into a new block, AutoCAD must make a list of all the objects that compose the new block. This means

AutoCAD must refer to any existing block definitions that are selected to be part of the new block. If you select an instance, or reference, of the block being redefined as a component object for the new definition, a problem occurs. You are trying to redefine a block name using a previous version of the block with the same name. In other words, the new block refers to a block of the same name, or *references itself*.

For example, assume you create a block named BOX that is composed of four line objects in the shape of a square, and insert it. You then decide the block needs to be changed so that it contains a small circle in the lower-left corner. If the original BOX block is exploded, all that is left are the four line objects. After drawing the required circle, you can enter the **BLOCK** command and recreate a block named BOX by selecting the four lines and the circle as the component objects. Redefining a block destroys the old definition and creates a new one. Any blocks with the same name are redefined with the updated changes. Make sure you want to redefine the block before agreeing to do so. Otherwise, give the block a new name. The correct way to redefine a block is shown in **Figure 22-21.**

Alternately, assume you do not explode the block, but still draw the circle and try to redefine the block. By selecting the BOX block *and* the circle, a new block named BOX would now be a block reference of the BOX block with a circle. The old block definition of BOX has not been destroyed, but a new definition has been attempted. Thus, AutoCAD is trying to define a new block named BOX by using an instance of the BOX block. This is referred to as a ***circular reference***, and is what is meant by a block referencing itself. Refer to **Figure 22-21.**

Figure 22-21.
A—The correct procedure for redefining a block. B—Redefining a block that has not first been exploded creates an invalid circular reference.

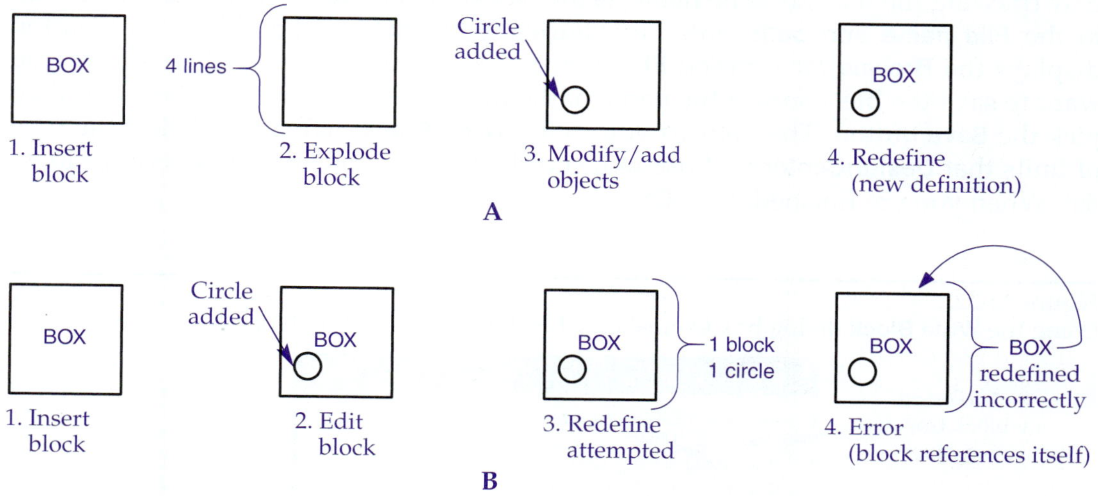

Creating a Block from a Drawing File

You can create a block from any existing drawing. This allows you to avoid redrawing the object as a block, thus saving time. Remember, if something has already been drawn, try to use it as a block rather than redrawing it.

To define a block named BOLT from an existing drawing file named fastener.dwg, enter the **INSERT** command and use the **Browse...** button to select the fastener file. The selected file is then displayed in the **Name:** text box. Use this text box to change the name from fastener to BOLT and pick **OK**. The file can be inserted into the drawing, or you can press the [Esc] key to exit the command. A block named BOLT has now been created from the file and can be used as desired.

EXERCISE 22-7 Complete the Exercise on the Student CD.

Creating Blocks As Drawing Files

Blocks created with the **BLOCK** command are stored in the drawing in which they are made. The **WBLOCK** (write block) command allows you to create a drawing (DWG) file out of a block. You can also use the **WBLOCK** command to create a global block from any object (it does not have to be first saved as a block). The resulting drawing file can then be inserted as a block into any drawing.

There are several ways to use the **WBLOCK** command. To see how the first method works, open drawing EX22-1. Convert the CIRCLE block to a permanent block by making it a separate drawing file. Use the following procedure:

Command: **W** *or* **WBLOCK**↵

The **Write Block** dialog box appears, Figure 22-22. This dialog box is similar to the **Block Definition** dialog box. Pick the **Block:** radio button, and then select the CIRCLE block from the drop-down list in the **Source** area. Specify where you want to save the wblock by typing in a path or picking the ellipsis (**...**) button next to the **File name and path:** drop-down list (if the path shown is not the desired location). By default, the new drawing file has the same name as the block. This is shown with the folder path in the **File name and path:** entry in Figure 22-22. Picking the ellipsis (**...**) button displays the **Browse for Drawing File** dialog box. Navigate to the folder where you want to save the file, confirm the name of the file in the **File name:** text box, and then pick the **Save** button. This returns you to the **Write Block** dialog box. Select the type of units that **DesignCenter** will use to insert the block in the **Insert units:** drop-down list. When you are finished, pick **OK**.

Figure 22-22.
Using the **Write Block** dialog box to create a wblock from an existing block.

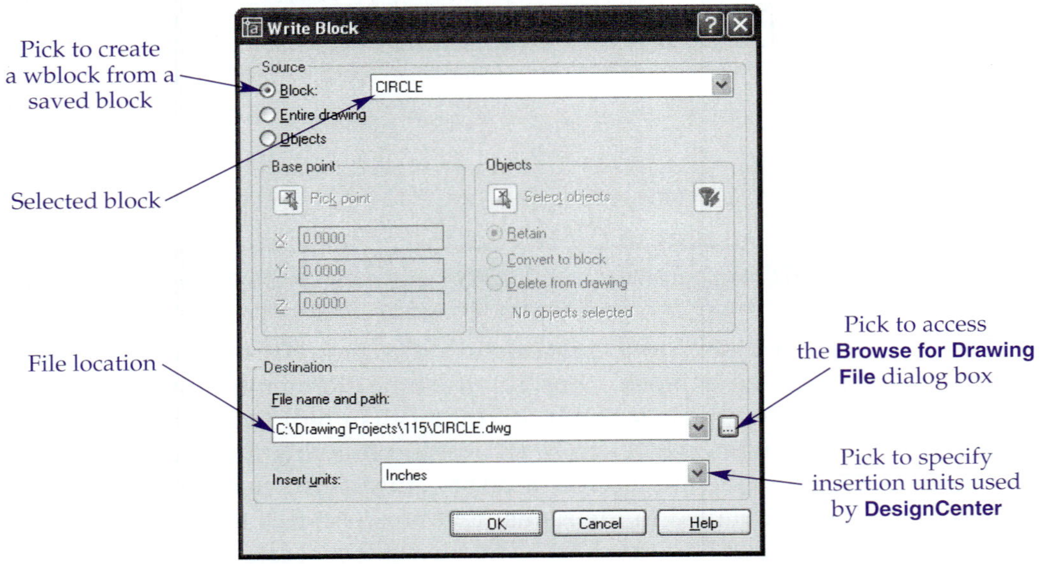

Creating a New Wblock

Suppose you want to create a wblock from a shape you have just drawn, but you have not yet made a block. The following sequence is used to save a selected object as a drawing file. First, enter the **WBLOCK** command and select the **Objects** radio button in the **Write Block** dialog box (it is active by default). Pick the **Select objects** button to select the objects for the drawing file. Next, pick the **Pick point** button to select the insertion point. You can also enter coordinates in the **X:**, **Y:**, and **Z:** text boxes. If the path shown in the **File name and path:** text box is not where you want to save the file, access the **Browse for Drawing File** dialog box by picking the ellipsis (**...**) button. Navigate to the folder where you want to save the file. Specify the name of the file in the **File name:** field and then pick the **Save** button. In the **Write Block** dialog box, select the type of units that **DesignCenter** will use to insert the block in the **Insert units:** drop-down list. When you are through, pick **OK**. See Figure 22-23.

This sequence is the same as that used with the **BLOCK** command. However, the wblock is saved to disk as a drawing file, *not* as a block in the current drawing. Be sure to specify the correct file path in the **File name and path:** text box when using the **Write Block** dialog box. A drawing file named desk that is to be saved in the blocks folder on the C: hard drive, for example, would be saved as c:\blocks\desk.

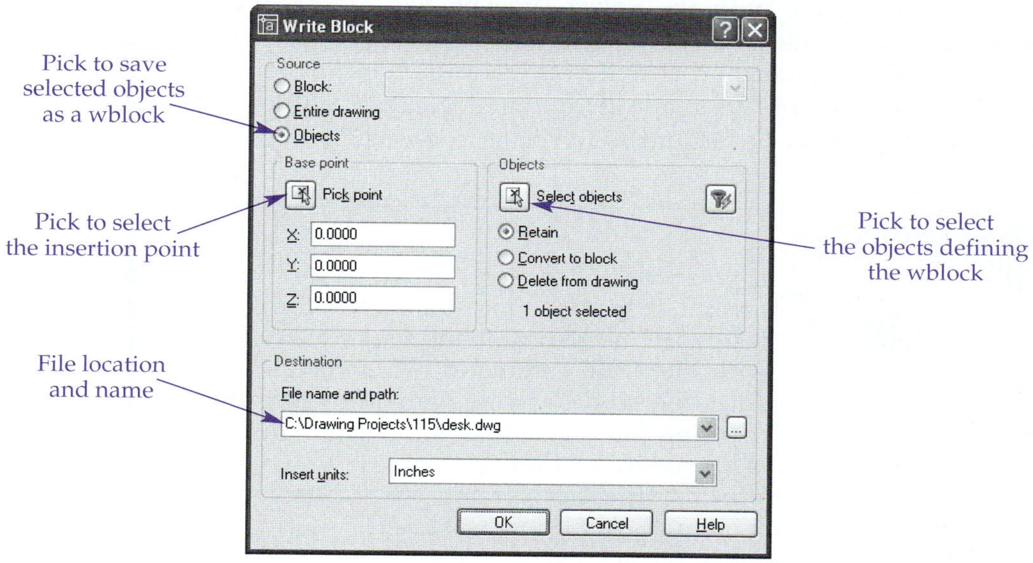

Figure 22-23.
Using the **Write Block** dialog box to create a wblock from selected objects without first defining a block.

Storing a Drawing As a Wblock

An entire drawing can also be stored as a wblock. To do this, pick the **Entire drawing** radio button in the **Write Block** dialog box. Specify the location to save the wblock and give it a name using the **File name and path:** text box. Select the type of units **DesignCenter** will use to insert the block in the **Insert units:** drop-down list, and pick **OK** when you are through.

In this case, the whole drawing is saved to disk as if you had used the **SAVE** command. The difference is that all unused blocks are deleted from the drawing. If the drawing contains any unused blocks, this method reduces the size of a drawing considerably.

PROFESSIONAL TIP

Using the **Entire drawing** wblock option is a good way to remove named objects that are unused in your drawing to reduce the file size. Use this routine when you have completed a drawing and decide the unused blocks, layers, styles, and other unused objects are no longer needed. The **PURGE** command can also be used to remove any unused objects. The process is slower than using the **Entire drawing** wblock option. The **PURGE** command is discussed later in this chapter.

EXERCISE 22-8 Complete the Exercise on the Student CD.

Revising an Inserted Drawing

You may find that you need to revise a drawing file that has been used in other drawings. If this happens, you can quickly update any drawing in which the revised drawing is used. For example, if a drawing file named pump was modified after being used several times in a drawing, simply enter the **INSERT** command and access the original drawing file with the **Select Drawing File** dialog box. Then, activate the **Specify On-screen** check box in the **Insertion point** area and pick **OK**. When a message from AutoCAD appears and asks if you want to redefine the block, pick **Yes**. All of the pump references are automatically updated. Next, press the [Esc] key. By canceling the command, no new insertions of the pump drawing are made.

PROFESSIONAL TIP

If you work on projects in which inserted drawings may be revised, it may be more productive to use reference drawings instead of inserted drawing files. Reference drawings are used with the **XREF** command, which is discussed in Chapter 24. All referenced drawings are automatically updated when a drawing file that contains the externally referenced material is loaded into AutoCAD.

Symbol Libraries

As you become proficient with AutoCAD, you will want to start constructing symbol libraries. A ***symbol library*** is a collection of related shapes, views, symbols, and other content used repeatedly in drawings. Some drafters incorporate symbols into screen and tablet menus. These customization methods are discussed in detail in ***AutoCAD and Its Applications—Advanced.*** Arranging a storage system for frequently used symbols increases productivity and saves time. First, you need to establish how the symbols are stored (as blocks or drawing files) and then determine where they will be stored for insertion into different drawings.

Blocks versus Separate Drawing Files

As discussed earlier, the main difference between the **BLOCK** and **WBLOCK** commands is that a block is saved with the drawing in which it is created and the **WBLOCK** command saves the block as a separate drawing file. A complete drawing file occupies more disk space than a block. Also, a drawing file can contain many blocks; once the drawing file is inserted into the current drawing, all the blocks in the drawing file are also inserted into the drawing.

If you decide to use blocks, each person in the office or class must have access to the drawing that contains the blocks. This is often done by creating the blocks in a template file or a separate drawing file. If individual drawing files are used rather than blocks, each student or employee must have access to the files.

Creating a Symbol Library

Once a set of related block definitions is created, you can arrange the blocks in a symbol library. This can consist of a single drawing file or several files. Each block should be identified with a name and insertion point location. Whether the symbols are being stored in a single drawing file or as individual files, several guidelines can be used to create the symbol library:

- Assign one person to initially create the symbols for each specialty.
- Follow class or company symbol standards.
- When using blocks, save one group of symbols per drawing file. When using individual drawing files, name the files accordingly so they can be assigned to separate folders on the hard drive. For example, you may want to create several different symbol libraries based on the following types of symbols:
  - ✓ Electronic
  - ✓ Electrical
  - ✓ Piping
  - ✓ Mechanical
  - ✓ Structural
  - ✓ Architectural
  - ✓ Landscaping
  - ✓ Mapping
- Print a hard copy of the symbol library. Include a representation of each symbol, its insertion point, any other necessary information, and where it is located. A sample is shown in **Figure 22-24.** Provide all users of the symbols with a copy of the listing.
- If a network drive is not in use, copy the symbol library file(s) to each workstation in the class or office.
- Keep backup copies of all files in a secure place.
- When symbols are revised, update all files containing the edited symbols.
- Inform all users of any changes to saved symbols.

Figure 22-24.
A printed copy of piping flow diagram blocks stored in a symbol library. Each colored dot indicates the insertion point, and is not part of the block.

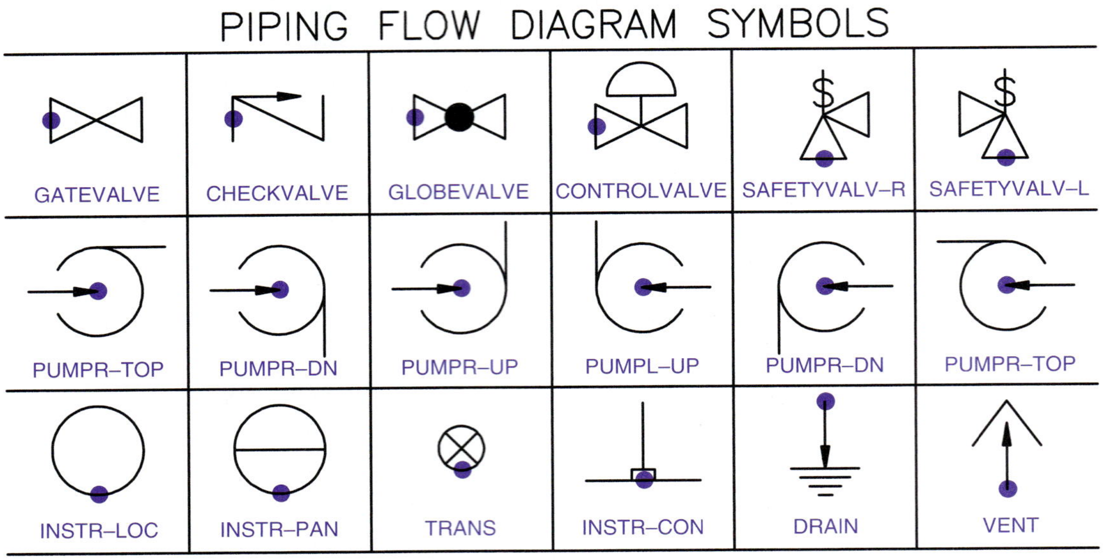

Storing Symbol Drawings

The local or network hard disk drive is one of the best places to store a symbol library. It is easily accessed, quick, and more convenient to use than portable media. Writable CDs or other media can be used for backup purposes if a network drive with an automatic backup function is not available. In the absence of a network or modem, portable media can be used to transport files from one workstation to another.

There are several methods of storing symbols on the hard drive. Symbols can be saved as wblocks and organized within folders. It is recommended to store symbols outside of the AutoCAD 2005 folder. This will keep the system folder uncluttered and allow you to differentiate which folders and files were originally installed with AutoCAD. A good idea is to create a Blocks folder for storing your blocks, as shown in **Figure 22-25.**

Figure 22-25.
An efficient way to store blocks saved as drawing files is to set up a Blocks folder containing folders for each type of symbol on the hard drive.

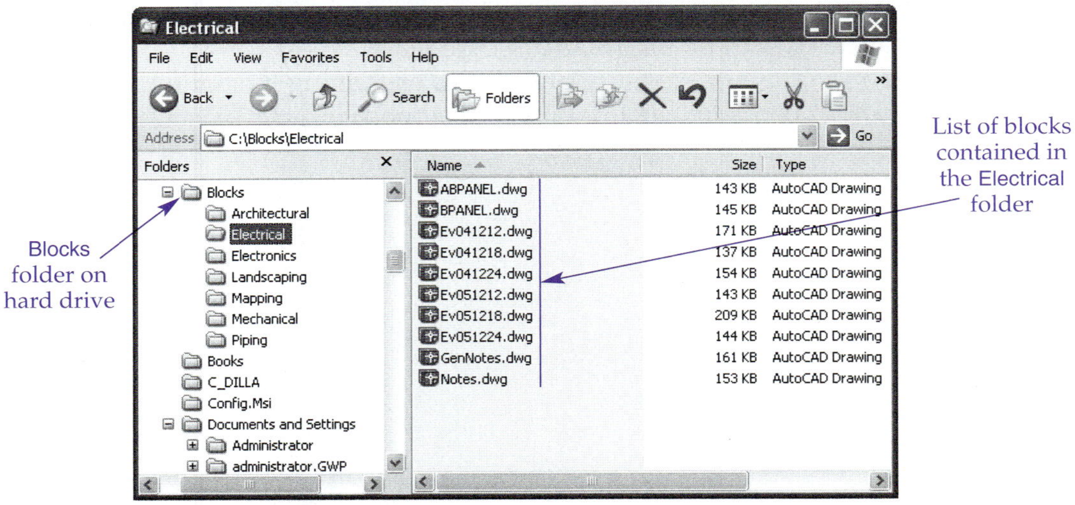

Symbols can also be saved as blocks within a drawing. The symbols are then inserted using **DesignCenter** or the **Tool Palettes** window. When using this system, symbols can be grouped within several drawing files. For example, electrical symbols can be saved in an electrical.dwg drawing, and piping symbols can be saved in a piping.dwg drawing. Limit the number of symbols within a drawing to a reasonable amount so the symbols can be found relatively easily. If there are too many blocks within a drawing, it may be difficult to locate the desired symbol.

Drawing files saved on the hard drive should be arranged in a logical manner. The following guidelines also apply:

- All workstations in the class or office should have folders with the same names.
- One person should be assigned to update and copy symbol libraries to all workstation hard drives.
- Drawing files should be copied onto each workstation's hard drive from a master CD or network server.
- The master and backup versions of the symbol libraries should be kept in separate locations.

Renaming Blocks

RENAME
REN

Format
➥ Rename...

Blocks can be renamed using the **RENAME** command. Access this command by selecting **Rename...** from the **Format** pull-down menu or entering REN or RENAME at the Command: prompt. This displays the **Rename** dialog box, Figure 22-26.

To change the name of the CIRCLE block to HOLE, select Blocks from the **Named Objects** list. A list of block names defined in the current drawing then appears in the **Items** list. Pick CIRCLE to highlight it in the list. When this name appears in the **Old Name:** text box, enter the new block name HOLE in the **Rename To:** text box. Pick the **Rename To:** button and the new block name appears in the **Items** list. Pick **OK** to exit the **Rename** dialog box.

Figure 22-26.
The **Rename** dialog box allows you to change the name of a block and other named objects.

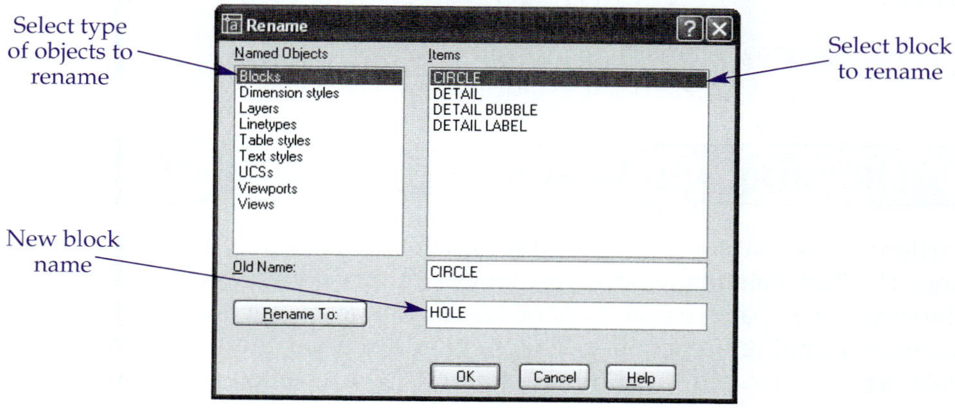

Deleting Named Objects

As discussed in the previous section, a block is a named object. In many drawing sessions, not all of the named objects in a drawing are used. For example, your drawing may contain several layers, text styles, and blocks that are not used. Since these objects occupy disk space, it is good practice to delete or *purge* the unused objects with the **PURGE** command.

PURGE
PU

File
➥ Drawing Utilities
➥ Purge...

The **PURGE** command accesses the **Purge** dialog box, **Figure 22-27.** To access this dialog box, select **Purge...** from the **Drawing Utilities** cascading menu in the **File** pull-down menu or enter PU or PURGE at the Command: prompt.

Select the appropriate radio button at the top of the dialog box to view content that can be purged or to view content that cannot be purged.

Before purging, select the **Confirm each item to be purged** check box to have an opportunity to review each item before it is deleted. If you wish to purge nested items, check the **Purge nested items** check box.

If you want to purge only some items, use the tree view to locate and highlight the items, and then pick the **Purge** button. If you want to purge all unused items, pick the **Purge All** button.

Figure 22-27.
The **Purge** dialog box.

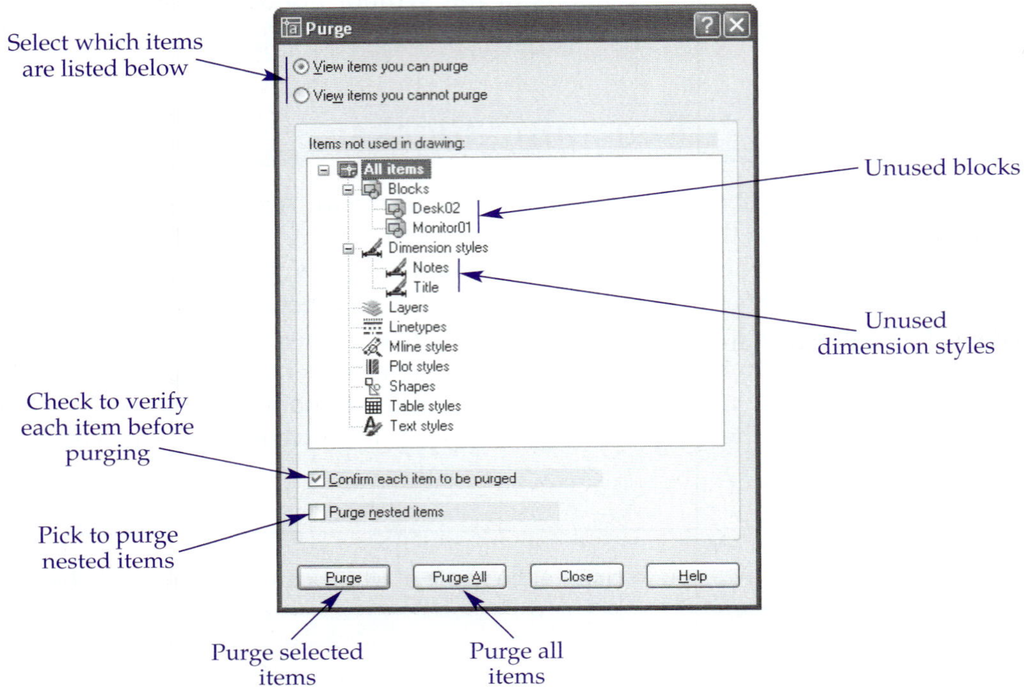

Using and Customizing Tool Palettes

Earlier in this chapter, you used the **Tool Palettes** window to insert blocks into a drawing. The **Tool Palettes** window provides a number of ways to manage frequently used blocks, hatch patterns, and other types of objects, such as gradients, images, tables, and external reference files. This section discusses the various features in the **Tool Palettes** window and the different methods available to customize tool palettes.

NOTE

Tool palettes can be used to store many different types of drawing content and tools, such as AutoCAD drawing and editing commands, customized commands, user-defined macros, script files, and AutoLISP routines. Examples of custom tools are provided in the **Command Tools** tool palette. For more discussion on AutoCAD customization, refer to *AutoCAD and Its Applications—Advanced*.

Modifying the Appearance of the Tool Palettes Window

As with other AutoCAD windows, such as **DesignCenter** and the **Properties** window, the **Tool Palettes** window can take up valuable drawing space. You can alternate the display of this window by using the **Auto-hide** setting. Turning on the **Auto-hide** setting hides the palette area of the window when it is not being used. This setting can be toggled on and off by picking the **Auto-hide** button on the **Tool Palettes** window title bar or by right-clicking on the title bar and picking **Auto-hide** from the shortcut menu. See Figure 22-28. The shortcut menu can also be accessed by picking the **Properties** button on the title bar. When **Auto-hide** is on, and the cursor is moved over the title bar, the tool palettes are displayed. When the cursor is moved outside the window, the tool palettes are hidden.

The title bar shortcut menu contains several other options that affect the appearance of the **Tool Palettes** window. The **Allow Docking** option controls whether the window can be docked. When this option is checked, the window is dockable. The **Tool Palettes** window is docked and resized in the same manner as any AutoCAD toolbar. You can also move, resize, or close the window by using the related option in the title bar shortcut menu. The **Rename** option allows you to rename the **Tool Palettes** window. The **Transparency...** option allows you to adjust the transparency of the **Tool Palettes** window. When you pick this option, the **Transparency** dialog box is displayed. See Figure 22-29. To adjust the transparency, move the **Transparency Level** slider. The lowest transparency setting is active by default. Moving the slider to the right makes the window more transparent.

The **New Tool Palette** and **Customize...** options in the title bar shortcut menu allow you to create new palettes, import or export palettes, and create tool palette groups. These options are discussed in later sections.

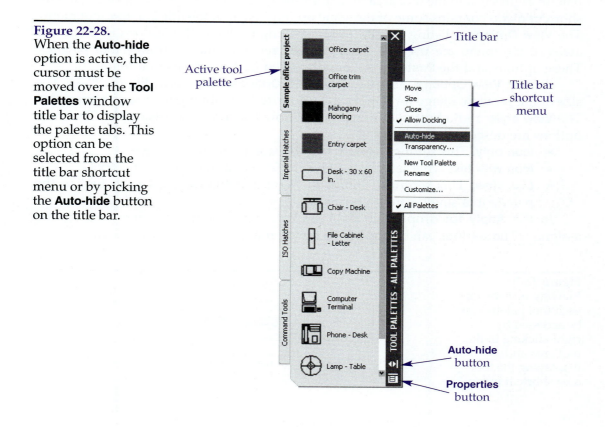

Figure 22-28.
When the **Auto-hide** option is active, the cursor must be moved over the **Tool Palettes** window title bar to display the palette tabs. This option can be selected from the title bar shortcut menu or by picking the **Auto-hide** button on the title bar.

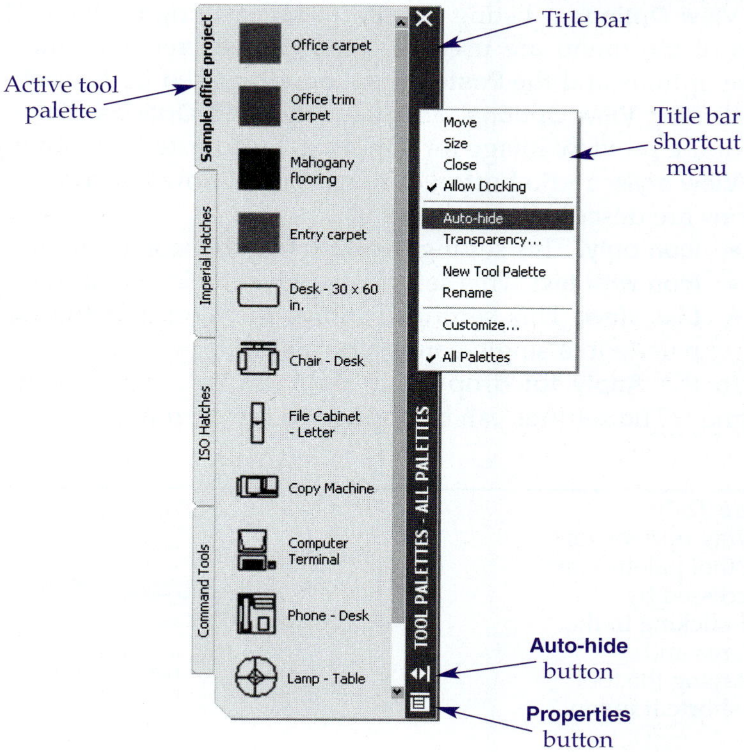

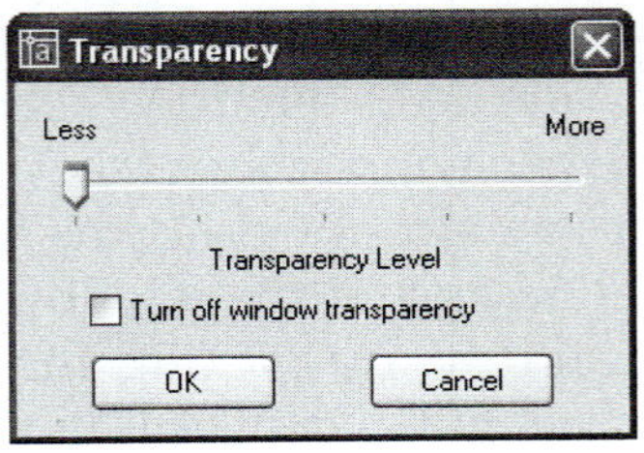

Figure 22-29. The transparency level of the **Tool Palettes** window is set in the **Transparency** dialog box.

Locating and Viewing Content

As previously discussed, each tool palette in the **Tool Palettes** window has its own tab. There are a number of ways to navigate through the tools, or content, in each palette. In addition, viewing options are available to display the content in different ways.

To view the content in a tool palette, click on the related tab to open it. If the **Tool Palettes** window contains more palettes than what is displayed on screen, pick on the edge of the lowest tab to display a selection menu listing the palette tabs. Locate the name of the tab to access the related tool palette.

The tool area in each palette can be navigated by using one of two scroll methods. If all of the content of a selected palette does not fit in the window, the remainder can be viewed by using the scroll bar or the scroll hand. The scroll hand appears when the cursor is placed in an empty area in the tool area. Picking and dragging scrolls the tool area up and down.

By default, the tools in each palette are represented by icons. The appearance of the tools can be adjusted to suit user preference. To access the viewing options in a palette, right-click in the tool area to display the shortcut menu. See Figure 22-30. This shortcut menu contains some of the same options listed in the title bar shortcut menu. The **View Options...** listing is used to set viewing options. The options in the lower areas of the menu are used to create, delete, rename, and rearrange tool palettes. These options and the **Paste** option are discussed in the sections that follow.

Picking **View Options...** displays the **View Options** dialog box, Figure 22-31. The size of the preview image for a tool can be adjusted by moving the **Image size:** slider. The **View style:** radio button options control how the content is displayed. The three options are described as follows:

- **Icon only.** This setting displays just the icon (a preview image).
- **Icon with text.** This setting displays the icon and the name of the tool.
- **List view.** This setting displays the icon and the name of each tool in the palette in a single-column format.

In the **Apply to:** drop-down list, you can specify how the view settings are assigned. The settings can be applied to the current palette only or to all palettes.

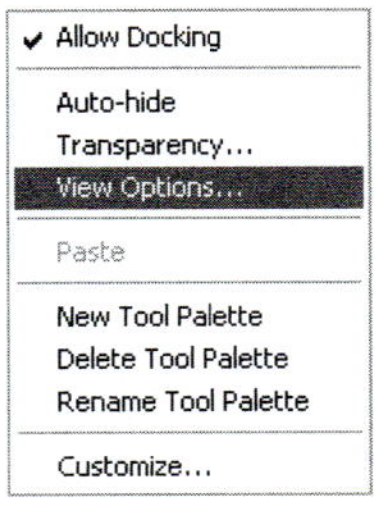

Figure 22-30. Viewing options for each tool palette can be accessed by right-clicking in the tool area and displaying the tool area shortcut menu.

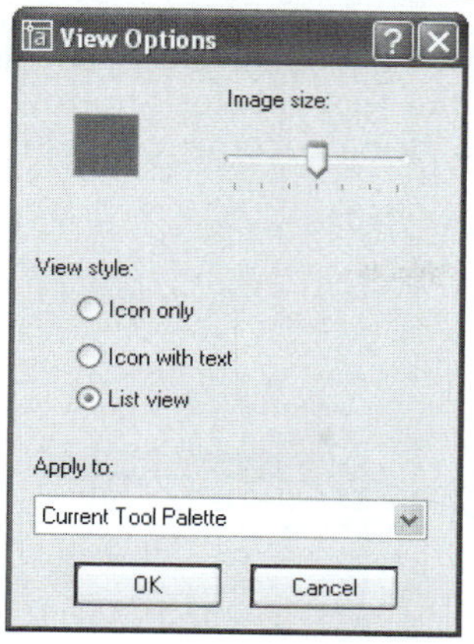

Figure 22-31.
Settings in the **View Options** dialog box control how the content is displayed in each tool palette.

Creating Palettes and Adding Blocks

There are four sample palettes provided by AutoCAD in the **Tool Palettes** window. Using a simple procedure, you can quickly create new palettes and assign blocks to them. To create a new palette, right-click on the **Tool Palettes** title bar or in a tool area. Select **New Tool Palette** from the shortcut menu. You are then prompted to enter a name for the tool palette tab. Choose a name that identifies the content the palette will store. The new palette appears at the bottom of the **Tool Palettes** window.

To add blocks to the palette, you can use one of two methods. If the blocks are located in a file on the hard drive, you can use **DesignCenter** to locate the file and access the blocks. You can then use drag-and-drop to add the blocks to the palette. If the blocks you want to add are displayed in the current drawing, you can drag and drop them to the desired palette.

If you are using **DesignCenter**, you can create individual tools as well as a new palette. For example, a palette can be created with all the blocks in a single drawing file by right-clicking on the drawing file name in **DesignCenter** and selecting **Create Tool Palette** from the shortcut menu. See Figure 22-32. In the example shown, a new palette is created from the Analog Integrated Circuits file. The resulting palette consists of all the blocks in the file and has the same name as the file. A palette can also be created in this manner by expanding the contents of a drawing file in the **Tree View** area and right-clicking over the **Blocks** listing in either the **Tree View** area or the **Content** area. When the shortcut menu appears, select **Create Tool Palette.**

Individual blocks can be added to a tool palette from **DesignCenter** by using a drag-and-drop operation. First, display the blocks to be added in the **Content** area of **DesignCenter**. Then, open the **Tool Palettes** window and display the tool palette that will store the blocks. Finally, drag each block from **DesignCenter** and drop it into the tool palette. If the palette is not already created, you can right-click on the block icon and select **Create Tool Palette** from the shortcut menu. This creates a new palette containing the selected block in a single operation. You are then prompted for a new name for the palette.

If you have a block in the current drawing that you want to add to a tool palette, you can use drag-and-drop. Open the **Tool Palettes** window and select the tool palette where the block is to be located. Next, pick the block once to highlight it. Then pick the block anywhere over a highlighted part of the block and drag it onto the tool palette. Do not pick the grip of the block for this step. If you pick the block grip, AutoCAD thinks you are trying to move the block in the drawing area.

An entire drawing file can be added to a tool palette from **DesignCenter** by picking the folder where the file resides in the **Tree View** area and then dragging the file from the **Content** area into a tool palette. When the file is inserted into a drawing from the **Tool Palettes** window, it becomes a block in the drawing.

Figure 22-32.
Right-clicking on a drawing name in **DesignCenter** and selecting **Create Tool Palette** will create a new palette in the **Tool Palettes** window with the name of the drawing file. All the blocks defined in the drawing become tools in the palette.

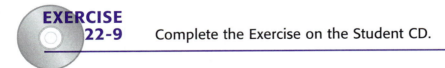

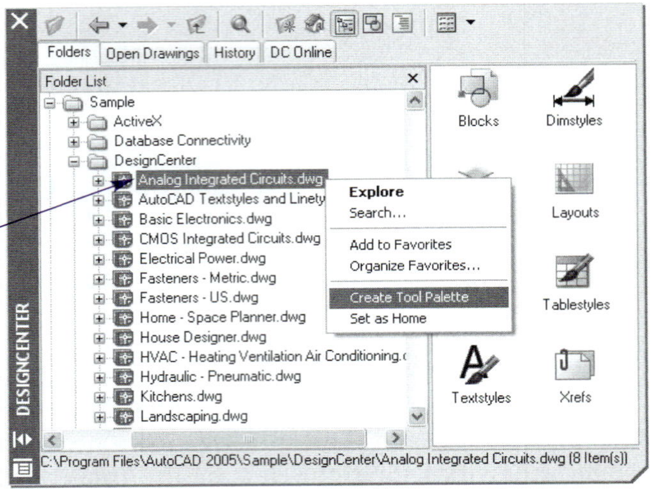

If you have multiple drawing files in a folder and want to create a tool palette that consists of all of the blocks combined from all of the drawing files, navigate to the folder in the **Tree View** area of **DesignCenter**. Next, right-click over the folder and select **Create Tool Palette of Blocks**. A new palette is created in the **Tool Palettes** window with the name of the folder.

NOTE

A block that has been added to a tool palette is directly linked to the drawing file in which it resides. If the block has been modified in the source file, inserting it from a tool palette inserts the updated block. The preview image in the palette does not reflect changes to the block. To update the icon, the tool must be deleted and then reinserted, or its properties must be changed in the **Tool Properties** window. This procedure is discussed later in this chapter.

EXERCISE 22-9 Complete the Exercise on the Student CD.

AutoCAD 2005 NEW FEATURE

Adding Hatch Patterns to a Tool Palette

Hatch patterns and gradient fills can be added to tool palettes using the same drag-and-drop procedures involved with blocks. The pattern must be in the current drawing or defined in an AutoCAD hatch pattern file. If you are adding a hatch pattern or gradient fill to a tool palette from the current drawing, first open the desired palette in the **Tool Palettes** window. Select the hatch pattern or gradient object in the drawing to highlight it. Then pick anywhere over the hatch pattern or gradient (do not select the grip) and drag it onto the tool palette.

As discussed in Chapter 21, the predefined hatch patterns provided with AutoCAD are stored in the acad.pat and acadiso.pat files. If you want to add a predefined pattern to a tool palette, one of the files must be located in **DesignCenter**. By default, these files are AutoCAD support files stored in the Support File Search Path folder. This path location can be determined by accessing the **Files** tab in the **Options** dialog box and identifying the path listed under Support File Search Path.

Once a hatch pattern file is located, its contents can be displayed in the **Content** area of **DesignCenter**. You can then add one or more hatch patterns to a tool palette.

To create a palette that contains all of the hatch patterns in a single PAT file, right-click on the hatch pattern file in the **Tree View** area and select **Create Tool Palette of Hatch Patterns** from the shortcut menu. To add an individual hatch pattern to a palette, drag-and-drop the pattern from the **Content** area into the desired palette.

Arranging and Customizing Tool Palettes

AutoCAD 2005
NEW FEATURE

Once you have created a set of tool palettes, there are a number of customization options that can be used to organize them in the **Tool Palettes** window. You can arrange different palettes into groups so that they can be quickly identified and accessed. If you are working in a multiple user environment, you can import additional tool palettes from other sources. This is a way to access drawing tools that meet company or school standards (such as symbol libraries). You can also export palettes so that they are available to others.

You can rename or delete existing palettes and change the order in which they appear in the **Tool Palettes** window. To rename or delete a tool palette, right-click in a tool area and select the appropriate shortcut menu option. To move a tool palette up or down in the **Tool Palettes** window, right-click on the palette tab and select **Move Up** or **Move Down** from the shortcut menu. The window immediately updates with the change.

Tool palettes can also be arranged into groups. A tool palette group consists of a number of named palettes. For example, it may be useful to have an Architectural tool palette containing individual tabs for doors, windows, details, symbols, and notes. An Electrical tool palette can be created in the same manner, with tabs for outlets, switches, and lighting fixtures. Tool palette groups can also be divided into subgroups.

To create a tool palette group, right-click in a palette and select **Customize...** from the shortcut menu. This displays the **Customize** dialog box with the **Tool Palettes** tab active. See Figure 22-33. In the **Palette Groups** area, right-click and select **New Group**. Enter a name for the new group. To add a palette to the group, select the palette in the **Tool Palettes** area and drag it to just below the group name in the **Palette Groups** area. Examples of tool palette groups are shown in Figure 22-34.

Figure 22-33.
Tool palette groups can be created in the **Customize** dialog box.

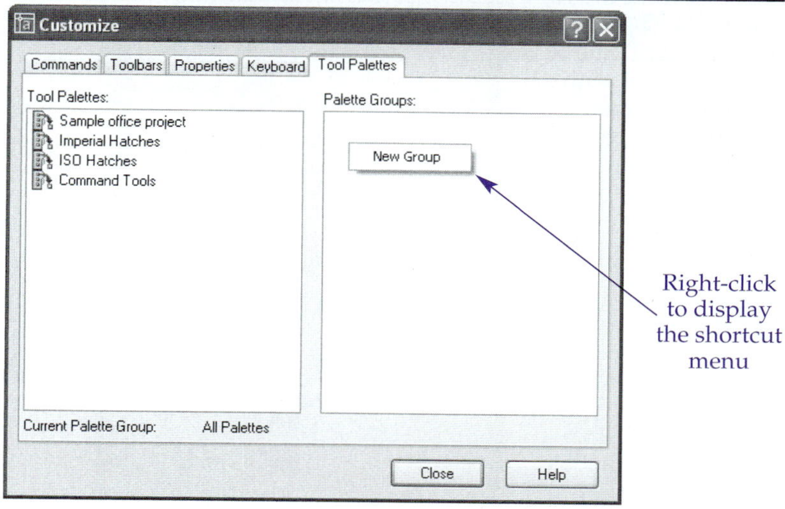

Editing options for tool palette groups can be accessed by right-clicking over a group name. Refer to **Figure 22-34B.** Selecting **New Group** from the shortcut menu allows you to create a new tool palette group within the selected group (a subgroup). You can also rename or delete the selected group. If the selected group is current in the **Tool Palettes** window, the **Delete** option is not available. Selecting **Set Current** switches the **Tool Palettes** window to display the selected tool palette group.

To remove a tool palette from a group, select the tool palette in the **Palette Groups** area and then right-click and select **Remove** from the shortcut menu. You can also drag the tool palette from the **Palette Groups** area back to the **Tool Palettes** area.

After closing the **Customize** dialog box, you can switch between tool palette groups in the **Tool Palettes** window by picking the **Properties** button on the title bar or selecting **Properties** from the title bar shortcut menu. See **Figure 22-35.** Select a tool palette group to display its tool palettes. The **All Palettes** option displays all tool palettes and palette groups.

Figure 22-34.
Tool palettes are added to a group by dragging them from the **Tool Palettes** area to the **Palette Groups** area. A—The Doors tool palette is selected for the Architectural palette group. B—Palettes are added to the Architectural and Electrical groups. Right-clicking over a group name accesses a shortcut menu with management options.

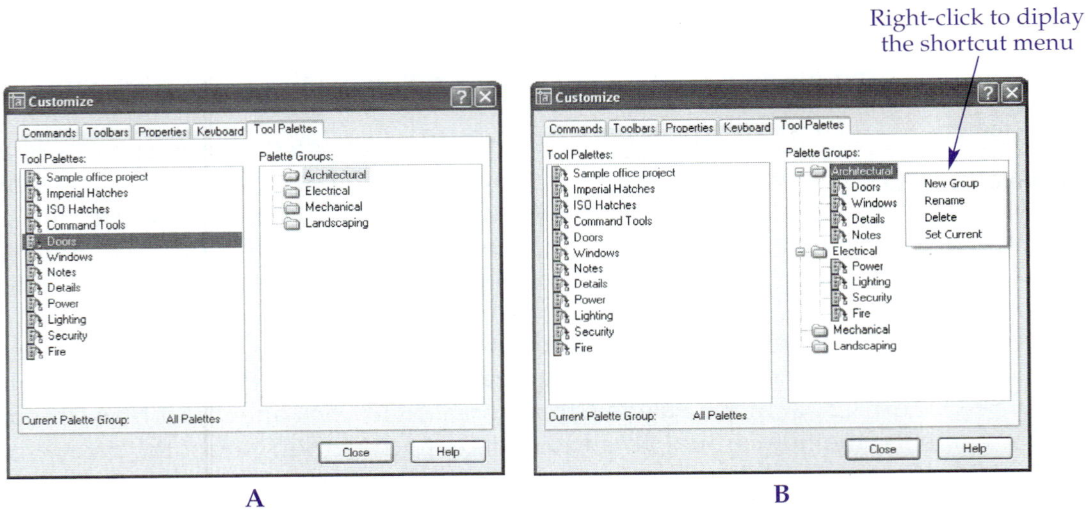

Figure 22-35.
Setting a tool palette group current with the **Tool Palettes** window title bar shortcut menu.

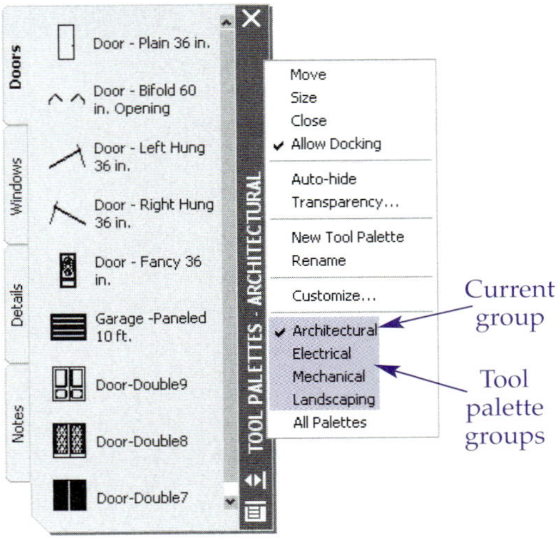

When you create a new tool palette, it is good practice to export it as a file to create a backup copy. Exporting a tool palette saves it to a file with an XTP extension. You can also import a tool palette saved as a file and place it in the **Tool Palettes** window.

To import or export a tool palette, open the **Customize** dialog box and right-click in the **Tool Palettes** area. See Figure 22-36. Selecting **Import** from the shortcut menu allows you to import a tool palette that has been saved using the **Import Tool Palette** dialog box. To export a tool palette, select the palette in the **Tool Palettes** area, right-click, and select **Export**. This allows you to export the selected palette as a file using the **Export Tool Palette** dialog box.

When new content is added to or deleted from a tool palette, you can export it again to update the saved file. In a multiple user environment, tool palettes can be imported and exported to maximize efficiency. For example, on one workstation, tool palettes can be created and then exported to a network drive. The tool palettes can then be imported by other users of the network.

> **NOTE**
> The path for AutoCAD's default tool palette files is specified in the Tool Palettes File Locations listing. To verify the location of this path, access the **Files** tab in the **Options** dialog box and check the path listed under Tool Palettes File Locations.

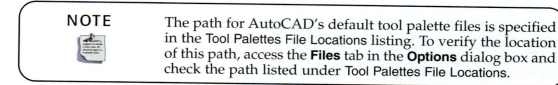

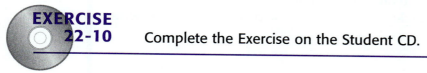

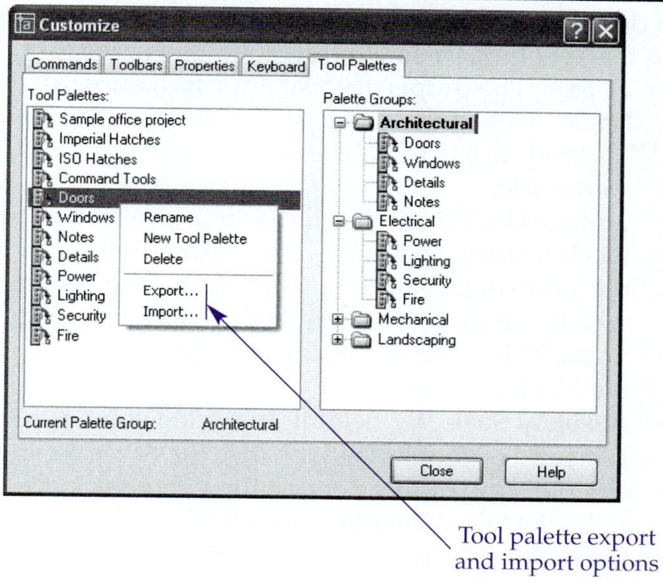

Figure 22-36. Tool palettes can be imported or exported using the **Customize** dialog box.

EXERCISE 22-10 Complete the Exercise on the Student CD.

Modifying Tools and Tool Properties

When working with several different palettes in the **Tool Palettes** window, it may be useful to copy or move the content of one palette to another. In addition, you may want to change the properties of blocks in certain palettes so that they vary from those in the source file or other palettes. Blocks residing in tool palettes can be modified to have different properties when inserted, such as different scales and rotation angles. Hatch patterns can be modified in the same manner. For example, you may want to specify a different angle for an inserted pattern. The properties override the defined object properties when the object is inserted.

A tool within a palette can be copied, moved, deleted, or renamed by right-clicking on the tool icon. This displays a tool shortcut menu, Figure 22-37. Property changes can be made by first displaying the same menu. The **Cut** option is used to remove a tool from one palette and move it to another. After picking **Cut**, select another palette tab, right-click in the tool area, and select **Paste** from the shortcut menu to move the tool to the new palette. The **Copy** option is used in the same way as the **Cut** option, except a copy is placed in the new palette and the tool remains in the original palette.

To delete a tool, right-click on its icon and select **Delete Tool** from the shortcut menu. When this option is selected, an alert dialog box appears. Selecting **OK** permanently deletes the tool.

To rename a tool, right-click on its icon and select **Rename** from the shortcut menu. Depending on the viewing option set in the **View Options** dialog box, the name of the tool may be displayed with the tool in the **Tool Palettes** window. If the name is not displayed, picking **Rename** temporarily displays the tool name so it can be renamed.

The properties of a tool can be viewed and modified by right-clicking on its icon and selecting **Properties...** from the shortcut menu. This opens the **Tool Properties** window. See Figure 22-38. The properties displayed depend on what type of tool is selected. A preview of the tool appears in the **Image:** area, and the name appears in the **Name:** text box. A description may be entered for the object in the **Description:** text box if desired.

In the **Tool Properties** window for a block, the first category is labeled **Insert**. See Figure 22-38A. The properties that appear are described as follows:

- **Name.** This is the name of the block in the source drawing file that will be inserted. It has to be the exact name of a block that has been defined in the source file.
- **Source file.** This is the location and name of the drawing file in which the block resides. To modify this setting, select the **Source file** setting. Then pick the ellipsis (**...**) button. This opens the **Select Linked Drawing** dialog box, which allows you to change the source drawing file.
- **Scale.** This value specifies the scale of the block in relation to the size at which the block was created.
- **Auxiliary Scale.** By default, this scale value is set to **None**. Setting the value to **Dimscale** or **Plot scale** overrides the **Scale** setting. The **Dimscale** option specifies the scale of the block as the value set in the **Use overall scale of:** text box in the **Fit** tab of the **Dimension Style** dialog box. The **Plot scale** option specifies the scale of the block as the **Scale:** setting in the **Page Setup** or **Plot** dialog box.
- **Rotation.** This value specifies the rotation angle used when the block is inserted.
- **Prompt for Rotation.** This setting determines whether you are prompted for the rotation angle when inserting the block. The default setting is **No**.

Figure 22-37.
A tool shortcut menu with modification options is displayed by right-clicking on a tool in a palette. Selecting **Properties...** opens the **Tool Properties** window.

Figure 22-38.
A—The **Tool Properties** window for a block tool. B—The **Tool Properties** window for a hatch pattern tool.

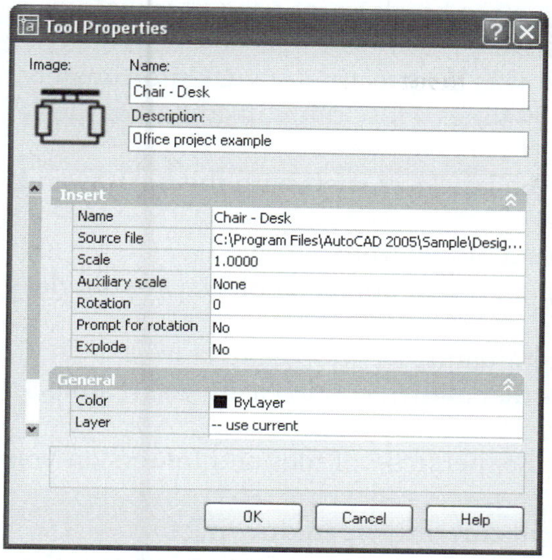

A

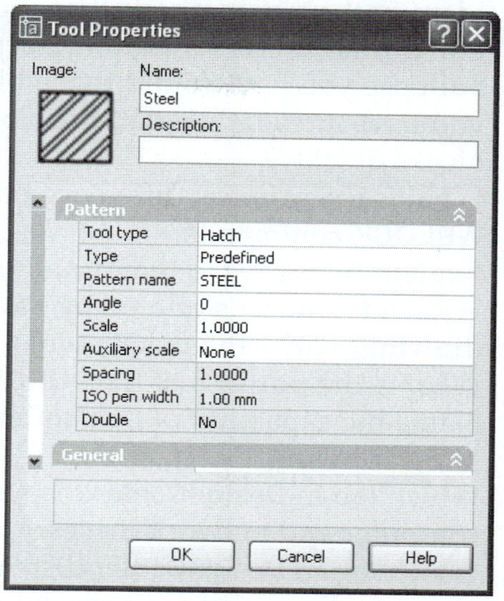

B

- **Explode.** This setting determines whether the block is exploded when inserted. The default setting is **No**.

In the **Tool Properties** window for a hatch pattern, the first category is labeled **Pattern**. The settings correspond to the options specified in the **Boundary Hatch** dialog box. Hatch patterns are discussed in Chapter 21.

The **Tool Properties** window has identical property settings in the **General** category for blocks and hatch patterns. These are the **Color**, **Layer**, **Linetype**, **Plot style**, and **Lineweight** settings. As with other object properties, these settings may be modified to produce different results when inserting a block or hatch pattern from a tool palette.

EXERCISE 22-11 Complete the Exercise on the Student CD.

Chapter Test

Answer the following questions on a separate sheet of paper.

1. Define *symbol library*.
2. Which color and linetype settings should be used if you want a block to assume the current color and linetype when it is inserted into a drawing?
3. When should a block be drawn to fit inside a one-unit square, and what type of block is this called when it is inserted?
4. A block name cannot exceed _____ characters.
5. What are two ways to access a listing of all blocks in the current drawing?
6. Describe the term *nesting* in relation to blocks.
7. How do you preset block insertion variables using the **Insert** dialog box?
8. Describe the effect of entering negative scale factors when inserting a block.
9. What properties do blocks drawn on a layer other than layer 0 assume when inserted?

10. Why would you draw blocks on layer 0?
11. What is a limitation of an array pattern created with the **MINSERT** command?
12. What is the purpose of the **BASE** command?
13. Identify the two methods that allow you to break an inserted block into its individual objects for editing purposes.
14. Suppose you have found that a block was incorrectly drawn. Unfortunately, you have already inserted the block 30 times. How can you edit all of the blocks quickly?
15. What is the primary difference between blocks created with the **BLOCK** and **WBLOCK** commands?
16. Explain two ways to remove all unused blocks from a drawing.
17. What advantage is offered by having a symbol library of blocks in a single drawing, rather than using wblocks?
18. What is the purpose of the **PURGE** command?
19. Name the capability of **DesignCenter** that allows you to easily insert a block into a drawing.
20. Which tab in **DesignCenter** displays the hierarchy of files and folders on your computer and network drives?
21. Which tab in **DesignCenter** displays all currently open drawings?
22. Give the dimensions of a block when it is inserted from **DesignCenter** if the original block was a 1″ × 1″ square and the inserted units were specified in feet.
23. Identify two ways to add blocks and hatch patterns to tool palettes.
24. Briefly describe how to insert a block from a tool palette into a drawing.
25. What is the best way to create a tool palette that consists of all the blocks in a drawing file?
26. Briefly explain how to create a tool palette group.

Drawing Problems

1. Create a symbol library for one of the drafting disciplines listed below, and then save it as a template or drawing file. Then, after checking with your instructor, draw a problem using the library. If you save the symbol library as a template, start the problem with the template. If you save it as a drawing file, start a new drawing and insert the symbol library into it.
   Specialty areas you might create symbols for include:
   - Mechanical (machine features, fasteners, tolerance symbols).
   - Architectural (doors, windows, fixtures).
   - Structural (steel shapes, bolts, standard footings).
   - Industrial piping (fittings, valves).
   - Piping flow diagrams (tanks, valves, pumps).
   - Electrical schematics (resistors, capacitors, switches).
   - Electrical one-line (transformers, switches).
   - Electronics (IC chips, test points, components).
   - Logic diagrams (AND gates, NAND gates, buffers).
   - Mapping, civil (survey markers, piping).
   - Geometric tolerancing (feature control frames).

   Save the drawing as P22-1 or choose an appropriate file name, such as ARCH-PRO or ELEC-PRO.
2. Display the symbol library created in Problem 1 on screen and print a hard copy. Put the printed copy in your notebook as a reference.

3. Open P12-20 from Chapter 12. The sketch for this drawing is shown below. Erase all copies of the symbols that were made, leaving the original objects intact. These include the steel column symbols and the bay and column line tags. Then do the following:
   A. Make blocks of the steel column symbol and the tag symbols.
   B. Use the **MINSERT** command or the **ARRAY** command to place the symbols in the drawing.
   C. Dimension the drawing as shown in the sketch.
   D. Save the drawing as P22-3.

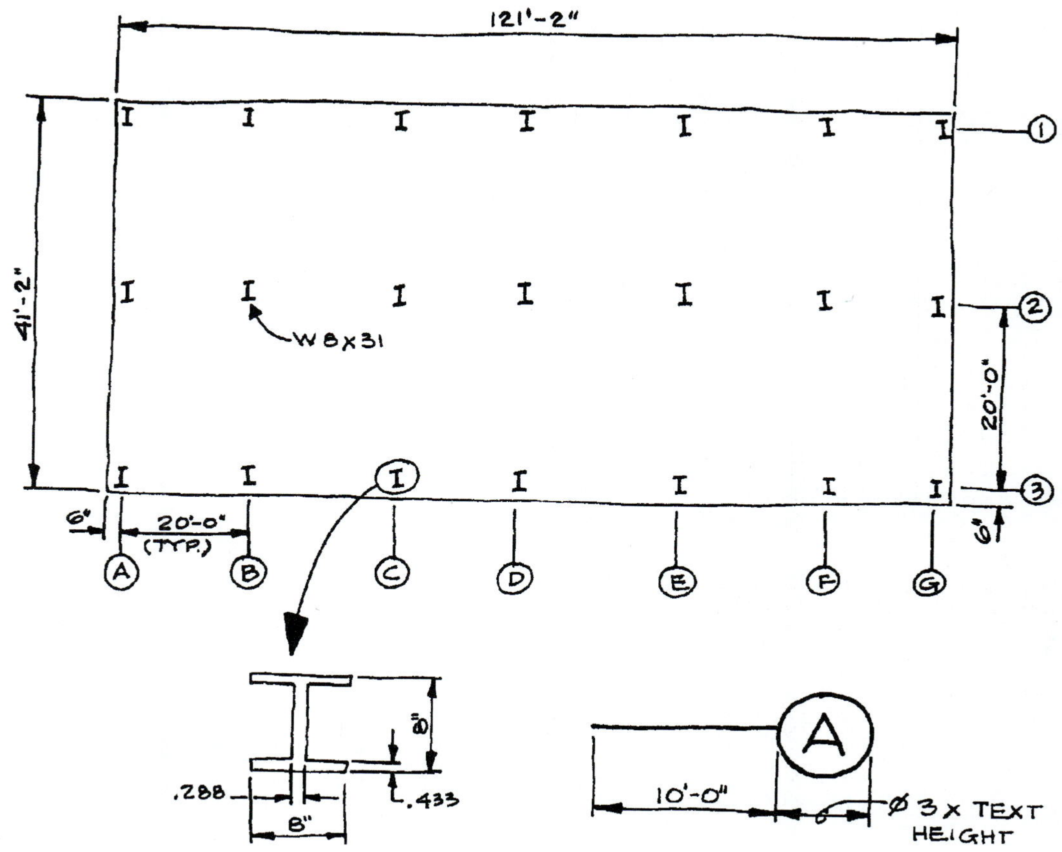

Problems 4–6 represent a variety of diagrams created using symbols as blocks. Create each drawing as shown (the drawings are not drawn to scale). The symbols should first be created as blocks or wblocks and then saved in a symbol library using one of the methods discussed in this chapter. Place a border and title block on each drawing. Save the drawings as ***P22-4, P22-5,*** *and so on.*

4.

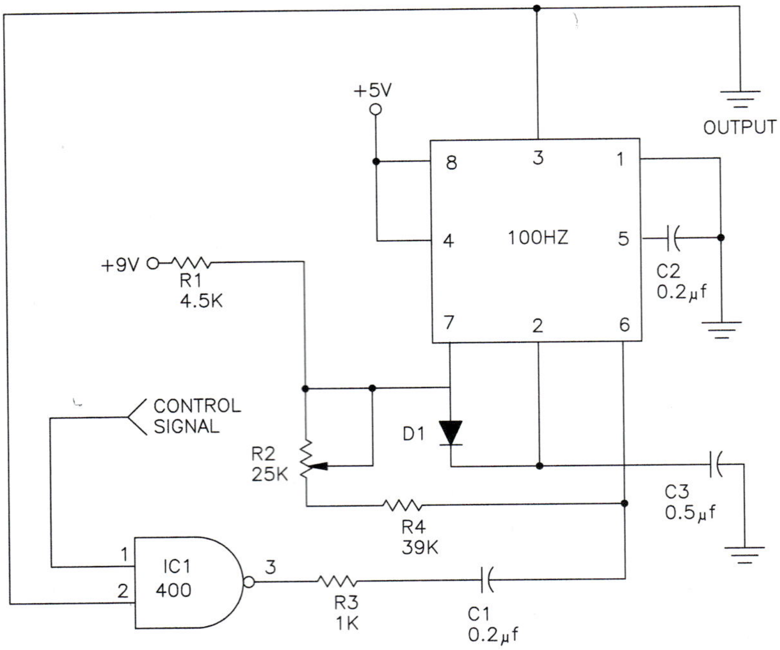

Integrated Circuit for Clock

5.

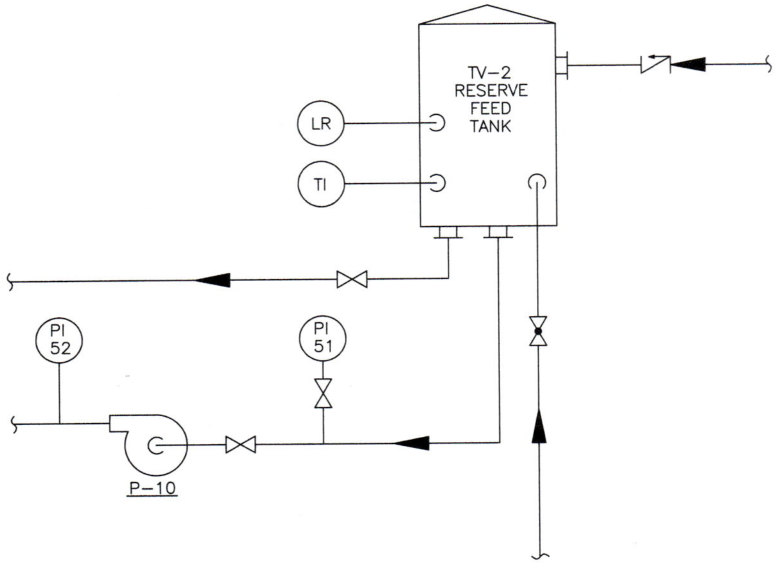

Piping Flow Diagram

6.

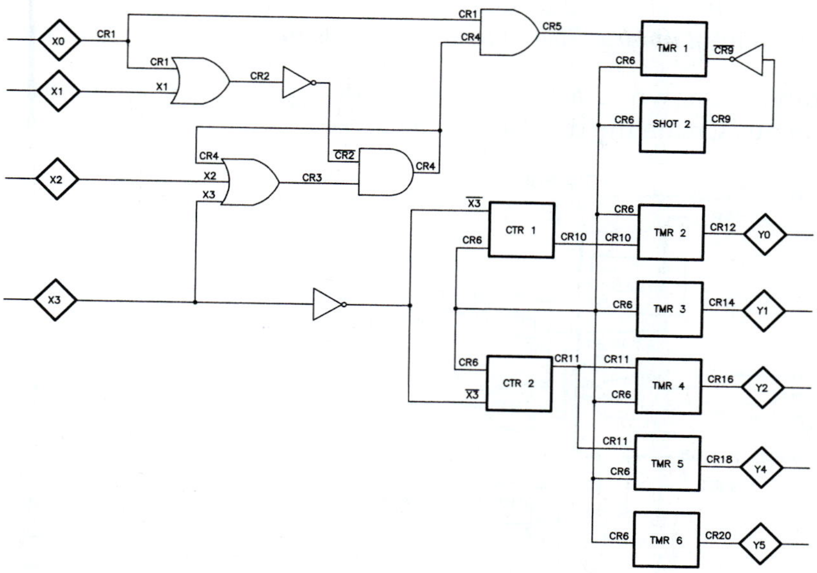

Logic Diagram of Marking System

7. Open P12-21 from Chapter 12. The sketch for this drawing is shown below. Erase all of the desk workstations except one. Then do the following:
   A. Create a block of the workstation.
   B. Insert the block into the drawing using the **MINSERT** command.
   C. Dimension one of the workstations as shown in the sketch.
   D. Save the drawing as P22-7.

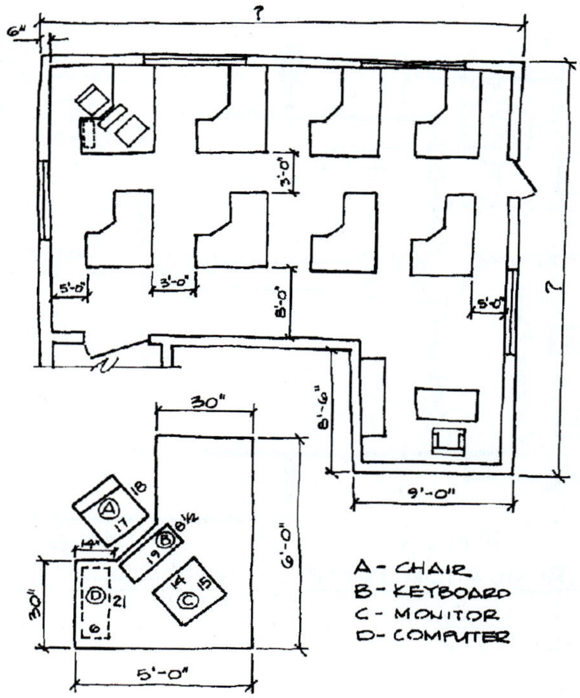

Problems 8–12 are presented as engineering sketches. They are schematic drawings created using symbols and are not drawn to scale. The symbols should first be drawn as blocks and then saved in a symbol library. Place a border and title block on each of the drawings.

8. The drawing shown is a logic diagram of a portion of a computer's internal components. Create the drawing on a C-size sheet. Save the drawing as P22-8.

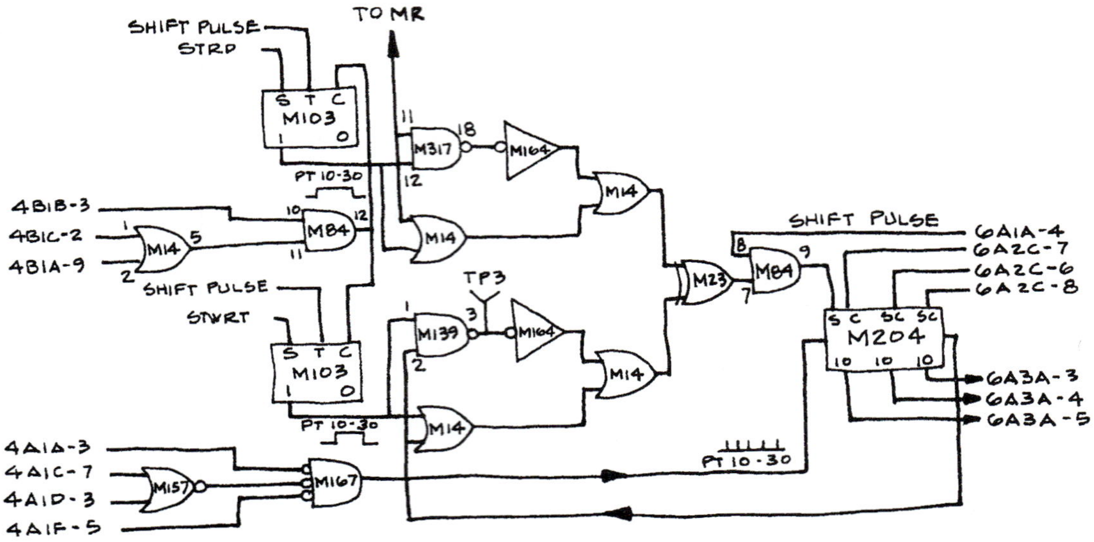

9. The drawing shown is a piping flow diagram of a cooling water system. Create the drawing on a B-size sheet. Look closely at this drawing. Using blocks and the correct editing commands, it may be easier to complete than you think. Draw the thick flow lines with polylines. Save the drawing as P22-9.

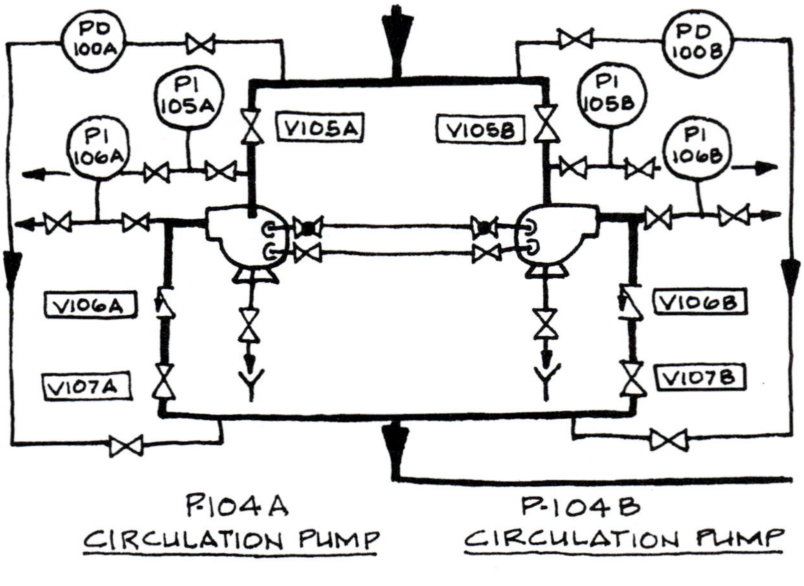

10. The drawing shown is the general arrangement of a basement floor plan for a new building. The engineer has shown one example of each type of equipment. Use the following instructions to complete the drawing:
   A. Create the drawing on a C-size sheet.
   B. All text should be 1/8″ high, except the text for the bay and column line tags, which should be 3/16″ high. The line balloons for the bay and column lines should be twice the diameter of the text height.
   C. The column and bay line steel symbols represent wide-flange structural shapes, and should be 8″ wide × 12″ high.
   D. The PUMP and CHILLER installations (except PUMP #4 and PUMP #5) should be drawn per the dimensions given for PUMP #1 and CHILLER #1. Use the dimensions shown for the other PUMP units.
   E. TANK #2 and PUMP #5 (P-5) should be drawn per the dimensions given for TANK #1 and PUMP #4.
   F. Tanks T-3, T-4, T-5, and T-6 are all the same size, and are aligned 12′ from column line A.
   G. Plan this drawing carefully and create as many blocks as possible to increase your productivity. Dimension the drawing as shown, and provide location dimensions for all equipment not shown in the engineer's sketch.
   H. Save the drawing as P22-10.

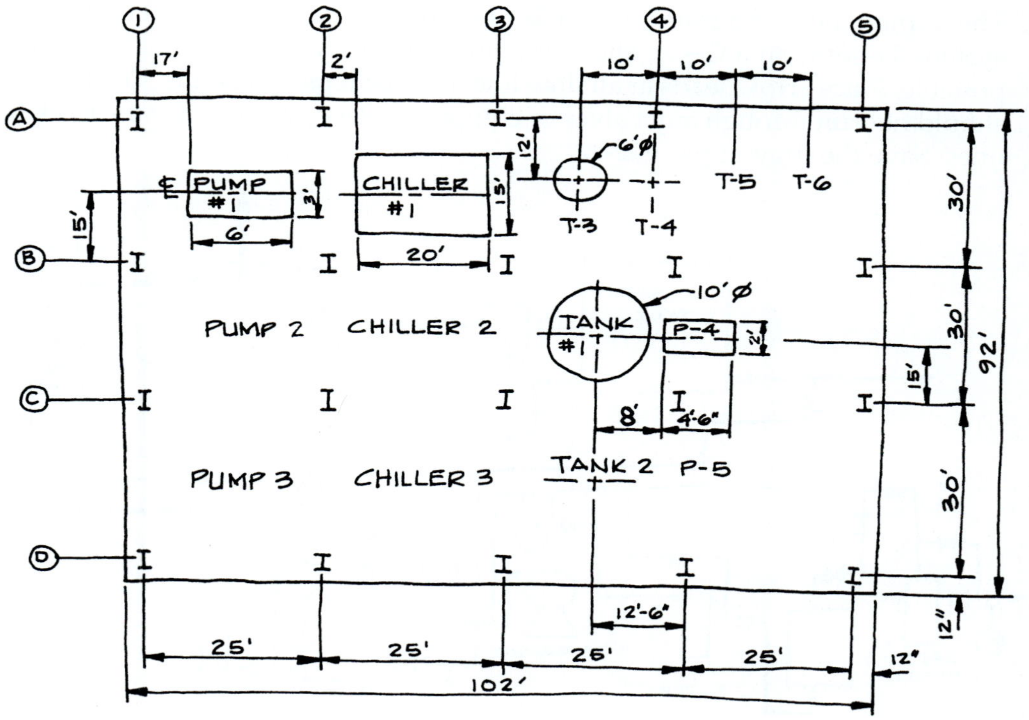

11. The drawing saved as P22-10 must be revised. The engineer has provided you with a sketch of the necessary revisions. It is up to you to alter the drawing as quickly and efficiently as possible. The dimensions shown on the sketch below *do not* need to be added to the drawing; they are provided for construction purposes only. Revise P22-10 so that all chillers and the four tanks reflect the changes. Save the drawing as P22-11.

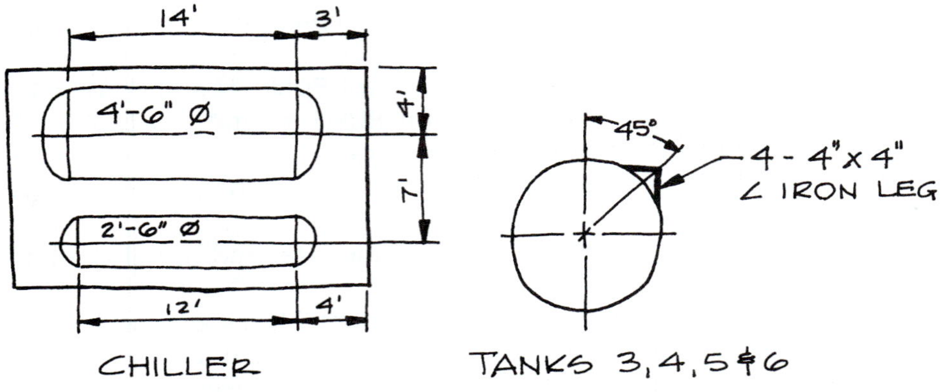

12. The piping flow diagram shown is part of an industrial effluent treatment system. Draw it on a C-size sheet. Eliminate as many bends in the flow lines as possible. Place arrowheads at all flow line intersections and bends. The flow lines should not run through any valves or equipment. Use polylines for the thick flow lines. Save the drawing as P22-12.

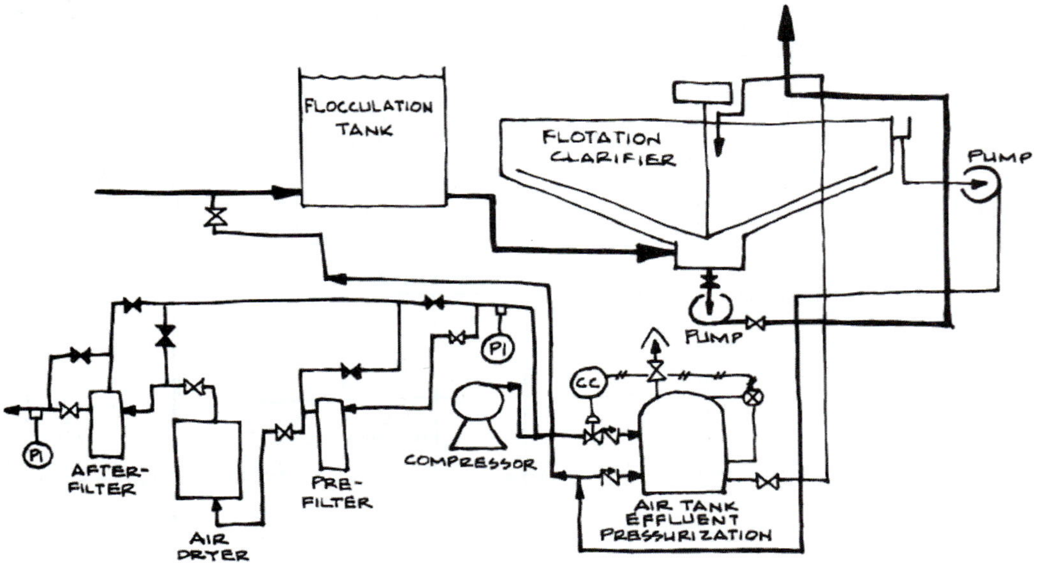

CHAPTER 23

Assigning Attributes and Generating a Bill of Materials

Learning Objectives

After completing this chapter, you will be able to do the following:

- Assign attributes to blocks.
- Edit attributes defined for existing blocks.
- Create a template file for the storage of block attribute data.
- Extract attribute values to create a bill of materials.

Blocks become more useful when written information is provided with them. It is even more helpful to be able to assign information to a block and make it either visible (for display) or hidden. From this data, a list very similar to a bill of materials can be requested and printed.

Written or numerical values assigned to blocks are called ***attributes*** by AutoCAD. In addition to being used as text, attribute information can be *extracted* from a drawing. Several blocks with attributes are shown in Figure 23-1.

Attributes are created using the **Attribute Definition** dialog box. Inserted attribute values can be modified using the **Enhanced Attribute Editor**. Attribute definitions are modified using the **Block Attribute Manager**. Finally, block and attribute text data can be exported into other applications using the **Attribute Extraction** wizard.

Assigning Attributes to Blocks

The first step in defining attributes for a block is to determine the information needed for the block. In most cases, the name of the object should be your first attribute. This could be followed by other attribute items, such as the manufacturer, type, size, price, and weight. After you determine which attributes to assign, decide how you should be prompted to enter a value for each attribute. A typical prompt, for example, might be What is the size?

Suppose you are drawing a valve symbol for a piping flow diagram. You might want to list all the product-related data along with the symbol. The number of attributes needed is limited only by the project requirements.

Once the symbol is drawn, you can use the **ATTDEF** (attribute define) command to assign attributes. To access this command, pick **Define Attributes...** from the **Block** cascading menu in the **Draw** pull-down menu, or enter ATT or ATTDEF at the Command: prompt. This displays the **Attribute Definition** dialog box, Figure 23-2.

ATTDEF
ATT

Draw
➥ Block
➥ Define Attributes...

Figure 23-1.
Examples of blocks with defined attributes.

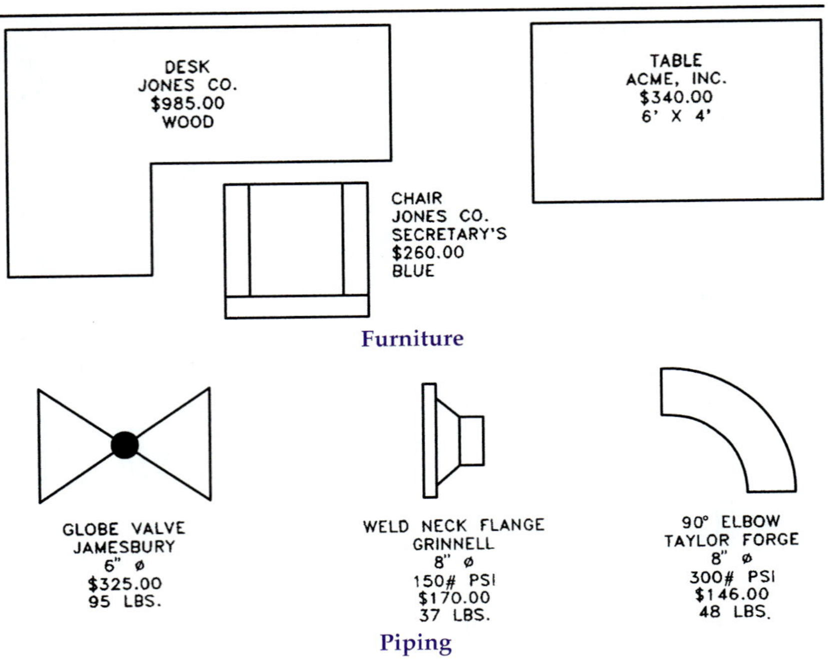

Figure 23-2.
Attributes can be assigned to blocks using the **Attribute Definition** dialog box.

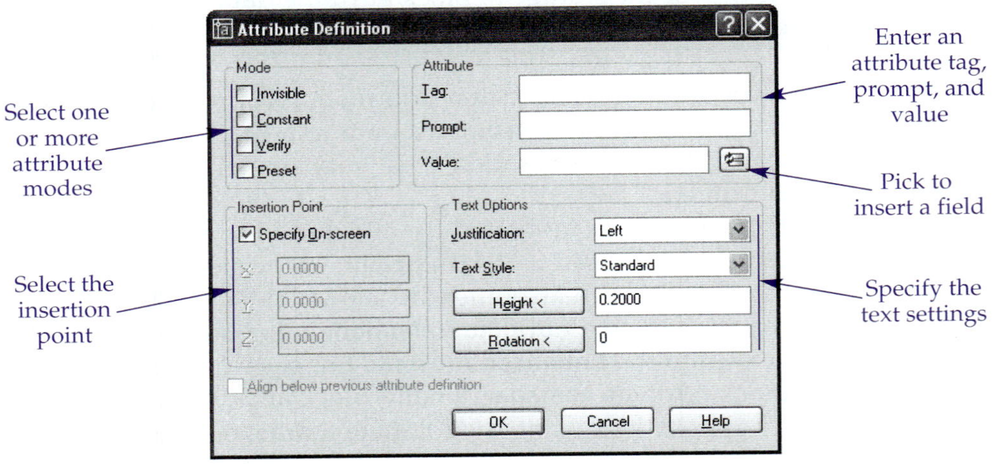

This dialog box is divided into four areas. Each area allows you to set the specific aspects of an attribute. The four areas, their components, and other features in the **Attribute Definition** dialog box are described as follows:

- **Mode area.** Use this area to specify any of the attribute modes you wish to set. The following is a description of each mode option:
  - **Invisible.** If you want the attribute to be shown with the inserted block, leave the **Invisible** check box inactive. If you activate this check box, the attribute will not be displayed when the block is inserted.
  - **Constant.** If the value of the attribute should always be the same, activate the **Constant** check box. All future uses of the block will display the same attribute value, and you will not be prompted for a new value. If you wish to use different attribute values for inserted blocks, leave this check box inactive.
  - **Verify.** Activate the **Verify** check box if you want a verification prompt to ask you whether the specified attribute value is correct when you insert the block.

- **Preset.** If you want the attribute to assume preset values during insertion, activate the **Preset** check box. This option disables the attribute prompt. Leave this check box inactive if you wish to display the normal prompt.

  If you do not activate any of the attribute modes, you will be prompted to enter values for all attributes, and they will be visible when inserted with a block.

- **Attribute area.** This area lets you assign a tag, prompt, and value to the attribute in the corresponding text boxes. The entries in these text boxes can contain up to 256 characters. If the first character in an entry is a space, start the string with a backslash (\). If the first character is a backslash, begin the entry with two backslashes (\\). Each feature is described as follows:
  - **Tag: text box.** Use this text box to enter the name, or tag, of the attribute. You must enter a name or number. Any characters can be used except spaces. All text is displayed in uppercase.
  - **Prompt: text box.** Use this text box to enter a statement for AutoCAD to prompt with when the block is inserted. For example, if Size is specified as the attribute tag, you might enter What is the valve size? or Enter valve size: as the prompt. If the **Constant** attribute mode is set, this option is inactive.
  - **Value: text box.** The entry in this text box is used as a *default* attribute value when the block is inserted. You do not have to enter anything in this text box. You might decide to enter a message regarding the type of information needed, such as 10 SPACES MAX or NUMBERS ONLY. The default value is displayed in chevrons (< >) when you are prompted for the attribute value. Use the **Insert field** button to include a field in the default value.
- **Text Options area.** This area allows you to specify the justification, style, height, and rotation angle for attribute text. The options in this area are described as follows:
  - **Justification.** You can use the **Justification:** drop-down list to select a justification option for the attribute text. The default option is Left.
  - **Text Style.** Access the **Text Style:** drop-down list to select one of the text styles in the current drawing. The default style is Standard.
  - **Height.** Use the text box to the right of the **Height** button to specify the height of the attribute text. Selecting the **Height** button temporarily returns you to the drawing area and allows you to indicate the text height by picking points on screen. Once the points are picked, the dialog box returns and the corresponding height is shown in the text box.
  - **Rotation.** To specify a rotation angle for the attribute text, enter an angular value in the text box next to the **Rotation** button. This button and the text box work in the same manner as the **Height** button and text box.
- **Insertion Point area.** This area is used to select the location for the attribute. Selecting the **Pick Point** button temporarily returns you to the drawing area and allows you to pick a point on screen. You can also enter coordinates in the text boxes.
- **Align below previous attribute definition check box.** When you first access the **Attribute Definition** dialog box, this check box is grayed out. After you create a block attribute, you can press [Enter] to reissue the **ATTDEF** command and create another attribute. If you want the next attribute to be placed below the first with the same justification, pick this check box. When you do this, the **Text Options** and **Insertion Point** areas become inactive.

When you are finished defining the attribute, pick **OK**. The attribute tag is then placed on screen. If you set the attribute mode to **Invisible**, do not be dismayed; this is the only time the tag appears. When the block is inserted, you are prompted for information based on the attribute definition.

Once you have created attributes for an object, you can use the **BLOCK** or **WBLOCK** command to define the object as a block. Blocks are discussed in Chapter 22. When creating the block, be sure to select all of the objects and attributes that go with the block. Select the attribute definitions in the order that you would like to be prompted or have them appear in the **Enter Attributes** dialog box. If you select the attribute definitions using either the **Window** or **Crossing** selection method, you will be prompted for the attribute values in the *reverse* order of creation of the attribute definitions. When creating the block, activate the **Delete** option button in the **Block Definition** dialog box. When the block is created, the selected objects should disappear, as well as the attributes. If any attributes remain on screen, undo the command and try again, making sure that all of the attributes are selected.

NOTE

Attributes can be defined at the Command: prompt using the **-ATTDEF** command. To access this command, enter -ATT or -ATTDEF at the Command: prompt. The command sequence then provides all the options found in the **Attribute Definition** dialog box.

PROFESSIONAL TIP

If you create attributes in the order in which you want to be prompted for their values, and the **Window** or **Crossing** selection method is used to select them for inclusion in the block, the attribute prompting will be in the *reverse* order of the desired prompting. This can be rectified by inserting the block, exploding it, and redefining the block. When specifying the new definition, pick the attributes by using the **Window** or **Crossing** selection method. This will reverse the order of the attribute prompting once again, thereby placing the prompts in the initially desired order.

Editing Attribute Definitions

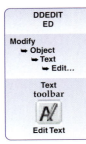

DDEDIT
ED

Modify
➡ Object
➡ Text
➡ Edit...

Text toolbar

Edit Text

Occasionally, you may need to change certain aspects of text attributes *before* they are included in a block or definition. If you only want to change the tag, prompt, or default value assigned to a text attribute, you may do so quickly using the **DDEDIT** command. To access the **DDEDIT** command, pick the **Edit Text** button on the **Text** toolbar, select **Text** and then **Edit...** from the **Object** cascading menu in the **Modify** pull-down menu, or enter ED or DDEDIT at the Command: prompt. When you select the attribute, the **Edit Attribute Definition** dialog box is displayed, Figure 23-3. Revise the **Tag:**, **Prompt:**, or **Default:** values. If the value contains a field, highlight the field and right-click to modify it or convert it to text.

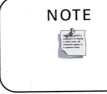

Figure 23-3.
The **Edit Attribute Definition** dialog box is used to change the tag, prompt, or default value of an attribute.

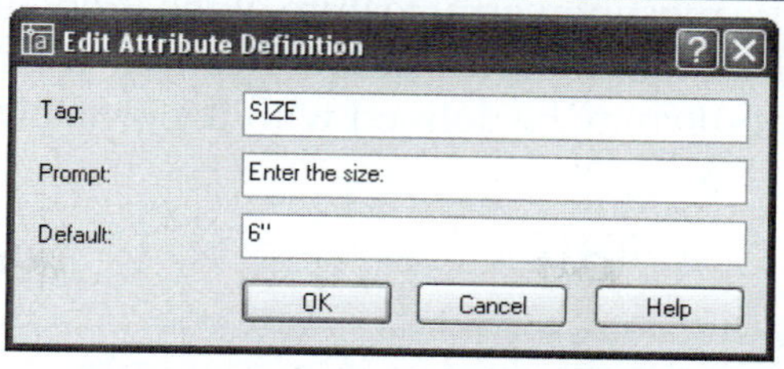

Using the Properties Window

PROPERTIES
PROPS
CH,
MO
[Ctrl]+[2]

Modify
➥ Properties

Standard toolbar

Properties

The **Properties** window provides expanded editing capabilities for attributes. To activate the **Properties** window, pick the **Properties** button on the **Standard** toolbar, pick **Properties** from the **Modify** pull-down menu, enter CH, MO, PROPS, or PROPERTIES at the Command: prompt, or use the [Ctrl]+[2] key combination. You can also select the attribute to be edited, while no command is active, and then right-click and select **Properties** from the shortcut menu to display the **Properties** window.

Figure 23-4 shows the **Properties** window with an attribute selected. You can change the color, linetype, or layer of the selected attribute in the **General** section. The attribute tag, prompt, and default value entries are listed in the **Text** section. You can select **Tag**, **Prompt**, or **Value** to change the corresponding values. If the value contains a field, it appears as normal text in the **Properties** window. If you modify the field text, it is automatically converted to text. There are also options to change the text style, justification, height, rotation angle, width factor, and obliquing angle in the **Text** section. You can change the insertion point of the text attribute in the **Geometry** section by using the **Position** options to enter new coordinates. Additional text options are available in the **Misc** section.

Figure 23-4.
The **Properties** window can be used to modify attributes.

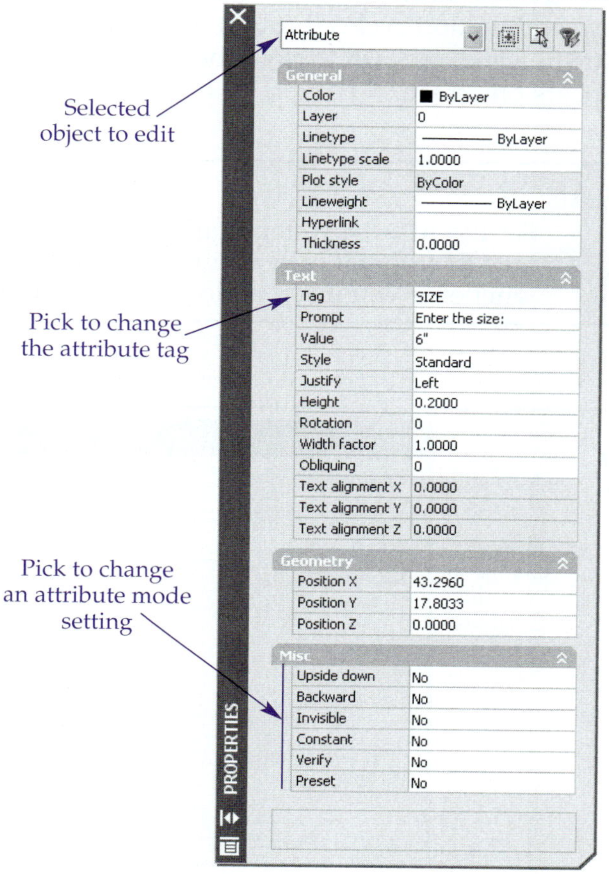

Perhaps the most powerful feature of the **Properties** window for editing attributes is the ability to change the attribute modes that were originally defined. As discussed earlier, an attribute may be defined with the **Invisible**, **Constant**, **Verify**, or **Preset** modes active.

Inserting Blocks with Attributes

When you use the **INSERT** command to place a saved block with attributes in your drawing, you are prompted for additional information after the insertion point, scale factors, and rotation angle are specified. The prompt statement that you entered with the **ATTDEF** command appears, and the default attribute value appears in brackets. Accept the default by pressing [Enter], or provide a new value. If the attribute value includes a field, you must accept the default to maintain the field—if you change the value at the Command: prompt, the field is lost. The attribute is then displayed with the block.

Attribute prompts may be answered using a dialog box if the **ATTDIA** system variable is set to 1 (on). After issuing the **INSERT** command and entering the insertion point, scale, and rotation angle of a block, the **Enter Attributes** dialog box appears. See Figure 23-5. This dialog box can list up to eight attributes. If the block has more than eight attributes, you can display the next page of attributes by clicking the **Next** button.

Responding to attribute prompts in a dialog box has distinct advantages over answering the prompts on the command line. With the dialog box, you can see at a glance whether all the attribute values are correct. To change a value, simply move to the incorrect value and enter a new one. If a value includes a field, you can right-click on the field to edit it or convert it to text. You can quickly move forward through the attributes and buttons in the **Enter Attributes** dialog box by using the [Tab] key. Using the [Shift]+[Tab] key combination cycles through the attributes and buttons in reverse order. When you are finished, pick **OK** to close the dialog box. The inserted block with attributes then appears on screen.

PROFESSIONAL TIP

Set the **ATTDIA** system variable to 1 in your template drawings to automatically activate the **Enter Attributes** dialog box whenever you insert a block with attributes.

Figure 23-5.
The **Enter Attributes** dialog box allows you to enter or change attribute definitions when a block is inserted.

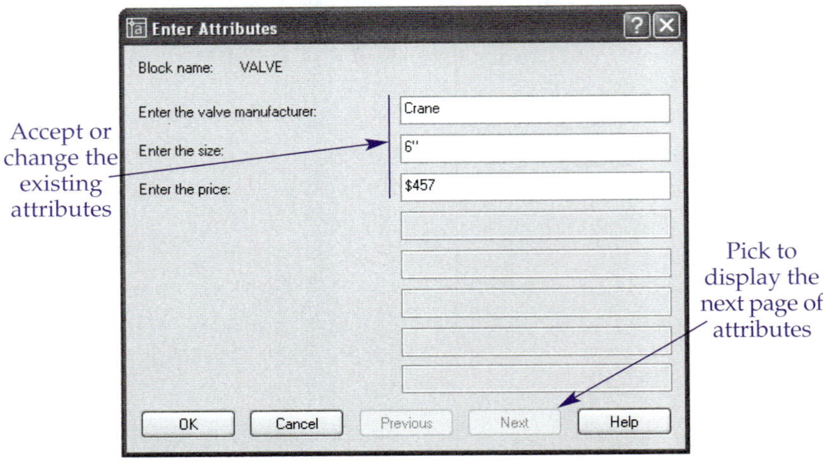

EXERCISE 23-1 Complete the Exercise on the Student CD.

Attribute Prompt Suppression

Some drawings may use blocks with attributes that always retain their default values. In this case, there is no need to be prompted for the attribute values when inserting a block. You can turn off the attribute prompts by setting the **ATTREQ** system variable to 0.

After making this setting, try inserting the VALVE block. Notice that none of the attribute prompts appear. The **ATTREQ** system variable setting is saved with the drawing. To display attribute prompts again, change the setting back to 1.

PROFESSIONAL TIP

Part of your project and drawing planning should involve the setting of system variables such as **ATTREQ**. Setting **ATTREQ** to 0 before using blocks can save time in the drawing process. Always remember to set **ATTREQ** back to 1 when you want to use the prompts instead of accepting defaults. When anticipated attribute prompts are not issued, you should check the current **ATTREQ** setting and adjust it if necessary.

Controlling the Display of Attributes

Attributes are intended to contain valuable information about the blocks in your drawings. This information is normally not displayed on screen or during plotting. The principal function of attributes is to generate materials lists and to speed accounting. In most cases, you can use the **TEXT** and **MTEXT** commands to create specific labels or other types of text. To control the display of attributes on screen, use the **ATTDISP** (attribute display) command. This command can be accessed by picking **Attribute Display** from the **Display** cascading menu in the **View** pull-down menu, or by entering ATTDISP at the Command: prompt. There are three options:

- **Normal.** This option displays attributes exactly as you created them. This is the default setting.
- **ON.** This option displays *all* attributes, including those defined with the **Invisible** mode.
- **OFF.** This option suppresses the display of all attributes.

PROFESSIONAL TIP

After attributes have been drawn, defined with blocks, and checked for correctness, hide them by entering the **Off** option of the **ATTDISP** command. If attributes are left on, they clutter the screen and lengthen regeneration time. In a drawing where attributes should be visible but are not, check the current setting of **ATTDISP** and adjust it if necessary.

Changing Attribute Values

EATTEDIT

Modify
➥ Object
➥ Attribute
➥ Single...

Modify II toolbar

Edit Attribute

As discussed earlier, you can edit attributes before they are included in a block using the **DDEDIT** command or the **Properties** window. However, once a block with attributes is inserted in a drawing, different commands are used to edit the inserted attributes. Inserted attribute values can be modified using the **Enhanced Attribute Editor**.

The **Enhanced Attribute Editor** is used to modify attributes within a single block. To access this dialog box, pick the **Edit Attribute** button on the **Modify II** toolbar, select **Attribute** and then **Single...** from the **Object** cascading menu in the **Modify** pull-down menu, or enter EATTEDIT at the Command: prompt. You are then prompted to select a block. Pick the block containing the attributes you wish to modify, and the **Enhanced Attribute Editor** is displayed. See Figure 23-6.

The **Enhanced Attribute Editor** contains three tabs. The **Attribute** tab is displayed when the dialog box is initially accessed, with the attributes within the selected block listed in the window. If you want to select a different block to modify, pick the **Select block** button. Pick the attribute to be modified. Enter a new value for the attribute in the **Value:** text box.

Other properties of the selected attribute can be modified using the two other tabs. The **Text Options** tab allows you to modify the text properties of the attribute. See Figure 23-7. The **Properties** tab, Figure 23-8, contains settings for the object properties of the attribute.

Figure 23-6.
Select the attribute to be modified and change its value in the **Attribute** tab of the **Enhanced Attribute Editor**.

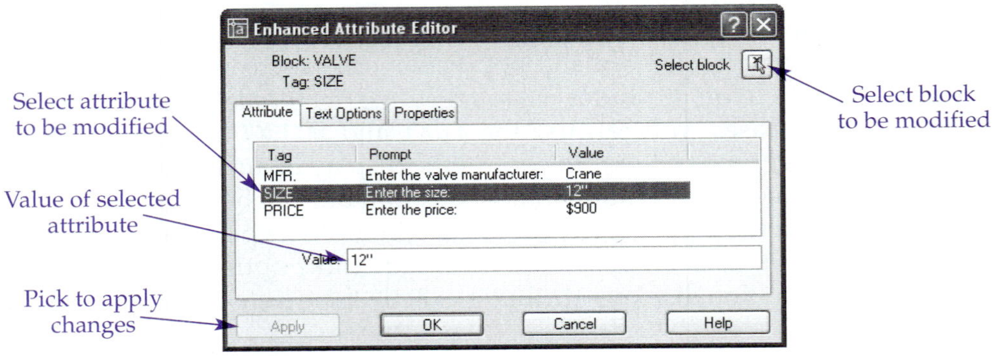

Figure 23-7.
The **Text Options** tab provides options in addition to those set in the **Attribute Definition** dialog box.

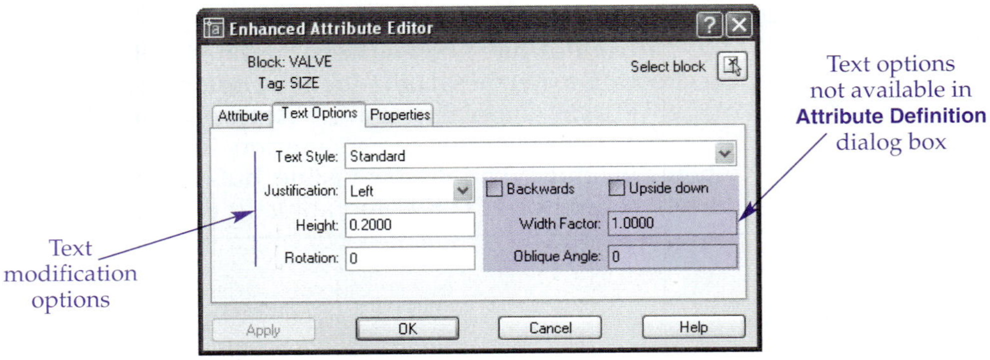

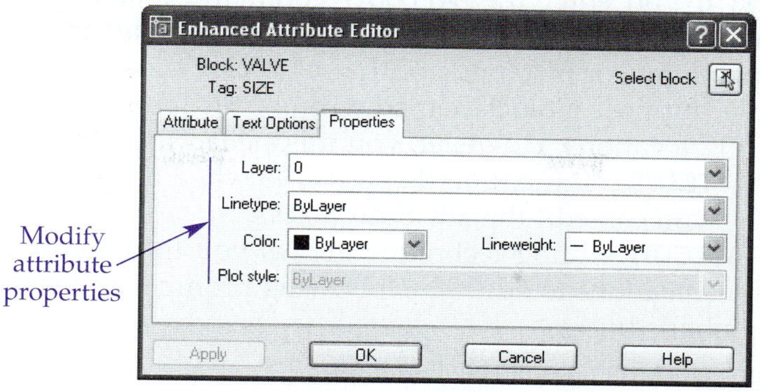

Figure 23-8.
The **Properties** tab can be used to modify an attribute's object properties.

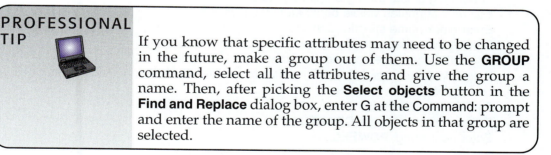

After editing the attribute values and properties, pick the **Apply** button to have the changes reflected on screen. Pick the **Select block** button to modify another block, or pick the **OK** button to close the dialog box.

EXERCISE 23-2 Complete the Exercise on the Student CD.

Using the FIND Command to Edit Attributes

One of the quickest ways to edit attributes is to use the **FIND** command. With no command active, right-click and select **Find...** from the shortcut menu to access the **Find and Replace** dialog box. You can then search the entire drawing for an attribute, or you can search a selected group of objects. The **Find and Replace** dialog box is discussed in detail in Chapter 8.

PROFESSIONAL TIP

If you know that specific attributes may need to be changed in the future, make a group out of them. Use the **GROUP** command, select all the attributes, and give the group a name. Then, after picking the **Select objects** button in the **Find and Replace** dialog box, enter G at the Command: prompt and enter the name of the group. All objects in that group are selected.

Editing Attribute Values and Properties at the Command Line

-ATTEDIT
-ATE

Modify
➡ Object
➡ Attribute
➡ Global

The **Enhanced Attribute Editor** allows you to edit attribute values by selecting blocks one at a time. You can also edit several block attributes at once or edit attributes individually by answering prompts on the command line. This type of attribute editing is done with the **-ATTEDIT** command. To access this command, select **Attribute** and then **Global** from the **Object** cascading menu in the **Modify** pull-down menu, or enter -ATE or -ATTEDIT at the Command: prompt:

Command: **-ATE** *or* **-ATTEDIT**↵
Edit attributes one at a time? [Yes/No] <Y>:

This prompt asks if you want to edit attributes individually. Pressing [Enter] at this prompt allows you to select any number of different block attributes for individual editing. AutoCAD lets you edit them all, one at a time, without leaving the command. It is also possible to change the same attribute on several insertions of the same block. If you enter the **-ATTEDIT** command and respond with No, you may change specific letters, words, and values of a single attribute. This lets you change all other insertions, or instances, of the same block, and is known as ***global editing***. For example, suppose a block named with the attribute RESISTOR was inserted on a drawing in 12 locations. However, you misspelled the attribute as RESISTER. If you enter the **-ATTEDIT** command and specify No when asked whether to edit attributes individually, you can edit the attribute *globally*.

Each **-ATTEDIT** editing technique allows you to determine the exact block and attribute specifications to edit. The following prompts appear after you specify individual or global editing:

Enter block name specification <*>:
Enter attribute tag specification <*>:
Enter attribute value specification <*>:

To selectively edit attribute values, respond to each prompt with the correct name or value. You are then prompted to select one or more attributes. Suppose you receive the following message after entering an attribute value and selecting an attribute:

0 found

You have picked an attribute that was not specified correctly. It is often quicker to press [Enter] at each of the three specification prompts and then *pick* the attribute you need to edit.

In **Figure 23-9,** the VALVE block was inserted three times with the manufacturer's name specified as CRANE. Unfortunately, the name was supposed to be POWELL. To change the attribute for each insertion, enter the **-ATTEDIT** command and specify global editing. Then, press [Enter] at each of the three specification prompts and respond to the prompts that follow:

Command: **-ATE** *or* **-ATTEDIT**↵
Edit attributes one at a time? [Yes/No] <Y>: **N**↵
Performing global editing of attribute values.
Edit only attributes visible on screen? [Yes/No] <Y>: ↵
Enter block name specification <*>: ↵
Enter attribute tag specification <*>: ↵
Enter attribute value specification <*>: ↵
Select Attributes: *(pick* CRANE *on each of the* VALVE *blocks and press* [Enter] *when completed)*
3 attributes selected.
Enter string to change: **CRANE**↵
Enter new string: **POWELL**↵

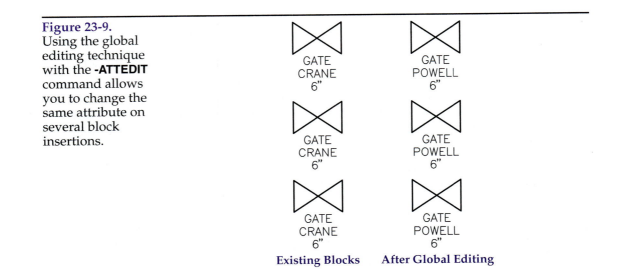

Figure 23-9.
Using the global editing technique with the **-ATTEDIT** command allows you to change the same attribute on several block insertions.

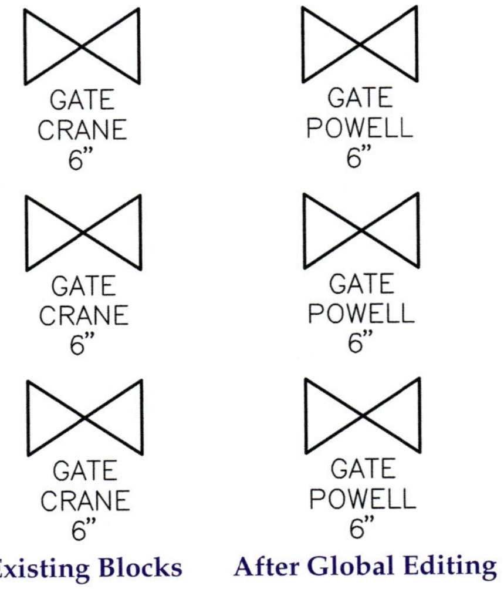

After pressing [Enter], each of the CRANE attributes on the blocks selected is changed to the new value POWELL.

PROFESSIONAL TIP

Use care when assigning the **Constant** mode to attribute definitions. The **-ATTEDIT** command displays 0 found if you attempt to edit an inserted block attribute with a **Constant** mode setting. The inserted block must then be exploded and redefined. Assign the **Constant** mode only to attributes you know will not change.

NOTE

The **-ATTEDIT** command can also be used to edit individual attribute values and properties. However, it is more efficient to use the **Enhanced Attribute Editor** for changing individual attributes.

EXERCISE 23-3

Complete the Exercise on the Student CD.

Changing Attribute Definitions

BATTMAN

Modify
➥ **Object**
➥ **Attribute**
➥ **Block Attribute Manager...**

Modify II toolbar

Block Attribute Manager

Before saving an attribute within a block, you can modify the tag, prompt, and default value using the **DDEDIT** command. Once an attribute is saved in a block definition, you must use the **Block Attribute Manager** to change the attribute definition.

The **Block Attribute Manager** is accessed by picking the **Block Attribute Manager** button from the **Modify II** toolbar, selecting **Attribute** and then **Block Attribute Manager...** from the **Object** cascading menu in the **Modify** pull-down menu, or by entering BATTMAN at the Command: prompt. The **Block Attribute Manager** is shown in Figure 23-10.

Figure 23-10.
Use the **Block Attribute Manager** to change attribute definitions, delete attributes, and change the order of attribute prompts.

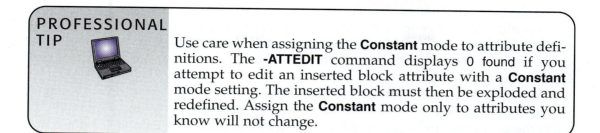

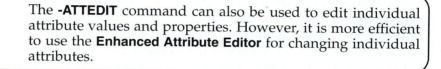

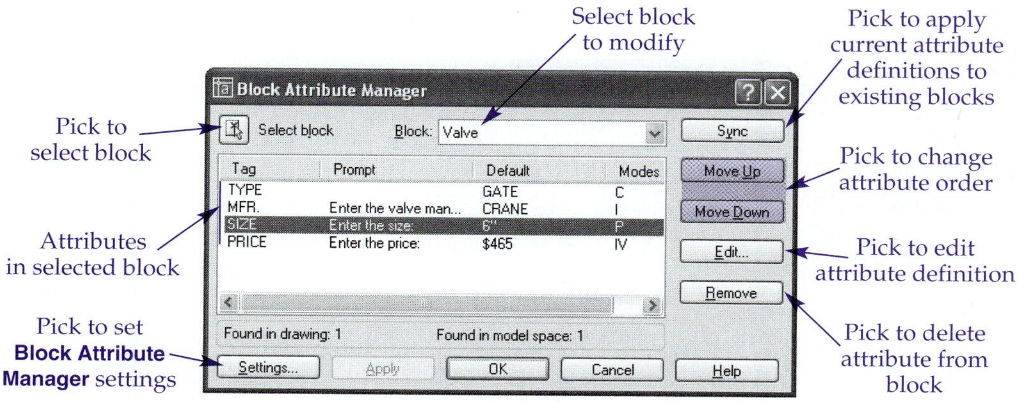

The **Block Attribute Manager** lists the attributes for the selected block. To select a block, select it from the **Block:** drop-down list or pick the **Select block** button to return to the drawing area and pick the block. By default, the tag, prompt, default value, and modes for each attribute are listed.

The attribute list reflects the order in which prompts appear when a block is inserted. To change the order, use the **Move Up** and **Move Down** buttons to change the location of the selected attribute within the list. To delete an attribute, pick the **Remove** button.

You can select the attribute properties to be listed in the **Block Attribute Manager** by picking the **Settings...** button. This accesses the **Settings** dialog box, Figure 23-11. Select the properties to list in the **Display in list** area. When the **Emphasize duplicate tags** setting is active, attributes with identical tags are highlighted in red. Select the **Apply changes to existing references** option if you want the changes applied to existing blocks.

To modify an attribute definition, select the attribute in the **Block Attribute Manager** and then pick the **Edit...** button. This displays the **Edit Attribute** dialog box, Figure 23-12. The **Attribute** tab allows you to modify the modes, tag, prompt, and default value. Use the check boxes in the **Mode** area to select the desired modes. Enter new text strings in the **Tag:**, **Prompt:**, and **Default:** text boxes. The **Text Options** and **Properties** tabs are identical to the same tabs found in the **Enhanced Attribute Editor** with the exception of the **Auto preview changes** check box. These tabs allow you to modify the object properties of the attributes. If the **Auto preview changes** check box is checked, changes to attributes are displayed in the drawing area immediately. After

Figure 23-11.
The **Settings** dialog box controls the display of the attribute list in the **Block Attribute Manager**.

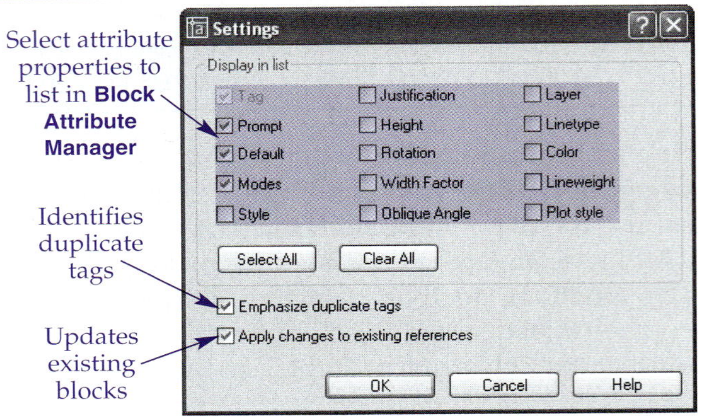

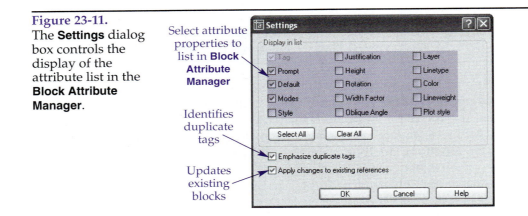

Figure 23-12.
Use the **Edit Attribute** dialog box to modify attribute definitions and properties.

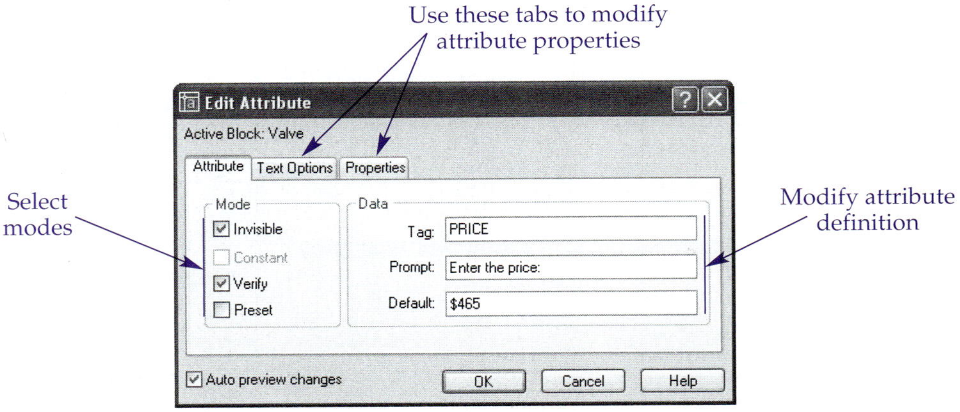

modifying the attribute definition in the **Edit Attribute** dialog box, pick the **OK** button to return to the **Block Attribute Manager**.

After modifying attributes within a block, all future insertions of the block will reflect the changes. Existing blocks are updated if the **Apply changes to existing references** option is selected in the **Settings** dialog box. If this option is not selected, the existing blocks retain the original attribute definitions.

> **NOTE**
>
> The **Block Attribute Manager** modifies attribute definitions—it does not modify attribute values. Attribute values are modified with the **Enhanced Attribute Editor**, which was discussed in the previous section.

Redefining a Block and Its Attributes

You may encounter a situation in which an existing block and its associated attributes must be revised. You may need to delete existing attributes, or add new ones, in addition to revising the geometry of the block itself. This could normally be a time-consuming task, but it is made easy with the **ATTREDEF** command. To access this command, enter AT or ATTREDEF at the Command: prompt. You are then prompted to select the attribute to be redefined.

When redefining a block and its attributes, a copy of the existing block must be exploded prior to using the **ATTREDEF** command, or completely new geometry must be used. If this is not done, the following error message will be displayed:

New block has no attributes.

Once you explode the existing block, or draw new geometry, you can use the **ATTREDEF** command. The sequence is as follows:

Command: **AT** *or* **ATTREDEF**↵
Enter name of the block you wish to redefine: *(enter the block name and press* [Enter]*)*
Select objects for new Block...
Select objects: *(select the block geometry and all new and existing attributes and press* [Enter]*)*
Specify insertion base point of new Block: *(pick the insertion base point)*

After you pick the insertion point, all existing instances of the redefined block and attributes will be immediately updated. If any of the old attributes were omitted from the redefined block, they will not be included in the new version.

> **NOTE**
>
> All objects within a block, including attributes, can be edited using the **REFEDIT** command. This command is discussed in Chapter 22. When using **REFEDIT** to modify attributes, be sure to select the **Display attribute definitions for editing** option in the **Reference Edit** dialog box. Attribute definitions can then be modified using the **DDEDIT** command. You cannot change attribute values with this method.

Using Attributes to Automate Drafting Documentation

So far you have seen that attributes are extremely powerful tools for assigning textual information to drawing symbols. However, attributes may also be used to automate any detailing or documentation task that requires a great deal of text. Such tasks include the creation of title block information and revision block data, as well as the generation of a parts list or list of materials.

Attributes and Title Blocks

After a drawing is completely drawn and dimensioned, it is then necessary to fill out the information used in the drawing title block. This is usually one of the more time-consuming tasks associated with drafting documentation, and it can be efficiently automated by assigning attributes. The following guidelines are suggested:

1. The title block format is first drawn in accordance with industry or company standards. Use the correct layer(s), and be sure to include your company or school logo in the title block. If you work in an industry that produces items for the federal government, also include the applicable FSCM code in the title block. A typical A-size title block drawn in accordance with the ASME Y14.1, *Decimal Inch Drawing Sheet Size and Format* standard is illustrated in **Figure 23-13.**

Figure 23-13.
A title block sheet must adhere to applicable standards. This title block is for an A-size sheet and adheres to the ASME Y14.1, *Decimal Inch Drawing Sheet Size and Format* standard.

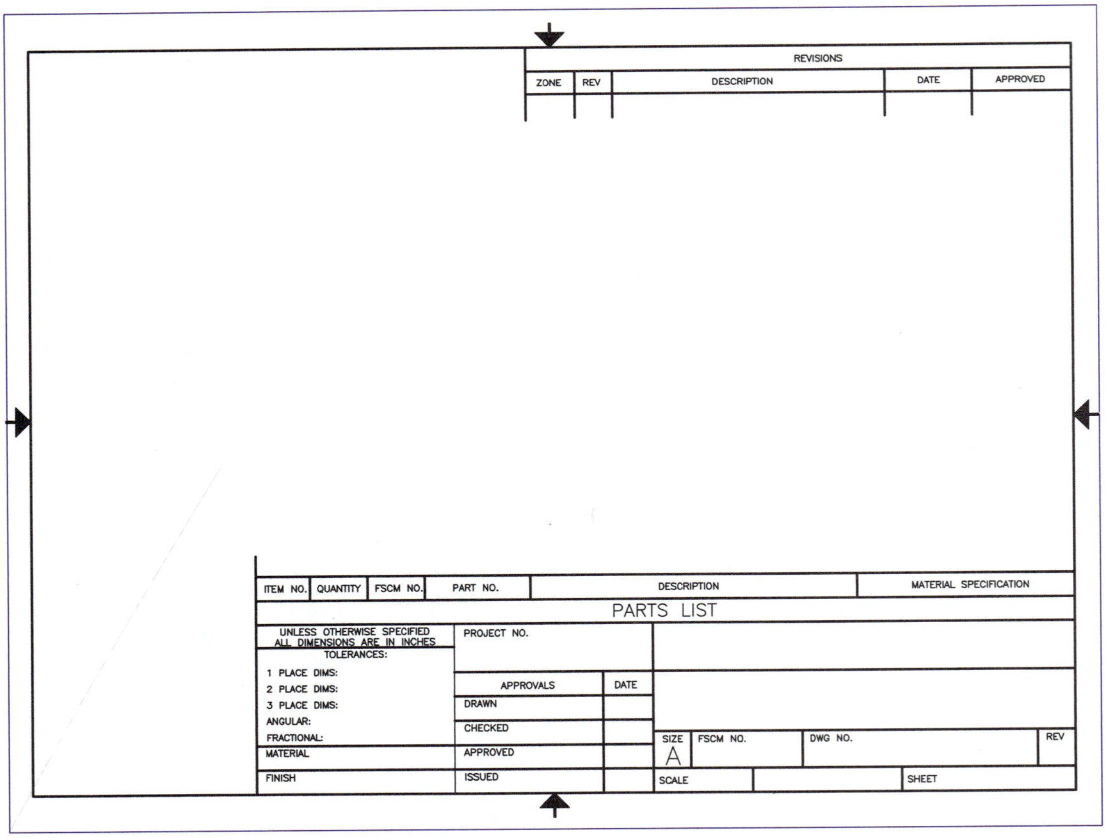

NOTE

The FSCM (Federal Supply Code for Manufacturers) is a five-digit numerical code identifier applicable to any organization that produces items used by the federal government. It also applies to government activities that are responsible for the development of certain specifications, drawings, or standards that control the design of items.

2. After drawing the title block, create a separate layer for the title block attributes. By placing the attributes on a separate layer, you can easily suppress the title block information by freezing the layer that contains the attributes. This can greatly reduce redraw and regeneration times. When you are ready to plot the finished drawing, simply thaw the frozen layer.
3. Define attributes for each area of the title block. As you create the attributes, determine the appropriate text height and justification for each definition. Attributes should be defined for the drawing title, drawing number, drafter, checker, dates, drawing scale, sheet size, material, finish, revision letter, and tolerance information. See **Figure 23-14.** Include any other information that may be specific to your organization or application.
4. Assign default values to the attributes wherever possible. As an example, if your organization consistently specifies the same overall tolerances on drawing dimensions, the tolerance attributes can be assigned default values.

Figure 23-14.
Attributes should be defined for each area of the title block.

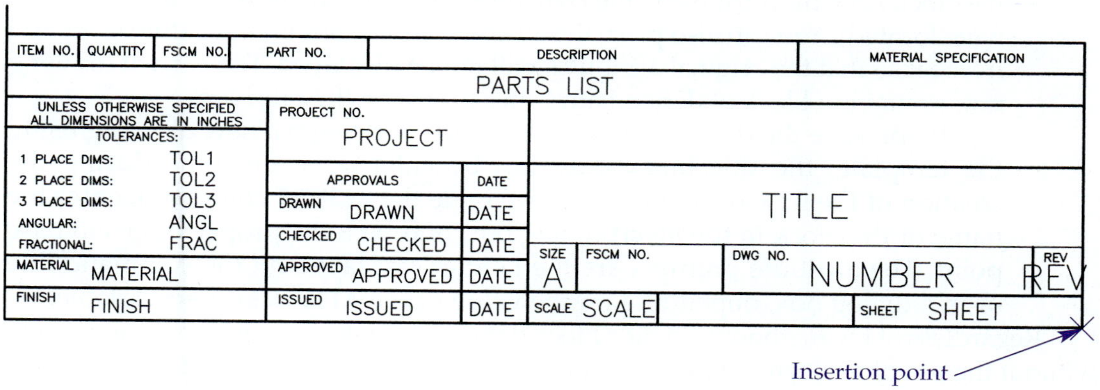

PROFESSIONAL TIP

The size of each title block area imposes limits on the number of characters you can have in a line of text. You can provide a handy cue to yourself by including a reminder in the attribute. When defining an attribute in which you wish to place a reminder, include the information in the attribute prompt. For example, the prompt could read Enter drawing name (15 characters max):. Each time a block or drawing containing the attribute is used, the prompt will display the reminder.

Once you have defined each attribute in the title block, the **WBLOCK** command can be used to save the drawing as a file to disk so that it can be inserted into a new drawing. You can also use the **BLOCK** command to create a block of the defined attributes within the current file, which can then be saved as a template or wblock file. Both methods are acceptable and are explained as follows:

- **WBLOCK method.** The **WBLOCK** command saves a drawing file to disk so that it can be inserted into any drawing that is currently open. Be sure to use 0,0 as the insertion point for the title block. Drawings used in this manner should be given descriptive names. An A-size title block, for example, could be named TITLEA or FORMATA. To utilize the wblock file, begin a new drawing and insert the template drawing. After locating and scaling the drawing, the attribute prompts are displayed. If the **ATTDIA** system variable is set to 1, all of the attributes can be accepted or edited in the **Enter Attributes** dialog box. When you pick **OK** to close the dialog box, the attributes are placed in the title block. This method requires that you begin with a new drawing, and that you know the information requested by the attribute prompts.
- **BLOCK method.** If you use the **BLOCK** command, you can use the **Block Definition** dialog box to create a block of the defined attributes in the title block. When you select the objects for the block, be sure to select *only* the defined attributes you have created. Do not select the headings of the title block areas, or any of the geometry in the title block. When you pick the insertion base point, select a corner of the title block that will be convenient to use each time this block is inserted into a drawing. The point indicated in Figure 23-14 shows an appropriate location for the insertion base point. Finally, activate the **Delete** option button in the **Block Definition** dialog box so the attribute definitions will be removed from the title block (when you insert the block later, the attribute values will be inserted where the attribute definitions were located). You can also place the attribute definitions on a separate layer and freeze it so that the original attributes will not be displayed. The current drawing now contains a block of defined attributes for use in the title block.

  If you save the drawing as a template file and begin a new drawing using the template, the title block data can be entered at any time during the creation of the new drawing. To do so, issue the **INSERT** command, enter the name of the block in the **Insert** dialog box, and pick the proper insertion base point. The attribute prompts are then either displayed on the command line or in a dialog box, depending on the value of the **ATTDIA** system variable.

Regardless of the method used, title block data can be entered quickly and accurately without the use of text commands. If the attributes are entered using the **Enter Attributes** dialog box, all the information can be seen at once, and mistakes can be corrected quickly. Attributes can be easily edited at a later date if necessary. The completed title block after insertion of the attribute block created in Figure 23-14 is shown in Figure 23-15.

Attributes and Revision Blocks

It is almost certain that a detail drawing will require revision at some time in the use of a product. Typical changes that occur include design improvements and the correction of drafting errors. The first time that a drawing is revised, it is usually assigned the revision letter *A*. If necessary, revision letters continue with *B* through *Z*, but the letters *I*, *O*, and *Q* are not used, because they might be confused with numbers.

Title block formats include an area specifically designated to record all drawing changes. This area is normally located at the upper-right of the title block sheet, and is commonly called the ***revision block***. The revision block provides space for the revision letter, a description of the change, the date, and approvals. These items are entered in columns. A column for the zone is optional, and need only be added if

Figure 23-15.
The title block after insertion of the attributes. When the drawing is complete, dates and approvals can be added.

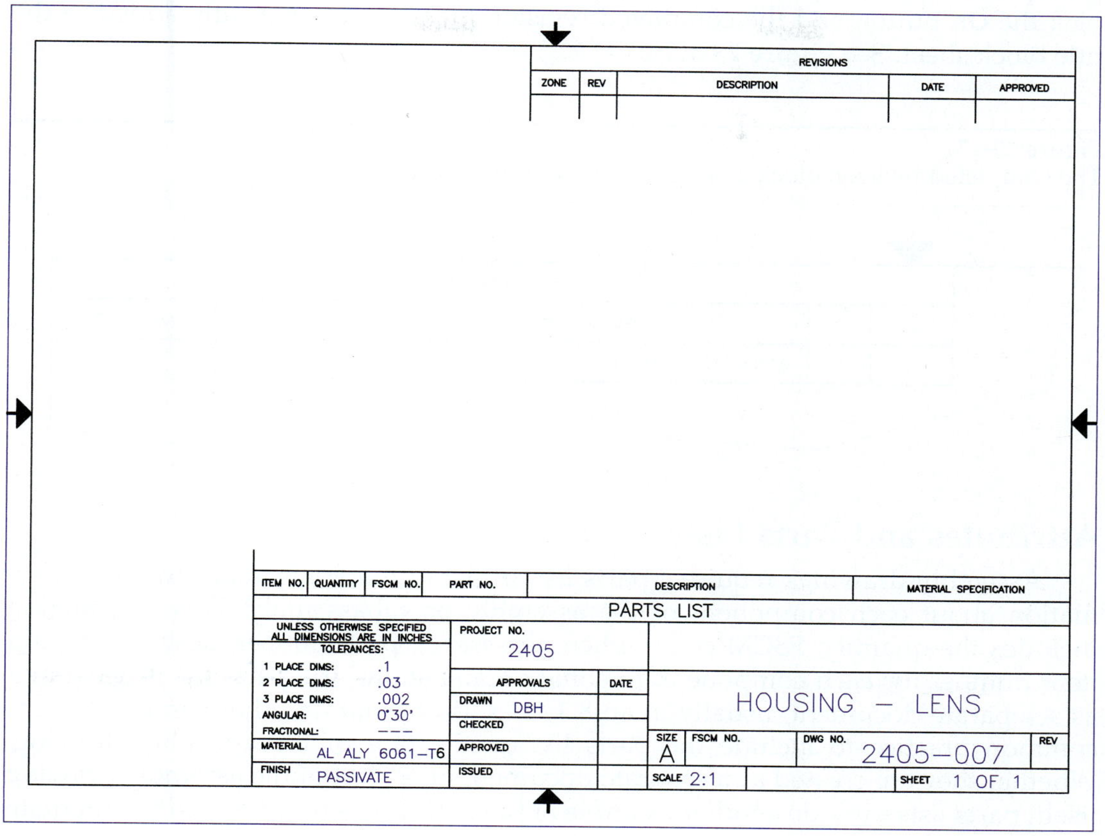

applicable. *Zones* appear in the margins of a title block sheet and are indicated by alphabetical and numeric entries. They are used for reference purposes the same way reference letters and numbers are used to identify a street or feature on a road map. Although A-size and B-size title blocks may include zones, they are rarely needed.

Block attributes provide a handy means of completing the necessary information in a revision block. Refer to Figure 23-16 as you follow these steps:

1. First, create the drawing geometry for the revision block using the appropriate layer(s).
2. Define attributes that describe the zone (optional), revision letter, description of change, date, and change approval on a separate layer.
3. Use left-justified text for the change description attribute, and middle-justified text for the remainder of the attributes.
4. Use the **WBLOCK** command to save the revision block and attributes as a drawing file. Use a descriptive name such as REVBLK or REV. Keep in mind that each line of the revision block has its own border lines. Therefore, the borders must be saved with the attributes. Use the upper-left endpoint of the revision block as the insertion point.

Figure 23-16.
The revision block consists of lines and defined attributes. The border lines must be drawn as part of the block, and the upper-left corner is used as the insertion point.

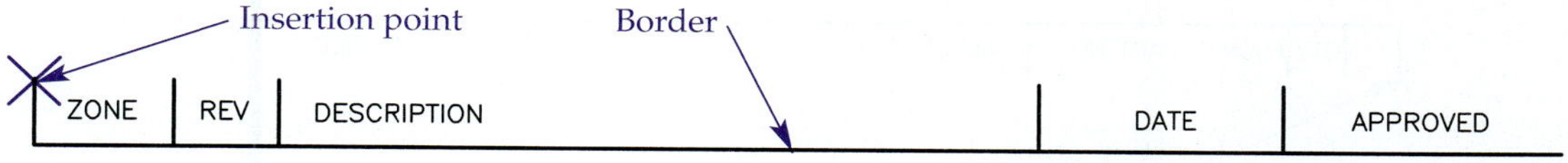

Now, after a drawing has been revised, simply insert the revision block at the correct location. If the **ATTDIA** system variable is set to 1, you can answer the attribute prompts in the **Enter Attributes** dialog box. After providing the change information, pick the **OK** button and the completed revision block is automatically added to the title block sheet. See Figure 23-17.

Figure 23-17.
The completed revision block after it is inserted into the drawing.

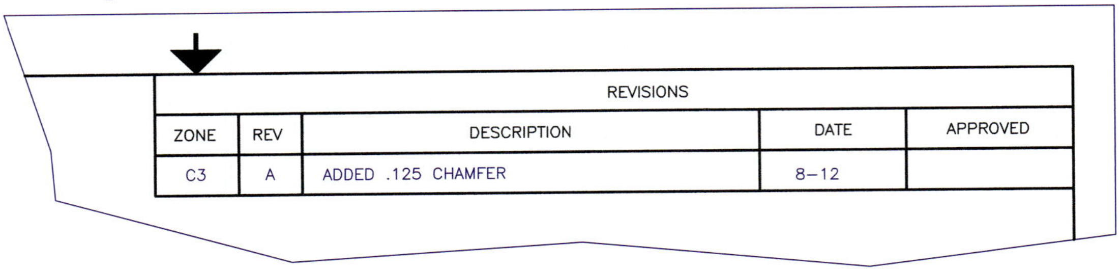

Attributes and Parts Lists

Assembly drawings require a parts list, or list of materials, that provides information about each component of the assembly or subassembly. This information includes the quantity, FSCM code (when necessary), part number, description, and item number for each component. In some organizations, the parts list is generated as a separate document, usually in an 8 1/2″ × 11″ format. In other companies, it is common practice to include the parts list on the face of the assembly drawing. Whether they are created as a separate document or as part of the assembly drawing itself, parts lists provide another example of how attributes may be used to automate the documentation process.

Refer once again to the title block in Figure 23-13. Observe the section specifically designated for a parts list, located just above the title block area. Now, consider a similar example, illustrated in Figure 23-18, as you follow these guidelines:

1. First, create a parts list block using the appropriate drawing layer(s).
2. On a separate layer, define attributes that describe the quantity, FSCM code (when necessary), part number, item description, material specification, and item number for the components of an assembly drawing.
3. Use left-justified text for the item description attribute and middle-justified text for the other attributes.
4. Use the **WBLOCK** command to save the parts list block to disk with a descriptive name, such as PL for parts list or BOM for bill of materials. You can also use the **BLOCK** command to create a block of the parts list in the current drawing. Use the lower-left endpoint of the parts list block as the insertion point, as shown in Figure 23-18.

Now, after an assembly drawing has been completed, simply insert the parts list block into the drawing at the correct location. If the **ATTDIA** system variable is set to 1, you can answer the attribute prompts in the **Enter Attributes** dialog box. After

Figure 23-18.
The parts list block is drawn with defined attributes and the insertion point located at the lower-left endpoint.

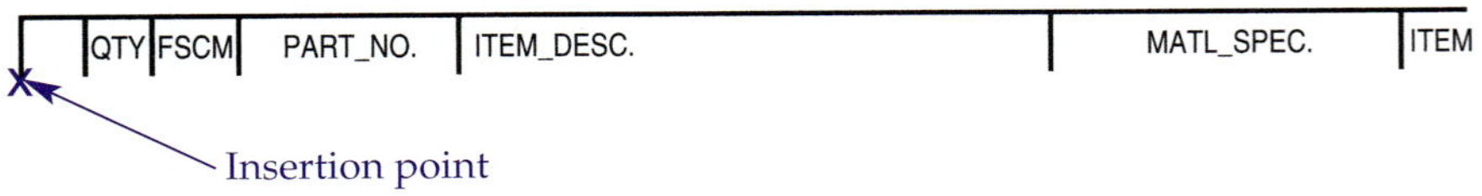

providing the necessary information, click **OK** and the completed parts list block is automatically added to the title block sheet. See **Figure 23-19.** Repeat the procedure as many times as required for each component of the assembly drawing.

From the preceding examples, you can see that block attributes are powerful objects. Their applications are virtually endless. Can you think of any other drafting procedures that could be similarly automated?

Figure 23-19.
The completed parts list block after it is inserted into the drawing.

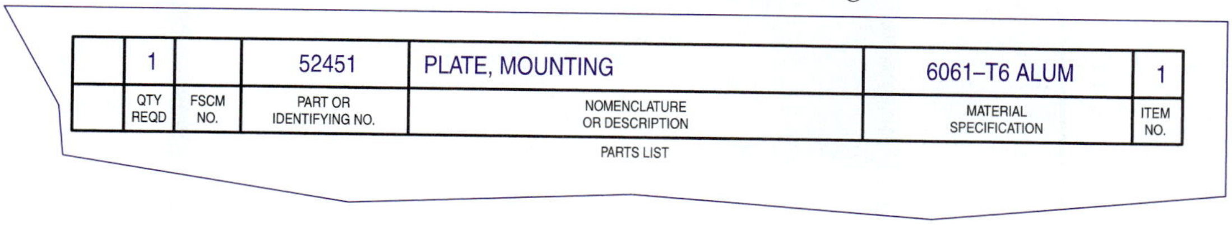

1
52451
PLATE, MOUNTING
6061–T6 ALUM
1
QTY REQD
FSCM NO.
PART OR IDENTIFYING NO.
NOMENCLATURE OR DESCRIPTION
MATERIAL SPECIFICATION
ITEM NO.
PARTS LIST

Attributes in Fields

AutoCAD 2005
NEW FEATURE

You can list attributes in fields. This allows you to display the value of an attribute in a location away from the block.

To display an attribute value in a field, access the **Field** dialog box from the **MTEXT** command, **TEXT** command, or by selecting **Field...** from the **Insert** pull-down menu. In the **Field** dialog box, pick **Objects** from the **Field category** drop-down list, and then pick **Object** in the **Field names** list box. Pick the **Select object** button to return to the drawing window and pick the block containing the attribute.

When you select the block, the **Field** dialog box reappears with the available properties listed. Attribute tags are at the bottom of the list. Pick the desired attribute tag, and the corresponding value is displayed in the text box. Select the format and pick **OK** to have the field inserted in the text object.

Collecting Attribute Information

Attribute values and definitions can be extracted from a drawing and organized in a text file. This process, called *attribute extraction*, is useful for creating bills of materials, schedules, and parts lists. AutoCAD creates a text file containing the attribute information in a tabular format. You can select the specific blocks, attributes, and values to be extracted.

EATTEXT

Tools
➥ Attribute Extraction...

Modify II toolbar

Attribute Extract

Attributes are extracted using the **Attribute Extraction** wizard. To access this wizard, pick the **Attribute Extract** button from the **Modify II** toolbar, select **Attribute Extraction...** from the **Tools** pull-down menu, or enter EATTEXT at the Command: prompt.

The first step in extracting attributes is to select the objects or drawings from which the information is to be gathered. The **Select Drawing** page of the **Attribute Extraction** wizard, shown in **Figure 23-20,** provides three options:

- **Select Objects.** Use this option if you want to include only some of the blocks in the current drawing. After selecting the radio button, the **Select Objects** button is activated. Pick this button to return to the drawing area and select the blocks to be included. You can select blocks from the current drawing only.
- **Current Drawing.** Pick this option to include all blocks in the current drawing.

Figure 23-20.
Select the blocks from which to extract information using the **Select Drawing** page.

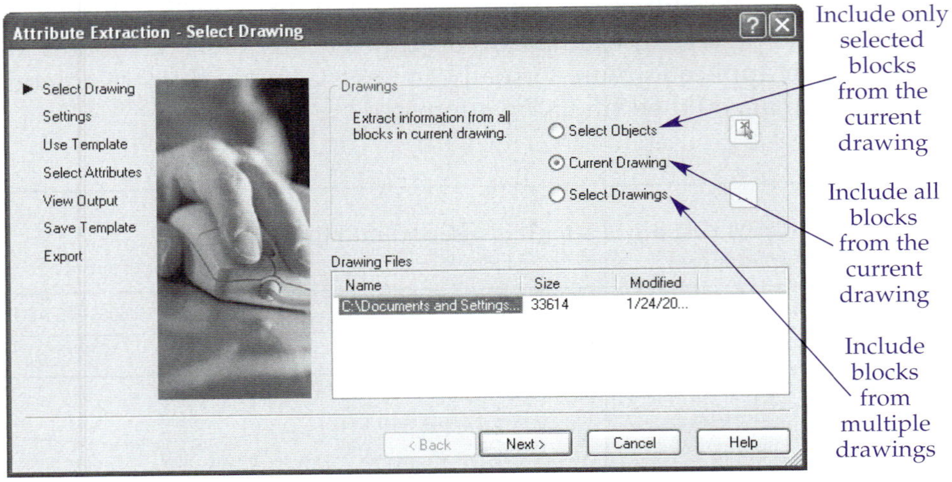

- **Select Drawings.** Use this option to gather information from blocks from multiple drawings. After picking the radio button, the ellipsis (...) button is activated. Pick the ellipsis (...) button to access the **Select Files** dialog box. Selected drawings are listed in the **Drawing Files** list.

After selecting the blocks to be included, pick the **Next** button to advance to the **Settings** page. The options on this page allow you to include blocks from external reference files and blocks nested within other blocks. These boxes are checked by default. Uncheck the **Include xrefs** and **Include nested blocks** check boxes if you wish to exclude either type of object.

The **Use Template** page allows you to select a template file to automatically select the attributes to be extracted. See Figure 23-21. If this is the first use of the **Attribute Extraction** wizard, there will not be a template file saved and available for use. However, if attribute and block information have been extracted, a saved template file could be used. To select a template, pick the **Use template** radio button, which activates the **Use Template...** button. Pick this button to access the **Open** dialog box and select the BLK file.

Figure 23-21.
Select a template of preset block and attribute values to be extracted using the **Use Template** page.

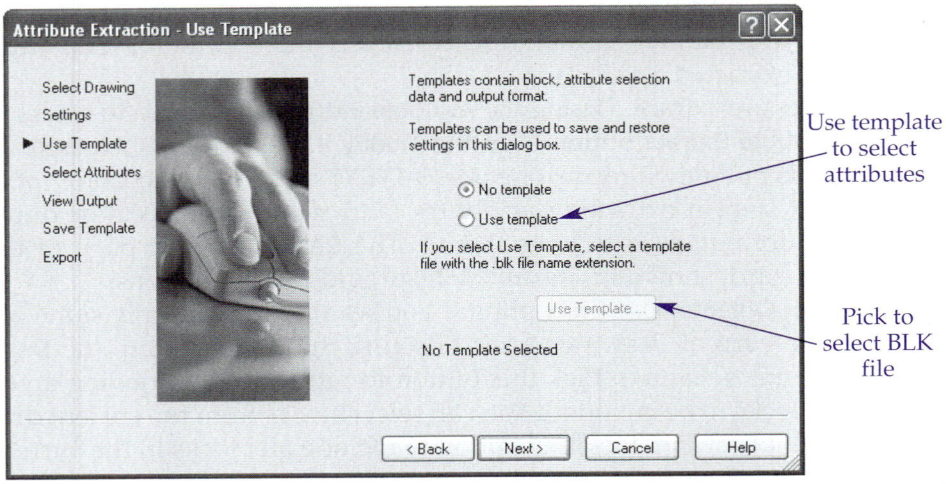

The **Select Attributes** page, Figure 23-22, lists the selected blocks and the attributes contained in those blocks. This page is divided into two tables. On the left is a list of all selected blocks. This list shows the block name and the number of times the block appears in the drawing. You can enter an alias for the block in the **Block Alias Name** column. On the right is a list of the attributes for the selected block. By default, all attributes are selected. Uncheck all attributes by selecting the **Uncheck All** button and then check only those attributes to be extracted to the output file. If a template file was selected in the previous step, the blocks and attributes are automatically selected to match the template.

You often need to be selective when listing blocks and attributes. In most cases, only certain types of attribute data need to be extracted from a drawing. This requires guidelines for AutoCAD to use when sorting through a drawing for attribute information. The guidelines for picking out specific attributes from blocks are specified using the **Select Attributes** page. This information is then used by AutoCAD to list the attributes when you create an extract file.

In addition to extracting attributes, AutoCAD can extract information about certain block characteristics. These include the following:

- **Name.** The block name.
- **Number.** The number of block insertions made.
- **X insertion point.** The X coordinate of the block insertion point.
- **Y insertion point.** The Y coordinate of the block insertion point.
- **Z insertion point.** The Z coordinate of the block insertion point.
- **Layer.** The name of the layer the block is inserted on.
- **Orient.** The rotation angle of the block.
- **X scale.** The insertion scale factor for the X axis.
- **Y scale.** The insertion scale factor for the Y axis.
- **Z scale.** The insertion scale factor for the Z axis.
- **X extrude.** The X value of the block extrusion direction.
- **Y extrude.** The Y value of the block extrusion direction.
- **Z extrude.** The Z value of the block extrusion direction.

After selecting the attributes to be extracted, pick the **Next** button to access the **View Output** page, Figure 23-23. A table displaying the results of the query is presented on this page. Two views of the information are available. Switch between the two views by selecting the **Alternate View** button. The view you select determines the format of the information when it is extracted. The information can also be copied

Figure 23-22.
Use the **Select Attributes** page to check the items to be extracted.

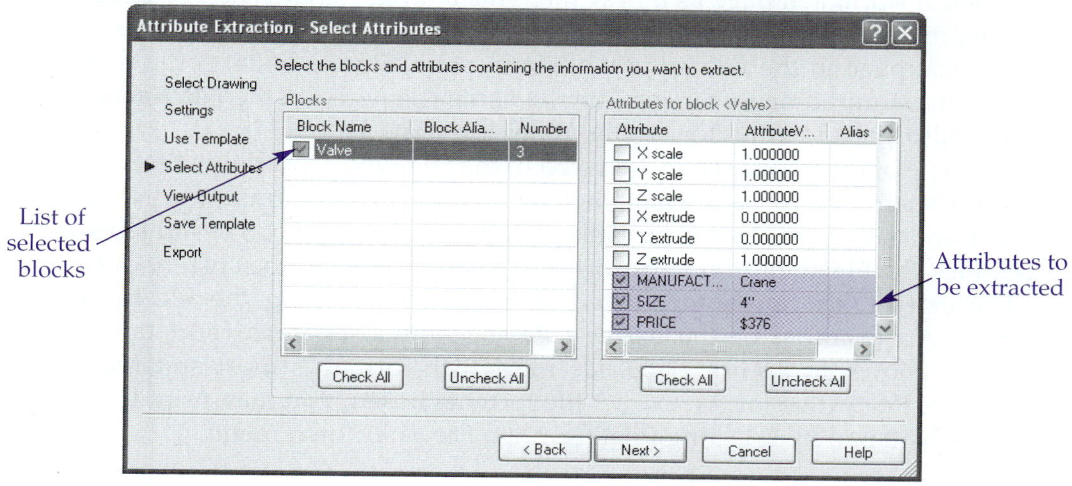

Figure 23-23.
Use the **View Output** page to select the format of the information being extracted.

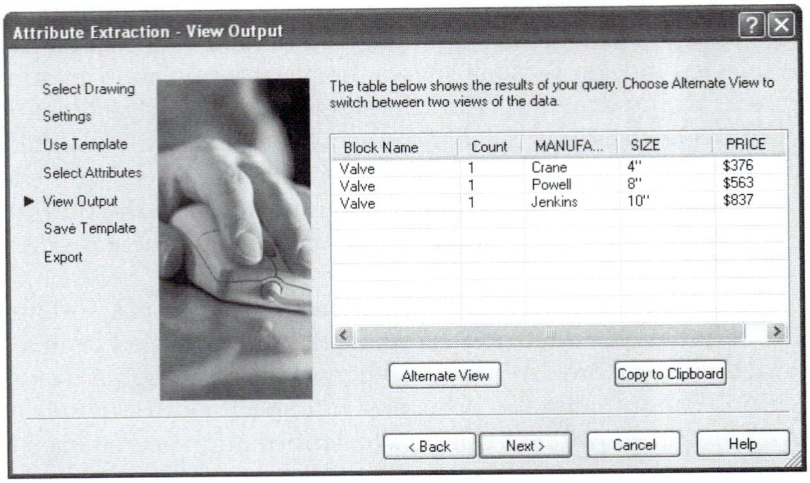

Initial View

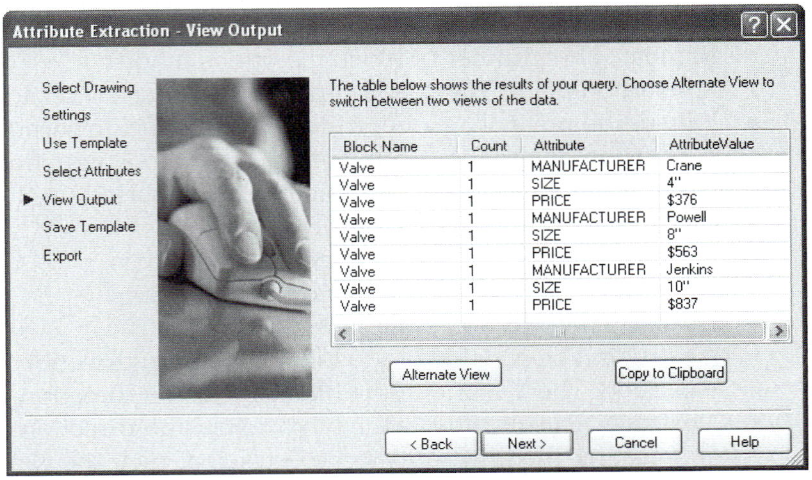

Alternate View

to the Clipboard. To do this, select the **Copy to Clipboard** button. The information is copied to the Clipboard in the same format as that displayed in the table.

After viewing the output, the **Save Template** page provides an opportunity to save a template file. The template file stores the block and attribute selections made in the **Select Attributes** page as a BLK file. This template could then be used to automatically make the attribute selection for similar extractions in the future.

The last page in the wizard is the **Export** page, **Figure 23-24.** A file name and a file type are required on this page. The file name is entered in the **File Name** text box. Pick the ellipsis (**...**) button to select a folder location.

The type of file to be saved is selected in the **File Type** drop-down list. If Microsoft Excel and Microsoft Access are installed, the XLS and MDB formats are available. The default formats that are always available are comma-separated (CSV) and tab-separated (TXT). Pick the **Finish** button to export the file and return to the current drawing.

The extract file can be displayed on screen by opening the file in Windows Notepad. An example of the extract file in comma-separated and tab-separated formats is shown in **Figure 23-25.** Decide which format is most suitable for your application. Regardless of the extract file format chosen, you may print the file from Windows Notepad by selecting Print from the File pull-down menu.

Figure 23-24.
Enter the file name and select the file type using the **Export** page.

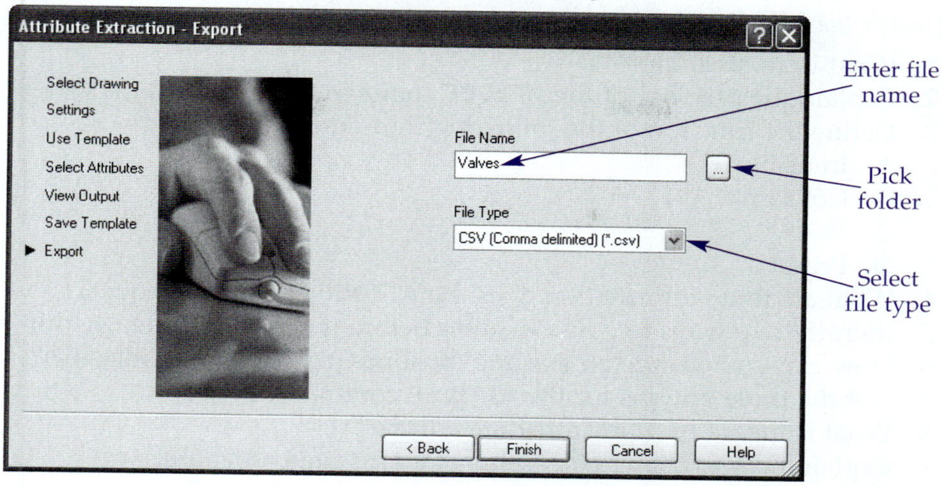

Figure 23-25.
Extract files opened in Windows Notepad.

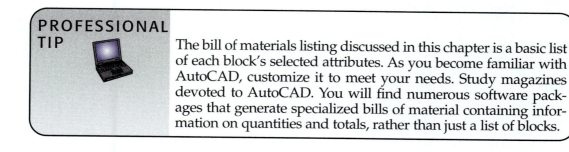

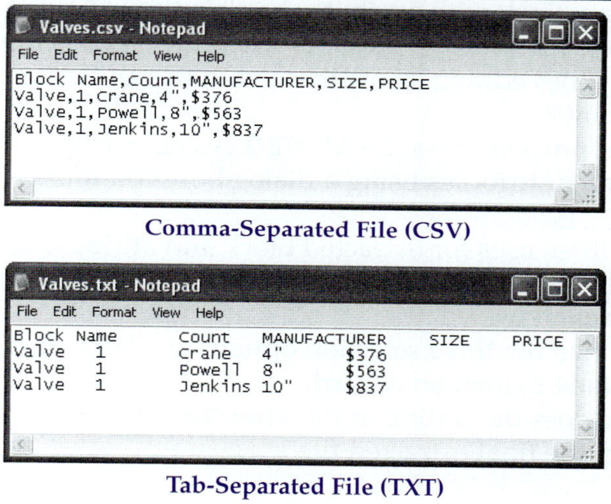

NOTE

If an attribute contains a field, the field is automatically converted to text during the extraction process.

PROFESSIONAL TIP

The bill of materials listing discussed in this chapter is a basic list of each block's selected attributes. As you become familiar with AutoCAD, customize it to meet your needs. Study magazines devoted to AutoCAD. You will find numerous software packages that generate specialized bills of material containing information on quantities and totals, rather than just a list of blocks.

EXERCISE 23-4

Complete the Exercise on the Student CD.

Chapter Test

Answer the following questions on a separate sheet of paper.

1. What is an attribute?
2. Explain the purpose of the **ATTDEF** command.
3. Define the function of the following four attribute modes:
   A. Invisible
   B. Constant
   C. Verify
   D. Preset
4. What attribute information does the **ATTDEF** command request?
5. Identify two ways to edit attributes before they are included within a block.
6. How can you change an existing attribute from **Visible** to **Invisible**?
7. List the three options for the **ATTDISP** command.
8. What is meant by *global* attribute editing?
9. Explain how to change the value of an inserted attribute.
10. How do you modify the prompt statement for an attribute that is saved within a block?
11. After a block with attributes has been saved, what method can you use to change the order of prompts when the block is inserted?
12. How does editing an attribute with **DDEDIT** differ from using the **Properties** window?
13. What purpose does the **ATTREQ** system variable serve?
14. To enter attributes using a dialog box, you must set the **ATTDIA** system variable to _____.
15. List three uses for extracted block and attribute data.
16. Explain the function served by a template file when using the **Attribute Extraction** wizard.
17. Describe the three selection options available in the **Select Drawing** page of the **Attribute Extraction** wizard.
18. How does the setting in the **View Output** page of the **Attribute Extraction** wizard affect the final extracted file?

Drawing Problems

1. Start AutoCAD and start a new drawing. Draw the structural steel wide flange shape using the dimensions given. Do not dimension the drawing. Create attributes for the drawing using the information given. Make a block of the drawing and name it W12 X 40. Insert the block once to test the attributes. Save the drawing as P23-1.

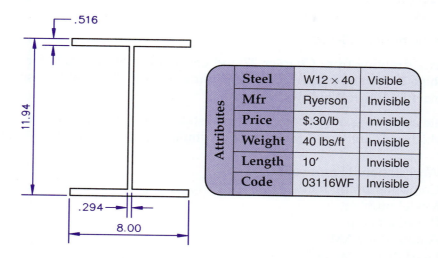

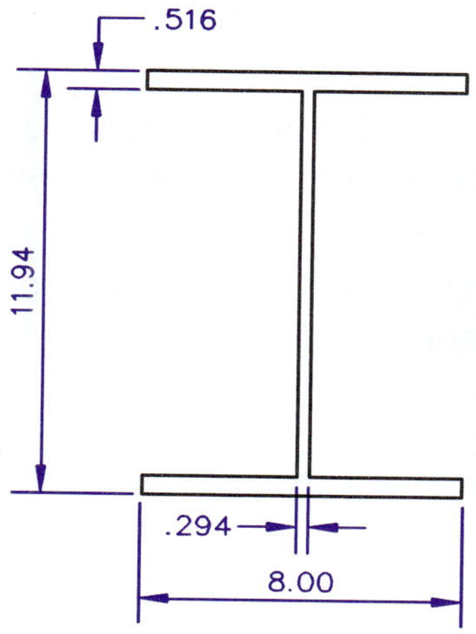

Attributes			
	Steel	W12 × 40	Visible
	Mfr	Ryerson	Invisible
	Price	$.30/lb	Invisible
	Weight	40 lbs/ft	Invisible
	Length	10′	Invisible
	Code	03116WF	Invisible

2. Open the drawing in Problem 1 (P23-1) and construct the floor plan shown using the dimensions given. Dimension the drawing. Insert the block W12 X 40 six times as shown. Required attribute data is given in the chart below the drawing. Enter the appropriate information for the attributes as you are prompted. Note the steel columns labeled 3 and 6 require slightly different attribute data. You can speed the drawing process by using **ARRAY** or **COPY**. Save the drawing as P23-2.

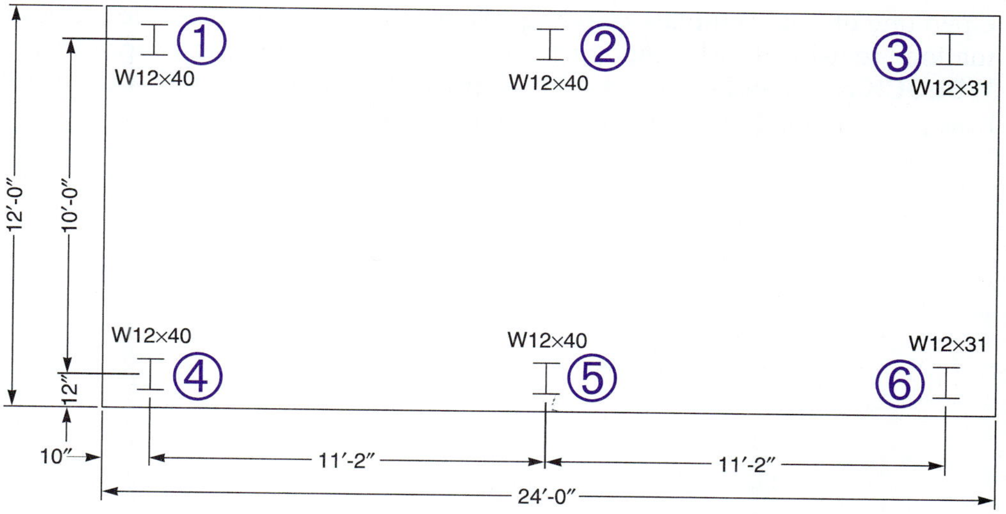

	Steel	Mfr	Price	Weight	Length	Code
Blocks ①, ②, ④, & ⑤	W12 × 40	Ryerson	$.30/lb	40 lbs/ft	10′	03116WF
Blocks ③ & ⑥	W12 × 31	Ryerson	$.30/lb	31 lbs/ft	8.5′	03125WF

3. Open Problem 2 (P23-2). Create a tab-separated extraction file for the blocks in the drawing. Extract the following information for each block:
   - Block name
   - Steel
   - Manufacturer
   - Price
   - Weight
   - Length
   - Code

   Save the file as P23-3.txt.

4. Select a drawing from Chapter 22 and create a bill of materials for it using the **Attribute Extraction** wizard. Use the comma-separated format to display the file. Display the file in Windows Notepad.

5. Create a drawing of the computer workstation layout in the classroom or office in which you are working. Provide attribute definitions for all the items listed here.
   - Workstation ID number
   - Computer brand name
   - Model number
   - Processor chip
   - Amount of RAM
   - Hard disk capacity
   - Video graphics card brand and model
   - CD-ROM speed
   - Date purchased
   - Price
   - Vendor's phone number
   - Other data as you see fit

   Generate an extract file for all the computers in the drawing.

6. Open one of your template drawings. Define attributes for the title block information, revision block, and parts list as described in this chapter. Use the **WBLOCK** command to save the entire drawing to disk using 0,0 as the insertion base point. Repeat the procedure for other templates.

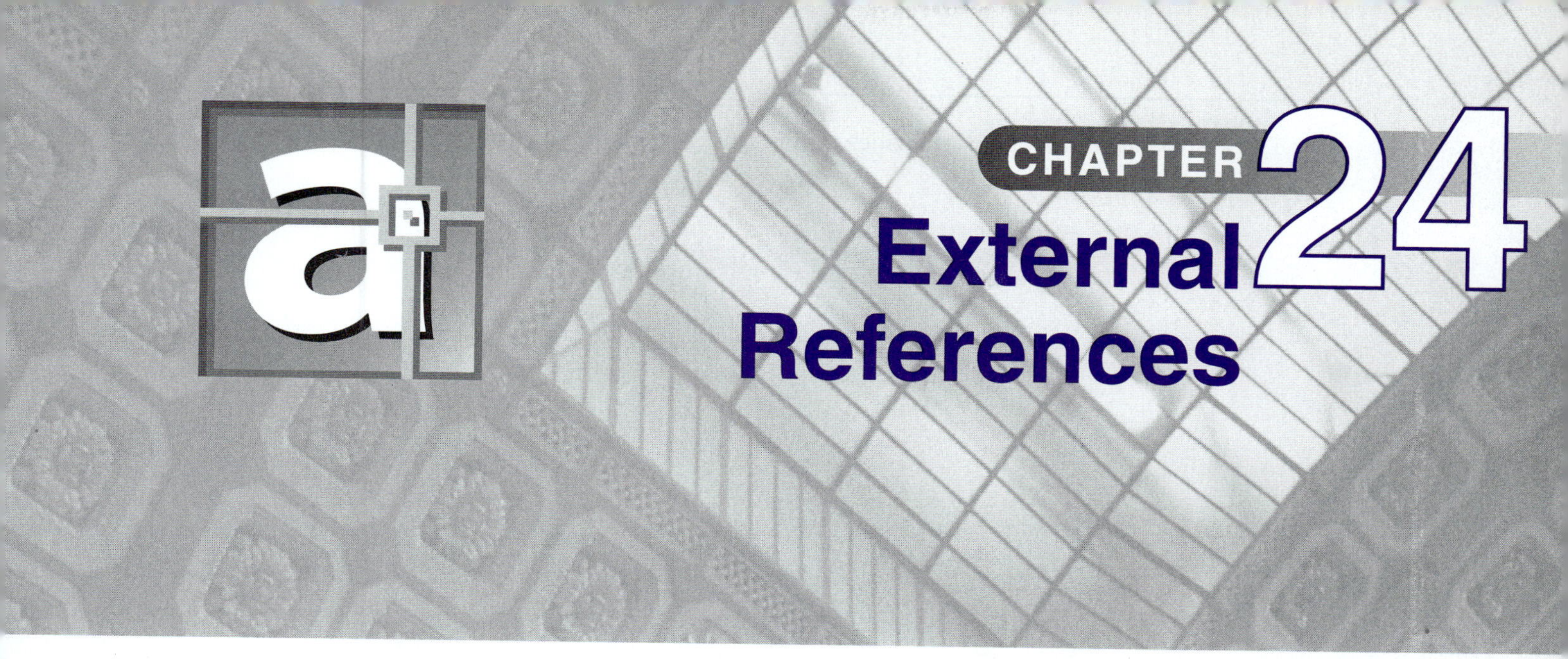

CHAPTER 24 External References

Learning Objectives

After completing this chapter, you will be able to do the following:

- Define the function of external references.
- Reference an existing drawing into the current drawing using the **XREF** command.
- Bind external references and selected dependent objects to a drawing.
- Use **DesignCenter** and tool palettes to attach external references.
- Edit external references in the current drawing.
- Use external references to create a multiview layout.
- Control the display of layers in viewports using the **Layer Properties Manager** dialog box.

When you create multiple objects in a drawing by copying them, the drawing file grows in size. This is because AutoCAD must maintain a complete description of the geometry of each copied object. On the other hand, when you use a block to represent multiple objects, AutoCAD maintains only one description of the block's geometry. All other instances of the block are recorded as X, Y, and Z coordinates, and AutoCAD refers to the original block definition to obtain the block's data. The size of a drawing is decreased considerably if blocks are used rather than copied objects.

AutoCAD enables you to go further in your efforts to control the size of drawing files. The **XREF** command allows you to incorporate, or *reference*, existing drawings into the current drawing without adding the drawing data. This procedure is excellent for applications in which existing base drawings or complex symbols and details must be shared by several users, or are used often. This chapter discusses the **XREF** command and introduces the different applications for reference drawings.

Using Reference Drawings

Any machine or electrical appliance contains a variety of subassemblies and components. These components are assembled to create the final product. The final product occupies a greater amount of space and weighs more than any of the individual parts. In the same way, a drawing composed of a variety of blocks and inserted drawings is larger than the individual components.

Figure 24-1.
The **Xref Manager** dialog box provides access to all options for externally referenced files.

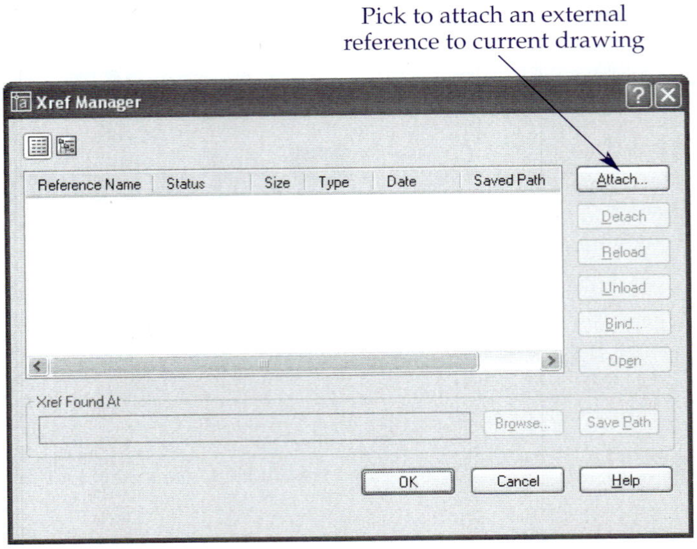

AutoCAD allows you to *reference* existing drawings to the master drawing you are currently working on. When you externally reference (xref) a drawing, the drawing's geometry is not added to the current drawing (unlike the geometry of inserted drawing files), but it is displayed on screen. This makes for much smaller files. It also allows several people in a class or office to reference the same drawing file, with the assurance that any revisions to the reference drawing will be displayed in any drawing where it is used.

XREF
XR

Insert
➥ Xref Manager...

Reference or Insert toolbar

External Reference

The **XREF** command is used to reference another drawing file into the master drawing. To access this command, pick the **External Reference** button from either the **Reference** or **Insert** toolbar, pick **Xref Manager...** from the **Insert** pull-down menu, or enter XREF or XR at the Command: prompt. This displays the **Xref Manager** dialog box, Figure 24-1. This dialog box is a complete management tool for your external references.

Reference drawings can be used in two basic ways:

- To construct a drawing using predrawn symbols or details, a method similar to the use of blocks.
- During a drawing project, to lay out drawings composed of multiple views or details, using different existing drawings. When working with sheet sets, external references can be used to arrange sheet views in paper space layouts. Sheet sets are discussed in Chapter 25.

Benefits of External References

One of the most important benefits of using xrefs is that whenever the master drawing is opened, the latest versions of the xrefs are displayed. If the original externally referenced drawings are modified between the time you revise the master drawing and the next time you open and plot it, all revisions are automatically reflected. This is because AutoCAD reloads each xref whenever the master drawing is loaded.

There are other significant advantages to using xrefs. They can be nested, and you can use as many xrefs as needed for any drawing. This means that a detail referenced to the master drawing can be composed of smaller details that are themselves xrefs. You can also attach other xrefs to the referenced drawing and have such updates automatically added to the master drawing when it is opened.

Attaching an External Reference to the Current Drawing

Using the **XREF** command is similar to using the **INSERT** command. A referenced drawing that is inserted into the current drawing is said to be *attached.* To attach the reference to the current drawing, enter the **XREF** command and pick the **Attach...** button in the **Xref Manager** dialog box. This displays the **Select Reference File** dialog box. This is a standard file dialog box. Use this dialog box to access the appropriate folder and select the desired drawing file to attach. Pick **Open** when you are finished.

Once a file to attach has been specified, the **External Reference** dialog box is displayed, Figure 24-2. This dialog box is used to indicate how and where the reference is to be placed in the current drawing. The name and the path of the currently selected xref are shown in the upper-left corner of the dialog box. To change the drawing to be attached, pick the **Browse...** button and select the new file in the **Select Reference File** dialog box. When attaching an xref, pick the **Attachment** option in the **Reference Type** area. This option is active by default. Working with the **Overlay** option is discussed later in this chapter.

If there is more than one external reference already in the current drawing, you can attach another copy of an xref by picking the **Name:** drop-down list arrow. You can also attach an existing xref by highlighting the desired reference name in the **Xref Manager** dialog box and picking the **Attach...** button.

The lower portion of the **External Reference** dialog box contains the options for the xref insertion location, scaling, and rotation angle. The text boxes in the **Insertion point** area allow you to enter 2D or 3D coordinates for insertion of the xref if the **Specify On-screen** check box is inactive. Activate this check box if you wish to specify the insertion location on screen. Scale factors for the xref can be set in the **Scale** area. By default, the X, Y, and Z scale factors are set to 1. You can enter new values in the corresponding text boxes, or activate the **Specify On-screen** check box to display scaling prompts on the command line. Checking the **Uniform Scale** check box tells AutoCAD to use the X scale factor for the Y and Z scale factors. The rotation angle for the inserted xref is 0 by default. You can specify a different rotation angle in the **Angle:** text box, or activate the **Specify On-screen** check box if you wish to be prompted at the command line.

The **Path type** drop-down list is used to set how the path to the xref file will be stored by AutoCAD. This path is then used to find the xref file when the master file is opened. The resulting path is displayed in the **Xref Manager** dialog box, Figure 24-3.

Figure 24-2.
The **External Reference** dialog box is used to specify how an external reference is placed in the current drawing.

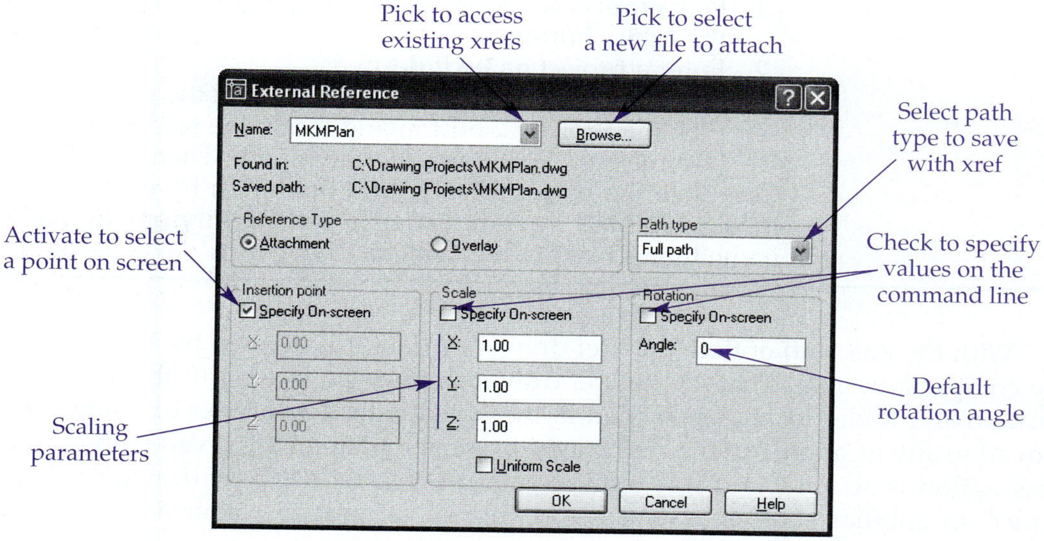

Figure 24-3.
An xref file attached to the current drawing can be referenced with a full path, a relative path, or no path. The type of path used is displayed in the **Saved Path** column in the **Xref Manager** dialog box.

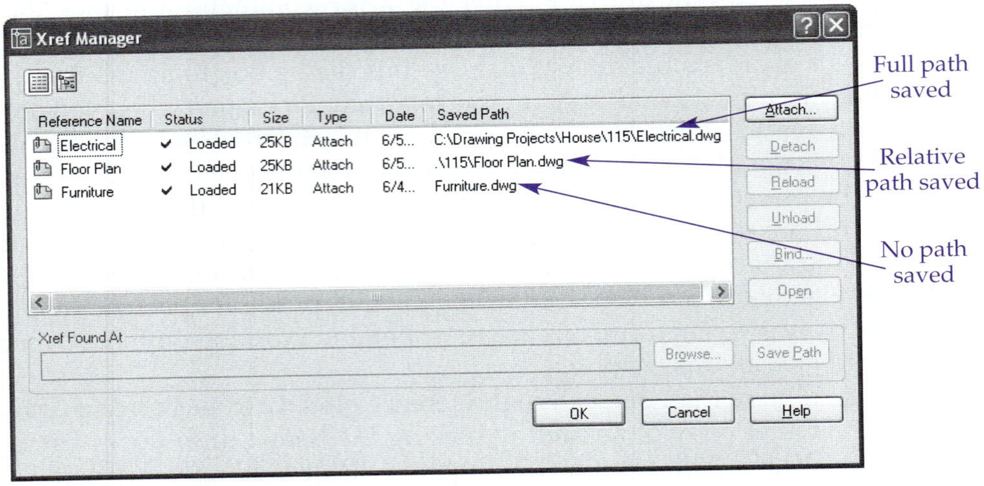

It also appears under the xref name in the **Saved path:** listing in the **External Reference** dialog box. There are three path options. They are described as follows:

- **Full path.** This option saves the full path to the xref drawing file. It is active by default. It specifies an *absolute path.*
- **Relative path.** This option saves the path relative to the file it is being referenced into (the current file). This option cannot be used if the xref file is on a local or network drive other than the drive that stores the master file.
- **No path.** This option does not save the path to the xref file. When this option is used, the xref file can only be found and loaded if the path to the file is included in one of the Support File Search Path locations or if the xref file is in the same folder as the master file. The Support File Search Path locations are specified in the **Files** tab of the **Options** dialog box.

NOTE

AutoCAD also searches for xref files in all paths of the current project name. These paths are listed under the Project Files Search Path in the **Files** tab of the **Options** dialog box. You can create a new project as follows:

1. Pick Project Files Search Path to highlight it, and then pick the **Add...** button.
2. Enter a project name if desired.
3. Pick the plus sign icon (+), and then pick the word Empty.
4. Pick the **Browse...** button and locate the folder that is to become part of the project search path. Then pick **OK**.

Complete the project search path definition by entering the **PROJECTNAME** system variable and specifying the same name that is used in the **Options** dialog box.

With the **Full path** option, the xref drawing location is defined by its location on the computer system. That is, the xref drawings must be located in the same drive location and folder location specified in the saved path. The master drawing can be moved to any location, but the xref drawings must remain in the saved path location. This option is acceptable if it is unlikely that the master and xref drawings will be copied to another computer or drive or moved to another folder. If you will be sharing your drawings with a client or eventually archiving the drawings, the **Relative path** option is more appropriate.

The **Relative path** option defines the saved path relative to the location of the master drawing. If the master drawing and xref files are contained within a single folder and subfolders, this folder can be copied to any location without losing the connection between files. For example, the folder can be copied from the C: drive of one computer to the D: drive of another computer, to a folder on a CD, or to an archive server. If these types of transfers were performed with the **Full path** option, you would need to open the master drawing after copying and redefine the saved paths for all xref files.

In the **Saved Path** list in the **Xref Manager** dialog box, AutoCAD uses prefixes to describe the relative paths to xref files. Referring to Figure 24-3, the path to the Floor Plan reference file is preceded by the characters .\. The period (.) represents the folder containing the master drawing. From that folder, AutoCAD "looks in" the 115 folder, where the Floor Plan drawing is found. A similar specification is used for the Elevation reference file in Figure 24-4. In this instance, the Elevation file is found in the same folder as the master drawing. The specification for the Wall reference file is preceded by the characters ..\. The double period (..) instructs AutoCAD to move up one folder level from the current location. The double period can be repeated to move up multiple folder levels. For example, the Panel reference file in Figure 24-4 is found by moving up two folder levels from the folder of the master drawing and then opening the Symbols folder.

Figure 24-4.
This figure shows the relationship between symbols in the **Saved Path** list and file locations within the folder structure.

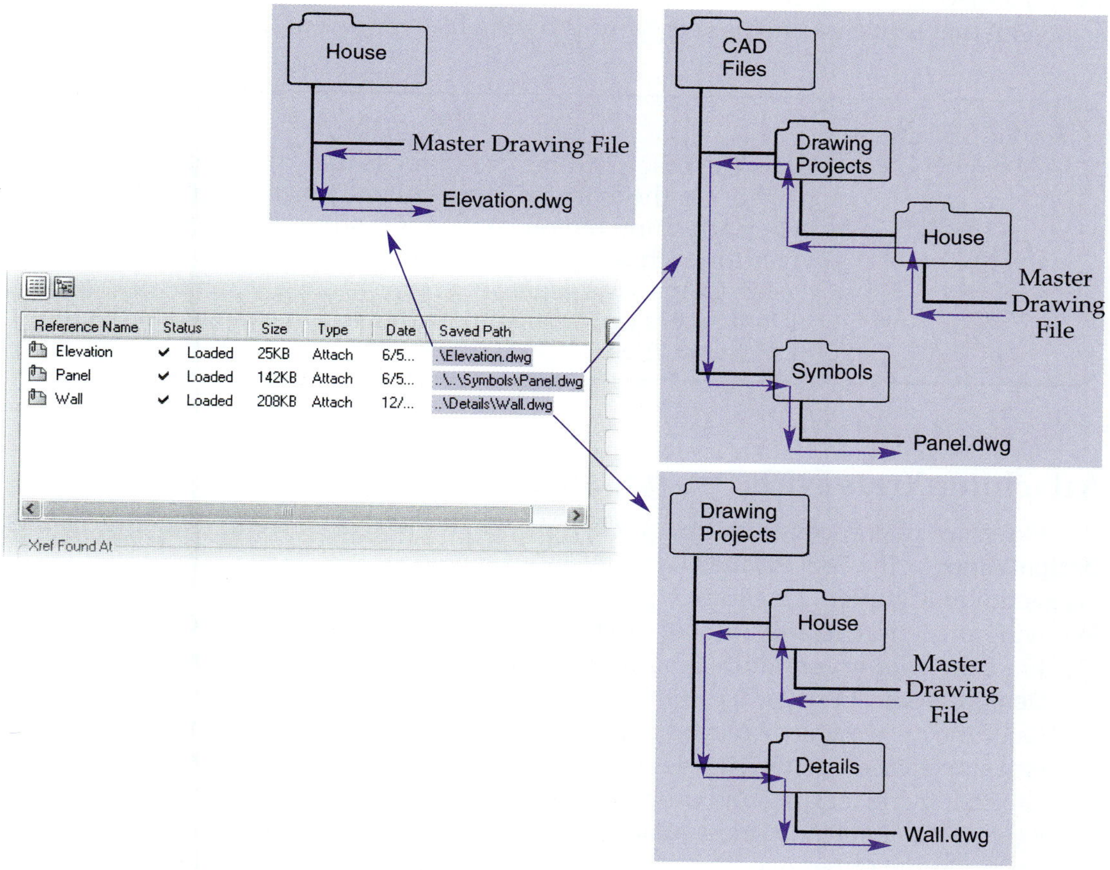

NOTE

The path saved to the xref is one of several locations searched by AutoCAD when a master drawing is opened and an xref must be loaded. When a file containing xrefs is opened, AutoCAD will try several ways to load each xref. The order in which AutoCAD searches path locations for loading xref files is as follows:

1. The path associated with the xref (the full path or a relative path).
2. The current folder of the master drawing.
3. The project paths specified in the Project Files Search Path.
4. The support paths specified in the Support File Search Path.
5. The Start in: folder path specified for the AutoCAD application shortcut (accessed with the **Properties** option in the desktop icon right-click menu).

After specifying a path type and reference type for an xref in the **External Reference** dialog box, the xref may be inserted into the current drawing. In the example given in **Figure 24-2,** the file C:\Drawing Projects\MKMPlan.dwg is selected for attachment. Because the **Specify On-screen** check box in the **Insertion point** area is activated, the dialog box disappears when you pick **OK**. The xref is attached to your cursor and you are prompted for the insertion point. You can use any valid point specification option, including object snap modes.

As you can see, the insertion options for attaching an xref are essentially the same as those used when inserting a block. Both commands function in a similar manner, but the internal workings and results are different. Remember that externally referenced files are not added to the current drawing file's database, as are inserted drawings. Therefore, using external references helps keep your drawing file size to a minimum.

PROFESSIONAL TIP

As is the case with inserted blocks and drawings, an xref is placed on the current layer when attached to a drawing. When attaching reference files, it is advisable to create an xref layer for each reference that you plan on using. This makes it easier to manage xrefs in your drawing because the individual layers can be frozen or thawed to change the display of different files.

Attaching Xrefs with DesignCenter and Tool Palettes

External references can be quickly attached to the current drawing using **DesignCenter** or the **Tool Palettes** window. Inserting blocks with both of these features is discussed in Chapter 22. Similar procedures are used for attaching xrefs. Use the following procedure to attach an xref to the current drawing with **DesignCenter**:

1. Find the folder containing the drawing to be attached in the **Tree View** area of **DesignCenter**. Display the contents of the folder in the **Content** area.
2. Once the drawing is displayed in the **Content** area, you can attach it as an xref using either of two methods. Right-click on the file and select **Attach as Xref…** from the shortcut menu, or drag and drop the drawing into the current drawing area *using the right mouse button* and select **Attach as Xref…** from the shortcut menu displayed.
3. The **External Reference** dialog box is displayed. Enter the appropriate values and pick **OK**.

A drawing file can also be attached to the current drawing as an xref from the **Tool Palettes** window. To add an xref to a tool palette, you can drag an existing xref from the current drawing or an xref file from the **Content** area of **DesignCenter**. The xref can then be attached to the current drawing from the palette by using drag and drop.

Xref files in tool palettes are identified with an external reference icon. If a drawing file is added to a tool palette from the current drawing or **DesignCenter**, it is designated as a block tool. You can check the status of a tool by right-clicking on the image and selecting **Properties...** to display the **Tool Properties** dialog box. The status is listed in the **Insert as** field.

Overlaying the Current Drawing with an External Reference

There are many situations in which you may want to see what your drawing looks like with another drawing overlaid on it. Overlaying the current drawing with an external reference file allows you to temporarily view the xref without attaching it. This is accomplished by activating the **Overlay** option button in the **External Reference** dialog box after selecting an xref.

The difference between an overlaid xref and an attached xref is related to the way in which nested xrefs are handled. ***Nesting*** occurs when an externally referenced file is referenced by an xref file that has been attached to the current drawing. The xref file that is attached is known as the ***parent xref***. When an xref is overlaid, any nested xrefs that it contains are displayed if those xrefs were *attached*, but not if they were *overlaid*. In other words, any nested overlays are not carried into the master drawing with the parent xref.

Detaching, Reloading, and Unloading

As discussed earlier, each time you open a master drawing containing an attached xref, the xref is also loaded and appears on screen. This attachment remains permanent until you remove or *detach* it. This is done by highlighting the reference name in the **Xref Manager** dialog box and picking the **Detach** button. When you detach an externally referenced file, all instances of the xref are erased, and all referenced data is removed from the current drawing. All xrefs nested within the detached file are also removed. The actual detachment does not occur until you press **OK** and close the dialog box. This is helpful if you accidentally detach an xref, because you can simply press **Cancel** to prevent the detachment and return to the drawing.

There may be situations where you need to update or ***reload*** an xref file in the master drawing. For example, if an externally referenced file is edited by another user while the master drawing is open, the version on disk may be different than the version currently displayed. To update the xref, highlight the reference name in the **Xref Manager** dialog box and pick the **Reload** button. This forces AutoCAD to read and display the most recently saved version of the drawing.

When you need to temporarily remove an xref file without actually detaching it, you can ***unload*** the xref. To do so, highlight the reference name in the **Xref Manager** dialog box and pick the **Unload** button. When an xref is unloaded, it is not displayed or regenerated, and AutoCAD's performance is increased. To display the xref again, access the **Xref Manager** dialog box and pick the **Reload** button.

Using the Xref Manager Dialog Box

In addition to attaching xref files, you can use the **Xref Manager** dialog box to access current information about any referenced file in the master drawing. Each of the labeled columns in this dialog box lists information, Figure 24-5. The file names in the **Reference Name** column can be displayed in either list view or tree view. The list view display mode is active by default. It can be activated by picking the **List View** button, located at the upper-left corner of the dialog box, or by pressing the [F3] key. The labeled columns displayed in list view are described as follows:

- **Reference Name.** This column lists the names of all existing external references.
- **Status.** This column describes the current status of each xref. The xref status can be classified as one of the following:
  - **Loaded.** The xref is attached to the drawing.
  - **Unloaded.** The xref is not displayed or regenerated.
  - **Unreferenced.** The xref has nested xrefs that are not found or are unresolved. An unreferenced xref is not displayed.
  - **Not Found.** The xref file was not found in valid search paths.
  - **Unresolved.** The xref file is missing or cannot be found.
  - **Orphaned.** The parent of the nested xref cannot be found.
  - **Reload.** The xref is marked to be reloaded. Loading and unloading both occur after the dialog box is closed.
  - **Unload.** The xref is marked to be unloaded.
- **Size.** The file size for each xref is listed in this column.
- **Type.** This column indicates whether the xref was attached or referenced as an overlay.
- **Date.** The last modification date for the file being referenced is indicated in this column.
- **Saved Path.** This column lists the path name saved with the xref. If only a file name appears here, the path has not been saved.

Figure 24-5.
Additional information on referenced files is displayed in the **Xref Manager** dialog box.

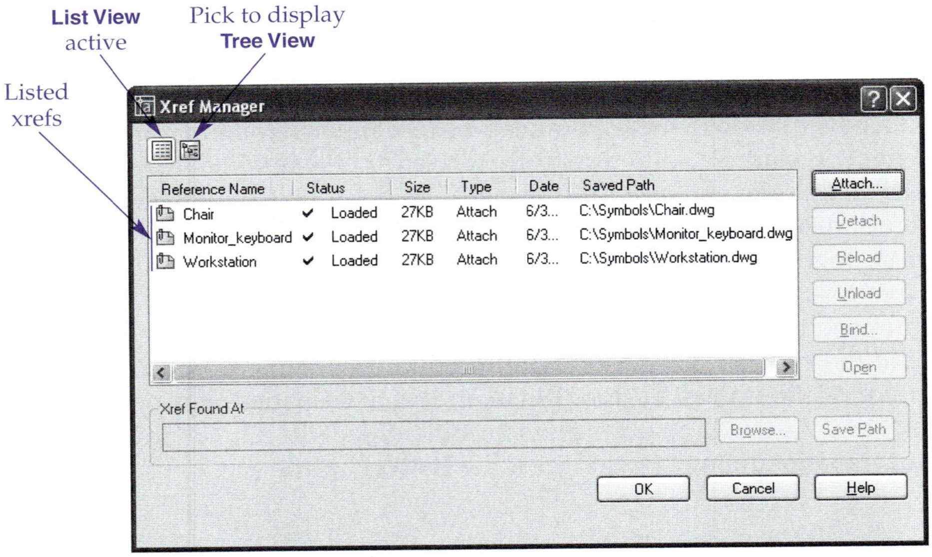

PROFESSIONAL TIP

In the list view display mode, the column widths can be adjusted as necessary to view incomplete information. To adjust the width of a column, move your cursor to the edge of the button at the top of the column until the cursor changes to a horizontal resizing cursor. Press and hold your left mouse button and drag the column to the desired width. The column width adjustments you make are used for subsequent displays of the dialog box. If the columns extend beyond the width of the dialog box window, a horizontal scroll bar appears at the bottom of the list.

To quickly see a listing of your externally referenced files that shows nesting levels, pick the **Tree View** button or press the [F4] key. See Figure 24-6. In the tree view display mode, the drawing is indicated with the standard AutoCAD drawing file icon, and xrefs appear as a sheet of paper with a paper clip. Nesting levels are shown in a format that is similar to the arrangement of folders. The xref icon can take on different appearances, depending on the current status of the xref. An xref whose status is unloaded or not found will have an icon that is grayed out. An upward arrow shown with the icon means the xref has just been reloaded, and a downward arrow means the xref has just been unloaded.

Figure 24-6.
The tree view display mode shows nested xref levels and the status of each xref.

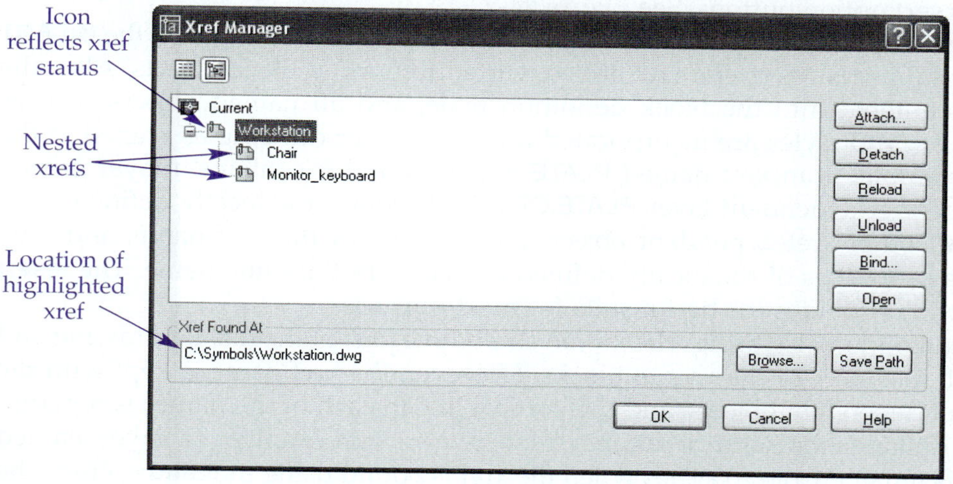

Updating the Xref Path

As previously discussed, a file path saved with an externally referenced file is displayed in the **Saved Path** column of the **Xref Manager** dialog box. If an xref file is not found in the **Saved Path** location when the master drawing is opened, AutoCAD searches along the *library* path, which includes the current drawing folder and the Support File Search Path locations set in the **Files** tab of the **Options** dialog box. If a file with a matching name is found, it is resolved. In such a case, the **Saved Path** location differs from where the file was actually found. You can check this in the **Xref Manager** dialog box by highlighting an xref name and then comparing the path listed in the **Saved Path** column with the listing in the **Xref Found At** area. To update the **Saved Path** location, pick the **Save Path** button.

When a referenced drawing has been moved and the new location is not on the library path, its status is indicated as Not Found. You can update the path to refer to the new location by selecting the **Browse...** button in the **Xref Found At** area. Using the **Select new path** dialog box, go to the new folder and select the desired file. Then, press **Open** to update the path. When you pick **OK**, the xref is automatically reloaded into the drawing.

Binding an External Reference

An externally referenced file can be made a permanent part of the master drawing as if it had been inserted with the **INSERT** command. This is called *binding* an xref. Binding is useful when you need to send the full drawing file to another location or user, such as a plotting service or a client.

Before an xref is bound, all dependent objects in the externally referenced file, such as blocks, dimension styles, layers, linetypes, and text styles, are named differently by AutoCAD. When an xref is attached to the master drawing, dependent objects are renamed so the xref name precedes the actual object name. The names are separated by a vertical bar symbol (|). For example, prior to binding, a layer named Notes within an externally referenced drawing file named Title comes into the master drawing as Title|Notes. This is done to distinguish the xref-dependent layer name from the same layer name in the master drawing. When an xref file is bound to the master drawing, the dependent objects are renamed again to reflect that they have become a permanent part of the drawing. There are different renaming methods, depending on the type of binding that is performed.

To bind an xref using the **Xref Manager** dialog box, highlight the xref to bind and select the **Bind...** button. This displays the **Bind Xrefs** dialog box, which contains the **Bind** and **Insert** option buttons. See Figure 24-7.

The **Insert** option brings the xref into the drawing as if you had used the **INSERT** command. All instances of the xref are converted to normal block objects. Also, the drawing is entered into the block definition table, and all named objects such as layers, blocks, and styles are incorporated into the master drawing as named in the xref. For example, if an xref named PLATE is bound and it contains a layer named OBJECT, the xref-dependent layer PLATE|OBJECT becomes the locally defined layer OBJECT. All other xref-dependent objects are stripped of the xref name, and they assume the properties of the locally defined objects with the same name. The **Insert** binding option provides the best results for most purposes.

The **Bind** option also brings the xref in as a native part of the master drawing and converts all instances of the xref to blocks. However, the xref name is kept with the names of all dependent objects, and the vertical line in each of the names is replaced with two dollar signs with a number in between. For example, a layer named Title|Notes is renamed Title0Notes when the xref is bound using the **Bind** option. The number inside the dollar signs is automatically incremented if a local object definition with the same name exists. For example, if Title0Notes already exists in the drawing, the layer is renamed to Title1Notes. In this manner, unique names are created for all xref-dependent object definitions that are bound. Any of the named objects can be renamed as desired using the **RENAME** command.

Figure 24-7.
The **Bind Xrefs** dialog box allows you to specify how the xref is incorporated into the master drawing.

In some cases, you may only need to incorporate one or more specific named objects from an xref into the master drawing, rather than the entire xref. If you only need selected items, it can be counterproductive to bind an entire drawing. In this case, you can bind only the named objects you select. This technique is covered later in this chapter.

Clipping an External Reference

A frequent need with externally referenced files is to display only a specific portion of a drawing. AutoCAD allows you to create a boundary that displays a subregion of an external reference. All geometry occurring outside the border is invisible. Objects that are partially within the subregion appear to be trimmed at the boundary. Although these objects appear trimmed, the referenced file is not changed in any way. Clipping is applied to a selected instance of an xref, and not to the actual xref definition.

XCLIP
XC

Modify
➥ Clip
➥ Xref

Reference toolbar

External Reference Clip

The **XCLIP** command is used to create and modify clipping boundaries. To access the **XCLIP** command, pick the **External Reference Clip** button from the **Reference** toolbar, pick **Xref** from the **Clip** cascading menu in the **Modify** pull-down menu, or enter XC or XCLIP at the Command: prompt. The prompt sequence for creating a rectangular boundary for an xref is as follows:

Command: **XC** *or* **XCLIP**↵
Select objects: *(select any number of xref objects)*
Select objects: ↵
Enter clipping option
[ON/OFF/Clipdepth/Delete/generate Polyline/New boundary] <New>: ↵

The Select objects: prompt allows you to select any number of xrefs to be clipped. Then press [Enter] to accept the default **New boundary** option. This option allows you to select the clipping boundary. The other options of the **XCLIP** command include the following:

- **ON and OFF.** The clipping feature can be turned on or off as needed by using these options.
- **Clipdepth.** This option allows a front and back clipping plane to be defined. The front and back clipping planes define what portion of a 3D drawing is displayed. An introduction to 3D drawing techniques is given in Chapter 27 of this text. Clipping of 3D models is discussed in ***AutoCAD and Its Applications—Advanced.***
- **Delete.** To remove a clipping boundary completely, use this option.
- **generate Polyline.** This option allows you to create a polyline object to represent the clipping border of the selected xref.

After the **New boundary** option is selected, the **XCLIP** command sequence continues as follows:

Specify clipping boundary:
[Select polyline/Polygonal/Rectangular] <Rectangular>: *(press* [Enter] *to create a rectangular boundary)*
Specify first corner: *(pick the first corner)*
Specify opposite corner: *(pick the other corner)*

An example of using the **XCLIP** command is illustrated in Figure 24-8. Note the geometry outside of the clipping boundary is no longer displayed after the command is completed. A clipped xref can be edited just like an unclipped xref. The clipping boundary moves with the xref. Note also that nested xrefs are clipped according to the clipping boundary for the parent xref.

Figure 24-8.
A clipping boundary is used to clip selected areas of an xref. A—Using the **Rectangular** boundary selection option. B—The clipped xref.

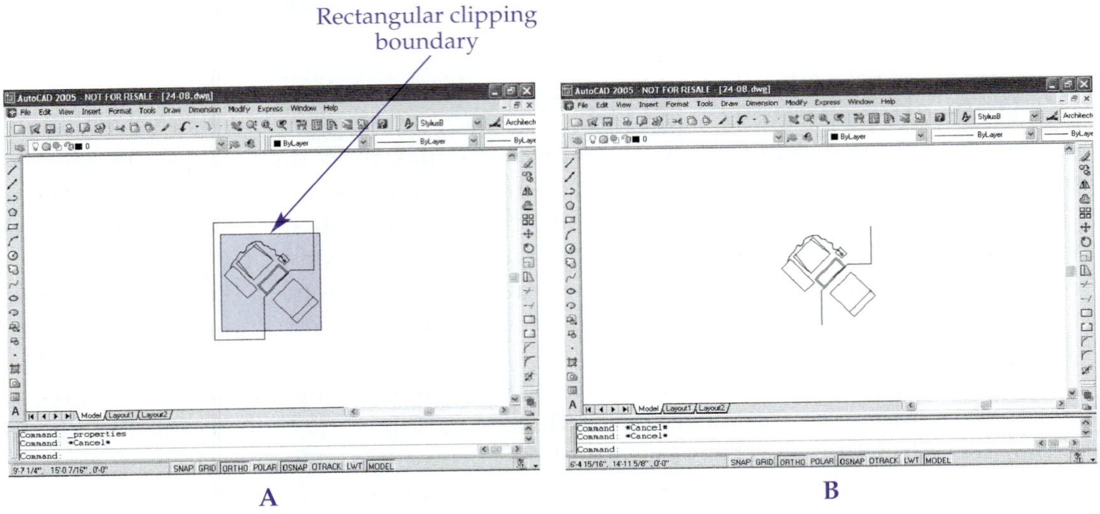

If you do not wish to create a rectangular clipping boundary after selecting an xref, there are two other options for defining a boundary. These options are described as follows:

- **Select polyline.** This option allows you to select an existing polyline object as a boundary definition. The border can be composed only of straight line segments, so any arc segments in the selected polyline are treated as straight line segments. If the polyline is not closed, the start and end points of the boundary are connected.
- **Polygonal.** This option allows an irregular polygon to be drawn as a boundary. This option is similar to the **WPolygon** selection option, and allows a fairly flexible boundary definition.

The clipping boundary is invisible by default. The boundary can be displayed by setting the **XCLIPFRAME** system variable to 1.

PROFESSIONAL TIP

If a drawing will be used as an external reference, it is good practice to save the file with spatial and layer indexes. ***Spatial indexes*** and ***layer indexes*** are lists that organize objects by their location in 3D space and their layer name. These lists help improve the performance of AutoCAD when referencing drawings with frozen layers and clipping boundaries. Layers that are frozen are not loaded when demand loading is enabled, and any areas outside clipping boundaries are also not loaded. (Demand loading is discussed in the next section.)

You can create spatial and layer indexes using the **Save Drawing As** dialog box. The procedure is as follows:

1. Pick **Options...** from the **Tools** menu and make sure the **DWG Options** tab is active in the **Saveas Options** dialog box.
2. In the **Index type:** drop-down list, pick the type of index required. The default option is **None**.
3. Pick **OK**, and then save the drawing.

Using Demand Loading and Xref Editing Controls

Demand loading controls how much of an external reference file is loaded when it is attached to the master drawing. When demand loading is enabled, the only portion of the xref file loaded is the part necessary to regenerate the master drawing. This improves performance and saves disk space because the entire xref file is not loaded. For example, any data on frozen layers, as well as any data outside of clipping regions, is not loaded.

Demand loading is enabled by default. To check or change the setting, open the **Open and Save** tab of the **Options** dialog box. The three demand loading options are found in the **Demand load Xrefs:** drop-down list in the **External References (Xrefs)** area. The options are described as follows:

- **Enabled with copy.** When this option is active, demand loading is turned on, and other users can edit the original drawing because AutoCAD uses a copy of the referenced drawing.
- **Enabled.** When this option is active, demand loading is turned on. While the drawing is being referenced, the xref file is kept open and other users cannot edit the file.
- **Disabled.** Enabling this option turns off demand loading.

Two additional settings in the **Open and Save** tab of the **Options** dialog box control the effects of changes made to xref-dependent layers and in-place reference editing. (Reference editing is discussed later in this chapter.) The settings are controlled by check boxes in the **External References (Xrefs)** area. Each option is explained as follows:

- **Retain changes to Xref layers.** This option allows you to keep all changes made to the properties and states of xref-dependent layers. Any changes to layers take precedence over the layer settings in the xref file. The edited properties are retained even if an xref is reloaded. This option is active by default.
- **Allow other users to Refedit current drawing.** This option controls whether the current drawing can be edited in place by others while it is open and when it is referenced by another file. This option is active by default.

Binding Dependent Objects to a Drawing

As discussed earlier, binding allows you to make all dependent objects in an xref file a permanent part of the master drawing. Dependent objects include named items such as blocks, dimension styles, layers, linetypes, and text styles. Before binding, you cannot directly use any dependent objects from a referenced drawing in the master drawing. For example, a layer that exists only in a referenced drawing cannot be made current in the master drawing. The same applies for text styles.

When a drawing is referenced to the master drawing, all dependent named objects are renamed. All xref-dependent layer names are given the name of the referenced drawing, followed by the vertical bar symbol (|), and then the name of the layer. This naming convention enables you to quickly identify which layers belong to a specific referenced drawing. In Figure 24-9, the **Layer Properties Manager** dialog box shows how layer names in the master drawing are distinguished from those belonging to different xref files.

There may be cases where you wish to individually bind an xref-dependent named object, such as a layer or block, rather than the entire xref file. This can be done using the **XBIND** command.

Figure 24-9.
Xref dependent layer names in the master drawing are preceded by the xref drawing name and the vertical bar symbol (|).

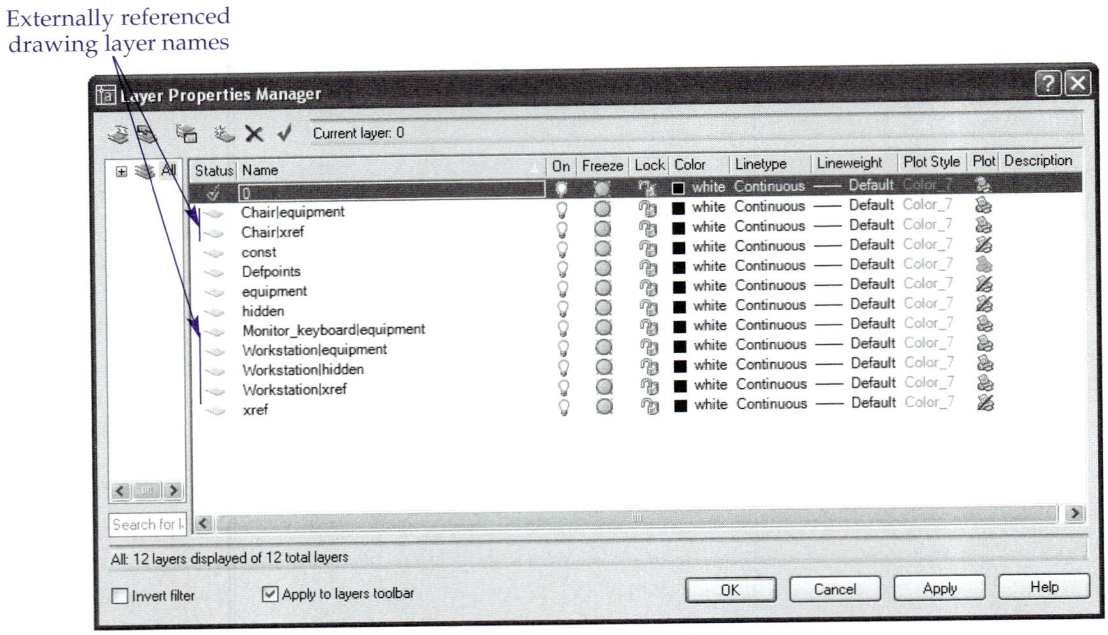

XBIND
XB

Modify
➥ Object
➥ External Reference
➥ Bind...

Reference toolbar

External Reference Bind

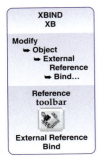

To access the **XBIND** command, pick the **External Reference Bind** button from the **Reference** toolbar, pick **Object** from the **Modify** pull-down menu and then pick **Bind...** from the **External Reference** cascading menu, or enter XB or XBIND at the Command: prompt. This displays the **Xbind** dialog box, Figure 24-10. This dialog box allows you to select individual xref-dependent objects for binding.

The xrefs shown are indicated by the AutoCAD drawing file icons. Click the plus sign to expand the listing and display the contents of the xref file.

To select an individually named object from a group, you must first expand the group listing by clicking on the plus sign next to the corresponding icon. To select an object for binding, highlight it and pick the **Add** button. The names of all objects selected and added are displayed in the **Definitions to Bind** list. When all desired objects have been selected, pick the **OK** button. A message displayed on the command line indicates how many objects of each type were bound.

Figure 24-10.
The **Xbind** dialog box is used to individually bind xref-dependent objects to the master drawing.

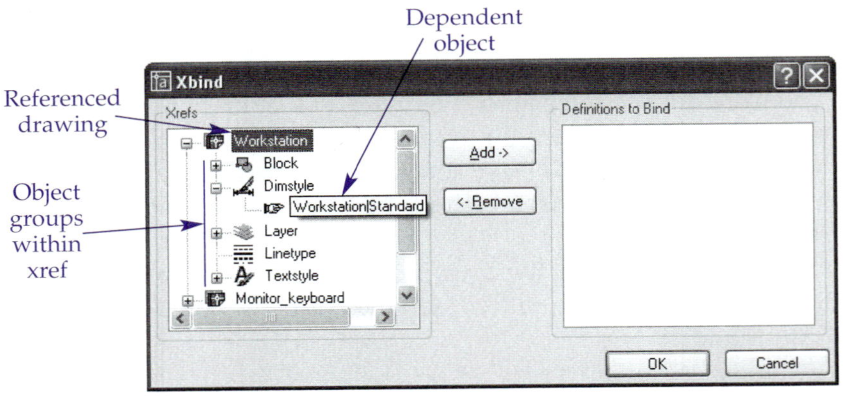

Individual objects that are bound using the **XBIND** command are renamed in the same manner as objects that are bound using the **Bind** option in the **Bind Xrefs** dialog box. In addition to being renamed, a bound layer can also be assigned a linetype that was not previously defined in the master drawing. An automatic bind is performed so the required linetype definition can be referenced by the new layer. A new linetype name, such as xref1$0$hidden, is created for the linetype. In similar fashion, a previously undefined block may be automatically bound to the master drawing as a result of binding nested blocks.

As discussed earlier, bound objects can be renamed as desired. This is done using the **RENAME** command.

NOTE

You can instruct AutoCAD to create and maintain a log file of the attaching, detaching, and reloading functions used in any drawing containing xrefs. Simply set the **XREFCTL** system variable to 1. At this setting, AutoCAD creates an XLG file having the same name as the current drawing, and the file is saved in the same folder. Each time you load a drawing that contains xrefs, or use the attaching, detaching, or reloading options provided by the **XREF** command, AutoCAD appends information to the log file. A new heading, or title block, is added to the log file each time the related drawing file is opened. The log file provides the following information:

- The drawing name, plus the date, time, and type of each xref operation.
- The nesting level of all xrefs affected by the operation.
- A list of xref-dependent objects affected by the operation, and the names of the objects temporarily added to the drawing.

Editing Reference Drawings

Reference drawings can be edited *in place*, or within the master drawing. This function, called *reference editing*, allows you to edit reference drawings without opening the original xref file. Any changes can then be saved to the original drawing while remaining inside the master drawing.

NOTE

In-place reference editing is best suited for minor revisions. Larger revisions should be done inside the original drawing. Making major changes with in-place editing can decrease the performance of AutoCAD because additional disk space is used.

REFEDIT
Modify
➥ **Xref and Block Editing**
➥ **Edit Reference In-Place**
Refedit toolbar
Edit block or Xref

The **REFEDIT** command is used to edit externally referenced drawings in place. To issue this command, pick the **Edit block or Xref** button from the **Refedit** toolbar, pick **Edit Reference In-Place** from the **Xref and Block Editing** cascading menu in the **Modify** pull-down menu, or enter REFEDIT at the Command: prompt.

```
Command: REFEDIT↵
Select reference:
```

This prompt asks you to select a reference to edit. After you make a selection, the **Reference Edit** dialog box is displayed with the **Identify Reference** tab active, Figure 24-11. A preview of the selected xref is shown in the **Preview** panel, and the name of the file is highlighted. In the example shown, the Workstation reference drawing has been selected.

In the **Path:** area, the radio button labeled **Automatically select all nested objects** is active by default. Using this option makes all the xref objects available for editing. If you wish to only edit certain xref objects, then the **Prompt to select nested objects** option can be used. When this option is selected, the Select nested objects: prompt is displayed after picking **OK**. This prompt asks you to pick objects that belong to the previously selected xref. Pick all lines and any other geometry of the object to be edited, and then press [Enter]. The nested objects that you select make up the ***working set***. If multiple instances of the same xref are displayed, be sure to pick objects from the one you originally selected.

Additional options for reference editing are available in the **Settings** tab of the **Reference Edit** dialog box. The **Create unique layer, style, and block names** option controls the naming of selected layers and objects that are *extracted*, or temporarily removed from the drawing, for editing purposes. If this check box is selected, layer and object names are given the prefix $*n*$, with *n* representing an incremented number. This is similar to the renaming method used when an xref is bound.

The **Display attribute definitions for editing** option is only available if a block object is selected in the **Identify Reference** tab of the **Reference Edit** dialog box. Checking this option allows you to edit any attribute definitions included in the reference. Attributes are covered in detail in Chapter 23.

To prevent accidental changes to objects that do not belong to the working set, you can check the **Lock objects not in working set** option. This makes all objects outside of the working set unavailable for selection when in reference editing mode.

If the selected xref file contains other references, the **Reference name:** area lists all nested xrefs and blocks in tree view. In the example given, Chair is a nested xref in the Workstation xref. If you pick the drawing file icon next to Chair in the tree view, an image preview is displayed. See Figure 24-12.

When you are through making settings, pick **OK** to begin editing the xref file. The **Refedit** toolbar is displayed in the drawing area, Figure 24-13. This toolbar displays the name of the selected reference drawing and is left on screen for the remainder of the reference editing session. You can use the toolbar to add objects to the working set, remove objects from the working set, and save or discard changes to the original xref file.

Figure 24-11.
The **Reference Edit** dialog box lists the name of the selected reference drawing and displays an image preview.

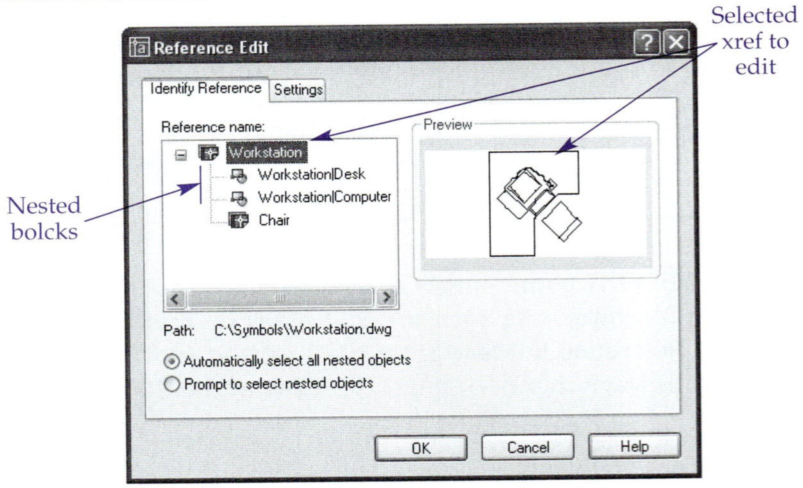

Figure 24-12.
The **Preview** panel displays the Chair xref after it is selected in tree view.

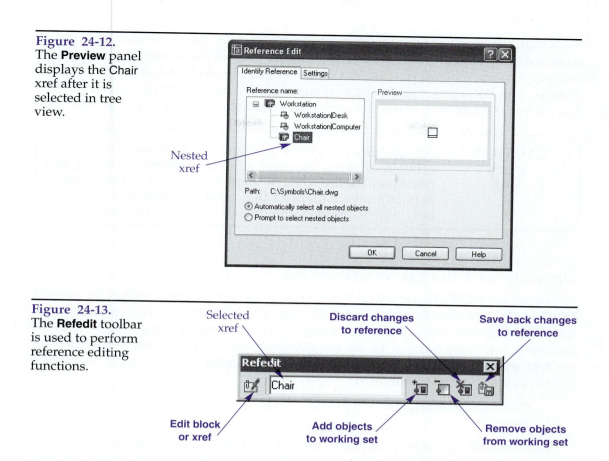

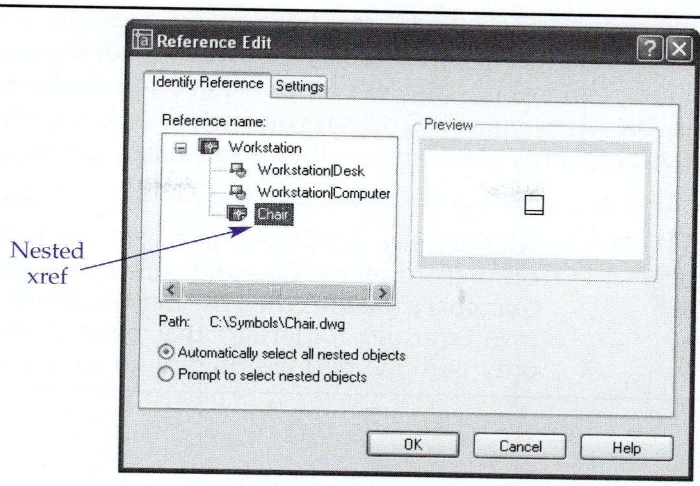

Figure 24-13.
The **Refedit** toolbar is used to perform reference editing functions.

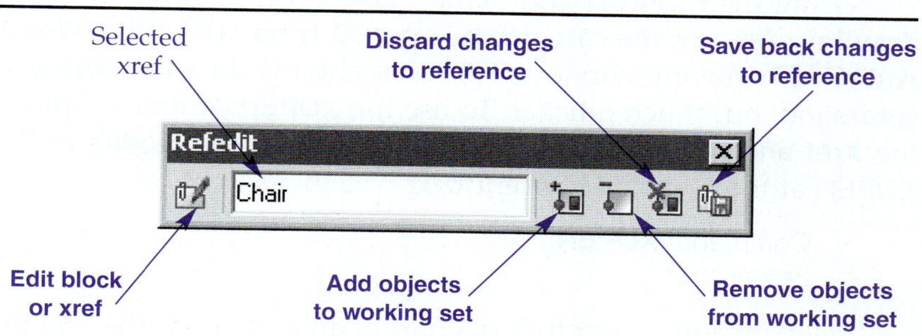

Any object that is drawn during the in-place edit is automatically added to the working set. Additional existing objects can also be added to the working set by using the **Add objects to working set** button. If an object is added to the working set, it is extracted, or removed, from the host drawing. The **Remove objects from working set** button allows you to remove selected objects from the working set. When a previously extracted object is removed, it is added back to the host drawing.

After you define the working set, it appears differently from the rest of the drawing. All nonselected objects are faded, or grayed out, Figure 24-14A. The objects in the working set appear in the normal display mode. Once the working set has been defined, you can use any drawing or editing commands to alter the object. In the example given in Figure 24-14A, the chair has been selected from the workstation so that arms can be added.

Figure 24-14.
Reference editing. A—Objects in the drawing that are not a part of the working set are grayed out during the reference editing session. B—All instances of the xref are immediately updated after reference editing.

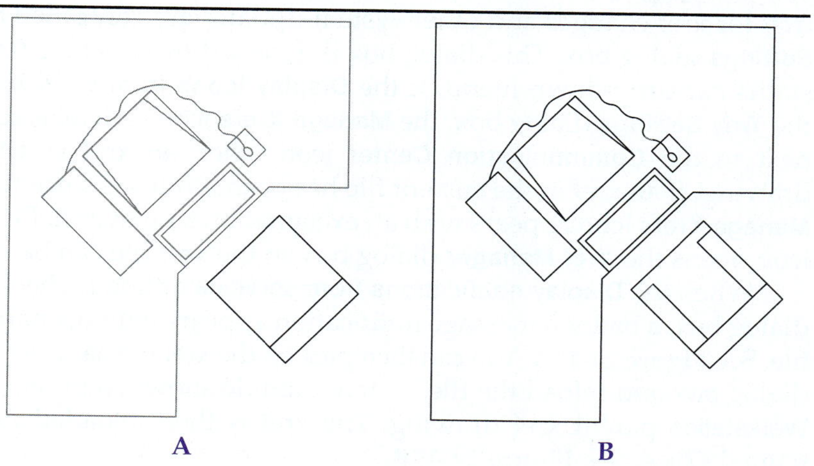

Once the necessary changes have been made, pick the **Save back changes to reference** button from the **Refedit** toolbar. If you wish to exit the reference editing session without saving changes, pick the **Discard changes to reference** button. If you save changes, pick **OK** when AutoCAD asks if you wish to continue with the save and redefine the xref. All instances of the xref are then immediately updated. See Figure 24-14B.

> **CAUTION**
>
> All reference edits made in this manner are saved back to the original drawing file, and affect any master drawing that references the file when the master is opened. For this reason, it is critically important that external references be edited only with the permission of your instructor or supervisor.

Opening an External Reference File

Using the **REFEDIT** command allows you to edit xref objects within the current drawing. An xref file can also be opened from within its parent drawing into a new AutoCAD drawing window. This is essentially the same procedure as using the **OPEN** command, but much quicker. To use the **XOPEN** command, pick **Open Reference** from the **Xref and Block Editing** cascading menu in the **Modify** pull-down menu or enter XOPEN at the Command: prompt.

> **XOPEN**
>
> **Modify**
> ➥ **Xref and Block Editing**
> ➥ **Open Reference**

```
Command: XOPEN↵
Select Xref:
```

Selecting any object that is a part of an xref opens the xref drawing file into a new AutoCAD drawing window. Picking the **Window** pull-down menu shows all the drawing files that are open in the AutoCAD session.

Once changes are made to the xref file and saved, the xref file needs to be reloaded in the master drawing file. Use the **Xref Manager** dialog box to reload the modified xref file. This ensures that the master file you are working in is up-to-date.

Xref files can also be opened by selecting an object that is part of the xref file in the drawing area and selecting **Open Xref** from the right-click menu. You can also select an xref in the **Xref Manager** dialog box and pick the **Open** button.

The Manage Xrefs Icon

When changes are made to parent drawings for xrefs used in a master drawing, a notification appears in the AutoCAD status bar tray. This tray is located in the lower-right corner of the drawing window. Changes are indicated by the appearance of the **Manage Xrefs** icon, a balloon message, or both. Notifications in the status bar tray for xref changes and other system updates are controlled by settings in the **Tray Settings** dialog box. This dialog box is accessed by selecting **Tray Settings...** from the status bar drop-down menu. If the **Display icons from services** option is checked in the **Tray Settings** dialog box, the **Manage Xrefs** icon is displayed in the status bar tray next to the **Communication Center** icon when an xref is attached to the current drawing. If an xref in the current file has been modified since the file was opened, the **Manage Xrefs** icon appears with an exclamation sign over it. Picking the **Manage Xrefs** icon opens the **Xref Manager** dialog box so the xref file can be reloaded.

When the **Display notifications from services** option is checked in the **Tray Settings** dialog box, a balloon message notification appears with the name of the modified xref file. See Figure 24-15A. You can then pick on the xref file name to access the **Xref Manager** dialog box and reload the file. In the example shown, a phone has been added to the Workstation parent xref drawing. The xref is then reloaded in the current drawing named Office. See Figure 24-15B.

Figure 24-15.
The **Manage Xrefs** icon in the AutoCAD status bar tray provides a notification when an xref file has been modified and saved. A—A balloon message is displayed with an exclamation point over the icon. B—Reloading the xref file updates the current drawing and changes the appearance of the icon.

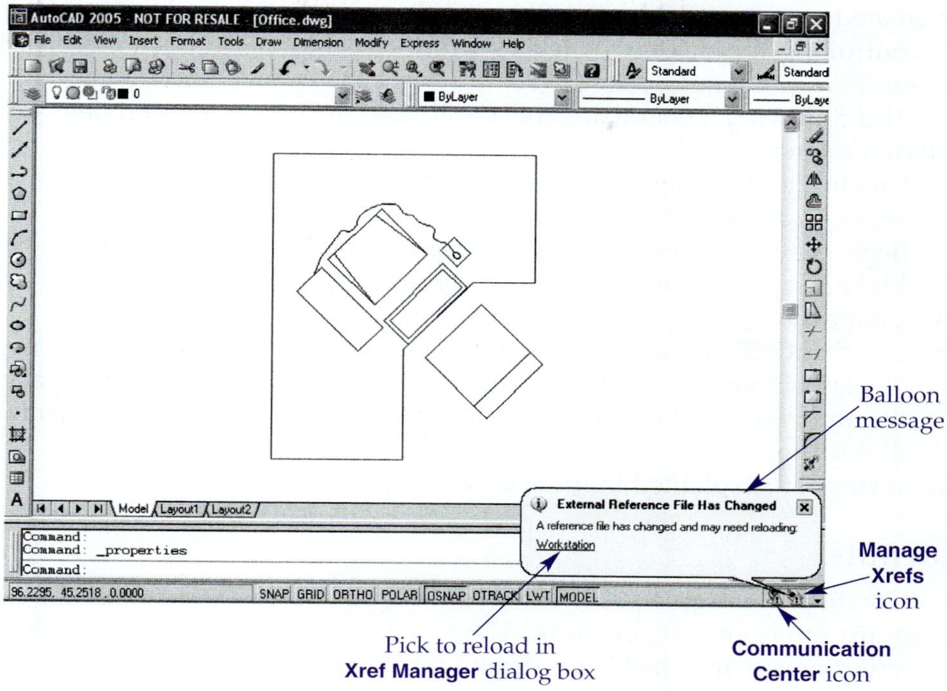

A

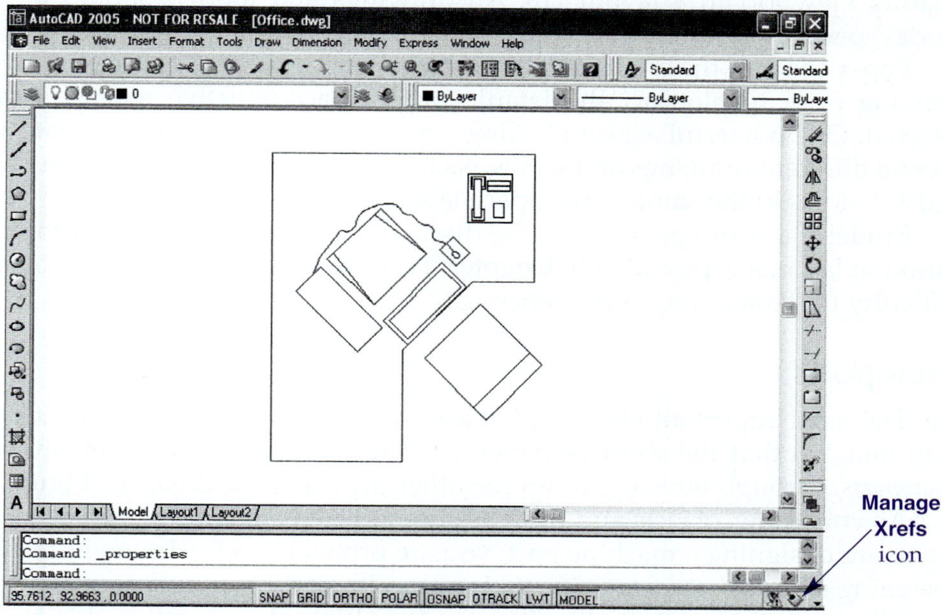

B

Using Xrefs in Multiview Layouts

Multiview mechanical drawings and architectural construction drawings often contain sections and details drawn at different scales. These sections and details can be created as separate drawing files and then attached as xrefs to a master drawing. By controlling the display of layers within viewports, you can create a multiview layout.

The following general procedure is used to create a multiview layout using external references:

1. Create the drawings and details to be displayed in the multiview drawing as separate drawing files.
2. Begin a new master drawing based on a template containing a title block.
3. Make a layer for referenced drawings and a layer for viewports.
4. Create viewports in a layout tab.
5. Use the **XREF** command to reference one drawing into each viewport. Adjust the display within the viewports using the **XP** option of the **ZOOM** command. Control the drawing display within the viewports using the **Layer Properties Manager** dialog box.

These steps are explained in more detail in the following sections.

Layouts

Creating a multiple viewport layout requires a basic understanding of the two designing environments in AutoCAD: model space and paper space. Model space is the environment in which you draw and design. When the **Model** tab is selected, model space is active. Model space is also accessed by double-clicking inside a floating viewport in a layout tab. All drawings and models should be created in model space.

Paper space is the environment you use when you wish to create a layout of the drawing prior to plotting. By default, paper space is active when a layout tab is selected. One powerful aspect of using paper space is that you can create a layout of several different drawings and views, each with different scales. You can even mix 2D and 3D views in the same paper space layout.

Model space and paper space are discussed in Chapter 10, and a thorough explanation of layouts is provided in Chapter 11. Review those chapters if you are having difficulty understanding these concepts.

Viewports

The most important visualization aspect involved in creating a multiview layout is to imagine that the sheet of paper you are creating will contain several cutouts *(viewports)* through which you can see other drawings *(models).* See **Figure 24-16.**

As you know, objects and designs should be created at full size in model space. If you are designing a machine part, you are probably using decimal units. If you are designing a house, you are using architectural units.

When creating a multiview layout of multiple drawings, double-click inside a viewport to make it active and then ***reference*** (insert) the drawing to be displayed. This procedure will be explained later in this chapter.

Now, imagine the C-size paper is hanging up in front of you, and the first viewport is cut 12″ wide and 12″ high. You want to display the floor plan of a house inside the opening. If you then place the full-size model of the floor plan directly behind the C-size paper, the house will extend many feet beyond the edges of the paper. How can you place the drawing within the viewport? You know the floor plan should be displayed inside the viewport at a scale of 1/4″ = 1′-0″. The scale factor of 1/4″ = 1′–0″ is 48.

Figure 24-16.
Views of other drawings can be seen through viewports cut into paper space.

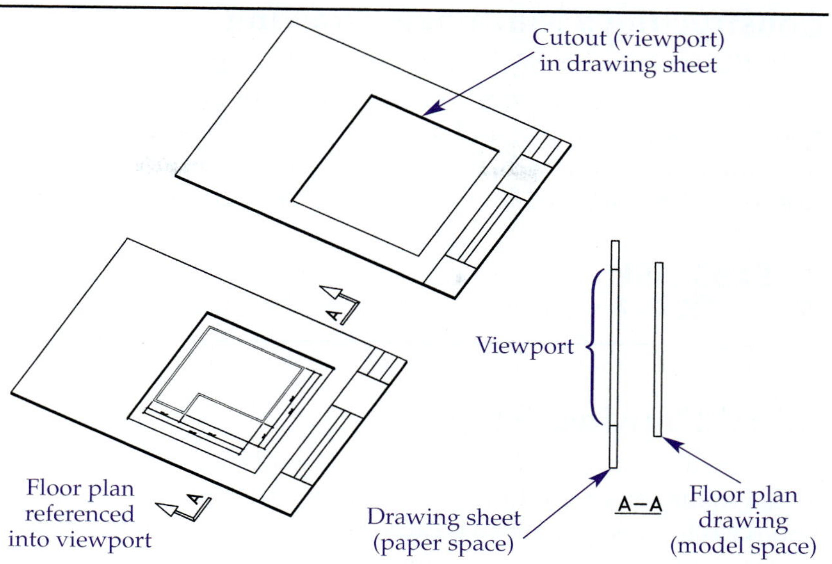

Therefore, you need to move the floor plan model away from the C-size paper until it is 1/48 (the reciprocal of 48) the size it is now. When you do that, the entire floor plan fits inside the viewport you cut. This is accomplished with the **XP** (times paper space) option of the **ZOOM** command, which is discussed later in this chapter. See **Figure 24-17.**

Figure 24-17.
A floor plan placed inside a viewport.

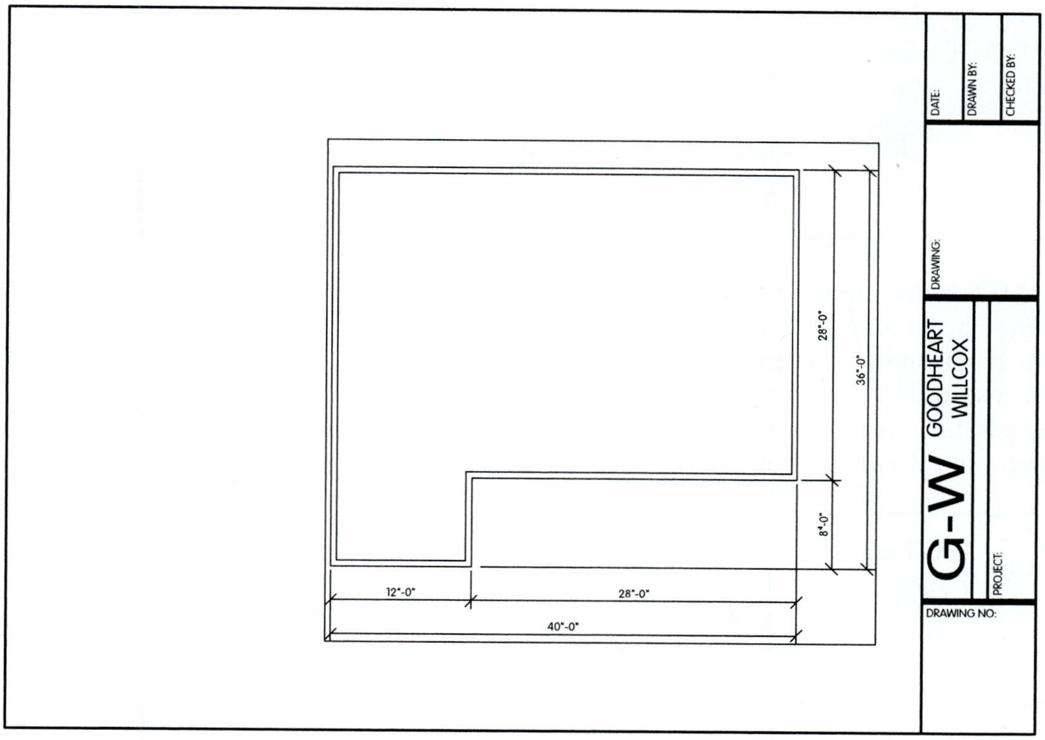

Constructing a Multiview Drawing

Now that you have a good idea of the multiview layout process, the following example leads you through the details of the procedure. This example uses a house floor plan, a stair detail, and a footing detail. This drawing is *not* among the sample drawings furnished with AutoCAD. Instead, the drawing is based on Exercise 24-1. Complete Exercise 24-1 before working through the example.

EXERCISE 24-1 Complete the Exercise on the Student CD.

Initial Drawing Setup

The first aspect of drawing setup is to place a border and title block on the screen. These items are created in the layout tab. They should be the proper size for the plot you wish to make. This can be accomplished in one of the following ways, depending on the depth of your preparation:

- Draw a border on a separate layer, then draw a title block.
- Draw a border and insert a predrawn title block.
- Open or insert a predrawn standard border and title block template containing all constant text and attributes for variable information. The Architectural, English units template drawing is a D-size sheet, but is appropriate for this example. It contains one viewport, which shows as a thin line just inside the left border line. Erase this viewport before creating a new one.

The method you use is not of primary importance for this example, but it is always best to use existing borders and title blocks to maximize efficiency and consistency.

PROFESSIONAL TIP

This initial setup phase is unnecessary if your school or company uses preprinted border and title block sheets. You might use a *phantom* border and title block sheet on the screen for layout purposes, and to add additional information to the title block. This phantom information can be frozen before plotting.

When setting up a drawing, first display a paper space layout, then set the units to match the type of drawing you are creating. Be sure the extents of your border and title block match the maximum active plotting area, or ***clip limits***, of your plotter. This example uses a standard architectural C-size sheet (18″ × 24″), and assumes that the plotter's active area is .75″ less along the top and bottom and 1.25″ less on the sides, for a total plotting area of 16.5″ × 21.5″.

NOTE

Use the page setup options to accurately create an appropriate layout based on a specific plotter or printer and its available paper sizes. Settings selected in the **Page Setup** dialog box are immediately reflected in the selected layout. See Chapter 11 for information on the **Page Setup** dialog box.

Set the units for the new layout as follows (if you do not use a template):

1. Pick a layout tab.
2. Set the following in the **Drawing Units** dialog box:
   - Architectural units.
   - Units precision = 1/2″.

- System of angle measure = Decimal degrees.
- Angle precision = 0.
- Direction for angle 0 = East.
- Angles measured counterclockwise.

3. Perform a **Zoom all**.

Creating New Layers

The border and title block should be on a separate layer, so you may want to create a new layer called Border or Title and assign it a separate color. Be sure to make this new layer current before you draw the border. If you wish to use an existing border and title block, insert it now.

One of the principal functions of this example is to use existing drawings in a layout. The house floor plan, stairs, and footing drawings will not become a part of the new drawing, but they will be *referenced* to the current drawing in order to save drawing file space. Therefore, you should also create a new layer for these drawings and name it Xref. Assign the Xref layer the color of 7.

The referenced drawings will fit inside viewports. These viewports can be any shape. They can be edited like any other AutoCAD object. Create a layer called Viewports for these entities and assign it a color.

The layers of any existing drawings that you reference (xref) into your new drawing remain intact. Therefore, you do not have to create additional layers unless you want to add information to your drawing.

If you do not have an existing C-size architectural border and title block, you can draw a border at this time. Make the Border layer current and draw a polyline border using the **RECTANG** command at the dimensions of 16.5″ × 21.5″. Draw a title block if you wish. Your screen should look similar to **Figure 24-18.**

Figure 24-18.
The border and title block in paper space.

Creating Viewports

The process of creating viewports is completed in a paper space layout because viewports are *cut* out of the paper. When creating a drawing in a layout, your screen represents a sheet of paper. You will now create an opening through which you can view a referenced drawing.

Methods of creating viewports are explained in Chapter 10. For this example, you can select the **Single Viewport** button in the **Viewports** toolbar to create each viewport. Be sure to set the Viewports layer current before creating the viewport. This allows the viewports to be turned off for plotting. Select two points to create a 12″ × 12″ viewport positioned as shown in Figure 24-19.

At this point, you can continue creating as many viewports as required. However, this example continues the process and references a drawing into the new viewport.

Figure 24-19.
A viewport added to the drawing in paper space.

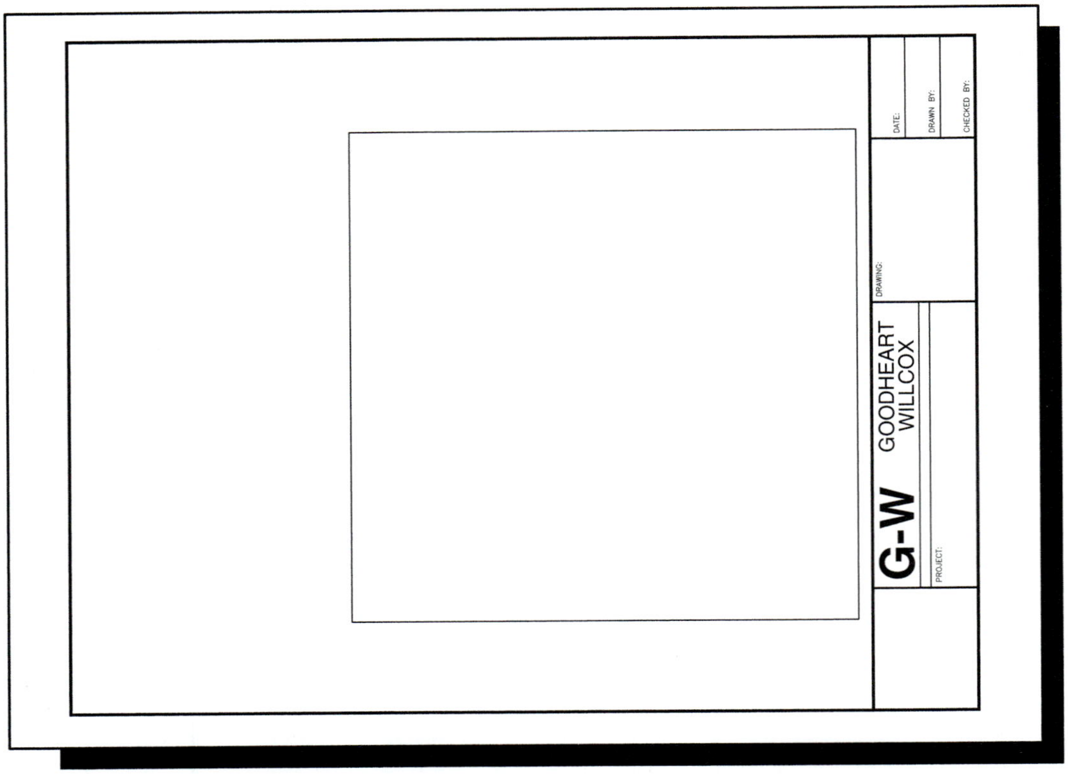

Placing Views in the Drawing

You will use the new viewport to insert the drawing of the floor plan named Floor. Instead of using the **INSERT** command, which combines an existing drawing with the new one, use the **XREF** command so that AutoCAD creates a *reference* to the Floor drawing. This allows the size of the new drawing to remain small because the Floor drawing has not been combined with it.

The following procedure allows you to enter model space, reference an existing drawing to the new one, and zoom the view to see the referenced drawing.

1. If the layout tab is active, double-click inside the viewport to activate model space within the viewport.
2. Set the Xref layer current.

3. Pick **External Reference...** from the **Insert** pull-down menu. The **Select Reference File** dialog box is displayed. See **Figure 24-20.**
4. Select Floor.dwg in the dialog box, and pick the **OK** button.

The **External Reference** dialog box is displayed. Set the insertion point to 0,0,0, the X, Y, and Z scale to 1.0, and the rotation angle to 0. Pick the **OK** button and perform a **ZOOM Extents**. Your drawing should now resemble the one shown in **Figure 24-21.**

Figure 24-20.
The Floor.dwg drawing is selected in the **Select Reference File** dialog box.

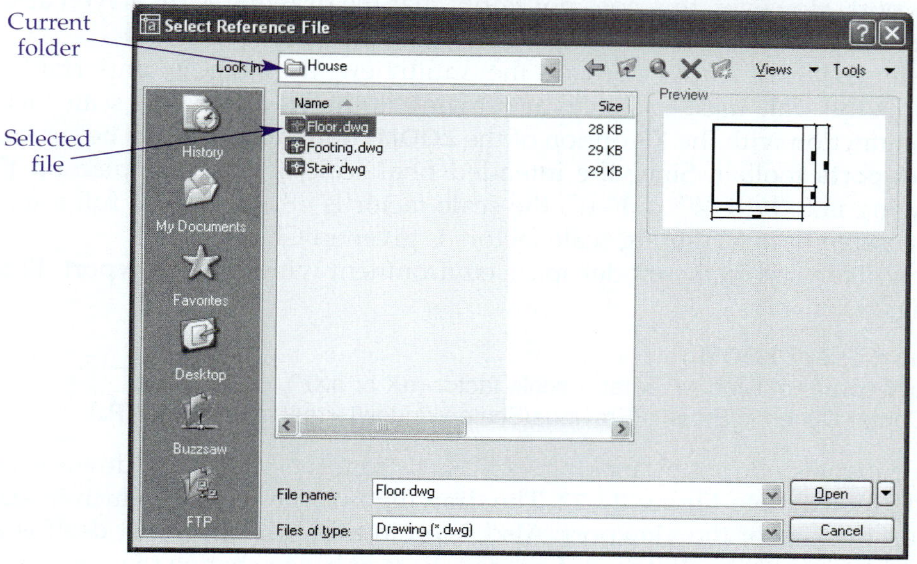

Figure 24-21.
The floor plan is referenced into the first viewport.

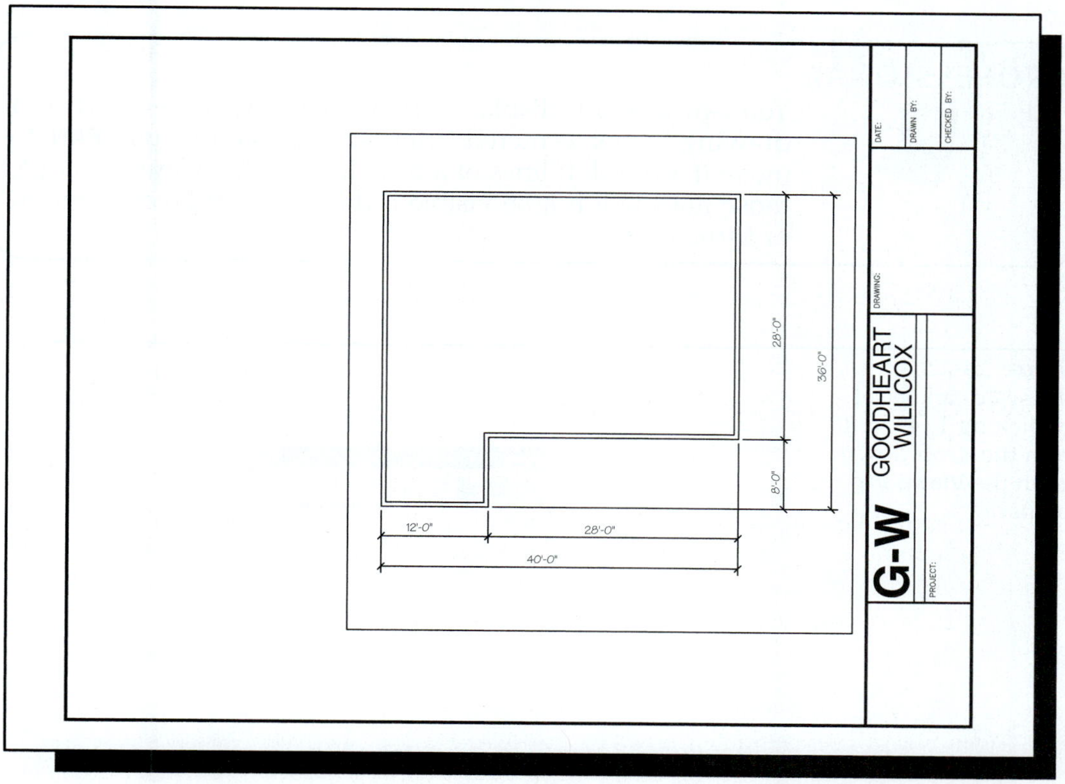

All layers on the referenced drawing are added to the new drawing. These layers can be distinguished from existing layers because the drawing name is automatically placed in front of the layer name and separated by a vertical bar symbol (|). This naming convention is shown in the **Layer Control** drop-down list in the **Object Properties** toolbar and in the **Layer Properties Manager** dialog box.

Scaling a Drawing in a Viewport

When a drawing has been referenced and placed in a viewport, it is ready to be scaled. After using the **Extents** option of the **ZOOM** command, the referenced drawing fills the viewport. However, this does not imply that the drawing is displayed at the correct scale.

The scale factor of each view of the multiview drawing is important to remember; it is the scale used to size your drawing in the viewport. The scale factor is used in conjunction with the **XP** option of the **ZOOM** command, or it can be selected from the **Viewports** toolbar. Since the intended final scale of the floor plan on the plotted drawing is to be 1/4″ = 1′–0″, the scale factor is 48, or 1/48 of full size. A detailed discussion of determining scale factors is given in Chapter 11.

Be sure you are still in the model space environment within the viewport. Enter the following:

Command: **Z** *or* **ZOOM**↵
Specify corner of window, enter a scale factor (nX or nXP), or
[All/Center/Dynamic/Extents/Previous/Scale/Window] <real time>: **1/48XP**↵

The scale can also be set by picking 1/4″ = 1′ from the scale drop-down list in the **Viewports** toolbar. See Figure 24-22. The drawing may not change much in size, depending on the size of the viewport. Also, keep in mind the viewport itself is an object that can be moved or stretched if needed. Remember to change to paper space when editing the size of the viewport. If part of your drawing extends beyond the edge of the viewport after applying the scale, simply use grips or the **STRETCH** command to change the size of the viewport.

PROFESSIONAL TIP

You can use any display command inside a viewport. If a drawing is not centered after scaling, simply use **PAN** to move it around. If lines of a drawing touch a viewport edge, those lines will not be visible if the viewport layer is frozen or turned off.

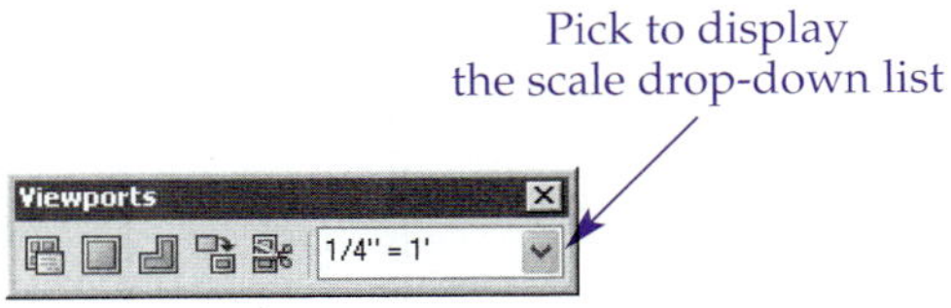

Figure 24-22.
The scale can be set by picking 1/4″ = 1′ from the drop-down list in the **Viewports** toolbar.

Controlling Viewport Layer Visibility

If you create another viewport, the floor plan will immediately fill it. This is because a viewport is just a window through which you can view a drawing or 3D model that has been referenced to the current drawing. One way to control what is visible in subsequent viewports is to freeze all layers of the Floor drawing in any new viewports that are created. Access the **Layer Properties Manager** dialog box and set all layers from the Floor xref to be frozen in new viewports by picking the icons in the **New VP Freeze** column. When the snowflake icon appears in this column, the layer is not displayed in any new viewports.

The frozen or thawed status in the current viewport is controlled by the icons in the **Current VP Freeze** column.

> **PROFESSIONAL TIP**
>
> Use the [Shift] and [Ctrl] keys in combination with picking to select multiple layer names. When multiple layers are selected, toggling one setting makes the same new setting apply to all highlighted layer names.

> **NOTE**
>
> The **New VP Freeze** and **Current VP Freeze** settings in the **Layer Properties Manager** dialog box can also be set using the **VPLAYER** command at the Command: prompt.

Creating Additional Viewports

The previous example of creating a viewport and referencing a drawing to it is the same process that is used to create the additional two viewports for the Stair and Footing drawings. In this case, two viewports are created before using the **XREF** command. If you know the number, size, and location of all viewports needed on a multiview drawing, it may save time to create them all at once.

> **PROFESSIONAL TIP**
>
> Viewports can always be added, deleted, or resized on a drawing. So, if your class or company uses standard sheet layouts containing several views, create and save templates that contain viewports.

Now that the floor plan layers will be frozen in new viewports, the other two viewports can be created. Use the following procedure:

1. Double-click outside the viewport to activate paper space.
2. Set the Viewports layer current.
3. Draw a viewport to the dimensions shown in Figure 24-23 using the **Polygonal Viewport** button in the **Viewports** toolbar.
4. Draw a third viewport 6″ wide and 5″ high.

The final arrangement of the three viewports is shown in Figure 24-24.

Now that the viewports are complete, you can begin referencing the remaining two drawings. The following procedure uses **DesignCenter** to reference the Stair drawing:

1. Set the current layer to Xref, and double-click in the lower-left viewport to make model space active.

Figure 24-23.
Draw this polygonal viewport.

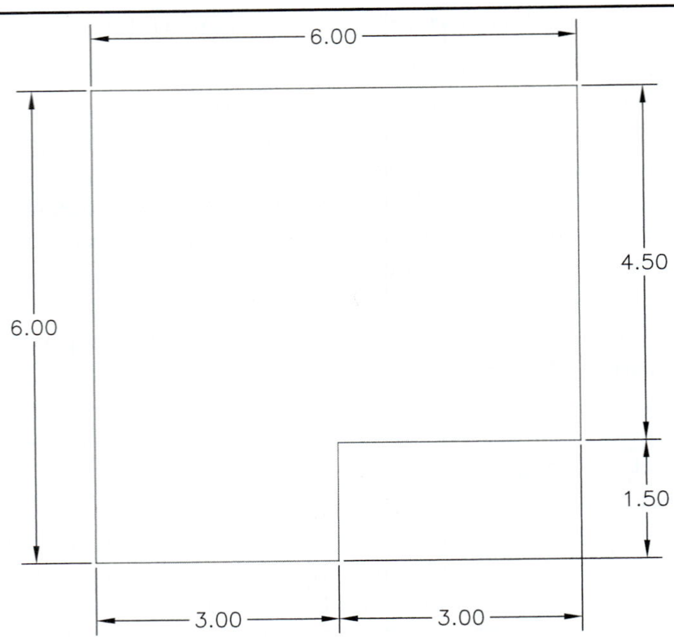

Figure 24-24.
Two additional viewports are placed and sized in the drawing.

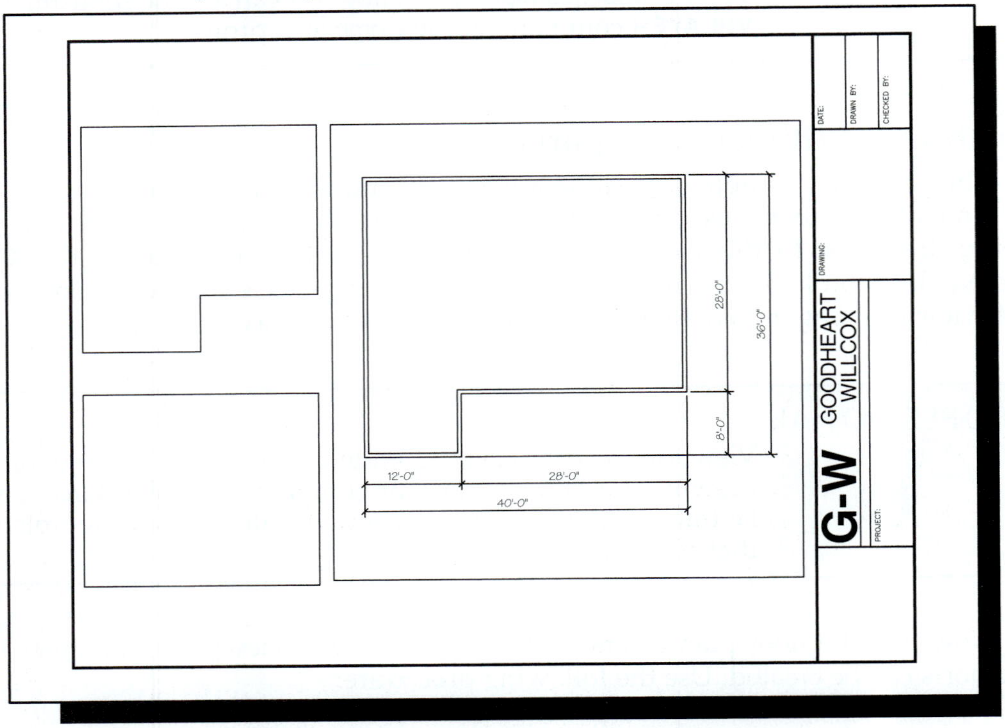

2. Activate **DesignCenter**. Locate the folder that contains the Stair.dwg file and pick it. Files contained in the selected folder are displayed in the **Content** area.
3. Right-click on the Stair.dwg file and select **Attach as Xref...** from the shortcut menu. The **External Reference** dialog box is displayed. Use 0,0,0 for the insertion point, 1.0 for the scale, and 0 for the rotation angle.
4. Press [Ctrl]+[2] to temporarily dismiss **DesignCenter**.
5. The scale factor for the Stair drawing is 32. Use the **ZOOM** command and enter 1/32XP to scale the drawing correctly.

The drawing now appears as shown in Figure 24-25. Notice the Stair drawing is shown in all three viewports. Use the **Layer Properties Manager** dialog box to freeze the stair layers in selected viewports using the following procedure:

1. Pick in the large viewport to make it active.
2. Open the **Layer Properties Manager** dialog box.
3. Select all layers that begin with the name of the referenced drawing you wish to freeze in the active viewport. In this case, all layers that begin with Stair are selected.
4. Pick the sun icon in the **Current VP Freeze** column of one of the selected layers. All selected icons change to a snowflake. Pick **OK**. The Stair drawing is now removed from the large viewport.

Repeat this procedure to freeze the stair layers in the upper-left viewport.

The final drawing can now be inserted into the last viewport. Prepare the third view by following these steps:

1. Double-click in the upper-left viewport.
2. Set the Xref layer current.
3. Attach the Footing drawing as an xref using one of the methods explained earlier in this chapter.
4. Freeze the Footing layers in the other two viewports.
5. Use the **ZOOM** command and enter 1/16XP.

   The drawing should now appear as shown in Figure 24-26.

NOTE

Be sure to set the current layer to Xref when referencing a drawing so the inserted drawing is not placed on another layer, such as Viewports.

Figure 24-25.
The reference drawing Stair is displayed in all viewports. Use the **Layer Properties Manager** dialog box to restrict its visibility.

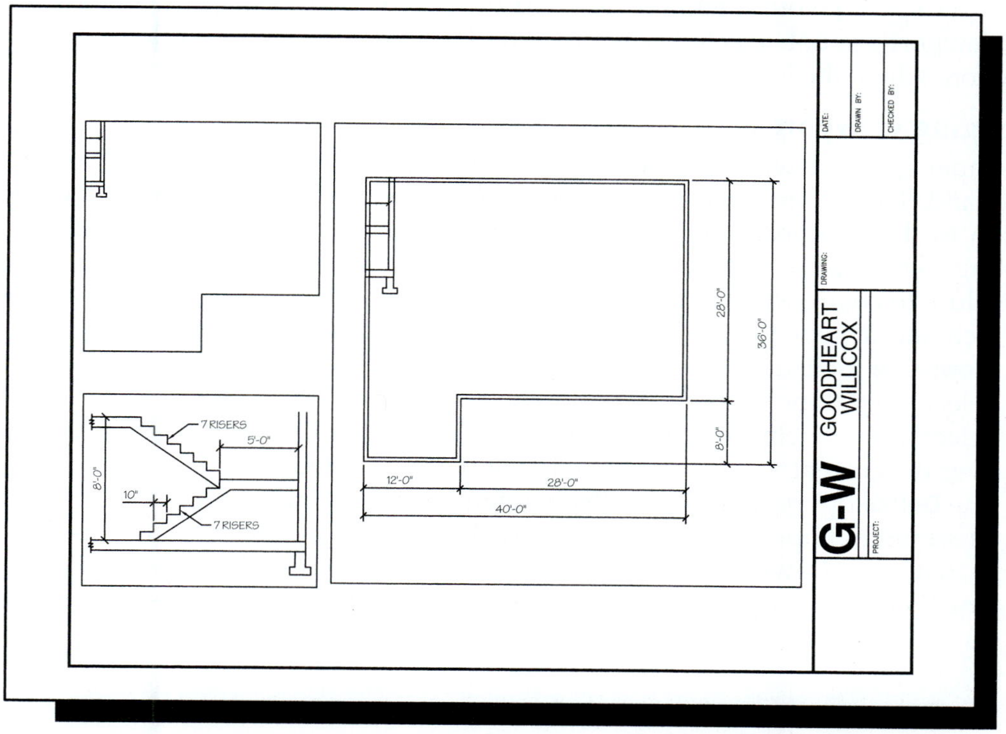

Figure 24-26.
The drawing is completed by referencing the Footing drawing.

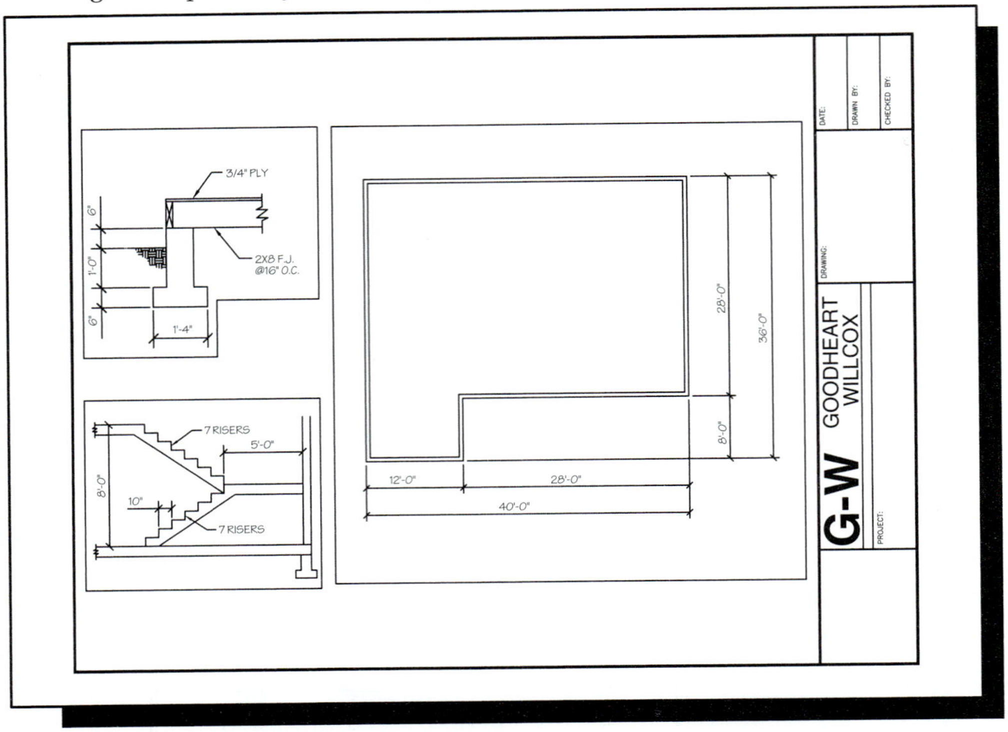

Adjusting Viewport Display, Size, and Location

If you need to adjust a drawing within a viewport, first be sure that model space is current. Then, pick the desired viewport to make it active, and use an appropriate display command, such as **ZOOM** or **PAN**.

The entire viewport can be moved to another location, but you must first activate the paper space layout. Pick the viewport border to display its grips. Objects inside the viewport are not selected when picking because they are in model space. After selection, adjust the location of the viewports.

Changing viewport shape and size

Paper space viewport shape and size can be quickly changed using the **VPCLIP** command. This command can also be accessed by selecting the **Clip Existing Viewport** button in the **Viewports** toolbar. A viewport can be clipped by either selecting an existing shape that has been drawn or by drawing a new polygon. Use the following procedure to change the shape of a viewport.

1. Activate a paper space layout. Pick the **Clip Existing Viewport** button in the **Viewports** toolbar.
2. Select the outline of the viewport to be resized.
3. Select the new clipping object, such as a circle that has been previously drawn over the current viewport. The old viewport is deleted.

The **Delete** option of the **VPCLIP** command enables you to delete a viewport that was previously clipped. It prompts you to select the clipping object, which is the new shape that was drawn to clip the old viewport. After selecting the viewport and pressing [Enter], the original viewport is redrawn and the clipped version is deleted.

Locking the viewport scale

Once a drawing has been scaled properly inside a viewport, it is important to avoid using a zoom again prior to plotting. AutoCAD provides a viewport locking feature that helps prevent inadvertent zooms. To lock the display in a viewport, access the **Properties** window and then select the viewport from paper space. Change the Display locked property to Yes. Repeat the procedure for all viewports you wish to lock.

Adding notes and titles

There are two ways in which titles and notes can be added to a multiview drawing with referenced drawings. The first method is to add the notations to the original drawing. In this manner, all titles and notes are referenced to the new drawing. This is the best system to use if the titles, scale label, and notes will not change.

However, titles may change. You may want to be sure that all titles of views use the same text style, or you might want to add a special symbol. This is easily completed after the drawings are referenced. The most important thing to remember is that the paper space layout must be active to add text. You can use new and existing text styles to add titles and notes to a drawing using the **TEXT** or **MTEXT** command. See **Figure 24-27.**

Removing viewport outlines

The viewport outlines can be turned off for plotting purposes, as shown in **Figure 24-27.** Open the **Layer Properties Manager** dialog box and click on the plot icon for the appropriate layer. A diagonal slash is placed over the symbol, indicating that the layer will not plot.

Figure 24-27.
The completed drawing with titles added and viewport outlines turned off.

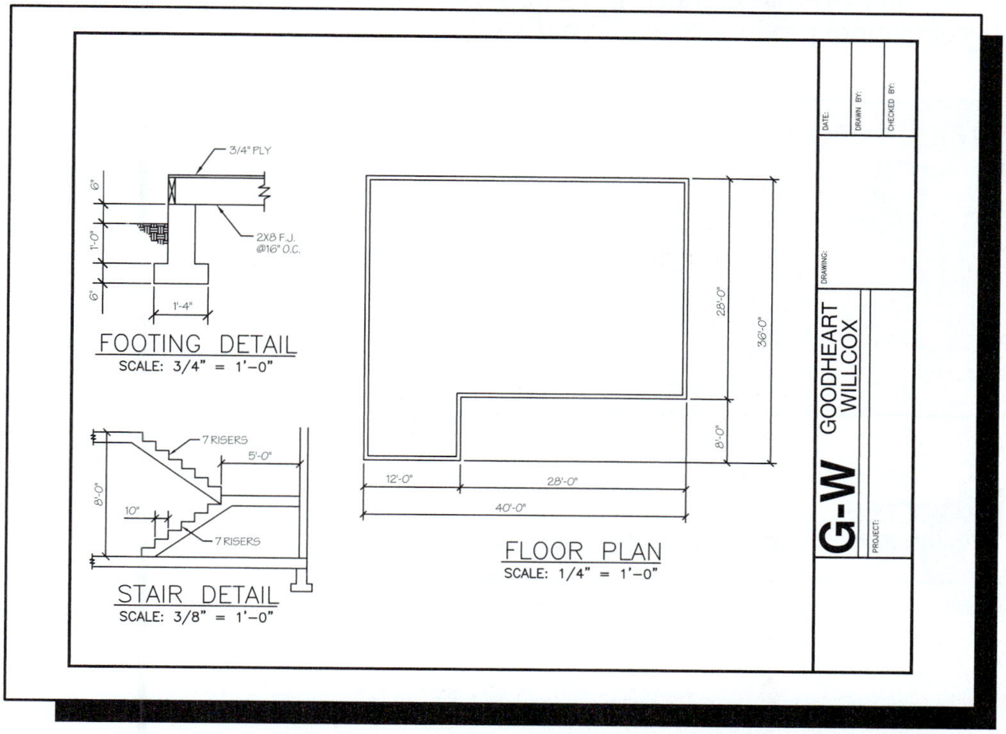

NOTE

If you freeze the Viewports layer and a box still surrounds one of the views, you are probably still in model space. Remember that a box outlines the current viewport in model space. Enter PS at the Command: prompt or pick the **Model** button on the status bar to enter paper space and the outline disappears.

Plotting a Multiview Drawing

You have already taken care of scaling the views because you used the **XP** option of the **ZOOM** command when you referenced them. The drawing that now appears on your screen in paper space can be plotted at full scale, 1 = 1, with the PLOT command.

Using the **PLOT** command in this manner is a simple procedure, but only if you planned your drawing at the start of the project. The process of creating a properly scaled multiview layout will go smoothly if you have planned the project. Review the following items, and keep them in mind when starting any drawing or design project—especially one that involves the creation of a multiview paper space layout.

- Determine the size of paper to be used.
- Determine the type of title block, notes, revision blocks, parts lists, etc., that will appear on the drawing.
- Prepare a quick sketch of the view layouts and their plotted scales.
- Determine the scales to be used for each viewport.
- Establish proper text styles and heights based on the drawing scale factors.
- Set the **DIMSCALE** variable using the proper scale factor when creating drawings in model space.

There is no substitute for planning a project before you begin. It may seem like an unnecessary expense of time, but it will save time later in the project, and may help you become more productive in all your work.

PROFESSIONAL TIP

You may never have to specify a scale other than full (1 = 1) when plotting. Any object or design, whether 2D or 3D, can be referenced into a border and title block drawing, scaled with **ZOOM XP**, and then plotted. Try using the paper space layout procedure for all your drawings, even if they are just a single view. You will find that you need fewer border and title block template drawings, and the process will become quicker.

EXERCISE 24-2 Complete the Exercise on the Student CD.

Chapter Test

Answer the following questions on a separate sheet of paper.

1. When inserting an xref, how does the **Overlay** option differ from the **Attach** option?
2. What effect does the use of referenced drawings have on drawing file size?
3. When are xrefs updated in the master drawing?
4. Why would you want to bind a dependent object to a master drawing?
5. What does the layer name WALL0NOTES mean?
6. What is the purpose of the **Detach** option in the **Xref Manager** dialog box?
7. What are spatial and layer indexes, and what function do they perform?
8. What are the three types of paths that can be used for storing an xref?
9. What command is used to edit external references in place?
10. What command allows you to open a parent xref drawing into a new AutoCAD drawing window by selecting the xref in the master drawing?
11. What is the function of the **VPCLIP** command?
12. What is the purpose of locking a viewport?
13. Indicate the command and value you would use to specify a 1/2″ = 1′-0″ scale inside a viewport.
14. How do you freeze all layers of a referenced drawing inside any new viewports?
15. Do you need to be in paper space or model space in order to resize a viewport?
16. Explain why you should plan your plots.

Drawing Problems

1. Open one of your dimensioned drawings from Chapter 19. Construct a multiview layout and generate a plot on C-size paper.
   A. Create four viewports of equal size, separated by 1″ of empty space.
   B. Select each viewport and display a different view of the drawing.
   C. Plot the drawing and be sure to use the scale of 1:1.
   D. Save the drawing as P24-1.
2. Open one of your dimensioned drawings from Chapter 19. Construct a multiview layout and generate a plot on C-size or B-size paper. Plot at the scale of 1:1.
3. Open one of your dimensioned drawings from Chapter 20. Construct a multiview layout and generate a plot on C-size or B-size paper. Plot at the scale of 1:1.
4. Open one of your dimensioned drawings from Chapter 21. Construct a multiview layout and generate a plot on C-size or B-size paper. Plot at the scale of 1:1.

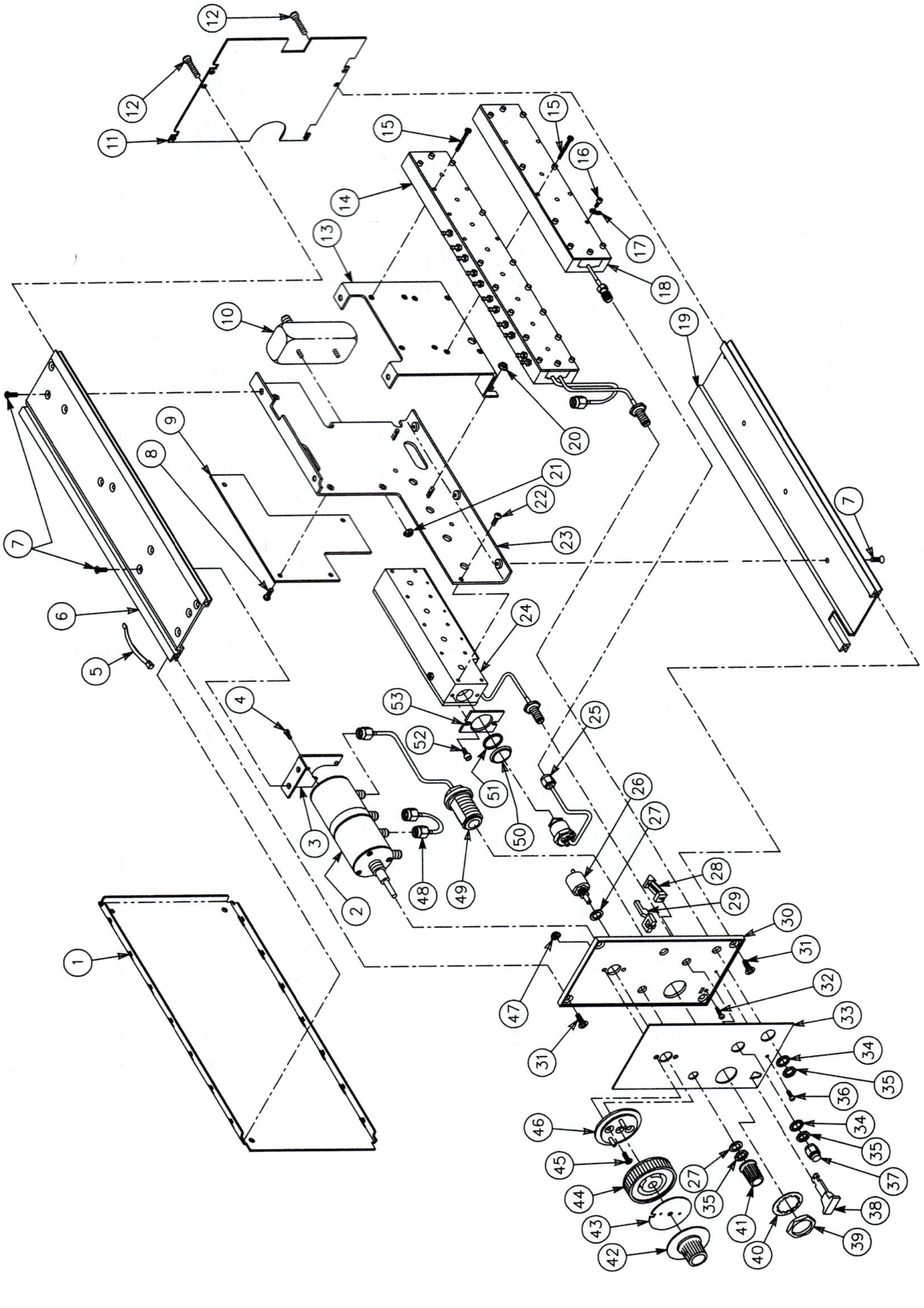

Assembly drawing. (Tektronox, Inc.)

CHAPTER 25

Sheet Sets

Learning Objectives

After completing this chapter, you will be able to do the following:

- Identify and describe the functions of the **Sheet Set Manager**.
- Create sheet sets.
- Add sheets and sheet views to a sheet set.
- Plot and publish a set of sheets.
- Insert callout blocks and view labels into sheet views.
- Set up custom properties for a sheet set.
- Create a sheet list table.
- Archive a set of electronic files for a sheet set.

Organizing and distributing drawings during the course of a design project can involve a wide range of tasks. Drawings often need to be shared with clients and other personnel to make sure the design is accurate and any changes are incorporated. As the project is developed, a set of drawings is used to build the design. The design can be relatively simple, such as the views for a mechanical part, or complex, such as the plans for a building or new highway off-ramp. While a simple mechanical part may only call for one drawing sheet for manufacturing, a 10-story office building may require a set of 100 sheets or more. Although design needs vary, the ability to organize drawings for exchange purposes is important because any project typically involves input from a number of sources. This capability becomes critical at the end of the project, when delivery of the drawings must take place in an orderly manner.

AutoCAD provides a tool that helps simplify the management of a project with multiple drawings and views. This tool is the **Sheet Set Manager**. This chapter discusses how to use the **Sheet Set Manager** to structure different drawing layouts into groups of files for reviewing, plotting, and publishing purposes.

NOTE

Sheet sets combine many AutoCAD features to automate and organize the entire drawing set for a project. To understand and effectively apply sheet sets, you must understand templates (Chapter 2), fields (Chapter 8), views (Chapter 10), layouts (Chapter 11), blocks (Chapter 22), attributes (Chapter 23), and external references (Chapter 24). If you encounter difficulties in understanding an aspect of sheet sets, it may be helpful to review the underlying concept being applied.

AutoCAD 2005 NEW FEATURE

Sheet Sets Overview

A ***sheet set*** is a collection of drawing sheets for a project. The term ***sheet*** refers to a drawing produced for the project. A sheet is a layout tab in a drawing file, and can have additional project-specific properties.

All sheets in a sheet set can use a single template. The template can contain a title block with attributes containing fields. The field values may include items such as project name and sheet number. Thus, if the project name changes during the course of the project, the field can be modified in the template, and the change is automatically applied to all sheets within the set. If a new sheet is inserted into the sheet sets, the sheet numbers and all sheet references update automatically. This automation can save a great deal of time and improve the accuracy of the set of drawings.

Sheets can contain ***sheet views***. A sheet view is any referenced portion of a drawing set, such as an elevation, a section, or a detail. Sheet views can be automatically labeled, placed on separate sheets, and referenced to each other through the use of blocks with attributes containing fields. Like the title block fields discussed in the previous paragraphs, these sheet view field values update automatically to reflect changes in sheet numbering.

Once the sheet set is complete, you can easily print, publish, and archive the entire set in a single operation. This is very efficient. For example, it is far easier to plot a sheet set containing twenty sheets than to open and print twenty separate drawings.

AutoCAD 2005 NEW FEATURE

Introduction to the Sheet Set Manager

SHEETSET
SSM
[Ctrl]+[4]

Tools
➡ **Sheet Set Manager**

Standard toolbar

Sheet Set Manager

Sheet sets are created, organized, and accessed using the **Sheet Set Manager**. To open the **Sheet Set Manager,** pick the **Sheet Set Manager** button on the **Standard** toolbar, select **Sheet Set Manager** from the **Tools** pull-down menu, enter SSM or SHEETSET at the Command: prompt, or use the [Ctrl]+[4] key combination. See **Figure 25-1A.** The window is divided into three tabs: the **Sheet List** tab, the **View List** tab, and the **Resource Drawings** tab. The **Sheet Set Control** drop-down list is used to open and create sheet sets. See **Figure 25-1B.** The buttons next to the drop-down list are used to control and manage the items listed in the **Sheet Set Manager** window. These buttons vary depending on the currently selected tab. The area at the bottom of the window (labeled **Details** or **Preview**) is used to show a text description or preview image of a selected sheet or view.

The **Sheet Set Manager** is a modeless dialog box. It can be resized, docked, and set to auto-hide. The Expand/Collapse buttons in the upper and lower portions of the **Sheet Set Manager** window can be used to hide or display the information. The **Details** and **Preview** areas can be toggled by picking the appropriate button on the title bar.

Figure 25-1.
The **Sheet Set Manager**. A—The window contains the **Sheet List**, **View List**, and **Resource Drawings** tabs. B—The **Sheet Set Control** drop-down list contains options for creating and opening a sheet set.

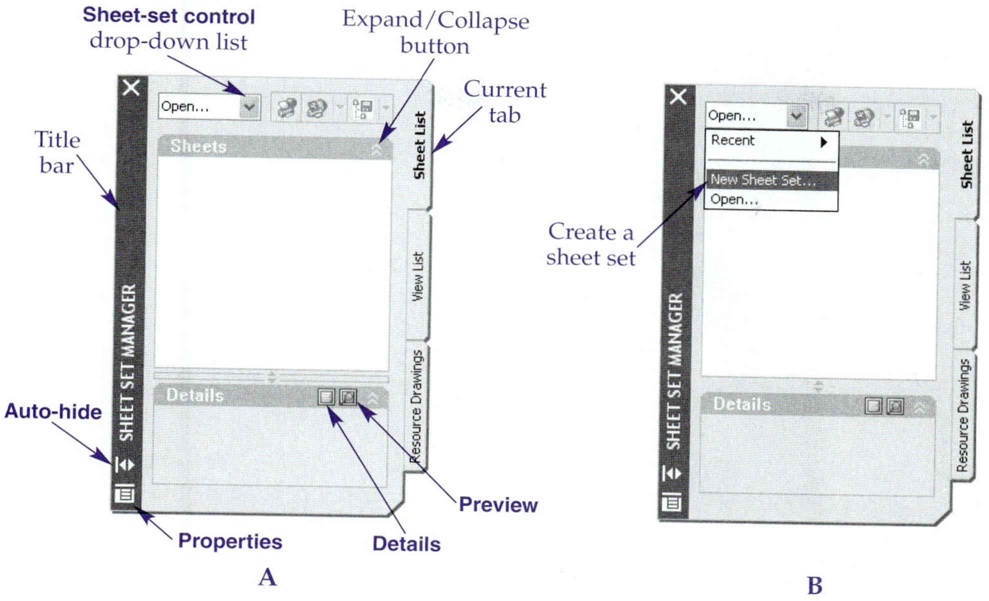

Creating Sheet Sets

AutoCAD 2005 NEW FEATURE

Sheet sets are created with the **Create Sheet Set** wizard. They can be created from an example sheet set or from existing drawing files.

Creating a Sheet Set from an Example Sheet Set

When you create a new sheet using an example sheet set, you select an existing sheet set as a model, and then modify it as needed to fit the needs of the new sheet set. AutoCAD provides several example sheet sets based on different drafting disciplines. You are not limited to the provided examples—you can use any sheet set as the example sheet set.

To create a new sheet set from an example sheet set, open the **Sheet Set Manager** and select **New Sheet Set...** from the **Sheet Set Control** drop-down list. Refer to **Figure 25-1B.** This opens the **Create Sheet Set** wizard. See **Figure 25-2.** This wizard steps you through the process of creating a sheet set.

The **Begin** page of the **Create Sheet Set** wizard provides two options. Pick **An example sheet set** to start your sheet set using an example sheet set. The second option, **Existing drawings**, is discussed in the next section. Pick the **Next** button to display the **Sheet Set Example** page, **Figure 25-3.**

Sheet set information is saved in a DST file (sheet set data file). When creating a sheet set from an example sheet set, you are starting from the existing DST file. The list box on the **Sheet Set Example** page lists all DST files in the default Templates folder. You can pick one of these sheet sets, or select the second option and select a DST file from another folder.

After selecting the DST file for the example sheet set, pick the **Next** button to display the **Sheet Set Details** page. See **Figure 25-4.** This page allows you to modify the existing sheet set data and create settings for your new project.

Enter the name of the sheet set in the **Name of new sheet set** text box. This is typically the project number or a short description of the project. A description for the

Figure 25-2.
Select **An example sheet set** on the **Begin** page to use an AutoCAD sheet set template.

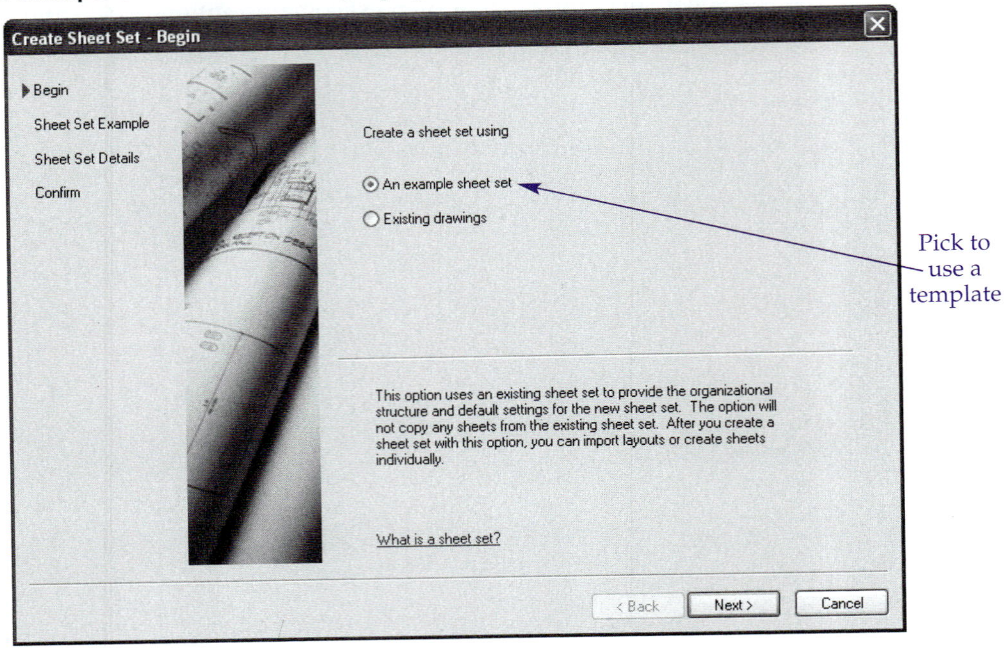

Figure 25-3.
Use the **Sheet Set Example** page to select an example sheet set.

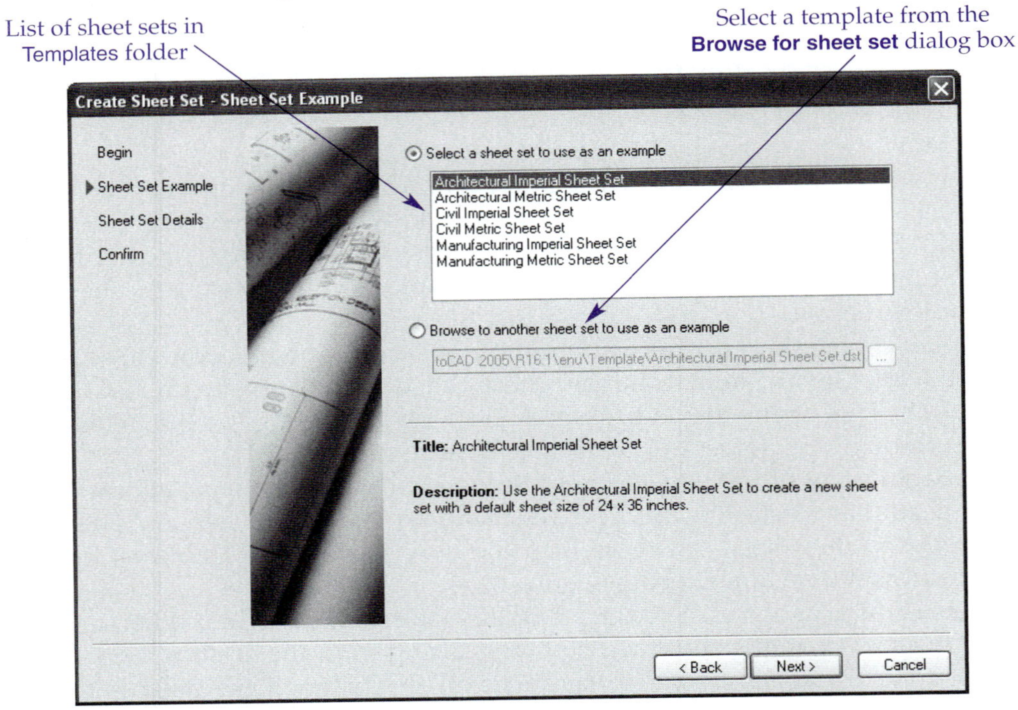

Figure 25-4.
Enter a name, description, and file path location for the new sheet set on the **Sheet Set Details** page.

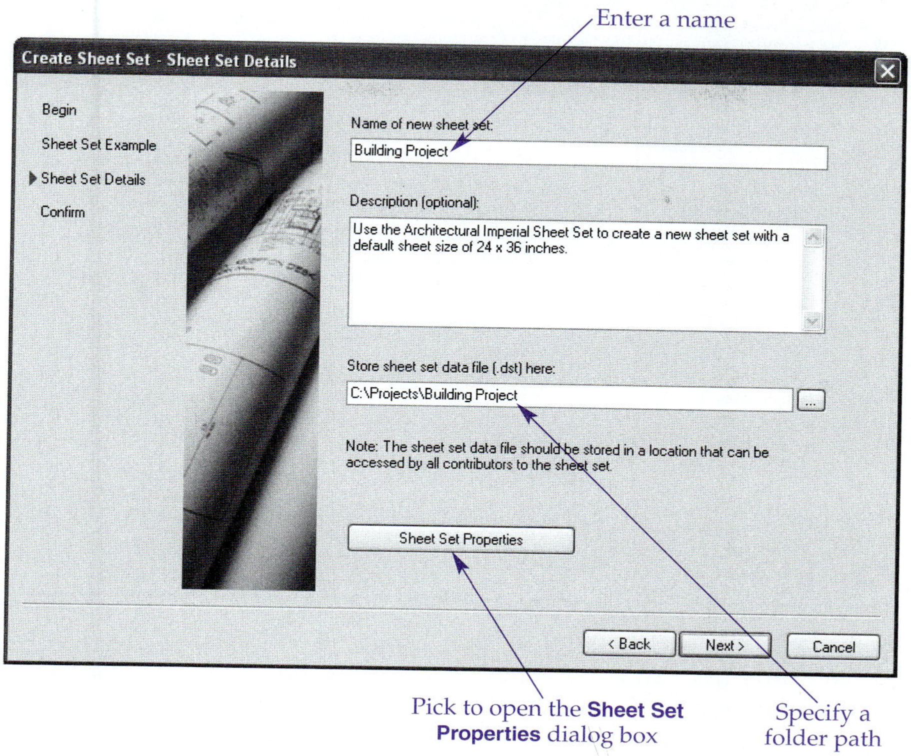

sheet set can be entered in the **Description** area. The **Store sheet set data file (.dst) here** text box determines where the sheet set file is saved on the hard drive. Picking the **Sheet Set Properties** button opens the **Sheet Set Properties** dialog box. See Figure 25-5. The main settings for the sheet set are specified in this dialog box. There are three sections. The properties in the **Sheet Set** section are explained as follows:

- **Name**. This is the title for the sheet set. This can be changed by clicking in the field and modifying the current name.
- **Sheet set data file**. This is the location of the DST file for the sheet set.
- **Description**. This is the description of the sheet set.
- **Resource drawing location(s)**. This text box specifies the folder(s) containing drawing files that are used for the sheet set. To modify this setting, pick in the text box, pick the ellipsis (...) button, and select a folder in the dialog box. Objects and views from resource drawings are inserted into sheets as views. This is discussed later in this chapter.
- **Label block for views**. Specifies the block used to label views. This is discussed later in this chapter.
- **Callout blocks**. Specifies blocks available for use as callout blocks. This is discussed later in this chapter.
- **Page setup overrides file**. Specifies the location of an AutoCAD template file (DWT file) containing a page setup to be used to override the existing sheet layout settings.

The properties in the **Sheet Creation** section determine the location for the drawing files for new sheets and the template used to create them. When a new sheet is added to a sheet set, AutoCAD creates a new drawing file based on the template and layout specified in the **Sheet creation template** setting. The folder path in the **Sheet storage location** field determines where the new file is saved. It is important to specify the correct location so you know where the files are being saved.

Figure 25-5.
The main properties of a sheet set are stored in the **Sheet Set Properties** dialog box.

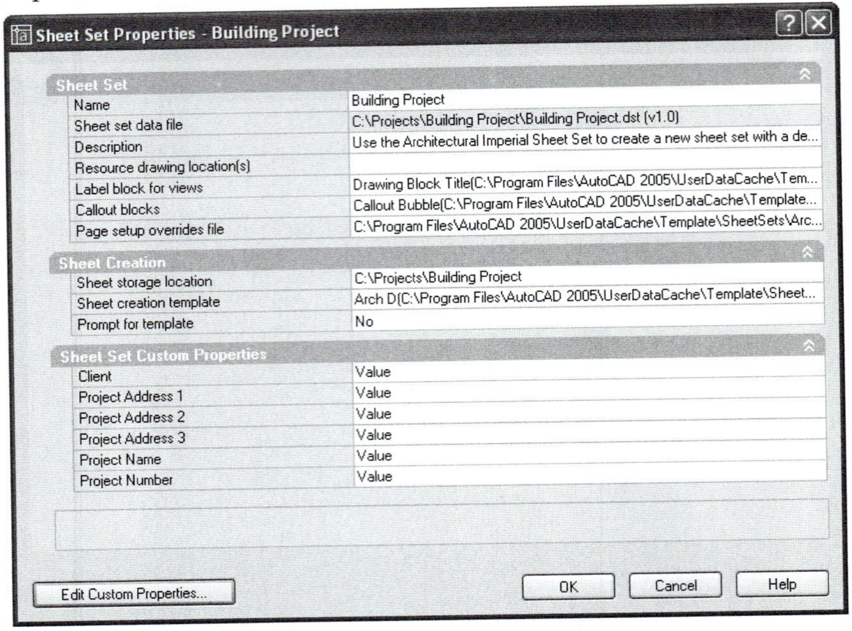

When selecting the **Sheet creation template** value, you must specify both a template file and a layout. To modify this setting, pick in the text box and then pick the ellipsis (**...**) button. This displays the **Select Layout as Sheet Template** dialog box, Figure 25-6. All layouts in the selected template are displayed in the list box. Select the layout and then pick **OK**.

If the value in the **Prompt for template** field is set to **No**, the template layout specified in the **Sheet creation template** field is automatically used when a new sheet is created. This is the default setting. If the field value is set to **Yes**, you can select a different layout when creating a new sheet.

Information specific to the project can be set up in the **Sheet Set Custom Properties** section. This topic is discussed later in this chapter.

Once all the values are set in the **Sheet Set Properties** dialog box, pick **OK**. This returns you to the **Sheet Set Details** page. Pick the **Next** button to continue creating the new sheet set. The **Sheet Set Preview** area on the **Confirm** page displays all of the information associated with the sheet set. See Figure 25-7. In the example shown, a sheet set named Building Project has been created. This sheet set contains a number of

Figure 25-6.
An existing layout is used as a template for new sheets in a sheet set.

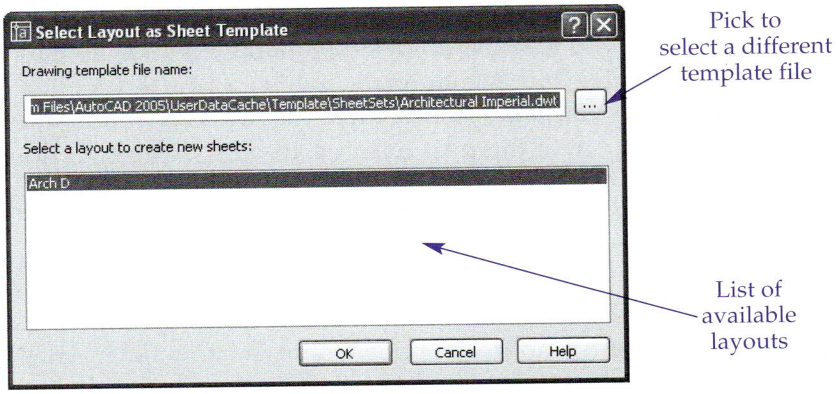

Figure 25-7.
Use the **Confirm** page to preview settings before creating the sheet set.

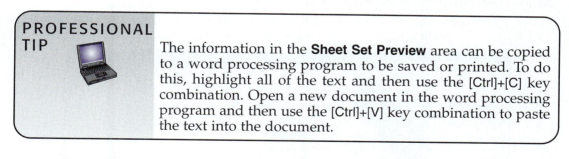

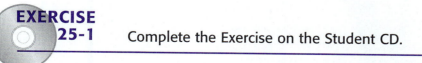

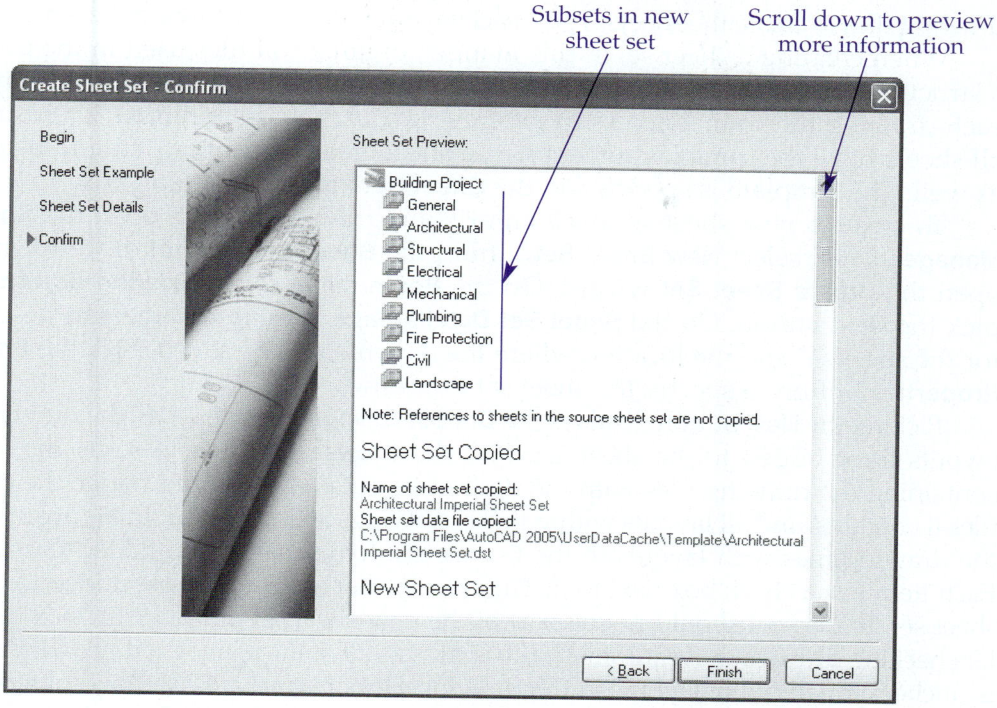

subgroups related to the project, such as **General** and **Architectural**. These are called *subsets*. After the sheet set is created, sheets can be added to each subset.

After reviewing the information on the **Confirm** page, pick the **Finish** button to create the sheet set. If a setting needs to be changed, use the **Back** button.

PROFESSIONAL TIP

The information in the **Sheet Set Preview** area can be copied to a word processing program to be saved or printed. To do this, highlight all of the text and then use the [Ctrl]+[C] key combination. Open a new document in the word processing program and then use the [Ctrl]+[V] key combination to paste the text into the document.

When the **Finish** button is picked, the sheet set data file is saved to the specified location. The sheet set can then be opened in the **Sheet Set Manager**. Since a sheet set is not associated with a particular drawing file, any sheet set can be opened, regardless of the open drawing file.

EXERCISE 25-1

Complete the Exercise on the Student CD.

AutoCAD 2005
NEW FEATURE

Creating a Sheet Set from Existing Drawing Files

You can use existing drawings to create a sheet set. Layouts are imported from the drawing files to create the sheets. Thus, each layout within the drawings becomes a sheet.

When creating a sheet set in this manner, organize all files used in the project in a structured hierarchy of folders. Also, it is recommended to have only one layout in each drawing file so that access to different layout tabs is simplified. To ensure that all sheets have the same layout settings, a sheet creation template should be created as well. The template is specified in the **Sheet Set Properties** dialog box.

To create a new sheet set from an existing drawing project, open the **Sheet Set Manager**. Then select **New Sheet Set...** from the **Sheet Set Control** drop-down list to open the **Create Sheet Set** wizard. On the **Begin** page, select **Existing drawings** and pick the **Next** button. On the **Sheet Set Details** page, specify a name and description for the sheet set and the location where the data file will be saved. Pick the **Sheet Set Properties** button to specify the sheet set properties.

Picking the **Next** button displays the **Choose Layouts** page. Specify the drawings and layouts to be added to the sheet set. Pick the **Browse...** button to select the folder(s) containing the drawing files with the desired layouts. The selected folder, the drawing files it contains, and all layouts within those drawings are displayed. In **Figure 25-8,** all of the drawing files with layouts in the Commercial folder have been added for selection. Each item has a check box next to it. The layouts that are checked are added to the new sheet set. If a layout should not be part of the new sheet set, uncheck the box next to it. Unchecking a drawing file automatically unchecks all of the layouts within it. If the folder is unchecked, all of the layouts in the drawing files are unchecked. More folders can be added to the **Choose Layouts** page by using the **Browse for Folder** dialog box.

Figure 25-8.
Existing layouts can be imported to a new sheet set from the **Choose Layouts** page. Layouts from drawing files in the Commercial folder are imported for addition to the new sheet set. The layouts must have a check next to them to be added to the sheet set.

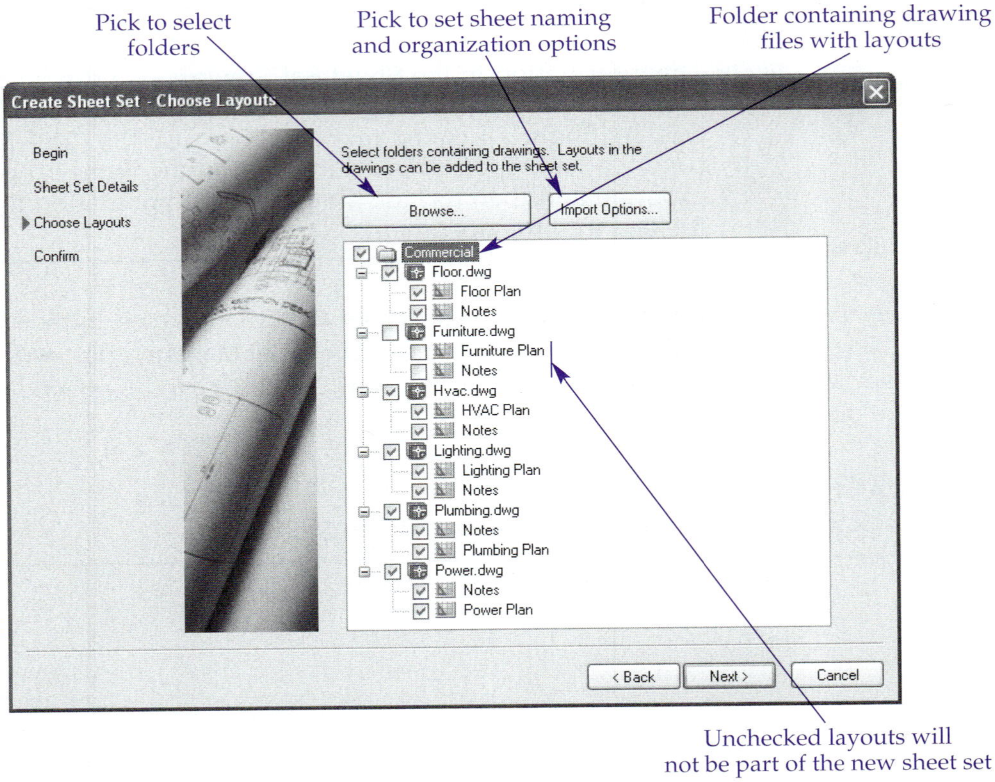

When a sheet set is created using existing layouts, the name for a new sheet can be the same as the layout name, or it can be the drawing file name combined with the layout name. Sheet naming options can be accessed by picking the **Import Options...** button to display the **Import Options** dialog box. See Figure 25-9. If the **Prefix sheet titles with file name** check box is checked, the layouts that become sheets are named with the drawing file name and the name of the layout. For example, if a layout named First Floor Electrical is imported from the drawing file Electrical Plan.dwg, the sheet that is created is named Electrical Plan – First Floor Electrical. To have the sheets take on only the layout name, uncheck this check box.

When importing layouts, a sheet set can be organized so that the folders are grouped into subsets of the sheet set. If the **Create subsets based on folder structure** option is checked in the **Import Options** dialog box, all of the folder names added to the sheet set become subsets. The layouts in the folders are added under each subset. The **Ignore top level folder** option determines whether a subset in the sheet set is created for the folder name at the top level. The example in Figure 25-10A shows the **Choose Layouts** page with layouts imported from the Residential folder for the Residential Project sheet set. This sheet set has been created with the **Create subsets based on folder structure** and **Ignore top level folder** options checked in the **Import Options** dialog box. The result of this configuration is shown in the **Sheet Set Manager** in Figure 25-10B. Creating subsets for sheet sets helps organize the sheets.

Notice how the sheets are named in Figure 25-10B. Each sheet has a number preceding its name. By default, a sheet is displayed in the **Sheet Set Manager** with its number, a dash, and then the name of the sheet. In the example shown, the drawing file name is used as a prefix for the sheet name.

When all folders and layouts have been selected for the new sheet set, and all settings have been specified, pick the **Next** button on the **Choose Layouts** page. This displays the **Confirm** page. In the **Sheet Set Preview** area, review the sheet set properties. Pick the **Finish** button to create the new sheet set. If a setting needs to be changed, use the **Back** button.

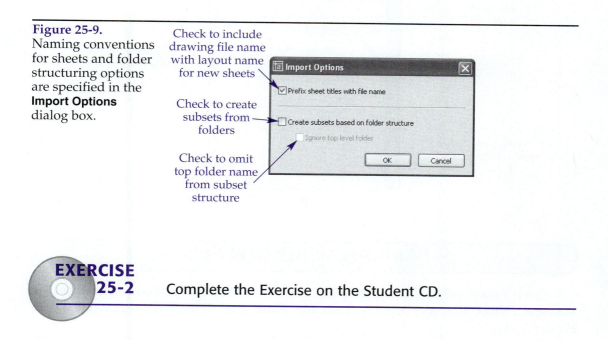

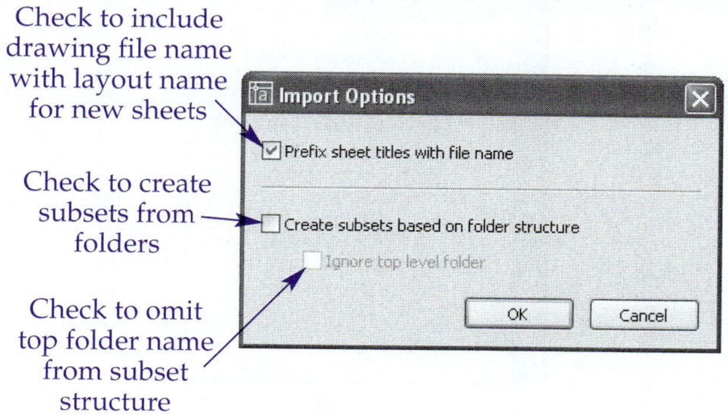

Figure 25-9.
Naming conventions for sheets and folder structuring options are specified in the **Import Options** dialog box.

EXERCISE 25-2 Complete the Exercise on the Student CD.

Figure 25-10.
Creating a sheet set named Residential Project with subsets. A—Layouts are imported from the Residential folder. The drawing files are stored in the Architectural and Structural subfolders. The subfolders are designated as subsets for the new sheet set. B—After creating the sheet set and opening it in the **Sheet Set Manager**, the subsets are shown. Notice that the Residential folder is not included as a subset. This was set in the **Import Options** dialog box.

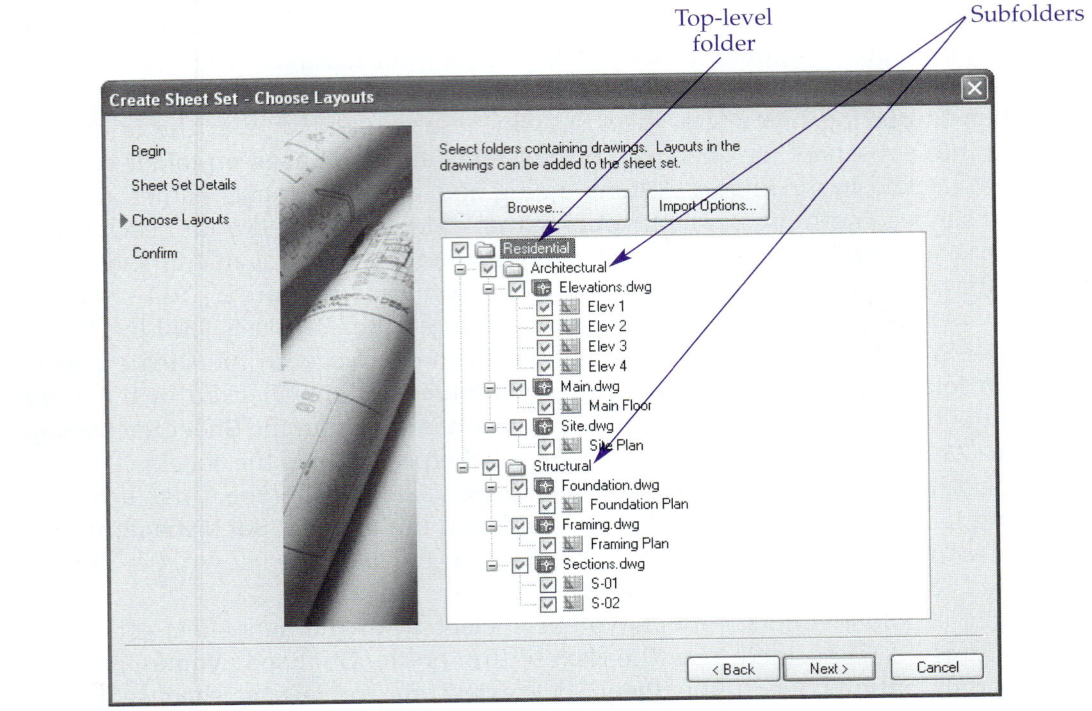

A

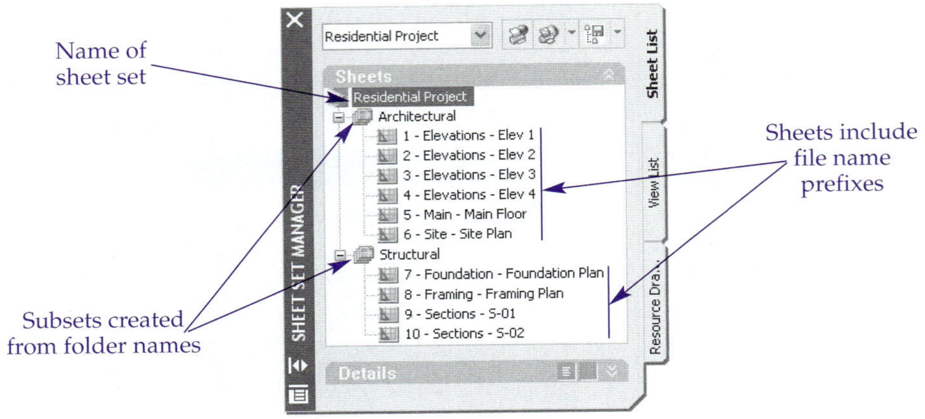

B

AutoCAD 2005 NEW FEATURE

Working with Sheet Sets

Once a sheet set has been created, it can be accessed and edited in the **Sheet Set Manager**. Sheet sets are opened from the **Sheet Set Control** drop-down list. See **Figure 25-11.**

The top area lists the sheet sets that have been opened in the current AutoCAD session. When AutoCAD is closed, this area is cleared. Selecting **Recent** displays a list of the most recently opened sheet sets. Selecting **Open...** displays the **Open Sheet Set** dialog box. You can then navigate to a sheet set data file (DST file) and open it in the

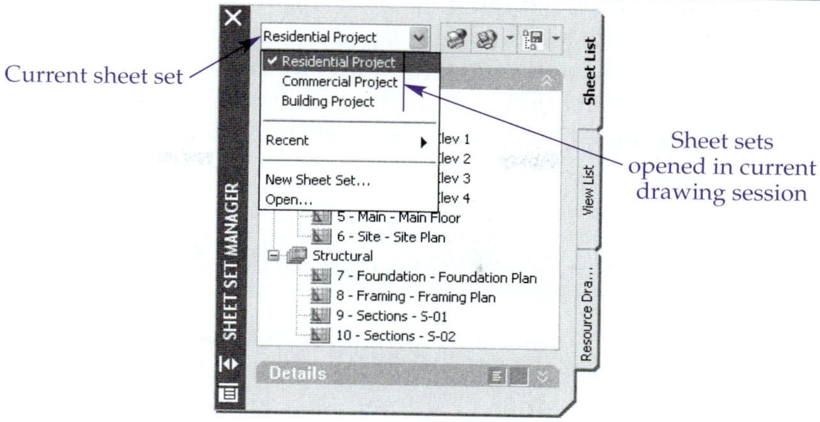

Figure 25-11.
The **Sheet Set Control** drop-down list displays recently opened sheet sets. Picking **Open...** allows you to browse for a sheet set that is not in the list.

Sheet Set Manager. A sheet set can also be opened by selecting **Open Sheet Set...** from the **File** pull-down menu.

Sheets in a sheet set are managed in the **Sheet List** tab of the **Sheet Set Manager**. Sheet views are managed in the **View List** tab, and drawing files with layouts are managed in the **Resource Drawings** tab. Almost all of the options for working with sheet sets are available from shortcut menus. Right-clicking over a sheet set displays the shortcut menu shown in **Figure 25-12.** The menu options are explained as follows:

- **Close Sheet Set.** Removes the sheet set from the **Sheet Set Manager** window.
- **New Sheet.** Creates a new sheet in the sheet set.
- **New Subset.** Creates a new subset in the sheet set.
- **Import Layout as Sheet.** Creates a new sheet containing an existing layout.
- **Resave All Sheets.** Updates the drawing files that are part of the current sheet set. All of the drawing files that are part of the sheet set need to be closed first. An open drawing file cannot be updated.
- **Archive.** Saves all drawing files and associated files to one location. Archiving a sheet set is discussed later in this chapter.
- **Publish.** Displays the **Publish** cascading menu. Different options for publishing and plotting a sheet set are available. These options are discussed later in this chapter.
- **eTransmit.** Displays the **Create Transmittal** dialog box for use with the **eTransmit** feature. This option is very similar to the **Archive** option. It is used to package together files and associated files for Internet exchange. The **eTransmit** feature is discussed in detail in *AutoCAD and Its Applications—Advanced*.
- **Transmittal Setups.** Displays the **Transmittal Setups** dialog box, which is used to configure **eTransmit** settings.

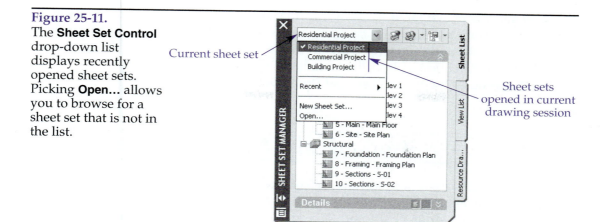

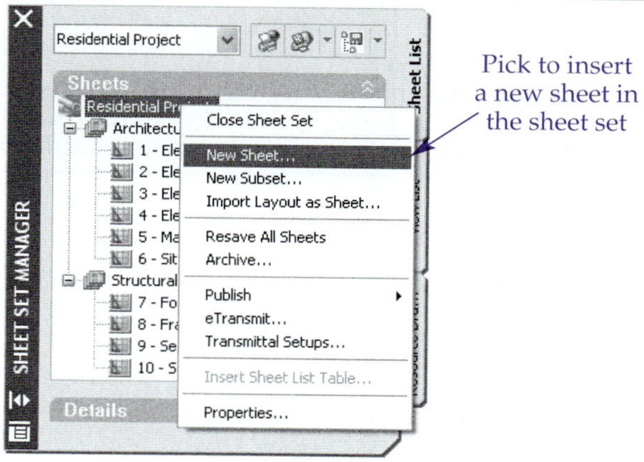

Figure 25-12.
This shortcut menu is displayed by right-clicking over a sheet set name in the **Sheet List** tab.

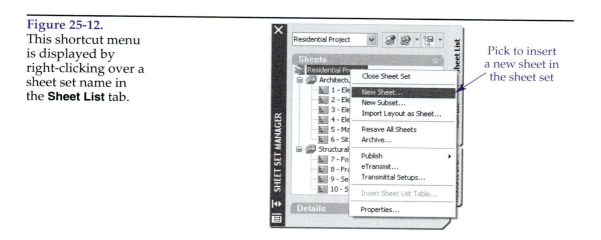

- **Insert Sheet List Table.** Gathers information about all the sheets in the sheet set and inserts the data into the drawing as a table. This option is only available when a drawing file with a layout in the sheet set is open with the layout tab current. Creating a sheet list table is discussed later in this chapter.
- **Properties.** Opens the **Sheet Set Properties** dialog box.

AutoCAD 2005 NEW FEATURE

Working with Subsets

As previously discussed, subsets are subgroups within a sheet set created to help organize the sheets. Creating subsets is similar to creating subfolders under a top-level folder in Windows Explorer. The subsets are created to help manage the contents of the sheet set. For example, if there are ten architectural sheets, ten electrical sheets, and ten plumbing sheets in a sheet set, the three subsets Architectural, Electrical, and Plumbing can be created to store the related sheets.

AutoCAD 2005 NEW FEATURE

Creating a New Subset

A new subset can be created by right-clicking over the sheet set name or an existing subset in the **Sheet Set Manager** and selecting **New Subset…** from the shortcut menu. This opens the **Subset Properties** dialog box. See Figure 25-13. The name of the new subset is entered in the **Subset name** text box. If a subset is being created for all of the electrical sheets in a sheet set, for example, then the subset can be named Electrical. When a new sheet is added to the subset using a template, the sheet is saved as a drawing file to the hard drive. The **Store new sheet DWG files in** setting determines the path to which new sheets are saved. The default value is the location specified when the sheet set was initially created.

Each subset can also have its own template and layout for new sheets. This is specified in the **Sheet creation template for subset** setting. For example, if the electrical sheets use their own title block and notes, a template sheet with these settings should be used. Specify the template and layout for a subset is identical to the procedure used in selecting the sheet set properties.

Figure 25-13.
Settings for a new subset are made in the **Subset Properties** dialog box.

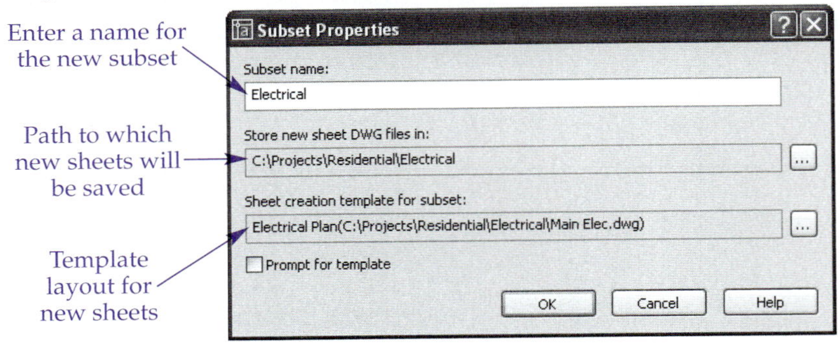

Modifying a Subset

AutoCAD 2005 NEW FEATURE

After a subset has been created, its settings can be modified by right-clicking over the subset and selecting **Properties...** from the shortcut menu. This displays the **Subset Properties** dialog box. The **Rename Subset...** shortcut menu option also opens the **Subset Properties** dialog box.

A subset can be deleted by right-clicking over the subset and selecting **Remove Subset** from the shortcut menu. If the subset contains sheets, this option is grayed out. In this case, the sheets need to be moved to a different subset or deleted before the subset can be removed.

EXERCISE 25-3 Complete the Exercise on the Student CD.

Working with Sheets

AutoCAD 2005 NEW FEATURE

One of the most useful features of the **Sheet Set Manager** is the ability to open a sheet quickly for reviewing or modifying. A sheet can be opened by double-clicking on the sheet, or by right-clicking over the sheet and selecting **Open** from the shortcut menu. The drawing file that contains the referenced layout tab is then opened in AutoCAD, and the layout is set current.

NOTE When files are opened from the **Sheet Set Manager**, they are added to the open files list. If many files are opened, it can affect the performance of AutoCAD. Use the **Window** pull-down menu to view all of the open files. Save and close files that are no longer needed.

Adding a Sheet Using a Template

AutoCAD 2005 NEW FEATURE

A new sheet can be added to a sheet set by using the template layout sheet or by importing an existing layout. To add a sheet using the template, right-click on the sheet set name or the subset where the sheet needs to be added, and then select **New Sheet...** from the shortcut menu. This displays the **New Sheet** dialog box. See **Figure 25-14.**

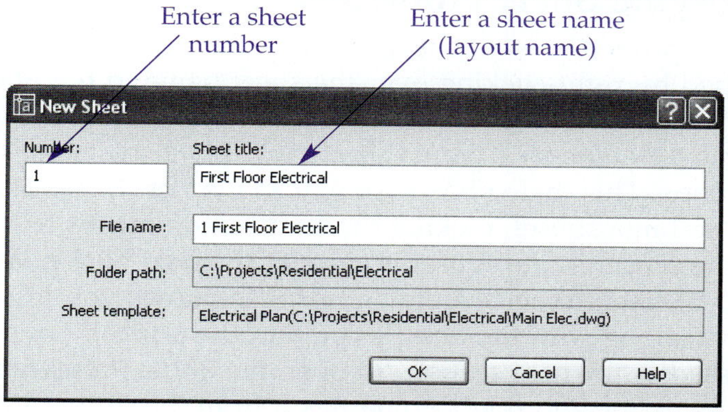

Figure 25-14. When creating a new sheet from a template, the sheet is defined in the **New Sheet** dialog box.

Enter the sheet number in the **Number** text box and the sheet name in the **Sheet title** text box (for example, First Floor Electrical). A new drawing file is created. The sheet title becomes the name of the layout in the drawing file. Enter the name for the file in the **File name** text box. By default, this is the sheet number and title. The **Folder path** field shows where the drawing file will be saved. This path is specified in the **Subset Properties** or **Sheet Set Properties** dialog box.

AutoCAD 2005
NEW FEATURE

Adding an Existing Layout as a Sheet

To add an existing layout to a sheet set, right-click on the sheet set name or the subset in which the sheet needs to be added. Then select **Import Layout as Sheet** from the shortcut menu. This displays the **Import Layouts as Sheets** dialog box. See Figure 25-15. Pick the ellipsis (**...**) button to select a drawing file. The layouts from the drawing file are then listed in the list box. The **Status** field indicates whether the layout can be imported into the sheet set. If a layout is already part of a sheet set, it cannot be imported. To import a layout, select the layout and then pick **OK**. Multiple sheets can be selected by holding the [Ctrl] key or [Shift] key down and selecting the different layouts. If the **Prefix sheet titles with file name** check box is checked, the name of the file is included in the sheet title.

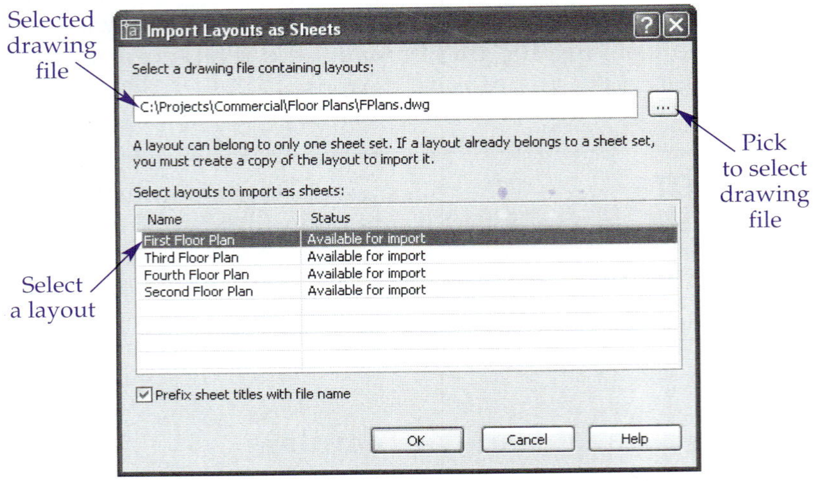

Figure 25-15. Existing layouts can be added as sheets to a sheet set from the **Import Layouts as Sheets** dialog box. The layouts from the selected drawing file are listed.

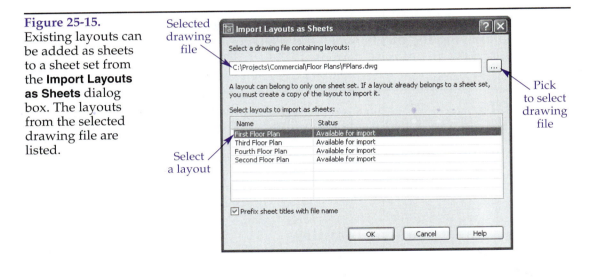

EXERCISE 25-4 Complete the Exercise on the Student CD.

AutoCAD 2005
NEW FEATURE

Modifying Sheet Properties

The properties of a sheet, such as the name, number, and description, can be modified by right-clicking over the sheet name in the **Sheet Set Manager** to display the sheet shortcut menu. The sheet name and number can be changed by selecting **Rename & Renumber...** from this menu. This displays the **Rename & Renumber Sheet** dialog box. This dialog box is similar to the **New Sheet** dialog box. If the sheet is one of several in a subset, picking the **Next** button moves to the next sheet in the subset. If the last sheet in the subset is current, the **Next** button is grayed out.

The **Sheet Properties** dialog box also allows you to change the sheet name and number, along with the description and the publish option. Publishing a sheet set is discussed in the next section. To open the **Sheet Properties** dialog box, right-click on the sheet name and select **Properties...** from the shortcut menu. The **Sheet Properties** dialog box is shown in Figure 25-16. A description of the sheet can be entered in the

Figure 25-16.
The properties of a sheet can be modified in the **Sheet Properties** dialog box.

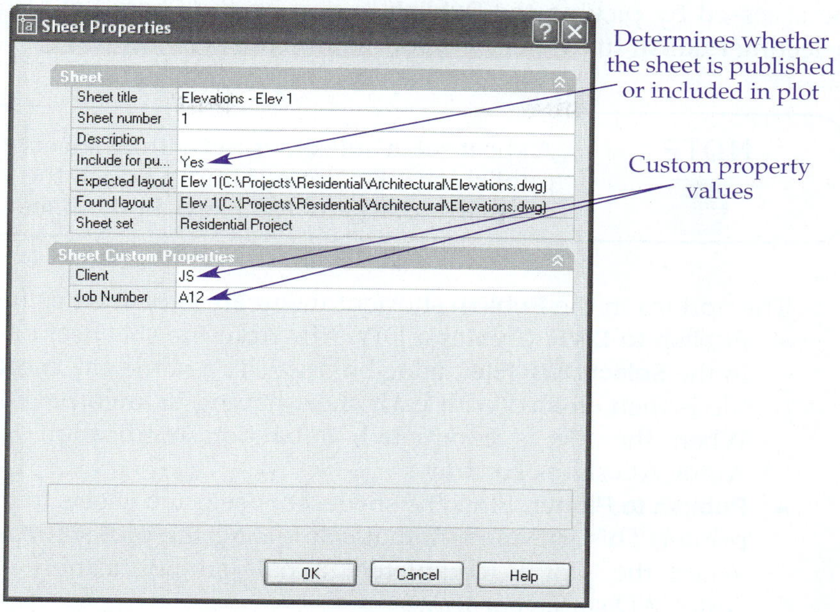

Description text box. The **Include for publish** option determines whether the sheet is included when the sheet set is published or plotted. The default value is **Yes**.

The **Expected layout** and **Found layout** text boxes display the file path where the sheet was originally saved and the file path where the sheet was found. If the paths are different, you can update the **Expected layout** field by picking the ellipsis (...) button.

If custom property fields have been set up for the sheet, they are displayed in the **Sheet Custom Properties** area. Custom property fields are discussed later in this chapter.

A sheet can be deleted from a sheet set by selecting **Remove Sheet** from the sheet shortcut menu. This does not delete the drawing file from the hard drive, it only removes the sheet from the sheet set.

> **NOTE**
>
> If the hard drive location of a drawing file is modified, and the drawing file has layouts that are associated with a sheet set, the association is broken. The layouts need to be reimported into the sheet set, or the specified path to the drawing file must be updated in the **Sheet Properties** dialog box.

Publishing a Sheet Set

AutoCAD 2005 NEW FEATURE

In AutoCAD, ***publishing*** refers to the creation of electronic files for distribution purposes or the plotting of hard copy prints. As is the case with other collections of drawing files, sheet sets can be published by creating drawing web format (DWF) files. DWF files are compressed, vector-based files that can be viewed with the Autodesk DWF Viewer, which is installed with AutoCAD. A sheet set can also be published by sending it to a plotter. AutoCAD's plotting and publishing functions were introduced in Chapter 11. For more information about outputting DWF files, refer to ***AutoCAD and Its Applications—Advanced***.

An entire sheet set can be published to a DWF file or plotted using the options in the **Publish** shortcut menu in the **Sheet Set Manager**. The **Publish** shortcut menu can be accessed by picking the **Publish** button on the **Sheet Set Manager** toolbar or by selecting **Publish** from the sheet shortcut menu. See **Figure 25-17.**

> **NOTE** A sheet set, a subset, or individual sheets can be selected for publishing at a time. Simply select the appropriate items using the [Shift] and [Ctrl] keys in the **Sheet Set Manager**.

The options in the **Publish** shortcut menu are explained as follows:

- **Publish to DWF.** Creates a DWF file from the sheet set or the selected sheets. In the **Select DWF File** dialog box, specify a name and location for the file. The file is then created with each sheet having its own page in a multisheet file. When the file is completed, a balloon notification is displayed in the AutoCAD status bar tray.
- **Publish to Plotter.** Plots the sheet set or selected sheets to the default plotter or printer. This is done automatically using the plot settings from each layout. When the plot is completed, a balloon notification is displayed in the AutoCAD status bar tray.
- **Publish using Page Setup Override.** Displays the page setups that are available for use as overrides. Selecting a page setup from the list forces the sheet to use the selected page setup settings instead of the plot settings that are saved with the layout. If a page setup override has not been specified for the sheet set or subset, this option is grayed out.
- **Include Plot Stamp.** If checked, places the plot stamp information for the layout on the sheet when it is plotted.
- **Plot Stamp Settings.** Opens the **Plot Stamp** dialog box to specify the plot stamp settings.
- **Manage Page Setups.** Opens the **Page Setup Manager**. A new page setup can be created or an existing one can be modified.
- **Sheet Set Publish Options.** Displays the **Sheet Set Publish Options** dialog box. This displays the available settings for creating a DWF file.
- **Publish Dialog box.** Opens the **Publish** dialog box. All of the sheets that are in the current sheet set or the sheet selection are listed.

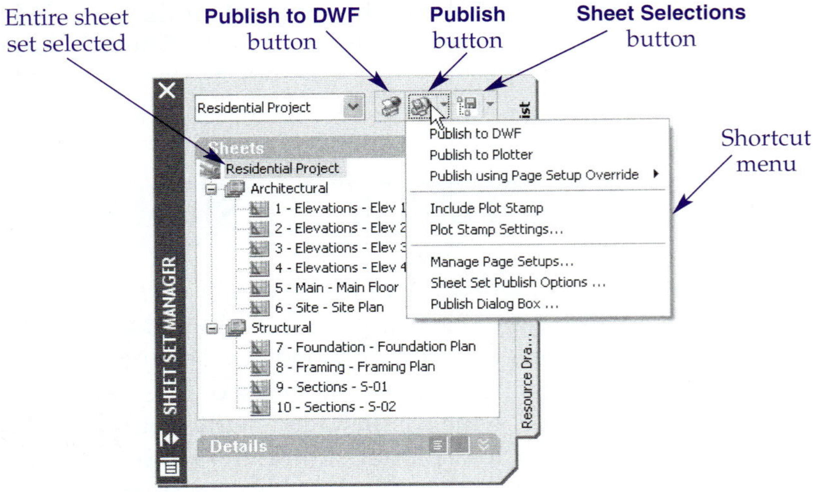

Figure 25-17. The **Publish** shortcut menu options are used to prepare a sheet set for publishing or plotting.

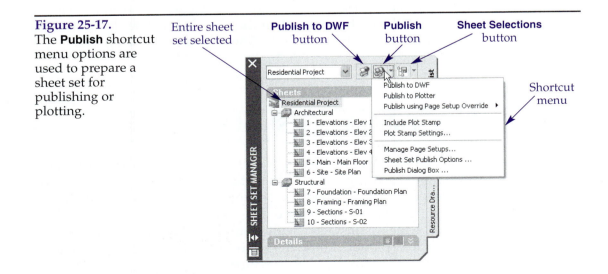

Creating Sheet Selection Sets

AutoCAD 2005 NEW FEATURE

During the course of a project, the same set of sheets may need to be published many times. A selection of sheets can be saved so that it can be accessed again quickly for publishing. To save a sheet selection set, select the sheets to be included in the set. Remember, if you want to select all of the sheets in a subset, simply select the subset. Then pick the **Sheet Selections** button on the **Sheet Set Manager** toolbar and select **Create...** from the shortcut menu. In the **New Sheet Selection** dialog box, enter a name for the selection set and pick **OK**. The new selection set is then listed when the **Sheet Selections** button is picked. In **Figure 25-18,** three different sheet selection sets are shown. When a selection set is selected from the shortcut menu, the sheets are automatically highlighted in the **Sheet Set Manager**.

To rename or delete a sheet selection set, pick **Manage...** from the **Sheet Selections** shortcut menu. In the **Sheet Selections** dialog box, select the sheet selection set and then pick the **Rename** or **Delete** button.

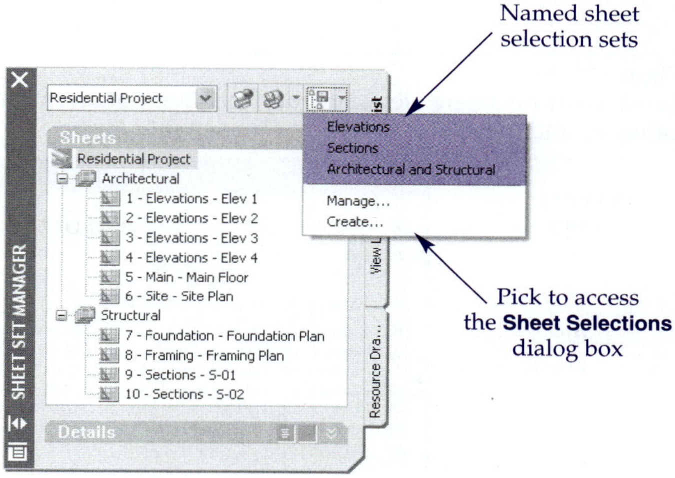

Figure 25-18. Sheet selection sets can be created from selected sheets or subsets in a sheet set. They are accessed from the **Sheet Selections** shortcut menu.

Sheet Views

AutoCAD 2005 NEW FEATURE

As previously discussed, sheet views are views within sheets that are typically referenced at another location in the sheet set. Sheet views are typically sections, elevations, and details. The **View List** tab of the **Sheet Set Manager** is used to manage sheet views. Using this tab, views can be grouped by category and opened for viewing and editing.

Special tools in the **Sheet Set Manager** can be used to identify views with numbers, labels, and callout blocks. This section discusses the methods used to create and manage views in the **Sheet Set Manager**.

Adding a View Category

AutoCAD 2005 NEW FEATURE

View categories are used to organize views in the **View List** tab. View categories are similar to subsets created in the **Sheet List** tab. To create a new view category, make the **View List** tab current. See **Figure 25-19.** Pick the **New View Category** button or right-click on the sheet set name and select **New View Category...** from the shortcut menu. This opens the **View Category** dialog box. See **Figure 25-20.** In the **Category name** text box, enter a name for the category. For example, if there are going to be four elevation views added to the new category, it could be named Elevations.

Figure 25-19.
View categories and views are created in the **View List** tab of the **Sheet Set Manager**.

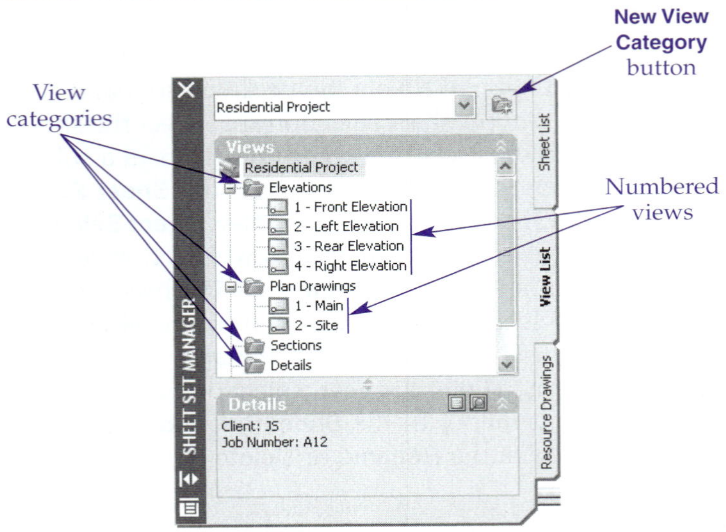

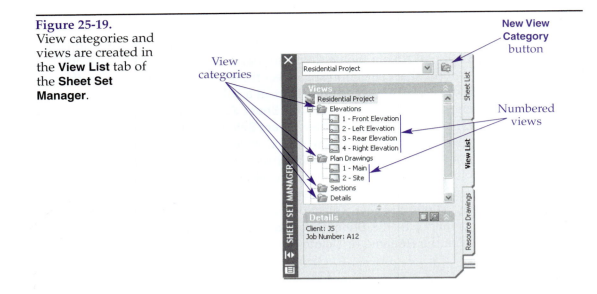

Figure 25-20.
When creating a new view category, the **View Category** dialog box is used to name the category and select callout blocks for use with views.

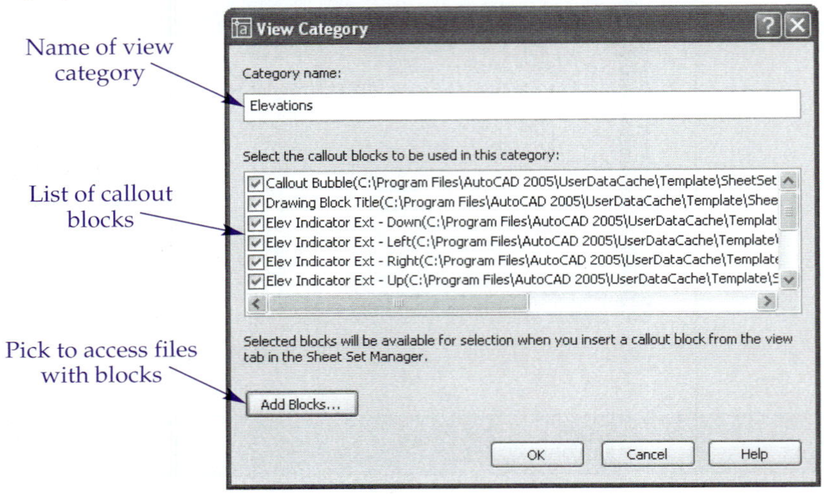

The **View Category** dialog box lists all of the available callout blocks for the current view category. Check the box next to the callout block to have it available for all of the views that are added to this category. If a block is not in the list, use the **Add Blocks...** button to select it from a drawing file. Once the necessary callout blocks are selected, pick the **OK** button to create the new category. Callout blocks are discussed later in this chapter.

AutoCAD 2005 NEW FEATURE

Modifying a Category

The properties for a category can be modified by right-clicking over the category name in the **Sheet Set Manager** and selecting **Rename...** or **Properties...** from the shortcut menu. Selecting either one of these options opens the **View Category** dialog box. The category name can be changed and different callout blocks can be added to the category.

A category can be deleted by right-clicking over the category name and selecting **Remove Category** from the shortcut menu. If there are views under the category, this option is grayed out. In this case, the views need to be removed before the category can be deleted.

Creating Sheet Views in an Existing Sheet

AutoCAD 2005 NEW FEATURE

New views can be added to sheets and organized within sheet sets from the **Sheet Set Manager**. Use the following procedure to add a view to an existing sheet set:

1. Open the desired sheet set and add a category for the view if it is not already created.
2. To add a view to a sheet, the sheet has to be a part of the sheet set. If the sheet has not been added to the sheet set, add it now.
3. Open the drawing file and set the layout tab current where the new view will be created.
4. Use display commands to orient the view as needed and then enter the **VIEW** command.
5. In the **View** dialog box, pick the **New...** button to open the **New View** dialog box.
6. Select the category that you want the view to be a part of from the **View category** drop-down list. See **Figure 25-21.**
7. Specify the rest of the view settings and pick **OK** to save the view.

The newly saved view now appears in the **Sheet Set Manager** under the view category that was selected in the **New View** dialog box.

Once a view has been added to a sheet set, it can be displayed from the **Sheet Set Manager** by double-clicking on the view name or by right-clicking over the name and selecting **Display** from the shortcut menu. If the drawing file is already open, the view is set current. If the file is not open, the drawing file is opened so that the view can be set current.

Figure 25-21.
The **View category** drop-down list displays the available view categories for the view being defined.

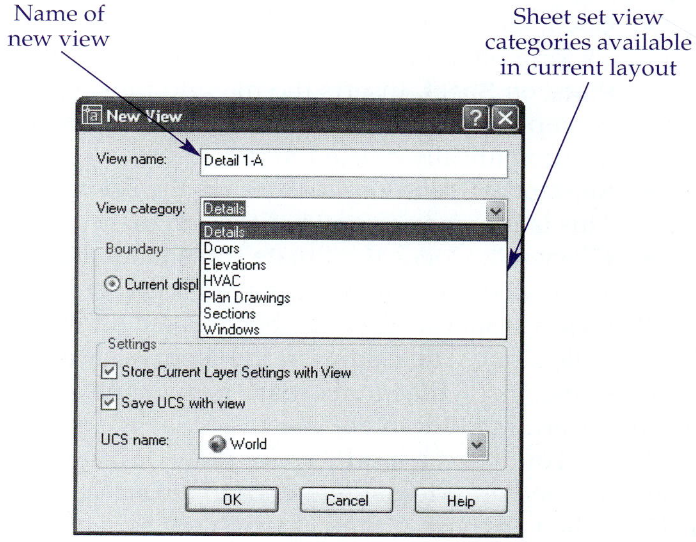

Creating Sheet Views from Resource Drawings

AutoCAD 2005 NEW FEATURE

Sheet views can be created from drawing files listed in the **Resource Drawings** tab. The sheet view can be the entire model space drawing or a model space view. When a model space view or drawing is inserted into a sheet, the resource drawing becomes an external reference of the sheet drawing.

The **Resource Drawings** tab is shown in **Figure 25-22.** Folders containing reference drawings are listed. To add a new folder, double-click on the Add New Location entry or pick the **Add New Location** button and select a folder. You cannot specify specific drawing files—you must select the folder containing the drawing.

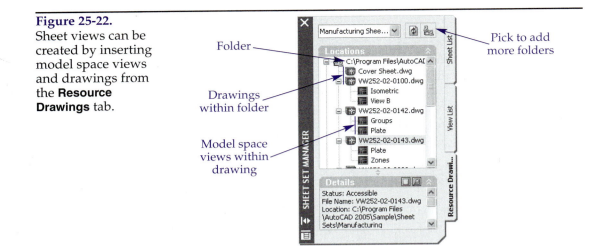

Figure 25-22.
Sheet views can be created by inserting model space views and drawings from the **Resource Drawings** tab.

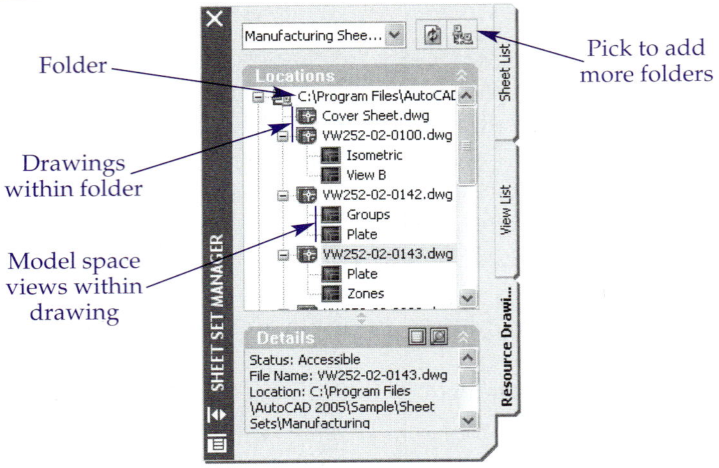

Only drawings listed in the **Resource Drawing** tab can be inserted into a sheet to create a new sheet view. If the drawing you wish to use is not listed, you must add the folder containing the drawing to the resource drawing list.

The folder and all of the drawing files that are in it are now listed in the **Locations** list area. The model space views saved in the drawing are listed under the drawing file.

The options available for a drawing file are located in the drawing file shortcut menu. To display the menu, right-click on a drawing file. The options are explained as follows:

- **Open.** Opens the drawing file and sets the model space tab current. Double-clicking on the drawing file also opens the file.
- **Place on Sheet.** Inserts the file into the current sheet as a sheet view. You are prompted to specify an insertion point. When the point is selected, a viewport is automatically created in the sheet.
- **See Model Space Views.** Expands the list of model space views in the drawing. This is the same as picking the + sign next to the drawing file.
- **eTransmit.** Opens the **Create Transmittal** dialog box, so the selected file and its associated files can be packaged together.

If a model space view has been saved in the drawing, it is listed under the drawing file name. You can insert the model space view as a sheet view in a sheet. To do so, right-click on the model space view name and select the **Place on Sheet** option. Pick an insertion point in the sheet.

When you insert a model space view or drawing into a sheet, AutoCAD creates a viewport and an external reference to the selected drawing. AutoCAD will assign a scale for the viewport, or you can right-click before selecting the insertion point and select the scale for sheet view. The scale for the sheet view is stored as the **ViewportScale** property of the **SheetView** field, and is often displayed in the view label block.

When sheet views are created from resource drawings, an entry is added to the **View List**. If you insert a model space view, the view name is added to the **View List** tab. If you insert a drawing, the drawing name is added to the **View List** tab. You can modify the sheet view name and add a sheet view number in the **View List** tab. This is discussed in the next section.

To delete a location from a sheet set, right-click on the location and select **Remove Location** from the shortcut menu.

Naming and Numbering Sheet Views

AutoCAD 2005 NEW FEATURE

In most projects, you will have several elevations, sections, or details. These items are typically numbered within the drawing set for easier reference. For example, the drawing set may include a foundation plan and a sheet with foundation details. On the foundation detail sheet, each detail is identified by a unique number. The foundation plan includes references to these numbers.

Once a sheet view has been assigned a number, view label blocks and callout blocks can use the number as part of the identification. These blocks are discussed in the next section.

To change the name or number of a sheet view, right-click on the sheet view name in the **Sheet Set Manager** and select **Rename & Renumber...** from the shortcut menu. The **Rename & Renumber View** dialog box is displayed, Figure 25-23. Enter a number for the view in the **Number** text box. The name of the view can be modified in the **View title** text box. Picking the **Next** button moves to the next view in the view category. Pick **OK** when you are done. The view number is displayed in front of the view name in the **Sheet Set Manager**.

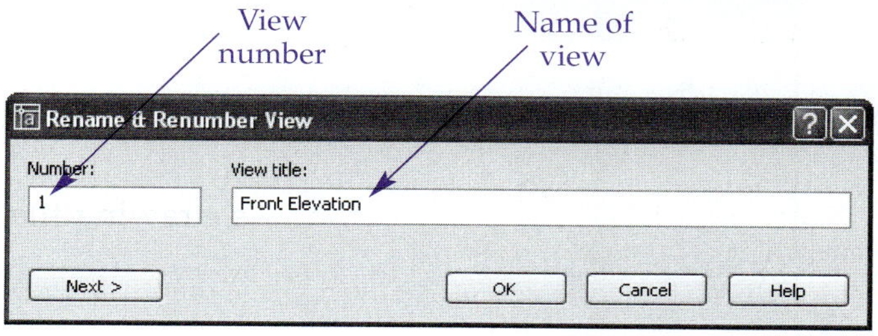

Figure 25-23.
A view can be numbered in the **Rename & Renumber View** dialog box.

EXERCISE 25-5

Complete the Exercise on the Student CD.

Sheet View Callout and Label Blocks

Sheet views are used for elevations, sections, and details. Often, these drawing components are located on one sheet and referenced on a different sheet. When using sheet views, you can insert blocks to identify the sheet view name, number, and scale on both the sheet with the sheet view and also the sheet that refers to the sheet views.

Typically, two types of blocks are used: callout blocks and view label blocks.

Callout blocks

A callout block is used to refer to the sheet view. For example, when a section line is drawn through a building, a callout block is placed at the end of the section line. The callout block indicates the sheet or location where the section view is found and information about the viewing direction. A callout block would also be used on a foundation plan to identify an area addressed by a detail drawing. The callout block is typically located on a different sheet than the sheet view it references.

AutoCAD provides several styles of callout blocks for use in different types of sheet views. See Figure 25-24. The upper value in a callout block is typically the sheet view number, and the lower value is the drawing on which the sheet view appears. For the default callout blocks, the upper value is an attribute containing the **ViewNumber** property of the **SheetView** field. See Figure 25-25. This lists the sheet view number specified for the sheet view. The lower value is the **SheetNumber** property of the **SheetSet** value. This lists the sheet number of the sheet containing the sheet view.

Figure 25-24.
Callout blocks provide reference information for views and sheets. A—An elevation symbol identifying the viewing direction, view number, and sheet number. B—A sampling of predefined callout blocks available in AutoCAD. Elevation and section blocks are selected based on the type of view and the viewing direction for the reference view.

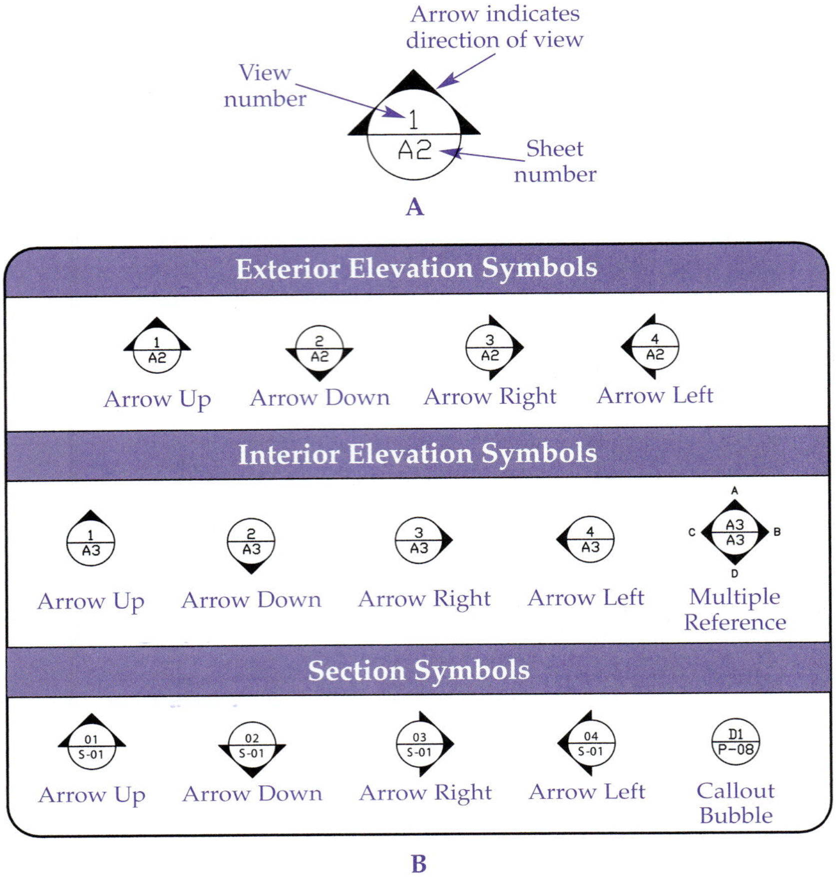

Figure 25-25.
The **ViewNumber** property displays the sheet view number. This field property is used in callout blocks.

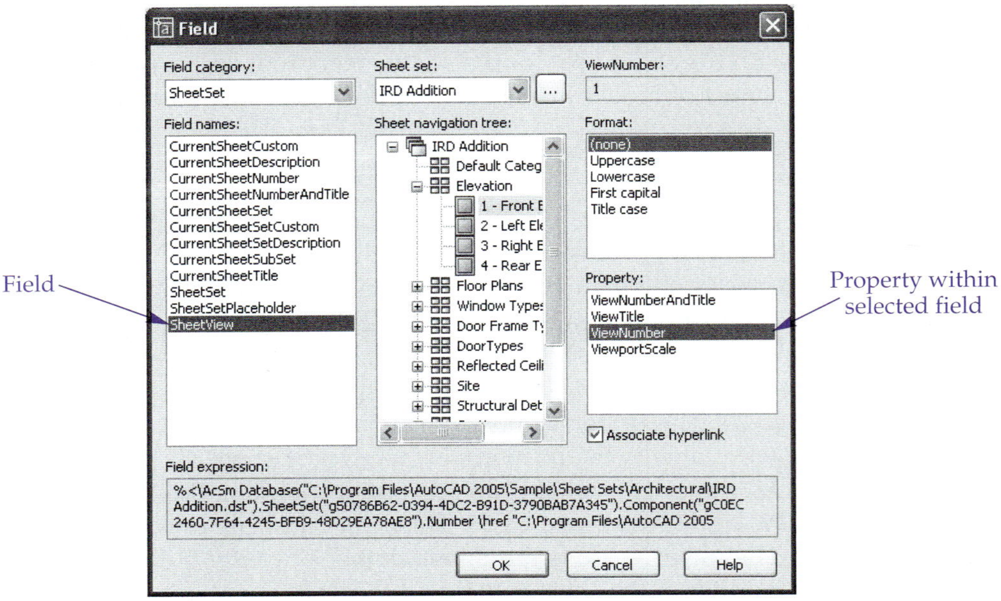

By using fields in the sheet view blocks, the values displayed are automatically updated if there are changes in the sheet set. For instance, if a new sheet is added in the middle of a sheet set, all subsequent sheets may need to be renumbered. The sheet view block values will update automatically as the sheet numbers change.

View label blocks

View label blocks are placed below the sheet view. The view label typically includes the name and number of the section, elevation, or detail and the scale. See **Figure 25-26.** Like callout blocks, view label blocks include attributes containing fields that automatically update to reflect changes to the sheet set or sheet views. View label blocks typically include three properties of the **SheetView** fields: **ViewNumber**, **ViewTitle**, and **Viewport Scale**.

Figure 25-26.
View labels normally appear below the view on a sheet. They indicate information such as the view name, number, and scale.

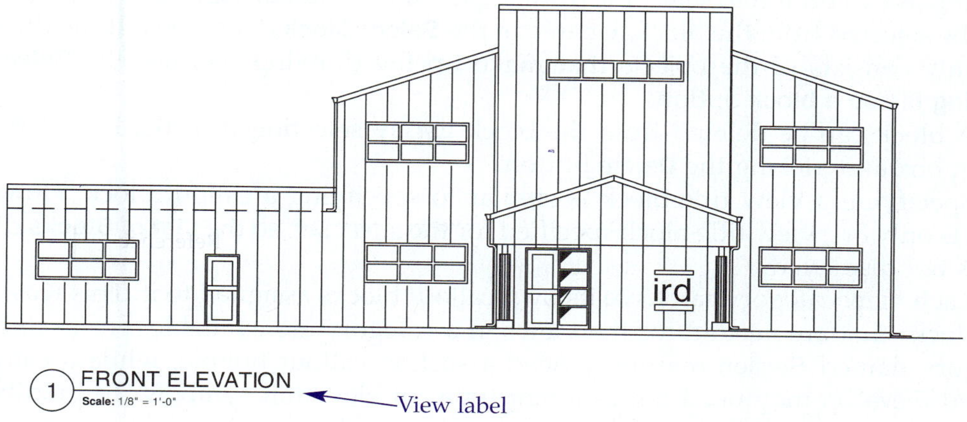

Block hyperlinks

The sample callout and view label blocks provided with AutoCAD also include hyperlink fields. You can pick the hyperlink on a callout block to instantly access the detail, section, or elevation being referenced. This greatly simplifies the process of accessing sheet views.

Associating Callout and View Label Blocks

To insert a callout or view label block from the **Sheet Set Manager,** the block first needs to be available to the sheet set in which the view is defined. These blocks are specified in the **Sheet Set Properties** dialog box. To access this dialog box, right-click on the sheet set name in the **Sheet Set Manager** and select **Properties...** from the shortcut menu. The available blocks are specified in the **Callout blocks** text box and **Label block for views** text box. The name of each block is listed, followed by the path to the drawing file where the block is saved.

> **PROFESSIONAL TIP**
>
> A sheet set or view category can have multiple callout blocks available, but only one view label block.

To add a callout block to a sheet set, pick in the **Callout blocks** text box and then pick the ellipsis (...) button. This opens the **List of Blocks** dialog box. See **Figure 25-27.**

Figure 25-27.
All callout blocks available to a sheet set are listed in the **List of Blocks** dialog box.

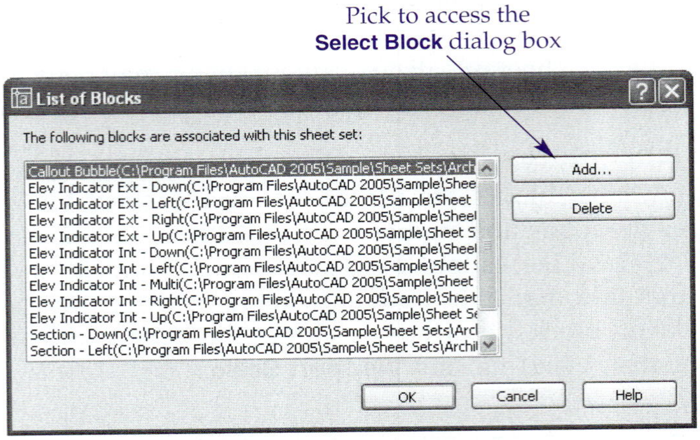

Pick the **Add...** button to display the **Select Block** dialog box. In this dialog box, pick the ellipsis (**...**) button to select the drawing file that contains the block. The block can then be selected from the block list area of the **Select Block** dialog box. If the drawing file only consists of the objects that make up the drawing file, use the **Select the drawing file as a block** option.

A block can be deleted from the block list by selecting it in the **List of Blocks** dialog box and picking the **Delete** button.

Specifying a view title block is similar to specifying a callout block. However, there is only one view title block specified for the sheet set, so the **List of Blocks** dialog box is not displayed.

Each view category can have its own callout blocks assigned to it. This way, only the blocks that are needed for the views in a category are available. For example, a category named Section may only need a section callout bubble, while a category named Elevation may need ten different types of elevation symbols. To modify the callout blocks available for a view category, right-click on the category name and select **Properties...** from the shortcut menu. This opens the **View Category** dialog box.

By default, the callout blocks and view title block assigned to the sheet set are displayed in the block list area. To make a block available to the view category, check the box next to the block. Refer to Figure 25-20. This makes the block available to all of the views within the view category.

New blocks can be added to the view category by picking the **Add Blocks...** button and accessing the **Select Block** dialog box.

Inserting Callout and View Label Blocks

To insert a callout block into a drawing, open the sheet where the reference is to be placed. In the **View List** tab of the **Sheet Set Manager**, right-click on the sheet view name and select the block from the **Place Callout Block** shortcut menu. See Figure 25-28A. You are then prompted to specify an insertion point for the block. The block can be scaled or rotated by using the options on the command line. When the block is inserted, it is given the same sheet view number and sheet number as the reference view and sheet. See Figure 25-28B. If the reference information changes, the block is automatically renumbered by AutoCAD.

The process of inserting a view label block is similar to that for inserting a callout block. In the **Sheet Set Manager,** right-click on the sheet view name and select **Place View Label Block** from the shortcut menu. You are then prompted to specify an insertion point. The block can be scaled or rotated by using the options on the command line. When the block is inserted, the label appears with the view name and number. If the view name or number is later changed in the sheet set, the information is automatically updated by AutoCAD.

Figure 25-28.
Placing callout blocks in a view. A—Right-click on the reference view name and select **Place Callout Block** to display a shortcut menu with all of the callout blocks available. B—Callout blocks are placed in the 1-Main Floor Plan view in the A-01 sheet to reference the section view named 1-Section in the A-05 sheet.

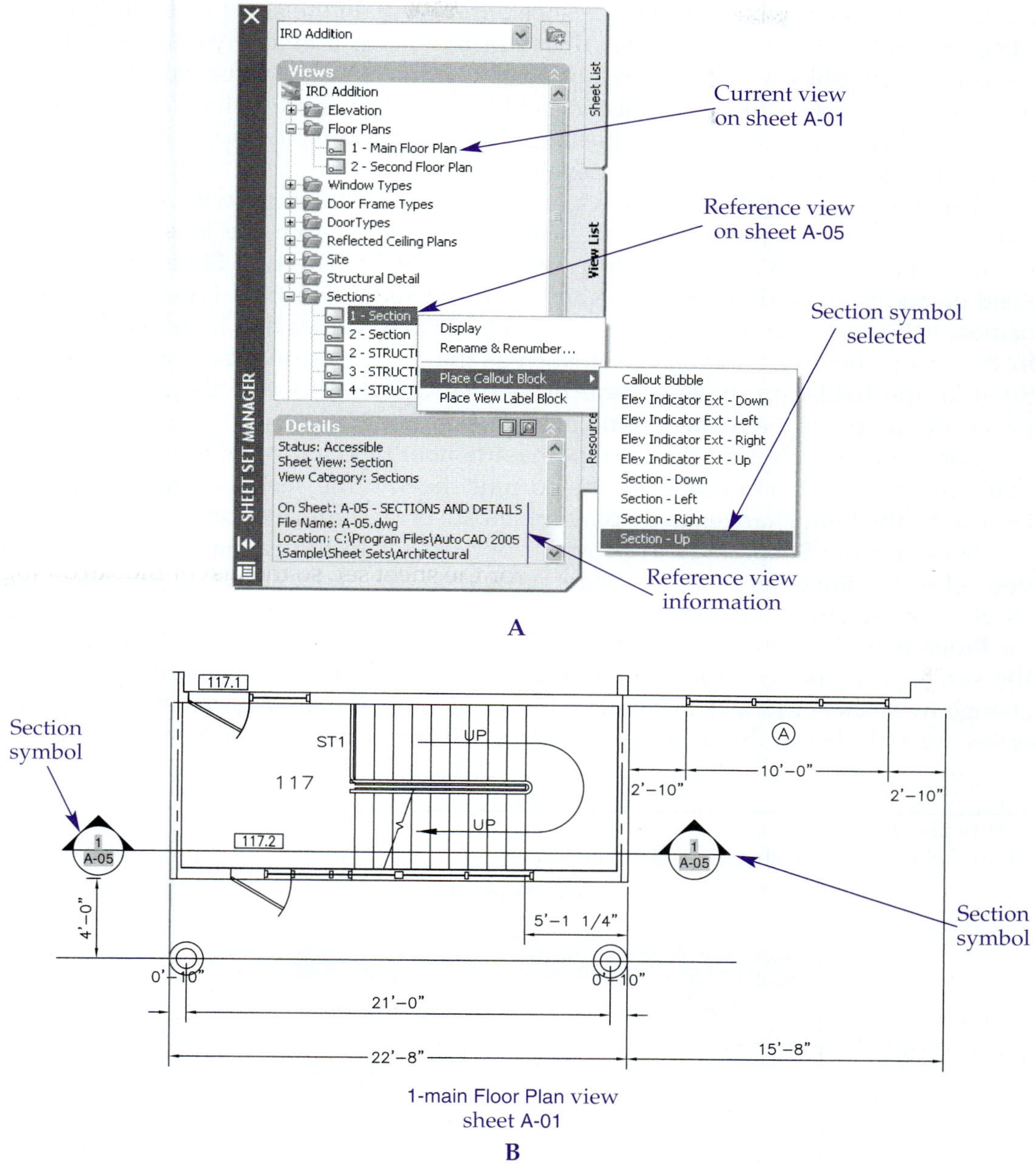

EXERCISE 25-6 Complete the Exercise on the Student CD.

Sheet Set Fields

Information about a sheet is usually placed in the title block area of the drawing. The information may include items such as the client's name and address, the project number, the person who checked the sheet, and the date the sheet was plotted. You can create fields on sheets to display this information. As previously discussed, fields are special text objects that display updateable values. A field value can change as a result of a change to the value of the field setting. Fields are valuable features for sheet sets, because text items on sheets can be set up to display up-to-date information if changes occur as the project develops.

There are specific field types available in AutoCAD for use with sheet sets. To create a field for a text value on a sheet, select **Field...** from the **Insert** pull-down menu. This displays the **Field** dialog box, **Figure 25-29.** Selecting **SheetSet** from the **Field category:** drop-down list displays a list of predefined field types in the **Field names:** list box. These fields can be inserted to display values that have been defined in the sheet, sheet view, or sheet set, such as the sheet title, number, or description. Some of the fields also have several properties. Selecting one of the field types or properties displays the related value in the **Field** dialog box.

For example, selecting the **CurrentSheetNumber** field allows you to insert a field that displays the sheet number of the current sheet. If the sheet is renumbered at a later date, the field changes to display the most current information.

Selecting the **SheetSet** field provides options for inserting many values. When you select the **SheetSet** field, the **Sheet navigation tree** is displayed. If you select the sheet set at the top of the tree, a set of properties related to the entire set is displayed in the **Property** list box. These properties include settings that can be applied to all sheets in the set, such as project information and client information. These setting will not change from sheet to sheet, but will be the same on all sheets. When these field properties are included in the sheet set title block, all sheets display the same values.

Figure 25-29.
Many fields related to sheet sets are available.

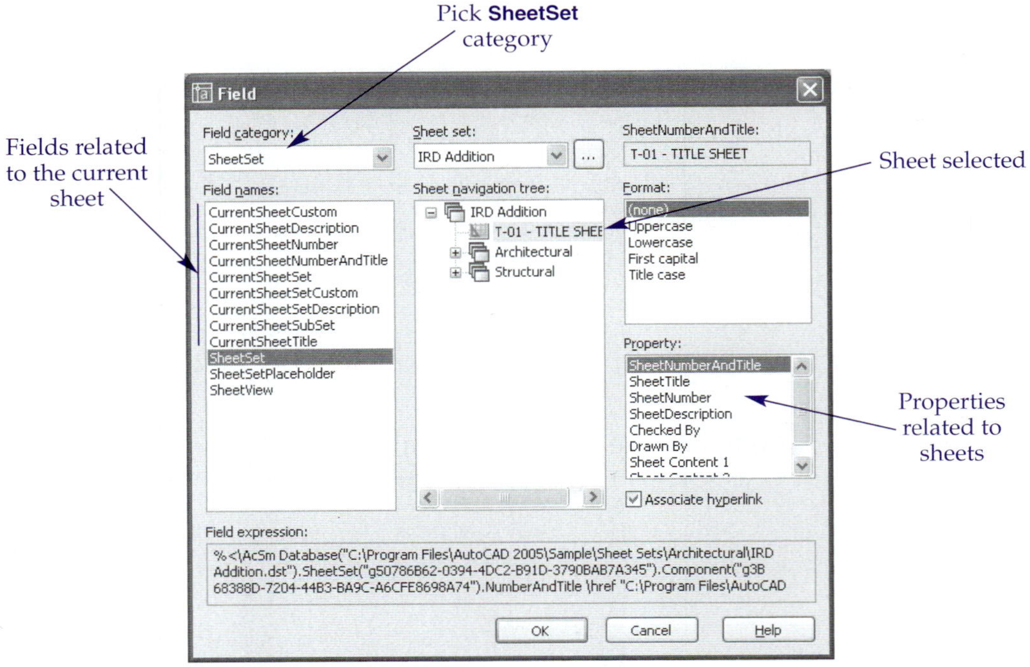

If you select a sheet in the **Sheet navigation tree**, properties related to sheets are displayed. These properties include **SheetTitle**, **SheetNumber**, **Drawn By**, and **Checked By** settings. When these field properties are included in the sheet set template title block, each sheet can have a unique value displayed. If a new sheet is added to a sheet set, the fields automatically update.

Selecting the **SheetSetPlaceholder** field allows you to insert a field that acts as a placeholder. A ***placeholder*** is a temporary value for a field. Selecting a placeholder in the **Placeholder type:** list box assigns a temporary value to the associated field, such as SheetNumber. Placeholders can be used to insert temporary field values in user-defined callout blocks and view labels. When defined with attributes in a callout block, placeholders are updated to display the correct values automatically when the block is inserted onto a sheet from the **Sheet Set Manager**.

Like the **SheetSet** field, the **SheetView** field has many options. When you select the **SheetView** field, the **Sheet navigation tree** displays the view list for the sheet set. If you pick the sheet set name in the **Sheet navigation tree**, the sheet set properties are displayed. These properties are identical to those displayed with the **SheetSet** field. If you pick a sheet view name in the **Sheet navigation tree**, sheet view properties are displayed. These properties are specific to a sheet view, and include **ViewTitle**, **ViewNumber**, and **ViewScale**. As discussed earlier in this chapter, these field properties are used in callout and view label blocks.

Selecting the **CurrentSheetCustom** or **CurrentSheetSetCustom** field allows you to insert a field that is linked to a custom property defined for a sheet or sheet set. Custom property fields for sheet sets are discussed in the next section.

Custom Properties

Information about a sheet is usually included in the title block area of the drawing. This may include information such as the client's name and address, the project number, the person who checked the sheet, and the date the sheet was plotted. Information about the sheet set or a specific sheet can be stored electronically with fields and custom properties. This information can then be viewed from the **Sheet Set Manager**. The data can also be inserted into the drawing using the **Field** command, which creates a link between the text data and the custom field data. By doing this, the data can be modified in the **Sheet Set Manager** and the linked data is updated in the drawing files.

Adding a custom property field

Custom properties are managed in the **Sheet Set Properties** dialog box. To add a custom property field to a sheet set, right-click on the sheet set name in the **Sheet Set Manager** and select **Properties...** from the shortcut menu. In the **Sheet Set Properties** dialog box, pick the **Edit Custom Properties...** button to open the **Custom Properties** dialog box. This dialog box is shown in Figure 25-30.

To add a custom property field to the sheet set, pick the **Add...** button. This displays the **Add Custom Property** dialog box. Enter a name for the custom property in the **Name** field. See Figure 25-31. Some examples of a custom property may be Job Number, Client Name, Checked By, and Date. If the data for the custom property is usually the same value, this can be entered in the **Default value** field. For example, if the custom property is Checked by, and most of the sheets in this project are checked by ST, then ST could be entered in as the default value. The **Owner** area has two options: **Sheet Set** and **Sheet**. If the custom property pertains to the entire project, then **Sheet Set** should be selected. If the custom property pertains to each individual sheet, select **Sheet**. When **Sheet** is selected, the custom property is available in the **Sheet Properties** dialog box. This way, the data is attached to each individual sheet. Pick the **OK** button to add the custom property to the sheet set. The custom property is then listed in the **Sheet Set Properties** dialog box.

Figure 25-30.
Information can be attached to a sheet set in the **Custom Properties** dialog box.

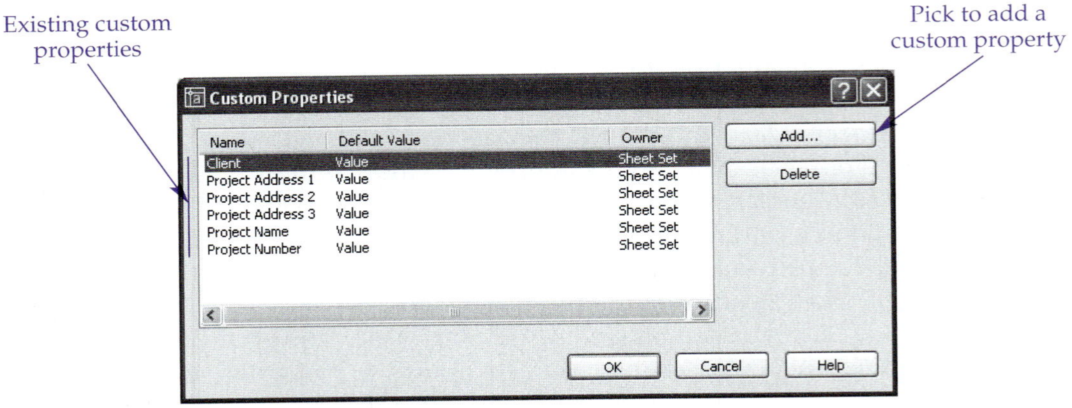

Figure 25-31.
Enter the information for the custom property in the **Add Custom Property** dialog box.

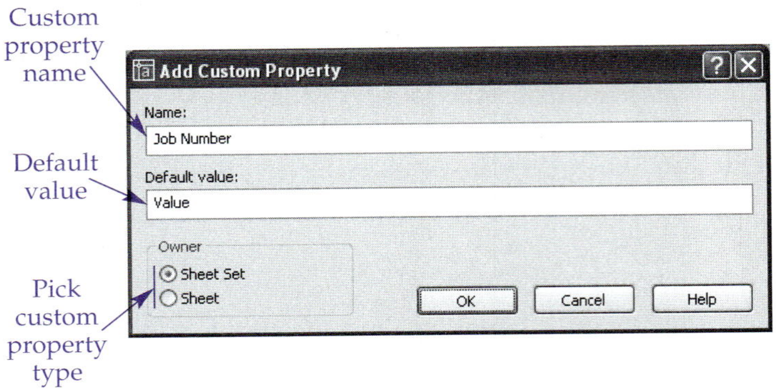

Entering custom property data

To modify or enter information into a custom property field for a sheet set, open the **Sheet Set Properties** dialog box. Modify the value.

If custom properties have been added for a sheet, the individual sheets display the custom property fields. To modify or enter information into a sheet custom property field, right-click on the sheet and select **Properties...** from the shortcut menu. The custom properties are listed under the **Sheet Custom Properties** heading of the **Sheet Properties** dialog box. See **Figure 25-32.**

Deleting a custom property

If a custom property field is no longer needed, it can be deleted from the sheet set. To do this, right-click on the sheet set and select **Properties...** to open the **Sheet Set Properties** dialog box. Pick the **Edit Custom Properties...** button. In the **Custom Properties** dialog box select the custom property and then pick the **Delete** button.

NOTE

If a sheet set is created from an example sheet set, any custom properties from the example sheet set are added to the new sheet set.

Figure 25-32.
Sheet custom properties are available in the **Sheet Properties** dialog box after they have been added to the sheet set.

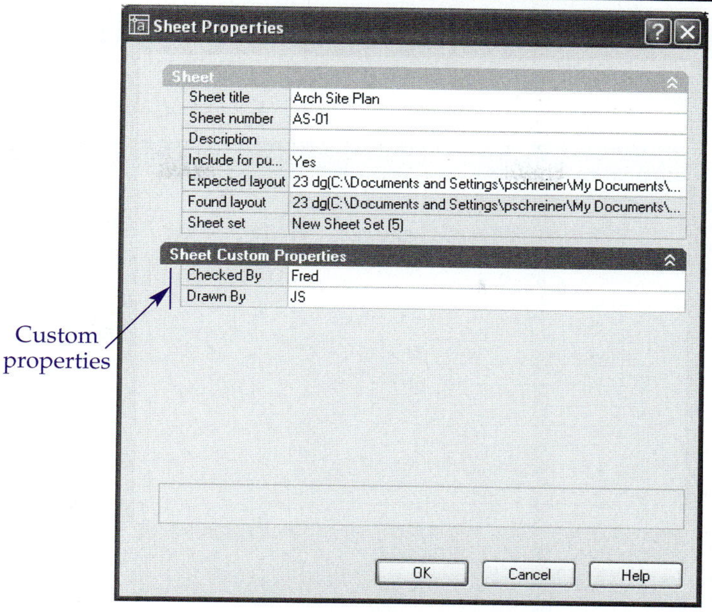

EXERCISE 25-7 Complete the Exercise on the Student CD.

Creating a Sheet List Table

One of the first pages of a sheet set typically includes a sheet list. A *sheet list* is like the table of contents for the sheet set. It lists all of the pages in the sheet set and what type of information can be found on the sheet. The **Sheet List Table** command inserts a table object using information from the sheet properties. The information in the table is directly linked to the sheet properties, so if the sheet information is updated in the **Sheet Set Manager** the sheet list table will be automatically updated also.

Inserting a Sheet List Table

A sheet list table can only be inserted into a drawing from the **Sheet Set Manager**. To insert a sheet list table, open the **Sheet Set Manager** and open the sheet where a table needs to be inserted. Right-click on the sheet set name and select **Insert Sheet List Table...** from the shortcut menu. This opens the **Insert Sheet List Table** shown in Figure 25-33.

A preset table style for the sheet list can be selected from the **Table Style name** drop-down list. A preview of the table is displayed in the preview area. The **Show Subheader** check box determines if the table will include a subheader row.

The information displayed in the table is set in the **Table Data Settings** area. The title for the sheet list is entered into the **Title Text** text box. The information the table contains is specified in the **Column Settings** area. Pick the **OK** button to insert the table. You are then prompted to specify the insertion point for the table. Figure 25-34 shows a sheet list table that uses the sheet number and sheet description fields.

NOTE

A sheet list table can only be inserted into a layout tab of a drawing file that is a part of the sheet set. The **Insert Sheet List Table...** options are grayed out if the drawing file is not part of the sheet set or if model space is current.

Figure 25-33.
Properties for the sheet list table are set up in the **Insert Sheet List Table** dialog box.

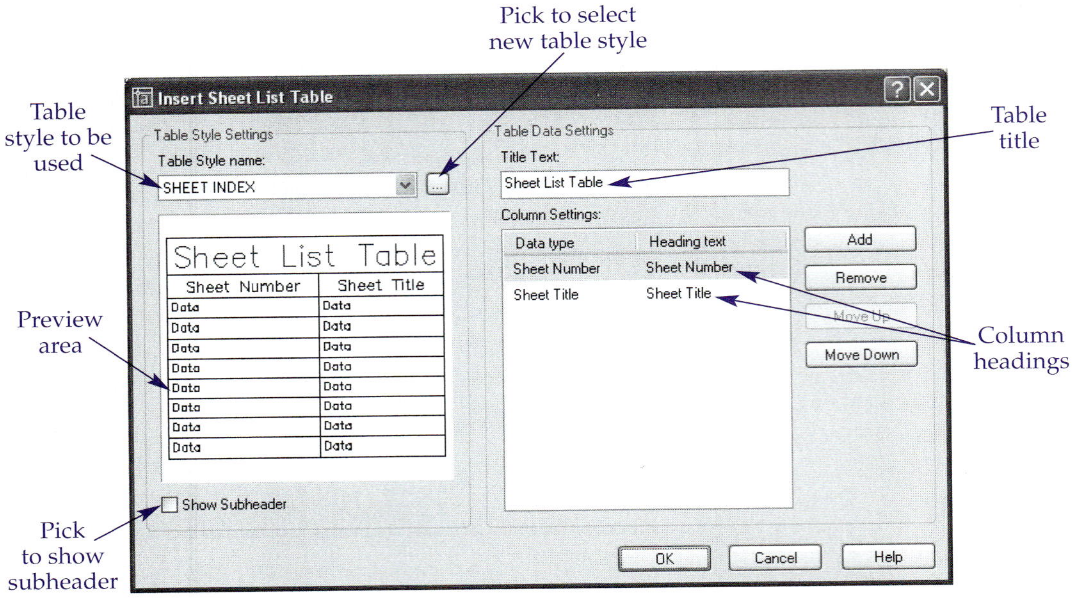

Figure 25-34.
A sheet list table displays information about each sheet in the sheet set.

SHEET INDEX	
Sheet Number	Sheet Description
T-01	SHEET INDEX, VICINITY MAP, BUILDING CODE ANALYSIS
Architectural	
AS-01	ARCHITECTURAL SITE PLAN, NOTES
A-01	MAIN FLOOR PLAN, SECOND FLOOR PLAN, WALL TYPE NOTES
A-02	EXTERIOR ELEVATIONS
A-03	DOOR & FRAME SCHEDULE, ROOM FINISH SCHEDULE, DOOR, DOOR FRAME & WINDOW TYPES
A-04	MAIN & SECOND FLOOR REFLECTED CEILING PLANS
A-05	STAIR SECTIONS AND DETAILS
Structural	
S-01	FOUNDATION PLAN, PILE SCHEDULE, PILE TYPICAL DETAIL
S-02	STRUCTURAL SECTIONS AND DETAILS
S-03	FLOOR FRAMING PLAN AND SECTIONS
S-04	STRUCTURAL SECTIONS

Modifying the Column Heading Data

A sheet list table can include various information from the drawing file and the sheet set. By default, the Sheet Number and Sheet Title fields are included. The sheet list table information is specified in the **Column Settings** area of the **Insert Sheet List Table** dialog box.

A new column can be added to the sheet list by picking the **Add** button. The new column is then placed under the last column in the list. To specify the data type, pick on the name in the **Data type** column to activate the drop-down list. Pick the drop-down list button to display the information that can be used in the sheet list table. Select the type of data you want to include. Then type the heading for the sheet list column in the **Heading text** column. The data types that are available in the drop-down list come from sheet set properties and drawing properties. To have a different data type added to the list, you need to add a custom property to the sheet set.

To delete a data column from the list, select the data column and pick the **Remove** button. To reposition the order of the columns, use the **Move Up** and **Move Down** buttons. The column at the top of the list is inserted as the first column in the sheet list table.

Editing a Sheet List Table

The information in the sheet list table is directly linked to the data source field. For example, if the sheet numbers are modified in the **Sheet Set Manager**, the sheet list table can be updated to reflect those changes. To do this, select the sheet list table in the drawing file, then right-click and select **Update Sheet List Table** from the shortcut menu.

The properties for the table can be modified by selecting the table, right-clicking, and selecting **Edit Sheet List Table Settings...** from the shortcut menu. This opens the **Edit Sheet List Table Settings** dialog box. After making the changes, pick the **OK** button to update the sheet list table.

> **NOTE** A sheet list table can be modified the same as any other table. For example, text can be modified, and columns and rows can be added. When the **Update Sheet List Table** command is used on the modified table, a warning dialog box is displayed stating that any manual modifications will be discarded.

Sheet List Table Hyperlinks

If the **Sheet Number** or **Sheet Title** columns are included in the sheet list table, hyperlinks are automatically assigned to the data. *Hyperlinks* are links in a text document connected to related information in other documents or to the Internet. To use a hyperlink, move the crosshairs over a sheet number or sheet title. Hold the pointing device still for a moment and the hyperlink icon and tool tip appear. The tool tip displays the message CTRL + click to follow link. Hold the [Ctrl] key on the keyboard and pick the hyperlink. The selected sheet is opened. This is another way to open a sheet quickly.

EXERCISE 25-8 Complete the Exercise on the Student CD.

Archiving a Sheet Set

At different periods throughout a project, you may want to gather up all of the electronic drawing files that pertain to a project and store them. This is called *archiving* the drawing set. For example, when a set of drawings in a project is presented to the client for the first time, the client probably wants to make some changes. At this point it may be wise to archive the files for future reference, before the modifications are made.

All files in a sheet set can be archived by using the **ARCHIVE** command. This copies all of the drawing files and their related files to a single location. *Related files* include external references, font files, plot style table files, and template files.

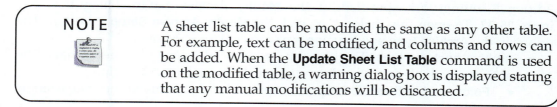

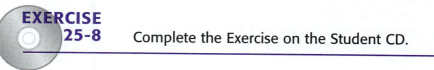

Setting up an Archive

To archive a sheet set, right-click on the sheet set name and select **Archive...** from the shortcut menu, or type **ARCHIVE** at the Command: prompt. The **Archive a Sheet Set** dialog box opens. See **Figure 25-35.**

The **Sheets** tab displays all of the subsets and sheets in the sheet set. Check the sheets to be archived. The drawing files and their related files are listed in the **Files Tree** tab. Pick the + sign next to a file to display its related files. A file that is not part of the sheet set can be included in the archive by picking the **Add a File** button. See **Figure 25-36.** This opens the **Add File to Archive** dialog box. Any type of a file can be added to the archive. The archive is not limited to only AutoCAD files. Notes can be included in the archive by typing them in the **Enter notes to include with this archive** text box. The **View Report** button lists all of the files included in the archive. This information can be saved to a text file by picking the **Save As...** button.

The location where the archive is saved, the type of archive that is created, and additional settings are specified in the **Modify Archive Setup** dialog box. See **Figure 25-37.** To open this dialog box, pick the **Modify Archive Setup...** button. The options in the **Archive type and location** area are explained below:

- **Archive package type.** The files can be archived in one of three formats. The options available from the drop-down list are explained as follows:
  - **Folder (set of files).** This option copies all of the archived files into a single folder.
  - **Self-extracting executable (*.exe).** This option compresses all of the files into a self-extracting zip (EXE) file. The files can be extracted at a later time by double-clicking on the file. A *zip file* is a file that has been compressed to take up less file space. The utility is used to unzip, or return the file to its original size.
  - **Zip (*.zip).** With this option, all of the files are compressed into a ZIP file. A program that works with ZIP files must be used to extract the files.
- **File Format.** The files can be converted to an earlier version of AutoCAD by selecting one of the options from the drop-down list.
- **Archive file folder.** This is the location where the archive is saved. Pick the **Browse...** button to select a different location.
- **Archive file name.** The drop-down list gives the options for how the archive package is named. The following options are available:
  - **Prompt for a filename.** The **Specify Zip File** dialog box is displayed, and a name for the archive package can be specified.

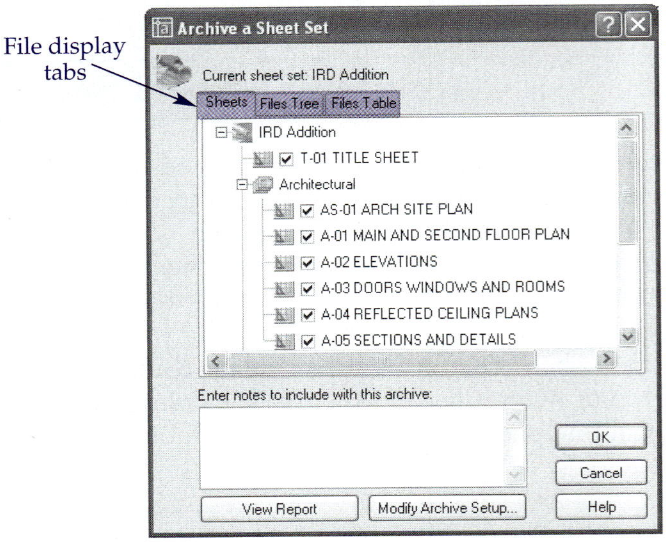

Figure 25-35.
The files to be archived and the archive settings are specified from the **Archive a Sheet Set** dialog box.

Figure 25-36.
Documents that relate to a project can be archived along with the AutoCAD files.

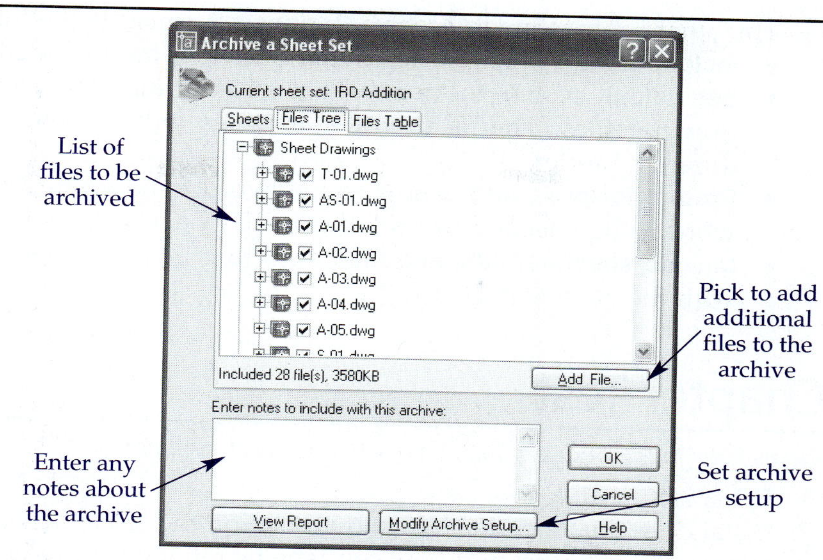

Figure 25-37.
The archive file settings are specified in the **Modify Archive Setup** dialog box.

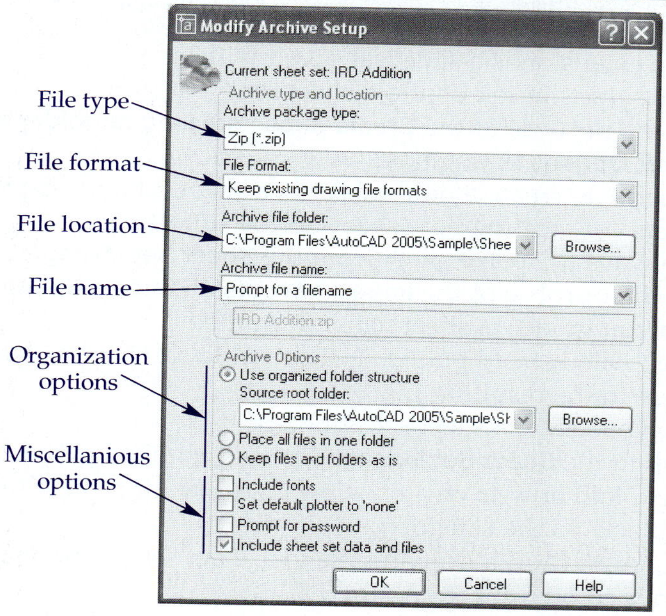

- **Overwrite if necessary.** The name for the resulting archive file can be entered in the text box below the drop-down list. If a file with the same name already exists, that file is automatically overwritten.
- **Increment file name if necessary.** The name for the resulting archive file can be entered in the text box below the drop-down list. If a file with the same name already exists, a new file is created and an incremental number is added to the file name. With this option, multiple versions of the archive package are saved.

Additional settings for the archive package are specified in the **Archive Options** area. The first option determines how the folder structure is saved. If **Use organized folder structure** is selected, the archive file duplicates the folder structure for the files. When this option is selected, the **Source root folder** setting is used to determine the root folder for files that use relative paths, such as xrefs. To archive all of the files into one single folder, use the **Place all files in one folder** option. The **Keep files and folders as is** option uses the same folder structure for all the files that are in the sheet set.

The other settings in the **Archive Options** area include the following:

- **Include fonts.** All fonts used in the drawings are included in the archive.
- **Set default plotter to 'none'.** This disassociates the plotter name from the drawing files. This is useful if the files will be sent to someone using a different plotter.
- **Prompt for password.** Allows a password to be set for the archive. The password is then needed to open the archive package.
- **Include sheet set data and files.** Selecting this includes the sheet set data file with the archive package.

Chapter Test

Answer the following questions on a separate sheet of paper.

1. What is a *sheet set*?
2. What does the term *sheet* refer to in relation to a sheet set and a drawing file?
3. What are *sheet views* and how can they be referenced to each other within a sheet set?
4. What wizard is used to create a sheet set? What two types of ways can a new sheet set be created?
5. What file extension is a sheet set saved with?
6. What are *subsets* in relation to a sheet set?
7. What is the purpose of the **Create subsets based on folder structure** option in the **Import Options** dialog box?
8. Explain how to create a new subset in a sheet set and specify a template file and layout for creating new sheets in the subset.
9. List two ways to open a sheet from the **Sheet Set Manager**.
10. What is the purpose of the **Import Layouts as Sheets** dialog box?
11. How do you modify a sheet name or number?
12. Briefly explain how to publish a sheet set to a DWF file. How are the sheets organized in the resulting file?
13. How do you create a sheet selection set?
14. What tab in the **Sheet Set Manager** is used to manage sheet views?
15. Briefly explain how to create a view category for a sheet set and associate callout blocks to the category.
16. Explain how to add a drawing file to a sheet set so that views in the drawing can be placed on a sheet.
17. Explain why AutoCAD callout blocks and view labels are automatically updated when they appear on sheets and changes are made to the related sheet set.
18. What information is typically provided by the upper and lower values displayed in a callout block?
19. Explain how to insert a callout block into a drawing.
20. Give three examples of fields that can be used in a sheet set.
21. What is the purpose of custom sheet set properties?
22. How do you add a custom property to a sheet set?
23. What is a *sheet list table*?
24. Can column headings be added to a sheet list?
25. How is a table updated to reflect changes that are made in the **Sheet Set Manager**?
26. If a sheet list table is edited manually, will the edits be preserved if the **Update Sheet List Table** command is used? Explain.
27. What is the purpose of archiving a sheet set?
28. List the three packaging types available for archiving a sheet set.
29. What is a *zip file*?
30. How can you password-protect an archive?

Drawing Problems

1. Create a new sheet set using the **Create Sheet Set** wizard and the **Existing drawings** option. Name the new sheet set Schematic Drawings. On the **Choose Layouts** page, pick the **Browse...** button and browse to the folder where the P11-10.dwg file from Chapter 11 is saved. Import all of the layouts from the file into the new sheet set. Continue creating the sheet set as follows:
   A. In the **Sheet Set Properties** dialog box, assign the ISO A2 Title Block layout from the ISO A2-Color Dependent Plot Styles.dwt template file in the AutoCAD 2005 Template folder as the sheet creation template.
   B. Open a new drawing file using the template of your choice and create a block for a view label. Save the drawing file and then assign the block to the sheet set using the **Label block for views** setting in the **Sheet Set Properties** dialog box.
   C. Create a new view category and name it Schematics.
   D. Open the 3 Wire Control layout, create a new view, and add it to the Schematics view category. Double-click on the new view name in the **View List** tab and then insert the view label block you previously created. Renumber the view and save the drawing.
   E. Add a custom property to the sheet set named Checked by and set the **Owner** type to **Sheet**. Add another custom property named Client and set the **Owner** type to **Sheet Set**.

2. Create a new sheet set using the **Create Sheet Set** wizard and an example sheet set. Use the Architectural Imperial Sheet Set example sheet set. Name the new sheet set Floor Plan Drawings. Finish creating the sheet set. Under the Architectural subset, create a new sheet named Floor Plan. Number the sheet A1. In the **Resource Drawings** tab, add a new location by browsing to the folder where the P17-17.dwg file from Chapter 17 is saved. Next, open the P17-17.dwg file and continue as follows:
   A. Create three model space views named Kitchen, Living Room, and Dining Room. Orient each display as needed to describe the area of the floor plan. Save and close the drawing.
   B. Open the A1-Floor Plan sheet. Create a new layer named Viewport and set it current.
   C. In the **Resource Drawings** tab, expand the listing under the P17-17.dwg file. For each view name, right-click on the name and select **Place on Sheet**. Insert each view into the layout. Delete the default view labels inserted with the views. Double-click inside each viewport and set the viewport scale as desired.
   D. In the **View List** tab, renumber the views. Insert a new view label block under each view and save the drawing.
   E. Close the drawing.

3. Open the Floor Plan Drawings sheet set created in Problem 25-2. Create an archive of the sheet set using the self-extracting zip executable (EXE) file format.

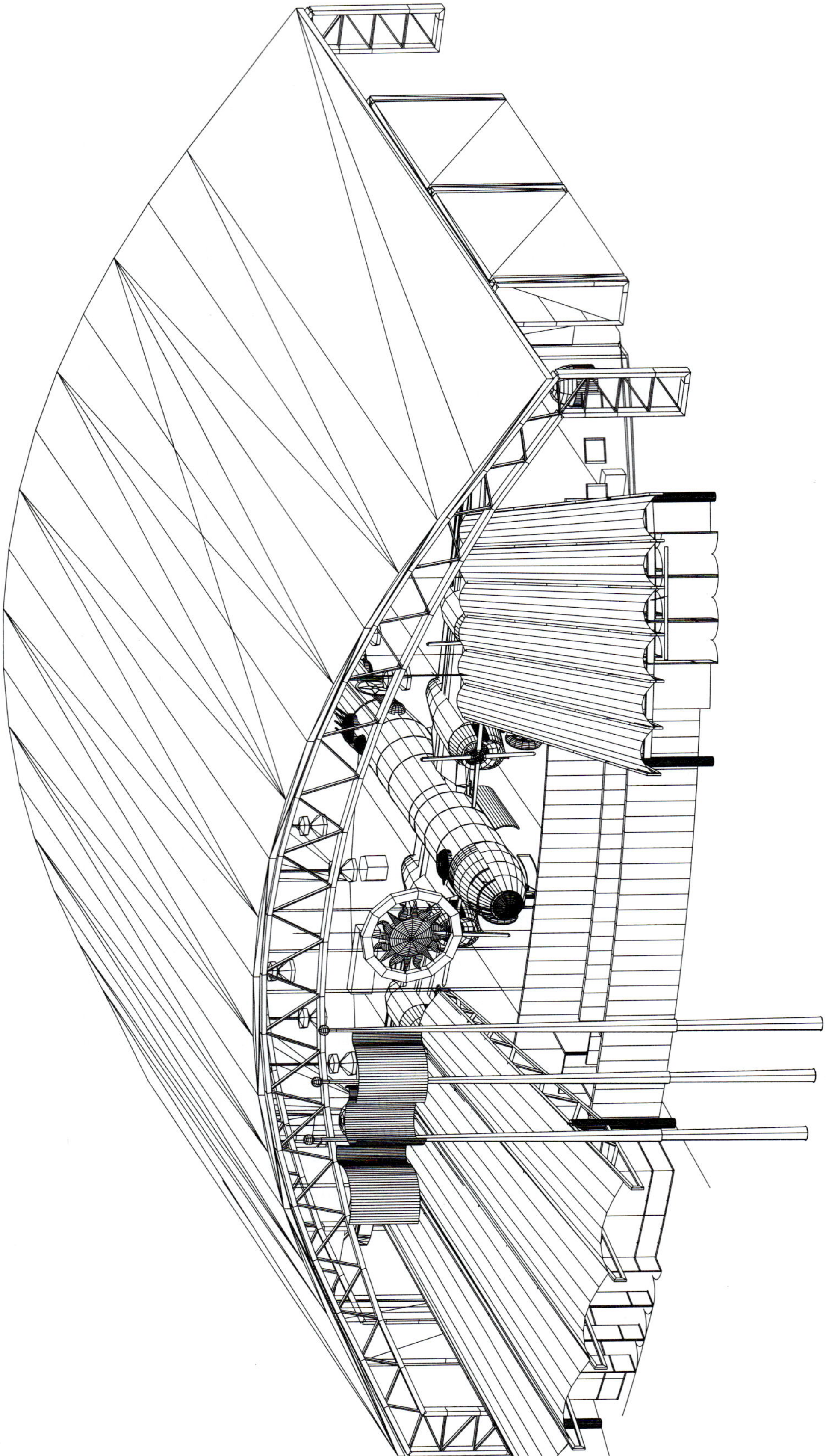

Drawing of an airplane hanger. (David Ward)

CHAPTER 26

Isometric Drawing

Learning Objectives

After completing this chapter, you will be able to do the following:

- Describe the nature of isometric and oblique views.
- Set an isometric grid.
- Construct isometric objects.
- Create isometric text styles.
- Demonstrate isometric and oblique dimensioning techniques.

Being able to visualize and draw three-dimensional shapes is a skill that every drafter, designer, and engineer should possess. This is especially important in 3D modeling. However, there is a distinct difference between drawing a view that *looks* three-dimensional and creating a *true* 3D model.

A 3D model can be rotated on the display screen and viewed from any angle. The computer calculates the points, lines, and surfaces of the objects in space. Chapter 27 introduces the methods of creating three-dimensional models. The focus of this chapter is creating views that *look* three-dimensional using some special AutoCAD functions and two-dimensional coordinates and objects.

Pictorial Drawing Overview

The word *pictorial* means "like a picture." It refers to any realistic form of drawing. Pictorial drawings illustrate height, width, and depth. Several forms of pictorial drawings are used in industry today. The least realistic is oblique. However, this is the simplest type. The most realistic, but also the most complex, is perspective. Isometric drawing falls midway between the two as far as realism and complexity are concerned.

Oblique Drawings

An *oblique drawing* shows objects with one or more parallel faces having true shape and size. A scale is selected for the orthographic, or front faces. Then, an angle for the depth (receding axis) is chosen. The three types of oblique drawings are *cavalier, cabinet,* and *general.* See **Figure 26-1.** These vary in the scale of the receding axis. The receding axis is drawn at half scale for a cabinet view and at full scale for a cavalier. The general oblique is normally drawn with a 3/4 scale for the receding axis.

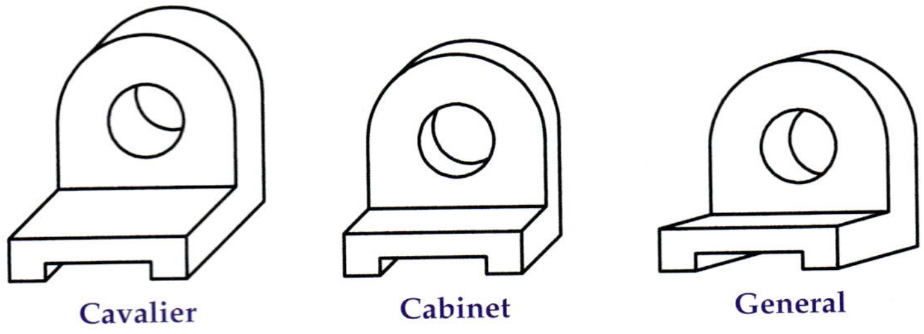

Figure 26-1.
The three types of oblique drawings differ in the scale of the receding axis.

Isometric Drawings

Isometric drawings are more realistic than oblique drawings. The entire object appears as if it is tilted toward the viewer. The word *isometric* means "equal measure." This equal measure refers to the angle between the three axes (120°) after the object has been tilted. The tilt angle is 35°16′. This is shown in **Figure 26-2.** The 120° angle corresponds to an angle of 30° from horizontal. When constructing isometric drawings, lines that are parallel in the orthogonal views must be parallel in the isometric view.

The most appealing aspect of isometric drawing is that all three axis lines can be measured using the same scale. This saves time, while still producing a pleasing pictorial of the object. This type of drawing is produced when you use Isometric Snap mode, discussed later.

Closely related to isometric drawing are dimetric and trimetric. These forms of pictorial drawing differ from isometric in the scales used to measure the three axes. ***Dimetric*** drawing uses two different scales and ***trimetric*** uses three scales. Using different scales is an attempt to create ***foreshortening.*** This means the lengths of the sides appear to recede. The relationship between isometric, dimetric, and trimetric drawings is illustrated in **Figure 26-3.**

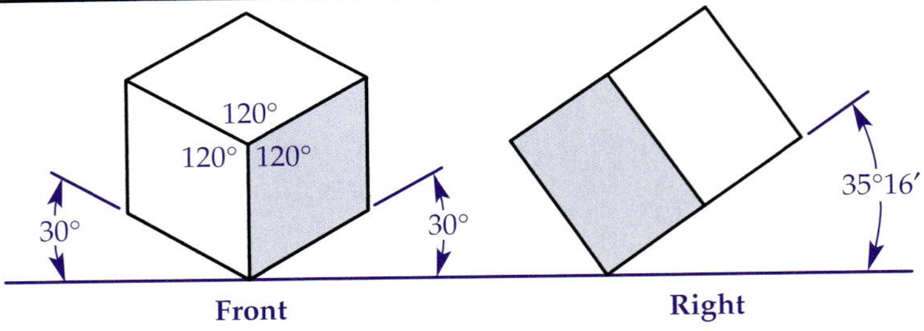

Figure 26-2.
An object is tilted 35°16′ to achieve an isometric view having 120° between the three axes. Notice how the highlighted face corresponds to each view.

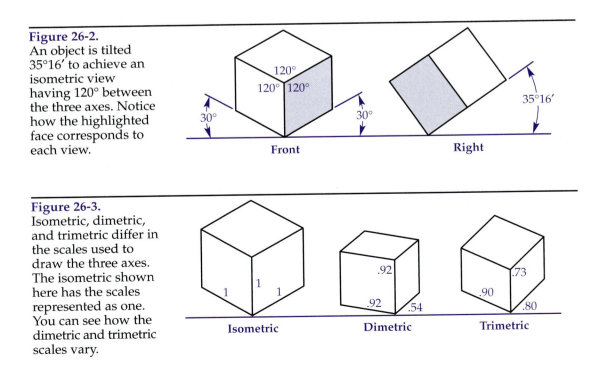

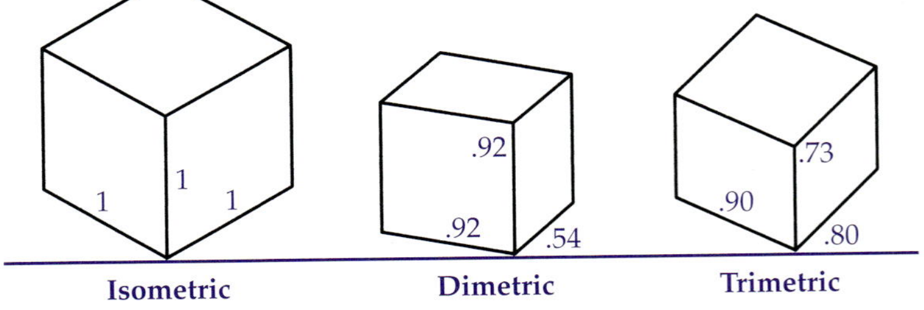

Figure 26-3.
Isometric, dimetric, and trimetric differ in the scales used to draw the three axes. The isometric shown here has the scales represented as one. You can see how the dimetric and trimetric scales vary.

Perspective Drawing

The most realistic form of pictorial drawing is a *perspective drawing.* The eye naturally sees objects in perspective. Look down a long hall and notice that the wall and floor lines seem to converge in the distance at an imaginary point. That point is called the *vanishing point.* The most common types of perspective drawing are *one-point* and *two-point.* These forms of pictorial drawing are often used in architecture. They are also used in the automotive and aircraft industries. Examples of one-point and two-point perspectives are shown in **Figure 26-4.** A perspective of a true 3D model can be produced in AutoCAD using the **DVIEW** and **3DORBIT** commands. See ***AutoCAD and its Applications—Advanced*** for complete coverage of **DVIEW** and **3DORBIT**.

Figure 26-4.
An example of one-point perspective and two-point perspective.

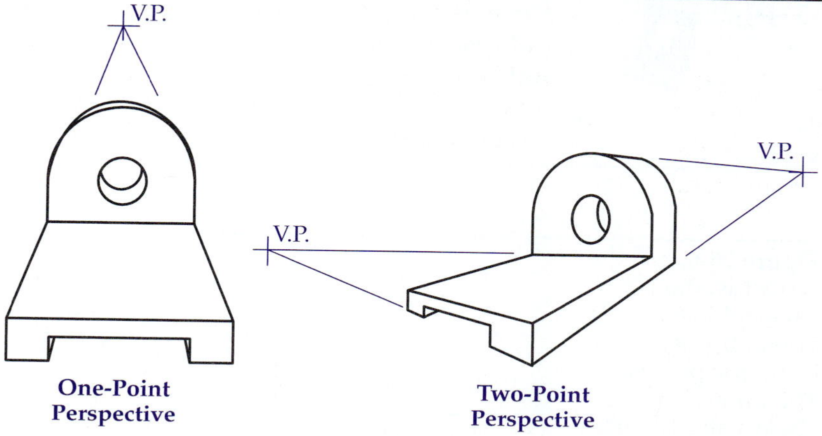

Isometric Drawing

The most common method of pictorial drawing used in industry is isometric. These drawings provide a single view showing three sides that can be measured using the same scale. An isometric view has no perspective and may appear somewhat distorted. Two of the isometric axes are drawn at 30° to horizontal; the third at 90°. See **Figure 26-5.**

The three axes shown in **Figure 26-5** represent the width, height, and depth of the object. Lines that appear horizontal in an orthographic view are placed at a 30° angle. Lines that are vertical in an orthographic view are placed vertically. These lines are parallel to the axes. Any line parallel to an axis can be measured and is called an ***isometric line.*** Lines that are not parallel to the axes are called ***nonisometric lines*** and cannot be measured. Note the two nonisometric lines in **Figure 26-5.**

Figure 26-5.
Layout of the isometric axes. Lines that are not parallel to any of the three axes are called nonisometric lines.

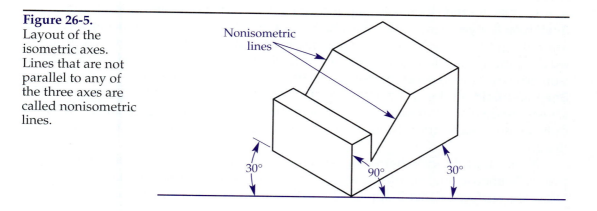

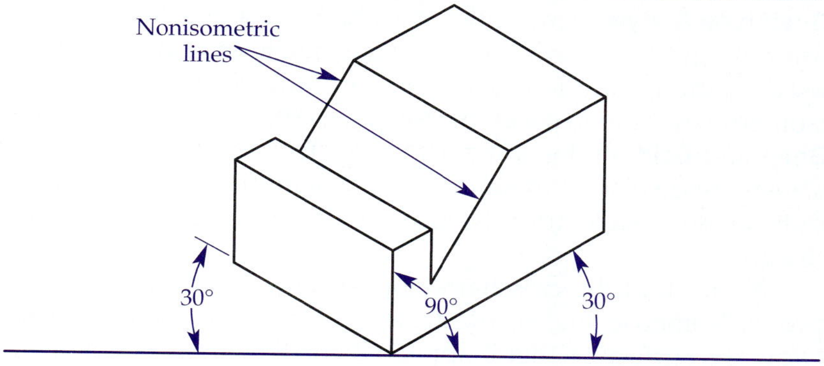

Circular features shown on isometric objects must be oriented properly or they appear distorted. The correct orientation of isometric circles on the three principle planes is shown in **Figure 26-6.** Circles appear as ellipses on an isometric. The small diameter (minor axis) of the ellipse must always align on the axis of the circular feature. Notice that the centerline axes of the holes in **Figure 26-6** are parallel to one of the isometric planes.

A basic rule to remember about isometric drawing is that lines parallel in an orthogonal view must be parallel in the isometric view. AutoCAD's **ISOPLANE** feature makes that task, and the positioning of ellipses, easy.

> **PROFESSIONAL TIP**
>
> If you are ever in doubt about the proper orientation of an ellipse in an isometric drawing, remember that the minor axis of the ellipse must always be aligned on the centerline axis of the circular feature. This is shown clearly in **Figure 26-6.**

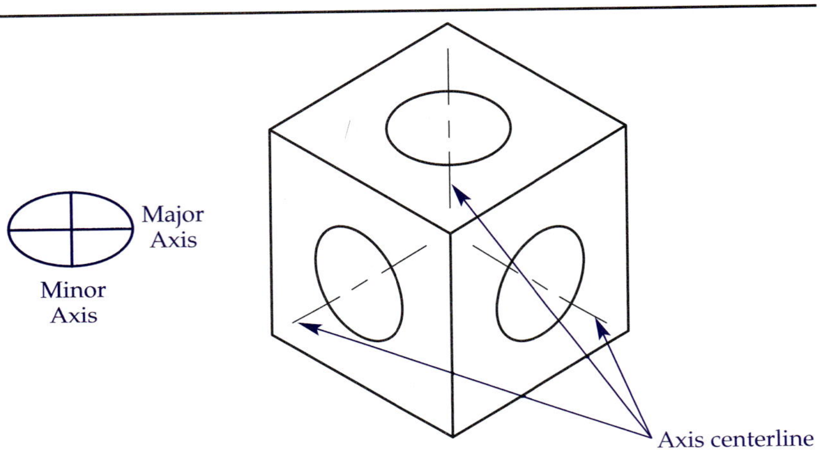

Figure 26-6. Proper isometric circle (ellipse) orientation on isometric planes. The minor axis always aligns with the axis centerline.

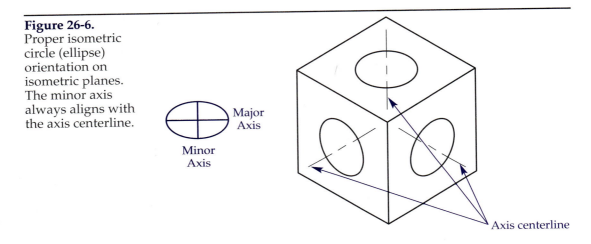

Settings for Isometric Drawing

DSETTINGS
DS
SE
DDRMODES

Tools
➡ Drafting Settings...

You can quickly set your isometric variables in the **Snap and Grid** tab of the **Drafting Settings** dialog box. See **Figure 26-7.** To access this dialog box, enter DS, SE, DSETTINGS, or DDRMODES at the Command: prompt, or select **Drafting Settings...** from the **Tools** pull-down menu. This dialog box can also be accessed by right-clicking on the **SNAP** or **GRID** status bar button and then selecting **Settings...** from the shortcut menu.

To activate the isometric snap grid, pick the **Isometric snap** radio button in the **Snap type & style** area. Notice that the **Snap X spacing** and **Grid X spacing** text boxes are now grayed-out. Since X spacing relates to horizontal measurements, it is not used in the isometric mode. You can only set the Y spacing for grid and snap in isometric. Be sure to check the **Snap On (F9)** and **Grid On (F7)** check boxes if you want **Snap** and **Grid** modes to be activated. Pick the **OK** button and the grid dots on the screen are displayed in an isometric orientation, as shown in **Figure 26-8.** If the grid dots are not visible, turn the grid on. You may also need to zoom in or out to display the grid.

Notice that the crosshairs appear angled. This aids you in drawing lines at the proper isometric angles. Try drawing a four-sided surface using the **LINE** command. Draw the surface so that it appears to be the left side of a box in an isometric layout.

Figure 26-7.
The **Drafting Settings** dialog box allows you to make settings needed for isometric drawing.

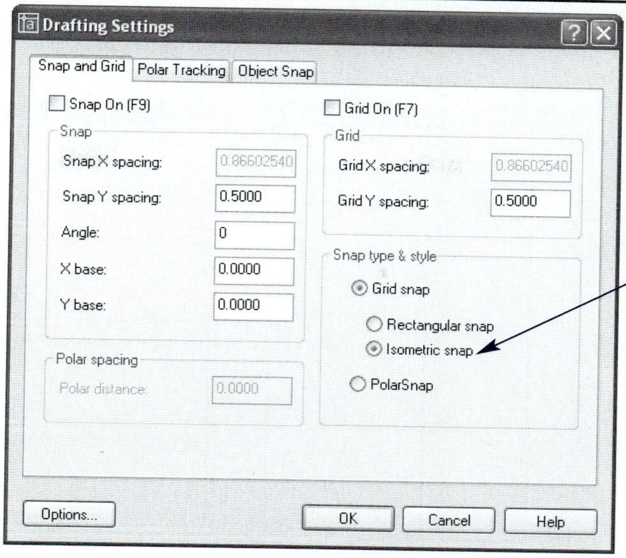

Figure 26-8.
An example of an isometric grid setup in AutoCAD.

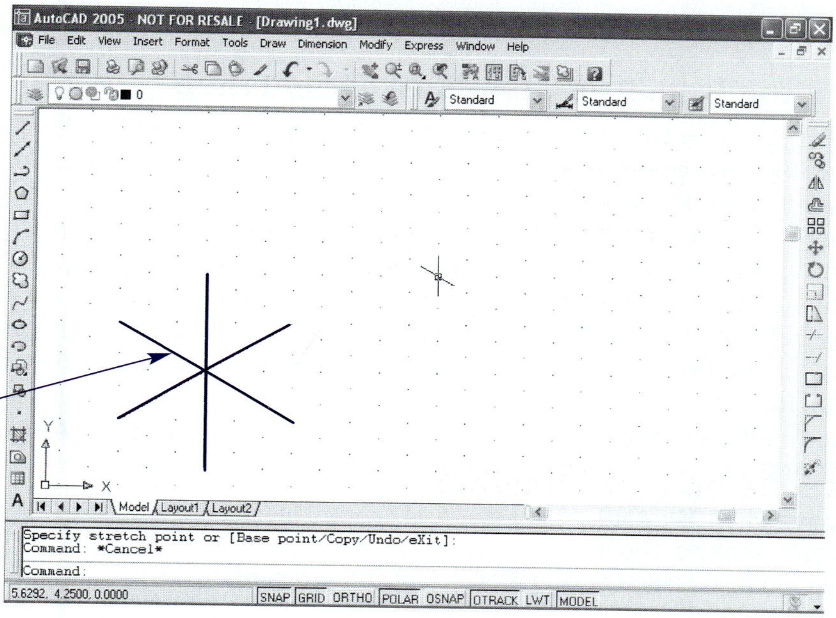

See **Figure 26-9.** To draw nonparallel surfaces, you can change the angle of the crosshairs to make your task easier, as discussed in the next section.

To turn off the Isometric Snap mode, pick the **Rectangular snap** radio button in the **Snap type & style** area. The Isometric Snap mode is turned off and you are returned to the drawing area when you pick the **OK** button.

> **NOTE**
>
> You can also set the Isometric Snap mode at the Command: prompt with the **SNAP** command. Type SNAP or SN, select the **Style** option, and then type I to select **Isometric**.

Figure 26-9.
A four-sided object drawn with the **LINE** command can be used as the left side of an isometric box.

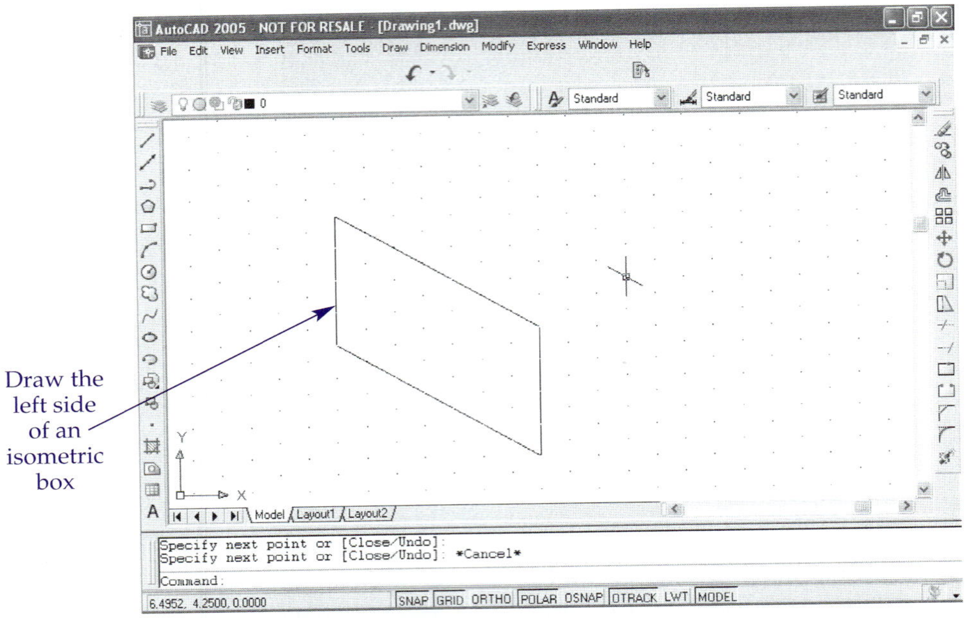

Changing the Isometric Crosshairs Orientation

Drawing an isometric shape is possible without ever changing the angle of the crosshairs. However, the drawing process is easier and quicker if the angles of the crosshairs align with the isometric axes.

Whenever the isometric snap style is enabled, simply press the [F5] key or the [Ctrl]+[E] key combination and the crosshairs immediately change to the next isometric plane. AutoCAD refers to the isometric positions or planes as ***isoplanes.*** As you change between isoplanes, the current isoplane is displayed on the prompt line as a reference. The three crosshairs orientations and their angular values are shown in **Figure 26-10.**

Another method to toggle the crosshairs position is with the **ISOPLANE** command. Enter ISOPLANE at the Command: prompt as follows.

Command: **ISOPLANE**↵
Current isoplane: Right
Enter isometric plane setting [Left/Top/Right] <*current*>: ↵

Press [Enter] to toggle the crosshairs to the next position. The command line displays the new isoplane setting. You can toggle immediately to the next position by pressing [Enter] at the Command: prompt to repeat the **ISOPLANE** command and pressing [Enter]

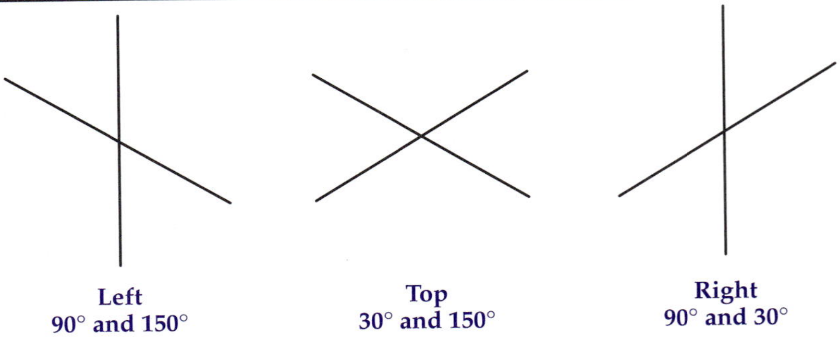

Figure 26-10.
The three isometric crosshairs positions can be changed using the [F5] function key, the [Ctrl]+[E] key combination, or using the **ISOPLANE** command.

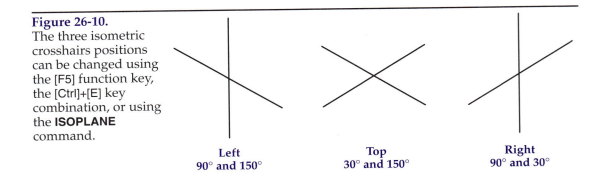

again. To specify the plane of orientation, type the first letter of that position. The **ISOPLANE** command can also be used transparently.

The crosshairs are always in one of the isoplane positions when Isometric Snap mode is in effect. An exception occurs during a display or editing command when a multiple selection set method (such as a window) is used. In these cases, the crosshairs change to the normal vertical and horizontal positions. At the completion of the display or editing command, the crosshairs automatically revert to their former isoplane orientation.

PROFESSIONAL TIP

The quickest way to change the isoplane is to press the [F5] function key or press the [Ctrl]+[E] key combination.

EXERCISE 26-1 Complete the Exercise on the Student CD.

Isometric Ellipses

ELLIPSE
EL

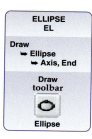

Draw
➥ **Ellipse**
➥ **Axis, End**

Draw toolbar

Ellipse

Placing an isometric ellipse on an object is easy with AutoCAD because of the **Isocircle** option of the **ELLIPSE** command. An ellipse is positioned automatically on the current isoplane. To use the **ELLIPSE** command, first make sure you are in Isometric Snap mode. Then, pick the **Ellipse** button on the **Draw** toolbar, select **Axis**, **End** from the **Ellipse** cascading menu in the **Draw** pull-down menu, or enter EL or ELLIPSE at the Command: prompt. Once the **ELLIPSE** command is initiated, the following prompts appear.

Specify axis endpoint of ellipse or [Arc/Center/Isocircle]: **I**↵
Specify center of isocircle: *(pick a point)*
Specify radius of isocircle or [Diameter]:

Once you select the **Isocircle** option, pick the center point and then set the radius or diameter. The **Center** option does not allow you to create isocircles. Also, the **Isocircle** option only appears when you are in Isometric Snap mode.

Always check the isoplane position before placing an ellipse (isocircle) on your drawing. You can dynamically view the three positions that an ellipse can take. Initiate the **ELLIPSE** command, enter the **Isocircle** option, pick a center point, and press [F5] to toggle the crosshairs orientation. See **Figure 26-11.** The ellipse rotates each time you toggle the crosshairs.

Figure 26-11.
The orientation of an isometric ellipse is determined by the crosshairs orientation.

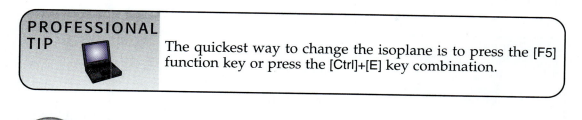

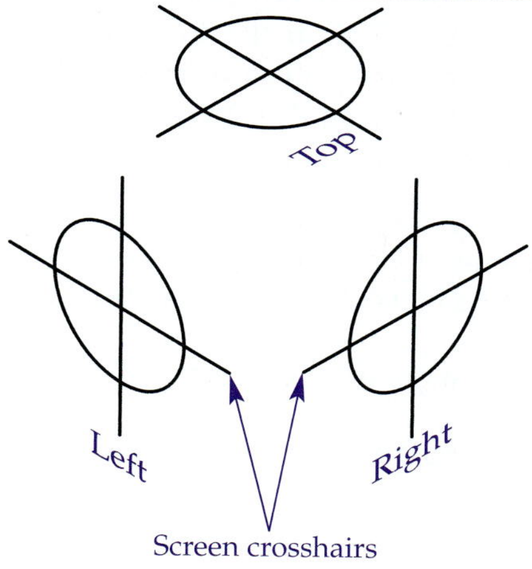

The isometric ellipse (isocircle) is a true ellipse. If selected, grips are displayed at the center and four quadrant points. See **Figure 26-12.** However, do not use grips to resize or otherwise adjust an isometric ellipse. As soon as you resize an isometric ellipse in this manner, its angular value is changed and it is no longer isometric. You can use the center grip to move the ellipse. Also, if you rotate an isometric ellipse while Ortho mode is on, it will not appear in a proper isometric plane. You *can* rotate an isometric ellipse from one isometric plane to another, but you must enter a value of 120°.

PROFESSIONAL TIP

Prior to drawing isometric ellipses, it is good practice to first place a marker at the ellipse center point. A good technique is to draw a point at the center using an easily visible point style. This is especially useful if the ellipse does not fall on grid or snap points.

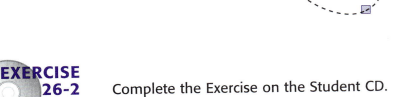

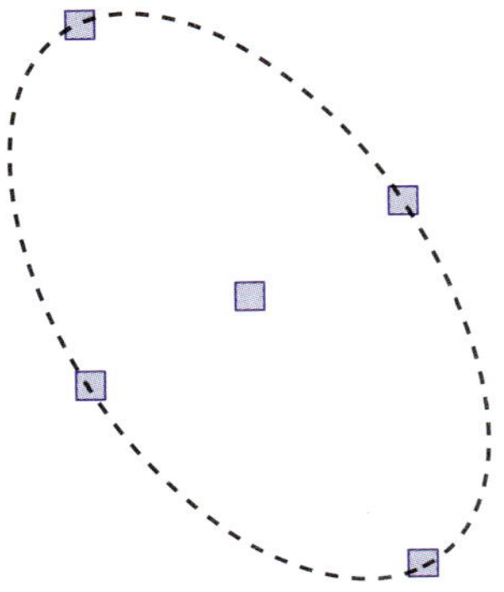

Figure 26-12.
An isometric ellipse has grips at its four quadrant points and center.

EXERCISE 26-2 Complete the Exercise on the Student CD.

Constructing Isometric Arcs

The **ELLIPSE** command can also be used to draw an isometric arc of any included angle. To construct an isometric arc, use the **Arc** option of the **ELLIPSE** command while in **Isometric mode**. To access the **Arc** option, pick the **Ellipse** button on the **Draw** toolbar, enter EL or ELLIPSE at the Command: prompt, or select **Arc** from the **Ellipse** cascading menu in the **Draw** pull-down menu. If you use the toolbar button or command line, you must then type A at the Command: prompt to enter the **Arc** option. Once the **Arc** option is initiated, the following prompts appear:

Specify axis endpoint of elliptical arc or [Center/Isocircle]: **I**↵
Specify center of isocircle: *(pick the center of the arc)*
Specify radius of isocircle or [Diameter]: *(pick the radius or type a value and press* [Enter]*)*
Specify start angle or [Parameter]: *(pick a start angle or type a value and press* [Enter]*)*
Specify end angle or [Parameter/Included angle]: *(pick an end angle or type an included angle value and press* [Enter]*)*
Command:

A common application of isometric arcs is drawing fillets and rounds. Once a round is created in isometric, the edge (corner) of the object sits back from its original, unfilleted position. See **Figure 26-13A.** You can draw the complete object first and then trim away the excess after locating the fillets. You can also draw the isometric arcs and then the connecting lines. Either way, the center point of the ellipse is a critical feature, and should be located first. The left-hand arc in **Figure 26-13A** was drawn first and copied to the back position. Use Ortho mode to help quickly draw 90° arcs.

The next step is to move the original edge to its new position, which is tangent to the isometric arcs. You can do this by snapping the endpoint of the line to the quadrant point of the arc. See **Figure 26-13B.** Notice the grips on the line and on the arc. The endpoint of the line is snapped to the quadrant grip on the arc. The final step is to trim away the excess lines and arc segment. The completed feature is shown in **Figure 26-13C.**

Rounded edges, when viewed straight on, cannot be shown as complete-edge lines that extend to the ends of the object. Instead, a good technique to use is a broken line in the original location of the edge. This is clearly shown in the figure in Exercise 26-3.

Figure 26-13.
Fillets and rounds can be drawn with the **Arc** option of the **ELLIPSE** command.

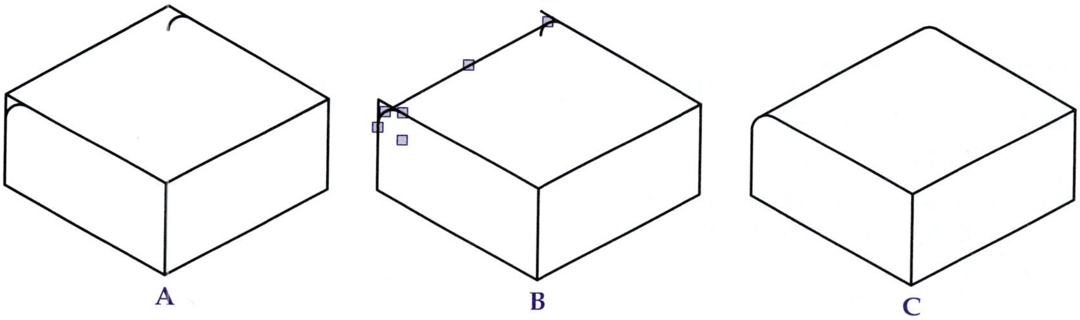

EXERCISE 26-3 Complete the Exercise on the Student CD.

Creating Isometric Text Styles

Text placed in an isometric drawing should appear to be parallel to one of the isometric planes. Text should align with the plane to which it applies. Text may be located on the object or positioned away from it as a note. Drafters and artists occasionally neglect this aspect of pictorial drawing and it shows on the final product.

Properly placing text on an isometric drawing involves creating new text styles. **Figure 26-14** illustrates possible orientations of text on an isometric drawing. These examples were created using only two text styles. The text styles have an obliquing angle of either 30° or –30°. The labels in **Figure 26-14** refer to the chart below. The angle in the figure indicates the rotation angle entered when using one of the **TEXT** commands. For example, ISO-2 90 means that the ISO-2 style was used and the text was rotated 90°. This technique can be applied to any font.

Name	Font	Obliquing Angle
ISO-1	Romans	30°
ISO-2	Romans	–30°

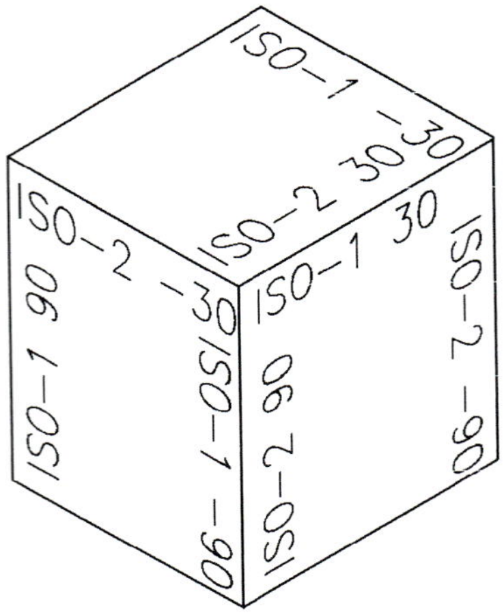

Figure 26-14.
Isometric text applications. The text shown here indicates which ISO style and angle were used.

EXERCISE 26-4

Complete the Exercise on the Student CD.

Isometric Dimensioning

An important aspect of dimensioning in isometric is to place dimension lines, text, and arrowheads on the proper plane. Remember these guidelines:

- ✓ Extension lines should always extend the plane being dimensioned.
- ✓ The heel of the arrowhead should always be parallel to the extension line.
- ✓ Strokes of the text that would normally be vertical should always be parallel with the extension lines or dimension lines.

These techniques are shown on the dimensioned isometric part in **Figure 26-15.** AutoCAD does not automatically dimension isometric objects. You must first create isometric arrowheads and text styles. Then, manually draw the dimension lines and text as they should appear in each of the three isometric planes. This is time-consuming when compared to dimensioning normal 2D drawings.

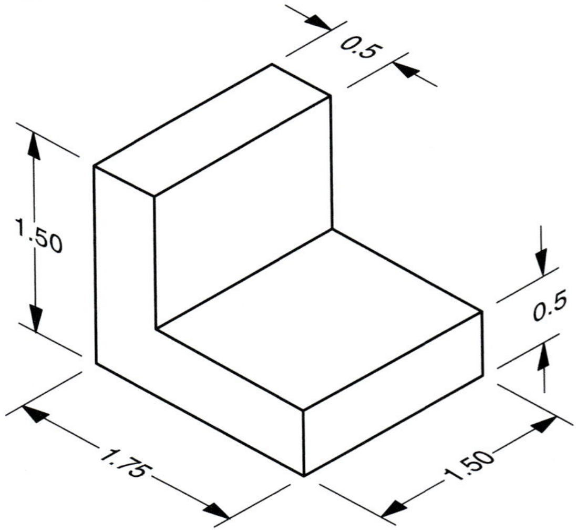

Figure 26-15.
A dimensioned isometric part. Note the text and arrowhead orientation in relation to the extension lines.

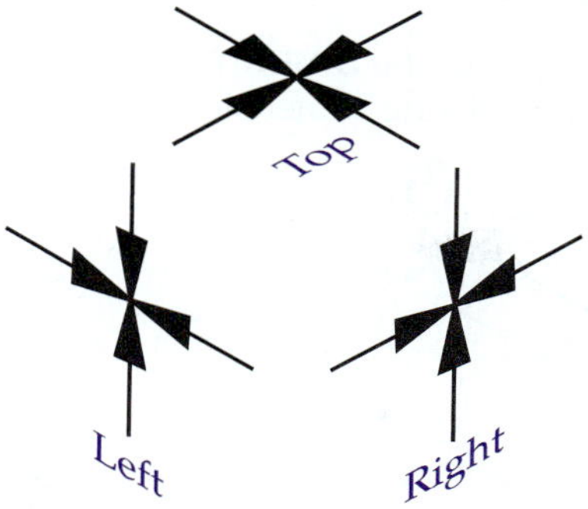

Figure 26-16. Examples of arrowheads in each of the three isometric planes.

You have already learned how to create isometric text styles. These can be set up in an isometric template drawing if you draw isometrics often. Examples of arrows for the three isometric planes are shown in **Figure 26-16.**

Isometric Arrowheads

Arrowheads can be drawn and filled-in with a solid hatch pattern, or you can use the **SOLID** command to create a filled arrowhead. A variable-width polyline cannot be used because the heel of the arrowhead will not be parallel to the extension lines.

Every arrowhead does not need to be drawn individually. First, draw two isometric axes, as shown in **Figure 26-17A.** Then, draw one arrowhead like the one shown in **Figure 26-17B.** Use the **MIRROR** command to create additional arrows. As you create new arrows, move them to their proper plane.

Save each arrowhead as a block in your isometric template or prototype. Use block names that are easy to remember.

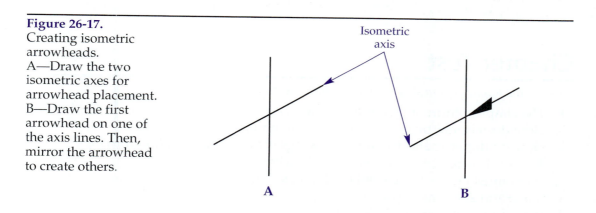

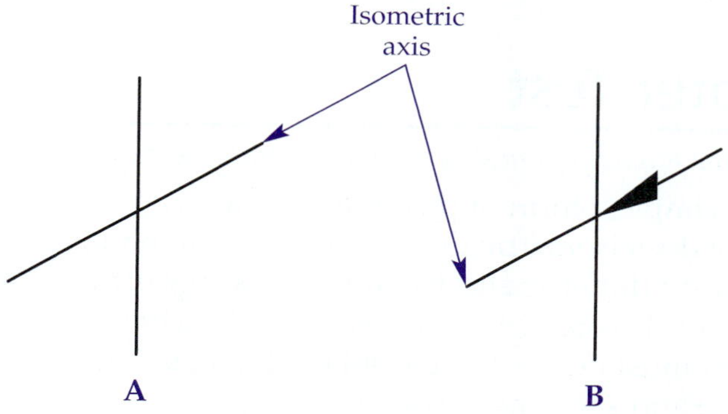

Figure 26-17. Creating isometric arrowheads. A—Draw the two isometric axes for arrowhead placement. B—Draw the first arrowhead on one of the axis lines. Then, mirror the arrowhead to create others.

Oblique Dimensioning

AutoCAD has a way to semiautomatically dimension isometric and oblique lines. First, the dimensions must be drawn using any of the linear dimensioning commands. **Figure 26-18A** illustrates an object dimensioned using the **DIMALIGNED** and **DIMLINEAR** commands. Then, use the **Oblique** option of the **DIMEDIT** command to rotate the extension lines. See **Figure 26-18B.**

To access the **Oblique** option, enter DED or DIMEDIT at the Command: prompt and then enter O for **Oblique**. You can also select **Oblique** from the **Dimension** pull-down menu. When prompted, select the dimension and enter the obliquing angle.

This technique creates suitable dimensions for an isometric drawing and is quicker than the previous method discussed. However, this method does not rotate the arrows so the arrowhead heels are aligned with the extension lines. It also does not draw the dimension text aligned in the plane of the dimension.

Figure 26-18.
Using the **Oblique** option of the **DIMEDIT** command, you can create semiautomatic isometric dimensions by editing existing dimensions.

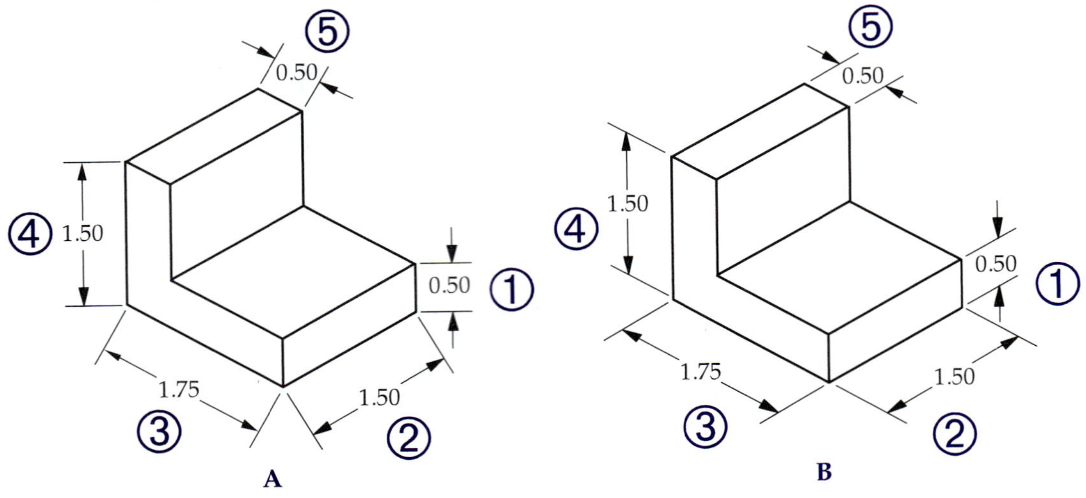

Dimension	Obliquing Angle
1	30°
2	-30°
3	30°
4	-30°
5	30°

Chapter Test

Answer the following questions on a separate sheet of paper.

1. The simplest form of pictorial drawing is _____.
2. How does isometric drawing differ from oblique drawing?
3. How do dimetric and trimetric drawings differ from isometric drawings?
4. The most realistic form of pictorial drawing is _____.
5. What must be set in the **Drafting Settings** dialog box to turn on Isometric Snap mode and set a snap spacing of 0.2?
6. What function does the **ISOPLANE** command perform?
7. Which pull-down menu contains the command to access the **Drafting Settings** dialog box?
8. What factor determines the orientation of an isometric ellipse?
9. Name the command and option used to draw a circle in isometric.
10. Which text style setting allows you to create text that can be used on an isometric drawing?
11. Which command and two options must you select in order to draw isometric arcs?
12. Where are grips located on a circle drawn in isometric?
13. Can grips be used to correctly resize an isometric circle? Explain your answer.
14. What technique does AutoCAD provide for dimensioning isometric objects?

Drawing Problems

Create an isometric template drawing. Items that should be set in the template include grid spacing, snap spacing, ortho setting, and text size. Save the template as isoproto.dwt. *Use the template to construct the isometric drawings in Problems 1–10. Save the drawing problems as* P26-*(problem number).*

1.

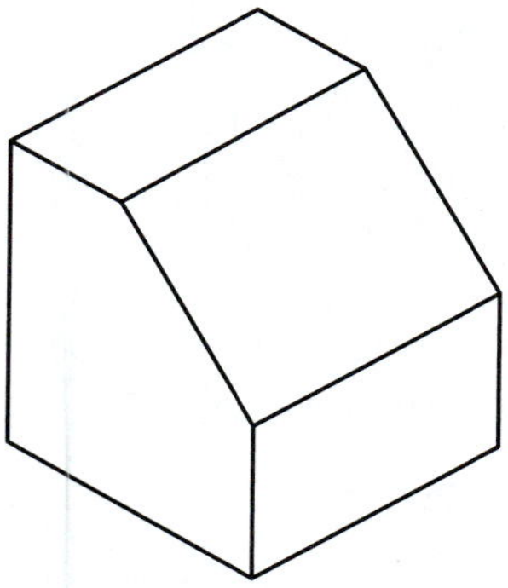

2.

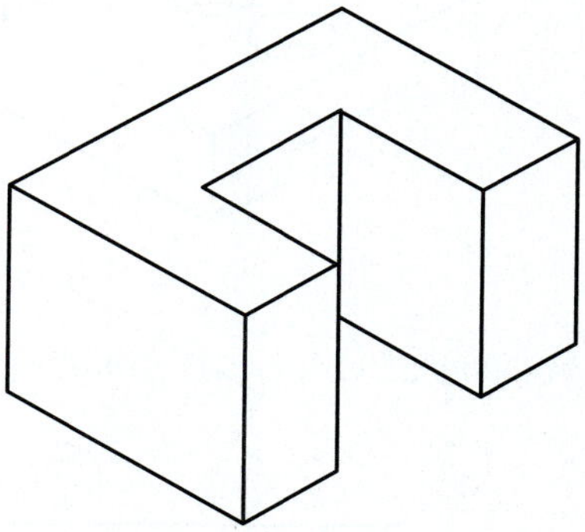

3.

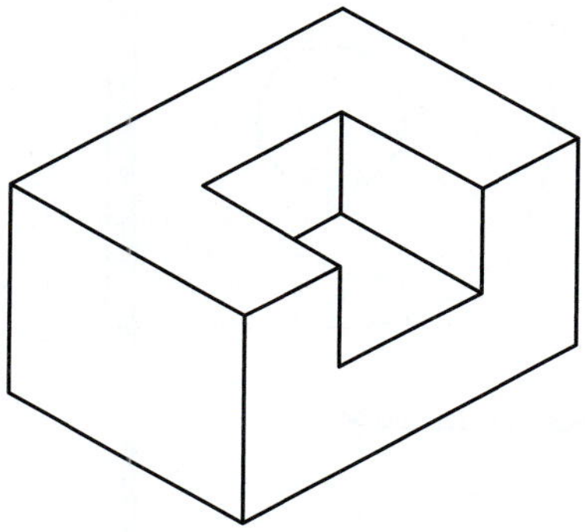

4.

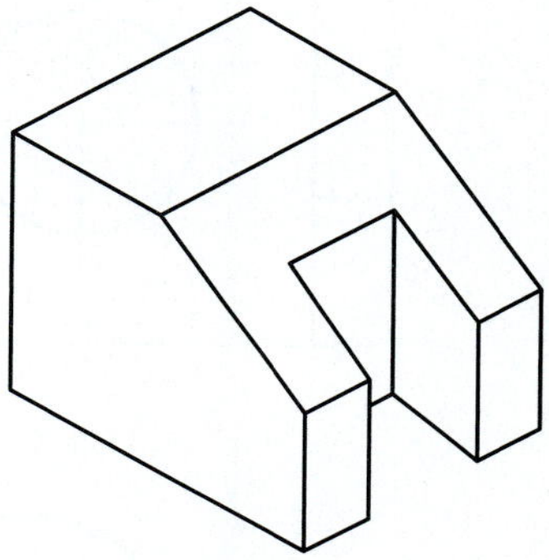

5.

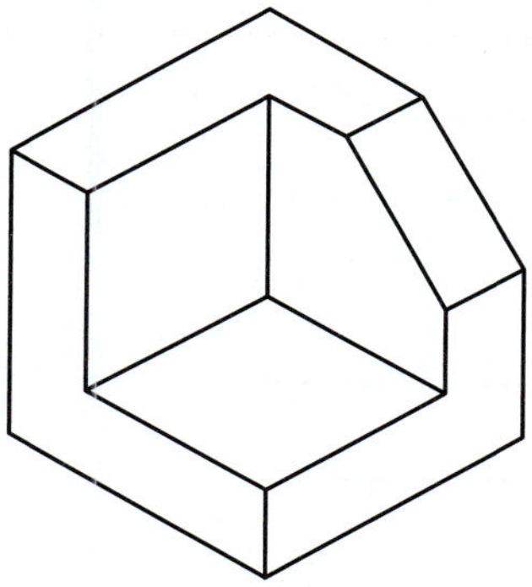

6.

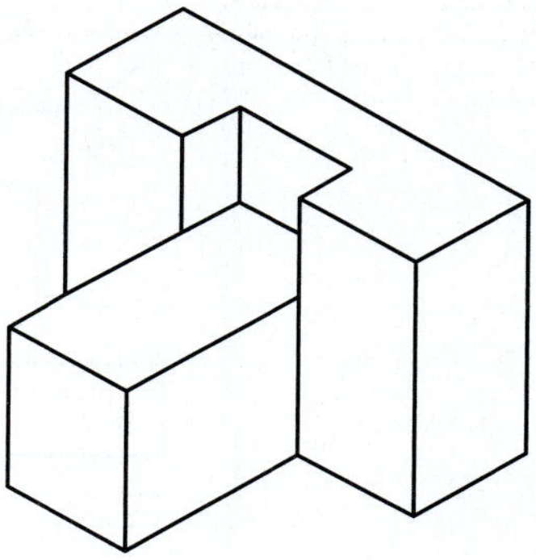

7.

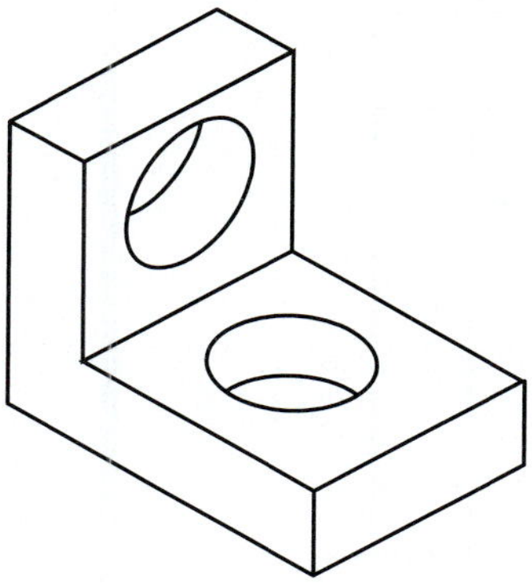

8.

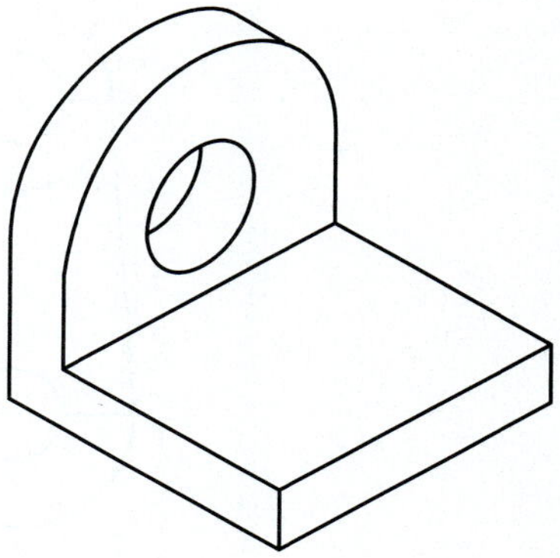

9.

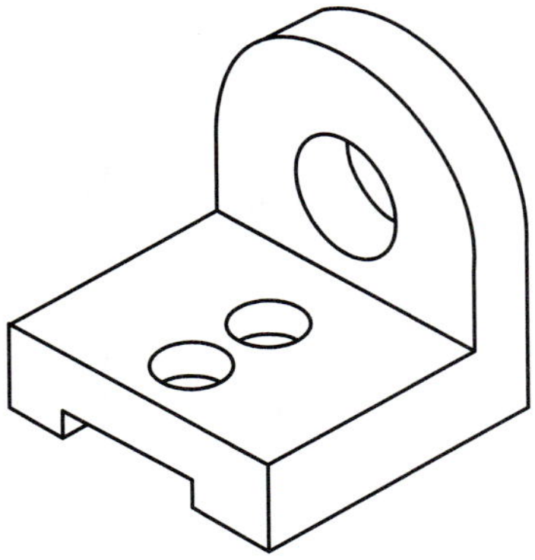

10.

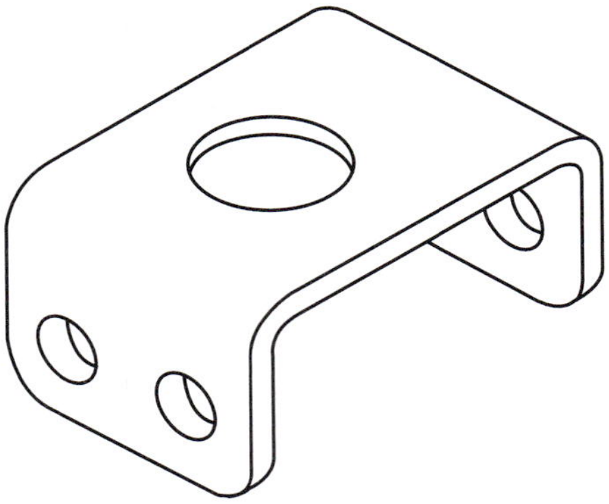

For Problems 11–14, create isometric drawings using the views shown.

11.

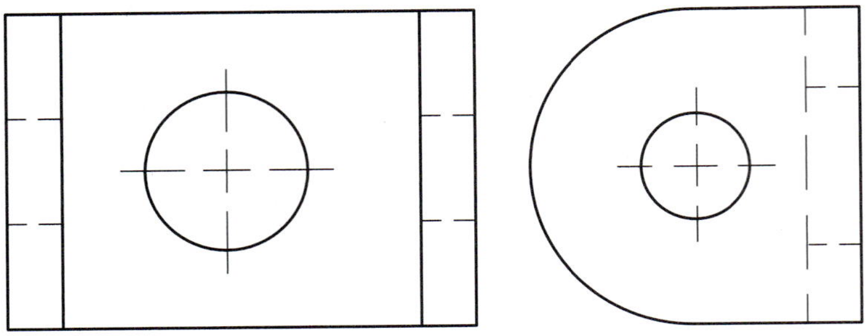

12.

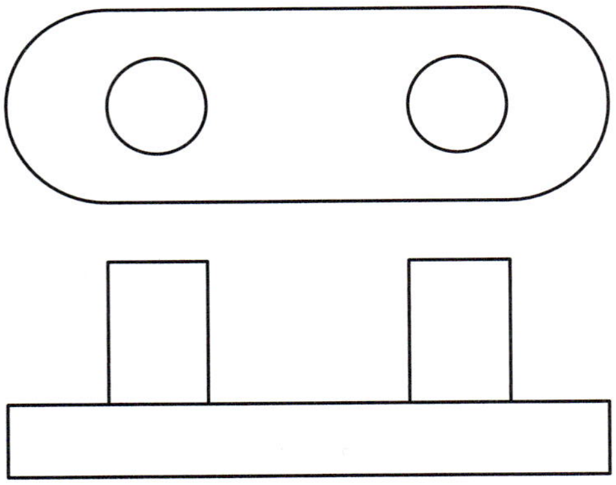

13.

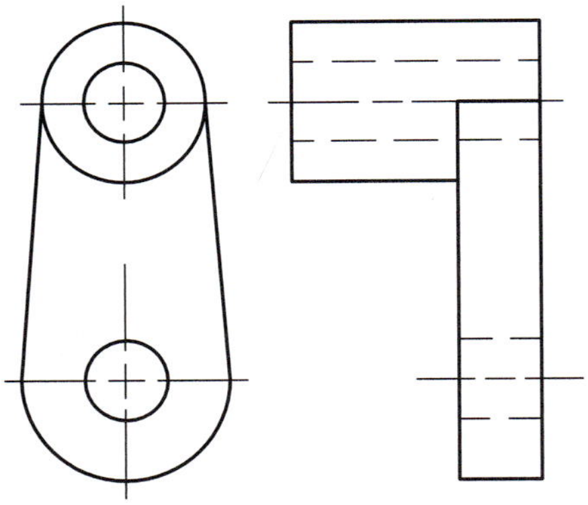

14.

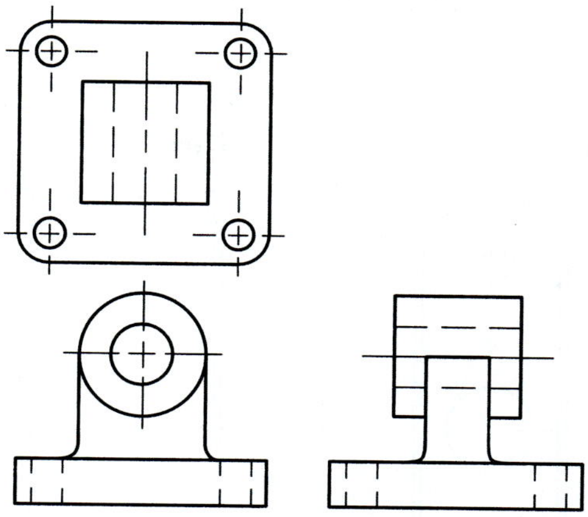

15. Construct a set of isometric arrowheads to use when dimensioning isometric drawings. Load your isometric template drawing. Create arrowheads for each of the three isometric planes. Save each arrowhead as a block. Name them with the first letter indicating the plane: T for top, L for left, and R for right. Also, number them clockwise from the top. See the example below for the right isometric plane. Do not include the labels in the blocks. Save the template again when finished.

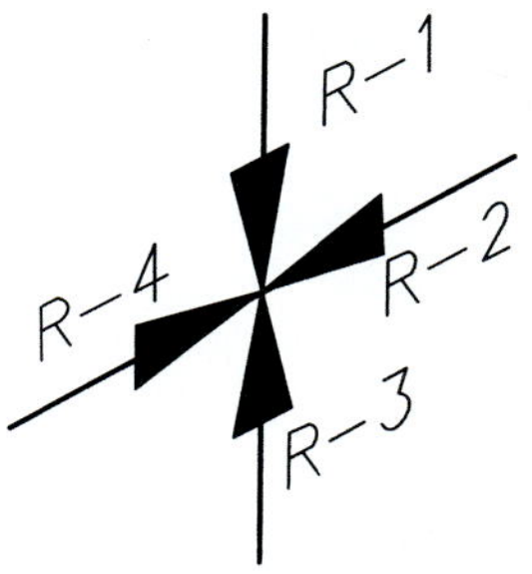

16. Create a set of isometric text styles like those shown in **Figure 26-14.** Load your template drawing and make a complete set in one font. Make additional sets in other fonts if you wish. Enter a text height of 0 so that you can specify the height when placing the text. Save the template when finished.

17. Begin a new drawing using your isometric template. Select one of the following problems from this chapter and dimension it: Problem 5, 7, 8, or 9. When adding dimensions, be sure to use the proper arrowhead and text style for the plane on which you are working. Save the drawing as P26-17.

18. Create an isometric drawing of the switch plate shown below. Select a view that best displays the features of the object. Do not include dimensions. Save the drawing as **P26-18**.

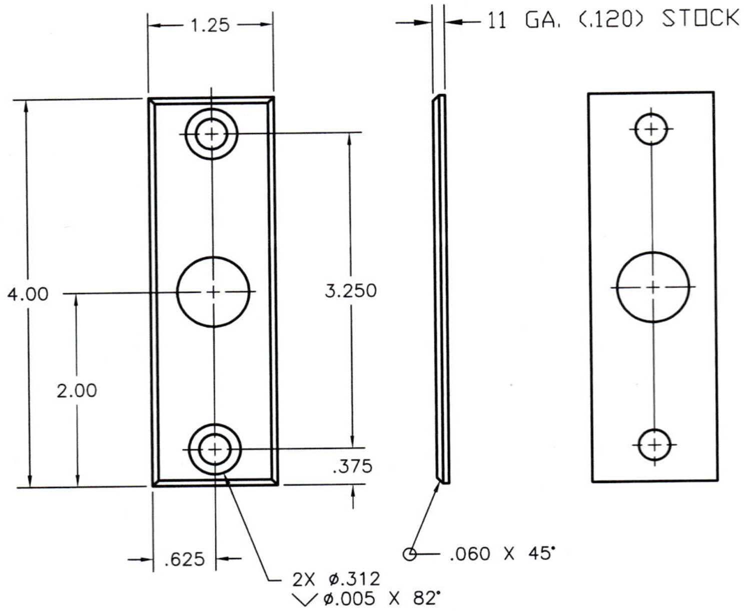

19. Create an isometric drawing of the retainer shown below. Select a view that best displays the features of the object. Do not include dimensions. Save the drawing as **P26-19**.

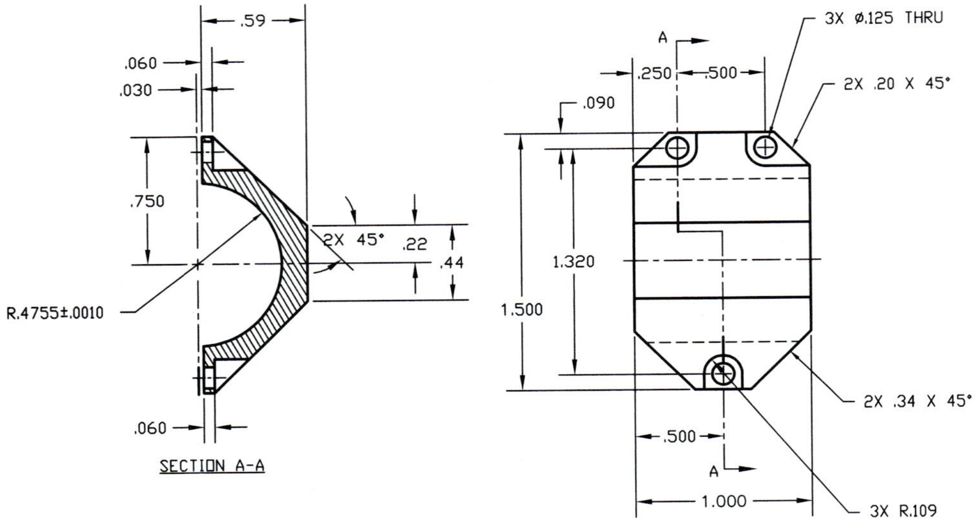

CHAPTER 27

Introduction to Three-Dimensional Drawing

Learning Objectives

After completing this chapter, you will be able to do the following:

- Describe how to locate points in 3D space.
- Use the right-hand rule of 3D visualization.
- Display 3D objects from preset isometric viewpoints.
- Display 3D objects from any desired viewpoint.
- Construct wireframe objects.
- Construct solid primitives.
- Construct surface primitives.
- Create hidden displays.
- Create shaded displays.

Drafters and designers must have good three-dimensional (3D) visualization skills, such as the ability to see an object in three dimensions and to visualize it rotating in space. These skills are acquired by using 3D techniques to construct objects and by trying to picture two-dimensional sketches and drawings as 3D models.

Chapter 26 explained a method of representing a 3D object in two-dimensional space. This chapter provides an introduction to several aspects of true 3D drawing and visualization. A thorough discussion of 3D drawing, modeling, visualization, and display techniques is provided in ***AutoCAD and its Applications—Advanced***.

3D Coordinates

To this point, you have been drawing in two dimensions (2D) in relation to X and Y coordinates. When drawing in 3D, however, a third coordinate measured along the Z axis is required. For 2D drawings, the Z coordinate is 0. Using X, Y, and Z coordinates, you can locate any point in 3D space.

Look at **Figure 27-1.** Note that the positive Z values come up from the XY plane. Consider the surface of your computer screen as the XY plane. Anything behind the screen is negative Z and anything in front of the screen is positive Z.

Figure 27-1.
A comparison of 2D and 3D coordinate systems.

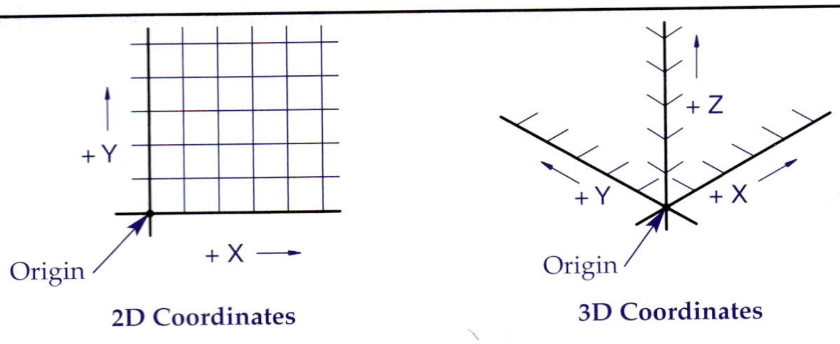

Figure 27-2A shows a 2D drawing of the top of an object. The XY coordinate values of each point are shown. However, this is actually a 3D object. When displayed in a pictorial view, the Z coordinates can be seen. Notice in **Figure 27-2B** that the first two values of each coordinate match the X and Y values of the 2D view. Three-dimensional coordinates are always expressed as (X,Y,Z).

Study the nature of the 3D coordinate system. Be sure you understand Z values before you begin constructing 3D objects. It is important that you visualize and plan your design when working with 3D constructions.

PROFESSIONAL TIP

All points in three-dimensional space can be drawn using one of three coordinate entry methods—rectangular, spherical, or cylindrical. This chapter uses the rectangular coordinate entry method. For complete discussions on the spherical and cylindrical coordinate entry methods, please refer to ***AutoCAD and its Applications—Advanced.***

Figure 27-2.
Each vertex of a 3D object must have an X, Y, and Z value.

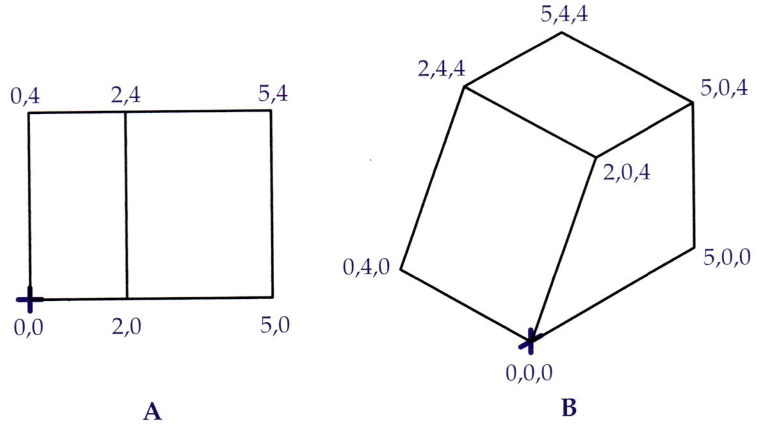

EXERCISE 27-1 Complete the Exercise on the Student CD.

The Right-Hand Rule

The *right-hand rule* is a representation of positive coordinate values in the three axis directions of a coordinate system. This rule requires that you hold the thumb, index finger, and middle finger of your right hand in front of you as shown in **Figure 27-3.** Although this may seem a bit unusual to do, especially if you are sitting in the middle of a school library or computer lab, it can help you understand the nature of the three axes. If you discover that your 3D visualization skills are weak or that you are having trouble working with different UCSs, do not be afraid to use the right-hand rule. It is a useful technique for improving your 3D visualization skills.

Imagine that your thumb represents the X axis, your index finger the Y axis, and your middle finger the Z axis. Holding your hand in front of you, rotate your wrist so your middle finger is pointing directly at you. Now you see the plan view of the XY plane. The positive X axis is pointing to the right, the positive Y axis is pointing up, and the positive Z axis comes toward you. The origin (0,0,0) of this system is the palm of your hand.

The concept behind the right-hand rule can be visualized even better if you are sitting at a computer and the AutoCAD drawing area is displayed. If the UCS icon is not displayed in the lower-left corner of the screen, turn it on:

Command: **UCSICON**↵
Enter an option [ON/OFF/All/Noorigin/ORigin/Properties] <*current*>: **ON**↵

Now, orient your right hand as shown in **Figure 27-3** and position it next to the UCS (or WCS) icon. Your thumb and index finger should point in the same directions as the X and Y axes, respectively, on the UCS icon. Your middle finger will be pointing out of the screen. See **Figure 27-4.**

The right-hand rule can also be used to eliminate confusion when rotating the UCS. The UCS can rotate about any one of the three coordinate axes, just as a wheel rotates on an axle. Therefore, if you want to rotate about the X axis, keep your thumb stationary and turn your hand either toward or away from you. If you wish to rotate about the Y axis, keep your index finger stationary and turn your hand to the left or right. When rotating about the Z axis, keep your middle finger stationary and rotate your entire arm.

Figure 27-3.
Try positioning your hand as shown to understand the relationship of the X, Y, and Z axes.

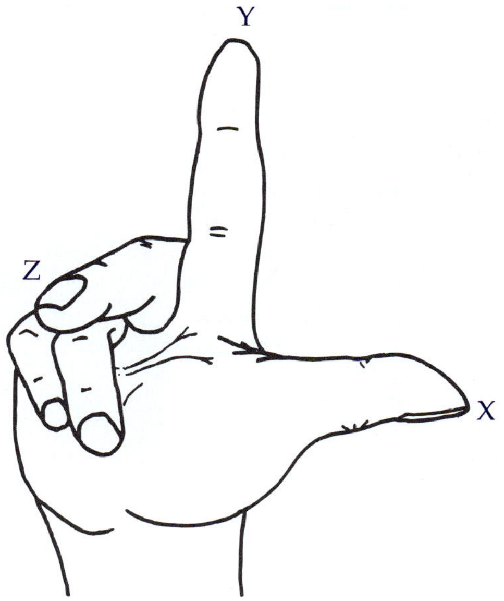

Figure 27-4.
Using the right-hand rule to view the WCS.

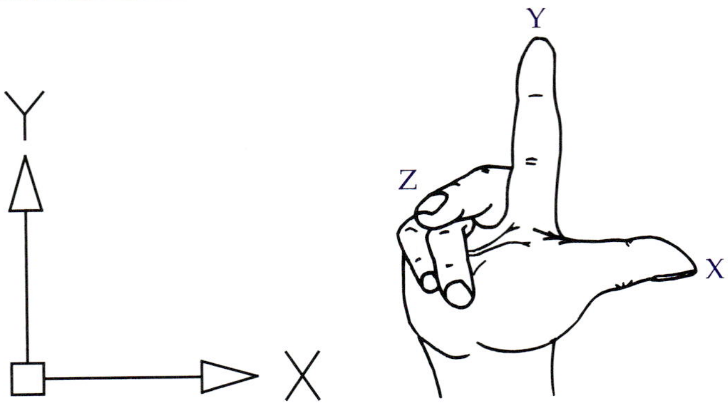

Working with UCSs is introduced in Chapter 6 of this text. A complete discussion of working with and managing UCSs is provided in ***AutoCAD and its Applications—Advanced***.

Displaying 3D Views

It does not do much good to understand how to draw in 3D space if you cannot see what you draw in three dimensions. To this point, you have been looking at a plan, or top, view of the XY plane. AutoCAD provides several methods of changing your viewpoint to produce a 3D, or pictorial, view. The *viewpoint* is the location in space from which the object is viewed. Two methods of changing your viewpoint are discussed here.

Isometric and Orthographic Viewpoint Presets

As you learned in Chapter 26, a 2D isometric drawing is based on angles of 120° between the three axes. AutoCAD provides preset viewpoints that allow you to view a 3D object from one of four locations. See **Figure 27-5.** Each of these viewpoints produces an isometric view of the object. In addition, AutoCAD has presets for the six standard orthographic views of an object. The isometric and orthographic viewpoint presets are based on the WCS.

Figure 27-5.
There are four preset isometric viewpoints in AutoCAD. This illustration shows the direction from which the cube will be viewed for each of the presets. The grid represents the XY plane of the WCS.

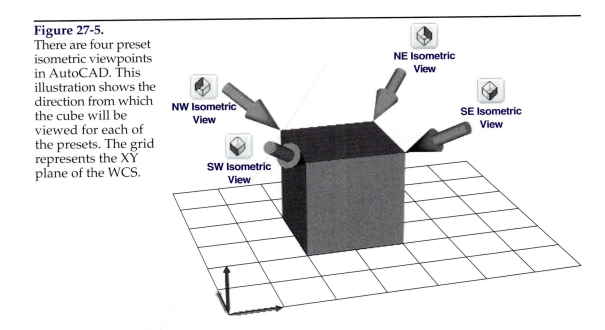

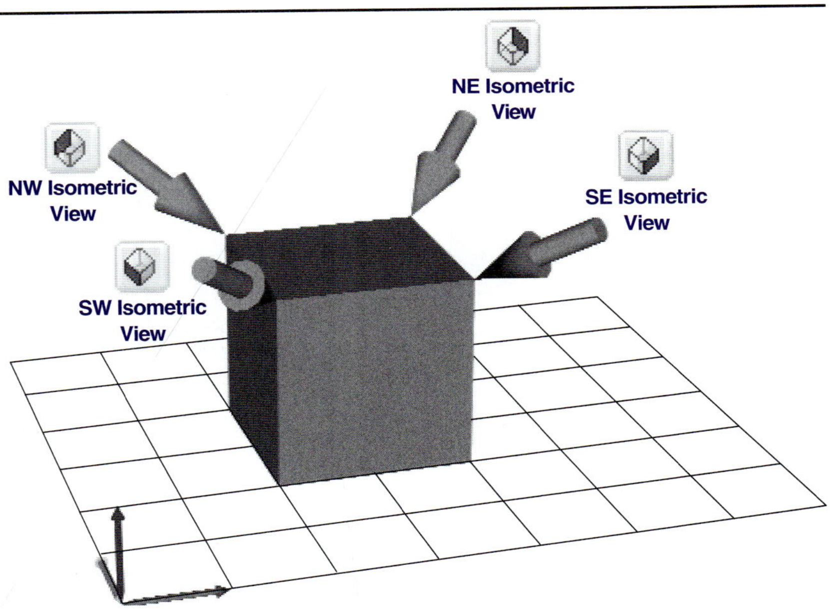

The four preset isometric views are southwest, southeast, northeast, and northwest. To switch your viewpoint to one of these presets, select **3D Views** from the **View** pull-down menu. Then, select **SW Isometric**, **SE Isometric**, **NE Isometric**, or **NW Isometric** from the cascading menu. You can also select the **SW Isometric**, **SE Isometric**, **NE Isometric**, or **NW Isometric** button on the **View** toolbar. This toolbar is not displayed by default.

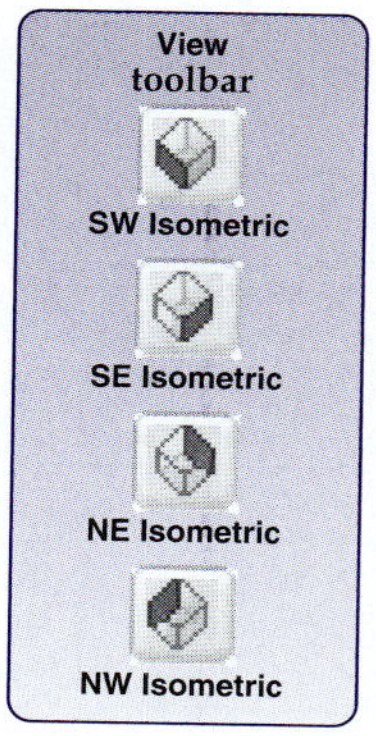

Once you select the command, the viewpoint in the current viewport is automatically changed to display an appropriate isometric view. Since these presets are based on the WCS, selecting a preset produces the same isometric view of the object regardless of the current UCS.

A view that looks straight down on the current drawing plane is called a ***plan view.*** For example, the default view when you start AutoCAD is a plan view of the WCS. When an isometric or other 3D view is displayed, you can easily switch to a plan view of the current UCS using the **PLAN** command. Type PLAN at the Command: prompt:

PLAN

View
➥ **3D Views**
➥ **Plan View**
➥ **World UCS**

Command: **PLAN**↵
Enter an option [Current ucs/Ucs/World] <Current>: **W**↵ *(if you press* [Enter]*, a plan view of the current UCS is displayed; the current UCS may or may not be the WCS)*
Regenerating model.
Command:

You can also create a plan view of the WCS by selecting **3D Views** in the **View** pull-down menu. Then, select **Plan View** in the cascading menu and **World UCS** in the next cascading menu.

The six orthographic presets are top, bottom, left, right, front, and back. To switch your viewpoint to one of these presets, select **3D Views** from the **View** pull-down menu. Then, select **Top**, **Bottom**, **Left**, **Right**, **Front**, or **Back** from the cascading menu. You can also select the **Top View**, **Bottom View**, **Left View**, **Right View**, **Front View**, or **Back View** button on the **View** toolbar. Once you select a preset, the view is changed to the corresponding orthographic view. Like the isometric presets, the orthographic presets are based on the WCS so the same view is displayed regardless of the current UCS.

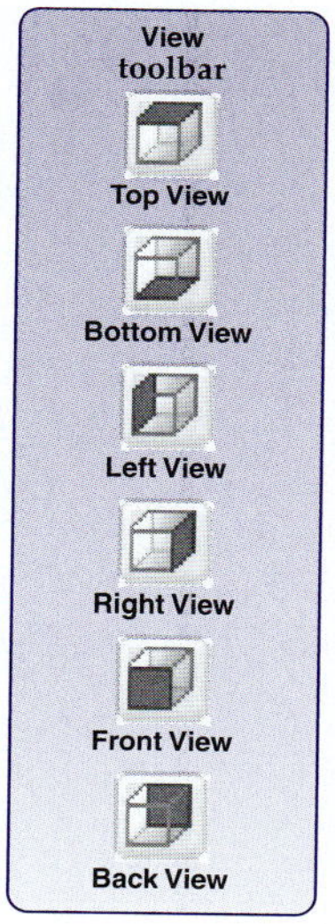

An important aspect of the orthographic presets is that selecting one not only changes the viewpoint, it changes the UCS to be plan to the orthographic view. All new objects are created on that UCS instead of the WCS (or previous UCS). Working with UCSs is explained in detail in ***AutoCAD and its Applications—Advanced***. For the activities in this text, do not use the orthographic presets. However, the command sequence to change the UCS to the WCS is:

Command: **UCS**↵
Current ucs name: *LEFT* *(this name will match the name of the orthographic preset used to display the view)*
Enter an option [New/Move/orthoGraphic/Prev/Restore/Save/Del/Apply/?/World] <World>: **W**↵
Command:

EXERCISE 27-2 Complete the Exercise on the Student CD.

Unlimited Viewpoints

3DORBIT
3DO

View
➥ 3D Orbit

You are not limited to the preset isometric viewpoints. In fact, you can view a 3D object from an unlimited number of viewpoints. The **3DORBIT** command allows you to dynamically rotate the view of the objects to create a new viewpoint.

To start the **3DORBIT** command, pick **3D Orbit** from the **View** pull-down menu or type 3DORBIT or 3DO at the Command: prompt. A green circle appears in the middle of the current viewport. See **Figure 27-6.** This is called the trackball, or arcball. Also, notice that the cursor changes. If you move it inside the trackball, it appears as two intersecting circles, as shown in **Figure 27-6.** If you move it outside of the trackball, the cursor appears as a single circle.

To change the view, pick anywhere inside the trackball and drag the cursor. The view is dynamically changed as you move the cursor. However, you are not rotating the *objects,* just the view. When you get the view you want, release the mouse button. The command remains active and you can further adjust the view. When done, right-click to display the shortcut menu. Then, select **Exit** from the menu. You can also press [Esc] to end the command. The **UNDO** command reverses the effects of the **3DORBIT** command.

Picking outside the trackball and dragging rotates the view about an axis extending out of the screen. Also, notice the circle "handles" at the four quadrants of the trackball. Picking in the right or left handle and dragging rotates the view about the vertical axis in the viewport. Picking in the top or bottom handle and dragging rotates the view about the horizontal axis in the viewport.

The **3DORBIT** command has many options. This discussion is merely an introduction to the command. The command options are covered in detail in ***AutoCAD and its Applications—Advanced.***

PROFESSIONAL TIP

AutoCAD has other commands for changing the viewpoint whose functionality has largely been replaced by the more useful **3DORBIT** command. These commands include **VPOINT**, **DDVPOINT**, and **DVIEW**.

Figure 27-6.
Using the **3DORBIT** command to change the viewpoint.

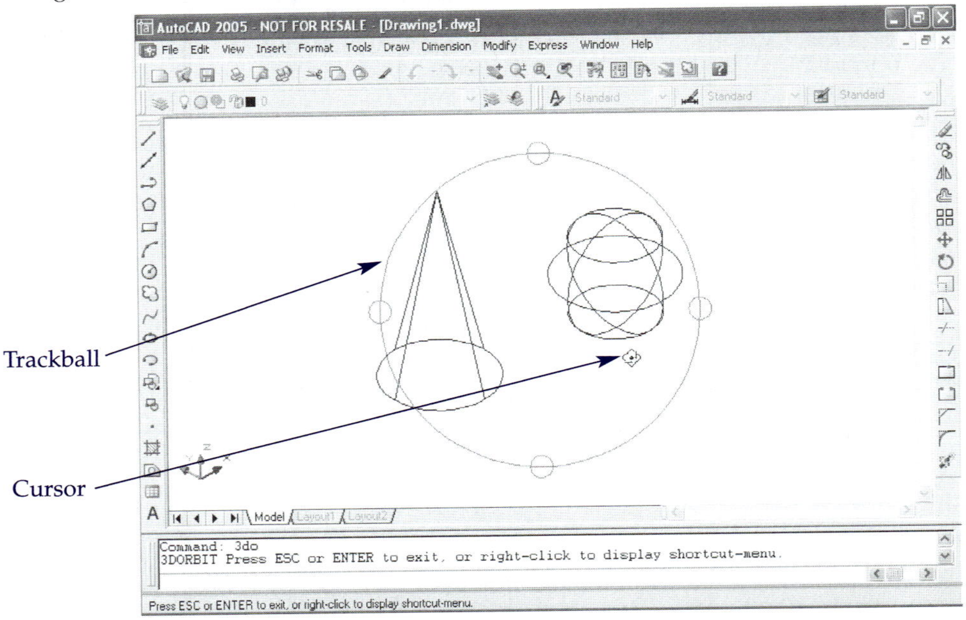

EXERCISE 27-3 Complete the Exercise on the Student CD.

Hiding Lines

When you display a 3D object in a pictorial view, such as from one of the isometric presets, AutoCAD displays all lines on the object. This includes the lines that represent the back of the object. See **Figure 27-7A.** This type of display is called a *wireframe display.* Often, it can be confusing looking at all of the lines. The **HIDE** command can be used to create a *hidden display* in which hidden lines are removed. See **Figure 27-7B.** The command is covered later in this chapter. However, to create a hidden display, simply type HIDE at the Command: prompt. Then, to return to a wireframe display, type REGEN at the Command: prompt.

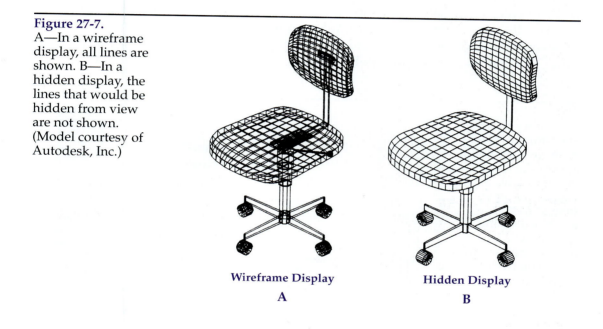

Wireframe Display
A

Hidden Display
B

Figure 27-7.
A—In a wireframe display, all lines are shown. B—In a hidden display, the lines that would be hidden from view are not shown. (Model courtesy of Autodesk, Inc.)

3D Construction Techniques

Before constructing a 3D model, you should determine the purpose of your design. What will the model be used for—presentation, analysis, or manufacturing? This helps you determine which tools should be used to construct the model. Three-dimensional objects can be drawn in three basic forms—wireframe objects, solid models, and surface models.

A ***wireframe object***, or model, is an object that is constructed of lines in 3D space. Wireframe models are hard to visualize because it is difficult to determine the angle of view and the nature of the surfaces. The **HIDE** command has no effect when used on a wireframe model because there is nothing to hide. All lines are always visible because there are no surfaces. There are not many practical applications for wireframe models. However, one application is to draw a wireframe and then place a skin, or surface, over the wireframe.

Surface modeling represents solid objects by creating a skin in the shape of the object. However, there is nothing inside the object. Think of a surface model as a hollow object. A surface model looks more like the real object than a wireframe and can be used for rendering. However, while more useful than wireframe models, surface models have limited applications.

Like surface modeling, ***solid modeling*** represents the shape of objects, but also provides data related to the physical properties of the objects because it is composed of solid material. Solid models can be analyzed to determine mass, volume, moments of inertia, and centroid location. Some third-party programs allow you to perform finite element analysis on the model. In addition, solid models can be rendered. Most 3D objects are created as solid models.

In AutoCAD, both solid and surface models can be created from primitives. ***Primitives*** are basic shapes used as the foundation to create complex shapes. These basic shapes in AutoCAD include boxes, cylinders, spheres, and cones. Primitives can be modified to create a finished product. See **Figure 27-8.**

Surface and solid models can be exported from AutoCAD for use in animation and rendering software, such as 3ds max® or Autodesk VIZ®. Rendered models can be used in any number of presentation formats, including slide shows, black and white or color prints, and animation recorded to videotape, CD-ROM, or DVD.

The discussions and examples in this chapter provide an introductory view of 3D constructions. Further study of solid and surface modeling techniques is presented in ***AutoCAD and its Applications—Advanced.***

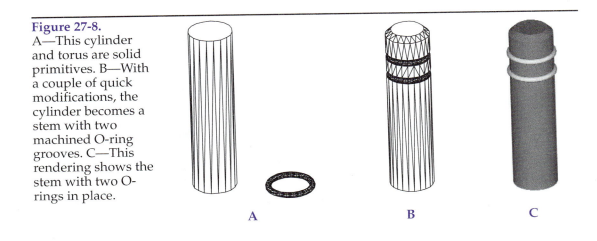

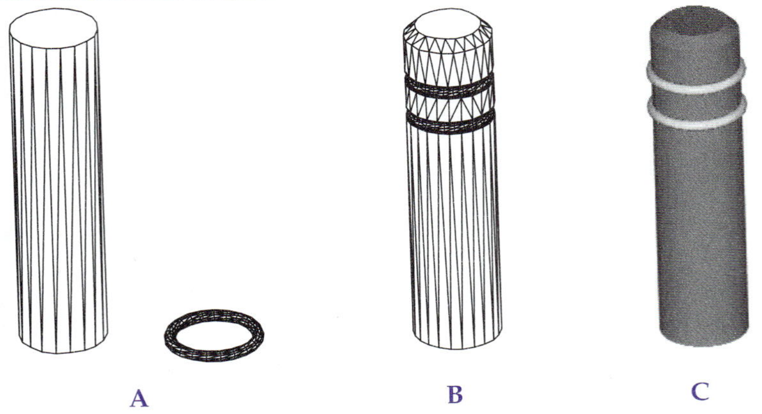

Figure 27-8. A—This cylinder and torus are solid primitives. B—With a couple of quick modifications, the cylinder becomes a stem with two machined O-ring grooves. C—This rendering shows the stem with two O-rings in place.

Constructing Wireframe Objects

Wireframe objects, or wireframes, can be created with any combination of AutoCAD line objects, such as lines, polylines, circles, polygons, and so on. While the applications for wireframes are limited, drawing wireframes is a fundamental 3D skill that should be learned. Learning to draw wireframes provides valuable practice working in 3D space. In addition, the fundamentals of drawing wireframes can be applied to other 3D modeling techniques, such as creating a profile and axis for a revolved solid.

In this section, you will draw the object shown in **Figure 27-9** as a 3D wireframe. First, start a new drawing in AutoCAD and draw the top view using the dimensions shown. Use lines, polylines, circles, arcs, and rectangles as needed. Do not draw centerlines or dimensions. Next, display the drawing using the southwest isometric preset.

The "surfaces" of the part are imaginary planes between the lines that make up the wireframe. What you drew as the top view is actually the bottom surface of the part. You now need to add a thickness to the part. The base of the part is 0.50 thick, as shown in **Figure 27-9.** The four ∅0.60 circles are actually holes through the base.

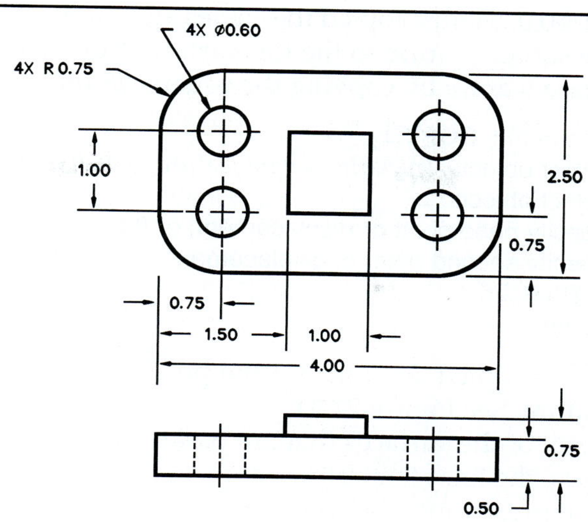

Figure 27-9.
You will use this orthographic drawing to create a wireframe object.

Therefore, the top and bottom surfaces of the base are represented by the outline and the four circles. Use the **COPY** command and relative displacement to create the top surface:

Command: **COPY**↵
Select objects: *(select the four circles and all lines that make up the outline of the part)*
Select objects: ↵
Specify base point or displacement, or [Multiple]: *(pick a point anywhere on screen)*
Specify second point of displacement or <use first point as displacement>: **@0,0,.5**↵
Command:

By specifying @0,0,.5 you tell AutoCAD that the second displacement point is 0 units on the X axis, 0 units on the Y axis, and .5 units on the Z axis from the first point. In other words, you have just copied the objects .5 units straight up the positive Z axis. See **Figure 27-10.**

Notice in **Figure 27-9** that the square feature is not a hole, but rather is extended from the top surface of the base. However, the square is currently on the bottom surface of the object. Therefore, you need to move the square to the top surface:

Command: **MOVE**↵
Select objects: *(select the square feature)*
Select objects: ↵
Specify base point or displacement: *(pick a point anywhere on screen)*
Specify second point of displacement or <use first point as displacement>: **@0,0,.5**↵
Command:

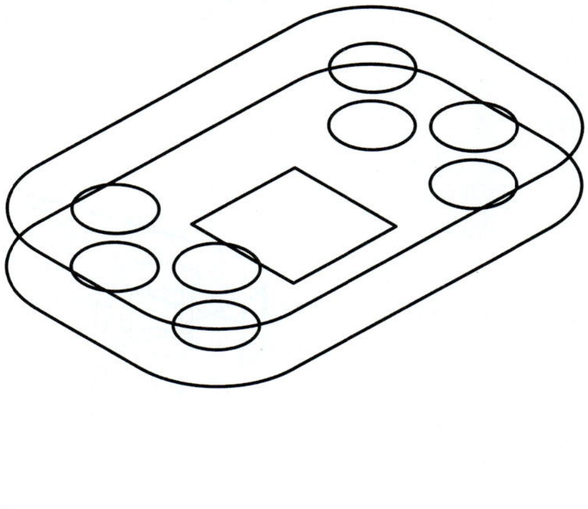

Figure 27-10.
The lines representing the bottom and top surfaces of the base are created.

Just as the @0,0,.5 entry copied the circles and outline up the positive Z axis, this entry moves the square feature to the top surface. Now, you need to create the top surface of the square feature by copying the square .25 units up the positive Z axis:

> Command: **COPY**↵
> Select objects: *(pick the square feature, which is now on the top surface of the base)*
> Select objects: ↵
> Specify base point or displacement, or [Multiple]: *(pick any point on screen)*
> Specify second point of displacement or <use first point as displacement>:
>   **@0,0,.25**↵
> Command:

The square is copied .25 units up the positive Z axis to create the top surface of the square feature. See Figure 27-11.

Now, all of the surfaces that are parallel to the XY plane have been "created." In other words, the lines that represent these surfaces are all correctly located. However, the lines representing the vertical surfaces need to be added. Set the **Endpoint**, **Midpoint**, and **Quadrant** object snaps and turn **OSNAP** on. Then, use the **LINE** command to connect endpoints and quadrants, as shown in Figure 27-12A.

The final wireframe is shown in Figure 27-12B after the viewpoint is changed using the **3DORBIT** command. Using the **HIDE** command has no effect on the display. This is because there are no actual surfaces in the model. The lines you see represent

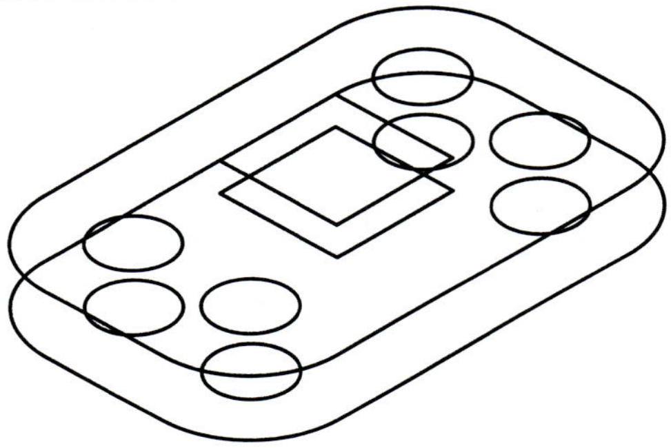

Figure 27-11.
The lines representing the bottom and top surfaces of the square feature are created.

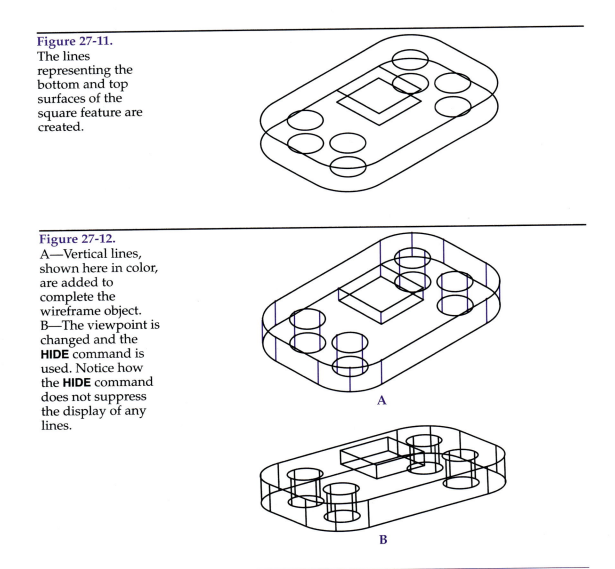

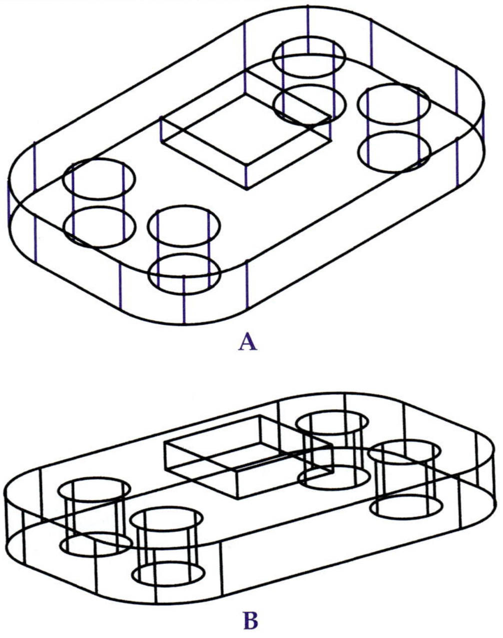

Figure 27-12.
A—Vertical lines, shown here in color, are added to complete the wireframe object. B—The viewpoint is changed and the **HIDE** command is used. Notice how the **HIDE** command does not suppress the display of any lines.

the edges of surfaces. Obviously, this type of 3D model has many drawbacks. However, you can now use this wireframe to create a surface or solid model. This approach to 3D modeling is covered in ***AutoCAD and its Applications—Advanced.***

PROFESSIONAL TIP

Do not confuse a wireframe *object* with a wireframe *display,* which is a 3D surface or solid object with all lines displayed. Often, a drafter may say a 3D object is "displayed in wireframe." This means that the view of the object shows all lines, visible and hidden, not that the object is drawn as a wireframe object. If the **HIDE** command is used on a 3D object displayed in wireframe, the hidden lines will be removed to create a *hidden display.* The **HIDE** command has no effect when used on a wireframe *object.*

Constructing Solid Primitives

As mentioned earlier, most 3D models are constructed as solids. This section provides an introduction to creating solid primitives. However, there are many more solid modeling techniques and methods available in AutoCAD. Extensive coverage of solid modeling is well beyond the scope of this text. Refer to ***AutoCAD and its Applications—Advanced*** for complete coverage of solid modeling.

The solid primitives that can be constructed in AutoCAD include a box, sphere, cylinder, cone, wedge, and torus. The commands to draw these primitives can be entered by selecting **Solids** in the **Draw** pull-down menu and then selecting the command in the cascading menu. You can also pick the appropriate button on the **Solids** toolbar or type the name of the solid, such as BOX, at the Command: prompt. See **Figure 27-13.** The **Solids** toolbar is not displayed by default.

Draw
➥ Solids
Solids
toolbar

The information required to draw a primitive depends on the type of primitive being drawn. See **Figure 27-14.** For example, to draw a solid cylinder you must provide a center point for the base, a radius or diameter of the base, and the height of the cylinder:

Command: **CYLINDER↵**
Current wire frame density: ISOLINES = 4
Specify center point for base of cylinder or [Elliptical] <0,0,0>: **0,0,1↵**
Specify radius for base of cylinder or [Diameter]: **2↵**
Specify height of cylinder or [Center of other end]: **4↵**
Command:

The cylinder is drawn with, normally, its base on the XY plane of the current UCS. However, notice that the center of the base was specified as 0,0,1. This locates the center one unit up the positive Z axis from the XY plane of the current UCS. Also, notice that there are other options, such as creating a cylinder that is elliptical instead of round, specifying a diameter instead of a radius, and locating the center of the opposite end rather than providing a height. The command sequence for the other solid primitives is similar to that for a cylinder.

Certain familiar editing commands can be used on solid primitives. For example, you can fillet or chamfer the edges of a solid primitive. In addition, there are other editing commands that are specifically for use on solids. These are covered in detail in ***AutoCAD and its Applications—Advanced.*** The following is an example of placing a .125 chamfer on a cylinder:

Figure 27-13.
A comparison of solid and surface primitives. Notice the differences in wireframe displays.

Basic Primitive Shape	Solid			Surfaces		
	Command	Wireframe All Lines/Hidden	Shaded	Command	Wireframe All Lines/Hidden	Shaded
Box	BOX Draw Solids Box Box	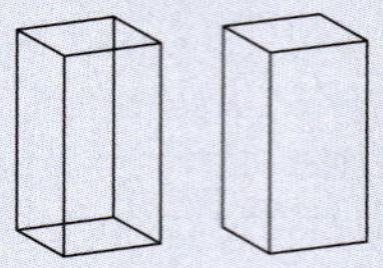		3D>Box Draw Surfaces 3D Surfaces... Box	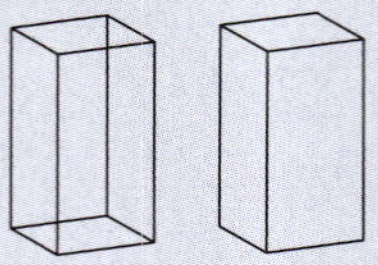	
Sphere	SPHERE Draw Solids Sphere Sphere	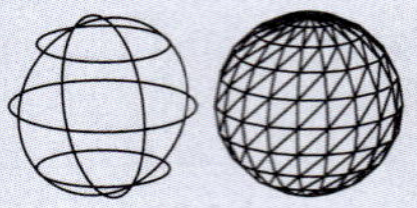		3D>Sphere Draw Surfaces 3D Surfaces... Sphere	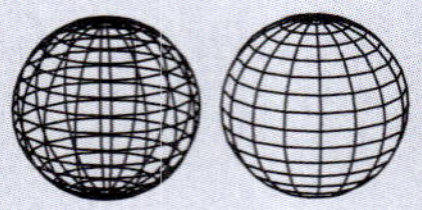	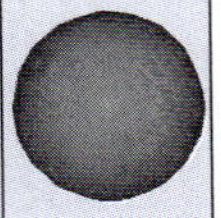
Cylinder	CYLINDER Draw Solids Cylinder Cylinder	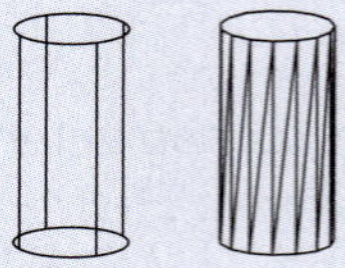		—	—	—
Cone	CONE Draw Solids Cone Cone	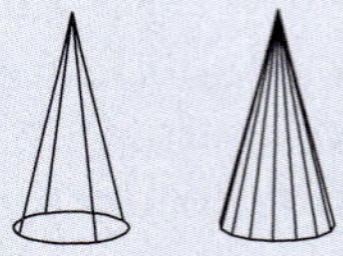		3D>Cone Draw Surfaces 3D Surfaces... Cone	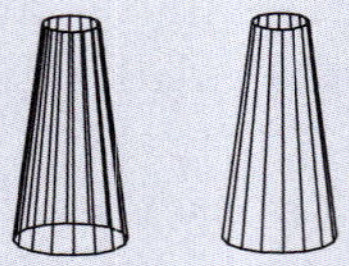	
Wedge	WEDGE Draw Solids Wedge Wedge			3D>Wedge Draw Surfaces 3D Surfaces... Wedge		
Torus	TORUS Draw Solids Torus Torus	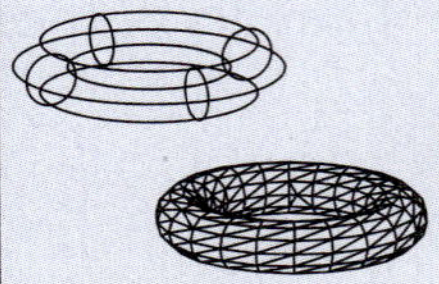		3D>Torus Draw Surfaces 3D Surfaces... Torus	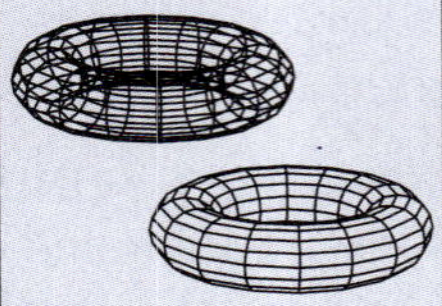	
Pyramid	—	—	—	3D>Pyramid Draw Surfaces 3D Surfaces... Pyramid	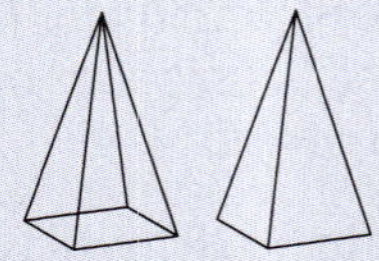	
Dome	—	—	—	3D>DOme Draw Surfaces 3D Surfaces... Dome	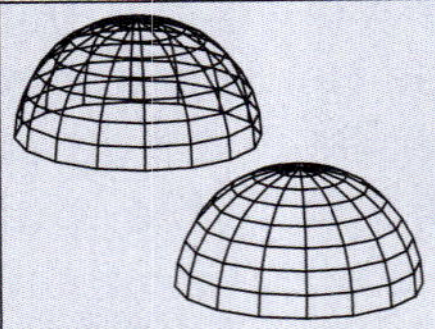	
Dish	—	—	—	3D>DIsh Draw Surfaces 3D Surfaces... Dish	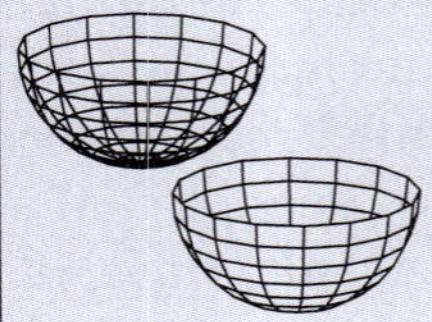	

Figure 27-14.
The basic information required to draw solid primitives.

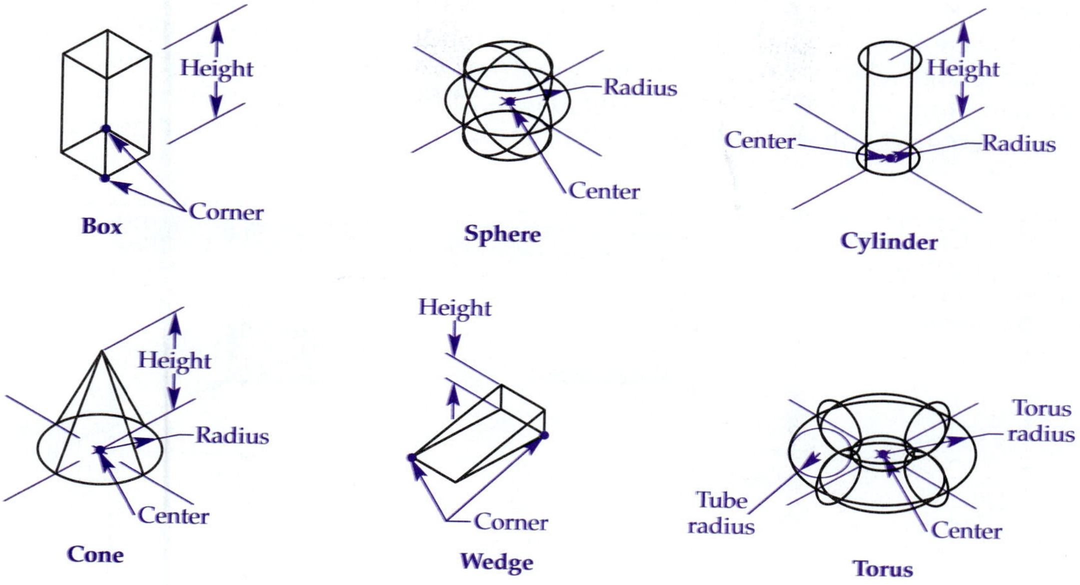

Command: **CHAMFER**↵
(TRIM mode) Current chamfer Dist1 = 0.0000 Dist2 = 0.0000
Select first line or [Polyline/Distance/Angle/Trim/Method/mUltiple]: *(pick the edge of the cylinder)*
Base surface selection...
Enter surface selection option [Next/OK/ (current)] <OK>: ↵
Specify base surface chamfer distance: ↵
Specify other surface chamfer distance <0.1250>: ↵
Select an edge or [Loop]: *(pick the edge again)*
Select an edge or [Loop]: ↵
Command:

PROFESSIONAL TIP

To see the object in 3D, use one of the isometric presets or the **3DORBIT** command. If you need to display a plan view of the current UCS, use the **PLAN** command.

EXERCISE 27-4 Complete the Exercise on the Student CD.

Constructing Surface Primitives

In addition to solid primitives, AutoCAD has several surface primitives. These primitives can be used to create more complex objects and features. However, surfaces are not nearly as easy to modify as solids. Remember, a surface is just a "skin" without volumetric data.

The commands for drawing surface primitives can be entered by selecting **Surfaces** from the **Draw** pull-down menu and then **3D Surfaces...** in the cascading menu. You can also enter the **3D** command at the Command: prompt or select the appropriate button on the **Surfaces** toolbar. Refer to **Figure 27-13.**

3D
Draw
➥ **Surfaces**
➥ **3D Surfaces...**
Surfaces toolbar

Using the pull-down menu displays the **3D Objects** dialog box, **Figure 27-15.** Notice the list box on the left of the dialog box and the image tiles on the right. The names correspond to the primitives shown on the image tiles. A primitive can be selected by picking either the name or the image. When selected, the image and the name are highlighted.

Once you select a surface primitive to draw, whether in the dialog box, on the command line, or from the toolbar, you are asked for certain information. The information required will depend on which primitive is being drawn. See **Figure 27-16.**

Figure 27-15.
Surface primitives can be drawn using the **3D Objects** dialog box.

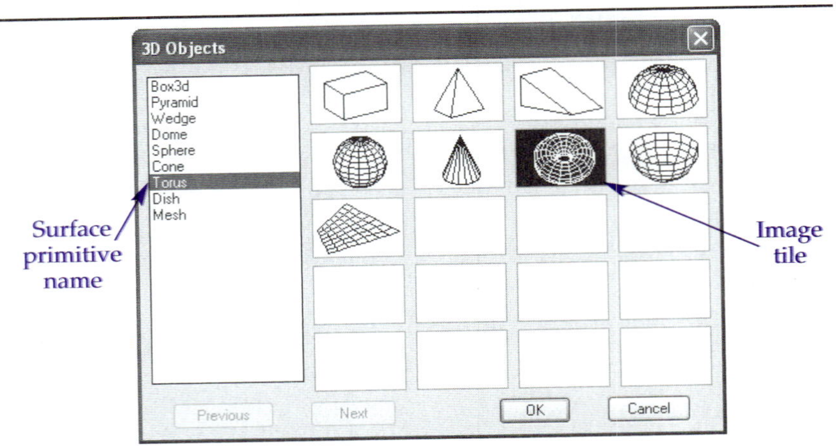

Figure 27-16.
The basic information required to draw surface primitives.

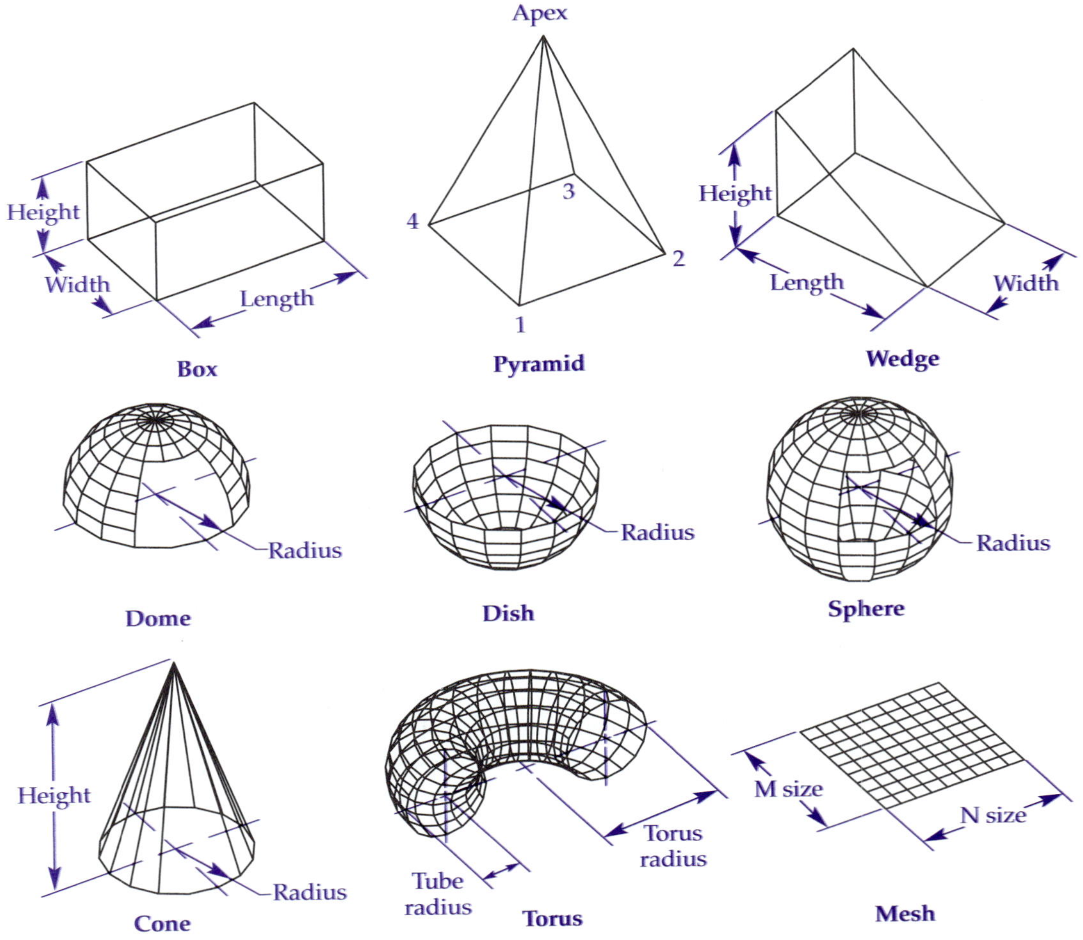

For example, to draw a dome, you must provide a center, radius, and the number of segments for the dome:

Command: **3D**↵ *(do not type the name of the surface primitive at the Command: prompt; you will draw a solid if you do)*
Enter an option
[Box/Cone/DIsh/DOme/Mesh/Pyramid/Sphere/Torus/Wedge]: **DO**↵
Specify center point of dome: *(pick a point)*
Specify radius of dome or [Diameter]: *(enter a radius or pick on the screen)*
Enter number of longitudinal segments for surface of dome <16>: ↵
Enter number of latitudinal segments for surface of dome <8>: ↵
Command:

The dome is drawn with its base on the XY plane of the current UCS. To see a 3D view of the object, use the **3DORBIT** command or an isometric viewpoint.

Notice in the previous command sequence that you are asked for longitudinal and latitudinal segments. Longitudinal segments are around the circumference of the dome. Latitudinal segments are the north-south segments on the height of the dome. See **Figure 27-17.** For the surface primitives that contain curved surfaces—sphere, cone, dome, dish, torus—you must provide the number of segments for the object. The more segments used to define a curved surface, the smoother the surface appears. However, more segments also increases screen regeneration times.

PROFESSIONAL TIP

The number of segments for solids is controlled by the **FACETRES** system variable. Refer to ***AutoCAD and its Applications—Advanced.***

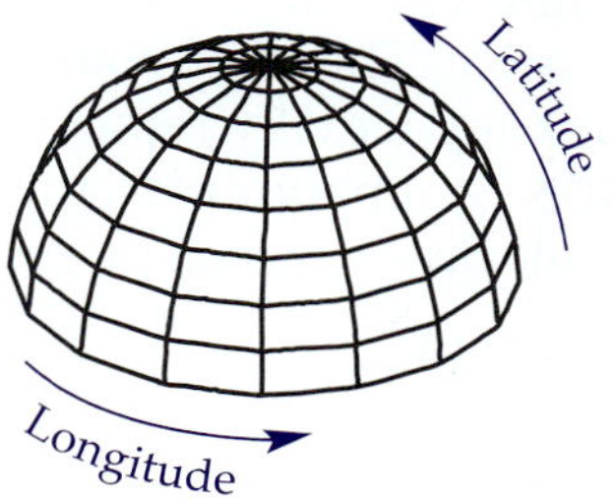

Figure 27-17.
Longitudinal segments are around the circumference of the dome. Latitudinal segments are on the height of the dome.

EXERCISE 27-5

Complete the Exercise on the Student CD.

Hiding and Shading

The ability to change your viewpoint is only one aspect of displaying 3D drawings. As you learned earlier in this chapter, you can use the **HIDE** command to remove hidden lines. Doing so makes the objects appear "solid," but the display is still a group of lines that define the edges and surfaces. In AutoCAD, you have four basic levels of display for 3D objects—wireframe, hidden, shaded, and rendered. See **Figure 27-18.** Creating hidden and shaded displays are discussed in this section. For complete coverage of rendering with AutoCAD, refer to ***AutoCAD and its Applications—Advanced.***

Figure 27-18.
The four basic levels of display available for a 3D model—wireframe, hidden, shaded, and rendered. (Model courtesy of Autodesk, Inc.)

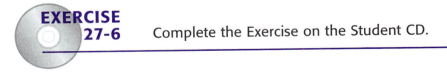

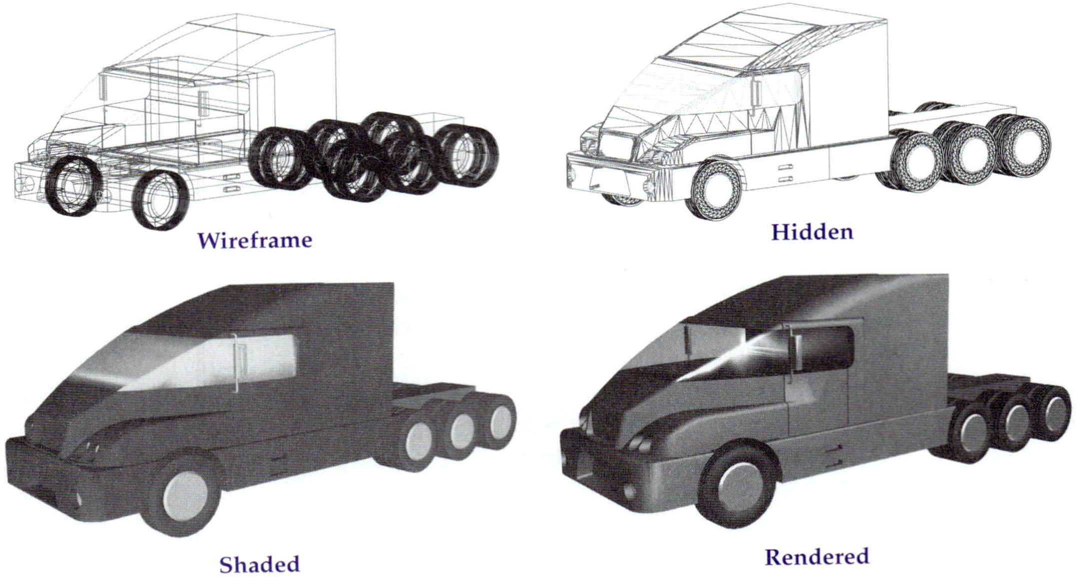

HIDE Command

The **HIDE** command was introduced earlier in this chapter. It is used to display a 3D object with hidden lines removed. Hidden lines are those lines on an object that would not be visible if the object were truly solid. For example, the features on the opposite side, or back, of the object would not be visible. Some internal features may also be hidden by the object. In a traditional 2D isometric drawing, these lines are drawn in a hidden linetype. In a wireframe display, all of the lines representing hidden features are visible. The **HIDE** command suppresses the display of these lines. However, the lines are not actually removed from the object.

HIDE
HI

View
➡ Hide

Render toolbar

Hide

To access the **HIDE** command, pick the **Hide** button in the **Render** toolbar, select **Hide** from the **View** pull-down menu, or enter HI or HIDE at the Command: prompt:

Command: **HI** *or* **HIDE**↵
Regenerating model.
Command:

The size and complexity of the drawing and the speed of your computer determines how long you must wait for the lines to be hidden. To redisplay the 3D object in a wireframe display, use the **REGEN** command. In addition, any command that performs a regeneration, such as **ZOOM Extents**, redisplays the hidden lines.

EXERCISE 27-6 Complete the Exercise on the Student CD.

Hidden Line Settings

By default, the **HIDE** command removes hidden lines from the display. However, you can have hidden lines displayed in a different linetype and color instead of having them removed. To set this, open the **Options** dialog box by right-clicking in the viewport and selecting **Options...** from the shortcut menu. You can also select **Options...** from the **Tools** pull-down menu or type OP or OPTIONS at the Command: prompt.

Once the **Options** dialog box is open, pick the **User Preferences** tab. See Figure 27-19. Then, pick the **Hidden Line Settings...** button at the bottom of the tab. The **Hidden Line Settings** dialog box is displayed, Figure 27-20. In the **Obscured Lines** area of the dialog box are drop-down lists from which you can select a linetype and color.

When the **Linetype** drop-down list is set to **Off**, the display of hidden lines is suppressed by the **HIDE** command. When a linetype is selected from the drop-down list, hidden lines are displayed in that linetype after the **HIDE** command is used. The linetypes available in the drop-down list are not the same as the linetypes loaded into your drawing.

When a linetype is selected, you can also change the display color of the hidden lines. Simply pick a color in the **Color** drop-down list. To have the hidden lines displayed in the same color as the object, select **ByEntity**, which is the default. The color setting has no effect when the **Linetype** drop-down list is set to **Off**.

When done making settings, pick the **OK** button to close the **Hidden Line Settings** dialog box. Then, pick the **OK** button to close the **Options** dialog box.

Figure 27-19. The **Hidden Line Settings...** button is located in the **User Preferences** tab of the **Options** dialog box.

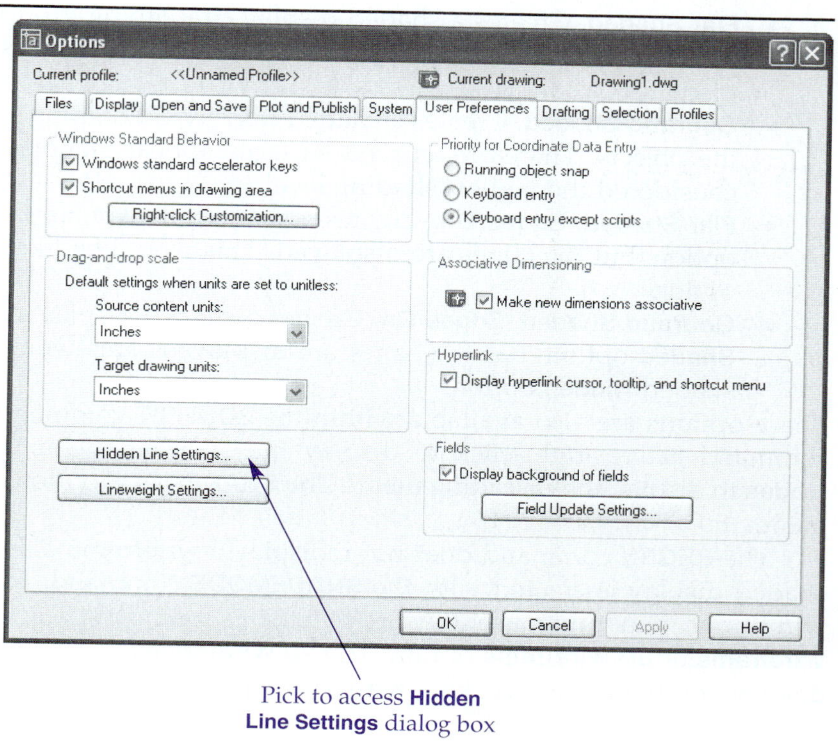

Figure 27-20. Changing how hidden lines are displayed when the **HIDE** command is used.

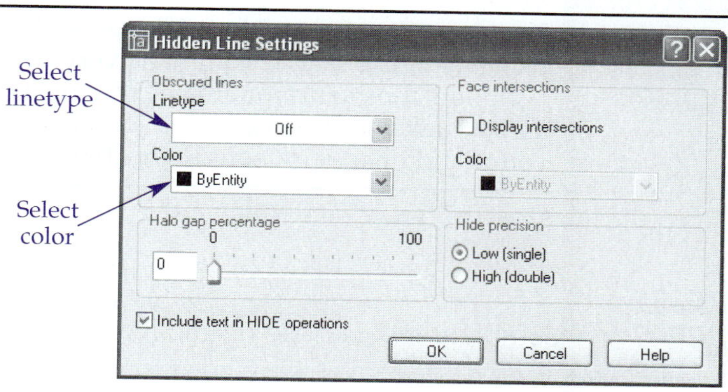

SHADEMODE Command

The **SHADEMODE** command is used to create both hidden and shaded displays. In a shaded display, hidden lines are removed as with the **HIDE** command. In addition, the surfaces of the object are shaded in the same color as the object's display color. Refer to **Figure 27-18.** The **SHADE** command can also be used to shade an object. However, its functionality has been replaced by the **SHADEMODE** command, which offers much more flexibility.

To access the **SHADEMODE** command, select **Shade** from the **View** pull-down menu. Then, select a level of shading in the cascading menu. You can also type SHADEMODE at the Command: prompt and select an option. The **SHADEMODE** command options, or levels of shading, are:

- **2D Wireframe.** Creates a wireframe display in which all lines are displayed in their correct linetype and line weight.
- **3D Wireframe.** Creates a wireframe display in which all lines are displayed in a thin, continuous linetype regardless of their setting.
- **Hidden.** Creates a hidden display in which all lines are displayed in a thin, continuous linetype.
- **Flat Shaded.** Creates a shaded display. Smoothing groups are not applied to the objects. Therefore, all objects with curved surfaces appear faceted, or made up of flat faces.
- **Gouraud Shaded.** Creates a shaded display. Smoothing groups are applied to the objects. Therefore, curved surfaces appear smooth, not faceted. This is considered the highest shading level.
- **Flat Shaded, Edges On.** Creates a shaded display similar to the **Flat Shaded** option, but the edges are displayed. This would be like a flat-shaded **Hidden** option.
- **Gouraud Shaded, Edges On.** Creates a shaded display similar to the **Gouraud Shaded** option, but the edges are displayed. This would be like a gouraud-shaded **Hidden** option.

These options are also available within the **3DORBIT** command. With the **3DORBIT** command active, right-click to display the shortcut menu. Then, select **Shading Modes** to display the cascading menu. The **SHADEMODE** options are in this cascading menu.

The **REGEN** command does not redisplay a wireframe display after a hidden or shaded display is created with the **SHADEMODE** command. In order to redisplay a wireframe, you must use the **SHADEMODE** command and select either the **2D Wireframe** or **3D Wireframe** option. The **2D Wireframe** option is the type of wireframe display you have been working with to this point.

PROFESSIONAL TIP

If you do a lot of drawing in 3D, you will probably find yourself using the **SHADEMODE** command very frequently. **SHADEMODE** is a good command for an alias. Using a command alias such as SM makes it much easier to enter the command. Creating command aliases is covered in Chapter 28.

EXERCISE 27-7

Complete the Exercise on the Student CD.

Chapter Test

Answer the following questions on a separate sheet of paper.

1. What are the three coordinates needed to locate any point in 3D space?
2. In a 2D drawing, what is the value for the Z coordinate?
3. What purpose does the right-hand rule serve?
4. Which three fingers are used in the right-hand rule?
5. Which command controls the display of the UCS icon?
6. What is the definition of a *viewpoint?*
7. How many preset isometric viewpoints does AutoCAD have? List them.
8. How does changing the UCS impact using one of the preset isometric viewpoints?
9. List the six preset orthographic viewpoints.
10. When using a preset orthographic viewpoint, what happens to the UCS?
11. Which command allows you to dynamically change your viewpoint using an on-screen trackball?
12. Define *wireframe display.*
13. Define *hidden display.*
14. Define *wireframe object.*
15. Define *surface model.*
16. Define *solid model.*
17. Define *primitive.*
18. List the six solid primitives available in AutoCAD.
19. List the four surface primitives for which you must set the number of segments.
20. What are the four basic levels of display for 3D objects in AutoCAD?
21. Briefly describe how to have hidden lines displayed in red when the **HIDE** command is used.
22. List the seven options available with the **SHADEMODE** command.
23. What is the difference between a 2D wireframe and a 3D wireframe display created with the **SHADEMODE** command?
24. After the **SHADEMODE** command is used to create a shaded display, how do you redisplay a wireframe display?
25. Which shading level is considered the highest?

Drawing Problems

1. Choose Problem 4, 5, or 6 from Chapter 26 and draw it using solid primitives. You will need to use the primitives as "building blocks" to create the object. Use object snaps and the **COPY**, **MOVE**, and **ROTATE** commands as needed. Change viewpoints to help in construction. Save the drawing as P27-1.

For Problems 2–5, draw the objects in 3D form. Use solid primitives and object snaps with the **COPY**, **MOVE**, *and* **ROTATE** *commands as needed. You will need to use the primitives as "building blocks" to create the object. Display the drawings from three different viewpoints. Use the* **HIDE** *and* **SHADEMODE** *commands as you draw to help in visualization. Save the drawings as* P27-2, P27-3, P27-4, *and* P27-5.

2.

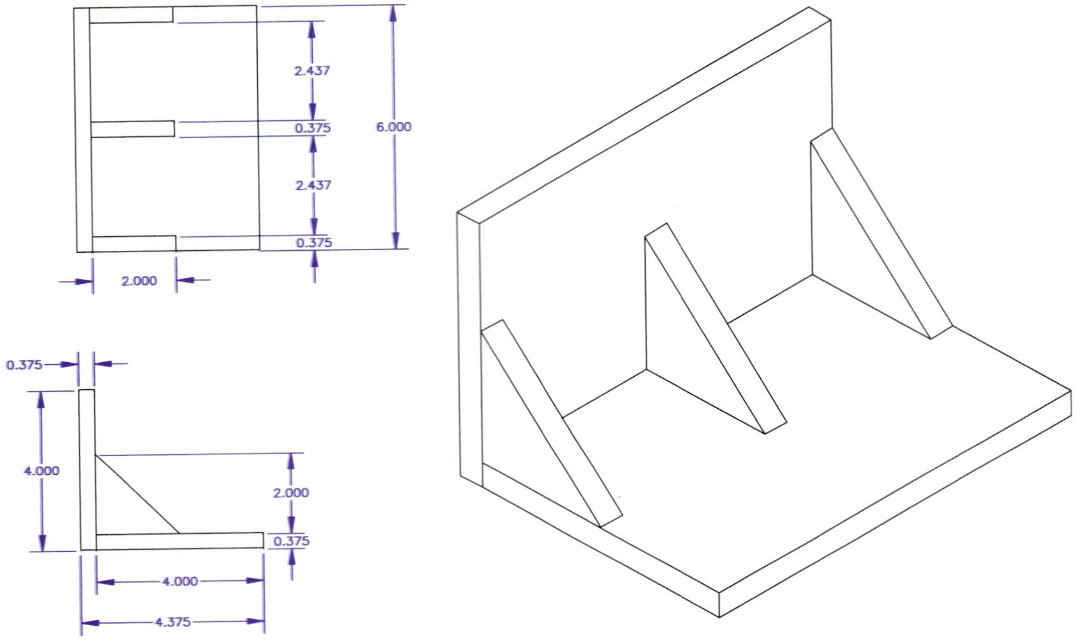

3.

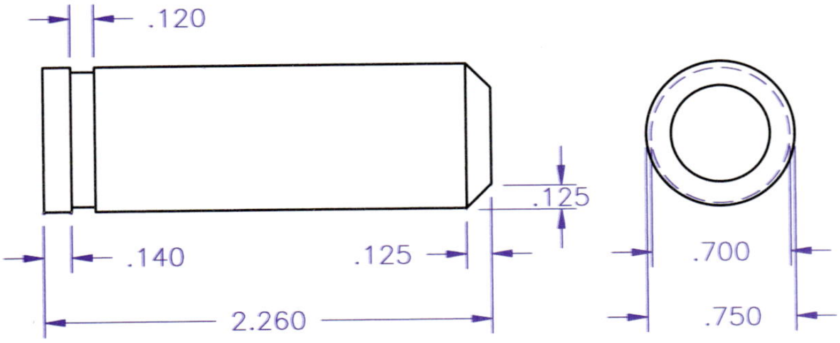

4.

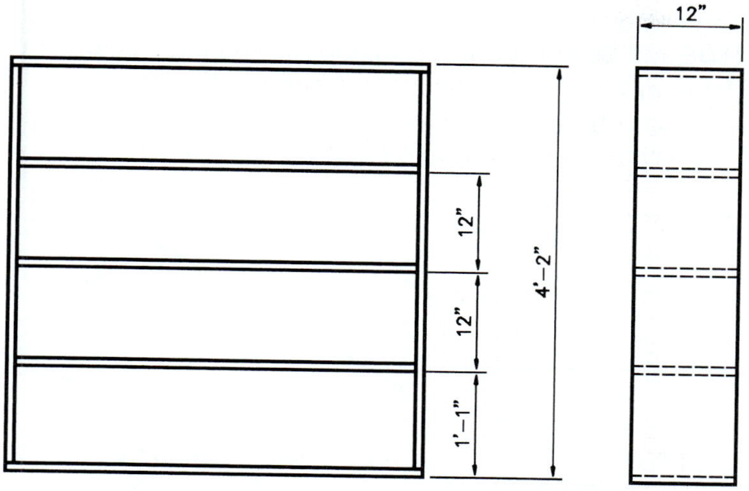

5.

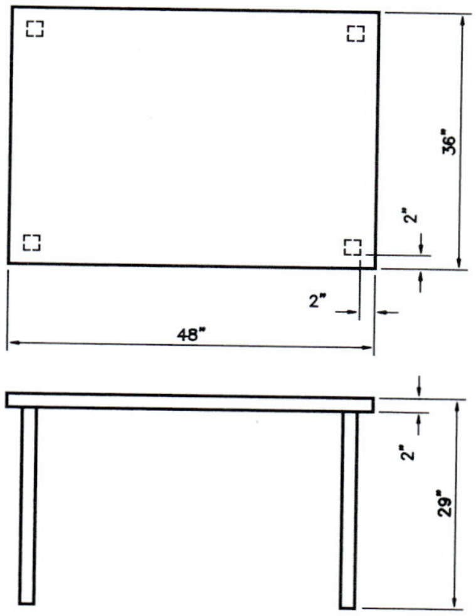

6. Construct a 3D model of the table shown.
   A. Use solid and/or surface primitives.
   B. Use the dimensions given.
   C. Use the **HIDE** and **SHADEMODE** commands as you go to help with visualization.
   D. Plot the table in wireframe display and hidden display.
   E. Alter the design of the table to include rounded tabletop corners or rounded feet. Try replacing the rectangular feet with spherical feet.

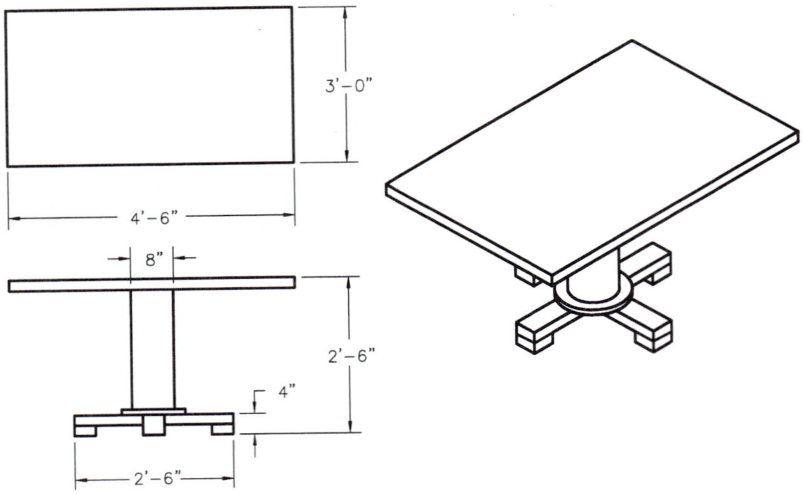

CHAPTER 28

External Commands, Script Files, and Slide Shows

Learning Objectives

After completing this chapter, you will be able to do the following:

- Edit the acad.pgp file.
- Use a text editor to create script files.
- Create a continuous slide show of existing drawings.
- Use the **SLIDELIB** command to create a slide library.

This chapter introduces you to the use of scripts. A ***script*** is a series of commands and variables listed in a text file. When the script file is activated by AutoCAD, the entire list of commands is performed without additional input from the user. One useful script is a continuous slide show. It is excellent for client presentations, demonstrations, and grading drawings.

Scripts can be written with word processing and text editor programs. The Windows operating system includes three tools for writing ASCII (American Standard Code for Information Interchange) text files: MS-DOS EDIT, Notepad, and WordPad.

Using Text Editors

As you become more experienced with AutoCAD, you will want to alter the program to suit your specific needs. Most of these alterations are done with a text editor program. Although Notepad lacks many formatting functions found in word processing programs, it can perform the text editing tasks required to customize AutoCAD.

Word Processors

Many AutoCAD users rely on full-fledged word processing programs to create their text files. There are dozens of word processing programs commercially available. WordPad is a word processor included with Microsoft Windows. Like Notepad, WordPad can be accessed by picking Accessories in the Programs group of the Start menu. See **Figure 28-1.**

Figure 28-1.
Both the Windows Notepad text editor and the Windows WordPad word processor can be accessed from the Accessories menu.

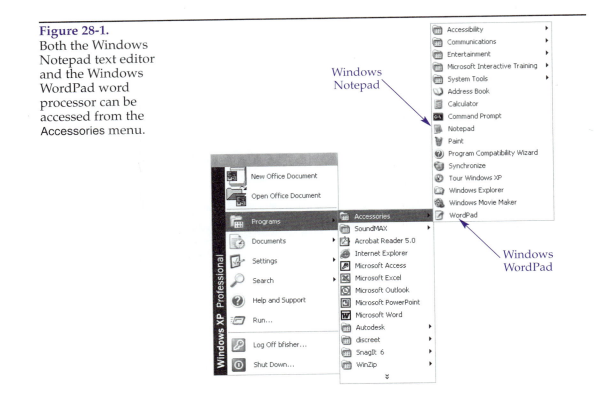

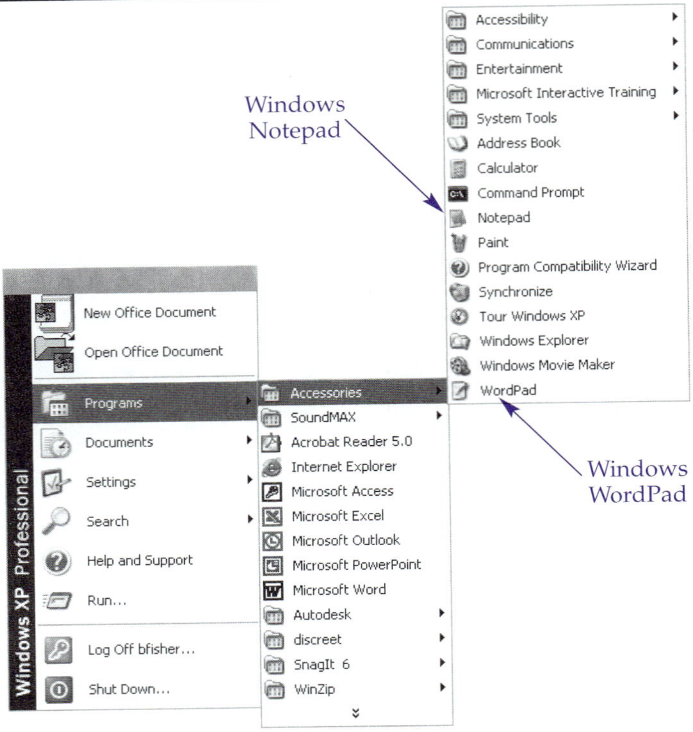

Other familiar Windows-compatible word processors include WordPerfect and Microsoft Word. These are excellent writing tools, but are far more sophisticated than is necessary to create text files for AutoCAD. If you create your AutoCAD text files with a word processor, save the document as a text-only (ASCII) file. This prevents the inclusion of special formatting codes, which makes the file unreadable by AutoCAD.

Programmer's Text Editors

The best type of text editor, however, is a programmer's text editor. There are a wide variety of inexpensive yet powerful text editors available. These programs are designed for creating the type of files needed to customize AutoCAD. Programmer's editors are recommended over word processors because of their design, size, function, ease of use, and price. Norton Editor and Text Pad are excellent examples of programmer's editors available.

The Visual LISP Editor is a very good editor and is included with AutoCAD. It can be accessed by selecting **Visual LISP Editor** from the **AutoLISP** cascading menu in the **Tools** pull-down menu.

The ACAD.PGP File

The acad.pgp (program parameters) file controls such features of AutoCAD as command aliases and external commands. The acad.pgp file is simply a text file, which can be edited with a word processor text editor. During the AutoCAD installation procedure, this file is placed in the Documents and Settings*User*\Application Data\Autodesk\AutoCAD 2005\R16.1\enu\Support folder. A portion of the acad.pgp file is shown in Notepad in **Figure 28-2.**

Modifying the acad.pgp file can be accomplished through the **Tools** pull-down menu. Go to **Tools**, then **Customize**, then **Edit Custom Files**, and then select **Program Parameters (acad.pgp)**. This procedure opens Notepad and displays the acad.pgp file.

Figure 28-2.
The acad.pgp file opened in Notepad.

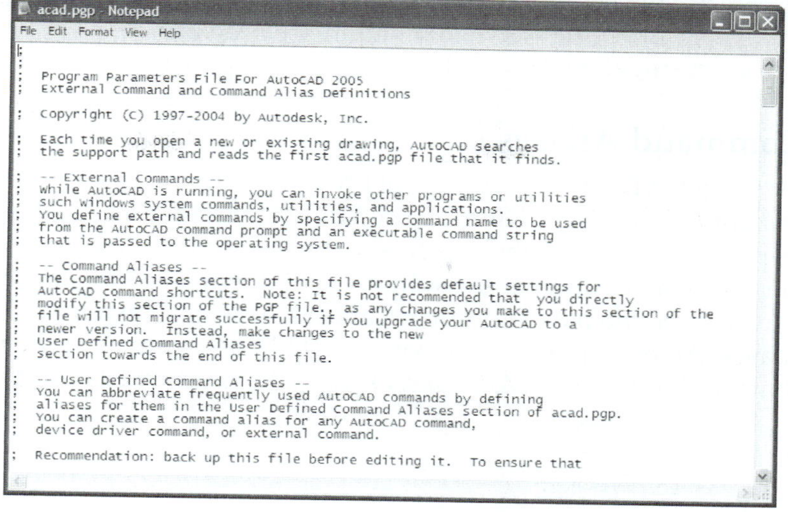

External Commands

External commands carry out functions that are not part of AutoCAD. Each of these external commands is defined in the acad.pgp file. AutoCAD contains eleven external commands in the acad.pgp file, beginning with **CATALOG**. The first word on each line is the text that is entered at the Command: prompt in order to execute the external command. The second word represents the DOS command or program to be executed.

You can see in **Figure 28-3** that entering EDIT at the Command: prompt runs MS-DOS EDIT, a text editor. A comma separates each field in the EDIT entry. The fields are defined as follows:

- **EDIT.** The command entered at the AutoCAD Command: prompt.
- **START EDIT.** The command or program name executed after the external command name is entered. This is the text that would normally be entered at the DOS prompt (Windows command prompt) to run the text editor. Later in this chapter, instructions are provided for editing the acad.pgp file so you can run your favorite text editor.

Figure 28-3.
External commands are defined in the acad.pgp file.

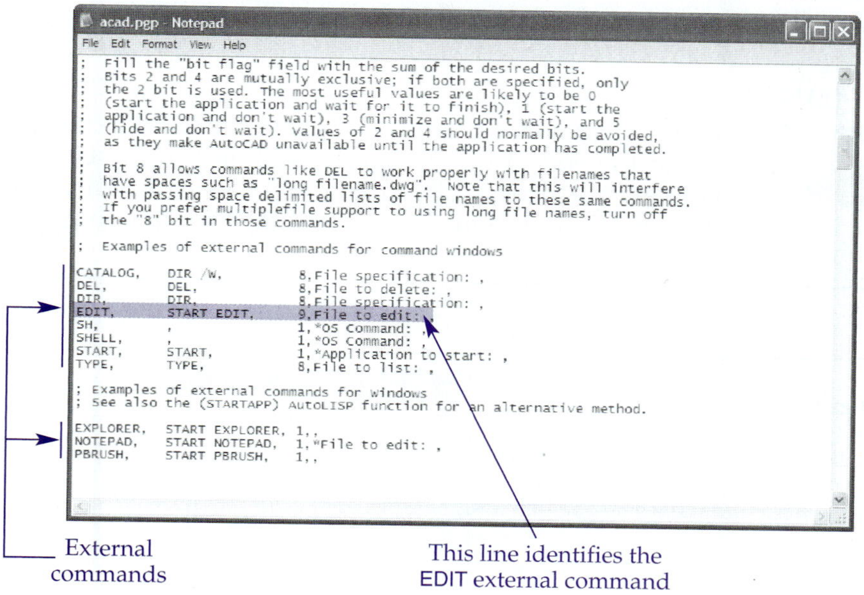

- **9.** This bit flag value specifies certain program parameters. The meanings of the bit values are explained in the acad.pgp file.
- **File to edit:.** This is the prompt that appears after the command is typed.

Command Aliases

AutoCAD allows you to abbreviate command names. This feature is called ***command aliasing***. A list of predefined aliases furnished with AutoCAD can be displayed by viewing the contents of the acad.pgp file. You can do this by loading the file into Notepad or another text editor. Scroll down past the list of external commands and you will see the list of command aliases. This is an extensive list containing over 200 aliases. An example of some command aliases is provided here. See *Command Aliases* chart in the *Reference Material* section of the Student CD for the complete listing.

```
CO,  *COPY
E,   *ERASE
L,   *LINE
P,   *PAN
Z,   *ZOOM
```

You can easily create your own aliases by editing this file. For example, if you want to add an alias **PP** for the **PLOT** command, enter the following below the **POLYGON** command in the acad.pgp file:

```
PP,  *PLOT
```

Be sure to include the asterisk since it indicates to AutoCAD that this is an alias. Save the Notepad file. The revised acad.pgp file will not work until you restart AutoCAD or reload the acad.pgp file by entering the **REINIT** command. This displays the **Re-initialization** dialog box, shown in **Figure 28-4.** Pick the **PGP File** check box in this dialog box and then pick **OK** to reinitialize the acad.pgp file. After you reinitialize the acad.pgp file, your new command alias will work.

NOTE

The **Re-initialization** dialog box can also be used if you have one of your serial ports, such as COM1, configured for both a plotter and a digitizer. If you change the cable from plotter to digitizer, pick the **Digitizer** check boxes in both areas of the dialog box to reinitiate the digitizer.

PROFESSIONAL TIP

In a professional environment, place additions to the acad.pgp file at the end of the file, in the section titled -- User Defined Command Aliases --. By doing so, you can easily find the modifications and migrate the settings when you upgrade to a new version of AutoCAD.

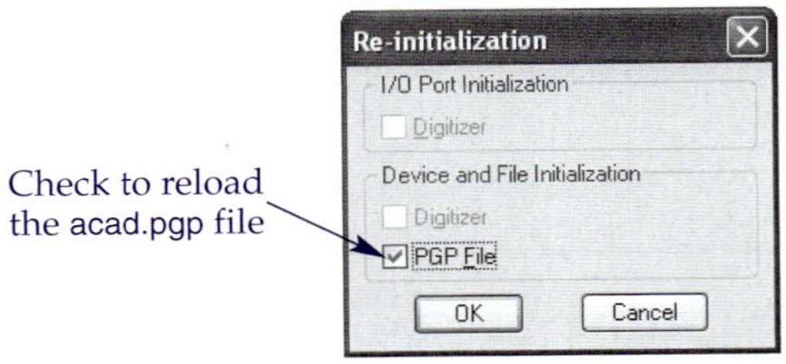

Figure 28-4.
The **Re-initialization** dialog box.

Editing the ACAD.PGP File

There are several tools available to edit the acad.pgp file. Notepad, MS-DOS EDIT, WordPad, or another text editor may be used. The easiest method of editing is to open the file with Notepad using the **Program Parameters (acad.pgp)** selection from the **Edit Custom Files** cascading menu from the **Customize** menu selection from the **Tools** pull-down menu.

> **PROFESSIONAL TIP**
>
> Always make backup copies of AutoCAD text files before editing them. If you "corrupt" one of these files through incorrect editing techniques, simply delete that file and restore the original.

The acad.pgp file can be easily altered to specify your personal text editor instead of the default MS-DOS EDIT. For this example, we will set up an external command to access an imaginary editor called TextEditor. If you are currently running AutoCAD, use the method described above to open the acad.pgp file in Notepad.

Once the acad.pgp file is displayed in Notepad, you can move the flashing text cursor around the screen with the left, right, up, and down arrows, as well as the [Home], [Page Up], [Page Down], [Insert], [Delete], and [End] keys. You can also move the text cursor with your pointing device. Use the down arrow key or your pointing device to move the text cursor to the end of the line labeled:

```
EDIT,    START EDIT,    9,File to edit: ,
```

Hit the [Enter] key to start a new line in the file. Type in the following new line of text:

```
TE,      START TEXTEDIT,      9,File to edit: ,
```

Use the space bar to line up the new text with the text on the previous line to make it easier to read. These changes allow you to run TextEditor by entering TE at the AutoCAD Command: prompt. When you are done, the acad.pgp file should appear as shown in **Figure 28-5.**

Figure 28-5.
TE has been added as a new command that will execute the TextEditor program.

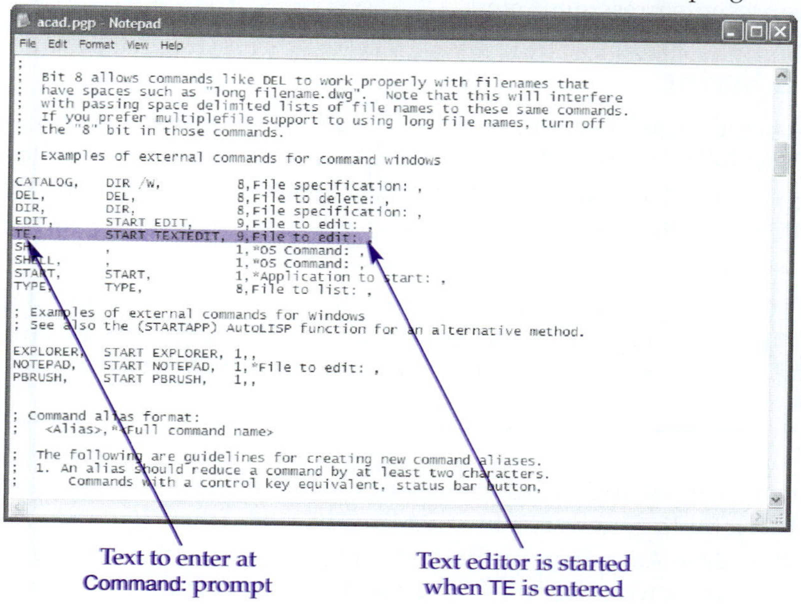

acad.pgp - Notepad
File Edit Format View Help
; Bit 8 allows commands like DEL to work properly with filenames that
; have spaces such as "long filename.dwg". Note that this will interfere
; with passing space delimited lists of file names to these same commands.
; If you prefer multiplefile support to using long file names, turn off
; the "8" bit in those commands.
; Examples of external commands for command windows
CATALOG, DIR /W, 8,File specification: ,
DEL, DEL, 8,File to delete: ,
DIR, DIR, 8,File specification: ,
EDIT, START EDIT, 9,File to edit: ,
TE, START TEXTEDIT, 9,File to edit: ,
SH , 1,*OS Command: ,
, 1,*OS Command: ,
START, 1,*Application to start: ,
TYPE, 8,File to list: ,
; Examples of external commands for Windows
; See also the (STARTAPP) AutoLISP function for an alternative method.
EXPLORER, START EXPLORER, 1,,
NOTEPAD, START NOTEPAD, 1,*File to edit: ,
PBRUSH, START PBRUSH, 1,,
; Command alias format:
; <Alias>,*<Full command name>
; The following are guidelines for creating new command aliases.
; 1. An alias should reduce a command by at least two characters.
; Commands with a control key equivalent, status bar button,
Text to enter at Command: prompt
Text editor is started when TE is entered

To save the edited file, activate the pull-down menus at the top of the screen. Select **Save** from the **File** pull-down menu. To return to AutoCAD, press [Alt]+[Tab] to display the Task List, and then hold the [Alt] key while repeatedly pressing the [Tab] key. This cycles through the icons. When AutoCAD is highlighted, release the [Alt] key.

If you try using the new **TE** command in AutoCAD now, it will not work because AutoCAD is still using the original version of the acad.pgp file. Before the **TE** command can function, you must reinitialize the acad.pgp file by restarting AutoCAD or executing the **REINIT** command.

NOTE

If you add an external command that references a new program, such as the text editor example on the previous page, you must make sure that the path to the program is listed in the **Support File Search Path** area in **Files** tab of **Options** dialog box. If the path to the program is not listed, it must be added before the command will work.

EXERCISE 28-1 Complete the Exercise on the Student CD.

Creating Script Files to Automate AutoCAD

A *script file* is a list of commands that AutoCAD executes in sequence without input from the user. Scripts enable nonprogrammers to automate AutoCAD functions. Scripts can be used for specific functions, such as plotting a drawing with the correct **PLOT** command values and settings, or creating a slide show. A good working knowledge of AutoCAD commands is needed before you can confidently create a script file.

When writing a script file, use one command or option per line in the text file. This makes the file easier to fix if the script does not work properly. A return is specified by pressing [Enter] after typing a command. If the next option of a command is a default value to be accepted, press [Enter] again. This leaves a blank line in the script file, which represents pressing [Enter].

Creating a Script

The following example shows how a script file can be used to save a drawing in AutoCAD 2000 DWG format. Write the script with Notepad or another text editor. Save the file as convert.scr in the Documents and Settings*User*\Application Data\Autodesk\AutoCAD 2005\R16.1\enu\Support folder.

CAUTION

A single incorrect entry in a script file can cause it to malfunction. Test the keystrokes at the keyboard as you write the script file and record them for future reference.

Many text editors and word processors save documents with .txt or .doc file extensions by default. Since scripts must end with the .scr file extension, you may have to use the Save As option in the text editor or word processor. Then, select All Files from the Save as type: menu in the Save As dialog box and save the file.

A comment can be inserted in a script file to provide information to the reader. Simply place a semicolon as the first character on the line and AutoCAD will not process that line. For example, the first line in the following script is a comment for information only:

; Saves the current drawing in AutoCAD 2000 DWG format. *(comment only)*
FILEDIA *(sets the system variable that controls file dialog boxes)*
0 *(disables file dialog boxes)*
SAVEAS *(command that saves the drawing in a format of your choice)*
2000 *(specifies the drawing is to be saved in the AutoCAD 2000 DWG format)*
(Enter accepts default file name and location)
Y *(replaces the original file with the converted file)*
FILEDIA *(sets the system variable that controls file dialog boxes)*
1 *(enables file dialog boxes)*

Figure 28-6 shows how the script file appears in the Windows Notepad.

PROFESSIONAL TIP

Avoid pressing the space bar at the end of a line in the script file. This adds a space, and can cause the script to crash. Plus, finding spaces in a script file can be tedious work.

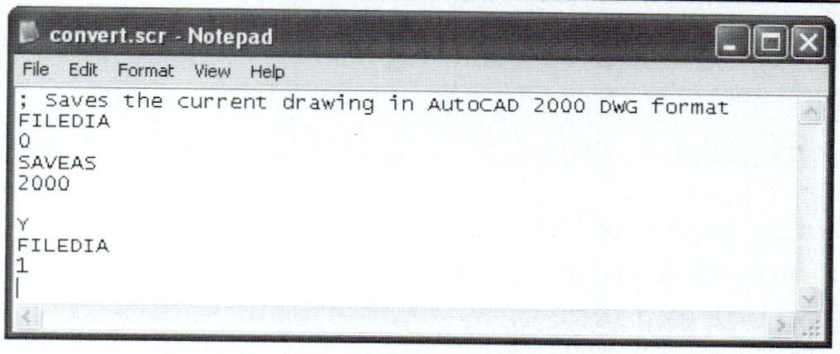
convert.scr - Notepad
File Edit Format View Help
; Saves the current drawing in AutoCAD 2000 DWG format
FILEDIA
0
SAVEAS
2000

Y
FILEDIA
1

Figure 28-6.
The conversion script file as it appears in Windows Notepad.

Running a Script

SCRIPT
SCR
Tools
➡ Run Script...

To run the script, select **Run Script...** from the **Tools** pull-down menu or enter SCR or SCRIPT at the Command: prompt. Next, select the file name convert.scr from the **Select Script File** dialog box. See **Figure 28-7.** Then sit back and watch the script run.

All the commands, options, and text screens associated with the commands in the script are displayed in rapid succession on the screen. If the script stops before completion, a problem has occurred. Flip the screen to the **AutoCAD Text Window** ([F2]) to determine the last command executed. Return to your text editor and correct the problem. Most often, there are too many or too few returns. Another problem is spaces at the end of a line. If you suspect these errors, retype the line.

Figure 28-7.
The **Select Script File** dialog box.

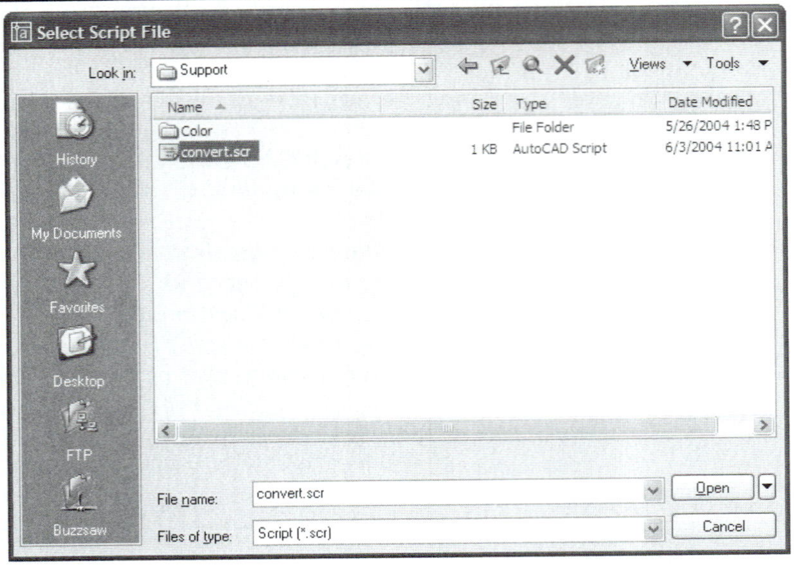

EXERCISE 28-2 Complete the Exercise on the Student CD.

Slides and Slide Shows

A ***slide*** in AutoCAD, similar to a slide in photography, is a snapshot of the drawing area display. Because of its nature, it cannot be edited or plotted. Slides can be viewed one at a time or as a continuous show. This is why slides are excellent for demonstrations, presentations, displays, and evaluation procedures.

You can create an impressive portfolio using a slide show. A ***slide show*** is a group of slides that are displayed at preset intervals. The slide show is controlled by a script file, which, as you learned from the previous examples, is a list of commands. Each slide is displayed for a specific length of time. The show can be continuous or can display each slide only once.

Making and Viewing Slides

Creating slides is easy. First display the drawing for which you need a slide. You might display the entire drawing or zoom to a specific area or feature. AutoCAD creates a slide of the current screen display. Make as many slides of one drawing as you want. For each, use the **MSLIDE** command and provide a file name for the slide. Do not enter a file type, as AutoCAD automatically attaches an .sld file extension. If **FILEDIA** is set to 1, a dialog box appears. Use **MSLIDE** at the Command: prompt as follows:

MSLIDE

Command: **MSLIDE**↵

The **Create Slide File** dialog box is displayed. This is the standard file dialog box. Pick the drive and folder in which the file is to be stored, enter the name in the **File name:** text box, and pick the **Save** button.

Slide names should follow a pattern. Suppose you are making slides for a class called cad1. File names such as cad1sld1 and cad1sld2 are appropriate. If working on project #4305 for the Weyerhauser Company, you might name the slide to reflect the client name or project number, such as weyersld1 or 4305sld1.

PROFESSIONAL TIP

To create a slide file at the highest resolution, set **VIEWRES** to its maximum value of 20000 before using the **MSLIDE** command. After making the slide, restore **VIEWRES** to its previous value.

Viewing a slide is as simple as making one. Enter VSLIDE at the Command: prompt to initiate the **VSLIDE** command.

VSLIDE

Command: **VSLIDE**↵

The **Select Slide File** dialog box appears. Pick the slide you want to display and pick **OK**. The slide is displayed in the graphics window.

PROFESSIONAL TIP

Keep the AutoCAD 2005 folder free of drawings, slides, and AutoLISP files. This speeds the computer's access to AutoCAD files. Create a separate folder for slides or save slides on a diskette. If using diskettes, be sure to give the appropriate file name when creating slides.

EXERCISE 28-3 Complete the Exercise on the Student CD.

Writing a Slide Show Script File

A slide show script file contains only two or three commands. This depends on whether it is a single pass or continuous show. A slide show script file typically contains the following commands:

- **VSLIDE.** This command is used to display a slide. The name of the slide follows the command. If the slide name is preceded by an asterisk (*), the slide is preloaded and displayed at the following **VSLIDE** command. This second command is not followed by a slide name, since the slide is already preloaded.
- **DELAY.** Any slide file can be displayed for up to approximately 33 seconds using this command. Delays are given in milliseconds. A delay of four seconds is written as DELAY 4000.
- **RSCRIPT.** This command is used at the end of a continuous script file. It causes the script to repeat.

To create a slide show, begin by writing a script file with a text editor. The script in **Figure 28-8** creates a slide show with four slides. Each slide appears for three seconds, and the script repeats. Notice that the next slide is preloaded while the previous one is viewed.

In order to display the slides, AutoCAD must first locate them. If the slide files are located in one of the folders listed in the **Support Files Search Path** area of the **Files** tab of the **Options** dialog box, AutoCAD can locate them automatically. If the slide files are not in one of the folders listed, you must either add the folder to the list or supply the full paths (drive letter:\folder\file name) of the slide files in the **VSLIDE** commands in the script.

Figure 28-8.
The show.scr script file as it appears in the Windows Notepad.

Full path to the slide

```
SHOW.SCR - Notepad
File  Edit  Format  View  Help
VSLIDE C:\SLIDES\CAD1SLD1
VSLIDE *C:\SLIDES\CAD1SLD2
DELAY 3000
VSLIDE
VSLIDE *C:\SLIDES\CAD1SLD3
DELAY 3000
VSLIDE
VSLIDE *C:\SLIDES\CAD1SLD4
DELAY 3000
VSLIDE
DELAY 3000
RSCRIPT
```

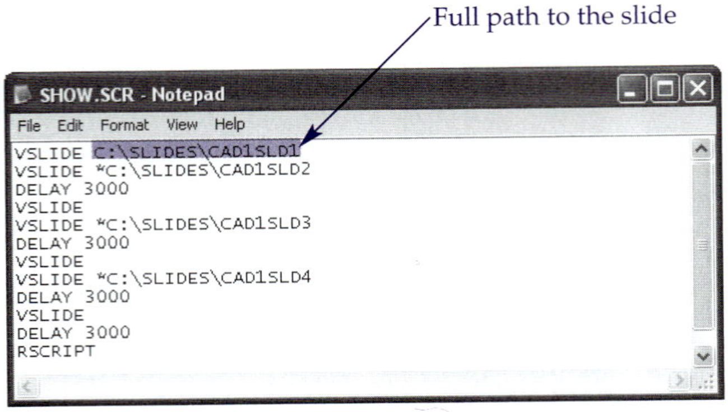

Viewing the Slide Show

SCRIPT
SCR

Tools
↳ Run Script...

The slide show is started by entering SCR or SCRIPT at the Command: prompt or by picking **Run Script...** from the **Tools** pull-down menu. Select the script file name show.scr from the **Select Script File** dialog box.

The show begins and the commands in the script file are displayed at the Command: prompt as the slides appear. To stop the show, press the [Backspace] key. You can then work on a drawing, use DOS commands, or work with a text editor on another script file. When finished, resume the slide show where it left off by entering RESUME. Any script file can be interrupted and restarted in this manner.

If your slide show encounters an error and fails to finish the first time through, do not panic. Take the following steps to "debug," or correct, problems in your script file.

1. Run the script to see where it crashes (quits working).
2. Check the command line for the last command that was executed.
3. Look for error messages, such as:
 - **Can't open slide file** *xxxxx*. This indicates an incorrect slide file name.
 - *xxxxx* **Unknown command.** A command may be spelled incorrectly or a space may be left at the end of the line.
 - **Requires an integer value.** The delay value contains characters other than numerals or ends with a space.
4. Correct the problem in the script file and save the file.
5. Test the script.

The most common errors are misspelled commands and spaces at the end of lines. If you suspect there is a space at the end of a line, it is best to delete the line and retype it. If you use Notepad, it is easy to see if a space exists. The flashing cursor, when placed at the end of a line, does not rest on the last character.

**EXERCISE
28-4** Complete the Exercise on the Student CD.

Creating and Using Slide Libraries

In addition to being displayed in slide shows, slide files are also used to create image tile menus. Image tile menus are groups of slides or vector images displayed in a dialog box. The 3D surfaces displayed after selecting **3D Surfaces...** from the **Surfaces** cascading menu in the **Draw** pull-down menu is an example of an image tile menu. Constructing image tile menus is discussed in *AutoCAD and its Applications—Advanced*.

Creating a Slide Library

To create a slide library, you must use a utility program called slidelib.exe, which operates from the DOS prompt. By default, the slidelib.exe utility program is installed in the Program Files\AutoCAD 2005 folder.

SLIDELIB

After entering the **SLIDELIB** command, list the paths and filenames of the slides that are to be included in the slide library. For example, suppose you have four slides of pipe fittings in the \pipe subdirectory of the AutoCAD 2005 folder. Compile these files in a slide library called PIPE in the following manner:

Command: **SH**↵
OS Command: **SLIDELIB PIPE**↵
SLIDELIB 1.2 (6/4/2003)
(C) Copyright 1987-1989, 1994-1996, 2003 Autodesk, Inc.
All Rights Reserved
\Program Files\AutoCAD 2005\PIPE\90elbow↵
\Program Files\AutoCAD 2005\PIPE\45elbow↵
\Program Files\AutoCAD 2005\PIPE\tee↵
\Program Files\AutoCAD 2005\PIPE\cap↵
↵
↵
Exit
Command:

After entering the last slide, press [Enter] three times to end the **SLIDELIB** command. The new slide library file is saved as pipe.slb.

Viewing Slide Library Slides

VSLIDE

The **VSLIDE** command is also used to view slides contained in a slide library. First change **FILEDIA** to 0. Then, enter the **VSLIDE** command and provide the library name plus the slide name in parentheses as follows:

Command: **FILEDIA**
New value for FILEDIA <1>: **0**

Command: **VSLIDE**↵
Enter name of slide file to view: <*current directory*> **PIPE(90ELBOW)**

Use the **REDRAW** command to remove the slide from the screen to display the previous drawing.

> **NOTE** The path for the slide libraries must be listed in the **Support Files Search Path** area of the **Files** tab of the **Options** dialog box.

Using the Slide Library in a Slide Show

The advantage of using a slide library for a slide show is that you do not need to preload slides. The script for a slide show of the four slides in the pipe.slb file would appear as follows:

```
VSLIDE PIPE(90ELBOW)
DELAY 1000
VSLIDE PIPE(45ELBOW)
DELAY 1000
VSLIDE PIPE(TEE)
DELAY 1000
VSLIDE PIPE(CAP)
DELAY 1000
REDRAW
```

The **REDRAW** command at the end of the slide show clears the screen and replaces the previous display. An **RSCRIPT** command instead of **REDRAW** repeats the show continuously.

Chapter Test

Answer the following questions on a separate sheet of paper.

1. What precautions should you take when using a word processor to create text files for AutoCAD?
2. How do you activate Windows Notepad from the AutoCAD Command: prompt, and what is the name of the file that allows you to do it?
3. If you edit the acad.pgp file from within AutoCAD, what must you do for the new file definitions to take effect?
4. Describe *external commands*.
5. Commands located in the acad.pgp file are executed by _____.
6. Name the parts of a command listing found in the acad.pgp file.
7. What is a command alias, and how would you write one for the **POLYGON** command?
8. Define *script file*.
9. Why is it a good idea to put one command on each line of a script file?
10. List two common reasons why a script file might not work.
11. What two commands allow you to make and view slides?
12. What file extension is assigned to slide files?
13. Explain why it is a good idea to keep slide files in a separate folder rather than in the AutoCAD 2005 folder.
14. List the three commands used when writing a slide show.
15. To stop a slide show, press the _____ key.
16. How do you begin a slide show that has been stopped?
17. Briefly explain the method used to create a slide library.
18. Suppose you want to view a slide named VIEW1, which is in a slide library file called VIEWS. How must you enter its name at the Enter name of slide file to view: prompt?
19. What is the principal difference between a slide show script file written for a slide library and one written for a group of slides?

Problems

1. If you use a text editor or word processor other than MS-DOS EDIT or Notepad, create a new command in the acad.pgp file that loads the text editor.

2. Create a new command for the acad.pgp file that activates the Windows Calculator.

3. Write a script file called notes.scr that does the following:
   A. Executes the **TEXT** command.
   B. Selects the **Style** option.
   C. Enters a style name.
   D. Selects the last point using the "@" symbol.
   E. Enters a text height of .25.
   F. Enters a rotation angle of 0.
   G. Inserts the text: NOTES:.
   H. Selects the **TEXT** command again.
   I. Enters location coordinates for first note.
   J. Enters a text height of .125.
   K. Enters a rotation angle of 0.
   L. Inserts the text: 1. INTERPRET DIMENSIONS AND TOLERANCES PER ASME Y14.5.
   M. Enters an [Enter] keystroke.
   N. Inserts the text: 2. REMOVE ALL BURRS AND SHARP EDGES.
   O. Enters the [Enter] twice at the Command: prompt to exit the command.
   Immediately before this script file is used, select the **ID** command and pick the point where you want the notes to begin. That point will be the "last point" used in the script file for the location of the word NOTES:. The script file, when executed, should draw the following:

   NOTES:
   1. INTERPRET DIMENSIONS AND TOLERANCES PER ASME Y14.5.
   2. REMOVE ALL BURRS AND SHARP EDGES.

4. Create a slide show of your best AutoCAD drawings. This slide show should be considered as part of your portfolio for potential employers. Place all of the slides and the script file on a floppy disk. Make two copies of the portfolio disk on separate diskettes. Keep the following guidelines in mind:
   A. Do not delay slides longer than 5 seconds. You can always press the [Backspace] key to view a slide longer.
   B. One view of a drawing is sufficient unless the drawing is complex. If so, make additional slides of the drawing's details.
   C. Create a cover slide or title page slide that displays your name.
   D. Create an ending slide that says THE END.

5. Create a slide show that illustrates specific types of drawings. For example, you might make a slide show for dimensioned mechanical drawings or for electrical drawings. Having these specialized slide shows in your portfolio is useful if you apply for a job in a specific discipline. Store all slide shows on the same disk. Identify slide shows by their content as follows:

   mech.scr—Mechanical
   arch.scr—Architectural
   pipe.scr—Piping
   struct.scr—Structural
   elect.scr—Electrical or Electronics
   map.scr—Mapping
   civil.scr—Civil

Index

@ symbol, 95, 162, 244, 428
3D command, 897–899
3D coordinates, 885–886
3D drawing, 885–902
3D Objects dialog box, 898
3DORBIT command, 362–365, 871, 890
3D views, 888–891
  hiding lines, 891
  isometric and orthographic viewpoint presets, 888–889

A

absolute coordinates, 93
acad.pgp file, 908–912. *See also* scripts
  editing, 911–912
accelerator keys, 46
acquired point, 198, 202
Add Plot Style Table wizard, 389–392
Add Plotter wizard, 384
Aerial View window, 352–353
ALIGN command, 440–441
aligned dimensioning, 569–570, 574, 613
aligned sections, 699–700
alignment path, 192
alternate units, 618
American Institute of Architects (AIA), 119
ANGBASE system variable, 279
ANGDIR system variable, 279
ANG function, 251–252
angular dimensioning, 574–577
annotation, 593
ANSI
  line conventions, 86
  sheet sizes, 53
  templates, 53
APBOX system variable, 206
aperture, 206–207
Apparent Intersection snap, 198
ARC command, 162–169
ARCHIVE command, 863–866
arcs, 162–169
  center dashes or centerlines, 587–588
  dimensioning, 591–593
  elliptical, 172–173
  isometric, 876–877
  polyline arcs, 521–525
area, 552–554
  calculating for plotting, 405
AREA command, 552–554
Array dialog box, 441–445
arrowheads, isometric, 879
arrowless dimensioning, 599
ASME
  line conventions, 86
  linetypes, 128
  multiview drawings, 221
  sheet sizes, 53, 786
  text, 275
ASSIST command, 44–45
associative dimensions, 642
  editing, 648–649
  exploding, 649
associative hatch patterns, 709, 719
ATTDEF command, 773–775
ATTDIA system variable, 778
ATTDISP command, 779
ATTREDEF command, 785
ATTREQ system variable, 779
Attribute Definition dialog box, 773–774
Attribute Extraction wizard, 791–795
attributes, 20, 773–795
  assigning to blocks, 773–776
  changing definitions, 783–785
  changing values, 780–783
  collecting information, 791–795
  editing definitions, 776–778
  fields, 791
  parts lists, 790–791
  redefining, 785
  revision blocks, 788–790
  title blocks, 786–788
AutoCAD 2005 Help window, 42–43
AutoCAD Color Index (ACI), 125
AutoCAD window, 28–39
AutoLISP, 257
automatic saves, 60–61
AutoSnap™, 191, 205–207
AUTOSNAP system variable, 206
AutoStack Properties dialog box, 292–293
AutoTracking, 209–214
auxiliary views, 224–227
AV command, 352–353
axis control, 670

B

Background Mask dialog box, 291–292
backgrounds, importing, 290–292
BAK files, 60
BASE command, 740
baseline, 582, 599
baseline dimensioning, 581–584
basic dimensions, 673
basic tolerance method, 661
BATTMAN command, 783–785
bearing, 79
BHATCH command, 702–720
Big Fonts, 297
bilateral tolerance, 655
bill of materials, 773–795
Bind Xrefs dialog box, 808
binding
  dependent objects, 811–813
  xrefs, 808–809
blip, 110, 337–338
BLIPMODE system variable, 110, 337–338, 559
BLK files, 792
Block Attribute Manager, 783–785
BLOCK command, 729–733, 776, 788
Block Definition dialog box, 732–733
blocks, 219, 469, 596, 729–765
  adding to **Tool Palettes**, 759–760
  attributes, 778–779
  creating wblocks, 751
  editing, 744–749
  exploding, 748
  inserting, 734–744
  redefining, 748
  renaming, 755
  revision, 788–790
BOUNDARY command, 544–546
Boundary Creation dialog box, 544
Boundary Definition Error alert box, 714
boundary edges, 431–432
boundary errors, 714–715
Boundary Hatch and Fill dialog box, 702–719
boundary hatching speed, 715–717
boundary set, 544
BREAK command, 427–429
break lines, 88
broken-out sections, 699–700

C

CAL command, 241–258
callout blocks, 853–857
Cartesian coordinate system, 20, 92
cascading menu, 32
CECOLOR system variable, 141
Cell Border Properties dialog box, 328
CELTYPE system variable, 142
CELWEIGHT system variable, 141
centerlines, 87
Center object snap, 196
chain dimensioning, 581–584
chain lines, 89
CHAMFER command, 420–424
CHAMFERA system variable, 421
CHAMFERB system variable, 421
CHAMFERC system variable, 423
CHAMFERD system variable, 423
chamfers, 176–177, 420–424
CHANGE command, 306, 433–434, 481
Change Dictionary dialog box, 312
Character Map dialog box, 290–291
chart dimensioning, 600
check box, 33
Check Spelling dialog box, 311
child, 607
CHPROP command, 481
CIRCLE command, 158–162
CIRCLERAD system variable, 159
circles, 158–162
    center dashes or centerlines, 587–588
    dimensioning, 588–590
    solid, 179
circular reference, 748–749
circumference, 158
circumscribed, 174
CLAYER system variable, 138
Clean Screen tool, 367
clip limits, 820–821
CLOSE command, 69
closed cross, 508
closing a drawing, 69
CMLJUST system variable, 501
CMLSCALE system variable, 501
CMLSTYLE system variable, 503
Color Books tab, 126–127
color-dependent plot style, 389
command alias, 90, 910
command buttons, 33
command line, 40
command window, 28
commands, 39–42, 351–352
    3D, 897–899
    3DORBIT, 362–365, 871, 890
    ADCENTER, 144, 301–302, 380–381, 646, 711–713, 741–743
    ALIGN, 440–441
    ARC, 162–169
    ARCHIVE, 863–866
    AREA, 552–554
    ARRAY, 441–445
    ASSIST, 44–45
    ATTDEF, 773–775
    ATTDISP, 779
    -ATTEDIT, 781–783
    ATTREDEF, 785
    AV, 352–353
    BASE, 740
    BATTMAN, 783–785
    BHATCH, 702–720
    BLOCK, 729–733, 776, 788
    -BLOCK, 733
    BOUNDARY, 544–546
    BREAK, 427–429
    CAL, 241–258
    CHAMFER, 420–424
    CHANGE, 306, 433–434, 481
    CHPROP, 481
    CIRCLE, 158–162
    CLOSE, 69
    COPY, 435–436, 473, 893
    DBLIST, 558
    DDEDIT, 303, 640–641, 689, 776–778
    DDGRIPS, 467–475
    DDIM, 656–658
    DDOSNAP, 203–205
    DDTYPE, 220–221
    DDVPOINT, 364
    DELAY, 915
    DIMALIGNED, 574, 879
    DIMANGULAR, 574–577
    DIMBASELINE, 582–584
    DIMCENTER, 587–588
    DIMCONTINUE, 584
    DIMDIAMETER, 588–590
    DIMEDIT, 592, 644
    DIMLINEAR, 570–573, 879
    DIMORDINATE, 601–603
    DIMOVERRIDE, 622
    DIMRADIUS, 591–593
    DIMREASSOCIATE, 649
    DIMSTYLE, 605–623
    DIMTEDIT, 642–643
    DISASSOCIATE, 649
    DIST, 558–559
    DIVIDE, 218–219
    DONUT, 179
    DRAWORDER, 366, 708–709
    DSETTINGS, 872–873
    DTEXT, 278
    DVIEW, 364, 871
    EATTEDIT, 780–781
    EATTEXT, 791–795
    ELLIPSE, 170–174, 875–876
    ERASE, 103–110
    EXIT, 70
    EXPLODE, 176, 535–536, 649, 748
    EXTEND, 431–433
    FILLET, 425–427
    FILTER, 260–266
    FIND, 313–314, 781
    GRAPHSCR, 560
    GRID, 72–73
    GROUP, 781
    HATCHEDIT, 709–710, 712–713, 718–719
    HELP, 42–44
    HIDE, 891, 900–901
    ID, 559
    INSERT, 729–730, 734–736, 778, 801
    ISOPLANE, 872, 874–875
    JUSTIFYTEXT, 307
    LAYER, 119–120, 397
    LAYERP, 139
    LAYOUT, 377–382
    LEADER, 597, 681–682
    LENGTHEN, 449–452
    LIMITS, 79–80
    LINE, 90–101
    LINETYPE, 131
    LINEWEIGHT, 132
    LIST, 556–558
    MATCHPROP, 483–484, 647
    MEASURE, 219
    MINSERT, 739–740
    MIRROR, 437–438, 475
    MLEDIT, 508–511
    MLINE, 500–511
    MLSTYLE, 502–503
    MOVE, 434–435, 472–473, 893
    MSLIDE, 914–915
    MTEXT, 283–294, 791
    MULTIPLE, 97
    MVIEW, 360–362
    NEW, 52
    OFFSET, 217–218
    OOPS, 110
    OPEN, 61–69
    OPTIONS, 499
    OSNAP, 191–207
    PAGESETUP, 382–383
    PAN, 343–345, 824
    PEDIT, 175–176, 525–526
    PLAN, 889
    PLINE, 491–499, 521–525
    PLOT, 148
    PLOTTERMANAGER, 384
    POINT, 220
    POLYGON, 174–175
    PROPERTIES, 140, 304–306, 477–480, 621
    PURGE, 639, 752, 755–756
    QDIM, 585–586, 641–642
    QLEADER, 593–598, 681–682
    QNEW, 55
    QSAVE, 58–59
    QSELECT, 258–266
    QTEXT, 302–303
    RAY, 230
    RECTANGLE, 175–178
    REDO, 499
    REDRAW, 110, 337–338, 918
    REDRAWALL, 365
    REFCLOSE, 747
    REFEDIT, 745–748, 785, 813–817
    REFSET, 747
    REGEN, 337–338, 891, 900
    REGENALL, 365
    REGENAUTO, 365
    REINIT, 910–912
    RENAME, 755, 813
    REVCLOUD, 180–181
    ROTATE, 438–440, 474
    RSCRIPT, 915, 918
    SAVE, 59–60
    SAVEAS, 59
    SCALE, 446–447, 474–475
    SCALETEXT, 307
    SCRIPT, 913, 916
    SELECT, 452
    SHADEMODE, 902
    SHEETSET, 834
    SKETCH, 512–515
    SLIDELIB, 917
    SNAP, 74–76
    SOLID, 719–720
    SPELL, 311–313
    SPLINE, 537–539
    SPLINEDIT, 539–544
    STATUS, 560–561
    STRETCH, 447–448, 470–471
    STYLE, 296–299
    -STYLE, 302
    TABLE, 323–335
    TABLEDIT, 326–331
    TABLESTYLE, 331–335
    TEXT, 277–282, 791
    TEXTSCR, 560
    TIME, 559–560
    TOLERANCE, 678–682

TOOLPALETTES, 713
TRACE, 495
TRIM, 429–431
U, 110, 494
UCS, 226, 889
UCSICON, 887
UNDO, 495–498
UNITS, 77–79, 91
UPDATEFIELD, 310
VIEW, 347–350
-VIEW, 350–351
VPCLIP, 828
VPLAYER, 825
VPOINT, 364
VPORTS, 355–359
VSLIDE, 915, 917
WBLOCK, 750–752, 776, 788
XBIND, 811–813
XCLIP, 809–810
XLINE, 227–230
XREF, 800–830
ZOOM, 339–343, 714
construction lines, 227–230
context oriented help, 43
control keys, 46
coordinate dimensioning, 574
coordinate display, 97
coordinate filters, 214–217
COORDS system variable, 97
COPY command, 435–436, 473, 893
copying objects, 435–436
with grips, 473
counterbore, 589
countersink, 589
Create New Dimension Style dialog box, 606
Create New Table Style dialog box, 332
Create Sheet Set wizard, 835–842
crosshairs orientation, 874–875
CSV files, 794
CTB files, 389
cubic curve, 536
CUR function, 245
cursor menus, 36
curve fitting, 532–533
curves, 537–539, 592–593. *See also* splines
Customize dialog box, 761–763
cutting edge, 429–430
cutting-plane line, 88, 697
CVUNIT function, 243
cycling, 112

D

dashed lines, 87
datum, 599, 671
datum dimensioning, 581–584
datum feature symbols, 675–677, 686–688
DBLIST command, 558
DCTCUST system variable, 313
DCTMAIN system variable, 313
DDEDIT command, 303, 640–641, 689, 776–778
DDGRIPS command, 467–475
DDIM command, 656–658
DDOSNAP command, 203–205
DDTYPE command, 220–221
DDVPOINT command, 364
deferred perpendicular, 199
deferred tangency, 200
definition points, 500, 650
defpoints, 650
DELAY command, 915
demand loading, 811
dependent blocks, 733
dependent symbols, 729
DesignCenter, 38, 143–146, 301–302, 380–381, 646, 711–713, 729, 741–743, 759–760, 804–805
detach, 805
deviation tolerance method, 659–660
dialog box, 29, 33–36
diametric, 870
DIMADEC system variable, 618
DIMALIGNED command, 574, 879
DIMALT system variable, 618
DIMALTD system variable, 616
DIMALTF system variable, 618
DIMALTRND system variable, 617
DIMALTU system variable, 616
DIMALTZ system variable, 618
DIMANGULAR command, 574–577
DIMAPOST system variable, 617
DIMASSOC system variable, 642, 648–649
DIMASZ system variable, 611
DIMATFIT system variable, 614
DIMAUNIT system variable, 618
DIMAZIN system variable, 618
DIMBASELINE command, 582–584
DIMBLK1 system variable, 610
DIMBLK2 system variable, 610
DIMCEN system variable, 611
DIMCENTER command, 587–588
DIMCLRD system variable, 608
DIMCLRE system variable, 610
DIMCLRT system variable, 612
DIMCONTINUE command, 584
DIMDEC system variable, 616
DIMDIAMETER command, 588–590
DIMDLI system variable, 609
DIMDRBLK system variable, 610
DIMDSEP system variable, 617
DIMEDIT command, 592, 644
dimensioning, 567–623, 667–677
aligned, 569–570
angles, 574–577
architectural features, 578
arcs, 591–593
arrowless, 599
chamfers, 598
circles, 588–590
cones and hexagonal shapes, 579–580
curves, 592–593
cylindrical shapes, 579
datum and chain, 581–584
editing dimensions, 639–650
fillets and rounds, 591–592
flat surfaces, 578
holes, 589
isometric, 878–880
leader lines, 593–598
linear, 570–573
location dimensions, 580–581
notes, 577–578
oblique, 879–880
ordinate, 601–603
practices, 577–580
primary units, 656–658
quick dimension, 585–586
repetitive features, 590
size dimensions, 577–578
square and rectangular features, 579
symbols, 586–587
tabular, 599–600
thread drawings and notes, 603–604
tolerances, 653–662
unidirectional, 569
WCS and UCS, 600–601
dimension lines, 88
Dimension Style Manager dialog box, 605–606, 656
dimension style override, 620
dimension styles, 605–623, 645–646
Dimension toolbar, 645
DIMEXE system variable, 610
DIMEXO system variable, 610, 622
DIMFRAC system variable, 616
DIMGAP system variable, 612–613, 688–689
DIMJUST system variable, 613
DIMLFAC system variable, 617
DIMLIN system variable, 658–659
DIMLINEAR command, 570–573, 879
DIMLUNIT system variable, 616
DIMLWD system variable, 608
DIMLWE system variable, 610
DIMORDINATE command, 601–603
DIMOVERRIDE command, 622
DIMPOST system variable, 617
DIMRADIUS command, 591–593
DIMREASSOCIATE command, 649
DIMRND system variable, 617
DIMSCALE system variable, 615, 830
DIMSD1 system variable, 609
DIMSD2 system variable, 609
DIMSE1 system variable, 610
DIMSE2 system variable, 610
DIMSOXD system variable, 615
DIMSTYLE command, 605–623
DIMTAD system variable, 612
DIMTDEC system variable, 661
DIMTEDIT command, 642–643
DIMTFAC system variable, 612, 662
DIMTIH system variable, 614
DIMTIX system variable, 615
DIMTM system variable, 658–659
DIMTMOVE system variable, 615
DIMTOFL system variable, 616
DIMTOH system variable, 614
DIMTOL system variable, 658–659
DIMTOLJ system variable, 662
DIMTP system variable, 658–659
DIMTXSTY system variable, 612
DIMTXT system variable, 612
DIMTZIN system variable, 661
DIMUPT system variable, 616
DIMZIN system variable, 618
DIN, 53
Direction Control dialog box, 78
DISASSOCIATE command, 649
DIST command, 558–559
DIST function, 248
dithering, 386
DIVIDE command, 218–219
dividing objects, 218–219
DMDLE system variable, 608
docked, 28
DONUT command, 179
DONUTID system variable, 179
DONUTOD system variable, 179
donuts, 179
double feature control frame, 685–686
DPL function, 248
DPP function, 248
Drafting Settings dialog box, 872–873
Object Snap tab, 203–204
Polar Tracking tab, 211
Snap and Grid tab, 72–74, 213

DRAGMODE system variable, 157–158, 448
drawing data, 556–558
drawing limits, 79–80
drawing order, 708–709
drawing orientation, 401
drawing plan sheets, 24–25
drawing status, 560–561
drawing templates. *See* templates
Drawing Units dialog box, 77–79
drawing windows, 66–69
drawings
closing, 69
inserting, 740
naming, 57
opening, 61–69
revising inserted, 752
saving, 57–61
starting new, 51–56
storing as wblocks, 751–752
DRAWORDER command, 366, 708–709
drop-down list box, 34
DSETTINGS command, 872–873
DST files, 835
DTEXT command, 278
dual dimensioning, 618
DVIEW command, 364, 871
DWF files, 410–412, 847–849
DWG files, 58
DWT files, 52
DXF files, 65

E

EATTEDIT command, 780–781
EATTEXT command, 791–795
EDGEMODE system variable, 430
Edit Attribute Definition dialog box, 776–777
Edit Attribute dialog box, 784
editing, 102–112
blocks, 744–749
cycling through objects, 112
dimensions, 639–650
erasing, 103–110
hatch patterns, 718–719
objects, 419–454
reference drawings, 813–817
selecting objects, 111
Edit Text dialog box, 303
Element Properties dialog box, 504–505
elements, 491, 500
ELLIPSE command, 170–174, 875–876
ellipses, 29, 170–174
isometric, 875–876
elliptical arcs, 172–173
Endpoint object snap, 194–195
Enhanced Attribute Editor, 780–781
Enter Attributes dialog box, 778
equal bilateral tolerance, 655
ERASE command, 103–110
escape key, 46
EXIT command, 70
EXPLODE command, 176, 535–536, 649, 748
EXTEND command, 431–433
extension lines, 87
Extension object snap, 198–199
extension path, 192, 198
external command, 909–910
External Reference dialog box, 801
external references, 733, 799–830. *See also* xrefs

F

FACETRES system variable, 899
feature, 577
feature control frame, 671–673
Field dialog box, 308, 554–555, 854, 858
fields, 308–310
attributes, 791
displaying information with, 554–556
editing, 310
inserting, 308–309
sheet sets, 859–861
updating, 310
Field Update Settings dialog box, 310
FILEDIA system variable, 57, 914
files
accessing, 62–63
finding, 63–64
read-only, 65–66
FILLET command, 425–427
FILLETRAD system variable, 425
fillets, 177, 425–427
dimensioning, 591–592
FILL mode, 179, 499, 719–720
FILTER command, 260–266
filters, 260–266
coordinate, 214–217
creating named, 264
editing, 264
layers, 135–138
using on drawings, 264–265
Find and Replace dialog box, 313–314
FIND command, 313–314, 781
Find dialog box, 63
fit points, 540–542
floating viewports, 359–362
layouts, 375–377
flyouts, 29
fonts, 295–296
foreshortened, 224
foreshortening, 870
front view, 223
FSCM, 786–787
full sections, 699
function keys, 47

G

gap tolerance, 714
geometric characteristic symbols, 668–669
geometric dimensioning and tolerancing
basic dimensions, 673, 688–689
datum feature symbols, 675–677, 686–688
double feature control frame, 685–686
feature control frame, 671–673, 688
material condition symbols, 669–671
placing symbols, 681–682
projected tolerance zones, 682–685
sample applications, 689–690
symbols, 668
Geometric Tolerance dialog box, 678–682, 684–685
geometry calculator, 241–258
advanced math functions, 255
angles, 251–252
basic math functions, 242–243
combining functions, 253–254
distances, 248–249
intersection points, 249–250
numeric entries, 242
object snap modes, 245–247
point entry, 244–245
points, 250
radius, 252
shortcut functions, 254–255
system variables, 257
trigonometric functions, 255–256
unit conversions, 243
GETVAR system variable, 257
global change, 143
grab bar, 28
gradient, 79
gradient fill, 709
graphical user interface, 33
GRAPHSCR command, 560
GRID command, 72–73
grid units, 73–74
GRIPBLOCK system variable, 469
GRIPCOLOR system variable, 469
GRIPHOT system variable, 469
GRIPHOVER system variable, 469
grips, 467–475. *See also* automatic editing
GRIPSIZE system variable, 468
GRIPS system variable, 469
GRIPTIPS system variable, 469
GROUP command, 781

H

half sections, 699
HATCHEDIT command, 709–710, 712–713, 718–719
Hatch Pattern Palette dialog box, 703
hatch patterns, 701–720
adding to **Tool Palettes**, 760–761
associative, 709
custom, 704
editing, 718–719
predefined, 703
scale, 704–705
user defined, 703–704
help, 35, 42–44
Info Palette, 44–45
online product support, 45
HELP command, 42–44
hidden features, 223
hidden line, 87, 900–901
Hidden Line Settings dialog box, 901
HIDE command, 891, 900–901
HSL color model, 126

I

icon, 26
ID command, 559
ILL function, 249–250
image tile, 34
image tile menus, 37
implied intersection, 430–433
included angle, 164, 251, 522–523
Indents and Tabs dialog box, 288
Index Color tab, 124–126
Info Palette, 44–45
inscribed, 174
INSERT command, 729–730, 734–736, 778, 801
Insert dialog box, 734–735
Insert Sheet List Table dialog box, 861–862
Insert Table dialog box, 323–324
integer, 243
Intersection object snap, 197–198
islands, 545, 707

ISO, 53
isometric drawings, 869–880
arcs, 876–877
arrowheads, 879
crosshairs orientation, 874–875
dimensioning, 878–880
ellipses, 875–876
settings, 872–874
text styles, 877–878
viewpoint presets, 888–889
isometric line, 871
isometric views, 363
isometrics, 20
ISOPLANE command, 872, 874–875
isoplanes, 874

J

JIS, 53
joints, 505
justify, 277
JUSTIFYTEXT command, 307

K

keyboard shortcuts, 90
keys, 45–47

L

label blocks, 853–857
landscape, 401
LAS files, 134–135
LASTPOINT system variable, 162, 244
LAYER command, 119–120, 397
Layer Control drop-down list, 146
Layer Filter Properties dialog box, 135–138
layer filters, 135–138
layer indexes, 810
LAYERP command, 139
Layer Properties Manager dialog box, 119–139, 811–812
layers, 117–139
creating, 120–121
current, 118, 121
deleting, 121
naming, 119
restoring settings, 139
states, 133–135
visibility in viewports, 825
Layer States Manager dialog box, 133–134
Layers toolbar, 31, 118
LAY files, 135
LAYOUT command, 377–382
layouts, 372–383
adding as sheets, 846
creating new, 378–380
deleting, 381
inserting title blocks, 374–375
managing, 377–382
saving, 381–382
working in **Layout** tabs, 374
xrefs in multiview, 818–830
layout space, 79
Layout tab, 148, 354
LEADER command, 597, 681–682
leader lines, 88, 593–598
Leader Settings dialog box, 594–598
least material condition (LMC), 671
LENGTHEN command, 449–452
library path, 807–808
limits, 654
calculating for plotting, 405
dimensioning, 654
tolerance method, 660
LIMITS command, 79–80
LINE command, 90–101
linear dimensioning, 570–573
lines, 85–101
break, 88
center, 87
chain, 89
construction, 227–230
cutting-plane and viewing-plane, 88
dimension, 88
extension, 87
hidden, 87, 900–901
leader, 88
object, 87
phantom, 89
section, 88, 700–702
LINETYPE command, 131
Linetype Control drop-down list, 142
Linetype Manager dialog box, 131, 731
linetypes, 128–133
changing assignments, 129–130
copying with **DesignCenter**, 144–147
lineweight, 131–133
managing, 131
scale, 143
LINEWEIGHT command, 132
Lineweight dialog box, 131–133
lineweights, 131–133
Lineweight Settings dialog box, 132–133
LIN files, 128–129
list box, 33
LIST command, 556–558
listing drawing data, 556–558
location dimensions, 580–581
LTSCALE system variable, 143, 406, 479
LWDEFAULT system variable, 132
LWDISPLAY system variable, 399

M

Manage Xrefs icon, 816–817
markers, 192
MATCHPROP command, 483–484, 647
Material Condition dialog box, 679
material condition symbols, 669–671
axis control, 670
least material condition control, 671
maximum material condition control, 671
surface control, 669–670
MAXACTVP system variable, 358
maximum material condition (MMC), 671
MAXSORT system variable, 121
MBUTTONPAN system variable, 345
MDB files, 794
MEASURE command, 219
MEASUREMENT system variable, 659
menu accelerator keys, 32
metric dimensioning, 656
Midpoint object snap, 195
MINSERT command, 739–740
MIRROR command, 437–438, 475
mirroring objects, 437–438
with grips, 475
MIRRTEXT system variable, 438
miters, 505
MLEDIT command, 508–511
MLINE command, 500–511
MLSTYLE command, 502–503
MNU files, 345
modeless dialog boxes, 37
model space, 79, 148, 354
Model tab, 148, 354
models, 79
MOVE command, 434–435, 472–473, 893
Move or Copy dialog box, 380
moving objects, 434–435
with grips, 472–473
MSLIDE command, 914–915
MTEXT command, 283–294, 791
Multiline Properties dialog box, 505–506
multilines, 491, 500–511
Multiline Styles dialog box, 503
multiline text, 283–294
multiline text editor, 277
MULTIPLE command, 97
multiple copies, 436
multiple datum reference, 671
Multiple Design Environment (MDE), 66
multiple document interface (MDI), 66
multiview drawings, 221–224, 820
front view, 223
hidden features, 223
layers, 821
one-view drawings, 223
placing views, 822–824
plotting, 830
viewports, 822
xrefs, 818–830
MVIEW command, 360–362

N

named plot style, 389
naming drawings, 57
naming layers, 119
nesting, 453, 734, 805
NEW command, 52
New View dialog box, 347–348, 851
nonisometric lines, 871
Notepad, 907–909
noun/verb format, 476
numeric expression, 242
NURBS, 537–539

O

Object Grouping dialog box, 453–454
object lines, 87
object linking and embedding, 410
object properties, 140
Object Selection Filters dialog box, 260–265
object snap, 191–207
geometry calculator, 245–247
modes, 192–203
multiple, 204–205
running, 203–205
tracking, 209–210
object snap override, 192
Object Snap shortcut menu, 193
Object Snap toolbar, 192–193
oblique dimensioning, 879–880
oblique drawings, 869–870
OFFSET command, 217–218
offset sections, 699
OLE, 410
OLEQUALITY system variable, 410
OLESTARTUP system variable, 410
one-view drawings, 223
OOPS command, 110
OPEN command, 61–69
opening drawings, 61–69
OPTIONS command, 499

Options dialog box
    Display tab, 346, 374
    Drafting tab, 205–206
    Files tab, 55
    Open and Save tab, 60
    Plot and Publish tab, 395
    Selection tab, 468, 476
    System tab, 56
    User Preferences tab, 309, 901
order, 543
ordinate dimensioning, 601–603
origin, 92
ortho, 97
orthographic multiview drawings. *See* multiview drawings
orthographic projection, 222
orthographic viewpoint presets, 888–889
orthographic views, 363
OSMODE system variable, 206
OSNAP command, 191–207
OSNAPCOORD system variable, 205
overlay system, 117
override, 607

P

PAGESETUP command, 382–383
Page Setup dialog box, 382–384, 399–400, 820
Page Setup Manager dialog box, 382–383
PAN command, 343–345, 824
pan displacement, 344
Pantone color books, 126
paper space, 148, 354
PAPERUPDATE system variable, 409
parallel alignment path, 202
Parallel object snap, 202
parent, 607
parent xref, 805
partial auxiliary view, 224
parts lists, 790–791
PAT files, 711
PDMODE system variable, 220–221
PDSIZE system variable, 220–221
PEDIT command, 175–176, 525–526
    Spline option, 533–534
PELLIPSE system variable, 173
perfect form, 669
Period subcommand, 513
Perpendicular object snap, 199–200
perspective drawings, 871
phantom lines, 89
pi, 256
PICKADD system variable, 477
PICKAUTO system variable, 104, 107, 477
pick box, 207
PICKBOX system variable, 468
PICKDRAG system variable, 477
PICKFIRST system variable, 472
pictorial drawings, 869–871
    isometric, 870
    oblique, 869–870
    perspective, 871
pixels, 206
placeholder, 859
PLAN command, 889
PLD function, 250
PLINE command, 491–499, 521–525
PLINEGEN system variable, 535
PLINEWID system variable, 525
PLOT command, 148
plot device selection and management, 384–386
Plot dialog box, 148–149, 399–400, 412
plot offset, 402
plot spooler, 385
Plot Stamp dialog box, 407–408
plot styles, 386–399
plot style table, 386
Plot Style Table Editor dialog box, 392–394
Plot Style Table Settings dialog box, 395
Plotter Configuration Editor dialog box, 385
PLOTTERMANAGER command, 384
plotters, 147
plotting, 147–151, 371–373
    adding plot stamp, 407–409
    calculating drawing area and limits, 405
    drawing scale factors, 403–406
    options, 403, 409–410
    page setups, 382–383
    paper size, units, and drawing orientation, 401
    plot device selection and management, 384–386
    plot offset, 402
    previewing, 406–407
    scaling, 404–405
    settings, 399–410
    shaded viewport options, 402
    specifying plot style table, 386
    styles, 386–399
PLT files, 410, 412
PLT function, 250
plus-minus dimensioning, 654
POINT command, 220
point entry, 90, 92–96
    absolute coordinates, 93
    direct distance entry, 98
    polar coordinates, 95–96
    relative coordinates, 94
    screen cursor, 96
point locations, 559
point of tangency, 161
points, 220–221
point specification prompt, 192
Point Style dialog box, 220
point-to-point dimensioning, 581–584
POLARADDANG system variable, 212
POLARANG system variable, 211
polar array, 441
polar coordinates, 95–96
polar coordinate system, 580
POLARMODE system variable, 214
polar tracking, 211–214
POLYGON command, 174–175
polygons, 174–175
polyline arcs, 521–525
polylines, 491–499
    arcs, 521–525
    boundary, 544–546
    breaking, 529–530
    chamfers, 422
    curve fitting, 532–533
    exploding, 535–536
    fillets, 426
    filling, 499
    joining to other objects, 527
    opening and closing, 526
    revising, 525–535
    smoothing, 536–537
    straightening segments or arcs, 531, 534
    tapered, 493
    vertices, 528–532
    width, 492–493, 528, 532
POLYSIDES system variable, 175
portrait, 401
prefixes, 617
preview box, 34
primary units, 656–658
primitives, 892
printers, 147
printing, 147–151
produced size, 669
program icon, 26
projected tolerance zones, 682–685
    drawing, 684–685
    representation, 683–684
projection plane, 222
PROJECTNAME system variable, 802
PROJMODE system variable, 431, 433
Properties toolbar, 31
Properties window, 38, 140, 304–306, 330–331, 403, 478–480, 646, 738, 777–778
Property Settings dialog box, 484
PSLTSCALE system variable, 406
PSTYLEPOLICY system variable, 123, 396
Publish dialog box, 411–412
publishing, 847–849
pull-down menus, 29, 32
PURGE command, 639, 752, 755–756
Purge dialog box, 756

Q

QDIM command, 585–586, 641–642
QLEADER command, 593–598, 681–682
QNEW command, 55
QSAVE command, 58–59
QSELECT command, 258–266
QTEXT command, 302–303
Quadrant object snap, 196–197
quadratic curve, 536
Quick Help, 44–45
quick save, 58
Quick Select dialog box, 258–259
Quick Text mode, 302–303

R

RAD function, 252
radian, 79
radio buttons, 33
radius, 158
RAL color books, 126
raster image, 366
RAY command, 230
read-only files, 65–66
real block, 736
record increment, 512
RECTANGLE command, 175–178
rectangles, 175–178
rectangular array, 441
rectangular coordinates, 20, 22, 580
REDO command, 499
REDRAW command, 110, 337–338, 918
REDRAWALL command, 365
REFCLOSE command, 747
REFEDIT command, 745–748, 785, 813–817
Refedit toolbar, 745, 814–815
Reference Edit dialog box, 745–746, 814
references, 799–830, 818
REFSET command, 747
regardless of feature size (rfs), 669–670
REGENAUTO command, 365
REGEN command, 337–338, 891, 900
regeneration
    controlling automatic, 365
    screen, 337–338
    viewports, 365

region, 717
REINIT command, 910–912
Re-initialization dialog box, 910
relative coordinates, 94
relative operators, 263
reload, 805
removed sections, 699–700
Rename & Renumber View dialog box, 853
RENAME command, 755, 813
Rename dialog box, 755
rendered, 20
repetitive features, 590
Replace dialog box, 289
resizing controls, 66–67
resource drawings, 851–852
REVCLOUD command, 180–181
revision blocks, 788–790
revision cloud, 180–181
revolved sections, 699–700
RGB color model, 126
right-hand rule, 887–888
root point, 228
ROTATE command, 438–440, 474
rotating objects, 438–440
    with grips, 474
rounds, 591–592
RSCRIPT command, 915, 918
rubberband, 157
running object snap mode, 192, 203–205

S

SAVEAS command, 59
SAVE command, 59–60
Save Drawing As dialog box, 58, 70–71
Save Multiline Style dialog box, 507
saving drawings, 57–60
    automatically, 60–61
scaleable, 295
SCALE command, 446–447, 474–475
scale factors, 403–406
SCALETEXT command, 307
scaling objects, 446–447
    hatch patterns, 704–705
    referencing, 447
    with grips, 474–475
schematic block, 736
SCR files, 915–916
screen layout, 28–31
SCRIPT command, 913, 916
script file, 912–914
scripts, 907–914
    command aliases, 910
    creating, 912–914
    editing acad.pgp file, 911–912
    external commands, 909–910
    running, 913
    slide show, 915–916
scroll bars, 34
section lines, 88
sections, 697–702
Select Color dialog box, 124–125, 731
SELECT command, 452
Select File dialog box, 61–63
selecting objects, 452
selection sets, 102, 849, 258–266
    filters, 260–266
Settings dialog box, 784
SETVAR, 258
shade, 710
shaded viewport options, 402
SHADEMODE command, 902
sheet list tables, 861–863
    column heading data, 862–863
    editing, 863
    hyperlinks, 863
    inserting, 861–862
Sheet Properties dialog box, 846–847, 860–861
sheets
    adding existing layouts, 846
    adding using templates, 845–846
    modifying properties, 846–847
SHEETSET command, 834
Sheet Set Control drop-down list, 842–843
Sheet Set Manager window, 29, 38, 834–835
Sheet Set Properties dialog box, 837–838
sheet sets, 29, 833–866
    archiving, 863–866
    creating, 835–842
    custom property fields, 859–861
    fields, 858–861
    overview, 834
    publishing, 847–849
    sheet list tables, 861–863
    sheet selection sets, 849
    Sheet Set Manager, 834–835
    sheet views, 849–858
    subsets, 844–845
    working with, 842–847
sheet size, 52
sheet views, 834, 849–858
    callout and label blocks, 853–856
    creating, 851–852
    modifying category, 850
    naming and numbering, 853
    view category, 849–850
shortcut menus, 36
SHX files, 295–299
size dimensions, 577–578
SKETCH command, 512–515
sketching, 512–515
SKPOLY system variable, 513
SLIDELIB command, 917
slide libraries, 916–918
slides, 914–918
slide shows, 914–916
SNAP command, 74–76
snap grid, 74–76
    horizontal and vertical units, 74
    rotating, 75
    setting grid spacing, 76
    type and style, 76
snap resolution, 74
soft copy, 147
SOLID command, 719–720
solid fills, 719–720
solid modeling, 892
solid primitives, 895–897
spatial indexes, 810
SPELL command, 311–313
SPLINE command, 537–539
SPLINEDIT command, 539–544
splines, 537–539
    closed, 538
    control points, 543
    converting from polylines, 539
    editing, 539–544
    fit data, 540–542
    moving vertices, 542
    opening or closing, 542
    smoothing or reshaping, 542–543
    tangents, 538–539
    tolerance, 538
    undoing changes, 543
SPLINESEGS system variable, 537
SPLINETYPE system variable, 536
spotface, 589
stacked objects, 112
Stack Properties dialog box, 293
standards, 23
Standard toolbar, 30, 498
starting a new drawing, 51–56
starting AutoCAD, 26–28
Startup dialog box, 56
startup wizards, 56
statistical process control (SPC), 674
statistical tolerancing, 674
STATUS command, 560–561
STB files, 389
STRETCH command, 447–448, 470–471
stretching objects, 447–448
    displacement, 448
    with grips, 470–471
STYLE command, 296–299
Styles toolbar, 30–31
subsets, 844–845
suffixes, 617
surface control, 669
surface modeling, 891
surface primitives, 896–899
Symbol dialog box, 679
symbol libraries, 688, 752–754
    blocks and drawing files, 753
    creating, 753–754
    storing symbol drawings, 754–755
symbols, 674–675, 729–765. *See also* blocks
    datum feature, 675–677
    dimensioning, 668
    geometric characteristic, 668–669
    importing, 290–292
    including with dimension text, 586–587
    inserting, 282
    libraries, 752–755
    material condition, 669–671
    placing, 681–682
    section, 700–702
symmetrical tolerance method, 658–659
system variables, 57, 257–258, 608

T

tab, 33
TABLE command, 323–335
TABLEDIT command, 326–331
tables, 323–335
    editing, 326–331
    entering text, 325–326
    inserting, 323–326
TABLESTYLE command, 331–335
Table Style dialog box, 331
table styles, 331–335
    creating and formatting, 332–335
    working with, 331–332
tablet menu, 41–42
tabular dimensioning, 599–600
tangent, 161
Tangent object snap, 200–201
Template Description dialog box, 71
templates, 51–54
    adding sheets, 845–846
    ANSI, 53
    creating and using, 70–72
    planning, 72
temporary lines, 514
temporary tracking, 207–209
    From point selection option, 208
    Mid Between 2 Points option, 209

text, 275–315
composition, 277
dictionaries, 312–313
editing dimensions, 640–641
entering into table, 325–326
fields, 308–310
finding and replacing, 313–314
fonts, 295–296
importing, 290–292
mirroring, 438
revising, 303
scale factors for height, 276–277
scaling, 307
single-line, 277–282
spelling, 311–313
standards, 275–276
symbols, 282
underscored or overscored, 282
text boundary, 283
text box, 33
TEXT command, 277–282, 791
text editor, 283, 907–908
TEXTFILL system variable, 295
Text Formatting toolbar, 283–284, 325–326
TEXTSCR command, 560
TEXTSIZE system variable, 286, 297
Text Style dialog box, 296–297
text styles, 296–302
changing, renaming, and deleting, 300–301
importing from existing drawings, 301–302
isometric, 877–878
selecting and modifying, 296–299
thread drawings, 603–604
three-dimensional drawing. *See* 3D drawing
tiled viewports, 355–359
TIME command, 559–560
tint, 710
title blocks, 786–788
TOLERANCE command, 678–682
tolerances, 653–662
assigning decimal places, 655–656
basic, 661
deviation, 659–660
fundamentals, 654–655
height, 662
justification, 662
limits, 660
method review, 661
precision and zero suppression, 661
symmetrical, 658–659
tolerance stack, 287
toolbars, 28
TOOLPALETTES command, 713
Tool Palettes window, 29, 38, 713, 743–744, 804–805
adding hatch patterns, 760–761
arranging and customizing, 761–763
creating palettes and adding blocks, 759–760
locating and viewing content, 758–759
modifying appearance, 757–758
modifying properties, 763–765
Tool Properties window, 764–765
Tools pull-down menu, 551–552
tooltip, 30
TRACE command, 495
trace segments, 495
TRACEWID system variable, 495
tracking, 207
TRACKPATH system variable, 214
Transparency dialog box, 757–758
transparent commands, 351–352
Tray Settings dialog box, 816
TRIM command, 429–431
trimetric, 870
trimming, 429–431
TRIMMODE system variable, 424, 426
True Color tab, 126–127
TrueType, 295
TXT files, 295, 794

U

U command, 110, 494
UCS command, 226, 889
UCSICON command, 887
UNDO command, 495–498
unidirectional dimensioning, 569
unilateral tolerance, 655
unit block, 736
unit cell, 443
unit conversions, 243
UNITS command, 77–79, 91
unload, 805
unnamed blocks, 733
unselected grips, 468
UPDATEFIELD command, 310
updating, 310
user blocks, 733
user coordinate system (UCS), 225–227, 600–601

V

variable, 257
vector expression, 242
vector image, 366
verb/noun format, 476
VIEW command, 347–350
View dialog box, 347–349
viewing-plane lines, 88, 225
View Options dialog box, 758–759
viewports
creating, 825–828
display, 828–830
floating, 359–362
layer visibility, 825
multiview layouts, 822
notes and titles, 829
outlines, 829
redrawing and regenerating, 365
scale, 829
scaling drawings, 824
tiled, 355–359
Viewports dialog box, 356, 360
Viewports toolbar, 824
View pull-down menu, 337–367
view resolution, 345–347
VIEWRES setting 346, 915
views
aerial, 352–353
creating, 347–351
virtual reality, 21
visible lines, 87
Visual LISP Editor, 908
VPCLIP command, 828
VPLAYER command, 825
VPOINT command, 364
VPORTS command, 355–359
VSLIDE command, 915, 917

W

walkthrough, 21
wblock, 729
WBLOCK command, 750–752, 776, 788
welding multilines, 511
window control buttons, 66–67
Window pull-down menu, 68
Windows Explorer, 65
wireframe objects, 891–895
wizards
Attribute Extraction, 791–795
Create Sheet Set, 835–842
startup, 56
working set, 814
world coordinate system (WCS), 225, 600–601
Write Block dialog box, 750–751

X

XBIND command, 811–813
Xbind dialog box, 812–813
XCLIP command, 809–810
XCLIPFRAME system variable, 810
XLG files, 813
XLINE command, 227–230
xline object, 227
XLS files, 794
XREF command, 800–830
XREFCTL system variable, 813
Xref Manager dialog box, 799–802, 806–807
xrefs, 799–830
attaching, 801–805
binding, 808–809
clipping, 809–810
detaching, 805
editing, 811–817
layers, 821
layouts, 818–830
overlaying current drawing, 805
reloading, 805
unloading, 805
updating path, 807–808
viewports, 818–819
XTP files, 763
XYZ coordinate system, 22

Z

zero suppression, 661
ZOOM command, 339–343, 714
Dynamic option, 342–343
Realtime option, 340–341
Window option, 341–342
ZOOMFACTOR system variable, 345